A GUIDE to GRANTS *for* INDIVIDUALS *in* NEED

2002/03

Alan French
Dave Griffiths
Tom Traynor
Sarah Wiggins

DIRECTORY OF SOCIAL CHANGE

A Guide to Grants for Individuals in Need
2002/2003 Edition

Published by
Directory of Social Change
24 Stephenson Way
London NW1 2DP
Tel: 020 7209 5151; Fax: 020 7209 4804
e-mail: books@dsc.org.uk; website: www.dsc.org.uk
from whom further copies and a full publications list are available.

Directory of Social Change is a registered charity no. 800517

First published 1987
Second edition 1990
Third edition 1992
Fourth edition 1994
Fifth edition 1996
Sixth edition 1998
Seventh edition 2000

Copyright © Directory of Social Change 2002

All rights reserved. No part of this book may be stored in a retrieval system or reproduced in any form whatsoever without prior permission in writing from the publisher. This book is sold subject to the condition that it shall not, by way of trade or otherwise, be lent, re-sold, hired out or otherwise circulated without the publisher's prior permission in any form of bindiong or cover other than that in which it is published, and without a similar condition including this condition being imposed on the subsequent purchaser.

ISBN 1 903991 25 0

British Library Cataloguing in Publication Data
A catalogue record for this book is available from the British Library

Cover design by Gabriele Kern
Text design by Gabriele Kern
Typeset by Tradespools, Frome

Other Directory of Social Change departments in London:
    Courses and Conferences: 020 7209 4949
    Charity Centre: 020 7391 4860
    Charityfair: 020 7391 4860
    Publicity: 020 7391 4900
    Research: 020 7391 4880

Directory of Social Change Northern Office:
    Federation House, Hope Street, Liverpool L1 9BW
    Courses and conferences: 0151 708 0117
    Research: 0151 708 0136

Contents

Introduction	5
How to use this guide	13
How to make an application	15
Occupational charities	19
Service and ex-service charities	71
Sickness and disability charities	89
National and general charities	105
Local charities	125
Advice organisations	383
Index	397

Introduction

Welcome to the eighth edition of *A Guide to Grants for Individuals in Need*. The main concern of the book is to list all sources of non-statutory help for people in financial need.

This guide continues to grow with every edition; it now contains 2,203 trusts with £289 million available each year, compared to 1,400 trusts giving £66 million in the first edition (1987). There are 229 trusts new to the guide, giving £4.7 million a year in total.

Help given by grant-making trusts is very small compared to the £100 billion given in non-contributory statutory benefits each year (figures from Department of Work and Pensions – which has replaced the Department of Social Security).

Grants made by charities in this guide range from £10 food vouchers to larger contributions such as grants for domestic items like washing machines, wheelchairs and house adaptations – although few will cover the whole cost of these. This kind of help does not overcome long-term financial problems, but it can be extremely valuable in helping to meet immediate needs, which the state does not currently cover.

This introduction looks at the trusts included in this guide and how to locate them, before discussing what help is available from them and how they can improve their roles. It also briefly looks at other funding sources for individuals, highlighting the need to explore all statutory sources available. Ashley Wood of Gaddum Centre has again provided a helpful section explaining how to make your application once the relevant trusts have been identified, see page 15.

At the end of the guide is a list of welfare agencies that can provide advice (not necessarily financial aid) to individuals. We have extended this from previous editions, which detailed sickness and disability organisations only, to include general welfare needs such as social circumstances.

Which trusts are included?

We aim to include all publicly registered charities (including those in Scotland and Northern Ireland, where there is no Charity Commission) which give at least £500 a year to individuals in need, although most give considerably more than this.

With a few exceptions, we do not include:
- ✗ organisations which give grants solely for educational purposes
- ✗ organisations which give grants to members only and not to dependants
- ✗ individual employer or company welfare funds
- ✗ Friendly Societies
- ✗ local branches of national charities, although they may raise money locally for cases of need
- ✗ organisations only providing services (such as home visiting) rather than cash (or in kind) grants.

Many of the trusts support individuals for educational purposes as well. These are all included in the sister guide to this book *The Educational Grants Directory*, which includes details of funding opportunities for all forms of education up to the end of a first degree, including apprenticeships, personal development and expeditions. Some trusts support organisations such as community groups. Others have large ongoing financial commitments (often providing housing). The entries in this guide concentrate solely on the trusts' grants to individuals in need.

How trusts are ordered in this guide

The trusts are separated into five sections: four UK-wide sections followed by a local section, broken down into nine countries/regions. The flow chart on page 14 shows how the guide works.

UK-wide trusts

Nearly 90% of the money in this book (over £254 million) is given by the 604 UK-wide trusts. They are divided into four sections:

Occupational charities   p19

This section contains about 333 charities which have a combined annual grant total of £66 million. These trusts benefit not simply the people who worked in a particular trade but also, in many cases, their widows/widowers and dependent children. Membership or previous membership of the particular institute can be required, but many are open to non-members. Length of service can sometimes be taken into account. Many of these trusts are members of Occupation Benevolent Fund Association, an umbrella organisation which represents this area of the sector. There are some occupations which have a number of funds covering them, and others which have none. For example, there are five trusts providing support to accountants in this guide, but none supporting personnel officers.

Service and ex-service charities   p71

This section includes 48 charities giving a total of £46 million. There is exceptionally thorough charitable provision for people who have served in the forces, whether as a regular or during national service. These are different from the other occupational funds as they support a large percentage of the male population over retirement age (many of them would have undertaken national service). Again, these usually also provide for the widows, widowers and dependent children of the core beneficiaries. Many of these funds have local voluntary workers who provide advice and practical help, and who in turn are backed up by professional staff and substantial resources. SSAFA Forces Help is an influential member of this sector, providing the well-used model, and often the initial contact and application form, for many of the regimental funds.

Sickness and disability charities   p89

These 82 charities together give about £114 million in grants to people with specific illnesses or disabilities. (This total includes over £66 million donated by The Independent Living Fund.) These trusts can help people (and often their families/carers) who are in financial need as a result of a particular illness or disability. Many of these also give advisory and other support, although for a fuller list of organisations providing these functions please see the list of advice organisations at the end of the guide.

National and general charities   p105

About 141 charities which operate UK-wide (or at least in more than one country or more than one region in England) and which are not tied to a particular trade, occupation or disability are included in this section. These range from those that have very wide objects, such as 'people in need', 'older people' or 'children' to members of particular religions or ethnic groups, and even people with particular dietary habits. They are among the best known and tend to be heavily oversubscribed. Together their grants total about £28 million.

Local charities

Included in this section are those trusts that only support individuals in Northern

INTRODUCTION

Ireland or Scotland or Wales or just one region of England. Trusts which are eligible for two of these geographical subsections have generally been given a full entry in one subsection and a cross reference in the other; trusts relevant to three or more of the subsections have generally been included in the national section. Charitable help is unequally distributed across the UK, with more money available in London and the south east of England than the rest of the UK. However, many of the main centres of population have at least one large trust able to give over £50,000 a year.

About 92% (1,869) of the trusts in this book are local charities giving over £34 million between them. Many are quite small (under £10,000 income a year).

The local section starts with details on how to use this section.

Unfortunately the section for Northern Ireland is very small, containing only 17 trusts (although they do give around £1.5 million a year). Very little information is available on charities in Northern Ireland, with no Charity Commission there and no proviso for charities to make information publicly available. Any further information would be gratefully received.

Who can receive help?

The Charity Commission leaflet CC4 entitled *Charities for the Relief of the Poor* includes the following information under the heading 'Modern meaning of "poor"'.

A person does not have to be destitute to qualify as 'poor'. Anyone who is in need, or suffering hardship or distress may be eligible for help. It is up to the trustees to make their own judgement as to whether a particular person qualifies for assistance. Generally speaking, anyone who cannot afford the normal things in life which most people take for granted would probably qualify for help. A person who normally has an acceptable standard of living but is suffering temporary hardship, perhaps because of an accident, a death in the family, or other setback, could also qualify for help.

People may qualify for help from the charity whether or not they are eligible for state benefits. Some people who already receive their full entitlement of state benefits may need additional help. Equally, some people who are not entitled to state benefits may sometimes need help because of particular circumstances. Each person's actual needs and financial circumstances must be assessed individually.

People who are unable to claim state benefits should not believe that charitable trusts will not support them. Similarly, people in paid employment on a low income should not be afraid to apply just because they are working. The New Policy Institute has found that half of all children and adults below retirement age have incomes beneath the low-income threshold, despite living in households where at least one adult works. Many welfare organisations have complained the minimum wage has not been set at a level that gives a liveable income to many of the people who receive it. Indeed, the London School of Economics says there were 1.4 million children in the UK living in poverty in 2001, despite having a working parent.

Some trusts complain that the people they wish to support refuse to accept charity and want to maintain their independence. A charitable trust is public money being held for the benefit of a specific group of people; just as people are encouraged to access any statutory funds they can, they should also accept all charitable money which has been set aside for them.

But it is not just people who are classified as 'poor' who are eligible for support from trusts. The Charity Commission leaflet CC6 *Charities for the Relief of Sickness* includes the following information under the question 'Who can be helped?':

Trustees can provide or pay for items, services and facilities to ease the suffering or assist the recovery of people who are:

- *sick*
- *convalescent*
- *disabled*
- *or infirm.*

The words sick and sickness include those suffering from:

- *a mental disorder, or*
- *an addiction*

unless the charity's governing document makes it clear that this is not permitted.

Before giving any assistance, we strongly advise the trustees to satisfy themselves that in each case the applicant has:

- *a clear need for the assistance*
- *that the benefits proposed are related to that need*
- *and that the benefit or assistance proposed is not readily available from other non-charitable sources.*

What is interesting is the omission of any mention of the ability of the applicant to cover the costs of the need. This is not because grants for relief of sickness are not means-tested, but simply because these trusts exist to relieve physical need. Many trusts believe that people should not lose their life savings and standard of living to buy an essential item they could afford, but which would leave them financially vulnerable for the future. CC6 differentiates between organisations that attempt to relieve sickness and organisations for the relief of the sick poor, which can only support people who are both sick and poor.

Although these are the areas trusts may support, it would be wrong to believe that any given trust will support all of these needs. Each trust in this guide has a trust deed, a legal document stating who can and cannot be supported. As mentioned earlier, we have broken down the trusts in this guide to aid the reader in identifying those which might be of relevance to them, and under no circumstances should an individual approach a trust they are not eligible for.

Many trusts have complained to us that they receive applications outside their scope, which their trust deed prevents them from supporting, even if they would like to do so. These applicants have no chance of being supported and bring two responses from the trustees: annoyance at the number of applicants who waste their time and resources, and sorrow at the needs they are made aware of but unable to relieve. It is not the number of trusts that you apply to which affects your chance of support but the relevance of them.

What types of help can be given?

Here are examples of help available from charities taken from the leaflet CC4. It should not be seen as a comprehensive list.

Grants of money in the form of:

- *weekly allowances for a limited period to meet a particular need*
- *special payments to relieve sudden distress*
- *payments of travelling expenses for visiting people, for example in hospital, convalescent home, children's home, prison or other similar place, particularly where more frequent visits are desirable than payments from public funds will allow*
- *payment to meet expenses associated with visiting people (as mentioned above) for example, childminding, accommodation and refreshments etc.*
- *donations to other charities accommodating those in need in the area of the charity, such as almshouses, homes or hostels for the old, infirm or homeless*
- *payments to assist in meeting electricity, gas and water bills*
- *payment of television licence fees.*

The provision of items *(either outright or, if expensive and appropriate, on loan) such as:*

- *furniture, bedding, clothing, food, fuel, heating appliances*
- *washing machines and fridges*
- *radio or television sets for the lonely, the bedridden or the housebound.*

Payment for services *such as:*

- *essential house decorating*

INTRODUCTION

- *insulation and repairs*
- *laundering*
- *meals on wheels*
- *outings and entertainment*
- *childminding.*

The provision of facilities such as:

- *the supply of tools or books; or payment of fees for instruction or examinations, or of travelling expenses to help the recipients to earn their living; or equipment and funds for recreational pursuits or training intended to bring the quality of life of the beneficiaries to a reasonable standard.*

Charities for the relief of the poor may give extra help for poor people who are also **sick, convalescent, infirm, or with disabilities,** *whether mentally or physically.*

Grants of money in the form of:

- *special payments to relieve sickness or infirmity*
- *payment of travelling expenses on entering or leaving hospitals, convalescent homes, or similar institutions, or for outpatient consultations*
- *payment towards the cost of adaptations to the homes of disabled people*
- *payment of telephone installation charges and rentals.*

The provision of items such as:

- *expensive food for special diets*
- *medical items, or equipment such as wheelchairs either outright or, if expensive but appropriate, on loan.*

The provision of services such as:

- *exchange of library books*
- *gardening*
- *bathing, hair washing, shaving, foot care*
- *help in the home*
- *nursing aid, physiotherapy in the home*
- *shopping*
- *reading, sitting-in, audio tapes for the housebound*
- *travelling companions.*

The provision of facilities such as:

- *arrangements for a period of rest or change of environment*
- *treatment at convalescent homes or other institutions*
- *transport.*

Many of the larger benevolent funds in this book are members of the Association of Charity Officers (ACO). An ACO report entitled *The assessment of applicant's needs for grants* said:

The most common items for which ACO member funds give grants to applicants are beds, washing machines and washer/dryers, vacuum cleaners, cookers, home repairs and redecorations, clothing including clothing for children, wheelchairs and stairlifts, and holidays, which appear to be seen as one of the most useful subjects of grants.

The report went on to state:

ACO member funds differed most greatly in their attitudes to giving grants in the cases of buildings insurance, clearance of debts, small business start-up, newspapers, and adaptations. Some funds make grants for these purposes whilst other funds refuse such applications.

Most trusts in this guide cannot provide all the help listed above. Generally their help falls into three categories:

One-off grants

Some trusts will only give one-off cash payments. This means that they will award a single lump sum (say £50) which is paid by cheque/postal order either direct to the applicant, to the welfare agency applying on the person's behalf, or to another suitable third party. No more help will be considered until the applicant has submitted a new application, and trusts are usually unwilling to give more than one such grant per person per year.

Recurrent grants

Other trusts will only pay recurrent grants, usually weekly allowances, often of up to the current 'disregard' level. (The disregard level is the maximum income a person on Income Support can receive in addition to their state benefit before it affects their Income Support calculations. The current disregard level is £20 a week in most cases.) These payments can be made quarterly (so each year the applicant receives four grants of up to £260 each), or in smaller, more regular amounts.

Weekly payments can be higher than this, particularly if the applicant requires expensive treatment/medicine on a regular basis, or has some other high ongoing cost.

Some trusts will give either one-off or recurrent payments according to what is more appropriate for the applicant.

Grants in kind

Occasionally grants are given in the form of vouchers or are paid directly to a shop or store in the form of credit to enable the applicant to obtain food, clothing or other prearranged items. Some charities still deliver coal!

More commonly, especially with disability aids or other technical equipment, the charity will either give the equipment itself to the applicant (rather than the money) or loan it free of charge or at a low rental as long as the applicant needs it. More common items, such as telephones and televisions, can also be given as equipment because the charity can get better trade terms than the individual.

Ex-gratia payments

Some trusts also make ex-gratia payments. The Charity Commission leaflet CC7 *Ex Gratia Payments by Charities* describes them as being where:

- the trustees believe that they are under a moral obligation to make the payment
- but the trustees are not under any legal obligation to make the payment
- and the trustees have no power under the governing document of the charity to make the payment
- and the trustees cannot justify the payment as being in the interests of the charity.

Although this suggests that charities should not make such payments, the leaflet goes on to advise trustees that if it is a payment that they feel an individual would be morally obliged to make, the trust can make the payment. These payments are usually set out in the will from which the trust was established.

Statutory funding

Whilst there is a wide range of types of grants that can be given and a variety of reasons they can be made, there is one area trusts cannot support. No charitable trust is allowed to provide funds which replace statutory funding. The reason for this is that if a trust gives £100 say, to an individual who could have received those much needed funds from statutory sources, then it is the state rather than the individual who is benefiting from the grant.

However, it could be argued that the lines defining statutory funding are slightly blurred. An ACO report in 1997 (*Charities Helping People in Need*), based on a small study of members and their working with local authorities, concluded: *Help from the Government via the Social Fund with essential needs for the poor is now discretionary. There is no consistency over the use of Section 17 funds to help with children's needs. Charities face an almost impossible task in trying to assess how to relieve need without replacing statutory funds.*

In July 2002, Health Secretary Alan Milburn announced a plan to give older people a choice between provision of services and a cash grant towards home help. This funding should relieve many trusts that provide grants to enable people to remain in their own home. But since the payments will only be of 'hundreds of pounds a week', quite where state help ends and trust helps begin is unclear.

The Citizens Advice Bureau Service, which provided advice on problem debt totalling £1.2 billion in 2000/01, stated in October 2001 that it found over half the people in England and Wales are unaware of their

Introduction

basic welfare rights, including access to statutory funds. These concerns have been echoed by Help the Aged, which claimed in June 2002 that £1.8 billion a year of statutory funds available to low-income older people is being left unclaimed. We suggest individuals should contact a welfare agency to check they are claiming all the assistance they are entitled to. A list of advice organisations is included on page 383, broken down into organisations such as Citizen's Advice Bureaux who can perform a check on any individual, to more specialist organisations dealing with only, for instance, older people, single parents or disability groups.

What trusts should do

Given the estimated levels of state funding not claimed, it would appear justified to suggest that some trusts have inadvertently been supporting the state with their donations. The Charity Commission aims to curb this by providing the following advice to trustees in leaflet CC4:

We recommend that trustees familiarise themselves with the system of state benefits, including how a person's state benefits may be affected by receiving a grant by a charity. For example, 'one off' charitable payments may be treated as capital for Income Support purposes and may affect a person's benefit entitlement if by receiving a payment their capital exceeds current capital thresholds. When assessing a person's income or financial circumstances, trustees need to count as part of that income any state benefits they know the person is entitled to receive. Trustees should not make payments to a person simply to replace unclaimed benefits. Instead we suggest that trustees encourage potential beneficiaries to claim their full entitlement of state benefits. Leaflets are available from local offices of the Benefits Agency about the benefits available to: people who are elderly, disabled, sick or unemployed; those on low incomes; and single parent families.

Where a charity identifies a service affecting its users which is not being provided to the required statutory level out of public funds, it is entitled to consider whether there is anything it can reasonably do to persuade the public body to provide funds for that service. Our guidance Charities and Contracts (CC37) provides some more information on this.

We advise trustees to keep in regular contact with local Benefits Agency offices and with the Social Service Department of the local authority. By consulting about specific cases trustees can find out how to help a person with charitable funds without affecting the state benefits which that person may be receiving. Similarly the Benefits Agency and local authority can develop an understanding of the work of the charity.

Whilst this advice relates in a large part to the maximum disregard level of £20 a week (or £1,040 a year) that individuals can receive before their benefits are cut, it should be read in relation also to other sources of funding, such as the Minimum Income Guarantee which Help the Aged claim many eligible people are unaware of. This requirement of trustees to make sure they are aware of how people can help themselves should not be seen as an additional burden on the trusts; it is merely a way of enabling the trusts to help their beneficiaries without making grants, thus allowing them to give the maximum possible assistance to the maximum number of applicants.

But it is not just statutory funding that trusts should be monitoring; the needs of their beneficiaries also have to be taken into account. Just as the Charity Commission has defined a modern meaning of 'poor', trusts should evaluate the needs of the people they are aiming to benefit.

The leaflet CC4 offers the following advice to trustees to make their charities more effective:

Trustees of some charities for the relief of the poor may find it difficult to spend all the charity's income in the way the governing document demands. This may be because the level of poverty in the charity's area of benefit has decreased significantly in recent times, and there are fewer needy people. In these circumstances trustees must take positive steps to search for potential beneficiaries, for example by:

- *asking the local Benefits Agency office and Social Services Department to let them know of any people living within the charity's area of benefit whose needs cannot fully be met by state payments*
- *advertising in the local newspaper*
- *or contacting trustees of other charities and voluntary organisations, particularly those involved in welfare.*

Whilst these measures might work for trusts working in one community, those working over a larger region might have to look for a wider picture. The New Policy Institute, in conjuction with The Joseph Rowntree Foundation, has set-up a website, www.poverty.org.uk, which publishes their findings on the changing face of poverty in the UK. It aims to remain as up-to-date as possible and provides links to all other relevant documents and sites on the internet. It is well worth looking at to assess the most pressing needs.

The National Association of Citizens Advice Bureaux have investigated the reasons why people get into debt, and have found that whilst job loss and low incomes were the key factors, other issues such as relationship breakdown and illness were also significant factors. Indeed, the study found that a change in personal circumstances was a larger factor in pushing people into debt than general overspending.

The Refugee Council has researched the financial situations brought to the attention of refugee organisations. It found that most organisations had clients who were: experiencing hunger; unable to purchase clothes or shoes; maintain good health; stay in touch with their families; and pay for children's bus fares to school. Indeed, every organisation they consulted had at least one client unable to meet a special dietary need. Research of this nature is something which trusts should be looking at if they are to maintain a knowledge of need amongst the people they are intended to benefit.

Trusts should also assess what difference their grants make. One or two trusts in this guide are restricted to making grants to inhabitants of relatively wealthy parishes and appear to have great difficulty finding individuals in need of financial support.

Most trusts, however, receive a constant flow of applications for worthy causes. Where the objects of the trust permit it, we would like to see trusts increasingly forming clear policies on who they do support, targeting those most in need.

Again, the Charity Commission leaflet CC4 states:

We recommend that trustees of all charities regularly review their use of the charity's funds, so as to ensure that the money is spent most effectively in carrying out the purpose of the charity. These reviews are particularly important for trustees of charities for the relief of the poor. This is because of continuing change in economic and social circumstances, changes in the nature of public provision and the vulnerability of the poor. Trustees should ask themselves whether they are in fact relieving poverty, and whether they are spending the charity's funds in the way most helpful way.

Some charities persist in their policy of dividing their income by the number of pensioners in their area of benefit and giving them all a Christmas gift, usually of less than £10 each. The Charity Commission states:

Rather than trying to spread the charity's resources thinly among as many people as possible, trustees could consider whether it might be more effective to target their funds, by giving larger benefits to a smaller number of people who are most in need.

There are trusts we have come across that bemoan a lack of applicants, yet only give 'a drop in the ocean' rather than a large enough sum to relieve need.

However, some trusts are taking steps in the right direction. South Ayrshire Council, for instance, administers nearly 100 trusts, which they are hoping to streamline into just three.

Improving charities

While some, particularly national, charities produce clear guidelines, others, especially local charities, do not. We would encourage all charities to consider at least the following:

- trusts should publish a policy setting out how they assess applications, to improve the profile of their work, and to limit unsuccessful appeals
- local charities could seek to expand their resources to meet new or more widespread needs
- if trustees can only meet twice a year, they should aim to cover the peak periods. For example, if a trust gives heating grants these would be most useful if distributed in early winter
- charities should also aim to ensure that needs can be met as rapidly as possible, for example by empowering the clerk or a small number of trustees to make payments up to a certain limit (say £100)
- charities should ensure they are very well known in their area of benefit. We recommend that each charity (depending on its eligibility restrictions) writes to at least the following: all welfare agencies (especially the citizen's advice bureaux); all churches, community centres and other public meeting points, and the offices of the relevant local authority.

There are also a few trusts where the need in the area of benefit is not sufficient for all the income to be spent and/or the needs have changed from those that the trust was originally set up to meet. In this case the trust, in consultation with the Charity Commission, can consider extending its area of benefit or altering (expanding) the type of help it can give.

We did come across one or two worrying practices during our research. One trust asks applicants to include an employer's certificate of earnings, expecting applicants to ask their manager for proof they are low paid. Another trust told us they send a uniformed police officer to interview applicants. We feel that individuals should be free to apply to trusts without having to justify their situation to their neighbours and colleagues. Trusts should make sure that their procedures are open and equal to everybody, especially those least able to communicate their needs. Indeed, one trust asked to be omitted from the guide, telling us it knows exactly who is in need. It has not received an application in over 13 years and we believe that accepting unsolicited applications might open the trustees' eyes to the hidden hardship amongst other potential beneficiaries. Similarly, we came across many trusts in our research that told us that the local vicar, for instance, tells them who is in need and the trustees act accordingly – a practice we feel may deter eligible applicants with different religious beliefs.

The Charity Commission has produced a number of leaflets providing excellent advice to charity trustees and administrators. Ones of particular relevance to this guide are: CC4 – *Charities for the Relief of the Poor*; CC6 – *Charities for the Relief of Sickness*; and RR3 – *Charities for the Relief of Unemployment*. They are available at the Charity Commission's website (www.charity-commission.gov.uk).

Are trusts the answer?

So far, all the information contained in this introduction has presumed that individuals should approach trusts for funding, but what are the other options?

Statutory sources

There are a lot of funding opportunities available to individuals from the state. As the exact details of these sources are different in different countries in the UK, and in some instances amongst different local authorities, comprehensive details are beyond the scope of this guide. Full details should be available from government departments such as benefits agencies and social services, as well as many of the welfare agencies listed on page 383. The Department for Work and Pensions' website (www.dwp.gov.uk) also has a comprehensive list with full information on who is eligible and how they can apply. Whilst many of the programmes are well-known, some of them have not received the same levels of publicity. Did you know, for instance, that people disabled as a result of a vaccination can apply for a large one-off payment from the government? Or that people widowed over the age of 45 without dependent children can claim a bereavement allowance for a year based on their late partner's National Insurance contributions?

However, there are two potential sources of funding which we will cover briefly. The Social Fund is a discretionary system of lump sum payments, grants and loans of up to £1,000 towards important costs that are difficult to afford from regular income to people who are either receiving some form of income support or who are improving an essential health and safety risk. The fund operates within a budget, meaning that if it is fully subscribed then no additional loans can be made. One Parent Families have criticised the fund for helping the best timed applications rather than the most needy, and have also questioned the relevance of the state making loans, rather than grants, to those in the greatest need.

The Minimum Income Guarantee ensures people aged over 60 with savings of less than £12,000 (£16,000 if in residential care or a nursing home) who work for less than 16 hours (24 if they have a partner) have a weekly income of at least £98.15 if they are single and £149.80 for couples. Top-up figures are available for: people who are disabled and living alone or with another disabled person; a carer receiving Invalid Care Allowance; housing costs not covered by Housing Benefit; people receiving Housing Benefit towards rent from the local council; or people who receive, or whose partner receives, Child Benefit. Further information for this support can be found by telephoning 0800 028 1111. (These details were correct as of August 2002; figures usually change each April.)

Disaster appeals

If there has been a large unexpected hardship that is beyond the scope of being relieved from statutory or charitable sources, then one possibility is to establish a disaster appeal. These are commonly established as a public response to a well publicised event, such as the Hillsborough football disaster in 1989, where the public wish to show their support. They can also be established in response to a personal misfortune. The Mark Davies Injured Riders Fund, for instance, was established to support injured riders by the parents of a talented rider killed during the Burghley Horse Trials. Appeals can also be established to aid a particular individual if they have needs which gain high levels of public sympathy and little time to apply for statutory or charitable sources, such as the appeal for Cheshire childcarer Louise Woodward in the 1990s. Disaster appeals can be to relieve an epidemic rather than an individual case, or to leave a lasting legacy.

There are many issues concerning the relevance of a disaster appeal, and whether it can claim charitable status. For an appeal to be charitable, it must be for the public benefit, not just for the benefit of an individual or a collective. Generally speaking, for an appeal to be charitable, it must be possible for people to become eligible in the future and it must be to relieve a financial need. The Penlee Lifeboat Disaster Appeal, for instance, received much public support after a great loss of life off the Penlee shores, but was rejected for charitable status for two reasons: firstly, it was only supporting a closed selection and families; and secondly, some of the families benefiting were not in financial need. Had the appeal been established to support the close relatives of people killed at sea who are in financial need it would have been charitable, but not under the noted terms. This is why there was much controversy about the post September 11 appeal funds in the US, which raised money for a select number of families in the heart of Manhattan.

Receiving charitable status for the appeal will make tax benefits available to the appeal itself and its donors. It would also

INTRODUCTION

make the appeal more enticing to corporate donors. However, any charity in England and Wales receiving an income of over £1,000 in any single year has to register with the Charity Commission or it is committing an illegal act. This means that any trustee raising £1,001 and putting it to good use is actually breaking the law if it has not registered with the Commission. This situation is not particularly helped by the Charity Commission itself, which rejects half of all applications for registration, often for administrative reasons rather than because the aims of the organisation are not charitable. However, the government report *Private Action, Public Benefit*, published in September 2002, suggests that this may change, recommending that charities with an income of less than £10,000 should no longer be obliged to register.

There can be advantages to being non-charitable. The Charity Commission leaflet CC40 *Disaster Appeals* states:

Charitable funds, being essentially public in their nature, cannot be used to give individuals benefits over and above those appropriate to their needs; and the operation of a charitable trust will be subject to our [Charity Commission's] scrutiny.

This restriction does not apply to non-charitable appeals, which may give as much funding to beneficiaries as they wish, regardless of levels of need. However, thought must be given to the moral implications of this and how the fund's surplus will be spent; non-charitable appeals have the same obligation as charitable appeals to act in accordance what they were legally established to do. CC40 raises the issues around how surplus funds should be spent, saying:

It sometimes happens that publicity given to individual suffering moves people to give. In such a case it is particularly desirable for those who make appeals to indicate whether or not the appeal is for a charitable fund.

It is also desirable for those who give to say whether their gift is meant for the benefit of the individual, or for charitable purposes including helping the individual so far as is charitable. If no such intention is stated, then the donation should be acknowledged with an indication how it will be used if the donor does not dissent.

Those who make appeals should bear in mind the possibility that generous response may produce more than is appropriate for the needs of the individual, and should be sure to ask themselves what should be done with any surplus.

Thus, if a child has a disease, the alternatives are:

- to appeal for the benefit of the child
- or to appeal for charitable purposes relating to the suffering of the child, such as may help them and others in the same misfortune, for example by helping to find a cure.

It may be that the child will not live long, in which case, that child may not be able to enjoy the generosity shown to them as an individual; alternatively, the child may be intended to receive as much as possible because they face a lifetime's suffering.

Disaster appeals are only really relevant in extreme circumstances, and after much thought or enquiry. For further information please see CC40 available on the Charity Commission website, or telephone their helpline on 0870 333 0123. The British Red Cross has its own disaster appeal helpline offering advice, which is 020 7201 5027.

Companies

Many employers are unhappy to see former members of staff, or their dependants, living in need or distress. Few have formal arrangements but a letter or telephone call to the personnel manager should establish if help is possible.

Most large companies give charitable grants, although most have a policy of only funding organisations (possibly because charities have more ways of publicising this support than individuals do). Many that will support individuals have their own charitable trusts, and therefore are included in this guide.

A growing trend is the recent rise in water companies setting up their own charitable trusts, which give to individuals who are struggling to pay their utility bills. This provides much relief to the individuals involved, lessening the financial burden upon them, and ensuring that no legal action will be taken against them for non-payment. However, questions could be asked about who the major beneficiaries of this practice are. The water companies are using the tax incentives attached to giving to reclaim bills that could not otherwise be paid. Whilst many have recently started supporting organisations providing debt advice, it appears this could be seen as another strategy to improve the ability of the less-well-off to afford their prices.

One of the trusts in this guide, Marham Poor's Land Trust, informed us that a water company, whose trust is contained within this guide, is still paying a peppercorn rent on its land despite the lease ending, and being renewable, in October 1999. The water company has refused to discuss increasing the rent, despite it being the land-owning charity's right, and it is also refusing to pay the £240 a year shooting rights on the land. Here is one case where a water company is taking money off the local voluntary sector and pumping it straight back into its profits.

Community foundations

A relatively new trend amongst grantmaking circles is the development of community foundations. These are community groups which are generally countywide (although Scotland and Wales have their own countrywide foundations, and the spread throughout England is currently uneven). They consist of many small trusts, which have pooled their resources to gain maximum levels of income whilst retaining their independence in considering applications and policies. The Community Foundation (serving Tyne and Wear and Northumberland) is a good example of this, allowing anybody able to donate £30,000 to the foundation to have their own trust, supporting whatever causes in the region they wish. A growing number of small businesses are investing in these schemes, and opportunities for funding are growing all the time. Whilst most of these trusts only support organisations, many of them also have funds available for individuals and therefore are included in this guide. In August 2002, there were many foundations across the country building up the funds to establish themselves, and many established funds that were not yet giving to individuals. Community Foundation Network have a list of existing and emerging foundations on their website (www.communityfoundations.org.uk).

Vicars, priests and ministers of religion

There may be informal arrangements within a church, mosque etc. to help people in need. Church of England vicars are often trustees of local charities which are too small to be included in the guide or which we have missed.

Hospitals

Most hospitals have patient welfare funds, but they are little known even within the hospitals and so are little used. It may take some time to locate an appropriate contact. Start with the trust fund administrator or the treasurer's department of the health authority.

Local organisations

Rotary Clubs, Lions Clubs and Round Tables etc. are active in welfare provision. Usually they support groups rather than individuals and policies vary in different towns, but some welfare agencies (such as citizen's advice bureaux) have a working relationship with these organisations and keep up-to-date lists of contacts. All enquiries should be made on behalf of the individual by a recognised agency.

Orders

Masonic and Buffalo lodges, Foresters Associations and other organisations exist for the mutual benefit of their members. Spouses and children of members (or deceased members) may also benefit, but people unconnected with these orders are unlikely to. Applications should be made to the lodge where the parent/spouse is or was a member.

Hobbies and interests

People with a particular hobby or interest should find out whether this offers any opportunities for funding. Included in this guide are a number of county bowling and football associations which exist to relieve people who are in need, but there may be many more which are not registered with the Charity Commission, or have less than £500 a year to give, but are of great value to the people they can help. It is likely that other sports and interests have similar governing bodies wish to help their members.

Educational support

This guide only deals with grants for the relief of need, ignoring trusts that can support individuals for educational purposes. However, many educational trusts are prepared to give grants to schoolchildren for uniforms, for instance. Receiving financial support for the cost of uniforms would obviously enable parents to spend the money budgeted for that purpose on other needs, so people with children of school age should check for any educational grants available to them. For information on statutory funds, contact your local educational authority or enquire for information at the office of the individual's school. For charitable funding, this guide's sister publication, *The Educational Grants Directory*, should provide the relevant information.

Charity shops

Some charity shops will provide clothing if the applicant has a letter of referral from a recognised welfare agency.

Getting help

Unfortunately, none of these methods can offer the quick fix that many people would want to relieve the stress and mounting debt that may be engulfing individuals. Applying for grants can be a daunting experience, especially if you are unfamiliar with the process; it is probably worth starting with the help of a sympathetic advisor. Most citizens advice bureaux have money advice workers or volunteers trained in basic money advice work. If you find that you are in financial need try going to the nearest citizen's advice bureau and talk to them about your financial difficulties. They may be able to help write an application to an appropriate charity, know of a welfare benefit you could claim or be able to re-negotiate some of your debt repayments on your behalf. They will certainly be able to help you minimise your expenditure and budget effectively.

Whilst waiting for funding to come through, here is some advice that Citizens Advice Bureau Network published in September 2001 to help people dealing with debt.

- Don't panic and don't ignore the problem – it can seem tempting to stuff bills and threatening letters unopened into a drawer, but they won't go away.
- Avoid borrowing further to try and pay off existing debt – this is likely to lead to more problems in the long run.
- Talk to your creditors – don't just stop payments without explaining why. They can sometimes be more understanding than you'd expect.
- Work out which debts are your priorities – mortgage, rent, council tax, child maintenance, utilities – and pay them first. Don't fall into the trap of paying whoever shouts loudest first.
- Work out a budget that covers all your income and essential outgoings. Only offer to pay off debts at a rate you can keep up – it is easy to be panicked into offering more than you can afford.
- Think twice before paying for debt advice – the CAB has outlets all over the country and many years of experience helping with debt problems and negotiating with creditors.

So you've decided trusts are for you?

When you have found relevant trusts that may be worth looking into further, read the entries through carefully. Many trusts have several criteria which potential applicants must meet. Some trusts publish guidelines to assist applicants. If so, get hold of them before making an application, along with an application form if there is one.

Some trusts welcome an initial telephone call from the individual or a third party, to enquire whether the application is suitable. Many of the correspondents for local trusts, however, administer the trust in their free time from home and may not be available during the day.

Many of the trusts in this guide state that unsolicited applications are not considered, or that only applicants known to the trustees are supported. This should not be seen as a reason to avoid approaching the trust. Some of the trusts in this guide receive many applications and can only help a small percentage of them, if any, in any one year. This means a particularly suitable unsolicited application, or from somebody unknown to the trustees, could be supported.

However, applicants should fear the worst if they are applying to these trusts, and should indicate in their letters that if they are unsuccessful they do not expect a response.

How to make an application on p15 goes into these issues in more detail.

Acknowledgements

Throughout this introduction, we have commented on the Charity Commission's guidelines and advice. Whilst we are aware that the Charity Commission only has rule over England and Wales, readers in Northern Ireland and Scotland (as well as the Isle of Man and the Channel Islands) should note that although the exact nature of charitable law differs in these countries, the spirit and guidance remains the same throughout the UK, and the Charity Commission's advice should be seen as being just as relevant.

We are extremely grateful to the many people, trust officers and others who have helped compile this guide. To name them all would be impossible. Over 95% of the trusts in this guide either replied to our letters or spoke to us on the telephone, the vast majority of whom were very helpful. We are also once again indebted to the staff of the Liverpool office of the Charity Commission.

However, although drafts of all the entries were sent to the charities concerned, and any corrections noted and incorporated, the text – and any mistakes within it – remain ours rather than theirs. We are similarly grateful to Ashley Wood of Gaddum Centre for his continued help with parts of the editorial text and model application form.

Request for further information

The research for this book was done as carefully as we were able, but there will be relevant charities that we have missed and some of the information is incomplete or will become out-of-date. If any reader comes across omissions or mistakes in this guide, please let us know so we can rectify them in future. A telephone call or e-mail to the Research Department of the Directory of Social Change Northern Office (0151 708 0136; e-mail: north@dsc.org.uk) is all that is needed. We are also always looking for ways to improve other guides and would appreciate any comments, positive or negative, about this guide, or suggestions on what other information would be useful for inclusion when we research the ninth edition.

How to use this Guide

Below is a typical trust entry, showing the format we have used to present the information obtained from each of the trusts.
On the following page is a quick reference flow chart to sources of help. We recommend that you follow the order indicated on the flow chart, to look at each section of the guide and find trusts that are relevant to you.

Eligibility
This states who is eligible to apply for a grant. It can include restrictions on age, family circumstances, occupation, ethnic origin, place of residence and so.

Annual grant total
The total amount of money given in grants to individuals in the last financial year for which figures were available. Other financial information may be given where relevant.

Correspondent
The main person to contact, nominated by the trustees. Often the correspondent is the trust's solicitor or accountants, who may just pass applications on to the trustees and therefore will not be able to help with telephone enquiries.

The Fictitious Trust

Eligibility: Children and young people up to 25 years of age who are in need. Preference is given to children of single parent families and/or those who come from a disadvantaged or unstable family background.

Types of grants: Small one-off grants, to help in cases of short-term need. The trust gives grants for a wide range of needs, including payment of utility bills, furniture, tv licence fee and medical equipment. The maximum grant is £250.

No grants for rent arrears or debts.

Annual grant total: 140 grants totalled £25,000 in 2001.

Applications: On a form available from the correspondent, submitted either directly by the individual or via a welfare agency or citizen's advice bureau. Applications are considered in January, April, July and October.

Correspondent: Mrs I M Helpful, Charities Administrator, 7 Pleasant Road, London SN0 0ZZ (020 7123 4567; Fax: 020 7123 4568).

Other information: The trust also gives grants to local organisations.

Types of grants
Specifies whether the trust gives one-off, recurrent grants or pensions, the size of grants given and what grants are actually given for, such as utility bills, household equipment, travel expenses to hospital, mobility aids and medical equipment.

Applications
Including how to apply, who should make the application (for instance, the individual or a third party) and when to submit an application.

Other information
This contains miscellaneous further information about the trust.

How to USE THIS GUIDE

How to identify sources of help – Quick reference flowchart

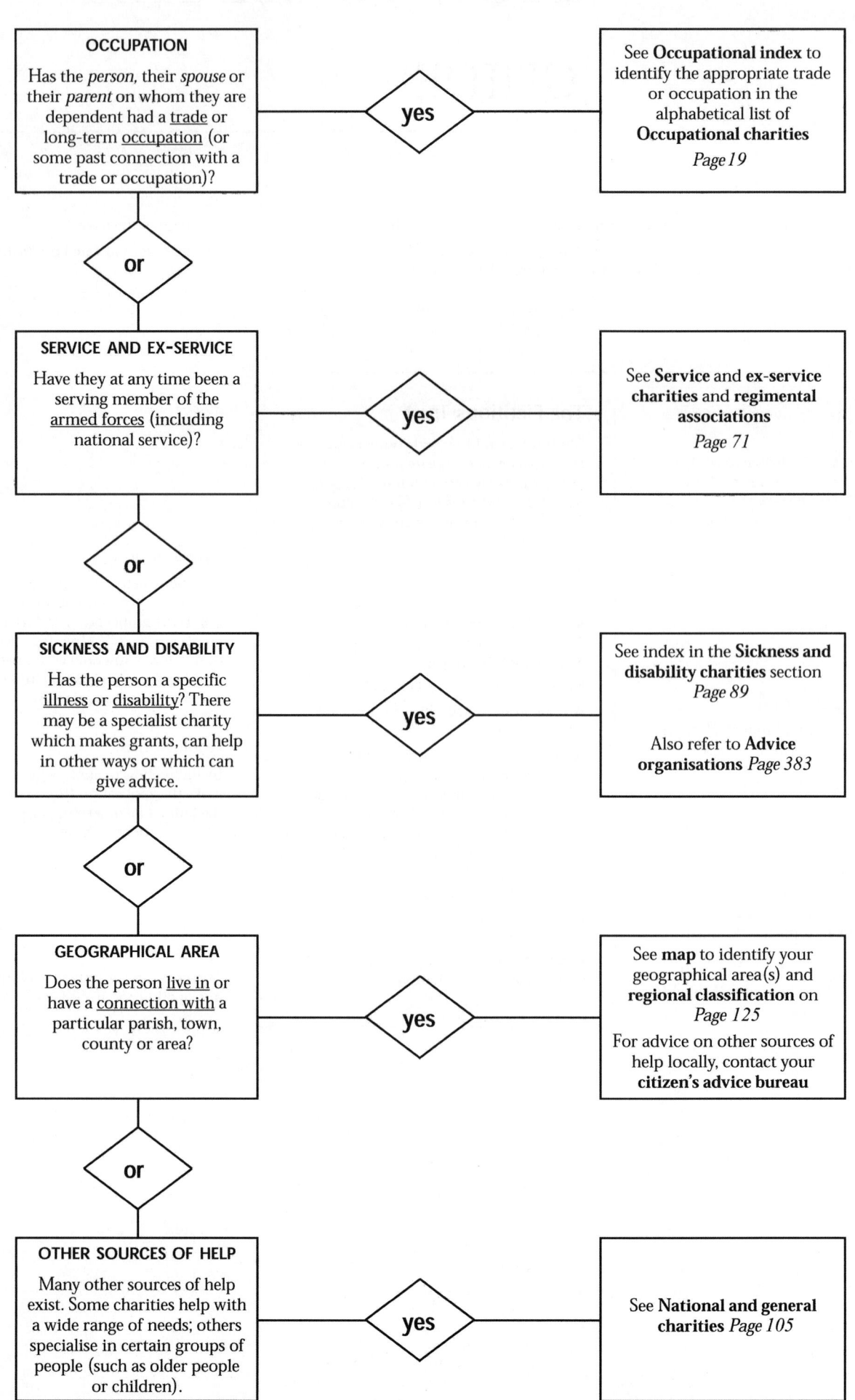

How to make an application

Ashley Wood, Gaddum Centre

Once the appropriate charities have been identified, the next stage is the application itself. People often find making applications difficult and those who might benefit sometimes fail to do so because of the quality of the application submitted.

This article gives guidelines both to individuals applying directly and to welfare agencies applying on behalf of individuals on how to make good, clear and relevant applications.

The application form

The first stage in submitting an application is the question of application forms.

Applications on agency letter headings or personal letters direct from the applicant, no matter how well presented, are fairly pointless if the charity being approached has a specific application form which must be completed. This obvious point is often overlooked. It is frustrating when the application is returned with a blank form requesting substantially the same information as has already been submitted. The resulting delay mean missing a committee meeting where the application would have been considered and a considerable wait until the next one.

Trust entries in this guide usually indicate when a particular application form is needed, but if there is any doubt the applicant should make a preliminary telephone call to the trust.

Who submits the application?

Again, it is important that the application is sent by an appropriate person. The guide usually indicates whether an individual in need can apply on his/her own behalf, or whether a third party (professional or otherwise) must apply for them.

With the current trend towards 'empowerment' of service users, advisory bodies sometimes simply advise families of funds they can approach themselves. However, most charities now require applications to be made by, for example, a professional person. Therefore, the individual in need may need to press the agency to make an application on his/her behalf.

The questions

When application forms are used, the questions asked sometimes cause problems, often because they don't appear relevant. Applications sometimes fail to realise all charities are governed by criteria laid down in their trust deeds and usually specific questions are designed to ensure these criteria are met.

For example, questions concerning date and place of birth are often answered very vaguely. 'Date of birth' is sometimes answered with 'late 50's' or, even worse, 'elderly'. Such a reply reflects the appearance of the person in question and not their age! If the charity can only consider applications for those below a pensionable age, and the request was on behalf of a women, then the above answers would be too imprecise.

Equally 'Place of birth' is sometimes answered with 'Great Britain' which is not precise enough for funds whose area of benefit is regional or local. It is always better to state the place of birth as well as town and county, even if they are different from the current home address.

Where application forms are not requested, it is essential to prepare clear, concise applications which provide the following.

1. A description of the person or family and the need which exists

Although applications should be concise, they must provide sufficient detail, such as:

(a) the applicant's name, address, place and date of birth

(b) the applicant's family circumstances (i.e. married/partners, separated/divorced/single parent, widow/widower, the number and ages of dependent children)

(c) the applicant's financial position (i.e. breakdown of weekly income and expenditure and, where appropriate, DWP/housing benefit awarded/refused, savings, credit debts, rent/gas/electricity arrears, etc.)

(d) other relevant information, such as how the need arose (e.g. illness, loss of job, marital separation, etc.) and why other sources (especially DWP/housing departments) have not helped. If applying to a disability charity, applicants should include details of the nature and effects of the disability (although see Medical information below); if applying to a local charity, how long have they lived in the locality.

The application which says 'this is a poor family who need their gas reconnecting' is unlikely to receive proper consideration. It is also worth mentioning that applications are dealt with in the strictest of confidence, so applicant's should aim to provide as much information as is relevant. The form printed after this article may serve as a useful checklist to ensure that all relevant information is included for the particular application.

2. How much money is requested and what it will be used for

This second point appears to cause the most difficulty. Applications are often received without any indication of the amount required or without sufficient explanation as to the desired use of the money.

For example, an applicant may have multiple debts totalling over £1,000. A grant of £100 would clear one of the debts and free much-needed weekly income. So the applicant approaches a suitable charity for a grant of £100. If the applicant explains the situation clearly, trustees can see that a £100 grant in this instance would be an effective use of their charities resources. However, if it is not made clear, trustees can only guess at the possible benefits of the grant. Because they are unwilling to take undue risks with charitable money, trustees may either turn down an incomplete application or refer it for more information which inevitably means delays.

Charity and the State

Charities are not supposed to give grants for items that are covered by statutory sources. However, the introduction of the Community Fund and other changes have made it increasingly difficult to say where statutory provision ends and charitable provision begins.

How to make an application

Similarly, the introduction of assesments and means testing under Disabled Facilities Grants procedures is creating shortfalls between the amount that statutory sources will pay and the full costs of equipment and adaptations to houses. Sometimes assessments of what families can pay appear unrealistic.

Changes arising from tightening of eligiblity criteria and Community Care legislation are creating new areas of unmet need. Where the identified need is not met, following the assessment process, any application for alternative finance should make the reasons clear.

If individuals are applying to charity because statutory provision is clearly no longer adequate, they should make it clear in the application that they have exhausted all possible statutory sources of funding but they are still left with a shortfall. A supporting reference from a knowledgable agency may be helpful.

Realism

It helps to be realistic. Sometimes families have contributed to their own situation. The applicant who admits this and seems not to expect miracles but rather seeks to plan afresh – even if with fingers crossed – will often be considered more sympathetically than the applicant who philosophises about the deprivation of the family and the imperfections of the political regime of the day.

Likewise, the application which tries to make the trustees feel guilty and responsible for the impending doom which is predicted for the most vunerable members of the family is unlikely to impress experienced trustees, however sympathetic.

In general, be clear and factual, not moralising and emotional. In effect, a good application attempts to identify the need and promote possible resolutions.

Applications to more than one charity

Where large amounts are being sought, it can take months to send applications one at a time and wait for the outcome of each before applying to another. However, if a number of applications are being sent out together, a paragraph explaining that other charities are being approached should be included together with a commitment to return any surplus money raised.

The same application should not be sent off indiscriminately. For example, if somebody is applying to a trade charity on behalf of a child whose deceased father had lengthy service in that particular trade, then a detailed description of the deceased father's service would be highly relevant. If an application for the same child was being made to a local charity, it would not.

Sometimes people who are trustees of more than one charity receive three or four identical letters, none tailored to that particular trust and none indicating that other trusts have been approached. The omission of such details and the neglect of explanations raise questions in the minds of trustees which in the end can result in delays or even refusal.

Timing

When applying to charities, remember the time factor, particularly in cases of urgent need. Committees often sit monthly, or even quarterly. Without knowledge but with 'luck', an application can be received the day before the meeting – but if Murphy's Law operates it will always arrive the day after. For the lack of a little homework, applications may not be considered in time.

From experience, few organisations object to a telephone call being made to clarify criteria, dates of meetings or requests for application forms. So often it seems that applications leave the whole process to chance, which leads to disillusionment, frustration and wasted time for all concerned.

Savings

When awarding a grant, most trustees take the applicant's savings into account. Some applicants may think this unnecessarily intrusive, but openness and honesty make for a better presented application and save time. However, sometimes savings may not need to affect trustees' calculations.

For example, if a women has a motor accident in which she was not at fault but which leaves her permanently disabled, she will receive compensation (often a one-off lump sum) through the guilty party's insurance company based on medical prognoses at the time. If her condition deteriorates faster and further than anticipated, requiring her to obtain an expensive item of equipment, it could well be argued that this should not be paid for out of the compensation awarded. The compensation was paid to cover factors such as loss of earnings potential, a reduced quality of life, reduced ability to easily fulfil basic household tasks and a general loss of future security, not to pay for unexpected and expensive pieces of equipment.

In such circumstances, the applicant should include a paragraph in the application to explain why his/her savings are not relevant to grant calculations.

In conclusion

Two final points should be borne in mind.

1. Be clear

Firstly, social workers in particular often resort to the use of jargon when plain English would be more effective. There appears to be two extremes; one to present a report on the basis that the trustees are not very intelligent lay people who need to be educated, or alternatively that they are all psychotherapists who need to be impressed. Usually, this only causes confusion.

2. Medical information

Secondly, medical information should not be presented without an accurate medical diagnosis to support it. Applicants' or social workers' presumptions on medical matters are not relevant. Often what is necessary is to explain why a financial need arises from a particular condition. This may be because of the rarity of the condition or the fluctuating nature of it.

The medical information should be presented by a professional in that field. The task of the applicant or the sponsor is to explain the implications of the condition.

Using the model application form for financial assistance

Over the page is a general purpose application form. It has been compiled with the help of Gaddum Centre. It can be photocopied and used whenever convenient and should enable applicants (and welfare agencies applying on behalf of individuals) to state clearly the basic information required by most trusts.

Alternatively, applicants can use it as a checklist of points to include in the letter. Applicants using this form should note the following things in particular:

1. It is worth sending a short letter setting out the request in brief, even when using this application form.

2. Because this form is designed to be useful to a wide range of people in need, not all the information asked for in the form will be relevant to every application. For example, not all applicants are in receipt of state benefits, nor do all applicants have HP commitments. In such cases, applicants should write N/A (not applicable) in the box or on the line in question.

3. Filling out the weekly income and expenditure parts of the form can be worrying or even distressing. Expenditure when itemised in this way is usually far higher than people expect. It is probably worth filling out this form with the help of a trained welfare rights worker.

4. You should always keep a copy of the completed form in case the trust has a specific query.

5. This form should not be used where the trust has its own form which must be completed.

A model application form for financial assistance

PURPOSE FOR WHICH GRANT IS SOUGHT	AMOUNT SOUGHT FROM THIS APPLICATION £
APPLICANT (Name)	Occupation/School
Address Tel. no	
Date of birth · Age	Place of birth
Nationality	Religion (if any)
☐ Single ☐ Married ☐ Divorced ☐ Partnered ☐ Separated ☐ Widow/er	

FAMILY DETAILS: Name	Age	Occupation/School
Husband/Wife	....	....
Partner	....	....
Children	....	....
Others (specify)	....	....

INCOME (weekly)	£ p	EXPENDITURE (weekly)	£ p
Father/husband's wage	....	Rent/mortgage	....
Mother's/wife's wage	....	Council tax	....
Partner's wage	....	Water rate	....
Income Support	....	Electricity	....
Job Seeker's Allowance	....	Gas	....
Sickness/invalidity benefit	....	Coal	....
Child benefit	....	Insurance	....
Family credit	....	Fares/travel	....
Attendance allowance	....	Household expenses (food, laundry etc.)	....
Disability living allowance	....	Clothing	....
Housing benefit	....	Maintenance	....
Maintenance payments	....	Childcare fees	....
Retirement pension	....	HP commitments	....
Occupational pension	....	Telephone	....
Other income (specify)............	....	TV rental	....
....	....	TV licence	....
....	....	Other expenditure (specify)..........	....
....	....	....	....
		....	....
		....	....
TOTAL WEEKLY INCOME	£	**TOTAL WEEKLY EXPENDITURE**	£

SAVINGS £	
DEBTS/ARREARS Rent, fuels, loans, HP etc. Specify in detail .... Amount owed .... £ .... £ .... £ .... £ .... £ .... TOTAL £ _____	Has applicant received help from any other source? YES/NO (If YES, please include details below) Sources of grant obtained .... Amount .... £ .... £ .... Other sources approached .... TOTAL STILL REQUIRED £ _____

Has applicant ever received previous financial help from this trust? YES/NO   If so, when?

REASON FOR THE APPLICATION

Continue on a separate sheet if necessary

FOR APPLICATIONS BEING SUBMITTED THROUGH A WELFARE AGENCY

Name of agency ....

Case worker ....

Address ....

....

Telephone ....

How long has the applicant been known to your department/organisation? ....

FOR ALL APPLICATIONS

Signature: Date:

Occupational Charities

This section contains:

- An index of particular trades or professions. The categories of trades/professions are listed alphabetically.

- After the index, the charities themselves are arranged alphabetically within each trade/profession. Charities include both independent charities and benevolent funds associated with trade unions or professional bodies.

Trusts included are those which support both members of the occupation listed, and their dependants. Individuals should also check for any trade unions listed which cover the area of work, sometimes they have resources available for workers in their sector who are not members of the union. When a possible occupation has been identified, people should turn to the relevant page and read the entries carefully. There may be criteria which makes individuals ineligible, despite being a member of the profession. (Trusts such as Hull Fishermen's Trust Fund, which support a particular occupation but only in a particular locality, are included in the relevant local section of this guide.)

Paid work is not essential for all the trusts, for instance there are trusts for certain amateur sportspeople as well as one for people who have been involved in charitable work.

We have grouped together certain occupations to make relevant trusts easier to identify. For instance, dance, magic, music, painting, theatre and writing have all been put under arts and entertainment, as there are some trusts which support arts generally (which would give to a number of these categories) and some which give to just one specific branch (only supporting one category). Sports are listed individually rather than collectively, this is because we have found no trusts which support sportspeople in general.

We have placed all medical and health workers in the same category, as again there are trusts which support these workers generally and some which only support certain areas. Similarly, clergy and missionaries have been placed under the religion category. The category 'food, drink and provision trade' contains a lot of different individual roles within the industry.

Index of funds for particular trades or occupations

A
Accountancy 21
Advertising and marketing 21
Agriculture 21
Air travel 22
Antique dealers 22
Architecture 22
Arts & entertainment 23
Athletics 27
Atomic energy 27

B
Banking 28
Book retail 28
Bookbinding 28
Bookmakers 29
Boxing 29
Building 29

C
Caravan industry 29
Ceramic industry 30
Chartered surveyors 30
Chemical engineers 30
Civil Service 30
Clayworking 32
Clothing/footwear/headwear 32
Coal industry 32
Commerce 33
Commercial travellers 33
Cooperative officials 33
Coopers 34
Corn exchange 34
Cricket 34
Customs & excise 34

D
Domestic service 34
Driving instructors 35

E
Electrical & electronic industry 35
Engineering 35
Environmental health 37

F
Farriers 37
Fire service 37
Food, drink & provision trades 38
Football 40
Fur trade 41
Furniture & furnishing 41

G
Gardening 41
Golf 42

H
Hairdressing 42
Horse racing 42
Hotel & catering 43

I
Insurance 43

J
Jewellery/giftware (including manufacture of raw materials involved) 44

L
Laundry 44
Leather trades 44
Legal profession 44
Librarians 45
Lock-keeping 45
Loss adjusters 45

M
Market research 45
Match manufacture 46
Media 46
Medicine & health 46
Metal trades & metallurgy 50
Motor industry 51
Motor sports 51

N
Naval architecture 52
Newsagents 52

19

P

Patent agents 52
Pawnbrokers 52
Petroleum industry 53
Police 53
Post office 54
Pottery & Glass 54
Printing 54
Probation officers 54
Public relations 55
Public sector 55
Public transport 55

Q

Quarrying 55

R

Railways 56
Religion 56
Removal trade 60
Retail trade 60
Road haulage 61
Rugby 61

S

School inspectors 61
Science 61
Seafaring & fishing 62
Secretaries 64
Self-employed/small businesses 64
Sewing machine trade 64
Snooker and billiards 65
Social workers 65
Stationery 65
Stock exchange 65

T

Tax inspectors 66
Teaching (including governessess) 66
Telecommunications 67
Textiles 68
Tobacco trade 68
Travel industry 69

V

Veterinary surgeons 69
Voluntary sector 69

W

Watch & clock makers 69
Water conservators 69

Accountancy

The Certified Accountants' Benevolent Association

Eligibility: Members, and former members, of the ACCA, and their dependants.

Types of grants: Grants range from £250 to £5,000. Recurrent grants are available to help with telephone bills, insurance and TV rental and so on; one-off grants in tragic circumstances to help beneficiaries get back on their feet; and low-interest or interest-free loans on property. Grants are not available for the education of children.

Annual grant total: In 2001 the trust had assets of £804,000 and an income of £89,000. Total expenditure was £31,000.

Applications: On a form available from the correspondent or downloadable from the website. Applications can be submitted directly by the individual or through a social worker, citizen's advice bureau, welfare agency or other third party, and are considered four or five times a year.

Correspondent: Lorraine Morrow, 64 Finnieston Square, Glasgow G3 8DT (0141 309 4157; Fax: 0141 309 4120; e-mail: morrowl@accaglobal.com; website: www.accaglobal.com).

The Chartered Accountants' Benevolent Association

Eligibility: Members and former members of the Institute of Chartered Accountants in England and Wales and their dependants. Also former articled clerks disabled as a result of the 1939–45 war and their dependants.

Types of grants: One-off and recurrent grants depending on need.

Annual grant total: In 2000 the association had assets of £15 million, an income of £1.5 million and a total expenditure of £1.7 million. Grants totalled £1.4 million.

Applications: In writing to the correspondent.

Correspondent: D A Barker, 3 Cottesbrooke Park, Heartlands, Daventry NN11 5YL (01327 314830; e-mail: caba.enquiries@icaew.co.uk).

The Chartered Institute of Management Accountants Benevolent Fund

Eligibility: Present and past fellows and associates of the institute, their widows/widowers and dependants anywhere in the world.

Types of grants: Grants are generally one-off for specific needs such as television licence/rental, telephone rental, motor insurance/tax, some repairs, house/contents insurance and necessary household items such as fridges, cookers and so on.

No grants are provided for private medical care or education, to enhance property, or for investment in business ventures. Loans may be provided in exceptional circumstances.

Annual grant total: In 2000 the trust had assets of £2.1 million, an income of £97,000 and a total expenditure of £70,000. Grants to 59 individuals totalled £68,000.

Applications: On a form available from the correspondent. Applications can be submitted directly by the individual or through a recognised referral agency (citizen's advice bureau, doctor, social worker etc.), or via a third party. They are considered monthly/as necessary.

Correspondent: Penny Rushton, CIMA, 26 Chapter Street, London SW1P 4NP (020 7663 5441).

The Institute of Company Accountants Benevolent Fund

Eligibility: Fellows and associates of the institute, and their close dependants, who are in need.

Types of grants: One-off grants according to need.

Annual grant total: In 1999 the fund had assets of £6,600 and a total expenditure of £4,400.

Applications: In writing to the correspondent.

Correspondent: B T Banks, 40 Tyndalls Park Road, Clifton, Bristol BS8 1PL (0117 973 8261; Fax: 0117 923 8292).

The Institute of Financial Accountants & International Association of Book-Keepers Benevolent Fund

Eligibility: Members or former members of the institute or the association and their dependants.

Types of grants: One-off grants according to need. Grants are normally only given in real cases of hardship and destitution, and usually range between £150 and £2,000. Every single application is considered on its merits.

Annual grant total: About £3,500.

Applications: On a form available from the correspondent. Applications can be submitted directly by the individual or on their behalf by a spouse or child. Details of full income and expenditure for the previous 12 months must be included.

Correspondent: J M Dean, Burford House, 44 London Road, Sevenoaks, Kent TN13 1AS (01732 458080; website: www.ifa.org.uk).

Advertising and marketing

NABS

Eligibility: People who work or have worked in advertising, marketing, marketing services and related industries, and their dependants.

Types of grants: One-off and recurrent grants according to need. Welfare advice is available through a NABS helpline.

Annual grant total: In 2000/01 the trust had assets of £3.8 million, an income of £2.2 million and a total expenditure of £2.3 million. 'Counselling and charitable grants' totalled £613,000, and included grants to individuals for educational and welfare purposes and grants to organisations.

Applications: On a form available from the correspondent.

Correspondent: Kate Harris, Chief Executive, 32 Wigmore Street, London W1U 2RP (020 7299 2888; Fax: 020 7299 2887; e-mail: nabs@nabs.org.uk; website: www.nabs.org.uk).

Other information: The society also provides sheltered housing, residential care and nursing accommodation for the elderly.

Agriculture

Association of Professional Foresters Education and Provident Fund

Eligibility: Forestry and Timber Association (or Association of Professional Foresters or Timber Growers Association) members and their dependants who are in need.

Types of grants: Grants are made according to need.

Annual grant total: In 2002 the trust had £3,300 available to give in welfare grants and £5,300 for education grants.

Applications: In writing to the correspondent.

Correspondent: Ms J Karthaus, Woodland Place, West Street, Belford, Northumberland NE70 7QA (01668 213937; e-mail: jane@apfs.demon.co.uk).

The Royal Agricultural Benevolent Institution

Eligibility: Farmers, farm managers and farm workers who are retired or disabled, and their families in need, who live in England, Wales or Northern Ireland and have worked in the industry for at least 10 years.

There is an emergency fund available for working farmers and farmworkers who are experiencing financial hardship.

Types of grants: One-off grants and regular financial assistance (paid quarterly) plus a Christmas and winter bonus if funds permit for applicants over 60 (or earlier if they have permanent ill health or disability). Grants can be towards white goods, disability equipment, TVs and licences, telephone rental, lifelines and so on. No grants can be given towards business debts and expenses or medical or educational costs.

Annual grant total: In 2001 the trust had assets of £34 million and an income of £23 million. Total expenditure was £12 million. £10 million was given in around 10,000 grants, of which around £8 million was given in connection to foot and mouth disease.

Applications: On a form available from the correspondent. Applications should include full details of farming experience, financial situations and referees (one for one-off grants, two for recurrent grants). They can be submitted directly by the individual or through a social worker, citizen's advice bureau, other welfare agency or any other third party. The grants committee meets every six weeks, although emergency needs can be met immediately.

Correspondent: Mrs Patricia Pickford, Shaw House, 27 West Way, Oxford OX2 0QH (Emergency helpline: 01865 727888; Tel: 01865 724931; Fax: 01865 202025; e-mail: welfare@rabi.org.uk; website: www.rabi.org.uk).

The Rural, Agricultural & Allied Workers' Benevolent Fund

Eligibility: Rural and agricultural members of the organisation (now a trade group within the Transport and General Workers Union).

Types of grants: One-off grants with an average value of £150.

Annual grant total: £3,000 to £4,000 each year is given in total in about 30 grants.

Applications: In writing to the correspondent.

Correspondent: Peter Allenson, TGWU, Transport House, 128 Theobalds Road, London WC1X 8TN (020 7611 2500; Fax: 020 7611 2555).

The Timber Trades Benevolent Society

Eligibility: People engaged in the timber trade in the UK for at least 10 years, and their dependants, who are in need. Furniture manufacturers and carpenters servicing the building trade are not eligible.

Types of grants: Grants have been awarded towards heating installation, adaptation of cars for disabled use, domestic appliances, phone rentals, TV rental or licences, hampers, house repairs or essential car maintenance. No grants are made towards care or nursing home fees.

Annual grant total: £101,000 in 2001.

Applications: On a form available from the correspondent. Applications can be either submitted directly by the individual or through a social worker, citizen's advice bureau, welfare agency or other third party. Applications are considered in January, May, July and October.

Correspondent: Malcolm Job, General Manager, 31 Chelthorn Way, Solihull B91 3FW (0121 705 5686; Fax: 0121 705 5802; e-mail: info@ttbs.org.uk).

Air travel

The British Airline Pilots' Association Benevolent Fund (BALPA)

Eligibility: Serving and retired commercial pilots, flight engineers and navigators who are or have been members of BALPA, and their dependants.

Types of grants: One-off and recurrent grants and interest-free loans. The fund prefers to give grants for specific needs such as electricity bills, school books for children and so on.

Annual grant total: About £15,000.

Applications: In writing to the correspondent requesting an application form. Applications are considered quarterly.

Correspondent: Peter Smith, Hon. Secretary, 81 New Road, Harlington, Hayes, Middlesex UB3 5BG (020 8476 4000; Fax: 020 8476 4077).

The Guild of Air Pilots Benevolent Fund

Eligibility: Members of the guild and those who have been engaged professionally as air pilots or air navigators in commercial aviation, and their dependants.

Types of grants: Grants or loans can be given towards, for example, debts, fuel bills, school fees and nursing care. Grants range between £250 and £2,000. Loans above about £2,000 may need some security. Training and higher education is not usually supported.

Annual grant total: In 1998/99 the trust had assets of £878,000 and an income of £32,000. Total expenditure was £44,000 with grants totalling £29,000.

Applications: On a form available from the correspondent. Applications are considered in January, April, July and October. The fund has helpers and visitors who can help applicants fill in the form (details required include the individual's financial situation and proof of an aviation career). The trust attaches great importance to the comments and recommendations of helpers.

Correspondent: Peter Davis, Secretary, Cobham House, 9 Warwick Court, Gray's Inn, London WC1R 5DJ (020 7404 4032; Fax: 020 7404 4035; e-mail: gapan@gapan.org).

Other information: The fund works closely with the other aviation trusts for individuals (both military and civilian). If an applicant has approached another such trust, they should say so in their application to this fund.

Antiques

The British Antique Dealers' Association Benevolent Fund

Eligibility: People closely related to, or having worked for, members or former members of the association.

Types of grants: One-off or recurrent grants for needs such as assistance with household bills.

Annual grant total: About £4,200.

Applications: On a form available from the correspondent. Applications are considered in May and November, or as necessary. Applicants should provide two references from members or former members of the association.

Correspondent: Mrs Elaine Dean, 20 Rutland Gate, London SW7 1BD (020 7589 4128; Fax: 020 7581 9083; website: ww.bada.org).

Architecture

The Architects Benevolent Society

Eligibility: People engaged or formerly engaged in the practice of architecture, and their dependants.

Types of grants: Recurrent grants and occasional one-off grants and loans. No educational grants.
Annual grant total: In 2000/01 the society had assets of £15 million and an income of £422,000. Grants totalled £458,000.
Applications: On a form available from the correspondent, with details of income and expenditure. Applications can be submitted directly by the individual or through a social worker, citizen's advice bureau or other welfare agency. They are considered throughout the year.
Correspondent: Keith Robinson, Charity Secretary, 43 Portland Place, London W1N 3AG (020 7580 2823; Fax: 020 7580 7075; e-mail: mail@theabs.org.uk).
Other information: The society also runs sheltered accomodation.

The Architecture & Surveying Institution Benevolent Trust

Eligibility: Members and former members of the institute and their dependants. Also past members of the Faculty of Architects and Surveyors, the Construction Surveyors Institute or the Guild of Incorporated Surveyors.
Types of grants: Grants and loans have been given, for example, to allow a widow to remain in her home after the death of her husband, towards ground floor accommodation for somebody with a progressive illness and disability aids.
Annual grant total: In 2000/01 the trust had an income of £4,800 and its total expenditure was £1,300.
Applications: On a form available from the correspondent at any time.
Correspondent: Janet Nuthall, Secretary, 15 St Mary Street, Chippenham, Wiltshire SN15 3WD (01249 444505; Fax: 01249 443602; e-mail: mail@asi.org.uk).

Arts & entertainment

The Artists' General Benevolent Institution

Eligibility: Professional artists in England, Wales and Northern Ireland whose work has been known to the public for some time, and their widows/widowers and orphans.
Types of grants: One-off and recurrent grants to artists who through old age, illness or accident are unable to work and earn.

The trust cannot help with career or legal difficulties, or (except in exceptional circumstances) student fees.

Annual grant total: In 2000/01 the trust had assets of £8.1 million, an income of £626,000 and a total expenditure of £652,000. Grants totalled £459,000.
Applications: Applications should initially be in writing and can be submitted directly by the individual, or through a recognised referral agency (citizen's advice bureau, doctor, social worker etc.). Appropriate applicants will then receive a form which they will need to complete.

The council meets eight times a year to consider applications.
Correspondent: April Connett-Dance, Secretary, Burlington House, Piccadilly, London W1J 0BB (020 7734 1193; Fax: 020 7734 9966).

The Entertainment Artistes' Benevolent Fund

Eligibility: Entertainment artistes (that is professional performers in variety, pantomime, revue, circus, concert party, cabaret, clubs, television, radio, making of records and light entertainment in general), and their dependants.
Types of grants: Regular allowances, one-off grants and loans towards, for example, gas, electricity and fuel bills, television licences and rentals, and telephone bills. Also help with funeral costs where necessary.
Annual grant total: In 2000 the fund had an income of £1.2 million and a total expenditure of £1.4 million. Grants totalled £87,000.
Applications: On a form available from the correspondent. Applications can be made directly or through a social worker/welfare agency.
Correspondent: Peter Elliott, Executive Administrator, Brinsworth House, 72 Staines Road, Twickenham TW2 5AL (020 8898 8164).
Other information: The fund has its own home for elderly entertainment artistes in need of care.

Equity Trust Fund

Eligibility: Professional performers (with special reference to members past and present of British Actors Equity), stage managers and directors, and their dependants.
Types of grants: One-off grants for general welfare purposes. Recent grants have been given towards repairs and renewals and essential equipment such as wheelchairs and medical costs. No grants are given towards repaying overdrafts, credit cards, loans or other debts.
Annual grant total: In 2000/01 the fund had assets of £8.5 million and an income of £376,000. 80 welfare grants to individuals totalled £88,000. 60 educational grants to individuals totalled £135,000. Grants to organisations totalled £86,000.

Applications: On a form available from the correspondent. Applications are considered every six weeks.
Correspondent: Keith Carter, Secretary, 222 Africa House, 64 Kingsway, London WC2B 6BD (020 7404 6041; Fax: 020 7831 4953; e-mail: keith@equitytrustfund.freeserve.co.uk).
Other information: The trust also gives grants for re-training.

Grand Order of Water Rats Charities Fund

Eligibility: People who are or have been connected with light entertainment, and their dependants, who are in need through sickness or age.
Types of grants: One-off and recurrent grants according to need. No grants are given towards students fees, taxes, overdrafts, credit card bills or building projects.
Annual grant total: In 2000 the fund had assets of £901,000 and an income of £426,000. Grants to individuals and organisations totalled £124,000.
Applications: On a form available from the correspondent, to be returned with a cv of professional career. They are considered monthly.
Correspondent: John Adrian, Secretary to the Trustees, 328 Gray's Inn Road, London WC1X 8BZ (020 7407 8007; Fax: 020 7403 8610; e-mail: jadrian675@aol.com).
Other information: This trust also supports organisations (see *A Guide to the Major Trusts Volume Two*).

The Guild of Motoring Writers Benevolent Fund

Eligibility: People in need who are motoring writers, photographers and historians, and are or have been members of the guild. Their dependants who are in need can also be supported.
Types of grants: One-off and recurrent grants according to need. Low-interest loans can also be made.
Annual grant total: In 2000 the trust's income totalled about £27,000. Grants to individuals totalled £20,000.
Applications: In writing to the trustees, care of the correspondent, at any time. Applications can be made either directly by the individual, or via a third party on behalf of the individual.
Correspondent: Frank Page, Trustee/Adminstrator, Shene House, Longtown, Herefordshire HR2 0LS (Tel & Fax: 01873 860213; e-mail: frankpage@tesco.net).

Occupational Charities

The Evelyn Norris Trust

Eligibility: Members or ex-members of the concert or theatrical profession who are elderly, sick, disabled or in need.

Types of grants: One-off grants of between £330 and £500. Grants are given to: convalescence or recuperative holidays following illness, injury or surgery; people who are elderly or infirm for fuel bills, telephone installation, household bills, TV licences; and people who are disabled towards the cost of adaptations to their homes, buying invalid chairs or similar aids.

Annual grant total: In 2001 grants to 40 individuals totalled £14,000.

Applications: On a form available from the correspondent. Applications are considered monthly and can be submitted directly by the individual or through a social worker, citizen's advice bureau, welfare agency or any third party.

Correspondent: Max Beckmann, Secretary to the Trustees, Equity, Guild House, Upper St Martin's Lane, London WC2H 9EG (020 7670 0223; Fax: 020 7379 7001; e-mail: mbeckmann@equity.org.uk).

The Royal Opera House Benevolent Fund

Eligibility: People who work, or have worked, for the Royal Opera House or Birmingham Royal Ballet, and their widows, widowers, partner or children. Applicants must have savings of less than £10,000 if single and £15,000 if married.

Types of grants: Grants range from £50 per month to £3,000 as a one-off grant. Monthly allowances are towards food and clothing. One-off grants are towards essential home maintenance, domestic equipment, urgent medical costs, education, holidays and so on.

Annual grant total: About £134,000 in 85 grants.

Applications: On a form available from the correspondent, providing details of income, expenditure, assets and liabilities. They should submitted directly by the individual for consideration quarterly.

Correspondent: David Pilcher, Royal Opera House, Covent Garden, London WC2E 9DD (020 7212 9128; Fax: 020 7212 9644; e-mail: ben.soc@roh.org.uk).

The Scottish Artists' Benevolent Association

See entry on page 140.

Valentine Memorial Pension Fund

Eligibility: Actors and actresses who are over 60 years old and members of Equity.

Types of grants: Pensions are available to two beneficiaries.

Annual grant total: £520.

Applications: The trust advertises on the rare occasions when funds are available.

Correspondent: Ann Maguire, Guild House, Upper St Martin's Lane, London WC2H 9EG (020 7379 6000).

Dance

The Dance Teachers' Benevolent Fund

Eligibility: Dance teachers or ex-dance teachers who are experiencing short or long-term hardship.

Types of grants: Grants of £100 to £1,000 are usually awarded as 'disregard allowance', clothing grants or assistance with home improvements. Other possibilities could be considered. No grants are given towards training.

Annual grant total: In 2000/01 the fund had assets of £250,000 and an income of £24,000. Total expenditure was £21,000, with 10 grants totalling £9,700.

Applications: On a form available from the correspondent. Forms can be submitted by the individual or any third party, and are considered all year.

Correspondent: Heather Knight, Secretary, c/o The Dancing Times Ltd, 45-47 Clerkenwell Green, London EC1R 0EB (020 7223 4034; Tel & Fax: 020 7223 8636; e-mail: hka@globalnet.co.uk; website: www.dancing-times.co.uk).

The International Dance Teachers' Association Benevolent Fund

Eligibility: Members and retired members of the association, other dancers, former dancers, teachers or former teachers of dance, employees or former employees of the association, and their dependants.

Types of grants: One-off grants only. 'Grants are made of a benevolent nature for people in need during times of crisis or ill health. Grants are not for the purpose of developing career training or prospects.'

Annual grant total: Up to £2,000 in 10 grants.

Applications: In writing to the correspondent.

Correspondent: J Dearling, Company Secretary, International House, 76 Bennett Road, Brighton BN2 5JL (01273 685652; e-mail: info@idta.co.uk; website: www.idta.co.uk).

The Royal Ballet Benevolent Fund

Eligibility: Members/former members of classical ballet and contemporary dance companies, and in special cases dependants of such people after their death. Ballet students are not eligible.

Types of grants: One-off grants are available to relieve any form of hardship. This includes financial assistance to people who are elderly, aids to people who are disabled, or specialist surgery/therapy to injured dancers. The fund claims it is 'not just a cash dispenser but takes personal interest and care of those for whom they are responsible'. No grants to students training to be dancers.

Annual grant total: In 1998/99 the fund had assets of £3 million, and an income of £300,000. Total expenditure was £110,000, with a total of £75,000 being awarded in 50 grants.

Applications: On a form available from the correspondent, to be submitted directly by the individual for consideration at any time.

Correspondent: Michael Dreyfoos-Crookes, 54 Crankton Close, Hounslow, Middlesex TW3 3DQ (020 8570 7569).

Magic

The Magic Circle Benevolent Fund

Eligibility: Members/former members of the Magic Circle and their dependants.

Types of grants: One-off grants according to need.

Annual grant total: The fund's annual income is generally between £4,000 and £5,000.

Applications: In writing to the correspondent either directly by the individual or by a third party. They can be considered at any time.

Correspondent: Richard Stupple, Fund Secretary, The Centre for the Magic Arts, 12 Stephenson Way, London NW1 2HD (Tel & Fax: 01234 851607; e-mail: richardstupple@ismagic.fsnet.co.uk).

Music

The Concert Artistes' Association Benevolent Fund

Eligibility: Members of the association who are over 18 and in need.

Types of grants: One-off grants towards, for example, telephone bills, insurance for a chair lift, raising of electrical sockets and sickness grants.

Annual grant total: In 2000/01 the fund had assets of £414,000, an income of £38,000 and a total expenditure of £24,000. Grants totalled £38,000.

Applications: In writing to the correspondent or any of the trustees.

Correspondent: Barbara Daniels, 20 Bedford Street, Strand, London WC2E 9HP (Tel & Fax: 020 7836 3172).

The English National Opera Benevolent Fund

Eligibility: People who are or have been employed by the English National Opera and/or Saddlers Wells Companies.

Types of grants: Applicants for recurrent grants must be over 58 years and grants '... would normally be to reimburse telephone, TV and insurance costs with small monthly cash payments or to reimburse such special expenses as are appropriate. One-off support is considered on a case by case basis.' Grants range between £150 to £3,000.

Medical/dental treatment is not normally supported, except where delay would affect a performing career. The fund will help with payments for treatment which is not generally available through the NHS.

Annual grant total: In 2000/01 the fund had assets of £295,000, an income of £73,000 and a total expenditure of £52,000. Grants totalled £49,000. A further £1,300 was spent on visiting expenses.

Applications: Submitted directly by the individual on a form available from the correspondent, to be considered in March, June, September and December.

Correspondent: Anthony Bennett, London Coliseum, St Martin's Lane, London WC2N 4ES (020 7845 9245).

The Incorporated Association of Organists Benevolent Fund

Eligibility: Organists and/or choirmasters who are members/former members of any association or society affiliated to the Incorporated Association of Organists, and their dependants, who are in need.

Types of grants: Recurrent grants of £20 a week. Welfare grants are mainly given to older organists who have fallen on hard times.

Annual grant total: In 2000 the fund had an income of £13,000 and a total expenditure of £15,000.

Applications: On a form available from the correspondent. Applications can be submitted by the individual or the secretary of the local organists' association. They are considered throughout the year.

Correspondent: Anthony J Cooke, Hon. Secretary, 8 Wrenbury Avenue, Cookridge, Leeds LS16 7EQ (Tel & Fax: 0113 267 1903; e-mail: acooke1174@aol.com).

ISM Members Fund (The Benevolent Fund of The Incorporated Society of Musicians)

Eligibility: Members and former members of the society and their dependants who are in need.

Types of grants: One-off and recurrent grants according to need. No grants towards professional training.

Annual grant total: In 2000/01 the trust had assets of £2.4 million and an income of £262,000. Total expenditure was £86,000, including grants to 68 individuals which totalled £64,000.

Applications: On a form available from the correspondent, to be submitted directly by the individual at any time.

Correspondent: Members Fund Officer, 10 Stratford Place, London W1C 1AA (020 7629 4413; Fax: 020 7408 1538; e-mail: membership@ism.org).

The Musicians Benevolent Fund

Eligibility: Professional musicians, and people who are working, or have worked, in an occupation closely related to the music industry. Applicants must be UK citizens, although they are eligible if they live overseas.

Types of grants: Recurrent grants of up to the charitable disregard level are given to people who are elderly or disabled towards telephones, TV licences, car expenses, insurance and holidays. One-off grants are given towards a wide range of needs, including household goods, home maintenance, mobility aids and adaptations, retraining and career aids. Help can be considered for private medical treatment if it avoids a long wait for NHS treatment.

Annual grant total: In 2001 grants totalled £1.7 million.

Applications: On a form available from the correspondent. They should be submitted directly by the individual and can be considered at any time.

Correspondent: Sara Dixon, 16 Ogle Street, London W1W 6JA (020 7636 4481; Fax: 020 7637 4307; e-mail: casework@mbf.org.uk; website: www.mbf.org.uk).

Other information: The fund also runs a residential home on the outskirts of Bromley in Kent.

Musicians' Social & Benevolent Council

Eligibility: Musicians who are or were members of the London branches of the Musicians' Union who are facing sickness or distress. Members of other branches who have performed for a long run in London, such as the West End, are also eligible.

Types of grants: Monthly grants of £20 are given to older, retired members. One-off grants of up to £170 are available to any members in need.

Annual grant total: About £18,000.

Applications: In writing to the correspondent, including the musicians union branch and membership number. Applications should be submitted directly by the individual or by spouse or friend.

Correspondent: Miss Geraldine Chalmers, 100a Weston Park, London N8 9PP (020 8348 9358).

The Organists' Benevolent League

Eligibility: Organists, and their dependants, who are in need.

Types of grants: One-off payments are given. Recent grants have included contributions towards an electric wheelchair, rethatching of a roof and the installation of a ramp into the home of a person who is disabled.

Annual grant total: In 2001 the league had assets of £207,000 and an income of £12,000. From a total expenditure of £8,200, grants totalled £5,600.

Applications: On a form available from the correspondent. Applications should be submitted directly by the individual and are considered all year round.

Correspondent: Richard Lyne, 10 Stratford Place, London W1N 1BA.

The Geoffrey Parsons Memorial Trust

Eligibility: Concert pianists and people with the ability to become concert pianists, who are in need. There is a preference for people under 35.

Types of grants: One-off and recurrent grants of £500 to £2,000 towards piano lessons with pre-eminent teachers and the purchase of music (i.e. sheet music and scores).

Annual grant total: In 2000/01 the trust had assets of £56,000 and an income of £2,800. Total expenditure was £3,000, all of which was given in four grants.

Applications: On a form available from the correspondent. Unsolicited applications will not be considered.

Correspondent: B P Griffin, 50 Broadway, Westminster, London SW1H 0BL (020 7227 7000; Fax: 020 7222 3480).

The Performing Right Society Members' Fund

Eligibility: Composers, authors and publishers of music who are or were members of the society, and their dependants.

OCCUPATIONAL CHARITIES

Types of grants: Regular grants to older members or dependants whose income has proved inadequate to maintain basic living standards. Recurring grants are a minimum of £20 per week. Temporary assistance by way of a loan to meet an unexpected financial crisis. Emergency assistance by way of outright money grants for financial difficulties caused by serious illness or accident. Help is also given to older members towards holidays, telephone and television rental, television licences and insurances.

Annual grant total: In 2000 the fund had an income of £1.1 million and a total expenditure of £489,000. Grants to individuals and organisations totalled £413,000.

Applications: On a form available from the correspondent. Applications can be submitted by the individual, through a social worker, citizen's advice bureau or other welfare agency, or by next of kin or associate. They are considered each month.

Correspondent: John Logan, General Secretary, 29-33 Berners Street, London W1T 3AB (020 7580 5544).

The Royal Society of Musicians of Great Britain

Eligibility: Professional musicians and their families who are in need through illness, accident or age. Membership of the society is not a requirement. No grants are given to students or people whose only claim for relief arises from unemployment.

Types of grants: One-off grants from £50 to £5,000.

Annual grant total: In 2000/01 the trust had assets of £12 million, an income of £644 and a total expenditure of £513,000. Grants totalled £340,000.

Applications: On a form available from the correspondent. Enquiries from welfare organisations are welcomed as is the identification of need from any concerned individual. An application for financial assistance must have the support of a member, honorary member or officer of the society. A copy of a current membership list is supplied to an applicant. Applications are considered monthly.

Correspondent: Mrs Maggie Gibb, Secretary, 10 Stratford Place, London W1C 1BA (Tel & Fax: 020 7629 6137).

Other information: Specialist advice is also available from honorary officers, which include medical consultants.

Painting

The Eaton Fund for Artists, Nurses & Gentlewomen

Eligibility: Artists (painters only in this respect), nurses or gentlewomen in need of financial help.

Types of grants: Modest one-off grants for one specific item or purpose which are limited to one per person/family. Grants range between £100 and £500. Consideration cannot be given to any matters relating to education, courses and so on. No recurrent grants are made.

Annual grant total: In 2000/01 the trust had an income of £40,000 and a total expenditure of £35,000, all of which was given in 150 grants.

Applications: On a form available from the correspondent on written request. Forms should be submitted directly by the individual or through a social worker, citizen's advice bureau or other welfare agency. They are considered four or five times a year.

Correspondent: A A H Selwood, 28 Windermere Road, Ealing, London W5 4TD.

Theatre

The Actors' Benevolent Fund

Eligibility: Members of the theatrical profession which includes actors and actresses, theatrical managers and people who have sung or spoken words professionally on the stage in English, including chorus singers whose efforts are devoted entirely to theatrical work, their spouses and dependants.

Types of grants: Recurrent grants of £20 per week, plus help, for example, with bills, TV licences and insurance. One-off grants for convalescence or items such as wheelchairs or stairlifts. No grants are available for students.

Annual grant total: In 2000 the fund had assets of £7.4 million, an income of £637,000 and a total expenditure of £322,000. Grants to 150 individuals totalled £193,000.

Applications: On a form available from the correspondent. Applications are to be submitted directly by the individual, and are considered on the last Thursday of every month.

Correspondent: Jane Skerrett, 6 Adam Street, London WC2N 6AD (020 7836 6378; Fax: 020 7836 8978; e-mail: office@abf.org.uk; website: www.actorsbenevolentfund.co.uk).

The Actors' Charitable Trust

Eligibility: Children (aged under 19) of people in the theatrical profession who are in financial need.

Types of grants: One-off and recurrent grants of up to £2,000 towards general maintenance including clothing, shoes and holidays. No grants are made towards school fees.

Annual grant total: In 2001 the trust had assets of £4.9 million and both an income and a total expenditure of £250,000. Grants to 100 families totalled £79,000.

Applications: On a form available from Rowena Armstrong. Applications can be considered at any time, and can be submitted either by the individual or a parent.

Correspondent: Robert Ashby/Rowena Armstrong, Africa House, 64-78 Kingsway, London WC2B 6BD (020 7242 0111, Fax: 020 7242 0234; e-mail: advice@tactactors.org; website: www.tactactors.org).

Peggy Ramsay Foundation

Eligibility: Writers for the stage who have been produced publicly, are 'of promise' and are in need of time to write which they cannot afford, or are in need of other assistance.

Types of grants: One-off grants. Individual awards rarely exceed £5,000 for writing time or £1,000 for word processors. No grants towards production costs or to writers who have not been produced.

Annual grant total: In 2000 the trust had assets of £5.7 million, an income of £271,000 and a total expenditure of £223,000. Grants to 44 individuals totalled £59,000. A further £131,000 was given to organisations.

Applications: Apply by writing a short letter to the correspondent, submitted with a cv directly by the individual. Scripts and publicity material do not help. Applications are considered throughout the year.

Correspondent: G Laurence Harbottle, Trustee, Hanover House, 14 Hanover Square, London W1S 1HP (020 7667 5000; Fax: 020 7667 5100; e-mail: laurence.harbottle@harbottle.com; website: www.harbottle.com).

Other information: No grants are made for productions or writing not for the theatre.

The Royal Theatrical Fund

Eligibility: People in need who have professionally practised or contributed to the theatrical arts (on stage, radio, films or television or any other medium by which such arts may be presented in future), and the relief of families or dependants of such people.

Types of grants: One-off and recurrent grants of £250 to £3,000 are given towards domestic bills, monthly allowances, shortfall in nursing and residential fees, car tax, insurance, TV licences and so on. No grants are made to students or towards courses or projects.

Annual grant total: In 2000/01 the fund had assets of £4.9 million, an income of £351,000 and a total expenditure of £375,000. Grants to 11,000 individuals totalled £142,000.

Applications: On a form available from the correspondent, to be returned with a cv and a medical letter if appropriate. Applications can be submitted at any time, either directly by the individual or through any third party such as social workers, citizen's advice bureaux and people with power of attorney.

Correspondent: The Secretary, 11 Garrick Street, London WC2E 9AR (020 7836 3322; Fax: 020 7379 8273; e-mail: admin@trtf.com; website: www.trtf.com).

The Theatrical Guild (formerly The Theatrical Ladies Guild of Charity)

Eligibility: People who have worked either backstage or front of house in a professional theatre and have retired through age or health.

Types of grants: Regular and one-off grants, mostly towards a shortfall in nursing fees but also covering a wide range of needs. No grants are made to students.

Annual grant total: In 2000 the trust had assets of £1.2 million and an income of £49,000. Total expenditure was £92,000, including £85,000 given in grants.

Applications: On a form available from the correspondent. Applications must be submitted by the individual or somebody with power of attorney. They are considered every month except August.

Correspondent: Miss Karen Nichols, PO Box 22712, London N22 5AG (020 8889 7570; e-mail: admin@the-theatrical-guild.org.uk; website: www.the-theatrical-guild.org.uk).

Writing

The Authors' Contingency Fund

Eligibility: Professional authors and their dependants in an emergency.

Types of grants: One-off grants of between £300 and £750 to relieve a temporary financial emergency.

Annual grant total: In 2000 the fund had assets of £233,000, an income of £18,000 and a total expenditure of £8,100. Grants to eight individuals totalled £3,900.

Applications: On a form available from the correspondent or downloadable from the website.

Correspondent: The Awards Secretary, The Society of Authors, 84 Drayton Gardens, London SW10 9SB (020 7373 6642; Fax: 020 7373 5768; e-mail: info@societyofauthors.org; website: www.societyofauthors.org).

The Francis Head Bequest

Eligibility: Professional authors over the age of 35 who live and were born in the UK.

Types of grants: Emergency grants of £1,000 to £2,500.

Annual grant total: In 2000 the bequest had assets of £611,000, an income of £44,000 and a total expenditure of £18,000. Grants to eight individuals totalled £11,000.

Applications: On a form available from the correspondent or downloadable from the website.

Correspondent: The Awards Secretary, 84 Drayton Gardens, London SW10 9SB (020 7373 6642; e-mail: info@societyofauthors.org; website: www.societyofauthors.org).

The Royal Literary Fund

Eligibility: Authors of published work of literary merit, or their dependants. The work must be written in English.

Types of grants: Awards range between £3,000 to £10,000. Most grants are outright grants which means there can be no reapplication within three years. Pensions run for five years. In special circumstances the trust gives interim grants which allow reapplication after one year. Dependants are also eligible to apply. The trust does not make loans. Recent examples of beneficiaries include (a) an older lady living on a low income who received a grant of £3,000 savings plus £20 per week for three years and (b) a writer living abroad recovering from a severe stroke who received a grant of £10,000.

Annual grant total: In 2000/01 the trust had assets of £86 million, an income of £7 million and a total expenditure of £7.5 million. Grants to 204 individuals totalled £2 million.

Applications: On a form available from the correspondent. Applications are considered every month except August. Applicants are asked to supply copies of their published work which is then read by two members of the committee who decide on the question of literary merit. If this is approved, a grant/pension may be made based on an assessment of need.

Correspondent: Eileen Gunn, General Secretary, 3 Johnson's Court, London EC4A 3EA (020 7353 7159; e-mail: egunnrlf@globalnet.co.uk; website: www.rlf.org.uk).

The Society of Authors Pension Fund

Eligibility: People aged over 65 who have been a member of the Society of Authors for at least 10 years.

Types of grants: Pensions of £1,500 a year are given.

Annual grant total: In 2000 it had assets of £370,000 and an income of £23,000. Grants to 12 individuals totalled £18,000.

Applications: In writing to the correspondent when vacancies are announced in the society's journal.

Correspondent: The General Secretary, 84 Drayton Gardens, London SW10 9SB (020 7373 6642; Fax: 020 7373 5768; e-mail: info@societyofauthors.org; website: www.societyofauthors.org).

Athletics

The British Athletics Benevolent Fund

Eligibility: Current and former athletes, athletic officials and employees of UK Athletics Ltd and the British Athletic Federation or any of their regional and national members and their dependants who are in need.

Types of grants: One-off and recurrent grants, for medical and rehabilitation assistance and the relief of poverty.

Annual grant total: In 1999 the trust had assets of around £120,000, with grants totalling under £10,000.

Applications: In writing to the correspondent.

Correspondent: The Trustees, 10 Harborne Road, Edgbaston, Birmingham B15 3AA.

Other information: This entry was not confirmed by the trust, but the address was correct according to the Charity Commission database.

Atomic energy

UBA Benevolent Fund

Eligibility: Past, present and future members of the non-industrial staff of UKAEA, AEA Technology plc, British Nuclear Fuels plc and Amersham plc and their dependants, who are in need. (Where single status has been adopted, all employees are eligible.) People who left the company as industrial employees are not eligible. Applicants do not need to have been a subscriber to the fund.

Types of grants: Single and continuing (including weekly) grants and allowances. Grants are given for most purposes, except where this would affect state benefits. Loans against property and for serving officers are possible.

Grants are given towards furniture, disability aids (stair lifts, wheelchairs, alarms etc.), holidays, nursing home fees, Christmas grants, television licences and sets, repairs, fuel bills (to prevent disconnection), telephone bills, removal costs, debts (in some cases), minor repairs and child minding.

Grants are NOT given for private health care (excluding convalescence and residential home fees) or private education.

Annual grant total: In 2000/01 the trust had assets of £3 million. It gave £97,000 in grants and £93,000 in loans.

Applications: Initially by letter or phone call, followed by a personal visit from a representative where possible. Applications can be made directly by the individual, or through a third party on their behalf and are considered every two months from January onwards.

Correspondent: Marie Sims, Secretary and Manager, c/o British Nuclear Fuels plc, Hinton House, Risley, Warrington WA3 6AS (01925 833288; Fax: 01925 832671; e-mail: marie.sims@bnfl.com).

Banking

The Bankers Benevolent Fund

Eligibility: People in need who are working or who have worked in a bank in the UK for at least two years, and their families and dependants. Applicants must not have capital in excess of the DWP limit for full entitlement to income support.

Types of grants: (a) Regular grants, plus other non-recurring grants within the DWP rules to those on Income Support and living in their own homes.
(b) Regular grants to help with the cost of residential care or nursing home fees.
(c) One-off grants to meet items of a capital nature such as urgent house repairs or special equipment for disabled people.
(d) Any grant agreed for an individual aged over 60 living in their own home which has a significant unencumbered value would not be by way of an outright grant but as interest free loan.

(A significant proportion of the help provided by the fund is directed towards the education and maintenance of the children of deceased or ill-health retired bank employees. See entry in *The Educational Grants Directory*).

Annual grant total: In 2001/02 the trust had an income of £1.4 million. It made grants totalling £1.1 million towards child-related causes, such as for clothing (£230,000), maintenance (£250,000), school fees and expenses (£450,000) and to students for studying (£140,000). Grants to older people totalled £380,000.

Applications: On a form available from the correspondent. Applications can be submitted directly by the individual or a relative, or through a social worker or other welfare agency. The trustees meet four times a year to consider grant applications.

Correspondent: Peter G Oliver, Secretary, St Mary-le-Bow House, 54 Bow Lane, London EC4M 9DJ (020 7236 6428).

The Alfred Foster Settlement

Eligibility: Employees and former employees of banks and their dependants who are in need.

Types of grants: One-off grants according to need

Annual grant total: In 2001/02 grants to 64 individuals totalled £27,000.

Applications: By the employee's bank, to their local regional office or directly to the correspondent.

Correspondent: Miss M Bertenshaw, Barclays Bank Trust Co. Ltd, Executorship & Trustee Service, Osborne Court, Gadbrook Park, Rudheath, Northwich CW9 7UE (01606 313000).

UNIFI Benevolent Fund

Eligibility: Members, employees or ex-employees of the union or dependants in need, or people who work or have worked in the banking, insurance or finance industries and their dependants.

Types of grants: One-off grants of between £100 and £1,000 to people who have fallen on hard times through being absent from work through prolonged sickness, retirement through ill-health, family bereavements or a change in domestic circumstances. Grants have included payment towards a riser/recliner for person with back problems, help to somebody dismissed while on sick leave, heating grants for older people, Christmas bonuses for people who are elderly or have young children, and general assistance with bills. Help with legal fees, educational grants and credit card bills is not usually available.

Annual grant total: In 2001 the fund had assets of £245,000 and an income of £19,000. Grants totalled £15,000.

Applications: Application forms are available from the correspondent and applications are considered in March, June, September and December. Forms are to be submitted directly by the individual, and be countersigned by UNIFI accredited representative, seconded representative, organiser or official. Financial statements must be sent with applications.

Correspondent: T Ayres, Secretary, Sheffield House, Amity Grove, Raynes Park, London SW20 0LG (020 8879 4248).

Book retail

The Book Trade Benevolent Society

Eligibility: People in need who have worked in the book trade in the UK for at least one year (normally publishing/distribution/book-selling), and their dependants. Priority will be given to people who are chronically sick, redundant, unemployed or 50 years of age or over.

Types of grants: One-off and recurrent grants of up to £1,500, are given according to need. Recurrent grants are generally of £1,300 a year. Grants are generally to supplement weekly/monthly income for housekeeping and help with fuel bills in long spells of cold weather. Other support is given in a variety of ways (e.g. assistance with telephone and television rental, medical aid, aids for disabled people and house repairs/redecoration). There is a holiday fund to help a number of people who have not had a break for many years with the cost of a holiday or to visit family or friends. Grants are also given to help retrain people from the book trade who have been made redundant.

Grants are not given for nursing home fees but 'pocket money' grants may be available.

Annual grant total: In 2001 the society had assets of £1.2 million and an income of £164,000. From a total expenditure of £220,000, grants to nearly 100 individuals totalled £77,000.

Applications: On a form available from the correspondent. Applications can be submitted by the individual or through a recognised referral agency (social worker, citizen's advice bureau, doctor, and so on) and are considered quarterly.

Correspondent: David Hicks, Chief Executive, The Foyle Centre, The Retreat, Abbots Road, Kings Langley, Hertfordshire WD4 8LT (01923 263128; Fax: 01923 270732; e-mail: btbs@booktradecharity.demon.co.uk; website: www.brooktradecharity.demon.co.uk).

Bookbinding

The Bookbinders' Charitable Society

Eligibility: Retired people in need who have worked in the bookbinding, printing and allied trades, and their dependants.

Applicants must be able to live independently.

Types of grants: Pensions of £50 a quarter are available. One-off grants of up to £250 can also be given towards specific items such as showers, carpets, furniture, stairlifts, motorised vehicles and so on.

Annual grant total: In 2001 it had assets of £1.4 million and an income of £56,000. Total expenditure was £49,000, including eight grants to individuals totalling £2,000.

Applications: On a form available from the correspondent. Applications should be submitted either directly by the individual or through a relative, social worker, citizen's advice bureau or other welfare agency and should include full details of employment and financial details, as well as a GP's letter if appropriate. Applications are considered on the last Tuesday of every month.

Correspondent: Mrs H Harris, 11 Bookbinders Cottages, Bawtry Road, London N20 0SS (Tel & Fax: 020 8368 4770).

Other information: The society also has accommodation (26 homes/flats) in Whetstone for eligible people in need. Residents pay a small contribution towards maintaining the property.

Bookmakers

The Archie Scott Benevolent Fund for Bookmakers' Employees

Eligibility: Bookmakers, former bookmakers and their employees or ex-employees. Applicants are usually people over 65.

Types of grants: Grants are given each year at Christmas to retired bookmakers and their employees. One-off grants can be awarded in times of proven need such as help with medical expenses or a bereavement. Grants range between £75 and £100.

Annual grant total: In 1998/99 the trust had assets of £30,000 and an income of £11,000. Total expenditure was £13,000, of which £8,000 was given in grants.

Applications: In writing to the correspondent either directly by the individual, or through a working bookmaker.

Correspondent: Jennifer Govier, Secretary, 665 Chester Road, Wylde Green, Sutton Coldfield, West Midlands B73 5JP.

Other information: This entry was not confirmed by the trust, but the address was correct according to the Charity Commission database.

Boxing

The Jack Solomons' Charity Fund

Eligibility: Ex-boxers, and their families, who are in need.

Types of grants: One-off grants according to need, for needs such as clothing and holidays.

Annual grant total: In 2000/01 the fund had an income of £270 and a total expenditure of £2,200.

Applications: In writing to the correspondent.

Correspondent: Malcolm Frith, Trustee, 101 Borough High Street, London Bridge, London SE1 1NL.

Building

Builders' Benevolent Institution

Eligibility: Those who are or who have been master builders (employers in the building industry), and their dependants. Applicants with fewer than 10 years experience are not eligible, nor are those who have been employees.

Types of grants: Grants are available in the form of pensions, Christmas vouchers and telephone rental. Birthday greetings are also given.

Annual grant total: In 1998 the trust had assets of £486,000 and an income of £86,000. Total expenditure was £59,000 with grants to individuals totalling £43,000.

Applications: On a form available from the correspondent, submitted directly by the individual, through a social worker, citizen's advice bureau, other welfare agency or third party. Applications are considered throughout the year.

Correspondent: The Secretary, Construction House, 51 St Mary's Road, Tonbridge TN9 2LE.

Other information: This entry has not been confirmed by the trust, but the address was correct according to the Charity Commission database.

The Chartered Institute of Building Benevolent Fund

Eligibility: Past and present members of the institute and their dependants ONLY who are in need.

Types of grants: Small recurrent pensions and one-off grants towards, for example, travel to an interview, car tax or a holiday.

Annual grant total: In 2001 grants totalled £6,000. This is a reduction of £16,000 on the grant total the previous year due to fewer eligible applications being received.

Applications: In writing to the correspondent. Applications are considered as they arrive.

Correspondent: Franklin MacDonald, Secretary, Englemere, Kings Ride, Ascot, Berkshire SL5 7TB (0141 638 3828; e-mail: fmacdonald@ciob.org.uk; website: www.ciob.org.uk).

Other information: The bulk of the charitable expenditure is spent on providing practical advice, information and advocacy, for example, help with a tribunal or with retraining for people out of work.

The Lighthouse Club Benevolent Fund

Eligibility: People, or families of people, who are working in the building and civil engineering industry in UK or Republic of Ireland. Nobody over 65 years of age will be supported.

Types of grants: One-off or recurrent grants for those in need through accident, disability or ill-health and for those in need because a member of their family (who was in the construction industry) has died or has a fatal illness.

Annual grant total: About £480,000.

Applications: In writing to the correspondent. The fund has 20 honorary welfare officers in the UK and Ireland to liaise with beneficiaries.

Correspondent: Peter Burns, Armstrong House, Swallow Street, Stockport, Cheshire SK1 3LG (0161 429 0022; Fax: 0161 477 1022).

Caravan industry

The National Caravan Council Benevolent Fund

Eligibility: People who work or have worked in caravan retail or manufacture, or on caravan sites, and their dependants.

Types of grants: Usually one-off grants, although occasionally recurrent grants may be given. Grants are usually towards redecoration, medical expenses, food, education or special equipment such as computers for people who are housebound or disabled.

Annual grant total: In 1999/2000 the trust had an income of £6,100 and a total expenditure of £5,000, all of which was given in grants.

Applications: In writing to the correspondent. Applications can be submitted directly by the individual,

OCCUPATIONAL CHARITIES

through a social worker, citizen's advice bureau, other welfare agency, or via a third party on their behalf.

Correspondent: Debbie Wyatt, 74-76 Victoria Road, Aldershot, Hampshire GU11 1SS (01252 318251).

Ceramic industry

The Ceramic Industry Welfare Society

Eligibility: People who are or have been employed in the ceramics industry. Membership of the Ceramic and Allied Trades Union is a condition as is payment when in work of 50p a year premium, deducted from annual holiday pay. No grants are payable beyond 12 months of the date of retirement.

Types of grants: Recurrent grants are fixed at £45 per six week period depending on the circumstances of the applicant as confirmed by the visit of the society's representative. About 500 grants are given each year, that is about 60 people per six week period.

Annual grant total: In 1999 the society had assets of £55,000, an income of £11,000 and a total expenditure of £29,000. Grants totalled £26,000.

Applications: In the first instance applications should be made through the Ceramic & Allied Trades Union, Hillcrest House, Garth Street, Hanley, Stoke-on-Trent ST1 2AB.

Correspondent: A McRae, Federation House, Station Road, Stoke-on-Trent ST4 2SA (01782 744631).

Chartered surveyors

Lionheart (The Royal Institution of Chartered Surveyors Benevolent Fund)

Eligibility: Members/former members of the Royal Institution of Chartered Surveyors or organisations it has merged with, and their dependants.

Types of grants: One-off and recurrent grants and loans are available for any purpose. Recent grants have been given towards insurance, telephone, car and travel expenses, care in the community, residential and nursing care, childcare, education and retraining, TV licences, holidays, aids and equipment, furnishings and redecoration.

Annual grant total: In 2001 the fund had assets of £9 million and both an income and a total expenditure of £1.2 million. Grants to 225 individuals totalled £543,000.

Applications: On a form available from the correspondent with evidence of RICS membership or details of the member of whom the applicant is a dependant. Applications should write, telephone, fax or e-mail a welfare advisor, who will arrange a volunteer to visit them at home to complete an application. Applications are considered quarterly, in January, April, July and October, although urgent cases can be considered between meetings.

Correspondent: M J Carter, Surveyor Court, Westwood Way, Coventry CV4 8BF (024 7646 6696; Fax: 020 7647 4701; e-mail: info@lionheart.org.uk; website: www.lionheart.org.uk).

Other information: This trust now incorporates The Incorporated Society of Valuers and Auctioneers Benevolent Fund and The IBC Benevolent Fund.

The fund offers confidential advice, counselling, information and help in kind to members of the profession and their dependants on a range of social welfare, financial, employment and property-related matters. A helpline is operated on 0845 603 9057.

Chemical engineers

The Chemical Engineer's Benevolent Fund

Eligibility: Chemical engineers and their dependants. This includes all chemical engineers worldwide, not simply members or former members of the Institution of Chemical Engineers.

Types of grants: One-off and recurrent grants, and loans, for example, towards medical treatment, special equipment, nursing home fees, special education needs and general expenses.

No grants for students.

Annual grant total: In 1998 the trust had assets of £153,000 and an income of £12,000. Total expenditure was £13,000 with two grants totalling £11,000.

Applications: In writing to the correspondent, to be submitted either directly by the individual, or through a third party such as a social worker, citizen's advice bureau or other welfare agency or another third party. Applications are considered in April and November, and should include proof of employment as a chemical engineer, such as a passport descriptor or company document.

Correspondent: Ms E Lawson, Davis Building, 165-189 Railway Terrace, Rugby, Warwickshire CV21 3HQ (01788 578214; Fax: 01788 560833).

Civil Service

British Association of Former United Nations Civil Servants Benevolent Fund

Eligibility: Former employees of the United Nations organisation or its specialised agencies and their dependants who are in need. Applicants must be resident in the UK, but do not have to be UK nationals.

Types of grants: One-off grants of between £100 and £500, and loans of up to £1,000. Grants can be made towards a wide range of needs, including health and convalescence needs, aids for people who are disabled or elderly and assistance towards hospital visits. Loans have been made to help the newly widowed until their pension rights are established.

Annual grant total: In 2001 the trust had assets of £30,000 and an income of £2,100. Grants to four individuals totalled £600.

Applications: In writing in the first instance, to the correspondent. Applications are normally referred to appropriate BAFUNCS registered welfare officer for immediate follow-up. Applications are considered throughout the year.

Correspondent: Clerk/Treasurer, 41 Riverine, Grosvenor Drive, Maidenhead, Berkshire SL6 8PF.

Century Benevolent Fund

Eligibility: Employees and ex-employees of the Government Communications Bureau and its associated organisations, and their dependants.

Types of grants: One-off or recurrent grants and loans towards telephone bills, house repairs and so on. No grants for education.

Annual grant total: In 2000/01 the fund had assets of £895,000, an income of £80,000 and a total expenditure of £112,000. Grants to about 150 individuals totalled £95,000.

Applications: In writing to the correspondent, although applications are often submitted through word of mouth. Applications are generally considered four times a year, although the trustees can be flexible over this.

Correspondent: S Barnes, 85 Albert Embankment, London SE1 7TP.

Other information: This entry was not confirmed by the fund, but the information was correct according to the public files at the Charity Commission.

OCCUPATIONAL CHARITIES

The Civil Service Benevolent Fund

Eligibility: Serving, former and retired staff of the civil service and associated organisations, and their dependants, who are in need.

Types of grants: Grants, loans and allowances according to need. Grants have been given towards daily living expenses, items of essential equipment, and in some cases towards household bills and funeral expenses. Allowances can be given towards the cost of community support services, nursing or residential home fees (by topping-up a local authority payment) or childcare.

In 1999 grant totals and numbers of beneficiaries were broken down as follows: community support services (£6,900 in eight grants), control commission Germany allowances and grants (£4,700 in 21 grants), childcare (£73,000 in 154 individual), repayable grants and loans against property (£160,000 in 147 grants), residents in private nursing homes (£74,000 in 110 grants), community care (£297,000 in 270 grants), retired staff (£185,000 in 514 grants), Christmas grants (£30,000 in 1,206 grants), sick and disabled staff (£753,000 in 2,404 grants), serving staff (£883,000 in 2,476 grants) and widows and dependants (£604,000 in 2,046 grants).

Annual grant total: In 1999 the fund had assets of £22 million, an income of £11 million and a total expenditure of £7 million. Grants to 9,356 individuals totalled £2.9 million.

Applications: Phone 0800 056 2424 (Freephone number) between 8.30am and 8pm every day of the year to request assistance. An application form is available from 'Help and Advisory Services' at the address below or the website. The fund can assist with the completion of the form, by either giving advice over the telephone or by sending one of its volunteer visiting officers to the applicant. The trust aims to consider completed application forms within five days of receipt, although they may occasionally take a little longer. In urgent cases payment can be made within 24 hours.

Correspondent: The Help and Advisory Team, Fund House, 5 Anne Boleyn's Walk, Cheam, Sutton, Surrey SM3 8DY (020 8240 2400; Fax: 020 8240 2401; Minicom: 020 8770 0572; e-mail: help@csbf.org.uk; website: www.csbf.org.uk).

Other information: The fund also helps people by providing an information service on a range of community-based services, a confidential visiting service to aid and advise on funding opportunities, and an advocacy service to tell the individual what services are available to them.

Overseas Civil Service Benevolent Fund

Eligibility: People, or their dependants, who have served in HM Overseas Civil Service or in the local civil service in a former British colonial territory and who are in need.

Types of grants: Usually quarterly grants ranging between £50 and £1,500. Fees at nursing homes or residential care homes are not funded.

Annual grant total: In 2000 the trust had an income of £4,200 and a total expenditure of £6,500. In the previous year grants totalled £5,000.

Applications: In writing directly by the individual or via a third party such as a close relative or a legal representative.

Correspondent: D F B Le Breton, Hon. Secretary, 138 High Street, Tonbridge, Kent TN9 1AX.

Overseas Service Pensioners' Benevolent Society

Eligibility: Members or potential members of the Overseas Service Pensioners' Association and other people with other relevant service in a former British dependent (colonial) territory, and their dependants, who are in need.

Types of grants: Generally quarterly grants to meet normal living expenses. Grants are not available to pay residential care or nursing home fees.

Annual grant total: In 2001 the trust had assets of £478,000 and an income of £74,000. Total expenditure was £91,000, including £79,000 given in 110 grants.

Applications: On a form available from the correspondent. Applications should normally be submitted directly by the individual.

Correspondent: D F B Le Breton, Secretary, 138 High Street, Tonbridge, Kent TN9 1AX (01732 363836; Fax: 01732 365070).

Prospects Benevolent Fund (formerly The Institution of Professionals, Managers & Specialists Benevolent Fund and The Engineers' & Manager's Association (EMA) Benevolent Fund)

Eligibility: Members and retired members of the union (and the former Institution of Professional Civil Servants), and their spouses, families, widows or widowers.

Types of grants: Generally one-off grants. Recurrent grants do not exceed £1,500. The trust does not make loans. The trustees aim to relieve immediate problems and point applicants to other channels and agencies for long-term solutions. Grants are usually sent to the applicant, but for speed and/or reliability, some awards are sent direct to the utility/body owed money. Occasionally this is processed through an agency or second party (such as welfare officer, debt counsellor, branch officer or relative).

Annual grant total: In 2000 the fund had assets of £182,000, an income of £40,000 and a grant total of £33,000.

Applications: On a form available from the correspondent. Applications can be submitted directly by the individual, through employer's welfare officers or branch representatives. Applications are considered throughout the year. Payments are usually made to successful applicants within a week of receiving the application (if a trustee is available urgent cases may only take one or two days).

Correspondent: Administrator, Prospects House, 75–79 York Road, London SE1 7AQ (020 7902 6600; Fax: 020 7902 6667).

Other information: In May 2002 The IPMS Benevolent Fund and The EMA Benevolent Fund agreed to merger. This entry is produced from information provided in July 2002 and covers the scope of the new fund.

The Public and Commercial Services Union Benevolent Fund

Eligibility: Members and associate members of the union who are in severe financial distess caused by domestic problems such as sickness or family troubles.

Applications will be rejected if they are not fully paid-up members, or associate members, of the union.

Types of grants: One-off grants to a maximum of £500 for domestic problems such as utility arrears. No grants are given towards private medical expenses, credit cards, debts, overdrafts or loans.

Annual grant total: In 2001 grants to 740 people totalled £140,000.

Applications: Applications should be made on a form, either through local area offices of the union and recommended by the branch officer, or directly by the individual to the national headquarters. The grants panel meets every two weeks to consider applications.

Correspondent: Mel Edwardes, 160 Falcon Road, London SW11 2LN (020 7801 2601, option 3; Fax: 020 7801 2630; e-mail: mel@pcs.org.uk).

The Staines Trust

Eligibility: Former civil servants employed by the British government overseas, and their dependants.

Types of grants: Quarterly, recurrent grants of £520 per year to help with things like telephone bills, nursing home fees, living expenses, rent, travel, and home and

Occupational Charities

vehicle repairs. One-off grants are also available at the trust's discretion, ranging from £50 to £250. No loans are given.

Annual grant total: In 2000 the trust had assets of £920,000, an income of £29,000 and a total expenditure of £31,000. Grants totalling £28,000 were given to 36 individuals, 34 of whom were supported in the previous year.

Applications: On a form available from the correspondent, accompanied by substantiated evidence of need. Applications can be submitted either directly by the individual or through a social worker, citizen's advice bureau, other welfare agency or a third party, and are usually considered in April and November.

Correspondent: Ms Shirley Farmer, Chair, Briar House, 3 King Street, Emsworth, Hampshire PO10 7AX.

Other information: This entry was not confirmed by the trust, but the information was correct according to the public files at the Charity Commission.

Clayworking

The Institute of Clayworkers Benevolent Fund

Eligibility: People in need who had to retire early from the clay-working industry through accident or ill-health. Dependants of deceased clayworkers may also be eligible. The fund covers brick-making, roof tiles, clay drainage pipes and refractory industries, but not pottery workers.

Types of grants: One-off grants, usually of £250. In exceptional cases where applicants have been identified by other charitable bodies as being in extreme need, larger grants may be given.

Annual grant total: Grants in 2000 totalled £3,000.

Applications: In writing to the correspondent, including age, length of service, date of termination of employment (if applicable), brief description (two or three sentences) of circumstances leading to application, and brief testimonial (a sentence or two) from a supervisor/manager if appropriate. The fund only accepts applications made through a former employer, but not usually those made directly by the individual. Applications may be made at any time.

Correspondent: A McRae, Secretary, Federation House, Station Road, Stoke-on-Trent ST4 2SA (01782 744631).

Clothing

The Feltmakers Charitable Foundation

Eligibility: Employees or former employees of the hatting trade who are in need.

Types of grants: One-off or recurrent grants according to need.

Annual grant total: In 2000 the foundation had an income of £21,000 and a total expenditure of £20,000.

Applications: Applicants must be nominated in the first place by their employer or former employer, or in exceptional circumstances by a welfare organisation.

Correspondent: Maj. Jollyon Coombs, The Old Post House, Bidden Road, Upton Grey, Basingstoke, Hampshire RG25 2RL (01256 862025).

Footwear Benevolent Society (formerly The Boot Trade Benevolent Society)

Eligibility: People who are working or have worked in the boot trade and footwear industry, and their dependants.

Types of grants: One-off grants and quarterly allowances with a Christmas bonus to supplement low income or to purchase a specific item such as a new cooker.

Annual grant total: In 2000/01 the society had assets of £1 million, an income of £106,000 and a total expenditure of £134,000. Grants to 309 individuals totalled £85,000.

Applications: On a form available from the correspondent. Applicants are considered every two months.

Correspondent: Ms V H S Jacob, Secretary, Suite 38–39, 3rd Floor, New House, 67–68 Hatton Gardens, London EC1N 8JY (020 7242 1364).

Master Tailors' Benevolent Association

Eligibility: Master tailors in the UK who have worked as a master tailor for ten years employing workers. People who meet this criteria but live elsewhere in the Commonwealth or Eire are also considered if they were born in the UK or Eire.

No grants are given to 'ladies [in the] dressmaking trade'.

Types of grants: One-off grants and recurrent grants of £20 to £40 a week.

Annual grant total: In 2000/01 the trust had assets of £590,000 and an income of £33,000. Total expenditure was £34,000, including £29,000 in grants.

Applications: On a form available from the correspondent, to be submitted directly by the individual or another master tailor known to the trust. They should include the names of woollen merchants the applicant has used for buying suit lengths.

Correspondent: C H R Garner, 35 Dewlands, Godstone, Surrey RH9 8BS (01883 743469).

The Tailors' Benevolent Institute

Eligibility: Tailors, tailoresses and their near relatives who were employed in the bespoke (made to measure) tailoring trade for at least 10 years. Preference is given to past and present members of the institute but help can be given to other eligible applicants. Factory tailors are not eligible.

Types of grants: Typically one-off grants of about £50 or allowances up to £20 a week.

Annual grant total: In 2000 the institute had assets of £2.3 million, an income of £99,000 and a total expenditure of £148,000. Grants totalled £115,000.

Applications: On a form available from the correspondent. Applications should preferably be submitted through a social worker. However, those submitted directly by the individual or through another third party will be considered. Applications are considered monthly except for August.

Correspondent: C M R Garner, 35 Dewlands, Godstone, Surrey RH9 8BS (01883 743469).

Coal industry

The Coal Industry Benevolent Trust

Eligibility: Dependants of people who were killed as a result of working in the mining industry. People attending hospital due to accidents at work are also eligible. The trust interprets this as widely as possible, supporting pulmonary and cardio-pulmonary disease, spectacles and dental work.

Types of grants: General hardship grants of up to £500 towards, for example, buying a motorised wheelchair, repairs, conversion of a heating system and debt arrears; grants of up to £1,400 to the dependants of miners who die as a result of their work made soon after the death and £400 for the following four years, if his widow remains single, and £200 to the children; grants of £50 every four weeks to miners who are in hospital as a result of their work, up to £200 a year; and grants of £5 per journey up to £200 for miners who have to travel to a outpatients centre as a result of an accident at work.

OCCUPATIONAL CHARITIES

Annual grant total: In 2000 the trust had assets of £20 million, an income of £876,000 and a total expenditure of £1.4 million. Grants totalled £1 million.

Applications: In writing to the correspondent for consideration by the trustees. The trust sends one of its own social workers to visit the individual to assess need and assist with the application form.

Correspondent: V O S Jones, Secretary, The Old Rectory, Rectory Drive, Whiston, Rotherham, South Yorkshire S60 4JG (01709 728115; Fax: 01709 839164).

The Coal Trade Benevolent Association

Eligibility: Non-manual workers of the coal industry in England, Wales and Northern Ireland, who have worked in the production or distribution sectors and allied trades and their widows, children and dependants.

Types of grants: Both regular and one-off grants for most kinds of needs. Assistance is given to people in nursing homes, for travel to hospital for treatment and towards special dietary needs.

Annual grant total: In 2001 £147,000 was given in total to 350 beneficiaries.

Applications: On a form available from the correspondent for consideration throughout the year.

Correspondent: T R Cloke, Secretary, 6 Bridge Wharf, 156 Caledonian Road, London N1 9UU (020 7278 3239; Fax: 020 7278 2720; e-mail: coalbenev@aol.com).

Mining Institute of Scotland Trust

Eligibility: Members of the Mining Institute of Scotland and their dependants.

Types of grants: One-off and recurrent hardship grants of up to £1,000 a year. Widows of members can receive Christmas and summer holiday grants.

Annual grant total: The trust has about £25,000 available to give in grants each year, for both education and hardship purposes. It has difficulty in finding enough eligible applicants to support.

Applications: In writing to the correspondent in the first instance, to request an application form.

Correspondent: Keith Donaldson, Hon. Secretary, Flat 4, 15 Baird Road, Ratho, Midlothian EH28 8RU.

Other information: Schools are also supported.

Commerce

The George Drexler Foundation

Eligibility: People in need who have a direct link with commerce, that is, who have owned and run their own commercial business. Applicants whose parents or grandparents have this link can also be supported. This does not include professional people such as doctors, lawyers, dentists, architects or accountants. No exceptions can be made.

Types of grants: One-off and recurrent grants according to need.

Annual grant total: In 2000/01 the trust had assets of £5.2 million and an income of £234,000. Grants to individuals for education and relief-in-need purposes totalled £45,000. In that year most grants were made to organisations (a total of £237,000), but in 2002 the trust decided to no longer make grants to organisations and now all its grant total is donated to eligible individuals.

Applications: On a form available from the correspondent, submitted directly by the individual, enclosing an sae. Applications should be submitted in May for consideration in June.

Correspondent: Mrs Carol Phillips, Trustee, PO Box 338, Granborough, Buckinghamshire MK18 3YT.

The Ruby & Will George Trust

Eligibility: People in need who have been or who are employed in commerce, and their dependants. Preference is given to people who live in the north of England.

Types of grants: One-off or recurrent grants for items which are needed but cannot be afforded, usually related to sickness and disability, for example, wheelchairs, washing machines and clothes.

Annual grant total: In 2000/01 the trust had an income of £144,000 and its total expenditure was £128,000. About £100,000 is given to individuals each year for welfare and educational purposes.

Applications: In writing to the correspondent in the first instance, requesting an application form. Applications are considered at quarterly trustees' meetings in July, October, January and April.

Correspondent: David John Simpson, Administrator, 18 Ghyll Edge, Lancaster Park, Morpeth, Northumberland NE61 3QZ (01670 516657).

Commercial travellers

The Commercial Travellers' Benevolent Institution

Eligibility: Commercial travellers, representatives and agents, and their dependants. Applicants must have been employed in commercial sales for a minimum of five years. It is not necessary to have been a member of any commercial travellers association, but grants are only given to suppliers, not door to door salespeople or those involved in direct selling to the public.

Types of grants: Grants usually of up to £20 a week paid quarterly in advance, plus gifts in kind. One-off grants will be considered.

Annual grant total: About £360,000 to over 300 regular beneficiaries.

Applications: On a form available from the correspondent. Applications are considered quarterly and can be submitted directly by the individual, through a welfare agency or another third party (e.g. citizen's advice bureau, nursing home and so on).

Correspondent: Mandy Leonard, 2 Fletcher Road, Ottershaw, Surrey KT16 0JY (Tel & Fax: 01932 429636; e-mail: sec.cbti@ntworld.com; website: www.ctbi.org).

Cooperative

The National Association of Cooperative Officials' Benevolent Fund

Eligibility: Members and retired members of the association and their families; also widows and children of deceased members.

Types of grants: One-off grants up to a maximum of about £500.

Annual grant total: In 2000 the fund had an income of £4,700 and a total expenditure of £1,500, all of which was given in grants.

Applications: On a form available from the correspondent to be submitted directly by the individual and considered in February, May, September and November. Applications should include details of personal finance.

Correspondent: Lindsay Ewing, 6a Clarendon Place, Hyde, Cheshire SK14 2QZ (0161 351 7900).

Coopers

William Alexander Coopers Liverymen Fund

Eligibility: Members of the Coopers' Company, their widows and other dependants, who are in need.

Types of grants: Money can be given to supplement relief or assistance provided out of public funds, in the form of one-off grants and Christmas grants.

Annual grant total: In 2000/01 the fund had an income of £4,800 and a total expenditure of £2,900.

Applications: This trust states that it does not respond to unsolicited applications.

Correspondent: The Clerk, Coopers' Hall, 13 Devonshire Square, London EC2M 4TH (020 7247 9577; Fax: 020 7377 8061; e-mail: clerk@coopers-hall.co.uk).

Corn exchange

The Bristol Corn Trade Guild

Eligibility: People who work in the corn and feed trade and their dependants, who are in need.

Types of grants: One-off grants ranging from £200 to £840. Recent grants have been given towards utility bills, medical equipment, repairs and as food vouchers.

Annual grant total: In 2001 the trust had assets of £144,000 and an income of £3,800. Total expenditure was £3,100, including £2,600 given in total in five grants.

Applications: In writing to the correspondent. Applications can be submitted directly by the individual or through a social worker, citizen's advice bureau or other welfare agency.

Correspondent: A C Gulland, 2 Blenheim Court, Stanfort Park, Woodlands, Almondsbury, Bristol BS32 4NE (01454 618008; Fax: 01454 617806; e-mail: gm@bctfa.fsnet.co.uk; website: www.bctfa.org.uk).

The Corn Exchange Benevolent Society

Eligibility: Members of the society and their dependants. Limited funds are available for people who work or have worked in the corn, grain, seed, animal feed stuffs, pulses, malt, flour or granary-keeping trades, and their dependants.

Types of grants: Recurrent grants according to need. Additional one-off grants are also made to meet unexpected items of expense, such as hospitalisation or going into a nursing home, and are made for three or four weeks.

Annual grant total: In 2000 the society had assets of £2.3 million, an income of £97,000 and a total expenditure of £83,000. Grants totalled £57,000.

Applications: On a form available from the correspondent.

Correspondent: R J M Butler, 20 St Dunstan's Hill, London EC3R 8HL (020 7283 6090).

Cricket

The Cricketers Association Charity

Eligibility: Members and former members of the association and any person who has played cricket on at least one occasion for any county which at the relevant time was recognised by the English Cricket Board (formerly the Test and County Cricket Board), and their dependants.

Types of grants: One-off or recurrent grants according to need.

Annual grant total: In 1999 grants totalled over £20,000.

Applications: In writing to the correspondent, to be considered as they arrive.

Correspondent: David Graveney, 34 High Street, Westbury-on-Trym, Bristol BS9 3DZ.

Other information: This entry was not confirmed by the trust, but the address was correct according to the Charity Commission database.

The Hornsby Professional Cricketers Fund Charity

Eligibility: Former professional cricketers and their dependants who are in need.

Types of grants: Monthly, holiday, Christmas, winter, medical and educational grants are given.

Annual grant total: In 2000/01 the charity had an income of £26,000 and a total expenditure of £28,000.

Applications: In writing to the correspondent. Applications can be submitted either directly by the individual or by the county cricket club.

Correspondent: A K James, Clerk, Dunroamin, 65 Keyhaven Road, Milford-on-Sea, Lymington, Hampshire SO41 0QX (01590 644720).

Customs & excise

The Customs & Excise Family Fund

Eligibility: Members and former members of the Customs & Excise Department and their dependants who are in need.

Types of grants: One-off or recurrent grants according to need. Loans can also be given to assist with long-term needs. Recent grants have gone to help with a parent's travel costs incurred when her child needed specialist medical care and to help support the daughter of a former member after his ill-health retirement. Children are given high priority. Numerous widows and former members also receive financial support, some with urgent replacement, repair or redecoration bills.

Annual grant total: In 2001/02 the trust had assets of £1.7 million and an income of £151,000. Expenditure was £144,000 and 197 grants totalling £139,000 were made.

Applications: On a form available from the correspondent. Applications are normally considered each month but there is provision for emergency grants in exceptional circumstances.

Correspondent: Mrs Jan Devine, 2nd Floor, New Kings Beam House, 22 Upper Ground, London SE1 9PJ (020 7865 4951; e-mail: jan.devine@hmce.gsi.gov.uk).

Domestic service

Domestic Servants Benevolent Institution

Eligibility: People in need who have been in domestic service or who are existing pensioners, members and former members of the institution.

Types of grants: One-off and recurrent grants according to need.

Annual grant total: In 2000/01 the trust had an income of £2,100 and its total expenditure was £1,500, all of which went on grants to individuals.

Applications: In writing to the correspondent at any time.

Correspondent: S G Robertson, Springboard Housing, 2a Claughton Road, London E13 9PN (020 8548 2545; Fax: 020 8470 9504; e-mail: mail@springboardha.org.uk).

Driving Instructors

The Driving Instructors Accident & Disability Fund

Eligibility: Driving instructors or former driving instructors (members of the Driving Instructors Association) who have been injured or disabled and their dependants. The association has about 10,000 members.

Types of grants: One-off grants of £150 to £250.

Annual grant total: Grants total £1,500 to £2,000.

Applications: In writing to the correspondent.

Correspondent: Graham Fryer, DIA, Safety House, Bedding Farm Road, Croydon, Surrey CR0 7XZ (020 8665 5151).

Electrical

The Amalgamated Engineering & Electrical Union

Eligibility: Members and former members of the union and their dependants, who are in financial distress caused by unemployment, ill-health or age. No grants to aid political or industrial action.

Types of grants: Usually one-off grants. The union's central office in Bromley does not have a benevolent fund, but is responsible for allocating resources to the 840 local branches, each of which has its own fund.

Annual grant total: In 1996 the funds had assets of £706,000 and an income of £531,000. Expenditure totalled £491,000, but not all of this was given in grants to individuals for relief-in-need.

Applications: In writing to the correspondent, who forwards the application to the relevant branch.

Correspondent: General Secretary, Hayes Court, West Common Road, Bromley, Kent BR2 7AU (020 8462 7755; Fax: 020 8315 8234).

Electrical and Electronics Industries Benevolent Association

Eligibility: Employees and former employees of the UK electrical and electronic industries and allied sciences, including mechanical engineering, and their dependants. There are no age limits.

Types of grants: Grants are: 'To provide practical help and support in any form most appropriate to each individual applicant including one-off grants, ongoing budget balancing grants, clothing, house repairs (specific criteria), aids for disabled people, holidays, wheelchairs (specific criteria), television and telephone rental, etc.'

Grants are not normally given to cover the costs of private medical care, educational fees or nursing/residential fees.

Annual grant total: In 2001 the trust had assets of £5.3 million and an income of £1.8 million. Grants to 8,300 people totalled £635,000.

Applications: On a form available from the head of welfare. They can be submitted directly by the individual or through a social worker, citizen's advice bureau, other welfare agency or a human resources department. They are considered throughout the year.

Correspondent: Ken Hadley, 8 Station Parade, Balham High Road, London SW12 9BH (020 8673 0131; Fax: 020 8675 2259).

Other information: The association also runs a sheltered housing scheme in Sellyoak, Birmingham.

The Incorporated Benevolent Fund of The Institution of Electrical Engineers

Eligibility: Members or former members, for not less than five consecutive years membership, of the institution, and their dependants.

Types of grants: Regular weekly grants, holidays, respite care, home adaptations, special equipment and loans.

Annual grant total: In 2000/01 the fund had assets of £14 million, an income of £1.6 million and a total expenditure of £1.4 million. Grants totalled £491,000.

Applications: On a form available from the benevolent fund office at the adress below. Applications are sent to a local welfare visitor who will visit the applicant to discuss the request and report the findings to the care committee.

Correspondent: Thomas Bennett, IEE, Savoy Place, London WC2R 0BL (020 7344 5497/8; Fax: 020 7240 0786; website: www.ieebenfund.org.uk).

Other information: The fund also owns a residential home in New Malden, Surrey, for the benefit of its members and their dependants.

The RTRA Benevolent Fund

Eligibility: People in need who are directly connected with the electronic and electrical retailing industry.

Types of grants: One-off grants to give relief to individuals in need.

Annual grant total: In 2000/01 the fund had an income of £8,700 and a total expenditure of £6,000.

Applications: In writing to the correspondent at any time.

Correspondent: The Secretary, Retra Ltd, Retra House, St John's Terrace, 1 Ampthill Street, Bedford MK42 9EY (01234 269110).

Engineering

The Chartered Institution of Building Services Engineers Benevolent Fund

Eligibility: Members of the institution and their dependants (on death of member), who are in need.

Types of grants: About 40 grants of £100 are made each quarter.

Annual grant total: Grants total £20,000 to £30,000 each year.

Applications: On a form available from the correspondent, including financial status. Applications are considered in February, May, August and November.

Correspondent: Julian Amey, CIBSE, 222 Balham High Road, London SW12 9BS.

Other information: This entry was not confirmed by the trust, but the address was correct according to the Charity Commission database.

The Benevolent Fund of the Engineering Employers' Federation (including the Dyer Memorial Funds)

Eligibility: 'The purpose of the fund is to enable federated employers to obtain financial assistance for their employees or their dependants. In order to be eligible the relevant employee should be or have been employed in a position of trust and this is normally taken to mean under-foreman or equivalent status.'

Types of grants: Grants fall into the following categories:
(i) Income grants, where the applicant's income, after certain deductions, has fallen below the equivalent of a state pension (this can be increased when the applicant is elderly, infirm or has dependants). These grants range from £200 to £1,040.
(ii) Property grants, generally for modifications to the applicant's home due to their physical condition.
(iii) Convalescent grants, for the costs of a short stay in a convalescent home. The application must be accompanied by a doctor's certificate.
(iv) Bereavement grants, payable in respect of the death of an employee or their spouse, to assist with funeral costs.
(v) Mobility grants to help applicants in

need of a wheelchair or to adapt other forms of transport.

The fund does not give loans.

Annual grant total: In 2000/01 the fund had assets of £1.7 million and an income of £67,000. Grants totalled £230,000.

Applications: All new applications must be submitted through the applicant's former employer and federated association on a form available from the correspondent. Applications are considered in January and June and must be submitted by May or December. Urgent cases will be dealt with throughout the year. Applications for property or mobility grants must be accompanied by written estimates or receipts and a letter forwarded from the applicant's GP advising why the applicant's condition necessitates the work. Applicants who have previously applied do not have to provide proof of their former employment.

Correspondent: Paul Reynolds, Fund Manager, Broadway House, Tothill Street, London SW1H 9NQ (020 7654 1563; Fax: 020 7222 2782; e-mail: preynolds@eef-fed.org.uk).

The Worshipful Company of Engineers Charitable Trust Fund

Eligibility: Engineers who are in need. Applicants do not necessarily have to be members of the Worshipful Company.

Types of grants: Grants of between £500 and £1,000 for welfare purposes.

Annual grant total: In 2001 the trust's assets totalled £282,000, its income was £24,000 and its total expenditure was £35,000. Grants to individuals and organisations for educational purposes totalled £14,000. Other grants were made to individuals for welfare purposes.

Applications: In writing to the correspondent at any time, directly by the individual, providing as much detail about your circumstances as possible. Applications are considered in January, April, July and October.

Correspondent: Commander Bryan D Gibson, The Worshipful Company of Engineers, Wax Chandlers Hall, Gresham Street, London EC2V 7AD (020 7726 4830; Fax: 020 7726 4820; e-mail: clerk@engineerscompany.org.uk; website: www.engineerscompany.org.uk).

Other information: Grants are also made to organisations and individuals for educational purposes.

The Guild of Benevolence of The Institute of Marine Engineering Science and Technology

Eligibility: Qualified marine engineers, or their dependants, who are in need. Scientists and technologists are also eligible if members of the institute.

Types of grants: Regular grants of £20 per week are given to supplement a low income. One-off grants, to a maximum of £2,500, for equipment for disabled people, debt relief, funeral costs, home maintenance and respite care. No grants for educational costs.

Annual grant total: In 2000/01 the guild had assets of £2.8 million, an income of £149,000 and a total expenditure of £202,000. Grants to 87 individuals totalled £151,000.

Applications: On a form available from the correspondent. Evidence of service or qualifications as a marine engineer must be produced if not already a member of the Institute of Marine Engineers, as well as full disclosure of financial situation. Applications are considered every two months.

Correspondent: The Chair, 80 Coleman Street, London EC2R 5BJ (020 7382 2600; Fax: 020 7382 2670; e-mail: guild@imarest.org; website: www.imarest.org/gob).

Other information: This fund was launched as a response to the sinking of the Titanic in 1912, a disaster which no marine engineer abroad survived. From 1989 the guild has administered the Marine Engineers Benevolent Fund. The guild also gives a grant to the Royal Merchant Navy School Foundation.

The Benevolent Fund of the Institution of Civil Engineers

Eligibility: Past and present members of the institution and their dependants. Also dependants of former members of the Institution of Municipal Engineers.

Types of grants: Regular or one-off grants to bring income up to a suitable level after receipt of state benefits, to top up nursing/care home fees, to buy equipment for people who are disabled or to help with temporary financial difficulties. Loans are also made, generally against security.

No grants towards funeral expenses or higher education. Education grants are only given in very exceptional circumstances and then only to those under 16.

Annual grant total: In 2001 the trust had assets of £13 million and an income of £893,000. Expenditure totalled £612,000 including £346,000 in grants to 134 individuals.

Applications: On a form available from the correspondent, sponsored by two members of the institution, or by solicitors, accountants and such like. Applications can be submitted directly by the individual or through a social worker, citizen's advice bureau or other welfare agency, or through a close relative, solicitor or similar third party. The trust requires information about the applicant's income, expenditure and capital. Grant-giving is considered throughout the year.

Correspondent: Mrs K Barnett, Administrative Secretary, 30 Mill Hill Close, Haywards Heath, West Sussex RH16 1NY (01444 417979; Fax: 01444 453307; e-mail: benfund@ice.org.uk).

Other information: Accommodation in West Sussex is offered to those in housing and financial difficulty. The fund also has nomination rights to the Hanover Housing Association.

The Institution of Gas Engineers Benevolent Fund

Eligibility: Members and ex-members of the Institution of Gas Engineers, and their dependants. Please note that other people in the gas industry who have no such connection with the institution are not eligible.

Types of grants: One-off and recurrent grants according to need.

Annual grant total: In 2000 the income was £17,000 and total expenditure was £5,000.

Applications: In writing to the correspondent.

Correspondent: Institute of Gas Engineers and Managers (Igem), 12 York Gate, London NW1 4QG (020 7487 0650; Fax: 020 7224 4762; e-mail: general@igem.org.uk; website: www.igaseng.com).

Other information: This entry, apart from the address, was not confirmed by the trust.

The Benevolent Fund of the Institution of Mechanical Engineers

Eligibility: Past and present members of the Institution and their dependants, who are in need.

Types of grants: One-off and monthly grants are available towards a variety of needs, including house repairs and maintenance, lifeline community alarms, disability equipment, cookers, washing machines, fridges, beds and bedding, furniture and residential care and nursing home fees.

No grants are given for education, private medical equipment or religious purposes.

Annual grant total: In 2001 the trust had assets of £12 million and both an income and expenditure of £750,000. Grants to 3,000 individuals totalled £553,000.

Applications: On a form available from the correspondent. Applications should be submitted by the individual in February, May, August or November for consideration in the following month.

Occupational Charities

Correspondent: R I Money, 3 Birdcage Walk, London SW1H 9JJ (020 7304 6812; Fax: 020 7973 1262; e-mail: benfund@imeche.org.uk; website: www.imeche.org.uk).

Other information: To confirm eligibility, phone a caseworker and welfare officer on 020 7304 6816.

The Institution of Plant Engineers Benevolent Fund

Eligibility: Members/former members of the institution, and their dependants living in England, Scotland and Wales.

Types of grants: Most grants are given to people who are financially stressed through serious illness, unemployment or bereavement. A recent grant for example went to a young member no longer able to work due to multiple sclerosis. Grants can range from £50 to £1,000.

Annual grant total: In 1999 the fund had assets of £250,000 and an income of £21,000. Total expenditure was £13,000 with 100 grants totalling £11,000.

Applications: In writing to the correspondent. Applications can be submitted directly by the individual or by a relative or close friend. They are considered in March, July and November.

Correspondent: Francis David Chapman, 22 Greencoat Place, London SW1P 1PR (020 7630 1111).

The Institution of Structural Engineers Benevolent Fund

Eligibility: Members of the institution and their dependants.

Types of grants: One-off and recurrent grants and loans according to need.

Annual grant total: In 2001 the fund had assets of £832,000 and an income of £104,000. Total expenditure was £100,000 with 33 grants totalling £88,000.

Applications: On a form available from the correspondent which can be submitted by the individual for consideration in March and November. The trust likes to visit an applicant before a grant is made.

Correspondent: H S Kitching, 11 Upper Belgrave Street, London SW1X 8BH (020 7235 4535; Fax: 020 7235 4294; e-mail: benfund@istructe.org.uk; website: www.istructe.org.uk).

The Lighthouse Club Benevolent Fund

See entry on page 29

Environmental health

Environmental Health Officers Welfare Fund

Eligibility: Past and present members of Chartered Institute of Environmental Health Officers, Association of Public Health Inspectors or The Guild of Public Health Inspection and their dependants, who are in need.

Types of grants: One-off and recurrent grants according to need.

Annual grant total: In 2000 the trust had an income of £4,900 and its total expenditure was £3,800, all of which was given in grants to individuals in need.

Applications: In writing to the correspondent, usually via centre or branch networks.

Correspondent: Andrew Gardner, Chadwick Court, 15 Hatfields, London SE1 8DJ (020 7928 6006; e-mail: membership@cieh.org; website: www.cieh.org.uk).

Farriers

The Worshipful Company of Farriers Charitable Trust

Eligibility: Registered farriers, their widows and dependants who are in need.

Types of grants: One-off or recurrent grants according to need. Grants are usually given to people who are unable to work through injury or sickness.

Annual grant total: In 2000 the trust had assets of £1.2 million, an income of £52,000 and a total expenditure of £51,000. Grants to 20 individuals totalled about £2,000.

Applications: In writing to the correspondent.

Correspondent: Mrs C C Clifford, Clerk, 19 Queen Street, Chipperfield, Kings Langley, Hertfordshire WD4 9BT (01923 260747; Fax: 01923 261677; e-mail: theclerk@wcf.org.uk; website: www.wcf.org.uk).

Fire service

The British Fire Services Association Widows Orphans and Benevolent Fund

Eligibility: Fire-fighters and ex-fire-fighters who have held BFSA membership, and their dependants.

Types of grants: One-off and recurrent maintenance grants according to need. One-off grants are made towards, for example, cookers, refrigerators and repairs and decoration. Recurrent grants are of up to £335 a year and are made to people who receive Income Support.

Annual grant total: In 2000 the fund had assets of £623,000, an income of £30,000 and a total expenditure of £37,000. Grants to 39 individuals totalled £19,000.

Applications: In writing to the correspondent. All applicants are subject to a home visit by a representative of the fund. The trustees require full details of applicants income and expenditure, and proof of eligibility, e.g. record of fire service employment. One-off grants of up to £250 are authorised by a subcommittee. Requests exceeding £250 are submitted to the full management committee which sits in March, July and November.

Correspondent: The Secretary & Treasurer, 86 London Road, Leicester LE2 0QR (Tel & Fax: 0116 254 2879).

The Fire Services National Benevolent Fund

Eligibility: People who are, or have been over a specified minimum period, active fire-fighters (including volunteers and those in the wartime National Fire Service) and non-uniform members. Widows, widowers, young dependants and young children with special needs of serving fire-fighters are also eligible.

Types of grants: Grants according to need. Local county committees can pay immediate hardship grants of up to £400; regional committees can make grants of up to £1,000; and grants of up to £5,000 can be made at national level. Some allowances are paid to people who are disabled and in need. Limited assistance may be given to people in residential care homes or nursing homes if they are already in receipt of Income Support and/or local authority assistance.

Annual grant total: In 2000 the trust had an income of £3.9 million and its total expenditure was £4.2 million. Further financial information was not available for this year.

In 1999 grants totalled £1.1 million. A further £81,000 was given in educational grants.

OCCUPATIONAL CHARITIES

Applications: Applications should be made to the Fund Secretary at the local fire brigade headquarters on a form available from them. Applicants should contact the fund before they apply.

Correspondent: Angela Suwell, Marine Court, Fitzalan Road, Littlehampton, West Sussex BN17 5NF (01903 736062; Fax: 01903 731095; e-mail: administration@fsnbf.org.uk; website: www.fsnbf.org.uk).

Other information: This fund was founded in 1943 to help all types of fire-fighters and their widows or widowers and young dependants. It also provides short-term convalescence, rehabilitation, therapy and sheltered housing, but does not have residential or nursing homes.

Food, drink and provision trades

The Bakers' Benevolent Society

Eligibility: People who are retired and have worked in the baking industry and its allied trades, and their spouses.

Types of grants: Small one-off grants and pensions.

Annual grant total: About £24,000.

Applications: On a form available from the correspondent. Applications are considered once a month.

Correspondent: F G Allen, Clerk to the Society, The Mill House, 23 Bakers Lane, Epping, Essex CM16 5DQ (01992 575951; Fax: 01992 561163).

Other information: The society also manages almshouses and sheltered housing in Congleton and Epping.

Barham Benevolent Foundation

Eligibility: People who have been employed in the milk business, and possibly their dependants, who are in need.

Types of grants: One-off and monthly grants according to need.

Annual grant total: In 2000 the trust's income was £145,000 and its total expenditure was £108,000, nearly all of which was given in grants to individuals in need.

Applications: In writing to the correspondent.

Correspondent: Mrs E Coombe, Barham Manor, 32 Western Parade, Southsea, Hampshire PO5 3JG (023 9281 1896).

The Butchers' & Drovers' Charitable Institution

Eligibility: People in the UK, normally those who are retired or medically certified unfit to work, who have worked in any aspect of the meat industry whether wholesale, retail or otherwise, usually for at least 10 years, and their close family members.

Types of grants: Pensions and one-off grants, recurrent grants or loans. One-off grants range from £100 to £1,000 and are made towards, for instance, heating bills, house repairs and clothing. Recurrent grants are of £13 a week. Grants of up to £50 a week are made to top-up nursing home fees.

Annual grant total: In 2000/01 the trust had assets of £3.1 million and an income of £294,000. Total expenditure was £425,000 with about 240 grants to individuals totalling £188,000.

Applications: On a form available from the correspondent with details of employment and savings and signatures of trade members supporting the application. Applications can be submitted directly by the individual or through a social worker, citizen's advice bureau, other welfare agency or third party and are considered monthly, with the exception of August and December.

Correspondent: Martyn Craddock, Butchers' Hall, 87 Bartholomew Close, London EC1A 7EB (020 7606 4106; Fax: 020 7606 4108).

Caravan (the trading name of The National Grocers Benevolent Fund)

Eligibility: People living in the UK who have spent at least 15 years of their adult working life (after the age of 18) in the grocery, provision and off-licence industries, and their dependants. This includes food manufacturing, wholesaling and retailing in all its aspects and the retail off-licence trade.

Types of grants: Quarterly payments plus two annual bonuses of £80 at Christmas and £50 for heating on 1 March, totalling £620 per annum.

Emergency grants for specific financial problems such as house repairs, disability equipment and household equipment are also available.

Annual grant total: In 2001/02 the trust had assets of £6.2 million and an income of £1.4 million. Total expenditure was £870,000, most of which was given in grants.

Applications: On a form available from the correspondent. Applications can be submitted directly by the individual, through a social worker, citizen's advice bureau, other welfare agency, or via a third party such as a relative. Applications are considered throughout the year.

Correspondent: Graham Kirker, Director General, 17 Farnborough Street, Farnborough, Hampshire GU14 8AG (01252 515946; Fax: 01252 377842; e-mail: ngbf@dial.pipex.com).

The Confectioners' Benevolent Fund

Eligibility: People engaged in the manufacture, wholesale or retail of chocolates and sweets for 10 years, usually those who have retired through ill health or old age.

Types of grants: Recurrent grants of up to £10 a week, plus assistance with TV licences. One-off grants of up to £250 are also available. No grants towards funeral payments or nursing home fees.

Annual grant total: In 2000/01 the trust had assets of £2.1 million and an income of £905,000. Total expenditure was £791,000, including £426,000 in grants

Applications: On a form available from the correspondent, submitted directly by the individual or through a social worker, citizen's advice bureau or welfare agency. Applications are considered in February, May, August and November. The trust has a team of paid field welfare offices who visit potential and existing beneficiaries. There are also 100 volunteer visitors who befriend and visit beneficiaries on a quarterly basis.

Correspondent: Liz Hartill, Director of Welfare, 37-41 Bedford Row, London WC1R 4JH (020 7404 5222; Fax: 020 7404 5221; e-mail: info@sweetcharity.net; website: www.sweetcharity.net).

The Fishmongers' & Poulterers' Institution

Eligibility: People who are or who have been in the fish or poultry trades from dock workers or processors to retailers, and their dependants.

Types of grants: Pensions, nursing home fees top-ups, or one-off grants for needs such as home repairs, orthopaedic beds, clothing/furniture following a fire, or debt clearance. Grants range between £250 and £700.

Annual grant total: In 2001 the institution had assets of £546,000 and an income of £34,000. Total expenditure was £53,000, with grants to individuals totalling £41,000.

Applications: On a form available from the correspondent. Applications can be submitted directly by the individual or by a third party such as a social worker or citizen's advice bureau. They are usually considered in January, May and September.

Correspondent: Martyn Craddock, Butchers' Hall, 87 Bartholomew Close, London EC1A 7EB (020 7606 4106; Fax: 020 7606 4108; e-mail: fpi@butchershall.com).

Other information: This charity also gives grants for educational purposes.

Sir Percival Griffiths' Tea Planters Trust

Eligibility: People who live in the UK who are or have been involved in tea planting in India and their dependants.

Types of grants: Monthly allowances and ad-hoc payments three or four times a year. In 1996, grants ranged from £300 to £1,500.

Annual grant total: In 2000 the trust had assets of £88,000. The income was £12,000, all of which was given in grants.

Applications: On a form available from the correspondent, to be submitted directly by the individual, through a social worker, citizen's advice bureau, welfare agency, or third party. Applications are considered at any time.

Correspondent: Mrs A Wilson, Wrotham Place, Wrotham, Sevenoaks, Kent TN15 7AE (01732 884488; Fax: 01732 885724).

The Incorporated Brewers' Benevolent Society

Eligibility: People employed or formerly employed in the brewing production profession, and their dependants, who are in need.

Types of grants: Regular and one-off grants according to need.

Annual grant total: The amount given varies each year.

Applications: On a form available from the correspondent. Applications can be submitted at any time.

Correspondent: The Secretary, 8 Ely Place, London EC1N 6SD (020 7405 4565).

The National Association of Master Bakers

Eligibility: Ex-master bakers from England or Wales (whether members of the association or not) and their families who are in need.

Types of grants: Pensions, one-off grants and loans according to need. No grants for business debt or towards nursing home fees. Recent grants have included help with household expenses (e.g. telephone, gas), purchase or loan of equipment (e.g. stair lifts, wheelchairs, smoke detectors), grants in case of special hardship (e.g. to pay-off loans, funeral costs) and Christmas food hampers. Recurrent grants are usually for £5 a week and are paid quarterly. About 150 individuals receive help; some receive more than one grant.

Annual grant total: In 2000 the trust had an income of £24,000 and a total expenditure of £143,000. The trust has been regularly overspending in recent years, but not usually to this degree.

Applications: On a form available from the correspondent, which can be submitted by the individual or through a recognised referral agency (social worker, citizen's advice bureau, doctor etc.) and are considered every month.

Correspondent: Karen Dear, 21 Baldock Street, Ware, Hertfordshire SG12 9DH (01920 468061).

The National British & Irish Millers' Benevolent Society

Eligibility: Members of the Incorporated National Association of British and Irish Millers, master millers and other flour milling employees from the UK, their widows and, in certain special cases, their dependants.

Types of grants: Donations and grants are awarded annually following a review of each individual's circumstances. Christmas cash gifts and hampers are also given, as is help with heating bills.

Annual grant total: In 1998 about £13,000 was given in grants.

Applications: On a form available from the correspondent. Unsolicited applications are not considered.

Correspondent: Linda Sinclair, Millers Mutual Assurance NAB, 21 Arlington Street, London SW1A 1RN (020 7493 2521).

National Dairymen's Benevolent Institution

Eligibility: People who have worked in the dairy trade in the UK for a continuous period of seven years and have since retired through age or ill health.

Types of grants: One-off grants of up to £1,500. Recent grants have included those towards replacement furniture, domestic appliances, necessitous healthcare aids, clothing, house repairs. Grants are not available for assistance with nursing home fees.

Annual grant total: In 2000/01 the trust had assets of £1.2 million and an income of £384,000. Total expenditure was £468,000, including £79,000 given in total in 242 grants.

Applications: On a form available from the correspondent, submitted directly by the individual or through a social worker, citizen's advice bureau or other welfare agency. Applications should include any relevant invoices or cost estimates and are considered in January, March, May, July, September and November.

Correspondent: Mrs Tina Scott, Secretary, First Floor, Front Office, 8 High Street, Worthing, Sussex BN11 1NU (01903 213065; Fax: 01903 203353; e-mail: tinascott@ndbi.freeserve.co.uk).

The National Federation of Fish Friers Benevolent Fund

Eligibility: Members or former members of the federation and their dependants, living in the UK.

Types of grants: One-off grants only for necessities, including convalescent holidays in the UK (up to £200 per week for two people for two weeks). Grants range from £150 to £300.

No grants for debts due to poor business practice or convalescence outside the UK.

Annual grant total: In 2000 the fund had an income of £3,900 and a total expenditure of £3,400, all of which was given in grants.

Applications: On a form available from the correspondent. Applications can be submitted by the individual, through a recognised referral agency (social worker, citizen's advice bureau or AFF Associations/branches etc.) or by the individual's family, and are considered throughout the year.

Correspondent: Mrs Ann M Kirk, General Secretary, New Federation House, 4 Greenwood Mount, Leeds LS6 4LQ (0113 230 7044).

The Provision Trade Charity

Eligibility: People in need in the provision trade, and their dependants. Applicants are normally retired and must have been employed in the trade for at least 10 years.

Types of grants: Quarterly payments; guidelines for 1999/2000 were £100 each week (single) and £130 each week (couple). Summer and winter gifts are awarded as appropriate. Loans are not given.

Annual grant total: In 2000 the charity had an income of £65,000. Grants to 49 individuals totalled £50,000.

Applications: On a form available from the correspondent. Applications are usually considered in February, May, August and November. They can be submitted directly by the individual or through a social worker, citizen's advice bureau, other welfare agency or through a relation or friend. Prospective beneficiaries are visited by the trust's welfare officer.

Correspondent: Peter Denhard, Secretary & Treasurer, 17 Clerkenwell Green, London EC1R 0DP (020 7253 2114; Fax: 020 7608 1645).

Other information: This trust was founded as the Cheesemonger's Benevolent Institution in 1835 'for pensionary relief of indigent or incapacitated members of the Provision Trade and their widows'. It was included in the last edition of the guide as The Provision Trade Benevolent Institution.

OCCUPATIONAL CHARITIES

The Society of Licensed Victuallers

Eligibility: Members and associate members of the society and their widows or widowers, who are in need. Ex-associate members are only eligible if they held membership for a minimum of three consecutive years.

Types of grants: Recurrent grants of up to: £20 for full members who are single; £40 for full members who are married; £10 for single associate members; and £20 for married associate members. One-off grants are also made towards convalescent care, Christmas gifts, winter allowances, TV licences, funeral expenses, mobility aids and so on.

Bursaries are also available for the members' children at the Licensed Victuallers Schools in Ascot – Berkshire and Ilkley – West Yorkshire.

Annual grant total: In 2000 the society had assets of £47 million, an income of £7.4 million and a total expenditure of £8.2 million. Welfare grants totalled £236,000. Bursaries totalled £5.9 million.

Applications: On a form available from the welfare secretary, at the address below, with proof of membership, personal details, personal history and full financial circumstances. Applications are considered monthly and can be submitted either directly by the individual or through a social worker, citizen's advice bureau or other welfare agency.

Correspondent: C J Wheeler, Heatherley, London Road, Ascot, Berkshire SL5 8DR (01344 884440; Fax: 01344 884703; e-mail: info@slv-online.org.uk; website: www.slv-online.org.uk).

The Wine & Spirits Trades' Benevolent Society

Eligibility: People living in England, Northern Ireland or Wales who have worked for some years, directly or indirectly, in the buying, selling, producing or distributing of wines and spirits, and their dependants. Applicants are mainly of pensionable age.

Types of grants: Regular grants of £15 a week paid monthly. One-off grants of up to £250 for a variety of items, including cookers, fridges, other household equipment, electric scooters and stairlifts. No grants are given towards business equipment.

Annual grant total: In 2001 the trust had assets of £3.1 million and an income and a total expenditure of £800,000. Grants to 400 individuals totalled £260,000.

Applications: On a form available from the correspondent. Applications can be submitted directly by the individual, or through a social worker or welfare agency. They are considered throughout the year and should include history of employment within the drinks industry.

Correspondent: M D Campbell, Chief Executive, Five Kings House, 1 Queen Street Place, London EC4R 1QS (020 7248 1343; Fax: 020 7248 1601; e-mail: ws.bensoc@virgin.net; website: www.winespiritbensoc.org).

Other information: The society also has two residential estates and a care home.

The Wine Trade Foundation

Eligibility: People in need who are or were employed in the wine and spirit and ancilliary trades in the UK and Republic of Ireland, and their dependants.

Types of grants: One-off grants for the general relief of poverty.

Annual grant total: Around £10,000.

Applications: In writing to the correspondent, preferably submitted directly by the individual. Applications are considered throughout the year.

Correspondent: M H R Hasslacher, Trustee, Broomwood, Kettlewell Hill, Woking, Surrey GU21 4JJ.

Football

The Football Association Benevolent Fund

Eligibility: People who have been involved in football in any capacity, such as players and referees, and their dependants, who are in need. The fund interprets people involved in football as broadly as possible, although it tends not to support professional footballers, passing their details on to the occupational benevolent funds which they can apply to.

Types of grants: One-off and recurrent grants ranging from £250 to £2,000 are given to meet any need.

Annual grant total: In 2000 the fund had assets of £2.9 million and an income of £256,000. Total expenditure was £54,000, most of which was given in grants. This surplus of over £200,000, which has often occurred in recent years, was all available in grants to eligible applicants.

Applications: On a form available from the correspondent. Applications should be submitted directly by the individual and are considered on a regular basis. The fund regularly advertises amongst county federations in order to boost the number of applicants.

Correspondent: Mike Appleby, 25 Soho Square, London W1D 4SA (020 7745 4589; e-mail: mike.appleby@thefa.com).

The Institute of Football Management & Administration Charity Trust

Eligibility: Members or former members of the institute (formerly the Football League Executive Staffs Association) who have worked for a Football League or Premier League Club and who are in need, and their dependants.

Types of grants: One-off grants in particular cases of need, and Christmas hampers.

Annual grant total: In 1998/99 the trust had an income of £7,800. Expenditure totalled £6,500.

Applications: In writing to the correspondent. Applications can be submitted directly by the individual or through a family member, friend or colleague.

Correspondent: O Dixon, Secretary, Camkin House, 8 Charles Court, Budbrooke Road, Warwick CV34 5LZ.

The League Managers Benevolent Trust

Eligibility: People in need who have been members of the League Managers Association and their wives, widows and children.

Types of grants: One-off and recurrent grants according to need.

Annual grant total: In 2000 the trust had an income of £2,300 and its total expenditure was £5,500.

Applications: In writing to the correspondent. Applications are considered throughout the year.

Correspondent: O Dixon, Trustee, Camkin House, 8 Charles Court, Budbrooke Road, Warwick CV34 5LZ.

Professional Footballers Association Accident Insurance Fund

Eligibility: Members or former members of the association in England and Wales who need mecial treatment or who have been forced to retire from the game through injury and need help towards operations as a result of injuries received in football.

Types of grants: Grants are to provide private medical treatment for all members and for members unable to claim under the terms of the PFA accident insurance policy due to the nature/circumstances of the injury. Grants are also given to meet operation costs which may not be covered by the insurance.

Grants are available to former members for treatment on injuries received as a result of their playing career.

Annual grant total: In 2000/01 the trust had assets of £3.5 million and an income of £1.5 million. Grants totalled £5.6 million.

Applications: On a form available from the correspondent. Completed applications, addressed to Gordon Taylor, should be returned directly by the individual or by a family member/social worker on their behalf.

Correspondent: Gordon Taylor, Chief Executive, 20 Oxford Court, Bishopsgate, Manchester M2 3WQ (0161 236 0575; Fax: 0161 228 7229; e-mail: info@thepfa.co.uk).

Professional Footballers Association Benevolent Insurance Fund

Eligibility: Current and former members of the association in England and Wales who are experiencing financial hardship and are on a low income.

Types of grants: One-off grants to help relieve financial difficulties such as threat of losing one's home due to mortgage/rent arrears or threat of bailiffs in respect of debts. Loans are not available to former members and there are no recurrent grants. Grants for cars, holidays or to set up a business are not available.

Annual grant total: In 2000/01 the fund had assets of £7.8 million and an income of £2.6 million. 740 grants totalled £1.1 million.

Applications: On a form available from the correspondent. Completed applications, addressed to Gordon Taylor, should be returned directly by the individual or by a family member/social worker on their behalf.

Correspondent: Gordon Taylor, Chief Executive, 20 Oxford Court, Bishopsgate, Manchester M2 3WQ (0161 236 0575; Fax: 0161 228 7229; e-mail: info@thepfa.co.uk).

The Referees' Association Members Benevolent Fund

Eligibility: Members or former members of the association, and their dependants, who are in need and live in England, Northern Ireland and Wales.

Types of grants: One-off and recurrent grants to relieve an immediate financial need such as food, clothing, hire purchases and so on.

Annual grant total: In 2001/02 the fund had assets of £126,000 and an income of £10,000. Total expenditure was £5,800, all of which was given in grants.

Applications: On a form available from the correspondent. Applications should be submitted directly by the individual for consideration at any time.

Correspondent: The General Secretary, 1 Westhill Road, Coundon, Coventry CV6 2AD (024 7660 1701; Fax: 024 7660 1556; e-mail: ra@footballreferee.org; website: www.footballreferee.org).

Fur trade

Fur Trade Benevolent Society

Eligibility: People in need who are or have been involved in the fur industry in the UK and their dependants.

Types of grants: Weekly grants of £5 or £10, which are reviewed every six months. One-off payments can also be made.

No loans are made.

Annual grant total: Around £7,500

Applications: In writing to the correspondent directly by the individual, with information about the type of grant being requested and an outline of the applicant's employment in the fur trade. Applications are usually considered within a month.

Correspondent: Mrs E Lockyer, Bellside House, 4 Elthorne Road, London N19 4AG (01322 281 2526).

Furnishing

Furnishing Trades Benevolent Association

Eligibility: People who are or have been employed in any capacity in the furnishing industry or allied trades for two years and who now face personal or financial hardship.

Types of grants: Grants can be towards, for instance, essential household equipment, medical or mobility equipment, funeral expenses, clothing, TV licences, computers, debt clearance, holiday and respite breaks (at the trust's holiday hotel in Lancashire). Weekly grants of £5 per person, which are reviewed annually. No contribution can be made towards residential or nursing care fees.

Annual grant total: In 2001 the association had assets of £2.4 million, an income of £587,000 and a total expenditure of £678,000. Welfare grants to 105 individuals totalled £108,000. Educational grants to six individuals totalled £1,400.

Applications: On a form available from the benefits coordinator at the address below. Applications can be submitted directly by the individual, or by a third party such as a family member or a welfare agency. Applications are considered in February, May, August and November. However, emergency applications can be dealt with quickly, if necessary.

Correspondent: John Seddon-Brown, Chief Executive, 8 Fulwood Place, Gray's Inn, London WC1V 6HG (020 7405 7633; Fax: 020 7405 7644; e-mail: jsb@ftba.freeserve.co.uk; website: www.ftba.co.uk).

Gardening

The Gardeners' Royal Benevolent Society

Eligibility: People who have made their living through gardening and horticulture, and their surviving spouses. Applicants should be of retirement age, unless retired early through disability.

Types of grants: Beneficiary payments: Regular allowances of £14 a week paid quarterly.
Holidays: People who are disabled receive grants to attend special holidays; able-bodied people attend the society's own holidays, which are run every year in the UK for 50 beneficiaries in rotation (approximately every four/five years).

One-off grants towards personal or household items such as clothing, kitchen equipment, funeral expenses, removal expenses, telephone and television rental. The society also provides bed linen and towels.

Grants range between £20 and £2,000. No grants for items not allowable under DWP regulations, with special reference to people receiving Income Support. No help towards maintaining council or other rented property.

Annual grant total: In 2000/01 the society had assets of £16 million. The income was £3.8 million, which was higher than usual due to the receipt of a large legacy. Grants totalled £415,000.

Applications: On a form available from the correspondent along with medical evidence if retired early due to acccident or ill health. Applications can be submitted directly by the individual or through a social worker, citizen's advice bureau, other welfare agency or other third party. Applications are considered in January, March, May, July, September and November, although urgent applications can be considered between meetings.

Correspondent: Sheila Thomson, Director of Services, 139 Kingston Road, Leatherhead, Surrey KT22 7NT (01372 373962; Fax: 01372 384055).

Other information: The society also has its own nursing/residential home and various other types of sheltered accommodation.

OCCUPATIONAL CHARITIES

The Horticultural Trades Association Benevolent Fund

Eligibility: Nurserymen and seedsmen and their dependants who are in need.

Types of grants: Usually one-off grants.

Annual grant total: In 2000 the fund had an income of £3,000 and a total expenditure of £1,000.

Applications: In writing to the correspondent.

Correspondent: David Gwyther, 19 High Street, Theale, Reading, Berkshire RG7 5AH.

Other information: This entry was not confirmed by the trust, but the address was correct according to the Charity Commission.

Royal Gardeners' Orphan Fund

Eligibility: Children in need, particularly orphans, whose parents are or have been employed full-time in horticulture. Applicants should be under 25. Assistance is also given to children of horticulturists who are mentally or physically disabled.

Types of grants: Quarterly allowances to orphaned children still in full-time education. One-off grants for items such as clothing, beds, bedding, holidays and so on, to needy qualifying children. Grants range from £50 to £500.

Annual grant total: In 2001 the trust had assets of £672,000 and an income of £100,000. Grants to 80 individuals for educational and welfare needs totalled £78,000.

Applications: On a form available from the correspondent, with details of parents' and/or applicant's income and expenditure. Applications can be submitted either directly by the individual, or through a social worker, citizen's advice bureau or other welfare agency. Ideally, this should be at least two weeks before one of the committee meetings which take place in March, July and November each year.

Correspondent: Mrs Kate Wallis, Secretary, 14 Scholars Mews, Welwyn Garden City, Hertfordshire AL8 7JQ (Tel & Fax: 01707 333663; e-mail: rgof@btopenworld.com).

Golf

Hampshire Golfers Benevolent Fund

Eligibility: Priority is given to people who are members of Hampshire Professional Golfers Association and their dependants. When funds are available the trust may also fund other people who have been employed as professional golfers and their dependants.

Types of grants: One-off and recurrent grants according to need.

Annual grant total: In 1998 the trust had both an income and total expenditure of £1,300.

Applications: In writing to the correspondent.

Correspondent: M J Dyer, Dyer Burdett & Co., 64 West Street, Havant, Hampshire, PO0 1PA (023 9249 2472).

The PGA European Tour Benevolent Trust

Eligibility: Members and former members of the PGA European Tour and other people whose main livelihood is or has been earned by providing services to professional golf, and their dependants.

Types of grants: One-off or recurrent grants according to need.

Annual grant total: In 1999 seven grants to individuals totalled £38,000.

Applications: In writing to the correspondent at any time. Applications can be submitted directly by the individual or through a social worker, citizen's advice bureau, other welfare agency or another third party.

Correspondent: The Secretary, Wentworth Drive, Virginia Water, Surrey GU25 4LX (01344 840400; Fax: 01344 840500).

Hairdressing

The Barbers' Amalgamated Charity

Eligibility: Poor members of the medical, dental or nursing professions, the barbers or hairdressing trades, and their widows and children.

Types of grants: Pensions and one-off grants.

Annual grant total: In 1998/99 the charity had assets of £225,000 and both an income and a total expenditure of £17,000. It gave £16,000 in pensions and £1,000 in supplementary assistance to pensioners.

Applications: In writing to the correspondent at any time. Most of the money is already committed.

Correspondent: The Clerk, The Worshipful Company of Barbers, Barber-Surgeons' Hall, Monkwell Square, Wood Street, London EC2Y 5BL (020 7600 0950).

The Professional Hair and Beauty Benevolent Fund (formerly British Hairdressers' Benevolent & Provident Institution)

Eligibility: Hairdressers or barbers over 18 years of age who are in need, and their dependants. Also eligible are people who have worked in associated industries, such as hairdressing retail and manufacture or the beauty industry, and their dependants. Children of hairdressers (up to 16 years old) are especially invited to apply.

Types of grants: One-off and recurrent grants and loans according to need. Grants range from £260 to £520 and are given to (i) people in nursing homes, needing help with a shortfall in fees: (ii) people in their own homes on very low incomes to help with television licence/rental and so on; (iii) recurrent grants to children for pocket money, winter clothing, Christmas presents and so on; and (iv) one-off grants can also be given towards holidays, wheelchairs, computers or specialist equipment for children who are disabled.

The trust does not help with funeral expenses or towards tertiary education.

Annual grant total: In 2001 the trust had assets of £1.2 million which generated an income of about £300,000. Total expenditure was £200,000 with grants totalling £151,000.

Applications: On a form available from the correspondent. Applications are considered in any month except August. They should include full details of hairdressing employment details. A supporting letter from a doctor/social worker etc. would be useful but not essential.

Correspondent: Alan Rapkin, Secretary, 28 Roseberry Avenue, Benfleet, Essex SS7 5HJ (01268 754620; Fax: 01268 754627).

Horse Racing

The Injured Jockeys Fund

Eligibility: Jockeys who have been forced to give up their career through injury, and their families. Applicants must hold (or have held) a licence to ride under the Rules of Racing.

Types of grants: Weekly or periodical grants to injured jockeys whose current income only gives them/their families a bare subsistence level of living (up to DWP disregard level); loans on mortgage to help buy a house or set up a small business; annual holidays for those who would otherwise never get a chance to leave home; help with the cost of education where children have special needs (e.g.

dyslexia); suitable transport for older or infirm jockeys (where necessary cars are adapted to the needs of people who are disabled).

The fund has a bulk account with a leading television rental company through which colour sets are hired for beneficiaries who, for some reason, are largely or totally confined to their home. This costs over £10,000 a year.

Annual grant total: In 2000/01 the trust had an investment income of £365,000.

Applications: On a form available from the correspondent.

Correspondent: Jeremy Richardson, Chief Executive, 1 Lynx Court, Victoria Way, Newmarket, Suffolk CB8 7SH (01638 662246; Fax: 01638 668988).

Racing Welfare

Eligibility: People who work or have worked in the thoroughbred horse-racing and breeding industry and their dependants. Applicants must usually be in receipt of a low income.

Types of grants: Mainly relief-in-need quarterly allowances, but also one-off grants to people who have been injured or who are disabled, for motorised wheelchairs, beds, stairlifts and adaptations to houses. The trust runs a holiday scheme – taking people on trust organised holidays. It also funds people to go on independent holidays.

Annual grant total: In 2001 the total income was £2.3 million and grants were made to individuals totalling £291,000.

Applications: On a form in the first instance, available from the welfare officer at most racing centres, or from the trust. Applicants are visited by a welfare officer, before the application is considered by the trustees.

Correspondent: Sir John Kemball, 20b Park Lane, Newmarket, Suffolk CB8 8QD (01638 560763; Fax: 020 7203 0202; e-mail: info@racingwelfare.co.uk).

Hotel & catering

Hospitality Action (formerly Hotel And Catering Benevolent Association)

Eligibility: Former and current workers in the hospitality industry in the UK. The individuals or the company they work for would need to have been involved in the direct provision of food, drink and accommodation away from home.

Types of grants: One-off grants for essential needs, including short-term crisis grants.

Annual grant total: £300,000 was available in 2002.

Applications: On a form available from the correspondent. Applications should be submitted via a social worker, citizen's advice bureau or other welfare agency. They are usually considered within a month.

Correspondent: Grants and Advisory Team, Second Floor, 166 High Holborn, London WC1V 6TT (020 7301 2977; Fax: 020 7301 2940; e-mail: info@hospitalityaction.org.uk; website: www.hospitalityaction.org.uk).

Other information: The association has a residential club in London for young people entering the hospitality industry.

Insurance

Crusader Benevolent Fund

Eligibility: Past and present employees of Crusader Insurance Company, and their spouses, who are in need and live in Essex and Surrey.

Types of grants: One-off grants according to need. No grants towards long-term care.

Annual grant total: In 2000/01 the trust had assets totalling £43,000, an income of £3,800 and the total expenditure was £6,000. Grants were made to 52 individuals and totalled £4,200.

Applications: In writing to the correspondent directly by the individual.

Correspondent: John Douglas McDonald, 54 Brooklands Way, Redhill RH1 2BW (01737 769538).

The Insurance Charities – The Benevolent Fund

Eligibility: Insurance employees, retired ex-employees and their dependants experiencing financial hardship as a result of misfortune, who live in the UK or Eire. Applicants or dependent relatives must usually have spent five years in the insurance industry with service taking place not more than 10 years before retirement or another event prompting the application.

Types of grants: Grants or interest-free or low-interest loans towards day-to-day expenses or special needs such as domestic appliances, disability aids, property maintenance and holidays.

Annual grant total: In 2000/01 the fund had assets of £8.1 million, an income of £640,000 and a total expenditure of £702,000. Grants to 398 individuals totalled £560,000.

Applications: In writing to the correspondent, requesting an applicaiton form. Forms can be submitted directly by the individual or through a social worker, citizen's advice bureau, a welfare agency or other third party. They are considered in February, May, August and November.

Correspondent: Mrs A J Thornicroft, Secretary, 20 Aldermanbury, London EC2V 7HY (020 7606 3763; Fax: 020 7600 1170; e-mail: info@theinsurancecharities.com).

The Insurance Charities – The Orphans' Fund

Eligibility: Children of people who have spent at least five years working in the insurance industry in UK or Eire. Adult children of insurance people can be considered where personal resources are insufficient to meet reasonable expenditure.

Types of grants: Ongoing grants and interest-free or low interest loans towards day-to-day expenses and one-off grants towards special needs such as domestic appliances, disability aids and property maintenance. Help is also given to students on first degree courses.

Annual grant total: In 2000/01 the trust had an income of £550,000, all of which was given in grants to 169 individuals, mostly for welfare purposes.

Applications: In writing to the correspondent with brief details in the first instance. The fund will then contact you, for example, with an application form or a visit from a fund representative.

Correspondent: Mrs A J Thornicroft, 20 Aldermanbury, London EC2V 7HY (020 7606 3763; Fax: 020 7600 1170).

The Lloyd's Benevolent Fund

Eligibility: People who work or have worked in the Lloyd's insurance market and their dependants, anywhere in the world.

Types of grants: One-off grants can be given towards normal household expenses but not medical costs or school fees.

Annual grant total: In 2000/01 the trust had assets of £6.4 million, an income of £269,000 and a total expenditure of £236,000.

Applications: On a form available from the correspondent. Applications can be submitted by the individual or through a social worker, citizen's advice bureau, other welfare agency or other third party. They are considered throughout the year.

Correspondent: R G Domney, c/o Lloyd's, 1 Lime Street, London EC3M 7HA (020 7327 6453).

OCCUPATIONAL CHARITIES

Jewellery

The British Jewellery & Giftware Federation Benevolent Society

Eligibility: People who have worked in the trades embraced by the federation, and their dependants who are in need. Eligible trades are jewellery manufacture or wholesale (not retail), leather goods manufacture, brass and copperware manufacture or surface engineering.

Types of grants: Regular allowances within the DWP 'disregard' limit. One-off grants are also given towards the provision of essential needs such as a second-hand fridge/freezer/washing machine or towards bed linen, clothes and so on.

Annual grant total: In 2001 grants totalled £67,000. In the previous year, when the grant total was the same, it had assets of £485,000, an income of £78,000 and a total expenditure of £80,000.

Applications: On a form available from the correspondent. Applications can be submitted either directly by the individual or through a social worker, citizen's advice bureau, welfare agency or other third party such as another charity. Applications are considered in March, June, September and December.

Correspondent: Lynn B Snead, Federation House, 10 Vyse Street, Birmingham B18 6LT (0121 236 2657).

The Goldsmiths', Silversmiths' & Jewellers' Benevolent Society

Eligibility: Members of trades connected with gold and silver smithing (including for example retail jewellers and jewellery designers) and their dependants; Liverymen Freemen of the Goldsmiths' Company and their dependants; Londoners in need, and some people who are blind and partially-sighted who are connected with the trade.

Types of grants: Regular payments of £500 a year. Over 100 one-off grants usually of £55 to £500 are given for cookers, washing machines, bedding, redecoration and so on. Special grants can be given, for example, £700 for a special electric bed to somebody who is disabled.

Payments are not usually made for holidays or to pay off debts.

Annual grant total: Over £66,000 was given in 2001.

Applications: On a form available from the correspondent. For individuals not connected with the trade or the Goldsmiths' Company, applications should be made through the appropriate social services department of the London area.

Correspondent: Malcolm Pullen, Maxet House, Liverpool Road, Luton LU1 1RS (01582 482161).

Laundry

The Worshipful Company of Launderers Benevolent Trust

Eligibility: People who are older and infirm who are connected with the laundry industry and their dependants.

Types of grants: Grants can be paid annually (towards fuel bills); bi-annually (fuel bills and a summer grant – maximum £75), or monthly (towards general living expenses – up to £10 a week).

Annual grant total: About £5,000 to individuals and £4,000 to organisations.

Applications: In writing to the correspondent.

Correspondent: Mrs Jacqueline Polek, 24 Borough High Street, London SE1 9QG (020 7403 3300).

Leather trades

The Leather & Hides Trades' Benevolent Institution

Eligibility: People who work or have worked in the leather trade (i.e. in the production of leather or in the handling of hide and skin), and their dependants. Applicants are usually over 60; people under 60 are considered in exceptional circumstances.

Types of grants: Annuities of £500 a year (paid quarterly) plus bonuses at Christmas and in summer. Also, one-off grants to annuitants and others for special needs, and help towards shortfall in nursing home fees.

Annual grant total: About £70,000 in about 80 grants each year.

Applications: On a form available from the correspondent. Applications can be submitted directly by the individual, through a welfare agency or other appropriate third party. The committee meets in March and October although urgent appeals can be considered between meetings.

Correspondent: Karen Harriman, Secretary, 2 Chapel House, Chapel Street, Oadby, Leicester LE2 5AD (0116 271 7316).

The Saddlery and Leather Goods Retailers Benevolent Fund

Eligibility: Employees or retired employees of saddlery, leather goods retailers, manufacturers, or individual craftsmen and their spouses.

Types of grants: Mainly one-off grants to help with specific problems.

Annual grant total: In 2000 the trust had an income of £1,700, and a total expenditure of £2,600, all of which was given in 12 grants.

Applications: In writing to the correspondent, either directly by the individual or through a social worker, citizen's advice bureau, welfare agency or, with their permission, a third party. Applications are considered as they are received, and should include full details of need.

Correspondent: The Secretary, Kettles Farm, Mickfield, Stowmarket, Suffolk IP14 6BY (Tel & Fax: 01449 711642).

Legal profession

The Barristers' Benevolent Association

Eligibility: Past or present practising members of the Bar in England and Wales, and their spouses, former spouses and dependants. No grants to those who when qualified went straight into commerce.

Types of grants: One-off grants, maintenance allowances and loans. The correspondent states that some form of grant is given in most cases.

Annual grant total: In 2000 the trust had an income of £795,000 and its total expenditure was £579,000. £375,000 was given in welfare and educational grants.

Applications: On a form available from the correspondent. Applications can be submitted by the individual or through a social worker or other welfare agency. They are considered at monthly meetings of the management committee.

Correspondent: Linda C Carlier, 14 Gray's Inn Square, London WC1R 5JP (020 7242 4761; Fax: 020 7831 5366; e-mail: linda@thebba.swinternet.co.uk).

The Institute of Legal Executive Benevolent Funds

Eligibility: Members and former members of the institute (including associates, fellows and student members), present and former solicitors' managing clerks, and the dependants of any of the above.

Types of grants: The fund usually gives one-off grants for specific purposes such as telephone/fuel bills, nursing/residential care, medical equipment and so on. Grants can also be made to members who are unable to pay their membership subscriptions through redundancy or illness etc.

Annual grant total: In 2001 the fund had an income of £10,000 and gave £4,800 in grants.

Applications: On a form available from Teresa Miller, Senior Liaison Officer at the address below. They should be submitted directly by the individual or a dependant and can be considered at any time.

Correspondent: Diane Burleigh, Secretary General, Kempston Manor, Kempston, Bedford MK42 7AB (01234 841000; Fax: 01234 854817; e-mail: info@ilex.org.uk; website: www.ilex.org.uk).

The Solicitor's Benevolent Association

Eligibility: Solicitors on the Roll for England and Wales, and their dependants, who are in need. Solicitors who have been considered to have brought the profession into disrepute are not eligible.

Types of grants: One-off and recurrent grants and interest-free loans (if sufficient equity is available). They can be made towards living expenses, TV licences, telephone rental, essential travel, emergency repairs or replacement of household appliances, holidays and medical or special equipment not provided for by the state.

Annual grant total: In 2001 the association had assets of £12 million and an income of £1.3 million. 390 grants totalling £803,000 were broken down as follows: £375,000 in living allowances; £301,000 for special grants; £38,000 for nursing home fees; and £89,000 towards education.

Applications: By application form available on request from the correspondent.

Correspondent: Cmdr A H Lorimer, 1 Jaggard Way, Wandsworth Common, London SW12 8SG (020 8675 6440; Fax: 020 8675 6441; e-mail: solben@btclick.com; website: www.sba.org.uk).

The United Law Clerks Society

Eligibility: People employed or who were employed in the legal profession in any capacity in England, Scotland and Wales, and their dependants.

Types of grants: One-off and recurrent grants according to need, mainly to pensioners and people who are sick. Recurrent grants are usually for £5 to £10 a week, but can be for up to £720 a year. One-off grants can be for up to £500 or £600 a year, for example, towards cookers, roof repairs, special chairs/beds and so on. No grants for students.

Annual grant total: The income of this trust varies greatly each year dependent on donations, ranging from less than £10,000 to over £20,000.

Applications: On a form available from the correspondent at any time.

Correspondent: The Secretary, Innellan House, 109 Nutfield Road, Merstham, Surrey RH1 3HD (01737 643261).

Librarians

The Chartered Institute of Library and Information Professionals (CILIP) (formerly known as The Library Association Benevolent Fund)

Eligibility: Members and former members of CILIP and their dependants.

Types of grants: Usually one-off grants or interest free loans according to need. No regular grants are made to supplement income over an extended period, or to assist librarianship students with fees or maintenance.

Annual grant total: In 2000 the trust had assets of £63,000 and an income of £16,000. Total expenditure was £26,000, including £18,000 given in 47 grants.

Applications: In writing to the correspondent either directly by the individual or through a social worker, citizen's advice bureau or other welfare agency. Applications are considered throughout the year.

Correspondent: Eric Winter, Secretary, 7 Ridgmount Street, London WC1E 7AE (020 7255 0648; Fax: 020 7255 0501; e-mail: eric.winter@cilip.org.uk).

Lock-keeping

The Myrtle Cohen Trust Fund

Eligibility: Lock-keepers, relief lock-keepers and boatmen either in active service on the non-tidal River Thames or who have retired from such service, and their wives/husbands, widows/widowers who are in need.

Types of grants: One-off grants according to need, ranging from £100 to 500 towards needs such as medical equipment and house moves.

Annual grant total: In 2001/02 the trust had assets of £5,000 and an income of £450. There was no expenditure during the year.

Applications: In writing to the correspondent, to be submitted at any time directly by the individual or an immediate relative.

Correspondent: Ben Cohen, 716 Endsleigh Court, Upper Woburn Place, London WC1H 0HW.

Loss adjusters

The Chartered Institute of Loss Adjusters Benevolent Fund

Eligibility: Members of the institute and their dependants.

Types of grants: One-off and recurrent grants according to need. Recent grants have been given to people diagnosed with terminal illnesses.

Annual grant total: About £3,000.

Applications: In writing to the correspondent. If a member passes away, the fund notifies his/her partner of the financial assistance available.

Correspondent: Graham Cave, Executive Director, Penisular House, 36 Monument Street, London EC3R 8LJ (020 7337 9960; Fax: 020 7929 3082; e-mail: info@cila.co.uk).

Market research

The Market Research Benevolent Association

Eligibility: People who are or have been engaged in market research, and their dependants.

Types of grants: Generally one-off grants.

Annual grant total: In 2001/02 the association had an income of £35,000 and gave grants totalling £20,000.

Applications: On a form available from the correspondent. Applications can be submitted either directly by the individual or by a third party and are considered throughout the year.

Correspondent: Mrs Gill Wareing, Secretary, 6 Walkfield Drive, Epsom Downs, Surrey KT18 5UF (01737 379261).

OCCUPATIONAL CHARITIES

Match manufacture

The Joint Industrial Council & the Match Manufacturing Industry Charitable Fund

Eligibility: People who are or have been involved in the manufacture of matches, and their dependants.

Types of grants: One-off grants towards, for instance, medical expenses, dental and optical expenses, home security, removal costs (to sheltered accommodation) and winter fuel costs. Grants at Christmas of £40 are also available.

Annual grant total: In 2000/01 the fund had assets of £129,000, an income of £6,500 and a total expenditure of £15,000. Grants to 600 individuals totalled £24,000.

Applications: In writing to the correspondent, directly by the individual. Applications are considered throughout the year.

Correspondent: Shila Dharma, Swedish Match, Sword House, Totteridge Road, High Wycombe, Buckinghamshire HP13 6EJ (01494 556127).

Media

The Chartered Institute of Journalists Orphan Fund

Eligibility: Orphaned children of institute members who are in need, aged between 5 and 22 and in full-time education.

Types of grants: Monthly grants (plus birthday/Christmas/ summer holiday payments).

Annual grant total: About £30,000 in eight grants.

Applications: In writing to the correspondent.

Correspondent: The Honorary Treasurer, 2 Dock Offices, Surrey Quays Road, London SE16 2XU (020 7252 1187; Fax: 020 7232 2302; e-mail: memberservices@ioj.co.uk).

Other information: This fund also gives grants for educational purposes.

The Cinema & Television Benevolent Fund

Eligibility: Anyone who has worked in any capacity, for a minimum of two years, behind the cameras (in any position other than actor/actress) in the British film, cinema or independent television industries, and their dependants.

Types of grants: Weekly allowances up to the DWP disregard level, and help with television licences and television rental. Capital grants are given towards: helping people stay in their own homes by buying household appliances, removals, utility arrears, wheelchairs and convalescence. Grants range between £200 and £1,000. Grants towards fees shortfall, of up to £30, are available to permanent residents at the fund's residential home in Gleblelands.

No grants towards private health care, mortgage repayments, education and training fees unless at final stage (i.e. last two years of GCSE or A-Level) in exceptional cases.

Annual grant total: In 2000/01 the fund had assets of £27 million, an income of £1.5 million and a total expenditure of £2.1 million. Grants totalled £1.3 million.

Applications: On a form available from the Welfare Department at the address below. Applications should be submitted either directly by the individual or through a social worker, citizen's advice bureau or other welfare agency. Applicants will be visited to help assess eligibility and need.

Correspondent: Mark Roberts, 22 Golden Square, London W1F 9AD (020 7437 6567).

The Grace Wyndham Goldie (BBC) Trust Fund

Eligibility: Employees and ex-employees worldwide engaged in broadcasting or an associated activity, and their dependants.

Types of grants: One-off grants to help relieve continuing hardship not covered by aid from other sources.

Annual grant total: About £25,000 was given in grants for educational and welfare purposes in 2001.

Applications: On a form available from the correspondent, for consideration in September. As the income of the fund is limited, and to ensure help can be given where it is most needed, applicants must be prepared to give full information about their circumstances.

Correspondent: Christine Geen, BBC Pension and Benefits Centre, Broadcasting House, Cardiff CF5 2YQ (029 2032 3772; Fax: 029 2032 2408).

The National Union of Journalists Provident Fund

Eligibility: Members or dependants of deceased or former NUJ members, living in the UK or Republic of Ireland. Members who left owing the union contributions are not eligible.

Types of grants: Mostly top-up grants of £110 per week. One-off grants can also be given.

Annual grant total: In 2001 the fund had assets of £1.2 million, an income of £123,000 and a total expenditure of £89,000. Grants totalled £57,000.

Applications: On a form available from the correspondent, submitted by the individual or through an NUJ welfare officer or other third party. Applications are considered throughout the year.

Correspondent: The Administrator, Headland House, 308-312 Gray's Inn Road, London WC1X 8DP (020 7833 2766).

Newspaper Press Fund

Eligibility: British journalists, their widows and dependants who are in need.

Types of grants: One-off grants, typically of £500 but to a usual maximum of £5,000. Weekly allowances of up to £20 a week.

Annual grant total: In 2001 the fund had assets of £15 million and an income of £1.1 million. Total expenditure was £1.3 million, with £777,000 being given in 322 grants to individuals.

Applications: On a form available from the correspondent, including details of career in journalism. Applications are considered monthly.

Correspondent: David Ilott, Director, Dickens House, 35 Wathen Road, Dorking, Surrey RH4 1JY (01306 887511; Fax: 01306 888212).

Other information: The fund also runs residential homes in Dorking.

Medicine and health

The 1930 Fund for District Nurses

Eligibility: Qualified nurses who have worked in the community as a district nurse.

Types of grants: One-off and recurrent grants ranging from £100 to £300 for a variety of needs, including bathroom and kitchen equipment, spectacles, dentures and disability aids. Consideration is given to recurrent quarterly grants for older people. Grants are also available for nursing home top-up fees.

Annual grant total: In 2000/01 the fund had assets of £1.3 million, an income of £65,000 and a total expenditure of £66,000. Grants to about 100 nurses totalled £44,000.

Applications: On a form available from the correspondent. Applications can be submitted directly by the individual, through a social worker, citizen's advice bureau, other welfare agency or third party. They are considered throughout the year and should include details of nursing experience.

Correspondent: Verona Boreland, Secretary, 5th Floor, 20 Cavendish Square,

London W1G 0RN (020 7499 1930; e-mail: verona.boreland@rcn.org.uk).

Ambulance Service Workers Hardship Fund

Eligibility: Employees and ex-employees in the ambulance service and their dependants.

Types of grants: One-off and recurrent grants according to need.

Annual grant total: In 1999 the fund had an income of £12,000 and a total expenditure of £20,000.

Applications: On a form available from the ambulance service trade union.

Correspondent: Margaret Dunn, UNISON, 1 Mabledon Place, London WC1H 9AJ (020 7388 2366).

Ambulance Services Benevolent Fund

Eligibility: Present and former ambulancemen/women, who have been employed by the NHS ambulance services of England, Wales, Scotland, Ireland (North or South) and the Channel Islands, and their dependants. People who only served for a couple of years before seeking other employment for the rest of their working life are not usually considered.

Types of grants: One-off grants of £100 to £1,000 are awarded to relieve genuine hardship, poverty or distress, or to assist medically.

Annual grant total: In 2000/01 the trust had assets of £150,000 and an income of £24,000. Total expenditure was £23,000, including £21,000 given in total in 52 grants.

Applications: Applications are considered throughout the year and should be made in writing to the correspondent by a recognised referral agency (social worker, citizen's advice bureau, doctor or ambulance officer/manager). The application should include: age, length of service with dates, specific details of hardship, support received from other agencies and other relevant financial or other information to support the claim.

Correspondent: Simon Fermor, Secretary, Cherith, 150 Willingdon Road, Eastbourne, East Sussex BN21 1TS (Tel & Fax: 01323 721150).

The Barbers' Amalgamated Charity

See entry on page 42

Benevolent Fund of the British Psychoanalytical Society

Eligibility: People in need who are or have been members or associate members of the British Psychoanalytical Society, and their dependants.

Types of grants: One-off and recurrent grants according to need.

Annual grant total: In 2000/01 the trust had an income of £3,400 and its total expenditure was £200. Up to £10,000 is available for grants to individuals a year.

Applications: In writing to the correspondent.

Correspondent: K Riddle, 112a Shirland Road, Maidavale, London W9 2EQ (020 7563 5018; e-mail: keithriddle@compuserve.com).

The British Dental Association Benevolent Fund

Eligibility: Dentists who are or have been on the UK dental register and their dependants.

Types of grants: One-off grants towards TVs, fridges, household repairs, holidays and respite care. Regular grants to supplement income are also available as are interest-free loans to relieve difficulties with a limited time span.

Help is not usually given with private medical fees or private school fees. The trust does not generally help people with a considerable amount of capital (it generally uses the DWP regulations as a guide, but this is flexible, especially in nursing home cases).

Annual grant total: In 2000 the fund had assets of £4.8 million, an income of £257,000 and a total expenditure of £312,000. Grants to 93 individuals totalled £262,000.

Applications: On a form available from the correspondent. Applications are considered as they are received. Enquiries can be made directly by the individual or through a social worker, citizen's advice bureau, welfare agency or another third party.

Correspondent: Mrs Sally Atkinson, 64 Wimpole Street, London W1M 8AL.

Other information: This entry was not confirmed by the fund, but the address was correct according to the Charity Commission database.

The Cameron Fund

Eligibility: General practitioners and their dependants who are in need.

Types of grants: One-off and recurrent grants towards general expenses, holidays, house repairs, replacement of household equipment, children's needs, nursing home fees and so on. Each application is considered on its own merits. No grants can be made towards items which should be provided through statutory sources.

Annual grant total: In 2000 the fund had assets of £4.1 million, an income of £286,000 and a total expenditure of £356,000. Grants totalled £326,000.

Applications: On a form available from the correspondent with career details. Applications can be submitted directly by the individual, through a social worker, citizen's advice bureau or welfare agency, or through a solicitor or person holding power of attorney. Applications are considered quarterly.

Correspondent: Mrs L Dluska-Miriura, Tavistock House North, Tavistock Square, London WC1H 9HR (020 7388 0796; Fax: 020 7554 6334; e-mail: info.cameronfund@bma.org.uk).

The Edith Cavell & Nation's Fund for Nurses

Eligibility: Registered nurses who are retired or unable to continue their chosen career owing to severe disability, with a minimum of five years service following qualification. VADs are also assisted. Nursing auxiliaries must have had at least 10 years' service.

Types of grants: One-off and recurrent grants are available to nurses of limited means who are already claiming all appropriate state benefits. Help is given towards household repairs and equipment, and to provide convalescence and respite care on medical recommendation. Help is also given with the provision of specialist aids and equipment. Grants usually range from £100 to £500, but are occasionally up to £1,000.

No help with debt repayment, loans, rent, mortgages, holidays, funerals or fee top-ups.

Annual grant total: In 2001 grants totalled approximately £130,000. In the previous year grants were made to 39 individuals totalling £140,000.

Applications: On a form available from the correspondent. Applications can be submitted by the individual, by a friend or relative or through a recognised referral agency (social worker, citizen's advice bureau, lawyer or other charitable organisation etc.). Applications are considered in January, March, May, July, September and November.

Correspondent: Mrs Ann Rich, Flints, Petersfield Road, Winchester, Hampshire SO23 0JD (Tel & Fax: 01962 860900; e-mail: natnurses.fund@virgin.net).

Other information: This fund incorporates 'The Groves Trust for Nurses'.

The Chartered Society of Physiotherapy Members' Benevolent Fund

Eligibility: Members, past members, assistant members and student members of the society.

Types of grants: One-off grants for emergency needs such as respite care or house repairs. Recurrent grants to help with living expenses, telephone rental, household repairs, heating bills and road tax (where car use is essential). The fund also supplements low income. Grants can range from £80 a month to £220 a month. No grants towards private acute care or payment of debts.

Annual grant total: In 2001 the trust had an income of £68,000 and it made grants totalling £133,000.

Applications: On a form available from the correspondent. Applications should be submitted directly by the individual or by a third party such as a carer or partner. Applications are considered in January, April, July and October.

Correspondent: Christine Cox, 14 Bedford Row, London WC1R 4ED (020 7306 6641; Fax: 020 7306 6643; e-mail: coxc@csphysio.org.uk; website: www.csp.org.uk).

The Benevolent Fund of the College of Optometrists and the Association of Optometrists

Eligibility: Members and former members of the College of Optometrists; former members of the British Optical Association; other members and former members of the optical/optometric profession, and their dependants who are in need.

Types of grants: According to need, some grants are paid monthly. Bills can be paid such as those for electricity, gas and telephone. Christmas grants are given. Help is occasionally given towards residence/nursing fees top-ups and towards major items such as house repairs or a wheelchair. Grants usually range from £20 to £200.

No grants to students.

Annual grant total: About £15,000.

Applications: Application forms are available from the correspondent and a financial form must be completed. Applications are considered all year round and applicants are usually visited by a member of the profession.

Correspondent: David Lacey, Administrative Secretary, PO Box 10, Swanley, Kent BR8 8ZF (01322 660388; Fax: 01322 665938; e-mail: davidflacey@aol.com).

The Eaton Fund for Artists, Nurses & Gentlewomen

See entry on page 26

Ethel Mary Fund For Nurses

Eligibility: Registered, or retired, state nurses over 40 years of age who are sick and disabled who live in the UK.

Types of grants: Pensions are given.

Annual grant total: In 2001 the fund had assets of £75,000, an income of £3,400 and a total expenditure of £3,200. Grants totalled £1,500.

Applications: On a form available from the correspondent. Applications are considered quarterly.

Correspondent: Miss Campbell, Vice President, Duke of York's Headquarters, 424 Left Wing, Turks Row, Chelsea, London SW3 4RY (020 7730 0624).

The Groves Trust for Nurses

Eligibility: Older retired registered, enrolled or auxiliary nurses in need, or those who are unable to work through disability.

Types of grants: Recurrent bi-monthly cash grants, and one-off payments for equipment, repairs, convalescence and therapeutic breaks.

Annual grant total: In 2000 the trust had an income of £29,000 and a total expenditure of £35,000.

Applications: In writing to the correspondent.

Correspondent: Mrs M A Rich, Flints, Petersfield Road, Winchester, Hampshire SO23 0JD (Tel & Fax: 01962 860900).

The Hastings Benevolent Fund

Eligibility: Medical doctors, and their dependants, who are in need.

Types of grants: One-off payments as grants or interest-free loans. The trust also helps refugee doctors to take the PLAB test.

Annual grant total: In 2001 the fund had assets of £985,000, an income of £66,000 and a total expenditure of £68,000. Grants to 31 individuals totalled £60,000.

Applications: On a form available from the correspondent. Applications can be submitted directly by the individual or through a social worker, citizen's advice bureau, welfare agency or other third party. Applications are considered all year round.

Correspondent: Mrs L Dluska-Miziura, BMA Charities, BMA House, Tavistock Square, London WC1H 9JP (020 7383 6142; Fax: 020 7554 6334; e-mail: info.bmacharities@bma.org.uk; website: www.bma.org.uk).

The Helena Benevolent Fund

Eligibility: State registered nurses, aged over 40, in the UK who are in need.

Types of grants: One-off grants towards nursing care.

Annual grant total: In 2001 the trust had assets of £26,000, an income of £820 and a total expenditure of £790.

Applications: In writing to the correspondent at any time.

Correspondent: Miss H M Campbell, Vice President, Duke of Yorks Headquarters, 424 Left Wing, Turks Row, London SW3 4RY.

The Institute of Healthcare Management Benevolent Fund

Eligibility: Members and former members of the institute and their dependants.

Types of grants: Emergency one-off grants (usually around £200); monthly grants (variable according to circumstances, presently £40 to £100 a month); special Christmas and summer holiday grants usually paid to people receiving regular grants (variable but with emphasis on dependent children); and top-up nursing/residential home fees and similar.

Generally no grants given to students but some educational grants may be given to members of the institute, not their children.

Annual grant total: £11,000 in 1999.

Applications: Should be submitted through a regional representative on the national council of the institute. Applications are considered on receipt.

Correspondent: M Stoneham, Hon. Secretary, 139 Hever Avenue, West Kingsdown, Sevenoaks, Kent TN15 6DT (Tel & Fax: 01474 853014; e-mail: ihmfund@stoneham.org).

The Junius S Morgan Benevolent Fund for Nurses

Eligibility: Members of the nursing profession.

Types of grants: One-off grants to relieve immediate hardship, with help towards domestic bills, household appliances and contributions towards capital items. Grants are not given towards educational fees, residential/nursing home fees or private medical healthcare.

Annual grant total: In 2001 the trust had an income of £43,000 and a total expenditure of £79,000. In 1999 grants to 396 individuals totalled £75,000.

Applications: On a form available from the correspondent. Applications should be submitted either directly by the individual or through a social worker, citizen's advice bureau, welfare agency or other third party. Applications are considered monthly.

Correspondent: Mrs Kim Gozzett, SG Hambros Trust Co. Ltd, SG House, 41 Tower Hill, London EC3N 4SG (020 7597 3000; Fax: 020 7702 9263).

The NHS Pensioners' Trust

Eligibility: i) Any person who has retired from service in any capacity in the NHS in England, Wales or Scotland.
ii) Any person who has retired from service in England, Wales or Scotland for any of the related health service organisations or caring professions prior to the creation of

OCCUPATIONAL CHARITIES

the NHS.

iii) Any person who is the wife, husband, widow, widower or other dependant of those specified above.

Types of grants: Grants, mostly of £250, for general up-keep to ease financial difficulty in cases of hardship, including the cost of disabled living, aids and equipment, repairs to the home and fuel bills. Larger grants can be considered in particular circumstances. Grants are one-off, but individuals can reapply in the following year.

Annual grant total: In 1999/2000 the trust had assets of £1.6 million, an income of £101,000 and a total expenditure of £118,000. Grants to individuals totalled £5,000. Grants to organisations totalled £81,000.

Applications: On a form available from the correspondent following receipt of an sae. Applications containing supporting information and/or the backing of social work agencies, will be processed more quickly. A trust representative may follow up applications to verify information.

Correspondent: Frank Jackson, Director, 11-13 Cavendish Square, London W1G 0AN (020 7307 2506; Fax: 020 7307 2800; e-mail: enquiries@nhspt.org.uk; website: www.nhspt.org.uk).

The Nurses Fund for Nurses

Eligibility: Nurses who are sick or elderly.

Types of grants: One-off grants towards, for example, fuel bills, telephone rental and installation (but not calls), beds, wheelchairs, special equipment not obtainable on the NHS and convalescent holidays. Help with nursing home fees is seldom given. Grants range from £50 to £250 for a single grant.

No grants to: dependants of the above; auxiliary nurses; repay debts such as credit cards, overdrafts, mortgages or catalogues; cover funeral expenses; or providing holidays without a respite element at its core. Loans are not given.

Annual grant total: In 2000 the fund had assets of £252,000, an income of £23,000 and a total expenditure of £45,000. Grants to 495 individuals totalled £27,000, broken down as follows: quarterly nursing and retirement home grants (£5,100 in 101 grants); quarterly telephone rental grants (£5,500 in 177 grants); other quarterly grants (£120 in 5 grants); and single grants (£19,000 in 212 grants).

Applications: On a form available from the correspondent. Applications should include precise details of need, and are considered every six weeks.

Correspondent: Rita Barry, Secretary, 2nd Floor, 380 Harrow Road, London W9 2UH (Tel & Fax: 020 7266 4747; e-mail: nursesfund@aol.com).

The Princess Royal Trust for Carers

Eligibility: Carers in the UK who live near a Princess Royal Trust for Carers Centre.

Types of grants: One-off grants of up to about £400, for example towards driving lessons or domestic items.

Annual grant total: Information unavailable.

Applications: Applications are made via your local Princess Royal Trust for Carers Centre.

Correspondent: The Clerk, 142 Minories, London EC3N 1LB (020 7480 7788).

The Queen's Nursing Institute

Eligibility: Qualified district nurses and Queen's nurses, usually who are unable to work due to age, illness or disability.

Types of grants: One-off and recurrent grants ranging between £300 and £3,500 to help with household expenses, essential equipment, bills, specialist aids and equipment, holiday breaks and building works. No assistance with loans, overdrafts or debts.

Annual grant total: In 2001 680 grants were awarded totalling £155,000.

Applications: On a form available from the correspondent, with estimates for the grant required. Applications can be submitted by the individual, or through a recognised referral agency (social worker, citizen's advice bureau or doctor) or other third party and are considered in February, May, August and November.

Correspondent: Miss Sarah Perry, 3 Albemarle Way, Clerkenwell, London EC1V 4RQ (020 7490 4227; Fax: 020 7490 1269).

The Royal College of Midwives Benevolent Fund

Eligibility: Midwives, former midwives and student midwives who are in need. Dependants of the above are not eligible.

Types of grants: Usually one-off grants for emergency or other unexpected needs (typically £50 to £200); very occasionally regular allowances where needed. Grants are given, for instance, towards the cost of a wheelchair, removal expenses, furniture, disability chairs, personal items and household equipment.

Annual grant total: About £5,000 in 50 to 70 grants.

Applications: On a form available from the correspondent. Applications should be submitted either directly by the individual or through a third party such as a nursing organisation. They are considered every six to eight weeks.

Correspondent: The Administrator, The Royal College of Midwives, 15 Mansfield Street, London W1G 9NH (020 7312 3535).

The Royal College of Nursing Charitable Trust

Eligibility: Registered nurses in membership of the Royal College of Nursing and retired nurses who were RCN members, who are sick or in need.

Types of grants: One-off grants ranging from £50 to £350. Grants can be given towards aids for daily living; mobility and communication; household repairs or equipment, if health, safety or well-being are at risk; payment of gas, electricity, phone and water bills; and respite care and convalescence.

No grants towards unqualified nurses (except student members who are in ill health), care home fees, regular grants, costs of study or further education or private medical treatment and care.

Annual grant total: In 2001/02 165 grants were awarded totalling £48,000.

Applications: On a form available from the correspondent, providing details of income, savings and outgoings, nursing career history, confirmation of need for a grant and information to assist in advising on other sources of grant aid and welfare. Applications can be submitted directly by the individual or through a social worker, citizen's advice bureau, other welfare agency, a nurse, a care worker or spouse or relative. Applicants are normally notified of the outcome within two weeks.

Correspondent: The Adviser, Nurseline, 20 Cavendish Square, London W1G 0RN (020 7647 3894; Fax: 020 7647 3589; website: www.rcn.org.uk).

The Royal Medical Benevolent Fund

Eligibility: Registered medical practitioners whose names are on the UK General Medical Council (GMC) register, their wives, husbands, widows, widowers and dependent children who are in need and are resident in Great Britain.

Types of grants: One-off gifts/loans and regular grants are only provided for the relief of poverty and are made entirely at the discretion of the fund's case committee.

No grants for school/higher education fees/maintenance, although occasionally one-off gifts are given in exceptional circumstances to dependants of current beneficiaries. Working doctors and their dependants are not normally considered.

Annual grant total: In 2000 the trust's income and expenditure both totalled £1.3 million. Grants were made to 630 doctors and their dependants totalling £800,000; most of this was given for welfare rather than educational purposes.

Applications: On a form available from the correspondent, which can be submitted either directly by the individual or through a social worker, citizen's advice bureau,

OCCUPATIONAL CHARITIES

other welfare agency, medical colleague or other medical and general charities. Applications are considered almost every month. Two references are taken up (at least one of which should be from a medical practitioner). All applicants are visited before a report is submitted to the case committee. Income/capital and expenditure are fully investigated, with similar rules applying as for those receiving Income Support.

Correspondent: The Senior Caseworker, 24 King's Road, Wimbledon, London SW19 8QN or FREEPOST, London SW19 8BR (020 8540 9194; Fax: 020 8542 0494; e-mail: info@rmbf.org; website: www.rmbf.org).

Other information: Voluntary visitors liaise between beneficiaries and the office.

The Royal Medical Foundation

Eligibility: Medical practitioners and their dependants who are in need.

Types of grants: One-off grants, monthly pensions and maintenance grants of £100 to £5,000.

Annual grant total: In 2000/01 the foundation had assets of £3.2 million, an income of £345,000 and a total expenditure of £359,000. Grants to 95 individuals for welfare and educational purposes totalled £283,000.

Applications: On a form available from the correspondent, for consideration on receipt. Applications can be submitted by the individual or a social worker. The trust advises applicants to be honest about their needs.

Correspondent: John Higgs, Epsom College, Epsom, Surrey KT17 4JQ (01372 821011; Fax: 01372 821013; e-mail: rmf@epsomcollege.org.uk; website: www.epsomcollege.org.uk/rmf/).

Royal Pharmaceutical Society's Benevolent Fund

Eligibility: Pharmacists, former pharmacists and their dependants In Great Britain (but not Northern Ireland).

Types of grants: One-off and recurrent grants (to a maximum of £25 a week, paid quarterly) towards daily living expenses. Recent grants have included a recliner chair for somebody with multiple sclerosis, nursing home fees shortfalls and interest free loans for drug/alcohol treatment. No grants are given to students or for medical care or expenses.

Annual grant total: £180,000 in 2001.

Applications: On a form available from the correspondent, to be considered throughout the year.

Correspondent: Mrs Beverley A Nicol, Benevolent Fund Coordinator, 1 Lambeth High Street, London SE1 7JN (01926 315994; Tel & Fax: 01323 890135; e-mail: benevolentfund@rpsgb.org.uk).

The Society for Relief of Widows & Orphans of Medical Men

Eligibility: Widows, widowers or orphans of any doctor (of either sex) who was at the time of his/her death, and for the preceding two years, a member of the society. In certain circumstances members and their dependants may also be eligible. Any surplus income may be used to help medical practitioners and their dependants who are in need but are not members of the society.

Types of grants: One-off and recurrent grants of between £500 and £5,000 towards: helping family hardship at times of illness or loss of 'bread-winner'; debt repayments; home alterations to accommodate wheelchairs; household repairs; retraining; and for medical students who are the children of doctors where the family is in need. No grants are made towards nursing home fees, loans, long-term assistance or second degrees.

Annual grant total: In 2001 grants totalled over £60,000.

Applications: On a form available from the correspondent. Applications should be submitted directly by the individual and are considered in February, May, August and November.

Correspondent: Mrs C Darby, Secretary, Lettsom House, 11 Chandos Street, Cavendish Square, London W1M 9DE (Tel & Fax: 01234 217522; e-mail: wandomed@ntlworld.com).

Benevolent Fund of The Society of Chiropodists

Eligibility: Members/former members of the society or one of its constituent bodies, and their dependants.

Types of grants: One-off according to need, ranging from £50 to £500.

Annual grant total: In 2001 the fund had an income of £21,000 and a total expenditure of £7,000.

Applications: On a form available from the correspondent, to be submitted directly by the individual or through a third party. Applications are considered monthly.

Correspondent: Andrew Forrester, 1 Fellmongers Path, Tower Bridge Road, London SE1 3LY (020 7234 8623; e-mail: af@scpod.org).

The Society of Radiographers Benevolent Fund

Eligibility: Radiographers and their dependants in need, with a possible preference for people who are sick, elderly or incapacitated.

Types of grants: One-off grants of £250 upwards. Grants have been awarded towards stairlifts, adaptations, car repairs and washing machines. No grants for further education.

Annual grant total: £6,000 a year.

Applications: In writing to the correspondent, requesting an application form. Applications can be submitted directly by the individual or through a third party such as a colleague or relative.

Correspondent: Mrs Gill Smith, Secretary, 207 Providence Square, Mill Street, London SE1 2EW (020 7740 7200; Fax: 020 7740 7233; e-mail: info@sor.org).

The Trained Nurses Annuity Fund

Eligibility: Nurses aged 40 or over who are disabled and have at least seven years service.

Types of grants: Annuities and occasionally one-off grants. Each year beneficiaries of recurrent grants send a short report explaining whether financial circumstances have changed and whether they are still in need of assistance. No grants for education or house improvements.

Annual grant total: About £20,000.

Applications: On a form available from the correspondent. These should normally be submitted by doctors or social workers along with a doctor's certificate or by the individual. Applications are considered at executive meetings and payments are made in July and December.

Correspondent: Miss H M Campbell, Royal British Nurses Association, Duke of York's Headquarters, 424 Left Wing, Kings Road, Chelsea, London SW3 (020 7730 0624).

Metal trades

The Benevolent Fund of the Institution of Mining & Metallurgy

Eligibility: Members of the institution and former members and their dependants.

Types of grants: One-off and recurrent grants and loans, according to need.

Annual grant total: In 2000 the fund had assets of £922,000, an income of £33,000 and a total expenditure of £58,000. Grants totalled £46,000.

Applications: On a form available from the correspondent for consideration at any time.

Correspondent: The Hon. Secretary, 77 Hallam Street, London W1W 5BS (020 7580 3802; Fax: 020 7436 5388).

OCCUPATIONAL CHARITIES

London Metal Exchange Benevolent Fund

Eligibility: People in need who are members of or have been connected with the London Metal Exchange, and their dependants.

Types of grants: One-off grants, and recurrent grants of about £900 over 12 months, according to need.

Annual grant total: In 2000/01 the fund had assets of £177,000 and an income of £46,000. It paid allowances totalling £15,000 and grants totalling £3,800.

Applications: On a form available from the correspondent, for consideration throughout the year.

Correspondent: Philip Needham, Secretary, 56 Leadenhall Street, London EC3A 2DX (020 7264 5555; Fax: 020 7680 0505).

Royal Metal Trades Benevolent Society

Eligibility: People in England and Wales who were employed in any capacity, for over 10 years, in manufacturing, distributing, wholesaling or retailing of products in hardware, housewares, DIY, brushware or builders merchants enterprises, and their spouse or widow/widower. Beneficiaries are typically of retirement age or over.

No grants are given to children, or for people working in the steel and motor industries.

Types of grants: A range of grants are given for different purposes: annual grants of up to £1,040; holidays (up to £100); TV licence assistance (up to £50 TV licence stamps); telephone bill assistance; and one-off grants for specific items and cold weather payments.

Annual grant total: In 2001 the trust had assets of £1.6 million, an income of £80,000 and a total expenditure of £128,000. 170 grants totalled £100,000.

Applications: On a form available from the correspondent, making full disclosure of income, expenses and state of health, and employment history. Applications can be submitted directly by the individual or through a social worker, citizen's advice bureau, other welfare agency or other third party. The applicant may be visited by the board while the case is under review. Applications can be considered at any time.

Correspondent: Mrs Donna Webb, General Secretary, Brooke House, 4 The Lakes, Bedford Road, Northampton NN4 7YD (01604 622023; Fax: 01604 631252; e-mail: rmtbs@brookehouse.co.uk).

Motor industry

Ben – Motor & Allied Trades Benevolent Fund

Eligibility: People from the UK or Republic of Ireland employed or formerly employed in the motor, agricultural engineering and cycle trades and allied industries.

Types of grants: Mostly one-off grants of £50 to £500 towards house repairs for health and safety reasons, white goods, heating, clothing, debts, disability equipment, home adaptations, respite breaks and so on. A few annuities are also given. No grants are made towards private medical expenses, private education or nursing/residential fee shortfalls.

Annual grant total: In 2001/02 grants to 5,700 individuals totalled £823,000.

Applications: On a form available from the correspondent, for consideration on the second Tuesday of every month. Applications can be submitted directly by the individual or through a social worker, citizen's advice bureau or other welfare agency.

Correspondent: Miss Jenny Brown, Lynwood, Sunninghill, Ascot, Berkshire SL5 0AJ (01344 620191; Fax: 01344 622042; e-mail: jenny.brown@ben.org.uk; website: www.ben.org.uk).

Other information: The fund also manages an extensive range of residential and nursing accommodation for people who are elderly or disabled, including sheltered accommodation.

The H T Pickles Memorial Benevolent Fund

Eligibility: Members, and ex-members, for five years of the Vehicle Builders' and Repairers' Association Limited, their employees and their dependants, in the UK and Republic of Ireland.

Types of grants: One-off and recurrent grants according to need.

Annual grant total: In 2000 the fund had assets of £42,000 and had an income of £4,400. Total expenditure was £3,100, all of which was given in 15 grants.

Applications: On a form available from the correspondent, to be submitted by another member of VBRA on behalf of the individual.

Correspondent: David C Hudson, The Vehicle Builders' & Repairers' Association Ltd, Belmont House, 102 Finkle Lane, Gildersome, Leeds LS27 7TW (0113 253 8333; Fax: 0113 238 0496; e-mail: cosec@vbra.co.uk; website: www.vbra.co.uk).

The Society of Motor Manufacturers & Traders Charitable Trust Fund

Eligibility: People in need who were senior executives in the motor industry, and their dependants.

Types of grants: One-off and recurrent grants and loans according to need.

Annual grant total: In 2000 the society had assets of £950,000, an income of £39,000 and a total expenditure of £25,000. £17,000 was given to BEN (see separate entry on page 51). No individuals were directly supported during the year.

Applications: In writing to the correspondent.

Correspondent: S Samuels, Forbes House, Halkin Street, London SW1X 7DS (020 7235 7000).

Motor Sports

The Auto Cycle Union Benevolent Fund

Eligibility: Past and present members of the Auto Cycle Union and their dependants, who are in need through accident, illness or hardship in England, Scotland or Wales.

Types of grants: Monthly grants, of between £150 and £260, to supplement low income.

Annual grant total: Over £40,000 in 2001.

Applications: On a form available from the local ACU officer. Applications should be made directly by the individual and include contain current income and expenses and they are considered monthly.

Correspondent: Robert William Smith, Treasurer, ACU House, Wood Street, Rugby CV21 2YX (01788 566400; Fax: 01788 573585; e-mail: admin@acu.org.uk; website: www.motorcyclinggb.com).

Other information: For details of the nearest ACU officer, please contact the correspondent.

British Motor Cycle Racing Club Benevolent Fund

Eligibility: Members of the club and their dependants, who are in need.

Types of grants: One-off grants towards subsistence, travel and medical care costs.

Annual grant total: In 2001 the trust's assets totalled £23,000, its income was £12,000 and it made grants to over 40 individuals totalling £8,800.

Applications: In writing to: David Stewart, c/o British Motor Cycle Racing Club Ltd, Lydden Motor Racing Circuit, Wootton,

OCCUPATIONAL CHARITIES

Canterbury, Kent CT4 6RX. Applications can be submitted at any time, either directly by the individual, or through a third party such as a spouse or next of kin.

Correspondent: John Wilson, 13 Watchet Lane, Holmer Green, High Wycombe HP15 6UA (01494 711210; Fax: 01494 717410).

The British Motoring Sport Relief Fund

Eligibility: People worldwide who have been injured through participating or assisting in motor car racing, testing, trials and competitions, and their dependants.

Types of grants: One-off and recurrent grants or loans, according to need, offering short term help. Grants are generally towards medical/rehabilitation expenses, car/transport costs or occasionally towards bills. Grants are usually for short-term relief until other assistance can be found.

Annual grant total: In 2000/01 the trust had assets of £106,000 and an income of £6,000. Total expenditure was just £28 as no grants were made.

Applications: Applications should be made by the individual in writing giving details of the event at which the injury or disability occurred. Applications are considered as they arrive.

Correspondent: The Trustees, c/o Rawlinson & Hunter, Eagle House, 110 Jermyn Street, London SW1Y 6RH (020 7451 9000; Fax: 020 7451 9090).

British Racing Drivers Club (BRDC) Benevolent Fund

Eligibility: Members of the club and their dependants, who are in need.

Types of grants: Grants according to need.

Annual grant total: Information not available.

Applications: In writing to the correspondent.

Correspondent: The Trustees, Silverstone Circuits Ltd, Silverstone, Towcester, Northamptonshire NN12 8TN (01327 857271).

The Grand Prix Mechanics Charitable Trust

Eligibility: Past and present Grand Prix mechanics and their dependants who are in need.

Types of grants: The trust pays the annual insurance costs of mechanics at Grand Prix meetings. Medical support has also been given.

Annual grant total: In 1999/2000 the trust had assets of £1.3 million, an income of £45,000 and a total expenditure of £6,300. Insurance cover for mechanics at Grand Prix meetings totalled £6,300. No other grants were made during the year, although £11,000 was given towards an individual's medical costs in the previous year.

Applications: In writing to the correspondent.

Correspondent: Christopher Bliss, Eagle House, 110 Jermyn Street, London SW1Y 6RH (020 7451 9000; Fax: 020 7451 9090).

Naval architecture

The Royal Institution of Naval Architects Benevolent Fund

Eligibility: Members and their dependants who are in need.

Types of grants: One-off grants for a variety of needs.

Annual grant total: About £15,000.

Applications: In writing to the correspondent, to be considered as they arrive.

Correspondent: The Chief Executive, 10 Upper Belgrave Street, London SW1X 8BQ (020 7235 4622; Fax: 020 7259 5912; e-mail: hq@rina.org.uk; website: www.rina.org.uk).

Newsagents

The National Federation of Retail Newsagents Convalescence Fund

Eligibility: Members of the federation and their spouses. Other people in the retail newsagents trade who are not members of the federation are not eligible.

Types of grants: Grants are given for relief-in-need, including convalescent holidays. They can be up to a maximum of £150 (inc. VAT) per person, per week for no more than six weeks in any five-year period.

Annual grant total: About £37,000.

Applications: On a form available from the correspondent. Applications must go through the district office of the federation. They should include confirmation of federation fees paid and confirmation from a doctor of the need for convalescence.

Correspondent: D Sheikh, Yeoman House, Sekforde Street, Clerkenwell Green, London EC1R 0HF (020 7253 4225).

NewstrAid Benevolent Society

Eligibility: Retired people and their dependants, and those who cannot work through ill health, who have been engaged in the distribution and sale of newspapers and magazines in the UK for at least 10 years and are not currently trading or working.

Types of grants: Regular monthly benefits to people who live in their own homes and one-off grants for various items including washing machines, cookers, special chairs and disability items. No grants for private medicine or school or college fees.

Annual grant total: £381,000 in 2001.

Applications: On a form available from the correspondent. Applications can be submitted directly by the individual, through a social worker or other welfare agency, or any third party who can vouch for the individual and their background. Applications are considered every two months from January.

Correspondent: Mrs B Davidson, Welfare Officer, PO Box 306, Great Dunmow, Essex CM6 1HY (01371 874198; Fax: 01371 873816).

Patent agents

The Chartered Institute of Patent Agents' Incorporated Benevolent Association

Eligibility: British members and former members of the institute, and their dependants.

Types of grants: One-off and recurrent grants or loans according to need.

Annual grant total: In 2000/01 the association had an income of £46,000 and a total expenditure of £30,000.

Applications: In writing to the correspondent, marked 'Private and Confidential'. Applications can be submitted at any time.

Correspondent: D R Chandler, Secretary of The Chartered Institute of Patent Agents' Incorporated Benevolent Association, c/o Chartered Institute of Patent Agents, Staple Inn Building, London WC1V 7PZ.

Pawnbrokers

The Pawnbrokers' Charitable Institution

Eligibility: Pawnbrokers who have been employed for at least five years, their widows, widowers and children who are convalescent, disabled or otherwise infirm or in need of financial assistance.

Types of grants: Annual grants and regular allowances. Recurrent grants generally of

OCCUPATIONAL CHARITIES

£520 are paid monthly (for those on Income Support) and grants of over £1,000 are available to meet emergency needs. Recent grants have been given towards new furniture, a cooker and a reclining chair.

Annual grant total: In 1999/2000 the institution had assets of £2.8 million, an income of £89,000 and a total expenditure of £88,000. Grants to 43 individuals totalled £52,000.

Applications: On a form available from the correspondent. The trustees meet on the first Tuesday of every month.

Correspondent: Mrs K Way, Secretary, 184 Crofton Lane, Orpington, Kent BR6 0BW (Tel & Fax: 01689 811978).

Petroleum

The Institute of Petroleum 1986 Benevolent Fund

Eligibility: Members and former members of the institute, and their dependants.

Types of grants: One-off grants according to need.

Annual grant total: In 2001 grants totalled £6,000.

Applications: In writing to the correspondent requesting an application form. Applications can be submitted by the individual, a social worker, citizen's advice bureau, welfare agency or a third party such as a carer or relative. Applications are considered throughout the year.

Correspondent: The Hon. Secretary, c/o Jenny Sandrock, Institute of Petroleum, 61 New Cavendish Street, London W1G 7AR (020 7467 7100; Fax: 020 7255 1472).

Police

The Gurney Fund for Police Orphans

Eligibility: Children under 18 of deceased or incapacitated police officers from 22 subscribing forces in southern and south midland areas of England and South and Mid-Wales, excluding the Metropolitan Police.

Types of grants: Grants are available for students up to 18 years old, applications from older students will be considered in certain circumstances at the discretion of the trustees. Grants can be for books, uniforms, equipment, educational travel, school trips, music lessons, sport and other extra-curricular activities. No grants for school fees, but consideration may be given to children with special needs. Grants range from £7 to £30 per week.

Annual grant total: In 2000/01 the fund had an income of £526,000 and a total expenditure of £357,000. About £300,000 to about 400 beneficiaries, for relief-in-need and for advancement in education.

Applications: A parent can apply by letter. A force welfare officer or local representative will then assess the application for a later decision by the trustees. Applications can be made at any time and are considered in February, May, August and November.

Correspondent: The Director, 9 Bath Road, Worthing BN11 3NU (01903 237256).

Indian Police Benevolent Fund

Eligibility: Former members of the Indian police, and their widows and children, worldwide.

Types of grants: One-off and recurrent grants according to need.

Annual grant total: In 2000/01 the fund had assets of £101,000 and an income of £7,400. Total expenditure was £21,000, all of which was given in 18 grants.

Applications: On a form available from the correspondent, for consideration throughout the year. Completed forms should be submitted directly by the individual.

Correspondent: Paul Dean, Executive Trustee, 97 Verulam Road, St Albans, Hertfordshire AL3 4DL (01727 845229; Fax: 01727 863896).

Metropolitan Police Civil Staff Welfare Fund

Eligibility: Members and past members of the Metropolitan Police Civil Staff and their families and dependants who, through poverty, hardship or distress, are in need. Past members include staff who have retired, resigned or been 'outsourced'.

Types of grants: One-off grants according to need. Loans may also be made, repayable within two years. No grants are made towards private healthcare, private education fees, legal costs, business debts or bills that have already been paid.

Annual grant total: In 2000/01 the fund had an income of £13,000 and a total expenditure of £9,200.

Applications: On a form available from the correspondent.

Correspondent: K J Castle, Metropolitan Police Service, Welfare Funds Unit, Room 1026, New Scotland Yard, 10 Broadway, London SW1H 0BG (020 7230 4413; Fax: 020 7230 4672).

Other information: Welfare counselling is also available.

The Metropolitan Police Combined Benevolent Fund

Eligibility: Metropolitan Police officers, ex-officers, their widows and orphans.

Types of grants: Generally one-off grants according to need.

Annual grant total: In 2000 the fund had both an income and a total expenditure of £1.1 million. It gave £774,000 throguh the Metropolitan Police Convalescent Home Fund and £277,000 through the Metropolitian and City Police Orphans Fund.

Applications: In writing to the correspondent directly by the individual. Applications are considered throughout the year.

Correspondent: Miss C Hulme, Head of Charities, Cobalt Square, 1 South Lambeth Road, London SW8 1SU.

Other information: This entry was not confirmed by the fund, but the address was correct according to the Charity Commission database.

Northern Police Orphans' Trust

Eligibility: People with at least one parent who was a member of a police force in northern England, or associated with the police, and who is now deceased or incapacitated due to their work.

Types of grants: One-off and recurrent grants according to need. Grants are made towards holidays, clothing, birthday and Christmas grants and so on.

Annual grant total: In 2000 the trust had assets of £2.9 million, an income of £112,000 and a total expenditure of £44,000. Grants to 108 individuals totalled £32,000.

Applications: Applications should be submitted via the police force in which the parent served. Applications are considered as they arrive.

Correspondent: A Outhwaite, St Andrews, Harlow Moor Road, Harrogate, North Yorkshire HG2 0AD (01423 04448 or 01423 567667; Fax: 01423 527543).

Police Dependants' Trust

Eligibility: (i) Dependants of current police officers or former police officers who died from injuries received in the execution of duty.
(ii) Police officers or former police officers incapacitated as a result of injury received in the execution of duty, and/or their dependants.

Types of grants: Annual maintenance and one-off grants are made. They can be given towards home alterations, wheelchairs, orthopaedic beds, education, holidays, care home fees and general maintenance.

Annual grant total: In 2000/01 the trust had assets of £26 million, an income of £1.9 million and a total expenditure of £783,000.

Applications: On a form available from the chief executive, to be submitted through one of the force's welfare officers. Applications are generally considered every two months although urgent decisions can be made between meetings.

Correspondent: David French, Chief Executive, Room 103, Clive House, Petty France, London SW1H 9HD (020 7273 2921; Fax: 020 7273 3300; e-mail: david.french@homeoffice.gsi.gov.uk)

Other information: The trust also gave £500,000 to a police convalescence home.

Post office

The Rowland Hill Memorial And Benevolent Fund

Eligibility: Past and present Post Office employees and their dependants.

Types of grants: One-off grants are made to people in need for disability aids, essential household items and so on. Recurrent cost of living grants are given of £45 a month with a £50 Christmas bonus (£80 a month to people in a care or nursing home). Loans can also be made, repayable either from salary or from the estate of retired people.

Weekly grants (sometimes loans) to supplement living expenses. Normally up to £10 a week, except for people in residential/nursing homes where the maximum is £20 a week.

Loans (but not grants) are either repayable from salary in the case of serving officers or from the estate in the case of pensioners or widows who own their own home. All loans are interest free.

The fund also sponsors nominees for places in certain rest and nursing homes and in sheltered accommodation schemes.

Annual grant total: In 2000/01 the fund had assets of £1.3 million, an income of £607,000 and a total expenditure of £532,000. Grants totalled £445,000, comprised of £232,000 in hardship grants, £164,000 in lump sum payments and £50,000 in residential homes fees.

Applications: In writing to the correspondent. Applications can be received from the applicant or any third party and are considered twice every calendar month.

Correspondent: Barry Higginson, 49 Featherstone Street, London EC1Y 8SY (020 7320 4285; Fax: 020 7320 4286).

The National Federation of Sub-Postmasters Benevolent Fund

Eligibility: (i) Serving or retired sub-postmasters and sub-postmistresses; (ii) serving or retired full-time employees of the NFSP; and (iii) the widows, widowers and children of the above.

Types of grants: One-off grants according to need. Recent examples include: fencing; a secondhand scooter; a downstairs shower for a person who is disabled; house and roof repairs; an adjustable bed; a reconditioned stairlift; and a holiday for somebody who is disabled.

Annual grant total: In 2001 the trust had assets of £1.4 million, an income of £185,000 and a total expenditure of £52,000. Grants to 76 individuals totalled £27,000.

Applications: On a form available from the correspondent, submitted directly by the individual or a welfare charity. Applications are considered in January, March, June and November, but emergency cases are dealt with as they arise.

Correspondent: Colin Baker, Evelyn House, 22 Windlesham Gardens, Shoreham-by-Sea, West Sussex BN43 5AZ (01273 452324; Fax: 01273 465403; e-mail: nfcp@subpostmasters.org.uk; website: www.subpostmasters.org.uk).

Pottery & glass

The Pottery & Glass Trade Benevolent Institution

Eligibility: People who were or are employed in manufacturing, wholesale or retail aspects of china or glass.

Types of grants: Weekly allowances and one-off grants.

Annual grant total: In 2000/01 the institution had an income of £31,000 and a total expenditure of £25,000.

Applications: On a form available from the correspondent.

Correspondent: Audrey Smith, 57 Whitley Court, Coram Street, London WC1N 1HD (Tel & Fax: 020 7837 2231).

Printing

Printers' Charitable Corporation

Eligibility: People who are aged, poor or distressed, who are, or were, either printers or employed in the printing or allied trades such as ink-making, paper-making, book binding, the warehousing of ink, paper, books or printing and binding materials or the manufacture of typesetting, foundry, printing or binding machinery. Also widows, widowers and children of deceased members who are in need.

Types of grants: One-off and recurrent grants and loans of between £100 and £1,000 which have included purchase of electric wheelchairs, furniture, decorating and clothing. Grants for general living expenses are available although there are no grants towards private medical treatment or payment of debts.

Annual grant total: In 2001 the trust had assets of £31 million, an income of £1.7 million and a total expenditure of £2 million. £538,000 was given in 450 regular grants and over 100 one-off grants.

Applications: On a form available from the correspondent, to be submitted either directly by the individual or through a social worker, citizen's advice bureau or other third party. Applications are considered monthly.

Correspondent: The Director, 7 Cantelupe Mews, Cantelupe Road, East Grinstead, West Sussex RH19 3BG (01342 318882; Fax: 01342 318887; e-mail: sandra@pccorp.fsnet.co.uk; website: www.printerscharitable corporation.co.uk).

Other information: The corporation provides sheltered homes for older people at Basildon and Bletchley plus a nursing home at Bletchley. It also advises people of pensionable age on their statutory entitlements.

Probation

The Edridge Fund

Eligibility: Members, and ex-members, of the probation service who are (or were) eligible to be members of NAPO or CAFCASS, their bereaved partners, spouses and dependants.

Types of grants: Financial and welfare support, generally in a one-off grant of up to £300 to alleviate cases of distress and hardship such as debt, relationship breakdown, accident or ill health. No grants are given towards further education or other courses.

Annual grant total: In 2000/01 the trust gave 120 grants totalling £30,000.

Applications: On a form available from the correspondent or local representative. Applications can be submitted either directly by the individual or through the local representative of the fund. They are considered at regular trustees' meetings, and at other times if the case is an emergency. Applicants should discuss their situation with their local representative if possible.

Correspondent: Richard Martin, Secretary, The Limes, Lynn Road, Gayton, King's Lynn, Norfolk PE32 1QJ (Tel &

Fax: 01553 636570;
e-mail: edridge@btinternet.com;
website: www.edridgefund.org).

Public relations

Iprovision (formerly The Institute of Public Relations Benevolent Fund)

Eligibility: Members of the institute and dependants of members or deceased members.
Types of grants: One-off and recurrent grants according to need.
Annual grant total: About £10,000.
Applications: In writing to the correspondent. Applications are considered every two months, although urgent applications can be considered at any time.
Correspondent: Alan Dadd, Administrator, The Old Trading House, 15 Northburgh Street, London EC1V 0PR (01227 749963; e-mail: iprovision@aol.com).

Public Sector

Corporation of London Benevolent Association

Eligibility: People in need who are, or have been, members of the Court of Common Council, and their dependants.
Types of grants: One-off and recurrent grants according to need.
Annual grant total: In 2000 the income of the trust was £8,100 and its total expenditure was £3,200.
Applications: In writing to the correspondent.
Correspondent: David Haddon, Town Clerk's Department, Corporation of London, PO Box 270, London EC2P 2EJ (020 7332 1432).

Corporation of London Staff Association Benevolent Fund

Eligibility: People in need who are or have been members of the Corporation of London Staff Association, and their dependants.
Types of grants: One-off and recurrent grants according to need.
Annual grant total: In 1997/98 the income of the trust was £4,400 and its total expenditure was £2,900.

Applications: In writing to the correspondent.
Correspondent: Tim Kelt, Chamberlain's Department, Corporation of London, PO Box 270, London EC2P 2EJ (020 7332 1331; e-mail: tim.kelt@ms.corpoflondon.gov.uk).

UNISON Welfare

Eligibility: Members and former members of UNISON, and their dependants, who are in need.
Types of grants: The trust stated it supports: 'a wide range of needs. A grant could be made to help with household bills, ease debts or to pay for a much needed break for a family experiencing stressful times or a member recovering from illness. We can often help with the costs of coping with a disability or caring for someone with special needs including hospital visits.'

No grants are given towards: travel abroad; legal costs; private medical treatment; private education; house purchase or sale; residential or nursing home fees; consumer credit debts; care purchase or maintenance (except for people who are disabled); and industrial action.
Annual grant total: In 2001 the charity had assets of £4 million, an income of £1.4 million and a total expenditure of £761,000. Grants to 1,200 individuals totalled £311,000.
Applications: On a form available from the welfare secretary, or the retired members secretary, of the local UNISON branch. Applications can also be submitted through the correspondent. They can be considered at any time.
Correspondent: Julie Grant, 1 Mabledon Place, London WC1H 9AJ (020 7391 9170; Fax: 020 7383 2617; e-mail: welfare@unison.co.uk; website: www.unison.org.uk/welfare).

Public Transport

The Worshipful Company of Carmen Benevolent Trust

Eligibility: People in need in the UK.
Types of grants: One-off grants according to need, where the grant will make an exceptional difference to the individual. A recent grant was given, for example, to a disabled person who needed computer equipment.
Annual grant total: In 1999/2000 the trust had an income of £80,000 and made grants totalling £55,000, mostly to organisations.
Applications: In writing to the correspondent. Please note, this trust only occasionally makes grants to individuals.

Correspondent: Lt Col G T Pearce, Secretary, 8 Little Trinity Lane, London EC4V 2AN (01784 452385).

The Transport Benevolent Fund

Eligibility: Employees and former employees of the public transport industry who are in need (sick, disabled or convalescent), their partners and dependants. Only members of the benevolent fund are supported.
Types of grants: Grants are to meet unexpected one-off situtations, where help is not available from other sources. Grants can be given towards medical equipment, complementary medical treatments and other needs.
Annual grant total: In 2000/01 the trust gave £52,000 in grants to individuals and spent a further £131,000 on other charitable expenditure.
Applications: On a form available from the correspondent. Applications are considered throughout the year.
Correspondent: Chris Godbold, Chief Executive, 87a Leonard Street, London EC2A 4QS (0870 0000 172/173; Fax: 0870 831 2882; e-mail: help@tbf.org.uk; website: www.tbf.org.uk).

Quarrying

The Institute of Quarrying Educational Development and Benevolent Fund

Eligibility: Members or former members of the Institute of Quarrying, and/or their dependants. People involved in the quarrying industry but are not members of the institute are not considered.
Types of grants: One-off grants ranging from £390 to £4,700. No recurrent grants are made, although most beneficiaries successfully reapply each year, with one individual having been supported each year since 1974.
Annual grant total: In 2000/01 grants to eight individuals totalled £33,000.
Applications: On a form available from the correspondent. Applications may be submitted at any time.
Correspondent: Roger Allen, Hon. Secretary, 7 Regent Street, Nottingham NG1 5BS (0115 941 1315).
Other information: Projects which advance the education and research of quarrying are also supported.

OCCUPATIONAL CHARITIES

Railways

Associated Society of Locomotive Engineers & Firemen (ASLEF) Hardship Fund

Eligibility: Members of ASLEF, and their dependants, who are in need.

Types of grants: One-off grants for reasons of hardship.

Annual grant total: £4,400 in 1999.

Applications: In writing to the correspondent.

Correspondent: The General Secretary, ASLEF, 9 Arkwright Road, Hampstead, London NW3 6AB (020 7317 8600; Fax: 020 7794 6406).

Railway Benevolent Institution

Eligibility: Railway employees (active or retired) and their dependants in the UK and Republic of Ireland. Unless there are very special circumstances, grants are not made to anyone with capital in excess of £16,000.

Types of grants: One-off grants of £100 to £2,500 to assist any need, including aids for the disabled, funeral costs and convalescence. Grants can also be used towards shortfalls in fees for people in care. Grants are also given to the children of employees for school aids or clothing or maintenance for higher education students.

Annual grant total: In 2001 the institution had assets of £3.3 million, an income of £327,000 and a total expenditure of £996,000. Grants to 1,700 individuals totalled £904,000.

Applications: On a form available from the correspondent, submitted by the individual, or through a social worker, citizen's advice bureau or other welfare agency. Applications are considered monthly.

Correspondent: B R Whitnall, Director, Electra Way, Crewe Business Park, Crewe, Cheshire CW1 6HS (01270 251316; Fax: 01270 503966).

The Railway Housing Association & Benefit Fund

Eligibility: People who are working or who have worked in the railway industry, and their dependants, in England, Scotland and Wales.

Types of grants: One-off grants, which have been given towards house repairs, care attendants, respite care, essential household items, aids and adaptations and general financial assistance.

Annual grant total: About £25,000 in 2001.

Applications: On a form available from the correspondent. Applications should be submitted through a social worker, citizen's advice bureau, or other welfare agency, and include proof of railway employment. There are regular meetings throughout the year.

Correspondent: Mrs Lathan, Director, Bank Top House, Garbutt Square, Neasham Road, Darlington DL1 4DR (01325 482125; Fax: 01325 384641).

RMT (National Union of Rail, Maritime & Transport Workers) Orphan Fund

Eligibility: The children (aged under 22) of deceased members of the union.

Types of grants: Grants are made of £8.50 a week for children up to 16 years of age, and £12.75 a week for young people aged 16 to 22 who are continuing in full-time education. An additional £4.25 a week may be paid to people under 16 if they had lost both of their parents.

Annual grant total: In 1999 relief-in-need grants totalled £234,000 to 418 individuals.

Applications: Through the local union branch.

Correspondent: The Benefits Section, Unity House, 39 Chalton Street, London NW1 1JD (020 7387 4771; Fax: 020 7387 4123; website: www.rmt.org.uk).

Other information: This entry was not confirmed by the fund, but the information was correct according to their website.

Religion

Frances Ashton's Charity

Eligibility: Serving and retired Church of England clergy, or their widows/widowers, who are in need.

Types of grants: Grants vary between £210 and £530 and are paid once a year in September.

Grants are not given towards property purchase, school fees, parochial expenses or office furniture/equipment.

Annual grant total: In 2001 the trust had assets of £1.3 million and both an income and a total expenditure of £52,000. Grants to 110 individuals totalled £44,000.

Applications: On a form available from the correspondent, to be submitted directly by the individual by 1 June each year.

Correspondent: Mrs Barbara Davis, Receiver, CAF, Kings Hill, West Malling, Kent ME19 4TA (01732 520081; Fax: 01732 520001).

The Auxiliary Fund of the Methodist Church

Eligibility: Retired ministers of the Methodist church and their dependants.

Types of grants: All kinds of need (including emergencies) are considered.

Annual grant total: £250,000.

Applications: In writing to the correspondent at any time.

Correspondent: Noel Rajaratnam, 25 Marylebone Road, London NW1 5JR (020 7486 5502; Fax: 020 7467 5237).

Archdeaconry of Bath Clerical Families Fund

Eligibility: Widows and children, of clergymen who have died and who last served in the deaneries of Bath, Chew Magna and Portishead.

Types of grants: One-off and recurrent grants according to need.

Annual grant total: In 1999/2000 the trust's income was £2,300 and its total expenditure was £1,700.

Applications: In writing to the correspondent.

Correspondent: John Bruce Eyers, Honorary Secretary and Treasurer, St Anthony's, The Barton, Corston, Bath BA2 9AL (01225 873607).

The Bible Preaching Trust

Eligibility: Ministers of the Evangelical Christian faith who are in need. Theological students may occasionally benefit.

Types of grants: Usually one-off ranging from £250 to £2,000. Funding is not given for social causes, group projects, or to any person who cannot agree to the trust's doctrinal statement.

Annual grant total: In 2000/01 the trust had an income of £13,000 and a total expenditure of £11,000.

Applications: This is usually either by recommendation or by letter; application forms and trust deed extracts are then sent out. Trustees' meetings are held every four months at which applications will be considered. 'Mass-targeting' applications or those outside the terms of the trust may not be answered.

Correspondent: Richard Mayers, Secretary and Treasurer, 5 The Crescent, Egham, Surrey TW20 9PQ (01784 436139).

Buckingham Trust

Eligibility: People in need who are missionaries or Christian workers, or people with some Christian connection. Applicants must be known to the trustees.

Types of grants: One-off and recurrent grants according to need.

Annual grant total: In 1998/99 it had assets of £689,000 and an income of

£164,000. Grants to individuals totalled £6,600, organisations received £84,000 and churches £48,000.

Applications: In writing to the correspondent.

Correspondent: The Secretary, Messrs Foot Davson & Co., 17 Church Road, Tunbridge Wells, Kent TN1 1LG.

The Chasah Trust

Eligibility: Missionaries who are known to the trustees, or to a contact of the trustees.

Types of grants: One-off and recurrent grants according to need.

Annual grant total: In 1999/2000 the trust had an income of £23,000, all of which was given in grants to individuals and organisations.

Applications: In writing to the correspondent, via the contact.

Correspondent: R D Collier-Keywood, Trustee, Glydwish Hall, Fontridge Lane, Burwash, East Sussex TN19 7DG (020 7213 3997).

Children of the Clergy Trust

Eligibility: Children of deceased ministers of the Church of Scotland, based anywhere.

Types of grants: One-off or recurrent grants to relieve poverty, hardship or distress, or to advance education.

Annual grant total: In 2001 the trust had assets of £40,000 and an income of £2,600. Total expenditure was £1,400.

Applications: In writing to the correspondent. Applications should be submitted directly by the individual to be considered at any time, and should include information about the applicant's ministerial parent, general family circumstances and other relevant information.

Correspondent: Revd Iain U Thomson, The Manse, Manse Road, Kirkton of Skene, Westhill, Aberdeenshire AB32 6LX (Tel & Fax: 01224 743277).

The Church of England Pensions Board

Eligibility: Retired clergy and licensed layworkers of the Church of England, their widows, widowers and dependants.

Types of grants: Allowances to supplement low incomes and assistance with fees in residential or nursing homes. There are about 900 recipients of allowances and supplementary pensions.

Annual grant total: About £1.9 million.

Applications: On a form available from the correspondent.

Correspondent: R G Radford, Secretary, 29 Great Smith Street, London SW1P 3PS (020 7898 1800; Fax: 020 7898 1801; e-mail: enquiries@cept.c-of-e.org.uk).

Other information: The trust's main concern is the welfare of retired clergy and their spouses or widow(er)s, who need sheltered accommodation. It runs eight residential and nursing homes for these beneficiaries.

The Collier Charitable Trust

Eligibility: Retired Christian missionaries and teachers in the UK and overseas.

Types of grants: One-off and recurrent grants of around £300 each.

Annual grant total: In 2000 the trust's income was £18,000 and its total expenditure was £35,000. Further information was not available for this year.

In 1998 the trust had an income of £19,000 and gave grants totalling £22,000 of which £3,900 went to 13 individuals.

Applications: In writing to the correspondent.

Correspondent: M A Blagden, Secretary, Cherry Tree Cottage, Old Kiln Lane, Churt, Farnham, Surrey GU10 2HX.

The Corporation of the Sons of the Clergy

Eligibility: Anglican clergy of the dioceses of the UK and Ireland and the diocese in Europe, their widows/widowers and dependants under 25, separated or divorced spouses of such clergy and elderly unmarried daughters of such clergy.

Types of grants: Grants cover a range of subject matters, including heating, maintenance of property, counselling, nursing home fees, child maintenance, child-minding, removal and resettlement of debts. Grants are also made for certain educational purposes. No grants for holidays, convalescence, courses, property or car purchase, sabbaticals, clerical clothing or TV licences.

Annual grant total: In 2001 the corporation had an income of £1.7 million and its total expenditure was £2.1 million. Grants to individuals in need totalled £725,000. Grants were also made for educational purposes.

Applications: An information leaflet and application form are available from the correspondent. All applications are means-tested.

Correspondent: Robert Welsford, Registrar, 1 Dean Trench Street, Westminster, London SW1P 3HB (020 7799 3696 or 020 7222 5887; Fax: 020 7222 3468).

Other information: This charity incorporates The Clergy Orphan Corporation.

Cross House Trust

Eligibility: Individuals in full-time Christian ministry.

Types of grants: One-off and recurrent grants according to need.

Annual grant total: In 1998/99 the trust had assets of £1.9 million, an income of £255,000 and a total expenditure of £92,000. Grants to individuals totalled £1,300. Grants to churches and Christian charities totalled £28,000.

Applications: In writing to the correspondent at any time. The trust commits most of its money early, giving the remaining funds to eligible applicants.

Correspondent: Gavin Croft Wilcock, 74 The Close, Norwich, Norfolk NR1 4DR (01603 610911).

Domine Trust

Eligibility: Children, young people and clergy who are in need.

Types of grants: One-off grants of £50 to £250.

Annual grant total: About £6,000 to individuals.

Applications: In writing to the correspondent for consideration monthly. The trust states that it receives hundreds of applications and can no longer reply to those whom it cannot help.

Correspondent: Barry Dinan, Chalkpit House, Knotty Green, Beaconsfield, Buckinghamshire HP9 2TY (e-mail: bdinan@hansongreen.co.uk).

Other information: Organisations are also supported.

The Four Winds Trust

Eligibility: Evangelists, missionaries and ministers, including those who have retired, and their widows, widowers and other dependants.

Types of grants: Usually ongoing grants.

Annual grant total: In 2000/01 the trust had both an income and a total expenditure of £35,000, after sales and purchase of investments. Grants to 32 individuals totalled £5,000. Grants to 58 organisations totalled £23,000.

Applications: In writing to the correspondent, although the trust states that it does not consider unsolicited applications. Applications without an sae will not receive a response. Applications with an sae will receive a rejection letter.

Correspondent: P A Charters, Trustee, Four Winds, Ashbury, Swindon, Wiltshire SN9 8LZ.

The Friends of the Clergy Corporation

Eligibility: Ordained Anglican ministers, their widows, children or other dependants, including separated or divorced wives and their children.

Types of grants: One-off cash grants for bereavement expenses, removal expenses, holidays, general welfare, pensions, Christmas grants, debts, retirement,

OCCUPATIONAL CHARITIES

repairs, school clothing and pre-school nursery fees.

Annual grant total: In 2000/01 grants totalled £920,000.

Applications: On a form available from the correspondent to be submitted directly by the individual or by a social worker, dependant etc. if the individual is unable to do so. Applications are considered each month.

Correspondent: B P Smith, Secretary, 27 Medway Street, Westminster, London SW1P 2BD (020 7222 2288; Fax: 020 7233 1244; e-mail: focc@btinternet.com; website: www.friendsoftheclergy.org).

The Groves Charitable Trust

Eligibility: Christian missionaries who are in need.

Types of grants: Grants ranging between £200 and £1,000 may be spent to support the work of Christian missionaries.

Annual grant total: In 2001 grants totalling £16,000 were made for welfare and educational purposes.

Applications: Applications should be made in writing, explaining the purpose for which the grant is being sought.

Correspondent: R Humphrey, Messrs Grant Thornton, 125 High Street, Crawley, West Sussex RH10 1DQ (01293 561383).

Other information: Support is also given to individuals undertaking Christian education or training.

Thomas Harley Relief in Need Charity

See entry on page 232

Harnish Trust

Eligibility: People who normally live in the UK who are carrying out Christian work in the UK or overseas.

Types of grants: One-off and recurrent grants ranging from £500 to £1,000. Grants are not made in response to unsolicited applications.

Annual grant total: In 2000/01 the trust's assets totalled £347,000, its income was only £14,000, while grants totalled £85,000. Grants were made to 15 individuals of £500 to £1,000 each.

Applications: The trust is very clear that unsolicited applications are not considered; it is recommended that you do not approach this trust for a grant.

Correspondent: Mrs Jill Dann, Trustee, The Cottage, 21 St Mary Street, Chippenham, Wiltshire SN15 3JW.

Other information: Grants are also made to individuals for educational purposes, and to organisations.

Lady Elizabeth Hastings' Non-Educational Charity

Eligibility: Licensed clergy of the Church of England working in the former counties of York, Cumberland or Northumberland as constituted on the 31 March 1974, and their dependants.

Types of grants: One-off and recurrent grants for welfare purposes.

Annual grant total: In 2000/01 Lady Elizabeth Hastings' Estate Charity had assets of £6.1 million, an income of £33,000 and a total expenditure of £421,000. 50% of the income was given to this non-educational branch, which gave 223 grants totalling £132,000.

Applications: In writing to the correspondent. The trustees meet four times a year, though grants can be made between the meetings, on the agreement of two trustees.

Correspondent: E F V Waterson, Clerk, Carter Jonas, 82 Micklegate, York YO1 1LF.

Other information: The trust is managed by Lady Elizabeth Hasting's Estate Charity.

The Lady Hewley Trust

Eligibility: Present or retired ministers of the Baptist or United Reformed Church and their widows who are in need. This is a national trust, although preference is given to applicants whose ministry is in the northern counties of England.

Types of grants: Grants to a usual maximum of about £1,000 (unless outside the scope of social security payments) to help with the relief of hardship or distress.

Annual grant total: About £100,000 given to a maximum of 100 people.

Applications: On a form available from the correspondent. Applications should be submitted by 15 March for the June meeting of the trustees and by 15 July for the October meeting.

Correspondent: D R Wharrie, Clerk, Woodside House, Ashton, Chester CH3 8AE (01829 751544).

The Arthur Hurst Will Trust

Eligibility: Distressed gentlewomen and needy clergy who have been forced to give up their work because of ill health.

Types of grants: One-off grants according to need.

Annual grant total: In 1998/99 the trust had assets of £720,000, and both an income and total expenditure of £23,000.

Applications: Applications can be submitted directly by the individual or through a social worker, citizen's advice bureau, a welfare agency or another third party. Applications can be considered at any time, although there is not always available funding to make payments.

Correspondent: Thomas Fitzgerald, Public Trust Officer, Stewart House, 24 Kingsway, London WC2B 6JX.

Other information: This entry was not confirmed by the trust, but the address was correct according to the Charity Commission database.

The Lyall Bequest

Eligibility: Ministers of the Church of Scotland.

Types of grants: Grants of up to £140 are given towards holidays.

Annual grant total: £700.

Applications: In writing to the correspondent. Applications for holiday grants should be made before the holiday begins.

Correspondent: Miss E L Calderwood, Secretary, c/o Pagan Osborne, 106 South Street, St Andrews, Fife KY16 9QD (01334 475001; Fax: 01334 476332; e-mail: enquiries@pagan.co.uk).

The Methodist Local Preachers Mutual Aid Association

Eligibility: Accredited Methodist or Wesleyan Reform Union Local Preachers, their widowed spouses and dependants living in the UK.

Types of grants: One-off grants (usually between £50 and £500) and weekly payments (up to £20 a week) according to need. The trust does not make loans.

Annual grant total: In 2000/01 the trust had assets of £624,000 and an income of £552,000. Total expenditure was £700,000 with grants totalling £46,000.

Applications: On a form available from the correspondent. Applications should include details of weekly income and expenditure and capital resources.

Correspondent: Godfrey C Talford, General Secretary, Head Office, 89 High Street, Rickmansworth, Hertfordshire WD3 1EF (01923 775856; Fax: 01923 710075; e-mail: headoffice@lpma.demon.co.uk).

Other information: The association also has four residential care homes.

Ministers' Relief Society

Eligibility: Protestant ministers, their widows and dependants who are in need.

Types of grants: One-off and recurrent grants ranging between £150 and £350. Grants have been for: ministers, including missionaries, whose congregation cannot fully support them; ministers who are retired or disabled, and their widows, with inadequate income or savings; specific emergencies, such as serious illness, removal costs, enforced resignation or dismissal by congregation; and candidates and students seeking vocational training in the ministry.

Annual grant total: In 2001 the society had an income of £22,000 and a total expenditure of £19,000. Grants to about 55 individuals totalled £18,000.

Applications: On a form available from the correspondent. Applications should be submitted directly by the individual, and are considered five or six times a year.

Correspondent: A Lathey, 8 Marston Avenue, Chessington, Surrey KT9 2HF (01372 226300; Fax: 01372 386705).

The Nadezhda Charitable Trust

Eligibility: People in need who are in Christian work in the UK and abroad.

Types of grants: One-off and recurrent grants according to need.

Annual grant total: In 1999/2000 the trust had an income of £92,000 and a total expenditure of £100,000. In previous years about a third of the grant total has been given to individuals and two-thirds to organisations.

Applications: In writing to the correspondent.

Correspondent: A R Collins, Trustee, Messrs Anthony Collins Solicitors, St Philips Gate, 5 Waterloo Street, Birmingham B2 5PG.

The Paton Trust

Eligibility: Ministers of the Established Church of Scotland who are elderly or infirm.

Types of grants: One-off grants ranging from £300 to £500. Grants are given to ministers requiring a holiday to recuperate from ill health and to ministers who are retiring to provide them with a holiday at time of retiral.

Annual grant total: In 2001 the trust had assets of £54,000, an income of £3,100 and a total expenditure of £7,800. £6,900 was given in 18 grants.

Applications: On a form available from the correspondent. Applications are considered throughout the year and should be submitted directly by the individual.

Correspondent: Iain A T Mowat, c/o Alexander Sloan, Chartered Accountants, 144 West George Street, Glasgow G2 2HG (0141 354 0354; Fax: 0141 354 0355; e-mail: iatm@alexandersloan.co.uk).

Lady Peel Legacy Trust

Eligibility: Priests in the anglo-catholic tradition who, due to ill health or age, have had to resign their work or livings.

Types of grants: One-off or recurrent grants according to need.

Annual grant total: Between £3,000 and £4,000, for both educational and welfare purposes.

Applications: In writing to the correspondent. The closing dates for applications are 1 April and 1 November each year. Telephone contact is not invited.

Correspondent: Revd Preb J Trevelyan, Ashmeadow, Barbon, Carnforth LA6 2LW.

The Podde Trust

Eligibility: Individuals involved in Christian work in the UK and overseas.

Types of grants: One-off and recurrent grants.

Annual grant total: In 2000/01 the trust had assets of £6,900 and an income of £20,000. Total expenditure was £21,000, with 34 grants to individuals totalling £7,900. 22 of these applicants were awarded grants in the previous year. A further £13,000 was given to organisations.

Applications: In writing to the correspondent: please note, the trust states that it has very limited resources, and those it does have are mostly already committed. Requests from new applicants therefore have very little chance of success.

Correspondent: P B Godfrey, 68 Green Lane, Hucclecote, Gloucester GL3 3QX (01452 613563).

Other information: Organisations involved in Christian work are also supported.

The Pyncombe Charity

Eligibility: Serving clergy in the Church of England and their immediate families who are in financial need resulting from a serious illness or accident to themselves or immediate family.

Types of grants: One-off grants of £200 to £2,000, although they are rarely of over £1,000.

Annual grant total: In 2000/01 the charity had assets of £297,000 and an income of £13,000. Grants to 25 individuals totalled £14,000.

Applications: Applications must be made through the diocesan bishop on a form available from the correspondent. They are considered in April. No direct applications can be considered.

Correspondent: Mrs Kate Jonas, Priory Cottage, Crowcombe TA4 4AD (01984 618665; e-mail: katejonas@hotmail.com).

The Retired Ministers' and Widows' Fund

Eligibility: Retired ministers, and ministers' widows, of Unitarian, Independent (i.e. Congregational and United Reformed) and Baptist churches who are over 50 years of age, live in the UK and are not on a high income.

Types of grants: Recurrent grants totalling £235 a year, paid in two equal instalments.

Annual grant total: In 2001 grants totalled £20,000.

Applications: On the fund's application form, to be submitted by the individual but signed by the local minister.

Correspondent: Arthur G Smith, 5 Crown Lea Avenue, Malvern, Worcestershire WR14 2DR (01684 899123; e-mail: arthurgsmith@hotmail.com).

The Rev Dr George Richards Charity

Eligibility: Church of England clergy who through sickness or infirmity have become incapable of performing their duties. Widows and other dependants can also be helped.

Types of grants: One-off grants of between £100 and £1,400 for general need, which have included 'top-up' grants.

Annual grant total: In 2000 the charity had assets of £159,000, an income of £20,000 and a total expenditure of £16,000. One pension of £1,500 was awarded. 57 Christmas gifts totalled £5,700, while general grants to clergy and dependants totalled £6,200.

Applications: On a form available from the correspondent. Applications should be submitted directly by the individual. They are considered in June and November.

Correspondent: D J Newman, Secretary, 27 Fifth Avenue, Frinton-on-Sea, Essex CO13 9LG (01255 676509).

The Silverwood Trust

Eligibility: Christian missionaries in need through illness or retirement.

Types of grants: One-off or small recurrent grants according to need. (Normally restricted to people known to the trustees.)

Annual grant total: Around £1,000 is allocated each year in grants to individuals in need.

Applications: In writing to the correspondent, directly by the individual.

Correspondent: J N Shergold, Trustee, 35 Orchard Grove, New Milton, Hampshire BH25 6NZ.

The Henry Smith Charity

Eligibility: Clergy of the Church of England in need within the UK (normally with the 13 dioceses traditionally supported by the charity).

Types of grants: Christmas gifts.

Annual grant total: About £600,000 each year.

Applications: On a form available from the trust secretary at the address below.

Correspondent: Miss J Portrait, Treasurer, 5 Chancery Lane, London EC4A 1BU (020 7320 6216; Fax: 020 7320 3842).

Other information: The 13 traditional dioceses cover the counties of Gloucestershire, Hampshire, Kent,

OCCUPATIONAL CHARITIES

Leicestershire, Suffolk, Surrey and East and West Sussex.

The Society for the Relief of Poor Clergymen

Eligibility: Evangelical ordained ministers and accredited lay workers and their dependants or widows/widowers in the Church of England and the Church in Wales.

Types of grants: One-off grants for illness or financial support when it can be shown that it has caused distress and hardship to the individual or family. Grants are not given towards educational costs or travel expenses. Grants range from £100 to £500.

Annual grant total: Around 50 grants totalling £20,000.

Applications: On a form available from the correspondent. The committee meets twice yearly (normally in March and September). Applications can be submitted directly by the individual, or through a third party without the knowledge of the individual and in confidence if the individual is not inclined to apply.

Correspondent: The Hon. Secretary, c/o CPAS, Athena Drive, Tachbrook Park, Warwickshire CV34 6NG (01926 458460).

The Foundation of Edward Storey

Eligibility: There are two branches, both of which support women in need. They are:

(a) Clergymen's Widows Branch: in the following order of priority:
(i) widows of clergymen of the Church of England
(ii) dependants of clergymen of the Church of England
(iii) women priests, deacons and deaconesses of the Church of England
(iv) missionaries of the Church of England
(v) other women closely involved with the work of the Church of England (including divorced and separated wives of clergymen of the Church of England).

(b) Parish Almspeople's Branch (no connection with the Church of England): 'unsupported' women in need living in Cambridgeshire, with preference for those in the city of Cambridge.

Types of grants: Grants and pensions (which are annually reviewable and renewable).

Annual grant total: In 2000/01 the foundation had assets of £10 million, an income of £818,000 and a total expenditure of £881,000. Grants totalled £161,000 whilst pensions totalled £44,000. A further £458,000 was spent on almshouse costs.

Applications: By application form and sponsorship by, for example, Diocesan Widows' Officers, Diocesan Visitors, clergy, social workers and so on.

Applications are considered bi-monthly by trustees.

Correspondent: The Clerk to the Trustees, Storey's House, Mount Pleasant, Cambridge CB3 0BZ (01223-364405; Fax: 01223-321313; e-mail: storeyscharities@aol.com).

Tancred's Charity for Pensioners

Eligibility: Men aged 50 or over who are UK citizens and clergy of the Church of England or Church in Wales or officers in the armed forces.

Types of grants: Annual pensions of £1,600 a year paid quarterly to 13 to 15 beneficiaries.

Annual grant total: In 2001 Tancred's Charity had an income of £1.7 million and both an income and a total expenditure of £61,000. Grants to older people totalled £22,000. Grants to students totalled £34,000.

Applications: In writing to the correspondent. Individuals may apply at any time, but applications can only be considered when a vacancy occurs, which is approximately once a year.

Correspondent: Andrew Hugh Penny, Clerk, 67 Grosvenor Street, London W1K 3JN (020 7863 8522; Fax: 020 7863 8444; e-mail: ahpenny@forsters.com).

Other information: Tancred's Charity also has an educational branch, giving help to some specified categories of medical and theological students and pupil barristers, but they must have attended Christ's College or Gonville & Caius College, Cambridge or be students at Lincoln's Inn. These grants are allocated by the colleges and Lincoln's Inn. Further information is available to students of those bodies who should approach the senior tutor (of either Cambridge College) or the student administrator at Lincoln's Inn.

The Thornton Fund

Eligibility: Ministers and ministerial students of the Unitarian church and their families who are in need.

Types of grants: One-off grants ranging from £250 to £1,000. Recent grants have been given towards convalescence, counselling, replacement of equipment not covered by insurance and taxis for somebody unable to drive for medical reasons.

Annual grant total: In 2000 the fund had assets of £360,000, an income of £17,000 and a total expenditure of £16,000. Three welfare grants to individuals totalled £1,500. Eight educational grants to individuals totalled £5,500. Grants to organisations totalled £10,000.

Applications: In writing to the correspondent, including an sae. Applications may be submitted directly by the individual or through the general

secretary of the Unitarian and Free Christian Churches in London.

Correspondent: Dr Jane Williams, 93 Fitzjohn Avenue, Barnet, Hertfordshire EN5 2HR (020 8440 2211).

The Widows Fund

Eligibility: Widows and orphans of Protestant dissenting ministers, and the ministers themselves, who are in need.

Types of grants: Recurrent grants according to need.

Annual grant total: In 2000/01 the trust's income was £37,000 and its total expenditure was £52,000.

Applications: In writing to the correspondent.

Correspondent: M F Marsden, Josolyne & Co., Silk House, Park Green, Macclesfield, Cheshire SK11 7QW (01625 442800).

Removal trade

The Removers Benevolent Association

Eligibility: People in need who are or were employed (for a minimum of one year) by a member or a retired member of the British Association of Removers Ltd, and their dependants.

Types of grants: One-off emergency grants, to tide people over a temporary period of difficulty, such as an inability to work due to illness.

Annual grant total: In 2001 the association gave grants totalling £9,000. In the previous year they totalled £14,000. This difference was caused by the receipt of fewer eligible applications.

Applications: In writing to the correspondent, to be submitted by the member company the employee has worked for. Applications are considered as they arrive.

Correspondent: R D Syers, Hon. Secretary, British Association of Removers, 3 Churchill Court, 58 Station Road, North Harrow HA2 7SA (020 8861 3331; Fax: 020 8861 3332; e-mail: info@bar.co.uk; website: www.bar.co.uk).

Retail trade

Retail Trust (formerly Cottage Homes)

Eligibility: People who have worked in the retail, wholesale, manufacturing and distribution trades for at least two years if still in the trade, or for at least ten years if

OCCUPATIONAL CHARITIES

retired, and their dependants, who are in need.

Types of grants: One-off and recurrent grants ranging from £300 to £1,000 towards medical needs, household equipment and so on. No grants are given to students or for items purchased prior to the application.

Annual grant total: In 2000/01 the trust had assets of £34 million and an income of £5.5 million. Total expenditure was £5.8 million, including £57,000 given in total in 153 grants.

Applications: On a form available from the correspondent, to be submitted either directly by the individual or through a social worker, citizen's advice bureau or other welfare agency. Applications are considered in February, April, June, October and December.

Correspondent: Geraldine Nurney, Marshall Estate, Hammers Lane, London NW7 4EE (020 8201 0117; Fax: 020 8959 4425; e-mail: gnurney@retailtrust.org.uk; website: www.retailtrust.org.uk).

Other information: This trust also runs a help and support line for its beneficiaries (0845 766 0113), offers respite care and runs sheltered, residential and nursing homes and a day centre.

Road haulage

The Road Haulage Association Benevolent Fund

Eligibility: Current and former members, and employees/ex-employees of members, of the association, and their dependants.

Types of grants: One-off grants according to need. Grants are not usually awarded towards holidays (unless there are exceptional circumstances).

Annual grant total: In 2000/01 the trust had assets of £560,000, an income of £57,000 and a total expenditure of £40,000. Grants to 50 individuals totalled £26,000.

Applications: On a form available from the correspondent, which can be submitted directly by the individual or through a social worker, citizen's advice bureau or other welfare agency or third party. Applications are considered throughout the year.

Correspondent: Derek Witcher, Secretary, 35 Monument Hill, Weybridge, Surrey KT13 8RN (01932 841515; Fax: 01932 852516; e-mail: d.witcher@rha.net).

Rugby

The Rugby Football Union Charitable Fund

Eligibility: Individuals injured while participating in any sport and any dependant of any person who was killed while participating in any sport.

Types of grants: One-off grants towards, for instance, hospital visits, personal and domestic expenses and computer packages or equipment for people who are housebound.

Annual grant total: In 2000 the fund had assets of £502,000, an income of £52,000 and a total expenditure of £28,000. Grants to 10 individuals totalled £13,000. Grants to 25 organisations totalled £9,800.

Applications: On a form available from the correspondent.

Correspondent: Michael J Christie, 41 Station Road, North Harrow, Middlesex HA2 7SX.

Other information: This entry was not confirmed by the trust, but the address was correct according to the Charity Commission database.

School inspectors

HM Inspectors of Schools Benevolent Fund

Eligibility: Present and retired HM Inspectors of schools in England and Wales and their dependants who are in need or distress.

Types of grants: One-off grants of £500 to £5,000 and loans of up to £10,000.

Annual grant total: In 2002 the trust had an income of £17,000. Grants and loans to individuals totalled £5,500.

Applications: In writing to the correspondent, either directly by the individual or through a third party such as a friend or colleague. Applications are considered as they arise, and should include the applicant's financial situation, and for example, arrangements for repaying loans.

Correspondent: R Kepadia, OHMCI, 29-33 Kingsway, London WC2B 6SE.

Science

The Institute of Physics Benevolent Fund

Eligibility: Physicists and members of their family in need, whether members of the institute or not.

Types of grants: One-off and recurrent grants according to need.

Annual grant total: 16 grants totalling £33,000.

Applications: In writing to the correspondent, marked 'Private and Confidential'.

Correspondent: Mrs Susan Dowling, Secretary, 76 Portland Place, London W1N 3DH (020 7470 4800; Fax: 020 7470 4861; e-mail: benfund@iop.org.uk; website: www.iop.org.uk).

The John Murdoch Trust

Eligibility: People in need who, either as amateurs or professionals, have pursued science in any of its branches, and who are at least 50 years old.

Types of grants: Yearly allowances and one-off grants, on average of about £500 to £1,000. Grants are given for relief-in-need rather than scientific needs.

Annual grant total: The grant total varies each year, but is usually in the range of about £4,000 a year. The trust is currently looking for more eligible applicants.

Applications: On a form available from the correspondent. Applications are considered twice a year, in May and November.

Correspondent: Don Henderson, c/o The Royal Bank of Scotland plc, Trust and Estate Services, 2 Festival Square, Edinburgh EH3 9SU (0131 523 2658; Fax: 0131 228 9889).

The Scientific Relief Fund of the Royal Society

Eligibility: Scientists professionally involved in the natural sciences, or their families in need of assistance, and retired scientists who need help to continue their research. Whilst there is no nationality requirement, the scientist concerned must have some connection with British or Irish science.

Types of grants: One-off grants of between £1,000 and £10,000. Recent grants have been made for travel to and from hospital, residential care costs, a sighted assistant to aid scientific research, computer equipment for scientific reasons, medical and surgical treatment and therapeutic drugs.

No grants are given towards scientist's salaries.

OCCUPATIONAL CHARITIES

Annual grant total: In 2000/01 the trust had assets of £1.4 million and an income of £95,000. Grants to six individuals totalled £15,000.

Applications: Applications can be submitted directly by the individual or through a third party such as a social worker or an officer of any nationally recognised scientific society within the British Commonwealth or the Republic of Ireland. Applicants should contact the correspondent for instructions about what they should put in their application. They can be considered at any time.

Correspondent: Miss Jane E C Lewis, 6–9 Carlton House Terrace, London SW1Y 5AG (020 7451 2538; Fax: 020 7451 2543; e-mail: jane.lewis@royalsoc.ac.uk; website: www.royalsoc.ac.uk).

Royal Society of Chemistry Benevolent Fund

Eligibility: People who have been members of the society for the last three years, or ex-members who were in the society for at least 10 years, and their dependants, who are in need.

Types of grants: Regular allowances, one-off grants and loans. Recent grants have been towards essential home maintenance, help with transport costs, household equipment and furniture, school uniforms, Christmas bonuses and funeral costs. Anything which should be provided by the government or local authority is ineligible.

Annual grant total: In 2001 the fund had assets of £7.5 million, an income of £374,000 and a total expenditure of £451,000. About 1,000 grants totalled £294,000.

Applications: In writing or by telephone in the first instance, to the correspondent. Applicants will be requested to provide a financial statement (forms supplied by the secretary) and include a covering letter describing their application as fully as possible. Applications can be made either directly by the individual, or through a third party such as a social worker or citizen's advice bureau. They are considered every other month, although urgent appeals can be considered at any time.

Correspondent: Christine Couchman, Benevolent Fund Manager, Thomas Graham House, Science Park, Milton Road, Cambridge CB4 0WF (01223 420066; Fax: 01223 432269; e-mail: couchmanc@rsc.org; website: www.rsc.org).

Seafaring & Fishing

The Baltic Exchange Charitable Society

Eligibility: Members of the society and their dependants.

Types of grants: One-off and regular grants paid quarterly, according to need. Additional grants are made to meet unexpected expenses, such as hospitalisation or a nursing home stay for three or four weeks.

Annual grant total: In 2000 the society had assets of £5.3 million, an income of £235,000 and a total expenditure of £470,000. 65 recurrent and 22 one-off grants totalled £395,000.

Applications: On a form available from the correspondent. Applications can be submitted at any time.

Correspondent: The Secretary, The Annexe, 20 St Dunstan's Hill, London EC3R 8HL (Tel & Fax: 020 7283 6090).

The Honourable Company of Master Mariners

Eligibility: British Master Mariners, navigating officers of the merchant navy, and their wives, widows and dependants who are in need.

Types of grants: One-off and quarterly grants according to need.

Annual grant total: In 1998 the trust had an income of £24,000 and grants to individuals totalled £14,000, including £7,000 in one-off grants, £2,900 in weekly and monthly allowances and £4,100 in special Christmas grants.

Applications: On a form available from the correspondent. Applications can be submitted directly by the individual, through a social worker, citizen's advice bureau, or other welfare agency, or by a friend or relative. They are considered throughout the year.

Correspondent: The Clerk to the Honourable Company, HQS Wellington, Temple Stairs, Victoria Embankment, London WC2R 2PN (020 7836 8179; Fax: 020 7240 3082; e-mail: info@hcmm.org.uk; website: www.hcmm.org.uk).

The London Shipowners' & Shipbrokers' Benevolent Society

Eligibility: Shipowners and shipbrokers and their dependants.

Types of grants: One-off and recurrent grants, plus Christmas bonuses.

Annual grant total: In 1999 the society had assets of £1 million, an income of £62,000 and a total expenditure of £89,000. A total of £74,000 was given in 11 recurrent grants and four one-off grants.

Applications: On a form available from the correspondent.

Correspondent: R J M Butler, 20 St Dunstan's Hill, London EC3R 8HL (020 7283 6090).

The Marine Society

Eligibility: Professional seafarers, active and retired, who are in need.

Types of grants: Bursaries, scholarships, one-off grants and loans; no recurrent grants. Interest-free loans rather than grants are given where the need is short-term and the applicant expects to be earning again.

Annual grant total: In 2001 relief-in-need grants and loans to individuals totalled £85,000, some of which was given in educational grants.

Applications: In writing to the correspondent in the first instance, requesting an application form.

Correspondent: Jeremy Howard, Director, 202 Lambeth Road, London SE1 7JW (020 7261 9535; Fax: 020 7401 2537; e-mail: enq@marine-society.org; website: www.marine-society.org).

The NUMAST Welfare Fund

Eligibility: Seafarers, former seafarers and their dependants. The union manages a number of different funds mainly for the welfare of former seafarers (Merchant Navy) all of which have slightly different eligibility criteria. In most cases of need or distress, the individual will be eligible for help from at least one of these. Applicants should normally be over 50 but exceptions are made, for example in cases of ill-health.

Types of grants: Relief-in-need grants and pensions, ranging from £100 to £1,000. Grants have been given towards clothing, replacement cookers, fridges, home repairs, decoration, mobility aids, wheelchairs, furniture and carpets.

Annual grant total: In 2001 the fund had assets of £17 million, an income of £1.5 million and a total expenditure of £1.2 million. Grants to 500 individuals totalled £202,000.

Applications: On a form available from the correspondent, submitted directly by the individual or through a social worker, citizen's advice bureau or other welfare agency, or through a third party (e.g. family, doctor or union official). Proof of sea-service, details of income and expenditure, bills and so on are required to support request for grant.

Applications are usually considered immediately.

Correspondent: Peter McEwen, Secretary, Nautilus House, Mariners' Park, Wallasey CH45 7PH (0151 639 8454; Fax: 0151 346 8801; e-mail: welfare@numast.org; website: www.numast.org).

Other information: The trust also runs the Mariners Park welfare complex in Wallasey, which accommodates independent older seafarers and their dependants in bungalows and flats, and older seafarers and their dependants assessed for residential or nursing care in the NUMAST Mariners Park Care Home which opened in 2002 (replacing an earlier home) and has 32 rooms. The management and maintenance of this site takes up a large proportion of the trust's income.

Royal Liverpool Seamen's Orphan Institution

Eligibility: Dependent children of deceased British merchant seafarers, who are of pre-school age or in full-time education (including further education).

Types of grants: Monthly maintenance and annual clothing grants. Grants range from £87 to £290 a month for each child. They are reviewed annually. Help may be given for school fees.

Annual grant total: In 2000, from a total expenditure of £750,000, welfare grants to individuals totalled £642,000 whilst educational grants totalled £18,000.

Applications: On a form available from the correspondent, to be considered at any time. Applications can be submitted either directly by the individual, or by the surviving parent or guardian.

Correspondent: Mrs Linda Gidman, Secretary, 3a, Ground Floor, Tower Building, 22 Water Street, Liverpool L3 1AB (Tel & Fax: 0151 227 3417; e-mail: enquiries@rlsoi-uk.org; website: www.rlsoi-uk.org).

Royal National Mission to Deep Sea Fishermen

Eligibility: Commercial fishermen, including retired fishermen, and their wives and widows who are experiencing unforeseen tragedy or hardship.

Types of grants: Immediate one-off payments to widows of fishermen lost at sea. There are also other individual grants to alleviate cases of hardship (e.g. provision of basic furniture for impoverished older fishermen). Grants are almost always one-off.

Annual grant total: In 1999 the trust had an income of £2.6 million and a total expenditure of £2.3 million.

Applications: In writing to the correspondent or the local superintendent, either directly by the individual or through a social worker, citizen's advice bureau or other welfare agency. Record of sea service and names of fishing vessels and/or owners is required.

Correspondent: The Mission Secretary, 43 Nottingham Place, London W1V 5BX (020 7487 5101; Fax: 020 7224 5240; e-mail: rnmdsf@charity.vfree.com; website: www.rnmdsf.moonfruit.com).

The Royal Seamen's Pension Fund

Eligibility: Masters and seamen (including women) who are over 60 or permanently unfit who have sea service in the British Merchant Navy of at least 15 years (hostility service counting double) and have little income other than the state pension.

Types of grants: Grants of £7 a week, plus Christmas and birthday bonuses.

Annual grant total: In 2000 the fund had assets of £2.9 million, an income of £135,000 and a total expenditure of £337,000. Grants to 665 beneficiaries totalled £266,000, with a further £18,000 being given as birthday bonuses.

Applications: On a form available from the correspondent.

Correspondent: Capt. J E Dykes, 1 North Pallant, Chichester, West Sussex PO19 1TL (01243 789329).

The Sailors' Families' Society

Eligibility: Seafarers from the UK or who sail on UK ships, or their dependants, who are in one-parent families with children aged below 16 years. Grants can also be given if the seafarer is in a two-parent family but is permanently disabled. Usually, the only source of income for the family is Income Support or Incapacity Benefit.

Types of grants: (i) Recurrent grants of £46 per month to families with children under 16 (18 if they remain at school/college). If the young person continues in further/higher education after they are 18, they can claim £46 per month until they complete their first degree or equivalent, or reach the age of 22; (ii) annual clothing grants of £75 per child in August and £40 per child in January until child reaches 16 (or 18 if they remain in school/college); (iii) Christmas grant of £35 per child paid in November for Christmas presents; (iv) holiday grants of between £80 and £100 to cover cost of travel to one of the society's six holiday caravan camps around the country for a free break, or £150 per family to those who cannot use the holiday caravans or prefer to take the children for a holiday with relatives; (v) one-off grants of up to £250 for unforeseen financial problems; (vi) special equipment grants of up to £250 to purchases items to develop 'non academic abilities' such as musical or sporting equipment, or special vocational training; (vii) Househlod replacement grants of £50 to £250 to help with debt relief, electrical items, beds, furniture, DIY and clothing; and (viii) educational grants of up to £250 for an educational holiday such as a sailing trip where the character building experience is beneficial.

Annual grant total: In 2000/01 the society had assets of £4.5 million, an income of £2.2 million and a total expenditure of £2.4 million. Grants to 410 families totalled £250,000.

Applications: On a form available from the correspondent, with details about children, income and expenditure, home environment and with copies of relevant certificates, for example, birth certificates and proof of seafaring service. Applications can be submitted directly by the individual or through a social worker, citizen's advice bureau, other welfare agency, or through seafaring organisations. Applications are considered every other month, beginning in February.

Correspondent: Ian Scott, Welfare Manager, Newland, Cottingham Road, Hull HU6 7RJ (01482 342331; Fax: 01482 447868; e-mail: info@sailors-families.org.uk; website: www.sailors-families.org.uk).

The Seamen's Hospital Society

Eligibility: Merchant seafarers, fishermen and anybody who earns their living from the sea, including deep sea fishermen and their dependants. Applicants must be seafarers with long service except where accident or illness interrupted intended long-term service. They may have worked anywhere in the UK and be of any nationality. Members, and former members, of the Royal Navy are not eligible.

Types of grants: Preference for applications of a medical or welfare nature. One-off grants can be up to £300 towards council tax, fuel charges, cookers, washing machines, clothing, convalescent breaks, funeral costs or medical equipment such as nebulizers. Larger grants need approval by the committee. No grants are given towards study costs or re-training costs.

Annual grant total: In 2001 grants to individuals totalled £70,000 and grants to organisations totalled £145,000.

Applications: On a form available from the correspondent, making a request for some kind of specific help and giving full details of sea service. Applications can be submitted directly by the individual or through a social worker, citizen's advice bureau, other welfare agency or other third party. Applicants must receive a visit from a third party before a grant can be made.

Correspondent: General Secretary, 29 King William Walk, Greenwich, London SE10 9HX (020 8858 3696; Fax: 020 8293 9630; e-mail: shs@btconnect.com).

Other information: The SHS supports priority medical treatment for seafarers via

OCCUPATIONAL CHARITIES

the Dreadnought Unit at Guys/St Thomas' Hospital in London.

The Shipwrecked Fishermen & Mariners' Royal Benevolent Society

Eligibility: Fishermen, merchant seamen, their widows and dependants, who are on a low income, especially those who are over 60, sick or disabled. Priority is given to widows with young children. There is a minimum sea service of eight years (15 for recurrent grants), although war service is given special consideration. Grants are available in the UK and Republic of Ireland.

Applicants must be receiving all the state benefits they are entitled to.

Types of grants: Mainly regular support of £520 a year (usually to people aged over 60) and, less frequently, one-off crisis grants averaging £350.

Activities are not confined to shipwreck relief. Relief of distress amongst the seafaring community includes:
(i) immediate financial aid to the dependants of seamen lost at sea
(ii) assistance to seamen shipwrecked on the coasts of the British Isles
(iii) financial aid to needy seamen and their widows and orphans, including regular grants to seamen or their widows
(iv) other objects for the benefit and welfare of seafarers. Awards are made for skill and gallantry in preventing loss of life at sea.

No grants are given towards funeral expenses. All grants are discretionary and are not pensions.

Annual grant total: Over £1.4 million in about 4,000 grants in 2001/02. In the previous year the trust had assets of £20 million, an income of £1.9 million and it gave 900 grants totalling £1.5 million.

Applications: In the first instance, contact the correspondent for information on how to apply and request an application form. The application will then need to be made through the society's honorary agent. Applications are considered weekly.

Correspondent: Capt. J E Dykes, General Secretary, 1 North Pallant, Chichester, West Sussex PO19 1TL (01243 787761; Fax: 01243 530853; e-mail: grants@shipwreckedmariners.org.uk; website: www.shipwreckedmariners.org.uk).

Other information: There is a Scottish office for the society: Beveridge & Kellas, Hon. Agents, 52 Leith Walk, Edinburgh EH6 5HB (0131 554 6321).

The Trinity Homes and Mariners' Charities

Eligibility: Former mariners over 65 who have normally served at least 15 years in UK or Commonwealth vessels, their wives and dependent children.

Types of grants: One-off grants of between £100 and £500 and annuities not exceeding £520 a year.

Annual grant total: In 1999 the trust had assets of £39 million and an income of £2.3 million. Grants totalled £295,000, but not all of them were for welfare purposes.

Applications: On a form available from the correspondent. Applications are considered quarterly and can be submitted directly by the individual, through a recognised referral agency (citizen's advice bureau, doctor, social worker etc.), or via another charity. In all cases proof of sea service and rank must be provided.

Correspondent: R F Dobb, Trinity House, Tower Hill, London EC3N 4DH (020 7481 6900; Fax: 020 7480 7662).

Other information: The primary objects are to provide almshouse accomodation for mariners and their dependants who are in need and to provide financial assistance to individuals in need.

The secondary objects are to advance the education and training of mariners and cadets in all matters pertaining to navigation and seamanship; research for the safety and welfare of mariners; cooperation with other charities and similar causes and the promotion of any matter for the advancement of education in navigation, shipping and seamanship.

Secretaries

The Institute of Chartered Secretaries & Administrators Benevolent Fund

Eligibility: Members and former members of the institute and their dependants who are in need, living in UK, Eire and associated territories.

Types of grants: Weekly allowances and regular support according to need, for example towards telephone line rental, rental for emergency alarm systems and TV rental and licences. One-off grants are given for clothing, clearance of debts and property repairs. Interest free loans are also considered.

Annual grant total: In 2000/01 the trust had assets of £3.6 million and an income of £220,000. Total expenditure was £142,000, including £87,000 given in grants.

Applications: On a form available from the correspondent, indicating full current income and expenditure details. Institute members (volunteers) visit beneficiaries where necessary. Applications can be made throughout the year. They are usually considered in February, June and October, but special consideration can be made at other times for urgent requests. Contact the correspondent if assistance in making the application is required.

Correspondent: Elizabeth Howarth, Charities Officer, 16 Park Crescent, London W1B 1AH (020 7580 4741; Fax: 020 7323 1132; e-mail: info@icsa.co.uk; website: www.icsa.org.uk).

The Secretary Heads Association Benevolent Fund

Eligibility: Members or former members of the Secretary Heads Association and their wives, widows, widowers, children or dependants, who are in need.

Types of grants: One-off and recurrent grants according to need. Grants cannot be given for long-term residential care.

Annual grant total: The income varies each year, averaging around £10,000.

Applications: In writing to the correspondent.

Correspondent: Carole Wright, 130 Regent Road, Leicester LE1 7PG (0116 299 1122; e-mail: carole.wright@sha.org.uk).

Self employed & small businesses

The Prime Charitable Trust

Eligibility: Members or former members of the National Federation of Self-Employed and Small Businesses Ltd and their family and dependants, who due to illness or incapacity are unable to look after themselves.

Types of grants: One-off and recurrent grants according to need.

Annual grant total: In 2000/01 the fund had an income of £9,300 and a total expenditure of £5,000.

Applications: In writing to the correspondent.

Correspondent: J Dickin, Federation of Small Businesses, Whittle Way, Blackpool FY4 2FE (01253 336000).

Sewing machine

The Sewing Machine Association Trade Benevolent Society

Eligibility: Members or former members of the Sewing Machine Trade Association,

the partners and employees of such members, and their dependants.
Types of grants: One-off and recurrent grants according to need.
Annual grant total: In 1998/99 the society had an income of £2,100, although no grants were made.
Applications: In writing to the correspondent at any time.
Correspondent: Michael Cohen, Administrator, 70 Walmington Fold, Woodside Park, London N12 7LL (020 8346 6854; Fax: 020 8343 4127; e-mail: mikecohen@ntlworld.com).

Snooker and billiards

The Professional Billiards & Snooker Players Benevolent Fund

Eligibility: Members of the World Professional Billiards and Snooker Association and their dependants, who are in need.
Types of grants: One-off and recurrent grants according to need.
Annual grant total: In 1998/99 the fund had assets of £225,000 and an income of £12,000. Total expenditure was £39,000 with 14 grants totalling £17,000.
Applications: In writing to the correspondent, to be considered within one month.
Correspondent: Eileen Goldsmith, Ground Floor, Albert House, 111–117 Victoria Street, Bristol BS1 6AX (0117 317 8200).

Social Workers

The Social Workers' Benevolent Trust

Eligibility: Social workers who are in need due to illness, age or marital breakdown.
Types of grants: One-off grants of up to £500. No grants are given towards training, car expenses, private healthcare or income maintenance.
Annual grant total: In 2000/01 the trust had assets of £150,000 and an income of £15,000. Grants to 37 individuals totalled around £14,000.
Applications: On a form available from the correspondent. Applications should be submitted directly by the individual and are usually considered in alternate months.
Correspondent: The Hon. Secretary, 16 Kent Street, Birmingham B5 6RD (website: www.basw.co.uk).

Stationery

The British Office Systems & Stationery Federation Benevolent Fund

Eligibility: People in the UK who work or have worked in the stationery and office products sector and their dependants who are elderly or infirm with inadequate income.
Types of grants: Most grants are regular quarterly payments totalling £520 a year. One-off payments are also made e.g. contributions towards wheelchairs or property repair.
Annual grant total: In 1999 the trust had an income of £53,000 and a total expenditure of £26,000.
Applications: On a form available from the correspondent. Applications can be submitted directly by the individual or through a social worker, citizen's advice bureau or other welfare agency, or by another third party. A team of visitors assess the need and offer support to beneficiaries.
Correspondent: J S Roscoe, Secretary, 6 Wimpole Street, London W1G 9SL (020 7637 7692; Fax: 020 7436 3137; e-mail: info@bossfed.co.uk).

The Stationers Social Society Benevolent Fund

Eligibility: People in need or distress who are or have been employed in the paper trade or paper industry, and their widows or children.
Types of grants: One-off and recurrent grants according to need. Grants have included pensions, TV licences, roof repairs and coal.
Annual grant total: In 2001 around £4,000 was given to individuals and organisations.
Applications: In writing to the correspondent. The trust stated that resources are fully committed, although they can often find a couple of hundred pounds in cases of real emergency.
Correspondent: John Garlick, 126 Larkspur Way, West Ewell, Epsom, Surrey KT19 9LU.

Stock Exchange

The Claude Lemon Memorial Fund

Eligibility: Members of the stock exchange or the stockbroking trade who are in need.
Types of grants: One-off grants of £100 to £500. Recent grants have been given towards topping up nursing home fees, replacing a uPVC front door and replacing money taken by a mugger.
Annual grant total: In 2000/01 the fund had assets of £141,000, an income of £5,700 and a total expenditure of £4,500. Grants to 10 individuals totalled £3,900.
Applications: On a form available from the correspondent. Applications can be submitted directly by the individual or through any third party.
Correspondent: A V Barnard, Secretary, 19th Floor, The Stock Exchange, London EC2N 1HP (020 7797 4373; Fax: 020 7410 6808).

The Stock Exchange Benevolent Fund

Eligibility: Ex-members of the Stock Exchange and their dependants. In exceptional circumstances, existing members and children of education age (i.e. last year of schooling, not further/ higher education) of ex-members.
Types of grants: Annual grants paid quarterly. The maximum grant is £6,000. Cases are regularly visited and their situations reviewed. There is a strict capital ceiling above which help cannot be given; otherwise the fund is extremely flexible financially and in its advisory services.
Annual grant total: About £400,000.
Applications: On a form available from the correspondent at any time.
Correspondent: The Secretary, The Stock Exchange, London EC2N 1HP (020 7797 1092/3120; Fax: 020 7410 6845; e-mail: sebf@beeb.net).

The Stock Exchange Clerks Fund

Eligibility: Members, and ex-members, of the Stock Exchange and the stockbroking trade who are in need.
Types of grants: Recurrent grants of £10 to £20 per week are given towards, for instance, holidays, decoration, digital TV, travel tickets, replacement windows, gardening and chiropody. No grants are given towards education or items provided for by Income Support.
Annual grant total: In 2001 the trust had assets of £1.2 million, an income of £51,000 and a total expenditure of £88,000. Grants to 47 individuals totalled £54,000.

Applications: On a form available from the correspondent at any time. Applications can be submitted directly by the individual or through any third party.
Correspondent: Alfred Barnard, The Stock Exchange, London EC2N 1HP (020 7797 4373; Fax: 020 7410 6808; website: www.secpf.com).

Tax inspectors

The Association of Her Majesty's Inspectors of Taxes Benevolent Fund

Eligibility: Current and former tax inspectors and other senior officers in the Inland Revenue who are members of the association, and their dependants, who are sick or in other necessitous circumstances. Clerical grade inspectors are not normally eligible.
Types of grants: Grants are given to people on sick leave towards the costs of their sickness, such as equipment, hospital travel and medicines.
Annual grant total: In 1999 the trust gave 11 grants totalling £1,100.
Applications: Can be submitted by the individual, in writing to the correspondent at any time.
Correspondent: Stephen Bibby, President, 2 Caxton Street, London SW1H 0QH (020 7438 6105; Fax: 020 7438 6148).

Teaching

Association of Principals of Colleges Benevolent Fund

Eligibility: Members and ex-members of the association, and their dependants, who are in need.
Types of grants: One-off and recurrent grants according to need. Grants have been given to widows and dependants of members who have died.
Annual grant total: In 1999/2000 the fund had an income of £2,300 and a total expenditure of £1,000.
Applications: In writing to the correspondent.
Correspondent: Michael Blagden, Southgate College, High Street, London N14 6BS.
Other information: This entry was not confirmed by the fund, but the address was correct according to the Charity Commission database.

The Association of Teachers & Lecturers Benevolent Fund

Eligibility: Members and former members of the association, and their dependants, who are in need.
Types of grants: One-off grants of up to £250 for things such as respite care, funeral costs and disability aids such as wheelchairs. Weekly grants of £20 are also available.
Annual grant total: In 2001 the fund had assets of £487,000 and an income of £122,000. Out of a total expenditure of £65,000, grants totalled £61,000.
Applications: On a form available from the correspondent. Applications can be submitted either directly by the individual or through a social worker, citizen's advice bureau or other welfare agency, for consideration in January, March, June and October.
Correspondent: Valerie Shield, 7 Northumberland Street, London WC2N 5RD (020 7930 6441; Fax: 020 7930 1359).

The Association of University Teachers Benevolent Fund

Eligibility: Present or past members or employees of the Association of University Teachers and dependent children or close relatives.
Types of grants: One-off grants most likely to be given for items such as essential household equipment or repairs, and to widows or former members left without occupational pension provision because of defects in the university pension scheme generally applicable before 1975. Grants are also made in connection with disablement, for example, home or car adaptations. No loans are given.
Annual grant total: £10,000 to £30,000 each year.
Applications: In writing to the correspondent, describing the help needed, details of financial circumstances and evidence of eligibility. Guidelines on applying are available (ask for form BF 4S).
Correspondent: Martin Machon, Unit 6, 133-137 Newall Street, Birmingham B2 5BN (0121 212 2713; Fax: 0121 212 2714; e-mail: bham.office@aut.org.uk).

Church School Masters and School Mistresses Benevolent Institution

Eligibility: Retired teachers throughout the UK who are in need.
Types of grants: One-off grants of £50 to £150 may be spent to relieve the hardship of retired teachers and to subsidise the fees of residents of the institution's own nursing home.
Annual grant total: About £500.

Applications: On a form available from the correspondent, for consideration throughout the year.
Correspondent: B Latham, Administrator, Glenarun Nursing Home, 9 Athelstan Way, Brighton Road, Horsham, West Sussex RH13 6HA (01403 253881).
Other information: In addition, the institution runs a registered nursing home and subsidises residents who are unable to meet the full cost of their fees.

The Headmasters' Association Benevolent Fund

Eligibility: Headteachers and ex-headteachers who are or were members of the association and the widows and dependants of such people who have died. Grants are usually given to people who are ill.
Types of grants: One-off and recurrent grants according to need.
Annual grant total: In 2001 grants totalled £15,000.
Applications: In writing to the correspondent. Applications are considered as they arrive.
Correspondent: J R Searle, Honorary Secretary, 5 St John's Gardens, Romsey SO51 7RW (01794 514166).

The Incorporated Association of Preparatory Schools Benevolent Fund

Eligibility: Past and present members of the association, or their staff, and their dependants, who are in need.
Types of grants: One-off and recurrent grants according to need.
Annual grant total: In 2001 the trust had an income of over £10,000.
Applications: In writing to the correspondent.
Correspondent: R T Fisher, Executive Trustee, 73 Overslade Lane, Rugby, Warwickshire CV22 6EE (01788 522011).

The Liverpool Governesses' Benevolent Institution

Eligibility: Women in need who are or have been governesses or schoolmistresses, or other women engaged in the education or care of the young, or whose husbands have held a similar position. The trust operates nationally but has a preference for those born or who lived in Merseyside, or who have connections with the area.
Types of grants: Mainly pensions of about £60 to £180 per quarter to regular beneficiaries. One-off grants of up to £500 are also given.
Annual grant total: In 1999/2000 the trust had an income of £2,700 and a total expenditure of £5,900.

Applications: By letter to the correspondent, considered in April and November.
Correspondent: Richard A Davies, Rathbones, Port of Liverpool Building, 4th Floor, Pier Head, Liverpool L3 1NW (0151 236 6666).
Other information: The correspondent stated in July 2002 that the institution only has four regular beneficiaries and is unlikely to add to the list, adding that he expected the charity to wind up towards the end of 2003. However, he did state that the institution could potentially still give one-off grants.

The National Association of Schoolmasters Union of Women Teachers Benevolent Fund

Eligibility: Members/former members of the association and their dependants.
Types of grants: One-off and recurrent grants and interest-free loans according to need. Grants/loans have been given to people with terminal illnesses to visit relatives; to pay for the services of an occupational therapist to assess disability home conversion needs; to buy a converted vehicle for a member who is paralysed; and a monthly grant to a member's widow with no occupational pension.
No grants/loans for private health care/ treatment, private school fees or costs incurred through legal action, or when state benefit entitlements would be reduced as a result.
Annual grant total: Around £250,000 each year.
Applications: On a form available from the address below. Forms should be filled in by the local association secretary. Applications are considered each month except August.
Correspondent: Annette Greening, Benevolent Department, NASUWT, Hillscourt Education Centre, Rose Hill, Rednal, Birmingham B45 8RS (0121 453 6150; Fax: 0121 457 6208).

The Ogilvie Charities

Eligibility: People who are, or have been, teachers or governesses in England and Wales.
Types of grants: One-off grants of £100 to £250.
Annual grant total: In 2002 the trust had assets of £1.8 million and an income of £88,000. One individual received a grant of £200. Grants to organisations totalled £135,000.
Applications: In writing to the correspondent, to be submitted through a social worker, citizen's advice bureau or other welfare agency. The referring agency may telephone the trust if there are doubts about their client's eligiblity. Applications can be considered at any time.
Correspondent: Trevor Last, The Gate House, 9 Burkitt Road, Woodbridge, Suffolk IP12 4JJ (01394 388746; e-mail: ogilviecharities@btinternet.com).

Schoolmistresses & Governesses Benevolent Institution

Eligibility: Women who work, and have worked, as a schoolmistress, matron or bursar in the private sector of education.
Types of grants: All types of help including annuities, one-off grants for help with telephone bills, TV licences, household items and so on.
Annual grant total: In 2000/01 the trust had assets of £4.3 million, an income of £744,000 and a total expenditure of £831,000. Grants to 70 individuals totalled £150,000.
Applications: On a form available from the correspondent, to be submitted at any time either directly by the individual or a third party.
Correspondent: Case Secretary, SGBI Office, Queen Mary House, Manor Park Road, Chislehurst, Kent BR7 5PY (020 8468 7997).
Other information: The institution arranges annual visits to beneficiaries.

The Society of Schoolmasters and Schoolmistresses

Eligibility: Schoolmasters or schoolmistresses (employed/retired) of any independent or maintained school who have 10 years of continuous service, and their dependants.
Types of grants: One-off and recurrent grants up to a maximum of £600 per year. Grants are normally made to retired schoolmasters or schoolmistresses who have no adequate pension, but there are exceptions to this.
Annual grant total: About £5,000 is given in about eight grants each year.
Applications: On a form available from the correspondent. Applications can be submitted directly by the individual or through a social worker, citizen's advice bureau, welfare agency or a third party such as a relative. They are considered in March, June and November.
Correspondent: Dr R B Mallion, Hon. Secretary, The King's School, Canterbury, Kent CT1 2ES (01227 595546; e-mail: rbma@kings-school.co.uk).

Teacher Support Network (formerly The Teachers Benevolent Fund – TBF)

Eligibility: Serving, former and retired teachers (regardless of teacher union affiliation) and their dependants. Applicants must have less than £5,000 in savings. Student teachers are not eligible for financial support.
Types of grants: One-off grants, of between £300 and £3,000, towards a range of needs including low income, illness and injury. Grants can be for special needs equipment, care home grants, clothing, white goods, household furniture, removal costs and household repairs. Loans can also be made. No grants for private school fees, educational course fees, school trips, unsecured debts, house purchases or private medical treatment. Student loans are not made.
Annual grant total: In 2000 the trust had assets of £6.9 million and an income of £3.2 million. Total expenditure was £4.2 million and it gave grants totalling £450,000 to 690 individuals.
Applications: On a form available from the correspondent. Applications are usually considered on a monthly basis, and can be submitted directly by the individual. Applications are means tested so financial information is needed, alongside other supporting information (such as proof of need).
Correspondent: Welfare Manager, Teacher Support Services, Hamilton House, Mabledon Place, London WC1H 9BE (020 7554 5222; Fax: 020 7554 5239; e-mail: support@teachersupport.info; website: www.teachersupport.info).
Other information: Grantmaking is just one aspect of the work of this trust, hence the change of name. In 1999 it established Teacher Support Line (formerly Teacherline), 'providing day-to-day support for teachers in both their personal and professional lives'. There is also a money and welfare benefits advice service and a dedicated service for retired teachers. (These non-grantmaking services are also available to student teachers.)

Telecommuni- cations

The BT Benevolent Fund

Eligibility: People who work or have worked for British Telecom or its predecessors (GPO/ Post Office Telephones), and their dependants.
Types of grants: One-off grants of up to £1,500 towards: aids for people who are disabled, priority debts; costs of moving home; and essential household items such as furniture and clothing. Weekly grants of up to £20 are also available for families on low income or to cover residential/ nursing home fees. No grants for legal expenses or for private medicine or education.

OCCUPATIONAL CHARITIES

Annual grant total: In 2000 the trust had assets of £2 million, an income of £407,000 and a total expenditure of £412,000. Grants to 505 individuals totalled £185,000.

Applications: On a form available from the case secretary at the address below. Applications are considered monthly and can be submitted either directly by the individual or through a third party such as a welfare agency.

Correspondent: Phil Jennings, Room 313, Telecoms House, Friar Street, Reading RG1 1BA (0118 952 1114; Fax: 0118 952 1117).

Other information: Originally set up in 1853 as the Post Office Clerks Charitable Fund, this fund was formed when the Post Office and Telecommunications businesses separated in 1981.

Textiles

The City of London Linen and Furnishings Trades Association

Eligibility: Members and former members of the association and their dependants.

Types of grants: One-off grants only (subject to review). The trust can contribute towards the cost of a holiday at one of the Textile Benevolent Association holiday homes.

Annual grant total: In 2000 the association had an income of £3,400 and a total expenditure of £3,000.

Applications: The correspondent has previously stated that 'all people who are eligible are known to the trustees'.

Correspondent: Geoffrey Blake, Secretary, 69a Langley Hill, Kings Langley WD4 9HQ.

Other information: This entry was not confirmed by the association, but the address was correct according to the Charity Commission database.

The Cotton Industry War Memorial Trust

Eligibility: People who have worked in the cotton textile industry in the last 20 years. This includes weaving, spinning and dyeing. Clothing, footwear, hosiery and other man-made fabrics are not eligible.

Also, people who became disabled whilst fighting for HM Forces in wartime.

Types of grants: One-off grants ranging between £100 and £2,000 according to need. Convalescence grants are available to people who have become sick, ill or disabled due to their work in the cotton textiles industry.

Annual grant total: In 2001 the trust had assets of £5.6 million, an income of £291,000 and a total expenditure of £120,000. Grants to nine individuals totalled £2,900. Grants to seven organisations totalled £76,000.

Applications: On a form available from: an employee or trade union for cotton workers; or SSAFA for ex-service personnel. The correspondent is not allowed to send forms directly to applicants, just to employers, trade unions or SSAFA for them to pass on to potential applications. Completed forms can be considered at any time.

Correspondent: Robert G Morrow, 5 Brampton Close, Platt Bridge, Wigan WN2 5HS (01942 735097).

Other information: The trust also gives very substantial grants to educational bodies to assist eligible students in furtherance of their textile studies, to other bodies which encourage recruitment into or efficiency in the industry and to organisations furthering the interests of the industry by research and so on.

Scottish Retail Credit Association Benevolent Fund

Eligibility: People who have worked in the drapery trade in Scotland, and their widows or dependants, who are in need.

Types of grants: One-off and recurrent grants according to need.

Annual grant total: About £1,400 is given each year to individuals and organisations.

Applications: In writing to the correspondent.

Correspondent: I H Campbell, 98 West George Street, Glasgow G2 1PJ (0141 332 0070).

Sydney Simmons Pension Fund

Eligibility: People in need who are or have been employed in the carpet trade.

Types of grants: One-off grants of £100 to £800 towards, for instance, household items, respite care, property repairs, wheelchairs and other aids.

Annual grant total: In 2001 the fund had assets of £115,000 and an income of £4,500. Total expenditure was £5,000, all of which was given in eight grants.

Applications: On a form available from the correspondent, to be submitted through a social worker, citizen's advice bureau or other welfare agency.

Correspondent: David Matanle, Homefield, Fortyfoot Road, Leatherfield KT22 8RP (01372 370073; Fax: 01372 361466; e-mail: luchare@btinternet.com).

The Textile Benevolent Association (1970)

Eligibility: People in need who are employees and former employees of: wholesalers and retailers engaged in the textile trade; and of manufacturers in the trade which distribute to retailers as well as manufacture. The wives, widows, husbands and widowers of such people can also benefit.

Types of grants: Grants are towards holidays, winter fuel bills, clothing, cookers and washing machines and so on.

Annual grant total: About £20,000 is available for grants to individuals each year.

Applications: On a form available from the correspondent, usually via employers, doctors or social services.

Correspondent: Mrs Sandra Tullet, 72a Lee High Road, Lewisham, London SE13 5PT (020 8852 7239).

Textile Industry Children's Trust

Eligibility: Children and young people under 20 (including orphaned children) whose parents work or have worked for at least five years in the retail, wholesale or manufacturing sectors of the textile and allied trades in the UK (for example, drapers, footwear, hosiers, clothiers, textile manufacturers etc.).

Types of grants: The trust concentrates its grant giving on 'the essential costs of education'. It also makes some welfare grants, especially towards equipment for people who are disabled.

Annual grant total: In 2000/01 the trust had assets of £6.4 million and an income of £406,000. Total expenditure was £378,000, with 135 grants being awarded to individuals totalling £226,000.

Applications: On a form available from the correspondent. Applications should be submitted directly by the individual for consideration at any time.

Correspondent: G Sullivan, Director, Lynnhaven House, Columbine Way, Gislingham, Eye, Suffolk IP23 8HL (Tel & Fax: 01379 788644).

Tobacco trade

Tobacco Trade Benevolent Association

Eligibility: People who have been engaged in the manufacture, wholesale or retail sections of the tobacco industry and their dependants, who are in need.

Types of grants: Monthly allowances and one-off grants for household items and house repairs.

Annual grant total: £150,000

Applications: Application forms are available from the correspondent to be considered in January, March, May, July, September and November, and can be submitted directly by the individual or through a social worker, citizen's advice

OCCUPATIONAL CHARITIES

bureau, welfare agency or other third party. Applicants are asked to provide details of the length of their service in the tobacco trade, financial position and whether they own their own home.

Correspondent: Dianne Jennings, Secretariat, Forum Court, 83 Copers Cope Road, Beckenham, Kent BR13 1NR (020 8663 3050; Fax: 020 8663 0949; e-mail: ttba@geotechnical.demon.co.uk).

Travel industry

The ABTA Benevolent Fund

Eligibility: People who are or have been employed by ABTA members and their dependants.

Types of grants: One-off and recurrent grants unrestricted in size, previously ranging from £130 to £16,000. Grants have been given for holidays, wheelchairs, children with disabilities, bills, decoration and so on. The fund cannot help with costs arising fro the failure of a business.

Annual grant total: In 2001 grants totalled £20,000.

Applications: On a form available from the correspondent, to be submitted directly by the individual at any time.

Correspondent: David N Parish, 68–71 Newman Street, London W1T 3AH (020 7307 1917; Fax: 020 7636 1425; e-mail: dparish@abta.co.uk).

The Guild of Registered Tourist Guides Benevolent Fund

Eligibility: Tourist Board registered (blue badge) guides, qualified for at least one year who are in need, and dependants of guides qualified for at least three years.

Types of grants: One-off grants to relieve need and enable a guide to work of up to £700, but normally between £300 and £400. Grants are not given for 'gambling debts, riotous living, or private hospital care'.

Annual grant total: £3,500 in 2000.

Applications: In writing to the correspondent, including the tourist board with which the applicant was registered, whether any statutory bodies have been approached and the specific need. Applications can be made directly by the individual or by a third party to one of the trustees or the committee. They can be considered at any time. Each trustee has a portfolio of clients and is responsible for checking how the beneficiaries are getting on, sometimes through home visits.

Correspondent: Robert Leon, Treasurer, The Guild House, 52d Borough High Street, London SE1 1XN (020 7403 1115; Fax: 020 7378 1705).

Veterinary

The Veterinary Benevolent Fund

Eligibility: Members and former members of the Royal College of Veterinary Surgeons, Registered Veterinary Practitioners and their dependants. Veterinary students are not eligible.

Types of grants: Monthly and one-off grants and short-term loans are given towards TV licences, telephone rental, vehicle taxes, wheelchairs and to enable people to find employment. Grants range from £36 to £1,000.

Annual grant total: In 2001 the trust had assets of £348,000, an income of £265,000 and a total expenditure of £159,000. Recurrent grants totalled £67,000, while one-off grants totalled £42,000.

Applications: On a form available from the correspondent. Applications can be made directly by the individual, through a social worker, citizen's advice bureau or other welfare agency, or through a third party such as a relative or colleague. Applicants applying for assistance will be required to provide details of their financial status, i.e. monthly income and expenditure, plus assets and liabilities.

Correspondent: Amanda Coleman, Administrative Manager, 7 Mansfield Street, London W1G 9NQ (020 7636 6541; Fax: 020 7637 0053; e-mail: info@vbf.org.uk; website: www.vbf.org.uk).

Voluntary Sector

The Andrew Anderson Trust

Eligibility: People who are, or were, involved in charitable activities, and their dependants, who are in need.

Types of grants: One-off and recurrent grants according to need.

Annual grant total: In 1998/99 the trust had assets of £8.5 million and an income of £290,000. Grants to individuals for relief-in-need purposes totalled £37,000. Students of theology received £3,500 in total. Grants to organisations amounted to £287,000.

Applications: The trust states that it rarely gives to people who are not known to the trustees or personally recommended by people known to the trustees. Unsolicited applications are therefore unlikely to be successful.

Correspondent: The Trustees, 84 Uphill Road, Mill Hill, London NW7 4QE.

Watch & clock makers

The National Benevolent Society of Watch and Clockmakers

Eligibility: People aged over 65 who previously worked in any branch of the watch and clock trade for a number of years, and their widows and dependants.

Types of grants: Recurrent grants paid quarterly.

Annual grant total: In 2000/01 the trust had assets of £2.1 million and an income of £122,000. Total expenditure was £146,000, including £132,000 given in 217 grants.

Applications: On a form available from: Mrs A Baker, Secretary, 18a Westbury Road, New Malden, Surrey KT3 5DE. Fully completed forms should be submitted to Mrs Baker directly by the individual. They are usually considered in March, June, September and December.

Correspondent: K E Angliss, 122 Parkway, London SW20 9HG (020 8540 3137; e-mail: keith@kangliss.freeserve.co.uk).

Water

Water Conservators Charitable Trust Fund

Eligibility: People in need, working in or who have worked in the field of water and environmental management and their dependants. In particular, members and former members of the Institution of Public Health Engineers and of the Chartered Institution of Water and Environmental Management and their dependants, who are in need.

Types of grants: Recurrent grants paid on a monthly basis and one-off grants for particular items. Loans can also be given, e.g. to deal with emergencies.

Annual grant total: In 1997 the trust had assets of £131,000, an income of £7,800 and its total expenditure was £5,000. Grants to five individuals totalled £4,200.

Applications: In writing to the correspondent, either directly by the individual or by a third party. Applications are normally considered in March, June and September, but urgent applications can be considered at other times.

Correspondent: The Clerk, 22 Broadfields, Headstone Lane, Hatch End, Middlesex HA2 6NH (Tel & Fax: 020 8421 0305; e-mail: clerk@waterconservators.org; website: www.waterconservators.org).

Service & Ex-Service Charities

Unlike other occupations, the service/ex-service charities have been given their own section in this guide as there are many more trusts available and they can support a large number of people. This branch of the sector is committed to helping anyone who has at least one day's paid service in any of the armed forces, including reserves and those who did National Service, and their husbands, wives, children, widows, widowers and other dependants. It is estimated that this covers a quarter of the UK's population.

These charities are exceptionally well organised. Much of this is due to the work of SSAFA Forces Help, which has an extensive network of trained caseworkers around the country who act on behalf of SSAFA Forces Help and other service charities. Many of the trusts in this section use the same application forms and procedures as SSAFA Forces Help and assist a specified group of people within the service/ex-service community, while others (such as Royal British Legion) have their own procedures and support the services as a whole.

There is a standard application form which is used by many service and ex-service charities. This form should not be filled in by the applicant, rather by a trained caseworker at the applicant's home. The completed form is sent to the appropriate service, regimental or corps benevolent fund (and where appropriate, copies may be sent to other relevant funds, both service and non-service).

Although many service benevolent funds rely on trained SSAFA Forces Help volunteer caseworkers to prepare application forms, some do have their own volunteers who can complete the form. However, these may not be spread so comprehensively around the country. Alternatively, some funds ask applicants to write to a central correspondent. In such cases, applicants may like to follow the guidelines in the article 'How to make an application' earlier in this guide. Most entries in this section state whether the applicant should apply directly to the trust or through a caseworker. If in doubt, the applicant should ring up the trust concerned or the local SSAFA Forces Help office.

Some people may prefer to approach their, or their former spouse's regimental or corps association. Each corps has its own entry in this guide and the regimental associations are listed at the end of this section. Many of them have their own charitable funds and volunteers, especially in their own recruiting areas. In other cases they will work through one of the volunteer networks mentioned above. Again, if in doubt or difficulty, the applicant should ring up the regimental/corps association or the local SSAFA Forces Help office.

SSAFA Forces Help is much more than just a provider of financial assistance, providing advice, support and training. It can assist members of the service and ex-service communities on many issues, ranging from how to replace lost medals to advice on adoption. Its website (www.ssafa.org.uk) is an excellent source of reference for the members of the community, giving a wide range of useful information and links. Local SSAFA Forces Help offices can generally be found in the local telephone directories (usually under Soldiers', Sailors' & Airmen's Families Association – Forces Help) or advertised in such places as citizen's advice bureaux, doctor's waiting rooms or libraries. Alternatively, the central office is based at: 19 Queen Elizabeth Street, London SE1 2LP (020 7403 8783; e-mail: info@ssafa.org.uk; website: www.ssafa.org.uk).

The Airborne Forces Security Fund

Eligibility: Serving and former members of all ranks of the Parachute Regiment, the Glider Regiment and other units of airborne forces, and their dependants.

Types of grants: Grants according to need.

Annual grant total: In 2000 the fund had an income of £350,000 and a total expenditure of £316,000.

Applications: On SSAFA Form A 2001.

Correspondent: The Controller, Browning Barracks, Aldershot, Hampshire GU11 2BU (01252 320772).

The Aircrew Association Charitable Fund

Eligibility: Serving or ex-serving aircrew of the allied forces, and their dependants.

Types of grants: One-off grants of up to £1,000. Grants have included debt relief (£84), help towards the purchase of a wheelchair (£300), decorating costs (£310), car repairs (£76) and assistance with funeral costs (£400).

Annual grant total: In 2000/01 the fund had an income of £23,000 and a total expenditure of £11,000.

Applications: On a form available from the correspondent. Applications can be submitted either directly by the individual or through a third party such as SSAFA, RAFA, RBC etc. Applications are considered on receipt, and are assessed according to need.

Correspondent: John Laister Guy, The Staithe, 43 Farmadine, Saffron Walden, Essex CB11 3HR.

Other information: This entry was not confirmed by the fund, but was correct according to the Charity Commission database.

AJEX Charitable Foundation (formerly known as The Association of Jewish Ex-Servicemen & Women)

Eligibility: Jewish ex-servicemen and women and their dependants who are in need.

Service & Ex-Service Charities

Types of grants: One-off grants and recurrent grants paid three times a year are available. Help can be given towards furnishings, bed linen, clothing, household appliances and so on.
Annual grant total: Over £45,000 in over 300 grants.
Applications: On a form available from the correspondent, to be returned directly by the individual or through a social worker, citizen's advice bureau, SSAFA or other welfare agency. Evidence of services in the British army and of Jewish religious status is required.
Correspondent: The Honorary Welfare Secretary, Ajex House, 3a–5a East Bank, Stamford Hill, London N16 5RT (020 8800 2844; Fax: 020 8880 1117; e-mail: ajexuk@talk21.com; website: www.ajexuk.org.com).

The Army Benevolent Fund

Eligibility: Members and ex-members of the British Army, and their dependants who are in need.
Types of grants: All types of emergency grant. Also monthly allowances for people over retirement age, who live alone and are on a very low income.
Annual grant total: In 1999/2000 the trust had assets of over £30 million and gave grants totalling £4.3 million to individuals and 85 charitable organisations which support ex-service personnel.
Applications: The fund does not deal directly with individual cases, which should be referred initially to the appropriate corps or regimental association. (Enquiries about the appropriate association can be made to the Army Benevolent Fund.) See also, in particular, the entries for SSAFA Forces Help and the Royal British Legion.
Correspondent: The Controller, 41 Queen's Gate, South Kensington, London SW7 5HR (020 7591 2060 Grants Department; Fax: 020 7584 0889).
Other information: This trust also gives educational grants to individuals.

Army Catering Corps Benevolent Association

Eligibility: Members of the Army Catering Corps between 1941 and 1993 (excluding Territorial Army service) and their dependants who are under 16. Divorced wives or husbands who remarry are not eligible.
Types of grants: One-off grants of between £100 and £750. Recent grants have been given towards mobility aids, household appliances, furniture, carpets, clothing, respite holidays, nursing home contributions, extra allowances for low pensions and grants to low-income families to reinstate a sustainable budget. No grants are given towards debts from credit cards or 'irresponsible expenditure'.

Annual grant total: In 2001 the trust had assets of £1.4 million, an income of £115,000 and a total expenditure of £142,000. Grants to 307 individuals totalled £96,000.
Applications: On a form available from the correspondent, to be submitted through SSAFA Forces Help or Royal British Legion Caseworkers. Applications can be considered at any time.
Correspondent: The Controller, Dettingen House, Princess Royal Barracks, Deepcut, Surrey GU16 6RW (01252 833394; Fax: 01252 833393; e-mail: controller@accassociation.org; website: www.accassociation.org).

The Association of Royal Navy Officers (ARNO)

Eligibility: Officers and retired officers of the Royal Navy, Royal Marines, WRNS, QARNNS and their Reserves, who have joined and are members of the association, and their dependants.
Types of grants: One-off grants towards, for example, household repairs and decoration, emergency gifts of money, mortgage repayment, buying a vehicle (e.g. to accommodate a wheelchair), travel (e.g. to visit relative in hospital) or a Christmas cheque.
Annual grant total: In 2000 the trust had an income of £181,000 and its total expenditure was £174,000, all of which was given in grants for relief-in-need and educational purposes.
Applications: In writing to the correspondent.
Correspondent: Lt Cdr I M P Coombes RN, 70 Porchester Terrace, Bayswater, London W2 3TP (020 7402 5231; e-mail: arno@eurosurf.com).

ATS & WRAC Benevolent Fund

Eligibility: Former members of the Auxiliary Territorial Service and the Women's Royal Army Corps. Also former members of the QMAAC (Queen Mary's Auxiliary Army Corps 1914/1918 War).
Types of grants: One-off grants towards furniture, clothing, respite care, disability aids, removal expenses and so on. Help towards rent and rates difficulties is also given. Recurrent grants are also given of £11 a week plus a Christmas bonus of £60. No loans are available.
Annual grant total: In 2000/01 the trust had assets of £4 million and an income of £409,000. 786 one-off grants totalled £170,000 whilst grants to 120 annual beneficiaries totalled £74,000.
Applications: On a form available from the correspondent. Most cases are investigated by an honorary representative of SSAFA or the RBL. The grants committee meets every month to consider requests over £400; cases recommending grants of less than £400 are dealt with by the joint secretaries of the fund outside the grants committee.
Correspondent: Case Secretary, Gould House, AGC Centre, Worthy Down, Winchester SO21 2RG (01962 887612; Fax: 01962 887478).

British Limbless Ex-Service Men's Association (BLESMA)

Eligibility: Serving and ex-serving members of HM or auxiliary forces who have lost a limb or eye or have a permanent loss of speech, hearing or sight, and their widows/widowers. Despite the association's name, it serves members of both sexes.
Types of grants: One-off and recurrent grants according to need. Recent grants have been made towards rehabilitation, disability equipment such as wheelchairs and stairlifts, gardening, decoration and vehicle adaptation.
Annual grant total: In 2000 the association had an income of £2.6 million and a total expenditure of £2.7 million. Grants to 901 individuals totalled £626,000.
Applications: On a form available from the correspondent, although a letter is acceptable if preferred. Applications can be submitted at any time, either directly by the individual or through their local BLESMA representative, SSAFA Forces Help, citizen's advice bureaux or other welfare agencies.
Correspondent: Jerome W Church, General Secretary, Frankland Moore House, 185-187 High Road, Chadwell Heath, Romford, Essex RM6 6NA (020 8590 1124; Fax: 020 8599 2932; e-mail: blesma@btconnect.com; website: www.blesma.org).
Other information: The association provides permanent residential and respite accommodation through its two nursing and residential care homes at Blackpool and Crieff in Perthshire.

The Burma Star Association

Eligibility: People who were awarded the Burma Star Campaign Medal during the second world war, and their immediate dependants, who live in the UK, other Commonwealth countries or Republic of Ireland. Grandchildren, great-grandchildren and other 'non-dependants' are not eligible (except in certain circumstances where the child is disabled).
Types of grants: One-off grants ranging between £10 to £520 towards: top-up fees for nursing, care and residential homes; respite care and holidays; travel to and from hospital; wheelchairs; stairlifts; riser/reclining chairs; lifeline telephones and telephone installation; repairs to homes; furniture; household items such as fridges; funeral costs; clothing; utility bills, general debts; blind and deaf aids; nebulizers; and

installation of showers, baths and bath aids.

No grants are given towards private medical treatment, headstones or plaques. No loans are given.

Annual grant total: In 2001 the trust had assets of £1.6 million and an income £264,000. Total expenditure was £356,000, of which £213,000 was given in total in 775 grants.

Applications: Applications can be made by the individual or through a third party such as a citizen's advice bureau or other welfare agency and should be submitted direct to the correspondent or to the correspondent via branches of the association or other ex-service organisations. Grants are made through branches of the association, SSAFA, the Royal British Legion or other ex-service organisations after investigation and completion of application form giving full particulars of circumstances and eligibility (including service particulars verifying the award of the Burma Star). Applications are considered throughout the year.

Correspondent: Miss R D Patrick, National Welfare Secretary, 4 Lower Belgrave Street, London SW1W 0LA (020 7823 4283; Fax: 020 7730 7882).

The Commandos' Benevolent Fund

Eligibility: Army commandos who served in World War Two, and their dependants, wives or widows.

Types of grants: One-off grants towards e.g. hospital transport, electricity and gas debts, stairlifts, wheelchairs, holidays and home repairs.

No grants towards the costs of private medicine.

Annual grant total: About £16,000.

Applications: In writing with service details to the correspondent, directly by the individual or through a social worker, citizen's advice bureau or other welfare agency such as SSAFA Forces Help. Applications are considered as soon as possible after receipt.

Correspondent: The Honorary Secretary, 190 Hammersmith Road, London W6 7DL (020 8746 3491).

The Commonwealth Ex-Services League

Eligibility: Ex-servicemen of the crown, their widows or dependants, who are living outside the UK. There are 57 member organisations in 48 countries.

Types of grants: All types of help can be considered. Grants are one-off, renewable on application. Grants are generally for medically related costs such as hearing aids, wheelchairs, artificial limbs, food or repairs to homes wrecked by floods or hurricanes etc. Grants usually range from £40 to £260 per year.

Annual grant total: In 2001 the league gave grants to 264 individuals totalling £22,000. It also gave bulk grants to organisations totalling £350,000 and to projects totalling £20,000.

Applications: Considered daily on receipt of applications from member organisations or British Embassies/High Commissions, but not directly from individuals.

Correspondent: Col. Brian Nicholson, 48 Pall Mall, London SW1Y 5JG (020 7973 7263; Fax: 020 7973 7308).

Other information: The league has members or representatives in most parts of the world through whom former servicemen or their dependants living abroad can seek help. The local British Embassy or High Commission can normally supply the relevant local contact. In a Commonwealth country the local ex-service association will probably be affiliated to the league.

W J & Mrs C G Dunnachie's Charitable Trust

Eligibility: People who are experiencing sickness, infirmity and disability as a result of service during the second world war. There is a preference for Scotland.

Types of grants: One-off grants usually of between £300 and £500, for example, towards a stairlift and recurrent payments of £140 a quarter.

Annual grant total: About £50,000 a year is given, mainly to individuals but also to organisations.

Applications: In writing to the correspondent at any time. Most applications are submitted via SSAFA Forces Help or through a regimental association.

Correspondent: The Trustees, Low Beaton Richmond, 20 Renfields Street, Glasgow G2 5AP (0141 221 8931).

Greenwich Hospital

Eligibility: Members and former members of the Royal Navy and Royal Marines and their dependants.

Types of grants: Pensions of £10 a week to: (i) older retired officers of the Royal Navy or Royal Marines and to ratings, who by reason of age or ill health are unable to contribute to their own support (ii) older widows of Royal Navy or Marine Petty Officers and ratings who served at least 22 years or died or were invalided out whilst serving for pension.

Applications may also be made for a Jellicoe Annuity by elderly and retired Royal Navy or Marines and their widows, who had served less than pensionable service and are in need. They must be on Income Support.

The charity also make educational grants.

Annual grant total: In 1999/2000 the trust had assets of about £130 million and an income of £5.1 million. Grants of between £50 and £1,500 per year were given to 12 people and totalled £18,000.

Applications: On a form available from the correspondent. Applications will then be reviewed by the Royal Naval Benevolent Trust or SSAFA.

Applications for Jellicoe Annuities should be made to the Grant's Secretary of The Royal Naval Benevolent Trust (see separate entry) who administer the annuities on behalf of Greenwich Hospital.

Correspondent: The Director, 40 Queen Anne's Gate, London SW1H 9AP (020 7396 0150; Fax: 020 7396 0149).

Other information: Greenwich Hospital is a charity responsible to the Admiralty Board. Its main functions are supporting the Royal Hospital School near Ipswich (an independent boarding school for the children and grandchildren of seafarers) through meeting the cost of fees, building sheltered housing for elderly naval families, and granting pensions and bursaries to those in need.

The Hampshire & Isle of Wight Military Aid Fund (1903)

Eligibility: People who serve or have served in a Hampshire army unit and his/her dependants.

Types of grants: One-off grants and monthly allowances for rent, utilities, clothing, education, furniture and removals and so on. Grants range from about £50 to £250.

Annual grant total: In 2001 grants totalled £50,000.

Applications: Normally through the local branch of SSAFA. Applications are considered fortnightly.

Correspondent: Lt Cdr G L Eddis RN, Serle's House, Southgate Street, Winchester SO23 9EG (01962 852933; Fax: 01962 888302).

The Kelly Holdsworth Artillery Trust

Eligibility: Retired officers in need who have served in the Royal Regiment of Artillery and their dependants.

Types of grants: One-off emergency grants of about £1,000 and recurrent grants ranging from £20 to £60 a week.

Annual grant total: In 2000 the trust had an income of £85,000 and a total expenditure of £81,000, nearly all of which was given in grants to individuals.

Applications: On a form available from the correspondent. Sometimes a representative from the Officers Association visits applicants.

Correspondent: Lt. Col. N G W Lang, Hon. Secretary, Artillery House, Front

Parade, RA Barracks, Woolwich, London SE18 4BH (020 8781 3003; e-mail: gensec.rhqra@army.mod.uk.net).

The Household Division Queens Jubilee Trust

Eligibility: Children who are physically and/or mentally disabled whose parents are officers, warrant officers, non-commissioned officers and soldiers of the Household Division, and other such children. Applicants must have been born while their fathers were serving in the Household Division unless they died whilst serving in it.

Types of grants: One-off and recurrent grants 'to assist in the care, upbringing, maintenance and education' of such children.

Annual grant total: In 2000/01 the trust had an income of £5,000, all of which was given in six to eight grants.

Applications: In the first instance ring 020 7930 4466 and ask for the assistant regimental adjutant of the regiment concerned who will tell you how to contact the relevant headquarters. In some cases SSAFA Forces Help will be asked to investigate and make recommendations on grants.

Correspondent: The Treasurer, Household Division Funds, Horse Guards, Whitehall, London SW1A 2AX (020 7414 2271; Fax: 020 7414 2207).

The Kinloch Bequest

Eligibility: Retired Scottish ex-servicemen who have served in the Royal navy, army or airforce.

Types of grants: Annuities of £8 to £10 per week paid quarterly.

Annual grant total: In 1998/99 the trust had assets of £104,000 and an income of £5,400. Total expenditure was £8,000, all of which was given to 19 individuals.

Applications: On a form available from the correspondent. Applications must be submitted through SSAFA or Royal British Legion.

Correspondent: The Chief Executive, 37 King Street, Covent Garden, London WC2E 8JS (020 7240 3718; Fax: 020 7497 0184).

Lloyd's Patriotic Fund

Eligibility: Ex-servicemen and women (Royal Navy, Army, Royal Marines and Fleet Air Arm, but excluding Royal Air Force personnel) who have served for at least five years, or less if they served during war-time, and their dependants.

Types of grants: One-off grants ranging from £100 to £500 towards essential items such as wheelchairs, stair lifts, domestic bills and so on. No grants for holidays, funeral expenses, home improvements, council tax, loans or debts.

Annual grant total: In 2000/01 the fund had assets of £1.9 million and an income of £89,000. Total expenditure was £92,000, all of which was given in 350 grants.

Applications: Through SSAFA, using their application form with details of income, expenditure and nature of need and background.

Correspondent: Mrs Linda Harper, Secretary, Lloyd's Building, One Lime Street, London EC3M 7HA (020 7327 5925; Fax: 020 7327 6368; e-mail: linda.harper@lloyds.com; website: www.lloydsoflondon.com).

The Metcalfe Shannon Trust

Eligibility: Canadian ex-servicemen and their dependants who are in need.

Types of grants: One-off grants ranging between £25 and £500, but generally of £60 each.. Grants are available for such things as appliances, removal costs, service bills and mobility chairs, but not to improvements to property resulting in gain in capital value.

Annual grant total: In 2000 the trust had assets of £167,000 and an income of £7,100. Grants to 320 individuals totalled £54,000.

Applications: In writing to the correspondent, submitted by either the individual or through a social worker, citizen's advice bureau or other welfare agency. Applications are considered quarterly.

Correspondent: Mrs J I Morton, Secretary, Canadian High Commission, 1 Grosvenor Square, London W1X 4AB (020 7258 6339).

Other information: This trust states in its 2000 accounts that it is gradually winding down. The reduction in assets over the previous few years would suggest that the trust, if continuing to overspend by the same amount, would cease to exist around 2005.

The Nash Charity

Eligibility: Wounded or disabled ex-service personnel.

Types of grants: Grants are usually paid through social services, citizen's advice bureaux or other welfare agencies to purchase specific items that are needed.

Annual grant total: In 2000/01 the charity had an income of £16,000 and a total expenditure of £18,000.

Applications: In writing to the correspondent at any time. Applications can be submitted directly by the individual or through a social worker, citizen's advice bureau, other welfare agency or other third party.

Correspondent: The Secretary, Messrs Peachey & Co., 95 Aldwych, London WC2B 4JF (020 7316 5200; Fax: 020 7316 5222).

The Navy Special Fund

Eligibility: Limited financial assistance for relief of temporary hardship or distress amongst those serving or who have served in the Royal Navy and the Royal Marines, and their dependants.

Types of grants: Small cash grants, usually of up to £500 although grants over this amount may be considered.

Annual grant total: In 2000 the fund had assets of £832,000, an income of £34,000 and a total expenditure of £16,000. Grants to 25 individuals totalled £10,000.

Applications: Applications should be made initially to the Royal Naval Benevolent Trust (see separate entry) or the Womens Royal Naval Service Benevolent Trust (for ex-WRNS). Applications should be submitted through SSAFA Forces Help, Royal Navy or British Legion case workers, or through a social worker, citizen's advice bureau or other welfare agency.

Correspondent: Lt Com A J Cooper RN, Room 49, Old Naval Academy, HM Naval Base, Portsmouth, Hampshire PO1 3LS (023 9272 4506; Fax: 023 9272 7212).

Other information: This fund works closely with The Royal Naval Benevolent Trust and The Women's Royal Naval Service Benevolent Trust.

The 'Not Forgotten' Association

Eligibility: Service and ex-service men and women who are disabled. Applicants must have served in the Armed Forces of the Crown (or Merchant Navy during hostilities). The association cannot help wives, widows or families (unless they are themselves ex-members of the forces or they are acting as carers).

Types of grants: The association does not give financial grants direct to applicants, rather it gives help in kind of between £100 and £250 in the following areas:

TV rental (£140 including insurance) and licences (£109) for those with restricted mobility or who are otherwise largely housebound; holidays (accompanied by carers if required) and day outings to events and places of interest; and entertainments at ex-service residential and nursing homes.

The association does not give cash grants, but in certain cases cheques may be sent to individual applicants for holidays or to office holders of bona fide ex-service organisations. The association does not have the resources to undertake case work.

Annual grant total: In 2001/02 the association had assets of £2.7 million and an income of £585,000. Total expenditure was £649,000 with over 3,000 grants totalling £501,000.

Applications: Applications should be submitted through SSAFA Forces Help, Royal British Legion, Combat Stress or the

Welfare Service of the War Pensions Agency. These agencies will complete the common application form on behalf of the applicant and then make the appropriate recommendation to the association, with the applicant's income and expenditure details and degree of disability. Applications are considered throughout the year. Successful applicants can reapply after a three-year gap.

Correspondent: The Director, 2 Grosvenor Gardens, London SW1W 0DH (020 7730 2400/3660; Fax: 020 7730 0020; e-mail: director@nfassociation.freeserve.co.uk; website: www.nfassociation.freeserve.co.uk).

Other information: The association holds a summer garden party and Christmas party for war pensioners in London each year.

The Officers' Association

Eligibility: People who have held a commission in HM Forces, their widows and dependants. Officers on the active list will normally be helped only with resettlement and employment.

Types of grants: Small annual grants to older ex-officers or their dependants who are trying to cope on very small pensions and state benefits. In addition to this standard allowance, the association gives grants for a wide spectrum of problems ranging from telephone bills to buying disability aids which are not provided by the NHS. Help also with small items, residential care and nursing home fees, as well as very limited assistance with education.

Annual grant total: In 2000/01 the trust had assets of £8 million, an income of £2 million and a total expenditure of £2.5 million. Grants to 1,020 individuals totalled £1 million.

Applications: On a form available from the Benevolence Secretary at the address below. Applications can be submitted either directly by the individual or via a third party. The association has a network of honorary representatives throughout the UK who will normally visit the applicant.

Correspondent: General Secretary, 48 Pall Mall, London SW1Y 5JY (020 7930 0125; Fax: 020 7930 9053; e-mail: postmaster@oaed.org.uk; website: www.officersassociation.org.uk).

Other information: For applicants in Scotland: See entry for the Officers' Association Scotland in the Scotland general section of this guide.

For applicants in Eire, contact: Captain D J Mooney, 26 South Frederick Street, Dublin 2 (00 353 1677 2554).

The association has a residential home at Bishopsteignton, South Devon, for ex-officers (male and female) over the age of 65 who do not need special care. It also provides a series of advice leaflets on finding accommodation in residential care or nursing homes, how to get financial assistance and how to find short-term convalescence accommodation and sheltered accommodation for older people who are disabled.

It also has an employment department to help ex-officers up to the age of 60 find suitable employment. It helps not only those just leaving the services but also those who have just lost their civilian jobs.

Polish Air Force Association Benevolent Fund

Eligibility: Ex-servicemen of the Polish Air Force who fought during World War II under British Command, its members who have settled in the west, and their widows, who are in need.

Types of grants: One-off grants of £150 to £300 for food, clothing and medical care.

Annual grant total: In 2002 the trust had assets of £200,000 and an income of £91,000. Total expenditure was £86,000, of which £40,000 was given in total to 80 individuals.

Applications: On a form available from the correspondent, to be submitted either directly by the applicant or a welfare officer from a local branch of the association. RAF service number is required as proof of service with the Polish Air Force. Applications are considered every second month.

Correspondent: T J Krzyster, Secretary, 238–246 King Street, London W6 0RF (020 8846 9487; Fax: 020 8748 6169).

The Polish Soldiers Assistance Fund

Eligibility: People in need who are former Polish comrades-in-arms who were prisoners of war, soldiers' families both inside and outside Poland, Polish children, former Polish combatants, widows and orphans or war invalids.

Types of grants: One-off or recurrent grants according to need, ranging from £25 to £75.

Annual grant total: In 2000/01 the fund had an income of £43,000 and a total expenditure of £72,000.

Applications: In writing to the correspondent.

Correspondent: Mrs Zychowecki, 240 King Street, London W6 0RF (020 8741 1911).

The Queen Adelaide Naval Fund

Eligibility: The orphan sons and daughters of officers of the Royal Navy and the Royal Marines (an orphan son or daughter may be a person of any age whose father is dead and who, in the case of a daughter, is unmarried or a widow).

Types of grants: One-off grants according to need (but typically £400) and assistance with nursing/residential home fees. Occasional help with boarding school fees.

Annual grant total: About £8,800 each year.

Applications: In writing to the correspondent, for consideration three times a year, in March, July and November. Emergency cases can be considered by the chair between these meetings.

Correspondent: Lt Cdr I M P Coombes, ARNO, 70 Porchester Terrace, Bayswater, London W2 3TP (020 7402 5231; Fax: 020 7402 5533).

Other information: This fund was established in 1850 in memory of Queen Adelaide, widow of King William IV. There are special arrangements whereby eligible girls can have subsidised places as Queen Adelaide pupils at the Royal School, Haslemere. The Admiral of the Fleet Sir Frederick Richards Memorial Fund is now part of this fund.

The REME Benevolent Fund

Eligibility: People who are serving or who have served in the corps, and their immediate dependants.

Types of grants: Generally one-off grants of up to £1,000 for any need except funeral expenses or debts. In 1998/99, a grant was made to a REME staff sergeant who lost a leg in a traffic accident towards buying an automatic car.

Annual grant total: In 2000 the fund had assets of £379,000, an income of £302,000 and a total expenditure of £303,000. Grants to 552 individuals totalled £299,000.

Applications: Generally on a form available from the correspondent or the local branch of SSAFA or Royal British Legion. Grants are only made through a third party (e.g. SSAFA/RBL), and applications made direct will be referred to a welfare agency for investigation. Applications are screened immediately on receipt and are either rejected on sight, referred back for more information or to a committee which meets on alternate Tuesdays. Grants of under £200 can be paid immediately on receipt of a suitable application.

Correspondent: The Secretary, HQ REME (A), Issac Newton Road, Arbourfield, Reading, Berkshire RG2 9NJ (0118 976 3220).

The RN & RM Children's Fund

Eligibility: People under 25 who are the dependants of people who have served in the Royal Navy or Royal Marines and are in need.

Types of grants: One-off and recurrent grants for general welfare needs.

Service & Ex-Service Charities

Annual grant total: In 2001/02 the fund had assets of £8.3 million, an income of £770,000 and a total expenditure of £706,000. Grants totalled £656,000, and were made for both education and welfare purposes.

Applications: On a form available from the correspondent. Applications can be submitted directly by the individual or through a social worker, citizen's advice bureau, other welfare agency or another third party. They are considered at any time.

Correspondent: Ms Monique Bateman, 311 Twyford Avenue, Portsmouth PO2 8PE (023 9263 9534; Fax: 023 9267 7574; e-mail: xvpsi@dial.pipex.com; website: www.rnrmchildsfund.org.uk).

Royal Air Force Benevolent Fund

Eligibility: Past and present members of the Royal Air Force or associated forces and their immediate dependants.

Types of grants: Almost all types of assistance can be considered in the form of grants or loans. Common types of award cover house repairs or modifications, mobility aids, maintenance and immediate need grants, specialist equipment and, in some cases, education and housing.

Annual grant total: In 2001 the trust had assets of £164 million, an income of £24 million and a total expenditure of £29 million. Grants to individuals totalled £22 million, including £336,000 in educational grants.

Applications: By telephoning the fund or through RAFA, SSAFA or other ex-service welfare agencies. Applications are considered weekly.

Correspondent: The Director Welfare, 67 Portland Place, London W1B 1AR (020 7580 8343; Fax: 020 7636 7005; e-mail: mail@rafbt.org.uk; website: www.raf-benfund.org.uk).

Other information: The fund maintains a residential and convalescent home in Sussex and a residential/nursing home in Aberdeenshire. It also jointly maintains respite homes in Northumberland, Avon and Lancashire with RAFA.

The Royal Air Forces Association

Eligibility: Serving and former members of the Royal Air Force (including National Service) and their dependants, the spouses, widows and widowers and dependants of those that died in service or subsequently.

Types of grants: Emergency grants, generally between £50 to £500. Grants are typically for gas and electricity bills, clothing, bedding, electrical goods and furniture. Also costs of transport to hospital for treatment or visiting. The trust may assist with nursing/convalescent/respite care costs. Credit card debts are not eligible, nor are medical fees 'other than those incurred when a GP completes a RAFA medical questionnaire'.

Annual grant total: Grants in excess of £2 million were disbursed during 1996 and over 52,000 cases were aided with either financial or care assistance by the Royal Air Forces Association and the Royal Air Force Benevolent Fund.

Applications: On a form available from the area welfare officer of the applicant's local branch. They are contactable at the addresses below, which can also be found on the association's website. There is an application form and confirmation of RAF service is required. Applications may be submitted directly by the individual, or through SSAFA Forces Help, Royal British Legion or other welfare agency.

Eastern Area: Area Welfare Officer, 1171/2 Loughborough Road, Leicester LE4 5ND (0116 266 2812).
Midland Area: Area Welfare Officer, 4 Park Road, Moseley, Birmingham B13 8AB (0121 449 3007).
North Eastern Area: Area Welfare Officer, 1 Cayley Court, George Cayley Drive, York YO3 4XE (01904 693686).
Northern Ireland Area: Area Welfare Officer, 2nd Floor, War Memorial Building, 9-13 Waring Street, Belfast BT1 2DW (028 9032 5718).
North Western Area: Area Welfare Officer, RAFA House, 58 Deepdale Road, Preston PR1 5AA (01772 555862).
Scotland Area: Area Welfare Officer, 20 Queen Street, Edinburgh EH2 1JX (0131 225 5221).
South Eastern Area: Area Welfare Officer, 3-5 Old Bridge Street, Hampton Wick, Kingston-upon-Thames KT1 4BU (020 8286 6667).
South Western Area: Area Welfare Officer, RAFA House, Chancel Lane, Pinhoe, Exeter EX4 8JU (01392 462088).
Wales Area: Area Welfare Officer, The Mayfield, Llanbadoc, Usk, Gwent NP15 1SY.
Overseas: Overseas Area Department, 43 Grove Park Road, Chiswick, London W4 3RX (020 8747 4134).

Correspondent: David Richardson, 43 Grove Park Road, London W4 3RX (020 894 8504; Fax: 020 8742 1927; e-mail: david.richardson@rafa.org.uk; website: www.rafa.org.uk).

The Royal Armoured Corps War Memorial Benevolent Fund

Eligibility: Ex-members of the disbanded wartime regiments of the Royal Armoured Corps, and their dependants.

Types of grants: One-off grants ranging between £50 and £350 to those in need through no fault of their own. Grants have been given for rent, gas, electricity and water rates arrears; clothing; buying a nebulizer; towards wheelchairs and stairlifts; convalescent holidays (up to 14 days maximum).

No loans. No grants for council tax arrears, funeral expenses, HP debt or bank loans, holidays (apart from the above), nursing or residential home fees, or requests to supplement a state pension with ongoing support.

Annual grant total: In 1998/99 the fund had assets of £1.1 million and an income of £50,000. Total expenditure was £44,000 with 83 grants being awarded totalling £18,000.

Applications: On a form available from the correspondent, to be submitted through SSAFA Forces Help or Royal British Legion. Applications are considered at any time. The name of the individual regiment in which the applicant served must be included. To enter RAC is not sufficient as all existing armoured regiments have their own regimental funds.

Correspondent: Secretary, c/o RHQ RTR, Stanley Barracks, Bovington, Dorset BH20 6JA (01929 403331; Fax: 01929 403488).

Other information: The Royal Armoured Corps is taken to include all cavalry, yeomanry, Royal Tank Regiment, reconnaissance corps, numbered RAC regiments and miscellaneous units of the RAC. Applications should specify the particular regiment or unit in which the applicant served.

The Royal Army Medical Corps Charitable Fund 1992

Eligibility: Members and former members of the Royal Army Medical Corps, and their dependants.

Types of grants: One-off and recurrent grants ranging from £100 to £2,000. Grants can go towards clothing, debts, household maintenance, fuel costs, household items, nursing/residential home fees, funeral costs, medical items, holidays, hospices and weekly supplementary grants and mobility items. Grants are not given towards debts or arrears owed to government bodies (such as rates).

Annual grant total: In 2001 the fund had assets of £3.2 million and an income of £205,000. Total expenditure was £140,000 with over 400 grants being awarded totalling £80,000.

Applications: On a form available from the correspondent and with confirmation of service in Royal Army Medical Corps. Applications are considered daily and must be submitted through SSAFA Forces Help or the Royal British Legion. The trustees meet monthly to consider grants, although the secretary can decide on applications for less than £400 on the day they arrive.

Correspondent: Lt Col (Retd) TA Reeves, RHQ RAMC, HQ Arms, Slim Road, Camberley GU15 4NP (01276 412752;

Fax: 01276 412793;
e-mail: ramc_assoc@hotmail.com).

The Royal Army Service Corps & Royal Corps of Transport Benevolent Fund

Eligibility: People in need who have at any time served in or with the former RASC or the former RCT, including people who so served and are now serving in the Royal Logistics Corp, and also members of the women's services and the dependants of any of the above, who are in need.

Types of grants: One-off grants according to need. Grants range from £50 to £500, and averaged £270 in 2000. No grants for repayment of general debts or loans with finance companies, banks, credit card companies or individuals. Applications for funeral expenses, convalescence, holidays, clothing, telephone aids and house repairs are only given in exceptional circumstances. For assistance with wheelchairs, telephone installation, alterations and repairs to property and stairlifts, further details for application are available from the correspondent.

Annual grant total: In 2000 the fund had assets of £10 million, an income of £476,000 and a total expenditure of £378,000. Grants to 1,032 individuals totalled £280,000, with a success rate for applicants of over 80%. A grant of £45,000 was made to Army Benevolent Fund.

Applications: On a form (RBL/SSAFA Form A 2001), through a SSAFA Forces Help caseworker, Royal British Legion or other welfare organisation (never directly by the individual). Grants will be given via the organisation that sponsored the applicant rather than directly to the individual.

Correspondent: Lt Col M J B Graham, Controller, RASC/RCT Association, Dettengen House, The Princess Royal Barracks, Deepcut, Camberley, Surrey GU16 6RW (Tel & Fax: 01252 833391; website: www.army-rlc.co.uk/rct_ass).

Royal Artillery Charitable Fund

Eligibility: Serving and ex-serving members of the Royal Regiment of Artillery and their dependants.

Types of grants: One-off and recurrent grants of £250 to £700 for essential needs such as household items, white goods and debts such as rent, water rates, electricity, gas and council tax.

No grants are made towards income tax, credit cards, loans, mortgages or legal fees.

Annual grant total: In 2001 the trust had assets of £12 million and both an income and a total expenditure of £1 million. Grants to 3,000 individuals in need totalled £750,000.

Applications: In writing to SSAFA Forces Help. Applications can also be made to the Royal British Legion in England and Wales or to Earl Haig Fund in Scotland (see Scotland section of this guide). Applications can be considered at any time.

Correspondent: The Welfare Secretary, Front Parade, Royal Artillery Barracks, Woolwich, London SE18 4BH (020 8781 3004; Fax: 020 8654 3617; e-mail: welfsec.rhqra@army.mod.uk.net).

The Royal British Legion

Eligibility: Serving and ex-serving members of the armed forces and their wives, widows, children and other dependants in England, Wales and Northern Ireland (for Scotland see the entry for the Earl Haig Fund [Scotland] in the Scotland section of the guide).

Types of grants: Grants can be given for any purpose within the scope of the Royal Charter.

In 2000/01 grants were broken down as follows: individual welfare cases (27,430 grants totalling £6.9 million), permanently incapacitated and widows (398 grants totalling £103,000), holidays for people who are severely disabled (229 grants totalling £139,000), rest and convalescence (35 grants totalling £14,000) and Polish ex-service personnel (960 grants totalling £192,000).

Annual grant total: In 2000/01 the legion had assets of £125 million, an income of £55 million and a total expenditure of £48 million. Welfare grants to 29,000 individuals totalled £7.4 million. Grants to service charities totalled £1.8 million.

Applications: Individual applications to any local branch or the county field officers. A local telephone number for an initial enquiry can usually be found in any telephone directory.

Correspondent: Head of Benevolent Department, 48 Pall Mall, London SW1Y 5JY (Telephone Legionline on 0845 772 5725. Tel: 020 7973 7200; Fax: 020 7973 7399; website: www.britishlegion.org.uk).

Other information: The Royal British Legion, one of the largest providers of charitable help for individuals in the country, is financed mainly by gifts from individuals, especially through its annual Poppy Day collection.

The Legion provides a comprehensive service for advising and helping all ex-servicemen and women and their dependants (though for ex-service women, wives, widows and dependants, see also the entry for Royal British Legion Womens Section). Direct financial assistance is but one aspect of this work. There are over 3,000 branches of the Legion, all of which can act as centres for organising whatever help the circumstances may require. The support of the Legion is available to all who served in the forces, whether in war or peace-time, as regulars or national-servicemen.

Most charities for ex-servicemen and women co-operate together in their work and the British Legion may also be approached through other service organisations, and vice versa.

There is a Property Repair Loan Scheme aimed at retired applicants or those who are disabled and cannot work to enable major property repairs to be completed. The maximum loan is £5,000 and interest is charged at 5% a year.

The Legion has seven homes for elderly or disabled people housing about 60 people in each and three rest homes to give a fortnight's break to those who have been ill/bereaved, or to relieve carers for 2 to 3 weeks of caring for very disabled ex-service people or widows/widowers.

Lifeline Alarm Units are available to certain categories of people who are medically in need but wish to retain independence by staying in their own homes and to give a fortnight's holiday to those who are too sick or disabled to stay at the British Legion's own homes.

The Royal British Legion Women's Section

Eligibility: Ex-servicewomen and the widows of ex-servicemen who are living in England, Wales and Northern Ireland and the Republic of Ireland. (For Scotland see the entry for the Earl Haig Fund (Scotland) in the Scotland General Section of the book.)

Types of grants: Grants are awarded for necessary items such as heating bills, clothing, lifelines, white goods, bedding and other household items. Annuities of £10 a week may be granted to women on low incomes or in real hardship owing to age, ill health or other difficulties. Support for periods of rest and convalescence may be granted for up to two weeks due to pre or post-hospitalisation, terminal illness, following a bereavement or any other exceptional case.

Annual grant total: In 2000/01 the trust's income was £980,000 and it had assets of £3.9 million. Total expenditure was £968,000.

Applications: Initial enquiry should be by telephone requesting a visit by a welfare visitor who will submit an application form, which includes a financial statement. Welfare grants are considered daily; allowances are considered four times a year.

Correspondent: Christine George, Welfare Advisor, 48 Pall Mall, London SW1Y 5JY (020 7973 7225; Fax: 020 7839 7917).

Other information: The Women's Section is an autonomous organisation within the Royal British Legion, concentrating on the needs of ex-servicewomen, widows of ex-servicemen and dependent children of ex-service personnel. It works in close association with the Legion but has its own funds and its own local welfare visitors.

Royal Military Police Central Benevolent Fund

Eligibility: People who are serving or have served in the Royal Military Police corps, or any of its predecessors, and their dependants.

Types of grants: One-off grants of £300 to £500 towards heating, funeral expenses, household furniture, debts, clothing and bedding, mobility aids, holidays, medical needs, special chairs, removals and other needs.

Annual grant total: In 1999/2000 the fund had assets of £2.2 million, an income of £227,000 and a total expenditure of £198,000. Grants totalled £192,000, with £94,000 going to individuals and the rest to service charities.

Applications: In writing to the correspondent. Applications must be made through Royal British Legion or SSAFA Forces Help.

Correspondent: Lt Col P H M Squier, Secretary, RHQ-RMP, Roussillon Barracks, Chichester, Sussex PO19 6BL (01243 534237; Fax: 01243 534288; e-mail: cbf@rhqrmp.freeserve.co.uk; website: www.rhqrmp.freeserve.co.uk).

The Royal Naval Benevolent Society for Officers

Eligibility: Officers, both active service and retired, of the Royal Navy, Royal Marines and QARNNS and their respective reserves, of the equivalent rank of Sub-Lieutenant RN and above, and their spouses, former spouses, families and dependants. There are no age limits.

Types of grants: Block grants to augment inadequate incomes or to meet specific unforeseen expenses. Grants have been given to help with: repairing houses; with car maintenance; removal costs; and nursing home fees. Education grants may be given to complete a particular stage of a child's education (not school fees).

The standard grant for a member of the society or his dependant is £3,900 a year paid in two six-monthly grants. The standard grant for an officer who is not a member (or his dependant) is £1,300 a year paid in two six-monthly grants of £650. The trust states that its object is to assist with the needs of the applicant and its grants are tailored accordingly.

Annual grant total: In 2001 the society had assets of £4.1 million and an income of £310,000. Total expenditure was £290,000, of which £180,000 was given in total in 225 grants.

Applications: On a form available from the correspondent. Applications can be submitted either directly by the individual, or through a third party e.g. a social worker or citizen's advice bureau. Applications are considered monthly.

Correspondent: Cmdr W K Ridley, Secretary, 1 Fleet Street, London EC4Y 1BD (Tel & Fax: 020 7427 7471; e-mail: rnbso@lineone.net).

Other information: The society was founded on 16 May 1739 by a group of naval officers suffering from unreasonable treatment by the admiralty. The benevolent function of the society emerged later and became its sole purpose in 1791.

Royal Naval Benevolent Trust

Eligibility: Serving and ex-serving men and women of the Royal Navy and Royal Marines (not officers) and their dependants.

Types of grants: Recurrent grants of £100 a quarter to older people and one-off grants towards a variety of needs, including rent and mortgage payments, food, clothing, fuel, childcare, medical treatment, disability aids, respite and recuperative holidays, household goods and repairs, removal expenses, debts and training for a second career.

Annual grant total: In 2000/01 the trust had assets of £31 million and both an income and a total expenditure of £3.4 million. Grants to 5,200 individuals totalled £2.1 million. Grants to organisations totalled £20,000.

Applications: On a form available from the correspondent, to be submitted through a social worker, welfare agency, SSAFA Forces Help, Royal British Legion or any Royal Naval Association branch. Applications are considered twice a week.

Correspondent: The Welfare Controller, Castaway House, 311 Twyford Avenue, Portsmouth PO2 8PE (023 9266 0296; Fax: 023 9266 0852; e-mail: rnbt@rnbt.org.uk; website: www.rnbt.org.uk).

Other information: The trust pays 1,050 annuities of up to £8 a week to elderly beneficiaries. These are called Jellicoe (Greenwich Hospital) Annuities. They cost about £437,000 a year.

The trust also runs a residential and nursing home for elderly ex-naval men (not women) namely, Pembroke House, Oxford Road, Gillingham, Kent.

The Royal Naval Reserve (V) Benevolent Fund

Eligibility: Members or former members of the Royal Naval Volunteer Reserve, Women's Royal Naval Volunteer Reserve, Royal Naval Reserve and the Women's Royal Naval Reserve, who are serving or have served as non-commissioned rates. The fund also caters for wives, widows and young children of the above.

Types of grants: One-off grants only, ranging from £50 to £350. Grants have been given for gas, electricity, removal expenses (i.e. to be near children/following divorce); clothing; travel to visit sick relatives or for treatment; essential furniture and domestic equipment; help on bereavement. Schoolchildren from poor families may very occasionally receive help for clothes, books or necessary educational visits, and help can also go to eligible children with aptitudes or disabilities which need special provision.

Annual grant total: In 2000/01 the trust had assets of £101,000, an income of £11,000 and a total expenditure of £2,300. Welfare grants to six individuals totalled £2,200.

Applications: In writing to the correspondent directly by the individual or through the local reserve division, Royal British Legion, SSAFA Forces Help or Royal Naval Benevolent Trust, which investigates applications.

Correspondent: Commander J M D Curteis, Hon. Secretary and Treasurer, The Cottage, St Hilary, Cowbridge, Vale of Glamorgan CF71 7DP (01446 771108; Fax: 01446 771109; e-mail: john.curteis@virgin.net).

The Royal Patriotic Fund Corporation

Eligibility: Widows, orphans and dependants of officers and men of the armed forces. Applicants are usually but not always over 60.

Types of grants: Quarterly allowances and one-off grants to meet specific needs. The corporation also provides televisions and/ or licences. Grants range from £50 to £500.

Annual grant total: In 2001 allowances totalled £197,000 and grants totalled £24,000.

Applications: Normally through services welfare organisations, social services departments or a similar body. Applications are considered fortnightly.

Correspondent: Col R Sandy, 40 Queen Anne's Gate, London SW1H 9AP (020 7233 1894; Fax: 020 7223 1799).

Royal Pioneer Corps Association

Eligibility: Serving Pioneer Services RLC and ex-serving Pioneers and their dependants who are under 18 who are in need.

Types of grants: Grants for a wide range of needs, on average of £230. The trust usually helps with clothing and bedding, fuel, utilities, household items and mobility. Normally no grants are given to pay off debts.

Annual grant total: £120,000 to 670 individuals.

Applications: People should apply on a form through SSAFA Forces Help, Royal British Legion, War Pensions Welfare Agency or a similar body. They are considered throughout the year. No applications should be made direct to the secretary.

Correspondent: Major G F Crook, Secretary, 51 St George's Drive, London SW1V 4DE (020 7834 0415; Fax: 020 7828 5860).

The Royal Signals Benevolent Fund

Eligibility: Members and former members of the Royal Signals, regular or territorial volunteer reserve, and their widows and other dependants.

Types of grants: One-off and recurrent grants according to need. Grants are given towards fuel and lighting costs, funeral expenses, domestic and medical appliances, convalescence, nursing home top-up fees, supplementary and Christmas allowances. No loans are made.

Annual grant total: In 2000 the fund supported 1,020 individuals, donating £335,000 in total. It also gave a total of £30,000 to service charities.

Applications: Applications should be made through SSAFA Forces Help or another charitable organisation, and are considered as required.

Correspondent: The Welfare Secretary, RHQ Royal Signals, Blandford Camp, Dorset DT11 8RH (01258 482081; Fax: 01258 482084; e-mail: rhq@rsignals.net).

SSAFA Forces Help

Eligibility: Service and ex-service men and women and their families in need.

Types of grants: Financial help is normally available to meet a specific and immediate problem, such as wheelchair, scooters, holidays, debts and so on. SSAFA Forces Help caseworkers always visit clients and either help directly or through other organisations.

Annual grant total: In 2000 the trust had assets of £30 million and an income of £31 million. Grants to individuals for welfare and education purposes totalled £330,000. A further £12 million was distributed on behalf of other charities.

Applications: Contact should normally be made by letter direct to the honorary secretary of the local branch. The appropriate address can usually be obtained from the citizen's advice bureau, the local telephone directory (under SSAFA Forces Help) and most main post offices. In case of difficulty, the local address can be obtained from the central office below.

Correspondent: Director of Welfare and Housing, 19 Queen Elizabeth Street, London SE1 2LP (020 7403 8783; Fax: 020 7403 8815; website: www.ssafa.org.uk).

Other information: SSAFA Forces Help operates throughout the British Isles and in garrisons and stations overseas. It is devoted to the welfare of the families of service and ex-service men and women.

All SSAFA Forces Help branches are empowered to give immediate help without reference to higher committees. Also, because of their unique coverage of the UK and Ireland, they act as agents for service and other associated funds. There are about 7,000 voluntary workers in the UK.

SSAFA Forces Help maintains a residential home on the Isle of Wight for older ex-service personnel and their dependants. Eligible men and women can be accepted from any part of the UK.

SSAFA Forces Help also maintains cottage homes for ex-service men and women and their spouses, some purpose-built for severely disabled people, for which residents pay no rent but make a modest maintenance payment. There are also short-stay apartments in the Isle of Wight providing recuperation and respite holidays for disabled ex-service men and women and their carers.

St Andrew's Scottish Soldiers Club Fund

Eligibility: Serving and ex-serving Scottish soldiers in need. Dependants of Scottish soldiers at their time of death may be considered.

Types of grants: One-off grants according to need.

Annual grant total: In 1998/99 the fund had assets of £88,000 and an income of £5,200. Total expenditure was £5,300 with 18 grants being given totalling £5,000.

Applications: In writing to the correspondent. Applications must be submitted through SSAFA Forces Help or Royal British Legion. Applications are considered monthly.

Correspondent: The Chief Executive, 37 King Street, Covent Garden, London WC2E 8JS (020 7240 3718; Fax: 020 7497 0184).

St Dunstan's

Eligibility: Ex-service men and women who are blind, irrespective of the cause of their loss of sight. Applicants must be ex-service personnel and meet St Dunstan's ophthalmic criteria.

Types of grants: Grants to allow applicants to develop their independence by a combination of training, rehabilitation, holiday and respite care. Grants are provided according to need once an applicant has become a beneficiary of St Dunstan's.

Annual grant total: In 1999/2000 the charity had assets of £116 million, an income of £14 million and a total expenditure of £12 million. General welfare, including grants and technical, medical and welfare visits, totalled £2.9 million.

Applications: On a form available from the correspondent, with details of which of the services the applicant belonged to, service number, dates of service and details of opthalmic physician.

Correspondent: The Head of Admissions, 12-14 Harcourt Street, London W1A 4XB (020 7723 5021; Fax: 020 7262 6199).

Other information: St Dunstan's provides lifelong aftercare to its beneficiaries and dependants. Its rehabilitation, training, nursing, residential and holiday centre is in Ovingdean – Brighton.

The Joint Committee of St John & Red Cross

Eligibility: People who have been disabled in war, particularly those disabled in the two world wars and subsequent recognised conflicts such as the Korean War. Also eligible are: ex-service personnel who are in receipt of War Disability Pensions; widows of people disabled in war; ex-members of HM Forces nursing services who are sick or elderly; and officers and members of VADs of the Red Cross and St John Ambulance who served people wounded in war.

Types of grants: Grants according to need.

Annual grant total: In 2000/01 the trust had assets of £6.3 million, an income of £928,000 and a total expenditure of £1.6 million. Grants to individuals totalled £260,000. Grants to organisations totalled £400,000.

Applications: Applications are made through the War Pensioners Welfare Service, Royal British Legion or similar organisations.

Correspondent: R S Aspinwall, Deputy Secretary, St John & Red Cross Joint Committee, 5 Grosvenor Crescent, London SW1X 7EH (020 7201 5130/5131; Fax: 020 7235 9350; e-mail: balwinder@jointcommittee.freeserve.co.uk).

Tancred's Charity for Pensioners

See entry on page 60

The WRNS Benevolent Trust

Eligibility: Ex-Wrens and female serving members of the Royal Navy (officers and ratings) who joined the service between 1 September 1939 and 1 November 1993 who are in need. People who deserted from the service are not eligible.

Types of grants: Recurrent grants of £130 a quarter for people of pensionable age who are living on a low income. These grants may also be awarded to younger people in exceptional circumstances. Amenity grants of £100 are made in June and December and £40 Christmas bonuses dependent on need, with an extra £25 per child being added to the Christmas bonus for parents of children of school age or below. There is also provision for recurrent grants to assist with telephone helpline rental and TV licences.

One-off grants are also available towards needs such as debts and arrears, household goods, medical aids, household repairs, funeral expenses, convalescent care, medical expenses, travel fares, education, removal costs, clothing and food.

Annual grant total: In 2001 the trust had assets of £2.6 million and an income of £293,000. Grants to 592 individuals totalled £209,000.

Applications: On a form, such as a SSAFA Form A, to be submitted by SSAFA Forces Help, Royal British Legion or other welfare organisation. Applications are considered twice monthly and must include full details of applicant and partner, children, financial details, debts, civilian employment, previous assistance, other charities approached and information on why help is needed. These details are important as often the funding arranged is a combined effort between various charities, and in cases where the application is above a certain limit, help is sought from other charities to meet the full amount required. Each and every case is taken on its own merits, and in 2001 out of 618 applications only 26 were turned down due to high incomes or savings.

Correspondent: Mrs Sheila Tarabella, General Secretary, 311 Twyford Avenue, Portsmouth, Hampshire PO2 8PE (023 9265 5301; Fax: 023 9267 9040; e-mail: wrnsbt@care4free.net).

SERVICE AND REGIMENTAL FUNDS

ROYAL NAVY AND ROYAL MARINES

Qarnns Trust Fund
Matron-in-Chief, QARNNS, Room 129, Victory Building, HM Naval Base, Portsmouth PO1 3LS (023 9272 7815).

Royal Marines Benevolent Fund
RM Corps Secretary, HMS Excellent, Whale Island, Portsmouth PO2 8ER (023 9265 1304; Fax: 023 9254 7207).

Royal Naval Association
82 Chelsea Manor Street, London SW3 5QJ (020 7352 6764; Fax: 020 7352 6764).

MERCHANT NAVY

Merchant Navy Welfare Board
19–21 Lancaster Gate, London W2 3LN (020 7723 3642; Fax: 020 7723 3643).

Royal Alfred Seafarers Society
SBC House, Restmor Way, Wallington SM6 7AH (020 8401 2889; Fax: 020 8401 2592).

ROYAL AIR FORCE

Princess Mary's Royal Air Force Nursing Services (PMRAFNS) Trust
Secretary, PMRAFNS Trust, HQ P&TC, Room G93, RAF Innsworth, Gloucester GL3 1EZ (01452 712612 ext. 5811; Fax: 01452 712612 ext. 5977).

Royal Air Force and Dependants Disabled Holiday Trust
BEM, 57 Junction Road, Ashford TW15 1NJ (01784 251968).

Royal Air Forces Ex-POW Association Charitable Fund
c/o Welfare Officer, Mill House, Great Bedwyn, Marlborough, Wiltshire SN8 3LY (01672 870529).

Royal Observer Corps Benevolent Fund
Dr H J G Dartnall, Copper Beeches, 76 Lewes Road, Ditchling, Hassocks BN6 8TY (01273 843237; Fax: 01273 841339).

ARMY

The Adjutant General's Corps Regiment Association
RHQ AGC, Gould House, Worthy Down, Winchester SO21 2RG (01962 887254; Fax: 01962 887690).

Argyll and Sutherland Highlanders' Regimental Association
RHQ A&SH, The Castle, Stirling FK8 1EH (01786 475165; Fax: 01786 446038).

Army Air Corps Fund (post Sept 1957)
RHQ AAC, HQDAAVV, Middle Wallop, Stockbridge, Hampshire SO20 8DY (01980 674426; Fax: 01980 674163).

Army Air Corps (Parachute Regiment and Glider Pilot Regiment) pre-1957
See Airborne Forces Security Fund on page 71

Army Cycle Corps
Applications should be forwarded directly to the Army Benevolent Fund – see entry on page 72.

Army Physical Training Corps Association
Army School of PT, HQ & Depot APTC, Fox Lines, Queen's Avenue, Aldershot GU11 2LB (01252 347131; Fax: 01252 340785).

Artists' Rifles Aid Fund
Leighton House, Regents Park Barracks, London NW1 4AL (01206 738273).

Ayreshire Yeomanry Charitable Trust
c/o D & J Dunlop Solicitors, 2 Barns Street, Ayr KA7 1XD (01292 264091).

Bedfordshire and Hertfordshire Regiment Association
Area HQ The Royal Anglian Regiment, Blenheim, Eagle Way, Warley, Brentwood CM13 3BN (Tel & Fax: 01227 213051).

Berkshire Regiment
(see Royal Gloucestershire, Berkshire & Wiltshire Regiment Association).

Berkshire and Westminster Dragoons Association
(see Westminster Dragoons Association).

Black Horse Association (7th Dragoon Guards)
(see Royal Dragoon Guards Benvolent Fund).

Blues and Royals Association
Combermere Barracks, Windsor, Berkshire SL4 3DN (01753 755297; Fax: 01753 755161).

Border Regimental Benevolent Fund
(see King's Own Royal Border Regimental Association).

Brecknockshire Regiment
(see Royal Regiment of Wales Benevolent Fund).

Buckinghamshire, Berkshire & Oxfordshire Yeomanry and Artillery Trust
Walnut Orchid, Chearsley, Aylesbury, Buckinghamshire HP18 0DA (Tel & Fax: 01844 201893).

Buffs Benevolent Fund
(see Queen's Own Buffs).

Cambridgeshire Regiment Association
HQ Royal Anglian Regiment, Britannia House, TA Centre, 325 Aylsham Road, Norwich NR3 2AD (01603 400290; Fax: 01603 401879).

Cameronians (Scottish Rifles) Benevolent Association
c/o Regimental HQ, The King's Own Scottish Borderers, The Barracks, Berwick-upon-Tweed, Northumberland TD15 1DG (01289 307426; Fax: 01289 331928).

Cheshire Regiment Association
RHQ, The Castle, Grosvenor Street, Chester CH1 2DN (01244 327617; Fax: 01244 401700).

Cheshire Yeomanry Association Benevolent Fund
Bowend, 3 Larchfields, Saughall, Chester CH1 6BU (01244 881037).

City of Glasgow Regiment
(see Royal Highland Fusiliers).

Coldstream Guards Association
RHQ Coldstream Guards, Wellington Barracks, Birdcage Walk, London SW1E 6HQ (020 7414 3246/3262; Fax: 020 7414 3444).

Connaught Rangers Association
Applications should be forwarded directly to the Army Benevolent Fund, see page 72.

Constable's Fund
(See Yeomanry Warders).

Corps of Army Music Trust
HQ Army Music, Kneller Hall, Twickenham TW2 7DU (020 8744 8642; Fax: 020 8893 8668).

County of London Yeomanry (3rd/4th) (Sharpshooters)
(see Yeomanry Benevolent Fund).

Derbyshire Yeomanry Old Comrades Association
50 Whitehurst Street, Allenton, Derby DE24 8LG (01332 343045).

Devonshire and Dorset Regiment Association
Wyvern Barracks, Exeter, Devon EX2 6AE (01392 492435/6; Fax: 01392 492469).

Devonshire Regiment Old Comrades' Association
(see Devonshire & Dorset Regiment Association).

Dorset Regiment Old Comrades Association
(See Devonshire and Dorset Regiment Association).

Dragoon Guards
1st Queen's Dragoon Guards Regimental Association Benevolent Fund, Maindy Barracks, Whitechurch Road, Cardiff CF4 3YE (029 2078 1213/1227; Fax: 029 2078 1344).

1st King's (see 1st Queen's above)

2nd (Queen's Bays) (see 1st Queen's above)

3rd Carabiniers (Prince of Wales's Dragoon Guards) (see Royal Scots Dragoon Guards)

4th/7th (see Royal Dragoon Guards Benevolent Fund)

SERVICE & EX-SERVICE CHARITIES

5th Royal Inniskilling Dragoon Guards (see Royal Dragoon Guards)

1st Royal (see Blues and Royals)

2nd Royal Scots Greys (see Royal Scots Dragoon Guards)

3rd Dragoon Guards (see Royal Scots Dragoon Guards)

6th Dragoon Guards (see Royal Scots Dragoon Guards)

22nd Dragoon Guards (see Royal Armoured Corps War Memorial Fund, page 76)

25th Dragoon Guards (see Royal Scots Dragoon Guards)

Westminster Dragoons (see Westminster Dragoons).

Duke of Albany's Seaforth Highlanders
(see Seaforth Highlanders).

Duke of Cambridge's Own Middlesex Regiment
(see Middlesex Regiment).

Duke of Cornwall's Light Infantry Association
Light Infantry Office (Cornwall), The Keep, Victoria Barracks, Bodmin PL31 1EG (Tel & Fax: 01208 72810).

Duke of Edinburgh's Royal Regiment Association (Berkshire & Wiltshire)
(see Royal Gloucestershire, Berkshire & Wiltshire Regiment Association).

Duke of Wellington's (West Riding) Regimental Association
RHQ DWR, Wellesley Park, Highroad Well, Halifax, West Yorkshire HX2 0BA (01422 361671; Fax: 01422 341136).

Durham Light Infantry Charitable Fund
(see Light Infantry Benevolent Association).

East Anglian Regiments
(see Royal Anglian Regiment).

East Kent Regiment
(see Queen's Own Buffs).

East Lancashire Regiment Benevolent Fund
(See Queen's Lancashire Regiment).

East Surrey Regiment
(see Queen's Royal Surrey Regiment).

East Yorkshire Regimental Association
(see Prince of Wales's Own [West & East Yorks] Regimental Association).

Essex Regiment Association
Area HQ, The Royal Anglian Regiment, Blenheim House, Eagle Way, Warley, Brentwood, Essex CM13 3BN (Tel & Fax: 01277 213051).

Fife and Forfar Yeomanry Association
Yeomanry House, Castlebank Road, Cupar, Fife KY15 4BL (01334 656195).

Fusiliers Aid Society
RHQ, The Royal Regiment of Fusiliers, HM Tower of London, London EC3N 4AB (020 7488 5606/9; Fax: 020 7488 5627).

Glasgow Regiment
(see Royal Highland Fusiliers).

Glider Pilot Regimental Association Benevolent Fund
26 North Quay, Abingdon Marina, Abingdon OX14 5RY (01235 200353; Fax: 01235 204053).

Gloucestershire Regimental Association
(see Royal Gloucestershire, Berkshire & Wiltshire Regiment Association).

Gordon Highlanders' Association
RHQ HLDRS, St Lukes, Viewfield Road, Aberdeen AB15 7XH (01224 313387; Fax: 01224 208652).

Green Howards Benevolent Fund
RHQ The Green Howards, Trinity Church Square, Richmond, North Yorkshire DL10 4QN (01748 822133; Fax: 01748 826561).

Green Jackets 1st, 2nd, 3rd, 43rd & 52nd
(see Riflemen's Aid Society).

Grenadier Guards Association
RHQ Grenadier Guards, Wellington Barracks, Birdcage Walk, London SW1E 6HQ (020 7414 3225/3285; Fax: 020 7222 4309).

Gurkha Brigade Association Trust
c/o HQ Brigade of Gurkhas, Airfield Camp, Netheravon, Salisbury Sp4 9SF (01980 678569; Fax: 01980 678564).

Gurkha Welfare Trust
PO Box 18215, Second Floor, 1 Old Street, London EC1V 9XB (020 7251 5234; Fax: 020 7251 5248).

Hampshire and Isle of Wight Military Aid Fund (1903)
Serles House, Southgate Street, Winchester SO23 9EG (01962 852933; Fax: 01962 883802).

Highland Light Infantry
(see Royal Highland Fusiliers).

Highlanders (Seaforth, Gordons & Camerons) Regimental Association
RHQ HLDRS, Cameron Barracks, Inverness IV2 3XD (Tel & Fax: 01463 224380).

Honourable Artillery Company Benevolent Fund
Armoury House, City Road, London EC1Y 2BQ (020 7382 1543; Fax: 020 7382 1538).

Hussars:
3rd The King's Own (see The Queen's Royal Hussars).

4th Queen's Own Hussars Regimental Association
Capt F R D Holland, 68 Ashley Road, Walton-on-Thames KT12 1HR (Tel & Fax: 01932 231535).

7th Queen's Own (see The Queen's Royal Hussars).

8th King's Royal Irish (see The Queen's Royal Hussars).

The King's Royal Hussars Welfare Fund
c/o Home Headquarters (North), Fulwood Barracks, Preston PR2 8AA (01772 260480; Fax: 01772-260553)

13th/18th Royal (Queen Mary's Own) Aid Fund (see The Light Dragoons Charitable Trust)

15th/19th King's Royal Hussars Regimental Association (see The Light Dragoons Charitable Trust)

The Queen's Own Hussars (see The Queen's Royal Hussars)

Queen's Royal Irish Hussars (see The Queen's Royal Hussars)

19th Royal Hussars Association (see 15th/19th King's Royal Hussars above).

Imperial Yeomanry
(see Yeomanry Benevolent Fund).

Indian Army Association
c/o British Commonwealth Ex-Services League, 48 Pall Mall, London SW1Y 5JY (020 7973 0633 ext. 262).

Inns of Court Regimental Association
10 Stone Buildings, Lincoln's Inn, London WC2 3TG (020 7831 6727).

Intelligence Corps Association
Defence Intelligence and Security Centre, Chicksands, Shefford, Bedfordshire SG17 5PR (01462 752340).

Irish Guards Association
RHQ Irish Guards, Wellington Barracks, Birdcage Walk, London SW1E 6HQ (020 7414 3295; Fax: 020 7414 3446).

King's and Manchester Regiments' Association (Liverpool Branch)
RHQ The King's Regiment, New Zealand House, Water Street, Liverpool L2 8TD (0151 236 6363; Fax: 0151 236 0439).

King's and Manchester Regiments' Association (Manchester Branch)
TA Centre, Ardwick Green, Manchester M12 6HD (0161 273 6191).

King's Own Royal Border Regimental Association
The Castle, Carlisle, Cumbria CA3 8UR (Tel & Fax: 01228 21275).

King's Own Royal Regiment
(see King's Own Royal Border Regimental Association).

King's Own Scottish Borderers Association
RHQ, The Barracks, Berwick-upon-Tweed, Northumberland TD15 1DG (01289 307426; Fax: 01289 331928).

King's Own Yorkshire Light Infantry Regimental Association
Light Infantry Office (Yorkshire), Minden House, Wakefield Road, Pontefract, West Yorkshire WF8 4ES (01977 703181; Fax: 01977 602070).

King's Royal Rifle Corps
(see Riflemen's Aid Society).

SERVICE & EX-SERVICE CHARITIES

King's Shropshire and Herefordshire Light Infantry Association
Light Infantry Office (Shropshire & Herefordshire), Copthorne Barracks, Shrewsbury SY3 8LZ (01743 262425/262430; Fax: 01743 262542).

Labour Corps
Applications should be forwarded directly to the Army Benevolent Fund, see page 72.

Lancashire Fusiliers' Compassionate Fund
Wellington Barracks, Bolton Road, Bury, Lancashire BL8 2PL (0161 761 2680 [Mon & Fri only]; Fax: 0161 764 2208).

Lancashire Regiment (Prince of Wales's Volunteers) Regimental Association
(See Queens Lancashire Regiment).

Lancers:
9th/12th Royal Lancers (Prince of Wales's) Regimental Association
TA Centre, Saffron Road, Wigston, Leicestershire LE18 4UX (0116 275 9577).

16th, 5th, 17th & 21st Lancers (see Queen's Royal Lancers)

16th/5th The Queen's Royal Lancers (see Queen's Royal Lancers).

Leicestershire Regiment
(see Royal Leicestershire Regiment).

Leinster Regiment (for those resident in UK)
Applications should be forwarded directly to the Army Benevolent Fund, see page 72.

The Life Guards Association
Combermere Barracks, Windsor, Berkshire SL4 3DN (01753 755297; Fax: 01753 755161).

Light Dragoons Charitable Trust
All enquiries on behalf of past members of 13th/18th Royal Hussars (Queen Mary's Own), the 15th/19th The King's Royal Hussars and The Light Dragoons should be directed to OC Home HQ, The Light Dragoons, Fenham Barracks, Newcastle upon Tyne NE2 4NP (0191 239 3140/3141/3138; Fax: 0191 239 3139).

Light Infantry Benevolent Association
RHQ The Light Infantry, Peninsula Barracks, Romsey Road, Winchester, Hampshire SO23 8TS (01962 828529; Fax: 01962 828534).

Lincolnshire Regiment
HQ Royal Anglian Regiment, Sobraon Barracks, Lincoln LN1 3PY (01522 525444).

Liverpool Regiment
(see King's and Manchester Regiments Association).

London Irish Rifles Benevolent Fund
Connaught House, 4 Flodden Road, London SE9 9LL (020 8647 5186; Fax: 020 7820 4060).

London Regiment
Applications should be forwarded directly to the Army Benevolent Fund, see page 72.

London Scottish Regiment Benevolent Fund
95 Horseferry Road, London SW1P 2DX (020 7630 1639).

Lothian & Border Regimental Association (1st Lothians & Border Yeomanry, 2nd Lothians & Border Horse)
c/o RHQ RTR, Stanley Barracks, Bovington Camp, Wareham BH20 6JB (01929 403331; Fax: 01929 403488).

Lovat Scouts Regimental Association
c/o W D Johnston & Carmichael, Commerce House, Souh Street, Elgin IV30 1JE (01343 547492; Fax: 01343 548896).

Loyal Regiment (North Lancashire) Regimental and Old Comrades' Association
(See Queens Lancashire Regiment).

Machine Gun Corps Old Comrades Association
Mrs J A Lappin, 305 Frobisher Road, Dolphin Square, London SW1V 3LL (Tel & Fax: 020 7976 5147) (For Heavy Branch Machine Gun Corps see Royal Tank Regiment Association and Benevolent Fund).

Manchester Regiment Aid Society and Benevolent Fund
(see King's and Manchester Regiment Association).

Mercian Volunteers Regimental Association
6 The Village, Kingswinford, West Midlands DY6 8AY (Tel & Fax: 01384 822135).

Middlesex Regiment (Duke of Cambridge's Own) Regimental Association
38 Traps Lane, New Malden, Surrey KT3 4SA (020 8949 7605; Fax: 020 8942 5610).

Military Police
(see Royal Military Police).

Military Provost Staff Corps Association
RHQ, MPSC, Berechurch Hall Camp, Colchester, Essex CO2 9NU (Tel & Fax: 01206 783527).

Monmouthshire Regiment
(see The Royal Regiment of Wales Benevolent Fund).

Norfolk Regiment
(see Royal Norfolk Regiment).

North Lancashire Regiment
(see Loyal Regiment).

North Staffordshire Regiment
(see Staffordshire Regiment).

Northamptonshire Regiment Benevolent Fund
TA Cente, Clare Street, Northampton NN1 3JQ (01604 35412).

Northamptonshire Yeomanry Association (1st and 2nd Regiments)
W J Hornsey, Regimental Secretary, 5 Southview, Kislingbury, Northampton NN7 3AR (01604 831627).

Nottinghamshire and Derbyshire Regiment
(see Worcestershire and Sherwood Foresters).

"Old Contemptibles"
Applications should be forwarded directly to the Army Benevolent Fund see page 72.

Oxfordshire and Buckinghamshire Light Infantry Regimental Association
(see Rifleman's Aid Society).

Oxfordshire Yeomanry Trust
5 (QOOH) Sgn Royal Signals, TA Centre, Oxford Road, Banbury OX16 9AN (01295 262178).

Parachute Regiment
See Airborne Forces Security Fund on page 71.

Post Office Rifles
Applications should be forwarded directly to the Army Benevolent Fund see page 72.

Princess Louise's Kensington Regimental Association
A E Easton, 17 Bowater Close, London NW9 0XD (020 8200 7264).

Prince of Wales Leinster Regiment
c/o Royal British Legion Ireland, 26 South Frederick Street, Dublin 2.

Prince of Wales's Own (West & East Yorkshire) Regimental Association
RHQ PWO, 3 Tower Street, York YO1 1SB (01904 662790; Fax: 01904 658824).

Prince of Wales' Royal Volunteers
(see Queen's Lancashire Regimental Association).

Princess of Wales's Royal Regiment Association and Benevolent Fund
RHQ, PWRR, Howe Barracks, Canterbury, Kent CT1 1JY (01227 818054).

Queen Alexandra's Royal Army Nursing Corps Association
RHQ QARANC, AMS Headquarters, Slim Road, Camberley GU15 4NP (01276 412754; Fax: 01276 412708).

Queen's Bay (2nd Dragoon Guards)
(see Dragoon Guards).

Queen's Bodyguard
(see Yeomen of the Guard and Yeoman Warders).

Queen's Dragoon Guards
(see Dragoons).

Queen's Lancashire Regiment Association
Fulwood Barracks, Preston PR2 4AA (01772 260362; Fax: 01772 260583).

83

Service & Ex-Service Charities

Queen's Own Buffs, The Royal Kent Regiment Benevolent Fund
RHQ, PWRR, Howe Barracks, Canterbury, Kent CT1 1JY
(01227 818052; Fax: 01227 818057).

Queen's Own Cameron Highlanders' Regimental Association
RHQ HLDRS, Cameron Barracks, Inverness IV2 3XD
(Tel & Fax: 01463 224380).

Queen's Own Highlanders (Seaforth and Camerons) Regimental Association
RHQ HLDRS, Cameron Barracks, Inverness IV2 3XD
(Tel & Fax: 01463 224380).

Queen's Own Royal West Kent Regiment Compassionate Fund
(see Queen's Own Buffs).

Queen's Own Yorkshire Dragoons
(see Yeomanry Benevolent Fund).

Queen's Regimental Association
RHQ PWRR, Howe Barracks, Canterbury CT1 1JU
(01227 818054/6; Fax: 01227 818057).

Queen's Royal Hussars (incorporating 3rd The King's Own Hussars, 7th Queen's Own Hussars, 8th King's Royal Irish Hussars, The Queens Own Hussars and Queen's Royal Irish Hussars)
Regent Park Barracks, Albany Street, London NW1 4AL
(020 7414 8717/9; Fax: 020 7414 8700).

Queen's Royal Lancers (incorporating 16th Lancers, 5th Lancers, 17th Lancers, 21st Lancers, 16th/5th The Queen's Royal Lancers, 17th/21st Lancers and The Queen's Royal Lancers)
c/o Regimental Secretary, Home HQ, The Queen's Royal Hussars, Regent's Park Barracks, Albany Street, London NW1 4AL
(020 7414 8717/9; Fax: 020 7414 8700).

Queen's Royal Regiment (West Surrey)
(see Queen's Royal Surrey Regiment).

Queen's Royal Surrey Regiment Regimental Association
RHQ PWRR, Howe Barracks, Canterbury, Kent CT1 1JY (01227 818053).

Reconnaisance Corps
See Royal Armoured Corps on page 76.

Rifle Brigade
(see Riflemen's Aid Society).

Riflemen's Aid Society
RHQ RGJ, Peninsula Barracks, Romsey Road, Winchester, Hampshire SO23 8TS
(01962 8285318; Fax: 01962 828500).
Includes: The Royal Green Jackets, The 43rd/52nd Oxfordshire & Buckinghamshire Light Infantry, The King's Royal Rifle Corps and The Rifle Brigade.

Ross-Shire Buffs, Duke of Albany's Seaforth Highlanders
(see Seaforth Highlanders).

Royal Anglian Regiment Association
The Keep, Gibraltar Barracks, Bury St Edmunds, Suffolk IP33 3RN
(01284 752394; Fax: 01284 752026).

Royal Army Chaplains' Department Centre
Amport House, Amport, Andover, Hampshire SP11 8BG
(01264 773144; Fax: 01276 773401).

Royal Army Dental Corps Association
RHQ RADC, The Former Staff College, London Road, Camberley GU15 4NP
(01276 412753).

Royal Army Educational Corps Association
Worthy Down, Winchester, Hampshire SO21 2RG (Tel & Fax: 01962 887624).

Royal Army Ordnance Corps Charitable Trust
Dettingen House, The Princess Royal Barracks, Deepcut, Camberley, Surrey GU16 6RW (01252 340514/340517).

Royal Army Pay Corps Regimental Association
RHQ, AGC, AGC Centre Worthy Down, Winchester, Hampshire SO21 2RG
(01962 887436; Fax: 01962 887074).
[Note: In cases where any application for help is received from a family of a serving member of the RAPC, it should be made through the Commanding Officer of the Unit in which the soldier is serving. In all other cases, to the Secretary at the above address.]

Royal Army Veterinary Corps Benevolent Fund
RHQ RAVC, c/o The Defence Animal Centre, Melton Mowbray, Leicestershire LE13 0SL
(01664 411811; Fax: 01664 410694).

Royal Berkshire Regiment Old Comrades' Association
(see Royal Gloucestershire, Berkshire & Wiltshire Regiment Association).

Royal Dragoon Guards Association
HHQ, RDG, 3 Tower Street, York YO1 1SB (01904 642036).
(Cases for The Royal Horse Guards, The Royals or The Royal Dragoons should be directed to the Blues and Royals Association.)

Royal Dublin Fusiliers
Applications should be forwarded directly to the Army Benevolent Fund see page 72.

Royal Dublin Fusiliers Old Comrades' Association
T Burke, c/o Civic Museum, South William Street, Dublin 2
(00 353 1706 1177).

Royal East Kent Regiment
(see Queen's Own Buffs).

Royal Engineers Association
RHQ Royal Engineers, Brompton Barracks, Chatham, Kent ME4 4UG
(01634 847005; Fax: 01634 822397).

Royal Fusiliers Aid Society
City of London Headquarters, The Royal Regiment of Fusiliers, HM Tower of London, London EC3N 4AB
(020 7488 5610; Fax: 020 7481 1093).

Royal Gloucestershire, Berkshire & Wiltshire Regiment Association
Gloucestershire: RHQ RGBW, Custom House, 31 Commercial Road, Gloucester GL1 2HE
(01452 5226852; Fax: 01452 311116).
Berkshire and Wiltshire: RHQ RGBW (Salisbury), The Wardrobe, 58 The Close, Salisbury SP1 2EX
(01722 414536; Fax: 01722 421626).

Royal Gloucestershire Hussars
(see Yeomanry Benevolent Fund).

Royal Green Jackets
(see Riflemen's Aid Society).

Royal Hampshire Regiment Comrades' Association
Serles House, Southgate Street, Winchester, Hampshire SO23 9EG
(01962 863658; Fax: 01962 888302).

Royal Highland Fusiliers Regimental Benevolent Association
518 Sauchiehall Street, Glasgow G2 3LW
(0141 332 5639; Fax: 0141 353 1493).

Royal Horse Guards (Blues) Comrades' Association
(see Blues and Royals Association).

5th Royal Inniskilling Dragoon Guards Association
(see Royal Dragoon Guards).

Royal Inniskilling Fusiliers Benevolent Fund
Regimental HQ, The Royal Irish Regiment, St Patrick's Barracks, Ballymena, Co Antrim BFPO 808
(028 2566 1380/2; Fax: 028 2566 1378).

Royal Irish Fusiliers (Princess Victoria's) Regimental Association
The Royal Irish Regiment, St Patrick's Barracks, Ballymena, Co Antrim BFPO 808
(028 2566 1382; Fax: 028 2566 1385).

Royal Irish Rangers Association
RHQ, The Royal Irish Rangers, 5 Waring Street, Belfast BT1 2EW (028 9023 2086).

Royal Irish Regiment Benevolent Fund
Regimental HQ, The Royal Irish Regiment, St Patrick's Barracks, Ballymena, Co Antrim BFPO 808
(028 2566 1380/2; Fax: 028 2566 1385).

Royal Irish Regiment & South Irish Horse Old Comrades' Association
c/o Royal Irish Rangers Association, 5 Waring Street, Belfast BT1 2EW
(028 9023 2086).

Royal Irish Rifles
c/o RHQ The Royal Irish Rangers, 5 Waring Street, Belfast BT1 2EW
(028 9023 2086).

SERVICE & EX-SERVICE CHARITIES

Royal Leicestershire Regiment Royal Tigers Association
TA Centre, Ulverscroft Road, Leicester LE4 6BY (0116 262 2749).

Royal Lincolnshire Regiment Association
Area HQ Royal Anglian Regiment (Lincolnshire), Sobraon Barracks, Lincoln LN1 3PY (01522 544886).

Royal Logistic Corps Association Trust
Regimental Headquarters, Dettingen House, The Princess Royal Barracks, Deepcut, Camberley, Surrey GU16 6RW (01252 833363; Fax: 01252 833375).

Royal Military Academy Sandhurst Band
Applications should be forwarded directly to the Army Benevolent Fund, see page 72.

Royal Munster Fusiliers Charitable Fund
Applications should be forwarded to the Army Benevolent Fund, see page 72.

Royal Norfolk Regimental Association
HQ Royal Anglian Regiment, Britannia House, TA Centre, 325 Aylsham Road, Norwich NR3 2AD
(01603 400290; Fax: 01603 401879).

Royal Northumberland Fusiliers Aid Society and Regimental Association
TA Centre, Lisburn Terrace, Alnwick, Northumberland NE66 1LA
(01665 510211; Fax: 01665 603320).

Royal Regiment of Fusiliers
(see Fusiliers Aid Society).

Royal Regiment of Wales (24th/41st) Benevolent Fund
RHQ The Royal Regiment of Wales, Maindy Barracks, Cardiff CF14 3YE (029 2078 1215).

Royal Scots Benevolent Society
RHQ The Royal Scots (The Royal Regiment), The Castle, Castle Hill, Edinburgh EH1 2YT
(0131 310 5016; Fax: 0131 310 5019).

Royal Scots Dragoon Guards Association (Carabiniers & Greys)
Home HQ, Royal Scots Dragoon Guards, The Castle, Edinburgh EH1 2YT
(0131 310 5102; Fax: 0131 310 5101).

Royal Scots Fusiliers Benevolent Association
(see Royal Highland Fusiliers).

Royal Scots Greys (2nd Dragoons)
(see Royal Scots Dragoon Guards).

Royal Sussex Regimental Association
Roussillon Barracks, Chicester PO19 4BN (01243 530852; Fax: 01243 530852).

Royal Tank Regiment Association and Benevolent Fund
RHQ Royal Tank Regiment, Stanley Barracks, Bovington Camp, Wareham BH20 7JA
(01929 403331; Fax: 01929 403488).

Royal Tigers' Association
(see Royal Leicestershire Regiment).

Royal Ulster Rifles Benevolent Fund
c/o RHQ The Royal Irish Rangers, 5 Waring Street, Belfast BT1 2EW (028 9023 2086).

Royal Warwickshire Regimental Association
RHQ, St John's House, Warwick CV34 4NF (01926 491653).

Royal Welch Fusilier Comrades' Association
RHQ, Hightown Barracks, Wrexham, Clwyd LL13 8RD (01978 264521).

Royal West Kent Regiment
(see Queen's Own Buffs).

Scots Guards Association
Wellington Barracks, Birdcage Walk, London SW1E 6HQ
(020 7414 3321/34; Fax: 020 7414 3445).

Scottish Rifles
see Cameronians (Scottish Rifles).

Seaforth Highlanders' Regimental Association
Cameron Barracks, Inverness IV2 3XD (01463 224380).

Sharpshooters Yeomanry Association (3rd/4th County of London Yeomanry)
10 Stone Buildings, Lincoln's Inn, London WC2A 3TG (020 7831 6727).

Sherwood Foresters
(see Worcestershire & Sherwood Foresters Regimental Welfare and General Charitable Fund).

Sherwood Rangers Yeomanry Regimental Association
20 Millington Road, Cambridge CB3 9HP (Tel & Fax: 01223 302535).

Small Arms School Corps Comrades' Association
HQ SASC, HQ Infantry, Warminster Training Centre, Warminster, Wiltshire BA12 0DJ
(01985 222487; Fax: 01985 222211).

Somerset Light Infantry Regimental Association
Light Infantry Office Somerset, 14 Mount Street, Taunton, Somerset TA1 3QE (01823 333434 ext. 4663/4665; Fax: 01823 351639).

South Lancashire Regiment (Prince of Wales's Volunteers)
c/o RHQ The Queen's Lancashire Regiment, Fulwood Barracks, Preston, Lancashire PR2 4AA
(01772 260362; Fax: 01772 260583).

South Staffordshire Regiment
(see Staffordshire Regiment).

South Wales' Borderers
(see The Royal Regiment of Wales Benevolent Fund).

Special Air Service Regimental Association (Benevolent Fund SAS)
Centre Block, Duke of York's Headquarters, Turks Row, London SW3 4SQ
(020 7414 5317; Fax: 020 7414 5447).

Staffordshire Regiment (Prince of Wales's) Regimental Association
Whittington Barracks, Lichfield, Staffordshire WS14 9PY
(0121 311 3229/3263; Fax: 0121 311 3205).

Staffordshire Yeomanry
(see Yeomanry Benevolent Fund).

Suffolk Regimental Old Comrades Association
HQ Royal Anglian Regiment, Britannia House, TA Centre, 325 Aylsham Road, Norwich NR3 2AD (01603 400290).

Sussex Regiment
(see Royal Sussex Regiment).

Ulster Defence Regiment Benvolent Fund
RHQ The Royal Irish Regiment, St Patrick Barracks, Ballymena BFPO 808
(028 2566 1381/2566 1311).

Welch Regiment
(see The Royal Regiment of Wales Benevolent Fund).

Welsh Guards Association & Benevolent Fund
Maindy Barracks, Whitchurch Road, Cardiff CF4 3YE
(029 2078 1219; Fax: 029 2078 1266).

West Kent Regiment
(see Queen's Own Buffs).

West Riding Regiment
(see Duke of Wellington's).

West Surrey Regiment
(see Queen's Royal Surrey Regiment).

West Yorkshire Regimental Association
(see Prince of Wales's Own – West & East Yorkshire Regimental Association).

Westminster Dragoons Benevolence Sub-Committee *(including The Berkshire & Westminster Dragoons)*
2 Amherst Road, Sevenoaks, Kent TN13 3LS (01732 458877).

Wiltshire Regiment Old Comrades' Association
(see Royal Gloucestershire, Berkshire & Wiltshire Regiment Association).

Women's Royal Army Corps Benevolent Fund
AGC Centre, Worthy Down, Winchester SO21 2RG
(01962 887612/887478/887570; Fax: 01962 887478).

Worcestershire Regiment
(see Worcestershire & Sherwood Foresters Regiment Welfare and General Charitable Fund).

Worcestershire & Sherwood Foresters Regiment Welfare and General Charitable Fund
Worcestershire Area Secretary: Norton Barracks, Worcester WR5 2PA
(01905 354359; Fax: 01905 353871). Nottinghamshire & Derbyshire Area Secretary: Foresters House, Chetwynd

Service & Ex-Service Charities

Barracks, Chilwell, Nottingham NG9 5HA
(0115 946 5415; Fax: 0115 946 5712).

Yeoman of the Guard – Queen's Bodyguard
St James's Palace, London SW1 1BA
(020 7930 3643).

Yeoman Warders
The Constable's Fund, HM Tower of London, London EC3N 4AB
(020 7488 5758; Fax: 020 7480 5543).

Yeomanry Benevolent Fund
10 Stone Buildings, Lincolns Inn, London WC2A 3TG (020 7831 6727) – this fund covers all Yeomanry Regiments except Oxfordshire Yeomanry and Queen's Own Oxfordshire Hussars.

York and Lancaster Regimental Association
Endcliffe Hall, Endcliffe Vale Road, Sheffield S10 3EU
(0114 266 2279; Fax: 01904 668251).

Yorkshire Hussars Regimental Association
(see Yeomanry Benevolent Fund).

Yorkshire Regiment (Alexandra, Princess of Wales's Own)
(see Green Howards).

ALL-SERVICE FUNDS

British Korean Veterans (1981) Relief Fund
D St John Griffiths, Secretary and National Welfare Officer, c/o 44 Lynton Terrace, Rumney, Cardiff CF3 4BS (029 2079 2485).

Requests for financial assistance should be sent to: Peter Crouch, Welfare Officer, B K V (1981) Relief Fund, c/o Royal British Legion, 48 Pall Mall, London SW1Y 5JY (020 7973 7200).

Fund for the relief of distress amongst men and women who served with the British Forces during the Korean Campaign between June 1950 and July 1954, who are holders of, or entitled to, the British Korean Medal or United Nations Medal, their widows and dependants. Each case is treated on its merits. No help can be made towards home fees, annuities or funeral expenses.

Cambridgeshire County Remembrance Fund
Mrs R B Bamford, Hon. Secretary, Vineyard Lodge, Market Place, Ely, Cambridgeshire CB7 4NP (01353 662817).

Grants to alleviate hardship among members of the Armed forces and Merchant Navy who served in World War I and II in the Cambridgeshire Regiment or were at the time of enlistment living in the old county of Cambridgeshire or the Isle of Ely, and their dependants. Application forms are available from the correspondent.

Canadian Veterans' Affairs
Welfare Officer, Department of Veterans' Affairs, Canadian High Commission, MacDonald House, 1 Grosvenor Square, London W1X 0BR (020 7258 6334).

Chindits Old Comrades Association
Capt B K Wilson, Secretary & Welfare Officer, c/o The TA Centre, Wolsley House, Park Lane, Fallings Park, Wolverhampton WV10 9QR
(01902 731841; Fax: 01902 303830).

The aim of the association is to provide and aid (including, in appropriate cases, financial aid) to people who served in Burma with the Chindit Forces in 1943 and 1944, and their widows.

Ex-Service Fellowship Centres
London Relief Centre, 8 Lower Grosvenor Place, London SW1W 0EP
(020 7828 2468; Fax: 020 7630 6784).

Help for ex-service (including ex-merchant service) men, women and dependants in need. Help is available daily and covers: small emergency cash grants, provision of clothing and footwear, food and travel warrants, hostel accommodation for people who are homeless and advice on employment and personal problems. It owns residential care homes for older people in Stepney, East London and in Bexhill-on-Sea, East Sussex which have facilities for people who are disabled and for married couples. It also owns a block of retirement flats in Bexhill.

Ex-Services Mental Welfare Society (Combat Stress)
Tyrwhitt House, Oaklawn Road, Leatherhead KT22 0BX
(01372 841600; Fax: 01372 841601).

The society is the only organisation specialising in helping men and women of all ranks with psychiatric disabilities who have served in the Armed Forces or the Merchant Navy, more particularly those with active or long regular service. Details of the regional offices can be found on the website (www.combatstress.com).

The Far East (Prisoners of War and Internees) Fund
Mrs J Denholm, Secretary, The Laurels, High Street, Child Okeford, Blandford Forum DT11 3EH
(Tel & Fax: 01258 863691).

Handles the cases of Far East prisoner of war and civilian internees only. (The Far East POW Central Welfare Fund at the above address has wider scope.)

Forces Pensions Society
68 South Lambeth Road, London SE8 1RL
(020 7820 9988; Fax: 020 7820 9948).

The fund was formed to help widows of people who served as officers of the Armed Forces of the Crown, who are in need. N.B. Applications should be sent on SSAFA Forces Help Form 9 to the Officers' Association.

Irish Ex-Service Trust
The Secretary, c/o The Benevolent Department, The Royal British Legion, 48 Pall Mall, London SW1Y 5JY
(020 7973 7200; Fax: 020 7973 7360).

This is a general fund for those ex-service persons of the British Armed Forces who are resident in Ireland, and their dependants. It can be approached direct or by asking the regimental fund to forward an application. They prefer to make long-term capital grants but will consider other needs, particularly those cases that might not normally be considered by other trusts/welfare organisations.

National Ex-Prisoners of War Association
99 Parlaunt Road, Langley, Slough SL3 8BE
(Tel & Fax: 01753 818308).

To relieve poverty and sickness among members of all ranks of the forces or nursing services and who during such service were prisoners of war in any theatre of war, and their widows and dependants.

1940 Dunkirk Veterans Association
Royal British Legion, 48 Pall Mall, London SW1Y 5JY
(020 7973 7200; Fax: 020 7973 7360).

Only veterans who are members of the 1940 Dunkirk Veterans Association, and their families, are eligible.

Normandy Veterans Association Benevolent Fund
27d Bilbrook Road, Codsall, Wolverhampton WV8 1EU
(01902 842479).

To give practical help to members, and to dependants of veterans, whose circumstances require it.

Regular Forces Employment Association
Head office: 49 Pall Mall, London SW1Y 5JG
(020 7321 2011; Fax: 020 7839 0970).

This national association, with 40 branches throughout the UK, exists to help men and women leaving the Armed Forces find employment in civil life.

South Atlantic Fund
The fund closed on 31 December 1992.

Residual monies have been handed over in appropriate shares to the Service Benevolent Funds who have given assurances that they will use the money to meet any future needs arising out of the Falklands Conflict for as long as it is necessary. Applications to meet such needs from dependants of those killed, and from those who were either injured in action during Operation Corporate 1982 or have, since the cessation of hostilities, been injured or mentally disabled in circumstances directly attributable to service during the Operations or to later service in the Falkland Islands directly linked to the conflict, should be addressed as follows:

SERVICE & EX-SERVICE CHARITIES

King George's Fund for Sailors
8 Hatherley Street, London SW1P 2YY (020 7932 0000; Fax: 020 7932 0095).

Supports serving and ex-serving RN & RM Officers, all Merchant Navy and Royal Fleet Auxiliary Seafarers including Hong Kong Chinese Seamen, civilians attached to or accompanying the Task Force and the wives, children and other dependants of such people.

Royal Naval Benevolent Trust
Supports serving and ex-serving ratings (or of equivalent rank) of the Royal Navy and Royal Marines, and their dependants. *See page 78.*

Army Benevolent Fund
Supports serving and ex-serving officers and soldiers, and their dependants. Applications in the first instance should be addressed to the appropriate corps or regimental association. *See page 72.*

Royal Air Force Benevolent Fund
Serving and ex-serving members of the RAF, and their dependants. *See page 76.*

Special Forces Benevolent Fund
c/o Roger Dillon, D Group, 13 The Ivory House, St Katherine's Docks, London E1 9AT (020 7480 5652).

Grants and pastoral support to 1939–1945 members of Special Operations Executive, and their dependants.

War Widows Association of Great Britain
Mrs D J Bowles, 11 Chichester Close, Bury St Edmunds IP33 2LZ (0870 2411 305).

The association, formed in 1971 to improve conditions for all service widows and their dependants, works with government departments and service and ex-service organisations to help with all matters of its members' welfare. There are 50 regional organisers. The association does not make grants.

Sickness & disability charities

There are many charities for people with illnesses or disabilities. The entries in this section are only for those which give financial help from their own resources. There are many others which do not have a large enough income to do this but may be the starting point for getting financial help. For this reason we have also printed on page 387 a list of organisations which provide advice and support.

This section starts with an index of sickness or disability. The entries are arranged alphabetically within each category, with those trusts supporting more than one illness or disability listed at the start of the chapter.

Local disability charities, such as Metropolitan Society for the Blind, are not included in this section but are listed in the relevant local section of the book. Northern Irish, Scottish and Welsh disability charities are also listed in the relevant locality rather than in this section.

Index of sickness and disability funds

A
AIDS/HIV   95
Alzheimer's disease   96
Arthritis and rheumatism   96
Ataxia   97

B
Blindness/partial sight   97
Brittle bones   98

C
Cancer and leukaemia   98
Cerebral palsy   99
Cystic fibrosis   99

D
Deafblind   100

H
Haemophilia   100
Huntington's disease   100

K
Kidney disease   100

L
Liver disease   100

M
Meningitis   101
Mental health   101
Motor neurone disease   101
Mucopolysaccharide diseases   101
Multiple sclerosis   101
Muscular dystrophy   102

N
Neurological disease   102

P
Parkinson's disease   102
Polio   103

S
Spina bifida   103
Spinal muscular atrophy   103
Stroke   103

T
Tuberous Sclerosis   103

Sickness & Disability Charities

Aldridge Charitable Trust

Eligibility: Young people under 21 who are physically or mentally disabled and in need.

Types of grants: One-off grants are made to four to six people a year, for example for computers, wheelchairs or special baths.

Annual grant total: In 2000 the trust's income was £9,200 and its total expenditure was £14,000.

Applications: In writing to the correspondent.

Correspondent: Edward Aldridge, Silca House, 32–34 Eagle Wharf Road, London N1 7EB (020 7324 3414).

Frederick Andrew Convalescent Trust

Eligibility: Professional women who are working or retired and are in need of convalescence.

Types of grants: One-off grants for convalescence of up to £750.

Annual grant total: In 2000 the trust had assets of £1.6 million and an income of £54,000. Total expenditure was £50,000, including £40,000 given in grants.

Applications: On a form available from the correspondent, to be submitted directly by the individual or through a social worker, citizen's advice bureau, other welfare agency or other third party.

Correspondent: Mrs D Genders, Clerk to the Trustees, Andrew & Co., St Swithin's Square, Lincoln LN2 1HB (01522 512123; Fax: 01522 546713; e-mail: andsol@enterprise.net).

ASPIRE (Association for Spinal Injury Research Rehabilitation and Reintegration) Human Needs Fund

Eligibility: People in need with a spinal cord injury and people with other disabilities.

Types of grants: One-off grants for the purchase of specialist equipment such as wheelchairs and computers.

Annual grant total: In 2000/01 the trust had both an income and a total expenditure of around £1.4 million. Grants were made to between 25 and 30 individuals, totalling £50,000.

Applications: On a form available from the correspondent, for consideration on an ongoing basis. Guidelines for applicants are available from the correspondent and on the website. Applications can be submitted either directly by the individual or through a third party such as a carer, parent or medical professional.

Correspondent: Kim Boughton, ASPIRE National Training Centre, Wood Lane, Stanmore, Middlesex HA7 4AP (020 8954 5759; Fax: 020 8420 6352; e-mail: info@aspire.org.uk; website: www.aspire.org.uk).

Other information: The charity also provides services for eligible individuals.

The Attlee Foundation

Eligibility: People who are disabled or disadvantaged anywhere in the UK.

Types of grants: One-off grants up to £100 towards travelling costs for therapeutic journeys, for example, to maintain family contacts with members in hospital, prison or rehabilitation a long way from home within the UK.

No grants are given towards funerals, holidays, travel outside the UK, wheelchairs or mobility adaptations.

Annual grant total: About £7,400.

Applications: On a form available from the correspondent. Applications must be made through a social worker, citizen's advice bureau or other welfare agency, to which the cheque will be payable on behalf of the individual. An sae must be enclosed.

Correspondent: Heléna Holt, Attlee House, 28 Commercial Street, London E1 6LR (020 7377 5836; Fax: 020 7377 5831; e-mail: info@attlee.org.uk; website: www.attlee.org.uk).

The Percy Bilton Charity

Eligibility: People who are: disabled; ill and receiving hospital or similar treatment; or aged over 65 and on a low income.

Types of grants: One-off grants of between £50 and £200. The charity stated: 'We consider all requests that are within our criteria, although the assistance given is more suitable for items in the £200 range or lower. If you are seeking a contribution towards larger items please ensure that you have raised at least 75% of the cost before applying to us. We can help with laundry equipment, cookers/microwaves, heating appliances, bedding, essential clothing, telephone installations (not rental), refrigerators, furniture and furnishings, communication aids (e.g. lightwriters), mobility aids and essential car adaptations.'

No grants are given towards: holidays or respite care; educational grants and computer equipment; debts of any kind, including gas, electricity and rent arrears; TV and car licences; nursing fees, respite care, medical treatment or therapy; funeral expenses; recurrent grants; vehicle purchase or deposit; house alterations and maintenance, including disability adaptations; removal expenses; sponsorship or course fees; or people outside the stated criteria.

Annual grant total: In 2000/01 the charity had assets of £18 million and an income of £636,000. Grants to 952 individuals totalled £112,000. Grants to organisations totalled £699,000.

Applications: On a form available from the administrator at the address below, to be submitted by qualified social workers or occupational therapists. Applications are considered weekly and the payment is made to the local, or health, authority and not to the individual. Applications are not accepted directly from individuals or any other agencies.

'We understand that speed of response is important in the case of essential items that are required urgently and our aim is to deal with all applications as quickly as possible. To help us achieve this objective, we would ask that you ensure that the beneficiary meets the charity's criteria and that all necessary information is provided in the application form. We shall be grateful if applications are not made in respect of items with which the charity cannot assist, as they can delay the administration of applications that are within our criteria.'

Correspondent: Mrs W A Fuller, Bilton House, 58 Uxbridge Road, Ealing, London W5 2TL (020 8579 2829; Fax: 020 8567 5459).

The Birchington Convalescent Benefit Fund

Eligibility: Children under the age of 18 who are chronically ill or recovering from surgery or long-term illness.

Types of grants: One-off grants of £100 towards part-payment of convalescent holidays for children. Grants are not given for reasons other than holidays. This includes no grants to allow ill parents to have a break from their children.

Annual grant total: In 2001 grants totalled £1,000.

Applications: In writing to the correspondent at any time. Applications should be made through a third party, for example, a doctor, social worker or hospital staff. Details of the sponsor of the application, type of illness or surgery, financial status and type and cost of holiday needed should be included.

Correspondent: David Phillips, Church Society, Dean Wace House, 16 Rosslyn Road, Watford WD18 0NY (01923 235111; Fax: 01923 800362).

The Margaret Champney Rest & Holiday Fund

Eligibility: Carers, particularly those caring for a severely disabled relative, who need a break away from the person they are caring for.

Types of grants: Generally one-off grants of between £75 and £250. Grants are not available towards 'normal' family holidays.

Annual grant total: In 2001 the fund had assets of £340,000 and an income of £14,000. Total expenditure was £16,000 with 60 awards totalling £12,000.

Applications: In writing to the correspondent, through a social worker or citizen's advice bureau etc. Applications can be considered at any time, and should include full details of weekly income and expenditure, details of other agencies being approached for funding and details of the holiday break and who will care for the person while the break is being taken.

Correspondent: Trevor Last, The Gate House, 9 Burkitt Road, Woodbridge, Suffolk IP12 4JJ (Tel & Fax: 01394 388746; e-mail: ogilviecharities@btconnect.com).

The Adele Chapman Foundation

Eligibility: Children in need experiencing I.N.D. and those undergoing small bowel, liver or pancreas transplants.

Types of grants: The trust provides funds and equipment not normally provided by the health authority. Up to £500 is given initially to each beneficiary in the first year of application; reapplications can be made for grants in subsequent years.

Annual grant total: About six individuals are supported with grants of £500 a year, totalling about £6,000.

Applications: On a form available either from the correspondent, or from Royal Belfast Children's Hospital or Birmingham Children's Hospital.

Correspondent: T Devanny, 69 Windermere Drive, Knottingley, West Yorkshire WF11 0LY (01977 678954; Mobile: 077142 73213; Fax: 01977 678954).

CommunicAbility – The John Powell (UK) Trust

Eligibility: People who are disabled and have communication problems.

Types of grants: Small grants towards equipment to enable communication.

Annual grant total: About £35,000 a year.

Applications: On a form available from the correspondent. All applications must be submitted through or supported by a professional adviser and proof provided that funding was not available from statutory or other sources. Applications are considered every four months. Telephone enquiries for application forms are not welcomed.

Correspondent: Bo Beolens, Director, 18 St Mildreds Road, Cliftonville, Margate, Kent CT9 2LT (website: www.communicability.org.uk).

The Community of the Presentation Trust

Eligibility: People who are disabled or infirm, particularly members of the Christian community. In practice, the trust only supports individuals known to the trustees.

Types of grants: One-off grants of between £250 and £500.

Annual grant total: In 2001 the trust had assets of £1.3 million and an income of £56,000. Grants to seven individuals totalled £2,700. Grants to organisations totalled £58,000.

Applications: Unsolicited applications are not considered.

Correspondent: Michael S MacDonald, 9 The Precincts, Canterbury, Kent CT1 2EE.

Other information: Grants are also given to organisations such as hospices.

The Alfred de Rothschild Charity

Eligibility: People unable to pay in full for medical treatment of a special nature.

Types of grants: Generally one-off grants ranging from £200 to £500, to help with medical and/or convalescent costs, for example, consultant's fees, nebulisers or physiotherapy costs. No grants for treatment outside the UK, or usually for clothing, furniture and so on.

Annual grant total: In 2000/01 the charity had an income of £31,000 and a total expenditure of £16,000.

Applications: On a form available from the correspondent, together with a consultant/doctor's report. Applications are considered every six weeks.

Correspondent: Ms Maggie Pound, Family Welfare Association, 501–505 Kingsland Road, London E8 4AU (020 7254 6251).

The Margaret de Sousa-Deiro Fund

Eligibility: Women who have, or have had, pulmonary tuberculosis or any other disease.

Types of grants: Generally one-off grants of between £100 and £300, depending on circumstances. Grants are restricted to aids for disability, extra comforts, clothing, extra nourishment, convalescent holidays and extra heating. No grants are made for debts or hire purchase liabilities.

Annual grant total: £60,000.

Applications: In writing from social workers, a registered charity or a hospital, providing full name, address, age, total income and expenditure, type of illness and the purpose of the grant.

Correspondent: Mrs K Gyngell, Administrator, PO Box 37900, London SW4 9YB.

The Family Fund Trust

Eligibility: Families who are caring at home for a child under 16 who is severely disabled. Eligible families must have a gross income of no more than £21,000 a year and savings of £8,000 or less. (These figures are for 2002 and are reviewed annually).

Types of grants: The help given must be related to the child's care needs. It may include help with a holiday, leisure activities, laundry equipment, bedding and clothing, transport, play equipment and other items.

The trust cannot provide items which are the responsibility of statutory agencies, such as medical or educational equipment or small items for daily living, such as bath aids, which are the responsibility of social services.

Annual grant total: In 2000/01 the trust helped 107,000 families with grants totalling £23 million. Almost 8,500 families were new applicants.

Applications: Applications can be made by parents or carers or, with parental consent, by a professional worker. An application form is available from the trust or applications can be by letter giving the child's full name and date of birth, and parent's name, address and telephone number. Brief details about the child's disability and how this affects daily life are also needed. Tell the trust what kind of help is being requested and whether an application has been made before (if so, quote the Family Fund Trust number if possible).

Correspondent: The Managing Director, PO Box 50, York YO1 9ZX (01904 621115; Fax: 01904 652625; Minicom: 01904 658085; e-mail: info@familyfundtrust.org.uk; website: www.familyfundtrust.org.uk).

Other information: The trust is funded entirely by the government administrations of England, Northern Ireland, Scotland and Wales, and works within guidelines agreed by the trustees. More information about the Family Fund Trust and a publications list are available from the Information Officer at the above address. This includes 'Introducing the Family Fund Trust' which outlines how the trust works and the guidelines are used.

Each family's application is looked at individually. If it is the first time a family has applied to the Family Fund Trust it is likely that a local visitor will arrange to call and discuss the request. The visitor will then report back to York, where a decision will be made about whether the trust can help.

The trust decides whether a child is 'severely disabled' by considering the child's age, how much his or her abilities are affected and how much care (s)he needs. The trust will ask for details of diagnosis, treatment and expected outcomes of the child's condition. However, it is the effects of these on the family rather than the actual diagnosis that is taken into account.

The Family Fund Trust also produces a number of information sheets: adaptations to housing, bedding and clothing, benefits checklist, equipment for daily living, hearing impairment, holidays, behaviour and attention difficulties and transport and a guide to the opportunities available to young disabled people over sixteen called 'After 16 – What's New?' is available free to young disabled people and their carers (£10 to professional workers). 'Taking Care' is a book for parents and carers based on parents' own experiences of caring for a child with a disability. It is available free to parents and carers (£4 to professional workers) from the address above.

The Farrell Charitable Trust

Eligibility: People who are disabled, including people who are blind, and their families or helpers.

Types of grants: Grants are given for the provision of holidays.

Annual grant total: In 1999/2000 the trust had an income of £6,300 and gave £2,300 to eight individuals, with £5,200 going to organisations.

Applications: In writing to the correspondent.

Correspondent: Mrs P K Farrell Tredinnick, Managing Treasurer, 6 Beaumont Court, Skeyne Drive, Pulborough, West Sussex RH20 2BA (01798 872131).

The David Finnie & Alan Emery Charitable Trust

Eligibility: People with disabilities in the UK who are in need and have exhausted all other avenues for funding, government or otherwise.

Types of grants: One-off grants ranging between £300 and £1,500. Examples of grants given are towards special needs motor vehicles or wheelchairs and help with travelling expenses where visiting a member of a family or where travelling somewhere to receive treatment.

No grants to building work of any nature, religious purposes, overseas projects, household repairs or goods, debt settlement, holidays, funeral expenses, housing deposits, loans or removal expenses.

Annual grant total: In 2000/01 the trust had assets of £2.1 million and an income of £83,000. Total expenditure was £61,000 with £11,000 being given in grants to individuals for welfare and educational purposes. Grants to organisations totalled £39,000.

Applications: Initially, in writing to the correspondent. Applications can be submitted directly by the individual or through a social worker, citizen's advice bureau, other welfare agency or other third party. They are considered in April and October each year, and, if successful, an application form is forwarded for completion.

Correspondent: John A Buck, 4 De Grosmont Close, Abergavenny, Monmouthshire NP7 9JN (01873 851048).

The Fox Memorial Trust

Eligibility: People who are disabled and in need, mainly in the UK.

Types of grants: Grants are normally for disability/mobility equipment, and are usually one-off; also occasionally contributions are made to the costs of holidays for people who are disabled as a means of respite care. Loans are never made.

Annual grant total: In 2000/01 the trust had assets of £1.5 million, an income of £95,000 and a total expenditure of £133,000. Information was not available as to how much was given to individuals in this year. In 1998/99 grants totalled £108,000, including £30,000 to individuals, mostly for educational purposes.

Applications: In writing to the correspondent, either directly by the individual or through a social worker, citizen's advice bureau, or other welfare agency or third party. The letter should be as brief as possible, outlining circumstances, how much has already been raised and from whom, and any other background the applicant feels is relevant.

Correspondent: Mrs C Hardy, Administrator, Hangover House, 3 Burford Lane, East Ewell, Surrey KT17 3EY (020 8393 1222).

Other information: Grants are also made for educational purposes and to a wide variety of charities.

The Megan and Trevor Griffiths Trust

Eligibility: People who are physically or mentally disabled. Preference is given to people living in the former administrative county of Carmarthen (Carmarthenshire and parts of Ceredigion and Pembrokeshire).

Types of grants: One-off grants of up to £200.

Annual grant total: In 2000 the trust had an income of £28,000 and a total expenditure of £22,000. Grants to individuals total about £2,000 a year.

Applications: On a form available from the correspondent.

Correspondent: Janet Griffiths, Secretary, 46 Partridge Road, Roath, Cardiff CF24 3QX.

Other information: The main activity of the trust is to provide respite breaks and holidays for people with disabilities and their carers.

Happy Days Children's Charity

See entry on page 113

The N & P Hartley Memorial Trust

Eligibility: Peopl who are disabled or terminally ill and live in Yorkshire, particularly West Yorkshire.

Types of grants: One-off grants according to need. Recent support has included grants towards specialist equipment for people who are disabled.

Annual grant total: In 2000/01 the trust had assets of £908,000 and an income of £47,000. Its total expenditure was £73,000. Grants were made to individuals and organisations.

Applications: In writing to the correspondent, preferably through a social worker, citizen's advice bureau or other welfare agency, for consideration on an ongoing basis. Reapplications from previous beneficiaries are welcomed.

Correspondent: J E Kirman, Trustee, c/o Monkgate House, 44 Monkgate, York YO61 3AL (01904 341200); Fax: 01904 341201; e-mail: jkirman@garbutt_elliott.co.uk).

Hospital Saturday Fund Charitable Trust

Eligibility: Individuals who live in the UK and the Republic of Ireland who are ill, disabled or receiving medical care.

Types of grants: One-off grants are made ranging from £25 to £250 towards medical care, medical equipment and appliances, and hospital travel. Grants are not made to anything without a medical connection.

Annual grant total: In 2000/01 the trust's income was £139,000 and grants totalled £130,000, including 90 grants to individuals totalling £9,000. Most of these were to people who are disabled or ill, and some were for medical students.

Applications: On a form available from the correspondent. If the application is made directly by the individual, a supporting letter from a welfare agency, social worker or other third party is appreciated. A third party can also apply on behalf of the individual.

Correspondent: K R Bradley, Administrator, 24 Upper Ground, London SE1 9PD (020 7928 6662); Fax: 020 7928 0446; e-mail: trust@hsf.eu.com).

Other information: Grants are also made to medical educational projects, medical charities and medical students taking overseas electives.

The Independent Living (1993) Fund

Eligibility: People between 16 and 65 years of age currently receiving the highest rate care component Disability Living Allowance rate. Applicants must not have savings over £18,500 and should be living alone or with another person who is unable to provide all the care they need, or be planning to move out of residential care.

Types of grants: Payments are of up to £395, provided the local authority firstly agrees to provide a minimum of £200 worth of services per week. They are towards the cost of buying in care to enable the applicant to continue living at home. Help is for people with ongoing needs, not short-term illness. Beneficiaries also have to be capable of living independently in the community for at least six months. The fund cannot help with the cost of any items of equipment or adaptations.

Annual grant total: The budget for 2000/01 is approximately £64 million for Great Britain and £2.5 million to Northern Ireland.

Applications: On a form available from the local authority social work department or the correspondent. Applicants are visited at home by one of the fund's social workers together with the local authority social worker to agree a joint care package to a maximum level of £665 per week.

Correspondent: Ian Lawrence, PO Box 183, Nottingham NG8 3RD (0115 942 8191/2; Fax: 0115 929 3156; e-mail: funds@ilf.org.uk; website: www.ilf.org.uk).

Other information: The old Independent Living Fund has now been split into two separate funds: (i) the Independent Living (extension) Fund which continues to administer payments to the 9,100 existing clients. No new names can be added to this list, and (ii) the Independent Living (1993) Fund which deals with all new claimants since 1993.

Invalids-at-Home

Eligibility: People who are substantially disabled or severely ill and who live at home or who wish to do so. Preference is given to people: with very severe disabilities; living on or just above Income Support level; or on very low incomes. No grants are made to people living in institutional care.

Types of grants: One-off grants towards specific additional costs associated with living at home with a disability, including equipment and emergencies. Grants range between £25 and £400 and priority is given for items directly related to needs arising from the disability or illness, such as wheelchairs, special beds/chairs and heating bills. The trust can only make a grant if adequate statutory provision is provided.

No grants are given towards medical treatment, telephone rental or call charges, televisions, holidays or new motor vehicles. Only one grant per person is given in any 12 months.

Annual grant total: In 2000/01 the trust had assets of £757,000, an income of £265,000 and a total expenditure of £249,000. Grants to 1,300 individuals totalled £207,000.

Applications: On a form available from the correspondent, to be submitted through a social worker, citizen's advice bureau or other welfare body. Applications are considered weekly.

Correspondent: Mary Rose, Executive Officer, Bamford Cottage, South Hill Avenue, Harrow, Middlesex HA1 3PA (020 8864 3818).

The Heinz & Anna Kroch Foundation

Eligibility: People who have a chronic illness and are in financial hardship.

Types of grants: One-off grants have been awarded towards travelling to hospital to visit individuals and towards payment of debts caused by chronic illness.

Annual grant total: In 2000/01 the foundation had assets of £2.1 million, an income of £144,000 and a total expenditure of £133,000. Grants totalled £84,000.

Applications: In writing to the correspondent, to be submitted through a social worker, citizen's advice bureau or a welfare agency. Applications are considered throughout the year, and should include full financial information including income and expenditure.

Correspondent: Mrs Heather Astle, PO Box 5, Bentham, Lancaster LA2 7XA (Tel & Fax: 01524 263001; e-mail: hakf50@hotmail.com).

Other information: This trust also gives money for medical research.

The League of the Helping Hand

Eligibility: People who are mentally or physically disabled and in financial need.

Types of grants: One-off grants ranging from £50 to £250, to help with; moving into the community, furniture replacement, telephone connection, heating costs, convalescent holidays after a stay in hospital, carers breaks, rent and utility arrears, travel to and from hospital, or any equipment not supplied through Health or Social Services.

Recurrent grants are given to regular beneficiaries as quarterly payments of between £65 and £195, as well as providing a small cheque at Christmas, giving £100 towards holidays, providing extra gifts and remembering their birthdays.

Annual grant total: In 2000/01 the trust had assets of £2.2 million and an income of £123,000. Grants totalled £89,000, of which £49,000 was given to 73 regular beneficiaries and £40,000 in 272 one-off grants.

Applications: On a form available from the correspondent, to be submitted through a social worker, carers' support centre, citizen's advice bureau or other welfare body. An sae must be enclosed. Supportive letters accompanying completed forms is not required. The trustees meet monthly to consider applications, although emergency needs can be met more quickly.

Correspondent: Mrs I Goodlad, 226 Petersham Road, Petersham, Richmond, Surrey TW10 7AL (Tel & Fax: 020 8940 7303; e-mail: inga@lhh.org.uk; website: www.lhh.org.uk).

Mobility Trust II

Eligibility: People with physical disabilities.

Types of grants: The trust will provide a piece of mobility equipment, such as wheelchairs or scooters. No cash is given, and grants are not given where the equipment can be purchased through statutory sources.

Annual grant total: In 1998/99 the trust had assets of £105,000 and an income of £84,000. Total expenditure was £46,000 with grants to individuals totalling £39,000.

Applications: On a form available from the correspondent. Applications can be submitted directly by the individual or through a social worker, citizen's advice bureau or other welfare agency. All applications must be countersigned by a social worker or responsible professional. They are usually considered in February, May, August and November.

Powered/manual wheelchairs: No application is considered without an assessment from an occupational therapist or physiotherapist as to the best type of chair, make, model, price and adaptations (if any). If an applicant is in receipt of mobility allowance they should, unless otherwise stated, apply to Motability (see separate entry).

The trust insures any equipment loaned for the first year against fire, theft or accident and in the second year expects the recipient to take over and to include parts in the insurance. The maintenance of the equipment will also be their responsibility, following the manufacturer's warranty period.

Correspondent: Andrew Mackintosh, Administrator, 50 High Street, Hungerford, Berkshire RG17 0NE (01488 686335 [24 hour answerphone]; Fax: 01488 686336).

Motability

Eligibility: People who receive one of the following benefits: higher rate mobility component of Disability Living Allowance; War Pensioners' Mobility Supplement (WPMS); or a government vehicle, trike or mini.

Sickness & Disability Charities

Types of grants: Grants can be given towards 'the least expensive suitable solution that meets basic mobility needs'. These are usually: vehicle advance payments; supplying and fitting adaptations, for instance hand controls to enable somebody with a lower body disability to drive an automatic car or hoists to load electric wheelchairs into estate cars; or driving lessons for people who are disabled, or whose children or spouses are disabled, especially people aged 16 to 24.

Annual grant total: In 2000/01 grants to 6,500 individuals totalled £9 million.

Applications: On a form available from the correspondent, giving social and financial circumstances and providing evidence of need. Applicants may be asked to visit a centre for assessment of transfer ability, give permission for third parties such as doctors to be contacted, and may receive a home visit.

Correspondent: Grants Directorate, Goodman House, Station Approach, Harlow, Essex CM20 2ET (01279 635666; Fax: 01279 632000; Minicom: 01279 632273; website: www.motability.co.uk).

Other information: Some of Motability's funds are administered on behalf of the government.

The Janet Nash Charitable Trust

Eligibility: People who are sick and in need and live in the UK.

Types of grants: One-off and recurrent grants according to need.

Annual grant total: In 1998/99 the trust had an income of £242,000 and grants totalled £266,000, comprised of £170,000 to individuals and £96,000 to organisations.

Applications: In writing to the correspondent. The trustees meet monthly.

Correspondent: R Gulliver, Trustee, Ron Gulliver and Co. Ltd, The Old Chapel, New Mill, Eversley, Hampshire RG27 0RA (0118 973 0300).

The National Association for Colitis and Crohn's Disease

Eligibility: People in need who have ulcerative colitis, Crohn's Disease or related inflammatory bowel diseases, or their carers.

Types of grants: One-off grants to meet special needs which have arisen as a direct result of their illness. Needs considered are, for instance, washing machines, telephone installation, special clothing, bedding and holidays. Grants will not usually exceed £300 and can be for the whole or part of the item. Only in exceptional circumstances will grants be made for more than three years in any five.

Ongoing grants for needs such as heating and food are not made.

Annual grant total: In 2000 the trust had an income of £1.2 million and a total expenditure of £1 million. About 12 welfare grants a year are made to individuals, usually of £300 each.

Applications: In writing to the correspondent.

Correspondent: The Clerk, 4 Beaumont House, Sutton Road, St Albans, Hertfordshire AL1 5HH (01727 830038; Fax: 01727 862550; e-mail: nacc@nacc.org.uk; website: www.nacc.org.uk).

The Florence Nightingale Aid-in-Sickness Trust

Eligibility: People who are sick, convalescent, disabled or infirm. Preference will be given to people with professional, secretarial, or administrative qualifications or experience.

Types of grants: One-off grants are available for convalescent or respite care, medical and other aids, household aids, telephone installation (or mobile phones in rare cases) and hospital visiting expenses. Grants are not available for: house alterations, adaptations, improvements or maintenance; car purchase or adaptations; electrical wheelchairs, scooters or buggies; holidays, carers breaks, exchange visits, nursing home fees; debts or repayments; general clothing; computers or software; or general house furnishing.

Partial funding may be provided where a large grant is requested.

Annual grant total: In 2000/01 the trust had assets of £6.7 million, an income of £363,000 and a total expenditure of £290,000. Grants to individuals totalled £123,000. Three organisations also received £30,000 each to donate to individuals.

Applications: In writing to the correspondent, to be submitted by a social worker, occupational therapist, doctor, health centre or one of the trust's country correspondents. Applications should include a brief medical history of the applicant and proof of need for assistance.

Letters should include sereval sub-headings giving the following information: name, age and address of the client with marital status; details of family living at home; weekly income of the household including all benefits; weekly expenditure of the household; precise nature of the illness, what is required as an aid – costs, suppliers etc; whether the client or family will contribute; and which other charities are being approached and what their response has been so far.

Normally assistance is only considered at intervals of three years for any one household.

Correspondent: The Administrator, 38 Ebury Street, London SW1W 0LU (020 7823 5673; Fax: 020 7823 5574; e-mail: fnaist@btinternet.com).

The Roger Pilkington Young Trust

See entry on page 118

React (Rapid Effective Assistance for Children with Potentially Terminal Illness)

Eligibility: Children, aged up to 18 years old, with potentially terminal illnesses.

Types of grants: One-off and occasionally recurrent grants of between £50 and £5,000. Grants are for a variety of needs, such as carpets, curtains, bedding, washing machines, tumble dryers, cookers, car seats, driving lessons, mobile phones, subsistence, travel expenses, holidays and funerals. The only exclusions are holidays overseas and home extensions.

The trust stated: 'React is a no fuss, no frills charity.'

Annual grant total: In 2000/01 the charity had an income of £268,000 and a total expenditure of £214,000. Grants to 650 people totalled £190,000.

Applications: On a form available from: Ms Vicky Andreas, Grants and Communications Manager, at the address below. Applications should be submitted through a social worker, GP or other welfare body. Applications are dealt with as soon as possible. Applications must be validated by a medical professional and declare the applicants financial status i.e. potential beneficiaries are means tested. Applicants are asked to phone if there is any doubt about eligibility.

Correspondent: Christopher Pulford, Development Director, St Luke's House, 270 Sandycombe Road, Kew, Richmond TW9 3NP (020 8940 2575; Fax: 020 8940 2050; e-mail: react@reactcharity.org; website: www.reactcharity.org).

Betty Rhodes Fund

Eligibility: People who have a physical or mental disability, and their families, anywhere in the UK. There is an additional programme specifically for the London boroughs of Croydon, Kingston, Lambeth, Merton, Richmond, Sutton and Wandsworth.

Types of grants: One-off grants of between £100 and £300 towards respite and holidays for carers and/or those being cared for. People in the above London boroughs may also claim up to £200 towards clothing for children and household equipment for people with mental/physical disabilities who are being rehoused in the community. No grants are available towards repaying debts.

Sickness & Disability Charities

Annual grant total: In 2001 the trust had an income of £25,000. It gave 123 grants totalling £22,000.
Applications: Direct applications are not considered. Applications must come from a social worker, care manager or recognised agency. They can be considered at any time and should include details of age, address and disability.
Correspondent: Mrs Katherine Bryne, 6 Rewley Road, Carshalton, Surrey SM5 1DB (Tel & Fax: 020 8685 0875; e-mail: katherinebryne@aol.com).

The Rosslyn Park Injury Trust Fund

Eligibility: Young people who are sick or disabled through a sports injury (amateur sports).
Types of grants: One-off grants for items such as computers which could enable somebody to restructure their life.
Annual grant total: Between four and six grants a year from an income of about £5,000.
Applications: In writing to the correspondent. Applications can be submitted by either the individual or through social services, and are considered as they are received.
Correspondent: Brian St J C Carr, Trustee, Charles Russell, 8–10 New Fetter Lane, London EC4A 1RS (020 7203 5162).

The Royal United Kingdom Beneficent Association (RUKBA)

See entry on page 118

The Rugby Football Union Charitable Fund

See entry on page 61

Miss Doreen Stanford Charitable Trust

Eligibility: People who are disabled, deaf or blind and in need. Also, children whose families are in financial need.
Types of grants: One-off and recurrent grants ranging between £500 and £1,500, mainly for equipment related to sickness or disability, not for items such as washing machines, clothes or repairs.
Annual grant total: About £25,000 a year.
Applications: Applications must be made through a charity, containing details of the individual's income and expenditure. The trustees meet once a year, in March, and applications must be submitted by the end of January.
Correspondent: Mrs G M B Borner, Secretary, 26 The Mead, Beckenham, Kent BR3 5PE (020 8650 3368).

The Starfish Trust

Eligibility: People who are disabled or ill and living in the UK; priority is given to those based within a 25-mile radius of central Bristol.
Types of grants: One-off and recurrent grants according to need.
Annual grant total: In 1998/99 the trust had assets of £4.8 million and an income of £4.3 million. This was due to a donation of £4 million from Dobson Family Settlement, which produced an income of £226,000. Grants totalled £30,000 including £16,000 in six grants to individuals. Grants are also made to organisations.
Applications: In writing to the correspondent.
Correspondent: Robert N Woodward and Charles Dobson, Trustees, PO Box 213, Patchway, Bristol BS32 4YY.
Other information: This entry was not confirmed by the trust, but the address was correct according to the Charity Commission database.

Support Paraplegics in Rugby Enterprise – SPIRE

Eligibility: Individuals living in England who have been injured while participating in rugby football and are, on a long-term or permanent basis, sick, convalescent, disabled, or in need of financial assistance as a result of (or partially due to) their injuries.
Types of grants: Mainly one-off grants, up to a maximum of £5,000 towards equipment to assist people in everyday living including computer equipment and home modifications and improvements.
Annual grant total: In 2000 the trust had an income of £327,000 and a total expenditure of £107,000. Grants to 31 individuals totalled £95,000, the largest of which was for £8,000.
Applications: On a form available from the correspondent.
Correspondent: Michael J Christie, Hon. Treasurer, 41 Station Road, North Harrow, Middlesex HA2 7SX.
Other information: This entry was not confirmed by the trust, but the address was correct according to the Charity Commission database.

The Victoria Convalescent Trust

Eligibility: People in medical need of convalescence, recuperative and respite care in England and Wales.
Types of grants: Grants ranging from £50 to £600 towards the cost of convalescence, respite care and recuperative holidays. Grants are not made for holidays.
Annual grant total: In 2000 the trust had an income of £136,000 and a total expenditure of £164,000.
Applications: On a form available from the correspondent. Applications must be submitted through a social worker, a health care worker or a welfare agency or another professional worker and will be considered every month. Medical and social reports supporting the need for the break must be provided.
Correspondent: Mrs Anita J Perkins, 11 Cavendish Avenue, Woodford Green, Essex IG8 9DA (Tel & Fax: 020 8502 9339).

Wireless for the Bedridden

Eligibility: People who are confined to their bed and housebound and older people, who are in financial need.
Types of grants: Radios are provided and sent to the organisation supporting the application. They are purchased by the society. Televisions are rented by the society on a full maintenance contract from a major rental company. The service is free to both recipient and sponsoring organisations. The sets remain the property of the society.
Annual grant total: In 2000/01 the trust had assets of £2 million and income of £267,000. There were 2,600 beneficiaries who received radios and televisions worth £221,000 in total.
Applications: On the official application form available from the correspondent and supported by a sponsor from an appropriate welfare agency. Applications are considered weekly.
Correspondent: John Parker, Secretary, 159a High Street, Hornchurch, Essex RM11 3YB (0800 018 2137; Fax: 01708 620816).

AIDS/HIV

The Crusaid Hardship Fund

Eligibility: People with HIV/AIDS, who face difficulty or extra expenditure because of their HIV status, and live in England, Northern Ireland or Wales.
Types of grants: One-off grants, usually of £40 but they can be up to £350, for items or services which cannot reasonably be afforded on current income, are not available from other sources and will improve the quality of life. Grants have been given towards, for example, telephone and other domestic bills (e.g. gas, electricity etc.), clothing, beds and bedding. Household equipment, such as refrigerators and washing machines, can also be given. Help can also be given towards the costs of respite care and alternative therapies, where statutory funding is not available.

Sickness & Disability Charities

No grants for council tax, rent, holiday expenses, air fares or funeral costs.

Annual grant total: In 2001/02 grants totalled £888,000.

Applications: On a form available from the correspondent or from many HIV specialist centres around the country. Applications should be submitted by a social worker, welfare rights worker, health adviser or THT buddy. A diagnosis letter from a consultant or doctor should be enclosed.

Correspondent: Steven Inman, Hardship Director, 73 Collier Street, London N1 9BE (020 7833 9707; Fax: 020 7833 8644; website: www.crusaid.org.uk).

Other information: For applicants living in Scotland, even if they are English, Welsh or Northern Irish, please see entry for Phace Scotland on page 138.

Paul Flynn Memorial Fund

Eligibility: People who have hearing difficulties and who have HIV/AIDS.

Types of grants: One-off grants of up to £300 from hardship funds. Grants have included helping with installing telephone lines with a minicom facility. Minicoms and textphones are also loaned to the immediate family. Grants are given for chairlifts, help with heating/telephone bills, travel to support groups, childcare for mothers with HIV/AIDS and hearing difficulties.

No grants to people with hearing difficulties who do not have HIV/AIDS, or towards communication support services or course fees. No grants for holidays or weekend breaks.

Annual grant total: About £1,700.

Applications: On a form available from the correspondent, with a certificate confirming HIV/AIDS status and audiological status. Applications should be either submitted directly by the individual or through social services departments, HIV/AIDS organisations, a member of the British Deaf Association Counselling Services Volunteer Group or another organisation for people with hearing difficulties. Applications can be considered at any time.

Correspondent: Michelle Simpson, Health & Counselling Service Manager, British Deaf Association Counselling Services, 13 Wilson Patton Street, Warrington, Cheshire WA1 1PG (01925 652520; Fax: 01925 652526; Minicom: 01925 652529; Videophone: 01928 630169;

Jewish AIDS Trust

Eligibility: Jewish people with HIV/AIDS.

Types of grants: One-off grants of up to £500 are available from the trust, which tries to share the cost of major items with other agencies. Recent grants have been given towards passover food, travel expenses for respite care, washing machines, cookers, moving costs and so on. No grants are given towards rent, mortgage arrears, luxury items or repayments of loans, debts or credit cards.

Annual grant total: In 2000/01 the trust had assets of £78,000, an income of £109,000 and a total expenditure of £128,000. Grants totalled £7,000.

Applications: On a form available from the correspondent. All referrals must be through a professional person i.e. social worker, health visitor and so on; buddies or befrienders are not considered appropriate. A referral must accompany every application and be on headed paper including client's name, date of birth, detailed breakdown of weekly income, details and nature of request, name, position and signature of referrer and details of whom the cheque should be made payable to. First applications require symptomatic proof of HIV diagnosis from the applicant's doctor.

Correspondent: Rosalind Collin, Walsingham House, 1331 High Road, London N20 9HR (020 8446 8228; Fax: 020 8446 8227; e-mail: admin@jat-uk.org; website: www.jat-uk.org).

Other information: The trust was established to educate Jewish people about HIV and also provide support for those affected by it.

The Macfarlane Trust

Eligibility: People with haemophilia who have been infected with HIV through blood products, and their dependants. No other people are eligible. The trust is in contact with those known to have haemophilia and to be HIV positive through infected blood products, and therefore any further eligibility to register with the trust seems unlikely.

Types of grants: One-off and recurrent grants and loans are available towards the additional costs associated with living with HIV. Grants can be given towards health-related needs such as convalescence, respite, travel, clothes, medical care, specialised equipment and so on.

Annual grant total: In 2000/01 the trust had assets of £7.9 million and an income of £2.8 million. A total of £2.7 million was given in 706 one-off grants and 635 recurrent grants.

Applications: Applications are made direct to the trust by those registered with the trust, or via a social worker or health professional. There is an application form, although requests by letter or telephone are equally considered. Medical reports and a supportive letter from a doctor or other medical staff is required.

Correspondent: Ann Hithersay, Chief Executive, Alliance House, 12 Caxton Street, London SW1H 0QS (020 7233 0342; Fax: 020 7233 0839; e-mail: ann@macfarlane.org.uk).

Alzheimer's disease

Alzheimer's Society

Eligibility: People with Alzheimer's disease and related illnesses, and their carers, who live in England, Northern Ireland and Wales.

Types of grants: One-off grants towards washing machines, clothing, telephone bills, respite breaks, aids, adaptations and replacement bedding, but not nursing home fees. Grants are usually of up to £500.

Annual grant total: Grants total £150,000 each year.

Applications: On a form available from the correspondent, to be considered weekly. Applications can be submitted at any time either directly by the individual, or through a social worker, recognised welfare agency or other third party. It is essential that all applications are supported by references from a doctor and a social worker endorsing the stated need.

Correspondent: Clive Evers, Director of Information & Education, Gordon House, 10 Greencoat Place, London SW1P 1PH (020 7306 0606; Fax: 020 7306 0808; e-mail: info@alzheimers.org.uk; website: www.alzheimers.org.uk).

Arthritis and Rheumatism

The Arthritic Association

Eligibility: People in need who have arthritis or a related disease.

Types of grants: One-off and recurrent grants and loans ranging from £50 to £300. Grants can be, for instance, for dietary supplements and remedial therapy.

Annual grant total: In 2000/01 the trust had assets of £2.9 million, an income of £600,000 and a total expenditure of £230,000. Grants were made to 113 individuals totalling £9,100 and grants for research totalled £19,000.

Applications: On a form available from the correspondent, for consideration in January, March, July and October. Applications can be submitted by the individual or through a social worker, citizen's advice bureau or other welfare agency.

Correspondent: Mrs K Fairhurst, The Membership Secretary, First Floor Suite, 2 Hyde Gardens, Eastbourne, East Sussex BN21 4PN (01323 416550;

Fax: 01323 639793;
e-mail: info@arthriticassociation.org.uk;
website: www.arthriticassociation.org.uk).

Other information: The association works to promote natural dietary treatments for arthritis and grants are also made for research in this area.

Betard Bequest

Eligibility: People in the UK who have arthritis or rheumatism. Preference is given to Scottish and French people who are isolated and also to older people.

Types of grants: Grants of £100 to £10,000 towards equipment, computers and so on. No grants are made to replace statutory funding.

Annual grant total: About £30,000.

Applications: In writing to the correspondent, through social services or a welfare charity. Applications are considered in February, May, September and November and should be received in the previous month.

Correspondent: CAF Grantmaking, CAF, Kings Hill, West Malling, Kent ME19 4TA (01732 520334; Fax: 01732 520159; e-mail: grants@cafonline.org; website: www.cafonline.org/grants).

Ataxia

Ataxia UK (formerly Friedreich's Ataxia Group)

Eligibility: Subscribed members of the Ataxia UK who are living in the UK and have Friedreich's Ataxia or Cerebellar Ataxia.

Types of grants: One-off grants usually between £200 and £1,000 towards, for instance, respite care, holidays, computers, equipment, aids and adapted furniture. No grants are given towards repaying loans, debts or credit cards.

Annual grant total: Grants totalled £17,000 in 1998/99.

Applications: On a form available from the correspondent, to be submitted directly by the individual or via any third party. Applications should be made at least three months before the grant is needed.

Correspondent: Julia Willmott, Rooms 10 & 10a, Winchester House, Kennington Park, Cranmer Road, London SW9 6EJ (020 7582 1444; Fax: 020 7582 9444; e-mail: offce@ataxia.org.uk; website: www.ataxia.org.uk).

Other information: The annual subscription fee is £15. The group also finances medical research.

Blindness

Action for Blind People

Eligibility: Registered blind or partially sighted permanent residents of the UK who are in need.

Types of grants: Low income grants are made to boost income generally or to meet specific bills such as heating and telephone costs. These can be applied for on an annual basis. Special grants up to £400 are available ONLY where all efforts to obtain statutory funding have failed. Grants are available for cookers, furniture, washing machines, refrigerators, computer equipment, medical equipment, beds, repairs/decoration, telephone installation, clothing, holidays and expenses related to children.

No grants towards nursing home fees and for conditions other than visual impairment. For example, no grants for hearing aids, wheelchairs or any vehicle costs. A welfare benefit check is carried out on all application forms and the referring agent advised if there appears to be any unclaimed entitlement to statutory benefit.

Annual grant total: In 2001 the trust gave £250,000 in total in over 1,000 grants.

Applications: On a form available from the correspondent. Applications are considered monthly and should be submitted through a social worker or local blind association.

Correspondent: Anna Slattery, Grants Officer, 14–16 Verney Road, London SE16 3DZ (020 7635 4800; Fax: 020 7635 4900; e-mail: info@afbp.org; website: www.afbp.org).

Other information: The organisation also has sheltered accommodation and employment, holiday hotels, and an information and support service for visually impaired people, their carers and professionals. A number of booklets and fact sheets are available from the address above.

Electronic Aids for the Blind

Eligibility: People who are registered blind or partially sighted and on a low income.

Types of grants: The equipment must be for personal or domestic communication purposes. The charity cannot help if there is a statutory obligation to provide the equipment.

The charity works on a one-off basis to raise funds on behalf of individuals to buy the specialised or specially adapted equipment each one needs. The charity does not make direct grants to individuals or to others acting on their behalf, but makes topping-up payments to the individual's appeal account so that the equipment can be purchased. Agreement to work on behalf of an individual is conditional on the charity purchasing the equipment direct from the supplier. The charity rarely joins in a fundraising appeal that has already been started.

Annual grant total: In 2000/01 the trust had an income of £209,000 and gave over £225,000 in grants.

Applications: On a form available from the correspondent with guidelines. Full information is needed as the trust considers the possibility of funding from other grant-making organisations. Applications are considered at any time and may be submitted directly by the individual, through a social or rehabilitation officer, welfare agency or other third party.

Correspondent: The Director, Suite 14, 71–75 High Street, Chislehurst, Kent BR7 5AG (020 8295 3636; Fax: 020 8295 3737; e-mail: admin@eabnet.org.uk; website: www.eabnet.org.uk).

Other information: The charity is entirely independent of equipment suppliers and manufacturers and happy to offer impartial advice and information on what is currently available. There is also a members' website and membership is open to anyone who has an interest in computers and IT in general as well as those who are interested in technology relating to sight loss.

Gardner's Trust for the Blind

Eligibility: Registered blind or partially sighted people in need who live in England or Wales.

Types of grants: One-off grants for domestic household tools and for educational purposes. No grants for holidays, residential or nursing home fees or for loan repayments.

Annual grant total: In 1999/2000 the trust had an income of £65,000 and its total expenditure was £55,000, including relief-in-need and educational grants.

Applications: In writing to the correspondent. Applications can be submitted either directly by the individual or by a third party, but they must also be supported by a third party who can confirm the disability and that the grant is needed. They are considered in March, June, September and December and should be submitted at least three weeks before the meeting.

Correspondent: Angela Stewart, Boundary House, 91–93 Charterhouse Street, London EC1M 6PN (020 7253 3757).

National Blind Children Society

Eligibility: People aged 0 to 25 years who are (or are eligible to be) registered blind or partially sighted and live in the UK.

Sickness & Disability Charities

Types of grants: One-off grants towards equipment, specialist software and recreation and other activities.

Annual grant total: In 2000 the trust's income was £1.2 million and its total expenditure was £1.1 million. Grants towards the provision of equipment to individuals totalled £304,000 and other grants to individuals totalled £15,000. In total 283 individuals received grants.

Applications: On a form available from the correspondent, for consideration at monthly meetings. Applications can be submitted either by the individual with a supporting letter, or via a social worker, welfare agency or qualified teacher of people who are visually impaired.

Correspondent: C Beaumont, Grants and Appeals Manager, NBCS House, Market Street, Highbridge, Somerset TA9 3BW (01278 764764; Fax: 01278 764790; e-mail: enquiries@nbcs.org.uk; website: www.nbcs.org.uk).

The Royal Blind Society for the UK

Eligibility: People who are registered blind or partially sighted and on a low income of £93 a week for single people and £140 a week for a couple.

Types of grants: One-off grants of £200 to £300. Recent grants have been given to meet the extra costs of visual impairment, such as talking aids and equipment, telephone and electricity bills and taxi fares. No grants are given towards household items, clothing or to supplement a low income.

Annual grant total: In 2000/01 the trust had assets of £1.7 million and an income of £111,000. Total expenditure was £231,000. About £94,000 was given in 375 grants.

Applications: On a form available from the correspondent. Applications should be submitted by a social worker, citizen's advice bureau or similar welfare agency on the individual's behalf. They are considered each month.

Correspondent: Mrs Gillian Pollard, Kent House, Romney Place, Maidstone, Kent ME15 6LH (01622 690756; e-mail: royalblindsoc@aol.com).

The Royal National Institute for the Blind

Eligibility: Registered blind and partially-sighted people who receive a means-test benefit or are on a very low income and who have savings of £3,000 or less.

Types of grants: One-off and recurrent grants according to need. Grants range between £50 to £350 and there is a limit of £500 for each individual over three years and there should be a gap of one year between grants. Priority is given to items essential for day-to-day living. Emergency grants are not available. No grants for recreational needs, nursing home fees, the costs of medical treatment, telephone installation, employment needs or repeatedly accruing debts.

Annual grant total: £60,000.

Applications: Application forms are available from the correspondent and must be supported by a social worker, rehabilitation officer or a worker from a voluntary society or citizen's advice bureau. Applications are considered throughout the year.

Correspondent: Community Care Advocacy Officer, Welfare Rights Services, RNIB, 105 Judd Street, London WC1H 9NE (020 7388 1266; Fax: 020 7388 2034; website: www.rnib.org.uk).

Other information: The RNIB provides over 60 services for blind and partially sighted people. Financial and other assistance is also available from the wide range of local charities for blind people, almost all of which work in close co-operation with the RNIB.

Brittle bones

The Brittle Bone Society

Eligibility: Children and others with osteogenesis imperfecta (brittle bones) or similar disorders.

Types of grants: Grants for wheelchairs and other equipment for personal care which are not available on the NHS.

Annual grant total: £66,000.

Applications: In writing to the correspondent at any time. Applications should include an occupational therapist's report showing a need for the item required.

Correspondent: Raymond Lawrie, Chief Executive, 30 Guthrie Street, Dundee DD1 5BS (01382 204446; Fax: 01382 206771; e-mail: bbs@brittlebone.org; website: www.brittlebone.org).

Cancer and Leukaemia

The Cancer & Leukaemia in Childhood Trust (CLIC)

Eligibility: Families in need as a result of their child (aged up to 21) having cancer or leukaemia.

Types of grants: One-off grants of between £100 and £500 for a wide variety of needs, including holiday expenses, computers, travel expenses, treats, carpets, telephone bills, bedding and furniture, childminding, clothing, funeral expenses, buggies and high chairs, washing machines and home improvements. No grants can be given towards private or overseas medical treatment.

Annual grant total: In 2001 the trust had assets of £4.7 million, an income of £5.8 million and a total expenditure of £5.1 million. Grants to 675 individuals and organisations totalled £100,000.

Applications: In writing to: Mrs Ros Padfield, Grants Officer at the address below. Applications should be submitted by a social worker, Macmillan/CLIC nurse or other suitable third party on behalf of the individual. Letters should include details of the total cost of the item or service, the amount required, clearly defined reasons for the application and receipts where appropriate. They are considered throughout the year.

Correspondent: Mrs Susan George, Services Director, 6 Emma-Chris Way, Abbey Wood, Bristol BS34 7JU (0117 311 2600; Fax: 0117 311 2649; e-mail: susan.george@clic-charity.demon.co.uk; website: www.clic.uk.com).

David Jenkinson Memorial Fund Child Cancer Concern

Eligibility: People under 21 who have non-Hodgkin's lymphoma, and their families, who are in need.

Types of grants: Grants are given for toys, holidays and educational needs. Grants are also given to families to help with debts accrued due to child's illness. Grants are of up to £1,000.

Annual grant total: In 2000/01 the fund had an income of £20,000 and a total expenditure of £28,000, all of which was given in grants.

Applications: Must be referred via a hospital oncology social worker attached to child's ward, to be considered at any time. Applications submitted from any other source will not be considered.

Correspondent: David Jenkinson, PO Box 123, Romford, Essex RM5 3DD (07941 184166; Fax: 01542 882004).

The Leukaemia Care Society

Eligibility: People with leukaemia and allied blood disorders.

Types of grants: The society gives limited financial assistance.

Annual grant total: In 1998/99 the society had assets of £480,000 and an income of £240,000. Total expenditure was £314,000 with £33,000 being awarded in grants.

Applications: On a form available from the correspondent, with details of diagnosis. Applications can be submitted directly by the individual/health professional, but normally through the local area secretary (if available). Membership of the society (which is free) is essential.

Correspondent: Marc Stowell, Communications Manager, 2 Shrubbery Avenue, Worcester WR1 1QH (01905 330003).

Christian Lewis Trust

Eligibility: Children with cancer who are under 18, and their families.

Types of grants: One-off grants ranging from £50 to £200. Grants are given towards needs such as toys, books, videos, beds, radio cassettes, holidays, headstones and funeral expenses. No grants towards purchasing, repairing or maintaining cars, buildings or computers.

Annual grant total: In 2001 grants to 178 individuals totalled £25,000.

Applications: In writing to the correspondent. Applications can be submitted either directly by the individual or through a social worker, citizen's advice bureau, welfare agency or other third party such as a nurse or health visitor. The trust promises to respond to every request within one calendar month.

Correspondent: Judith May, 62 Walter Road, Swansea, West Glamorgan SA1 4PT (01792 480500; Fax: 01792 480700).

Other information: The trust stated that consideration will be given to any request that will improve the quality of life of a child with cancer.

Macmillan Cancer Relief – Patients Grants Scheme

Eligibility: People, of any age, who have cancer, or who are still affected by the illness, and are in financial need.

'To qualify, patients must not have capital savings of more than £8,000 per couple, or £6,000 for a single person. Individual household members must not have more than £100 each to spend each week, after allowing for basic costs.'

Types of grants: One-off grants towards daily expenses, including travel, heating, clothing, furnishings, care, telephones, convalescence and so on.

Annual grant total: In 2001 grants to 14,420 individuals totalled £4.9 million, at an average of £340 each.

Applications: On a form available from the correspondent. No direct applications can be made, they must be made through a Macmillan or community nurse, health or social worker, hospital social worker or a health professional from another welfare charity. Welfare workers can receive more information about the scheme by calling Macmillan CancerLine on 0808 808 2020. Applications are usually processed within three days.

Correspondent: Rolf Millican, Manager of Patient Welfare, 89 Albert Embankment, London SE1 7UQ (020 7840 7840; website: www.macmillan.org.uk).

Other information: Grants to patients are only one feature of the fund's work. Others include funding Macmillan Nurses (who are skilled in providing advice and support on symptom control and pain relief), Macmillan buildings for in-patient and day care, and financing an education programme for professionals in palliative care. The fund also gives grants to three associated charities.

The Ada Oliver Will Trust

Eligibility: People with cancer or rheumatism in need of relief of poverty or distress.

Types of grants: Monthly and one-off grants up to £150 for any kind of need, including settling rent arrears, nursing home fees where there is a shortfall, and necessities. No grants towards holidays.

Annual grant total: In 2000/01 the trust had an income of £3,600 and a total expenditure of £7,400.

Applications: By letter, including details of income, family and dependants. Applications can be submitted throughout the year by a social worker, citizen's advice bureau or other welfare agency on behalf of the individual.

Correspondent: The Trustees, c/o Marshalls Solicitors, 102 High Street, Godalming, Surrey GU7 1DS (01483 416101).

Sargent Cancer Care for Children

Eligibility: Young people under the age of 21 living in the UK who have cancer, leukaemia or Hodgkin's disease, or have received treatment for one of these diseases in the last six months.

Types of grants: Grants of up to £170 are awarded to alleviate crises and to add to quality of life to the child and family during treatment. Grants have been given towards education and training, equipment, holidays, travel, telephone bills, heating, clothing and childminding. Funeral expenses, headstones, treatment and research are not eligible for grants.

Annual grant total: In 2000/01 the charity had a total expenditure of £9.9 million. 18% of this was spent on grants, totalling around £1.8 million.

Applications: On a form, to be completed by the individual's Sargent social worker, who will be automatically appointed by the hospital when the disease is diagnosed. Any applicants applying directly will be referred back to their Sargent social worker. Applications are considered daily, and a response is usually given within 48 hours. Applications concerning payment of bills should include supporting documentation.

Correspondent: Alison Wood, Griffin House, 161 Hammersmith Road, London W6 8SG (020 8752 2825; Fax: 020 8752 2805; e-mail: grants@sargent.org; website: www.sargent.org).

Tenovus Cancer Information Centre

Eligibility: People who have cancer, or are still affected by illness or treatment, who live in the UK. Applicants must have savings of less than £6,000 if single or £8,000 if a couple.

Types of grants: One-off grants of £50 to £150 can be given for a wide variety of needs, including fares to hospital for treatment, heating and lighting bills, telephone bills, washing machines, tumble dryers, bedding and clothing (especially mastectomy bras). No grants are made towards funerals or overseas holidays.

Annual grant total: About £12,000 a year.

Applications: Applications must be made through social workers or similar professional. They are processed within 10 working days of receipt.

Correspondent: Mrs Jo Jarman, Head of Social Work and Welfare Rights, Velindre NHS Trust, Velindre Hospital, Whitchurch, Cardiff CF14 2TL (029 2019 6100; Fax: 029 2019 6105; e-mail: tcic@tenovus.com; website: www.tenovus.com).

Cerebral Palsy

Hylton House Fund

See entry on page 117

Cystic fibrosis

The Cystic Fibrosis Trust

Eligibility: People who have cystic fibrosis.

Types of grants: One-off grants for urgent needs where a grant will have an immediate effect. The trust is reluctant to make grants for significant debts or to meet on-going costs.

Annual grant total: No information available.

Applications: On a form available from the correspondent. Applications must be supported by a social worker or other professional and should state whether the applicant has applied to other charities and the outcome, the general financial circumstances and the reason for the application.

Correspondent: Cystic Fibrosis Trust Research & Clinical Care, 11 London Road, Bromley, Kent BR1 1BY (020 8464 7211; Fax: 020 8313 0472).

Sickness & disability charities

Other information: Providing financial help to those in need is just part of the help available from the CF Trust Support Service department of the trust. Other services include welfare benefit advice, advocacy and local support workers.

Deafblind

Deafblind UK

Eligibility: Deafblind people in need, aged over 16 and living in the UK. 'Deafblind' includes those substantially deprived of hearing and sight.

Types of grants: One-off grants for telecommunications equipment, deafblind mothers' help, vibrating doorbells etc. Some small training/education grants may also be available. The trust builds/purchases/maintains flats, guesthouses and sheltered and other accommodation for benefit and use of people who are deafblind.

Annual grant total: About £6,000 a year.

Applications: In writing to the correspondent including confirmation that the applicant is deaf and blind. Applications can be submitted by the individual or through a recognised referral agency (social worker, citizen's advice bureau, doctor etc.) and are considered throughout the year.

Correspondent: Jackie Hicks, 100 Bridge Street, Peterborough, Cambridgeshire PE1 1DY (01733 358100; website: www.deafblinduk.org.uk).

Other information: The trust also participates in several other activities to further the interests of people who are deafblind, e.g. participating in national developmental and lobbying groups and linking people who are deafblind through magazines and newspapers in touch-based media.

Sense, the National Deaf-Blind & Rubella Association

Eligibility: People who are deafblind or multi-sensory impaired, and their families.

Types of grants: One-off emergency grants only, in exceptional circumstances. Grants are generally £50. Grants have been given towards clothing and travel fares to hospitals.

Annual grant total: £500.

Applications: In writing to the correspondent, to be considered as they arrive.

Correspondent: Eileen Boothroyd, 11-13 Clifton Terrace, Finsbury Park, London N4 3SR (020 7272 7774; Fax: 020 7272 6012).

Other information: Sense provides a complete range of support and services for people with dual sensory impairments, or a sensory impairment and another disability (and their families) including holidays.

Haemophilia

The Haemophilia Society

Eligibility: People with haemophilia and related bleeding disorders, and their families.

Types of grants: One-off grants up to a maximum of £500, for items relating to applicants bleeding problems, such as fridges to store treatment, floor coverings, washing machines and bedding. No grants for holidays, motor vehicles, ongoing bills such as gas or electricity, hospital travelling expenses or driving lessons.

Annual grant total: About £10,000 is given in grants each year.

Applications: On a form available from the correspondent. Applications should be submitted to the benefits adviser at the address below for consideration in February, April, June, August, October or December. Forms may be returned directly by the individual or via any third party, including welfare agencies.

Correspondent: Ruth Taylor/ Joan Adamson, Chesterfield House, 385 Euston Road, London NW1 3AU (020 8380 0600; Fax: 020 8387 8220; e-mail: info@haemophilia.org.uk; website: www.haemophilia.org.uk).

Huntington's disease

The Huntington's Disease Association

Eligibility: People with Huntington's Disease, their immediate families and those at risk, who live in England or Wales.

Types of grants: One-off grants only, typically of up to £200, although each application is considered on merit. Recent grants have been for clothing, furniture, domestic equipment (e.g. washing machines and cookers), telephone installation, respite care and holidays. No grants towards nursing home or day care fees, courses, rent or season tickets. No loans.

Annual grant total: About £18,000.

Applications: On a form available from the correspondent. Applications should be submitted through a social worker, doctor, citizen's advice bureau or other welfare agency. Applications made directly by the individual would need to be followed up by an association case worker. Requests are processed monthly although urgent cases will be considered as soon as possible.

Correspondent: Eileen Cook, 108 Battersea High Street, London SW11 3HP (020 7223 7000).

Kidney disease

The British Kidney Patient Association

Eligibility: Renal patients of UK nationality, whether on dialysis or not.

Types of grants: One-off grants can be given for all kinds of need caused by the condition, including fares for hospital visiting, clothing costs, gas/electric/water rates. Grants are not given to reimburse for bills already paid, make loans, pay court fines or pay for improvements or extensions to a patient's home.

Annual grant total: In 2001 the trust had assets totalling £29 million and an income of £2 million. Grants were made totalling £1.7 million, including £332,000 to individuals for education and welfare purposes.

Applications: On an application form available from the correspondent, via a social worker or medical staff. Applications are considered daily.

Correspondent: Mrs Elizabeth Ward, Bordon, Hampshire GU35 9JZ (01420 472021/2; Fax: 01420 475831; website: www.bkpa.org.uk).

Other information: The association also runs a holiday dialysis centre in Jersey where dialysis facilities are available free of charge.

Liver disease

The Ben Hardwick Fund

Eligibility: Low-income families of children and young people aged 18 or under who have primary liver disease.

Types of grants: One-off and recurrent grants of between £100 and £400 to help with costs which are the direct result of the child's illness, such as hospital travel costs, in-hospital expenses, telephone bills and childminding for other children left at home.

Annual grant total: In 2000/01 the trust had assets of £34,000 and an income of £6,100. Total expenditure was £7,000, including £5,700 given in 38 grants.

Applications: In writing to the correspondent with brief details of family circumstances. Applications should be submitted by a social worker, citizen's advice bureau or other welfare agency, and will be considered at any time.

Correspondent: Mrs Anne Auber, 12 Nassau Road, Barnes, London SW13 9QE (Tel & Fax: 020 8741 8499).

Meningitis

Meningitis Trust

Eligibility: UK residents in need with meningitis or meningococcal diseases, or who are disabled as a result of meningitis.

Types of grants: One-off and recurrent grants towards e.g. respite care, specialist aids and equipment, re-education and special training, refitting homes and vehicles, funeral expenses and healdstones, travel and subsistence costs.

No grants towards domestic bill arrears (such as gas, electricity, telephone or council tax), clothing, bedding, furniture, holidays and swimming pools.

Annual grant total: In 2001/02 the trust had net assets totalling £826,000, an income of £2.7 million and a total expenditure of £2.9 million. Grants were made to about 85 individuals and totalled £80,000 – including those for re-education and training.

Applications: Each applicant needs a third party professional representative (such as a GP, nurse, health visitor or social worker) who knows the applicant's background and history well. The representative needs to contact the trust for an application form.

Clients can also contact the helpline (0845 6000 800) in the first instance, requesting information regarding the application process.

Correspondent: Peter Kirby, Fern House, Bath Road, Stroud GL5 3TJ (01453 768000; Fax: 01453 768001; Minicom: 01453 768003; e-mail: info@meningitis-trust.org; website: www.meningitis-trust.org).

Mental health

The Matthew Trust

Eligibility: People who are mentally ill.

Types of grants: One-off grants of between £50 and £250 towards: counselling or medical bills; equipment and furniture to make a flat liveable; accommodation deposits; clothing; second chance learning and skills training opportunities; taking up housing issues with local authorities; travel costs for prison visits; respite breaks; and debt support in special circumstances.

Annual grant total: In 2000/01 the trust had assets of £123,000, an income of £222,000 and a total expenditure of £195,000. Grants to 427 individuals totalled £43,000.

Applications: Applications should be made by professional agencies only – not individuals. The Matthew Trust is a 'last-stop' agency and will only consider applications when all other avenues of funding, statutory and voluntary, have been exhausted and then only where a care programme has been established. The trust aims to provide a response within 14 days.

Correspondent: Jean Bailie, PO Box 604, London SW6 3AG (020 7736 5976; Fax: 020 7731 6961; e-mail: matthewtrust@ukonline.co.uk; website: www.matthew-trust.org).

Motor neurone

The Motor Neurone Disease Association

Eligibility: People with motor neurone disease, living in England, Wales and Northern Ireland.

Types of grants: One-off grants of up to £750 and recurrent grants of up to £2,000. Grants are usually given towards topping-up nursing/residential fees, equipment rental and purchase, holidays and similar needs which cannot be met by statutory sources.

Annual grant total: In 2000/01 the association had assets of £3.8 million, an income of £5.7 million and a total expenditure of £5.6 million. Grants totalled £282,000.

Applications: On a form available from the correspondent or a local regional care adviser. Applications must be submitted through a health or social care professional. In additional to stating what is requested, applications should include details of why the need is not available from statutory sources and where any payments should be made.

Correspondent: Care Services Manager, David Niven House, 10-15 Notre Dame Mews, Northampton NN1 2PR (01604 250505; Fax: 01604 624726; e-mail: enquiries@mndassociation.org; website: www.mndassociation.org).

Mucopoly-saccharide diseases

Society for Mucopolysaccharide Diseases

Eligibility: Children and young adults with mucopolysaccharide and related disorders. Applicants must be members of the society.

Types of grants: One-off grants and loans ranging between £50 and £200, primarily to enable members to access activities and conferences organised by the society. Grants for equipment, holidays and bereavement costs are also considered. No grants can be paid towards arrears or to non-members.

Annual grant total: In 2000/01 the society had assets of £862,000, an income of £707,000 and a total expenditure of £618,000. In previous years grants to individuals have totalled around £3,600.

Applications: On a form available from the correspondent, to be submitted directly by the individual. They are considered in February, May, July, September and November.

Correspondent: Mrs Christine Lavery, Director, 46 Woodside Road, Amersham, Buckinghamshire HP6 6AJ (01494 434156; Fax: 01494 434252; e-mail: mps@mpssociety.co.uk; website: www.mpssociety.co.uk).

Other information: The trust also funds research into mucopolysaccharide and related diseases.

Multiple sclerosis

The Multiple Sclerosis Society of Great Britain and Northern Ireland

Eligibility: People with multiple sclerosis and their families (where the person with MS benefits directly), living in the UK. People living in Scotland may be subject to other conditions, please contact MS Scotland (0131 472 4106).

Types of grants: One-off grants of up to £2,000, although different needs have different maximum amounts which may be beneath this figure. Grants are given towards particular items such as home adaptations and repairs, wheelchairs, special equipment and furnishings and up to one week's respite care. Holidays are only available to people who have not had a holiday in the last three years.

No grants are given towards medical equipment, conventional or complementary treatment, legal costs, insurance, residential fees, retrospective items (including where a deposit has been paid) or recurrent grants.

Annual grant total: In 2001 grants totalled £108,000.

Applications: On a form available from the correspondents. Applications should include quotes for the expenditure and a letter of support from a social worker, health professional or occupational therapist.

Correspondent: The Grants Team, MS National Centre, 372 Edgware Road, Cricklewood, London NW2 6ND (020 8438 0700; Fax: 020 8438 0701; e-mail: grants@mssociety.org.uk; website: www.mssociety.org.uk).

Other information: 'The above only relates to MS National Centre procedures; there are 370+ branches who have their own funds and make their own grants, MSNC can only consider applications which have the recommendation of the local branch and assessments are made locally in the first instance. Where possible, applications should be made to these local branches. MSNC grants are available as a "top up" for such grants.'

Muscular dystrophy

The Joseph Patrick Memorial Trust

Eligibility: People with muscular dystrophy or an allied neuromuscular condition.

Types of grants: One-off grants of between between £100 and £900 to partially fund the purchase of specialist/therapeutic equipment, adaptations to vehicles, heating and wheelchairs. In 2000 wheelchairs accounted for 38% of the grants.

Grants are not given towards items which statutory authorities should provide, equipment which has already been bought, structural building works, furniture, domestic appliances or insurance, maintenance or repairs of the equipment obtained.

Annual grant total: In 2000 the trust had assets of £397,000, an income of £150,000 and a total expenditure of £264,000. Grants to 280 beneficiaries totalled £136,000.

Applications: On a form available from the correspondent, which can be submitted directly by the individual or via a third party. Applications should be supported by a family care officer of Muscular Dystrophy Campaign and include professional assessment confirming the need and suitability of equipment for which assistance is being requested. Exceptionally, it may be necessary to obtain more than one assessment or provide further information than is included in an assessment report. Applications are considered every two months.

Correspondent: The Grants Administrator, 7–11 Prescott Place, London SW4 6BS (020 7720 8055; Fax: 020 7498 0670).

Neurological

The Chartered Society of Queen Square

Eligibility: People in the UK who have a neurological disorder and are in need.

Types of grants: One-off grants range from £100 to £300 and have been given for debts, furniture, telephone installation and towards computers, wheelchairs, vehicles and recuperative holidays. Pensions are also made, but the award of new pensions has been temporarily suspended owing to current financial constraints.

Annual grant total: In 2000 the society had assets of £3 million, an income of £132,000 and a total expenditure of £187,000. Grants to 239 individuals totalled £75,000. Grants for other purposes totalled £39,000.

Applications: Applications must be made through a social worker or professional equivalent on a form available from the correspondent. The society will not deal directly with the individual. Applications are considered in February, May, September and December.

Correspondent: M Theodorou, c/o CAF, Kings Hill, West Malling, Kent ME19 4TA (01732 520082; Fax: 01732 520001).

The Roald Dahl Foundation

Eligibility: Children and young people aged 25 or under who have a neurological or haematological condition and are from a low-income family. The only eligible cancer is benign brain tumour. Families must be in receipt of Income Support, working families tax credit or housing benefit. Families who do not qualify for these benefits, but are on a low-income or whose income has been interrupted by the child's illness may also be considered.

Types of grants: One-off grants of £20 to £500 each. Grants can be given towards household appliances, utility bills, clothing, beds and bedding, medical alert jewellery, travel and subsistence payments whilst children are in hospital, specialised equipment such as sensory toys, car seats, wheelchairs, motability vehicles, vehicle tax and insurance and respite care. Grants are only given towards holidays (within the UK) in exceptional circumstances. No grants are given towards debts (except utility bills) or items that should be provided by statutory sources.

Annual grant total: In 2000/01 the trust had assets of £1.6 million, an income of £674,000 and a total expenditure of £656,000. Grants to 346 individuals totalled £70,000.

Applications: On a form available from the correspondent. Applications must be submitted by a social worker or healthcare professional who is willing to see the application through to completion, supplying and confirming the information contained. Applicants need to provide details of income and expenditure if no state benefits are being claimed.

Correspondent: Mrs J Smith, Small Grants Manager, 92 High Street, Great Missenden, Buckinghamshire HP16 0AN (01494 890465; Fax: 01494 890459; e-mail: josmith@roalddahlfoundation.org).

Other information: This charity also supports charities and NHS hospitals working in the fields of neurology, haematology and literacy.

Parkinson's disease

Parkinson's Disease Society

Eligibility: People with Parkinson's disease, with savings of less than £3,000 (unless claiming Income Support).

Types of grants: One-off grants of about £150 each towards needs such as holidays, respite care, equipment and transport to and from hospital. No grants are given towards ongoing costs such as care fees, fuel bills, telephone bills and so on.

Annual grant total: About £25,000.

Applications: In writing to the correspondent, providing extensive details of the request. Applications can be submitted either directly by the individual or through any third party.

Correspondent: Rosie Hayward, 215 Vauxhall Bridge Road, London SW1V 1EJ (020 7931 8080; Fax: 020 7233 9908; e-mail: rhayward@parkinsons.org.uk; website: www.parkinsons.org.uk).

Polio

The British Polio Fellowship

Eligibility: People disabled through poliomyelitis (polio) living in the UK and Eire.

Types of grants: One-off grants according to need including help with heating bills, television licences, phone rental, household items, holidays, home improvements, mobility and disablity aids. The fellowship aims to alleviate all kinds of need among people with polio, not merely financial ones.

Annual grant total: In 2001 over £211,000 was given in grants.

Applications: On a form available from the correspondent with a medical certificate stating polio-disability. Applications should be submitted by the individual or by an appropriate third party on their behalf, and are considered throughout the year.

Correspondent: Dorothy Nattrass, Unit A, Eagle Office Centre, The Runway, South Ruislip, Middlesex HA4 6SE (020 8842 4999; Fax: 020 8842 0555; e-mail: info@britishpolio.org).

Other information: The fellowship's welfare department also provides support through (a) information on a wide range of issues affecting people disabled through polio and (b) advocacy/liaison with other agencies. The fellowship has over 50 local branches or groups, its own holiday accommodation and runs indoor sports championships.

Spina bifida

Association for Spina Bifida & Hydrocephalus (ASBAH) Welfare Grant

Eligibility: People with spina bifida and/or hydrocephalus living in England, Wales and Northern Ireland.

Types of grants: One-off grants towards the cost of wheelchairs, special trikes, driving assessments or lessons, hospital travel expenses, clothing, beds and bedding, car adaptations, house adaptations or household items.

Annual grant total: Around £10,000, with a further £2,000 in educational grants.

Applications: In writing to the correspondent directly by the individual or by a social worker, citizen's advice bureau or similar third party. Applications should include details of any other agencies approached and the outcome; whether the individual has spina bifida, hydrocephalus or both; whether the family know ASBAH has been contacted if the referral is by a third party; and when the amount requested is large, whether any other funds have been raised and how much. Applications are considered throughout the year.

Correspondent: Milly Rollinson, Assistant Director (Services), ASBAH House, 42 Park Road, Peterborough PE1 2UQ (01733 555988; Fax: 01733 555985; e-mail: postmaster@asbah.demon.co.uk; website: www.asbah.org).

Other information: ASBAH provides advisory and other specialised services. There are local associations in most parts of the country.

Spinal muscular atrophy

The Jennifer Trust

Eligibility: People diagnosed as having the genetic condition spinal muscular atrophy. (N.B. The trust cannot give grants to people with any other condition.)

Types of grants: One-off grants have been awarded for electric wheelchairs, beds, computers and chairs. No grants towards vehicles or their adaptations.

Annual grant total: In 1998/99 the trust had assets of £265,000 and an income of £214,000. Total expenditure was £221,000, with 25 relief-in-need grants being awarded totalling £14,000.

Applications: On a form available from the correspondent. Applications can be submitted by the individual, a social worker, citizen's advice bureau, welfare agency or any third party. Applications are considered four times a year.

Correspondent: Mrs Anita Macaulay, Director, Elta House, Birmingham Road, Stratford-upon-Avon CV37 0AQ (01789 267520; Fax: 01789 268371).

Other information: Financial grants to individuals is only one way in which the trust supports individuals. For more information, contact the trust and request an information pack.

Stroke

The Stroke Association

Eligibility: People living in England and Wales who have had a stroke. People with savings over £8,000 are not considered.

Types of grants: One-off grants are available, usually between £10 and £200. Grants have been given to purchase cookers, washing machines and washer/dryers. No grants for holidays abroad, motor expenses, telephone bills (except installation), private medicine, structural alterations, stairlifts, scooters, wheelchairs or nursing home fees.

Annual grant total: About £175,000 in about 1,000 grants each year.

Applications: On a form available from the correspondent to be completed by social workers or health professionals on the individual's behalf. Applications are considered monthly and must be supported by a doctor's letter confirming the stroke.

Correspondent: The Welfare Secretary, Stroke House, Whitecross Street, London EC1Y 8JJ (020 7566 1501; Fax: 020 7490 5086).

Tuberous sclerosis

Tuberous Sclerosis Association Benevolent Fund

Eligibility: People in need who have tuberous sclerosis.

Types of grants: Grants of up to £500 are given towards travel to clinics, special equipment and so on. Holidays are given in cases of specific need.

No grants are made for things which are the responsibility of a statutory service.

Annual grant total: In 2000/01 the trust had assets of £2.6 million and an income of £450,000. Total expenditure was £614,000, including £5,000 given in total in 25 grants.

Applications: In writing to the correspondent at any time, either directly by the individual or via a third party such as a social worker or citizen's advice bureau.

Correspondent: Janet Medcalf, Head of Support Service, PO Box 9644, Bromsgrove B61 0FP (01527 871898; Fax: 01527 579452; e-mail: support@tuberoussclerosis.org).

National & General Charities

This section includes all the entries which could not be tied to a particular occupation, disability or locality. It starts with an index of beneficiaries (e.g. children, older people etc.) with a separate category for trusts that specifically give grants for convalescence/holidays. Children and young people contains trusts for people aged 25 or under whilst older people contains trusts for people aged 50 or over – this reflects the criteria of some of the trusts in the guide, although not every trust will use these exact limits. We have also included refugees and asylum seekers under ethnic and foreign communities in the UK, as they may be eligible for support from other trusts in that section.

At the start of this section are those trusts which do not fit into any particular category. This is because they can give to a wide range of people, so if individuals are unable to find help from other sources in the guide then they should be able to approach one or more of these. However, most of these charities still have restrictions on who they can help; applicants should not simply send off indiscriminate applications to any charity under the general heading, rather they should first consider carefully whether they are eligible. Similarly, older people should not apply to all the trusts in the older people section, for instance, as there may be criteria will makes them ineligible for support.

After the index come the entries which are arranged alphabetically within each category.

Index of National and general charities

Children/young people 112

Convalescence *(see Holidays)*

Ethnic & foreign communities in the UK – including refugees and asylum seekers 113

Holidays 115

Homeless 116

Older people *(see also Widows/widowers/single people and women)* 116

Orders *(Buffaloes, Catenian, Masonic)* 119

Prisoners/former prisoners 120

Religion:

    Chrisitan 120

    Christian Science 121

    Church of England 121

    Jewish 121

    Protestant 122

    Roman Catholic 122

Sports 123

Vegetarians/Vegans 123

Women 123

The Alchemy Foundation

Eligibility: People in need in the UK and overseas.

Types of grants: One-off and recurrent grants according to need.

Annual grant total: In 1998/99 the trust had an income of £1.2 million and made grants totalling £860,000 of which £48,000 went to 213 individuals.

Applications: In writing to the correspondent.

Correspondent: Richard Stilgoe, Trustee, Trevereux Manor, Limpsfield Chart, Oxted, Surrey RH8 0TL (01883 730600; Fax: 01883 730800).

The Anglian Water Trust Fund

Eligibility: People in need whose only, or main, home is within the Anglian or Hartlepool Water regions.

Types of grants: The main emphasis of the trust is to receive a large annual grant from Anglian Water, which is then paid back to the company as one-off relief-in-need grants to households which are unable to pay their water/sewage bills to the company. Grants can also be given towards other important household bills and essential items, even if there is no application for help with water/sewage charges.

No grants are given towards: fines for criminal offences; education or training needs; medical equipment, aids and adaptations; holidays; debts to cental government departments such as tax and national insurance; business debts; overpayment of benefits; accommodation deposits; or catalogue, credit card, personal loan or other forms of unsecured lending.

Annual grant total: In 2000/01 the trust had assets of £688,000 and an income of £1.6 million, mostly from donations. Grants to 2,700 households totalled £1.4 million.

Applications: On a form available from the correspondent or local welfare agencies such as citizen's advice bureaux. Forms can also be downloaded from the trust's website.

Correspondent: The Administrator, PO Box 42, Peterborough PE3 8XH (01733 331177; Fax: 01733 334344;

NATIONAL & GENERAL CHARITIES

e-mail: admin@awtf.org.uk;
website: www.awtf.org.uk).

The Bagri Foundation

Eligibility: People in need worldwide.

Types of grants: One-off and recurrent grants according to need.

Annual grant total: In 1999/2000 it had an income of £116,000 and gave £11,000 in grants to individuals. Grants to organisations totalled £59,000.

Applications: In writing to the correspondent.

Correspondent: R Gatehouse, Trustee, 3rd Floor, 80 Cannon Street, London EC4N 6EJ (020 7280 0000).

Barony Charitable Trust

Eligibility: Individuals in need 'who are now entering, returning to, or struggling unaided within, society'.

Types of grants: 'Small grants to give individuals a fresh start, or often where unaided, financial assistance in society.'

Annual grant total: The trust's income is of around £10,000 a year and is wholly distributed in grants to individuals in need and to other causes.

Applications: On a form available from the correspondent, submitted preferably through a recognised referral agency such as a GP, health visitor, priest or minister, social worker or care worker. Applications will only be considered on receipt of a reference from such a referral agency.

Correspondent: Michael Coates, Hon. Secretary, 68 Newbattle Terrace, Edinburgh EH10 4RX (0131 447 5372).

Other information: Please note, this trust is a 'seed corn' subsidiary charitable trust of Barony Housing Association. Applications from Barony Housing Association's areas of activity may receive priority.

Thomas Betton's Charity for Pensions & Relief-in-Need

Eligibility: People in need.

Types of grants: One-off grants of £100 to £350 for household items such as furniture, kitchen equipment and bedding. No grants are given towards medical expenses, holidays, travel expenses, funerals, educational purposes, structural improvements to property or rent debts.

Annual grant total: In 2000/01 the trust had assets of £839,000 and an income and a total expenditure of £52,000. Grants to 70 individuals totalled £20,000. A further £25,000 was given to organisations.

Applications: Forms are available from the correspondent on receipt of an sae. They must be submitted with an sae by a social worker for consideration at any time.

Correspondent: Helen Sant, Charities Administrator, Ironmonger's Hall, Barbican, London EC2Y 8AA (020 7606 2725; Fax: 020 7600 3519).

The Carnegie Hero Fund Trust

Eligibility: Heroes and their families (that is people who have suffered financial loss or have been injured – or the families of people who have been killed – in performing acts of heroism in saving human life in peaceful pursuits in the UK, Eire, Channel Islands and territorial waters). About three to four new cases are recognised each year.

Types of grants: One-off and recurrent grants towards household bills, repairs, education, holidays and so on.

Annual grant total: In 2000 the trust had assets of £4 million and an income of £172,000. Expenditure totalled £163,000, including £100,000 in grants to individuals.

Applications: Direct applications are rare; recommendations are usually submitted by the police or by other organisations. The trustees also hear of suitable cases via a press agency.

Correspondent: Secretary, Abbey Park House, Abbey Park Place, Dunfermline, Fife KY12 7PB (01383 723638;
Fax: 01383 721862;
e-mail: herofund@carnegietrust.com;
website: www.carnegietrust.org.uk).

Other information: The trust was established in 1908 by Andrew Carnegie, who made a great fortune from steel. His Birthplace Museum in Dunfermline displays the Roll of Honour of the Hero Fund Trust, now containing the names of over 6,000 heroes and heroines.

Catholic Clothing Guild

Eligibility: People in need of clothing, regardless of denomination, in England and Wales.

Types of grants: The guild's aim is to give new clothing to people in need. It achieves this by donating clothing worth between £10 and £50, which has usually been knitted by one of its volunteers although it may also buy the goods on behalf of the individual. The required item of clothing is usually given in kind, cash grants are rarely given.

Annual grant total: About 4,500 items costing £3,800 to make are donated by the headquarters and regional branches every year.

Applications: No grants are given to applications submitted directly by the individual. They must have been referred by social services, welfare agencies or the clergy. It is helpful if the sex, age and size of the individual is given. Applicants may be referred by the headquarters to one of the regional groups for response.

Correspondent: Mrs F Ripper, Hon. Secretary, 3 Spring Way, Sible Hedingham, Halstead, Essex CO9 3SB (01787 460234).

Other information: The trust tends to give most of its support to organisations, such as older people's homes or schools, where a need has been identified which then distributes the clothing as relevant.

The Chamberlain Foundation

Eligibility: People in extreme need who are poor, injured, elderly and infirm and of limited educational means.

Types of grants: One-off grants ranging from £1,600 to £7,000.

Annual grant total: In 2000/01 the trust had an unusually high income of £624,000 and a total expenditure of £262,000. Grants totalled £48,000.

Applications: This trust has limited facilities for supporting new unsolicited cases but the trustees are proactive in finding beneficiaries; the trust therefore regrets that it is unable to respond to most unsolicited applications.

Applications are considered at the trustees' meetings in May and November. The trustees and secretary visit individuals who are shown to have long-term need of support from the foundation.

Correspondent: Christina Elmer, Devon House, 3c Wilson Street, Winchmore Hill, London N21 1BP (020 8882 9366).

Conservative and Unionist Agents' Benevolent Association

Eligibility: Individuals who are, or have been Conservative and Unionist Agents, or Women Organisers, and their dependants, who are in need. Support is also given to the dependants of deceased Conservative or Unionist Agents or Women Organisers.

Types of grants: One-off and annual grants. General grants may be spent on living expenses. Specific grants may be used for things such as holidays, telephone rental or television licences. They are also made towards the costs of: home adaptations for people who are disabled; medical emergencies; or moving house. Annual grants range from £240 to £2,400 a year. One-off grants have no limits.

Annual grant total: In 2000/01 the association had assets of £2.2 million, an income of £153,000 and a total expenditure of £128,000. Grants to 50 individuals for welfare and educational purposes totalled £106,000.

Applications: Initial telephone calls are welcomed and application forms are available on request. Applications can be made either directly by the individual, or through a member of a management committee or local serving agent. All beneficiaries are allocated a 'visiting agent' for their award reassessment. More frequent visits may be made as necessary. Applications are considered in February and July and should arrive in the preceding month.

Correspondent: The Secretary, Conservative Central Offices, 32 Smith Square, London SW1P 3HH (020 7984 8172; e-mail: jofarrell@conservatives.com).

The Worshipful Company of Cordwainers

Eligibility: The company administers a number of small trusts, the eligibility of which varies. Specific trusts exist for people who are blind, people who are deaf and dumb, widows of clergymen, unmarried women in the Church of England, ex-servicemen and widows of those who served in the merchant or armed forces.

Types of grants: Small annual grants depending on the trust and the circumstances.

Annual grant total: The annual grant total is about £20,000.

Applications: In writing to the correspondent supported, if possible, by referrals from welfare or other charitable bodies.

Correspondent: The Clerk, 8 Warwick Court, Gray's Inn, London WC1R 5DJ.

The Late Baron F A D'Erlanger's Charitable Trust

Eligibility: People in need, including people who are elderly, infirm or children. Preference is given to people who are disabled.

Types of grants: One-off grants ranging from £100 to £300, according to need. No grants for the relief of debts or for student grants. Grants are rarely given for holidays (99% are turned down).

Annual grant total: In 2000/01 the trust had assets of £6 million and an income of £127,000. Grants to 305 individuals totalled £126,000. Grants to eight organisations totalled £62,000.

Applications: In writing to the correspondent with full details about the family situation, financial situation, exact reasons for need and the amount of grant required. Applications received directly from the individual will generally not be successful; they should be submitted through a social worker, citizen's advice bureau or other welfare agency. Applications are considered throughout the year.

Correspondent: Philip Roderick Denman, 36 Upper Cheyne Row, London SW3 5JJ (020 7823 3432).

The Dibs Charitable Trust

Eligibility: People in need.

Types of grants: One-off grants for the relief of immediate distress only, ranging from £25 to £250. No pensions or annuities. Grants are not given for education, overseas travel, holidays, clothing, funeral expenses or group activities.

Annual grant total: Around £31,000.

Applications: Either in writing or on a form available from the correspondent. Applications should be made through a local social services department or citizen's advice bureau and are considered throughout the year.

Correspondent: Trustee Department, Coutts & Co., 440 Strand, London WC2R 0QS (020 7753 1000).

East Africa Women's League (UK) Benevolent Fund

Eligibility: People of UK origin who have previously lived and worked in East Africa.

Types of grants: One-off and recurrent grants according to need.

Annual grant total: In 2000 the trust had an income of £8,100 and its total expenditure was £7,500.

Applications: In writing to the correspondent. Members of a fund sub-committee may visit applicants.

Correspondent: Mrs J Considine, 37 Horwood Close, Headington, Oxford OX3 7RF (01865 764086; e-mail: joanconsidine@care4free.net; website: www.eawl.org.uk).

Family Welfare Association

Eligibility: People in need.

Types of grants: 'Almost every kind of need can be met, as a wide variety of trust funds are administered by the FWA. Fuel bills, clothing, particularly children's clothing and household needs are most commonly requested, but we can also help with more unusual needs such as electronic aids. We have limited funds to assist with holidays.

'We cannot help with rent arrears, council tax, funeral expenses, fines, or expenses already covered by statutory funds.

'The FWA also administers pensions to elderly people and the amalgamation of a number of old pension funds has enabled us to make half-yearly grants to approximately 150 pensioners.'

Most grants range between £100 and £200.

Annual grant total: In 2001 grants to over 5,000 individuals and families totalled £1 million.

Applications: 'Application must be made by a social worker on behalf of a client as part of an overall treatment plan. The grants manager is first contacted by letter and given a brief outline of the need. If funds are available and an application can be accepted, the application form is sent to the social worker. When this has been returned and processed it is then considered by the grants panel at its weekly meeting. Emergency applications will be accepted by telephone.

'Grants panel members are experienced workers from various branches of social work, who can also advise on additional statutory benefits to which the client may be entitled. Payment in all cases is made either to the referring agency or intermediary and not direct to the beneficiaries.'

Correspondent: Grants Manager, 501-505 Kingsland Road, Dalston, London E8 4AU (020 7254 6251; Fax: 020 7249 5443; website: www.fwa.org.uk).

The Farthing Trust

Eligibility: People in need. Those either personally known to the trustees or recommended by those personally known to the trustees have priority.

Types of grants: One-off and recurrent grants according to need.

Annual grant total: £21,000 in 2000/01, of which £9,000 was given outside of the UK.

Applications: In writing to the correspondent, including a reference from a third party such a social worker, citizen's advice bureau or other third party confirming the need. Applicants will only be notified of a refusal if an sae is enclosed.

Correspondent: H Martin, 48 Ten Mile Bank, Littleport, Ely, Cambridgeshire CB6 1EF.

Other information: The trusts states that it receives 10 letters a week and is able to help one in a hundred. There would seem little point in applying unless you can establish a personal contact with a trustee.

Elizabeth Finn Trust

Eligibility: British or Irish people from a professional or similar background or connection, and their dependants.

Types of grants: Recurrent grants are made towards daily living expenses. One-off grants are also available towards needs such as car expenses, household items, house repairs and adaptations, specialist equipment and help with nursing/residential fees. All grants are means-tested. The trust will not give grants for healthcare costs, computer equipment, school fees, respite care, debts or funeral expenses.

Annual grant total: In 2000/01 the trust had assets of £41 million, an income of £17 million and a total expenditure of £18 million. Grants to 1,733 individuals totalled £2 million.

Applications: On a form available from the correspondent. Applications can be considered at any time.

Correspondent: Mrs M E Yeats, Director of Casework, 1 Derry Street, London W8 5HY (020 7396 6700; Fax: 020 7396 6739).

NATIONAL & GENERAL CHARITIES

Other information: The association also runs its own residential and nursing homes. For information contact Miss Hilary Funston at the above number.

Friendship Community Trust

Eligibility: People who are living in poor or difficult circumstances.

Types of grants: One-off and recurrent grants according to need.

Annual grant total: In 1998/99 the trust had an income of £11,000 and a total expenditure of £9,000.

Applications: An application form and guidelines are available on request from the address below.

Correspondent: S McCorry, Secretary, 50 Newhall Hill, Birmingham B1 3JN.

Other information: This entry was not confirmed by the trust, but the address was correct according to the Charity Commission database.

Fund for Human Need

Eligibility: Refugees, asylum seekers, people who are homeless and anybody attempting to get over a short-term hurdle.

Types of grants: One-off grants of about £200.

Annual grant total: In 1999/2000 the fund had assets of £89,000, an income of £33,000 and a total expenditure of £42,000. Grants totalled £39,000, mostly given to organisations.

Applications: In writing to the correspondent.

Correspondent: Stan H Platt, 50 Leeds Road, Selby YO8 4HX (01757 706040).

Other information: This trust also gives money to organisations and for overseas projects.

The R L Glasspool Charity Trust

Eligibility: People in need who are on a low income.

Types of grants: Small one-off grants only, primarily for household equipment (including furniture, kitchen items, cookers, fridges and bedding), clothing and holidays. The trust no longer supports major kitchen appliances or beds but provides these items in kind. No grants for loans, debts, rent or rate arrears, funeral expenses, structural repairs, building work, education, research or project funding.

Annual grant total: In 2000/01 about 2,000 grants totalled £453,000.

Applications: In writing to the correspondent through the social services, a health visitor, probation service, citizen's advice bureau or hospital social work department. Applications should include the individual's: (a) full names, age and address of members of the household; (b) family circumstances and background; (c) breakdown of household income and expenditure, including any disability benefits; (d) other sources approached and other requests; and (e) detail of the need being requested e.g. cooker. Applications are considered throughout the year.

Correspondent: Mrs F Moore, Administrator, Second Floor, Saxon House, 182 Hoe Street, Walthamstow, London EH17 4QH (020 8520 4354).

The Grut Charitable Trust

Eligibility: 'Individuals suffering from the effects of illness or poverty.' Children in need and older people are given particular consideration.

Types of grants: Grants generally up to £100. No grants towards holidays.

Annual grant total: About £25,000.

Applications: In writing to the correspondent. Applications should be supported by a recognised body such as a local authority or social welfare organisation. Details of the individual's income/expenditure are required. If there has been no reply after eight weeks, the application has been unsuccessful.

Correspondent: The Secretary, Poole & Co. Solicitors, Mansion House, Prince's Street, Yeovil BA20 1EP (01935 846000).

Gurunanak Charitable Trust

Eligibility: People in financial need who live in the UK or overseas.

Types of grants: One-off grants according to need.

Annual grant total: In 1999/2000 the trust's income totalled £66,000, all of which was given in grants to organisations and individuals.

Applications: In writing to the correspondent at any time.

Correspondent: J S Kohli, Trustee, 11–12 Sherborne Street, Manchester M3 1JS (0161 831 7879).

The Margaret Jeannie Hindley Charitable Trust

Eligibility: People in 'reduced or destitute circumstances' and in need. In practice priority is given to people living in Godalming.

Types of grants: Recurrent grants of £30 to £90 each month are made. One-off grants are also available.

Annual grant total: In 2000/01 the trust had assets of £303,000 and both an income and a total expenditure of £23,000. Grants and donations to individuals totalled £23,000.

Applications: In writing to the correspondent. The trustees meet regularly throughout the year to consider applications.

Correspondent: Mrs C Burnett, Marshalls Solicitors, 102 High Street, Godalming, Surrey GU7 1DS (01483 416101).

Hunt & Almshouse Charities

Eligibility: These charities consist of a number of small trusts, each of which has different eligibility criteria. In general the trusts support the needs of single, older women. Applicants should be in receipt of a state pension or be an adult with a disability and receiving relevant benefits. One of the smaller trusts supports male applicants, although very little funds are available from this source. The charities only operate in England.

Types of grants: One-off grants of up to £500, although they usually range from £100 to £300. They are only made towards: essential household items, such as furniture, appliances, carpets and furnishings; computer equipment; and mobility equipment, such as wheelchairs, scooters and adapted vehicles.

Annual grant total: In 2000/01 the charities had assets of £324,000 and an income of £16,000. Grants to 42 individuals totalled £14,000.

Applications: On a form available from the correspondent, to be submitted through a citizen's advice bureau or other welfare agency. Written estimates or invoices should be included. The charities welcome initial discussions about whether an approach should be made. Applications are considered when received, although as the charities do not keep a reserve of funds the decisions may not be made until the funds are available; in these cases the applicant will be kept informed of when the application can be considered.

Correspondent: Charities Administrator, Skinners' Hall, 8 Dowgate Hill, London EC4R 2SP (020 7213 0562; Fax: 020 7236 6590; website: www.skinnershall.co.uk).

Other information: This trust is a part of the Skinners' Company and was included in the last edition of the guide as The Skinners Company Charities. The grant-making is made through Hunt & Almshouse charities and includes grants from some smaller trusts, including Sir Thomas Devitt Endowment Fund, Lady Tyrrell Giles Gift (both of which had separate entries in the previous edition), Sir Jeremiah Colman Fund and Frederic Holl-Morris Charity.

The Johnston Family Fund

Eligibility: Members of the upper and middle classes (and widows and daughters of such people) who, through no fault of their own, have fallen into impoverished circumstances. No men under 50 or women under 40 are supported.

Types of grants: Recurrent grants of £650 a year and one-off grants of around £100 each for TV licences and birthday gifts.

Annual grant total: In 2001 the fund had assets of £453,000 and an income of £29,000. Grants totalled £15,000.

Applications: In writing to the correspondent. Applications are considered throughout the year.
Correspondent: Tony Baylies, Rathbones, Port of Liverpool Building, Liverpool L3 1NW (0151 236 6666).

The William Johnston Trust Fund

Eligibility: People in need. Preference is given to older people.
Types of grants: Recurrent grants of £650 to £4,000 each. One-off grants for TV licences and birthdays can also be given.
Annual grant total: In 2001 the trust made 22 recurrent grants totalling £29,000 and 13 one-off grants totalling £1,200.
Applications: By letter ONLY to the correspondent. Applications are considered throughout the year.
Correspondent: Tony Baylies, Rathbones, Port of Liverpool Building, Liverpool L3 1NW (0151 236 6666).

Jordison and Hossell Animal Welfare Charity

Eligibility: People who are on low incomes and are in need of financial assistance in meeting vets bills for their pets.
Types of grants: One-off grants of up to £500 towards vets' bills. Vets' bills for larger animals such as horses and farm animals are not funded.
Annual grant total: In 2000/01 the trust had an income of £6,400 and a total expenditure of £6,600.
Applications: Applications must be made by the vet in question, rather than from the client. The charity does not deal with the client directly. Applications should be made by telephone in the first instance (rather than an invoice arriving).
Correspondent: Ms Sally Drabble, Administrator, 173 Tanworth Lane, Shirley, West Midlands B90 4BZ (0121 745 4274).

The Florence Juckes Memorial Trust Fund

Eligibility: People in need living within a 50-mile radius of Birmingham city centre.
Types of grants: One-off grants which range from £50 to £200, but are generally £100 or less. Recent grants have included £30 for shoes for a child who is disabled and £100 towards car insurance for a man who is disabled.
Annual grant total: In 2000/01 the fund had an income of £2,600 and a total expenditure of £860.
Applications: The correspondent stated that: 'the trust has very limited funds and we receive many applications. Generally speaking our grants are through personal recommendation from other members of Soroptimist clubs – not by general application'. The income is often earmarked before it is received, therefore even these applications are unlikely to be successful.
Correspondent: Miss A E Bond, 42 White House Way, Solihull, West Midlands B91 1SE (0121 704 3308).

Kangas Trust

Eligibility: People personally known to the trustees. Previously, the trust supported individuals in need, including ex-service and service people, seafarers and fishermen.
Types of grants: One-off and recurrent grants according to need.
Annual grant total: In 2000/01 the trust had an income of £2,100 and a total expenditure of £1,900. No grants were made to individuals during the year, although £50 was given to an organisation.
Applications: In writing to the correspondent.
Correspondent: Dr K N G Shaw, Trustee, 2 The Orchard, Kingston St. Michael, Chippenham, Wiltshire SN14 6JH.

The Longfields Trust

Eligibility: People who are in need who have a personal contact with the trust.
Types of grants: One-off grants of £10 to £100. The bulk of the funds are given in regular donations to organisations, the surplus is available in grants to individuals.
Annual grant total: In 2000/01 the trust had an income of £1,600 and a total expenditure of £2,200. Grants to four individuals totalled £340. Grants to organisations totalled £1,800.
Applications: In writing to the correspondent.
Correspondent: Dr A Lennard-Jones, Chair to the Trustees, 16 Wordsworth Road, Colchester CO3 4HR.

P & M Lovell Charitable Settlement

Eligibility: People in need.
Types of grants: One-off grants of £100 to £250.
Annual grant total: In 2000/01 the trust had an income of £29,000. Grants to eight individuals totalled £950 and a further £12,000 was given to organisations.
Applications: In writing to the correspondent.
Correspondent: c/o Matthew Bird, KPMG, 100 Temple Street, Bristol BS1 6AG.

The McKenna Charitable Trust

Eligibility: People in need in England and Wales.
Types of grants: One-off grants are occasionally made to individuals, according to need.
Annual grant total: In 1997/98 the trust had an income of £1,300 and a total expenditure of £1,100. Up-to-date information was not available, but the trust states that grants are mainly made to organisations.
Applications: In writing to the correspondent.
Correspondent: The Trustees, c/o Buzzacott, 12 New Fetter Lane, London EC4A 1AG (020 7556 1200).

Midhurst Pensions Trust

Eligibility: Older people who have been employed by the Third Viscount Cowdray or on the Cowdray Estate, and their dependants who are also over retirement age.
Types of grants: One-off and recurrent pensions are made ranging from £510 to £2,100, for day-to-day needs, for example clothing or food. Grants are not made to people with an income that is £1,000 greater than their personal allowance for income tax.
Annual grant total: In 2000/01 the trust had an income of £134,000 and grants totalling £49,000 to 57 individuals. No grants were made to organisations.
Applications: In writing to the correspondent for consideration by the trust on an ad hoc basis. Applications can be submitted either directly by the individual or through a social worker, citizen's advice bureau or other third party.

Unsuccessful applications will not be acknowledged.
Correspondent: Alan John Winborn, The Cowdray Trust Limited, Pollen House, 10-12 Cork Street, London W15 3LW (020 7439 9061).
Other information: This trust also gives grants to organisations.

NCDS (National Council for the Divorced & Separated Trust)

Eligibility: People in need in the UK. All applications are considered regardless of marital status.
Types of grants: One-off grants according to need.
Annual grant total: In 2000 the trust had an income of £3,300 and a total expenditure of £1,600.
Applications: On a form available from the correspondent. Applications can be submitted directly by the individual or through a social worker, citizen's advice bureau or other welfare agency. Applications are considered every six to eight weeks, although urgent cases can be considered between meetings.
Correspondent: The Secretary, PO Box 6, Kingswinford, West Midlands DY6 8YS (0114 272 6331).

NATIONAL & GENERAL CHARITIES

Professional Classes Aid Council

Eligibility: People of professional background who have no specific fund to turn to when in distress. Grants are also given for the welfare of children of the above.

Types of grants: Weekly allowances of £5 to £20, and one-off gifts according to need.

Annual grant total: In 2000 the trust had assets of £2.5 million, an income of £753,000 and a total expenditure of £272,000. Grants to 360 individuals totalled £245,000 and were made for education and welfare purposes.

Applications: On a form available from the correspondent, submitted either by the individual, or via a third party such as a social worker, citizen's advice bureau or other welfare agency.

Correspondent: Hugh David, Secretary, 10 St Christopher's Place, London W1U 1HZ (020 7935 0641).

The J C Robinson Trust No. 3

Eligibility: People in need in England, with a preference for those living in Sussex, Bristol and south Gloucester.

Types of grants: Grants were in the range of £50 to £1,000, about half were for £500 each.

Annual grant total: In 1999/2000 the trust had assets of £590,000 and an income of £20,000, all of which was distributed in 47 grants, about half going to individuals with the rest to organisations.

Applications: In writing to the correspondent, including some sort of supporting evidence of the need, such as from a doctor or social worker.

Correspondent: Dr C J Burns-Cox, Trustee, Southend Farm, Wotton-under-Edge, Gloucestershire GL12 7PB (01453 842243).

Other information: Grants are also made to organisations.

Mrs L D Rope's Second Charitable Settlement

Eligibility: People in need, with a preference for Suffolk.

Types of grants: Grants are given for the relief of poverty and for the support of religion. Almost all grants are made to or at the recommendation of charities or organisations with which the trust has long-term connections.

Annual grant total: In 1999/2000 the trust gave £8,700 to individuals. A further £11,000 was given to organisations.

Applications: The trust stated: 'The Charity does not accept unsolicited requests for grants, either from individuals or organisations.'

Correspondent: C M Rope, Trustee, Crag Farm, Boyton, Near Woodbridge, Suffolk IP12 3LH.

The Royal Scottish Corporation (also known as The Scottish Hospital of the Foundation of King Charles II)

See entry on page 362

The Salvation Army

Eligibility: People in need.

Types of grants: All grants are one-off, in the form of specific practical assistance such as for needs in the home. Subject to availability, it also provides holidays at a local caravan or at their centre in Westgate – Kent.

No grants are given for educational purposes, except to time-serving prisoners.

Annual grant total: In 1998/99 grants to individuals totalled £1.1 million, a further £828,000 being given to organisations.

Applications: In writing to the divisional director for business administration at the nearest regional office. The regional offices cover: Anglia; Central North; Central South; London Central; London North East; London South East; East Midlands; West Midlands; North West; Northern England; East Scotland; North Scotland; West Scotland; South Western; Southern; South and Mid Wales: and Yorkshire. Address can usually be found in any telephone directory, or by visiting the charity's website.

All applications must be supported by a caseworker's report from a social agency, welfare organisation, hospital or medical practice. Information about the applicant's social and financial background must be included in the report.

Correspondent: John Warner, Company Secretary, 101 Newington Causeway, London SE1 6BN (020 7367 4783; Fax: 020 7367 4716; website: www.salvationarmy.org.uk).

Other information: The Salvation Army is one of the largest welfare organisations in the UK. Its main feature is the provision of direct practical help. Financial assistance is usually only a small and incidental part of its work.

Mr William Saunders Charity for the Relief of Indigent Gentry and Others

Eligibility: 'Indigent gentry tutors, governesses, merchants and others'; and their dependants, who are in need.

Types of grants: One-off and recurrent grants according to need.

Annual grant total: In 2001 the trust's income was £6,800 and its total expenditure was £8,400.

Applications: In writing to the correspondent.

Correspondent: The Trustees, c/o Richard Charles Kirby, 6 St Andrew Street, London EC4A 3LX (020 7427 6400; e-mail: speechlys@speechlys.co.uk).

Other information: Grants are also made to local organisations caring for people in need.

The Severn Trent Water Charitable Trust

Eligibility: People who are unable to afford to pay charges owed to Severn Trent Water Limited, including people no longer in a property served by the company or if the charge is collected by a third party.

Types of grants: Grants are given to write-off people's bills to the company. Further assistance can also be given towards essential household items or other priority bills (i.e. utility bills). Further assistance grants are limited and will normally only be given if an application shows either that it will help the individual make a future sustainable weekly budget or it will make an important and significant difference to the individual's quality of life.

Annual grant total: £2.1 million was available to individuals in 2001/02.

Applications: On a form available from the correspondent, a citizen's advice bureau, money advice centres or other supporting agencies. Forms can also be requested by e-mail or downloaded from the trust's website. Unsuccessful applicants can reapply after six months.

Correspondent: S Braley, Chief Executive, PO Box 8778, Sutton Coldfield B72 1TP (e-mail: office@sttf.org.uk; website: www.sttf.org.uk).

Other information: This trust also supports organisations which provide debt counselling and money advice to individuals.

The Patricia and Donald Shepherd Trust

Eligibility: People in need, with preference to young people who live in Scotland or the north of England.

Types of grants: One-off and recurrent grants according to need.

Annual grant total: In 1999/2000 the trust had assets of £489,000 generating an income of £93,000. Grants to individuals totalled £3,000. A further £77,000 was given to organisations.

Applications: In writing to the correspondent.

Correspondent: Mrs Patricia Shepherd, Trustee, PO Box 10, York YO1 1XU.

Other information: This entry was not confirmed by the trust, but was correct according to information on file at the Charity Commission.

NATIONAL & GENERAL CHARITIES

Springboard Charitable Trust

Eligibility: People in the UK who are on a low income.

Types of grants: One-off and recurrent grants according to need, towards essential items, such as cookers and fridges. No grants are given to: students from overseas; people who are disabled and aged over 25; medical research; second degrees; further education; expeditions; and art and music projects.

Annual grant total: In 2000/01 the trust had assets of £342,000, an income of £132,000 and its total expenditure was £130,000. Grants totalled £27,000, and were probably mostly given to organisations.

Applications: In writing to the correspondent three months before the grant is needed.

Correspondent: C E Shannon, 38 Suffolk Street, Helensburgh G84 9PD (01436 673326).

The St Martin-in-the-Fields' Vicar's Relief Fund

Eligibility: People in need or hardship.

Types of grants: One-off grants of up to £250 to have a positive impact and help alleviate distress or avert a crisis. Grants have been given towards a range of needs, including furniture, child and adult clothing, domestic appliances, equipment for babies and toddlers, utility bills and household maintenance and repair.

No grants are given for travel, computers, education or holidays. Only one grant is usually made to an individual within 12 months.

Annual grant total: About £200,000, half of which is given through local groups, the remaining half given in about 500 grants.

Applications: On a form available from the correspondent. Applications should not be made directly by the individual but through agencies such as social services, probation, citizen's advice bureaux or other welfare agencies. They can usually be considered within two days.

Correspondent: The Administrator, VRF, St Martin-in-the-Fields, 6 St Martin's Place, London WC2N 4JJ.

The St Vincent de Paul Society (England & Wales)

Eligibility: Anyone in need in England and Wales. Although predominantly a Catholic charity, it is completely non-denominational in its operation. Grants are only offered following a visit from a member of the society.

Types of grants: Small one-off grants towards food, clothing, fuel bills or small holiday grants, dependent on local assessment and availability of funds. Friendship to anyone in need is a fundamental principle of the society, financial relief is incidental to this.

No grants for education.

Annual grant total: Around £2 million.

Applications: In writing to the correspondent at any time. Applications can be submitted directly by the individual or through any third party, such as advice centres or probation services.

Correspondent: Administration Manager, SVP, 14 Blandford Street, London W1U 4DR (020 7935 9126; Fax: 020 7935 9136; e-mail: terryk@svp.org.uk).

Other information: There are about 1,600 parish groups in England and Wales, with around 16,000 members. Most of the income is raised locally by members and distributed by them. The society runs several children's camps, holiday caravans and so on and a number of hostels, shops and furniture stores. Prison visitations take place in some areas, and a 'Catholic Cassette' for the blind and partially sighted is available. Considerable support is given to the developing world and Romania.

The Straits Settlement & Malay States Benevolent Society

Eligibility: Retired people who have lived in the Far East for a minimum of two years, and their dependants.

Types of grants: One-off and recurrent grants according to need. The society tends to support Europeans and dependants of Europeans, although this is not exclusively so.

Annual grant total: In 2001 the society had an income of £14,000 and a total expenditure of £17,000.

Applications: Applications should be sponsored by a subscriber.

Correspondent: Vince Cheshire, Ernst & Young, 400 Capability Green, Luton LU1 3LU (01582 643470).

Other information: The society's funds are fully committed and the society does not wish to incur further administration costs in replying to applications which cannot at present be considered.

Mary Strand Charitable Trust

Eligibility: People who are in need due to poverty, sickness or old age. The trustees publish the Mary Strand Column in each edition of Universe, a weekly Roman Catholic newspaper. The column contains details of deserving causes with names changed to preserve anonymity, and appeals are made for specific requirements. Donations from readers are received in answer to these appeals.

Types of grants: One-off and recurrent grants, towards the item or service specified in the appeal (see above).

Annual grant total: In 2000 the trust had an income of £72,000 and its total expenditure was £68,000. In 1999 the trust had an income of £78,000 and gave grants to individuals totalling £61,000.

Applications: In writing to the correspondent, usually by priests, charities or welfare agencies on behalf of the individual. Applications must be submitted with supporting evidence and a reference.

Correspondent: Mary Concannon, Gabriel Communications Ltd, First Floor, St James Buildings, Oxford Street, Manchester M1 6FP (0161 236 8856).

Sir John Sumner's Trust

Eligibility: People in need who are resident in the UK, with strong preference for the Midlands.

Types of grants: One-off grants ranging between £30 and £70. The trust will sometimes give an amount towards larger requests if other charities make up the rest. No grants towards religious or political causes.

Annual grant total: In 2000/01 the trust had assets of £795,000, an income of £39,000 and a total expenditure of £42,000.

Applications: On a form available from the correspondent, supported by an appropriate welfare agency. Applications can be considered at any time.

Correspondent: A C Robson, Secretary, 8th Floor, Union Chambers, 63 Temple Row, Birmingham B2 5LT.

Other information: This trust also gives grants for educational purposes.

The Vardy Foundation

Eligibility: People in need in who live in the UK.

Types of grants: One-off and recurrent grants according to need.

Annual grant total: In 1998/99 the foundation had assets of £5.4 million and an income of £267,000. Grants to 12 individuals and 31 organisations totalled £617,000.

Applications: In writing to the correspondent.

Correspondent: Sir Peter Vardy, Chair of the Trustees, Houghton House, Emperor Way, Doxford International Business Park, Sunderland SR3 3XR (0191 516 3636).

Edward Wilde Foundation

Eligibility: People who are in need.

Types of grants: One-off and recurrent grants according to need.

Annual grant total: In 2000/01 the trust had an income of £3,100 and an expenditure of £2,500.

Applications: In writing to the correspondent.

Correspondent: E Wilde, Durfold Cottage, Deerleap Road, Westcott, Dorking, Surrey RH4 3LE.

NATIONAL & GENERAL CHARITIES

Other information: Grants are also made to organisations.

S C Witting Trust

Eligibility: Individuals in need who live in England, Germany or Poland and are under 15 or over 60 years old.

Types of grants: One-off grants ranging from £100 to £170. Grants are not made for the payment of debts.

Annual grant total: In 2001 the trust's income was £18,000 and its total expenditure was £21,000. Grants to 150 individuals for education and relief-in-need purposes totalled £20,000. 40% of the grant total is given to individuals in England, with 40% to people in Germany and the remaining 20% to people in Poland. In 2001 there were 72 grants made to individuals in England, averaging £110 each.

Applications: In writing to the correspondent, at any time, through a social worker, citizen's advice bureau or other welfare agency. Unsuccessful applications are not acknowledged.

Correspondent: The Trustees, c/o Administrator, Friends House, 173 Euston Road, London NW1 2BJ.

You and Your Community Millennium Awards

Eligibility: The Millennium Commission is awarding grants to individuals in the UK with a bright idea for a community project that also benefits him/herself. Grants have included those to a writer in Northern Ireland to produce a book about his local community and to people to obtain first aid training and training in counselling, to enable them to serve their communities better, for example, at their sports club.

Grants are not given for career development, for example for academic study, or soley to help relieve financial need.

Applications: These awards are not directly for individuals in need, so we are only including a brief entry for them in this guide. The last applications for grants will be autumn 2003. For further information, see the website www.starpeople.org.uk, or telephone 020 7880 2072.

Children/young people

The Buttle Trust

Eligibility: Children under 21 who are either (i) looked after by adoptive parents; (ii) cared for by family members or friends; (iii) living with single parents; or (iv) estranged or orphaned and living independently.

The trust cannot help children who (i) are supported by two caring parents living in the home; (ii) are being looked after by a local authority (in accordance with the Children Act 1989); (iii) were in the care of statutory authority where the authority has unequivocal responsibility; (iv) have been in the UK for less than two years and have neither full refugee status or exceptional leave to remain; or (v) are living outside the UK.

Types of grants: One-off grants towards clothes, bedding, essential furniture and household equipment. No grants towards payment of debts, holiday and child care costs, computers or adaptations to houses and cars.

Annual grant total: In 2000/01 the trust made 3,111 grants totalling £818,000.

Applications: In writing, through a statutory agency or voluntary organisation that is capable of assessing the needs of the child and that can also administer a grant on behalf of the trust; where no such organisation exists, the trust will discuss alternative arrangements. Applications should include the facts of the case, highlighting the problems or misfortune experienced by the child. Eligible applicants will be sent an application form which will be considered monthly.

Applications should be sent to the relevant address below:

For applicants in England: The Director, The Buttle Trust, Audley House, 13 Palace Street, London SW1E 5HX (020 7828 7311; Fax: 020 7828 4724;
e-mail: director@buttletrust.org).

For applicants in Wales: The Regional Secretary, PO Box 7, Rhayader, Powys LD6 5WB (Tel & Fax: 01597 870060; e-mail: wales@buttletrust.org).

For applicants in Scotland: The Regional Secretary, PO Box 5075, Uplawmoor, Glasgow G78 4WA (Tel & Fax: 01505 850547; e-mail: scotland@buttletrust.org).

For applicants in Northern Ireland: The Regional Secretary, c/o Bryson House, 28 Bedford Street, Belfast BT2 7FE (Tel & Fax: 01232 641164; e-mail: nireland@buttletrust.org).

Other information: The trust was founded by the Rev W F Buttle in 1953. It publishes useful Notes for the guidance of social agencies or others applying for a Buttle Trust grant.

The J I Colvile Charitable Trust

Eligibility: Disadvantaged young people.

Types of grants: One-off grants of £50 to £250.

Annual grant total: In 2000 the trust had an income of £8,200 and a total expenditure of £4,000.

Applications: In writing to the correspondent.

Correspondent: M S Lee-Browne, Solicitor, Wilmot & Co. Solicitors, High Street, Fairford, Gloucestershire GL7 4AE (01285 712207).

Other information: Grants are also made to youth training projects.

Domine Trust

See entry on page 57

Ebb and Flow Charitable Trust

Eligibility: Pre-school children who are in need. Grants are made to all parts of the UK, but there is a preference for Oxford and the surrounding areas.

Types of grants: Grants ranging from £200 to £400 are made for children's pre-school education and development.

Annual grant total: In 2000/01 the trust had assets of £99,000, an income of £6,500 and grants to organisations and individuals totalled £6,700.

Applications: On a form available from the correspondent, submitted by the parent/guardian. Trustees meet at the beginning of March and September, and applications should be submitted in January and July.

Correspondent: Mrs M A Bickmore, 28 Northmoor Road, Oxford, OX2 6UR (01865 513100).

Other information: Grants are also made to organisations working in the fields of physical and mental disability and homelessness. Postgraduate or mature students can also be supported who are disabled or face an unusual degree of hardship or who are studying for qualifications in the therapy fields (art, music, speech, physio etc.). Postgraduate students from overseas are considered if they have been accepted by an institution for study in the UK.

The Glebe Charitable Trust

Eligibility: Children and young people up to the age of 25 who are disabled or disadvantaged in some way in addition to being in financial need. Please note, financial need alone is not sufficient.

Types of grants: One-off and recurrent grants according to need.

Grants are not made towards fees for higher education save in the most exceptional circumstances nor for gap year activities.

Annual grant total: In 2001 the trust had an income of £25,000 and it made grants totalling £20,000. Only £100 of this was given in grant to individuals in need, with £2,800 given to individuals for educational purposes.

Applications: The trust states that it: 'receives applications beyond its capacities, both administrative and financial. The trustees have therefore taken the reluctant decision that they can no longer consider unsolicited applications from either charities or individuals.'

Correspondent: T K H Robertson, Trustee, Tweedie & Prideaux, PO Box 38078, Wimbledon D.O., London SW19.

Happy Days Children's Charity

Eligibility: Children and young people aged 3 to 17 years inclusive who are disadvantaged and have special needs. Children who do not have special needs are not funded.

Types of grants: One-off grants ranging from £25 to £1,000 for family holidays in the UK (occasionally children who are terminally ill are funded for an overseas holiday). All funding is paid directly to the providers, i.e. venue/resort, transport provider etc. All trips are organised and funded directly by the charity, therefore cheques are not normally given directly to the family. Essential key carers are also funded who are necessary to support the needs of the children on the holiday (see below). No extra adults are funded.

Annual grant total: In 2000/01 the trust's assets totalled £13,000 and it had an income of £397,000 and a total expenditure of £406,000. Gifts in the form of payment for holidays and day trips were made to 2,620 families and groups totalling £124,000.

Applications: On a form available from the Families and Groups Bookings Welfare Officer at the address below. Applications are considered year round and can be submitted either directly by the family or through a social worker, citizen's advice bureau or other welfare agency. A telephone call is welcome for advice and guidance.

Correspondent: Miss Claire Simpson, Byron House, 43 Cardiff Road, Luton LU1 1PP (01582 755999; Fax: 01582 755900; e-mail: happydays@connect4free.net).

Other information: Grants are also made to groups of children and young people who have special needs for day trips.

The Jay Foundation

Eligibility: Children and young people up to the age of 25 years who are victims of physical, sexual or mental abuse, and their families, legal guardians, carers or educators.

Types of grants: One-off and recurrent grants, ranging between £100 and £500.

Annual grant total: In 2000 the trust had an income of £1,000 and its total expenditure was £780.

Applications: In writing to the correspondent.

Correspondent: P C Jackson, Chair, Stanhill, North Hill, Little Badden, Essex CM3 4TD.

Other information: Grants are also made for educational purposes.

Richard Langhorn Trust

Eligibility: Children who are disabled or underprivileged.

Types of grants: One-off and recurrent grants towards sporting opportunities, particularly rugby, sailing, basketball and skiing.

Annual grant total: In 1997 the trust's income totalled £150,000 and £50,000 was given in grants to individuals and organisations. More recent information was not available.

Applications: In writing to the correspondent, for consideration throughout the year.

Correspondent: The Trustees, c/o Harlequins Rugby Football Club, Stoop Memorial Ground, Langhorn Drive, Twickenham, Middlesex TW2 7SX (020 8410 6000).

Colonel Peter Murray Bequest – Clan Gregor Fund

Eligibility: Boys in need, aged between 7 and 16 when the grant starts, who have the surname MacGregor or whose mother's maiden name was MacGregor.

Types of grants: A recurrent grant of £150 is made each year to four boys until they reach the age of 21. The grant is given for educational rather than welfare purposes, therefore beneficiaries leaving education before 21 may be taken off the list.

Annual grant total: In 2000/01 the trust had assets of £16,000, an income of £920 and a total expenditure. Grants to four individuals totalled £600.

Applications: In writing to the correspondent by the individual or parent. Applications can only be considered when a vacancy on the list arises.

Correspondent: Alastair H Cruickshank, Judicial Factor, Messrs Condies, Solicitors, 2 Tay Street, Perth PH1 5LJ (01738 440088; Fax: 01738 441131; e-mail: enquiry@condies.co.uk).

Other information: The trust told us in March 2002 that the fund is fully committed until the end of 2014 and no vacancies will arise until then. Whilst this appears unlikely, potential applicants should be cautious about applying to this trust.

The Royal Eastern Counties Schools Limited

Eligibility: People under 25 with special educational needs, particularly those with emotional and behavioural difficulties. While support is given throughout the UK, preference will normally be given to people living in Essex, Suffolk, Norfolk, Cambridgeshire and Hertfordshire.

Types of grants: One-off grants are given for education, training, care and welfare purposes. Normally no grants are made for recurring costs.

Annual grant total: The trust has about £20,000 a year to distribute, mostly to organisations but individuals may also be considered.

In 2000/01 the trust's net assets totalled £1.7 million, its income was £97,000 and its total expenditure was £90,000. One grant was made to an individual of £2,200. Grants to organisations totalled £18,000.

Applications: Application forms can be obtained from the correspondent. Applications should normally be submitted during October for consideration between November and March, although urgent applications can be considered at other times. Applications can be made directly by the individual or through a social worker, citizen's advice bureau or other welfare agency. Unsuccessful applicants will not be informed unless an sae is provided.

Correspondent: A H Corin, Company Secretary, Brook Farm, Wet Lane, Boxted, Colchester, Essex CO4 5TN (01206 273295).

Ethnic & Foreign Communities in the UK – including refugees and asylum seekers

The Bestway Foundation

Eligibility: People who are ill and are of Indian, Pakistani, Bangladeshi or Sri Lankan origin.

Types of grants: One-off and recurrent grants according to need.

Annual grant total: In 1998/99 the trust had an income of £406,000 and it made grants to organisations and individuals for both welfare and educational purposes totalling £191,000.

Applications: In writing to the correspondent enclosing an sae. Telephone calls are not welcome.

Correspondent: D Taylor, Bestway Cash & Carry Ltd, 2 Abbey Road, Park Royal, London NW10 7BW.

NATIONAL & GENERAL CHARITIES

The Assyrian Charity and Relief Fund of UK

Eligibility: People of Assyrian descent living in UK or worldwide who are in need, hardship or distress.

Types of grants: The fund offers food, medicine and temporary shelter to people in need. One-off and recurrent grants are made usually ranging between £10 and £400.

No grants for rich people, business men, political organisations and people already settled in Europe, America, Australia and Canada.

Annual grant total: In 1998/99 the fund had an income of £2,500. Total expenditure was £2,400, all of which was given in 229 grants.

Applications: In writing to the correspondent, submitted through a social worker, citizen's advice bureau, welfare agency or other charity.

Correspondent: Andrious Mama Jotyar, Secretary, 108 Alderney Road, Erith, Kent DA8 2JD (01322 331711).

Other information: Ten university students were also sponsored in Iraq for the year 1999/2000.

The Croatian Relief Fund

Eligibility: Croatians and people of Croatian descent worldwide, who are sick, distressed or in need.

Types of grants: One-off and recurrent grants according to need.

Annual grant total: In 2000 the fund had an income of £310 and a total expenditure of £300.

Applications: In writing to the correspondent.

Correspondent: Count Louis Doimi de Lupis, 18 Eldon Road, London W8 5PT (e-mail: frankopan@dial.pipex.com).

Egyptian Community Association in the United Kingdom

Eligibility: People in need who are Egyptian or of Egyptian origin and are living in or visiting the UK.

Types of grants: Grants towards a broad range of needs, for example, help with the costs of medical treatment and gas bills.

Annual grant total: In 1996 the trust had an income of £39,000 and its total expenditure was £48,000. Recent information was unavailable.

Applications: In writing to the correspondent.

Correspondent: H Elsheriff, General Secretary, 100 Redcliffe Gardens, London SW10 9HH (020 7259 2801).

Other information: The association arranges seminars and national and religious celebrations, as well as offering other services. It also gives grants to individuals for educational purposes.

This entry was not confirmed by the trust. The address and financial information are the most recent available on the Charity Commission database.

Fund for Human Need

See entry on page 108

German Welfare Council

Eligibility: People who are of German origin, and their dependants who are aged under 18, who are on a low income and live in the UK.

Types of grants: One-off and recurrent grants of £20 to £250 are given towards heating, essential items and repairs. Holiday costs of up to £500 can also be met in certain circumstances.

Annual grant total: In 2001 the trust had an income of £99,000 and a total expenditure of £101,000. Grants totalled £36,000.

Applications: In writing to the correspondent, either directly by the individual or through a social worker, citizen's advice bureau or other welfare agency. Applications should include proof of income and expenditure where possible. The trustees consider applications monthly.

Correspondent: The Trustees, German Advice Centre, 4th Floor, 34 Belgrave Square, London SW1X 8QB (020 7235 4343; Fax: 020 7235 4355; e-mail: german.advice@btinternet.com; website: www.germanadvicecentre.btinternet.co.uk).

The Ibero-American Benevolent Society

Eligibility: Subjects or citizens of all Spanish or Portuguese speaking countries, whilst in the UK, and the wives or widows and children of the above.

Types of grants: One-off grants of up to £250 for a wide range of needs, including washing machines, cookers and telephone installation/bills in certain circumstances. No education grants are made.

Annual grant total: About £5,000.

Applications: In writing to the correspondent, at any time. Applications must be submitted through a social worker, citizen's advice bureau, a welfare agency or similar official worker, not directly by the individual.

Correspondent: Mrs I Talman, Secretary, c/o Banco Bilbao Vizcaya, 108 Cannon Street, London EC4N 6EU (020 7623 3060).

India Welfare Society

Eligibility: Members of the Indian community, who have membership with the society, who are in need.

Types of grants: One-off and recurrent grants according to need for hardship and welfare purposes only.

Annual grant total: In 2001 the society had an income of £9,000 and its total expenditure was £8,500.

Applications: In writing to the correspondent.

Correspondent: S K Gupta, President, 11 Kensal Road, London W10 5BJ (020 8960 2637).

The Netherlands Benevolent Society

Eligibility: People in need who are Dutch nationals or of Dutch extraction and living in the UK.

Types of grants: One-off grants ranging between £100 to £800 and regular allowances of £40 a month for each individual. Grants have included payments of debts to avoid legal action, essential home repairs, clothing, cost of training course and cost of tools or materials for work. Beneficiaries must not have access to financial help from other sources.

Annual grant total: In 2001 the society had assets of £500,000 and both an income and a total expenditure of £40,000. Grants to 50 individuals totalled £25,000.

Applications: On a form available from: Mrs M Schippers, c/o 19 Travertine Road, Walderslade, Chatham, Kent ME5 9LG. Applications should be submitted directly by the individual or through the consul section of the Dutch embassy, for consideration in any month except August. Information of the individual's financial situation including details of social security benefits received should be included.

Correspondent: Mrs M Schippers, The Administrator, 7 Austin Friars, London EC2N 2HA (01634 868989).

The Puri Foundation

Eligibility: Individuals in need living in Nottinghamshire who are from India (particularly the towns of Mullan Pur near Chandigarh and Ambala). Employees/past employees of the Melton Medes Group Ltd, Blugilt Holdings or Melham Inc and their dependants, who are in need, are also eligible

The trust wants to support people who have exhausted state support and other avenues, in other words to be a 'last resort'.

Types of grants: One-off and recurrent grants according to need, e.g. for items of furniture and clothes. The maximum donation is usually between £150 and £200.

Annual grant total: In 2000/01 the foundation had assets of £3.3 million, an income of £119,000 and a total expenditure of £53,000. 73 relief-in need and education grants to individuals

NATIONAL & GENERAL CHARITIES

totalled £3,300. Grants to organisations totalled £50,000.

Applications: In writing to the correspondent, either directly by the individual or through a social worker.

Correspondent: Nathu Ram Puri, Environment House, 6 Union Road, Nottingham NG3 1FH
(Tel & Fax: 0115 901 3000).

The Rhodesians Worldwide Assistance Fund

Eligibility: People formerly resident in Zimbabwe (previously Rhodesia) prior to 1980, and their dependants who are in need.

Types of grants: Grants for short term needs.

Annual grant total: In 1999, 113 grants totalled £62,000.

Applications: On a form available from the correspondent. Full financial and social circumstances plus complete reasons for applying must be included. Details will be verified.

Applications can be submitted directly by the individual or through another charity or close relative. Applications are considered in February, May, August and November. In cases of emergency, applications can be considered immediately.

Correspondent: Peter Hagelthorn, 42 Victoria Park, Great Cheverell, nr Devizes, Wiltshire SN10 5TZ (01380 818381).

The Royal Belgian Benevolent Society

Eligibility: Belgians who live in Britain, and their close dependants, who are in need.

Types of grants: Regular grants of £300 to £2,000.

Annual grant total: In 2001 the society had assets of £126,000, an income of £7,700 and a total expenditure of £10,000. Welfare grants to individuals totalled £3,000. Educational grants to individuals totalled £7,500.

Applications: On a form available from the correspondent, submitted either directly by the individual, or via a social worker, citizen's advice bureau or other welfare agency.

Correspondent: Patrick Bresnan, Anglo-Belgian Club, 60 Knightsbridge, London SW1X 7LF (020 7235 2121; Fax: 020 7245 9470).

The Scandinavian Benevolent Society

Eligibility: Norwegians and Danes who live in the UK. The society particularly helps older people and families who are in need. However, all applications for help will be considered. The society can also help with repatriation.

Types of grants: About 20 pensioners receive £5 or £10 a week. The trust also makes one-off payments of £50 to £200. No grants for educational purposes or to top up fees for nursing/residential homes.

Annual grant total: In 2000 the trust had assets of £247,000 and an income of £14,000. Total expenditure was £22,000, including £15,000 in grants.

Applications: Applications must be made through Norwegian or Danish churches/embassies, or a social services department, citizen's advice bureau, doctor, vicar or other such person or welfare agency. The trustees meet quarterly, but payments can be made more promptly in certain cases.

Correspondent: Mrs V K Goodhart, Secretary, 68 Burhill Road, Hersham, Walton-on-Thames, Surrey KT12 4JF (01932 244916;
e-mail: scanbensoc@freeuk.com).

The Society of Friends of Foreigners in Distress

Eligibility: People living in London or its surrounding area who are from countries not in the Commonwealth, the USA or which were once part of the British Empire.

Types of grants: One-off grants of up to £100 to families, refugees and asylum seekers.

Annual grant total: In 1999/2000 the trust had assets of £547,000, an income of £23,000 and a grant total of £17,000. Grants totalled £13,000.

Applications: In writing to the correspondent at any time. Applications should be submitted by a social worker, citizen's advice bureau or other welfare agency.

Correspondent: Mrs V K Goodhart, 68 Burhill Road, Hersham, Walton-on-Thames, Surrey KT12 4JF (01932 244916).

The Swiss Benevolent Society

Eligibility: Swiss nationals who live in the consular district of the Swiss Embassy in London (mainly the Greater London area and the south of England).

Types of grants: One-off and recurrent grants according to need (generally of not more than £10 per week) for help holidays, heating, travel to and from day centres, therapies, household equipment, telephone and TV licences and as Easter and Christmas presents.

No loans or student grants are made.

Annual grant total: In 2001 the society had assets of £803,000, an income of £69,000 and a total expenditure of £109,000. Grants totalled £25,000.

Applications: In writing to the social worker at the address below. Applications can be submitted directly by the individual or via any third party and are considered monthly.

Correspondent: The Secretary, 79 Endell Street, London WC2H 9DY (020 7836 9119; Fax: 020 7379 1096;
e-mail: swissbenevolent@aol.com).

Zimbabwe Rhodesia Relief Fund

Eligibility: Zimbabwe Rhodesians living worldwide who are distressed or sick.

Types of grants: One-off and recurrent grants of £70 to £300. Grants are not given for educational purposes or travel.

Annual grant total: In 2000/01 the trust had an income of £43,000 and a total expenditure of £51,000. Grants to 135 individuals totalled £49,000.

Applications: In writing to the correspondent. Applications should be made via somebody known to the charity and include proof of past or present Zimbabwean citizenship.

Correspondent: W Denis Walker, Secretary, PO Box 5307, Bishop's Stonford, Hertfordshire CM23 3DZ (01279 466300; Fax: 01279 466111).

Holidays

The Family Holiday Association

Eligibility: Families who are referred by social workers, health visitors or other caring agencies as desperate for a holiday break. Applicants must not have had a holiday within the past four years, unless there are exceptional circumstances; and at least one child must be aged between 3 and 18.

Types of grants: Either the family has an idea about where they want to go and the association decides how much to give towards the total cost, or the association funds the entire holiday at a holiday centre and gives money towards the costs of food, spending money and so on. Grants are generally from £250 upwards.

Annual grant total: About 1,000 families are supported each year.

In 1999/2000 the association had assets of £409,000, an income of £1 million and a total expenditure of £837,000. Grants totalled £445,000.

Applications: Applications should be submitted in November each year. The association usually has enough applications to commit all its funds by December. Social workers should apply by letter requesting an application form and enclose an sae. Applications must be referred by a welfare agency, voluntary organisation etc; those made directly by

NATIONAL & GENERAL CHARITIES

the individual are not accepted. Grants can be calculated on the basis of the kind of holiday the family would choose.

Correspondent: The Grants Officer, 16 Mortimer Street, London W1T 3JL (020 7436 3304; Fax: 020 7436 3302).

Pearson's Holiday Fund

Eligibility: Disadvantaged children and young people aged between 4 and 16 years (inclusive) who live in the UK.

Types of grants: Financial assistance for holidays and/or respite activities in the UK that give an opportunity for the child/young person to be way from their normal environment. The maximum grant per individual is £50 (£750 for groups of children and young people). Grants can be one-off and annual, although a new application is required each year. No grants for activities outside the UK, or for people who live outside the UK.

Annual grant total: In 2002 £113,000 was available to individuals and organisations in grants. In 2001 it had assets of £191,000, an income of £129,000 and gave grants to 554 individuals totalling £76,000, whilst grants to organisations totalled £67,000.

Applications: In writing to the correspondent, enclosing an sae. They should be submitted by an appropriate third party, such as social workers, health visitors, teachers, doctors, ministers of religion and so on. The fund does not deal directly with families or children/young people. Guidance Notes re Applications for Grants are available upon receipt of an sae.

Correspondent: The General Secretary, PO Box 3017, South Croydon, Surrey CR2 9PN (020 8657 3053).

The Lloyd Thomas Charity for Women & Girls

Eligibility: Women and girls on a low income in desperate need of a holiday.

Types of grants: Grants up to £130 for women and £65 for girls towards the cost of a holiday. Only in exceptional circumstances can a person be considered for a grant if they have had a holiday within the last four years.

Annual grant total: £5,000 in 2001.

Applications: In writing through a social worker or other welfare agency requesting an application form. Applications are considered all year, though generally from November to May.

Correspondent: Sacha Jewell/ Sheila Field, c/o FHA, 16 Mortimer Street, London W1T 3JL (020 7436 3304; Fax: 020 7436 3302).

Homeless People

Fund for Human Need

See entry on page 108

Housing the Homeless Central Fund

Eligibility: People who are homeless or have accommodation problems, especially expectant parents or those with children.

Types of grants: One-off grants of around £250 to £300 for household items. No recurrent grants are given, or grants for holidays, medical apparatus, funeral expenses, travel costs, removal costs, vehicles, educational expenses, structural improvements to property, computers or televisions.

Annual grant total: £70,000 in 2001.

Applications: Guidelines and applications should be requested by a social worker, on headed paper and enclosing an sae, who will receive the information. Decisions are usually made within a week, although no grants are made in March or December. No telephone calls can be accepted.

Correspondent: The Clerk to the Trustees, 2 Evershed House, Old Castle Street, London E1 7NU.

Older people

BCOP

Eligibility: People over 60 who are in need.

Types of grants: One-off grants to a limit of £350 each. Grants are no longer made towards funeral expenses.

Annual grant total: Less than £10,000 a year.

Applications: In writing to the correspondent. Applications are considered in March, June, September and December.

Correspondent: Marcus Fellows, Chief Executive, Onneley House, 109 Court Oak Road, Birmingham B17 9AA (0121 428 2234; Fax: 0121 428 2151).

The Percy Bilton Charity

See entry on page 90

Counsel & Care for the Elderly

Eligibility: People over 60 years old.

Types of grants: One-off grants of £100 towards special equipment, respite care, holidays, repairs, bills, debts, general living expenses and so on.

Annual grant total: Grants top 250 individuals totalling £25,000.

Applications: On a form available from the correspondent, to be submitted either directly by the individual or through a social worker, welfare agency, citizen's advice bureau or other third party. Applications are considered weekly.

Correspondent: Advice Work Department, Twyman House, 16 Bonny Street, London NW1 9PG (e-mail: advice@counselandcare.org.uk; website: www.counselandcare.org.uk).

Other information: This charity provides an advice service (including 24 fact sheets) for older people on matters such as help at home, accommodation, and finance (the latter to ensure older people are receiving their full DWP entitlements).

Friends of the Elderly

Eligibility: People in need who are over retirement age, on a low income and have no more than £3,000 in savings.

Types of grants: One-off and recurrent grants according to need, ranging from £50 to £500. Grants are given for most essential household items, clothing, household repairs, mobility aids and telephone installation. Weekly allowances are usually for £10. There is a special fund for winter comforts.

No grants for funerals, telephone bills or council tax. Loans are not given.

Annual grant total: In 2000/01 550 grants totalled £195,000.

Applications: On a form available from the welfare services department at the address below, to be submitted by the individual or through a social worker, citizen's advice bureau, welfare agency or other third party. Details of occupation of the applicant and spouse, as well as any military service history is required. Applications are continually considered.

Correspondent: Mrs Bridget Hollidge, Welfare Manager, 40–42 Ebury Street, London SW1W 0LZ (020 7730 8263; Fax: 020 7259 0154; e-mail: bridget.hollidge@fote.org.uk; website: www.fote.org.uk).

Other information: The charity also has eight residential homes, several of them with nursing wings, and a developing programme of community services.

Home Warmth for the Aged

Eligibility: People of pensionable age, at risk from the cold in winter. No grants are made to people who have younger members of their family living with them.

Types of grants: Provision of heating appliances, bedding, clothing and solid fuel, and to pay fuel debts where the supply has been disconnected. One-off grants only, ranging between £45 to £280.

Annual grant total: In 2000/01 the trust had assets of £163,000 and an income of £20,000. Total expenditure was £24,000, including £17,000 given in 125 grants.

Applications: On a form available from the correspondent and submitted through social workers, doctors, nurses etc. only, to whom grants are returned for disbursement. If there is an armed forces connection, applications should be made through SSAFA (see service section of this guide). Applications made directly by individuals are not considered. Applications are looked at from October through to April.

Correspondent: W J Berentemfel, 19 Towers Wood, South Darenth, Kent DA4 9BQ (01322 863836).

The William Johnston Trust Fund

See entry on page 109

The Lifespan Trust

Eligibility: Individuals over 50 years of age. Support is given in order to relieve sickness or disability, and also to assist people in life-affirming activities – 'adding life to years'.

Types of grants: One-off grants of up to £250. Grants have been given towards a new computer for somebody who was unemployed, an electrical wheelchair, a 'retired learner of the year award' and a retired person trekking in Peru for charity.

No grants are made towards travel or work overseas, general household costs or expenditure, or towards the replacement of statutory funding. It is unlikely to support home improvements or house repairs.

Annual grant total: In 1999 the trust had an income of £14,000 and made grants to six individuals totalling £1,500.

Applications: On a form available from the correspondent. Applications are usually considered in February, May, September and December and completed forms must be returned to the trust by the first day of the preceding month. Applications can be submitted directly by the individual, or through a third party.

Correspondent: D W Steele, Secretary, c/o ARP/O50, Windsor House, 1270 London Road, London SW16 4HD (020 7828 0500); Fax: 020 7233 7132; e-mail: lifespan@arp.org.uk; website: www.lifespan-trust.org.uk).

Other information: Grants are also made to organisations.

The trust is the grant-making arm of the Association of Retired and Persons Over 50 (ARP/O50) who contribute 1% of their subscription income each year.

Harry Livesey Charity

Eligibility: People in need who are of retirement age, on a low income and have total savings of no more than £3,000.

Types of grants: One-off and regular grants towards household equipment, clothing, holidays, home repairs and mobility aids. No grants for funerals, telephone bills or council tax. Loans are not given.

Annual grant total: £6,500 in 2000/01.

Applications: All applicants need to complete an application form which must be requested in their name. Applicants can either write to or telephone the welfare services department at the address below for an application form. They are considered throughout the year and can be submitted either directly by the individual or through a social worker, citizen's advice bureau, other welfare agency or other third party.

Correspondent: Mrs B Hollidge, Friends of the Elderly, 40–42 Ebury Street, London SW1W 0LU (020 7730 8263; Fax: 020 7259 0154; e-mail: bridget.hollidge@fote.org.uk; website: www.fote.org.uk).

Lady McCorquodale's Charity Trust

Eligibility: People who are over retirement age and live in the UK.

Types of grants: One-off and recurrent grants ranging from £300 to £1,800. Grants are for day-to-day needs, for example for clothing and food. Grants are not made to people with an income that is £1,000 greater than their personal allowance for income tax.

Annual grant total: In 2000/01 the trust had assets totalling £860,000, an income of £19,000 and made grants totalling £3,300 to six individuals. Grants to organisations totalled £11,000.

Applications: In writing to the correspondent. Applications can be submitted either directly by the individual, or via a social worker, citizen's advice bureau or other third party. They are considered on an ad hoc basis.

Unsuccessful applications will not be acknowledged.

Correspondent: Alan John Winborn, Pollen House, 10–12 Cork Street, London W1S 3LW (020 7439 9061).

Morden College

Eligibility: People in need who are aged over 50.

Types of grants: Quarterly allowances and one-off grants of between £150 and £750 towards household items, holidays and convalescence.

Annual grant total: In 2001/02 grants to 86 individuals totalled £63,000.

Applications: On a form available from the correspondent, for consideration throughout the year. Applications can be submitted either directly by the individual or through any third party.

Correspondent: Clerk to the Trustees, 19 St German's Place, Blackheath, London SE3 0PW (020 8858 3365; Fax: 020 8293 4887).

The National Benevolent Institution

Eligibility: Ladies and gentlemen who are elderly and of a professional background or equivalent. Applicants must be over 50 years old, and those under pensionable age are only considered if in receipt of the higher rate of the Care Component of Disability Living Allowance. Net income, after paying rent and council tax, should be less than £6,600 per year for a single person, and £10,200 for a couple. Applicants should be claiming full state benefits and have savings of less than £3,000.

Types of grants: Recurrent grants of up to £10 per week to allow people to live in their own homes in comfort and warmth. These grants may be supplemented by one-off donations for unexpected household costs.

Annual grant total: In 1998 the institution had assets of £126,000 and an income and a total expenditure of £7,600. Grants to individuals totalled £7,500.

Applications: On a form available from the correspondent, including an income form. Applications can be made through a social worker, citizen's advice bureau, GP or other referral agency, although direct applications will be considered. Applicants are asked to produce birth and marriage certificates if necessary, details of benefits being claimed, and the names and addresses of two character references.

Correspondent: Grp Capt D ST J Homer, 61 Bayswater Road, London W2 3PG (020 7723 0021; Fax: 020 7706 7035).

The Perry Fund

Eligibility: Women in the UK aged 65 or over who are 'of the artisan class'.

Types of grants: One-off and recurrent grants of £100 to £300.

Annual grant total: In 1999/2000 the trust had an income of £12,000 and a total expenditure of £10,000.

Applications: On a form available from the correspondent. Applications can be submitted directly by the individual or through a third party such as a social worker, nursing home manager or welfare organisation. The trustees meet in May and December to consider applications, which should be submitted by February and September respectively.

NATIONAL & GENERAL CHARITIES

Correspondent: W S C Carter, Clerk to the Trustees, St Leonard's House, St Leonard's Close, Bridgnorth, Shropshire WV16 4EJ.

The Roger Pilkington Young Trust

Eligibility: People who are of British birth and live in England, Scotland or Wales, whose income has been reduced through no fault of their own, but prior to application was enough for them to live in a 'reasonable degree of comfort'. Applicants must be over 60 unless their income has been reduced as a result of illness or accident.

Types of grants: Monthly pensions of about £45 for single people and £60 for married couples. The pensions are currently all allocated; should funds become available the trustees will advertise for applicants.

Annual grant total: About £90,000.

Applications: On a form available from the correspondent, after the pensions are advertised.

Correspondent: P B Miles, Trustee, Everys Solicitors, 104 High Street, Sidmouth, Devon EX10 8EF (01395 577983).

The Florence Reiss Trust for Old People

Eligibility: Women over 55 and men over 60 who are in need. Priority may be given to those who live in the parishes of Streatley in Berkshire and Goring-on-Thames in Oxfordshire.

Types of grants: One-off and recurrent grants according to need.

Annual grant total: In 2000/01 the trust had assets of £180,000 and an income of £10,000. Grants totalled £8,400.

Applications: In writing to the correspondent.

Correspondent: Dr Stephen Reiss, Trustee, 94 Tinwell Road, Stamford, Lincolnshire PE9 2SD.

The Royal United Kingdom Beneficent Association (RUKBA)

Eligibility: People in need and people who are older or infirm who come from a professional background and live in the UK or Eire, particularly those 'who have served their generation in a professional capacity, in devoted service to others or in one of many humanitarian causes. They need to be over 60, or be over 40 and permanently unable to work through disability. In addition, their assessed income needs to be below the limits set by RUKBA's committee. These levels are revised regularly and are currently £6,608 for a single person and £11,234 for a married couple.'

Types of grants: Annuities, which are granted for life (unless there is an unexpected and considerable improvement in the recipients circumstances), are £882 for single people and £1,500 for couples a year and are the main form of help. 482 new annuities were awarded in 2001.

The association does not award one-off grants to people who are not regular beneficiaries, nor provide funds for medical or educational costs.

Annual grant total: In 2001 the trust had assets of £140 million and an income of £9.6 million. Total expenditure was £11 million, including £5 million in grants to around 5,500 regular beneficiaries.

Applications: In the first instance the applicant should write to the correspondent describing their occupational background and give a brief description of their circumstances. Arrangements will then be made for the applicant to be visited by one of the association's 1,000 honorary secretaries. Applications can be submitted directly by the individual or through a social worker, citizen's advice bureau, other welfare agency or other third party. Applications are considered every other month beginning in February each year.

Applications can also be made from people in residential/nursing homes who are unable to meet the balance of "reasonable" fees. In such cases, the income limit is not necessarily applied but capital resources have to be reduced to £10,000 before a case can be considered.

Correspondent: Applicants Officer, 6 Avonmore Road, London W14 8RL (020 7605 4222; Fax: 020 7605 4201; e-mail: charity@rukba.org.uk; website: www.rukba.org.uk).

Other information: RUKBA has a residential and two nursing homes with 170 beds at present and has 24 flats and 8 bungalows for older people who are disabled. RUKBA also provide volunteers to assist people in their daily lives, and attempt to make it easier for people to remain in their own homes through adapting them for special needs.

The Universal Beneficent Society

Eligibility: People over 70 and living at home. Beneficiaries are usually housebound, living alone and have savings of less than £1,500. There is a preference for people in London and Merseyside.

Types of grants: The trust provides:
'A small additional income, paid quarterly and promised for life unless there is an improvement in a person's circumstances.
'Emergency payments to cover essential bills, buy medical equipment, replace household goods or install telephone or security devices. Where Universal Beneficent Society cannot afford the whole cost, we work with other charities or agencies to meet the need.
'Food hampers plus an additional cash gift of £35 for each single person, or £25 each for married couples, at Christmas.
'Bedding packs for new beneficiaries.
'A regular newsletter offering advice on health, useful contact details, stories, poems and news about UBS, providing a sense of belonging.'

It also provides, where possible, pastoral care and visits through its regional development officers or volunteer visitors to entend 'a feeling of belonging to the UBS family'. In practice, these visits can only be made in Liverpool and London.

Annual grant total: In 2001 the trust had assets of £2 million and an income of £387,000. Grants to 1,162 individuals totalled £341,000. The surplus was transferred to reserves as they are committed funds to provide the guaranteed grants for life.

Applications: On a form available from Mrs Lillian Artis, at the address below. Applications can be made directly, but are usually submitted through social workers or citizen's advice bureaux. Applications are considered at the beginning of every other month, starting with February.

Correspondent: Miss Natalie Stow, 6 Avonmore Road, London W14 8RL (020 7605 4200; Fax: 020 7605 4201).

Williamson Memorial Trust

Eligibility: People who are over 65 years of age.

Types of grants: One-off grants of between £20 and £100, given as gifts rather than maintenance. Grants are mainly given at Christmas.

Annual grant total: In 2001/02 the trust had an income and expenditure of £13,000. Welfare grants to 30 individuals totalled £2,000. Educational grants to 150 people totalled £5,600.

Applications: In writing to the correspondent, to be considered at any time. Applications should be submitted directly by the individual, and references may be required. As preference is given to cases known by the trustees, the likelihood of grants is small. No telephone calls are accepted.

Correspondent: C P Williamson, Little Cluny, The Street, Ightham, Sevenoaks, Kent TN15 9HE.

Other information: This trust also gives grants to religious and other organisations.

Francis Winham Foundation

Eligibility: Older people who live in England.

Types of grants: One-off grants for people in a time of crisis or need for needs such as medical care, equipment, house repairs/

improvements and respite for carers. No grants are given towards debts or administration costs.

Annual grant total: Grants total about £479,000, mostly to organisations.

Applications: In writing to the correspondent. Applications must be submitted through a citizen's advice bureau or other welfare agency and are considered throughout the year.

Correspondent: Miss Penelope Pepper, 35 Pembroke Gardens, London W8 6HU (020 7602 1261; Fax: 020 7602 5092).

Wireless for the Bedridden

See entry on page 95

Orders

Catenian Benevolent Association

Eligibility: Members of the association and their dependants who are in need.

Types of grants: One-off and recurrent grants according to need.

Annual grant total: In 1999/2000 the association had assets of £5.2 million, an income of £411,000 and a total expenditure of £210,000. Grants to 39 individuals totalled £109,000. A further £100,000 was given in non-secured loans.

Applications: In writing to the correspondent. Applications are considered four times a year.

Correspondent: Michael Cohen, 8 Chesham Place, London SW1X 8HP (020 7235 6671).

The Grand Charity (of Freemasons under the United Grand Lodge of England)

Eligibility: Personal petitioners must be indigent freemasons under the United Grand Lodge of England, or their dependents (i.e. widows, dependant children under 21, and unmarried daughters or sisters who are incapacitated or over 60).

Types of grants: Lump sums, which may be disbursed over not less than 12 months, are made available. The average grant to personal petitioners in 2001 was £1,350. Annuities are not granted.

Annual grant total: £1.9 million in 2001.

Applications: In writing to the correspondent at any time.

Correspondent: The Secretary, 60 Great Queen Street, London WC2B 5AZ (020 7395 9293).

Other information: 1. Personal applicants whose masonic link is not under the United Grand Lodge of England should apply to the appropriate Grand Lodge. If applicants do not have appropriate addresses, the Secretary above will be able to help.
2. Much practical help and financial support in personal distress and for local charity is given independently of the Grand Charity by individual lodges and Provincial Grand Lodges. Addresses are available from the Secretary above.
3. The Grand Charity gives substantial support to operating charities, including national (but not local) non-masonic charities, as well as to individuals.
4. There is also the Masonic Trust for Girls and Boys to help children of any age (including adopted children and step-children) of freemasons under the United Grand Lodge of England. See entry in *The Educational Grants Directory*.
5. See also the separate entries for the Royal Masonic Benevolent Institution and the New Masonic Samaritan Fund in this Guide.

The New Masonic Samaritan Fund

Eligibility: Freemasons, their families and dependants who are in both financial and medical need.

Types of grants: Grants are made to avoid a long wait on a NHS waiting list by providing private treatment where it would otherwise not be affordable. Grants average £5,900.

No grants can be made towards treatment which has already been provided privately, or which can be made through the NHS without undue delay or hardship.

Annual grant total: In 2000/01 the fund had an income of £5 million and a total expenditure of £3 million. Since the fund was formed in 1991 over 5,000 grants have been made totalling over £19 million.

Applications: On a form available from the correspondent. The trustees meet each month (usually the last Thursday) to consider applications received in the previous 30 days.

Correspondent: The Secretary, 26 Great Queen Street, London WC2B 5BL (020 7404 1550; Fax: 020 7404 1544; e-mail: mail@masonicsamaritan.org.uk; website: www.nmsf.org).

The Royal Antediluvian Order of Buffaloes, Grand Lodge of England War Memorial Annuities

Eligibility: Members of the order who are elderly or disabled and their dependants.

Types of grants: Annuities, though the Grand Lodge may have other charitable funds available for one-off grants.

Annual grant total: In 1999/2000 the trust had assets of £253,000, an income of £108,000 and a total expenditure of £104,000. Grants totalled £73,000.

Applications: Applications should be made through the member's lodge. All assistance originates at the local lodge level; if its resources are inadequate, the lodge may then seek assistance at provincial or ultimately national level. For dependants of deceased members, it is necessary to give the lodge to which the member belonged. If its name and number is known, the correspondent below will probably be able to identify a current local telephone number or address. If only the place is known, this may still be possible, but not in all cases, particularly when the lodge concerned does not belong to this Grand Lodge group.

Correspondent: The Secretary, Grove House, Skipton Road, Harrogate, North Yorkshire HG1 4LA (01423 502438).

Other information: The Grand Lodge of England is the largest of 15 separate and independent Buffalo groups in the country. They appear to exist for mutual sociability and support as well as the support of their local communities. There are over 3,500 local lodges, all of which may be concerned to help members, dependants and perhaps others in time of need or distress. This fund was established as a tribute to members of the order who died during the First World War.

The Royal Masonic Benevolent Institution

Eligibility: Freemasons (usually over 60 years of age, unless unemployed due to incapacity) of the English Constitution (England, Wales and certain areas overseas) and their dependants.

Types of grants: Regular assistance to beneficiaries living in their own homes. Annuities are paid quarterly and can be for life, up to the maximum disregard figure (currently £1,040 per year) for social benefit purposes. Annuitants living in their own house may also be eligible for low-interest loans to renovate their house.

Annual grant total: About £2.8 million.

Applications: On a form available from the correspondent, usually submitted through the lodge of the relevant freemason. Applications are considered every month.

Correspondent: The Chief Executive, 20 Great Queen Street, London WC2B 5BG (020 7405 8341; Fax: 020 7404 0724).

Other information: The institution has a team of welfare visitors covering the whole of England and Wales and also runs 18 homes catering for 1,100 older freemasons.

NATIONAL & GENERAL CHARITIES

Prisoners/former prisoners

The Aldo Trust

Eligibility: People in need who are being held in detention pending their trial or after their conviction. The applicant must still be serving the sentence. Applicants must have less than £25 in private cash.

Types of grants: Grants up to a maximum of £10 a year towards any needs except toiletries and training shoes.

Annual grant total: Around £18,000 a year for educational and welfare purposes.

Applications: On a form available from the correspondent. Applications must be made through prison service personnel (for example, probation, chaplaincy, education), and should include the name and number of the prisoner, age, length of sentence and expected date of release. No applications direct from prisoners will be considered.

Applicants may apply once only in each twelve-month period, and applications are considered monthly.

Correspondent: Sandra MacIntosh, Welfare Administrator, c/o NACRO, 169 Clapham Road, London SW9 0PU (020 7582 6500; Fax: 020 7840 6444).

Other information: NACRO also offers a fund for people on probation; see separate entry in this guide.

The Michael and Shirley Hunt Charitable Trust

Eligibility: Relatives and dependants of prisoners, such as their spouses and children.

Types of grants: Grants have been given, for example, towards helping a prisoner with disablties gain work experience and to help a prisoner buy essentials for her baby.

Annual grant total: In 2001/02 the trust had assets of £3.5 million and an income of £216,000. Grants totalled £64,000 including grants to individuals.

Applications: In writing to the correspondent.

Correspondent: Mrs D S Jenkins, Trustee, Ansty House, High Street, Henfield, West Sussex BN5 9DA (01273 492233; Fax: 01273 492273).

The National Association for the Care & Resettlement of Offenders (NACRO)

Eligibility: Ex-offenders and their partners and families.

Types of grants: One-off grants only, usually of around £50 to match a grant from the Probation Be-friending Fund. Only one grant can ever be made to an individual.

Annual grant total: About £50,000, including educational grants.

Applications: Either directly by the individual or through a probation service, social service department, citizen's advice bureau or registered charity. Applications are considered every two months.

Correspondent: Sandra MacIntosh, Welfare Administrator, 169 Clapham Road, London SW9 0PU (020 7582 6500; Fax: 020 7840 6444).

The Royal London Aid Society

Eligibility: Offenders, both before and after discharge from prison, their families and young people 'at risk' (that is young people under a supervision order or who have come to the attention of the police). Grants can be made UK-wide, but preference is given to London and the south east of England.

Types of grants: One-off grants, for example, for education, tools and specialist clothing. There is a preference for items that will help with employment. Grants have also been given for clothing, furniture, training courses and so on to people discharged from prison and their families.

Annual grant total: Between £20,000 and £30,000 a year.

Applications: On a form available from the correspondent. All applications must be supported by an authority, such as a welfare agency, and grants are made through that authority (not directly to the beneficiary). Applications are considered in March, June, September and December.

Correspondent: Miss Jude Cohen, 69 Felhampton Road, London SE9 3NP (020 8851 7209).

Religion

Christian

The Alexis Trust

Eligibility: Members of the Christian faith.

Types of grants: Grants of between £50 and £100 are available, mostly for Christian-based acitivities.

Annual grant total: In 1998/99 the trust had an income of £35,000. Grants to organisations totalled £30,000 and 58 grants to individuals totalled £3,600.

Applications: In writing to the correspondent.

Correspondent: Prof. D W Vere, 14 Broadfield Way, Buckhurst Hill, Essex IG9 5AG.

Other information: The grants given to individuals are usually from the surplus funds from the grants to organisations. Applicants should contact the correspondent for further information before making an application.

Christadelphian Benevolent Fund

Eligibility: Members of the Christadelphian body who are in need and live in the UK.

Types of grants: One-off and recurrent grants according to need.

Annual grant total: In 2001 the trust had an income of £118,000 and its total expenditure was £85,000.

Applications: In writing to the correspondent.

Correspondent: K H A Smith, 1 Sherbourne Road, Acocks Green, Birmingham B27 6AB (0121 706 6100; Fax: 0121 706 7193).

The Lavender Trust

Eligibility: Christians living in London, south east counties and Norfolk.

Types of grants: One-off and recurrent grants according to need.

Annual grant total: In 2000/01 the trust had an income of £4,900, all of which was given in grants. Grants are also made to organisations.

Applications: In writing to the correspondent at any time.

Correspondent: C D Leck, Trustee, Larchfield, Copt Hall Road, Ightham, Sevenoaks, Kent TN15 9DT (01732 885127).

The Sure Foundation

Eligibility: Christians seeking to share their faith in the UK or overseas and people needing a new start in employment, such as ex-offenders.

Types of grants: One-off and recurrent grants according to need.

Annual grant total: In 2000/01 the trust had assets of £30,000 and an income of £2,100. Grants for educational and welfare needs totalled £4,200.

Applications: In writing to the correspondent.

Correspondent: Andrew Ingrey-Senn, Trustee, Hobbs Green Farm, Odell, Bedfordshire MK43 7AB.

Arthur Townrow Pensions Fund

Eligibility: Spinsters, over 40 years of age who are in need, of good character and are members of the Church of England or of a Protestant dissenting church that acknowledges the doctrine of the Holy Trinity. One half of the pensions granted must be paid to women living in Chesterfield, Bolsover and north east Derbyshire. The remaining grants may be paid anywhere in England but only to spinsters over 40. Allowances will not be made to those with an income greater than £5,300 a year.

Types of grants: About 225 regular allowances of £30.50 a month are made. One half of the pensions granted must be paid to unmarried women and widows living in Chesterfield, Bolsover and north east Derbyshire. The remaining grants may be paid anywhere in England but only to eligible unmarried women over the age of 40.

Annual grant total: In 2000/01 the trust had assets of £1.2 million, an income of £120,000 and a total expenditure of £102,000.

Applications: In writing to the correspondent, requesting an application form. Applications should be submitted either directly by the individual or through a social worker, citizen's advice bureau or other welfare agency.

Correspondent: P I King, Secretary, PO Box 48, Chesterfield, Derbyshire S40 1XT (01246 208081).

Christian Science

The Morval Foundation

Eligibility: Older Christian Scientists who are members of The Mother Church, The First Church of Christ, Scientist in Boston, USA.

Types of grants: Grants of between £75 and £120 to allow Christian Scientists who are elderly to continue living independently in their own homes.

Annual grant total: In 1998/99 the foundation had assets of £864,000 and an income of £33,000. Total expenditure was £40,000 with 23 grants being awarded totalling £34,000.

Applications: On a form available from the correspondent, to be submitted directly by the individual for consideration in April, July or November.

Correspondent: Mrs D Holden, 32 Upper Grotto Road, Strawberry Hill, Middlesex TW1 4NF (020 8892 0004).

Church of England

The Deakin Institution

Eligibility: Ladies who live in the UK, who have never been married, are in reduced circumstances and who are members of the Church of England or of a church having full membership of the Council of Churches for Britain and Ireland. Grants are not given to ladies under 40 years of age and beneficiaries are usually over 55 years.

Types of grants: Annuities of £335 a year, paid half yearly. No one-off grants are made.

Annual grant total: In 2000/01 the institution had assets of £1.4 million, an income of £94,000 and a total expenditure of £66,000. Grants to 154 individuals totalled £50,000.

Applications: On a form available from the correspondent submitted directly by the individual. Applications are considered in April and October.

Correspondent: David Mangles, 56 Shoreham Street, Sheffield S1 4SP (0114 280 8980).

The Hounsfield Pension

Eligibility: Unmarried women, widows and widowers who are over 50 years old, live in England or Wales, are members of the Church of England and have never received parochial relief or public assistance.

Types of grants: Regular allowances of £500 a year paid in two instalments.

Annual grant total: Slightly less than £6,000 was given in 1999.

Applications: In writing to the correspondent. Only a limited number of pensions are available, and places become available at irregular intervals.

Correspondent: Karen Hobson, c/o DLA, Fountain Precinct, Balm Green, Sheffield S1 1RZ (0114 283 3283; Fax: 0114 278 1158).

Jewish

The AJR Charitable Trust

Eligibility: Jewish refugees from Nazi oppression, their dependants and descendants, who are settled in the UK. Potential applicants must be members of the AJR, or eligible to become members and be willing to join the association.

Types of grants: Regular allowances of up to £20 per week for members on very limited income and who cannot be helped from public funds. One-off grants to members in whole or part payment of a particular need, for example, necessities, debts or holidays.

Annual grant total: No information available, but see above.

Applications: In writing to the correspondent, together with statements of background and needs. Applications can be submitted directly by the individual, through a recognised referral agency (citizen's advice bureau, doctor, social worker and so on), or via a third party. The association generally likes to make home visits at some time. Applications are considered approximately every three months.

Correspondent: Carol Rossen, Administrator, 1 Hampstead Gate, 1a Frognall, London NW3 6AL (020 7431 6161; Fax: 020 7431 8454; e-mail: enquiries@ajr.org.uk; website: www.ajr.org.uk).

Carlee Ltd

Eligibility: Jewish people in need.

Types of grants: One-off and recurrent grants according to need.

Annual grant total: In 2000/01 the trust had an income of £200,000 and a total expenditure of £192,000. In previous years most of the expenditure was given in grants to individuals for relief of need and educational purposes, and to organisations.

Applications: In writing to the correspondent.

Correspondent: Mrs A Stroh, Secretary, 6 Grangecourt Road, London N16 5EJ.

Closehelm Ltd

Eligibility: People of the Jewish faith who are in need.

Types of grants: Grants and loans are given to needy families for wedding costs and other needs.

Annual grant total: In 1999/2000 the trust had an income of £326,000 and a total expenditure of £270,000.

Applications: In writing to the correspondent.

Correspondent: A Van Praagh, Trustee, 30 Armitage Road, London NW11 8RD.

Other information: This entry was not confirmed by the trust, but the address was correct according to the Charity Commission database.

The George Julian Egerton Fund

Eligibility: Jewish ladies and gentlemen of good family who are in reduced circumstances and in middle or old age.

Types of grants: One-off or recurrent grants according to need.

Annual grant total: £6,500.

Applications: In writing to the correspondent. Applications can be submitted directly by the individual.

Correspondent: The Trustees, Jewish Care, 221 Golders Green, London NW11 9DW (020 8922 2000).

Finnart House School Trust

Eligibility: Young people of the Jewish faith who are in need. Priority is given to people over 16, although all applicants are considered.

Types of grants: Grants to deprived or sick people, to provide care or education. Grants range between £100 and £1,000.

Annual grant total: In 2000/01 the trust had assets of £4.5 million and an income of

NATIONAL & GENERAL CHARITIES

£160,000. Total expenditure was £182,000, with grants totalling £138,000, although the majority of this was given in grants to organisations.

Applications: On a form available from the correspondent. Applications must be submitted through a school or social-work agency, and are considered three or four times a year.

Correspondent: Peter Shaw, 707 High Road, London N12 0BT (020 8445 1670; Fax: 020 8446 7370; e-mail: finnart@anjy.org).

Other information: This trust also gives grants for educational purposes and to organisations which work with children and young people of the Jewish faith who are in need.

The Nathan and Adolphe Haendler Charity

Eligibility: Jews who, as a consequence of religious persecution or other misfortune, have taken (or need to take) refuge in the UK, and are in need.

Types of grants: One-off or recurrent grants according to need.

Annual grant total: £13,000 in 1999.

Applications: In writing to the correspondent at any time.

Correspondent: The Clerk, Refugee Department, World Jewish Relief, 74–80 Camden Street, London NW1 0EG (020 7691 1771).

The Jewish Aged Needy Pension Society

Eligibility: Members of the Jewish community aged 60 or over, who have known better circumstances and have lived in the UK for at least 10 years or are of British nationality.

Types of grants: Up to 60 pensions of up to £10 per week for all kinds of need.

Annual grant total: In 2001 grants totalled £25,000.

Applications: In writing to the correspondent. Applications are considered quarterly.

Correspondent: Mrs S A Taylor, Secretary, 34 Dalkeith Grove, Stanmore, Middlesex HA7 4SG (020 8958 5390; Fax: 020 8958 8046).

MYA Charitable Trust

Eligibility: Individuals in need who are Jewish, worldwide.

Types of grants: One-off and recurrent grants according to need.

Annual grant total: In 1999/2000 the trust had an income of £272,000 and a total expenditure of £151,000. In previous years grants have mostly been made to organisations.

Applications: The correspondent has previously stated that all the trust's funds are fully committed.

Correspondent: M Rothfield, Trustee, 25 Egerton Road, London N16 6UE (020 8800 3582).

The Chevras Ezras Nitzrochim

Eligibility: Jewish people in need, especially in Greater London.

Types of grants: One-off and recurrent grants according to need.

Annual grant total: In 2000 the trust had an income of £201,000 coming mainly from funds raised by the trustees and voluntary helpers. Grants were made totalling £195,000 to organisations and individuals.

Applications: In writing to the correspondent.

Correspondent: H Kahan, Trustee, 53 Heathland Road, London N16 5PQ.

Other information: This entry was not confirmed by the trust, but the address was correct according to the Charity Commission database.

Norwood (formerly Norwood Ravenswood)

Eligibility: Mostly Jewish children and their families, although one-quarter of their clients are of mixed faith. This is a national trust but concentrates on London and the south east of England.

Types of grants: According to need, but no regular allowances. Grants towards the celebration of Jewish religious festivals, social need and occasional holidays.

Annual grant total: In 1999/2000 the trust made 246 grants totalling £55,000.

Applications: Grants are recommended by Norwood staff.

Correspondent: The Chief Executive, Broadway House, 80–82 The Broadway, Stanmore, Middlesex HA7 4HB (020 8954 4555; Fax: 020 8420 6859).

Other information: Grants are made in conjunction with a comprehensive welfare service. Norwood provides a range of social services for Jewish children and families, including social work, day facilities, residential and foster care.

The ZSV Trust

Eligibility: Jewish people in need.

Types of grants: One-off and recurrent grants according to need. Most of the trust's funds is spent on providing food parcels. Other recent grants have been given towards care for older people, families undergoing stress, clothing, shoes, weddings, healthcare and to help orphans and newly-born children.

Annual grant total: In 1998 the trust had an income of £235,000 and a total expenditure of £228,000. Grants totalled £224,000, of which £193,000 was given as food parcels.

Applications: In writing to the correspondent. Individuals need to apply through Social Services.

Correspondent: A Mordechai Fogel, 178 Osbaldeston Road, London N16 6NJ (020 8880 5622).

Protestant

The Mylne Trust

Eligibility: Members of the Protestant faith who are in need.

Types of grants: Annual and one-off grants.

Annual grant total: In 2000/01 the trust had assets of £1 million and an income of £50,000, all of which was given in grants for educational and welfare purposes.

Applications: In writing to the correspondent, requesting an application form and explaining why a grant is needed. Applicants must include a passport size photograph of themselves certified as a true likeness and a letter of support from their home church.

Correspondent: The Trustees, Bells Potter Solicitors, 11 South Street, Farnham, Surrey GU9 7QX (01252 733733; Fax: 01252 723718; e-mail: mail@bellspotter.co.uk).

Roman Catholic

The Hoper-Dixon Trust

Eligibility: People in need connected with or resident in Newcastle-upon-Tyne, Leicester and London.

Types of grants: One-off and recurrent grants according to need ranging from £100 to £500.

Annual grant total: In 1998/99 the trust had assets of £396,000 and an income of £18,000. Total expenditure was £21,000 with 21 grants to individuals totalling £11,000.

Applications: Only considered if made through the parish priest. Applications addressed to the correspondent below will NOT be processed.

Correspondent: The Provincial Bursar, St Dominic's Priory, Southampton Road, London NW5 4LB.

Other information: Grants are also made to groups.

This entry was not confirmed by the trust, but the address was correct according to the Charity Commission database.

NATIONAL & GENERAL CHARITIES

Sports

The Mark Davies Injured Riders Fund

Eligibility: People injured in horse-related accidents (excluding professional and amateur jockeys and those injured in the horse racing industry).

Types of grants: One-off and recurrent grants according to need. Grants are given towards travel expenses, physiotherapy, adapted motor cars, house adaptations and home and stable help.

Annual grant total: In 2000 the fund had assets of £582,000, an income of £261,000 and a total expenditure of £170,000. Grants to individuals totalled £102,000.

Applications: In writing to, or telephoning, the correspondent. Applications can be submitted directly by the individual or any third party, with a report by a MDIRF representative. They are considered at any time.

Correspondent: Mrs Jane Davies, Little Woolpit, Ewhurst, Cranleigh, Surrey GU6 7NP (01483 277344/268623; Fax: 01483 277899).

Other information: The fund also helps to collate information about safety standards for headgear and gives grants for research into head/spinal injuries.

The Francis Drake Fellowship

Eligibility: Widows and dependants of members of the fellowship who have died.

Types of grants: One-off and recurrent grants according to need. There is a sliding scale of grants depending on surplus income. If after general household/living expenses (excluding food, clothing etc.) the applicant has a surplus of under £70 per week, grants are £550; if the surplus income is between £70 and £90, grants are £450; between £90 and £110, grants are £350; between £110 and £130, grants are £200; and for incomes over £130, grants are £50.

Annual grant total: In 2000 the fellowship had assets of £132,000, an income of £51,000 and gave grants totalling £33,000.

Applications: In writing to the correspondent, requesting an application form. Applications should be submitted through the bowling club's Francis Drake Fellowship delegate.

Correspondent: Joan Jupp, 24 Haldane Close, London N10 2PB (020 8883 8725).

Richard Langhorn Trust

See entry on page 113

Vegetarians/vegans

The Vegetarian Charity

Eligibility: Children and young people under the age of 26 who are vegetarian or vegan and are sick or in need.

Types of grants: One-off and recurrent grants to relieve poverty and sickness, usually ranging from £100 to £1,000.

Annual grant total: In 2000/01 the trust had assets of £898,000 and an income of £41,000. It made grants to 102 vegetarians totalling £36,000.

Applications: On a form available from the correspondent, for consideration throughout the year.

Correspondent: Margaret Chatfield, 6 Cox Bank, Audlem, Cheshire CW3 0EU (e-mail: maggiechat@hotmail.com).

Other information: Grants are also made to organisations which promote vegetarianism among young people and to vegetarian children's homes.

Women

The Frederick Andrew Convalescent Trust

See entry on page 90

The Arbib Lucas Fund

Eligibility: Distressed gentlewomen in need, with a preference for women of the Jewish faith.

Types of grants: One-off grants according to need, of up to £200. Most grants are given to older people who cannot look after themselves, and also single parents.

Annual grant total: In 1999/2000 the fund had an income of £27,000 and a total expenditure of £32,000.

Applications: Applications should be made via a social worker, Jewish Care, other welfare agency, doctor or clergy. They are considered throughout the year.

Correspondent: Mrs Anita Kafton, Hon. Secretary, 16 Sunny Hill, London NW4 4LL (020 8203 3567).

Bircham Dyson Bell Charitable Trust – The Crossley Fund

Eligibility: Single women, including widows, of at least 50 years of age, who are in need.

Types of grants: Grants of £3 per week towards rent.

Annual grant total: About £4,100 in 26 grants.

Applications: Usually made with the assistance of welfare organisations or third parties such as vicars. A form is sent to likely applicants on request. Applications are considered in June and December.

Correspondent: Miss H Abbey, Bircham Dyson Bell, 50 Broadway, Westminster, London SW1H 0BL (020 7227 7000; Fax: 020 7227 3480

Other information: The correspondent states: 'We receive lots of inappropriate applications; we can only help older people with rent .'

The Eaton Fund for Artists, Nurses & Gentlewomen

See entry on page 26

The Morris Beneficent Fund

Eligibility: 'Distressed gentlewomen' recommended by members of the fund. Grants generally go to older people.

Types of grants: Recurrent grants according to need.

Annual grant total: In 1998 the trust had assets of £430,000 and its income was £27,000, all of which was given in grants.

Applications: On an application form supplied by a member. No unsolicited applications will be considered.

Correspondent: S Jamison, 15 Boult Street, Reading RG1 4RD.

Other information: There is at present a waiting list and no new applications can be considered.

The Royal Society for the Relief of Indigent Gentlewomen of Scotland

See entry on page 139

The Society for the Assistance of Ladies in Reduced Circumstances

Eligibility: British ladies living on their own, who are on a low income and who live in the British Isles.

Types of grants: One-off and recurrent grants according to need.

Annual grant total: In 2000 the society had assets of £24 million, an income of £849,000 and a total expenditure of £744,000. It gave 95 one-off grants and, on average, 584 monthly grants totalling £481,000. Grants to organisations totalled £42,000.

Applications: In writing or by telephone to the correspondent at any time.

Correspondent: J Sands, Lancaster House, 25 Hornyold Road, Malvern, Worcestershire WR14 1QQ (01684 574645).

123

St Andrew's Society for Ladies in Need

Eligibility: Single ladies aged over 60 from a well-educated and/or professional background who are in reduced circumstances and live alone.

Types of grants: Mainly recurrent grants of £10 to £20 a week for daily living expenses. One-off special grants are also given towards heating, domestic appliances, moving expenses, convalescence and so on. Help towards shortfall in residential home fees is also available.

Annual grant total: In 2001 the trust had assets of £1.5 million, an income of £78,000 and a total expenditure of £67,000. Grants to 80 individuals totalled £53,000.

Applications: On a form available from the correspondent, to be submitted either directly by the individual or through a social worker, citizen's advice bureau, other welfare agency or somebody with power of attorney. Applications should include as much background detail as possible, such as education, occupations and so on. They are considered in March, June and October.

Correspondent: Mrs M Pope, General Secretary, 20 Denmark Gardens, Holbrook, Ipswich, Suffolk IP9 2BG (01473 327408).

WRVS Benevolent Trust

Eligibility: Members of the WRVS who are in need and live in the Channel Islands, England, Scotland or Wales.

Types of grants: One-off grants for basic necessities which cannot otherwise be affordable.

Annual grant total: £19,000 in 2001.

Applications: In writing to the correspondent or through any of the trustees. Applications can be considered at any time.

Correspondent: Mrs Sylvia Hatchell, Hon. Secretary, 151 Clapham Road, London SW9 0PU (020 7793 1122/3;
Fax: 020 7793 1177;
e-mail: sylvia.hatchell@btinternet.com).

LOCAL CHARITIES

This section lists local charities giving grants to individuals for welfare purposes. The information in the entry applies only to welfare grants and concentrates on what the charity actually does rather than on what its trust deed allows it to do.

All the charities listed have a grant-making potential of £500 a year for individuals; most are giving considerably more than this.

Regional classification

We have divided the UK into nine geographical areas, as numbered on the map overleaf. Scotland, Wales and England have been separated into areas or counties in a similar way to previous editions of this guide. Overleaf, we have included a list under each such area/county of the unitary and local authorities they include. (Please note: not all of these unitary or local authorities have a trust included in this guide.)

The Northern Ireland section has not been subdivided into smaller areas. Within the other sections, the trusts are ordered as follows.

Scotland
- Firstly, the charities which apply to the whole of Scotland, or at least two areas in Scotland.
- Secondly, Scotland is sub-divided into five areas. The entries which apply to the whole area, or to at least two unitary authorities within, appear first.
- The rest of the charities in the area are listed in alphabetical order of unitary authority.

Wales
- Firstly, the charities which apply to the whole of Wales, or at least two areas in Wales.
- Secondly, Wales is sub-divided into three areas. The entries which apply to the whole area, or to at least two unitary authorities within, appear first.
- The rest of the charities in the area are listed in alphabetical order of unitary authority.

England
- Firstly, the charities which apply to the whole area, or at least two counties in the area.
- Secondly, each area is sub-divided into counties. The entries which apply to the whole county, or to at least two towns within it, appear first.
- The rest of the charities in the county are listed in alphabetical order of parish, town or city.

Please note, in the North East section, the former county of Cleveland has been incorporated under County Durham for Hartlepool and Stockton on Tees and North Yorkshire for Middlesbrough and Redcar and Cleveland.

London
- Firstly, the charities which apply to the whole of Greater London, or to at least two boroughs.
- Secondly, London is sub-divided into the boroughs. The entries are listed in alphabetical order within each borough.

Please note, within each county/area section, the trusts are arranged alphabetically by the unitary or local authority which they benefit in Scotland and Wales, while in England they are listed by the city/town/parish.

To be sure of identifying every relevant local charity, look first at the entries under the heading for your:
- unitary authority for people in Scotland and Wales
- city/town/parish under the relevant regional chapter heading for people living in England
- borough for people living in London.

People in London should then go straight to the start of the London chapter, where trusts which give to individuals in more than one borough in London are listed.

Other individuals should look at the sections for trusts which give to more than one unitary authority/town before finally considering those trusts at the start of the chapter which make grants across different areas/counties in your country/region.

For example, if you live in Liverpool, firstly establish which region Merseyside is in by looking at the map on page 127. Then having established that Merseyside is in region 5, look at the list overleaf and see which page entries for Merseyside are on. Then look under the heading for Liverpool to see if there are any relevant charities. Next check the charities which apply to Merseyside generally. Finally, check under the heading for the North West generally.

Having found the trusts covering your area, please read carefully any other eligibility requirements. While some trusts can and do give for any need for people in their area of benefit, most have other criteria which potential applicants must meet.

LOCAL CHARITIES

1. Northern Ireland *129*

2. Scotland *133*

Aberdeen & Perthshire *142*
 Aberdeen & Aberdeenshire; Angus; Dundee; Moray; Perth & Kinross

Central *150*
 Clackmannanshire; Falkirk; Fife; Stirling

Edinburgh, the Lothians & Scottish Borders *152*
 East Lothian; Edinburgh; Midlothian; Scottish Borders; West Lothian

Glasgow & West of Scotland *157*
 Argyll & Bute; Dumfries & Galloway; East, North & South Ayrshire; East & West Dunbartonshire; East Renfrewshire; Glasgow (city of); Inverclyde; North & South Lanarkshire; Renfrewshire

Highlands & Islands *163*
 Highland; Isle of Lewis; Orkney Islands; Shetland Islands; Western Isles

3. Wales *165*

Mid Wales *165*
 Ceredigion; Powys

North Wales *165*
 Anglesey; Conwy; Denbighshire; Flintshire; Gwynedd; Wrexham

South Wales *168*
 Blaenau Gwent; Bridgend; Caerphilly; Cardiff; Carmarthenshire; Merthyr Tydfil; Monmouthshire; Neath & Port Talbot; Newport; Pembrokeshire; Rhondda, Cyon, Taff; Swansea; Torfaen; Vale of Glamorgan

4. North East *175*

County Durham *180*
 Durham; Darlington; Hartlepool; Stockton-on-Tees

East Yorkshire *181*
 East Riding of Yorkshire; Kingston-upon-Hull

North Yorkshire *183*
 Middlesbrough; North Yorkshire; Redcar & Cleveland; York

Northumberland *186*

South Yorkshire *187*
 Barnsley; Doncaster; Rotherham; Sheffield

Tyne & Wear *190*
 Gateshead; Newcastle-upon-Tyne; North & South Tyneside; Sunderland

West Yorkshire *192*
 Bradford; Calderdale; Kirklees; Leeds; Wakefield

5. North West *201*

Cheshire *202*
 Cheshire; Halton; Warrington

Cumbria *205*

Greater Manchester *207*
 Bolton; Bury; Manchester; Oldham; Rochdale; Salford; Tameside; Trafford; Wigan

Isle of Man *212*

Lancashire *212*
 Blackburn & Darwen; Blackpool; Lancashire

Merseyside *216*
 Knowsley; Liverpool; St Helens; Sefton; Wirral

6. Midlands *223*

Derbyshire *227*
 Derby; Derbyshire

Herefordshire *230*

Leicestershire *231*
 Leicester; Leicestershire; Rutland

Lincolnshire *236*
 Lincolnshire; North East Lincolnshire; North Lincolnshire

Northamptonshire *241*

Nottinghamshire *246*
 Nottingham; Nottinghamshire

Shropshire *252*
 Shropshire; Telford and Wrekin

Staffordshire *255*
 Staffordshire; Stoke-on-Trent

Warwickshire *259*

West Midlands *264*
 Birmingham; Coventry; Dudley; Sandwell; Solihull; Walsall; Wolverhampton

Worcestershire *272*

7. South West *275*

Avon *276*
 Bath & North East Somerset; Bristol; North Somerset; South Gloucestershire

Cornwall *280*

Devon *281*
 Devon; Plymouth; Torbay

Dorset *289*
 Bournemouth; Dorset; Poole

Gloucestershire *292*

Somerset *295*

Wiltshire *298*
 Swindon; Wiltshire

8. South East *301*

Bedfordshire *304*
 Bedfordshire; Luton

Berkshire *305*
 Bracknell Forest; Newbury; Reading; Slough; Windsor & Maidenhead; Wokingham

Buckinghamshire *307*
 Buckinghamshire; Milton Keynes

Cambridgeshire *310*
 Cambridgeshire; Peterborough

East Sussex *314*
 Brighton & Hove; East Sussex

Essex *315*
 Essex; Southend; Thurrock

Hampshire *318*
 Hampshire; Isle of Wight; Portsmouth; Southampton

Hertfordshire *323*

Kent *325*
 Kent; Medway Council

Norfolk *330*

Oxfordshire *337*

Suffolk *340*

Surrey *345*

West Sussex *356*

9. London *359*

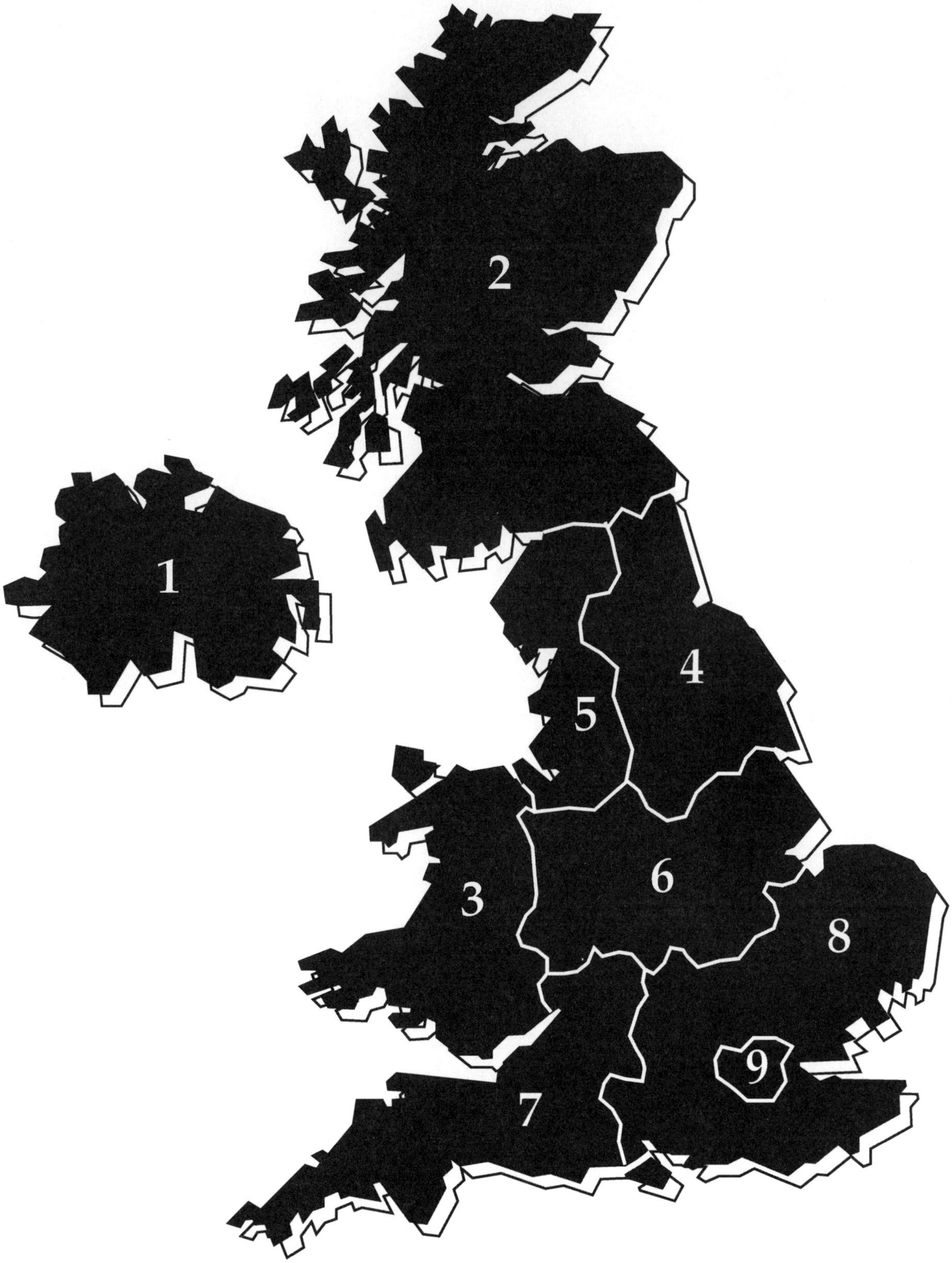
2
1
4
5
6
3
8
9
7

1. Northern Ireland

The Belfast Association for the Blind

Eligibility: People in Northern Ireland who are registered blind.

Types of grants: Grants of £250 to £350 towards holidays, house repairs, visual aids and so on as well as educational needs.

Annual grant total: In 2001 the trust had assets of £870,000 and an income of £63,000. Grants to individuals totalled £31,000. Grants for medical research and equipment totalled £35,000.

Applications: In writing to the correspondent, through a social worker or from the secretary of an organisation. Applications are considered throughout the year.

Correspondent: R Gillespie, Hon. Secretary, 30 Glenwell Crescent, Newtownabbey, County Antrim BT36 7TF (028 9083 6407).

The Belfast Central Mission

Eligibility: Children or senior citizens who are in need and live in Greater Belfast. It has started supporting children aged two to four years old with autism.

Types of grants: One-off gifts of food parcels and toys at Christmas.

Annual grant total: Approximately £15,000 worth of donations and gifts in kind.

Applications: On a form available from Mrs Janet Sewell at the address below. Applications are considered in October and November and the applicant's benefit or social security books should be shown to the mission.

Correspondent: Volunteer Coordinator, Grosvenor House, 5 Glengall Street, Belfast BT12 5AD (028 9024 1917; Fax: 028 9024 0577; e-mail: admin@belfastcentralmission.org; website: www.belfastcentralmission.org).

Other information: This charity also runs advice centres and residential homes.

The Belfast Sick Poor Fund

Eligibility: Families with children aged under 18 who are ill or disabled and are in receipt of benefits or on a low income and who are in need. Referrals are sometimes considered for older people.

Types of grants: One-off grants ranging from £50 to £200 for necessities and comforts.

Annual grant total: In 2001/02 the trust had an income of £3,000, all of which was given in 23 grants.

Applications: In writing to the correspondent by a social worker, for consideration within one week of submission. Applications should include: background information on applicant with a breakdown of needs; why the request is being made; how a grant will benefit the applicant; details of income and expenditure on a weekly or monthly basis; and details of other sources of financial assistance and outcomes of any applications.

Correspondent: Rosaleen Murray, c/o Bryson House, 28 Bedford Street, Belfast BT2 7FE (028 9032 5835; Fax: 028 9043 9156; e-mail: rosaleen.murray@brysonhouse.com).

The King George VI Youth Awards

Eligibility: Young people aged between 14 and 21 who live in Northern Ireland. Grants are also given to groups who work with this age group.

Types of grants: Grants towards the cost of travel within the UK or Ireland for cultural or social activities and towards the development of interaction between able-bodied and disabled young people. Grants are also given towards the local costs of organising self-help community or environmental projects where young people will be playing a major role. The largest grant is £350.

Annual grant total: About £6,500.

Applications: On a form available from the correspondent. The committee meets four times a year in February, May, September and December to discuss applications.

Correspondent: Linda Gordon, Youthnet, The Warehouse, 7 James Street South, Belfast BT2 8DN (028 9033 1880; Fax; 028 9033 1977; e-mail: linda@youthnet.co.uk).

Other information: Funding will not be given in retrospect and consecutive awards will only be given to the same group or individual if the application is for a different project. Grants are not given for uniforms or musical instruments and are only given to sports projects when they are part of a broad based youth work programme. Individuals applying for help with a sports activity or coaching must be able to demonstrate that they will pass on their skills to a group or community.

The Londonderry Methodist City Mission

Eligibility: People in need who live in Londonderry and the surrounding area.

Types of grants: One-off grants for necessities and some help at Christmas and holiday time.

Annual grant total: No information available.

Applications: By personal application or through a referral by a minister of religion, social worker or citizen's advice bureau, to the correspondent.

Correspondent: Revd Frederick L Munce, 11 Clearwater, Londonderry BT47 1BE.

Other information: This entry was not confirmed by the trust.

The Methodist Child Care Society

Eligibility: Children from families under stress and/or hardship due to a variety of factors, for example, single parents who have lost their partner through death, separation or divorce and families where there is a loss of income due to illness or unemployment. Applicants should be members of the Methodist Church in Ireland. The maximum age for benefit is normally 18, but can be extended to the young person if they are going into further education without a source of income.

Types of grants: Quarterly payments plus one-off payments in June and December. There is a list of maximum income levels to qualify for a grant which can be obtained from the correspondent.

Annual grant total: Grants totalled £54,000 in 2001.

NORTHERN IRELAND

Applications: Application forms must be completed and can only be considered when submitted to the Superintendent of a Methodist Circuit and passed by the circuit quarterly meeting. They are considered in March, June, September and December.

Correspondent: Joseph Edgar, Drum Lodge, 11 Drumhirk Road, Comber, County Down BT23 5LY (028 9187 0696).

The Newtownabbey Methodist Mission

Eligibility: Socially disadvantaged children, adults, families and older people who live in Rathcoole and the surrounding area and Newtownabbey.

Types of grants: One-off grants for food, clothing and fuel bills throughout the year, and food/toy parcels at Christmas.

Annual grant total: About £10,000 to around 450 people.

Applications: By personal application or through a referral by a minister of religion, social worker or citizen's advice bureau at any time.

Correspondent: Mrs Eleanor McIlvenna, Administrator, 35a Rathcoole Drive, Newtownabbey, County Antrim BT37 9AQ (028 9085 2546; Fax: 028 9085 9956; e-mail: nmm@nireland.com; website: www.nireland.com/nmm).

Other information: The mission also has a playgroup, a charity shop and provides hot meals for older people.

NICHS (Northern Ireland Children's Holiday Schemes)

Eligibility: Underprivileged children aged between 9 and 18 living in Northern Ireland or the Republic of Ireland.

Types of grants: Grants are NOT given. Community Relations Programmes are organised and paid for by the organisation. Beneficiaries are equally drawn from both sections of the community and nominated by local community contacts.

Annual grant total: About 600 children attend the programmes.

Applications: In writing to the correspondent by the community contact. Applications are considered throughout the year.

Correspondent: Paddy Doherty, Assistant Director, 547 Antrim Road, Belfast BT15 3BU (028 9037 0373; Fax: 028 9078 1161; e-mail: info@nichs.org; website: www.nichs.org).

The Presbyterian Old Age Fund, Women's Fund & Indigent Ladies Fund

Eligibility: Needy, elderly or infirm members of the Presbyterian Church who live in any part of Ireland.

Types of grants: Recurrent grants of up to £150 paid quarterly, plus a Christmas gift of £150; one-off grants are occasionally considered in emergencies.

The Women's Fund and Indigent Ladies Fund are administered with the Old Age Fund.

Annual grant total: In 2001 grants to 124 beneficiaries totalled £77,000.

Applications: In writing through a minister to the correspondent. Applications are considered in January, April, June and October.

Correspondent: The Secretary, Church House, Fisherwick Place, Belfast BT1 6DW (028 9032 2284; Fax: 028 9023 6609; e-mail: finance@presbyterianireland.org).

The Presbyterian Orphan and Children's Society

Eligibility: Children under the age of 23 in full- or part-time education, living in Northern Ireland and Republic of Ireland, usually in single parent families. One parent must be a Presbyterian.

Types of grants: One-off and recurrent grants according to need. A grant scale is used in which the current grant for one child and one adult is £560 (Northern Ireland) or £580 (Republic of Ireland).

Annual grant total: In 2001 the society had assets of £5.1 million and an income of £482,000. Total expenditure was £457,000 and grants to 870 individuals totalled £333,000. Grants to childcare organisations totalled £15,000.

Applications: Applications are made by Presbyterian clergy on a form available from the correspondent. They are considered in March and September and should be submitted with details of the applicant's income and expenditure. Applicants are means tested.

Correspondent: Paul Gray, Church House, Fisherwick Place, Belfast BT1 6DW (028 9032 3737; e-mail: orphans@presbyterianireland.org).

The Protestant Orphan Society for the Counties of Antrim & Down (Inc)

Eligibility: Orphan children who live in the counties of Antrim or Down and who are members of the Church of Ireland.

Types of grants: An annual grant of £500 with holiday and Christmas bonuses of £30 each; also one-off bereavement grants of £500 to a family on the death of a parent.

Annual grant total: About £73,000 is available each year.

Applications: Applications can be made at any time through the clergy of the parish in which the individual lives.

Correspondent: T N Wilson, Secretary, Church of Ireland House, 61–67 Donegall Street, Belfast BT1 2QH (028 9032 2268).

The Retired Ministers' House Fund

Eligibility: Retired full-time members and servants of the Presbyterian Church in Ireland, and those comtemplating retirement.

Types of grants: Provision of rented accommodation and loans. No grants.

Annual grant total: About £150,000, although this varies each year.

Applications: In writing to the correspondent. Applications are considered as they arrive.

Correspondent: Ian McElhinly, Secretary, Church House, Fisherwick Place, Belfast BT1 6DW (028 9032 2284; Fax: 028 9023 6609).

The Royal Ulster Constabulary Benevolent Fund

Eligibility: Members and ex-members of the Royal Ulster Constabulary and their dependants who are in need. 'Founded in 1969 with its main objectives being to look after widows and their dependants, injured officers, pensioners and serving police officers.'

Types of grants: One-off or recurrent grants according to need. The fund '... offers a wide range of assistance including adventure holidays for children, short breaks for widows, convalescence for injured officers and financial help when required. In short, it does its utmost to be "all things to all people" – if there is a need and it can assist it does". NHS treatment is excluded.

Annual grant total: Grants totalled over £600,000 in 2001.

Applications: In writing to the correspondent at any time. Applications must be submitted via a regional representative.

Correspondent: The Secretary, PSNI Garnerville, Garnerville Road, Belfast BT4 2NX (028 9076 0831; Fax: 028 9076 1367).

The Society for the Orphans and Children of Ministers & Missionaries of the Presbyterian Church in Ireland

Eligibility: Children and young people aged under 26 who are orphaned and whose parents were ministers, missionaries or deaconesses of the Presbyterian Church in Ireland.

Types of grants: One-off grants of £300 to £2,000 for general welfare purposes.

Annual grant total: In 2001 the trust had assets of £715,000 and an income of £40,000. Total expenditure was £41,000 and grants to individuals for educational and welfare purposes totalled £30,000.

Applications: On a form available from the correspondent. Applications should be submitted directly by the individual in March for consideration in April.

Correspondent: Paul Gray, Church House, Fisherwick Place, Belfast BT1 6DW (028 9032 3737).

Other information: The trust also gives educational grants to the children of living ministers and missionaries.

The Sydney Stewart Memorial Trust

Eligibility: People in Northern Ireland who are involved in voluntary work.

Types of grants: One-off grants of between £100 and £250 to individuals interested in volunteering in projects in developing countries for at least one month. Preference is given to people going to the Indian sub-continent.

Annual grant total: In 2001/02 the trust had assets of £108,000 and an income of £8,000. Total expenditure was £6,800, with 11 grants totalling £1,400.

Applications: On a form available from the correspondent.

Correspondent: The Correspondent, 9 Ailesbury Crescent, Belfast BT7 3EZ.

Other information: This trust also gives grants to organisations.

The Sunshine Society Fund

Eligibility: Families with children aged under 18 who are ill or disabled and are in receipt of benefits or on a low income and who are in need. Referrals are sometimes considered for older people.

Types of grants: One-off grants ranging from £100 to £150 for necessities and comforts.

Annual grant total: In 2001/02 the trust had an income of £3,000, all of which was given in 28 grants.

Applications: In writing to the correspondent by a social worker, for consideration within one week of submission. Applications should include: background information on applicant with a breakdown of needs; why the request is being made; how a grant will benefit the applicant; details of income and expenditure on a weekly or monthly basis; and details of other sources of financial assistance and outcomes of any applications.

Correspondent: Rosaleen Murray, c/o Bryson House, 28 Bedford Street, Belfast BT2 7FE (Tel & Fax: 028 9032 5835; e-mail: rosaleen.murray@brysonhouse.com).

The Victoria Homes Trust

Eligibility: Young people under 21 who live in Northern Ireland. The trust prefers to fund groups or organisations for a specific project involving young people under 21 years old, rather than funding individual young people.

Types of grants: One-off and recurrent grants of £200 to £2,500 to help with problems associated with homelessness, alcohol and drug abuse and towards the cost of counselling for young people. Grants are occasionally made for educational purposes.

Annual grant total: In 2000/01 the trust had assets of £1.2 million and an income of £51,000. Grants totalled £39,000.

Applications: On a form available from the correspondent. Applications should be submitted through a social worker, citizen's advice bureau or other welfare agency. They are considered throughout the year.

Correspondent: Derek H Catney, Secretary, 2 Tudor Court, Rochester Road, Belfast BT6 9LB (028 9079 4306; e-mail: derek.catney@btclick.com).

2. Scotland

The Adamson Trust

Eligibility: Children aged 16 or under who have a physical or mental disability.

Types of grants: Grants to help with the cost of holidays. No grants can be given towards the costs of accompanying adults.

Annual grant total: In 2000/01 the trust had assets of £939,000 and an income of £66,000. Grants to 146 individuals totalled £9,300. Grants to 42 organisations for similar purposes totalled £30,000.

Applications: On a form available from the correspondent, to be returned with: evidence from a family doctor, social worker and so on; booking confirmations; and evidence that the balance of the holiday can be met if the trust is not paying for the full cost of the holiday. Applications are considered in January, May and September.

Correspondent: The Trustees, c/o Messrs Miller Henry, 14 Comrie Street, Crieff, Perthshire PH7 4AZ (01764 655151; Fax: 01764 652903).

The Aged Christian Friend Society of Scotland

Eligibility: Christians in need living in Scotland who are over 60 years of age.

Types of grants: About 18 pensions of £220 a year.

Annual grant total: In 1999 relief-in-need grants to individuals totalled £4,000.

Applications: The trust was not inviting new applications at the time of publication of this guide. It was undergoing a change of policy and planned to award other types of grants and phase out the pensions; contact the correspondent for further information.

Correspondent: James Clark, Brodies WS, 15 Atholl Crescent, Edinburgh EH3 8HA (0131 228 3777).

Other information: The society's principal activity is in the provision of sheltered housing for older people in Scotland.

The Airth Benefaction Trust

Eligibility: People in need, 'who have seen better days and who are incapable of gaining a livelihood'.

Types of grants: Grants of £120 paid in December.

Annual grant total: £6,600. A maximum of 55 grants are given each year.

Applications: On a form available from the correspondent. These should be returned not later than 30 September for consideration in December. Beneficiaries are invited to reapply each year.

Correspondent: Douglas Munro Hunter, Henderson Boyd Jackson, 19 Ainslie Place, Edinburgh EH3 6AU (0131 226 6881; Fax: 0131 226 4027; e-mail: info@hbj.co.uk).

The Reverend Alexander Barclay Bequest

Eligibility: Female relatives (mother, daughter, sister or niece) of a current or deceased minister of the Church of Scotland, who are in need and, at the time of his death was acting as his housekeeper.

Types of grants: Beneficiaries receive a quarterly grant and bonuses three times a year, at Easter, September and Christmas.

Annual grant total: About £4,000.

Applications: In writing to the correspondent, to be submitted directly by the individual at any time.

Correspondent: The Trustees, Pomphreys Solicitors, 79 Quarry Street, Hamilton ML3 7AG (01698 891616; Fax: 01698 891617; e-mail: general@pomphreys.solicitors.co.uk).

The John Boyd Baxter Charitable Trust

Eligibility: Women over 55, who live in and around Dundee, or in and around Newport or Fife and have done so for at least 10 years.

Types of grants: About 18 individuals receive about £100 a year. Beneficiaries must be 'deserving respectable females to whom a little help may bring comparative comfort'.

Annual grant total: About £1,800 in 1999.

Applications: In writing to the correspondent. Applications can be submitted either directly by the individual or through a social worker, citizen's advice bureau or other welfare agency or other third party on behalf of an individual.

Correspondent: Dale Ross, Thorntons WS, Brothockbank House, Arbroath DD11 1NF (01241 872683).

The Benevolent Fund for Nurses in Scotland

Eligibility: Nurses who trained in Scotland and/or held professional posts there.

Types of grants: One-off and quarterly grants to applicants with limited income owing to illness or disability, or in the case of retired nurses, those with little or no superannuation pension. The fund can also help by buying furnishings or equipment.

Annual grant total: In 2001 grants to 170 regular beneficiaries totalled £170,000.

Applications: Application forms, available from the correspondent, can be submitted by the individual or through a recognised referral agency (social worker, citizen's advice bureau, doctor etc.) and are considered as they are received. The trust may decide to visit potential beneficiaries.

Correspondent: Margaret Sturgeon, 15 Camp Road, Motherwell ML1 2RQ (01698 252034; e-mail: magsturgeon@yahoo.co.uk; website: www.bfns.org.uk).

The Elizabeth Bibby Bequest

Eligibility: Seafarers or ex-seafarers in financial or other need who are either former employees of North of Scotland, Shetland and Orkney Shipping Company, native or one time residents of the counties of Aberdeen, Orkney or Shetland or residents of the Seamen's Institute Leith.

Types of grants: One-off grants according to need.

Annual grant total: £2,000.

Applications: On a form available from the correspondent.

Correspondent: Alan Smith, General Secretary, British and International Sailors' Society, Orchard Place, Southampton, Hampshire SO14 3AT (023 8033 7333; Fax: 023 8063 1789).

The Biggart Trust

Eligibility: People in need, with preference for people related to the founders and their descendants.

Types of grants: One-off and recurrent grants (half-yearly), ranging from £600 to £1,100.

Annual grant total: In 1998/99 the trust had assets of £248,000 and an income of £12,800. Its total expenditure was £8,900 of which £6,500 was given in seven grants.

Applications: In writing to the correspondent, directly by the individual.

Correspondent: Andrew S Biggart, McClay Murray & Spens, 151 St Vincent Street, Glasgow G2 5NJ (0141 248 5011).

The Black Watch Association

Eligibility: Serving and retired soldiers of the regiment, their wives, widows and families.

Types of grants: 1. Financial assistance for those eligible if they find themselves in adverse circumstances. Grants are made towards household bills, clothing, household equipment, mobility and sometimes debts.

2. Grants towards holidays for widows and dependent children and former members of the Regiment in necessitous circumstances.

Standard grants up to £250. No grants towards council tax arrears or large debts.

Annual grant total: About £100,000 in grants to individuals.

Applications: SSAFA Form 9 is used for welfare grants. Holiday applications should be made on a separate form. Applications are considered throughout the year.

Correspondent: Maj. A R McKinnell, Balhousie Castle, Hay Street, Perth PH1 5HR (01738 623214; Fax: 01738 643245).

The Blyth Benevolent Trust

Eligibility: Women aged over 60 and in need. Preference is given to people who are blind or partially sighted with the surname Bell or Blyth, and who live in or are connected with Newport-on-Tay, Fife or Dundee.

Types of grants: Annuities paid twice a year of £65 and a Christmas bonus of £25. Pensions are paid in June and December, alongside the bonus. Between 15 and 20 individuals are supported each year.

Annual grant total: Around £1,500.

Applications: In writing to the correspondent.

Correspondent: Mrs Elizabeth N McGillivray, Secretary, Bowman Scottish Lawyers, Solicitors, 27 Bank Street, Dundee DD1 1RP (01382 322267).

The Buchanan Society

Eligibility: People with the following surnames: Buchanan, McAuslan (any spelling), McWattie, and Risk.

Types of grants: Pensions of £640 for older people in need and bursaries for students in severe financial difficulties of about £700. One-off grants can also be given.

Annual grant total: About 70 people are supported each year.

Applications: On a form available from the correspondent, including the applicant's birth certificate. Applications are considered throughout the year.

Correspondent: Mrs Fiona Risk, Secretary, 18 Iddesleigh Avenue, Milngavie, Glasgow G62 8NT (Tel & Fax: 0141 956 1939).

Other information: The Buchanan Society is the oldest Clan Society in Scotland having been founded in 1725. Grantmaking is its sole function.

Challenger Children's Fund

Eligibility: Children aged under 18 who live in Scotland and are physically disabled.

Types of grants: One-off grants of up to £400 each towards a specific need such as clothing, bedding, washing machines, fridges, beds and so on.

Annual grant total: £34,000.

Applications: In writing to the correspondent. Applications are considered monthly. Individuals can apply more than once.

Correspondent: Wendy Dunn, Cunningham Unit, Astley Ainslie Hospital, Edinburgh EH9 2HL (0131 537 9093; Fax: 0131 537 9095; e-mail: ecas@theoffice.net).

The Commercial Travellers of Scotland Benevolent Fund for Widows & Orphans

Eligibility: Widows and orphans of commercial travellers in Scotland.

Types of grants: Quarterly grants totalling £600 a year are given for general financial assistance.

Annual grant total: In 2001 the trust had assets of £88,000 and an income of £19,000. Total expenditure was £18,000, including £12,000 given in 16 grants to individuals.

Applications: On a form available from the correspondent. Applications are considered in March, June, September and December.

Correspondent: David M Betts, c/o McCreath & Co. CA, Bank House, 20a Strathearn Road, Edinburgh EH9 2AB (0131 446 9292; Fax: 0131 446 9009).

The Craigcrook Mortification

Eligibility: People in need over the age of 60 who were born in Scotland and have lived there for most of their lives.

Types of grants: Annual pensions. One-off payments are not available.

Annual grant total: £22,000.

Applications: In writing to the correspondent. Applications should be supported by a member of the clergy.

Correspondent: R Graeme Thom, Clerk and Factor, 17 Melville Street, Edinburgh EH3 7PH (0131 473 3500).

Other information: The trust has limited capacity to take on new applicants.

The Alastair Crerar Trust for Single Poor

Eligibility: Single people aged 16 or over who are on low incomes. Applicants or the person applying on their behalf, must have an active Christian faith.

Types of grants: Help towards holiday accommodation, travel, Christmas meals, theatre and cinema outings, bus trips, household necessities, educational expenses, community projects and so on. Grants are rarely over £300.

Annual grant total: In 1998/99 the trust had assets of £235,000, an income of £9,800 and its total expenditure was £12,000. £10,000 was given in 60 grants.

Applications: On a form available from the correspondent (who has stated that 'the trust receives more applications than it is able to respond to'). Applications can be submitted either directly by the individual or through a social worker, citizen's advice bureau or other welfare agency or other third party.

Correspondent: Michael I D Sturrock, Secretary, The Garden Flat, 34 Mayfield Terrace, Edinburgh EH9 1RZ (0131 668 3524).

Other information: The object of the trust is to provide financial assistance for eligible people in order to improve their quality of life.

ECAS – Challenger Children's Fund

Eligibility: Children under 18 who live in Scotland and are physically disabled. The fund aims to help by meeting expenses where the child's disability is the cause or has a direct bearing on the child.

The following disabilities alone are not eligible: learning difficulties, developmental delay, Downs Syndrome, cystic fibrosis, autism and visual or hearing impairment.

Types of grants: One-off grants for essential items which directly benefit the applicant and are not covered by statutory sources. No grants to cover the cost of items already bought or to repay loans.

Annual grant total: In 1998/99 the budget was £34,000 and 242 applications were received. Grants were given for educational and welfare purposes.

Applications: On a form available from the correspondent with parental income and expenditure and a GP's report. Applications are normally received from the parent/guardian of the child through a social worker, health visitor or other professional who is currently aware of the child's needs. They are considered monthly.

Correspondent: Wendy Dunn, Cunningham Unit, Astley Ainslie Hospital, 133 Grange Loan, Edinburgh EH9 2HL (0131 537 9093; Fax: 0131 537 9095; e-mail: wendyd@ecasuk.demon.co.uk; website: http://theoffice.net/ecas).

Other information: Every six months £300 is given to hospital social work departments. Awards are made at the discretion of the social worker and can be used to cover a variety of needs such as travel expenses and subsistence.

Charities administered by the Educational Institute of Scotland

The correspondent for the following is: The General Secretary, Educational Institute of Scotland, 46 Moray Place, Edinburgh EH3 6BH (0131 225 6244).

(i) The James Clark Bequest Fund

Eligibility: Members of the institute and their widows/widowers and dependants who are ill or in need.

Types of grants: Three grants of £500 each are made a year.

Annual grant total: £1,500.

Applications: In writing to the correspondent.

(ii) The Educational Institute of Scotland Benevolent Fund

Eligibility: Members of the institute, their widows and dependants in need. They must have been in membership for at least one year prior to application.

Types of grants: One-off and recurrent grants according to need.

Annual grant total: About 60 grants are made totalling £65,000.

Applications: On a form available from the correspondent of the benevolent fund committee of the local association of which the applicant is a member or from the correspondent. Meetings are normally held in February, April, June, September and November.

(iii) The Catherine McCallum Memorial Fund

Eligibility: Women who are incapacitated by ill health and have been teachers or governesses. (It is not necessary to have been members of the institute.)

Types of grants: One-off grants are made and can be towards both essentials and 'comforts', e.g. nighties, toiletries.

Annual grant total: Between two and four grants are made each year, totalling about £6,000.

Applications: In writing to the correspondent.

The Faculty of Advocates 1985 Charitable Trust

Eligibility: 1. Widows, widowers, children or former dependants of deceased members of the Faculty of Advocates. 2. Members of the faculty who are unable to practise by reason of permanent ill health.

Types of grants: Single grants, annuities or loans appropriate to the circumstances. Grants range from £700 to £12,000.

Annual grant total: £60,000.

Applications: In writing to the correspondent.

Correspondent: J W Macpherson, Bursar, Advocate's Library, Parliament House, Edinburgh EH1 1RF (0131 332 1750).

The Emily Fraser Trust

Eligibility: People in need who work or worked in the drapery and allied trades, printing, publishing, bookselling, stationery and newspaper and allied trades and their dependants who live in Scotland.

Types of grants: One-off grants of £500 to £2,500.

Annual grant total: In 1999/2000 the trust had assets of £2.3 million and an income of £87,000. Grants to 26 individuals totalled £34,000. Grants to 21 organisations totalled £47,000.

Applications: In writing to the correspondent. The trustees meet on a quarterly basis.

Correspondent: Heather Thompson, Turcan Connell, Princes Exchange, 1 Earl Grey Street, Edinburgh EH3 9EE (0131 228 8111; Fax: 0131 228 8118).

Other information: Grants are also given to charitable organisations, concerned with the relief of poverty, elderly people and people who are ill.

The Glasgow Society of the Sons of Ministers of the Church of Scotland

Eligibility: Children of ministers of the Church of Scotland who are in need, particularly students and the children of deceased ministers.

Types of grants: One-off and recurrent grants according to need.

Annual grant total: About £40,000 a year is given in educational and welfare grants to individuals.

Applications: On a form available from the correspondent. Applications from the children of deceased ministers are considered in February; applications from students in August.

Correspondent: R Graeme Thom, Secretary and Treasurer, Scott-Moncrieff, 17 Melville Street, Edinburgh EH3 7PH (0131 473 3500; Fax: 0131 473 3535; e-mail: graeme.thom@scott-moncrieff.com).

The Governesses' Benevolent Society of Scotland

Eligibility: Older governesses in need living in Scotland.

Types of grants: Recurrent grants are given to older governesses in difficulties through poverty or ill-health. Grants are in the region of £10,000 a year, depending on personal circumstances.

Annual grant total: In 2000/01 the trust had assets of £740,000 with an income and a total expenditure of £29,000. Two grants totalled £22,000.

Applications: On a form available from the correspondent, to be submitted directly by the individual and certified by a professional person. Applications are considered in April, but new applications can be considered as received.

Correspondent: Allan Gibson, Secretary & Treasurer, Grant Thornton, 1/4 Atholl Crescent, Edinburgh EH3 8LQ (0131 659 8541; Fax: 0131 229 4506; e-mail: sue.m.melrose@gtuk.com).

The Grand Lodge of Antient, Free & Accepted Masons of Scotland

Eligibility: Members and their dependants, and the widows and dependants of deceased members.

Types of grants: One-off and recurrent grants according to need.

Annual grant total: About £155,000 is given in welfare grants and £25,000 in educational grants.

Applications: On a form available from the correspondent, or by direct approach to the local lodge.

Correspondent: C Martin McGibbon, Grand Secretary, Freemasons Hall, 96 George Street, Edinburgh EH2 3DH (0131 225 5304; Fax: 0131 225 3953; e-mail: glhomes@grandlodgescotland.org).

The Earl Haig Fund Scotland

Eligibility: Ex-serving members of the Armed Forces in Scotland and their widows/widowers and dependants.

Scotland – General

Types of grants: Annual and off-one grants of £25 to £1,000, are given towards repairs, clothing, white goods, powered vehicles, debts and household items. No grants are given towards funeral expenses, headstones or the replacement of medals. Loans are not available.

Annual grant total: In 2000/01 the fund gave £690,000 in 3,000 grants.

Applications: On a form available from the correspondent. Applications are considered weekly and should be submitted through a social worker, citizen's advice bureau, other welfare agency or one of the funds, or other ex-service charity's, own caseworkers. Applicants must have proof of service in HM Forces in writing (i.e. a discharge book).

Correspondent: The Secretary, New Haig House, Logie Green Road, Edinburgh EH7 4HR (0131 557 2782; Fax: 0131 557 5819).

Other information: The Earl Haig Scotland is in many respects the Scottish equivalent of the benevolence department of the Royal British Legion in the rest of Britain. Like the legion, it runs the Poppy Appeal, which is a major source of income to help those in distress. There is, however, a Royal British Legion Scotland, which has a separate entry in this guide. The two organisations share the same premises and work together.

The Douglas Hay Trust

Eligibility: Children aged under 18 who are physically disabled and live in Scotland.

Types of grants: One-off grants of £40 to £500 towards shoes, clothes, bedding, holidays, computers and equipment.

Annual grant total: In 2000/01 the trust had assets of £849,000, an income of £36,000 and a total expenditure of £30,000. Grants totalled £23,000 to 180 individuals.

Applications: On a form available from the correspondent, to be submitted through a social worker, citizen's advice bureau or other welfare agency. Applications are considered monthly.

Correspondent: John D Ritchie, Whitelaw Wells, 9 Ainslie Place, Edinburgh EH3 6AT (0131 226 5822; Fax: 0131 240 5498; e-mail: johnritchie@whitelawwells.co.uk).

The George Hogg Trust

Eligibility: People who live in Killin and district, who are in need.

Types of grants: One-off and recurrent grants according to need, for example £200 towards an electric wheelchair.

Annual grant total: In 2001 the trust's assets totalled £150,000 and its income was £10,000. No grants were made that year.

Applications: In writing to the correspondent via a third party such as a local doctor or minister.

Correspondent: C J McRae, Tayview House, Main Street, Killin, Perthshire FK21 8UT (01567 820719; e-mail: tayview@aol.com).

William Hunter's Old Men's Fund

Eligibility: Older men in need who were born in Scotland and are of Scottish parentage and who are/were merchants, manufacturers or master tradesmen.

Types of grants: Recurrent grants paid twice a year of £370 for people under 80, and £385 for those over 80.

Annual grant total: Between £5,000 and £5,500.

Applications: In writing to the correspondent.

Correspondent: Miss Heather Stevenson, Edinburgh Chamber of Commerce, 27 Melville Street, Edinburgh EH3 7JF (0131 477 7000).

The George Jamieson Fund

Eligibility: Widows and single women who are in need and live in the city of Aberdeen or the counties of Aberdeen and Kincardine.

Types of grants: Recurrent grants totalling £220 a year payable half yearly in May and November.

Annual grant total: In 2000/01 the trust had assets of £322,000 and an income of £6,600. Grants to 30 individuals totalled £2,600.

Applications: In writing to the correspondent. Applications can be submitted directly by the individual or through a social worker, citizen's advice bureau or other welfare agency or other third party on behalf of an individual. Applications should include details of circumstances and are considered all year round.

Correspondent: The Trustees, Wilsone & Duffus, 7 Golden Square, Aberdeen AB10 1EP (01224 651700; Fax: 01224 647329; e-mail: info@wilsoneduffus.co.uk).

Jewish Care Scotland

Eligibility: Jewish people in need living in Scotland.

Types of grants: One-off grants of £50 to £750 towards clothing, food, household goods, rent, holidays, equipment, travel and education.

Annual grant total: In 2000 the trust had an income of £515,000 and a total expenditure of £525,000. Grants to around 300 people totalled £12,000, including £3,000 in 10 educational grants.

Applications: In writing to the chief executive at the address below.

Correspondent: Ethne Woldman, May Terrace, Giffnock, Glasgow G46 6LD (0141 620 1800; Fax: 0141 620 2409; e-mail: admin@jcarescot.org.uk).

Other information: The board also helps with friendship clubs, housing requirements, clothing, meals-on-wheels, counselling and so on.

The Johnstone Wright Fund

Eligibility: Unmarried or widowed women who are in need and (a) were born in Scotland, (b) are preferably 'connected with Edinburgh' and (c) are 'of the professional classes'.

Types of grants: Grants are paid half-yearly in May and November, and are reviewed annually. Grants range from £300 to £700 and are given to between 17 and 20 individuals each year.

Annual grant total: About £10,000.

Applications: In writing to the correspondent, for consideration in March.

Correspondent: The Secretary, Messrs Morton Fraser, 30–31 Queen Street, Edinburgh EH2 1JX (0131 247 1000).

Key Trust

Eligibility: People in Scotland who have learning difficulties.

Types of grants: Grants and loans are given to help people setting up home gain independence and 'experience more out of life', such as towards furnishings such as carpets.

Annual grant total: In 2000 the trust had an income of £10,000, all of which was given in grants.

Applications: On a form available from the correspondent, submitted either directly by the individual or via a welfare agency. Applicants must approach every other source of funding before approaching this trust.

Applications are considered throughout the year, but more funds are available at the beginning of the financial year which runs April to March.

Correspondent: Gordon Taylor, Savoy Tower, 77 Renfrew Street, Glasgow G2 3BZ (0141 332 6672; Fax: 0141 332 7498).

The Law Society of Scotland Benevolent Fund

Eligibility: Members and former members of the society and their dependants.

Types of grants: One-off and recurrent grants according to need.

Annual grant total: No information available.

Applications: In writing to the correspondent.

Correspondent: Mrs Janice H Webster, The Scottish Law Agents Society, 11 Parliament Square, Edinburgh EH1 1RF (0131 225 5051).

SCOTLAND – GENERAL

The Benevolent Society of the Licensed Trade of Scotland

Eligibility: Members of the society and people who have been employed in the licensed trade in Scotland for at least three years.

Types of grants: One-off and recurrent grants according to need. One-off grants are up to a maximum of £300.

Annual grant total: £150,000 in 300 grants.

Applications: On a form available from the correspondent at any time. Applications can be made directly by the individual or through a social worker, citizen's advice bureau or other welfare agency.

Correspondent: Chris Gardener, Secretary, 79 West Regent Street, Glasgow G2 2AW (0141 353 3596).

John A Longmore's Trust

Eligibility: People who live in Scotland who have an incurable disease.

Types of grants: Annuities of £330 in two instalments. One-off grants of up to £1,000 to improve the quality of life on a day-to-day basis. Equipment sought can be either fixed or moveable such as a wheelchair. No grants are given towards holidays or house decoration.

Annual grant total: In 2000/01 the trust had assets of £466,000, an income of £23,000 and a total expenditure of £28,000. In the previous year grants to 70 individuals totalled £20,000.

Applications: On a form available from the correspondent, to be returned with a covering letter detailing income and expenses of the household and a breakdown of how the grant will be used. Applications are considered in the third week of every month and should be submitted by the 16th of the month.

Correspondent: Robin D Fulton, Trustee, Turcan Connell, Princes Exchange, 1 Earl Grey Street, Edinburgh EH3 9EE (0131 228 8111; Fax: 0131 228 8118; e-mail: rdf@turcanconnell.com).

The Catherine Mackichan Trust

Eligibility: People who are in need, with a preference for people who are unemployed, disabled or elderly.

Types of grants: One-off and recurrent grants, usually of up to £500 each.

Annual grant total: In 2000/01 the trust had assets of £45,000 and an income of £1,500, all of which was given in four grants.

Applications: On a form available from: I Fraser, School of Scottish Studies, 27 George Square, Edinburgh. Applications should arrive by 15 April for consideration in April/May.

Correspondent: N D Mackichan, Aros, Whittingham, Alnwick, Northumberland NE6 4RF (01665 574335; e-mail: neil.mackichan@care4free.net).

Other information: Grants are also given for education and research in archaeology and to schools and local history societies.

The Agnes Macleod Memorial Fund

Eligibility: Women in need who are over 60, living in Scotland and were born with the name Macleod or whose mothers were born Macleod.

Types of grants: To provide monetary grants or donations of gift vouchers when benefits from the state are either not sufficient or not appropriate. Grants range from £100 to £250 and are one-off.

Annual grant total: In 2000/01 the fund gave 30 grants totalling £4,500.

Applications: In writing to the correspondent. Advertisements are also put in newspapers. Applications are considered in May and November. Doctors, social workers, citizen's advice bureau, other welfare agencies, health visitors, ministers and priests may also submit applications on behalf of an individual.

Correspondent: Linda Orr, Secretary, 80 Stevenson Avenue, Edinburgh EH11 2SW (0131 337 6264).

The George McKenzie Fund

Eligibility: Members and former members of the British Linen Bank and their dependants who are in need of financial assistance.

Types of grants: One-off grants for capital items only. There are no payments to supplement income.

Annual grant total: About £700.

Applications: On a form available from the correspondent, submitted either directly by the individual or through Bank of Scotland pensioners associations or Bank of Scotland branches.

Correspondent: Miss Josie O'Connor, Bank of Scotland, 30 Queensferry Road, Edinburgh EH4 2UZ.

Other information: This entry was not confirmed by the trust.

The McLaren Fund for Indigent Ladies

Eligibility: Scottish widows/unmarried women (preferably over 40 years of age) and widows/unmarried daughters of commissioned officers in certain Scottish regiments.

Types of grants: Regular allowances of between £160 and £170 made twice a year. One-off grants are also available.

Annual grant total: There were 110 to 130 beneficiaries in 2001, although funds were available for more applicants.

Applications: On a form available from the correspondent. For new applicants, applications are considered twice yearly, in July and December. Applicants from the previous year will be contacted by the trust.

Correspondent: Elspeth J Talbot, BMK Wilson, Apsley House, 29 Wellington Street, Glasgow G2 6JA (0141 221 8004).

The George McLean Trust

Eligibility: People in Fife and Tayside who are mentally or physically disabled, elderly or infirm.

Types of grants: Grants are given towards holidays, clothing, furnishing, residential care and so on.

Annual grant total: In 2000/01 the trust had assets of £667,000. Its income was £34,000, all of which was given in 140 grants to individuals for educational and welfare purposes. A further £1,000 was given to organisations.

Applications: On a form available from the correspondent. Applications can be submitted directly by the individual or through any third party. They are considered monthly.

Correspondent: Mrs Beth Anderson, The Help Unit, Blackadders Solicitors, 30-34 Reform Street, Dundee DD1 1RJ (01382 229222; Fax: 01382 342220; e-mail: beth.anderson@blackadders.co.uk)

The Annie Ramsay McLean Trust for the Elderly

Eligibility: People aged 60 or over who live in Fife and Tayside.

Types of grants: One-off and recurrent grants of £100 to £1,000. Recent grants have been given towards a car hoist and residential care fees (£500 each), a holiday (£290) and winter clothing (£100). No grants are given towards debts.

Annual grant total: In 2000/01 the trust had assets of £750,000, an income of £42,000 and a total expenditure of £10,000. Grants to 31 individuals totalled £8,800. Grants to organisations totalled £1,400.

Applications: On a form available from the correspondent. Applications can be submitted directly by the individual or thorough any third party. They are considered monthly.

Correspondent: The Trustees, Blackadders Solicitors, 30-34 Reform Street, Dundee DD1 1RJ (01382 229222; Fax: 01382 342220; e-mail: beth.anderson@blackadders.co.uk).

The Morison Bequest

Eligibility: Members of the Congregational Churches in Scotland who are disabled, blind or infirm.

SCOTLAND – GENERAL

Types of grants: Recurrent grants of £30 every six months.
Annual grant total: In 1999 the trust had an income of about £800. Only one grant was made, of £60.
Applications: Applications should be sent to: W B Hampton, 4 The Square, Letham, Angus DD8 2PZ.
Correspondent: Mr Munton, Low Beaton Richmond, Sterling House, 20 Renfield Street, Glasgow G2 5AP (0141 221 8931).

The Alexander Naysmyth Fund

Eligibility: Scottish artists of established reputation in painting, sculpture, architecture or engraving who are in need.
Types of grants: One-off payments of up to £1,000.
Annual grant total: In 2000/01 the trust had assets of £240,000 and an income of £10,000. From a total expenditure of £7,600, grants were given to two individuals totalling £2,000.
Applications: In writing to the correspondent directly by the individual for consideration in May/June.
Correspondent: Prof. Isi Metzstein, Royal Scottish Academy, 17 Waterloo Place, Edinburgh EH1 3BG (0131 558 7097; Fax: 0131 557 6417; e-mail: info@royalscottishacademy.org; website: www.royalscottishacademy.org).

North of Scotland Quaker Trust

Eligibility: People who are associated with the Religious Society of Friends in the north of Scotland monthly meeting area, namely Aberdeen City, Aberdeenshire, Morar, Highland, Orkney, Shetland, Western Isles and that part of Argyll and Bute from Oban northwards.
Types of grants: One-off and recurrent grants according to need.
Annual grant total: In 2000 the trust had assets of £54,000 and an income of £14,000. Three welfare grants to individuals totalled £1,300. Educational grants to 13 individuals totalled £2,500.
Applications: In writing to the correspondent.
Correspondent: John M Melling, Clerk, 86 Culduthel Park, Inverness IV2 4RZ (01463 237686).
Other information: This trust was previously known as The Aberdeen Two Months' Meeting Trust.

The Nurses Memorial to King Edward VII Edinburgh Committee

Eligibility: Nurses with a strong connection to Scotland (including nurses who have worked in Scotland, or Scottish nurses working outside Scotland) who are retired, ill or otherwise in need. Retired nurses are given priority.

Types of grants: One-off and monthly grants. Help is given towards accommodation charges, domestic bills and to supplement inadequate income.
Annual grant total: Between 50 and 60 nurses are supported each year, with grants totalling around £50,000.
Applications: Details of present financial and other circumstances are required on a form available from the correspondent. The information given should be confirmed by a social worker, health visitor, doctor or similar professional.
Correspondent: Mr Byers, Byers & Company, 2b Roseburn Terrace, Edinburgh EH12 6AW (0131 313 5555).

The Officers' Association Scotland

Eligibility: Ex-officers of the armed forces of Great Britain, or of the merchant navy or Polish forces during World War Two, (including the women's and nursing services) and their widows/widowers and dependants who are in distress, and ex-officers of all ages seeking employment.
Types of grants: Normally annual grants in four quarterly payments of up to £20 a week. One-off grants are investigated and dealt with as they arise.
Annual grant total: In 2001/02 the association had assets of £5.5 million with an income of £395,000. Total expenditure was £459,000, with £277,000 given in 210 grants.
Applications: On a form available from the correspondent, submitted through SSAFA, a social worker, citizen's advice bureau or other suitable agency, or Officer's Association Honorary representatives.
Correspondent: Cmdr A C Herdman, Benevolence Secretary, New Haig House, Logie Green Road, Edinburgh EH7 4HR (0131 557 2782; Fax: 0131 557 5819).

The Mrs Jeane Panton and Miss Anne Stirling Trust

Eligibility: Ministers or pastors (not bishops) of the Scotch Episcopal Communion who were born in Scotland and have small incomes.
Types of grants: One-off grants are given to supplement the individual's regular income.
Annual grant total: Between £2,000 and £3,000 is given each year.
Applications: In writing via bishops of the dioceses, who are the trustees and recommend ministers in need. Ministers cannot apply directly.
Correspondent: John Stewart, General Synod, 21 Grovesnor Street, Edinburgh EH12 5EE (0131 225 6357).

Phace Scotland – Crusaid Hardship Fund In Scotland

Eligibility: People with HIV/Aids who live in Scotland, including people currently resident in prison. There are no citizenship or permanent residency requirements.
Types of grants: Generally, one-off grants of to £200 towards items such as white goods, start-up costs for a new home and needs directly related to the individual's condition. The level of support available is means-tested, with applicants with lower incomes and savings being able to receive multiple one-off grants during a twelve-month period, as well as being eligible for help with utility bills and living expenses such as food, toiletries and travel costs.

No grants can be towards: travel or accommodation of any kind outside of the UK; funeral costs; or luxury items such as dishwashers (except if required for medical purposes). Debts will only be supported if the applicant includes a budget plan with their application.
Annual grant total: In 2001/02 grants to 356 individuals totalled £50,000.
Applications: An application form must be completed with the help of a social worker, health advisor or welfare agency, who must send the application on behalf of the applicant. Completed forms must be sent to: The Crusaid Hardship Fund, Phace Scotland, Freepost SCO 307, Glasgow G2 2BR. Applications sent directly by the individual, or which are faxed or e-mailed, cannot be considered.

Applications must include proof of income (such as copies of benefit books, bank statements and wage slips), bills to be paid, proof of diagnosis (if a new applicant) and any other relevant documents. The referring agent making the application may telephone for further information between 1pm and 4pm, Tuesdays to Thursdays.

In most cases, cheques (made paid to the welfare agency or organisation to which the bill is payable) are sent out within a week of the receipt of successful applications.
Correspondent: Grants Officer, 49 Bath Street, Glasgow G2 2DL (0141 332 3838; Fax: 0141 332 3755; e-mail: contact@phacewest.org; website: www.phacescotland.org).
Other information: People with HIV/Aids living in other parts of the UK, even if of Scottish origin, should apply to The Crusaid Hardship Fund, see separate entry.

Radio Forth Help A Child Appeal

Eligibility: Children who have special needs and live in east central Scotland.
Types of grants: Grants are given towards medical equipment, treatment, toys and computers.

Annual grant total: In 1998/99 the trust gave £126,000 in grants to individuals and organisations.

Applications: On a form available from the correspondent. Applications are considered four times a year.

Correspondent: Lesley Fraser, Charity Coordinator, Forth House, Forth Street, Edinburgh EH1 3LE (0131 556 9255; Fax: 0131 475 1221; e-mail: lesley.fraser@srh.co.uk; website: www.forthonline.co.uk).

Radio Tay – Caring for Kids (Radio Tay Listeners Charity)

Eligibility: Children and young people aged under 19 who are in need and live in Tayside and North East Fife.

Types of grants: One-off grants of £300 to £5,000 towards needs such as clothing, beds, bedding, holidays and special needs equipment.

Annual grant total: In 2000/01 the trust had assets of £44,000 and an income of £98,000. Grants were given to 6,700 individuals and organisations totalling £90,000.

Applications: On a form available from the correspondent from the start of December, to be returned by the end of January for consideration in February. Applications have to be submitted with a letter from a social worker, doctor, teacher etc. Letter must be on headed paper. This is to confirm that the application form submitted by the individual is correct and accurate.

Correspondent: Mandy McLernon, Coordinator, Radio Tay Ltd, 6 North Isla Street, Dundee DD3 7JQ (01382 200800; e-mail: tay-cfk@radiotay.co.uk; website: www.radiotay.co.uk).

The Royal Air Force Benevolent Fund (Scottish Branch)

Eligibility: Ex-RAF people (and their direct dependants) in Scotland who are in need.

Types of grants: The type of grant is determined by the need of the eligible applicant and may consist of a one-off grant, small regular allowance, or loan. There are limitations on assistance to those dishonourably discharged, and for credit card debt (only after CAB advice accepted). No assistance is given for headstones and memorials.

Annual grant total: Just over £2 million in Scotland for educational and welfare purposes.

Applications: In writing to the correspondent. Applications can be made at any time, submitted either directly by the individual or through RAFA, SSAFA, war pensions or a social worker. Confirmation of RAF service, or sufficient details to allow a search of RAF service records, should be included.

Correspondent: The Director, 20 Queen Street, Edinburgh EH2 1JX (0131 225 6421).

Other information: Applications from serving RAF people and those involving sums over £7,500 (rare) are handled by the London HQ of the RAF Benevolent Fund, 67 Portland Place W1N 4AR (see separate entry).

The fund also operates a Residential Nursing Home on Deeside.

The Royal Incorporation of Architects in Scotland

Eligibility: Architects (and members of RIAS) and their dependants who are in need and live in Scotland.

Types of grants: Small one-off grants.

Annual grant total: No information available.

Applications: In writing to the correspondent.

Correspondent: Sebastian Tombs, Chief Executive, 15 Rutland Square, Edinburgh EH1 2BE (0131 229 7205).

The Royal Scottish Agricultural Benevolent Institution

Eligibility: People in need who are or have been engaged in agriculture, forestry, horticulture, fish farming or rural estate work in Scotland and their dependants.

Types of grants: The total number of beneficiaries in 2000/01 was 633. 437 people were given annual grants of £600 and had television licences paid. One-off grants towards television license fees, telephone and telephone alarm installation costs, debt and minor building repairs etc. were made to 196 individuals, varying greatly in size. Foot and mouth in 2001 resulted in 650 additional families seeking help and follow up work was expected to continue for at least three years.

Annual grant total: In 2000/01 the trust had assets of £6.3 million and an income of £1.1 million. Grants to individuals totalled £396,000. The income figure is higher than in previous years due to the trust receiving extra donations for foot and mouth disease support.

Applications: Write to or telephone the correspondent for an application form. Applications through referrals by local representatives, welfare organisations or social service departments are also welcomed. They are considered at any time. Applicants should include as much background about their working life, present financial situation and medical state.

Correspondent: John Macdonald, Director, South Bungalow, Ingliston, Edinburgh EH28 8NB (0131 333 1023; Fax: 0131 333 1027; e-mail: rsabi@rsabi.org.uk; website: www.rsabi.org.uk).

Other information: Grants are carefully tailored to match the needs of individual applicants. There is no set figure for one-off grants and annual grants are related to the DWP disregard level.

The Royal Scottish Corporation (also known as The Scottish Hospital of the Foundation of King Charles II)

See entry on page 362

The Royal Society for Home Relief to Incurables, Edinburgh (General Fund)

Eligibility: Adult people throughout Scotland under retirement age, who have earned a livelihood (or been a housewife) and are no longer able to do so because of an incurable illness.

Types of grants: An annuity is given quarterly (totalling £500 per year) to help provide extra comforts. The fund is not in a position to consider isolated requests to meet single emergencies.

Annual grant total: £90,000.

Applications: On a form available from the correspondent.

Correspondent: R Graeme Thom, Scott-Moncrieff, 17 Melville Street, Edinburgh EH3 7PH (0131 473 3500; e-mail: graeme.thom@scott-moncrieff.com).

The Royal Society for the Relief of Indigent Gentlewomen of Scotland

Eligibility: Single women, widows or divorcees over 50 years of age of Scottish birth or background, who have (or whose husband or father had) a professional or business background. Applicants' income must be less than £8,000 a year, with savings and investments below £16,000. Applicants need not live in Scotland.

Types of grants: Annuities, paid in quarterly instalments, of £1,000 a year, or less if the beneficiary receives help from other funds such as DWP. Beneficiaries may also receive one-off grants for TV licences, telephone rental, holidays, nursing, property maintenance and so on.

Annual grant total: In 2000/01 the trust had assets of £27 million and an income of £1.2 million. Grants to 830 women totalled £970,000.

Applications: On a form available from the correspondent, to be submitted directly by the individual or through a social worker, citizen's advice bureau or other welfare agency or third party. Applications are considered in May and November so completed forms must be received by 31

March and 30 September. Details of applicant's age, current financial position, personal family background and a copy of the divorce document (if appropriate) are required.

Correspondent: G F Goddard, Secretary & Cashier, 14 Rutland Square, Edinburgh EH1 2BD (0131 229 2308; Fax: 0131 229 0956; e-mail: admin@igfund.freeserve.co.uk).

SACRO Trust

Eligibility: Ex-offenders in Scotland who are in need.

Types of grants: Grants are usually to a maximum of £200, although applications for larger sums can be considered. No grants are made where financial help from other sources is available.

Annual grant total: £3,000 a year.

Applications: On a form available from the correspondent. Applications can only be accepted if they are made through a local authority, voluntary sector worker, health visitor or so on. No payment can be made directly to an individual by the trust; payment will be made to the organisation making the application.

Applications for grants up to £200 can be considered at any time; applications for larger sums will be considered in quarterly meetings held in March, June, September and December.

Correspondent: Trust Fund Administrator, 1 Broughton Market, Edinburgh EH3 6NU (0131 624 7270; Fax: 0131 624 7269; website: www.sacro.org.uk).

Sailors' Orphan Society of Scotland

Eligibility: Orphaned or fatherless children of sea-faring men throughout Scotland who are in need.

Types of grants: Grants are given to help towards the cost of clothes, food, education and other necessities.

Annual grant total: About £58,000 was given in grants in 1998/99 comprised of about 111 recurrent grants of £36 per month per child plus a £36 holiday gift and a £36 Christmas gift, per child.

Applications: In writing to the correspondent. There is a small management committee who decide all cases. The local representatives look after and report on the children in their area.

Correspondent: John Dow, 18 Woodside Crescent, Glasgow G3 7UL (0141 353 2090; Fax: 0141 353 2196).

The Scottish Artists' Benevolent Association

Eligibility: Scottish artists in need or their dependants, not necessarily living in Scotland.

Types of grants: Regular or one-off grants according to need, single payments can also be made to cover emergency situations. Grants are mainly given to people who are older or in ill health.

Annual grant total: In 2001/02 the trust had assets of £450,000 and an income of £21,000. Total expenditure was £29,000, of which £20,000 was given in total to five individuals.

Applications: On a form available from the correspondent. They should be returned directly by the individual for consideration in March or October, or at any time in emergencies.

Correspondent: G C McAllister, 2nd Floor, 5 Oswald Street, Glasgow G1 4QR (0141 248 7411; Fax: 0141 221 0417).

The Scottish Association of Master Bakers Benevolent Fund

Eligibility: Members or ex-members of the Scottish Association of Master Bakers and their families who are in need. Any other member of the Scottish baking industry can also be supported.

Types of grants: One-off and recurrent grants of up to £700 each towards replacement electrical goods, household repairs, repayment of small debts etc.

Annual grant total: £10,000.

Applications: On a form available from the correspondent.

Correspondent: Chief Executive, 4 Torphichen Street, Edinburgh EH3 8JQ (0131 229 1401; Fax: 0131 229 8239; e-mail: master.baker@samb.co.uk).

The Scottish Chartered Accountants' Benevolent Association

Eligibility: Members of the Institute of Chartered Accountants of Scotland, and their dependants.

Types of grants: Generally one-off grants or quarterly allowances. Occasional loans are also available.

Annual grant total: In 2001 the association had assets of £1.2 million and an income of £166,000. Grants to 52 individuals for relief-in-need and educational purposes totalled £123,000.

Applications: On a form available from the correspondent.

Correspondent: R Linton, Hon. Secretary, 141 West Nill Street, Glasgow G1 2RN (0141 333 6565; Fax: 0141 333 1116).

The Scottish Cinematograph Trade Benevolent Fund

Eligibility: People in need living in Scotland who are or have been involved in the cinema trade for a continuous period of one year, and their dependants.

Types of grants: One-off and recurrent grants according to need.

Annual grant total: In 1998 grants to 36 individuals totalled £17,000.

Applications: In writing to the correspondent. Applications can be submitted either directly by the individual, or through a social worker, citizen's advice bureau or other welfare agency or third party.

Correspondent: Mrs Pat Munro, c/o Grant Thornton, 95 Bothwell Street, Glasgow G2 7JZ (0141 223 0000; Fax: 0141 223 0001).

Scottish Grocers' Federation Benevolent Fund

Eligibility: Past members or employees of the grocery trade in Scotland who are in need.

Types of grants: One-off or recurrent grants of up to £780 a year.

Annual grant total: In 2001 the fund had assets of £240,000 and an income of £17,000. Its expenditure was £14,000, most of which was given in grants to individuals in need.

Applications: On a form available from the correspondent. Applicants are then visited to assess the most appropriate form of help.

Correspondent: Scott Landsburgh, Secretary, Federation House, 222-224 Queensferry Road, Edinburgh EH4 2BN (0131 343 3300; Fax: 0131 343 6147).

The Scottish Hide & Leather Trades Provident & Benevolent Society

Eligibility: People of retirement age who have worked in the Scottish hide and leather trades.

Types of grants: The society exists principally to provide pensions to its members. It also pays pensions to the widows and widowers of members who have survived their pensionable spouse. Donations equivalent to the annual pensions are also paid to people who have been employed in the trades but who are not members. Very occasionally one-off payments of about £100 to £200 are made for specific purposes, usually for the replacement of household equipment, such as a washing machine, fridge and so on.

Annual grant total: In 2000 it had a total expenditure of £10,000.

Applications: Most applicants have been recommended by other members of the society or local organisations. An application form is then sent to the individual. Applications can be submitted at any time.

Correspondent: The Secretary, c/o Mitchells Roberton Solicitors, George House, 36 North Hanover Street, Glasgow G1 2AD (0141 552 3422; Fax: 0141 552 2935; e-mail: darb@mitchells-roberton.co.uk).

SCOTLAND – GENERAL

Scottish Hydro Electric Community Trust

Eligibility: People living in the Scottish Hydro Electric supply area.

Types of grants: Grants are given for up to 30% of the costs of domestic electricity connections.

Annual grant total: Information was not available.

Applications: On a form available from the correspondent. Applications should be submitted directly by the individual and are considered about three times a year.

Correspondent: Alisa Stroud, Secretary, 200 Dunkeld Road, Perth PH1 3AQ (01738 455154; Fax: 01738 455281).

Other information: Grants are also given to community ventures for electricity connections.

Scottish Mining Disasters Relief Fund

Eligibility: People who are, or have been, employed in the Scottish mining or mining-related industries, their families and dependants who are in need.

Types of grants: In 1999/2000 grants included breakdown cover and insurance for drivers who are disabled (£690 in total), railcards for people who are disabled or elderly (£195), Christmas vouchers (£3,400), holidays for widows and orphans (£9,200) and grants to children who are mentally and physically handicapped (£1,500). Grants for other general needs, including holidays for people with special needs are also available.

Annual grant total: In 1999/2000 the trust had assets of £385,000, an income of £66,000 and a total expenditure of £97,000. Grants to individuals totalled £26,000, including £8,500 in educational grants. A further £60,000 was given in grants to organisations.

Applications: In writing to the correspondent.

Correspondent: Ian McAlpine, Secretary, CISWO, 2nd Floor, 50 Hopetoun Street, Bathgate, West Lothian EH48 4EU (01506 635550; Fax: 01506 631555).

The Scottish National Institution for the War-Blinded

Eligibility: Visually impaired ex-service personnel. Applicants must live in Scotland.

Types of grants: Mainly regular monthly grants for aftercare and workshop allowances. A few hardship grants are given.

Annual grant total: In 1998/99 the institution had assets of £54 million, an income of £3.4 million and its total expenditure was £2.4 million. Grants totalled £1.2 million.

Applications: Through the Workshops and After-Care Department (telephone 0131 333 1369). Applications are considered as required.

Correspondent: (See above for applications.) J B M Munro, Secretary, PO Box 500, Gillespie Crescent, Edinburgh EH10 4HZ (0131 229 1456; Fax: 0131 229 4060).

The Scottish Nautical Welfare Society

Eligibility: Active, retired and disabled seafarers who are in need and their widows.

Types of grants: Recurrent grants according to need.

Annual grant total: No information available.

Applications: In writing to the correspondent.

Correspondent: Mrs Gail Haldane, Administrator, 937 Dumbarton Road, Glasgow G14 9UF (Tel & Fax: 0141 337 2632).

Other information: This society was established in April 2002 as an amalgamation of Glasgow Aged Seaman Relief Fund, Glasgow Seaman's Friend Society and Glasgow Veteran Seafarers' Association.

Scottish Prison Service Benevolent Fund

Eligibility: Scottish prison officers, both serving and retired, and their families who are in need.

Types of grants: One-off and recurrent grants according to need.

Annual grant total: About £15,000 a year.

Applications: In writing to the correspondent.

Correspondent: The Governor, HM Prison Edinburgh, 33 Stenhouse Road, Edinburgh EH11 3LN (0131 444 3000; Fax: 0131 444 3045).

Scottish Secondary Teachers' Association Benevolent Fund

Eligibility: Members and retired members of the association and in certain circumstances their dependants who are in need.

Types of grants: Recurrent grants usually during a period of long-term illness. One-off grants can also be given.

Annual grant total: £16,000 to individuals and organisations.

Applications: In writing to the correspondent, submitted directly by the individual or referred by school representatives.

Correspondent: General Secretary, 15 Dundas Street, Edinburgh EH3 6QG (0131 556 5919; Fax: 0131 556 1419; e-mail: info@ssta.org.uk; website: www.ssta.org.uk).

The Scottish Solicitors' Benevolent Fund (incorporating The Scottish Law Agents' Society Benevolent Fund)

Eligibility: People in need who were members of the solicitor profession in Scotland and their dependants. Grants are generally awarded to minor dependent children, widows and widowers of solicitors who practised in Scotland and have died; occasional help is given to practising solicitors who are in need.

Types of grants: Grants are paid twice yearly in May and November. Grants can range from £100 to £750, but are mostly of £250 to £400.

Annual grant total: About £9,000.

Applications: On a form available from the correspondent, including financial details and two referees.

Correspondent: Mrs Janice H Webster, Secretary, Scottish Law Agents' Society, 11 Parliament Square, Edinburgh EH1 1RF (Tel & Fax: 0131 225 5051; e-mail: secretary@slas.co.uk).

The Scottish Women's Land Army Benevolent Fund

Eligibility: Former members of the Scottish Women's Land Army who worked in Scottish agriculture or forestry.

Types of grants: Christmas gifts, one-off grants to cope with illness and other types of financial need. About 30 individuals receive grants each year.

Annual grant total: About £1,000 in 2000/01.

Applications: Through referral from social services departments, welfare organisations, doctors or other professional people such as lawyers or bankers, or direct to the correspondent.

Correspondent: Director, c/o RSABI, South Bungalow, Ingliston, Edinburgh EH28 8NB (0131 333 1023; Fax: 0131 333 1027).

The Show Business Benevolent Fund (Scotland)

Eligibility: Members of The Show Business Association (Scotland), over 60 years old, their children and other dependants in need. People cannot become members after the age of 50.

Types of grants: Weekly or monthly grants towards clothing, fuel, funeral expenses and other grants according to need. Christmas/new year and Easter gifts are also given, as well as an all expenses paid holiday to Blackpool.

Annual grant total: Around £8,000 in grants, and £7,000 towards the trips to Blackpool.

Applications: In writing to the correspondent. Applications are considered monthly.

Correspondent: T Davies Brock, Secretary & Treasurer of Funds, Royal Bank Buildings, 55 Main Street, Callander, Perthshire FK17 8DZ (01877 330033).

Dr J R Sibbald's Trust

Eligibility: People living in Scotland who have an incurable disease and who are in financial need.

Types of grants: Usually £120 a year payable in two instalments in May and November. Occasional one-off grants are given in exceptional circumstances.

Annual grant total: About £2,700.

Applications: On a form available from the correspondent. Applications should be accompanied by a certificate from a surgeon or physician giving full details of the disease and certify that in their opinion it is incurable. As much background information about the applicant as possible is also required which can be in the form of a letter from a social worker or friend describing the family circumstances and giving other personal information. Applications are considered annually in December but can be made at any time.

Correspondent: H J Stevens, Brodies WS, 15 Atholl Crescent, Edinburgh EH3 8HA (0131 228 3777; Fax: 0131 228 3878).

The Stead Benefaction Trust

Eligibility: Older people born in Scotland who have an incurable disease and are in financial need.

Types of grants: A grant of £60 paid in May.

Annual grant total: £600 in 10 grants each year.

Applications: On a form available from the correspondent, to be returned by 31 March for consideration in May.

Correspondent: The Trustees, Henderson Boyd Jackson, 19 Ainslie Place, Edinburgh EH3 6AU (0131 226 6881; Fax: 0131 226 4027; e-mail: info@hbj.co.uk).

The Miss M O Taylor's Trust

Eligibility: Impoverished artists in Scotland of sufficient standing to deserve the title i.e. they must have had some measure of success in the profession that they have adopted and must have earned money in it.

Types of grants: One-off payments of up to £500.

Annual grant total: Two to three grants are given each year totalling £800.

Applications: In writing to the correspondent directly by the individual for consideration in May/June.

Correspondent: Prof. Isi Metzstein, Royal Scottish Academy, 17 Waterloo Place, Edinburgh EH1 3BG (0131 558 7097; Fax: 0131 557 6417; e-mail: info@royalscottishacademy.org; website: www.royalscottishacademy.org).

Mrs S H Troughton Charitable Trust

Eligibility: People in need who receive a pension and live on the estates of Ardchatten in Argyll, and Blair Atholl.

No grants are given to people whose income is £1,000 above their personal allowance for income tax.

Types of grants: One-off and recurrent grants ranging from £200 to £620.

Annual grant total: In 2001/02 the trust made grants totalling £1,900 to individuals. Grants to organisations totalled £35,000.

Applications: In writing to the correspondent at any time. Unsuccessful applications will not be acknowledged.

Correspondent: Alan John Winborn, Pollen House, 10–12 Cork Street, London W1S 3LW (020 7439 9061).

The Eliza Haldane Wylie Fund

Eligibility: People in need who are related to or associated with Eliza Haldane Wylie or her family and 'gentlefolk of the middle class' in need.

Types of grants: Small one-off payments.

Annual grant total: About £3,000.

Applications: In writing to the correspondent

Correspondent: A M Bowman, Solicitor, 9–11 Hill Street, Edinburgh EH2 3JT (0131 225 8371; Fax: 0131 225 2048/9065).

Aberdeen & Perthshire

The Brian & Margaret Cooper Trust

Eligibility: Journalists under 30, born or working in Aberdeen, the north east and north of Scotland (the area north of Stonehaven), and their dependants, who are in need.

Types of grants: Usually one-off payments according to need.

Annual grant total: £1,000, some of which was given in educational grants.

Applications: In writing to the correspondent.

Correspondent: Alan J Innes, Messrs Peterkins (Advocates), 100 Union Street, Aberdeen AB10 1QR (01224 428000).

The Neil Gow Charitable Trust

Eligibility: People in need who live in the district of Perth and Kinross or immediate neighbourhood.

Types of grants: Annuities of £87.50 each, paid quarterly at the start of January, April, July and October.

Annual grant total: There are about 22 annuitants. Grants are also made to organisations.

Applications: In writing to the correspondent at any time.

Correspondent: A G Dorward, Messrs Miller Hendry, 10 Blackfriars Street, Perth PH1 5NS (01738 637311; Fax: 01738 638685).

Grampian Police Diced Cap Charitable Fund

Eligibility: People who are ill or disabled and live in the Grampian police force area.

Types of grants: One-off and recurrent grants according to need.

Annual grant total: £35,000 a year to individuals and organisations.

Applications: In writing to the correspondent.

Correspondent: The Secretary, Grampian Police, Queen Street, Aberdeen AB10 1ZA.

The Anne Herd Memorial Trust

Eligibility: People who are blind or partially sighted who live in Broughty Ferry (applicants from the city of Dundee, region of Tayside or those who have connections with these areas and reside in Scotland will also be considered).

Types of grants: Grants are usually given for educational equipment such as computers and books. Grants are usually at least £50.

Annual grant total: In 2000/01 it had an income of £30,000. Grants to individuals and organisations totalled £78,000, which was higher than usual due to the spending of £56,000 from accumulated funds.

Applications: In writing to the correspondent, to be submitted directly by the individual in March/April for consideration in June.

Correspondent: The Trustees, Bowman Scottish Lawyers, 27 Bank Street, Dundee DD1 1RP (01382 322267).

The Gertrude Muriel Pattullo Trust for Handicapped Boys

Eligibility: Boys (generally under 18) who are physically disabled and live in the city of Dundee or the county of Angus.

Types of grants: One-off and recurrent grants of £50 to £500. Recent grants have been given towards a computer (£500), a car seat (£400) and a lighting system for somebody with a visual impairment (£230). No grants are given towards repayment of debts.

Annual grant total: In 2000/01 the trust had assets of £70,000, an income of £5,400 and a total expenditure of £6,300. Grants to 18 individuals totalled £4,500. Grants to organisations totalled £1,700.

Applications: On a form available from the correspondent at any time. Applications can be submitted directly by the individual or through any third party.

Correspondent: Mrs Beth Anderson, Help Unit, Blackadders Solicitors, 30–34 Reform Street, Dundee DD1 1RJ (01382 229222; Fax: 01382 342220; e-mail: beth.anderson@blackadders.co.uk).

The Gertrude Muriel Pattullo Trust for Handicapped Girls

Eligibility: Girls (generally under 18 years) who are physically disabled and live in the city of Dundee or the county of Angus.

Types of grants: One-off and recurrent grants of £100 to £1,000. Recent grants have been given towards a holiday (£500) and a door beacon (£220). No grants are given for the repayment of debts.

Annual grant total: In 2000/01 the trust had assets of £88,000, an income of £6,500 and a total expenditure of £6,100. Grants to 12 individuals totalled £4,300. Grants to organisations totalled £1,800.

Applications: On a form available from the correspondent at any time. Applications can be submitted directly by the individual or through any third party.

Correspondent: Mrs Beth Anderson, Help Unit, Blackadders Solicitors, 30–34 Reform Street, Dundee DD1 1RJ (01382 229222; Fax: 01382 342220; e-mail: beth.anderson@blackadders.co.uk).

The Gertrude Muriel Pattullo Trust for the Elderly

Eligibility: Older people (i.e. generally those of state pensionable age) in the city of Dundee and county of Angus.

Types of grants: General welfare including (a) help for people in reduced circumstances, particularly those with a physical disability; (b) financial provision in respect of admission to a residential home or similar; (c) provision of medical services not obtainable under National Health Service facilities; (d) financial provision for home nursing in appropriate cases; (e) provision of accommodation, furnishings, clothing and other necessities; and (f) provision of holidays.

Annual grant total: £5,000.

Applications: On a form available from the correspondent at any time.

Correspondent: Mrs Beth Anderson, Help Unit, Blackadders Solicitors, 30–34 Reform Street, Dundee DD1 1RJ (01382 229222; Fax: 01382 342220; e-mail: beth.anderson@blackadders.co.uk).

Aberdeen & Aberdeenshire

Charities Administered by the City of Aberdeen

Eligibility: The City of Aberdeen administers a large number of trusts for varying purposes, several are for the relief-in-need of poor people in the area of Aberdeen. Each trust will have its own eligibility requirements details of which can be obtained from the correspondent.

Types of grants: One-off and recurrent grants according to need.

Annual grant total: About £12,000 is available each year.

Applications: Applications should be made through: Voluntary Service of Aberdeen, 38 Castle Street, Aberdeen AB11 5YU (01224 212021).

Correspondent: Mr Fraser, Finance Department, Town House, Aberdeen City AB9 1AH (01224 522712).

The Aberdeen Disabled Person's Trust

Eligibility: People who are disabled and live in the city of Aberdeen.

Types of grants: One-off grants for aids/appliances (washing machines, mattresses and so on); special clothing and items not available through DWP; convalescence/holidays; and home repairs/alterations. Up to 25 grants are given annually. Grants frequently cover the full cost of the need, but the trust often joins other charities in raising the sum required e.g. for electric wheelchairs.

Annual grant total: In 1998/99 the trust had assets of £23,000 and an income of £3,600. Grants of £100 to £250 were given to 21 people totalling £2,300.

Applications: Applications must be in writing and submitted through a social worker, citizen's advice bureau or other welfare agency.

Correspondent: J I Rose, 68 Cornhill Road, Aberdeen AB25 2EH (01224 483855).

Aberdeen Indigent Mental Patients' Fund

Eligibility: People who live in Aberdeen and are, or have been, mentally ill on their discharge from hopsital.

Types of grants: One-off and recurrent grants according to need.

Annual grant total: About £700.

Applications: In writing to the correspondent.

Correspondent: Alan J Innes, Messrs Peterkins, 100 Union Street, Aberdeen AB10 1QR (01224 428000; Fax: 01224 644479).

The Aberdeen Widows' & Spinsters' Benevolent Fund

Eligibility: Widows and unmarried women over 60 years of age who live in the city or county of Aberdeen; in cases of special need and where surplus income is available, those between 40 and 60 are considered.

Types of grants: Generally yearly allowances of up to £360 paid in two instalments in June and December.

Annual grant total: £54,000 was given in total to 167 individuals in 2001.

Applications: On a form available from the correspondent.

Correspondent: Messrs Ledingham Chalmers, 52–54 Rose Street, Aberdeen AB10 1HA (01224 408408).

The James Allan of Midbeltie

Eligibility: Widows who live in Aberdeen and are in need.

Types of grants: Recurrent yearly allowances of £250 a year.

Annual grant total: In 2000/01 the trust had assets of £975,000 and an income of £42,000. Total expenditure was £32,000, including £13,000 in 54 grants.

Applications: On a form available from the correspondent. Applications should be submitted through a social worker, citizen's advice bureau or other welfare agency and are considered in April and October.

Correspondent: Michael D McMillan, Burnett & Reid, 15 Golden Square, Aberdeen AB10 1WF (01224 644333; Fax: 01224 632173; e-mail: mdmcmillan@burnett-reid.co.uk).

The Braemar Charitable Trust

Eligibility: People in need who live in the parish of Braemar.

Types of grants: Grants of £40 each are given.

Annual grant total: In 2001 the trust had assets of £10,000 and an income of £1,600. Total expenditure was £960, all of which was given in 24 grants.

Applications: In writing to the correspondent in November for consideration in December.

Correspondent: W Meston, Coilacriech, Ballater, Aberdeenshire AB35 5UH (Tel & Fax: 01339 755377).

Other information: This trust will also consider funding for medical equipment.

The Dr John Calder's Fund

Eligibility: People in need who live in the parish of Machar, or within the city of Aberdeen.

Types of grants: Grants of up to £500 (£1,000 in certain cases). This trust deals primarily with educational grants, although relief-in-need grants can be considered.

Annual grant total: Around £2,000 is available for individuals. A further £8,000 is given in grants towards educational projects or organisations.

Applications: In writing to the correspondent. Applications can be considered as they arrive, although the trust states more money is available early in the year.

Correspondent: Clive Phillips, Paull & Williamsons, Investment House, 6 Union Row, Aberdeen AB10 1DQ (01224 621621).

The Cameron Fund

Eligibility: People of pensionable age who live in the burgh of Laurencekirk and are in need.

Types of grants: Recurrent payments of £40. No grants to people in long-term care in hospital or nursing home.

Annual grant total: In 1998/99 the fund had assets of £120,000 and an income of £6,000. Its total expenditure was £6,500 and it gave £3,200 in grants to 80 individuals in need.

Applications: In writing to the correspondent, for consideration in November/December. Applications should be submitted directly by the individual.

Correspondent: Mr Banski, W J C Reed, Royal Bank Buildings, High Street, Laurencekirk, Kincardineshire AB30 1AF (01561 377245; Fax: 01561 378020).

The George, James & Alexander Chalmers Trust

Eligibility: Women living in Aberdeen who have fallen on hard times as a result of misfortune and not through any fault of their own.

Types of grants: Annuities are currently £450 a year, payable by half-yearly instalments in June and December. Up to 80 annuities are given.

Annual grant total: About £36,000.

Applications: On a form available from the correspondent.

Correspondent: J C Chisholm, Clerk, Factor, 2 Bon Accord Crescent, Aberdeen AB11 6DH (01224 587261).

The Gordon Cheyne Trust Fund

Eligibility: Widows and daughters of deceased merchants, shopkeepers and other businessmen, who are elderly natives of Aberdeen or who have lived there for at least 25 years.

Types of grants: Annual allowances of about £400, paid twice-yearly in May and November.

Annual grant total: In 2001 about £23,000 was given in total to 40 beneficiaries.

Applications: On a form available from the correspondent via a social worker, citizen's advice bureau or other welfare agency.

Correspondent: Messrs Ledingham Chalmers, 52–54 Rose Street, Aberdeen AB10 1HA (01224 408408).

The Crisis Fund of Voluntary Service Aberdeen

Eligibility: People in need who live in Aberdeen.

Types of grants: About 500 one-off grants each year according to need; typically £50.

Annual grant total: About £25,000.

Applications: By interview with Voluntary Service Aberdeen's social work team, or through a social worker or other professional welfare agency on an application form available from the correspondent.

Correspondent: Mrs Margaret McEwen, Voluntary Service Aberdeen, 38 Castle Street, Aberdeen AB11 5YU (01224 212021).

The Elisabeth Davidson Memorial Benevolent Trust

Eligibility: Sick, elderly, physically or mentally disabled residents of the parish of Bervie which includes the burgh of Inverbervie and the town of Gourdon.

Types of grants: Grants range from £20 to £150.

Annual grant total: In 1998/99 the trust had assets of £25,000 generating an income of £1,000. However, no grants were made that year.

Applications: In writing to the correspondent or via a committee member.

Correspondent: Miss F M Whyte, 10 Croftlands, St Cyrus, Montrose DD10 0AX (01674 850374).

George Davidson's Benevolent Fund

Eligibility: People in need who live in Aberdeen and Cults or their surrounding areas.

Types of grants: Annual grants of £60.

Annual grant total: £2,300.

Applications: In writing to the correspondent.

Correspondent: The Director, Voluntary Service Aberdeen, 38 Castle Street, Aberdeen AB11 5YU (01224 212021).

The Donald Trust

Eligibility: People in need who 'belong to' the city of Aberdeen and former county of Aberdeen. 'Advanced age, lack of health, inability to work, high character and former industry are strong recommendations.'

Types of grants: Annual allowances paid twice-yearly in May and November.

Annual grant total: In 2001 18 grants totalled about £5,000.

Applications: On a form available from the correspondent.

Correspondent: Messrs Ledingham Chalmers, 52–54 Rose Street, Aberdeen AB10 1HA (01224 408408).

Other information: The trustees do not feel that the balance of income is such as to enable them to consider further applications unless exceptionally deserving applications are received.

The Forbes Fund

Eligibility: Burgesses of Guild of the city of Aberdeen and their dependants; and widows or daughters of deceased merchants, shopkeepers and businessmen who have lived in Aberdeen for at least 25 years and who are in need.

Types of grants: Annual allowances paid twice-yearly in June and December.

Annual grant total: In 2001 grants to nine individuals totalled around £2,700.

Applications: On a form available from the correspondent.

Correspondent: Messrs Ledingham Chalmers, 52–54 Rose Street, Aberdeen AB10 1HA (01224 408408).

Garden Nicol Benevolent Fund

Eligibility: 'Ladies [of] birth, education and character, who, by birth and residence are inhabitants of the town or county of Aberdeen, and who, having been in a position of affluence, have, by circumstances beyond their control, been reduced to comparative poverty [and require financial help]'.

Types of grants: One-off and recurrent grants according to need.

Annual grant total: About £4,000.

Applications: In writing to the correspondent.

Correspondent: Alan J Innes, Messrs Peterkins, 100 Union Street, Aberdeen AB10 1QR (01224 428000; Fax: 01224 644479).

The Gordon District Charities

Eligibility: People in need who live in the area previously administered by Gordon District Council.

Types of grants: One-off and recurrent grants according to need. The council administers a number of funds details of

SCOTLAND – ABERDEEN & PERTHSHIRE

which are available from the correspondent.
Annual grant total: No information available.
Applications: In writing to the correspondent.
Correspondent: Amanda Rowe, Gordon House, Blackhall Road, Inverurie, Aberdeenshire AB51 3NB (0845 606 7000).

Miss Margaret Gray's Trust

Eligibility: Deserving widows or unmarried females living in the City and County of Aberdeen who are in need.
Types of grants: Recurrent grants of benefits disregard limits.
Annual grant total: About 20 grants totalling about £860.
Applications: In writing to the trustees c/o the correspondent. Applications can be submitted directly by the individual or through a social worker, citizen's advice bureau, other welfare agency or other third party and are considered in April and November.
Correspondent: Messrs Mackinnons, 379 North Deeside Road, Cults, Aberdeen AB15 9SX (01224 868687; Fax: 01224 861012).

John Harrow's Mortification

Eligibility: People in need who live in the parishes of Old Machar and Denburn, Aberdeen and attend the church in Denburn or St Machar Cathedral.
Types of grants: About £800 is given to the ministers of each parish at Christmas for distribution to older people.
Annual grant total: £1,600.
Applications: Applications are made via the ministers of the parishes of Old Machar and Denburn, not directly to the trust.
Correspondent: Alan J Innes, Peterkins (Advocates), 100 Union Street, Aberdeen AB10 1QR (01224 626300; Fax: 01224 428000).

The Henry John Jopp Fund

Eligibility: Widowed or single women in need living in the city or county of Aberdeen.
Types of grants: Recurrent grants totalling £500 per year each, paid in May and November.
Annual grant total: In 2000/01 grants totalled £14,000.
Applications: On a form available from the correspondent. Applications can be submitted directly by the individual or through a social worker, citizen's advice bureau or other welfare agency. They can be considered at any time.
Correspondent: Douglas M Watson, Adams Cochran Solicitors, 6 Bon-Accord Square, Aberdeen AB11 6XU

(01224 588913; Fax: 01224 581149; e-mail: dmwatson@adamcochran.co.uk).

The Malcolm Fund

Eligibility: Children aged up to 16 who are disabled and their carers and parents who live in Crimond and adjacent villages.
Types of grants: Grants are one-off and are given in the form of educational or recreational material or resources. In the past, they have been used for a holiday, a touch screen computer, and towards a house conversion. Help is not provided where it is available from statutory sources.
Annual grant total: The fund has a bank balance of up to £5,000 to £7,000 at any time, derived from donations and fundraising. Grants to individuals total about £300 to £400 a year on average, although can vary greatly from year to year.
Applications: Individuals should apply verbally or in writing to the correspondent. Most applications are forwarded by the local GP (the correspondent) or social services, although individuals can apply directly if they are within the beneficial area.
Correspondent: Dr R Murray, The Surgery, Crimond Medical Centre, Fraserburgh, Grampian AB43 4QJ (01346 532215).

The McRobert Mortification – Gamrie & Forglen

Eligibility: Residents over 60 of the parishes of Gamrie and Forglen in the Banff and Buchan district.
Types of grants: Recurrent grants are made.
Annual grant total: No information available.
Applications: On a form available from the correspondent.
Correspondent: Messrs Alexander George & Co., 24 Shore Street, Macduff, Banffshire AB44 1XT.
Other information: This entry was not confirmed by the trust.

The Mary Morrison Cox Fund

Eligibility: People in need in the parish of Dyce, Aberdeen.
Types of grants: Cash grants of £200 to £550 to help with general living expenses.
Annual grant total: In 2000/01 the trust had assets of £244,000 and an income of £13,000. Grants to individuals totalled £9,500.
Applications: On a form to the correspondent, to be submitted in November for consideration in early December.
Correspondent: W A Mitchell, 18 Bon-Accord Crescent, Aberdeen AB11 6XY

(01224 573321; Fax: 01224 576115; e-mail: wmitchell@acmr.co.uk).
Other information: This trust also supports Cornerstone Community Care.

The Matilda Murray Trust

Eligibility: People in need who have lived in Old Aberdeen for at least five years immediately before the date of application.
Types of grants: Annual grants only of £50 to £60.
Annual grant total: About £2,000.
Applications: On a form available from the correspondent. Applications must be submitted by mid-October for consideration in November and grants are distributed in December.
Correspondent: E Grant MacKenzie, Solicitor, Stronarchs, 34 Albyn Place, Aberdeen, AB10 1FW (01224 845845; Fax: 01224 845800).

The Peterhead Coal Fund

Eligibility: People in need who live in the parish of Peterhead.
Types of grants: Three deliveries of three bags of coal are given to the people on the lowest incomes in the parish between December and April.
Annual grant total: In 2000/01 the trust had assets of £86,000, an income of £7,100 and an expenditure of £6,100. 30 grants worth £1,500 in total were given.
Applications: In writing to the correspondent in October or November for consideration in December.
Correspondent: David Taylor, Hon. Secretary, 13 Skerry Drive, Peterhead, Aberdeenshire AB42 2YH (01779 478389).

Presbytery of Gordon Benevolent Fund

Eligibility: People in need in the parish of Alford.
Types of grants: One-off and recurrent grants according to need.
Annual grant total: Information was not provided.
Applications: In writing to the correspondent.
Correspondent: Revd I U Thomson, The Manse, Skene, Aberdeenshire AB32 6XX.
Other information: This entry was not confirmed by the trust, but the address was correct according to the Scottish Charities Index.

W H Shepherd Trust

Eligibility: Female widows and daughters aged over 25 of deceased merchants, shopkeepers or other businessmen who have live in Aberdeen for at least 25 years.
Types of grants: £220 a year payable half-yearly in March and September.

Annual grant total: In 2000/01 the trust had assets of £53,000 and an income of £1,800, all of which was given in nine grants.

Applications: In writing to the correspondent through a social worker, citizen's advice bureau or other welfare agency or third party for consideration in November. Direct applications are not considered.

Correspondent: The Trustees, Wilsone & Duffus, 7 Golden Square, Aberdeen AB10 1EP (01224 651700; Fax: 01224 647329; e-mail: info@wilsoneduffus.co.uk).

The James Sim of Cornhill Trust

Eligibility: Merchants, shopkeepers and businessmen who were either born in Aberdeen or who carried out business there, and their widows, daughters or unmarried sisters.

Types of grants: Annual allowances of up to £200 paid half-yearly in June and December.

Annual grant total: In 2001 the trust gave a total of £1,600 to eight individuals.

Applications: On a form available from the correspondent which can be obtained through a social worker, citizen's advice bureau or other welfare agency. Applicants can apply directly, although they will need to be recommended by a professional person such as a doctor or a social worker.

Correspondent: Messrs Ledingham Chalmers, 52–54 Rose Street, Aberdeen AB10 1HA (01224 408408).

Other information: The trustees state, 'we will continue to consider future applications but will be able to grant only any which are exceptionally deserving'.

The Simpson Trust

Eligibility: People of retirement age who are in need and live in the burgh of Macduff.

Types of grants: Annuities of £80 and £120, usually paid in two instalments in June and December.

Annual grant total: In 1998/99 the trust had assets of £61,000 and an income of £9,700. 40 grants totalled £5,500.

Applications: On a form available from the correspondent. When there are vacancies on the list of annuitants, applications are invited through the local press. Applications are usually considered in November/December.

Correspondent: Alexander George & Co., 24 Shore Street, Macduff, Banffshire AB44 1TX (01261 815678).

Miss Caroline Jane Spence's Fund

Eligibility: Widows or unmarried females living within the city or county of Aberdeen who are in need.

Types of grants: Recurrent grants are made. No grants are made where statutory funding is available.

Annual grant total: About £31,000.

Applications: On a form available from the correspondent. Applications can be submitted either directly by the individual, or through a social worker, citizen's advice bureau other welfare agency or other third party. Applications are considered in November, January and April.

Correspondent: The Trustees, c/o Messrs Mackinnons, 379 North Deeside Road, Cults, Aberdeen AB15 9SX (01224 868687; Fax: 01224 861012).

Verden Sykes Trust

Eligibility: People in need who live in Aberdeen. Preference is given to retired ministers.

Types of grants: One-off grants to people in need. Pensions to retired ministers.

Annual grant total: In 1998/99 the trust had assets of £11,000 and an income of £18,000. Grants totalled £16,000 with £400 being given to individuals and the rest to organisations.

Applications: On a form available from the correspondent. Applications should arrive in January, May and October for consideration in February, June and November.

Correspondent: Mrs Irene Merriless, Administrator, 20 Forvie Circle, Bridge of Don, Aberdeen AB22 8TA (01224 704907; e-mail: merrilees.forvie@dial.pipex.com).

Miss Jessie Ann Thomson's Trust

Eligibility: Women in need who live in the city of Aberdeen, with a preference for those whose maiden name is Thomson or Middleton.

Types of grants: Recurrent grants of £300 per year, paid in May and November.

Annual grant total: In 2001 grants totalled £5,300.

Applications: On a form available from the correspondent, for consideration at any time.

Correspondent: Douglas M Watson, Adam Cochran Solictors, 6 Bon-Accord Square, Aberdeen A11 6XU (01224 588913; Fax: 01224 581149; e-mail: dmwatson@adamcochran.co.uk).

The Fuel Fund of Voluntary Service Aberdeen

Eligibility: People living in Aberdeen who need help in maintaining a warm home, particularly older people, people with a disability and families with young children.

Types of grants: About 350 one-off grants typically of £20.

Annual grant total: £8,000.

Applications: By interview with Voluntary Service Aberdeen's social work team, or on an application form available from the correspondent, to be submitted through a social worker or other professional welfare agency.

Correspondent: Voluntary Service Aberdeen, 38 Castle Street, Aberdeen AB11 5YU (01224 212021).

Angus

Charities Administered by Angus Council

Eligibility: Residents of Arbroath, Brechin, Carnoustie, Forfar, Kirnemuir, Montrose, Kettins, Carmyllie and Arbirlot (particularly older people and people who are in need).

Types of grants: One-off grants generally of £30 upwards.

Annual grant total: The combined grant totals of these charities is about £2,500.

Applications: In writing to the correspondent.

Correspondent: Elaine Whittet or Fiona Anderson, Angus Council, St James's House, St James's Road, Forfar, Angus DD8 2ZE (01307 473466).

Other information: This entry includes the following charities: Brechin Charitable Funds, Arbroath Charitable Funds, Forfar Charitable Funds, Forfar Landward Charities, Carnoustie Charitable Funds and Kirriemuir Charitable Funds.

The Boath & Milne Trust

Eligibility: People in need who were born in or who have been resident in Kirriemuir for at least 10 years and are aged 70 and over. Preference is given to those who were bakers by profession.

Types of grants: Grants of £90 are given to around 30 people each year.

Annual grant total: £2,700.

Applications: There is a local press advertisement each year, further information can be gained from the correspondent.

Correspondent: Messrs Wilkie & Dundas Solicitors, 28 Marywellbrae, Kirriemuir, Angus DD8 4BP (01575 572608).

The Boyack Fund

Eligibility: Pensioners in need who live in Monifieth by Dundee.

Types of grants: £50 a year.

Annual grant total: £1,000.

SCOTLAND – ABERDEEN & PERTHSHIRE

Applications: In writing to the correspondent. Applicants must state how long they have lived in Monifieth and will be means tested. Anyone with significant assets/income will be excluded.

Correspondent: S J Cumming, 28 Wellmeadow, Blairgowrie, Perthshire PH10 6AX (01250 874441).

The Brechin Victoria Nursing Association

Eligibility: People who are sick, infirm, poor or distressed and live in the district of Brechin.

Types of grants: One-off or recurrent grants according to need for the provision of medical and surgical equipment and/or assistance, and the supply of comforts and necessities. Also help to people requiring, but unable to employ, a private nurse. Grants usually range from £50 to £100.

Annual grant total: About £500.

Applications: Applications should be submitted through a recognised referral agency (e.g. social worker, health visitor or doctor), and are usually passed through the local council. They are considered throughout the year.

Correspondent: I A McFatridge, Ferguson & Will, Solicitors, 24 Swan Street, Brechin, Angus DD9 6EJ (01356 622289).

The Colvill Trust

Eligibility: People in need living in the town of Arbroath and the parish of St Vigeans and surrounding area.

Types of grants: Grants range from £75 to £250 each. The main annual grants are given to older people on the basis of financial need, with half paid in May and the other half in November. Special one-off grants are given to meet medical needs or for specific needs in the case of young children.

Annual grant total: In 2000/01 the trust had assets of £294,000 and an income of £11,000. Total expenditure was £12,000, including £11,000 given in 94 grants to individuals.

Applications: On a form available from the correspondent. They should be submitted through a social worker, citizen's advice bureau or other welfare agency by May for payments in May and November.

Correspondent: Thorntons WS, Brothockbank House, Arbroath, Angus DD11 1NE (01241 872683).

Other information: The charity also has a special fund which gives one-off grants to people in need in Arbroath. These grants are made at the discretion of the trustees usually after recommendation from a doctor or social services.

The Mrs Marie Dargie Trust

Eligibility: People of pensionable age living within the city boundaries of Brechin.

Types of grants: One-off and recurrent grants according to need.

Annual grant total: Not known.

Applications: In writing to the correspondent.

Correspondent: David H Will, Trustee, Ferguson & Will, 24 Swan Street, Brechin, Angus DD9 6EJ (01356 622289).

The Jamieson Charity

Eligibility: Older people living in Arbroath and Arbirlot, Angus.

Types of grants: Grants range from £50 to £250. Most are recurrent and paid either in May or at Christmas. Other special one-off grants are available towards items of equipment which the applicant cannot afford and which are generally for medical purposes.

Annual grant total: In 2001 the trust had assets of £36,000 and an income and total expenditure of £2,100. It made 25 grants to individuals totalling £1,700.

Applications: In writing to the correspondent, to be submitted through a social worker, citizen's advice bureau or other welfare agency.

Correspondent: Messrs Thorntons WS, Brothockbank House, Arbroath, Angus DD11 1NJ (01241 872683).

The St Cyrus Benevolent Fund

Eligibility: People who are sick, infirm and in need and live in the parish of St Cyrus, Montrose only.

Types of grants: One-off grants of £25 to £100 are given. Recent grants have included those towards utility bills, phone installations, food, carpets, medical equipment and travel expenses for an older women to visit her sick son.

Annual grant total: In 2000/01 the trust had assets of £11,000 and an income of £1,000. Total expenditure was £560, including two grants to individuals totalling £130.

Applications: In writing to the correspondent. Recommendation by social worker, minister, doctor, nurse or similar is essential. Applications are considered at any time.

Correspondent: Miss M Singleton, Secretary, c/o Scott Alexander Solicitors, 46 High Street, Montrose, Angus DD10 8JF (01674 671477).

Other information: The trust has also supported medical equipment for use by a district nurse/GP and Kirk Hall for disability access.

The Angus Walker Benevolent Fund

Eligibility: People in need who live in Montrose.

Types of grants: Grants normally ranging from £20 to £100 per year.

Annual grant total: About £6,000 each year.

Applications: By formal application through a trustee, local district councillors, the minister of Montrose Old Church or the rector of St Mary's & St Peter's Episcopal Church, Montrose.

Correspondent: Messrs T Duncan & Co., Solicitors, 192 High Street, Montrose DD10 8NA (01674 672533).

The Wilson & Peter Bequest

Eligibility: Women in need who where born, educated or who live in the parish of Dunnichen.

Types of grants: Recurrent payments of £15.

Annual grant total: In 1999/2000 the trust had assets of £14,000 and an income of £300. Grants to 40 beneficiaries totalled £600.

Applications: In writing to: W B Hampton, 4 The Square, Letham, Angus DD8 2PZ. Applications are considered in mid-July.

Correspondent: Mr Munton, Low Beaton Richmond, Sterling House, 20 Renfield Street, Glasgow G2 5AP (0141 221 8931).

Dundee

The Andrew Adie and Margaret Thoms Fund

Eligibility: Women in need who live in Dundee or Broughty Ferry and who are protestants connected with the Church of Scotland. They must not be in receipt of any public assistance, except the state pension.

Types of grants: Grants do not exceed £45.

Annual grant total: In 1998 the trust gave £45 in grants and had a surplus of £890.

Applications: In writing to the correspondent.

Correspondent: J P C Clark, 34 Reform Street, Dundee DD1 1RJ (01382 229222; Fax: 01382 342220).

The Broughty Ferry Benevolent Fund

Eligibility: People in need living in Broughty Ferry, Dundee, who are not in residential care.

Types of grants: Cash payments are given twice a year, totalling £120.

Annual grant total: In 1999/2000 the trust had assets of £72,000 and an income of

SCOTLAND – ABERDEEN & PERTHSHIRE

£4,300. Total expenditure was £4,800, including £3,500 given in 29 grants to individuals.

Applications: In writing to the correspondent. Applications can be submitted either directly by the individual or through a social worker, citizen's advice bureau or other welfare agency. They are considered in May and November.

Correspondent: A F McDonald, Thorntons WS, 50 Castle Street, Dundee DD1 3RU (01382 229111; Fax: 01382 202288).

The Dundee Indigent Sick Society

Eligibility: People who live in Dundee and who are sick or infirm and in financial need.

Types of grants: One-off grants of up to £100, although more can be given in exceptional circumstances.

Annual grant total: In 2001/02 the trust had assets of £40,000 and an income of £4,100. Total expenditure was £6,100, including £5,600 given in 55 grants.

Applications: In writing to the correspondent or directly to the visitor for the area concerned. Potential applicants are usually visited by the trust.

Correspondent: Donald N Gordon, Secretary, Messers Blackadders, 34 Reform Street, Dundee DD1 1RJ (01382 229222; Fax: 01382 342220; e-mail:donald.gordon@blackadders.co.uk).

The Hospital Fund and Johnston Bequest

Eligibility: Older people who are infirm and in need who live in the old City of Dundee boundary.

Types of grants: Yearly pensions of £50 for up to 490 pensioners.

Annual grant total: In 2000/01 the trust had assets of £328,000 and an income of £75,000. Total expenditure was £18,000, including £15,000 given in 380 grants.

Applications: Individuals should first contact their councillor who will submit an application form on the individual's behalf to the Director of Finance of Dundee City Council.

Correspondent: Andrew Blakeman, Principal Accountant, Dundee City Council, Tayside House, 28 Crichton Street, Dundee DD1 3RF (01382 433967; Fax: 01382 433975).

John Normansell Kyd's Trust for Walton & Rashiewell Employees

Eligibility: Ex-employees of the former Walton Works and Rashiewell Works in Dundee (which closed over 20 years ago) and their dependants who are in need.

Types of grants: Currently £40 a year is given to each beneficiary.

Annual grant total: £500.

Applications: In writing to the correspondent.

Correspondent: The Trustees, P O Box 61, City House, 16 Overgate, Dundee DD1 9LB.

Other information: This entry was not confirmed by the trust.

The Misses Elizabeth & Agnes Lindsay Fund

Eligibility: Unmarried women aged 55 years or over who have been dependent on their own industry and are not in receipt of an old age pension. They must be natives of Dundee and living there, or born elsewhere but living in Dundee for at least 10 years preceding their application.

Types of grants: One-off and recurrent grants according to need. The maximum grant is £12 per year.

Annual grant total: £300.

Applications: In writing to the correspondent.

Correspondent: (Ref. SW), Blackadders Solicitors, 30-34 Reform Street, Dundee DD1 1RJ (01382 229222; Fax: 01382 342220).

The Mair Robertson Benevolent Fund

Eligibility: Elderly gentlewomen who live in Dundee, Blairgowrie and Broughty Ferry.

Types of grants: £250 payable in two grants in June and December.

Annual grant total: In 1999/2000 the trust had assets of £95,000, an income of £5,300 and its expenditure was £4,400. It gave £3,200 in grants to 16 individuals.

Applications: On a form available from the correspondent. Applications are considered in May and November and can be submitted directly by the individual or through a social worker, citizen's advice bureau, other welfare agency or other third party.

Correspondent: Ian R Steven, Rollo Steven & Bond Solicitors, 21 Dock Street, Dundee DD1 3DS.

Other information: This entry was not confirmed by the fund.

The Ouchterlony Old Men's Indigent Society

Eligibility: Deserving and indigent old men (generally over 60) belonging to or born in Dundee or neighbourhood.

Types of grants: 10 beneficiaries receive £50 each in May and November each year.

Annual grant total: In 1998/99 the trust had assets of £58,000, an income of £3,100 and its total expenditure was £2,100. £1,000 was given in grants.

Applications: In writing to the correspondent. Applications can be submitted either directly by the individual, through a social worker, citizen's advice bureau or other welfare agency, or by any person with close knowledge of the applicant's affairs. They are considered throughout the year.

Correspondent: Dale Ross, Thorntons WS, Brothockbank House, Arbroath DD11 1NF (01241 872683).

The Peter Benevolent Fund

Eligibility: Older gentlewomen who live in Dundee and Broughty Ferry.

Types of grants: £75 twice a year to each individual.

Annual grant total: In 1998/99 the fund had assets of £30,000, an income of £3,100 and its expenditure was £2,600. It gave £1,300 in grants to seven individuals.

Applications: On a form available from the correspondent. Applications are considered in May and November and can be submitted directly by the individual or through a social worker, citizen's advice bureau, other welfare agency or other third party.

Correspondent: Ian R Steven, Rollo Steven & Bond, Solicitors, 21 Dock Street, Dundee DD1 3DS.

Other information: This entry was not confirmed by the trust.

Mrs Margaret T Petrie's Mortification

Eligibility: Aged, infirm and indigent individuals over 55 years of age belonging to, or settled in, Dundee.

Types of grants: One-off and recurrent according to need.

Annual grant total: In 1998/99 the trust had assets of £93,000, an income of £4,500 and its total expenditure was £4,000. £2,800 was given in 14 grants ranging from £25 to £210.

Applications: In writing to the correspondent. Applications can be submitted either directly by the individual, or through a social worker, citizen's advice bureau or other welfare agency, or another third party.

Correspondent: Dale Ross, Thorntons WS, Brothockbank House, Arbroath DD11 1NF (01241 872683).

Miss Margaret J Stephen's Charitable Trust

Eligibility: People in need who live in Dundee.

Types of grants: One-off and recurrent grants according to need.

Annual grant total: Around £6,000 is given to organisations and individuals.

SCOTLAND – ABERDEEN & PERTHSHIRE

Applications: In writing to the correspondent. Applications are considered in March.

Correspondent: The Trustees, Maclay Murray & Spens, 151 St Vincent Street, Glasgow G2 5NJ (0141 248 5011).

The Hannah & Margaret Thomson Trust

Eligibility: 1. People who are war wounded from the Second World War or their spouses. Applicants must live in Dundee and be in need.
2. Ex-employees of Thomson Shepherd & Co. who are in need.

Types of grants: £300 per year.

Annual grant total: In 1998/99 the trust had assets of £308,000, an income of £27,000 and total expenditure was £27,000. £22,000 was given in 46 grants to individuals.

Applications: In writing to the correspondent. Applications can be submitted either directly by the individual, or through a social worker, citizen's advice bureau, other welfare agency or other third party.

Correspondent: Dale Ross, Thorntons WS, Brothockbank House, Arbroath DD11 1NF (01241 872683).

Moray

Charities Administered by the Moray Council – Welfare Grants

The correspondent for the following is: Chief Financial Officer, Finance and Information Technology Services, Moray Council, District Headquarters, High Street, Elgin IV30 1BX (01343 543451; Fax: 01343 540183).

(i) The Auchray Fund

Eligibility: People who are elderly or infirm and were in business in the burgh of Elgin and who are now in financial need.

Types of grants: Help with council house rent.

Annual grant total: Usually about £4,000, although no grants were given in 1999/2000.

Applications: Grants are advertised in the local press. Applications must be supported by a magistrate.
The council administers another 17 trusts for the benefit of residents of Elgin and surrounding area, most of which are very small. Further details can be obtained from the correspondent. This trust does not receive many applications and has not given grants for a few years.

(ii) The Forres Poor Fund & Others

Eligibility: People in need who live in Forres.

Types of grants: One-off and recurrent grants given once and twice a year.

Applications: Applications to the correspondent following an advertisement in a local paper. Cases are considered by a local councillor. Applicants are nominated by a local councillor for the Jonathon & Robert Anderson Funds when a vacancy arises.
The council administers other trusts for residents of Forres, including Dick & Smith Fund, Jonathon & Robert Anderson Funds and various smaller funds.

(iii) Other trusts

The council also administers various small charities (under £500 grant total) for residents of the following areas: Kirkmichael, Inveravon, Mortlach, Keith and Aberlour (Keith/Dufftown Poor Funds & Keith Nursing Fund); Dufftown (Watt Bequest); Lossiemouth; the parishes of Boharm, Deskford, Dibble, Knockando, Rothes and Speymouth; and the burgh of Cullen. Further details are available from the correspondent.

Perth and Kinross

The Anderson Trust

Eligibility: Women in need who live in the parish of Kinnoull or Perth and who belong to the established Church of Scotland.

Types of grants: Grants are limited to a maximum of £500 per person each year.

Annual grant total: About £5,600.

Applications: On a form available from the correspondent at any time.

Correspondent: A G Dorward, Messrs Miler Hendry, 10 Blackfriars Street, Perth PH1 5NS (01738 637311).

The Bertha Trust

Eligibility: People in need who live in Perth and Kinross.

Types of grants: Grants of up to £200 towards everyday needs such as clothes, cookers, electrical items and so on. No grants are made towards debts or holidays.

Annual grant total: About £10,000.

Applications: On a form available from the correspondent, who can also provide further information on the trust.

Correspondent: Care Together, Moncrieffe Ward, Perth Royal Infirmary, Perth PH1 1NX (01738 473121).

Mrs Agnes W Carmichael's Trust (incorporating Ferguson and West Charitable Trust)

Eligibility: The relief of poverty, sickness and distress of elderly and needy residents of Coupar Angus.

Types of grants: Normally payments of £40 to £50 are given to about 50 beneficiaries in December each year.

Annual grant total: Between £2,000 and £3,000.

Applications: On a form available from the correspondent. Applications should give details of individual's financial circumstances and are considered in November.

Correspondent: K Lancaster, Watson Lyall Bowie, Union Bank Building, Coupar Angus, Blairgowrie PH13 9AJ (01828 628395; Fax: 01828 627147).

Other information: The trust also supports older people's organisations.

The Trust of Mrs Mary Anne Forbes

Eligibility: Women in need who live in the parish of Kinnoull or, failing that, the parish of Perth.

Types of grants: One-off grants to assist with the relief of poverty, which have included help towards household items.

Annual grant total: In 2000 the trust had assets of £13,000 and an income of £640. Grants to two individuals totalled £300. There was also an exceptional and non-recurring administration expense of £300, which explains why the grant total was lower than in recent years.

Applications: In writing to the correspondent with details of the applicant's special or general need and his/her financial circumstances. Applicants can apply either directly, or through a social worker, citizen's advice bureau, other welfare agency or a third party. Applications are considered all year round.

Correspondent: Alastair H Cruickshank, Messrs Condies Solicitors, 2 Tay Street, Perth PH1 5LJ (01738 440088; Fax: 01738 441131).

The Guildry Incorporation of Perth

Eligibility: People in need who live in Perth.

Types of grants: One-off and recurrent grants usually ranging between £100 and £200.

Annual grant total: In 2000/01 the trust had an income of £174,000. Grants were broken down as follows: weekly pensions (£14,000); quarterly pensions (£11,000); coal allowances (£5,200); school prizes (£1,800); charitable donations (£34,000); bursaries (£19,000).

149

Applications: In writing to the correspondent, for consideration at the trustees' meetings on the last Tuesday of every month.
Correspondent: Lorna Peacock, Secretary, 42 George Street, Perth PH1 5JL (01738 623195).

Dr William Henderson's Mortification

Eligibility: Men over 60 years of age who live in Perthshire and are in need.
Types of grants: Recurrent grants are paid half-yearly in May and November.
Annual grant total: In 2000/01 the trust had assets of £22,000, an income of £2,600 and its expenditure was £470. The trust made four grants totalling £175.
Applications: On a form available from the correspondent directly by the individual, for consideration throughout the year.
Correspondent: Douglas Lamond, 48 Tay Street, Perth PH1 5TR (01738 635353; Fax: 01738 643773).

King James VI Hospital Fund

Eligibility: People in need aged over 60 who live in Perth.
Types of grants: Weekly grants totalling £250 a year
Annual grant total: In 2000/01 the trust gave 27 grants totalling £8,000.
Applications: On a form available from the correspondent. Applications are considered when a vacancy occurs.
Correspondent: Graham MacKenzie, Hospital Master, King James VI Hospital, Hospital Street, Perth PH2 8HP (01738 624660).

The Perth Indigent Old Men's Society

Eligibility: Men who are in need and live in Perth. Most beneficiaries are aged 55 or over.
Types of grants: Assistance with fuel costs, food and clothing.
Annual grant total: £11,000.
Applications: In writing to the correspondent. Distributions are usually made in autumn, although they can be made at other times.
Correspondent: Hamish G R Milne, Hon. Secretary, c/o Spirax Binding Scotland Ltd, Inveralmond Road, Perth PH1 3XA (01738 626281).

Scones Lethendy Mortifications

Eligibility: People in need who live in the burgh of Perth.
(i) *Butter Mortifications:* People over 60 years who have been industrious all their life.
(ii) *Jackson Mortifications:* Poor descendents of Alexander Jackson, or with the surname Jackson and other people who are in need.
Types of grants: Grants of about £60 a quarter.
Annual grant total: In 2000/01 grants to 35 people totalled £9,000.
Applications: On a form available from correspondent. Both trusts have a waiting list to which applications would be added, although successful applicants are judged on need rather than when they applied.
Correspondent: Graham MacKenzie, Treasurer, King James VI Hospital, Hospital Street, Perth PH2 8HP (01738 624660).
Other information: A third trust is the Cairnie Mortification: Recurrent grants lasting for 10 years can be given to two young men, starting when they are near the age of 14. Priority is given to those who are direct descendants of Charles Cairnie or any of his five brothers, otherwise grants can be given to people with the surname Cairnie.

Central Scotland

Clackmannanshire

The Clackmannan District Charitable Trust

Eligibility: People in need who live in the area administered by Clackmannanshire Council, and have either lived there at least 12 consecutive months immediately before receiving benefit, or have had three years' continuous residence in the district at any period and six months immediately before receiving benefit. People eligible for The Spittal Trust (see separate entry) should not apply.
Types of grants: One-off and recurrent grants, generally of between £80 and £150
Annual grant total: About £3,000.
Applications: On a form available from the correspondent, to be considered in March or September.
Correspondent: Administration Services, Clackmannanshire Council, Greenfield, Alloa FK10 2AD (01259 452108).

The Spittal Trust

Eligibility: People in need who have lived in Alloa for at least 10 years immediately before applying to the trust.
Types of grants: One-off and recurrent grants of between £80 and £150 for items such as beds, bedding, cookers and washing machines. The trust provides reconditioned cookers and washing machines with a one year guarantee. The cookers and washing machines remain the property of the trust and should be returned to the trust when they are no longer needed.
Annual grant total: £3,000.
Applications: On a form available from the correspondent. Applications are considered in January, April, July and October.
Correspondent: Administration Services, Clackmannanshire Council, Greenfield, Alloa FK10 2AD (01259 452108).

Falkirk

The Anderson Bequest

Eligibility: People in need who live in Bo"ness.
Types of grants: Annual grants of about £130 per year.
Annual grant total: In 1999 the bequest had an income of £17,000 and gave £7,600 in grants.
Applications: In writing to the correspondent.
Correspondent: J W Johnston, 11 Register Street, Bo"ness, West Lothian EH51 9AE (01506 822112).

Falkirk Temperance Trust

Eligibility: Individuals who have alcohol, drug or other substance abuse problems and live in the former burgh of Falkirk.
Types of grants: One-off grants according to need.
Annual grant total: The trust makes grants totalling up to £7,500 a year, most of which is given to organisations.
Applications: In writing to the correspondent at any time.
Correspondent: A Jannetta, Director of Finance, Falkirk Council, Municipal Buildings, Falkirk FK1 5RS (01324 506070; Fax: 01324 506363).

The Shanks Bequest

Eligibility: People in need who live in Denny.
Types of grants: There is a list of beneficiaries, which is updated each year, who receive a share of the income as a Christmas gift.
Annual grant total: About £850 a year.
Applications: In writing to the correspondent.
Correspondent: Irene Patterson, Finance Services, Falkirk Council, Municipal Buildings, Falkirk FK1 5RS (01324 506070).
Other information: Falkirk Council also administers other small trusts for individuals in need who live in the Falkirk area. Further details from the correspondent above.

Fife

The Bruce Charitable Trust

Eligibility: People in need who live in the burgh of Cupar.

Types of grants: Financial aid is given to people who are poor, aged, infirm or distressed in the burgh of Cupar, and/or to charitable institutions providing assistance to such people. Provision is also made to assist youth organisations, people needing but unable to afford a holiday and projects considered of benefit to the community.

Annual grant total: About £9,000.

Applications: In writing to the correspondent.

Correspondent: Miss E L Calderwood, Secretary, c/o Pagan Osborne, 106 South Street, St Andrews KY16 9QD (01334 475001).

Fife Council – Common Good Funds and Trusts (East)

Eligibility: People living in the various towns or villages in East Fife where there are funds available for residents.

Types of grants: Distributions are made each year from different charitable bequests. Details of exact funds and trusts available can be obtained from the correspondent.

Annual grant total: In 2000/01 the combined funds and trusts had assets of £170,000 and an income of £116,000. Grants to individuals and organisations totalled £45,000.

Applications: Contact the correspondent for further details. An application form is used for the funds but not for the trusts. The trustees meet monthly.

Correspondent: Area Law and Administration Manager (East), Fife Council, County Buildings, St Catherine Street, Cupar, Fife KY15 4TA (01334 412200; Fax: 01334 412940).

Charities Administered by Fife Council (West Fife Area)

Eligibility: The beneficial area differs from charity to charity, the largest of which are the McGregor Bequest and the Wildridge Memorial Fund. The majority refer only to Dunfermline, but smaller ones exist for Aberdour, Culross, Lochgelly, Limekilns, Kincardire, Ballingry and Tulliallan.

Types of grants: Generally one-off grants, usually to poor and/or older people, including help in the form of annual pensions, coal and groceries.

Annual grant total: In 2001/02 funds available totalled £6,100.

Applications: Applications should be made to one of the eight local panels in the communities. Enquiries in the first instance should be made to the correspondent.

Correspondent: David W Henderson, Team Leader (Administration), City Chambers, Kirkgate, Dunfermline KY12 7ND (01383 312700; Fax 01383 312732).

The Fleming Bequest

Eligibility: People living in the parish of St Andrews and St Leonards in the town of St Andrews who are poor, elderly, infirm or distressed.

Types of grants: One-off grants, generally of £100 each, for a specific household need, such as clothing, carpets, fridge/freezers, special chairs and so on.

Annual grant total: About £8,200 in about 600 grants.

Applications: In writing to the correspondent preferably through a social worker, citizen's advice bureau or other welfare agency. Applications are considered at any time.

Correspondent: Miss E L Calderwood, Pagan Osborne, 106 South Street, St Andrews, Fife KY16 9QD (01334 475001; Fax: 01334 476322; e-mail: enquiries@pagan.co.uk).

The Kirkcaldy Charitable Trust

Eligibility: Poor, sick, disabled and elderly people living in the former royal burgh of Kirkcaldy.

Types of grants: One-off grants made only for emergency circumstances. Grants range from £10 to £250 for heating/fuel, clothing, aids/appliances and food.

Annual grant total: £2,500 in grants to 35 to 40 individuals.

Applications: In writing to the correspondent either directly by the individual or through a social worker, citizen's advice bureau or other welfare agency. The trust requires evidence of Social Fund refusal before considering giving a grant.

Correspondent: N Geddes, Team Leader (Enquiry Information – Central), Fife Council, Social Work Office, 390 South St, Glenrothes, Fife KY7 5NL (01592 415210; Fax: 01592 415278).

Other information: This entry was not confirmed by the trust.

The Macdonald Bequest

Eligibility: Young people in need who live in the city of St Andrews or in the parish of St Andrews and St Leonards.

Types of grants: Provision of holidays or convalescence facilities for young persons experiencing or recovering from illnesses. Provision of grants towards Christmas parties, entertainment or treats for persons under 14 years.

Annual grant total: £700 to individuals and youth organisations.

Applications: In writing to the correspondent.

Correspondent: Miss E L Calderwood, Secretary, c/o Pagan Osborne, 106 South Street, St Andrews, Fife KY16 9QD (01334 475001).

Other information: The trust also gives grants to youth organisations in the area of benefit.

The Moonzie Parish Trust

Eligibility: People in need who live in the parish of Moonzie.

Types of grants: Pensions paid annually.

Annual grant total: About £1,000. Most of this is given to organisations, with only a few individuals supported.

Applications: In writing to the correspondent at any time.

Correspondent: The Trustees, c/o Messrs Rollo, Davidson & McFarlane, 67 Crossgate, Cupar, Fife KY15 5AS (01334 654081).

Other information: The same correspondent administers two smaller trusts, Dr Guland's Bequest and The Charles Skinner Trust. The former is restricted to people, particularly older people, who are in need and who live in the parish of Falkland, and the latter to people over 65 years of age in need who live in Dairsie.

The St Andrews Welfare Trust

Eligibility: Young and older people in need who live within a four mile radius of St Andrews.

Types of grants: One-off grants of up to £300 are given towards carpeting, cookers, clothing, fireguards and so on.

Annual grant total: About £10,000 is given to individuals and about £4,000 to organisations each year.

Applications: In writing to the correspondent through a social worker, citizen's advice bureau or other welfare agency. Applications are considered throughout the year.

Correspondent: Miss Calderwood, Pagan Osborne, 106 South Street, St Andrews, Fife KY16 9QD (01334 475001; Fax: 01334 476332; e-mail: enquiries@pagan.co.uk).

Other information: Grants are also given to playgroups and senior citizen Christmas teas.

Stirling

The Forth Valley Medical Benevolent Fund

Eligibility: People in need who are the families or relatives of General Practitioners living in Forth Valley.

Types of grants: One-off grants according to need.

Annual grant total: £2,000.

Applications: In writing to the correspondent.

Correspondent: Dr D I Selfridge, Treasurer, Health Centre, Kersiebank Avenue, Grangemouth FK3 9EL (01324 471511).

Edinburgh, the Lothians & Scottish Borders

The Avenel Trust

Eligibility: Children in need under 18 and students of nursery nursing living in the Lothians.

Types of grants: Small one-off grants for safety items such as fireguards and safety gates, also for shoes and clothing, bedding, cots and pushchairs.

Grants are not given for holidays or household furnishings.

Annual grant total: £10,000 a year.

Applications: Applications should be submitted through a recognised referral agency (e.g. a social worker, health visitor or doctor) to the correspondent. They are considered every two months.

Correspondent: Mrs Elizabeth Duncan, 101 Comiston Drive, Edinburgh EH10 5QU.

The Blackstock Trust

Eligibility: People who are elderly or sick and live in the counties of Roxburgh, Berwick and Selkirk.

Types of grants: Financial assistance (usually up to £500) with accommodation, maintenance or welfare, short holiday breaks, respite care and the provision of amenities.

Annual grant total: About £25,000 to over 100 individuals.

Applications: In writing to the correspondent. Applicants must provide details of financial position (income and capital).

Correspondent: William Windram, Secretary, Messrs Pike & Chapman, 36 Bank Street, Galashiels TD1 1ER (01896 752379).

The Capital Charitable Trust

Eligibility: People in need who live in the Edinburgh and Lothians area.

Types of grants: One-off payments of £10 to £20 for clothes, decorating, household goods and so on.

Annual grant total: £13,000.

Applications: Application forms are available from the Lothian Regional Council Social Work Departments and other responsible bodies who forward them to the correpondent. Applications are not accepted directly from the individual.

Correspondent: A W Stevenson, 7 Abercromby Place, Edinburgh EH3 6LA (0131 556 6644).

The Robert Christie Bequest Fund

Eligibility: People over 60 who are in need, live in the county of Edinburgh or Midlothian and have an acutely painful disease.

Types of grants: Yearly allowances of no more than £625. No one-off grants can be given.

Annual grant total: In 1998/99 the fund had assets of £468,000 and an income of £24,000. Total expenditure was £23,000 with 29 grants totalling £17,000.

Applications: On a form available from the correspondent, with details about the applicant's financial circumstances. Applications can be submitted directly by the individual or through a social worker, citizen's advice bureau or other welfare agency. Applications are usually considered in May and November.

Correspondent: A D Sheperd, J & R A Robertson WS, 15 Great Stuart Street, Edinburgh EH3 7TS (0131 225 5095).

The ECAS (Access/Holiday Fund)

Eligibility: Physically disabled people living in Edinburgh and the Lothian area. People with the following conditions do not fall within the fund's eligibility criteria: cancer, diabetes, epilepsy, HIV, learning difficulties, lower back pain, ME, or sensory impairments.

Types of grants: One-off grants range from £100 to £400 and are given to help with bedding, holidays, telephone installations and similar needs. These grants should not replace statutory provision, rather they should be seen as supplementary. No grants to pay for items which have already been bought, or to repay loans.

Annual grant total: £20,000 in about 100 grants.

Applications: Applications should be made through social workers, health visitors and doctors on the form available from the correspondent. Applications should include the individual's income and expenditure and a report from their GP. They are considered every month except August.

Correspondent: Wendy Dunn, Cunningham Unit, Astley Ainslie Hospital, 133 Grange Loan, Edinburgh EH9 2HL (0131 537 9093; Fax: 0131 537 9095).

Other information: ECAS administer another fund called The Challenger Children's Fund.

The Edinburgh Merchant Company Endowment Trust

Eligibility: People in need over the age of 55 (on 1 July) who are unable to work (certified on medical grounds) and who live in Edinburgh or Midlothian. Traditonally preference has been given to people with the name Gillespie, Gibb or Heriot or who were connected with the building trade in Edinburgh, although this is rarely still applied.

Types of grants: Mostly ex gratia payments of £400. Some one-off grants are also given towards clothing, furniture and so on.

Annual grant total: About £50,000.

Applications: On a form available from the correspondent. Applications can be submitted at any time.

Correspondent: Mrs Margaret Allan, Merchants' Hall, 22 Hanover Street, Edinburgh EH2 2EP (0131 225 7202).

The Edinburgh Voluntary Organisations' Trusts

Eligibility: Individuals in need who live within the Edinburgh and Lothian region.

Types of grants: Grants are one-off and up to £200. Grants are for a specific need such as clothing and urgent furnishings. They must not substitute grants from statutory sources. No grants for electrical equipment, holidays or students' fees or equipment.

Annual grant total: In 1999/2000 the trust had assets of £3.7 million and an income of £242,000. Grants to 513 individuals totalled £39,000. Grants to organisations totalled £102,000.

Applications: Only from social workers and others in the caring professions on behalf of the individual, on a form available from the correspondent. Applications are considered on the last day of each month.

Correspondent: Janette Scappaticcio, Trust Fund Administrator, 14 Ashley Place, Edinburgh EH6 5PX (0131 555 9100; Fax: 0131 555 9101; e-mail: janettescappaticcio@evoc.org.uk).

Other information: The council previously administered a number of small trust funds which have now been amalgamated into a new fund, The EVOT Trust. This entry covers this new fund and two other funds which have remained independent, William Thyne Trust and Miss Beveridge's Trust. In addition the council administers BBC Children in Need grants for the Edinburgh and Lothian region, of up to £75 per family.

Joseph Thomson Mortification

Eligibility: People in need who live in the Edinburgh and Lothian area.

Types of grants: One-off grants between £25 and £50 for food vouchers.

Annual grant total: About £3,000.

Applications: In writing to the correspondent.

Correspondent: George Clark, Morton Fraser, 30–31 Queen Street, Edinburgh EH2 1JX (0131 247 1000; Fax: 0131 247 1007).

Visual Impairment Services South East Scotland

Eligibility: People who have a significant visual impairment and live in Edinburgh, the Lothians or the Scottish borders.

Types of grants: One-off grants ranging from £25 to £200 towards holidays, transport costs, household equipment, clothing, household repairs and specific equipment e.g. watches, kitchen equipment, computers (to a maximum of £100) or communication aids.

No grants for running costs e.g. gas, electric or telephone bills.

Annual grant total: About £30,000 is given in grants each year.

Applications: On a form available from the correspondent with as much relevant information as possible, including details of the applicant's weekly income. Applications can be submitted directly by the individual or through a social worker, citizen's advice bureau or other welfare agency. They are considered every month.

Correspondent: Bryn Merchant, Chief Executive, 12–14 Hillside Crescent, Edinburgh EH7 5DZ (0131 557 1004; Fax: 0131 557 4001).

John Watt's Trust

Eligibility: (a) People over 55 who have the name Watt and who live in the parish of South Leith and have done so for at least 10 years prior to their application. (b) People in need who have lived in the City of Edinburgh or any part of Midlothian may apply.

Types of grants: Currently beneficiaries are receiving £70 per year in quarterly instalments.

Annual grant total: In 2000/01 the trust had assets of £2,400, an income of £1,400 and a total expenditure of £1,900. Grants to 12 individuals totalled £840.

Applications: Prospective applicants must respond to an advertisement in the local press or through the local Leith churches, but more information can be gained from the correspondent. Applications are generally requested in November for consideration in January, although the trust states that at present no further applications can be considered.

Correspondent: Mrs Elspeth Williamson, Mowat Dean WS, 45 Queen Charlotte Street, Leith, Edinburgh EH6 7HT (0131 555 0616; Fax: 0131 553 1523; e-mail: elspeth.williamson@mowatdean.co.uk).

Other information: The trust has a visitor who is a member of South Leith Parish Church. He visits the pensioners throughout the year and reports to the trustees on their state of health and needs.

The John Wilson Bequest Fund

Eligibility: People in need who are over 60 and live in Edinburgh, mid or east Lothian. Grants are also eligible to missionaries of any protestant church in Scotland.

Types of grants: Yearly allowances of £670. No one-off grants are made.

Annual grant total: In 1999 the trust had assets of £1.6 million, an income of £70,000 and a total expenditure of £63,000. 62 grants to individuals totalled £35,000.

Applications: On a form available from the correspondent. Applications can be submitted directly by the individual or a family member or friend, or through a social worker, citizen's advice bureau, other welfare agency or other third party. Applications are considered in April and November.

Correspondent: Alex Sheperd, Messrs J & R A Robertson, 15 Great Stuart Street, Edinburgh EH3 7TS (0131 225 5095).

City of Edinburgh

The Corstorphine & Cramond Bequests

Eligibility: Applicants must: (a) be over 55 or, on account of incurable disease, permanently incapacitated; (b) have lived within the boundaries of the former parishes of Corstorphine (postcode EH12) and Cramond (postcode EH4) for at least five years; and (c) be of good character and in necessitous circumstances which are not accounted for by their own improvidence or misconduct.

Types of grants: Recurrent grants totalling £100 are given twice a year.

Annual grant total: About £10,000 to about 100 individuals.

Applications: On a form available from the correspondent. Applications are considered in May and October.

Correspondent: The Trustees, City of Edinburgh Council, Department of Corporate Services, City Chambers, High Street, Edinburgh EH1 1YJ (0131 529 4273).

Alexander Darling Silk Mercer's Fund

Eligibility: Unmarried or widowed women, over 55, who were born in Edinburgh or lived there for the greater part of their life and have been involved in the women's or children's clothing trade. Women who were not involved in the Silk Mercer's trade but who were born, or have lived, in Edinburgh for the greater part of their lives will be considered. Preference is given to those with the name Darling, Millar, Scott or Small.

Types of grants: The fund gives ex gratia pensions which are reviewed every three years. Grants range from £100 to £400.

Annual grant total: About £40,000.

Applications: Applicants will be visited by a representative who will assist in filling in an application form and make recommendations to the fund.

Correspondent: Mrs Margaret Allan, The Merchant Company, The Merchants' Hall, 22 Hanover Street, Edinburgh EH2 2EP (0131 225 7202).

City of Edinburgh Charitable Trusts

Eligibility: People in need who live in Edinburgh, mostly people of pensionable age.

Types of grants: One-off and recurrent grants, generally of £10 to £110. The charity is made up of approximately 135 trusts, all of which give different types of grants with different eligibility criteria.

Annual grant total: In 2000/01 the trusts had assets of £15 million and an income of £582,000. Grants to individuals and organisations totalled £400,000.

Applications: Initially in writing to the correspondent. The application criteria for each trust varies.

Correspondent: Susan Sharkie, City Chambers, High Street, Edinburgh EH1 1VP (0131 469 3589).

Charities adminstered by Edinburgh City Council

The correspondent for the following trusts is: Susan Sharkie, Investment & Treasury, City of Edinburgh Council, 12 St Giles Street, Edinburgh EH1 1PT (0131 469 3895; e-mail: susan.sharkie@edinburgh.gov.uk).

(i) The Alexander Mortification Fund

Eligibility: People in need aged 50 and over. Preference is given to the relatives of Mr James Alexander Knockhill (who died in 1696) and to people with the surname (or maiden name) of Alexander. Other applicants must live in Edinburgh.

Types of grants: Regular allowances of £120 a year, paid in six equal instalments. A small funeral allowance is payable where there is insufficient funds in the estate to meet the costs. No loans are given.

Annual grant total: In 2000/01 the trust had assets of £717,000 and an income of £30,000. Total expenditure was £17,000, including £13,000 given in 118 grants.

Applications: On a form available from: Mary Pender, Trinity Hospital Visitor, City of Edinburgh Council, City Chambers, High Street, Edinburgh EH1 1YJ. Applications are considered in January and July.

(ii) The John McGibbon Fund

Eligibility: Governesses, female day-school teachers and women in business (e.g. shop or office) over 50 who live in Edinburgh. Applicants must also be of Scottish birth and the daughters of deceased businessmen, master tradesmen or professional men in the City of Edinburgh. Younger applicants who are unable to work for medical reasons may be considered if a medical certificate is supplied.

Types of grants: Regular allowances of £120 a year, paid in six equal instalments. A small funeral allowance is payable where there is insufficient funds in the estate to meet the costs. No loans are given.

Annual grant total: In 2000/01 the trust had assets of £1 million and an income of £43,000. Total expenditure was £29,000, including £23,000 given in 212 grants.

Applications: On a form available from: Mary Pender, Trinity Hospital Visitor, City of Edinburgh Council, City Chambers, High Street, Edinburgh EH1 1YJ. Applications are considered in January and July.

(iii) The Sir William Ramsay Watson Bequest

Eligibility: People in need who are over 50 and live in Corstorphine parish.

Types of grants: £100 in twice yearly payments.

Annual grant total: In 2000/01 the trust had assets of £382,000 and an income of £16,000. Total expenditure was £6,900, including £5,900 in grants to 59 individuals.

Applications: In writing to: Mary Pender, Trinity Hospital Visitor, City of Edinburgh Council, City Chambers, High Street, Edinburgh. Applications are considered in May and November.

(iv) The John Reid Mortification Fund

Eligibility: People in need who live in the former burgh of Leith, Edinburgh.

Types of grants: Annual award of £12.

Annual grant total: In 2000/01 the trust had assets of £85,000 and an income of £3,600. Total expenditure was £1,300, including £1,100 in 89 grants to individuals.

Applications: In writing to the correspondent for consideration in November.

(v) The Sir James Steel's Trust

Eligibility: Joiners, masons and other workers connected with the building trade, sometimes their daughters and widows are considered. Applicants must be over 50 and live in Edinburgh and district. Younger applicants are only accepted if they provide a medical certificate which confirms that they are unable to work.

Types of grants: Regular allowances of £120 a year, paid in six equal instalments. A small funeral allowance is payable where there is insufficient funds in the estate to meet the costs. No loans are made.

Annual grant total: In 2000/01 the trust had assets of £1 million and an income of £51,000. Total expenditure was £31,000, including £24,000 in grants to 204 individuals.

Applications: On a form available from: Mary Pender, Trinity Hospital Visitor, City of Edinburgh Council, City Chambers, High Street, Edinburgh.

Applications are invited twice a year by advertisement and are considered in January and July. Prospective applicants can apply directly or be nominated by a third party with the knowledge of the nominee. Emergency applications cannot be considered.

Applications must include name, age, address, occupation, family, all sources of income and main outgoings plus a statement regarding the health of the applicant.

(vi) The Surplus Fire Fund

Eligibility: Injured firefighters and widows and orphans of any who lost, or may lose, their lives through fires in Edinburgh.

Types of grants: One-off payments.

Annual grant total: In 2001 the trust had assets of £1 million generating an income of £54,000. No grants were given to individuals in this year, with grants mainly to organisations, such as for a burns unit in a hospital.

Applications: In writing to the correspondent.

(vii) Trinity Hospital Fund

Eligibility: People in need over 50 who have lived in Edinburgh for at least two years. Applicants should 'be in need through no fault of their own and be of good reputation'.

Types of grants: Regular allowances of £120 a year (paid in six equal instalments). A small funeral allowance is payable where there is insufficient in the estate to meet the costs. No loans.

Annual grant total: In 2000/01 the trust had assets of £6 million, an income of £240,000 and a total expenditure of £53,000. Grants to 210 individuals totalled £22,000.

Applications: On a form available from the correspondent. Applications should be submitted for consideration in January and July, either directly by the individual or through a local newspaper.

(viii) The George Valance Bequest

Eligibility: People in need who live in the City of Edinburgh who are or who have been Master Tailors.

Types of grants: Up to five grants are made each year. No further information was available.

Annual grant total: In 2001 the trust had assets of £23,000 and an income of £980. No grants were made.

Applications: In writing to the correspondent.

(ix) The John Watson of Saughton Fund

Eligibility: People in need who live in Cramond parish, Edinburgh.

Types of grants: £80 to £100 paid annually.

Annual grant total: The trust has assets of £473,000, an income of £20,000 and a total expenditure of £11,000. Grants to 103 individuals totalled £10,000.

Applications: In writing to: Mary Pender, Trinity Hospital Visitor, City of Edinburgh Council, City Chambers, High Street, Edinburgh EH1 1YJ. Applications are considered in May and November.

The Edinburgh Royal Infirmary Samaritan Society

Eligibility: Patients of NHS hospitals in Edinburgh who are in need.

Types of grants: Specific sums of money for clothing, bills, travel expenses or other help for patients while in these hospitals or on leaving (e.g. grants for travel expenses for members of families visiting or accompanying patients). Grants range from £5 to £150.

Annual grant total: In 2000/01 the trust had assets of £195,000 and an income of £17,000. Total expenditure was £10,000, all of which was given in 236 grants.

Applications: Through a medical social worker (at Edinburgh Royal Infirmary Social Work Department) on an application form. Applications should be sent to: Social Work Department, Edinburgh Royal Infirmary, 23 Chalmers Street, Edinburgh EH3 9EW. They are considered fortnightly.

Correspondent: Mrs Sheila Somerville, 23 Morningside Place, Edinburgh EH10 5ES (Tel & Fax: 0131 447 1618).

The Edinburgh Society for Relief of Indigent Old Men

Eligibility: Older men of good character resident in Edinburgh who usually have no pension apart from statutory sources, have capital of £3,000 or less and are experiencing hardship or disability. (Under exceptional circumstances, men under 65 will be considered.)

Types of grants: Monthly payments of £57.

Annual grant total: About £27,000 to about 45 individuals.

Applications: In writing to the correspondent.

Correspondent: R J Elliot, Secretary, Lindsays WS, 11 Atholl Crescent, Edinburgh EH3 8HE (0131 229 1212).

EMMS International Hawthornbrae Trust

Eligibility: People of good chararcter and in need of a convalescent or respite holiday (e.g. stress/depression after illness or major surgery) who live in Edinburgh city and who are unable to pay for one themselves.

Types of grants: Grants to help with the travel costs and accommodation for a convalescent holiday. The maximum grant for adults is £200 and £100 for children.

Annual grant total: In 2001 the trust had assets of £350,000 and an income of £13,000. Grants to 32 individuals totalled £12,000.

Applications: On a form available from the correspondent. Applications must be sponsored by a recognised social work agency and be supported by a medical reference from a GP. Applications are considered throughout the year.

Correspondent: Robin G K Arnott, Chief Executive, 7 Washington Lane, Edinburgh EH11 2HA (0131 313 3828; Fax: 0131 313 4662; e-mail: info@emms.org; website: www.emms.org).

Other information: Grants are not paid to individuals but to sponsoring agencies or accredited guesthouses or travel agents. Only one successful application per individual is allowed.

Miss Jane Campbell Fraser's Trust

Eligibility: People over 60 living in Leith.

Types of grants: One-off and recurrent grants of £300, normally paid at Christmas.

Annual grant total: In 2000/01 the trust had assets of £86,000 and an income of £4,100. Total expenditure was £4,500, all of which was given in 15 grants.

Applications: In writing to: Revd A MacGregor, North Leith Parish Church, Madeira Street, Edinburgh EH6 4AW. Applications are considered throughout the year.

Correspondent: Alan Anderson, Trustee, Wallace & Menzies, 21 Westgate, North Berwick EH39 4AE (01620 892307; Fax: 01620 895106).

The Leith Aged Mariners Fund

Eligibility: Needy older mariners and their widows, currently living in or connected with Leith or Edinburgh (and not receiving assistance from other seafaring charities).

Types of grants: Regular yearly allowances of £418.

Annual grant total: £42,000.

Applications: On a form available from the correspondent.

Correspondent: Alan Smith, General Secretary, British and International Sailors' Society, Orchard Place, Southampton, Hampshire SO14 3AT (023 8033 7333; Fax: 023 8063 1789).

Leith Benevolent Association Ltd

Eligibility: People in financial need who live in Leith.

Types of grants: One-off grants, usually of £10 to £15 per person.

Annual grant total: About £500 a year.

Applications: In writing to the correspondent with supporting evidence from a social worker.

Correspondent: James Bowers, Administrator, 6 Alemoor Park, Edinburgh EH7 6US (0131 554 7208, from 7am to 1pm).

Leith Holiday Home Committee

Eligibility: Children in Leith and north Edinburgh who are aged 16 or under (and occasionally up to 21 years) who are disabled or have experienced abuse, stressful home circumstances or are in financial need.

Types of grants: Grants are one-off and range from £25 to £100. They are primarily to help with holiday costs, including educational outings, but can also be towards clothing, pocket money and other associated items.

Annual grant total: In 2001 the trust's assets totalled £10,000 and its income was £1,500, nearly all of which was given to 60 individuals for holidays.

Applications: On a form available from the correspondent. Applications should be submitted via a third party such as a social worker, citizen's advice bureau, health visitor, doctor, youth club leader and so on, in time for consideration at the annual general meeting of the trustees in April.

Correspondent: Peter Gibb, 35 Barnton Park Crescent, Edinburgh EH4 6ER (0131 336 4371).

The William Brown Nimmo Charitable Trust

Eligibility: Women in need aged over 50 who were born and permanently live in Leith or Edinburgh and who are on a small income.

Types of grants: Annual grants, currently £65 paid in November.

Annual grant total: About £22,000. The trust usually accepts 10 to 15 new beneficiaries a year, but this is dependent on available income and existing beneficiaries failing to requalify for a grant.

Applications: On a form only available from 1 June from the correspondent. They should be returned by 31 July. Applicants are visited.

Correspondent: Mrs Fiona D Marshall, Secretary, Shepherd & Wedderburn, Saltire Court, 20 Castle Terrace, Edinburgh EH1 2ET (0131 473 5408; Fax: 0131 228 9900; e-mail: fiona.marsall@shepwedd.co.uk).

The Police Aided Clothing Scheme of Edinburgh

Eligibility: Children in need who live in the area administered by City of Edinburgh Council.

Types of grants: In-kind gifts of socks, shoes and a coat or jacket are given to children. No cash grants are made, or help towards school uniforms.

Annual grant total: About 300 children were supported in 2001, although funds were available for many more grants.

Applications: Applications can be submitted at any time, by the individual or any third party. All applicants are visited in their homes by a police officer in uniform.

Correspondent: Mr Sprott, Administrator, Lothian & Borders Police Headquarters, Fettes Avenue, Edinburgh EH4 1RB (0131 311 3001).

East Lothian

The Red House Home Trust

Eligibility: Young people who are aged under 22 and live in East Lothian.

Types of grants: Grants are given to help young disadvantaged people move into independent living. Educational grants are also made.

Annual grant total: In 2001 grants to individuals totalled £14,000, whilst £13,000 was given in total to organisations supporting young people.

Applications: In writing to the correspondent.

Correspondent: R Graeme Thom, Scott-Moncrieff, 17 Melville Street, Edinburgh EH3 7PH (0131 473 3500; e-mail: graeme.thom@scott-moncrieff.com).

155

Midlothian

The Cockpen Lasswade & Falconer Bequest

Eligibility: People who live in Cockpen and Lasswade and need help for medical expenses not covered by the NHS.

Types of grants: Grants can be given for any medical expense, including: treatment; nursing home fees; private wards in hospitals; medical and surgical costs; convalescent home fees; transport for any medical purpose not available from the NHS; food, clothing and other comforts; domestic help; and welfare of the children of parents who are ill.

Annual grant total: About £1,200.

Applications: In writing to the correspondent at any time.

Correspondent: Director, Corporate Services, Midlothian Council, Midlothian House, Buccleuch Street, Dalkeith, Midlothian EH22 1DN (0131 271 3162).

Charities Administered by Midlothian Council

There are various trusts administered by Midlothian Council. Most of them are small (under £500) and therefore do not warrant individual entries in this guide. However, together they are large enough to be included. The following entry gives basic details about the trusts; further information is available from the correspondent or from Dalkeith or Penicuik Citizens Advice Bureau.

All applications should be in writing to the correspondent. The correspondent for all the following trusts is: The Director, Corporate Services, Midlothian Council, Midlothian House, Buccleuch Street, Dalkeith EH22 1DN (0131 270 7500).

(i) The Ainslie, Sir Samuel Chisholm & Fraser Hogg Bequests

Eligibility: Poor people who live in the parish of Dalkeith.

Types of grants: Grants of £20 paid to 18 people in total at Whitsunday and Martinmas.

(ii) The Cockpen, Lasswade & Falconer Bequest

Eligibility: People in need who live in the formal burghal areas of Bonnyrigg and Lasswade, and in the immediate surrounding district.

Types of grants: One-off and recurrent grants generally for medical or convalescent expenses not covered by the National Health Service. Applications should be made through doctors or district nurses. About £25,000 is available each year.

(iii) The John & Margaret Haig Bequest

Eligibility: People in need over 70 who live in the former burghal area of Bonnyrigg.

Types of grants: Grants of £10 each totalling £310.

(iv) The Earl of Stair Bequest

Eligibility: People in need who live in the parish of Cranston.

Types of grants: Logs for the poor.

(v) The Tod Bequest

Eligibility: People in need who live in Loanhead or Polton.

Types of grants: One-off payments totalling £530 a year.

(vi) The Mrs E W Yorkston Bequest

Eligibility: Poor young people belonging to the former burghal area of Lasswade who have an infectious disease.

Types of grants: Grants to help with the cost of a suitable rest in the country or at a convalescent home. About £2,700 is available each year.

Scottish Borders

Christie Fund

Eligibility: People in need in Duns Parish.

Types of grants: One-off and recurrent grants according to need.

Annual grant total: £1,000.

Applications: In writing to the correspondent, through a social work department or other charitable body.

Correspondent: A Campbell, Trustee, Messrs Iain Smith & Partners, 11 Murray Street, Duns TD11 3DF (01361 882733; Fax: 01361 883517)

The R S Hayward Trust

Eligibility: People in need who have been employed in Galashiels for at least 10 years, and have retired or become incapacitated, either permanently or temporarily, from work, and their wives or widows.

Types of grants: There are 60 beneficiaries who receive £8 per week.

Annual grant total: About £25,000 in 2001.

Applications: In writing to the correspondent.

Correspondent: The Secretary, c/o Pike & Chapman, Solicitors, Bank Street, Galashiels, Selkirkshire TD1 1ER (01896 752379; Fax: 01896 754439).

The Elizabeth Hume Trust

Eligibility: Pensioners in need who live in the parish of Chirnside.

Types of grants: Grants range between £10 to £20 per household, given in the form of bags of coal or cash grants. Applicants may usually only receive one grant each year.

Annual grant total: Between £3,000 and £4,000.

Applications: On an informal approach to the parish minister.

Correspondent: Revd W P Graham, The Manse, Chirnside, Duns, Berwickshire TD11 3XL.

Other information: This entry was not confirmed by the trust, but the address was correct according to Scottish Charities Index's database.

Roxburghshire Landward Benevolent Trust

Eligibility: People in need who live in the landward area of the former Roxburgh County Council.

Types of grants: Grants are normally given to assist people with health and social problems where government assistance is not available. Financial help can be towards heating expenditure relating to home illness, travel to hospital, respite care, equipment such as wheelchairs and the purchase of domestic equipment. Grants are one-off and range from £10 to £250. No grants to settle debts.

Annual grant total: In 2001 the trust had an income of £4,500, all of which was given in grants.

Applications: In writing to the correspondent. Applications can be submitted directly by the individual, through a social worker, citizen's advice bureau or other welfare agency, or through other third party on behalf of an individual. They are considered in April and October.

Correspondent: B W Evans, Alderwood, Main Street, St Boswells, Melrose TD6 0AP.

Trusts administered by the Scottish Borders Council

For all the following trusts, apply in writing to the correspondent: David Quinn, Scottish Borders Council, Albert Place, Galashiels TD1 3DL (01361 882600).

(i) Black's Bequest

Eligibility: People in need who live in Coldstream and Coldstream Newton.

Types of grants: One-off grants according to need.

Annual grant total: £290 in 1994/95. No recent information was available.

(ii) The MacWatt Bequest

Eligibility: People in need who live in the former burgh of Duns.

Types of grants: Grants for coal and food.

Annual grant total: £250 was paid in grants in 1994/95. Recent information was unavailable.

(iii) The Watson Bequest

Eligibility: People in need who live in Cranshaws.

Types of grants: Probably one-off and recurrent grants according to need.

Annual grant total: No grants were made in 1994/95.

West Lothian

The James Wood Bequest and the James Wood & Christina Shaw Bequests

Eligibility: There are three separate James Wood Bequests: the first is for poorer people who live in Armadale; the second for poorer people who live in Blackridge and Torphichen; and the third for people who live in Blackridge and Torphichen who are sick or in need. The Christina Shaw Bequest is also for people who are sick and in need who live in Armadale and Blackridge/Torphichen. For all trusts, applicants must have an income of less than £130 per week.

Types of grants: One-off grants at Christmas. The Christina Shaw Bequest gives grants for comforts and home help, whilst the others are given for general relief in need.

Few grants have been made in recent years due to lack of applicants.

Annual grant total: In 2000/01 the trusts had combined assets of £46,000 and a combined income of £2,400. Total expenditure was £200, given in 40 grants of £5 each.

Applications: Advertisements for applicants are placed in the local papers in November each year. Further information can be obtained from the correspondent.

Correspondent: Finance Manager, West Lothian Council, West Lothian House, Almondvale Boulevard, Livingston, West Lothian EH54 6QG (01506 777091).

Glasgow & West of Scotland

The Association for the Relief of Incurables in Glasgow & the West of Scotland

Eligibility: People in financial need who are suffering from incurable diseases and are living at home. Applicants must be living in Glasgow and the West of Scotland.

Types of grants: Pensions of £378 a year paid quarterly. One-off grants totalling no more than £350 per person, for specific needs such as telephone installation, washing machines and cookers.

Annual grant total: In 2001 the trust had assets of £3.4 million and an income of £142,000. Grants totalled £128,000, mainly given in the form of pensions, but also including 23 one-off grants to individuals totalling £6,700 and a donation of £1,000 to City of Glasgow Society of Social Service. Management expenses totalled £16,000.

Applications: Applications must be made through social workers or welfare agencies, on a form available from the correspondent. They are considered quarterly.

Correspondent: BMK Wilson, Solicitors, Apsley House, 29 Wellington Street, Glasgow G2 6JA (0141 221 8004; Fax: 0141 221 8088).

Dr James Black's Trust

Eligibility: 'Faithful domestic servants' who have for 10 years or upwards been in one situation in Glasgow or the immediate neighbourhood. Preference is given to applicants over 60 years old.

Types of grants: Recurrent grants of £150 each are given twice a year.

Annual grant total: About seven grants totalling £2,100.

Applications: In writing to the correspondent either directly by the individual or via another third party, for consideration at any time.

Correspondent: J A M Cuthbert, Mitchells Roberton, George House, 36 North Hanover Street, Glasgow G1 2AD (0141 552 3422; Fax: 0141 552 2935; e-mail: info@mitchells-robertson.co.uk).

The Robert Hart Trust

Eligibility: Working men over 50 who live in Glasgow or the surrounding area who are in need.

Types of grants: Usually £5 per year.

Annual grant total: £700.

Applications: In writing to the Glasgow Society of Social Services, 30 George Square, Glasgow G2 1EG.

Correspondent: James Patrick & Muir, Solicitors, 44 New Street, Dalry, Ayrshire KA24 5AE (01294 832442).

Other information: The trust also gives small grants to institutions in Glasgow.

Merchants House of Glasgow

Eligibility: Pensioners who live in Glasgow and the West of Scotland.

Types of grants: Pensions.

Annual grant total: In 2001 pensions to 103 people totalled £82,000.

Applications: In writing to the correspondent at any time.

Correspondent: The Collector, 7 West George Street, Glasgow G2 1BA (0141 221 8272).

Other information: Grants are also given to organisations.

James Paterson's Trust

Eligibility: Women who have worked in factories or mills in the Glasgow area, consisting of the district of the City of Glasgow and the contiguous districts of Dumbarton, Clydebank, Bearsden and Milngavie, Bishopbriggs and Kirkintilloch, East Kilbride, Eastwood and Renfrew.

Types of grants: Grants are given to pay primarily for short term convalescent accommodation and occasionally for medical expenses and private accommodation in any private hospital. Grants are usually one-off payments of £150 to £300.

Annual grant total: About £15,000.

Applications: In writing to the correspondent. Applications should be submitted directly by the individual and are considered throughout the year.

Correspondent: Donald Reeves, Mitchells Roberton, Solicitors, George House, 36 North Hanover Street, Glasgow G1 2AD (0141 552 3422; Fax: 0141 552 2935).

Radio Clyde – Cash for Kids at Christmas

Eligibility: Children under 16 who live in west central Scotland and are sick or underprivileged.

Types of grants: Christmas grants of between £3 and £15.

Annual grant total: In 2000/01 the trust had assets of £167,000 and an income of £588,000. Grants totalled £507,000, mostly to organisations.

Applications: On a form available from the correspondent, to be submitted by a headteacher, priest or minister who is aware of the family circumstances and will take responsibility for cashing the cheque. The closing date is usually around the first week of December, although this may vary

some years; exact dates are broadcast regularly on the radio station each year.
Correspondent: Yvonne Wyper, Finance Officer, Clyde Action, 236 Clyde Street, Glasgow G1 4JH (0141 566 2827; Fax: 0141 248 2148).

Mairi Semple Fund for Cancer Relief & Research

Eligibility: People who live in Kintyre or the Island of Gigha and who have any type of cancer.

Types of grants: Provision of equipment and/or nursing help in the home, and grants for travelling to cancer treatment centres for patients or relatives. Grants of £60 a month can be awarded. No grants are given to students for research.

Annual grant total: £700 is given in grants each month, half to individuals, half to organisations.

Applications: In writing through the doctor, nurse or church minister of the patient, at the relevant address:
(i) Minister, Killean & Kilchenzie Church, Manse, Muasdale, Tarbert, Argyll.
(ii) Doctor, The Surgery, Muasdale, Tarbert, Argyll.
(iii) Nurse, The Surgery (same address as (ii)).

Correspondent: Mrs Margaret S Semple, Secretary, Rhonadale, Muasdale, Tarbery, Argyll PA29 6XD (01583 421234).

Strathclyde Police Benevolent Fund

Eligibility: Police officers, former police officers and their dependants who live in Strathclyde.

Types of grants: One-off and recurrent grants according to need.

Annual grant total: Grants total about £150,000 a year. Registered charities are also supported.

Applications: In writing to the correspondent. Applications should be received by the end of March for consideration at the annual meeting held in April.

Correspondent: Robert Waterston, Secretary, Strathclyde Police Federation, 151 Merrylee Road, Glasgow G44 3DL (0141 633 2020).

Tullochan Trust

Eligibility: People in need who live in Dunbartonshire, Bearsden, Milngavie and Helensburgh.

Types of grants: One-off and recurrent grants of up to £1,000 each.

Annual grant total: About £5,000 a year is given to individuals and youth clubs.

Applications: In writing to the correspondent by the end of January and the end of August.

Correspondent: Mrs Fiona Stuart, Chair, Tullochan, Gartocharn G83 8ND (01389 830205; Fax: 01389 830653).

Argyll and Bute

The G M Duncan Trust

Eligibility: People in need who live in the burgh of Campbeltown.

Types of grants: Vouchers for groceries of about £10.

Annual grant total: In 2000 240 grants totalled £2,400.

Applications: On a form available from Argyll & Bute Council, Dell Road, Campbeltown, Argyll. Adverts are placed in the local press.

Correspondent: T Armour, Treasury Manager, Argyll & Bute Council, Kilmory, Lochgilphead, Argyll PA31 8RT (01546 602127).

The Glasgow Bute Benevolent Society

Eligibility: 'Indigent persons belonging to Bute, particularly as are of advanced age and responsibility of character.' The length of time a person has lived in Bute and how long they have been connected with Bute are taken into consideration.

Types of grants: The society does not award grants as such; suitable applicants are admitted to the Society's Roll of Pensioners and receive a pension payable half-yearly in May and November and a Christmas bonus payment. The half-yearly pension is currently about £50; the value and availability of the bonus depends on income available.

Annual grant total: About 40 grants each year total £7,000.

Applications: On a form available from the correspondent, with supporting recommendation by a minister of religion, doctor, solicitor or other responsible person. Applications are considered in April, June and October.

Correspondent: Miss Wilson, Secretary, McLeish Carswell, 29 St Vincent Place, Glasgow G1 2DT (0141 248 4134).

Charles & Barbara Tyre Trust

Eligibility: People aged 18 to 25 who live in the former county of Argyll and are of the protestant faith.

Types of grants: Grants are given to provide recreative holidays for people who are mentally or physically disabled. Grants are also given for educational purposes.

Annual grant total: No information was available.

Applications: In writing to the correspondent by 31 May for consideration in July/August.

Correspondent: The Clerk, Dalriada House, Lochgilphead, Argyll PA31 8ST (01546 604511; Fax: 01546 604530).

Dumfries & Galloway

Elizabeth Armstrong Charitable Trust

Eligibility: People in need living in Canonbie.

Types of grants: One-off and recurrent grants according to need.

Annual grant total: About £800.

Applications: In writing to the correspondent.

Correspondent: R J B Hill, Secretary, Bank of Scotland Buildings, Langholm DG13 0AD (01387 380428; Fax: 01387 381144; e-mail: stevandj@nascr.net).

Charities Administered by Dumfries and Galloway Council

Correspondent: Alex Haswell, Deputy Secretary, Dumfries & Galloway District Council, Council Offices, English Street, Dumfries DG1 2DD (01387 260000).

(i) The Lockerbie Trust

Eligibility: People in need who live in Lockerbie.

Types of grants: One-off grants. Annual payments are only considered in exceptional circumstances. The availability of grants from other sources will be taken into account in assessing applications. Each grant is for no more than 50% of the total cost of any expenditure incurred. Education grants are not awarded where Scottish Office grants are available.

Annual grant total: In 2001/02 the trust's assets totalled £483,000, it had an income of £25,000 and its total expenditure was £44,000. Grants were made totalling £42,000 to individuals and organisations.

Applications: On a form available from the correspondent submitted directly by the individual.

(ii) The Henry McDonald Trust

Eligibility: Mothers and babies or young children who live in Stranraer and are in need.

Types of grants: One-off grants up to £500, according to need. In the past, a grant was given to a family to pay for furniture whose income was expended on travel to Glasgow to visit a premature baby.

Annual grant total: The trust has an income of about £500 and some grants were made.

Applications: In writing to the correspondent with as much information as possible; special circumstances and needs must be clearly identified. Applications can be submitted directly by the individual or through a social worker, citizen's advice bureau, other welfare agency or other third party. Applications are usually considered in April, at the start of the financial year.

(iii) Nithsdale District Charities

Eligibility: People in need who live in the former Nithsdale district.

Types of grants: The council administers a number of very small trusts. The largest has a grant total of £400.

Annual grant total: See above.

Applications: In writing to the correspondent.

(iv) The Nivison Trust

Eligibility: People in need who live in Sanquhar.

Types of grants: At present beneficiaries receive quarterly payments of £20.

Annual grant total: £1,200.

Applications: In writing to the correspondent.

The Holywood Trust

Eligibility: Young people aged 15 to 25 living in the Dumfries and Galloway region, with a preference for people who are mentally, physically or socially disadvantaged.

Types of grants: One-off and recurrent grants of £50 to £500. Applications which contribute to their personal development are more likely to receive support. This could include financial or material assistance to participate in education or training, access employment, establish a home or involve themselves in a project or activity which will help them or their community. No grants are given towards carpets or accommodation deposits.

Annual grant total: In 2000/01 the trust had assets of £11 million and an income of £630,000. Grants to individuals totalled £34,000 for welfare purposes and £40,000 for educational purposes. Grants to organisations totalled £120,000.

Applications: On a form available from the correspondent, to be submitted directly by the individual. Applications are considered at least four times a year. The trust encourages applicants to provide additional information about any disadvantage which affects them where their application form has not given them an opportunity to do so. It also welcomes ant supporting information from third party workers.

Correspondent: Peter Robertson, Director, Mount St Michael, Craigs Road, Dumfries DG1 4UT (01387 269176; Fax: 01387 269175; e-mail: funds@holywood-trust.org.uk; website: www.holywood-trust.org.uk).

Other information: The trust also supports groups and project applications which benefit young people.

Lockerbie & District Sick Benevolent Assocation

Eligibility: People in Lockerbie and the surrounding parishes who are in need, with a preference for older people.

Types of grants: Grants are given towards food, appliances, clothing, convalescence and so on.

Annual grant total: About £5,100 is given each year to individuals and organisations.

Applications: In writing to the correspondent in May or November.

Correspondent: Mrs Rosemary V Scott, c/o Royal Bank of Scotland, 47 High Street, Lockerbie DG11 2JH (01576 202230).

Other information: Grants are also given to homes and cottage hospitals in the region.

The James McKune Mortification

Eligibility: People in need who are natives of the parish of Kirkbean and have lived there for 20 years.

Types of grants: Annual pensions of £30 a year.

Annual grant total: In 2001 the trust had assets of £26,000 and an income of £1,000. Grants to 11 individuals totalled £330.

Applications: On a form available from the correspondent. Applications should be submitted directly by the individual in January for consideration in March.

Correspondent: George Fazakerley, Coniston, Carsethorn, Dumfries DG2 8DS.

The John Primrose Trust

Eligibility: People in need with a connection to Dumfries and Maxwelltown by parentage or by living there.

Types of grants: Grants of £100 to £150 are given twice a year to 10 to 20 older people.

Annual grant total: About £10,000, half of which is given to individuals for relief-in-need and educational purposes.

Applications: On an application form available from the correspondent, to be considered in June and December.

Correspondent: The Trustees, Primrose & Garden, 92 Irish Street, Dumfries DG1 2PF (01387 267316).

Other information: Local charities are also considered.

East Ayrshire

Charitable trusts administered by East Ayrshire Council

Correspondent: Administration Manager, East Ayrshire Council, Council Headquarters, London Road, Kilmarnock KA3 7BU (01563 576000; Fax 01563 576500).

(i) Matthew Cochrane Bequest

Eligibility: Older people who are in financial need and live in Kilmarnock.

Types of grants: One-off and recurrent grants of about £300 are given for the provision of holidays.

Annual grant total: Grants to two individuals totalled £650 in 2001/02. There was no income in the year and the assets totalled £1,300.

Applications: The trustees meet to consider grants on an ad hoc basis as necessary. Further details and application forms are available from the correspondent. Applications can be submitted either directly by the individual, or through a social worker, citizen's advice bureau or other welfare agency. Details of household income and employer's certificate of earnings should be included with the application.

Applications were not being sought in 2002 as funds were low.

(ii) The Robert Cummings Bequest

Eligibility: Young people aged under 21 who are orphans and originate from Kilmarnock.

Types of grants: One-off and recurrent grants of about £300 for maintenance, computers, holidays, clothes and medical costs. Grants are also made for educational purposes.

Annual grant total: In 2001/02 the trust gave grants totalling £4,500 to 19 individuals for relief-in-need and educational purposes. Its income was £1,200.

Applications: Further details and application forms are available from the correspondent. Applications can be submitted throughout the year, either directly by the individual or through a third party such as a social worker, citizen's advice bureau and guardian or curator. The following information should be submitted with the application: details of household income, employer's certificate of earnings, applicant's birth certificate, parent's death certificate and satisfactory evidence of the guardian's right to act in that capacity.

(iii) Miss Annie Smith Mair Bequest

Eligibility: People 'of good character' who are in need (i.e. in receipt of benefits) and originate from, or live in, the former burgh of Newmilns and Greenholm. Preference is given to unmarried women and orphaned children. Applicants must be in need either due to their age, bereavement, ill-health or similar misfortune, and must not be in receipt of relief from the Public Assistance Authority.

Types of grants: One-off and recurrent grants ranging from £50 upwards. Grants can be for holidays, redecoration expenses, clothes, various household equipment, daily living expenses, various medical equipment/aids to daily living and Christmas expenses.

Annual grant total: £12,000 was given in grants to 53 individuals in 2001/02.

Applications: On a form available from the correspondent. Applications can be made directly by the individual, or through a social worker, citizen's advice bureau or other welfare agency. Applicants not in receipt of statutory benefits may be required to provide details of personal income and expenditure.

The trustees meet to consider grants three times a year in February, June and November, although in an emergency applications can be considered between meetings.

(iv) The Archibald Taylor Trust

Eligibility: Unmarried women in need, who are aged 45 or over and originate from, or live in, Kilmarnock.

Types of grants: Grants are given for the provision of special nursing or convalescent treatment and convalescent holidays of up to three weeks.

Annual grant total: In 2001/02 the trust made grants to individuals totalling £1,400. In the previous year its income was £18,000 and one grant of £750 was given.

Applications: On a form available from the correspondent, for consideration throughout the year. Applications can be made either directly by the individual, or through a social worker, citizen's advice bureau or other third party such as a GP. The following should be submitted with the application: details of the proposed holiday and cost, household income, employer's certificate of earnings and a declaration by a medical attendant.

The Shearer Bequest

Eligibility: Spinsters and widows in need who are native to Kilmarnock.

Types of grants: Grants are given for general relief in need purposes.

Annual grant total: In 1995 the trust had an income of £760. More recent information was not available.

Applications: In writing to the correspondent.

Correspondent: Revd C G F Brockie, Grange Manse, 51 Portland Road, Kilmarnock, Ayrshire KA1 2EQ.

Other information: This entry was not confirmed by the trust.

East Renfrewshire

The Janet Hamilton Memorial Fund

Eligibility: People who are chronically sick or infirm, live in the former burgh of Barrhead and are of pensionable age.

Types of grants: Postal orders of £15, distributed at Christmas.

Annual grant total: In 1999 30 grants totalled £450.

Applications: Directly by the individual on a form available from the correspondent. A signature from a doctor confirming the person's physical state is necessary, as well as a signed copy of his/her life certificate. Grants are distributed in early December.

Correspondent: Robert Spencer, Principal Accountant, East Renfrewshire Council, Council Headquarters, Eastwood Park, Roukenglen Road, Giffnock, Glasgow, East Renfrewshire G46 6UG (0141 577 3070).

Glasgow (city of)

The City of Glasgow Native Benevolent Association

Eligibility: 'Worthy citizens, their widows and families, who from reverses of fortune are in need of assistance.' Beneficiaries must be members of the association or related to one (as above).

Types of grants: Grants for heating, lighting, television and telephone bills, and summer or Christmas gifts. Grants range from £150 to £600. The basic grant is £300 (a Christmas gift of £150 and a summer gift of £150). Adjusted payments can be made for heating, telephone and holidays.

Annual grant total: In 1996/97 27 grants totalled £20,000. More up-to-date information was not available.

Applications: On a form available from the correspondent. Applications are considered in April, September and October.

Correspondent: Robert F Frame, Hon. Secretary, Kidstons & Co., 1 Royal Bank Place, Buchanan Street, Glasgow G1 3AA (0141 221 6551; Fax: 0141 204 0507).

Charities administrated by The City of Glasgow Society of Social Service

Applications for the following trusts should be made in writing to the correspondent: James Smilie, General Secretary, City of Glasgow Society of Social Service, 30 George Square, Glasgow G2 1EG (0141 248 3535).

(i) Miss Christian Balmanno's Mortification

Eligibility: 'Unmarried ladies of irreproachable character; not under 40 years of age; daughters of gentlemen who shall have carried on some profession or extensive business in Glasgow. Ladies shall be natives of Glasgow.'

Types of grants: One-off and recurrent grants according to need.

Annual grant total: In 1999/2000 the mortification had assets of £7,300 and an income of £610. Grants totalled £580.

(ii) Fife, Kinross & Clackmannan Charitable Society

Eligibility: People living in or near Glasgow who were natives or are married to the descendants of natives, and are in need.

Types of grants: Annual pensions or single grants to help with heating bills etc.

Annual grant total: In 1995 grants totalled £3,500. More updated information was not available.

(iii) Foreigners' Relief Fund

Eligibility: People from overseas either travelling through, or living in, Glasgow.

Types of grants: One-off and recurrent grants according to need.

Annual grant total: In 1999/2000 the fund had assets of £2,300 and an income of £69. There was no expenditure.

(iv) Glasgow Angus & Mearns Benevolent Society

Eligibility: Life members of the society and their dependants, together with people in need who live in Glasgow and the surrounding area who are connected with the counties of Angus and Mearns by birth, marriage or long residence.

Types of grants: One-off and recurrent grants according to need.

Annual grant total: In 1999/2000 the society had assets of £39,000 and an income of £1,400. Grants totalled £1,500.

(v) Glasgow Benevolent Society

Eligibility: People who are poor or sick and live in Glasgow.

Types of grants: One-off grants through the society's almoners who are usually representatives of churches of Protestant denominations and various missions.
Annual grant total: In 1999/2000 the society had assets of £613,000 and an income of £26,000, all of which was given in grants.

(vi) Glasgow Dumfriesshire Society

Eligibility: People in need who were born in Dumfriesshire and are now living in Glasgow.
Types of grants: One-off and recurrent grants according to need for educational and welfare purposes.
Annual grant total: In 1999/2000 the society had assets of £29,000 and an income of £1,000. Grants totalled £440.

(vii) Glasgow Dunbartonshire Benevolent Association

Eligibility: People born in the county of Dumbarton, or their children, living in and around Glasgow who are in need.
Types of grants: One-off or recurrent grants according to need, to relieve poverty, sickness or a sudden emergency.
Annual grant total: In 1995 grants totalled £1,500. More updated information was not available.

(viii) Glasgow Kilmarnock Society

Eligibility: 'Honest and industrious' people who live in Glasgow but were born in or around Kilmarnock.
Types of grants: One-off and recurrent grants according to need.
Annual grant total: In 1999/2000 the trust had assets of £1,600 and an income of £44. There was no expenditure.

(ix) The Glasgow Kilmun Society

Eligibility: People in need.
Types of grants: Grants to pay for recuperative holidays and convalescent accommodation.
Annual grant total: In 1999/2000 the trust gave £20,000 to WRVS and rotaries, for distribution to individuals.
Applications: Individuals should not apply directly. Applications must be made through a social work department, or other agencies e.g. WRVS, Children First or Rotaries.

(x) Francis Lipton Memorial Fund

Eligibility: 'Poor working class mothers and their children under 16 or between 21 years who are physically or mentally handicapped and are substantially dependant on their parents. Motherless children excluded.' Applicants must live within the city of Glasgow.
Types of grants: One-off and recurrent grants according to need.
Annual grant total: In 1999/2000 the fund had assets of £149,000 and an income of £5,300. Grants totalled £3,300.

Lethbridge – Abell Charitable Bequest

Eligibility: People in Glasgow who are in need.
Types of grants: One-off grants of up to £300.
Annual grant total: Information unavailable.
Applications: In writing to the correspondent via social workers, who are made aware of the grants available by the trust.
Correspondent: The Private Secretary to the Lord Provost, Glasgow City Council, City Chambers, Glasgow G2 1DU (0141 287 4002).
Other information: Grants are also given to organisations.

The Andrew & Mary Elizabeth Little Charitable Trust

Eligibility: People in need whose sole source of income is income support, disability benefit or pension, and live in the city of Glasgow.
Types of grants: One-off and recurrent grants according to need.
Annual grant total: Grants total about £56,000 a year, of which 80% is given to individuals and 20% to organisations.
Applications: In writing to the correspondent, to be submitted through social services. Applications should include financial details and are considered monthly.
Correspondent: R Munton, Low Beaton Richmond Solicitors, 20 Renfield Street, Glasgow G2 5AP.

The Lord Provost Charities Fund, the D M Stevenson Fund & the Lethbridge Abell Fund

Eligibility: People in need who live in Glasgow.
Types of grants: One-off and recurrent grants of up to £300 each.
Annual grant total: Information was unavailable.
Applications: Applications should only be made through a welfare agency, social worker or another agency.
Correspondent: The Lord Provost, The Lord Provost's Office, Glasgow City Council, City Chambers, Glasgow G2 1DU (0141 287 4002).

Esther Ross' Bequest

Eligibility: People in need who live in Glasgow. Preference is given to people who are elderly or disabled.
Types of grants: One-off grants of £50 for clothes, bedding or other essentials. No grants are made towards holidays or respite care.
Annual grant total: In 2001/02 the trust had an income of £1,900, all of which was given in 37 grants.
Applications: In writing to the correspondent by a social worker, who should supervise how the grant is spent. Applications are considered as received and should contain details of weekly or monthly income and expenditure.
Correspondent: Paul McKenzie, Glasgow City Council, City Chambers, 285 George Street, Glasgow G2 1DU (0141 287 5343; Fax: 0141 287 3911).

The Trades House of Glasgow

Eligibility: People in need who live in Glasgow, especially those receiving only a pension.
Types of grants: One-off grants of between £5 and £3,000.
Annual grant total: In 1998/99 the charity had assets of £13 million and an income of £539,000. Grants to 301 individuals totalled £172,000. A further £5,200 was given in educational grants and £166,000 to organisations.
Applications: In writing to the correspondent.
Correspondent: The Clerk, 310 St Vincent Street, Glasgow G2 5QR (0141 228 8000).

The Ure Elder Fund for Widows

Eligibility: Widows in need who live in Glasgow, particularly Govan.
Types of grants: Annual grants of £190 are made in twice-yearly payments of £70 plus a Christmas bonus of £50.
Annual grant total: In 1999/2000 the trust had assets of £180,000 and an income of £25,000. Grants totalled £4,200.
Applications: On a form available from the correspondent. Applications can be submitted directly by the individual or through a third party. They are considered in April and October.
Correspondent: Eleanor Kerr, Maclay, Murray and Spens Solicitors, 151 St Vincent Street, Glasgow G2 5NJ (0141 248 5011).

Inverclyde

The Gourock Coal & Benevolent Fund

Eligibility: People who live in the former burgh of Gourock. There is a preference

161

SCOTLAND – GLASGOW & WEST OF SCOTLAND

for older people, especially people who live on their own.

Types of grants: Gas and electricity vouchers are given and coal deliveries are made. In 2001 the value of the donation was £40.

Annual grant total: In 2001 the trust gave gas vouchers totalling £880, electricity vouchers totalling £2,800 and deliveries of coal valued at £170 in total.

Applications: In writing to any minister or parish priest in the town, or the local branch of the WRVS (not to the correspondent). Applications are considered in early December and can be submitted either directly by the individual or through a social worker, citizen's advice bureau or other welfare agency.

Correspondent: D M Blair, Hon. Secretary and Treasurer, Woodside, 68 Reservoir Road, Gourock, Renfrewshire, PA19 1YQ (01475 632188).

Seamans' Friend Charitable Society

Eligibility: Seamen in need in Greenock and Port Glasgow.

Types of grants: One-off grants usually of about £150, distributed once a year at Christmas.

Annual grant total: About £1,200 a year.

Applications: In writing to the correspondent.

Correspondent: David Foggie, Patten & Prentice Solicitors, 2 Ardgowan Square, Greenock PA16 8PP (01475 720306; Fax: 01475 888127).

The Lady Alice Shaw-Stewart Memorial Fund

Eligibility: Female ex-prisoners recommended by the probation officer in the Inverclyde council area.

Types of grants: One-off grants are given for general welfare purposes, e.g. to purchase clothing or towards a holiday.

Annual grant total: In 1999/2000 the trust had an income of £1,600. No grants were given that year, with very few given in recent years.

Applications: In writing to the correspondent. Applications should be submitted by a probation officer on behalf of the individual.

Correspondent: Director of Finance, Inverclyde Council, Municipal Buildings, Greenock PA15 1JA (01475 717171).

Other information: The council administers about 20 other small trusts for people living in Greenock, Gourock, Inverkip and Kilmalcolm.

Mrs Mary Sinclair's Trust

Eligibility: Older seamen who were born or sailed out of Greenock, their widows and children, who are in need.

Types of grants: A twice yearly pension to each beneficiary of £12.

Annual grant total: About £1,700.

Applications: Application forms can be obtained from the correspondent.

Correspondent: D I Banner, Neill Clerk & Murray, Solicitors, 3 Ardgowan Square, Greenock PA16 8NG (01475 724522).

Renfrewshire

Provost's Fuel Fund

Eligibility: People in need who are over 70 years of age and who live in Paisley and are on a low income.

Types of grants: One-off grants of £5. The fund was originally established to help towards the cost of coal, but nowadays the grants can be spent as needed.

Annual grant total: £3,300.

Applications: On a form available from the correspondent in November each year.

Correspondent: The Director of Finance, Renfrewshire Council, Cotton Street, Paisley PA1 1JB (0141 842 5051).

Other information: The fund told us that it is currently oversubscribed. It is continuing to consider applications and awards £5 wherever appropriate, but was concerned that its fund may be totally spent in the near future.

The Jessie Williamson Bequest

Eligibility: People in need, usually of pensionable age, who are natives of, or who have lived in, the villages of Kilbarchan and Bridge-of-Weir for at least five years. Preference is given to people who live alone and have no family of their own. Annuities normally stop if the beneficiary goes into full-time care.

Types of grants: The trust has a list of about 11 annuitants who all receive £50 in total each year, paid in July and December.

Annual grant total: About £550.

Applications: The trust states 'we operate in two small villages and the trustees know who is most likely to be in need'. The trust reviews its list of annuitants in July and December.

Correspondent: James McIntyre, 2 Park View, Kilbarchan PA10 2LW (01505 702634).

South Ayrshire

The James and Jane Knox Fund

Eligibility: Older men in need, preferably bachelors, in the parish of Monkton and Prestwick

Types of grants: One-off and recurrent grants for the provision of comforts.

Annual grant total: In 2002 the trust had assets of £18,000, producing an income of about £900. No grants were made, although the whole income was available to be given.

Applications: In writing to the correspondent directly by the individual with as much information as possible. Applications are considered as and when required.

Correspondent: Dan Russell, Head of Legal and Administration Services, South Ayrshire Council, County Buildings, Wellington Square, Ayr KA7 1DR.

Other information: South Ayrshire Council administers 93 smaller trusts, details of which can be obtained from the correspondent.

The Loudoun Bequest

Eligibility: People in need who live in Monkton and Prestwick.

Types of grants: Gifts of coal to anyone who meets the criteria.

Annual grant total: In 2001 the trust had assets totalling £15,000, which generated an income of £700 – all of this was available for grants, but no grants were made.

Applications: In writing to the correspondent, directly by the individual, providing detailed information.

Correspondent: Dan Russell, Head of Legal and Administration Services, South Ayrshire Council, County Buildings, Wellington Square, Ayr KA7 1DR (01292 612132).

West Dunbartonshire

Dumbarton Children's Trust

Eligibility: Children in Dumbarton who are disadvantaged.

Types of grants: One-off and recurrent grants according to need. No grants for household equipment, foreign travel, medical expenses or debts.

Annual grant total: £6,000.

Applications: In writing to the correspondent by a social worker, health visitor or other third party.

Correspondent: Liz Cochran, Secretary, c/o Citizens Advice Bureau, 6–14 Bridge Street, Dumbarton G82 1NP (01389 841333).

Other information: Only the address for this trust was confirmed.

Lennox Childrens Trust

Eligibility: Children who are disadvantaged in Dumbarton.

Types of grants: One-off and recurrent grants according to need. No grants are given for household equipment, debts already incurred or items which should be provided from statutory funds.

Annual grant total: About £7,000 a year.

Applications: On a form available from the correspondent with guidelines. Applications must be submitted by a third party with a connection to the child.

Correspondent: Ms Liz Cochran, c/o Citizen's Advice Bureau, 6–14 Bridge Street, Dumbarton G82 1NP (01389 841333).

Other information: Only the address for this trust was confirmed.

Highlands & Islands

Highland

The Dr Forbes (Inverness) Trust

Eligibility: People with a medical or similar need who live in the former burgh of Inverness or surrounding areas.

Types of grants: Generally one-off grants to help with the cost of medical treatment and equipment, convalescence, food, clothing and travel expenses to visit sick relatives. Help has also been given with holidays for people who, from a medical point of view, would benefit from it.

Annual grant total: Usually around £6,000 to £8,000 with a maximum of £500 for individual grants.

Applications: Applications, on a form available from the correspondent, can be submitted by the individual or through a recognised referral agency (e.g. social worker, citizen's advice bureau or doctor) or other third party, and are considered throughout the year. Forms must be signed by the applicant's doctor. Supporting letters help the application.

Correspondent: D J Hewitson, Secretary & Treasurer, Munro & Noble Solicitors, 26 Church Street, Inverness IV1 1HX (01463 222687; Fax: 01463 225165; e-mail: legal@munronoble.com).

The Highland Children's Trust

Eligibility: Children and young people in need who are under 25 and live in the Highlands.

Types of grants: Grants are given towards the cost of family holidays. They range from £50 to £250.

Annual grant total: In 2000/01 the trust had assets of £797,000, an income of £52,000 and a total expenditure of £49,000. 100 relief-in-need grants totalled £8,000. There were also 88 educational grants which totalled £22,000.

Applications: On a form available from the correspondent. They can be submitted at any time either directly by the individual or through a social worker, citizen's advice bureau or other welfare agency. Applications must include details of income and savings.

Correspondent: Mrs Shirley A Grant, 105 Castle Street, Inverness IV2 3EA (01463 243872; Fax: 01463 243872; e-mail: hctrust@aol.com; website: www.hctrust.co.uk).

Highland Council – Ross & Comarty Area

Eligibility: People in need who live in the area administered by the Highland Council – Ross & Comarty Area (including Cromarty, Dingwall, Fortrose, Invergordon, Maryburgh, Rosemarkie, Tarbat and Tain).

Types of grants: Income generated by the charities is solely distributed at Christmas time. No one charity generates an income in excess of £500 a year.

Annual grant total: In 2001/02 the combined annual grant total for the charities was £1,800.

Applications: Each Christmas grants are distributed through local community councils or a local councillor. For further information, contact a local community council.

Correspondent: Alister McBain, Council Offices, The Highland Council, Dingwall IV15 9QN (01349 868577).

Other information: This council administers 97 different trusts for individuals and the relevant information about all of them is covered in this entry.

The Morar Trust

Eligibility: People who live in the community of Morar and environs.

Types of grants: Funds are used to support educational, social and charitable occasions in the local community. The trust has in the past assisted with payments for educational equipment, trips and festivities along with supporting the Hospital, ambulance, the blind and incapacitated. Grants are given in one-off payments.

Annual grant total: £1,000 for educational and welfare purposes.

Applications: In writing to the council via the correspondent or through a social or medical worker.

Correspondent: P J Ritchie, Morar Community Council, 11 Rhubana View, Morar, PH40 4PB.

Other information: This entry was not confirmed by the trust and is repeated from the previous edition of the guide.

The Scheme of Winter Payments to the Elderly and Disabled

Eligibility: Pensioners and disabled people who live within the Inverness area. Applicants must not have a wage-earning member of the family living with them, must have no other source of income other than the state pension apart from supplementary benefit or rent/community charge rebate and be the sole claimant for the household.

Types of grants: Recurrent grants are given in November/December each year. £22 to elderly people and £12 to disabled people.

Annual grant total: About £10,000 is available to be given in grants each year.

Applications: Forms are available from the local councillor for each ward, community councils and the library and should be submitted by the middle of November or the start of December each year. The exact date is advertised locally.

Correspondent: Alister Patterson, The Highland Council – Inverness Area, Town House, Inverness IV1 1JJ (01463 239111).

Other information: Other trusts
The council administers various smaller charities for residents of Inverness with a combined annual income of about £3,000. Further details from the correspondent.

Miss M C Stuart's Legacy

Eligibility: People in need who live in Grantown and district.

Types of grants: In practice Christmas donations are made to Senior Citizens Welfare Association and individual senior citizens.

Annual grant total: The trust has an income of about £850 a year.

Applications: In writing to the correspondent at any time.

Correspondent: Director of Finance, Finance Department, Highlands Council, Ruthven Road, Kingussie PH21 1EJ (01540 664500).

The Julie Wheatcroft Trust

Eligibility: Children (under 21) in Caithness whose medical conditions require treatment outside Caithness.

Types of grants: Financial assistance and advice is given to enable parents to remain with their children whilst undergoing medical treatment. Grants are one-off and recurrent and are usually made towards providing meals, telephone calls, accommodation (where this is not provided) and travel expenses.

Annual grant total: No information available.

Applications: In writing to the correspondent. Applications can be submitted directly by the individual, or through a social worker, health visitor, other medical personnel, citizen's advice bureau or other welfare agency. They can be submitted at any time.

Correspondent: Mrs Helen Allan, c/o The Community Education Office, Princess Street, Thurso, Caithness KW14 7DH (01847 895782; Fax: 01847 893156).

Orkney Islands

Dr Sutherland's Fund

Eligibility: People in need who live in the parishes of Olrig – Caithness and Kirkwall and St Ola in the Orkney Isles.

Types of grants: Grants generally of about £50 each.

Annual grant total: About £1,800 is available each year.

Applications: No grants given on application. The fund's administrators write to the relevant social work departments and ask for a list of eligible beneficiaries, who the administrators then contact.

Correspondent: Mrs Elizabeth Faith Cotter, Stewarts and Murdoch, 1 Royal Bank Place, Buchanan Street, Glasgow G1 3AA (0141 248 8810).

Shetland Islands

Georgeson Charitable Trust

Eligibility: People who are elderly, infirm or otherwise in need in the village of Walls, Shetland.

Types of grants: Annual payments are given at Christmas.

Annual grant total: Over £500.

Applications: Applications should be made via a councillor of the district of Walls, to arrive by mid-November.

Correspondent: The Branch Manager, Bank of Scotland, 117 Commercial Street, Lerwick, Shetland ZE1 0DN (01595 732200; Fax: 01595 732204).

The Gilbertson Trust

Eligibility: People who live in Lerwick and the Shetland Islands who are in need.

Types of grants: Recurrent grants of £20 each.

Annual grant total: In 2000/01 the trust had assets of £43,000 and an income of £1,600. Total expenditure was £620, all of which was given in 31 grants to individuals.

Applications: Applications should be in writing and submitted through a recognised referral agency (e.g. social worker, citizen's advice bureau or doctor) or other third party such as a councillor. They are considered in May.

Correspondent: Ruth Wood, Breiwick House, 15 South Road, Lerwick, Shetland ZE1 0RB (01595 744610; Fax: 01595 744667).

Shetland Islands Council Charitable Trust

Eligibility: Pensioners and people who are disabled who live in the Shetland Islands.

Types of grants: Grants and loans range from £300 to about £300,000. Grants made under the Independence at Home scheme are to assist people who are elderly or disabled to remain in their own homes. Nearly every pensioner or disabled person on the island also receives a bonus grant at Chrismas.

Annual grant total: In 2000 the trust had an income of £15 million and a total expenditure of £14 million. Assets totalled £327 million. Grants to individuals included: £910,000 to pensioners/disabled people as Christmas bonus grants; and £162,000 in Independence at Home scheme grants.

Applications: Applications directly from the general public are not considered. Projects are recommended by the various committees of the Shetland Islands Council. The trustees meet every six to eight weeks.

Correspondent: Mary Halcrow, Breiwick House, 15 South Road, Lerwick, Shetland ZE1 0TD (01595 744658; Fax: 01595 744667).

Western Isles

The William MacKenzie Trust

Eligibility: Older and infirm people who live in the old burgh of Stornoway.

Types of grants: One-off grants to enable people who are aged or infirm to continue living in their own homes. Particular support is given to necessary alterations to houses whilst the provision of items such as reclining chairs and domestic equipment such as washing machines is also provided.

No grants are given as an alternative to state funding. Local authorities and health boards must be approached first if they are statutorily required to help.

Annual grant total: In 2000/01 the trust had assets of £864,000 and an income of £39,000. Grants to individuals totalled £18,000. £10,000 was given to other organisations to pass on to individuals.

Applications: In writing to the correspondent at any time. Applications can be submitted directly by the individual, or through a social worker, citizen's advice bureau or other welfare agency.

Correspondent: Jack Kernahan, 26 Lewis Street, Stornoway, Isle of Lewis HS1 2JF (01851 702335; Fax: 01851 706132; e-mail: jack@mannjudd.co.uk).

3. Wales

The Cambrian Educational Trust Fund

Eligibility: Blind and partially sighted people under the age of 21 who were born in or live in Wales.

Types of grants: One-off grants to promote the education of blind and partially-sighted people, such as towards care and maintenance costs.

Annual grant total: In 2000 the trust made grants totalling £5,000 to individuals.

Applications: On a form available from the correspondent. Applications are considered quarterly.

Correspondent: Vanessa Webb, Wales Council for the Blind, 3rd Floor, Shand House, 20 Newport Road, Cardiff CF24 0DB (029 2047 3954).

Children's Leukaemia Society

Eligibility: Children in need who have leukaemia. Grants are made primarly to those living in Wales, although occasionally grants can also be made to people living in the West Country.

Types of grants: A gift of the child's choice is made to them while they are in hospital, for example, a TV, video, or a games console. These can range in value from about £60 to £350.

Annual grant total: In 2000/01 the society had an income of £54,000 and a total expenditure of £26,000. About 70 gifts are made each year.

Applications: Applications are usually made via the welfare office at Randock hospital. Parents or relatives can also apply in writing to the correspondent.

Correspondent: Peter Robinson, 49 Broadway, Cardiff CF24 1QE (029 2045 2483).

Other information: The society also makes caravans available for the children when they are well enough and their families, to have a free holiday.

This entry was not confirmed by the society but was correct according to information on file at the Charity Commission.

The Megan and Trevor Griffiths Trust

See entry on page 92

Help a South Wales Child

Eligibility: People in need who are under 18 years old and live within the Red Dragon listening area.

Types of grants: One-off grants of up to £5,000 each are made for educational and relief-in-need purposes 'where the grant will make a difference'.

Annual grant total: The trust's fundraising target in 2002 was £100,000, which would be available to distribute in grants to individuals and organisations.

Applications: In writing to the correspondent. The trustees meet four times a year.

Correspondent: Lisa Allen, Red Dragon FM, Atlantic Wharf Leisure Village, Hemingway Road, Cardiff CF10 4DJ (029 2066 2066).

The Welsh Rugby Charitable Trust

Eligibility: Amateur sportsmen and sportswomen, mainly of rugby union football, who live in or were born in Wales and are suffering sports injuries, and their dependants in need.

Types of grants: One-off grants for necessities, comforts and other needs. Grants have been made to help with transport, wheelchairs, computers and holidays.

Annual grant total: In 2000/01 the trust had an income of £162,000 and a total expenditure of £152,000. Grants to individuals totalled about £100,000.

Applications: In writing to the correspondent. Applications are usually considered in March, June, September and December and can be submitted either directly by the individual or by a representative of the player's club. Applications should normally set out the circumstances of the injury and the effect it has on the applicant's career. Information on the financial position before and after the accident should also be included.

Correspondent: Edward Jones, Hon. Secretary, 55 West Road, Bridgend CF31 4HQ (01656 653042; Fax: 01656 653042; e-mail:edwardjones@chartrust.freeserve.co.uk).

The Widows', Orphans' & Dependants' Society of the Church in Wales

Eligibility: Widows, orphans and dependants of deceased Anglican clergy of the Church in Wales only.

Types of grants: One-off grants in the form of birthday, Christmas and Easter bonuses.

Annual grant total: In 2001 grants to individuals for relief-in-need purposes totalled £105,000.

Applications: In writing to the correspondent with information regarding the applicant's income and relationship to relevant member of the clergy and the last parish they served in. Applications can be considered at any time. Grants should be made through one of the six diocesan committees of the Church in Wales.

Correspondent: Mrs Louise Davies, 39 Cathedral Road, Cardiff CF11 9XF (029 2034 8200; Fax: 029 2038 7835; e-mail: louisedavies@churchinwales.org.uk).

Mid Wales

Powys

The Brecknock Association for the Welfare of the Blind

Eligibility: Blind and partially-sighted people living in Brecknock.

Types of grants: One-off grants at Christmas and for special equipment/special needs, for example, cookers, talking books and college fees.

Annual grant total: In 2000/01 the association had an income of £2,600 and a total expenditure of £2,800.

Applications: In writing to the correspondent, to be considered when received.

Correspondent: Geoffrey Petty, 17 Woodlands, Cefnllys Lane, Llandrindod Wells, Powys LD1 5DE (01597 823963).

Other information: This entry was not confirmed by the association but was correct according to information on file at the Charity Commission.

The Brecknock Welfare Trust

Eligibility: People in need who live in the town of Brecon.

Types of grants: One-off grants according to need.

Annual grant total: About £1,000 is given to individuals each year.

Applications: In writing to the correspondent. Applications can be submitted by the individual or through a recognised referral agency (social worker, citizen's advice bureau or doctor etc.).

Correspondent: Mrs Gail Elizabeth Rofe, Secretary, The Guildhall, Lion Street, Brecon, Powys LD3 7AL (01874 622884; Fax: 01874 623609; e-mail: brecon.guildhall@btinternet.com; website: www.wiz.to/brecon).

Garthgwynion Charities

Eligibility: Principally people in need who have a strong connection with the mid-Wales or Machynlleth area.

Types of grants: One-off grants of £250 to £500.

Annual grant total: In 2000/01 the charity had assets of £1.3 million, an income of £60,000 and a total expenditure of £57,000. Grants for the year totalled £57,000, although just one grant of £250 was given to an individual.

Applications: In writing to the correspondent. Applications can be made at any time, and are usually considered quarterly in March, June, September and December.

Correspondent: Mrs J Baker, Garthgwynion Estate Ltd, 13 Osborne Close, Hanworth, Middlesex TW13 6SR (020 8890 0469).

Other information: The trust also supports organisations.

The Llanidloes & District Community Nurses' Comfort Fund Committee

Eligibility: People in need living in and around Llanidloes who are sick, disabled, housebound or infirm and who are being nursed at home.

Types of grants: One-off grants for medical aids and necessities such as purchase of disposable sheets, walking aids and payment towards special telephones to Age Concern etc. as recommended by the community nurses.

Recurrent grants are not made. No grants are made for aids which can be provided by the Social Services.

Annual grant total: In 2001/02 the trust had assets of £3,400. During the year £500 was given in grants. The trust stated in 2002 that it was winding down, and when the funds were spent the trust would cease to exist. Much of its work has been diverted towards other local organisations such as Age Concern.

Applications: In writing to any member of the trustees committee. Applications can be made by the individual, or through a relative or community nurse. Applications are considered throughout the year.

Correspondent: Mrs M Edwards, 23 Hafren Terrace, Llanidloes, Powys SY18 6AT (01686 412621).

The Llanidloes Relief-in-Need Charity

Eligibility: People in need who live in the communities of Llanidloes and Llanidloes Without only.

Types of grants: One-off grants for fuel, equipment for disabled people and to families and students in need.

Annual grant total: About £1,700 in 36 grants, although not all this was given to individuals in need.

Applications: In writing to the correspondent. Applications should be made through social service, doctors, citizen's advice bureaux or churches.

Correspondent: Mrs S J Jarman, Clerk, Llwynderw, Old Hall, Llanidloes, Powys SY18 6PW (01686 412636).

The Montgomery Welfare Fund

Eligibility: People in need who live permanently in the ecclesiastical parish of Montgomery (not the county).

Types of grants: One-off grants ranging from £10 to over £200. Reapplications can be made. Grants cover a wide range of needs.

No grants to pay rates, tax or other public funds.

Annual grant total: In 2000/01 the fund had an income of £4,600 and a total expenditure of £3,500. Grants to individuals totalled about £1,500.

Applications: In writing to the correspondent either directly by the individual, or by a third party such as a neighbour, social worker, citizen's advice bureau or other welfare agency. This should include, if possible, a brief note of financial circumstances and income. Applications can be received all year round.

Correspondent: Father A M Hirst, The Rectory, Montgomery, Montgomeryshire SY15 6PT (01686 668243; e-mail: ahirst@avnet.co.uk).

Other information: Grants can also be given to individuals for education, 'development in life' and so on.

North Wales

The Corwen College Pension Charity

Eligibility: Needy widows of clergymen of the Church in Wales whose husbands held office in the district of Merionydd in Gwynedd or the communities of Betws Gwerfil Goch, Corwen Gwyddeldern, Llandrillo, Llangar and Llansantffraid Glyndyfrdwy (all in Clwyd).

Types of grants: One-off and recurrent grants according to need.

Annual grant total: In 2000/01 the charity made five grants to individuals totalling about £2,000.

Applications: In writing to the correspondent, for consideration in January.

Correspondent: The Clerk, The Diocese of St Asaph, Diocesan Office, St Asaph, Denbighshire LL17 0RD (01745 582245; Fax: 01745 583566; e-mail: asaphdbf@cwcom.net).

The Owen Jones Charity

Eligibility: People in need who live in Northop, Northop Hall and Sychdyn.

Types of grants: One-off and recurrent grants according to need.

Annual grant total: In 2000/01 the charity had an income of £8,300 and a total expenditure of £15,000. Grants to individuals for welfare and educational purposes have previously totalled around £10,000.

Applications: In writing to the correspondent.

Correspondent: Mrs Lesley Evans, Bank House, London Road, Sychdyn, Mold CH7 6EL.

Other information: This entry was not confirmed by the trust but the address was correct according to information on file at the Charity Commission.

The North Wales Fund for Needy Psychiatric Patients

Eligibility: People with mental illness who live in North Wales.

Types of grants: One-off grants only ranging from £25 to £150 (for example, for clothes, furniture, holidays and learning courses). No grants for the payment of debts.

Annual grant total: About £3,000.

Applications: In writing to the correspondent, through a social worker or any health professional, including details of income and other possible grant sources. Applications are considered throughout the year.

Correspondent: Mrs J Rees, Clerk, Meadowslea Hospital, Vounog Hill, Penyffordd, Chester CH4 0ED (01978 762155).

The North Wales Police Benevolent Fund

Eligibility: Members of the North Wales Police Force and former members of this and previous forces amalgamated within constituent forces, and their families and immediate dependants who are in need.

Types of grants: One-off and recurrent grants according to need. Grants are also made at Christmas.

Annual grant total: In 2000/01 the fund made grants to individuals totalling £7,500.

Applications: In writing to the correspondent. Applications are considered quarterly, although urgent applicants can be considered as they arrive.

Correspondent: Inspector R Hughes, Chief Constable's Office, Glan-y-Don, Colwyn Bay LL29 8AW (01492 517171; Fax: 01492 511224).

The North Wales Society for the Blind

Eligibility: Blind and partially sighted people who live in Conwy, Ynys Mon, Gwynedd, Denbigh, Wrexham and the Montgomery district of Powys.

Types of grants: One-off grants for necessities, comforts, equipment, household grants, fares and other needs. The minimum award is £50.

Grants are not given if there is a statutory obligation to provide such items.

Annual grant total: In 2000/01 the society gave £17,000 in grants.

Applications: On a form available from the correspondent. Applications should be submitted through a social worker or rehabilitation officer and are considered monthly. 'All other sources should be explored before making an application.'

Correspondent: G C Williams, Director, 325 High Street, Bangor, Gwynedd LL57 1YB (01248 353604; Fax: 01248 371048).

The Evan & Catherine Roberts Home

Eligibility: People over 60 who live within a 40-mile radius of the Bethesda Welsh Methodist Church in Old Colwyn.

Types of grants: One-off grants ranging from £50 to £100.

Annual grant total: In 2000/01 grants to individuals totalled £2,000.

Applications: On a form available from the correspondent.

Correspondent: J Haines Davies, 24 Cadwgan Road, Old Colwyn, Clwyd LL29 9PY (01492 515463).

Elizabeth Williams Charities

Eligibility: People in need who live in the communities of St Asaph, Bodelwyddan, Cefn and Waen.

Types of grants: One-off grants, generally between £50 and £100, are given as Christmas bonuses for the elderly, to families with parents suffering serious illnesses and for particular needs such as hospital trips and washing machines.

Grants are not given for aid that can be met specifically by public funds, for private education or if the grants would affect a claimant's benefit from the DWP.

Annual grant total: In 2001/02 the charity had assets of £190,000 and an income of £6,700. Total expenditure was £7,200, with 126 grants totalling £6,500.

Applications: In writing to the correspondent, to be submitted either directly by the individual or through a social worker, citizen's advice bureau or other welfare agency. Applications can also be submitted via a trustee. They are generally considered in November, although specific cases can be considered at any time.

Correspondent: Mrs Alison R Alexander, Arfon Cottage, 19 Roe Parc, St Asaph, Denbighshire LL17 0LD (01745 583798; e-mail: alison.alexander@btinternet.com).

Anglesey

Anglesey Society for the Welfare of Handicapped People

Eligibility: People living in Anglesey who suffer from tuberculosis or any disease, illness, accident or disability.

Types of grants: One-off or recurrent grants according to need.

Annual grant total: In 1998 the society had an income of £8,300 and a total expenditure of £6,800. More recent information was not available.

Applications: In writing to the correspondent, normally via social services.

Correspondent: Mrs Glynis Aldcroft, 4 The Lodge Orchard, Amlwch, Anglesey LL68 9RX.

John Theodore Wood Charity

Eligibility: Pensioners in need, especially married couples, who live on the Island of Anglesey. Women must be over 60 and men over 65.

Types of grants: One-off grants towards warm clothing, bed linen, coal and towards heating bills and telephone installation in isolated houses. Help cannot be given where statutory provision is available.

Grants range from £100 to £200.

Annual grant total: In 2000/01 the charity made grants totalling £3,000.

Applications: On a form available from the correspondent. Applications can be submitted directly by the individual or through a social worker, citizen's advice bureau, other welfare agency or other third party. Applications are considered in March/October.

Correspondent: Mrs Brenda Randall, Trust Secretary, Trefnant, Chapel Street, Menai Bridge, Anglesey LL59 5HW (01248 712478).

Conwy

Conwy Welsh Church Acts Fund

Eligibility: People living in the County Borough of Conwy.

Types of grants: One-off grants, normally in the range of £50 to £2,000, for relief of poverty, relief in sickness, financial aid for older people, medical treatment, people on probation, people who are blind or visually impaired and to relieve emergencies and disasters.

Grants are not made to individuals for sport or education.

Annual grant total: In 2000/01 the fund had assets of £324,000 and an income of £16,000. Total expenditure was £12,000 with grants totalling £11,000, including one grant of £750 to an individual.

Applications: On a form available from the correspondent. Applications should be submitted directly by the individual any time before the beginning of October, for consideration in November.

Correspondent: K W Finch, Director of Finance and Property Services, Conwy County Borough Council, Bodlondeb, Conwy LL32 8DU (01492 576201; Fax: 01492 576203; e-mail: paulette.saturley@conwy.gov.uk).

Other information: The fund also supports organisations.

The North Wales Association for Spina Bifida & Hydrocephalus

Eligibility: People with spina bifida and/or hydrocephalus who live in North Wales, i.e. the counties of Conwy, Denbighshire, Gwynedd, Flintshire, Isle of Anglesey and Wrexham.

Types of grants: One-off grants of up to £300 to help with maximising 'opportunities for independence' for people with spina bifida or hydrocephalus in order to 'extend their choices and so help their integration into society'.

Grants are given to support mobility needs, funeral expenses, household items and travel expenses incurred when visiting members in hospital out of the area.

Grants are not given for housing adaptations and improvements, house purchase or pilgrimages.

Annual grant total: In 2001/02 the association had an income of £15,000 and a total expenditure of £14,000. Grants to individuals totalled £3,600.

Applications: Applications must be submitted by the association's area advisers and are considered every month. Applications for assistance must be related to the person's disability and the statutory authorities' responsibilty should be determined. Only one welfare grant can be given in 12 months, except in exceptional circumstances.

Correspondent: Mrs Carol Buxton, Canoflan Yr Orsedd, Ffordd Yr Orsedd, Llandudno, Conwy LL30 1LA (01492 860140; e-mail: nwasbah@zoom.co.uk).

Other information: This entry was not confirmed by the association but was correct according to information on file at the Charity Commission.

Denbighshire

The Freeman Evans St David's Day Denbigh Charity

Eligibility: Elderly, poor and chronically sick and disabled people who live in the former borough of Denbigh. Preference is given to schemes that will benefit groups of individuals over a long term.

Types of grants: One-off grants according to need. Grants are also given towards the assistance and care of groups of qualifying persons.

Annual grant total: About £15,000 is available for grants each year.

Applications: In writing to the correspondent with details about how the grant is to be used. Applications can be made directly by the individual if it is supported by a third party such as a doctor, teacher, social worker etc., or through a citizen's advice bureau or other welfare agency.

Correspondent: Medwin Jones, Town Hall, Crown Lane, Denbigh LL16 3PB.

Gwynedd

The Freeman Evans St David's Day Ffestiniog Charity

Eligibility: Elderly, disabled, chronically sick or poor people who have been living in the districts of Blaenau Ffestiniog and Llan Ffestiniog as they were on 31 March 1974 for at least three years.

Types of grants: One-off and recurrent grants of £30 to £1,500 for readaptation of bathrooms, disabled specialist chairs, stairlifts, battery operated wheelchairs and phone lifelines.

No grants to pay off debts.

Annual grant total: In 2001/02 the charity had assets of £644,000, and both an income and a total expenditure of £29,000. Grants to individuals totalled £23,000.

Applications: Applications can be submitted in writing directly by the individual or through a recognised referral agency (e.g. social worker, minister of religion, councillor, citizen's advice bureau or doctor) in March and September for consideration in April and October. Urgent cases are dealt with immediately if the need arises.

Correspondent: Elwyn Hughes, Council Office, Blaenau Ffestiniog, Gwynedd LL41 3ES (01766 831338).

Wrexham

The Ruabon & District Relief-in-Need Charity

Eligibility: People in need who live in the county borough of Wrexham, which covers the community council districts of Cefn Mawr, Penycae, Rhosllanerchrugog (including Johnstown) and Ruabon.

Types of grants: One-off and occasionally recurrent grants of up to £200. Grants can be towards installation of a telephone, heating costs, children's clothing, cookers, furniture, musical instruments, electric wheelchairs, clothing for adults in hospital, travel costs for hospital visits and books and travel for university students.

Grants are not given for instigating bankruptcy proceedings. Loans are not given.

Annual grant total: In 2001 the charity had both an income and a total expenditure of around £2,500. Grants to individuals for educational and welfare purposes totalled £1,500.

Applications: In writing to the correspondent or through a third party such as a social worker, citizen's advice bureau, doctor, trustee, trade union or clergy. Applicants should include age, marital status, work, address and reason for application. Applications are considered on the second Monday of every month but urgent cases can be considered at any time.

Correspondent: J R Fenner, Secretary, Cyncoed, 65 Albert Grove, Ruabon, Wrexham LL14 6AF (01978 820102; Fax: 01978 821595).

The Wrexham & District Relief in Need Charity

Eligibility: People in need who live in the former borough of Wrexham or the communities of Abenbury, Bersham, Bieston, Broughton, Brymbo, Esclusham Above, Esclusham Below, Gresford, Gwersyllt and Minera in Wrexham.

Types of grants: One-off or recurrent grants according to need. For example grants have been given towards the cost of maternity necessities, household equipment, wheelchairs, clothing and a stairlift.

Annual grant total: In 2001 the charity made 29 grants to individuals totalling £9,200.

Applications: In writing to the correspondent. Applications should be submitted directly by the individual, or by a third party, and should include full details of the applicant's weekly income and expenditure together with the cost of the item required where applicable. Applications are considered throughout the year.

Correspondent: P J Blore, Clerk, 49 Norfolk Road, Borras Park, Wrexham LL12 7RT (01978 356901).

South Wales

James Edward Harris Trust

Eligibility: People in need who live in South Wales. There is a preference for older 'people of good' character (described as 'gentlefolk'), who are in distressed circumstances and in need of regular assistance through no fault of their own.

Types of grants: Regular grants of between £100 and £1,200 a year, given in quarterly payments. One-off grants are very rarely given.

No grants for students.

Annual grant total: In 2000/01 the trust had assets of £284,000, an income of £15,000 and a total expenditure of £13,000. Grants were given to nine individuals and totalled £11,000.

Applications: In writing either directly by the individual, or through a recognised referral agency (e.g. social worker, citizen's advice bureau or doctor) or other third party. Grants are made in January, April, September and December.

Correspondent: Richard H Read, Llanmaes, St Fagans, Cardiff CF64 1AF (029 2067 5100; Fax: 029 2067 5105; e-mail:richard.read@culver-holdings.com).

The Honourable Miss Frances Horley Charity

Eligibility: 1. Widows of clergymen in the Church of England and Ireland who are in need and live in the counties of Hereford, Brecon and Radnor, or, failing any applicants, in the city of Monmouth.
2. People who are blind, in need and are members of the Church of England. Usually grants are given to those people living within the area defined above, although individuals living further afield may also be considered.

Types of grants: One-off grants, but individuals who receive a grant can reapply each year.

Annual grant total: In 2000/01 the charity had an income of £4,300 and a total expenditure of £2,300, all of which was given in grants to individuals.

Applications: In writing to the correspondent.

Correspondent: T Davies, Trustee, Elgar House, Holmer Road, Hereford HR4 9SF (01432 352222).

Trust of Arthur Linnecar

Eligibility: People who are registered blind and live in the counties of Ceredigion, Carmarthenshire and Pembrokeshire. No grants are made to people who are registered partially sighted or who are unregistered.

Types of grants: One-off grants in cases where needs are connected with sight loss. Grants have recently been given towards computer equipment, household equipment, holidays and for the relief of financial difficulties.

Annual grant total: In 2001/02 the trust had assets of £47,000, an income of £2,600 and gave grants to 10 individuals totalling £2,100.

Applications: On a form available from the correspondent, for consideration four times a year. Applications can be made through the local Social Services Department, directly by the individual or through one of the following three local voluntary societies for the blind: The Cardiganshire Blind Society, The Pembrokeshire Blind Society or The Carmarthenshire Blind Society. The completed form should be signed by a professional in the field.

Correspondent: Vanessa Webb, Wales Council for the Blind, 3rd Floor, Shand House, 20 Newport Road, Cardiff CF24 0DB (029 2047 3954; Fax: 029 2043 3920; e-mail: staff@wcbnet.freeserve.co.uk; website: www.wcb-ccd.org.uk).

Local Aid for Children & Community Special Needs

Eligibility: People with special needs/learning difficulties, between the ages of 3 and 30, who live in Swansea or Neath Port Talbot.

Types of grants: One-off grants ranging from £30 to £250 for specialist equipment such as a specialist bed, chair or bike. No grants are given for items which should be funded by statutory sources.

Annual grant total: In 2000/01 the trust had both an income and a total expenditure of £115,000. Grants were given to 30 individuals for welfare and educational purposes totalling £14,000.

Applications: In writing to the correspondent, including confirmation that the amount requested is not available from statutory sources. Applications should be submitted through a social worker, citizen's advice bureau or other welfare agency or professional. They are considered in December, March and July.

Correspondent: Mrs Denise Inger, Chairperson, 9 Linden Avenue, Westcross, Swansea SA3 5LE (01792 405041; e-mail: terrance.richardson@ntlworld.com).

The South Wales Association for Spina Bifida & Hydrocephalus

Eligibility: People who have spina bifida and hydrocephalus and live in South Wales.

Types of grants: Grants are for general welfare, travel expenses for visiting children/adults in hospital and car adaptations. Bereavement grants can also be made. Grants are one-off and range from £20 to £200. No grants for loans, driving lessons, car deposits or car phones.

Annual grant total: In 2000/01 grants totalled about £3,000.

Applications: By telephone or in writing to the correspondent. Applications can be submitted either directly by the individual or through a social worker, citizen's advice bureau or other welfare agency or third party. Applications are considered throughout the year.

Correspondent: Mrs A Jones, Hon. Secretary, 22 Heol Undeb, Yorkdale, Beddau, Mid Glamorgan CF38 2LB.

Benevolent Fund of the South Wales Institute of Engineers (Incorporated)

Eligibility: People in need who are, or at any time have been, members, associate members or students of South Wales Institute of Engineers, and their dependants and relatives.

Types of grants: One-off and recurrent grants according to need.

Annual grant total: In 2000/01 the trust's income was £5,200 and its total expenditure was £4,700. Five grants were made to individuals and charities totalling £4,500.

Applications: In writing to the correspondent, either directly by the individual, or through a third party on their behalf.

Correspondent: T H Rhodes, Secretary, 2nd Floor, Empire House, Mount Stuart Square, Cardiff CF10 5FN (029 2048 1726; Fax: 029 2045 1953; e-mail: swie@celtic.co.uk; website: www.swie.celtic.co.uk).

The South Wales Police Benevolent Fund

Eligibility: Serving or retired members of the South Wales Police or constituent force pre-1968 and their dependants, who are in need.

Types of grants: One-off and recurrent grants to meet relief in cases of financial need for those who are sick, convalescent, disabled, infirm, poor or aged. Recent grants have been made to assist with travel expenses to and from a police convalescent home; to assist in buying orthopaedic beds for disabled pensioners and specialist equipment for disabled children in hospitals; to assist in travel expenses for specialist treatment in hospitals; and to help for financial hardship 'not brought about by folly'.

Grants are not made for private medical treatment or for holidays of convalescence other than at a police home. Loans are not given.

Annual grant total: In 2000/01 the trust had assets of £450,000, an income of £29,000 and a total expenditure of £18,000. £17,000 was given in grants to individuals.

Applications: On a form available from the correspondent. Applications should be submitted either by the individual or by any committee member or member of the Force's Welfare Staff on behalf of the individual. Applications are considered quarterly, but emergency payments can be made within 14 days.

Correspondent: Supt. N R Lanagan, Communications Division, Police Headquarters, Bridgend CF31 3SU (01656 869370; Fax: 01656 869508; e-mail: nrlanagan@supanet.com).

The West Glamorgan County Blind Welfare Association

Eligibility: People who are registered visually impaired and live in the area of the former county of West Glamorgan.

Types of grants: One-off grants for special items for blind people (e.g. RNIB aids) and towards computer/technical equipment. Items costing less than £25 can not be considered, with the exception of big button telephones. In addition to these grants the association loans out equipment. Grants range from £25 to £300.

No grants for domestic/household equipment.

Annual grant total: In 2001/02 the association had assets of £79,000 and both an income and a total expenditure of £19,000. Grants to individuals totalled £12,000. A further £3,000 was spent on the provision of talking books and braille publications.

Applications: Applications should be made on a form via a specialist social worker for visual impairment based at the area Social Services Offices. If the grant is made as part of the total cost of items required, the association needs details of other sources/charities that will be making up the balance. Applications are considered continually, subject to funds available.

Correspondent: Alan Cuff, Room 2.3.31, County Hall, Oystermouth Road, Swansea SA1 3SN (01792 636073; Fax: 01792 636807).

Other information: Grants are also made to organisations for people who are visually impaired in the area of benefit.

Bridgend

The Laleston Relief-in-Sickness Charity

Eligibility: People who live in the civil parish of Laleston and who are sick, convalescing, disabled or infirm.

Types of grants: One-off and recurrent grants according to need.

Annual grant total: About £2,000 is available for grants.

Applications: In writing to the correspondent.

Correspondent: Ian Williams, 36 Shakespeare Avenue, Kefngalf, Bridgend CF31 4RY (01656 655956).

Caerphilly

The Rhymney Trust

Eligibility: People in need who live in Rhymney, Gwent.

Types of grants: One-off and recurrent grants ranging from £30 to £100.

Annual grant total: In 2000/01 the trust had an income of £4,200 and a total expenditure of £2,000, all of which was given in grants to individuals for both welfare and educational purposes and to organisations.

Applications: In writing to the correspondent directly by the individual. Applications should be submitted in June for consideration in August.

Correspondent: D Brannan, 11 Forge Crescent, Rhymney, Gwent NP22 5PR (01685 843094).

Other information: The trust also makes grants for educational purposes.

Carmarthenshire

The Abergwili Relief-in-Need Charity

Eligibility: People in need who live in the parish of Abergwili.

Types of grants: One-off cash grants.

Annual grant total: In 2000/01 the charity made grants to individuals totalling £600.

Applications: In writing to the correspondent by the individual or the parent/guardian. Applications are considered at any time.

Correspondent: Mrs Liz Harrison, 10 Cwm Ystrad Park, Johnstown, Camarthen SA31 3MZ. (01267 238995).

Maerdy Children's Welfare Fund

Eligibility: Children under the age of 17 living in the electoral ward of Maerdy Rhonda.

Types of grants: Primarily grants towards urgently required equipment. Grants have also been given towards travel expenses in cases where childrens' parents have to be present at hospital.

Annual grant total: About £3,500 is available each year for grants to individuals. The trust stated that in recent years few applications have been received.

Applications: In writing to the correspondent. Applications can be considered at any time, and a consultation takes place between the chair and the local senior doctor before any equipment is bought.

Correspondent: Emrys Evans, 29 Oxford Road, Maerdy, Ferndale, Mid Glamorgan CF43 4BG (01443 755652).

City of Cardiff

The Cardiff Caledonian Society

Eligibility: People of Scottish nationality and their families, who live in Cardiff or the surrounding district and are in need.

Types of grants: Grants are given for clothing, food, equipment, books for specialised studying and bedding. The trust states that grants can be one-off or recurrent, and loans are also made.

Annual grant total: In 2000/01 the trust had assets of £20,000, an income of £3,100 and a total expenditure of £1,400. Five grants were given to individuals for relief-in-need and educational purposes totalling £950.

Applications: In writing to the correspondent. Applications can be submitted directly by the individual or through a social worker, citizen's advice bureau or other welfare agency at any time. Applications are considered on the third Friday of every month.

Correspondent: Mrs Elizabeth Anne Elsbury, The Dingle, 9 Warren Drive, Caerphilly CF83 1HQ (Tel & Fax: 029 2088 2588).

Cardiff Charity for Special Relief

Eligibility: People in need who live in the city or county of Cardiff.

Types of grants: One-off grants, for example, for funeral expenses, clothes, specialist computer software and household appliances.

No grants are made for educational purposes.

Annual grant total: In 2001 the charity had assets of £13,000 and an income of £770. Total expenditure was £430, all of which was given in grants.

Applications: Applications, on a form available from the correspondent, can be submitted by the individual or through a recognised referral agency (e.g. social worker, citizen's advice bureau or doctor) or other third party. Evidence of special distress must be shown.

Correspondent: Paul Leverett, County Events Coordinator, City Hall, Cardiff CF10 3ND (02920 871796; Fax: 02920 871738; e-mail: p.leverett@cardiff.gov.uk).

The Poor's Charity of Margaret Evans

Eligibility: People in need who live in Cardiff.

Types of grants: One-off grants, Christmas gifts and heating allowances.

Annual grant total: In 2000/01 grants were made totalling £3,000.

Applications: In writing to the correspondent.

Correspondent: Mrs Susan Oxenham, 5 Melrose Avenue, Penylan, Cardiff CF23 9AR (029 2045 5272).

Marjorie Williams Bequest Fund

Eligibility: People in need and over the age of 50 who have lived in the city and county of Cardiff for at least 25 years.

Types of grants: One-off grants ranging from £100 to £400. Grants have been given towards the cost of funeral expenses, a caller-display telephone and alarms. Grants are only given towards repaying debts in exceptional circumstances.

Annual grant total: In 2001 the trust had assets of £24,000 and an income of £1,300. It had an expenditure of £440, all of which was given in grants.

Applications: On a form available from the correspondent. Applications can be submitted directly by the individual, although through a social worker, citizen's advice bureau or other welfare agency is preferred. Applications are considered throughout the year.

Correspondent: Paul Leverett, County Events Coordinator, City Hall, Cardiff CF10 3ND (02920 871769; Fax: 02920 871738; e-mail: p.leverett@cardiff.gov.uk).

Merthyr Tydfil

The Lord Buckland Trust

Eligibility: People in need over 30 years of age who were either born in the old county borough of Merthyr Tydfil or who have lived there for at least 10 years.

Types of grants: 'Distress payments'(presumably one-off payments for emergencies) and Christmas grants.

Annual grant total: In 1998/99 the trust had an income of £37,000 and a total expenditure of £25,000.

Applications: On a form available from the correspondent.

Correspondent: Roy James, St Jude, Glyn Bargoed Close, Trelewis, Merthyr Tydfil CF46 6AJ.

Other information: This entry was not confirmed by the trust but was correct according to information on file at the Charity Commission.

Merthyr Mendicants

Eligibility: People in need who live in the borough of Merthyr Tydfil.

Types of grants: One-off grants towards medical equipment not available from the national health (providing it is recommended by a medical authority); Christmas parcels; holidays for children aged 10 to 14 whose parents are caught in the poverty trap; telephone helpline for incapacitated people; help with domestic equipment such as cookers, refrigerators, washing machines, bedding and beds, quite often to invalids and unmarried mothers. Grants range from £50 to £500.

Annual grant total: Generally around £5,000 to individuals and £6,000 to organisations.

Applications: In writing to the correspondent, including information on other sources of income. Applications can be submitted directly by the individual or through a social worker, citizen's advice bureau or other welfare agency. They are considered monthly on the third Monday.

Correspondent: L A Goodwin, 1 York Close, Shirley Gardens, Heolgerrig, Merthyr Tydfil, Mid Glamorgan CF48 1SG (01685 385831).

Monmouthshire

Chepstow Charity Amalgamated

Eligibility: People over the age of 60 who are in need and live in Chepstow.

Types of grants: One-off grants to supplement low income.

Annual grant total: In 2001 the charity made 12 grants to individuals of £237.50 each, totalling £2,850.

Applications: Directly by the individual on a form available from the correspondent. Applications are considered in May/June.

Correspondent: Mrs S Bode, Secretary, 12 Badgers Meadow, Pwllmeyric, Chepstow, Monmouthshire NP16 6UE (01291 626069).

Llandenny Charities

Eligibility: People over 65 and in need who are in receipt of a state pension, live in the parish of Llandenny and have lived there for more than one year.

Types of grants: Pensions of £30 per year to people receiving a state pension.

Annual grant total: In 2001 the trust had an income of £1,200 and a total expenditure of £1,300. Pensions of £30 were given to 27 individuals totalling £810. Other grants were made totalling £400, to students in full-time education.

Applications: In writing to the correspondent, to be submitted directly by the individual. Applications should be submitted by 15 January for consideration in February.

Correspondent: Dr G K Russell, Forge Cottage, Llandenny, Usk, Monmouthshire NP15 1DL (01291 690380; e-mail: gsrussell@btinternet.com).

Monmouth Charity

Eligibility: People in need who live within an eight-mile radius of Monmouth and neighbourhood.

Types of grants: One-off grants usually up to a maximum of £500.

Annual grant total: In 2000/01 the trust had assets of £135,000, and both an income and an expenditure of £10,000. £5,000 was given in relief-in-need grants to individuals in need and a further £5,000 was given in grants for other purposes, including education.

Applications: The trust advertises in the local press each September/October and applications should be made in response to this advertisement for consideration in November. Emergency grants can be considered at any time. There is no application form. Applications can be submitted directly by the individual or through a social worker, citizen's advice bureau or other welfare agency.

Correspondent: T P Williams, Ambleside, 17A Monkswell Road, Monmouth NP5 3PF (01600 712653).

The Monmouthshire Welsh Church Acts Fund

Eligibility: People living in the boundaries of Monmouthshire County Council who are: in need as the result of emergencies or disasters; distressed; discharged prisoners; on probation; poor; sick; disabled; elderly; blind; convalescent or infirm; or children from community homes (or similar institutions) and their families.

Types of grants: Grants of money or payment for items, services or facilities. Accommodation can be provided to older people who need it because of infirmities or disabilities. People who are blind may also be given access to charitable homes and holiday homes. Grants range from £50 to £500.

Annual grant total: In 2000/01 the fund had an income of £162,000 and a total expenditure of £116,000. About 50 grants are made each year to individuals for relief-in-need and educational purposes and to organisations.

Applications: On a form available from the correspondent which can be submitted at any time, and must be signed by a County Councillor. Applications can be made either directly by the individual, or through a third party such as a social worker or citizen's advice bureau and are usually considered in June, September, December and March.

Correspondent: Mrs Caroline Davies, Corporate Accountancy, Monmouthshire County Council, County Hall, Cwmbran, Torfaen NP44 2XH (01633 644293; Fax: 01633 644276).

Other information: Following the reorganisation of local councils the funds from the Gwent Welsh Church Fund were divided and are now administered by five new councils. The above council is the only one which makes grants directly to individuals. The following councils give the funds to local organisations and churches: Newport County Borough Council (Jim Parsons, Tel: 01633 244491), Caerphilly County Borough Council (Douglas Jones, Tel: 01443 863361), Blaenau Gwent County Borough Council (Keith Jones, Tel: 01495 350 555) and Torfaen County Borough Council (Paul Rowles, Tel: 01495 766179).

Charity of Frederick William Smith

Eligibility: Widows in need who live in Monmouth Town.

Types of grants: One-off grants of between £40 and £100 towards winter heating costs.

Annual grant total: In 2001 the trust gave £850 in 14 grants to individuals.

Applications: In writing to the correspondent in January for consideration in the same month. Applications can be submitted directly by the individual, through a social worker, citizen's advice bureau, other welfare agency or a member of the clergy.

Correspondent: D H Jones, New Ways, 19 The Gardens, Monmouth, Monmouthshire NP5 3HF (01600 712221; e-mail: mojonesneways@aol.com).

Other information: The smaller Monmouth Relief-in-Need Charity and the John Trewen Vizard's Relief-in-Sickness Charity are also administered by the correspondent above.

Pembrokeshire

The Gild of Freemen of Haverfordwest

Eligibility: Hereditary freemen of Haverfordwest aged 18 years and over.

Types of grants: One-off grants according to need.

Annual grant total: In 2000/01 the trust stated that it had assets of £3,100, an income of £2,100 and a total expenditure of £1,500. It also stated that information regarding grants to individuals was confidential.

Applications: Freemen must be enrolled by the chairman of the local authority. The honour is hereditary being passed down through the male or female line.

Correspondent: Messrs R K Lucas & Son, The Tithe Exchange, 9 Victoria Place, Haverfordwest, Pembrokeshire SA61 2JX (01437 762538; Fax: 01437 765404; e-mail: mail@pembrokeshirecoast properties.co.uk; website: www.pembrokeshirecoast properties.co.uk).

The William Sanders Charity

Eligibility: 'Poor and deserving widows and spinsters' who live within a five-mile radius of St John's Church in Pembroke Dock.

Types of grants: Christmas gifts of £15 to £30 although it can be more.

Annual grant total: In 2000/01 the charity had an income of £7,000 and a total expenditure of £8,000. About £6,000 was given in grants to individuals.

Applications: In writing to the correspondent.

Correspondent: Revd Canon A Thomas, The Vicarage, Church Street, Pembroke Dock, Pembrokeshire SA72 6AR (01646 682943).

The Tenby Relief-in-Need & Pensions Charity

Eligibility: Pensioners in need who live in the community of Tenby and have lived there for over 15 years.

Types of grants: Monthly pensions of £12 only.

Annual grant total: In 2000/01 about 130 pensions were made totalling around £19,000.

Applications: In writing to the correspondent.

Correspondent: Clive Mathias, Clerk to the Trustees, County Chambers, Pentre Road, St Clears, Carmathen SA33 4AA (01994 231044; Fax: 01994 230791) or County Chambers, Warren Street, Tenby (01834 844844).

William Vawer's Charity

Eligibility: People in need who live in the town of Haverfordwest.

Types of grants: Pensions to existing pensioners. Other grants to those in need, hardship or distress.

Annual grant total: In 2000/01 the trust had assets of £114,000, an income of £6,900 and a total expenditure of £2,900. The trust stated that information regarding grants to individuals was confidential.

Applications: In writing to the correspondent.

Correspondent: Messrs R K Lucas & Son, The Tithe Exchange, 9 Victoria Place, Haverfordwest, Pembrokeshire SA61 2JX (01437 762538; Fax: 01437 765404; e-mail: mail@pembrokeshirecoast properties.co.uk; website: www.pembrokeshirecoast properties.co.uk).

Swansea

The Swansea & District Friends of the Blind

Eligibility: People who are registered blind and living in Swansea, of all ages. People who are partially sighted must be under 16 years old.

Types of grants: Grants towards aids and equipment, for example, talking watches, kitchen equipment and part payment towards computers. Most of the trust's funds go towards putting on events such as summer outings and a Christmas lunch.

Grants to individuals can be for up to £200.

Annual grant total: In 2000/01 the trust had an income of £35,000 and a total expenditure of £15,000. Grants to individuals totalled about £5,000.

Applications: In writing to the correspondent. Applications are considered at monthly meetings.

Correspondent: John Allan, Secretary, 3 De La Beche Street, Swansea SA1 3EY (01792 655424).

Torfaen

The Cwmbran Trust

Eligibility: People who are sick, poor and in need and live in the town of Cwmbran, Gwent.

Types of grants: One-off and recurrent grants, ranging from £125 to £2,500.

Annual grant total: In 2000 the trust had an income of £68,000 and a total expenditure of £51,000. The trust has previously divided funds between welfare and educational grants to individuals and grants to organisations.

Applications: In writing to the correspondent. Applications can be submitted directly by the individual or through a social worker, citizen's advice bureau, welfare agency or other third party. Applications are usually considered in March, May, July, October and December.

Correspondent: K L Maddox, c/o Meritor HVBS (UK) Ltd, Grange Road, Cwmbran, Gwent NP44 3XU.

Other information: This entry was not confirmed by the trust but the address was correct according to the Charity Commission database.

Vale of Glamorgan

The Cowbridge with Llanblethian United Charities

Eligibility: People in need who live in the town of Cowbridge with Llanblethian.

Types of grants: The provision of items, services or facilities that will reduce the person's need.

Annual grant total: In 2000/01 the charities had an income of £25,000 and a total expenditure of £32,000.

About £25,000 is available each year for grants to individuals for relief-in-need and education purposes, although there is more emphasis on relief-in-need.

Applications: In writing to the correspondent. Applications can be submitted directly by the individual or through a welfare agency.

Correspondent: H G Phillips, 66 Broadway, Llanblethian, Cowbridge, Vale of Glamorgan CF71 7EW (01446 773287; e-mail: unitedcharities@aol.com).

LATCH (Llandough Aim to Treat Children with Cancer and Leukaemia with Hope)

Eligibility: All children and adolescents (up to 21 at time of diagnosis) who suffer from cancer and leukaemia and who are referred to the Paediatric Oncology Unit at Llandough Hospital, and their families.

Types of grants: Grants for travel expenses, heating, telephone bills, car repairs, washing machines, special crisis break holidays, outings and financial difficulties.

Annual grant total: In 2001 the charity had an income of £383,000 and a total expenditure of £436,000. Grants to individuals totalled £130,000.

Applications: To one of the two LATCH social workers, who submite applications for consideration by the trust.

Correspondent: Mrs D A Henderson, LATCH Office, Llandough Hospital, Penarth, South Glamorgan CF64 2XX (029 2071 2217; e-mail: latch@aol.com).

The Neale Trust Fund for Poor Children

Eligibility: Schoolchildren in need who live in the district of Barry and are aged 16 or under.

Types of grants: One-off grants of up to £500 each for clothes, shoes or food. The trust will also consider books, equipment/instruments and educational outings in the UK.

Annual grant total: About £600 is available each year to distribute in grants.

Applications: In writing to the correspondent, who will then send out a form to be completed. The need for support has to be shown by the applicant. Applications are considered in January and September according to availability of funds or in special cases by home visit of the secretary. Applications can be made through the social services, citizen's advice bureau or local childcare officer, or directly by the individual.

Correspondent: Dr Anne Hughes, Court Road Surgery, 29 Court Road, Barry, Vale of Glamorgan CF63 4YD (01446 733181; Fax: 01446 420004).

The Norris (Penarth, Cogan, Llandough) Charity

Eligibility: Young people aged 10 to 19 years and widows, who live in Penarth, Cogan and Llandough.

Types of grants: One-off grants according to need. Grants of coal and tea are also available for widows, and prizes are given to allotment holders and people attending Sunday schools.

Annual grant total: In 2000/01 the charity had both an income and a total expenditure of about £1,400.

Applications: In writing to the correspondent, directly by the individual or by a parent/guardian or the school/college. The grant is based on parental income.

Correspondent: Mrs Pam Skone, 13 Despenser Road, Sully, Penarth, Vale of Glamorgan GF64 5JX.

4. North East

The Abbott Memorial Trust

Eligibility: Families with children up to the age of 18 who are in need and who live in Newcastle upon Tyne, Gateshead, Northumberland, North and South Tyneside and Sunderland.

Types of grants: One-off grants, usually up to £150, for all types of need. The trust has helped many children from one-parent families. Grants are not usually given to relieve debts or for holidays but have been used towards beds, bedding, children's clothing, cookers and school uniforms.

Annual grant total: In 2001 grants to individuals for relief-in-need and educational purposes totalled £6,000.

Applications: Must be made through the relevant social services department only (see below). Applications are considered monthly.

Correspondent: For applicants south of the Tyne: Alison Webster, Community Based Services, Civic Centre, Regent Street, Gateshead NE8 1HH (0191 477 1011; Fax: 0191 477 6544).

For applications north of the Tyne: Alan Dinning, Social Service Directorate, Civic Centre, Barras Bridge, Newcastle upon Tyne NE1 8PA (0191 232 8520).

The Christina Aitchison Trust

Eligibility: People who are blind or have any ophthalmic disease or disability, and people who have a terminal illness, who are in need, and live in north east or south west England.

Types of grants: One-off and recurrent grants for up to £200 to relieve blindness, ophthalmic disease or disability, and terminal illness.

Annual grant total: £1,500 in 1999/2000.

Applications: On a form available from the correspondent, to be submitted in March or September for consideration in April or November.

Correspondent: A P G Massingberd Mundy, The Old Rectory, Harrington, Spilsby, Lincolnshire PE23 4NH (01790 752234).

Other information: Grants are also given to organisations concerned with education, equitation, sailing and music.

The Sir Hugh & Lady Bell Memorial Fund

Eligibility: Iron and steel workers, or their families, who are in need and live in the Teeside area.

Types of grants: Usually one-off grants of about £150.

Annual grant total: About £4,000.

Applications: In writing to the correspondent or through social workers.

Correspondent: J C Sutcliffe, Punch Robson, 35 Albert Road, Middlesbrough, Cleveland TS1 1NU (01642 353753).

Blakeley-Marillier Annuity Fund

Eligibility: Ladies over 55 who are in need and are not of the Roman Catholic faith or members of the Salvation Army. Preference is given to women from the counties of Yorkshire and Devon and in particular the towns of Scarborough and Torquay.

Types of grants: Annuities of £520 a year, paid half yearly. Grants will not be given if the effect is to reduce income support or other benefits or to reduce debt.

Annual grant total: About £16,000.

Applications: On a form available from the correspondent. Applications are usually considered in November and May.

Correspondent: Miss Rowbottom, Messrs Hooper & Wollen, Carlton House, 30 The Terrace, Torquay, Devon TQ1 1BS (01803 213251; Fax: 01803 296871).

The Charity of Miss Ann Farrar Brideoake

Eligibility: Communicant members of the Church of England living within the dioceses of York, Liverpool and Manchester, who are in need. This includes clergy and retired clergy.

Types of grants: Recurrent grants of £500 to £1,500 are given to help in 'making ends meet'. Support is given towards household outgoings, domestic equipment, holidays, children's entertainment and so on as well as special medical needs. One-off payments are made in special circumstances; and debt relief can be supported in exceptional circumstances.

Annual grant total: In 2000/01 the trust had assets of £1.8 million and an income of £78,000. Grants to 65 individuals totalled £65,000.

Applications: On a form available from the correspondent, to be countersigned by the local vicar as confirmation of communicant status. They should be submitted in April or May for consideration in July/August.

Correspondent: Alexander B Anderson, 8 Blake Street, York YO1 8XJ (01904 625678; Fax: 01904 620214).

The Community Foundation (Serving Tyne & Wear and Northumberland)

Eligibility: This foundation comprises of over 100 other funds, all with their own independent grantmaking policies. See below for information on eligibility for a number of funds that support individuals in need. Note, one application to The Community Foundation counts as an application to all the funds.

Types of grants: (a) *Asylum Seekers Fund* Hardship grants are made to asylum seekers resettling in the north east of England.
(b) *Evening Chronicle Sunshine Fund* Individuals up to 16 years old who live within the Evening Chronicle circulation area can receive grants towards the purchase of equipment which will improve the quality of children's lives.
(c) *Lady Grey Memorial Fund* Grants are for individuals in need in the Chathill area.
(d) *The Brian Roycroft Fund* Young people aged between 16 and 25 who are in need in Tyne & Wear and Northumberland who have been in local authority care for at least six months. Grants of about £100 to £200 to help individuals to settle into independent living, for example towards white goods.
(e) *South Tyne Valley Fund* Individuals in need who live in the South Tyne Valley may receive a grant.

Annual grant total: In 2001/02 grants totalled £4.5 million, including £52,000 in total awarded to individuals for education and relief-in-need purposes.

Applications: In writing to the correspondent. Applications for (b) must be supported by a registered organisation or health authority.

Correspondent: Maureen High, Senior Grants Administrator, Percy House, Percy Street, Newcastle upon Tyne NE1 4PW (0191 222 0945; Fax: 0191 230 0689; e-mail: general@communityfoundation.org.uk; website: www.communityfoundation.org.uk).

Other information: More detailed information on this trust can be found in *A Guide to the Major Trusts Volume 1*.

The Cotton Districts' Convalescent Fund

See entry on page 201

Lord Crewe's Charity

Eligibility: Widows and other dependants of deceased clergy of the dioceses of Durham and Newcastle (i.e. the counties of Durham, Northumberland and Tyne & Wear) who are in need.

Types of grants: One-off and recurrent grants according to need.

Annual grant total: In 2000 the charity had an income of £576,000. Grants to individuals for welfare and educational purposes totalled £511,000. Grants to three organisations totalled £16,000.

Applications: On a form available from the correspondent for consideration in March or November.

Correspondent: The Clerk, The Chapter Office, The College, Durham DH1 3EH (0191 384 1690).

Susannah Fearnside's Charity

Eligibility: Preference will be given to people in need who have carried on the business of a farmer in the former county of York (all three ridings), or a dependant or former spouse of a farmer.

Types of grants: Recurrent grants of between £100 and £250. Grants are given towards the cost of heating bills and to meet an urgent need to provide household essentials when the farmer is running an unprofitable business and facing bankruptcy.

Annual grant total: In 2001 the trust had assets of £27,000, an income of £1,700, slightly lower than in previous years. Five grants of £50 each were given to individuals, totalling £250. £500 was given to an organisation to disburse to people in need due to the affects of foot and mouth.

Applications: On a form available from the correspondent. Applications can be submitted by the individual or through a social worker, citizen's advice bureau, welfare agency or any other third party. Applications are usually considered in March and October, although emergencies can be considered at any time. In cases of real difficulty a trustee will visit the applicant.

Correspondent: C N Hobson, Clerk, 3 Hengate, Beverley, East Yorkshire HU17 8BL (Fax: 01482 887343).

The Olive & Norman Field Charity

Eligibility: People who are sick, convalescent, disabled or infirm and live in the former North Riding of Yorkshire (now the counties of Durham and North Yorkshire and the unity authorities of Darlington, Hartlepool, Middlesbrough, Redcar & Cleveland, Stockton-on-Tees and York).

Types of grants: One-off grants towards holidays, clothing, household equipment and medical equipment. No grants are given towards debt repayments, computer equipment or loans.

Annual grant total: In 2001 £21,000 was given in grants to individuals.

Applications: On a form available from the correspondent or social services. The trust prefers applications to be submitted through a recognised referral agency (e.g. social worker, citizen's advice bureau, SSAFA or doctor). Applications are considered in March, June, September and December and should be received two weeks before the meeting.

Correspondent: D Harvey, British Red Cross, Red Cross House, Zetland Street, Northallerton, North Yorkshire DL6 1NB (01609 772186; Fax: 01609 777580).

Greggs Trust Hardship Fund

Eligibility: Individuals and families in need who live in the north east of England, i.e. Tyne and Wear, Northumberland, Durham and Teesside.

Types of grants: Grants range from £30 to £200 (average grant £100). Grants are given for essential items e.g. washing machines, fridges, cookers, furniture, baby equipment, decorating materials, carpets, clothing and school uniforms.

Applications for the payment of debts, holidays, medical equipment and funeral costs will only be considered if the client is in exceptional need, while applications for computer equipment or sponsorship and overseas expeditions will not be considered.

Annual grant total: In 2000 the trust had assets of £5.9 million and an income of £392,000. Grants to 720 individuals totalled £63,000. Grants to organisations totalled £449,000.

Applications: On a form available from the correspondent (which is a standard application form that a number of local trusts use). Applications should be submitted by a welfare agency, i.e. social services, probation office, citizen's advice bureau, victim support, health, disability and housing projects or other such organisations. Applications submitted directly by the individual will not be considered.

Applications are considered twice a month. Due to the large number received, rejected applications are not replied to.

Correspondent: Jenni Wagstaff, Trust Administrator, Fernwood House, Clayton Road, Jesmond, Newcastle-upon-Tyne NE2 1TL (0191 212 7626; Fax: 0191 281 1444; e-mail: jenniw@greggs.co.uk).

Other information: Through the Hardship Fund, Greggs Trust administers funds on behalf of a number of other local charitable trusts at no extra cost to them. These include The Brough Benevolent Association, The Hadrian Trust, The 1989 Willan Charitable Trust, The Sir James Knott Trust, The Joicey Trust and The R W Mann Trust. Greggs Trust allocated £63,000 towards the fund in 2000.

N.B. Only one form from each applicant should be submitted to the joint trusts, as the payment will be made from joint funds.

The N & P Hartley Memorial Trust

Eligibility: People who are disabled or terminally ill and live in Yorkshire, particularly West Yorkshire.

Types of grants: One-off grants according to need. Recent support has included grants towards specialist equipment for people who are disabled.

Annual grant total: In 2000/01 the trust had assets of £908,000 and an income of £47,000. Its total expenditure was £73,000. Grants were made to individuals and organisations.

Applications: In writing to the correspondent, preferably through a social worker, citizen's advice bureau or other welfare agency, for consideration on an ongoing basis. Reapplications from previous beneficiaries are welcomed.

Correspondent: J E Kirman, Trustee, c/o Monkgate House, 44 Monkgate, York YO61 3AL (01904 341200; Fax: 01904 341201; e-mail: jkirman@garbutt_elliott.co.uk).

The Bill & May Hodgson Charitable Trust

Eligibility: People in exceptional need who live in the north east of England.

Types of grants: Grants are usually between £50 and £100.

Annual grant total: In 1999/2000 the trust had assets of £362,000 and an income of £19,000. Grants totalled £14,000 and were mostly made to organisations.

Applications: In writing to the correspondent, for consideration in July and November.

Correspondent: Richard Wilson, Dickinson Dees, St Anne's Wharf, 112 Quayside, Newcastle upon Tyne NE99 1SB (0191 279 9000).

The Hospital of God at Greatham

Eligibility: People in need who live within the ancient diocese of Durham, i.e. between the rivers Tees and Tweed.

Types of grants: One-off grants of £50 to £350 for items and services to relieve need, hardship or distress. No grants are given for education or travel/adventure projects, nor usually for holidays or rent arrears.

Annual grant total: The trust gives around 120 grants each year totalling £40,000. Grants to organisations total about £11,000.

Applications: All applications must be made through the nominated officer in the local social services departments.

Correspondent: David Granath, Director, Estate Office, Greatham, Hartlepool TS25 2HS (01429 870247; e-mail: david.granath@greatham.co.uk).

The John Routledge Hunter Memorial Fund

Eligibility: Men who live in Northumberland and Tyne and Wear (north of River Tyne) who have (or recently have had) chest, lung or catarrhal complaints.

Types of grants: Grants of £200 to £530 towards a two or three week recuperative holiday in a hotel in Lytham St Annes or Southport (including rail travel expenses, bed, breakfast, evening meal and £25 in cash). Holidays are taken between Easter and September.

Annual grant total: In 1999/2000 the fund had assets of £395,000 and an income of £17,000. 36 grants totalled £16,000.

Applications: On a form available from the correspondent, supported by a certificate signed by a doctor. Applications should be submitted directly by the individual and are considered from January to April.

Correspondent: Mrs Cherry Gallon, Dickinson Dees (Solicitors), St Ann's Wharf, 112 Quayside, Newcastle upon Tyne NE99 1SB (0191 279 9248; Fax: 0191 279 9129).

Hylton House Fund

Eligibility: People with cerebral palsy and related disabilities, and their families and carers. Priority is given to people living in Durham, Darlington, Gateshead, South Shields and Sunderland, followed by those living in Hartlepool, Redcar, Cleveland, Middlesbrough and Stockton. (People living in the former North Riding of Yorkshire, or elsewhere in the UK can be considered, but should contact the correspondent before applying to check availability of funds.)

Types of grants: One-off grants of between £100 and £500. There are two types of grants:

(i) *welfare and holiday grants or respite support for carers*

Applicants must be on income support or low residual incomes and in a family where redundancy or unemployment has affected income; where the degree of disability creates a particularly heavy financial demand.

The maximum grant is for £150. Funding can be made for: domestic equipment (washing machine) or services; costs of setting up an independent home for an individual, but not those covered by a move from residential care into independent living if this is a SCOPE or Local Authority led move; debts if you can prove that this was incurred due to a member of your family's disability; holidays or respite support for carers of up to two weeks duration in this country or abroad – you must include details and the date of your proposed holiday.

(ii) *grants for buying specific items or activities and respite support*

Priority will be given to applications which address the following areas: education, training and therapy, e.g. sound and light therapy for people with cerebral palsy to improve quality of life; training and support for carers and self help groups (where no statutory support/provision is available); provision of aids and equipment, particularly specialist clothing, communication and mobility aids; travel costs e.g. taxi or rail fares to attend a specific activity if no alternative transport is available; respite support for an individual when the needs of the person requires them to either be accompanied by an employed carer or by visiting a specialist centre where full-time or extensive care is provided.

Exclusions: The trust will not fund legal costs, ongoing education, medical treatment, decorating and/or refurbishment costs unless the work has occurred due to circumstances associated with the applicant's disability, building adaptations, motor vehicle adaptations, motor insurance, deposits or running costs, TVs or VCRs. No grants for payment for assessments e.g. Scope Advisory Assessments or additional costs involved in the SCOPE Living Options Schemes. The trust will not make grants which are: retrospective, the responsibility of local government, or for activities recommended by SCOPE for which SCOPE has subsequently refused grant aid.

Annual grant total: In 2000/01 the trust had assets of £156,000, an income of £5,300 and a total expenditure of £8,700. 58 welfare grants to individuals totalled £8,100 and 3 educational grants to individuals totalled £600.

Applications: On a form available, with guidelines for applicants, from the correspondent. Applications can be made either directly by the individual, or through a third party such as a teacher, doctor, social worker, citizen's advice bureaux and so on. Only one grant can be made per family in each financial year.

See (i) above; grants will be assessed within two weeks. There is a limited number of grants and success will be determined upon availability of funds.

See (ii) above; you will need to provide full costings and show that you have researched and sought advice from an appropriate source such as SCOPE or an independent professional adviser, for example, a therapist, or teacher for specialist equipment and provision. These applications are considered in July, October, January and April.

Correspondent: Mel Caldwell, Jordan House, Forster Business Centre, Finchale Road, Durham DH1 5HL (0191 383 0055; Fax: 0191 383 2969; e-mail: info@countydurhamfoundation.co.uk; website: www.countydurhamfoundation.co.uk).

The Rose Joicey Fund

Eligibility: Families or individuals who live in the counties of Durham, Northumberland or Tyne & Wear and who are in need.

Priority for grants is given to groups which organise holidays for people in need. Requests from individuals will only be considered if made through a proper social work agency. Preference will be given in cases of hardship involving the sickness or disability of a family member.

Types of grants: One-off grants only, ranging from £50 to £200. Grants are not given for furniture, clothing, building restoration or medical care or equipment.

Annual grant total: In 2000/01 the trust had assets of £103,000 and an income of £4,700. 30 grants totalled £5,000.

Applications: In writing to the correspondent by a social worker at any time.

Correspondent: Carolyn Lamb, c/o Newcastle Council for Voluntary Service, Mea House, Ellison Place, Newcastle upon Tyne NE1 8XS (0191 232 7445; Fax: 0191 230 5640).

The Leeds Jewish Welfare Board

Eligibility: Jewish people who live in Leeds or North and West Yorkshire.

North East – General

Types of grants: Grants may be given as part of a 'support package'. They are rarely given as a one-off without a full assessment of the situation. Loans may also be given and depending on individual circumstances may be part-grant/part-loan. A flexible approach together with budgeting advice is offered. The majority of grants are given to families with children. These may be for clothes, bedding requirements and so on. Grants are also given at Jewish Festivals such as Passover and holiday grants are given towards a stay at their caravan on the east coast. Counselling and meals-on-wheels services along with a comprehensive range of services and resources are also offered to Jewish children, families and older people.

Annual grant total: About £15,000 is given to individuals in need.

Applications: Applications for help can be made at any time by individuals, welfare agencies, friends or relatives. The board can respond quickly in urgent cases. The applicant will be seen by a social worker who will assess the application and gather the relevant information.

Correspondent: Sheila Saunders, Chief Executive, 311 Stonegate Road, Leeds LS17 6AZ (0113 268 4211; Fax: 0113 203 4915; e-mail: ljbw@dial.pipex.co.uk).

The Merchant Taylors of York Charity

Eligibility: 'Decayed tailors' and people who worked in allied crafts, who are in need and live in Yorkshire, particularly in York and nearby.

Types of grants: One-off grants.

Annual grant total: In 1999/2000 the charity had assets of £74,000 and an income of £66,000. Grants to individuals and organisations totalled £1,200.

Applications: In writing to the correspondent. Applications are considered throughout the year.

Correspondent: Neil Pearce, Chancellor, 104 The Mount, York YO4 1GR (01904 655626; e-mail: n.pearce@calvertsmith.co.uk).

The North East Area Miners Welfare Trust Fund

Eligibility: People in need living in Durham, Northumberland and Tyne & Wear who are employed by the coal industry, or who have not been employed since retirement or redundancy from the coal industry.

Types of grants: One-off grants according to need.

Annual grant total: In 1998/99 the trust had assets of £488,000, an income of £84,000 and a total expenditure of £89,000. Grants totalled £64,000, and were mostly to organisations but included one to an individual for legal fees worth £910.

Applications: In writing to the correspondent. Applications can be submitted directly by the individual or through a social worker, citizen's advice bureau or other welfare agency. They are usually considered four times a year.

Correspondent: V B Clements, Coal Industry Social Welfare Organisation, 6 Bewick Road, Gateshead, Tyne & Wear NE8 4DP (0191 477 7242; Fax: 0191 477 1021).

The North East Area Mineworkers' Convalescent Fund

Eligibility: Workers, or their spouses, who are/were employed in the mining industry in County Durham, Northumberland or Tyne & Wear, and who are in need of convalescence.

Types of grants: For women, the fund provides a period of convalescence at an establishment in Richmond, North Yorkshire. Medical treatment is not provided and applicants should not be more than 80 years of age in the year of application or confined to a wheelchair.

For men, a period of convalescence is provided at an establishment in Scarborough. Medical treatment is not provided.

Annual grant total: In 1998 the fund had a total expenditure of £342,000.

Applications: On a form available from the correspondent, to be considered at any time.

Correspondent: V B Clements, c/o The Coal Industry Social Welfare Organisation, 6 Bewick Road, Gateshead, Tyne & Wear NE8 4DP (0191 477 7242; Fax: 0191 477 1021).

The North Eastern Prison After Care Society

Eligibility: People in need who live in Northumberland, Durham, Tyne & Wear, Cleveland and North Yorkshire who are suffering or who have suffered a legal restriction on their liberty in any penal or correctional establishment or through any means whatsoever, and their families.

Types of grants: The policy is described as follows: '(i) Particular consideration is given to the rehabilitative aspects of support needed at the point of discharge and beyond; (ii) Applications indicating an investment with some potential pay-off in someone's life, like accommodation, education, family welfare, receive priority; (iii) Help is also given to prisoners facing the loneliness and despair of incarceration without the support of family or friends.'

Grants are one-off and range from £10 to £100. They have been given towards, for example, accommodation, bicycles, cell furnishings, children's needs, education, employment needs, furniture, glasses, prison hobbies, tattoo removal, toiletries and typewriters.

Annual grant total: In 2000/01 the society had assets of £150,000 and an income of £147,000. Total expenditure was £116,000, including £9,800 given in total to 147 individuals.

Applications: On a form available from the correspondent, to be submitted and received by the probation service. They are usually considered in March, June, September and December. Applications directly by individuals will not be accepted.

Correspondent: Ruth Cranfield, Hon. Secretary, 22 Old Elvet, Durham DH1 3HW (0191 384 3096; e-mail: rcranfield@ukonline.co.uk).

Other information: As well as providing grants, the society provides holidays for prisoners' families, improves visitors centres for the benefit of children and adults and collects and publishes information relating to criminal justice and the prevention of crime.

The Northern Counties' Charity for the Incapacitated

See entry on page 202

Northern Counties Orphans' Benevolent Society

Eligibility: Children in need through sickness, disability or other causes with a preference for those who live in the counties of Cleveland, Durham, Tyne and Wear, Northumberland and Cumbria. There is a preference for orphaned children.

Types of grants: Both one-off and recurrent grants for education and clothing. In 1999: 'Assistance took the form of grants towards school fees, the cost of school clothing and equipment and, in a limited number of cases, the provision of special equipment of an educational or physical nature for disabled children. In almost every case, the need for assistance arises through the premature death of the major wage earner, or the break up of the family unit. Applications are treated in strict confidence and the financial circumstances of each applicant are fully and carefully considered by the trustees before an award is made.'

Annual grant total: In 1999 grants to 47 children for education and relief-in-need purposes totalled £77,000.

Applications: In writing to the correspondent.

Correspondent: Ms G Mackie, 30 Princes Road, Gosforth, Newcastle upon Tyne NE3 5AL.

The Northern Ladies Annuity Society

Eligibility: Single or widowed ladies in need who live in the northern counties of England and who are incapacitated from work. At present only those over 60 years of age are considered for financial assistance as annuitants.

Types of grants: Recurrent grants paid quarterly to annuitants of the society. One-off grants are also given to annuitants for needs such as vests, outings and Christmas gifts and hampers. All annuitants also receive a birthday card.

Annual grant total: In 1999/2000 the trust had assets of £4.6 million, an income of £257,000 and a total expenditure of £199,000. Grants and annuities totalled £94,000, including £8,700 given in holiday grants.

Applications: Applications to become an annuitant should be made on a form available from the correspondent. Completed forms can be submitted directly by the individual and are considered monthly except for February and August.

Correspondent: Mrs Susan Chilton, Secretary/Treasurer, 178 Portland Road, Jesmond, Newcastle upon Tyne NE2 1DJ (0191 232 1518; Fax: 0191 221 0661).

The Sir John Priestman Charity Trust

Eligibility: Clergy and their families in need who live in the historic counties of Durham and York (especially the county borough of Sunderland).

Types of grants: One-off or recurrent grants according to need. Grants range from £50 to £1,000.

Annual grant total: In 2000 the trust had assets of £8.5 million, an income of £301,000 and a total expenditure of £328,000. Grants to three individuals for welfare purposes totalled £2,200. Grants to six individuals for educational purposes totalled £4,000. Grants to organisations totalled £289,000.

Applications: In writing to the correspondent. Applications are considered quarterly.

Correspondent: P W Taylor, McKenzie Bell, 19 John Street, Sunderland, Tyne & Wear SR1 1JG (0191 567 4857; Fax: 0191 510 9347; e-mail: mckbell@dial.pipex.com).

Other information: The trust also assists charities serving County Durham (especially the Sunderland area) and helps maintain Church of England churches and buildings in the above area.

The Edward Ramsden Charitable Trust

Eligibility: Individuals in North and West Yorkshire who are in need.

Types of grants: One-off or recurrent grants according to need.

Annual grant total: In 2000/01 the trust had an income of £27,000 and a total expenditure of £17,000.

Applications: The trust stated in March 2002 that it was currently fully committed and would be unlikely to be making grants in the foreseeable future.

Correspondent: Mrs P Talbot, 7 Grove Park Court, Harrogate, North Yorkshire HG1 4DP.

The Rycroft Children's Fund

See entry on page 202

The Teesside Emergency Relief Fund

Eligibility: People in need who live in the former county borough of Teesside.

Types of grants: One-off grants of between £100 to £1,000 to meet a specific need. No grants are made for: rates, taxes or other public funds; existing loans and debts; holidays and associated costs; non-essential electrical goods such as TVs, videos, stereos and telephones; or household goods which could have been preserved by correct prevention and intervention.

Annual grant total: In 2000/01 the trust had assets of £171,000 and an income of £19,000. Grants totalled £59,000. The trust had been greatly overspending and its assets had nearly halved in the preceding three years. No explanation of this was given in the accounts.

Applications: On a form available from the correspondent, which should be supported by a letter from a social worker, health visitor, welfare officer, GP, probation officer, local tenancy office, citizen's advice bureau or other welfare agency representative. Proof of household income should be supplied. The trust needs to know which shop the vouchers can be made payable to if there is no welfare organisation to administer the cheque. The trustees meet every three weeks.

Correspondent: Tanya Harrison, Law and Democracy, Stockton-on-Tees Borough Council, PO Box 11, Municipal Buildings, Church Road, Stockton-on-Tees TS18 1LD (01642 393070; Fax: 01642 393076).

Other information: This trust includes The Mayor of Teesside Clothing Fund.

The Speck Walker Annuity Fund

Eligibility: Spinsters and widows in need who are over the age of 25 and have lived in the parish of Stockton-on-Tees or in the North Riding of Yorkshire for the last 12 months.

Types of grants: Recurrent grants of £60 a quarter, reviewed annually.

Annual grant total: In 1999/2000 the trust had assets of £551,000 and an income of £55,000. Grants totalled £7,500. There was also £28,000 spent on property maintenance and administration.

Applications: On a form available from the correspondent. Applications should be sent directly by the individual and are usually considered in January, April, July and October

Correspondent: Mrs J A Smith, Archers Solicitors, Barton House, 24 Yarm Road, Stockton-on-Tees TS18 3NB (01642 673431; Fax: 01642 613602).

York Division Medical Association Charities Fund

Eligibility: Widows, orphans and dependants of medical practitioners who resided or practised in the area of the above division.

Types of grants: One-off and recurrent grants according to need.

Annual grant total: In 1999 the trust had an income and a total expenditure of £810.

Applications: In writing to the correspondent.

Correspondent: Dr A Sweeny, Secretary, 190 Tang Hall Lane, York YO1 3RL (01904 411139).

Yorkshire County Bowling Association Benevolent Fund

Eligibility: Bowlers and their dependants from Yorkshire County EBA Clubs who are in need.

Types of grants: Christmas grants of £70.

Annual grant total: In 1999 17 grants totalled £1,200.

Applications: On a form available from the correspondent submitted via club secretaries. Applications are usually considered in November.

Correspondent: B H Reeve, 163 New Village Road, Cottingham, East Yorkshire HU16 4ND (01482 848276).

Yorkshire Water Community Trust

Eligibility: People who are in arrears with Yorkshire Water and have one other priority debt. Council and housing association tenants whose water charges are included with their rent may also apply.

Types of grants: No cash grants are given. One-off payments are made to Yorkshire Water and credited to the applicant's account.

Annual grant total: In 2000/01 the trust had an income of £333,000, all of which was given in grants to 961 households.
Applications: On a form available from the correspondent. Although applications can be submitted directly by the individual or a friend or relative, the trust prefers them to be submitted by a social worker, citizen's advice bureau or other welfare agency. Succesful applicants may not reapply within two years.
Correspondent: John P Cox, Trust Officer, Freepost BD3074, PO Box 405, Bradford BD3 7BR (0845 124 2426; Fax: 01274 262283; e-mail: john.cox@loop.co.uk).

County Durham

The Ferryhill Station, Mainsforth & Bishop Middleham Aid-in-Sickness Charity

Eligibility: People who are sick and in need and live in the parishes of Ferryhill Station, Mainsforth and Bishop Middleham.
Types of grants: One-off grants of £250 to £1,000 towards medical care and equipment, holidays for people who are disabled and their carers and for special needs arising from disability or illness.
Annual grant total: In 2001/02 the charity had assets of £57,000 and an income of £1,800. Grants to four individuals totalled £3,500.
Applications: In writing to the correspondent, either directly by the individual or via a third party such as a district nurse, social worker, citizen's advice bureau or other welfare agency. Applications are considered within six to eight weeks, usually as they are received.
Correspondent: Mrs Gladys Courtney, Nevilla, Mainsforth Village, Ferryhill, County Durham DL17 9AA.

The Hamsterley Poors' Land Charity

Eligibility: People in need who live in Hamsterley, South Bedburn, Lynesack and Softley.
Types of grants: Recurrents gifts of £30, usually made at Christmas.
Annual grant total: In 2001 33 grants totalled £990.
Applications: Applications by word of mouth (or in writing) to: J E Brown-Humes, Prospect House, Hamsterley, Bishop Auckland DL13 3PZ; or J P Chatsworth, West Rackwood Hill Farm, Hamsterley, Bishop Auckland DL13. Applications are considered in June or December.
Correspondent: Mrs A Layfield, Secretary, New Row Farm, Hamsterley, Bishop Auckland, Co. Durham DL13 3QX (01388 488358).

The Ropner Centenary Trust

Eligibility: People in need who are associated with seafaring and shipping and live in County Durham.
Types of grants: Recurrent grants according to need.
Annual grant total: In 1999/2000 the trust had an income of £29,000 and gave grants totalling £26,000 of which £20,000 went to individuals and £6,000 to organisations.
Applications: In writing to the correspondent.
Correspondent: Paul Scott, Company Secretary, 6 Stratton Street, London W1J 8LD (020 7408 0123).

The Sedgefield District Relief-in-Need Charity

Eligibility: People in need who live in the parishes of Bishop Middleham, Bradbury, Fishburn, Mordon, Sedgefield and Trimdon in County Durham.
Types of grants: Grants are one-off and have recently been given towards medical needs, disability equipment such as scooters, a stair lift, a tumble dryer, disability access, cooking instruction and educational bursaries to people aged over 25.
Annual grant total: In 2001 the charity had an income of £25,000 and a total expenditure of £27,000. Grants to 10 individuals totalled £4,500. Grants to organisations totalled £19,000.
Applications: On a form available from the correspondent, or in writing. Applications can be submitted directly by the individual or through a social worker, citizen's advice bureau, welfare agency or other third party such as a carer or relative. They are considered as they arise.
Correspondent: R Smeeton, Clerk, 13 North Park Road, Sedgefield, County Durham, TS21 2AP (01740 620009).
Other information: This charity was created by the amalgamation of The Sedgefield & District Relief-in-Need Charity, Thomas Cooper's Charity, The Sedgefield Poor Fund and Bishop Middleham Relief in Need Charities.

Darlington

The Thomas Metcalfe Barron Charity

Eligibility: Communicant members of the Church of England who have lived in the borough of Darlington for at least five years.
Types of grants: Christmas gifts of £35.
Annual grant total: In 2002 grants to 14 individuals totalled £490.
Applications: In writing to the correspondent through the relevant Church of England vicar in the area. Applications are considered in October for payment in December.
Correspondent: Joan Curran, Darlington Borough Council, Feethams, Darlington, County Durham DL1 5QT (01325 388323).

Hartlepool

Anglian Water Trust Fund

See entry on page 105

The Furness Seamen's Pension Fund

Eligibility: Seamen in need who are 50 or over and live in the borough of Hartlepool or the former county borough of West Hartlepool, or who had their permanent residence there during their sea service. All applicants must have served as deep-seamen for at least 15 years and with some part of the sea service in vessels registered in Hartlepool, West Hartlepool or the Port of Hartlepool, or vessels trading to/from any of these ports.
Types of grants: Regular allowances only.
Annual grant total: About £10,000 to about 50 pensioners.
Applications: On a form available from the correspondent. Advertisements are placed in the Hartlepool Mail when vacancies are available.
Correspondent: D N Williams, Secretary, c/o Horwatch Clark Whitehill, 40 Victoria Road, Hartlepool, Cleveland TS26 8DD (01429 234414; Fax: 01429 231263).

Middleton

Ralph Gowland Trust

Eligibility: People in need aged 60 or over who live in the parish of Middleton in Teesdale.
Types of grants: One-off and recurrent grants according to need.
Annual grant total: In 2000/01 the trust had an income of £1,700 and its total expenditure was £530.
Applications: In writing to the correspondent.
Correspondent: Ronald Corner, The Holt, 6 North Field, Barnard Castle, County Durham DL12 8HX (01833 637869).

East Yorkshire

The Joseph & Annie Cattle Trust

Eligibility: Primarily people who live in the Hull area and are in need. Preference is given to people who are older, disabled or disadvantaged, particularly children who are dyslexic.

Types of grants: One-off and recurrent grants according to need.

Annual grant total: In 1998/99 it had assets of £7.4 million and an income of £396,000. Grants to individuals totalled £61,000 whilst £237,000 was given to organisations.

Applications: In writing to the correspondent, only via a welfare organisation, for consideration on the third Monday of every month. Please note, if applicants approach the trust directly they will be referred to an organisation, such as Disability Rights Advisory Service, or social services.

Correspondent: Roger Waudby, Administrator, Morpeth House, 114 Spring Bank, Hull HU3 1QJ (Tel & Fax: 01482 211198).

The Hesslewood Children's Trust (Hull Seamen's & General Orphanage)

Eligibility: People under 25 and in need who are native to, or have family connections with, the former county of Humberside and North Lincolnshire. Students who have come to the area to study are not eligible.

Types of grants: One-off and recurrent grants according to need. Grants have been given for specified short periods of time at special schools, holiday funding for individuals and youth organisations in the UK and overseas, and for musical instruments and special equipment for children who are disabled.

Annual grant total: In 2000 the trust had assets of £1.6 million and an income of £70,000. Grants totalled £92,000, mostly to organisations.

Applications: On a form available from the correspondent. Applications can be made either directly by the individual or through the individual's school/college/welfare agency or another third party on their behalf. Applicants must give their own or their parental financial details, the grant required, and why parents cannot provide the money. If possible, a contact telephone number should be quoted. Applications must be accompanied by a letter from the tutor or an educational welfare officer (or from medical and social services for a disability grant). The deadlines are 16 February, 16 June and 16 September.

Correspondent: R E Booth, Secretary, 66 The Meadows, Cherry Barton, Beverley, East Yorkshire HU17 7SP.

The Hull Aid in Sickness Trust

Eligibility: People in need, on a low income, live in the city and county of Kingston-upon-Hull and are sick, disabled, infirm or convalescent.

Types of grants: One-off and recurrent grants, to a usual maximum of £500, to aid and improve quality of life. No grants are given towards debts or where funds are available from public funds.

Annual grant total: In 2000/01 the trust had an income of £32,000 and a total expenditure of £23,000. Grants to 82 individuals totalled £18,000.

Applications: On a form available from the correspondent, to be submitted directly by the individual or through a social worker, citizen's advice bureau, other welfare agency or other third party. Applications are considered in February, May, August and November.

Correspondent: Gerard A Conlin, 18 Oaklands Drive, Willerby, Hull HU10 6BJ (01482 656111; e-mail: haist@conlin.karoo.co.uk).

Humberside Police Welfare and Benevolent Fund

Eligibility: Serving and retired officers of the Humberside Police and retired officers from other forces who live in Humberside, and their partners and dependants; and civilian employees of Humberside Police Authority, retired civilian employees and their partners and dependants.

Types of grants: One-off and recurrent grants of up to £500.

Annual grant total: In 2000 the trust had assets of £171,000, an income of £32,00 and a total expenditure of £22,000. Grants totalled £6,100. £11,000 was spent on holiday home rent and £3,500 on welfare visits.

Applications: In writing to the correspondent at any time, through either the branch/divisional representative or the headquarters.

Correspondent: Graham Fisher, Humberside Police, Occupational Health and Welfare Section, 30 Derringham Street, Hull HU3 1EP (01482 220957/220994).

The Nafferton Feoffee Charity Trust

Eligibility: People in need who live in the parish of All Saints Nafferton with St Mary's Wansford.

Types of grants: One-off grants of £100 to £250 to help individuals and families travel to visit relatives in hospital, as Christmas and heating gifts to older people and in the form of food vouchers. Bursaries are also given to students for educational trips overseas.

Annual grant total: In 2001 the trust had assets of £8,500, an income of £6,900 and a total expenditure of £5,500. One grant, of £100, was given to an individual. Grants to organisations totalled £4,300.

Applications: In writing to the correspondent at any time, directly by the individual.

Correspondent: Mrs M A Buckton, South Cattleholmes, Wansford, Driffield, East Yorkshire YO25 8NW (01377 254293).

Ethel Maude Townend Charity

Eligibility: People in need who live in Hull and the East Riding of Yorkshire. Applicants should have been in the medical, nursing or legal professions or have been ministers of religion, accountants or architects, or members of other professions generally. Their widows can also be supported.

Types of grants: Usually weekly payments plus a Christmas bonus. Also one-off grants e.g. to pay a registration fee to enable a nurse to take up employment, to pay an outstanding telephone account, to buy a top loading washer for a nurse with a back injury, to pay for roof repairs, to buy a bed to meet a nurse's medical needs, to buy a TNS machine and towards the cost of replacing defective windows in a flat.

No grants for educational purposes.

Annual grant total: In 1998/99 the trust had an income of £9,100 and a total expenditure of £16,000.

Applications: On a form available from the correspondent following an advertisement. Applications can be submitted directly by the individual or through a social worker, citizen's advice bureau, doctor or other welfare agency. Applications are usually considered in March, July and November.

Correspondent: Stephen Walker, Gosschalks, 61 Queens Gardens, Hull HU1 3DZ (01482 324252).

Robert Towries Charity

Eligibility: People in need who live in Aldbrough, East Newton and West Newton.

Types of grants: One-off and recurrent grants for food, fuel and education.

Annual grant total: In 2001/02 the trust had assets of £30,000, an income of £6,100 and a total expenditure of £12,000. About £6,500 has been given in the past.

Applications: In writing to the correspondent. Applications should be submitted directly by the individual for consideration in November.

NORTH EAST – EAST YORKSHIRE

Correspondent: Mrs P M Auty, 6 Willow Grove, Headlands Park, Aldbrough, Hull HU11 4SH (Tel & Fax: 01964 527553).

Aldbrough

Aldbrough Poor Fields

Eligibility: People aged over 65 and widows who are in need and live in Aldbrough village.

Types of grants: Grants are given towards food and fuel.

Annual grant total: In 2001/02 the trust had assets of £2,700 and an income of £280. Total expenditure was £830 including £460 given in grants.

Applications: In writing to the correspondent for consideration in November.

Correspondent: Mrs P M Auty, 6 Willow Grove, Headlands Park, Aldbrough, East Yorkshire HU11 4SH
(Tel & Fax: 01964 527553).

Barmby on the Marsh

Garlthorpes Charity

Eligibility: People in need who live in the parish of Barmby on the Marsh.

Types of grants: One-off grants only.

Annual grant total: About £3,500.

Applications: In writing to the correspondent, submitted by the individual for consideration in July or December.

Correspondent: Roger Beattie, Clerk, 1 Vicar Lane, Howden, East Yorkshire DN14 7BP (01430 430209; Fax: 01430 432101).

Bridlington

The Bridlington Charities

Eligibility: People in need who live in the parish of Bridlington and Bridlington Quay.

Types of grants: Recurrent grants ranging up to £130 per year, for purchase of fuel (gas, coal, electricity). Payment is made direct to the suppliers. One-off grants towards school clothing can also be made. No loans or grants for meals or paid help.

Annual grant total: In 2000 the trust had an income of £17,000 and gave £37,000 in grants to individuals and £2,900 in grants to seven organisations.

Applications: In writing to the correspondent, usually for consideration in February, May, August and November. Applications can be submitted through a social worker, citizen's advice bureau or other welfare agency. The charity's field officers visit the applicants and report to the trustees in writing.

Correspondent: C E Leatham, Clerk Treasurer, 28 Eight Avenue, Bridlington YO15 2NA (01262 602644).

Kingston-upon-Hull

Hull Fisherman's Trust Fund

Eligibility: Widows, children and dependent relatives of:
1. deceased fishermen who sailed on a Hull fishing vessel, or
2. disabled fishermen who served on a Hull fishing vessel.

Types of grants: Regular weekly allowances only.

Annual grant total: In 2000 the trust had assets of £2.7 million and an income of £194,000. A total of £180,000 was given in 431 grants to individuals, of which 422 were given to widows and 7 to other dependent relatives and 2 to people who are disabled.

Applications: In writing to the correspondent.

Correspondent: R Brookes, Secretary, J Marr Ltd, St Andrews Dock, Hull HU3 4PN (01482 327873).

The Charity of Miss Eliza Clubley Middleton

Eligibility: Poor women of the Catholic faith who have lived in the Hull area for over 10 years.

Types of grants: Grants are distributed twice a year, at Christmas and in the summer.

Annual grant total: In 2000/01 the trust had assets of £350,000 and an income of £15,000. Grants totalled £14,000.

Applications: A list of current beneficiaries is circulated to all local priests each year. They then recommend any additions or note changes in circumstances.

Correspondent: Mr D M Scanlan, Rollits, Wilberforce Court, High Street, Hull HU1 1YJ (01482 323239; Fax: 01482 326239).

The 'Mother Humber' Memorial Fund

Eligibility: People in need who live in the city of Kingston upon Hull.

Types of grants: One-off grants ranging from £12 to £2,000.

No grants are made for: educational appeals and sponsorship e.g. of Duke of Edinburgh Award students; the payment of debts; the payment of wages or administration expenses.

Most of the larger grants are given to organisations.

Annual grant total: In 2000/01 the trust had assets totalling £442,000, an income of £29,000 and made grants totalling £30,000, about £18,000 of which was given to individuals.

Applications: On a form available from the correspondent, submitted through a social worker, citizen's advice bureau or other welfare agency.

Correspondent: Malcom Welford, Secretary, 7 Wright Street, Hull HU2 8HU (01482 328097).

National Amalgamated Stevedores & Dockers Union Building & Benevolent Fund

Eligibility: Retired (over 65) former members of the National Amalgamated Stevedores and Dockers Union, operating in Hull. On reaching the age of 65 all NASDU members are automatically entitled to a grant.

Types of grants: Grants of £400 each are paid in December.

Annual grant total: In 2001 grants totalled £8,000.

Applications: In writing to the correspondent, for consideration in December.

Correspondent: A D Atkinson, 484 Great Thornton Street, Anlaby Road, Hull HU3 2LU.

The Joseph Rank Benevolent Fund

Eligibility: Men aged 65 or over and women aged 60 or over who are retired and have lived in Hull for at least 10 of the last 15 years.

Types of grants: Small monthly allowances. Priority is given to people on income support.

Annual grant total: In 2001 grants to individuals totalled £104,000. A further £5,500 was given to local organisations.

Applications: On a form available from the correspondent. Applications are considered throughout the year.

Correspondent: Mrs M Burman, Clerk to the Trustees, 1 The Pathway, Alfred Gelder Street, Hull HU1 1XJ (01482 225542).

The Wilmington Trust

Eligibility: People in need who live in Kingston-upon-Hull (east of the river Hull).

Types of grants: One-off grants ranging from £50 to £100 towards, for instance, clothing, holidays, emergencies, furniture, white goods and other household goods.

The trust will not give grants for the relief of rates, taxes or other public funds, but may apply income and property in supplementing relief or assistance provided out of public funds.

Annual grant total: In 2001 the trust had an income of £6,000 and a total expenditure of £7,000. Grants to 38 individuals totalled £3,100.

Applications: On a form available from the correspondent. Applications must be made through a citizen's advice bureau or member of the clergy. The trustees meet twice a year to consider grants, although decisions can be made between meetings.

Correspondent: Miss S Outram, Clerk, The Church Room, 25 Church Street, Sutton-on-Hull, East Yorkshire HU7 4TL (01482 472899).

Newton on Derwent

Newton on Derwent Charity

Eligibility: People who are sick or elderly who live in the parish of Newton on Derwent.

Types of grants: One-off grants according to need.

Annual grant total: In 2000 the trust had assets of £30,000 and an income of £11,000. Welfare grants totalled £3,100. Educational grants totalled £5,100.

Applications: In writing to the correspondent.

Correspondent: The Clerk to the Charity, Messrs Grays, Duncombe Place, York YO1 7DY (01904 634771).

Ottringham

The Ottringham Church Lands Charity

Eligibility: People in hardship and/or distress who live in the parish of Ottringham.

Types of grants: Normally one-off grants, but recurrent grants may be considered. No grants are given which would affect the applicant's state benefits.

Annual grant total: In 2001/02 the trust had assets of £34,000 and an income of £4,900. Grants to 12 individuals totalled £4,400.

Applications: In writing to the correspondent at any time.

Correspondent: J R Hinchliffe, 'Hallgarth', Station Road, Ottringham, East Yorkshire HU12 0BJ (01964 622230).

Walkington

Sherwood and Waudby Charity

Eligibility: People of any age who are in need, due for example to hardship, disability or sickness and living in the parish of Walkington only.

Types of grants: One-off grants ranging between £200 and £500 towards items, services or facilities calculated to alleviate need.

Annual grant total: In 2000 the charity had an income of £39,000 and gave 18 grants to individuals and organisations totalling £5,600.

Applications: In writing to the correspondent for consideration in November.

Correspondent: Mrs Sue Sugars, 11 Waudby Close, Walkington, Beverley HU17 8SA (01482 861056).

North Yorkshire

The Aldborough, Boroughbridge & District Relief-in-Sickness Fund

Eligibility: People who are sick, mentally/physically disabled or infirm and live in the parishes of Aldborough, Boroughbridge, Dunsforth, Kirkby Hill, Langthorpe, Minskip, Skelton and Roecliffe. No other applicants can be considered.

Types of grants: One-off grants in kind (e.g. beds, pillows, coal and so on) and discretionary cash grants for approved purposes. Maximum grant is £200.

Annual grant total: In 2001 the trust had an income of £450 and gave £500 in grants.

Applications: Applications should be in writing and can be submitted by the individual or through a recognised referral agency (social worker, citizen's advice bureau or doctor etc.) Applications are considered when brought to notice.

Correspondent: Revd P Smith, The Vicarage, Church Lane, Boroughbridge, York YO51 9BA.

Bedale Welfare Charity

Eligibility: People who are elderly and/or infirm and/or in need who live in the parishes of Aiskew, Bedale, Burrill, Cowling, Crakehall, Firby and Leeming Bar.

Types of grants: One-off grants usually ranging from £20 to £500.

Annual grant total: In 2000/01 the trust had assets of £350,000 and an income of £13,000. Grants totalled £12,000.

Applications: On a form available from the correspondent, to be submitted at any time either directly by the individual or through a social worker, citizen's advice bureau or other welfare agency.

Correspondent: P J Hirst, 9 Hird Avenue, Bedale, North Yorkshire DL8 2UE (Tel & Fax: 01677 423376; e-mail: curlyhirst@aol.com).

Broughton, Kirkby & District Good Samaritan Fund

Eligibility: People who are over 65 years of age or infirm and resident in the parishes of Kirkby and Ingleby Greenhow.

Types of grants: A simple Christmas present and visit.

Annual grant total: In 2000 the trust had an income of £4,300 and a total expenditure of £4,600.

Applications: In writing to the correspondent.

Correspondent: R Cooper, Hon. Secretary, Roseworth House, Great Broughton, Middlesbrough, Cleveland TS9 7EN.

Other information: This entry was not confirmed by the trust, but the address was correct according to the Charity Commission database.

The Gargrave Poor's Land Charity

Eligibility: People in need who live in Gargrave, Banknewton, Coniston Cold, Flasby or Eshton.

Types of grants: One-off and recurrent grants and loans for specific items such as school uniforms, rent arrears, council tax, travel to hospital, household equipment, furniture, debt settlement, respite care, electrical goods and essential repairs.

Annual grant total: In 2000/01 the trust had assets of £345,000, an income of £25,000 and a total expenditure of £23,000.

Applications: On a form available from the correspondent. Applications can be submitted at any time.

Correspondent: Mrs B M Wood, 9 Meadow Croft, Gargrave, Skipton, North Yorkshire BD23 3SN (01756 749466).

The Goldsborough Poor's Charity

Eligibility: People over 70 who live, or used to live, in Goldsborough, Flaxby or Coneythorpe. Most of the recipients are widows and widowers.

Types of grants: Recurrent grants usually of £60 (and up to £120) to supplement pensions or low incomes. Distribution takes place half-yearly, in June and December.

Annual grant total: In 1999 the trust had assets of £32,000 producing an income of £1,700. Grants to 15 individuals totalled about £1,500.

Applications: In writing to the correspondent. Applications can be submitted either directly by the individual, through a social worker, citizen's advice bureau, other welfare agency or other third party such as a friend or relative. Applications are considered in May and November.

North East – North Yorkshire

Correspondent: J L Clarkson, 25 Princess Mead, Goldsborough, Knaresborough, North Yorkshire HG5 8NP (01423 865102).

Harrogate Good Samaritan Fund

Eligibility: People in need aged 55 or over who live within a 10-mile radius of Harrogate and are members of a Protestant church.

Types of grants: One-off grants towards e.g. hospital visits, holidays, telephone installations for housebound people and winter heating. Quarterly grants as agreed and reviewed at each trustees meeting.

Annual grant total: In 2000 the trust had an income of £11,000 and a total expenditure of £10,000.

Applications: On a form available from and submitted through the correspondent or through the minister of the relevant local church. Trustees meet quarterly.

Correspondent: J Ward, The Quoin, 3a Wheatlands Road East, Harrogate, North Yorkshire HG2 8PX (01423 884567).

Reverend Matthew Hutchinson Trust (Gilling and Richmond)

Eligibility: People who live in the parishes of Gilling or Richmond.

Types of grants: Recent grants have been given towards medical care, telephone rental, a violin, running shoes, students at college and university and children's nursery fees.

Annual grant total: In 2001 the combined trusts had assets of £28,000, an income of £14,000 and a total expenditure of £10,000. Grants totalled £3,800.

Applications: In writing to the correspondent before March or November. Applications can be submitted directly by the individual or through a trustee, social worker, citizen's advice bureau or other welfare agency.

Correspondent: Mrs E Williams, 21 Eastfield Avenue, Richmond, North Yorkshire DL10 4NH (01748 822831).

Other information: The Gilling and Richmond branches of this charity are administrated jointly, but with separate funding.

Grants are also made to local schools and hospitals.

The Purey Cust Fund

Eligibility: People with medical needs who live in York and the surrounding area.

Types of grants: One-off grants ranging between £50 and £1,000, for healthcare equipment, specialist medical equipment and medical education.

Annual grant total: In 1999/2000 the trust had assets of £31,000 and an income of £88,000. 21 grants to individuals and organisations totalled £11,000.

Applications: Applications must show evidence of the medical need and can be submitted directly by the individual or through a social worker, citizen's advice bureau, other welfare agency or third party. They are considered throughout the year.

Correspondent: The Secretary, 9 Muncastergate, York YO31 9JX (01904 422995; e-mail: pureycusttrust@hotmail.com).

The Rowlandson & Eggleston Relief-in-Need Charity

Eligibility: People in the parishes of Barton and Newton Morrell who are in need.

Types of grants: The trust provides the aid-call facility to older people. One-off grants are also given towards funeral, medical, sickness or disability costs.

Annual grant total: In 2000/01 the trust had assets of £80,000 and both an income and a total expenditure of £3,200. Grants to 17 people totalled £1,400.

Applications: In writing to the correspondent, for consideration throughout the year. Applications may be submitted directly by the individual, through a social worker, citizen's advice bureau or other welfare agency or any third party.

Correspondent: P E R Vaux, Chair, Brettanby Manor, Barton, Richmond, North Yorkshire DL10 6HD (01325 377233; Fax: 01325 377647).

The York Dispensary Charitable Trust

Eligibility: People experiencing poverty and ill health who live in York and surrounding districts.

Types of grants: Usually one-off grants for specific needs such as clothing, domestic equipment or holidays.

Annual grant total: In 2001 the fund had assets of £475,000, an income of £18,000 and a total expenditure of £16,000. Grants to about 100 people totalled £14,000.

Applications: In writing to the correspondent, preferably through social services or a similar welfare agency, though direct application is possible. Applications are considered regularly.

Correspondent: R W Miers, Secretary, 1 St Saviourgate, York YO1 8ZQ (01904 558600).

Carperby-cum-Thoresby

The Carperby Poor's Land Charity

Eligibility: People in need who live in the parish of Carperby-cum-Thoresby.

Types of grants: Quarterly grants of £21 to £54.

Annual grant total: In 2001 the trust had assets of £28,000 and an income of £1,400, all of which was given in 10 grants to individuals.

Applications: In writing to the correspondent, with details of the financial need. Applications are considered in January, April, July and October.

Correspondent: E R D Johnson, Messrs Johnsons Solicitors, Market Place, Hawes, North Yorkshire DL8 3QS (01969 667000; Fax: 01969 667888; e-mail: johnsons.hawes@dial.pipex.com).

Danby

The Joseph Ford's Trust

Eligibility: People who live within the original parish of Danby and are blind, aged or in poverty or misfortune.

Types of grants: One-off or recurrent grants according to need.

Annual grant total: About £1,800.

Applications: In writing to the correspondent or any other trustee, at any time.

Correspondent: David Bryan Hesletine, 25 Riverslea, Stokesley, Middlesbrough, Cleveland TS9 5DE (01642 711289).

Knaresborough

The Knaresborough Relief-in-Need Charity

Eligibility: People in need who live in the parish of Knaresborough, with a preference for people who have lived there for at least five years.

Types of grants: About 40 one-off grants ranging from £18 to £1,000 towards items such as a cooker and television licence. Also about 300 Christmas grants of £25.

Annual grant total: In 1999 the trust had assets of £370,000 and an income of £20,000. Grants to individuals totalled £7,100. Grants to 12 organisations totalled £14,000.

Applications: In writing to the correspondent.

Correspondent: Mike Dixon, Administrator, 9 Netheredge Drive, Knaresborough, North Yorkshire HG5 9DA (01423 863378).

Lothersdale

Raygill Trust

Eligibility: Older people who live in the ecclesiastical parish of Lothersdale.

Types of grants: One-off grants are made according to need.

Annual grant total: In 1999/2000 the trust had assets of £112,000 and an income of £24,000. Grants to individuals for welfare purposes totalled £3,200. Educational grants to individuals totalled £3,900. Grants to four organisations totalled £250.

Applications: In writing to the correspondent. Applications can be submitted directly by the individual and are considered in March, June, September and December.

Correspondent: Roger Armstrong, Secretary, Gordons Cranswick, 6-14 Devonshire Street, Keighley, West Yorkshire BD21 2AY (01535 218333; Fax: 01535 609748; e-mail: roger.armstrong@gordonscranswick.co.uk).

Middlesbrough

The Lady Crosthwaite Bequest Fund

Eligibility: Pensioners in need who live in the former county borough of Middlesbrough.

Types of grants: Small grants at Christmas, and occasional day trips, via the social services and community councils, together with one-off lump sums to organisations.

Annual grant total: In 1998/99 the fund had an income of £6,000 and gave no grants due to a lack of applications.

Applications: In writing to the correspondent, through social services.

Correspondent: Mark Taylor, Middlesbrough Council, Pensions Section, PO Box 340, Middlesbrough TS1 2XP (01642 262924; Fax: 01642 262947).

Northallerton

The Grace Gardner Trust

Eligibility: Senior citizens who live within the boundary of Northallerton parish.

Types of grants: One-off and recurrent grants according to need. The trust makes contributions towards various activities such as providing transport to the library once a fortnight and supporting a Christmas Carol Concert. It also subsidises payments for garden refuse bags, swimming, shopping trips and summer outings.

Annual grant total: About £6,000 is available each year.

Applications: Applications in writing can be submitted by the individual or through a recognised referral agency (e.g. social worker, citizen's advice bureau or doctor) at any time.

Correspondent: Mrs Kay Batterbee, c/o Town Hall, High Street, Northallerton, North Yorkshire DL7 8QR (01609 770735).

Other information: Grants can also be made to organisations working with older people in the parish.

Redcar and Cleveland

Anchor Aid

Eligibility: People who are elderly or disabled in Guisborough, Redcar and East Cleveland.

Types of grants: One-off and recurrent grants and Christmas hampers are given.

Annual grant total: In 1998/99 the trust had an income of £12,000 and an expenditure of £8,000. Grants to individuals and organisations totalled £2,900. Christmas hampers were also given totalling £450.

Applications: In writing to the correspondent.

Correspondent: Adrian Horner, Trustee, Anchor Inn, Belmangate, Guisborough, Cleveland TS14 7AB (01287 632715; e-mail: enquiries@anchoraid.co.uk; website: www.anchoraid.co.uk).

Other information: This entry was not confirmed by the trust, but the information was checked against the trust's website.

Scarborough

The John Kendall Trust

Eligibility: Children under 18 who live in Scarborough and who are orphaned, from single-parent families or whose parents receive income support.

Types of grants: Grants of £300 towards clothing and education.

Annual grant total: In 1999 the trust had an income of £16,000. Grants to six individuals totalled £1,700. Grants to four organisations totalled £5,000.

Applications: In writing to the correspondent for consideration in January, May and September.

Correspondent: Harold R Bedford, 76 Scalby Road, Scarborough, North Yorkshire YO12 5QN (01723 375212).

The Scarborough District Nursing Trust

Eligibility: People in need who are sick and/or convalescent and live in the borough of Scarborough.

Types of grants: One-off grants for £200 to £300 to relieve ill health, viewed as broadly as possible.

Annual grant total: In 2001/02 the trust had assets of £61,000, an income of £2,400 and a total expenditure of £850. Grants to three individuals totalled £600.

Applications: In writing to the correspondent, stating the amount needed, the purpose for the grant and the cost if known. The trustees meet in May and November to discuss grant applications, although urgent cases can be dealt with at other times.

Correspondent: Colin Barnes, Allatt House, 5 West Parade Road, Scarborough, North Yorkshire YO12 5ED (01723 362205; Fax: 01723 507570; e-mail: post@sdcvs.demon.co.uk).

The Scarborough Municipal Charities

Eligibility: People in need who are of retirement age and live in Scarborough.

Types of grants: Grants are one-off.

Annual grant total: Amount available varies each year.

Applications: In writing to the correspondent. Applications are considered quarterly.

Correspondent: W Temple, Accountant, 305a Scalby Road, Scarborough, North Yorkshire YO12 6TF (01723 362584).

St Margaret

The Robert Winterscale Charity

Eligibility: Older people who live in the ancient parish of St Margaret and are in need.

Types of grants: Pensions of £25, made twice a year.

Annual grant total: About £500.

Applications: In writing to the correspondent when vacancies arise, which are advertised within the parish.

Correspondent: Richard Watson, Crombie Wilkinson, 19 Clifford Street, York YO1 9RJ (01904 624 4185).

West Witton

The Smorthwaite Charity

Eligibility: Older people who live in West Witton. Applicants must be at least 70 if born in the parish or at least 75 if born elsewhere.

Types of grants: '£100 is given to any applicants who meet the criteria.'

Annual grant total: In 1998/99 the trust had an income of £10,000 and a total expenditure of £5,200.

Applications: The charity advertises in the local post office and on a telegraph pole. Most applications are submitted by word of mouth and through conversations with members of the trustees rather than through a formal application process.

Correspondent: Jeremy Guard, Bolton Dene, West Witton, Leyburn, North Yorkshire DL8 4LS.

York

The Micklegate Strays Charity

Eligibility: Freemen of the city of York and their dependants living in the Micklegate Strays ward. (This area is now defined as the whole of that part of the city of York to the west of the River Ouse.)

Types of grants: Pensions and medical grants of £30 a year.

Annual grant total: In 2001/02 the charity had assets of £21,000 and an income of £680. There were 20 welfare grants totalling £600 and 2 educational grants totalling £60.

Applications: On a form available from the correspondent. Applications should include the date of the freeman's oath and are considered in November.

Correspondent: Geoffrey Barraclough, 35 Queenswood Grove, Acomb, York YO24 4PN (01904 793533).

Other information: The trust was created by the 1907 Micklegate Strays Act. The city of York agreed to pay the freemen £1,000 a year in perpetuity for extinguishing their rights over Micklegate Stray. This sum has been reduced due to the forced divestment of the trust government stock, following the Charities Act of 1992.

The Charity of St Michael-le-Belfry

Eligibility: People in need who live in York, with priority for those living in the parish of St Michael-le-Belfry.

Types of grants: Grants range between £50 to £500 and take the form of quarterly pensions to older people and one-off payments to relieve special needs.

No grants for the purposes of education.

Annual grant total: In 2001 the trust had assets of £190,000 and an income of £8,800. Total expenditure was £7,700, including nine grants totalling £6,400.

Applications: On a form available from the correspondent, including evidence of financial circumstances. Applications can be submitted directly by the individual or through a social worker, citizen's advice bureau, other welfare agency or other third party.

Correspondent: C C Goodway, Clerk, Grays Solicitors, Duncombe Place, York YO1 7DY.

Other information: Grants are also given to organisations.

The Charity of Jane Wright

Eligibility: People in need who live in the city of York.

Types of grants: One-off and recurrent grants according to need.

Annual grant total: £26,000 in 2001.

Applications: Applications must be made directly or via recognised welfare agencies. They are considered within a few days.

Correspondent: P E Baines, Clerk, 18 St Saviourgate, York YO1 8NS (01904 655555).

York City Charities

Eligibility: People in need who live within the pre-1996 York city boundaries (the area within the city walls).

Types of grants: One-off grants of between £50 and £200. Recent grants have been given towards furniture and to people on probation to set up a new home.

Annual grant total: In 2002 welfare grants totalled £2,400 whilst educational grants to individuals totalled £2,000.

Applications: In writing to the correspondent, to be submitted by a doctor, occupational nurse, headteacher, social worker, citizen's advice bureau or other third party or welfare agency. Applications are considered throughout the year.

Correspondent: Mrs Carol Bell, 41 Avenue Road, Clifton, York YO30 6AY (Tel & Fax: 01904 645131; e-mail: carol@forthergil15.freeserve.co.uk).

The York Fund for Women & Girls

Eligibility: Women and girls younger than 50 years old, who live in York and who are in need.

Types of grants: Generally one-off grants, between £50 and £100, to help with essential household items and furnishings, baby equipment and children's clothes, and towards fuel bills.

No grants for education.

Annual grant total: In 2000/01 the trust had assets of £84,000 and an income of £3,300. Grants to 22 individuals totalled £1,700.

Applications: On a form available from the correspondent, only from recognised agencies on behalf of individuals. Applications should include details of the individual's income and are considered within a few days.

Correspondent: Colin Stroud, Clerk to the Trustees, c/o York Council for Voluntary Service, 15 Priory Street, York YO1 6ET (01904 621133; Fax: 01904 630361).

Northumberland

The Alnwick & District Relief-in-Sickness Fund

Eligibility: People who live in and around Alnwick who are sick, convalescing, disabled or infirm.

Types of grants: Grants of about £25 for gas, electricity and coal; food vouchers; help to buy new items such as mattress, children's fire guard and so on. Cash grants are rarely given.

Annual grant total: In 2001 the trust had assets of £10,000 and an income of £620. Grants to 19 individuals totalled £670.

Applications: By referral from a health visitor, doctor, social worker, nurse, minister etc. Direct applications are not encouraged. Applications are considered at any time.

Correspondent: Aileen B C White, 33 Swansfield Park Road, Alnwick, Northumberland NE66 1AT (01665 602718).

The Morpeth Dispensary

Eligibility: People who are sick or poor and live in or around Morpeth.

Types of grants: Grants are one-off and range from £40 to £400. Examples have included £300 for carpets to a 17 year old boy with learning difficulties who is living with his sister since the death of his mother; and £200 each to the family of an eight year old boy with a mental illness for decoration, the parents of a six-month old baby with a skin complaint for a washing machine, a single parent with mental health difficulties and a man with learning difficulties.

Annual grant total: In 2001 the trust had assets of £7,200 and an income of £2,200. Grants to 20 individuals totalled £2,400.

Applications: In writing to the correspondent through a social worker, GP, citizen's advice bureau or other welfare agency. Applications must include detail of the applicant's age, whether a single parent, whether on benefit, their address and any details regarding health matters. Money is not given directly to the applicant but through an agency such as social services.

Correspondent: M A Gaunt, 15 Bridge Street, Morpeth, Northumberland NE61 1NX (01670 512336; Fax: 01670 510471).

Berwick-upon-Tweed

The Berwick-upon-Tweed Nursing Amenities Fund

Eligibility: People who are sick, poor or in need and live in the borough of Berwick-upon-Tweed.

Types of grants: One-off grants according to need.

Annual grant total: In 2000/01 the trust had assets of £25,000 and an income of £860. Grants totalled £940.

Applications: In writing to the correspondent through a social worker, citizen's advice bureau or other welfare agency at any time.

Correspondent: A J Patterson, Greaves, West & Ayre, 1–3 Sandgate, Berwick-upon-Tweed TD15 1EW (01289 306688; Fax: 01289 307189; e-mail: ap@gwayre.co.uk).

East Chevington

The East Chevington Mining Community Aged & Sick Persons Fund

Eligibility: People in need in the parish of East Chevington who worked in the coal mining industry and have not found other employment.

Types of grants: One-off grants are given to people for hospital visits, either for treatment or to visit a patient who is in hospital for a reasonable time. Grants usually range from £30 to £60.

Annual grant total: In 2001 the fund had assets of £70,000 and an income of £2,000. Grants to 13 individuals totalled £780.

Applications: In writing to the correspondent or any of the trustees either directly by the individual or via a relative. Applications are considered throughout the year.

Correspondent: Mark Coleran, 22 Chibburn Avenue, Hadston Estate, South Broomhil, Morpeth, Northumberland NE65 9SS (01670 760351).

Morpeth

The Mary Hollon Annuity & Relief-in-Need Fund

Eligibility: People over 60 who have lived in the town of Morpeth (including Buller's Green) for the last 15 years and who are in need.

Types of grants: Quarterly annuities of £2.50 and an allowance of £30 in December in lieu of meat and coal. The trust also provides a liberal meat tea on 5 November each year, the anniversary of Mr and Mrs Hollon's wedding.

Annual grant total: In 2000/01 it had assets of £58,000, and income of £6,000 and a total expenditure of £4,400. Grants to 98 individuals totalled £3,400.

Applications: On a form available from the correspondent. Applications are invited by public advertisement, usually two or three times a year.

Correspondent: R Slater, Castle Morpeth Borough Council, Financial Services Unit, Council Offices, The Kylins, Loansdean, Morpeth, Northumberland NE61 2EQ (01670 514351; Fax: 01670 510348; e-mail: rslater@castlemorpeth.gov.uk; website: www.castlemorpeth.gov.uk).

Wansbeck

The Wansbeck Appeal Fund Trust

Eligibility: People in need who live in the administrative area of Wansbeck District Council. There is a preference for people who are disabled, elderly or sick, and for the relief of hardship.

Types of grants: Grants of up to £200 for almost any need.

Annual grant total: No grants were given during 1999 due to the trust receiving no eligible applications.

Applications: In writing to the correspondent, wither directly by the individual or through a social worker, citizen's advice bureau or other welfare agency. Applications can be considered at any time.

Correspondent: Caroline Foster, Wansbeck District Council, Town Hall, Ashington, Northumberland NE63 8RX (01670 532292 Fax: 01670 520136).

South Yorkshire

The Brampton Bierlow Welfare Trust

Eligibility: People in need who live in Brampton Bierlow and West Melton, and those parts of Wentworth and Elscar within the ancient parish of Brampton Bierlow.

Types of grants: One-off grants from £100 to £250 for necessities and comforts and Christmas grocery vouchers of £6.

Annual grant total: In 2000 the trust had an income of £8,000 and a total expenditure of £4,100.

Applications: Applications in writing to the correspondent can be submitted by the individual and are considered at any time.

Correspondent: Jill Leece, Newman & Bond, 35 Church Street, Barnsley S70 2AP (01226 213434; Fax: 01226 213435).

The Cooper & Lancaster Annuities

Eligibility: Women in need who live in Barnsley, Worsborough Dale and Worsborough Bridge (i.e. the Barnsley District).

Types of grants: Recurrent grants of £72 per year, paid quarterly.

Annual grant total: No information was available.

Applications: In writing to the correspondent.

Correspondent: Mrs Jill Leece, Messrs Newman & Bond, Solicitors, 35 Church Street, Barnsley S70 2AP (01226 289336).

The Fisher Institution

Eligibility: Unitarian and Roman Catholic widows and spinsters over 45 living in and around Sheffield who are in need.

Types of grants: Regular yearly allowances of £90 to £125 to supplement low incomes.

Annual grant total: In 2001 the trust had assets of £2,200 and an income of £1,200. Grants to 10 individuals totalled £1,300.

Applications: On a form available from the correspondent, to be submitted via the applicant's minister. The trustees meet in April and forms should be submitted before the end of March.

Correspondent: Mrs K Woodhouse, 22 Brooklands Crescent, Sheffield S10 4GE (0114 230 3027).

The George & Clara Ann Hall Charity

Eligibility: Widows and unmarried women over 45 who have lived in the city of Sheffield or the township and chapelry of Bradfield for the past five years and are in need.

Types of grants: Annuities of £400 a year.

Annual grant total: About £2,300 each year.

Applications: In writing to the correspondent. Applications are considered bi-monthly.

Correspondent: Nick Warren, Director, c/o Voluntary Action Sheffield, 69 Division Street, Sheffield S1 4GE (0114 249 3360 ext. 128; Fax: 0114 249 3361; e-mail: nick@vas.org.uk).

The Jeffcock Memorial Aid In Sickness Trust

Eligibility: People in need who are sick and live in Ecclesfield and neighbourhood.

Types of grants: One-off grants have been given to people who are bedridden for beds, kimodes and bedpans.

North East – South Yorkshire

Annual grant total: In 2001 the trust had an income of £4,000, all of which was given in grants.

Applications: In writing to the correspondent. Applications are considered each month.

Correspondent: David D Banham, 6 Priory Close, Ecclesfield, Sheffield S35 9TS (0114 246 0194; e-mail: juliebanham@gattyland.freeserve.co.uk).

Rebecca Guest Robinson Charity

Eligibility: People who live in the villages of Birdwell and Worsbrough, near Barnsley, and are in need. Preference is given to children, young people and older people.

Types of grants: One-off grants, usually ranging between £50 and £100, towards clothing, household equipment, disabled persons' equipment, holidays and childcare. Grants are also made for educational purposes.

Annual grant total: In 1998/99 the trust's assets totalled £48,000, it had an income of £1,600 and made seven grants totalling £950.

Applications: On a form available from the correspondent. Applications are usually considered in January and November and should be submitted either directly by the individual or by any local caring institution.

Correspondent: John Armitage, 10 St Marys Gardens, Worsbrough, Barnsley, South Yorkshire S70 5LU (01226 290179).

Other information: Local organisations are also supported.

The Sheffield West Riding Charitable Society Trust

Eligibility: Clergymen of the Church of England in the diocese of Sheffield who are in need. Also their widows, orphans or distressed families, and people keeping house, or who have kept house, for clergymen of the Church of England in the diocese or their families.

Types of grants: One-off and recurrent grants according to need.

Annual grant total: In 2001 the trust had assets of £234,000 and an income of £9,800. Grants totalling £9,000 were given to individuals, of which retired clergy received £4,800, stipendiary clergy received £3,700 and the widows of clergy received £500.

Applications: In writing to the correspondent.

Correspondent: C A Beck, Secretary and Treasurer, Diocesan Church House, 95-99 Effingham Street, Rotherham S65 1BL (01709 309116; Fax: 01709 512550).

Armthorpe

Armthorpe Poors Estate Charity

Eligibility: People who are in need and live in Armthorpe.

Types of grants: Grants towards items, services or facilities calculated to alleviate need.

Annual grant total: In 2000/01 the trust had assets of £204,000 and an income of £8,800. Grants to 29 individuals totalled £5,200, including £2,300 in educational grants. Welfare bodies supporting Armthorpe residents received £2,800.

Applications: Contact the clerk by telephone who will advise if a letter of application is needed. Applicants outside of Armthorpe will be declined.

Correspondent: Frank Pratt, 32 Gurth Avenue, Edenthorpe, Doncaster DN3 2LW (01302 882806).

Aston-cum-Aughton

The Aston-cum-Aughton Charity Estate

Eligibility: People in need who live in the parish of Aston-cum-Aughton.

Types of grants: One-off and recurrent grants according to need. Grants have in the past been given towards the cost of holidays for a single parent family and an unemployed couple and their three children. Help was given towards installing a phone for an older couple. The charity also supports local organisations.

The charity will not give to profit-making concerns, nor will it make loans.

Annual grant total: In 1999 the trust had assets of £34,000 and an income of £12,000. To celebrate the millennium it gave a china mug to every infant and junior schoolchild in the parish at a cost of £5,400. Grants to organisations totalled £5,200.

Applications: In writing to the correspondent or any trustee, directly by the individual or through a social worker, citizen's advice bureau or other welfare agency. Applications are considered in March and September, although a sub-committee can consider urgent requests at any time.

Correspondent: J Nuttall, Clerk, 31 Worksop Road, Aston, Sheffield S26 2EB (0114 287 6047; e-mail: jim_nuttall@lineone.net).

Barnsley

The Barnsley Prisoner of War Fund

Eligibility: Ex-servicemen and women (not necessarily ex-prisoners of war) living in the Barnsley Metropolitan area, and their dependants, who are in need.

Types of grants: One-off grants only of between £50 and £500. Applicants who receive a grant must wait one year before applying again.

Annual grant total: In 2000/01 grants totalled £1,500.

Applications: In writing to the correspondent either directly by the individual or through a social worker, citizen's advice bureau, other welfare agency, any representative of the trust such as a trustee or local branch of a forces welfare agencies. Applicants must include financial details and their service record. Applications are considered throughout the year.

Correspondent: Stephen Loach, Committee Section, Borough Secretary's Department, Barnsley Metropolitan Borough Council, The Town Hall, Barnsley S70 2TA (01226 773066; Fax: 01226 773099).

The Barnsley Tradesmen's Benevolent Institution

Eligibility: Merchants and traders, their widows and unmarried daughters, who are in need and have lived in the old borough of Barnsley for at least seven years.

Types of grants: Recurrent grants of £35 are given towards general daily living expenses such as food, medical care and equipment and travel to and from hospital.

Annual grant total: In 2001/02 the trust had an income of £1,200 and gave 24 grants totalling £840.

Applications: In writing to Linda Barber at the address below, either directly by the individual or through a third party such as a citizen's advice bureau or other welfare agency. Applications are considered monthly.

Correspondent: David Bishop Richards, Heseltine Bray & Welsh, 29 Church Street, Barnsley, South Yorkshire S70 2AL (01226 210777; Fax: 01226 210007; e-mail: l.barber@hbw-law.co.uk).

The Fountain Nursing Trust

Eligibility: People in need who live in Barnsley.

Types of grants: One-off or recurrent grants for needs such as travel and medical appliances.

Annual grant total: In 2000/01 the trust had an income of £780 and gave £750 in grants.

Applications: In writing to the correspondent for consideration in April or October.

Correspondent: The Trustees, Newman & Bond, 35 Church Street, Barnsley, South Yorkshire S70 2AP (01226 213434; Fax: 01226 213435).

Beighton

Beighton Relief-in-Need Charity

Eligibility: People in need who live in the former parish of Beighton.

Types of grants: Winter fuel grants of £15 per household are given to older people. Other grants include those towards bath lifts and child care seats for people who are disabled.

Annual grant total: In 2000/01 the trust had an income of £9,700. Welfare grants to 408 individuals totalled £8,500, of which 401 were for fuel and totalled £6,000. Educational grants to four individuals totalled £230. Grants to 14 organisations totalled £2,600.

Applications: In writing to the correspondent. Applications can be submitted directly by the individual or through a social worker, citizen's advice bureau, other welfare agency or a third party such as a relative, neighbour or trustee. Applications are considered throughout the year.

Correspondent: Michael Lowe, Elms Bungalow, Queens Road, Beighton, Sheffield S20 1AW (0114 269 2004).

Bramley

The Bramley Poors' Allotment Trust

Eligibility: People in need who live in the ancient township of Bramley, especially people who are elderly, poor and sick.

Types of grants: One-off grants (generally up to £200) for necessities such as reconditioned cookers, fireguards and other household essentials.

Annual grant total: About £1,400 is available each year.

Applications: In writing to the correspondent. The trust likes applications to be submitted through a recognised referral agency (social worker, citizen's advice bureau, doctor, headmaster or minister). They are considered monthly.

Correspondent: Len Barnett, 31 St Oswald's Terrace, Guiseley, Leeds LS20 9BD (01943 876033).

Cantley

The Cantley Poor's Land Trust

Eligibility: People in need who live in the ancient parish of Cantley with Branton (which now includes the areas known as Bessacarr and the Cantley Estates, together with the villages of Old Cantley and Branton).

Types of grants: One-off grants ranging from £50 to £500. Recent grants have been given towards debts such as utility bills and rent, redecoration of new accommodation, carpeting, furniture, medical equipment, repairs to household electrical equipment and children's educational trips.

No grants are given towards council tax, telephones, televisions or repairs/improvements to private accommodation.

Annual grant total: In 2000/01 the trust had assets of £688,000, an income of £30,000 and a total expenditure of £25,000. Grants to 156 individuals totalled £17,000.

Applications: On a form available from the correspondent for consideration monthly. They should be submitted directly by the individual.

Correspondent: Mrs M Jackson, Clerk to the Trustees, 30 Selhurst Crescent, Bessacarr, Doncaster, South Yorkshire DN4 6EF (01302 530566)

Doncaster

The John William Chapman Charitable Trust

Eligibility: People in need who live in the metropolitan borough of Doncaster.

Types of grants: One-off grants in kind, not cash, up to the value of £1,000 towards daily living expenses. No grants are given towards education, rent, debts or improvements on rented accommodation.

Annual grant total: In 2000/01 the trust had an expenditure of £72,000, of which £51,000 was given to individuals.

Applications: On a form available from the correspondent. Applications must be accompanied by a letter from a social worker, GP or welfare agency and they are considered monthly.

Correspondent: Rosemary Sharp, Jordans, 4 Priory Place, Doncaster DN1 1BP (01302 365374).

Other information: Grants are also given to organisations for the benefit of the Doncaster community.

Rotherham

The Common Lands of Rotherham Charity

Eligibility: People who are elderly or poor and live in Rotherham.

Types of grants: One-off and recurrent grants according to need.

Annual grant total: £5,000 in 1998.

Applications: In writing to the correspondent.

Correspondent: W B Copley, Barn Cottage, 7 Castlegate, Tickhill, Doncaster DN11 9QP (01302 759429).

The Stoddart Samaritan Fund

Eligibility: People aged 16 or over who have been ill and are in need of convalescence to help them recover and return to work. Applicants should be either living or working within a four-mile radius of Rotherham Town Hall. No grants are given to people with terminal illnesses.

Types of grants: One-off grants only, ranging from £100 to £500.

Annual grant total: In 2000/01 the fund had assets of £265,000 and an income of £10,000. It gave £6,400 in grants to 14 individuals.

Applications: On a form available from the correspondent, submitted by the applicant's doctor. They are considered every month.

Correspondent: Peter Wright, Secretary, 7 Melrose Grove, Rotherham, South Yorkshire S60 3NA (01709 376448).

Sheffield

The Ecclesfield Welfare Charities

Eligibility: People in need in the ancient parish of Ecclesfield (the area covers most of the city of Sheffield north of the Don, including Bradfield, Chapeltown, High Green, Wincobank, Stannington and Wadsley).

Types of grants: Grants range from £15 to £500, with half of the available funds being given in large grants to organisations and half in small grants to individuals.

Annual grant total: About £5,000 is given each year to individuals and organisations.

Applications: In writing to the correspondent for consideration in March, June/July and September.

Correspondent: David Banham, Secretary, 6 Priory Close, Ecclesfield, Sheffield S35 9TS (0114 246 0194).

Jane Fisher's Gift

Eligibility: People who have worked as merchants or manufacturers in any branch of the steel, or kindred, trades in Sheffield, and their dependants, who are in need.

Types of grants: Recurrent grants according to need.

Annual grant total: In 1997/98 the charity had an income of £7,600 and a total expenditure of £5,800. Payments to annuitants totalled £1,900 while special pension payments totalled £3,900. More up-to-date information was not available.

Applications: In wriitng to the correspondent at any time.

Correspondent: Col. Peter David Gardner, Cutlers Hall, Church Street, Sheffield S1 1HG (0114 272 8456).

Sir George Franklin's Pension Charity

Eligibility: People in need aged 50 and over who live in the city of Sheffield.

Types of grants: Annual allowances of £280.

Annual grant total: In 2000/01 the trust had assets of £51,000, an income of £1,900 and a total expenditure of £1,600. Grants to eight individuals totalled £800.

Applications: Vacancies arise infrequently and are publicised locally. Applications should only be made in response to this publicity. Speculative applications will not be successful.

Correspondent: R H M Plews, Clerk, Knowle House, 4 Norfolk Park Road, Sheffield S2 3QE (0114 276 7991).

Sir Samuel Osborn's Deed of Gift (Relief Fund)

Eligibility: First priority is given to people who live in Sheffield who were employees of the steel works Samuel Osborn Company Limited (which has not existed since 1978) and their dependants and descendants.

Types of grants: One-off and recurrent grants according to need.

Annual grant total: In 2000/01 the trust's income was £12,000 and its total expenditure was £30,000. About £15,000 is available each year to be given in grants to individuals.

Applications: In writing to the correspondent.

Correspondent: The Clerk, South Yorkshire Community Foundation, Clay Street, Sheffield S9 2PE (0114 242 4294).

Sheffield Church Burgesses Trust

Eligibility: People in need who live in Sheffield.

Types of grants: One-off and recurrent grants according to need.

Annual grant total: In 1999 the trust had assets of £26 million and an income of £1.9 million. Grants totalled £1.4 million, mostly to organisations.

Applications: On a form available from the correspondent, for consideration in January, April, July and October.

Correspondent: G J Smallman, c/o Dibb Lupton Alsop, Fountain Precinct, Balm Green, Sheffield S1 1RZ (0114 283 3268).

John Walsh Fund

Eligibility: Those working in or retired from the retail, fashion and department store trade who are in conditions of need, hardship or distress and live in Sheffield.

Types of grants: One-off grants ranging between £200 and £1,000 towards equipment or services.

Annual grant total: About £2,500 each year.

Applications: Applicants may telephone for an application form.

Correspondent: Welfare Services Department, Cottage Homes, Marshall Estate, Hammers Lane, London NW7 4EE (020 8201 0112; Fax: 020 8358 7209).

The Withers Pensions

Eligibility: Women in need who are single or widowed, members of the Church of England, over 50 years old and live in Sheffield.

Types of grants: Yearly allowances of £200 (paid in April and October).

Annual grant total: In 1998/99 the charity had assets of £118,000 and an income of £4,800. Total expenditure was £5,300, with 15 grants totalling £3,200.

Applications: Applications are considered in October each year.

Correspondent: D K P Mangles, RST Accountants, 56 Shornham Street, Sheffield S1 4SP (0114 280 8980).

Tyne & Wear

The Sunderland Guild of Help

Eligibility: People in need who live in the city of Sunderland and the surrounding area.

Types of grants: Support is given for the advancement of health and the relief of poverty, distress and sickness. Grants have been made in the past for clothing, fuel, holidays, household items and children's items. They range from £50 to £150 and are always one-off.

Annual grant total: In 2000/01 the trust had assets of £214,000 and an income of £88,000. From a total expenditure of £81,000, grants to individuals totalled £4,800.

Applications: Applications can only be considered if they are submitted on behalf of the client by a health visitor, social worker or other statutory agency. Applications must include an income/expenditure statement. They are considered throughout the year.

Correspondent: Norman Taylor, Chair, 4 Toward Road, Sunderland, Tyne & Wear SR1 2QG (0191 567 2895).

The Sunderland Orphanage & Educational Foundation

Eligibility: Young people under 25 who are resident in or around Sunderland who have a parent who is disabled or has died, or whose parents are divorced or legally separated.

Types of grants: Grants are given to children for clothing and living expenses. Grants are also made to students.

Annual grant total: In 1999/2000 the trust had assets of £308,000 and an income of £21,000. Grants totalled £12,000, of which £1,400 was given to students, £5,000 for clothing and £5,800 as 'pocket money'.

Applications: Applications should be made in writing and addressed to: D G Goodfellow, Administrator, 54 John Street, Sunderland SR1 1JG. They are considered every other month.

Correspondent: P W Taylor, McKenzie Bell, 19 John Street, Sunderland SR1 1JG (0191 567 4857; Fax: 0191 510 9347; e-mail: mckbell@dial.pipex.com).

The Thomas Thompson Poors Rate Gift

Eligibility: People in need who live in Byker and Monkchester.

Types of grants: One-off grants for items such as washing machines, furniture and cookers. Grants have also been given to replace Christmas presents and children's bikes which have been stolen.

Annual grant total: In 1999 the trust had £2,000 to distribute, of which £1,600 was given in grants.

Applications: In writing to the correspondent, for consideration throughout the year. Grants to replace stolen property are usually submitted through victim support.

Correspondent: I Humphreys, c/o Head of Democratic Services, Newcastle City Council, Civic Centre, Newcastle upon Tyne, NE99 2BN (0191 211 5116; Fax 0191 211 4942; e-mail: ian.humphreys@newcastle.gov.uk).

The Tyne Mariners' Benevolent Institution

Eligibility: Former merchant seamen who live in Tyneside (about five miles either side of the River Tyne) and their widows. Applicants must be: (a) at least 63 years old and have served at least 15 years at sea; (b) under the age of 63, but unable to work owing to ill-health; or (c) the widows of such people.

Types of grants: Grants of £35 a calendar month and two bonuses of varying value.

Annual grant total: In 2000 the trust had assets of £780,000 and an income of £145,000. Grants to 290 beneficiaries totalled £124,000. The number of grants made has been declining in recent years due to fewer applications being made.

Applications: On a form available from the correspondent, to be submitted either directly by the individual or through a social worker, citizen's advice bureau or other welfare agency. Applications can be considered at any time.

Correspondent: Timothy Duff, Messrs Hadaway & Hadaway, 58 Howard Street, North Shields, Tyne & Wear NE30 1AL (0191 257 0382; Fax: 0191 296 1904; e-mail: timothyd@hadaway.co.uk).

Other information: The institution also administers The Master Mariners Homes in Tynemouth which provides 30 flats for its beneficiaries.

Gateshead

The Davidson Charity Trust

Eligibility: People in need who live in the metropolitan borough of Gateshead.

Types of grants: One-off grants according to need. Top-up grants are occasionally given.

Annual grant total: About £8,000.

Applications: In writing to the correspondent. Applications should be submitted by 1 March or 1 September each year with details of the grant needed and how much money has already been received from other sources.

Correspondent: Mrs M Gillespie, 6 River Bank Road, Alnmouth, Alnwick, Northumberland NE66 2RH (01665 830123).

The Gateshead Blind Trust Fund

Eligibility: People who are registered blind or partially sighted and live in the borough of Gateshead.

Types of grants: One-off grants up to £500 towards household items such as cookers, fridges, washing machines, as well as furniture, computer equipment, educational expenses and any aids that will benefit people who are blind or partially sighted in their daily living.

Grants are not given for debts of any kind, television or car licences, cars, holidays, funeral expenses or nursing or residential home fees.

Annual grant total: In 2000/01 the trust had an income of £1,900 and a total expenditure of £5,000.

Applications: All applications must be submitted via the Technical Officers for the Blind, employed in the social services department, on the form available. Applications are considered throughout the year. Re-application for grants is not allowed for two years once a grant has been awarded.

Correspondent: Angela Todd, Civic Centre, Regent Street, Gateshead NE8 1HH (0191 433 3000; Fax: 0191 478 2224).

The Gateshead Relief-in-Sickness Fund

Eligibility: People who live in the metropolitan borough of Gateshead and who are sick, convalescent, disabled or infirm.

Types of grants: One-off and recurrent grants towards providing or paying for items, services or facilities which are calculated to alleviate need or assist the recovery of such persons in such cases but are not readily available to them from other sources.

Grants have been given to adapt a bathroom for a boy with learning and physical disabilities and for computers and talking typewriters for people who are registered blind.

Annual grant total: In 2001/02 it had an income of £11,000 and an expenditure of £8,800. Grants to four individuals totalled £1,000. Grants to organisations, such as the evening and night nursing service in Gateshead, totalled £7,500.

Applications: In writing to the correspondent. Applications can be submitted directly by the individual, through a social worker, citizen's advice bureau or other welfare agency. Applications are usually considered in March, June and September each year, although in urgent cases can be considered between meetings.

Correspondent: Ken Watson, Clerk to the Trustees, 23 Cloverdale Gardens, Whickham, Newcastle on Tyne NE16 5HT (0191 488 1332; e-mail: ken@khwatson.fsnet.co.uk).

Newcastle upon Tyne

The Non-Ecclesiastical Charity of William Moulton

Eligibility: People in need who have lived in the city of Newcastle upon Tyne for at least 12 months.

Types of grants: Grants range between £50 and £150 towards general household/personal needs such as washing machines, cookers, furniture, clothing and so on. No grants are given for education or training.

Annual grant total: In 2001 the trust had assets of £1 million and an income of £40,000, all of which was given in 300 grants to individuals.

Applications: On a form available from the correspondent. Applications should be submitted through a social worker, citizen's advice bureau or other welfare agency and are considered monthly.

Correspondent: G E Jackson, Clerk, 10 Sunlea Avenue, Cullercoats, Tyne & Wear NE30 3DS (0191 251 0971).

The Town Moor Money Charity

Eligibility: Freemen of Newcastle upon Tyne and their widows and daughters who are in need.

Types of grants: One-off and recurrent grants according to need. Grants are means tested and paid in June and December.

Annual grant total: In 1999/2000 the trust had assets of £599,000 and an income of £181,000. Total expenditure was £106,000, including £76,000 given in 202 grants to individuals.

Applications: In writing to the correspondent for consideration in May and November.

Correspondent: Mrs Patricia Ansell, Administrator, Moor Bank Lodge, Claremont Road, Newcastle upon Tyne NE2 4NL (0191 261 5970).

South Shields

The South Shields Indigent Sick Society

Eligibility: People in need who are sick, convalescent, disabled or infirm and live in South Shields parliamentary constituency.

Types of grants: One-off and recurrent grants according to need.

Annual grant total: The trust has an annual income of £2,500.

Applications: In writing to the correspondent.

Correspondent: M Robson, Director of Finance, South Tyneside Health Care Trust, South Tyneside General Hospital, Harton Lane, South Shields, Tyne & Wear NE34 0PL (0191 202 4006).

Sunderland

The Mayor's Fund for Necessitous Children

Eligibility: Children in need (under 16, occasionally under 18) who are in full-time education, live in the city of Sunderland and whose family are on a low income.

Types of grants: About £25 grants for provision of footwear paid every six months.

Annual grant total: In 2000/01 grants to 18 individuals totalled £900.

Applications: Applicants must go the civic centre, address below, and fill in a form with a member of staff. The decision is then posted at a later date.

Correspondent: Jo-anne Stewart, Financial Service Awards Team, Education Services, Civic Centre, PO Box 101, Sunderland SR2 7DN (0191 553 1415)

Wallsend

The Victor Mann Trust (also known as The Wallsend Charitable Trust)

Eligibility: People over 60 who are on or just above state benefit income levels and live in the former borough of Wallsend. Grants can be given to organisations provided that the majority of members meet the same criteria as apply to individuals.

Types of grants: One-off grants ranging between £10 to £500, to help meet extra requirements. The trust will not help with continuing costs such as residential care or telephone rentals and will not help a person whose income is significantly above state benefit levels. Applicants must have exhausted all statutory avenues e.g. DWP, Social Fund, Social Services department etc. Recent grants have been made for washing machines, cookers, carpets, home decoration and telephone installation.

Annual grant total: In 1999 the trust had an income of £59,000 and a total expenditure of £18,000. £810 was given in grants to individuals and £14,000 in grants to organisations.

Applications: In writing to the correspondent either directly by the individual or through a social worker, citizen's advice bureau or other welfare agency or third party, such as a friend or relative. Applications are considered quarterly in April, July, September and December. They must include details of the purpose of the grant and an estimate of the cost.

Correspondent: Ms S Watson, Secretary, Care in the Community, 126 Great Lime Road, West Moor, Newcastle upon Tyne NE12 7DQ (0191 200 8181).

West Yorkshire

Bradford & District Wool Association Benevolent Fund

Eligibility: Former workers in small businesses (offices) in the wool trade in Bradford and district or their spouses, who are in need.

Types of grants: Normally recurrent grants up to a maximum of £200 towards heating, electricity and telephone costs. Special cases (e.g. the need for an invalid chair) are considered.

Annual grant total: In 2001 grants totalled £4,000.

Applications: In writing to the correspondent either directly by the individual or through a relative or friend. Applications are considered at any time.

Correspondent: Sir James F Hill, Chair, c/o Suite 2, Baildon Mills, Northgate, Baildon, Shipley, West Yorkshire BD17 6JX (01274 532200).

The Bradford Jewish Benevolent Fund

Eligibility: Older people in need who are Jewish and live in the city of Bradford and district.

Types of grants: One-off and recurrent grants according to need. Grants are to relieve poverty and sickness.

Annual grant total: In 2000 the trust's income was £1,800 and its total expenditure was £2,100. Grants to individuals totalled £450, with the rest going to organisations.

Applications: In writing to the correspondent.

Correspondent: Albert Waxman, 11 Staveley Road, Shipley, West Yorkshire BD18 4HD (01274 581189).

The Calverley Charity

Eligibility: People in need who live in the parishes of Calverley, Farsley and Thornbury.

Types of grants: Small one-off grants to alleviate hardship.

Annual grant total: The trust tends to have an annual income of £500. No grants have been made in recent years as the trust has been building up its funds.

Applications: In writing to the correspondent.

Correspondent: Cllr Andrew Carter, Civic Hall, Leeds LS1 1UR (0113 247 4551).

The Clayton, Taylor & Foster Charity

Eligibility: People in need who live in the parish boundaries of Wakefield (city), Thornes with Alvertorpe and Wrenthorpe with Outwood.

Types of grants: Grants of £10, paid three times a year in March, September and December, to people over 60 and in need. Grants may be given to people under 60 in extreme circumstances.

Annual grant total: About £1,500.

Applications: For pension applicants aged over 60 a form is available from the correspondent. Other individuals should apply directly in writing. Trustees meet in March, September and November.

Correspondent: Colin M Towler, Clerk to the Trustees, 'Colmar', 84 Brandy Carr Road, Kirkhamgate, Wakefield, West Yorkshire WF2 0RJ (Tel & Fax: 01924 375897).

Combined Services Association (Wakefield) Benevolent Fund

Eligibility: People in need who live in Wakefield and the surrounding area.

Types of grants: One-off grants according to need.

Annual grant total: In 2000/01 the trust's assets were £3,700, its income was £1,000 and its total expenditure was £1,600. Most grants are made to local projects.

Applications: On a form available from the correspondent, submitted directly by the individual. Please note, local people who apply for a grant, where possible, are requested to join the association as members and help in the association's fundraising activities.

Correspondent: Andrew Dickson, 28 Silkstone Crescent, Wakefield, West Yorkshire WF2 7EX (01924 252932).

Dewsbury & District Sick Poor Fund

Eligibility: People who live in the county borough of Dewsbury and the ecclesiastical parish of Hanging Heaton.

Types of grants: One-off grants of up to £350 towards household items. Recent grants have been for cookers, washers and a bicycle for a child with cancer whose bike had been stolen.

Annual grant total: In 2001 the trust had assets of £142,000 and an income of £6,800. Total expenditure was £1,700, including three grants totalling £610.

Applications: In writing to the correspondent through a social worker, citizen's advice bureau or other welfare agency at any time.

Correspondent: John Alan Winder, 130 Boothroyd Lane, Dewsbury, West Yorkshire WF13 2LW (01924 463308).

Mary Farrar's Benevolent Trust Fund

Eligibility: Women of limited means who are not less than 55 years of age. They should be natives of, or have lived in, the ancient parish of Halifax (the current metropolitan borough of Calderdale and part of Fixby in the metropolitan borough of Kirklees) for at least five consecutive years.

Types of grants: Annual pensions paid quarterly from 1 January (at present £75 a quarter) plus an annual bonus (£70 in 2001). Grants are not given to people in residential care.

Annual grant total: £8,500 is available for grant making purposes.

Applications: On a form available from the correspondent. Applications can be submitted by the individual, through a recognised referral agency (such as social worker, citizen's advice bureau or doctor) or other third party such as a relative, friend or minister of religion. They are considered in March, June, September and December, although emergency applications can be considered at any time.

Correspondent: Peter Haley, P Haley & Co., Chartered Accountants, Poverty Hall, Lower Ellistones, Greetland, Halifax HX4 8NG (01422 376690).

The Heckmondwike & District Fund for the Needy Sick

Eligibility: People in need who are sick and live in and around Heckmondwike.

Types of grants: Usually one-off grants.

Annual grant total: Between £2,000 and £3,000 is given each year in total.

Applications: In writing to the correspondent, either directly by the individual or through a welfare organisation, Salvation Army contact or trustee. Applications are considered quarterly.

Correspondent: J E Pilkington, Clerk, Redferns Solicitors, HSBC Chambers, Heckmondwike, West Yorkshire WF16 0HZ (01924 403745; Fax: 01924 404913).

Huddersfield and District Army Veterans' Association Benevolent Fund

Eligibility: Veterans of the army, navy and air force who are in need, aged over 60 years, and were discharged from the forces 'with good character' and live in Huddersfield and part of Brighouse.

Types of grants: One-off and recurrent grants according to need.

Annual grant total: In 2000 the trust's income was £16,000 and its total expenditure was £15,000, divided between spending on grants and on events organised by the fund for its beneficiaries.

Applications: In writing to the correspondent, or on a form published in the fund's applications leaflet; the leaflet is available from doctor's surgeries, local libraries and so on.

Correspondent: David Morrell, 126 Ibbetson Oval, Churwell, Morley, Leeds LS27 7UL (0113 229 4176).

The Lucy Lund Holiday Grants

Eligibility: Present or former teachers (especially women teachers living in West Yorkshire) who need a recuperative holiday. No grants to dependants or to students.

Types of grants: Grants for recuperative holidays.

Annual grant total: Around 26 grants up to a maximum of £75 each.

Applications: On a form available from the correspondent to be submitted by the individual.

Correspondent: The Secretary, Tringham House, Wessex Fields, Deansleigh Road, Bournemouth, BH7 7DT.

The William & Sarah Midgley Charity

Eligibility: People over 65 who are in need and live in Lees, Cross Roads or Barcroft.

Types of grants: Christmas hampers are given to the residents of William & Sarah Midgley's Almshouses and to other local residents. Occasional one-off grants are also made to people in need. No grants are given towards rates, taxes or other public funds.

Annual grant total: In 2000/01 the trust had assets of £101,000 and an income of £5,900. Total expenditure was £1,600, including £690 given in grants.

Applications: In writing to the correspondent, for consideration in May or November.

Correspondent: Mrs Eileen J Proctor, 7 Lachman Road, Trawden, Colne, Lancashire BB8 8TA (01282 862757).

Sir Titus Salt's Charity

Eligibility: People in need who are over the age of 75 and live in Shipley, Baildon, Saltaire, Nab Wood and Wrose of Bradford.

Types of grants: Food vouchers of £3 paid once a year, available from Shipley Information Centre. The trust can make grants or loans of up to about £100 towards the supply of special foods or medicines, medical comforts, shoes and domestic help. No suitable applications for these one-off grants have been received recently.

Annual grant total: In 2000/01 the charity had an income of £1,700 and a total expenditure of £1,500, all of which was given in grants.

Applications: Applications are considered November/December each year. 'All applicants will receive the grant if they are of the correct age and live in the grant area.'

Correspondent: Alan Baldwin, Housing & Environmental Protection Administration, 5th Floor, Central House, Forster Square, Bradford BD1 1DJ (01274 754355; Fax: 01274 390076).

The Sanderson Charity for Women

Eligibility: Women in need who live in the diocese of Wakefield.

Types of grants: One-off grants of £50 to £250, mostly for household equipment but also for emergency holidays and clothing. Grants are only given to meet an immediate need.

Annual grant total: In 2001 the trust had assets of £63,000 and an income of £3,100. Grants to 31 individuals totalled £6,500.

Applications: On a form available from the correspondent for consideration in March or November/December. Applications can be submitted directly by the individual but are usually made via the incumbent of the parish.

Correspondent: Mrs Linda Mary Box, Dixon Coles & Gill Solicitors, Bank House, Burton Street, Wakefield WF1 3DA (01924 373467; Fax: 01924 366234; e-mail: box@dixon-coles-gill.co.uk).

The William Webster's Charity

Eligibility: People who are widowed or orphaned and live in Oulton and Woodlesford.

Types of grants: Annual payments in the second week of January.

Annual grant total: In 1999 grants totalled £2,400. A further £660 was given in educational grants.

Applications: In writing to the correspondent, to be considered by the second week of January. Applicants who turn up at the distribution will be considered.

Correspondent: C J Greaves, Solicitor, 34 Commercial Street, Rothwell, Leeds LS26 0AW (0113 282 7988; Fax: 0113 282 1010).

The West Riding Distress Fund

Eligibility: People in need who live in the area of the former county of the West Riding of Yorkshire. When the trust deed was written the former county of West Riding did NOT include the county boroughs of Barnsley, Bradford, Dewsbury, Doncaster, Halifax, Huddersfield, Leeds, Rotherham, Sheffield, Wakefield and York.

Types of grants: One-off grants for bedding, clothing, food, fuel, furniture or comforts or aids for people who are sick and their relatives, including holidays and travel expenses to hospital.

Annual grant total: In 2001/02 grants to 22 individuals totalled £2,500.

Applications: No direct applications from individuals. All requests must come through social services departments on the application form available, and they are considered in January, April, July and September.

Correspondent: Dianne Clothier, North Yorkshire County Council, County Hall, Northallerton, North Yorkshire DL7 8DD (01609 780780; Fax: 01609 532025).

West Yorkshire Police (Employees) Benevolent Fund

Eligibility: Employees and ex-employees of West Yorkshire Police Force and West Yorkshire Metropolitan County Council who are in need, and their widows, orphans and other dependants.

Types of grants: One-off and recurrent grants according to need.

Annual grant total: In 2000/01 the fund had assets of £96,000, an income of £5,500 and a total expenditure of £830. Grants to two individuals totalled £190.

Applications: In writing to the correspondent. Trustee meetings are held every three months, although urgent cases can be considered at any time.

Correspondent: The Secretary, West Yorkshire Police Occupational Health Unit, PO Box 9, Wakefield WF1 3QP (01924 292727).

Baildon

The Butterfield Trust

Eligibility: People in need who live in the parish of Baildon.

Types of grants: One-off grants for emergencies.

Annual grant total: In 1999 grants totalled £2,000.

Applications: In writing to the correspondent. Decisions can be made immediately.

Correspondent: Revd John Nowell, The Vicarage, Browgate, Baildon, West Yorkshire BD17 6BY.

Batley

Batley Town Mission

Eligibility: People who are sick, elderly or otherwise in need, and children, who live in the former borough of Batley.

Types of grants: One-off grants of about £100 each.

Annual grant total: About £3,000.

Applications: On a form available from the correspondent, to be processed through social workers or other welfare agencies at any time. No direct applications are considered.

Correspondent: P D Taylor, Secretary & Trustee, Batley Town Mission, Oakwood House, Upper Batley, Batley, West Yorkshire WF17 0AL.

Bingley

The Bingley Diamond Jubilee Relief-in-Sickness Charity

Eligibility: People who live in the parish of Bingley (as constituted on 14 February 1898) who are sick, convalescent, disabled or infirm.

Types of grants: Emergency payments or annual grants averaging £500.

Annual grant total: About £1,000.

Applications: In writing to the correspondent through a social worker, citizen's advice bureau, other welfare agency or a third party. For specific items, estimates of costs are required. The trustees meet in February and November. A sub-committee of trustees can deal promptly with emergency payments.

Correspondent: John Daykin, Clerk, Weatherhead & Butcher, Solicitors, 120 Main Street, Bingley BD16 2JJ (01274 562322; Fax: 01274 551558).

The Samuel Sunderland Relief-in-Need Charity

Eligibility: People who live in the former parish of Bingley (as constituted on 14 February 1898) and are in need, hardship or distress.

Types of grants: Emergency payments and annual grants averaging £500 each.

Annual grant total: About £4,000 to £5,000 each year.

Applications: In writing to the correspondent through a social worker, citizen's advice bureau, other welfare agency or any other third party on behalf of the individual. When specific items are required estimates of the cost must be provided. Applications are considered in February and November.

Correspondent: John Daykin, Clerk, Weatherhead & Butcher Solicitors, 120 Main Street, Bingley BD16 2JJ (01274 562322; Fax: 01274 551558).

Other information: Grants are also given to local organisations which serve a similar purpose.

Bradford

The Bradford & District Children's Charity Circle

Eligibility: Children in need under 16 who live in Bradford.

Types of grants: One-off grants of between £100 and £500. No grants are given towards domestic bills.

Annual grant total: In 2001 the trust had an income of £10,000. Grants to 120 individuals totalled £4,000. Other grants totalled £6,800.

Applications: In writing to the correspondent through a social worker, citizen's advice bureau or other welfare agency. They are considered monthly. Individuals should not apply directly.

Correspondent: Mrs M Seal, 24 Hazel Beck, Bingley, Bradford BD16 1LZ (01274 562000).

The City of Bradford Fund for the Disabled

Eligibility: People who are physically disabled (but not necessarily registered) of any age who live in Bradford. Applicants must be in need through lack of finance or low income.

Types of grants: One-off grants of up to £100 to cover a range of needs, including nebulisers, aids, medical equipment, clothing, bedding and household items. No grants are made towards holidays.

Annual grant total: In 2001 grants totalled £1,400.

Applications: On a form available from the correspondent. Applications can be submitted either directly by the individual or through a recognised referral agency (social worker, citizen's advice bureau or doctor). They are considered quarterly in March, June, September and December. Grant applications for medical equipment must be supported by a doctor's note. Applications should give as much detail as possible regarding the applicant's circumstances and special costs for the items needed.

Correspondent: Mrs A Sugden, Hon. Secretary, Community Initiatives, 1st Floor, Jacobs Well, Manchester Road, Bradford BD1 5RW (01274 757796; Fax: 01274 752954).

The Bradford Tradesmen's Homes

Eligibility: Unmarried women over the age of 60 who have lived in Bradford metropolitan district for at least seven years who are not in employment and are in need.

Types of grants: Pensions of £40 a quarter, plus a £70 Christmas grant.

Annual grant total: In 2000/01 the trust had assets of £421,000, an income of £143,000 and a total expenditure of £100,000. Grants to nine individuals totalled £1,800.

Applications: On a form available from the correspondent. Applications can be submitted directly by the individual or through a social worker, citizen's advice bureau, other welfare agency, doctor, clergy or other third party. Applicants will be visited before an award is made and they must provide the names of two referees. Applications are considered throughout the year.

North East – West Yorkshire

Correspondent: Colin Askew, Trust Administrator, 44 Lily Croft, Heaton Road, Bradford BD8 8QY
(Tel & Fax: 01274 543022).

Other information: The trust also runs almshouses.

The Emmandjay Charitable Trust

Eligibility: People in need who live in the city of Bradford, with preference to people who are disadvantaged, terminally ill or physically or mentally disabled, and their carers.

Types of grants: Generally one-off grants, although the payments can be spread over three years. No grants towards rent, utility or telephone bills or debts, or to students.

Annual grant total: In 2000/01 the trust had assets of £2.6 million generating an income of £265,000. Grants totalled £226,000, mostly to organisations. About £4,500 is given to individuals each year.

Applications: Applications must be submitted by a social services worker. Direct applications by the individual will not be considered or acknowledged.

Correspondent: Mrs A E Bancroft, PO Box 88, Otley, West Yorkshire LS21 3TE.

The Moser Benevolent Trust Fund

Eligibility: People in need who are 60 or over and have lived or worked in the former county borough of Bradford for at least three years.

Types of grants: Pensions of £45 a quarter.

Annual grant total: In 2000/01 it had assets of £124,000 and an income of £4,700. Total expenditure was £3,900, including £3,800 in 18 grants to individuals.

Applications: In writing at any time to: M Chappell, 56 Carr Lane, Shipley, West Yorkshire BD18 2LB. Applicants should include details of income and assets.

Correspondent: D C Stokes, 33 Mossy Bank Close, Queensbury, Bradford, West Yorkshire BD13 1PX
(Tel & Fax: 01274 817414).

Joseph Nutter's Foundation

Eligibility: People aged 18 or under who live in the metropolitan district of Bradford and have at least one parent who has died.

Types of grants: One-off grants of £100 to £250 are given towards clothing, bedding, beds and household equipment which specifically benefit the child, such as cookers, fires and washing machines. Other needs may occasionally be considered on an individual basis.

Annual grant total: In 2000/01 the trust had assets of £357,000, an income of £16,000 and a total expenditure of £19,000. Grants to individuals totalled £16,000.

Applications: In writing to the correspondent at any time.

Correspondent: Mrs J M Barraclough, Administrator, The Ballroom, Hawkswick, Skipton BD23 5QA (01756 770361; Fax: 01756 770363).

Paul and Nancy Speak's Charity (formerly The Bradford Gentlewomen's Pension Fund)

Eligibility: Women in need who are over the age of 50 and live in Bradford.

Types of grants: Regular allowances of £500 a year, paid quarterly.

Annual grant total: In 2000 the trust had assets of £363,000 and an income of £16,000. Grants to 16 individuals totalled £7,600.

Applications: In writing to the correspondent.

Correspondent: Michael Chapel, Secretary, 56 Carr Lane, Windhill, Shipley, North Yorkshire BD18 2LD
(01274 585301).

Calderdale

The Community Foundation for Calderdale

Eligibility: People in need who live in Calderdale.

Types of grants: One-off grants of up to £100 and occasionally small loans to meet urgent needs, such as household equipment, clothing and food which cannot be readily funded from other sources.

Annual grant total: In 2001 the foundation gave £85,000 in grants, mostly to organisations.

Applications: Individuals must apply through a referring agency, such as a citizen's advice bureau, on an application form available from the correspondent. Grants will only be awarded to individuals in the form of a cheque; cash is not given.

Correspondent: Grants Officer, Room 158, Dean Clough, Halifax HX3 5AX (01422 349700; Fax: 01422 350017; e-mail: enquiries@ccfoundation.co.uk; website: www.ccfoundation.co.uk).

The Halifax Childrens Welfare League

Eligibility: Children who live in Calderdale and who are in need. The parent/s or guardian/s of the child must first try to cover the cost themselves.

Types of grants: One-off grants towards needs such as holidays; holidays must be taken in mainland Britain (that is, not including the Channel Islands and so on) and grants will only cover the costs of children, not adults.

Grants are not made for clothing or education, nor are they made retrospectively. When a child is supported this cannot be taken as a guarantee that other children in the same family will also receive a grant.

Annual grant total: In 1999 the trust's income was £41,000 and grants to individuals totalled £8,700.

Applications: On a form available from the correspondent.

Correspondent: Neil Carter, 184 Rochdale Road, Willow Gardens, Halifax HX2 7JT.

The Halifax Society for the Blind

Eligibility: People who are registered visually impaired and live in Calderdale.

Types of grants: One-off grants of cash or equipment according to need. Grants can be given towards, for example, a bed, school equipment, a television or decorating costs.

Annual grant total: In 2000/01 the trust had assets of £603,000 and an income of £95,000. From a total expenditure of £119,000, grants totalled £8,500.

Applications: On a form available from the correspondent, to be submitted through one of the visiting staff of the society. The committee meets monthly and can act rapidly in urgent cases.

Correspondent: Graham Mitchell, Secretary, 3 Wards End, Halifax HX1 1DD (01422 352383).

Other information: The society visits each of its 730 members five or six times a year and also operates a minibus, holiday home, a resource centre and a hotel at Fleetwood.

The Halifax Tradesmen's Benevolent Institution

Eligibility: People in need aged 60 or over who live in the parish of Halifax and the surrounding area, who were self-employed or a manager of a business for at least seven years. Applicants should have no other income than a pension and have less than £11,000 in savings.

Types of grants: Quarterly allowances of £550 a year.

Annual grant total: In 2001/02 the trust had assets of £240,000 and an income of £26,000. Total expenditure was £28,000, including £24,000 in 43 grants to individuals.

Applications: In writing to the correspondent for consideration in June or November.

Correspondent: John R Robertshaw, 3 Wards End, Halifax HX1 1DB
(01422 365858; Fax: 01422 340277).

195

North East – West Yorkshire

A Pickles Charitable Trust

Eligibility: People who are elderly, disabled or infirm and live in Calderdale.

Types of grants: One-off and occasionally recurrent grants, ranging between £250 and £3,000.

Annual grant total: In 2000/01 grants to 17 individuals totalled £2,100. Grants to eight organisations totalled £3,700.

Applications: The trust states that it does not respond to unsolicited applications.

Correspondent: J D Turner, Trustee, Matthews Brooke Taylor & Co., 3 Wards End, Halifax HX1 1DD (01422 365858; Fax: 01422 340277).

Dewsbury

The Dewsbury Relief in Sickness Fund

Eligibility: People in need who are sick, convalescent, disabled or infirm and live in the county borough of Dewsbury.

Types of grants: One-off grants of up to £200 for needs such as ambilifts, refrigerators, washing machines, house cleaning and decoration, electronic aids for people who are blind and so on,

Annual grant total: In 2000/01 the trust had assets of £6,000 and an income of £340. Grants to six individuals totalled £950.

Applications: In writing to the correspondent either directly by the individual or through a social worker, citizen's advice bureau or other welfare agency. Applications are considered at any time.

Correspondent: G J Jones, 6 Crowlees Road, Mirfield, West Yorkshire WF14 9PJ (01924 492423).

The Whittuck Charity

Eligibility: People in need who live in the former county borough of Dewsbury (as constituted on 1 April 1974). There is a preference for people who are sick, convalescent or disabled.

Types of grants: One-off grants of between £50 and £500 for clothing, holidays, household equipment and other items, services or facilities where help is not readily available from other sources.

Annual grant total: About £2,600.

Applications: Applications can be submitted directly by the individual or through a social worker, citizen's advice bureau or other welfare agency or third party such as a parent, spouse or doctor. They are considered throughout the year.

Correspondent: G Swain, Clerk to the Trustees, 27 Union Street, Dewsbury, West Yorkshire WF13 1AY (01924 455391; Fax: 01924 469299; e-mail: gswain@whg.co.uk).

Halifax

The Goodall Trust

Eligibility: Widows and unmarried women in need who live in the parishes of St Jude and All Saints – Halifax (the ancient township of Skircoat).

Types of grants: Recurrent grants according to need. Grants range from about £100 to £175 a year.

Annual grant total: In 2000 the trust had assets of £70,000, an income of £2,600 and a total expenditure of £1,600. Grants to six individuals totalled £1,400.

Applications: On a form available from the correspondent, to be submitted between July and September for consideration in October. Advertisements are placed in the local press and parish magazines.

Correspondent: Charles Ross Woodward, 11 Fountain Street, Halifax HX1 1LU (01422 339600; Fax: 01422 339601; e-mail: crw@wilkinsonwoodward.co.uk).

Charity of Ann Holt

Eligibility: Single women who are over the age of 55 and in need and have lived in Halifax for at least five years.

Types of grants: Pensions, in 2000 of £74 a year, paid in quarterly instalments until the recipient dies, moves out of the area or moves into a residential home. About 110 grants are given each year.

Annual grant total: In 1999/2000 the trust had assets of £140,000 and an income of £14,000. Total expenditure was £13,000, including £12,000 given in pensions.

Applications: Directly by the individual in writing to the correspondent. Applicants will need to be prepared to provide two referees who are not relations, e.g. vicar, ex-employer or someone else they have known for a number of years.

Correspondent: G D Jacobs, Oak House, 9 Cross Street, Oakenshaw, Bradford, West Yorkshire BD12 7EA.

Other information: This entry was not confirmed by the trust, but the address was correct according to the Charity Commission database.

Horbury

St Leonards Hospital Charity

Eligibility: People in need, hardship or distress who live in the former urban district of Horbury.

Types of grants: Mostly one-off grants, ranging from £25 to £1,500. Grants have been given towards adaptations, convalescence, nursing, renovation and repairs to homes for disabled access and helping people who are homeless or having marriage problems. No grants are made towards maintenance of equipment already paid for. No loans are made although recurrent grants are considered.

Annual grant total: In 2001 the charity had assets of £6,000, an income of £2,900 and a total expenditure of £2,100. Welfare grants to individuals totalled £1,300. Grants to organisations totalled £800.

Applications: In writing to the following address: The Priest, St Peter's Vicarage, Northgate, Horbury, Wakefield WF4 6AS. Applications can be submitted directly by the individual, through a social worker, citizen's advice bureau or other welfare agency or through a church member. They are considered at any time and the trustees can act quickly in urgent cases.

Correspondent: I Whittell, 31 New Road, Horbury, Wakefield, West Yorkshire WF4 5LS (01924 272762).

Horton

The John Ashton Charity (including the Gift of Ellis Smethurst).

Eligibility: People in need who are 65 or over and live in the ancient townships of Great and Little Horton, and the Great Horton Municipal Ward.

Types of grants: Grants of £11 to £22 are made.

Annual grant total: In 2001 the charity had assets of £39,000 and an income of £2,600. Grants to 115 individuals totalled £1,800.

Applications: On a form available from the correspondent, to be submitted directly by the individual for consideration in May and November.

Correspondent: Clement Richardson, 262 Poplar Grove, Bradford BD7 4HU (01274 788616).

Huddersfield

The Beaumont & Jessop Relief-in-Need Charity

Eligibility: People in need who are over 65 and live in the ancient township of Honley (in Huddersfield).

Types of grants: One-off grants ranging from £60 to £500 towards, for instance, Winged Fellowship holidays, heating grants (nominated by doctors), medical equipment, spectacles, transport to luncheon clubs and so on.

Annual grant total: In 1999 the trust had assets of £78,000 and an income of £3,300. Total expenditure was £4,600. It gave £3,200 in grants to 22 individuals.

Applications: In writing to the correspondent, indicating the purpose of the grant. Applications can be submitted directly by the individual or through a social worker, citizen's advice bureau, other welfare agency or other third party (nurses or doctors). Applications are considered throughout the year.

Correspondent: Mrs Wendy Peach, 46 Westcroft, Honley, Holmfirth HD9 6JP.

Other information: This entry was not confirmed by the trust, but the address was correct according to the Charity Commission database.

The Charles Brook Convalescent Fund

Eligibility: People in need who live within the old Huddersfield Health Authority catchment area.

Types of grants: One-off grants for medical comforts, items essential to live independently and convalescent holidays. No loans.

Annual grant total: In 1998/99 the trust had an income of £12,000. Grants of up to £150 were given to 96 individuals and totalled about £10,000.

Applications: On a form available from the social work department at Royal Infirmary Huddersfield and St Luke's Hospital Huddersfield. Applications must be submitted through a social worker and include details of weekly income/expenditure and family situation. Applications sent directly to the correspondent cannot be considered.

Correspondent: Ms C Thompson, Mistal Barn, Lower Castle Hill, Almondsbury, Huddersfield HD4 6SZ.

The Henry Percy Dugdale Charity

Eligibility: People in need who live in the county borough of Huddersfield (comprising the urban districts of Colne Valley, Kirkburton, Meltham and Holmfirth).

Types of grants: One-off and recurrent grants according to need. In 2002 about 90 grants of between £11.50 and £25 a week and about 100 single payments (of between £50 and £500) were made

Annual grant total: In 2000/01 the charity had assets of £1.5 million, an income of £82,000 and a total expenditure of £85,000. Grants to 84 individuals totalled £67,000.

Applications: Applications must be made through a sponsor (e.g. social worker, vicar, citizen's advice bureau). There are two trustees meetings each year, although most applications are considered within a month of arrival rather than waiting for the meeting.

Correspondent: T J Green, Clerk, Bank Chambers, Market Street, Huddersfield HD1 2EW (01484 648482).

The Huddersfield School Children's Trust

Eligibility: Children under 16 who live in the former county borough of Huddersfield.

Types of grants: The trustees do not normally like to be the sole funders of the proposal. The trust stated that it is currently fully subscribed and any new beneficiaries would result in all beneficiaries receiving slightly less, although this is not something which would necessarily mean applications would be declined.

Annual grant total: In 2001 the trust had an income of £3,300.

Applications: In writing to the correspondent, preferably through a school, educational welfare agency or a social worker. Applications are considered in April/May.

Correspondent: Stephen Fox, For The Director of Lifelong Learning, 2 Oldgate, Huddersfield, West Yorkshire HD1 6QW (01484 225014; Fax: 01484 225264).

Keighley

Bowcocks Trust Fund for Keighley

Eligibility: People in need who live in the municipal borough of Keighley as constituted on 31 March 1974.

Types of grants: One-off grants ranging between £100 and £300. Grants are usually given by way of payments direct to suppliers of goods.

Annual grant total: In 2000/01 the trust had assets of £175,000 and an income of £12,000. Grants to students totalled £8,000. Grants to schools and charities totalled £2,500.

Applications: Initial telephone calls are welcomed. Applications should be made in writing to the correspondent by a social worker, citizen's advice bureau or other welfare agency, for consideration throughout the year.

Correspondent: Phillip Vaux, Clerk, Old Mill House, 6 Dockroyd, Oakworth, Keighley, West Yorkshire BD22 7RH.

Other information: This entry was not confirmed by the trust, but the address was correct according to information on file at the Charity Commission.

Leeds

The Bramhope Trust

Eligibility: People in need within the parish of Bramhope.

Types of grants: Gifts of varying amounts are given to organisations and individuals.

Annual grant total: In 2000/01 the trust had an income of £32,000 and a total expenditure of £25,000, most of which was given in grants.

Applications: In writing to the correspondent directly by the individual or through a doctor. Applications are considered throughout the year.

Correspondent: Mrs A R Schofield, 51 Breary Lane East, Bramhope, Leeds LS16 9EU.

The Chapel Allerton & Potternewton Relief-in-Need Charity (Leeds)

Eligibility: People who live in the parish boundaries of Chapel Allerton and Potternewton, Leeds.

Types of grants: One-off grants of £5 to £100 mainly for white electrical goods. Grants can also be to assist with arrears of fuel bills, rent (where housing benefit is not available); telephone (where required by people who are sick or housebound); to replace cookers beyond repair; and to provide food in emergencies when social security is not available.

No grants for furniture as there are two local furniture stores organised by churches.

Annual grant total: About £800.

Applications: Applications must be made through the Leeds or Chapeltown Citizen's Advice Bureau, a social services department, probation officers and so on. Trustees meet in March but applications can be dealt with at any time according to need.

Correspondent: D Milner, 8 Quarrie Dene Court, Leeds LS7 3PH (0113 262 9078) or the Vicar of Chapel Allerton, St Matthew's Vicarage, Wood Lane, Leeds LS7 3QF (0113 268 3072).

The Community Shop Holiday Fund

Eligibility: Families with a child of over three years old living with the Leeds boundaries for whom a holiday would be beneficial.

Types of grants: One-off grants for families to take a break away where circumstances show a need. Although children aged under three are not specifically eligible for a grant on their own, they may receive funding if they have an older sibling who the trust is supporting.

Annual grant total: In 2001 the trust had an income of £14,000 and a total expenditure of £13,000. Grants to 62 families (containing 176 children) totalled £13,000. A further grant of £150 was given to a school.

Applications: In writing to the correspondent through a social worker, citizen's advice bureau or other welfare agency. Potential applicants are then sent an application form to complete; for this reason the initial letter must give full details of the personal circumstances. Applications are considered as received between April and September.

Correspondent: Mrs L Higo, Unit 4, Clayton Wood Bank, West Park Ring Road, Leeds LS16 6QZ (0113 274 5551; Fax: 0113 278 3184; e-mail: info@thecommunityshop.fsnet.co.uk; website: www.thecommunityshop.org.uk).

Other information: The Community Shop is a charity shop and distributes its profits to local charities, groups and individuals in need, particularly people in vulnerable situations. Grants are also given for general welfare purposes (see previous entry).

The Community Shop Trust

Eligibility: People in need who live within the Leeds boundaries. Preference is given to people who are mentally or physically disabled, homeless people, victims of violence, poorer families and people who are severely ill.

Types of grants: One-off grants of £10 to £200 are given towards emergency items such as cookers, fridges, washers, beds and bedding. Help can also be given towards food and toys at Christmas (about £25 per child).

Annual grant total: In 2001 grants to 372 families (containing 918 children) totalled £38,000, excluding grants made from the Holiday Fund (see previous entry). A further £760 was given to organisations.

Applications: In writing to the correspondent, for consideration as received. Applications must be submitted through a social worker, citizen's advice bureau or other welfare agency. All other potential avenues of funding, such as Disabled Living Allowance, must have been explored first.

Correspondent: Mrs L Higo, Unit 4, Clayton Wood Bank, West Park Ring Road, Leeds LS16 6QZ (0113 274 5551; Fax: 0113 278 3184; e-mail: info@thecommunityshop.fsnet.co.uk; website: www.thecommunityshop.org.uk).

Other information: The Community Shop is a charity shop and distributes its profits to local charities, groups and individuals in need, particularly people in vulnerable situations.

The Harrison & Potter Trust (incorporating Josias Jenkinson Relief-in-Need Charity)

Eligibility: People in need who live within the pre-1974 boundaries of Leeds.

Types of grants: One-off grants ranging from £100 to £200 for items or services e.g. gas, electricity, rent, clothing, holidays and for particular items of furniture (excluding washing machines). Grants have also been made for essential repairs to owner-occupied properties. No grants are available for rates or taxes.

Annual grant total: In 2000 the trust had assets of £4.8 million, an income of £295,000 and a total expenditure of £263,000. Grants totalled £161,000, including £24,000 given in total to 196 individuals.

Applications: On a form available from the correspondent, supported by a detailed breakdown of income and expenditure. Applicants should indicate other charities approached. They should be submitted through a citizen's advice bureau, social worker or other welfare agency and are considered at the end of each month.

Correspondent: Miss A S Duchart, Clerk, Wrigleys, Solicitors, 19 Cookridge Street, Leeds LS2 3AG (0113 204 5710; Fax: 0113 244 6101).

Other information: The trust owns and operates two housing schemes for older people in Leeds. Eligible applicants must be within DWP income/capital limits and under the terms of the scheme preference must be given to women. Suitable applicants are eligible for grants to meet removal costs, furnishings etc.

The trust also makes grants to institutions or groups which provide services or facilities to those in need. (For further information please see *A Guide to Local Trusts in the North of England*.)

Kirke Charity

Eligibility: People in need who live in the ancient parish of Adel comprising Arthington, Cookridge and Ireland Wood. There must be evidence of real need/poverty.

Types of grants: One-off grants only, generally up to about £600.

Annual grant total: In 1998/99 the trust had an income of £7,100 and a total expenditure of £8,200.

Applications: Applications can be submitted directly by the individual or through a social worker, citizen's advice bureau or other welfare agency or third party. There is a quick response in cases of emergencies. Other applications are considered in January.

Correspondent: J B Buchan, 8 St Helens Croft, Leeds LS16 8JY.

Other information: This entry was not confirmed by the trust, but the address was correct according to the Charity Commission database.

The Leeds Benevolent Society for Single Ladies

Eligibility: Single ladies in need who are over 60 and live in the Leeds metropolitan area.

Types of grants: Mainly regular allowance of £5 a week paid quarterly. The society also pays telephone rental and television licence fees and also helps with holiday payments.

Annual grant total: Grants are paid to 120 beneficiaries totalling £31,000.

Applications: On a form available by telephoning the correspondent or writing to: Miss J Wenham, 36 Towers Way, Leeds LS6 4PJ.

Applications can be submitted directly by the individual or through a social worker, citizen's advice bureau, other welfare agency or other third party. Applicants are visited to assess the case. Applications are considered every month except August.

Correspondent: Mrs E A Stephens, Chair, 5 Scarcroft Grange, Wetherby Road, Scarcroft, Leeds LS14 3HJ (Tel & Fax: 0113 289 2482).

Other information: The society also runs a residential home (Madeleine Joy House, 10 Broomfield Crescent, Headingley, Leeds) with accommodation for 20 ladies.

The Leeds District Aid-in-Sickness Fund

Eligibility: People who live in the city of Leeds and are in need through unexpected illness or accident ('city of Leeds' refers to the Leeds boundaries as they were prior to the re-organisation of 1974 and the establishment of the metropolitan district of Leeds).

Types of grants: One-off grants of £50 to £250 towards domestic appliances, furnishings, food, medical aid, travel, holidays, adapted computers and so on. No recurrent grants or loans are given and there is no support for debts, rates or taxes.

Annual grant total: In 2001 the trust had an income of £2,400 and a total expenditure of £3,000, all of which was given in 14 grants.

Applications: On a form available from the correspondent, sent on behalf of the applicant by a social worker, welfare agency, doctor, teacher, clergyman or similar third party (personal applications will not be accepted). Applications of over £150 are considered quarterly, in March, June, September and December.

Correspondent: Mrs S Davies, 13 Primley Park Road, Leeds LS17 7HR (0113 269 3700; Fax: 0113 268 0887; e-mail: sallie.davies@lineone.net).

The Leeds Poors Estate

Eligibility: People in need who live within the pre-1974 boundary of Leeds.

Types of grants: One-off grants ranging from £50 to £200 for heating, lighting, furniture, carpets, TV licences, cookers, respite holidays and other essentials. No grants are given towards rates or taxes.

Annual grant total: In 2001 the trust had assets of £128,000, an income of £5,200 and its total expenditure was £6,600. Grants to 63 individuals totalled £3,900, whilst grants to 3 organisations totalled £2,200.

Applications: On a form available from the correspondent. Applications must be submitted through a social worker, citizen's advice bureau or other charity, which must verify and certify that the financial information is correct. Applications are considered monthly.

Correspondent: Miss A S Duchart, Wrigleys, Solicitors, 19 Cookridge Street, Leeds LS2 3AG (0113 204 5710; Fax: 0113 244 6101).

The Leeds Tradesmen's Trust

Eligibility: People over 50 who have carried on business, practised a profession or been a tradesperson for at least five years (either consecutively or in total) and who, during that time, lived in Leeds or whose business premises (rented or owned) were in the city of Leeds. Grants are also given to self employed business/professional people who 'have fallen upon misfortune in business'; normally older people. Widows and unmarried daughters of the former are also eligible.

Types of grants: Quarterly pensions of £10 to £500 a year, plus Christmas grants and spring fuel grants only to those already receiving a pension.

Annual grant total: In 2000 the trust had assets of £1.1 million and an income of £46,000. It distributed over £35,000. Over £18,000 was given in pensions; £4,300 was allocated to special grants; £700 for cash grants and gifts in kind, and £1,800 was for outings.

Applications: In writing to the correspondent, including details of the business or professional addresses, length of time spent there and financial position. All applicants are visited by the assistant secretary.

Correspondent: John C Suttenstall, Secretary, Centenary House, North Street, Leeds LS2 8AY (0113 289 3563).

The Metcalfe Smith Trust

Eligibility: People in need who are infirm, disabled, sick or convalescent and live in Leeds.

Types of grants: One-off grants, generally ranging from £50 to £75. Recent grant have been given towards convalescent holidays, children's clothing, travel expenses, second-hand washing machine and spin dryers to people with disabilities, certain educational equipment and small items of furniture.

Annual grant total: About £1,200 in 19 grants to individuals.

Applications: Applications should only be made by a social worker or similar third party and will be dealt with as received.

Correspondent: Keith Nathan, Chief Executive, Voluntary Action Leeds, Stringer House, 34 Lupton Street, Hunslet, Leeds LS10 2QW (0113 297 7920; Fax: 0113 297 7921; Minicom: 0113 297 7941; e-mail: info@val.org.uk; website: www.val.org.uk).

Other information: The above information concerns grants to individuals, which forms a small part of the trust's grant-making. For further information please see *A Guide to Local Trusts in the North of England*.

Sandal Magna

The Henry & Ada Chalker Trust

Eligibility: People in need who live in Sandal Magna. Most beneficiaries are retired members of the textile industry.

Types of grants: Recurrent grants of £10 a year are distributed in the first week of December. No emergency grants are made.

Annual grant total: Between 90 and 110 grants are made each year.

Applications: On a form available from the correspondent. Applications are stockpiled until a vacancy appears on the list of regular beneficiaries.

Correspondent: The Beaumont Partnership, 67 Westgate, Wakefield, West Yorkshire WF1 1BW (01924 291234; Fax: 01924 290350).

The Sandal Magna Relief-in-Need Charity

Eligibility: People in need who live in the old parish of Sandal Magna (this includes Sandal, Walton, Crigglestone, Painthorpe and West Bretton).

Types of grants: One-off grants of about £20 to £300 are made each year to 20 to 25 individuals. Grants have been used in the past for the purchase of a second-hand washing machine, decorating materials, bedding for a child and a safety gate for the stairs.

Annual grant total: In 2000 the charity had an income of £1,600 and a total expenditure of £1,700.

Applications: In writing to the correspondent. Applications can be sent directly by the individual or through a social worker, citizen's advice bureau or other welfare agency. Applicants must supply their name and address and the circumstances leading to the request.

Correspondent: M J Perry, 50 Dukewood Road, Clayton West, Huddersfield HD8 9HF.

Other information: This entry was not confirmed by the trust, but the address was correct according to the Charity Commission database.

Stanley

The Stanley St Peter Relief-in-Sickness Fund

Eligibility: People who are sick, convalescent, infirm or disabled and live in the ecclesiastical parish of St Peter, Stanley.

Types of grants: One-off and recurrent grants for items such as wheelchairs or medical equipment.

Annual grant total: Between £500 and £1,000.

Applications: In writing to the correspondent. Trustees meet quarterly but can act quickly in urgent cases.

Correspondent: Revd W E Henderson, The Vicarage, 379 Aberford Road, Stanley, Wakefield, West Yorkshire WF3 4HE (01924 822143).

Todmorden

Todmorden Needy Sick Fund

Eligibility: People who are sick or in need and are from and live in the former borough of Todmorden.

Types of grants: Grants are mostly one-off; recurrent grants are very occasionally given. TV licences are given to first and second world war families. Food vouchers, medicine, medical comforts, bedding, fuel, domestic help and convalescence expenses are also given.

Annual grant total: In 2000/01 the trust had assets of £118,000 and an income of £6,000. Grants to 15 individuals totalled £910. Grants to hospices totalled £4,000.

Applications: In writing to: Mrs M Gunton, Case Secretary, Stile House, Stilerd, Todmorden OL14 8NU. Applications must be through a welfare agency or similar organisation and they are considered monthly.

Correspondent: Mrs A Greenwood, Secretary, 22 Park Road, Todmorden OL14 5NJ (01706 812015).

Wakefield

The Brotherton Charity Fund

Eligibility: People in need over 60 who have lived in Wakefield for at least 15 years continuously or 25 years in broken periods.

Types of grants: Annual pension of £50 in April (to commemorate the birthdays of Lord Brotherton and Mrs Eva Greaves).

Annual grant total: In 2000 the fund had an income of £4,600 and a total expenditure of £4,100.

Applications: In writing to the correspondent. When vacancies arise an advert is placed in the Wakefield Express and a waiting list is then drawn up.

Correspondent: C Brotherton-Ratcliffe, PO Box 374, Harrogate HG1 4YW.

5. North West

The Charity of Miss Ann Farrar Brideoake

See entry on page 175

The Cotton Districts' Convalescent Fund

Eligibility: People who are convalescing or have a severe/incurable illness or disability and live in Lancashire, Greater Manchester or the districts of Craven in North Yorkshire, High Peak in Derbyshire, Macclesfield and Warrington in Cheshire, and Calderdale in West Yorkshire.

Types of grants: Grants are for a convalescent holiday of one week at hotels in Blackpool and St Annes. In 2001 applicants paid between £50 to £80 for a week's half board holiday with the fund paying the difference. Consideration will be given to making a contribution towards the costs of a special needs holiday proposed by the applicant.

Annual grant total: In 2001 the fund made grants to 105 individuals totalling £15,000.

Applications: On medical and income forms available from the secretary. Applications may be submitted directly by the individual or through a social worker, citizen's advice bureau or other welfare agency.

Correspondent: John Bardsley, Secretary, Cassons Bow Chambers, Third Floor, 8 Tib Lane, Manchester M2 4JB (0161 832 3074; Fax: 0161 819 8319).

The Grant, Bagshaw, Rogers & Tidswell Fund

Eligibility: Older people in need who live or were born in Liverpool, the Wirral, Ellesmere Port or Chester and who are in need.

Types of grants: Pensions, currently around £425 per annum paid half yearly. Occasional one-off grants may also be given.

Annual grant total: In 1999/2000 the fund had both an income and a total expenditure of £17,000.

Applications: On a form available from the correspondent. Applications should be returned by 31 March and 30 October for consideration in April and November respectively. Applications should be submitted through a social worker, citizen's advice bureau or other welfare agency, although direct applications will also be considered.

Correspondent: Paul R Clarke, Secretary, Mace & Jones, Drury House, 19 Water Street, Liverpool L2 0RP (0151 236 8989; Fax: 0151 227 5010; e-mail: paul.clarke@maceandjones.co.uk).

Other information: This entry was not confirmed by the fund, but the address is correct according to the Charity Commission database.

The Gregson Memorial Annuities

Eligibility: Female domestic servants who have worked for at least 10 years in one service within 10 miles of Liverpool, Southport or Chester or within five miles of Malpas, Cheshire and cannot now work for health reasons. Also, governesses, gentlewomen, widows and unmarried daughters or sisters of clergymen, physicians, lawyers or merchants. These applicants must be born within 10 miles of Liverpool, Southport or Chester, or within five miles of Malpas, be over 50 and members of the Church of England. They must be of limited means and have lived for at least seven years, since the age of 21, in one of the areas mentioned above. No grants are made to women whose husbands are alive.

Types of grants: Annuities of £300 a year, payable in two six-monthly instalments of £150 in advance in March and September.

Annual grant total: About £2,000 in grants each year.

Applications: Applications in writing to the correspondent are considered throughout the year.

Correspondent: G Robin Miller, Brabners Chaffe Street Solicitors, 1 Dale Street, Liverpool L2 2ET (0151 600 3000; Fax: 0151 600 3300).

The Lancashire Infirm Secular Clergy Fund

Eligibility: The secular clergy of the dioceses of Liverpool, Salford and Lancaster who are unable, through age or infirmity, to attend to their duties of office and are in need.

Types of grants: Annual grants mostly of £1,015 although smaller grants of around £500 are available.

Annual grant total: In 2000/01 the fund had an income of £180,000 and a total expenditure of £82,000. In previous years most expenditure was given in grants to individuals.

Applications: On a form available from the correspondent.

Correspondent: Revd Dunstan Harrington, St Hughs Presbytery, 53a Cranbourne Road, Liverpool L15 2HY.

Other information: This entry was not confirmed by the fund but the address is correct according to the Charity Commission database.

The North West Customs and Excise Benevolent Society

Eligibility: Present and former customs officials from the north west who are in need, their widows and other dependants.

Types of grants: One-off grants and loans according to need.

Annual grant total: In 2001 the trust had an income of £2,400 and a total expenditure of £3,200.

Applications: In writing to the correspondent.

Correspondent: Brian Roberts, Customs & Excise, 1st Floor, Queen's Dock, Liverpool L74 4AG (0151 703 1388; Fax: 0151 703 1400; e-mail: brian.roberts@hmce.gsi.gov.uk).

North West Police Benevolent Fund

Eligibility: Serving officers and pensioners of Cheshire County Constabulary, Greater Manchester and Merseyside Police Forces and amalgamated forces of those areas. Also their dependants.

Types of grants: Recurrent grants and loans for convalescence and medical equipment (but not for private health care), financial help for cases of need arising from unforeseen circumstances. Orphaned children of police officers can receive a weekly allowance. Christmas gift and holiday grants are made through the subsidiary St George's Fund.

No grants for private health or education fees.

Annual grant total: In 2001 the fund had assets totalling £2.9 million, an income of £1.4 million and a total expenditure of £813,000. Grants to individuals totalled over £200,000.

Applications: On a form available from the correspondent. Applications are usually made through a force welfare officer or a member of the management committee. They are considered each month and should be submitted by the second Wednesday in January or by the first Wednesday in any other month.

Correspondent: Trevor Williams, Secretary, Progress House, Broadstone Hall Road South, Reddish, Stockport SK5 7DE (0161 355 4420; Fax: 0161 355 4410; e-mail: twilliams@gmpf.polfed.org).

The Northern Counties' Charity for the Incapacitated

Eligibility: People who are totally and permanently incapacitated owing to an incurable or chronic disease, accident or deformity, and who live in the north of England. There is a preference for people living in Bolton and Greater Manchester.

Types of grants: Regular monthly allowances of £5 to £10 a week, paid quarterly to about 10 beneficiaries. Gifts in kind such as shoes and/or bonuses can also be paid to existing beneficiaries when money is available.

Annual grant total: In 2000/01 the charity had an income of £5,000 and a total expenditure of £6,000. Grants totalled £5,000.

Applications: On a form available from the correspondent. Applications should be submitted directly by the individual if possible, otherwise through a social worker, citizen's advice bureau or other welfare agency. They are considered three/four times a year.

Correspondent: The Clerk, 1 Westminster Drive, Cheadle Hulme, Cheadle, Cheshire SK8 7QX (0161 440 9407).

The Northern Counties Orphans' Benevolent Society

See entry on page 178

The Northern Ladies Annuity Society

Eligibility: Single or widowed ladies in need who live in the northern counties of England and who are incapacitated from work. At present only those over 60 years of age are considered. The applicant should have an annual income less than £7,000.

Types of grants: Allowances paid quarterly to annuitants of the society only.

Individuals not already in receipt of an annuity are ineligible for any other form of help from the society. The trust does NOT give one-off grants to non-annuitants, nor support students, and will ignore any such requests for assistance.

Annual grant total: In 2000/01 the trust had assets of £4.5 million, an income of £317,000 and a total expenditure of £184,000. Annuities and grants from the general fund totalled around £116,000.

Applications: Applications to become an annuitant should be made on a form available from the correspondent. Completed forms can be submitted directly by the individual and are considered monthly except for February and August.

Correspondent: Mrs Susan Chilton, Secretary, Mea House, Elephant House, Newcastle-upon-Tyne NE1 8XS (0191 232 1518; Fax: 0191 221 0661; e-mail: susan@nlas.org.uk).

The James Parrott Charity

Eligibility: People in need who live in the South Shore area of Blackpool and the boroughs of Manchester and Salford.

Types of grants: Monthly allowances of £5 per person per week.

Annual grant total: In 2000 the charity had an income of £2,300 and a total expenditure of £1,200, all of which was given in grants to individuals.

Applications: For applicants living in South Shore, Blackpool, applications should be processed through Wyre & Fylde Council for Voluntary Service, 95 Abingdon Street, Blackpool FY1 1PP.

For applicants living in Salford and Manchester, applications should be processed through the Gaddum Centre, Gaddum House, 6 Great Jackson Street, Manchester M15 4AX.

Correspondent: Ann Hudson, Pricewaterhouse Coopers, Abacus Court, 6 Minshull Street, Manchester M1 3ED (0161 236 9191).

The Rycroft Children's Fund

Eligibility: Children in need who live in Cheshire, Derbyshire, Greater Manchester, Lancashire, Staffordshire, South and West Yorkshire. There is a preference for children living in the cities of Manchester and Salford and the borough of Trafford. Applicants should be aged 18 or under.

Types of grants: One-off and recurrent grants according to need.

Annual grant total: In 2000/01 the trust had assets of £1.1 million, an income of £37,000 and a total expenditure of £24,000. Grants were made to 27 individuals totalling £9,500. Grants were also made to organisations.

Applications: On a form available from the correspondent either directly by the individual or through a social worker, citizen's advice bureau or other welfare agency. Details of the applicant's available income and contributions from other sources must also be included. Applications can be made at any time.

Correspondent: J N Smith, 10 Heyridge Drive, Northernden, Manchester M22 4HB (0161 998 3127).

Cheshire

The Cheshire Provincial Fund of Benevolence

Eligibility: People in need in Cheshire, especially, but not exclusively, freemasons and their dependants.

Types of grants: One-off and recurrent grants according to need.

Annual grant total: In 1999/2000 the trust had assets of £3.1 million and an income of £358,000. Grants to individuals totalled £151,000, with £140,000 given to masonic organisations and £83,000 to non-masonic organisations.

Applications: In writing to the corrrespondent.

Correspondent: Peter Carroll, Provincial Grand Secretary, Ashcroft House, 36 Clay Lane, Timperley, Altrincham WA15 7AB (0161 980 6090).

John Holford Charity

Eligibility: People in need who live in the parishes of Astbury, Clutton and Middlewich, and the borough of Congleton.

Types of grants: One-off and recurrent grants for a range of needs, ranging from £100 to £2,500. No grants for education, or for medical treatment.

Annual grant total: In 2001 the trust had both an income and a total expenditure of £58,000. Further information about grants was not available for this year. The previous edition of this guide stated that in 1998 the trust gave a total of £26,000 to 41 individuals in need.

Applications: On a form available from the correspondent. Applications should be submitted by a social worker, carer, citizen's advice bureau, other welfare agency or other third party such as a relative. They are considered at any time.

Correspondent: Birch Cullimore Solicitors, 20 White Friars, Chester CH1 1XS (01244 321066; Fax: 01244 312582; e-mail: info@birchcullimoresolicitors.co.uk; website: www.birchcullimoresolicitors.co.uk).

The Ursula Keyes' Trust

Eligibility: People in need who live in the area administered by Chester District Council and in particular those within the boundaries of the former City of Chester and the adjoining parishes of Great Boughton and Upton.

Types of grants: On-going and emergency grants can be made (although the trustees only meet four times a year to consider grantmaking). Grants can be towards, for example, washing machines for families in need or computers for children with disabilities.
No grants to repay debts or loans or to reimburse expenditure already incurred.

Annual grant total: In 2000 the trust had an income of £285,000 and a total expenditure of £266,000. Most grants are given to organisations, with grants to individuals totalling about £5,000.

Applications: In writing to the correspondent, with details of applicant's income and expenditure. Applications must be supported by a social worker, a doctor (if relevant) or another professional or welfare agency. Applications are considered at the beginning of January, April, July and October.

Correspondent: Peter Robinson Wise, Hillyer McKeown, 90–92 Telegraph Road, Heswall, Wirral CH60 0AQ (0151 342 6116).

The Weaverham & Acton Bridge Sick Poor Fund

Eligibility: People in need who live in Weaverham or Acton Bridge.

Types of grants: One-off grants in the form of money or gifts at Easter of £5 value and at Christmas of £10.

Annual grant total: In 2000/01 the fund had an income of £820 and an expenditure of £880.

Applications: In writing to the correspondent, with a letter of recommendation from a third party. Applications are considered before Easter and Christmas each year.

Correspondent: Mrs E A Glover, 61 Wallerscote Road, Weaverham, Northwich, Cheshire CW8 3JS (01606 852201).

Other information: This entry was not comfirmed by the fund but the address is correct according to the Charity Commission database.

The Wrenbury Consolidated Charities

Eligibility: People in need who live in the parishes of Chorley, Sound, Broomhall, Newhall, Wrenbury and Dodcott-cum-Wilkesley.

Types of grants: Payments on St Marks (25 April) and St Thomas (21 December) days to pensioners and students. Grants are also given for one-off necessities. Grants range from £120 to £130.

Annual grant total: In 2000 the charity had an income of £9,000 and a total expenditure of £8,500.

Applications: In writing to the correspondent either directly by the individual or through another third party on behalf of the individual. The Vicar of Wrenbury and the parish council can give details of the six nominated trustees who can help with applications. Applications are considered in December and April.

Correspondent: Mrs M H Goodwin, Eagle Hall Cottage, Smeatonwood, Wrenbury, North Nantwich CW5 8HD.

Other information: Grants are also given to churches and the village hall, and for educational purposes.

This entry was not confirmed by the trust but the address is correct according to the Charity Commission database.

Chester

The Chester Parochial Relief-in-Need Charity

Eligibility: People in need who live within the boundary of the Chester District Council, with preference given to the area of the ecclesiastical parish called the Chester Team Parish in the city of Chester.

Types of grants: One-off grants ranging from £50 to £1,000. Grants are mostly for household items such as furniture, electrical items and carpets. Occasionally beds and children's clothing are purchased. Vouchers are also distributed for Christmas.

Annual grant total: In 2001 the trust had both an income and a total expenditure of £45,000, and gave a total of £30,000 in grants to individuals in need.

Applications: On a form available from the correspondent. Applications can be made directly by the individual, through a recognised referral agency (e.g. social worker, citizen's advice bureau or other welfare agency) or through other third party such as relatives. Applications are considered at any time.

Correspondent: Birch Cullimore Solicitors, 20 White Friars, Chester CH1 1XS (01244 321066; Fax: 01244 312582).

Other information: Grants are also made to organisations.

Congleton

The Congleton Town Trust

Eligibility: People in need who live in the town of Congleton (this does not include the other two towns which have constituted the borough of Congleton since 1975).

Types of grants: Grants are given to individuals in need or to organisations who provide relief, services or facilities to those in need.

Annual grant total: In 2001 the trust gave £24,000 to organisations and individuals.

Applications: In writing to the correspondent. Small grants will be considered when they are received, large grants will be considered in June or November.

Correspondent: Ms J Money, Clerk, c/o Congleton Town Hall, High Street, Congleton CW12 1BN (01260 291156).

Other information: The trust also administers several smaller trusts, and has recently taken over the finances of the William Barlow Skelland Charity for the Poor which has been wound up.

Frodsham

Frodsham Nursing Fund

Eligibility: People in need of all ages, who are sick, convalescent, disabled or infirm and live in the town of Frodsham.

Types of grants: Cash grants are not made. Grants are given in the form of items such as bedding, clothing, medical aids, heating and other domestic appliances. Temporary relief may also be provided to those caring for somebody who is sick or disabled and help can be given towards relatives and friends visiting or caring for patients.

Annual grant total: In 2001/02 the fund had both an income and a total expenditure of around £2,500.

Applications: Applications may be made in writing to the correspondent at any time, either directly by the individual or on their behalf by a doctor, nurse or social/welfare worker. They should state briefly the circumstances and what help is being sought.

Correspondent: Robert Watson, Secretary/Treasurer, 5 Lansdowne, Frodsham WA6 6QB (01928 733063).

Macclesfield

The Macclesfield Relief-in-Sickness Fund

Eligibility: People in dire need who live in Macclesfield town and who have a chronic illness or a learning disability.

Types of grants: One-off grants only for necessary items such as washing machine, telephone installation, removals or specialist wheelchairs and especially for health related items that would improve the quality of the applicant's situation.

Annual grant total: About £1,000.

Applications: Applications must be made through a local social services office, doctor's surgery or other welfare agencies and they should verify the need of the applicant.

Correspondent: Mrs L Cookson, c/o Macclesfield Council of Voluntary Service, 81 Park Lane, Macclesfield, Cheshire SK11 6TX (01625 428301).

Mottram St Andrew

The Mottram St Andrew United Charities

Eligibility: People in need who live in the parish of Mottram St Andrew.

Types of grants: One-off grants ranging from £35 to £250 reviewed annually; recurrent grants according to need. Recent grants have been given in cases of illness and death, for travel to and from hospital and Christmas bonuses to pensioners.

Annual grant total: In 2000 the trust had assets of £85,000, an income of £3,500 and a total expenditure of £3,600, all of which was given in grants to 35 individuals.

Applications: In writing to the correspondent or to individual trustees. Applications can be submitted directly by the individual or through a social worker, citizen's advice bureau, other welfare agency or other third party. They are considered in November.

Correspondent: J D Carr, Thornlea, Oak Road, Mottram St Andrew, Macclesfield, Cheshire SK10 4RA (01625 829634).

Prestbury

The Prestbury, Harehill & District Nursing Association

Eligibility: People in need who are sick and convalescent and live in Prestbury, Harehill and Over Alderley.

Types of grants: Christmas bonuses to people who are sick or convalescing.

Annual grant total: In 2000 the charity had assets of £2,600 and an income of £750. Total expenditure was £1,100 with eleven grants to individuals made totalling £550.

Applications: The committee decides who in the area deserves the grants. Applications should not be made.

Correspondent: Miss Mary Shaw, 12 Bridge Green, Prestbury, Macclesfield, Cheshire SK10 4HR.

Other information: The charity also gives small grants to a local hospice.

Runcorn

The Runcorn General War Relief Fund

Eligibility: People in need who live in Runcorn. There is a preference for people in need as a result of service in World War II.

Types of grants: One-off grants for items such as cookers, beds, washing machines and so on.

Annual grant total: In 2001/02 the fund had an income of £1,300 and a total expenditure of £2,600. About £2,500 is given each year in grants to individuals.

Applications: On a form available from the correspondent.

Correspondent: Greg Yeomans, Secretary, Chief Executive's Department, Halton Borough Council, Municipal Buildings, Kingsway, Widnes, Cheshire WA8 7QF (0151 424 2061).

Warrington

The Charity of Letitia Beaumont

Eligibility: People in need who were born or who have lived for some time in the borough of Warrington or the parish of Moore.

Types of grants: Annual pensions of about £160 per person.

Annual grant total: About £1,000.

Applications: In writing to the correspondent.

Correspondent: Clifford Straw, Messrs Robert Davies & Co, 21 Bold Street, Warrington WA1 1DF (01925 650161).

The Joseph & Lucy Monk's Trust

Eligibility: People in need who were born or have lived for a long time in the county borough of Warrington or within three miles from Market Gate in Warrington. The number of pensions distributed must be, as far as possible, an equal number to both sexes.

Types of grants: Annual pensions of about £156 per person.

Annual grant total: In 2000/01 the trust gave grants to about seven individuals totalling around £1,000.

Applications: In writing to the correspondent.

Correspondent: Clifford Straw, Messrs Robert Davies & Co, 21 Bold Street, Warrington WA1 1DF (01925 650161).

The Police-Aided Children's Relief-in-Need Fund

Eligibility: Children in need who are under secondary school age and who live in the borough of Warrington. Applications from students of secondary school age and over will be considered in exceptional circumstances.

Types of grants: Grants of up to £40 to help with the cost of clothing and footwear.

Annual grant total: About £7,500 in about 210 grants each year.

In 2000/01 the fund had an income of £12,000 and a total expenditure of £17,000.

Applications: Via Warrington Council for Voluntary Services, or public authorities.

Correspondent: Garry Bradbury, Education Accountancy, Third Floor, New Town House, Buttermarket Street, Warrington WA1 2NJ.

Other information: This entry was not confirmed by the fund, but the address was correct according to the Charity Commission database.

The Warrington Sick & Disabled Trust

Eligibility: People in need, especially those who are disabled or infirm, who live in a six-mile radius of the Nurses' Home at 21 Arpley Street, Warrington.

Types of grants: One-off grants for holidays, Christmas parcels and other needs.

Annual grant total: In 2001 the trust had both an income and a total expenditure of £4,000. Grants to individuals totalled around £1,500.

Applications: In writing to the correspondent.

Correspondent: John Brian Naylor, Chairman, Ridgway Greenall Solicitors, 21 Palmyra Square, Warrington WA1 1BW (01925 654221;
e-mail: jnaylor@ridgeway.co.uk).

The Clara Westgarth Trust

Eligibility: Older people, over 60, who are in need and live in the borough of Warrington.

Types of grants: One-off grants to enable people to live independently and to improve their quality of life. Grants can be used for equipment or to improve the home situation, where statutory funding is unavailable.

Annual grant total: In 2000/01 the trust had assets of £210,000, an income of £16,000 and a total expenditure of £12,000. The grant total has previously been about £7,000.

Applications: On a form available from the correspondent, to be submitted through a social worker, citizen's advice bureau, welfare agency, clergy, advice worker or any professional or community group leader in contact with the individual. Applications are usually considered every two months. Individual applicants are not means tested and no financial income is asked for, but it helps the trustees in assessing an application to know what type of income the applicant has, e.g. pension, income support, disability allowance and so on, so that the amount of grant awarded assists in meeting the individual's needs.

Correspondent: E Lockett, Administrator, Warrington CVS, 5 Hanover Street, Warrington, Cheshire WA1 1LZ (01925 630239; Fax: 01925 630519).

Other information: Grants are also available to organisations who help older people within Warrington.

Widnes

The Knight's House Charity

Eligibility: People in need who live in Widnes, including as far as Hale Village.

Types of grants: One-off grants for a cooker, washing machine, fridge, other domestic items and clothing. Applications for second-hand furniture may also be successful, provided by a separate organisation, Justice and Peace.

Annual grant total: About £10,000 each year in grants to individuals.

Applications: On a form available from the correspondent.

Correspondent: Greg Yeomans, Secretary, Chief Executive's Department, Halton Borough Council, Municipal Buildings, Kingsway, Widnes, Cheshire WA8 7QF (0151 424 2061).

Wilmslow

The Lindow Workhouse Trust

Eligibility: People in need who live in the ancient parish of Wilmslow.

Types of grants: One-off grants to help with, for example, fuel bills, equipment repairs, property repairs. Any cases of real need are considered. No grants are made towards relief of rates, taxes or other public funds.

Annual grant total: In 2001 the trust had assets of around £226,000, and both an income and a total expenditure of around £8,000. Grants were made to 60 individuals totalling £5,900. Although the trust makes educational grants to individuals, none were made during the year.

Applications: In writing to the correspondent. Applications can be submitted directly by the individual or through a social worker, citizen's advice bureau or other welfare agency. They are considered at any time.

Correspondent: Grp Capt J Buckley, 10 Summerfield Place, Wilmslow, Cheshire SK9 1NE (01625 531227).

The Wilmslow Aid Trust

Eligibility: People in need who live in Wilmslow and neighbourhood.

Types of grants: One-off grants including furniture, bedding, comforts, food, fuel, medical aids, recuperative holidays and domestic help. Grants range from £5 to £150. Recent grants have included bedding/children's beds after a house fire; fridge/freezers to single parents; removal costs due to bankruptcy; heating system repairs; furniture, clothing, and decorating materials.

Annual grant total: In 2000/01 the trust had both an income and a total expenditure of £3,000. In previous years grants have been given to 80 individuals totalling £3,000.

Applications: Through a welfare agency, church, social worker or citizen's advice bureau or in writing to the correspondent including address, income and statement of what is needed and why.

Correspondent: Dr A R Anderson, 21 Edgeway, Wilmslow SK9 1NH (01625 535634).

Wybunbury

The Wybunbury United Charities

Eligibility: People in need who live in the 18 townships of the ancient parish of Wybunbury as it was in the 1600s and 1700s. The townships are Basford, Batherton, Blakenhall, Bridgemere, Chorlton, Checkley-cum-Wrinehill, Doddington, Hatherton, Hough, Hunsterson, Lea, Rope, Shavington-cum-Gresty, Stapeley, Walgherton, Weston, Willaston and Wybunbury.

Types of grants: The three administering trustees for each township are responsible for distribution of grants. Some make annual payments to individuals in need but funds are also kept in most townships to cover emergency payments for accidents, bereavement or sudden distress.

Annual grant total: In 2000/01 the trust had assets of about £62,000, and both an income and a total expenditure of £3,500.

Applications: By direct application to one of three administering trustees, one of which is the vicar.

Correspondent: Richard Elwood, Cockshades Farm, Wybunbury, Nantwich, Cheshire CW5 7HA (01270 841259).

Cumbria

Barrow Thornborrow Charity

Eligibility: People in need who are sick, convalescent, disabled or infirm, and live in the former county of Westmorland, the former county borough of Barrow, the former rural districts of Sedbergh and North Lonsdale, or the former urban districts of Dalton-in-Furness, Grange and Ulverston.

Types of grants: One-off grants ranging between £50 and £400 towards items, services or facilities which are calculated to alleviate suffering and assist recovery and which are not available from other sources, e.g. household equipment, assistance with travelling expenses in case of hospitalisation, clothing, computer aids and assistance with essential property repairs. No grants are given for debts.

Annual grant total: In 2000/01 the charity had assets of £129,000, and both an income and a total expenditure of £7,300. Grants to individuals totalled £7,100.

Applications: In writing to the correspondent including details of the applicant's circumstances. Applications can be submitted through a social worker, citizen's advice bureau or other welfare agency. Applications from individuals must be supported from an independent source. They are considered in January, April, July and October, although may be looked at between meetings in an emergency.

Correspondent: Mrs J M Walker, 6 Murley Moss, Kendal, Cumbria LA9 7RW (01539 722956).

The Cumbria Constabulary Benevolent Fund

Eligibility: Members and former members of the Cumbria Constabulary in need, and their widows and dependants.

Types of grants: One-off cash grants, usually for the purchase of medical equipment.

Annual grant total: In 2000 the fund had an income of £11,000 and a total expenditure of £7,000.

Applications: In writing to the correspondent.

Correspondent: Federation Representative, Police Headquarters, 1–2 Carleton Hall, The Green, Carleton Avenue, Penrith, Cumbria CA10 2AU (01768 217086).

The Cumbria Miners' Welfare Trust Fund

Eligibility: Miners and their families who are in need and live or work in Cumbria.

Types of grants: Grants are given mainly to miners' welfare schemes in the Cumbria area, but individuals may also apply. Mineworkers who have taken up other employment since leaving the industry are excluded from applying. No recurrent grants are made.

Annual grant total: In 2001 the trust had an income of £9,400 and a total expenditure of £57,000.

Applications: In writing to the correspondent either directly by the individual, through the union or via a CISWO social worker.

Correspondent: V B Clements, c/o CISWO, 6 Bewick Road, Gateshead, Tyne & Wear NE8 4DP.

Other information: This entry was not confirmed by the trust but the address is correct according to the Charity Commission database.

The Jane Fisher Trust

Eligibility: People in need over 50, and people who are disabled, who have lived in the the townships of Ulverston and Osmotherly or the parish of Pennington for at least 20 years.

Types of grants: Monthly payments of £14 to 24 beneficiaries. No lump sum payments have been made for many years.

Annual grant total: In 2000/01 the trust had an income of £4,500 and a total expenditure of £7,000.

Applications: On a form available from the correspondent. Applications are considered when they are received. They must include details of income, capital, age, disabilities, marital status and how long the applicant has lived in the area.

Correspondent: Steven Marsden, Secretary, Livingstons Solicitors, 9 Benson Street, Ulverston, Cumbria LA12 7AU (01229 585555; Fax: 01229 584950).

Ambleside

The Ambleside Welfare Charity

Eligibility: People in need who live in the parish of Ambleside, especially those who are ill.

Types of grants: One-off and recurrent grants according to need. Help is also given to local relatives for hospital visits.

Annual grant total: In 2000 the charity had an income of £36,000 and a total expenditure of £19,000.

Applications: In writing to the correspondent.

Correspondent: David Alexander Morton, 7 Loughrigg Avenue, Ambleside, Cumbria LA22 0DG (01539 431462).

Other information: The correspondent stated that this charity's activities are currently being reviewed by the trustees.

The Backhouse Fund

Eligibility: Unmarried women (widows and spinsters) aged over 50 who live in the parish of Ambleside.

Types of grants: Recurrent grants of £50.

Annual grant total: In 2001 the fund made grants totalling £5,000.

Applications: In writing to the correspondent.

Correspondent: J D Townend, Temple Heelis Solicitors, Plane Tree House, Rydal Road, Ambleside, Cumbria LA22 9AP (01539 433131).

Other information: The trust states that people who currently fit the above criteria should be receiving a grant, whether rich or poor.

Carlisle

The Carlisle Sick Poor Fund

Eligibility: People who are both sick and poor and in need, who live in and around the city of Carlisle.

Types of grants: One-off grants for necessities such as bedding, food, fuel, convalescence and medical needs.

Annual grant total: In 2000 the trust had both an income and a total expenditure of around £7,000.

Applications: In writing to the correspondent.

Correspondent: Brenda Newbegin, Atkinson Ritson Solicitors, 15 Fisher Street, Carlisle, Cumbria CA3 8RW.

Cockermouth

The Cockermouth Relief-in-Need Charity

Eligibility: People in need who live in Cockermouth.

Types of grants: One-off grants according to need.

Annual grant total: In 2000 the charity had an income of £1,600 and a total expenditure of £1,500.

Applications: In writing to the correspondent.

Correspondent: Rev Dr David Thomson, The Rectory, Lorton Road, Cockermouth, Cumbria CA13 9DU.

Other information: This entry was not confirmed by the charity but the address is correct according to the Charity Commission database.

Crosby Ravensworth

The Crosby Ravensworth Relief-in-Need Charities

Eligibility: People in need who have lived in the ancient parish of Crosby Ravensworth for at least 12 months. Preference is given to older people.

Types of grants: One-off and recurrent grants. Grants include £30 coal vouchers to senior citizens and a basket of fruit (or other gift) to people who have been in hospital.

Annual grant total: In 2001 the charity had an income of £9,000 and a total expenditure of £4,000. Grants to individuals total about £2,000 each year.

Applications: In writing to the correspondent submitted directly by the individual including details of the applicant's financial situation. Applications are considered in February, May and October.

Correspondent: James T Relph, Holly Cottage, Crosby Ravensworth, Penrith, Cumbria CA10 3JP (01931 715359).

Hunsonby and Winskill

The Joseph Hutchinson Poors Charity

Eligibility: People in need who are over 65 or widows, and live in the villages of Hunsonby and Winskill.

Types of grants: Grants of £45 according to need.

Annual grant total: In 2001 the trust had an income of £2,200 and a total expenditure of £1,900 Grants were given to 41 individuals totalling £1,800.

Applications: In writing to the correspondent.

Correspondent: S J Holliday, Trustee, South View Farm, Hunsonby, Penrith CA10 1PN (01768 881364).

Kirkby Lonsdale

The Kirkby Lonsdale Relief-in-Need Charity

Eligibility: People in need who live in the parish of Kirkby Lonsdale.

Types of grants: One-off or recurrent grants of £30, usually given just before Christmas.

Annual grant total: In 2000/01 the trust had assets totalling £25,000 and an income of £920. Grants were given to 28 individuals and totalled £840.

Applications: In writing to the correspondent directly by the individual, or by a third party on his or her behalf. Applications are considered in December for Christmas gifts.

Correspondent: Mrs M Quinn, 19 Fairgarth Drive, Kirkby Lonsdale, Carnforth, Lancashire LA6 2DT (01524 271985).

Workington

The Bowness Trust

Eligibility: People in need who live in Workington and live at home (not in institutions).

Types of grants: One-off grants only.

Annual grant total: About £1,000.

Applications: In writing to the correspondent.

Correspondent: Milburns, Oxford House, 19 Oxford Street, Workington, Cumbria CA14 2AW (01900 67363; Fax: 01900 65552).

Greater Manchester

The Barnes Samaritan Charity

Eligibility: People living in the county of Greater Manchester who are convalescing, have a severe/incurable disease, or are disabled or infirm, and are living in their own homes.

Types of grants: Monthly payments not exceeding £30 a month as long as the need continues. Applicants must be able to demonstrate an ongoing, rather than temporary, shortage of income.

Annual grant total: About £9,000 each year to individuals.

Applications: On medical and income forms available from the secretary. Applications can be submitted directly by the individual or through a social worker, citizen's advice bureau or other welfare agency.

Correspondent: John Bardsley, Secretary, Cassons, Bow Chambers, 3rd Floor, 8 Tib Lane, Manchester M2 4JB (0161 832 3074; Fax: 0161 819 8319).

The James Bayne Charitable Trust

Eligibility: People in need who live in Greater Manchester. Students and ex-offenders are not considered.

Types of grants: One-off grants ranging from £50 to £500. Recent grants have been for the purchase of an electric scooter, a stairlift, a child's car seat, a freezer and a computer. No grants are given towards holidays, or in response to requests for numerous household items, for example when someone has been offered accommodation and does not have any items at all.

Annual grant total: In 2000/01 the trust had an income of £6,300 and a total expenditure of £2,500. Grants were given to 12 individuals totalling £3,200.

Applications: In writing to the correspondent. Applications should be submitted through a social worker, citizen's advice bureau, other welfare agency or other third party. They are considered on receipt.

Correspondent: Michael Garret, CLB, 14 Wood Street, Bolton BL1 1DZ (01204 551100; Fax: 01204 551101).

J T Blair's Charity

Eligibility: People over 65 who live in Manchester and Salford and who are in need.

Types of grants: Weekly pensions of up to £5, paid at four-weekly intervals. One-off grants can also be made to eligible people who are in exceptional need.

Annual grant total: In 2000/01 the charity had an income of £15,000 and a total expenditure of £13,000. Grants to individuals totalled about £10,000.

Applications: On a form available from the correspondent. All applicants have an assessment visit by a social worker before their application is considered. Those in receipt of a pension are visited at least once a year.

Correspondent: Shirley Adams, Gaddum Centre, Gaddum House, 6 Great Jackson Street, Manchester M15 4AX (0161 834 6069; Fax: 0161 839 8574; e-mail: sma@gaddumcentre.co.uk; website: www.gaddumcentre.co.uk).

The Lawrence Brownlow Charity

Eligibility: People (usually older people) in need who live in the ancient townships of Tonge, Haulgh and Darcy Lever in Bolton.

Types of grants: One-off grants of £15 upwards, for gas, electricity, fuel, footwear, clothing and food.

Annual grant total: In 2000/01 the charity had assets of £10,000, an income of £1,300 and a total expenditure of £1,400, all of which was given in 70 grants to individuals in need.

Applications: In writing to the correspondent. Applications can be submitted through a social worker, citizen's advice bureau, other welfare agency or trustee. Applications are considered throughout the year subject to funds being available.

Correspondent: R Hill, 24 Exford Drive, Bolton BL2 6TB (01204 524823; e-mail: rae.hill@ntlworld.com).

The Manchester District Nursing Institution Fund

Eligibility: People with health related needs in the cities of Manchester and Salford and the borough of Trafford.

Types of grants: One-off grants. It is important that the request is directly related to the health issue of the applicant and is not related to a general condition of poverty.

Annual grant total: In 2001 the fund had an income of £26,000 and a total expenditure of £23,000.

Applications: On a form available from the correspondent which must be completed by a sponsor from a recognised social and/or health agency. Trustees meet monthly and the deadline for any meeting is the first Wednesday of the month.

Correspondent: Shirley Adams, Gaddum Centre, Gaddum House, 6 Great Jackson Street, Manchester M15 4AX (0161 834 6069; Fax: 0161 839 8574; e-mail: sma@gaddumcentre.co.uk; website: www.gaddumcentre.co.uk).

The Manchester Jewish Federation

Eligibility: Jewish people in need who live in Greater Manchester including Bury, Salford, South Manchester and North Manchester.

Types of grants: Small monthly grants of £5 to £150 to people on low income or one-off help with utility bills, childcare support, respite care, essential household items and the additional food costs of Passover and other religious festivals. The federation also provides help for children's holidays and playschemes and help to re-establish within the community i.e. removal.

Annual grant total: In 2000/01 the federation had an income of £288,000 and a total expenditure of £274,000. About £60,000 was given in grants to individuals.

Applications: On a form available from the correspondent, submitted directly by the individual or, with the applicant's permission, through a social worker, citizen's advice bureau, other welfare agency or other third party. Applications are considered throughout the year. Duty social worker is available each day from 9.30 to 12.30 to discuss requests for financial assistance.

Correspondent: Shelley Lewis, Team Manager, 12 Holland Road, Manchester M8 4NP (0161 795 0024; Fax: 0161 795 3688; e-mail: thefed@charity.vfree.com).

Other information: Other services are also provided, including a full social work service, a centre for people with mental health needs, respite support for parents of children with special needs, a carer's helpline, a luncheon club, a toy library and other help for people who are isolated or housebound.

North West – Greater Manchester

The Manchester Jewish Soup Kitchen

Eligibility: Poor, older and housebound Jewish people who live in the Greater Manchester area, who are in poor health and are unable to care for themselves.

Types of grants: Meals twice a week, and extra food for the Jewish holidays. A day out in St Annes is also arranged each year.

Annual grant total: In 1999/2000 the trust had an income of £34,000 and a total expenditure of £30,000. About £25,000 was spent in total on the food distributions.

Applications: In writing to the correspondent direct or through a hospital, social worker, member of the clergy, doctor or other welfare agency.

Correspondent: Mrs D Phillips, Hon. Secretary, 1 Singleton Lodge, Cavendish Road, Salford M7 4MB.

The Mellor Fund

Eligibility: People who are sick or in need and live in Radcliffe, Whitefield and Unsworth.

Types of grants: One-off grants towards fuel, food and clothing, domestic necessities, medical needs, recuperative breaks and so on. Recurrent grants are generally not given.

Annual grant total: In 2001 the fund had assets of £58,000 and an income of £4,400. Grants were made to 15 individuals totalling £3,200.

Applications: In writing to the correspondent. Applications can be submitted directly by the individual or through a social worker, citizen's advice bureau, other welfare agency or a relative, and should include brief details of need, resources, income and commitments. Applications are considered when received.

Correspondent: W H Mapp, 48 Ashbourne Grove, Whitefield, Manchester M45 7WL (0161 766 2770).

The Pratt Charity

Eligibility: Women over 60 who live in or near Manchester and have done so for a period of not less than five years.

Types of grants: Grants are given towards education, health and relief of poverty, distress and sickness.

Annual grant total: In 2000/01 the trust had an income of £680. Grants to individuals totalled about £1,000.

Applications: In writing to the correspondent via a social worker.

Correspondent: Shirley Adams, Gaddum Centre, Gaddum House, 6 Great Jackson Street, Manchester M15 4AX (0161 834 6069; e-mail: sma@gaddjmcentre.co.uk).

Bolton

The Bolton & District Nursing Association

Eligibility: People who are sick, convalescing, disabled or infirm and live in the area of Bolton Metropolitan Borough Council.

Types of grants: One-off grants for items and services, such as the provision of medical equipment and aids, ranging from £50 to £150.

Annual grant total: In 2001 the trust had an income of £3,200. Grants were made to eight individuals totalling almost £1,000.

Applications: On a form available from the correspondent. Applications can be submitted directly by the individual or through a third party such as a social worker or welfare agency.

Correspondent: Mrs M Watkins, Bolton Guild of Help (Inc.), Scott House, 27 Silverwell Street, Bolton BL1 1PP (01204 524858; Fax: 01204 520018).

The Bolton Poor Protection Society

Eligibility: People in need who live in the former county borough of Bolton.

Types of grants: One-off grants for emergencies and all kinds of need, ranging from £25 to £35.

Annual grant total: In 2000/01 the society had an income of around £2,000. Grants were made to 42 individuals totalling £1,300.

Applications: Initial telephone enquiries are encouraged to establish eligibility. Application forms are sent out thereafter.

Correspondent: Mrs M Watkins, Scott House, 27 Silverwell Street, Bolton BL1 1PP (01204 524858; Fax: 01204 520018).

The Louisa Alice Kay Fund

Eligibility: People in need who live in the area of Bolton Metropolitan Borough Council.

Types of grants: One-off grants for emergencies and all kinds of need, mostly for replacing household equipment and furniture. Grants usually range from £50 to £190.

Annual grant total: In 2001 the trust had an income of £72,000 and a total expenditure of £64,000. Grants were given to 343 individuals totalling £40,000.

Applications: On a form available from the correspondent.

Correspondent: Mrs M Watkins, Bolton Guild of Help (Inc.), Scott House, 27 Silverwell Street, Bolton BL1 1PP (01204 524858; Fax: 01204 520018).

Bury

The Bury Relief-in-Sickness Fund

Eligibility: People who live in the metropolitan borough of Bury and who are sick, convalescent, disabled or infirm.

Types of grants: One-off grants for convalescence and necessities in the home (not telephone installation), which are not available from other sources. No grants to pay debts.

Annual grant total: In 2000 the trust had an income of £5,000 and a total expenditure of £4,300, all of which was given in grants to individuals.

Applications: In writing to the correspondent. Applications should be made through a social worker, citizen's advice bureau or other welfare agency.

Correspondent: Mrs J P Fraser, Secretary, 245 Brandlesholme Road, Bury, Lancashire (0161 764 4947).

Denton

The Denton Relief in Sickness Charity

Eligibility: People in need who are sick, convalescent, disabled or infirm who live in the parish of Denton.

Types of grants: Grants to provide a medical need not available from the NHS.

Annual grant total: In 2001 the trust had an income of £3,800 and a total expenditure of £3,500.

Applications: In writing to the correspondent.

Correspondent: M D Dickin, Secretary, Booth, Ince & Knowles Solicitors, 1 Market Street, Denton, Manchester M34 2BN (0161 336 7011).

Dukinfield

The Emma Rowland Fund

Eligibility: People in need who have lived most of their lives in Dukinfield and are over pensionable age.

Types of grants: Pensions only, paid annually.

Annual grant total: About £700 allocated to 26 pensioners in 2002/03.

Applications: On a form available from the correspondent.

Correspondent: C W Viney, 7 Rochester Close, Dukinfield, Cheshire SK16 5DG (0161 304 9073).

Golborne

The Golborne Charities

Eligibility: People in need who live in the parish of Golborne as it was in 1892.

Types of grants: One-off and recurrent grants usually of between £35 and £50 but occasionally up to £100. Grants are usually cash payments, but are occasionally in kind, e.g. food, bedding, fireguards, clothing and shoes. Also help with hospital travel and necessary holidays. Loans or grants for the payments of rates are not made. Grants are not repeated in less than two years.

Annual grant total: In 2001/02 the trust had assets of £2,200, an income of £4,700 and a total expenditure of £6,300. Grants were given to 125 individuals totalling £5,600.

Applications: In writing to the correspondent through a social worker, citizen's advice bureau or other welfare agency or through the trustees, teachers, doctors, clergy, health visitors etc. Applications are considered throughout the year.

Correspondent: Paul Gleave, 56 Nook Lane, Golborne, Warrington WA3 3JQ.

Other information: Grants are also given to charitable organisations in the area of benefit, and for educational purposes.

Manchester

The Crosland Fund

Eligibility: People in need who live in central Manchester.

Types of grants: One-off grants, usually of £40 to £50, for basic necessities such as clothing, food, bedding, furniture, repairs and household materials.

Annual grant total: In 2000/01 the trust had an income of £5,500 and a total expenditure of £6,000. Grants of £40 to £50 are made to about 20 individuals each quarter.

Applications: In writing to the correspondent, through a social worker, citizen's advice bureau or other welfare agency. Applications are considered in June, September, December and March. Around 20 grants are given each time.

Correspondent: The Dean, Manchester Cathedral, Manchester M3 1SX (0161 833 2220; Fax: 0161 839 6226).

The Dr Garrett Memorial Trust

Eligibility: Families or groups in need who live in Manchester.

Types of grants: Grants towards the cost of convalescence or holidays for individual families and groups.

Annual grant total: In 2000/01 the trust had an income of £12,000 and a total expenditure of £13,000, most of which was given in grants to individuals.

Applications: Application forms available from the correspondent must be completed by social workers or other welfare agencies.

Correspondent: Shirley Adams, Gaddum Centre, Gaddum House, 6 Great Jackson Street, Manchester M15 4AX (0161 834 6069; Fax: 0161 839 8574; e-mail: sma@gaddumcentre.co.uk; website: www.gaddumcentre.co.uk).

The Gratrix Charity

Eligibility: People within a 15-mile radius of the Manchester Exchange who work as (or formerly worked as) plumbers, glaziers, brass workers, lead workers or gas fitters; also their dependants, widows or orphans.

Types of grants: Weekly pensions of up to £3 per week paid at four-weekly intervals.

Annual grant total: About £1,000.

Applications: On a form available from the correspondent. All applications have an assessment visit by a social worker. Those in receipt of a pension are visited at least once a year.

Correspondent: Shirley Adams, Gaddum Centre, Gaddum House, 6 Great Jackson Street, Manchester M15 4AX (0161 834 6069; Fax: 0161 839 8574; e-mail: sma@gaddumcentre.co.uk; website: www.gaddumcentre.co.uk).

The Manchester Relief-in-Need Charity and Manchester Children's Relief-in-Need Charity

Eligibility: People in need who live in the city of Manchester and who are over 25 (Relief-in-Need) or under 25 (Children's Relief-in-Need).

Types of grants: One-off grants only for emergencies, equipment for the home, clothing, home repairs, aids/appliances and other general necessities. Debts are very rarely paid and council tax, rent debts and funeral expenses are never met. Cash is never paid and in most cases items are given. Cheques are made out to the supplier of the goods or services.

Annual grant total: In 2000/01 both trusts had a combined expenditure of £78,000

Applications: On a form available from the correspondent which must be completed by a sponsor from a recognised social or health related agency. Applications are considered monthly and the closing date for each meeting is the 15th of the month.

Correspondent: Shirley Adams, Gaddum Centre, Gaddum House, 6 Great Jackson Street, Manchester M15 4AX (0161 834 6069; Fax: 0161 839 8574; e-mail: sma@gaddumcentre.co.uk; website: www.gaddumcentre.co.uk).

New Mills

John Mackie Memorial Ladies' Home

Eligibility: Widows or spinsters who are members of the Church of England, are over 50 and are in need.

Types of grants: Christmas gifts to 50 individuals of £50 each. Applicants will not receive help if they re-marry.

Annual grant total: In 2001 the trust had an income of £3,200 and a total expenditure of £3,900. Grants to individuals totalled £2,500.

Applications: In writing to the correspondent, with (i) evidence of the birth, marriage and death of the applicant's husband, (ii) references from three houseowners, confirming her character, respectability and needy circumstances, (iii) proof that she has a small income and (iv) evidence that she is a member of the Church of England. Applications should be submitted directly by the individual, and are considered throughout the year.

Correspondent: Mrs Margaret Wood, 27 Low Leighton Road, New Mills, High Peak SK22 4PG (01663 743243).

Oldham

The Charity of Arthur Vernon Davies for the Poor

Eligibility: People in need who live in the ecclesiastical parishes of St James, East Crompton; St Mary, High Crompton; and Holy Trinity, Shaw.

Types of grants: One-off grants only. Grants are not given towards council tax or other public funds.

Annual grant total: In 2000/01 the trust had an income of £13,000 and a total expenditure of £14,000, most of which was given in grants to individuals.

Applications: On a form available from the correspondent.

Correspondent: Christine Chester, Chief Executive's Department, PO Box 33, Civic Centre, West Street, Oldham OL1 1UL (0161 911 3000).

The Sarah Lees Relief Trust

Eligibility: People living in Oldham who are sick, convalescent, disabled or infirm.

Types of grants: One-off grants are made.

Annual grant total: In 2001/02 the trust had an income of £5,000 and a total expenditure of £6,000.

Applications: In writing to the correspondent through a social worker, citizen's advice bureau or other recognised welfare agency.

North West – Greater Manchester

Correspondent: Mrs Julia Mercer, Moorlands, 6 The Park, Grasscroft, Oldham OL4 4ES.

Other information: This entry was not confirmed by the trust, but the address was correct according to the Charity Commission database.

The Oldham Distress Fund

Eligibility: People in need who live in the borough of Oldham.

Types of grants: One-off grants for household items, services or facilities that will reduce need.

Annual grant total: In 2000/01 the fund had an income of £3,000 and a total expenditure of £5,800. Grants to individuals totalled about £3,000.

Applications: On a form available from the correspondent.

Correspondent: The Administrator, Chief Executive's Department, PO Box 33, Civic Centre, West Street, Oldham OL1 1UL (0161 911 3000).

The Oldham United Charities

Eligibility: People in need who live in the borough of Oldham.

Types of grants: One-off grants normally of £50 or over usually towards medical needs, for example, wheelchairs, and washing machines for people who are incontinent. Some grants are given to students towards educational expenses.

Annual grant total: The charities have an income of about £5,000, over £4,000 of which is available for relief-in-need purposes.

Applications: In writing to the correspondent. Trustees meet four times a year, in February, May, July and October.

Correspondent: B McKown, c/o Mills McKown, 85 Union Street, Oldham OL1 1PF (0161 624 9977).

Ramsbottom

The Ramsbottom Aid-in-Sickness Fund

Eligibility: People in need who are sick, convalescent, disabled or infirm and who live within the boundary of the Ramsbottom Urban District Council.

Types of grants: Grants are available for heating, food, telephone stamps, convalescence holidays, support of family if provider is hospitalised and clothing, all at the request of trained nurses or doctors. Grants are not paid in cash but in what is actually needed, arrangements can be made for the correspondent to travel to the shop to pay for the goods. No grants towards paying debts.

Annual grant total: In 2000/01 the fund gave grants totalling about £1,600.

Applications: On a form available from the correspondent. Applications are usually made through a social worker, citizen's advice bureau, a welfare agency or a member of the trustees or committee.

Correspondent: J P Dunne, Butcher & Barlow, 2-6 Bank Street, Bury, Lancashire BL9 0DL (0161 764 4062).

Other information: Applications made through Greater Manchester Voluntary Services for applicants outside Ramsbottom will not be considered.

Rochdale

The Nurses' Benefit Fund

Eligibility: Nurses or any other person formerly in the employment of Rochdale District Nursing Association and any retired or disabled nurse in the borough of Rochdale.

Types of grants: Recurrent grants, paid either once or twice a year.

Annual grant total: In 2000/01 the fund had an income of £2,000, all of which was given in grants to individuals.

Applications: In writing to the correspondent.

Correspondent: Miss Susan M Stoney, Clerk, Jackson Brierley Hudson Stoney, The Old Parsonage, 2 St Mary's Gate, Rochdale OL16 1AP (01706 644187/647094).

Charities Administered by Rochdale Borough Council

The address for the following is: Rochdale Metropolitan Borough Council, PO Box 15, Town Hall, Rochdale OL16 1AB.

(i) Heywood Relief-in-Need Trust Fund

Eligibility: People in need who live in the former municipal borough of Heywood.

Types of grants: One-off grants ranging from £50 to £400 particularly to help with fuel arrears, clothing and furniture. Grants have also been given towards baby clothing for single parents and for telephone installation.

Annual grant total: In 2000/01 the trust had an income of £7,000 and a total expenditure of £8,000. Grants to individuals totalled about £5,000.

Applications: On a form available from the correspondent. Applications should preferably be supported by a social worker, health visitor or similar professional. Applications are considered in January, March, May, July, September and November.

Correspondent: Moira Whitehead (01706 864713; Fax: 01706 864705).

(ii) The Middleton Relief-in-Need Charity

Eligibility: People in need who live in the former borough of Middleton.

Types of grants: One-off grants (typically £200) for emergencies, for example, travel expenses to visit people in hospital or similar institutions, fuel bills, television licence fees, arrears, holidays for disadvantaged families and general household necessities.

Annual grant total: In 2000/01 the charity had both an income and a total expenditure of £2,500.

Applications: Made by individual application and through social workers, health visitors, victim support schemes and citizen's advice bureaux.

Correspondent: Peter Thompson (01706 864715; Fax: 01706 864705).

(iii) Rochdale United Charity

Eligibility: People in need who live in the ancient parish of Rochdale (the former county borough of Rochdale, Castleton, Wardle, Whitworth, Littleborough, Todmorden and Saddleworth). The charity is made up of three funds; the United Charity is a general charity for people in need, the Ladies Charity is particularly for women, especially those who are pregnant or who have recently given birth, the Harold Shawcross Fund is for the benefit of people who are sick, ailing or those whose means are small.

Types of grants: One-off grants ranging from £50 to £250. Grants have been given to help with washing machines, cookers, fridges/freezers, bedding, clothing, recuperative holidays for people long deprived of such, special food, medical or other aids, and telephones, televisions or radios for people who are alone.

Annual grant total: In 2000/01 grants to individuals totalled £6,000.

Applications: On a form available from the correspondent. Applications can be submitted through a social worker, GP, health visitor, citizen's advice bureau or other welfare agency or directly by the individual if it includes a letter from any of those listed above. Applications are considered in March, June, September and December.

Correspondent: Peter Thompson (01706 864715; Fax: 01706 864705).

The Rochdale Fund for Relief-in-Sickness

Eligibility: People living in Rochdale who are sick, convalescent, disabled or infirm. This is not a charity for relief of poverty.

Types of grants: One-off grants only, usually of £50 to £1,000 for individuals. The trustees will consider any requests for items which will make life more comfortable or productive i.e. medical equipment such as nebulizers. Doctors surgeries or community nurses usually receive the larger payments of £1,000 to £5,000, for specialist equipment. Grants are not given to help with household bills, especially telephones. Cash grants are not given directly to individuals; individuals are given equipment or money is given via a social worker.

Annual grant total: In 2000/01 the fund had an income of £33,000 and a total expenditure of £20,000, all of which was given in grants.

Applications: Applications can be made either directly by the individual (if no other route is available) or through a social worker, citizen's advice bureau, other welfare agency or other third party such as a doctor. Individuals who are applying directly should use an application form, available from the correspondent.

Correspondent: Miss Susan M Stoney, Clerk, Jackson Brierley Hudson Stoney, The Old Parsonage, 2 St Mary's Gate, Rochdale OL16 1AP (01706 644187/647094).

Royton

The Royton Sick & Needy Fund

Eligibility: People in need who live in the district of Royton.

Types of grants: Supply of special food and medicines, medical comforts, extra bedding, fuel, and medical and surgical appliances; provision of domestic help and cash grants to obtain the benefits above or to defray the expenses of convalescence, obtaining change of air, special protection or treatment including the expense of any necessary transport. Grants are not given towards council tax or other public funds.

Annual grant total: In 2000/01 the trust had an income of £2,000 and a total expenditure of £2,500. Grants to individuals totalled about £2,000.

Applications: On a form available from the correspondent.

Correspondent: Ian Thorpe, Chief Executive's Department, PO Box 33, Civic Centre, West Street, Oldham OL1 1UL (0161 911 4716).

Salford

The Booth Charities

Eligibility: People who are retired, over 60, on a basic pension, live in the city of Salford and are in need.

Types of grants: Regular allowances of £6 to £8 a month paid directly to the electricity company. One-off grants are also made through a discretionary fund.

Annual grant total: In 2000/01 the charities had an income of £500,000.

About £100,000 was given in grants to around 1,000 individuals. The remainder was given to organisations.

Applications: On a form available from the correspondent. Applications for one-off grants must be made by Social Services, ministers of religion, doctors etc.

Correspondent: Mrs Sheila Jones, Midwood Hall, 1 Eccles Old Road, Salford, Manchester M6 7DE (0161 736 2989; Fax: 0161 737 4775).

The City of Salford Relief-in-Distress Fund

Eligibility: People in need who live in the City of Salford.

Types of grants: One-off grants to families and individuals of up to £250 (although grants over this amount may be considered). Applications will be considered for clothing, convalescence/holidays, furniture, special equipment for those with special needs, and bedding etc. Recent grants have included funds for a memorial to a young person's father, a grant to enable a family to partially equip their home after a fire, and a holiday for a family where the mother had terminal cancer. Grants cannot be considered for local authority rent or council tax arrears.

Annual grant total: In 2000/01 four grants were made totalling £1,000.

Applications: On a form submitted by a City of Salford social worker, who must be prepared to attend a meeting with the trustees to present the case. For information on how to apply through a social worker, contact the address below.

Correspondent: The Director of Community and Social Services, c/o Welfare Rights & Debt Advice Service, 12 Station Road, Swinton, Salford M27 6AF (0161 727 8235; Fax: 0161 727 9139).

Stockport

Sir Ralph Pendlebury's Charity for Orphans

Eligibility: Orphans in need who have lived (or whose parents have lived) in the borough of Stockport for at least two years.

Types of grants: Grants can be for £5 or £6 a week and orphans can also receive a clothing allowance twice a year.

Annual grant total: In 2000/01 the charity made grants for educational and relief-of-need purposes totalling £18,000. Most of the grants were for relief-of-need purposes.

Applications: In writing to the correspondent.

Correspondent: A Roberts, 32 Sevenoaks Avenue, Stockport SK4 4AW.

Sir Ralph Pendlebury's Charity for the Aged

Eligibility: Older people in need who have lived in the borough of Stockport for at least two years

Types of grants: Small pensions to older people.

Annual grant total: In 2000/01 the charity made grants to 40 to 50 individuals in need totalling around £15,000.

Applications: In writing to the correspondent.

Correspondent: A Roberts, 32 Sevenoaks Avenue, Stockport SK4 4AW.

The Stockport Sick Poor Nursing Association

Eligibility: People in need who are sick and poor or infirm and who live in the old county borough of Stockport.

Types of grants: One-off grants for specific items only.

Annual grant total: In 1999/2000 the association had an income of £4,400 and a total expenditure of £5,000. In previous years most of the expenditure was given in grants to individuals.

Applications: In writing to the correspondent through social services or a welfare agency. Direct applications from individuals are not accepted. The trustees meet on the third Wednesday of every other month to discuss applications. If grants are approved, cheques are sent out straight away. Cheques are made payable to the agency that supports the application who will then buy the items for the applicant.

Correspondent: Mrs Gwen Jackson, Secretary, 11 Heathfield Road, Davenport, Stockport, Cheshire SK2 6JL (0161 480 2915).

Tameside

The Mayor of Tameside's Distress Fund

Eligibility: People who live in the borough of Tameside and are deprived of the basic necessities of life. Applicants must use the fund as a last resort.

Types of grants: One-off grants of about £50 to £250.

Annual grant total: The fund usually has an income and an expenditure of around £4,000 to £5,000.

Applications: On a form available from the correspondent. Applications must be made through a social worker or similar third party. Applicants must include details of income, expenditure, reason for and amount of request and other organisations approached.

Correspondent: Ms Nazam Islam, Tameside M B C, Corporate Services Unit, Council Offices, Wellington Road, Ashton Under Lyne, Lancashire OL6 6DL (0161 342 3562; Fax: 0161 342 2187; e-mail: nazma.islam@mail.tameside.gov.uk).

Wigan

The Wigan Town Relief-in-Need Charity

Eligibility: People in need who live in the former county borough of Wigan (i.e. the pre-1974 boundaries). Operated under this charity is also the Mitton War Fund which gives grants to individuals who served in the two world wars.

Types of grants: One-off grants ranging from £50 to £250.

Annual grant total: In 1998 the trust's income was £12,000. Most grants are given to organisations, but grants to individuals are considered. £1,000 was given in grants to three individuals in need. A further £200 to £300 is available each year from the Mitton War Fund. No recent information was available.

Applications: In writing to the correspondent. Applications can be submitted directly by the individual or through a social worker, citizen's advice bureau, other welfare agency, or other third party (British Legion). They are considered in May.

Correspondent: G Shepherd, Clerk, Healds Solicitors, Moot Hall Chambers, 8 Wallgate, Wigan WN1 1JE (01942 241511; Fax: 01943 826639).

Isle of Man

The Manx Marine Society

Eligibility: Seafarers, retired or disabled seafarers and their widows, children and dependants, who live on the Isle of Man. Young Manx people under 18 who wish to attend sea school or become a cadet are also eligible.

Types of grants: One-off and recurrent grants of up to £416 according to need.

Annual grant total: In 2000 the trust made 12 grants to individuals totalling £5,000.

Applications: On a form available from the correspondent. Applications are considered at any time and can be submitted either by the individual, or through a social worker, citizen's advice bureau or other welfare agency.

Correspondent: Capt. R Cringle, Cooil Cam Farm, St Marks, Isle of Man IM9 3AG (01624 822828).

Lancashire

The Accrington & District Helping Hands Fund

Eligibility: People living in the former borough of Accrington, Clayton Le-Moors and Altham, who are in poor health and are either supported by benefits or are on a low income.

Types of grants: One-off grants towards the cost of:
(i) special foods and medicines, medical comforts, extra bedding, fuel, and medical and surgical appliances
(ii) provision of domestic help
(iii) provision of mobile physiotherapy service.
No recurrent grants can be made.

Annual grant total: In 2000 the fund had assets of £310,000, an income of £10,000 and a total expenditure of £27,000, all of which was given in 50 grants to individuals in need.

Applications: On a form available from the correspondent submitted either directly by the individual or through a social worker, citizen's advice bureau or other welfare agency. Applications should include evidence of income and state of health, as well as estimates of what is required. Applications are considered every six or seven weeks.

Correspondent: Mrs Mary-Ann Renton, The Coach House, Clitheroe Road, Waddington, Lancashire BB7 3HQ (01200 422062; e-mail: maryann.renton@zen.co.uk).

The Baines Charity

Eligibility: People in need who live in the ancient townships of Carleton, Hardhorn-cum-Newton, Marton, Poulton and Thornton.

Types of grants: One-off and recurrent Christmas grants of between £60 and £100.

Annual grant total: In 2001 the charity had an income of £16,000 and a total expenditure of £9,400. Grants to individuals in need totalled £4,900. One grant of £680 was given to a local school for educational purposes, although individuals can be supported if they are eligible.

Applications: On a form available from the correspondent. Applications should be submitted by 31 October each year, for consideration in November.

Correspondent: Duncan Waddilove, 2 The Chase, Normoss Road, Normoss, Blackpool, Lancashire FY3 0BF (01253 893459; e-mail: duncanwaddilove@hotmail.com).

The Blackpool, Fylde & Wyre Society for the Blind

Eligibility: People who are blind/visually impaired and live in Blackpool, Fylde and Wyre.

Types of grants: One-off grants of between £10 and £250 to relieve difficulties arising from visual impairment.

Annual grant total: About £2,500 is available each year.

Applications: On a form available from the correspondent to be submitted through a society welfare officer. Applications are considered throughout the year.

Correspondent: John Booth, Clifton Road, Marton, Blackpool FY4 4QZ (01253 792600; Fax: 01253 767590).

Brentwood Charity

Eligibility: Individuals in need who live in Lancashire (boundaries pre-1974).

Types of grants: One-off grants ranging from £50 to £100, towards such things as necessary household appliances, furnishings and special equipment. No grants to pay for debts or rent bonds.

Annual grant total: About £2,500 is available each year for grants to individuals.

Applications: On a form available from the correspondent, with information on the individual's income and expenditure. Applications should be submitted through a social worker, citizen's advice bureau or other welfare agency. No response is made without an sae. Applications are considered quarterly, around January, April, July and October.

Correspondent: Clerk to the Trustees, Community Futures, 15 Victoria Road, Fulwood, Preston PR2 8PS (01772 717461/718710; Fax: 01772 900250).

The Chronicle Cinderella Fund

Eligibility: Children who are disadvantaged, under 18 and live in the pre-1974 boundaries of Lancashire.

Types of grants: Grants range from £50 to £250 to enable single parent families to have a holiday. Grants are given to individual children to allow them to go on group holidays, and to children and mothers for family holidays on referral from agencies.

Annual grant total: In 2000/01 the fund had an income of £7,800 and a total expenditure of £14,000, all of which was given in grants to individuals.

Applications: On a form available from the correspondent. Direct applications are not considered, but are usually referred by schools, child guidance clinics or other welfare agencies or voluntary bodies. Applications are considered quarterly (about January, April, July and October). No response is made without an sae.

Correspondent: Marion Flemming, Clerk to the Trustees, Community Futures, 15 Victoria Road, Fulwood, Preston PR2 8PS (01772 718710/717461; Fax: 01772 718710; e-mail: ccl@communityfutures.org.uk; website: www.communityfutures.org.uk).

Other information: This trust also gives grants to organisations running holidays for children who are disadvantaged.

The Foxton Dispensary

Eligibility: People who are sick, disabled or infirm and in need who live in Blackpool and Poulton-le Fylde.

Types of grants: Food vouchers and other necessities such as household equipment. No cash grants are made.

Annual grant total: In 2000 the trust had an income of £50,000 and a total expenditure of £17,000.

Applications: In writing to the correspondent through doctors, healthcare professionals or social services departments. The trustees meet quarterly.

Correspondent: Jeffrey Meadows, Clerk, PO Box 27, Blackpool FY4 5GF (01253 760277).

The Goosnargh & Whittingham United Charity

Eligibility: Older people in need who have retired and live in the parishes of Goosnargh and Whittingham.

Types of grants: Recurrent grants of £100 paid twice each year.

Annual grant total: In 2000 the relief-of-need fund had assets of £59,000, an income of £5,200 and a total expenditure of £5,000. 23 grants were made to individuals totalling £4,500.

Applications: In writing to the correspondent, submitted directly by the individual, or by recommendation of the trustees, or through a third party such as a social worker or citizen's advice bureau. They are considered in May and November.

Correspondent: R S B Garside, Fleet House, Fleet Street, Preston PR1 2UT (01772 201117; Fax: 01772 561775).

Other information: The charity also makes educational grants from a separate fund.

The Harris Charity

Eligibility: People in need under 25 who live in Lancashire, with preference for the Preston district.

Types of grants: One-off grants according to need. No grants for course fees or to supplement living expenses, to meet salary costs or towards groups travelling overseas.

Annual grant total: In 2000/01 the charity had assets of £2.8 million and an income of £118,000. It had £258,000 available for grants, to be distributed between organisations and individuals, both for relief-of-need and educational purposes.

Applications: In writing to the correspondent with information about financial income and outgoings. Applications are considered during the three months after 31 March and 30 September and must be submitted before these dates by a third party on behalf of the individual.

Correspondent: P R Metcalf, Richard House, 9 Winckley Square, Preston PR1 3HP (01772 821021; Fax: 01772 259441).

Other information: The charity also supports charitable institutions that benefit individuals, recreation and leisure and the training and education of individuals.

Lancashire County Nursing Trust

Eligibility: (i) Retired nurses, who are sick or in need of financial support and have been employed in Lancashire.
(ii) People in need who are sick and live in the old county of Lancashire (excluding Preston) and who should not or cannot be assisted by Social Services.
Most of the income is for the benefit of retired nurses; the remaining income is to be distributed as the trustees think fit to sick and needy people.

Types of grants: One-off grants ranging from £50 to £250. Grants are not made where statutory funding is available. For retired nurses, grants can be for any purpose; for sick and needy people, grants are primarily for medical care, holidays and equipment to further earning prospects. The trust prefers not to give large grants to one person.

Annual grant total: In 2001 the trust had assets of £272,000, an income of £10,000 and a total expenditure of £9,000. Grants were given to 177 individuals totalling £8,500.

Applications: In writing to the correspondent. Applications should be submitted in March/April for consideration in May, and September/October for consideration in November, and must include background reasons for the application. Applications can be submitted directly by the individual or through a social worker, citizen's advice bureau or other welfare agency or nursing authority.

Correspondent: Mrs Margaret Bibby, Hon. Secretary, Deane Croft, Deane Hall Lane, Shaw Green, Euxton, Chorley, Lancashire PR7 6ER (01257 451553).

The Lancashire Football Association Benevolent Fund

Eligibility: People in need who are members of clubs associated with Lancashire Football Association and players or officials injured during, or travelling to or from, matches organised by the association.

Types of grants: One-off grants ranged from £100 to £300.

Annual grant total: In 2000/01 the trust had an income of £4,000 and a total expenditure of £5,000, most of which was given in grants to individuals.

Applications: In writing to the correspondent. Applications can be submitted directly by the individual or through a personal representative or a friend.

Correspondent: J Kenyon, The County Ground, Thurston Road, Leyland, Preston, Lancashire PR25 2LF (01772 624000; Fax: 01772 624700).

Peter Lathom's Charity

Eligibility: People in need living in the district of Chorley and West Lancashire.

Types of grants: One-off grants at Christmas.

Annual grant total: In 1999 the charity had an income and a total expenditure of £29,000.

Applications: On a form available from the correspondent.

Correspondent: Mark Abbott, The Kennedy Partnership, 15 Railway Road, Ormskirk, Lancashire L39 2DW.

Other information: This entry was not confirmed by the trust, but the address was correct according to the Charity Commission database.

Shaw Charities

Eligibility: People over 60 who are on low incomes and live in Rivington, Anglezarke, Heath Charnock and Anderton, Lancashire.

Types of grants: Recurrent grants at Easter and Christmas. Grants range from £15 to £20.

Annual grant total: In 2000/01 the charities had assets of £30,000, an income of £2,300 and a total expenditure of £2,400. Grants were given to 32 individuals totalling £780.

Applications: On a form available from the correspondent to be submitted by the individual for consideration in March and November.

Correspondent: Mrs E Woodrow, 99 Rawlinson Lane, Heath Charnock, Chorley, Lancashire PR7 4DE (01257 480515; e-mail: woodrows@tinyworld.co.uk).

Other information: Grants for the purchase of books by undergraduates are also given through the Shaw's Educational Endowment.

The Skelton Swindells Trust

Eligibility: Women in need who live in Lancashire (pre-1974 boundaries), usually women not supported by a partner.

Types of grants: One-off grants usually of £50 (£100 in special circumstances) for heating, furnishings, special equipment, household appliances, provision of services and so on.

Annual grant total: The trust makes grants totalling about £3,000 each year.

Applications: On a form available from the correspondent, via the social services department or other statutory or voluntary agencies. Applications are considered three times a year, and an sae must be included for a reply.

Correspondent: Marion Flemming, Clerk, Community Futures, 15 Victoria Road, Fulwood, Preston PR2 8PS (01772 718710/717461; Fax: 01772 900250; e-mail: ukinformation@communityfutures.org.uk).

The Swallowdale Children's Trust

Eligibility: People who live in the Blackpool area who are under the age of 25. Orphans are given preference.

Types of grants: Grants are given for a wide variety of educational and other purposes where a need can be established. Grants to students in further/higher education and people starting work can recieve help towards books and equipment/living expenses. Help is given to schoolchildren for cost of school uniform, other school clothing, books, equipment/instruments, educational outings and maintenance.

Annual grant total: In 2000/01 the trust had assets of £905,000 and an income of £42,000. It gave £3,500 in grants to five individuals. Grants to organisations totalled £17,000.

Applications: On a form available from the correspondent, with the financial details of the individual or family. Applications should be made through the individual's school/college/educational welfare agency or through a social worker, health visitor or similar recognised third parties. Applications are considered every two months.

Correspondent: Mrs M Bell, Secretary, 7 Arnold Avenue, Blackpool FY4 2EP (01253 345027).

Blackburn

The Irving Fund to Relieve Distress

Eligibility: People in need who live in the former county of Lancashire who are disabled.

Types of grants: One-off grants of up to £200 towards items such as fridges and heaters, given as goods rather than cash.

Annual grant total: In 2000/01 grants to individuals totalled £2,000.

Applications: On a form available from the correspondent, with the applicant's income and disability details. Applications can be made either directly by the individual or through a social worker, citizen's advice bureau, other welfare agency or any third party.

Correspondent: Ann Cartwright, 13 Buncer Lane, Blackburn BB2 6SE.

Blackpool

Blackpool Borough Council Services Welfare Fund (formerly The Mayor of Blackpool's Welfare Services Fund)

Eligibility: Ex-service men and women who lived in Blackpool and enlisted from there during World War II, and who live in Blackpool at the time of application.

Types of grants: One-off grants for emergencies, heating/fuel, clothing, aids/appliances, travel, home repairs/alterations and funeral costs. No fixed limit on grants to ex-service personnel; the maximum grant to widows is £300.

Annual grant total: About £1,000 is available each year for grants to individuals.

Applications: The Town Hall usually tells the correspondent of possible candidates. Individuals are visited as the first step in the application procedure.

Correspondent: Maj. Jim Houldsworth, 38 Halifax Street, Blackpool FY3 9QQ (01253 765676).

The Blackpool Ladies' Sick Poor Association

Eligibility: People in need who live in Blackpool.

Types of grants: Mainly food vouchers of £12 to £20 a month per family. Special relief grants can be made for immediate needs such as rent, second-hand cookers and washers, clothing, heaters, fireguards, stair gates and so on.

Annual grant total: In 2000/01 the association had an income of £34,000 and a total expenditure of £33,000. Grants to about 1,700 individuals totalled £31,000.

Applications: Applications must include proof of extreme hardship and must be in writing via health visitors, social workers, citizen's advice bureau or other welfare agencies such as Age Concern, MIND etc. Health visitors and social workers can write to the association's treasurer directly, otherwise letters should be sent to the correspondent. Applications are considered all year round, excluding August.

Correspondent: Mrs Colette Ardron, c/o Town Hall, Blackpool, Lancashire FY1 1GB (01253 477477).

Caton with Littledale

The Cottam Charities

Eligibility: People in need who are at least 50 and have lived in Caton with Littledale for at least five years.

Types of grants: One-off grants according to need.

Annual grant total: About £14,000 to individuals in 2001.

Applications: In writing to the correspondent. Grants are awarded in October each year. Applicants must reapply each year.

Correspondent: W J Harris, Blackhurst Swainson Solicitors, 3 & 4 Allborg Square, Lancaster LA1 1GG (01524 32471).

Clitheroe

The Clitheroe District Nursing Association Fund

Eligibility: People in need who are sick, convalescent, disabled or infirm and live in the borough of Clitheroe and the surrounding area.

Types of grants: One-off grants according to need.

Annual grant total: In 2000/01 the fund had an income of £2,400 and a total expenditure of £400.

Applications: In writing to the correspondent.

Correspondent: Dr W G MacKean, Castle Medical Practice, Clitheroe Health Centre, Railway View Road, Clitheroe, Lancashire BB7 2JG (01200 421850; Fax: 01200 421902).

Darwen

The W M & B W Lloyd Trust

Eligibility: People in need who live in the old borough of Darwen in Lancashire. Preference is given to single parents.

Types of grants: One-off grants of between £250 and £750 only for necessities, usually household equipment. Educational grants are given priority over social or medical grants.

Annual grant total: In 2000/01 the trust had assets of £1.7 million, an income of £75,000 and a total expenditure of £67,000. Almost £3,000 was given in 13 grants to individuals in need.

Applications: On a form available from the correspondent, only through a social worker, citizen's advice bureau, other welfare agency, doctor or health visitor. Applications are considered throughout the year.
Correspondent: J N Jacklin, The Lloyd Charity Committee, 10 Borough Road, Darwen, Lancashire BB3 1PL (01254 702111; Fax: 01254 706837).

Fleetwood

The Fleetwood Fishing Industry Benevolent Fund

Eligibility: People directly employed in all sections of the fishing industry at Fleetwood, and their dependants.
Types of grants: Recurrent grants usually of £415 a year (paid quarterly) and one-off grants according to need.
Annual grant total: In 2001/02 the fund had an income of £28,500 and a total expenditure of £23,000. Grants totalling £22,500 were given to 54 individuals in need.
Applications: In writing to the correspondent.
Correspondent: Mrs J Porter, 8 Leighton Avenue, Fleetwood, Lancashire FY7 8BP (01253 777343).

Lancaster

The James Bond Charity

Eligibility: People in need who live in the city of Lancaster, or within a 10-mile radius of Lancaster and have respiratory complaints.
Types of grants: Grants of £60 per quarter towards the cost of gas/electricity and other household bills; and one-off grants of up to £800 for nebulisers, and furniture, carpets and other household items. Ongoing grants are made to people with respiratory problems who are on a low income.
Annual grant total: About £5,000 is given in grants each year to individuals.
Applications: In writing to the correspondent, either directly by the individual or via a doctor or a social worker; applications are considered four times a year at a meeting of trustees. A charity officer may visit applicants.
Correspondent: The Clerk to the Trustees, c/o Administration Services, Lancaster City Council, Town Hall, Dalton Square, Lancaster LA1 1PJ (01524 582068).

The Gibson, Simpson & Brockbank Annuities Trust

Eligibility: Unmarried women or widows who are 50 or over, in need, and have lived in the former borough of Lancaster for the last two years.
Types of grants: Regular yearly allowances totalling £150 each, paid quarterly.
Annual grant total: About £2,000 to about 10 to 15 people.
Applications: On a form available from the correspondent.
Correspondent: W J Harris, Blackhurst Swainson Solicitors, 3 & 4 Allborg Square, Lancaster LA1 1GG (01524 32471).

The Lancaster Charity

Eligibility: People in need who live in the old city of Lancaster and have done so for at least three years, and are at least 60 years old (or under 60 but unable to work to maintain themselves due to age, accident or infirmity).
Types of grants: £26 a week paid monthly to each individual.
Annual grant total: In 2001 the charity had an income of £98,000 and a total expenditure of £103,000. About 12 individuals are supported at a time, with the rest of the income being spent on maintaining the charities' almshouses.
Applications: On a form available from the correspondent. Applications are considered when vacancies occur.
Correspondent: P E M Oglethorpe, Clerk, 16 Castle Park, Lancaster LA1 1YG (01524 846846).

Littleborough

The Littleborough Nursing Association Fund

Eligibility: People in need who are sick, convalescent, disabled or infirm and live in the former urban district of Littleborough.
Types of grants: Recurrent grants according to need. Grants are not given for costs which are normally covered by the DWP or NHS.
Annual grant total: In 2000/01 the fund gave about £2,000 to children's playgroups and organisations. No grants were made to individuals during the year.
Applications: In writing to the correspondent for consideration in October. Applications can be submitted directly by the individual or through a social worker, citizen's advice bureau, other welfare agency or other third party.
Correspondent: Marilyn Aldred, 26 Hodder Avenue, Shore, Littleborough OL15 8EU (01706 370738).

Lowton

The Lowton Charities

Eligibility: People in need who live in the parishes of St Luke's and St Mary's in Lowton.
Types of grants: One-off grants at Christmas and emergency one-off grants at any time.
Annual grant total: About £8,000 in 1999/2000 including £3,500 in Christmas grants. Most of the remainder was given in emergency grants and some educational grants to individuals.
Applications: Usually through the rectors of the parishes or other trustees.
Correspondent: J B Davies, Secretary, 10 Tarvin Close, Lowton, Warrington WA3 2NX (01942 678108).

Lytham St Anne's

The Lytham St Anne's Relief-in-Sickness Charity

Eligibility: People of all ages who are in need through sickness and who live in the borough of Fylde.
Types of grants: One-off grants, for example, towards fuel bills, washing machines, special beds/chairs, respite holidays and travel for medical treatment or to visit sick relatives. No grants for court fees or funeral costs.
Annual grant total: Grants to individuals totalled £6,000 in 2000/01.
Applications: In writing to the correspondent with financial details and information about the illness or the reason for need. Applications can be submitted directly by the individual or through a social worker, citizen's advice bureau, other welfare agency or other third party. Applications are considered bi-monthly.
Correspondent: Rosie Jolly, Secretary, 7 St George's Road, St Anne's, Lancashire FY8 2AE (01253 725563; Fax: 01253 781193).

Lytham Sick Aid Fund

Eligibility: People in need who are both sick and poor, and who live in Lytham St Anne's.
Types of grants: One-off and recurrent grants according to need, for e.g. special beds, washing machines and milk bills.
Annual grant total: About £1,000 in grants each year.
Applications: In writing to the correspondent, for consideration twice a year, around November and May.

Correspondent: C Stephen Chillito, Clerk, Bradshaws Hamer Park and Haworth Solicitors, 71 Adelaide Street, Blackpool FY1 4LQ (01253 621531).

Nelson

The Nelson District Nursing Association Fund

Eligibility: Sick poor people who live in Nelson, Lancashire.

Types of grants: One-off grants according to need.

Annual grant total: In 2000/01 the fund had an income of £6,500 and a total expenditure of £3,500, all of which was given in grants to individuals.

Applications: In writing to the correspondent.

Correspondent: Mrs Patricia A Hudson, Democratic & Legal Services, Borough of Pendle Town Hall, Market Street, Nelson, Lancashire BB9 7LG (01282 661633; e-mail: pat.hudson@pendle.gov.uk).

Preston

The Preston Relief-in-Need Charity

Eligibility: People who live in the area administered by Preston City Council who are in need through poverty, sickness, disability or convalescence.

Types of grants: One-off grants are given for cookers, fridges and washing machines. Other cases are considered such as help towards gas/electric arrears. Grants are not given to pay off statutory grants.

Annual grant total: In 2001/02 grants were made to 35 individuals totalling £4,500.

Applications: A full financial statement must be submitted with an application form, through a social worker, citizen's advice bureau or other welfare agency. Applications are considered every 10 to 12 weeks. The trustees ensure all statutory services and benefits have been exhausted.

Correspondent: The Town Clerk/Chief Executive, Preston City Council, Town Hall, Lancaster Road, Preston PR1 2RL (01772 906115; Fax: 01772 906195).

Merseyside

The Girls Welfare Fund

Eligibility: Girls and young women (usually aged 15 to 25) who are in need and were born, educated and live in Merseyside. Applications from other areas will not be acknowledged.

Types of grants: One-off and recurrent grants according to need. Grants range from £200 to £500. Grants are not made to charities that request funds to pass on and give to individuals.

Annual grant total: In 2001 the trust had both an income and a total expenditure of £7,000. Grants were given to 11 individuals in need totalling £3,900. The trust's assets were £142,000.

Applications: By letter to the correspondent (including full details of what is needed and for what purpose). Applications can be submitted directly by the individual or through a social worker, citizen's advice bureau, other welfare agency, youth justice agency, probation officer, victim support or housing organisation. Applications are considered quarterly in March, June, September and December.

Correspondent: Mrs S M O'Leary, West Hey, Dawstone Road, Heswall, Wirral CH60 4RP (e-mail: gwf_charity@hotmail.com).

Other information: The trust also gives grants to organisations benefiting girls and young women on Merseyside, and to eligible individuals for leisure, creative activities, sports, arts and education.

The Ladies Aid Fund

Eligibility: Women in need over the age of 40 who live within a 10-mile radius of Liverpool or Southport Town Halls.

Types of grants: Recurrent grants according to need. No grants for education or where there is evidence of debt.

Annual grant total: About £1,000 is available each year for grants.

Applications: In writing to the correspondent. Applications are considered throughout the year.

Correspondent: J N L Packer, Secretary to The Ladies Aid Fund, Port of Liverpool Building, Pier Head, Liverpool L3 1NW.

The Liverpool Caledonian Association

Eligibility: People of Scottish descent, or their immediate family, who are in need and who live within a 15-mile radius of Liverpool Town Hall. The association states that 'generally speaking we do not welcome applications from people who have fewer than one grandparent who was Scots born'.

Types of grants: Regular monthly payment of annuities, heating grants and a limited number of Christmas food parcels. Holidays are generally excluded. The usual maximum grant is £50.

Annual grant total: In 2000 the association had an income of £12,000 and a total expenditure of £15,000. Grants to individuals totalled £10,000.

Applications: In writing to the correspondent either directly by the individual, through a social worker, citizen's advice bureau, or other welfare agency or through any other third party. Applications are considered at any time and applicants will be visited.

Correspondent: John Thornhill, 5 Lynnbank Road, Liverpool L18 3HE (0151 722 1813).

The Liverpool Children's Welfare Trust

Eligibility: Children aged 16 or under who live in Merseyside. The trust mainly supports children of single-parent families and of long-term unemployed people.

Types of grants: One-off grants up to £100 for clothing, bedding, washing machines and other household equipment, etc. No grants for debts, telephone rental or installation, or medical equipment.

Annual grant total: About £800 to individuals in need.

Applications: On a form available from the correspondent. Applications are considered on the third Tuesday of every month except August. Applications must be submitted by a social worker or other professional. Direct applications from the client will not be considered.

Correspondent: Gill Gargan, Personal Service Society, 18–28 Seel Street, Liverpool L1 4BE (0151 707 0131).

The Liverpool Ladies Institution

Eligibility: Single women in need who were either born in the city of Liverpool or live in Merseyside. Preference is given to such women who are members of the Church of England, and to older women.

Types of grants: One-off and recurrent grants ranging from £75 to £230 are given in the form of pensions, donations, and Christmas and birthday bonuses.

Annual grant total: In 2000 the trust had an income of £5,700 and a total expenditure of £4,400. Grants were made to 19 individuals totalling £3,800.

Applications: On a form available from the correspondent. Applications should be submitted, at any time, through a social worker, citizen's advice bureau or other welfare agency. The trust has stated that it receives a lot of inappropriate applications.

Correspondent: David Anderton, Whiteacre, 15 Childwall Park Avenue, Childwall, Liverpool L16 0JE (0151 722 9823; Fax: 0151 475 8586; e-mail: da@rapid.co.uk).

The Liverpool Merchants' Guild

Eligibility: Retired, professional, clerical or self-employed people or their dependants who live on Merseyside (or who have lived there for a continuous period of at least 15 years), are aged 50 or over, and are in need or distress. Women whose husbands are still living are only eligible in exceptional circumstances.

Types of grants: Mainly pensions paid half-yearly. Occasional one-off grants for items of exceptional expenditure e.g. telephone bills, repairs, cooker, washing machine, holidays, decorating etc. for those already in receipt of a pension.

Annual grant total: In 2000 the trust had assets in excess of £29 million, an income of £916,000 and a total expenditure of almost £1 million. Grants were made to 585 individuals totalling £931,000.

Applications: On a form available from the correspondent, which requires countersigning by two unrelated referees. Applications can be submitted at any time; they are usually considered in January, April, July and October.

Correspondent: The Secretary, Moore Stephens, Barratt House, 47–49 North John Street, Liverpool L2 6TG (0151 236 9044; Fax: 0151 231 1267).

The Liverpool Provision Trade Guild

Eligibility: Members of the guild and their dependants who are in need. If funds permit, benefits can be extended to other members of the provision trade on Merseyside who are in need and their dependants.

Types of grants: Recurrent grants of £400 to £900 paid monthly, half-yearly or annually.

Annual grant total: In 2001 relief-in-need grants were given to 10 individuals totalling about £9,000.

Applications: In writing to the correspondent, directly by the indivdual. Meetings are held in May and December to discuss applications.

Correspondent: The Secretary, c/o Macfarlane & Co., Cunard Building, Water Street, Liverpool L3 1DS (0151 236 6161).

The Liverpool Queen Victoria District Nursing Association (LCSS)

Eligibility: People who are sick or disabled, live in Merseyside and are in need. No help is given where this should be provided by the 'public purse'.

Types of grants: One-off grants of between £8 and £250 to provide financial help towards food, appliances or other items to help alleviate suffering or assist the recovery of eligible people.

No grants for debts, pilgrimages, medical treatment or travel to hospital.

Annual grant total: In 2001 the trust had assets of £680,000, an income of £37,000 and a total expenditure of £56,000. Grants were given to 143 individuals totalling £34,000.

Applications: On a form only available from the Community Nursing Services of Merseyside Health Districts (not from the correspondent) via district nurses, health visitors or through a social worker. An initial telephone call to the correspondent to discuss eligibility and needs is welcomed. Applications are considered all year round.

Correspondent: Marje Staunton, Liverpool Council of Social Service, 14 Castle Street, Liverpool L2 0NJ (0151 236 7728; Fax: 0151 258 1153; e-mail: marje.staunton@liverpoolcss.org).

The Liverpool Queen Victoria Nursing Association (PSS)

Eligibility: People who are sick, convalescent, disabled or infirm and live in Merseyside.

Types of grants: One-off grants up to £100 for bedding, clothing and household equipment. No grants for medical equipment, telephones or debts.

Annual grant total: About £3,000.

Applications: On a form available from the correspondent. Applications must be made through a social worker, health visitor or district nurse. Appeals are considered on the third Tuesday of every month except August.

Correspondent: Gill Gargan, Personal Service Society, 18–28 Seel Street, Liverpool L1 (0151 707 0131).

Other information: A larger part of the charity's income is administered by the Liverpool Council of Social Service. See entry above.

The Mersey Mission To Seafarers

Eligibility: Active, retired or disabled seafarers and fishermen, their children, widows and dependants.

Types of grants: One-off and recurrent grants according to need.

Annual grant total: In 2001 the mission had an income of £503,000 and a total expenditure of £529,000, a small proportion of which was given in grants to individuals.

Applications: In writing to the correspondent.

Correspondent: Chaplain, Colonsay House, 20 Crosby Road South, Liverpool L22 1RQ (0151 920 3253; Fax: 0151 928 0244; e-mail: liverangel@aol.com; website: www.merseymissiontoseafarers.org).

The Merseyside Police Orphans' Fund

Eligibility: Children/adopted children of deceased police officers or police officers who are incapacitated and will never work again. The police officers must have been members of the Merseyside Police Force.

Types of grants: Allowances of £200 a quarter and a parting gift of £150. Allowances are paid until the child is 16 (unless he/she remains in full-time secondary education). No grants for students being educated at university level.

Annual grant total: In 1999/2000 the fund had an income of £23,000 and a total expenditure of £20,000.

Applications: In writing to the correspondent.

Correspondent: Welfare Department, Merseyside Police, PO Box 59, Liverpool L69 1JD. (0151 777 8745).

Other information: This entry was not confirmed by the fund, but the address is correct according to the Charity Commission database.

The South Moss Foundation

Eligibility: Children under the age of 18 who live in Merseyside and are in need of care or rehabilitation, particularly as a result of crime, deprivation, maltreatment or neglect, or who are in danger of lapsing into delinquency.

Types of grants: The foundation will consider applications for grants to benefit individual young people or small groups of young people who come within the above mentioned criteria. Trustees prefer to make grants where there is likely to be some lasting benefit to the child or young person concerned; for example, to help pursue a constructive interest or hobby, to take up educational or employment opportunities including the purchase of clothing for work and assisting those leaving care or custody to move into their own accommodation, including the purchase of household items. Grants are single payments; most are for less than £150.

The foundation does not make grants which would be a substitute for state benefits or to fund holidays.

Annual grant total: In 2000/01 the trust had assets of £34,000, an income of £1,700 and a total expenditure of £2,100. It gave £335 in grants to three individuals. The remaining funds were given to an organisation benefiting young people.

Applications: Applications should be made on a form available from the correspondent by a social worker, youth worker, probation officer, headteacher or representative of the agency/youth group working with the child concerned. Applications should include details of the money needed and for what purpose and a brief description of why the young person is eligible for funding, i.e. if they are in danger of being taken into care or custody, or involved in the criminal justice system. Applications are considered throughout the year and grants are made payable to the agency applying on behalf of the child. A copy of the grant letter or refusal letter is sent to the child concerned.

Correspondent: Tara Parveen, c/o John Moores Foundation, 7th Floor, Gostins Building, 32-36 Hanover Street, Liverpool L1 4LN (0151 707 6077; Fax: 0151 707 6066).

The Richard Warbrick Charities

Eligibility: Widows in need, with a preference for widows of seamen, who live in Merseyside.

Types of grants: Pensions of £140 a year (paid £35 quarterly).

Annual grant total: In 2000/01 the charities had an income of £17,000 and a total expenditure of £20,000. Grants were made to 120 individuals totalling about £17,000.

Applications: On a form available from Liverpool Parish Church, Our Lady & St Nicholas, Liverpool L2. Applications must be accompanied by the marriage certificate, the husband's death certificate and husband's sea record. A letter of support from a minister of religion should be included.

Correspondent: Helen Miller, Macfarlane & Co., 2nd Floor, Cunard Building, Water Street, Liverpool L3 1DS (0151 236 6161; Fax: 0151 236 1095).

Bebington

The Mayor of Bebington's Benevolent Fund

Eligibility: People 'who are in extreme need and distress' and live in the former borough of Bebington. Anyone living outside the post codes CH63 and CH62 will not be considered.

Types of grants: One-off grants for people in extreme poverty or distress. No grants for council tax payment, or on a regular basis to increase weekly or monthly income.

Annual grant total: About £1,500 is available each year.

Applications: On a form available from the correspondent. Applications can be submitted directly by the individual or through a social worker, citizen's advice bureau or other welfare agency or third party. They are considered at any time, subject to the availability of trustees.

Correspondent: Mrs M Aitken, 38 Wirral Gardens, Bebington, Wirral CH63 3BH.

Bidston

The Emily Clover Trust

Eligibility: Individuals and families who are in need and live within a 10-mile radius of Bidston Parish Church, Birkenhead.

Types of grants: One-off grants of between £70 and £200 for needs such as beds and bedding, lycra support suits, a disabled toilet, holidays for disadvantaged children and household grants. No grants towards further or adult education or adventure holidays.

Annual grant total: In 2001 the trust had assets of £35,000, an income of £3,000 and a total expenditure of £3,400. In previous years 12 grants have been given to individuals totalling £1,700. Some grants are made each year to other charities.

Applications: In writing to the correspondent; support from a social worker or other welfare agency is useful. Applications are considered when they are received.

Correspondent: L F Chettenden, 31 Brookside Crescent, Upton, Wirral CH49 4LE (0151 677 2119).

Billinge

John Eddleston's Charity

Eligibility: People in need who live in the ecclesiastical parish of Billinge.

Types of grants: One-off and recurrent grants according to need.

Annual grant total: In 2000 the trust had an income of £83,000 and a total expenditure of £70,000. Grants to individuals and organisations totalled £19,000.

Applications: In writing to the correspondent by the end of March, for consideration in June.

Correspondent: Mrs G Blundell, A H Leech Son & Dean, Greenbank House, 152 Wigan Lane, Wigan WN1 2LA (01942 740400; Fax: 01942 740401).

Birkenhead

The Birkenhead Relief-in-Sickness Charities

Eligibility: People in need through ill-health who are on a low income and live in the old county borough of Birkenhead. Applicants should have tried to obtain a social fund loan or approached any other source of grants before they then apply to the trust.

Types of grants: One-off grants to a usual maximum of £250. Grants are given for items such as clothing, electrical appliances, furniture (e.g. beds), travel costs and household items (e.g. bedding, towels).

Annual grant total: In 2000/01 the trust had assets of £15,000, an income of £5,300 and a total expenditure of £6,200, all of which was given in grants to 32 individuals.

Applications: Applications, in writing to the correspondent, can be submitted by the individual, through a recognised referral agency (e.g. social worker, citizen's advice bureau or doctor) or other third party, and are considered throughout the year. A doctor's note will be needed to certify the nature of the sickness. Potential recipients will be visited.

Correspondent: Viv Kenwright, Wirral CVS, 46 Hamilton Square, Birkenhead CH41 5AR (0151 647 5432; Fax: 0151 650 1402; e-mail: vivk@wirralcvs.fsnet.co.uk).

The Christ Church Fund for Children

Eligibility: Children in need up to the age of 17 whose parents are members of the Church of England and who live in the county borough of Birkenhead. Preference is given to children living in the ecclesiastical parish of Christ Church, Birkenhead.

Types of grants: Grants for any kind of need, but typically for bedding, furniture, clothing and trips.

Annual grant total: In 2000/01 the fund had an income of £3,000 and a total expenditure £2,000. In previous years all the expenditure was given in grants to individuals.

Applications: In writing through a recognised referral agency (for example, a social worker or citizen's advice bureau) or other third party. Applications are usually considered quarterly (around January, April, September and December), but emergency applications can be considered at any time.

Correspondent: Mrs N Corcoran, c/o Christ Church Parish Office, Bessborough Road, Birkenhead CH43 5RW (0151 652 2775).

Other information: This entry was not confirmed by the fund but is correct according to information on file at the Charity Commission.

Higher Bebington

The Thomas Robinson Charity

Eligibility: People in need who live in Higher Bebington.

Types of grants: One-off or recurrent grants of £10 to £100. Grants can be made for educational purposes.

Annual grant total: In 2000 the charity had both an income and a total expenditure of £2,700. Grants to individuals and organisations totalled around £2,000.

Applications: In writing to the correspondent directly by the individual, for consideration at any time.

Correspondent: Charles F Van Ingen, 1 Blakeley Brow, Wirral, Merseyside CH63 0PS.

Huyton with Roby

The Huyton with Roby Distress Fund

Eligibility: People in need who live in the former urban district of Huyton with Roby (in Knowsley).

Types of grants: One-off grants ranging from £100 to £350 towards the cost of items such as washing machines, carpets and beds. No grants for debts or fuel costs or to buy non-essential items.

Annual grant total: About £1,000.

Applications: In writing to the correspondent through a social worker, citizen's advice bureau or other welfare agency. A social worker would usually assess the need and should inform the trust about the applicant's full circumstances and give details about the item required (e.g. the cost). Applications are considered on receipt.

Correspondent: Maria Graham, Knowsley Metropolitan Borough Council, PO Box 24, Municipal Buildings, Archway Road, Huyton, Merseyside L36 9YZ (0151 443 3664; Fax: 0151 443 3661).

Liverpool

Channel – Supporting Family Social Work in Liverpool

Eligibility: Children living on Merseyside who are in need, where the need cannot be met by statutory grants from the social services.

Types of grants: One-off grants up to £100 for clothing, food, furniture, kitchen equipment and childcare.

Annual grant total: In 2000/01 the trust had an income of £17,000 and a total expenditure of £18,000.

Applications: Applications can only be made through a social worker, health worker or voluntary agency, who should contact the correspondent for advice on funding, an application form and guidelines. Applications are considered on an ongoing basis.

Correspondent: Rebecca Black, 109 Garston Old Road, Liverpool L19 9AE (0151 494 9297).

The Charles Dixon Pension Fund

Eligibility: Merchants who are married men, widowers or bachelors of good character, who are practising members of the Church of England, and widows of pensioners who are in reduced circumstances. Applicants must live in Bristol, Liverpool or London and must be over 60 years.

Types of grants: Pensions of between £520 and £2,000 a year.

Annual grant total: In 2000/01 the trust had an income of £6,200 and gave five grants totalling £5,700.

Applications: On a form available from the correspondent. Applications can be submitted directly by the individual or through a social worker, citizen's advice bureau, other welfare agency or a third party such as a clergyman. They are dealt with as received.

Correspondent: Brig. H W K Pye, Treasurer, The Society of Merchant Venturers, Merchants' Hall, The Promenade, Bristol BS8 3NH (0117 973 8058; Fax: 0117 973 5884; e-mail: hwkpye@btinternet.com).

The William Edmonds Fund

Eligibility: Married or divorced women and widows with dependent children who live in the archdeancory of Liverpool.

Types of grants: One-off grants, usually of between £50 and £200, for holidays, clothing, household necessities (e.g. fridges, gas fires, washing machines, beds/bedding), interior decorating, travel to hospital. Most women helped have several children, are often in poor health and are emotionally stressed and financially impoverished. The grant is intended to 'brighten their lives'.

Annual grant total: In 2001/02 the trust had assets of £64,000, an income of £6,300 and a total expenditure of £7,700, all of whch is given in grants to 53 individuals.

Applications: On a form available from the correspondent. This must be completed and signed by the applicant and a social worker, probation officer or priest in charge of the parish where the woman lives. A professional person must apply on the beneficiary's behalf and payment is made to this third party who is responsible for overseeing the spending of the grant. Applications are considered throughout the year.

Correspondent: Dr O McKendrick, Flat 2, 1 Ibbotson's Lane, Liverpool L17 1AL.

Other information: Grants cannot be made to women who have never been married, or to men. It is helpful for the applicant to state the beneficiary's marital status and also to whom the cheque is to be made payable to (not the beneficiary).

The Liverpool Corn Trade Guild

Eligibility: Members of the guild and their dependants who are in need. If funds permit benefits can be extended to former members and their dependants. Membership is open to anyone employed by any firm engaged in the Liverpool Corn and Feed Trade.

Types of grants: One-off and recurrent grants according to need.

Annual grant total: In 2000 the trust had an income of £14,000 and a total expenditure of £16,000.

Applications: In writing to the correspondent. Applications should be made directly by the individual.

Correspondent: Mr Groves, Secretary, Seafield House, Crosby Road North, Liverpool L22 0LG (0151 949 0955).

The Liverpool Wholesale Fresh Produce Benevolent Fund

Eligibility: People in need, who are or have been associated with the Liverpool fruit trade either as importers or wholesalers, and their families.

Types of grants: One-off and recurrent grants usually ranging from £50 to £80.

Annual grant total: In 2000/01 the fund had an income of £11,000. Total expenditure was £1,800, all of which was given in 20 grants.

Applications: In writing to the correspondent.

Correspondent: Thomas J C Dobbin, Secretary, Administration Office Block E, Wholesale Fruit & Vegetable Market, Edge Lane, Old Swan, Liverpool L13 2EP (0151 259 4973).

Merseyside Jewish Community Care

Eligibility: Poor people of Merseyside of the Jewish faith, including older people, one parent families, students and children.

Types of grants: One-off grants are given for holidays, medical equipment for the relief of pain and suffering and respite breaks. Grants are considered which will enable people to improve their lives. No grants are made for ongoing costs.

Annual grant total: In 2000/01 the trust had an income of £304,000 and a total expenditure of £277,000. Grants to individuals totalled £12,000.

Applications: By letter or telephone to the correspondent. A social worker may visit if necessary. Applications are considered at any time and can be submitted by the individual, and should only be submitted by a third party if the individual needs assistance and has consented to the application.

Correspondent: Mrs Lisa Dolan, Chief Executive, Shifrin House, 433 Smithdown Road, Liverpool L15 3JL (0151 733 2292; Fax: 0151 734 0212; e-mail: mjccshifrin@hotmail.com).

The Ann Molyneux Charity

Eligibility: Seamen living in the city of Liverpool. Preference for men who sailed from the city for most of the last five years that they were at sea. Applicants must receive Income Support, rent or council tax rebate.

Types of grants: Pensions of £140 a year (paid £35 quarterly).

Annual grant total: In 2000/01 the charity had both an income and a total expenditure of around £14,000. Grants were made to 88 individuals totalling £13,000.

Applications: On a form available form Liverpool Parish Church, Our Lady & St Nicholas, Liverpool 2. Applications should be accompanied by seamen's books, details of income and a testimonial from a person of good standing in the community.

Correspondent: Helen Miller, Macfarlane & Co., 2nd Floor, Cunard Building, Water Street, Liverpool L3 1DS (0151 236 6161; Fax: 0151 236 1095).

Pritt & Corlett Funds

Eligibility: Solicitors who are in need and have practised in the city of Liverpool or within the area of Liverpool Law Society, and their dependants.

Types of grants: One-off and recurrent grants and loans according to need.

Annual grant total: In 2000/01 the trust gave a total of £25,000 in grants to individuals

Applications: On a form available from the correspondent, for consideration at any time.

Correspondent: M Hill, Liverpool Law Society, Castle Chambers, Cook Street, Liverpool L2 9SH (0151 236 6998 – ask for Mrs Wright; Fax: 0151 236 0072).

Lydiate

John Goore's Charity

Eligibility: People in need living in the parish of Lydiate only.

Types of grants: Recurrent grants of about £50 distributed in summer and at Christmas to selected individuals. One-off grants for special needs, usually to a maximum of £500.

Annual grant total: In 2001/02 the charity had an income of £7,800 and a total expenditure of £1,400.

Applications: Applications should be made on a form available from the correspondent, through a social worker, teacher, probation officer, cleric, doctor or other responsible third party.

Correspondent: E R Bostock, 124 Liverpool Road, Lydiate, Merseyside L31 2NB (0151 526 4919).

Sefton

Southport & Birkdale Provident Society

Eligibility: People in need who live in the metropolitan borough of Sefton.

Types of grants: One-off grants only, after social services have confirmed that all other benefits have been fully explored. Grants are given towards clothing, bedding, cookers, washing machines and other special needs. Grants are not given for education, training experience, rental deposits, personal debt relief or hire purchase.

Annual grant total: In 2001 the trust had assets of £535,000 and its income was £23,000. Grants were given to 234 individuals totalling £24,000.

Applications: In writing to the correspondent with as much background information of family and reasons for request as possible. Applications can be submitted directly by the individual, through a social worker, citizen's advice bureau or other welfare agency or by letter from recognised agencies; otherwise via social services. Applications are considered every two months from January, and weekly for urgent cases.

Correspondent: The Secretary, Haigh Court, Peel Street, Southport PR8 6JL.

Other information: Local groups supporting people in need in the beneficial area will also be considered.

Wirral

The Conroy Trust

Eligibility: People in need who live (permanently) in the parishes of St Andrew's and Holy Trinity, Bebington and St Mark's, New Ferry. Applications from people outside these areas cannot be considered.

Types of grants: About half the income is distributed as bi-monthly payments to regular beneficiaries. The rest is used to make one-off grants for special needs. Grants range from £50 to £300. The trust also gives grants to other charities working within the beneficial area.

No grants are made for educational purposes.

Annual grant total: In 2001 the trust had an income of £4,400 and a total expenditure of £4,300. Grants were given to 18 individuals totalling £3,200. Grants to organisations totalled £900.

Applications: In writing to the correspondent directly by the individual in January. Applications are considered in February.

Correspondent: Wilfred Gordon Favager, 60 Tudorville Road, Bebington, Wirral CH63 2HU (0151 645 6593).

The John Lloyd Corkhill Trust

Eligibility: People with chest complaints who live in the metropolitan borough of Wirral.

Types of grants: Mostly for equipment (e.g. nebulisers). Help is also given towards services and amenities, for example, holidays and milk bills, and occasionally to buy domestic appliances such as fires, washing machines and so on.

Annual grant total: About £4,000 is available each year.

Applications: Clients are generally referred by their social worker or doctor and have a low income. Supporting medical evidence must be supplied. Applications are considered in June and December.

Correspondent: Mrs M Couche, Secretary, 4 Mere Farm Road, Oxton, Wirral CH43 9TT (0151 652 4179).

The Maud Beattie Murchie Charitable Trust

Eligibility: People in need who live on the Wirral.

Types of grants: One-off and recurrent grants according to need. Grants to organisations are mostly recurrent. No grants for educational purposes.

Annual grant total: In 2000 the trust had both an income and an expenditure of around £25,000. In previous years grants have totalled £20,000.

Applications: Should be made through Wirral Social Services. Applications are considered in June and December.

Correspondent: Mrs L S Mitchell, The Dormy House, Gayton Lane, Heswall, Wirral CH60 3RE.

The West Kirby Charity

Eligibility: People in need who have lived in the old Hoylake urban district (Caldy, Frankby, Greasby, Hoylake, Meols, and West Kirby) for at least three years and who can no longer look after themselves due to age, ill health, accident or infirmity.

Types of grants: Pensions of £5 per week, paid monthly, totalling £260 each year per individual. Christmas gifts and one-off grants are also made. No grants towards rates or taxes.

Annual grant total: In 2000 the charity had an income of £13,000 and a total expenditure of £2,000

Applications: On a form available from the correspondent; considered four times a year. Applications for emergency grants can be considered between meetings.

Correspondent: Roger B Brown, Clerk, 5 Claremont Road, West Kirby, Merseyside CH48 5EA (0151 625 5045).

The Wirral Sick Children's Fund

Eligibility: Children up to 18 who are receiving medical attention and live in the area covered by the former Wirral Health Authority.

Types of grants: One-off grants according to need for, in particular, playing equipment, essential medical equipment and occupational therapy. No grants can be given for medical treatment or medical research, repayment of loans, items that are needed before applications can be processed, or anything that is a statutory responsibility or of an unspecified nature.

Annual grant total: In 2001 the fund had assets of £8,000, an income of £16,000 and a total expenditure of £13,000. Grants were made totalling £12,000.

Applications: Applications should be made on behalf of the individual by a member of the medical profession or a social worker. An application form is available from the correspondent, along with guidelines, which can be submitted at any time. Applications made directly by the individual are not accepted.

Correspondent: Susan Unsted, Hon. Secretary, 17 Brimstage Road, Heswall, Wirral CH60 1XA (0151 342 8952; e-mail: steve.unsted@btopenworld.com).

Other information: The fund also gives grants to schools, centres and hospitals catering for sick children and those with special needs.

6. Midlands

The Birmingham & Midland Cinematograph Trade Benevolent Fund

Eligibility: Individuals and their dependants who are or have been employed for a reasonable period in the cinematograph industry in Birmingham or the Midland counties (i.e. West Midlands, Worcestershire, Herefordshire and parts of Shropshire but not Staffordshire). Applicants should have worked for independent cinemas rather than national circuits.

Types of grants: One-off or recurrent grants or loans according to need.

Annual grant total: In 2000 the fund had an income of £17,000 and a total expenditure of £10,000. About £6,000 a year is given to individuals.

Applications: In writing to the correspondent or through a member of the Committee of Cinema Proprietors or a cinema manager.

Correspondent: S W Clarke, Secretary, 8 Gate Lane, Sutton Coldfield, West Midlands B73 5TT (0121 355 2330; Fax: 0121 355 5032).

The Birmingham & Three Counties Trust for Nurses

Eligibility: Nurses on any statutory register, who have practiced or practice in the city of Birmingham and the counties of Staffordshire, Warwickshire and Worcestershire.

Types of grants: One-off or recurrent grants according to need but up to a maximum of £750. Grants are given to meet the costs of heating, telephone bills, cordless phones for the infirm, household equipment, household repairs, car repairs, electric scooters, wheelchairs, medical equipment and personal expenses such as spectacles and clothing. Grants are also made for convalescent care, recuperative holidays and to clear debt.

Annual grant total: In 2000/01 the trust had assets of £306,000 producing an income of £26,000. Its total expenditure was £36,000 including relief-in-need grants given to over 135 individuals totalling £27,000.

Applications: On a form available from the correspondent. Applications can be submitted either directly by the individual or through a friend, relative or a social worker, citizen's advice bureau or other welfare agency. Details of financial status including income and expenditure, reasons for application, and health status where relevant should be included. Applications are considered throughout the year.

Applicants are visited by a trustee (where distance allows) for assessment. Supportive visiting continues where considered necessary.

Correspondent: Mrs Mary Welsby, Hon. Secretary, 4 Haddon Croft, Halesowen, West Midlands B63 1JQ (Tel & Fax: 0121 550 9422).

Burton Breweries Charitable Trust

Eligibility: Individuals who through their voluntary efforts assist, care, support or develop young people. People are only considered who live in Burton and the East Staffordshire and South Derbyshire district (including a small area of north west Leicestershire).

Types of grants: One-off grants ranging from £100 to £500.

Annual grant total: In 2001/02 the trust had assets totalling £780,000, an income of £33,000 and it made grants to individuals and organisations totalling £35,000.

Applications: In writing to the correspondent. Awards for the benefit of individuals will not be made direct but will be made, in general, via organisations with a significant youth membership and will normally take the form of a one-off sponsorship for a person nominated by the organisation to the trustees.

The trustees meet in February, June and October and applications should be sent in January, May and September. A copy of the trust's guidelines are available on request.

Correspondent: Brian Edward Keates, Secretary to the Trustees, Gretton House, Waterside Court, Third Avenue, Centrum 100, Burton-on-Trent, Staffordshire DE14 2WQ (01283 740600; Fax: 01283 511899; e-mail: info@burtonbctrust.co.uk; website: www.burtonbctrust.co.uk).

Other information: Grants are also made to young people involved in character-building activities, see *The Educational Grants Directory*, and to organisations assisting them.

The Charities of Susanna Cole & Others

Eligibility: Quakers in need who live in parts of Worcestershire and most of Warwickshire and are 'a member or attender of one of the constituent meetings of the Warwickshire Monthly Meeting of the Society of Friends'. Preference is given to younger children, and retired people on inadequate pension.

Types of grants: One-off and recurrent grants according to need. Help may be given with domestic running costs, rent or accommodation fees, convalescence, recreation and home help, and to those seeking education or re-training.

Annual grant total: In 2000 the charities had an income of £9,900 and a total expenditure of £7,600.

Applications: In writing to the correspondent via the overseer of the applicant's Quaker meeting. Applications are considered early in March and October.

Correspondent: Bronwen Lilley, Secretary, Warwickshire Monthly Meeting Office, Friends Meeting House, 40 Bull Street, Birmingham B3 6AF.

Thomas Corbett's Charity

Eligibility: People in need who live in Worcestershire, Staffordshire and Birmingham.

Types of grants: One-off grants according to need. The income is mainly used to maintain and upgrade almshouses and recently so much has been spent on the almshouses that no extra has been available to give in grants to individuals.

Annual grant total: In 2000 the charity had assets of £233,000, an income of £28,000 and its total expenditure was £23,000.

Midlands – General

Applications: In writing to the correspondent directly by the individual for consideration in March and October.

Correspondent: A G Duncan, Clerk, 16 The Tything, Worcester WR1 1HD (01905 731731).

The Baron Davenport Emergency Grant

Eligibility: Needy widows, spinsters (over 18) and children whose fathers are dead (under 21). Applicants should not have savings over £1,000. Applicants must have lived within the old county boundaries of Warwickshire for at least 10 years (this includes Coventry).

Types of grants: One-off grants for emergencies only, particularly unexpected domestic expenses, heavy funeral expenses or similar instances where state benefit is not available or undue delay would cause hardship. Grants are normally between £60 and £150.

Annual grant total: In 2001/02 the charity had an income of £960 of which £920 was distributed in five grants.

Applications: On a form available from the correspondent. Applications can be submitted through a social worker, citizen's advice bureau or other welfare agency; or directly by the individual. They are considered at any time.

Correspondent: Tina Lowe, Coventry Carers Centre, 3 City Arcade, Coventry CV1 3HX (024 7663 2972;
Fax: 024 7683 7082;
e-mail: cov.carers@dial.pipex.com).

Other information: For information on Baron Davenport's Charity Trust, see entry in the Midlands general section.

Baron Davenport's Charity

Eligibility: Needy widows, spinsters and divorcees all aged 60 and over; ladies abandoned by their partners and their children; and people under 25 whose fathers are dead. Applicants must live in the West Midlands, Shropshire, Staffordshire, Warwickshire or Worcestershire. (Net income of applicant should not exceed £141 per week and savings should not be more than £3,000.)

Types of grants: Recurrent grants, typically of £180 to £220 a year, paid half yearly. In very special circumstances one-off grants of up to £250 are given for varying cases of need.

Annual grant total: In 2001 the trust had assets of £27 million, an income of £1 million and a total expenditure of £1.2 million. 4,400 grants to individuals were awarded totalling £437,000.

Applications: Except for emergency cases, applications should be made through local authority social services departments or recognised welfare agencies (when they will be considered at six-monthly intervals), but direct applications from individuals may also be considered. Application forms are available from the secretary and should be submitted by 15 March or 15 September. Grants awarded are paid in June and November.

Applications where prompt relief is needed should be addressed to the local Council of Voluntary Service, as listed under their separate entries.

Correspondent: J R Prichard, Secretary, Portman House, 5–7 Temple Row West, Birmingham B2 5NY (0121 236 8004; Fax: 0121 233 2500).

Other information: The trust and CVS regard as fatherless those whose fathers are dead, and in some cases children abandoned by their fathers. Similarly, although 'spinster' covers all women who have not married, they prefer elderly women who fit the traditional usage of the term.

For emergency needs, see the separate entries in: Staffordshire, Warwickshire, Worcestershire, and West Midlands.

The W E Dunn Trust

Eligibility: People who are in need and live in the West Midlands, particularly Wolverhampton, Wednesbury, north Staffordshire and the surrounding area. Preference is given to people who are very old or very young, who the trust recognises as possibly being the least able to fund for themselves.

Types of grants: One-off grants ranging from £100 to £1,000. Grants are not made to settle or reduce debts already incurred. Grants can be for: clothing and furniture; convalescence and holidays; domestic equipment, especially cookers and washing machines; radio and tv licences; subsistence grants; and welfare grants.

Annual grant total: In 2000/01 the trust had assets of £3.9 million and an income of £156,000. Grants to organisations totalled £107,000. 286 grants to individuals for relief-in-need and educational purposes totalled £49,000, and were broken down as follows:

clothing and furniture	123	£16,000
convalescence and holidays	31	£4,900
domestic equipment	55	£8,100
education	43	£14,000
radio, tv and licences	1	£150
social and welfare	30	£5,000
subsistence	3	£800

Applications: Applications should be made in writing via a social worker, citizen's advice bureau or other welfare agency. The trustees meet on a regular basis to consider applications.

Correspondent: Alan H Smith, The Trust Office, 30 Bentley Heath Cottages, Tilehouse Green Lane, Knowle, Solihull B93 9EL (01564 773407).

The Charles Henry Foyle Trust

Eligibility: Generally people aged 16 and over living in Birmingham and north-east Worcestershire (apart from medical degrees – pre-clinical years, intercalated and elective periods – which are considered nationally), who are in need. There is a preference for medical studies.

Types of grants: To promote and support social, cultural and educational developments, particularly those of a pioneering nature. Grants are also given to individuals for education and welfare purposes. Grants may be given to students in further/higher education towards books, fees/living expenses and study or travel abroad and to mature students towards books and fees. Grants to individuals (including education grants) range from £100 to £250. No grants to students in receipt of an LEA award.

Annual grant total: In 2000/01 the trust had an income of £108,000 and its total expenditure was £79,000. Grants totalled £67,000 and included major awards, mostly made to organisations, totalling £48,000. Smaller grants were listed as follows: general minor awards £8,400 (57 grants); educational awards £8,000 (36 grants); grants to people of pensionable age £3,000 (4 grants); and expeditions/overseas service £2,000 (11 grants).

Applications: In writing to the correspondent. Suitable applicants will be sent an application form to be returned by 30 September for consideration in October/November.

Correspondent: Mrs P Elvins, Trust Administrator, c/o Boxfoldia Ltd, Merse Road, Redditch B98 9HB 01527 68787; Fax: 01527 68810).

Friends Hall Farm Street Trust

Eligibility: Individuals with membership of or links with the Religious Society of Friends (Quakers) who live within 35 miles of the centre of Birmingham.

Types of grants: One-off grants ranging between £100 and £250 are given for academic courses, travel costs and learning experiences.

Annual grant total: In 2000/01 the trust's assets totalled £148,000, it had an income of £12,000 and made eight grants to individuals totalling £1,900. Total expenditure was £12,000.

Applications: In writing to the correspondent, directly by the individual. Applications should be submitted between March and October for consideration in October/November. Ineligible applications will not receive a reply.

Correspondent: Eric Adams, 36 Grove Avenue, Birmingham B13 9RY.

Francis Butcher Gill's Charity

Eligibility: Unmarried or widowed women aged over 50 in need, who are regular attenders of Christian worship, or prevented from being by bodily infirmity. Applicants must also be of good standing and live in Nottinghamshire primarily, but those living in Derbyshire or Lincolnshire may also be considered.

Types of grants: Pensions are given to a fixed number of pensioners. One-off grants may also occasionally be available for items such as gas fires.

Annual grant total: About £12,000.

Applications: On a form available from the correspondent. Applications should be submitted either through a doctor or member of the clergyman or directly by the individual supported by a reference from the one of the aforementioned. Applications can be submitted at any time for consideration in March and October, or at other times in emergency situations.

For pensions, applications will only be considered as a vacancy arises.

Correspondent: Charles Nigel Cullen, Clerk, Bramley House, 1 Oxford Street, Nottingham NG1 5BH (0115 936 9369; Fax: 0115 901 5500).

Dr Isaac Massey's Charity

Eligibility: Women who have lived in Nottinghamshire, Derbyshire or Lincolnshire for at least 10 years and who are either (a) widows over 50 who have not remarried, or (b) fatherless unmarried daughters of clergymen or professional or business people. Applicants must have an annual income (including this grant) of under £10,000.

Types of grants: Regular yearly allowances of up to £250 to supplement income. No capital grants.

Annual grant total: About £2,300.

Applications: On a form available from the correspondent.

Correspondent: J C Foxon, Blythens Accountants, Haydn House, 309-329 Haydn Road, Sherwood, Nottingham NG5 1HG (0115 960 7111; Fax: 0115 969 1313).

Melton Mowbray Building Society Charitable Foundation

Eligibility: Individuals in need who live in Leicestershire, Lincolnshire, Nottinghamshire and Rutland.

Types of grants: One-off grants, for example to provide security and protection for older people. No grants are made for circular appeals.

Annual grant total: In 2001/02 the trust had assets totalling £5,700 and an income of £15,000. Its total expenditure was £11,000. Grants were made to 22 individuals for education and relief-in-need purposes totalling £2,600, and other grants totalled £8,100.

Applications: In writing to: Miss M O Swainston, Secretary to the Trustees, at the address below. Applications can be submitted directly by the individual at any time and are considered in March, June, September and December, and at other times as necessary.

Correspondent: G F Wells, 39 Nottingham Street, Melton Mowbray LE13 1NR (01664 563937; Fax: 01664 480205; e-mail: g.wells@mmbs.co.uk).

Other information: Grants may also be given to organisations for education, disability, medical needs and safer communities.

Thomas Monke's Charity

Eligibility: Young individuals between the ages of 17 and 23 who live in Austrey, Mersham, Shenton and Whitwick.

Types of grants: One-off and recurrent grants according to need.

Annual grant total: In 2001 the charity had assets of £100,000 and an income of £4,300. Total expenditure for the year was £4,600. Educational grants to five individuals totalled £880.

Applications: Application forms are available from the correspondent and should be submitted directly by the individual, preferably in February and March, in time for the trustees' yearly meeting held in April.

Correspondent: C P Kitto, Steward, 20 St John Street, Lichfield, Staffordshire WS13 6PD (01543 262491; Fax: 01543 254986).

Other information: Grants are also made to organisations and to individuals for educational purposes.

The Newfield Charitable Trust

Eligibility: Girls and women (under 30) who are in need of care and assistance and live in Coventry or Leamington Spa.

Types of grants: 'The relief of the physical, mental and moral needs of, and the promotion of the physical, social and educational training of' eligible people. Most grants are under £500 towards things such as clothing, bed, bedding, essential household items and nursery fees. Grants are also given for educational purposes. No grants for rent arrears, council tax, utility bills, HP repayments or postgraduate education.

Annual grant total: In 2000/01 the trust had an income of £49,000 and it made grants totalling £33,000. Assets totalled £1.3 million. Grants were made for educational and welfare purposes.

Applications: Write to the correspondent for an application form. Applications are accepted from individuals or third parties e.g. social services, citizen's advice bureau, school/college etc. A letter of support/reference from someone not a friend or relative of the applicant (i.e. school, social services etc.) is always required. Details of income/expenditure and personal circumstances should also be given.

Applications are considered in January, March, April, June, July, September, October and December.

Correspondent: D J Dumbleton, Clerk, Rotherham & Co Solicitors, 8–9 The Quadrant, Coventry CV1 2EG.

Other information: This entry was not confirmed by the trust, but the information was correcct according to its Charity Commission file.

The Norton Foundation

Eligibility: Young people under 25 who live in Birmingham or Warwickshire and are in need of care or rehabilitation or aid of any kind, 'particularly as a result of delinquency, deprivation, maltreatment or neglect or who are in danger of lapsing or relapsing into delinquency'.

Types of grants: One-off grants ranging between £150 and £500 are given towards clothing, household items and so on.

Annual grant total: In 2000/01 the trust had assets of £3.5 million and an income of £152,000. Grants to 485 individuals totalled £81,000, including £2,800 for educational purposes. Grants to organisations totalled £67,000.

Applications: On a form available from the correspondent. Applications must be submitted through a social worker, citizen's advice bureau, other welfare agency or another third party. They are considered every month.

Correspondent: D F Perkins, PO Box 10282, Redditch, Worcestershire B97 5ZA (e-mail:correspondent@nortonfoundation.org; website: www.nortonfoundation.org).

The Pargeter & Wand Trust

Eligibility: Women who have never been married and are 55 or over and live in their own homes. There is a preference for those living in the West Midlands area, but other areas of the country are considered.

Types of grants: Annuities of £300, paid in quarterly instalments of £75, reviewed annually. One-off payments of £50 to £150 are also given.

Annual grant total: In 2001 the trust had assets of £264,000 and an income of £13,000 all of which was given in grants to individuals.

Applications: On a form available from the correspondent submitted directly by the individual, or through a social worker, citizen's advice bureau or other welfare agency or third party and including two references. Applications are considered in March and September.

Correspondent: Mrs Heddwen Hewis, 1 Little Blenheim, Yarton, Kidlington, Oxfordshire OX5 1LX (01865 372265; e-mail: peter.hewis@hcm.ox.ac.uk).

The Persehouse Pensions Fund

Eligibility: Elderly or distressed people belonging to the upper or middle classes of society who were born in the counties of Staffordshire or Worcestershire, or people who have lived in either county for 10 years or more.

Types of grants: Mainly pensions, but occasional one-off grants.

Annual grant total: In 2000/01 the trust had an income of £10,000 and its total expenditure was £6,400.

Applications: On a form available from the correspondent.

Correspondent: C S Wheatley, 12a Oakleigh Road, Stourbridge, West Midlands DY8 2JX.

The Rycroft Children's Fund

See entry on page 202

The Severn Trent Trust Fund

Eligibility: People with water or sewage services by Severn Trent Water Ltd (area bound by Wales, East Leicestershire, Humber Estuary and Bristol Channel) who are in need and are experiencing difficulty in meeting their water charges.

Types of grants: One-off grants are given to clear or reduce water and/or sewage debt.

Further assistance can be given through the purchase of essential household items or by the payment of other priority bills, for example utility bills. These grants are limited and will normally only be given if an application shows either that it will help the individual maintain a future sustainable weekly budget, or it will make an important and significant difference to the individual's quality of life. The average award is for £450.

Annual grant total: In 2000/01 the trust had an income of £2.7 million and a total expenditure of almost £3 million of which £2.2 million was given in relief-in-need grants to individuals. A further £300,000 was given to organisations towards money and debt advice.

Applications: On a form available from the correspondent, the trust's website or a citizen's advice bureau, money advice centres or other supportive agencies. Unsuccessful applicants may reapply after six months.

Correspondent: S Braley, Director, Emmanuel Court, 12–14 Mill Street, Sutton Coldfield B72 1TJ (0121 355 7766; Fax: 0121 354 8485; e-mail: office@sttf.org; website: www.sttf.org.uk).

Richard Smedley's Charity

Eligibility: People in need who live in the parishes of Breaston, Dale Abbey, Draycott with Church Wilne, Heanor, Hopwell, Ilkerton, Ockbrook and Risley (all in Derbyshire) and of Awsworth, Bilborough, Brinsley, Greasley and Strelley (all in Nottinghamshire).

Types of grants: Usually one-off grants of £50 to £350 towards items such as furniture, washing machines, mobility aids, clothing and carpets. No grants are given towards holidays.

Annual grant total: In 2000 the charity had assets of £201,000, an income of £9,200 and a total expenditure of £6,000. The sum of £5,700 was distributed in 28 relief-in-need grants. Grants are also given to organisations with similar objects.

Applications: On an application form available from the correspondent to be submitted either through a social worker, citizen's advice bureau or other welfare agency or directly by the individual. They can be submitted at any time and are considered in March, June, September and December.

Correspondent: M T E Ward, Clerk, c/o Messrs Robinsons, Market Place, Ilkeston, Derbyshire DE7 5RQ (0115 932 4101; e-mail: mauriceward@robinsons-solicitors.co.uk).

The Snowball Trust

Eligibility: Children and young people under 21 who are sick or disabled and live in Coventry and Warwickshire.

Types of grants: One-off grants to individuals ranging from £100 to £5,000. Grants are for equipment only, such as wheelchairs, tricycles, seating support systems, special toilet seating and nebulisers.

No grants are given for maintenance costs, respite care and holidays, or for any other items except the sort outlined above. Ongoing grants are not made.

Annual grant total: In 2000/01 the trust had assets of £200,000, an income of £110,000 and gave grants to 46 individuals in need totalling £52,000. Other grants to special schools and organisations totalled £36,000.

Applications: On a form available from the correspondent, to be submitted either by the individual or through a third party such as a special school, social worker or other welfare agency, with a firm quote for equipment to be supplied, a letter of support from the individual's school and/or a medical professional, and confirmation of the parents'/guardians' financial need. Applications can be made at any time and they are considered about six times a year.

Correspondent: Mrs P Blackham, Clerk to the Trustees, 11 Rotherham Road, Holbrooks, Coventry CV6 4FF (024 7672 9727).

Sir John Sumner's Trust

See entry on page 111

The Tenbury & District Nursing Association

Eligibility: People in need who live in the parishes of Bockleton, Brimfield, Burford Greete, Eastham, Hanley, Hope Bagot, Knighton-on-Tene, Kyre, Leysters, Little Hereford, Nash, Rochford, Stoke Bliss and Tenbury.

Types of grants: The provision or payment for items, services or facilities which will alleviate the suffering or assist the recovery of eligible people. Grants are generally of £50 to £200. Grants are also given to district nurses towards medical appliances and supplies.

Annual grant total: In 2000/01 the association had an income of £680 and a total expenditure of £960.

Applications: In writing to the correspondent. Applications usually come via a district nurse.

Correspondent: Mrs E Smith, Churchbridge, Nash, Near Ludlow, Shropshire SY8 3AX.

Other information: The correspondent also administers The Tenbury Dispensary which has similar eligibility criteria.

The Eric W Vincent Trust Fund

Eligibility: People in need living within a radius of 20 miles of Halesowen.

Types of grants: Grants range from £50 to £150 and can be for clothing, furniture, hospital travel expenses, equipment and holidays. The trust does not make loans or give grants for gap year projects, any educational purposes or to pay off debts.

Annual grant total: In 2000/01 the trust had assets of £1.1 million and an income of about £44,000, but only some of this was available for relief-in-need grants to individuals.

Applications: Trustees normally meet bimonthly. Applications should be in writing through a health professional, social worker, citizen's advice bureau or other welfare agency. Details of financial circumstances must be included.

Correspondent: Mrs Janet Stephen, Clerk, 4-5 Summer Hill, Halesowen, West Midlands B63 3BU.

The Anthony & Gwendoline Wylde Memorial Charity

Eligibility: People in need with a preference for residents of Stourbridge (West Midlands) and Kinver (Staffordshire).

Types of grants: One-off grants for items such as cookers, vacuum cleaners, washing machines, reclining or lifting chairs, computer packages for people who are blind, TVs, special needs trikes, sports wheelchairs, wheelchair powerpacks, mattresses and clothing etc. No grants are made towards bills or debts.

Annual grant total: In 2000/01 grants to individuals and organisations totalled £33,000.

Applications: In writing to the correspondent. Applications can be submitted directly by the individual, through a social worker, citizen's advice bureau or other welfare agency or through a third party such as a doctor or church minister. For people applying through social services, they would be responsible for administrating the grant. They are considered in January, May, July and September.

Correspondent: Mrs P Gardener, Clerk, Remlane House, 25–27 Hagley Road, Stourbridge, West Midlands DY8 1QH (01384 342100).

The Jonathan Young Memorial Trust

Eligibility: People who as a result of physical handicap, learning disability, long-term illness or educational disadvantage would benefit from access to computer technology. The trust operates primarily within the East Midlands but is also able to consider applications from further afield.

Types of grants: Contributions of up to £500 towards the cost of new computer equipment and the provision of refurbished computer systems suitable for wordprocessing/internet use.

Annual grant total: In 2001 the trust had assets of £65,000 and an income of £11,000. Over £12,000 was spent, of which £10,000 was distributed in 39 relief-in-need grants to individuals, with a further £2,400 to organisations.

Applications: In writing to the correspondent, preferably with supporting references. An information leaflet is available. Applications will be considered in April and October.

Correspondent: Mrs Armorel Young, 10 Huntingdon Drive, The Park, Nottingham NG7 1BW (0115 947 0493; e-mail: young@lineone.net).

Other information: Occasional grants are made to small organisations/voluntary groups with similar objects.

Derbyshire

The Chesterfield Municipal Charities

Eligibility: There are two charities, one for elderly and poor people who were born or live in Hasland; the other for respectable widows and elderly spinsters who were born or live in Chesterfield.

Types of grants: One-off grants and regular payments to seven people of about £100 made twice a year. These beneficiaries have remained the same for a number of years, although the charity welcomes new applicants.

Annual grant total: About £1,400 to £2,000.

Applications: In writing to the correspondent.

Correspondent: D Dolman, Shipton, Halliwell & Co., 23 West Bars, Chesterfield, Derbyshire S40 1AB (01246 232140).

Derbyshire Special Constabulary Benevolent Fund

Eligibility: Members of Derbyshire Special Constabulary, ex-members who resigned on the grounds of ill-health, injury or age, and their dependants, who are in need.

Types of grants: One-off and recurrent grants according to need.

Annual grant total: In 2000/01 the trust had an income of £2,100 and its total expenditure was £1,000, all of which was given in grants to individuals.

Applications: In writing to the correspondent.

Correspondent: The Chief Commandant, Derbyshire Special Constabulary Benevolent Fund, Police Headquarters, Butterlea Hall, Ripley, Derbyshire DE5 3RS (01773 570100).

Door of Hope Christian Trust

Eligibility: Children and young people who are in need and live in the Derby area.

Types of grants: One-off grants according to need.

Annual grant total: In 2000/01 welfare grants totalled £5,000.

Applications: In writing to the correspondent, for consideration throughout the year.

Correspondent: Carl Taylor, Hope Farm, Hedge Lane, Elwell, Derby DE65 6LS (01283 732414).

The Dronfield Relief-in-Need Charity

Eligibility: People in need who live in the ecclesiastical parishes of Dronfield, Holmesfield, Unstone and West Handley.

Types of grants: One-off grants, up to a value of £100, towards household needs (e.g. washing machines), food, clothing, medical appliances (e.g. nebulizer) and visitors' fares to and from hospital. No support for rates, taxes etc.

Grants are also given to local organisations.

Annual grant total: In 2000 the charity had an income of £3,900 and a total expenditure of £2,900. It gave grants to individuals totalling £940.

Applications: In writing to the correspondent though a social worker, citizen's advice bureau, other welfare agency, doctor, member of the clergy of any denomination or a local councillor. The applicants should ensure they are receiving all practical/financial assistance they are entitled to from statutory sources.

Correspondent: Dr A N Bethell, Ramshaw Lodge, Crow Lane, Unstone, Dronfield, Derbyshire S18 4AL (01246 413276; e-mail: tonyb@doctors.org.uk).

The Goldminers OAP Outing & Christmas Fund

Eligibility: People over 60 who buy 'Tote tickets' (to go in a local draw) and who live in Littlemoor, Dunston, Newbold and elsewhere in the area surrounding Chesterfield.

Types of grants: Subsidies of about £45 towards an annual weeks holiday for all eligible people. The trust states that all grants are given irrespective of whether the people are in need or not.

Annual grant total: In 1999, 500 subsidies of £45 totalled nearly £23,000.

Applications: The people who buy Tote tickets are given an application form, which will be collected with their tickets.

Correspondent: Mrs Goucher, 1 Edale Court, Newbold S41 8PB.

The Margaret Harrison Trust

Eligibility: 'Gentlewomen of good character' aged 50 or over who have lived within a 15-mile radius of St Giles Parish Church, Matlock for at least five years.

Types of grants: Pensions.

Annual grant total: In 2001 the trust had an income of £3,300 and a total expenditure of £2,300.

Applications: On a form available from the correspondent, although the trust is already spending all its income and will not be looking for applicants whilst interest rates remain low.

Correspondent: Ian Duff, Heny, Loveday & Keighley, Bank Road, Matlock, Derbyshire DE4 3AQ.

The Stanton Charitable Trust

Eligibility: People of any age or occupation who are in need, due for example to hardship, disability or sickness, and who live near Staveley Works in Chesterfield, Derbyshire, e.g. Staveley, Brimington, Barrowhill, Hollingwold and Inkersall.

Types of grants: Grants towards items, services or facilities.

Annual grant total: In 2000/01 the trust had assets of £32,000, an income of £2,100 and a total expenditure of £1,400.

Applications: In writing to the correspondent either through a social worker, citizen's advice bureau or other welfare agency, or a relevant third party.

Applications can be submitted at any time and are considered when they are received.

Correspondent: Miss S Wetton, Saint-Gobain Pipelines plc, Staveley Works, Chesterfield, Derbyshire S43 2PD (01246 280088; Fax: 01246 280061).

Other information: Grants are also made to schools, churches, scouts, guides and local fundraising events.

Arthur Townrow Pensions Fund

See entry on page 120

The Wirksworth and District Trust Fund

Eligibility: People in need who live in the parishes of Alderwasley, Ashleyhay, Callow, Cromford, Hopton, Ible, Idridgehay & Alton, Middleton-by-Wirksworth and Wirksworth.

Types of grants: Grants of between £20 and £100.

Annual grant total: Between £1,500 and £1,800 is given each year, depending on income.

Applications: In writing to the correspondent for consideration in February and November, although urgent needs can be considered at any time. Applications can be submitted either directly by the individual or through a social worker, citizen's advice bureau or other welfare agency.

Correspondent: Jill Hughes, Clerk, 8 Lady Flatts Road, Wirksworth, via Matlock, Derbyshire DE4 4BQ (01629 822706).

Other information: The Wirksworth Charities are made up of 21 smaller charities, the funds from which are distributed as one sum.

The Woodthorpe Relief-in-Need Charity

Eligibility: People in need who live in the ancient parishes of Barlborough, Staveley and Unstone.

Types of grants: One-off grants for fuel, beds, washing machines, furnishings, mobility chairs and so on. Generally cash grants are given although loans would be considered.

Annual grant total: In 2001 the charity had an income of £5,000 and a total expenditure of £940.

Applications: In writing to the correspondent, or contact Revd W Butt, 1 Eckington Road, Staveley, Derbyshire. Applications are considered monthly.

Correspondent: M Scott, Clerk, 8 Wigley Road, Inkersall, Chesterfield, Derbyshire S43 3ER (01246 274358).

Alfreton

The Alfreton Welfare Trust

Eligibility: People in need who live in the former urban district of Alfreton (i.e. the parishes of Alfreton, Ironville, Leabrooks, Riddings, Somercotes and Swanwick).

Types of grants: Grants have included travel expenses to hospital; provision of necessary household items and installation costs; recuperative holidays; relief of sudden distress (e.g. theft of pension or purse, funeral costs, marital difficulties); telephone installation; and outstanding bills. Support is also given to people who are disabled (including helping to buy wheelchairs etc.).

Grants are not given to organisations or for educational purposes.

Annual grant total: In 2000/01 the trust had an income of £2,500 and a total expenditure of £1,800.

Applications: In writing to the correspondent directly by the individual. Applications are considered throughout the year.

Correspondent: Mrs C Johnson, Clerk, 30 South Street, Swanwick, Alfreton, Derbyshire DE55 1BZ.

Other information: This entry was not confirmed by the trust, but was correct according to information on file at the Charity Commission.

Buxton

The Bingham Trust

Eligibility: People in need, primarily those who live in Buxton. Most applicants from outside Buxton are rejected unless there is a Buxton connection.

Types of grants: One-off grants ranging from £200 to £1,000. Grants are made for a wide variety of need, for example, to relieve poverty, to further education and for religious and community causes. No grants are made for higher education study.

Annual grant total: In 2000/01 the trust had assets of £1.3 million and an income of £64,000. Grants to 15 individuals totalled £7,800. Grants to organisations totalled £33,000.

Applications: In writing to the correspondent in March, June, September or December for consideration in the following months. Applications should be submitted through a third party such as a social worker, citizen's advice bureau, doctor or minister.

Correspondent: R Horne, Trustee, Brooke-Taylors Solicitors, 4 The Quadrant, Buxton, Derbyshire SK17 6AW (01298 22741).

Chesterfield and Dronfield Woodhouse

The Chesterfield General Charitable Fund

Eligibility: People in need in the parliamentary constituency of Chesterfield and Dronfield Woodhouse.

Types of grants: One-off and recurrent grants according to need.

Annual grant total: In 2000/01 the trust's assets totalled £136,000 and its income was £6,500. Total expenditure was £7,500.

In 1998/99 grants to six individuals for educational and welfare purposes totalled £1,700. Grants to 10 organisations totalled £5,000.

Applications: In writing to the correspondent, directly by the individual, for consideration at the start of January, April, August or October.

Correspondent: P B Robinson, Secretary, Bradbury House, Goytside Road, Chesterfield, Derbyshire S42 7LD (01246 505196).

Clay Cross

The Eliza Ann Cresswell Memorial

Eligibility: People in any kind of need who live in the former urban district of Clay Cross (now the civil parish of Clay Cross), particularly needy families with young children.

Types of grants: Usually one-off grants in whole or part payment of a particular need for example heating costs, housing, debts, replacement of bedding and damaged furniture, removal costs, and holidays.

The trust does not give cash directly to applicants nor does it usually pay the full amount of a debt unless any repayment is beyond the individual's means.

Annual grant total: In 2001 the charity had assets of £17,000 and an income of £2,700. A total of £600 was given in five relief-in-need grants to individuals.

Applications: In writing to the correspondent. A description of the person's financial position, the gaps in statutory provision, what contribution the applicant can make towards the need and what help can be given to prevent the need for future applications should be included. Applications are considered throughout the year. Grants are given on the recommendation of social workers, health visitors, probation officers, home nurses, doctors, clergy and welfare organisations (e.g. citizen's advice bureaux), and are paid through these bodies.

Correspondent: Dr S E Dilley, Correspondent Trustee, Blue Dykes, Eldon

Street, Clay Cross, Chesterfield, Derbyshire S45 6NR.

Derby

The Derby City Charity

Eligibility: People under 25 who live in the city of Derby and are in need.

Types of grants: One-off grants only according to need. No grants are given for the relief of taxes or other public funds.

Annual grant total: About £2,000 is given in grants each year. At least 5% of the trust's grant total must be used for educational purposes, the rest, for welfare grants.

Applications: On a form available from the correspondent on written request. Applications can be submitted either through a relevant third party such as a social worker, citizen's advice bureau or other welfare agency; or directly by the individual. The trustees must meet at least twice a year to consider applications.

Correspondent: The Director of Corporate Services, Derby City Council, The Council House, Corporation Street, Derby DE1 2FS (01332 255468; Fax: 01332 255500; Minicom: 01332 256666).

The Lavender's Charity

Eligibility: People in need who are elderly, convalescent, sick or disabled and live in the city of Derby.

Types of grants: One-off grants are given in cash or in kind for items, services or facilities which may alleviate an individual's suffering or assist their recovery, such as towards travel expenses to and from hospital, meals on wheels, outings, entertainments, childminding and payments towards holidays.

Grants are not given for the relief of taxes or other public funds. Recurrent grants are not made.

Annual grant total: Around £600 a year.

Applications: On a form available from the correspondent giving details of applicant's income/expenditure, illness/disability, family circumstances and support for the application. Applications can be submitted by the individual or a relevant third party such as a social worker, doctor, citizen's advice bureau or other welfare agency. They are normally considered twice a year, at the beginning of the year and towards the end, depending on how many applications are received.

Correspondent: The Director of Corporate Services, Derby City Council, Council House, Corporation Street, Derby DE1 2FS (01332 255468; Fax: 01332 255500; Minicom: 01332 256666).

The Liversage Trust

Eligibility: People in need who live in the city of Derby.

Types of grants: Cash grants for the relief of poverty, usually limited to a maximum of £150, although most grants are of between £30/£40 and £150. Grants can be towards clothing, food or consumer durables.

Annual grant total: In 2001/02 the trust gave £26,000 in 180 grants to individuals.

Applications: On a form available from the correspondent. Applications should be submitted through a recognised referral agency (e.g. social worker, citizen's advice bureau or doctor), and are considered throughout the year.

Correspondent: R Pike, Clerk, The Board Room, London Road, Derby DE1 2QW (01332 348155; Fax: 01332 349674; e-mail: kim@liversagetrust.fsnet.co.uk).

Glossop

The Mary Ellen Allen Charity

Eligibility: People over 60 who are in need and live in the former borough of Glossop (as it was in 1947). There is a preference for those who have lived in that area for at least five years in total.

Types of grants: One-off grants in the range of £50 to £300.

Annual grant total: In 2000/01 the charity had assets of £200,000 and an income of £7,800. A total of £10,000 was spent in the year and grants were made to both individuals and organisations.

Applications: In writing to the correspondent either through a social worker, citizen's advice bureau or other welfare agency, or directly by the individual. Applications can be submitted at any time for consideration in January, April, July and October.

Correspondent: Philip Sills, 1 Bowden Road, Glossop, Derbyshire SK13 7BD (01457 865885).

High Peak

The Cotton Districts' Convalescent Fund

See entry on page 201

Ilkeston

The Old Park Ward Old Age Pensioners Fund

Eligibility: People over 65 who are in need and live in the Old Park ward of the former borough of Ilkeston (now Erewash).

Types of grants: One-off cash grants, usually £5, at Christmas. The fund also provides recreational facilities i.e. dancing, bingo, Age Concern meals, WRVS meals and other outings.

Annual grant total: In 2001 the fund had an income of £14,000 and a total expenditure of £9,600.

Applications: Applicants are required to supply their address and date of birth. A register is kept of applicants. Beneficiaries are issued cards which must be presented to enable a grant to be claimed. Applications are considered from January to October.

Correspondent: Miss J Ellson, 16 Chaucer Street, Ilkeston, Derbyshire DE7 5JJ.

Matlock

The Ernest Bailey Charity

Eligibility: People who are sick, poor, elderly, in distress and in need and live in Matlock (this includes Bonsall, Darley Dale, South Darley, Tansley, Matlock Bath and Cromford).

Types of grants: Most applications have been from local groups, but individuals in need and those with educational needs are also supported. Each application is considered on its merits. Grants to individuals are one-off and usually of to a maximum of £200 or £250.

Annual grant total: In 2001 the sum of £7,400 was given in grants, of which £900 was given to individuals.

Applications: On a form available on written request from the correspondent. Applications are considered in October and must be returned by the end of September. They can be submitted directly by the individual and/or can be supported by a relevant professional. Applications should include costings (total amount required, funds raised, funds promised and grant requested). Previous beneficiaries may apply again, account being taken of assistance given in the past.

Correspondent: Corporate Services Department, Derbyshire Dales District Council, Town Hall, Matlock, Derbyshire DE4 3NN (01629 580580; Fax: 01629 581009).

Spondon

The Spondon Relief-in-Need Charity

Eligibility: People in need who live in the ancient township of Spondon.

Types of grants: Grants are made to people in need, as follows:
The garden tidy scheme is to help older people, especially widows. In 2000 18 people had grants of £138 each for work on

their gardens.

Christmas goodwill grants are made for older people and mothers with young children. In 2000 42 grants of £37 were made to families with young children, and 81 grants of £15 were made to older people.

Further grants are made for school uniforms and to students. Small grants are also available to young football enthusiasts towards sports equipment.

Annual grant total: In 2000 the trust had an income of £19,000 and made grants totalling £45,000, including at least £4,500 to individuals for relief-in-need.

Applications: On a form available from the correspondent. Each form must be accompanied by a letter of support from a sponsor such as a doctor, health authority official, social worker, city councillor, clergyman, headteacher, school liason officer, youth leader or probation officer. The sponsor must justify the applicant's need. The latter is particularly important. The applicant should provide as much information on the form as possible. It is better to ask for a visit by a trustee if possible.

The trustees meet four times a year and applications must be received by the end of January, April, July and October; grants are given one month later.

Correspondent: David A Oddie, Secretary/Treasurer, 37 Huntley Avenue, Spondon, Derby DE21 7DW (01332 662048).

Other information: This charity consists of several ancient charities now combined as one. The charities date from 1642 to 1929. Historically, over the centuries they have supported a schoolmaster in 1657, given two shillings to several poor people after church in 1662 and grants to purchase four yards of Coarse Yorkshire Flanel at Christmas in 1817 for poor widows. In 1895 poor people were given five shillings and half a ton of coal at Christmas.

Herefordshire

Becket Bulmer Charitable Trust

Eligibility: People in need who live in the Herefordshire area, with preference for those with special needs.

Types of grants: Mostly one-off grants of £10 to £1,000, but typically of £100 to £500. Grants may be spent on items, services or facilities calculated to alleviate need.

Annual grant total: In 1998/99 the trust had an income of £19,000 and made 27 grants to organisations and 13 grants to individuals for both educational and welfare purposes, totalling £15,000.

Applications: Guidelines can be issued. Applications should be by letter, typed, word-processed or hand-written, and submitted at any time to the correspondent. The trustees' meeting is held in May. An sae is appreciated.

Correspondent: S Bulmer, Trustee, The Old Rectory, Credenhill, Hereford HR4 7DJ.

The Hereford Corn Exchange Fund

Eligibility: People in Herefordshire who have been employed at one farm for over 30 years.

Types of grants: Grants of between £100 and £500.

Annual grant total: This trust has an income of £2,500, and gives about £1,000 to individuals and £1,000 to agricultural organisations.

Applications: In writing to the correspondent in March/April for consideration in May.

Correspondent: E P Edwards, Secretary, 7 Yew Tree Gardens, Kings Acre, Hereford HR4 0TH.

The Hereford Society for Aiding The Industrious

Eligibility: People in need who live in Herefordshire and are trying to better themselves by their own efforts.

The early history of the society involved aid to the 'industrious poor' and those who would not make an effort to help themselves were excluded. This is reflected today by priority being given to individuals who are trying to obtain training to get back to work, often as a mature student.

Grants will be considered when a person is required to fund a gap between formal education and training for a career. The society also considers postgraduate applicants and applications from girl guides and boy scouts for assistance with the cost of camp, but need must be proved in all cases.

Types of grants: Grants or interest free loans, of £50 to £1,000, according to need.

Annual grant total: In 1998/99 the charity had assets of £740,000 and an income of £62,000. Total expenditure was £66,000; with 23 grants awarded totalling £8,500. About 75% of the income is given to organisations each year.

Applications: On a form available from the correspondent. Trustees usually meet on the third Monday of every month.

Correspondent: R M Cunningham, 18 Venns Close, Bath Street, Hereford HR1 2HH (01432 274014 – Thursdays only).

Other information: The society also runs 28 almshouses.

The Honourable Miss Frances Horley Charity

See entry on page 169

Open House Darts League

Eligibility: People who are sick or mentally/physically disabled and live in Herefordshire.

Types of grants: Recurrent grants in the form of purchased goods only (not cash).

The charity does not sponsor students.

Annual grant total: In 2000/01 the trust had an income of £1,800 and a total expenditure of £2,300.

Applications: Applications can be submitted either directly by the individual or by a relevant third party such as a social worker, citizen's advice bureau or other welfare agency. They are considered between April and September on the first Sunday of each month.

Correspondent: Gwyn Davies, 3 Raglan Place, Newton Farm, Hereford, HR2 7DU.

Other information: Grants are also given to schools, hospitals and hospices.

The Rathbone Moral Aid Charity

Eligibility: People who live in Herefordshire who are under 25 and in need of rehabilitation, 'particularly as a result of crime, delinquency, prostitution, addiction to drugs or drink, maltreatment or neglect'.

Types of grants: One-off and recurrent grants according to need. No grants are given for nursery fees.

Annual grant total: In 2000 the trust's income was £7,700 and its total expenditure was £3,900. Further information was not available for this year. In 1997 the trust had an income of £9,000 and gave grants totalling £7,700. A total of £2,600 was given to individuals in need.

Applications: In writing to the correspondent. Individual applications are considered throughout the year. All individual applications must be supported by a welfare agency or doctor, social worker, teacher or other professional.

Correspondent: Mrs Carol A Thompson, Clerk, PO Box 181, Hereford HR2 9YN (01981 250899).

Other information: Grants are also made to organisations.

Hereford

All Saints Relief-in-Need Charity

Eligibility: Mainly individuals in need in the city of Hereford with a preference for the ancient parish of All Saints, Hereford.

Types of grants: The trust prefers to provide items rather than giving cash grants. The charity does not help to pay off debts.

Annual grant total: In 2000/01 the charity had an income of £6,300 and a total expenditure of £8,300.

Applications: On a form available from the correspondent. The trustees meet four times a year in March, June, September and December.

Correspondent: D G Harding, Clerk, 6 St Ethelbert's Street, Hereford HR1 2NG (01432 358075).

The Hereford Municipal Charity

Eligibility: The Eleemosynary Branch gives grants to people in need. Grants to prisoners, ex-prisoners and their families are made through the William Brydges Charity and educational grants through the Apprenticing & Educational Branch. Grants are only given to people who live in the city of Hereford.

Types of grants: One-off grants generally of £50 to £200. Grants are given to help with household equipment, clothes, educational equipment, emergencies etc. No grants towards debts or nursery fees.

Annual grant total: About £24,000 in total from all branches.

Applications: On a form available from the correspondent to be submitted directly by the individual or through a social worker, citizen's advice bureau or other welfare agency. All applicants are interviewed by the trustees who meet once a month (except for August) for this purpose.

Correspondent: Lance Marshall, Clerk to the Trustees, 147 St Owen Street, Hereford HR1 2JR (01432-354002).

Other information: This entry was not confirmed by the trust, but the address was correct according to the Charity Commission database.

The United Charity of All Saints (Relief-in-Need Branch)

Eligibility: People in need who live in the city of Hereford.

Types of grants: One-off grants ranging from £100 to £250 towards clothing, assistance with basic furniture, assistance with mobility, taxi costs and so on. No grants towards repayment of debt, rent or funeral costs and no loans.

Annual grant total: In 2000/01 the charity had an income of £6,300 and its total expenditure was about £8,300. The sum of £3,300 was given in 24 grants to individuals in need.

Applications: On a form available from the correspondent, submitted either directly by the individual or through a social worker, citizen's advice bureau or other welfare agency. Applications are considered in March, June, September and November.

Correspondent: D G Harding, 6 St Ethelbert Street, Hereford HR1 2NR (01432 267821).

Middleton-on-the-Hill

The Middleton-on-the-Hill Parish Charity

Eligibility: People living in the parish of Middleton-on-the-Hill.

Types of grants: One-off and recurrent grants according to need. Grants are given for both welfare and educational purposes.

Annual grant total: About £1,000 a year is given in grants.

Applications: In writing to the correspondent.

Correspondent: Clare Halls, Secretary, Leysters Garage, Leysters, Leominster, Herefordshire HR6 0HP (01568 750257).

Norton Canon

The Norton Canon Parochial Charities

Eligibility: People in need who live in the parish of Norton Canon.

Types of grants: One-off and recurrent grants according to need.

Annual grant total: In 2001 the sum of £4,600 was given in grants to individuals for educational and welfare purposes.

Applications: In writing to the correspondent at any time.

Correspondent: Mrs M L Gittins, Ivy Cottage, Norton Canon, Hereford HR4 7BQ (01544 318984).

Tenbury Wells

The Edmund Godson Charity

See entry on page 369

Leicestershire

The Ashby-de-la-Zouch Relief-in-Sickness Fund

Eligibility: People in need who live in Ashby-de-la-Zouch and Blackfordby.

Types of grants: Grants have included help with transport to hospital, a washing machine, a machine for a neck pain sufferer, bed linen, holiday expenses and appliance repairs. Cash grants are also given for general help. Grants are in the range of £50 to £100.

Annual grant total: In 2000/01 the trust had assets of £18,000 and an income of £920. A total of £670 was distributed in eight grants to individuals. Groups can also be supported.

Applications: In writing to the correspondent at any time directly from the individual, or through a social worker, citizen's advice bureau or other welfare agency. Anybody who thinks they know someone who needs help is welcome to submit an application. It is useful to know whether any other source of help has been approached. Applications are considered at all times.

Correspondent: The Correspondent, Crane & Walton, 30 South Street, Ashby-de-la-Zouch, Leicestershire LE65 1BT (01530 414111).

William Clayton Barnes Trust

Eligibility: People in need who are sick and infirm and live in Melton Mowbray, Eye Kettleby or Great Dalby and have lived there for three years.

Types of grants: One-off grants in the range of £25 and £500. Recent donations have included those towards wheelchairs, stairlifts (purchase and rental), household equipment for special needs, food and travel to hospital.

Grants are also made to organisations.

Annual grant total: In 2000/01 the trust had an income of £2,500 and made grants to 13 individuals totalling £3,200.

Applications: The trust welcomes an initial telephone call. Applications should be in writing to the correspondent either directly by the individual or through a doctor, church leader, social worker, citizen's advice bureau or other welfare agency. They are considered all year round.

Correspondent: John Thornton, The Old Rectory, Wyfordby, Melton Mowbray, Leicestershire LE14 4RY (01664 564437).

The John Heggs Bates' Charity for Convalescents

Eligibility: People requiring convalescence, with a preference for those living in Leicestershire.

Types of grants: One-off grants of about £100 to £600. Grants to convalescents in need, with priority to people who are not already receiving help. Where individuals have already received help, priority is probably given to people living in Leicestershire.

Annual grant total: In 2001 the sum of £11,000 was distributed in 32 grants.

Applications: On a form available from: Leicester Charity Organisation Society, 20a Millstone Lane, Leicester LE1 5JN.

Applications should be submitted through a social worker, citizen's advice bureau, doctor or church and are considered throughout the year.

Correspondent: Mrs Wendy Faulkner, 4th Floor, Norwich House, 26 Horsefair Street, Leicester LE1 5BD (0116 204 6620; e-mail: wf@stwcharity.co.uk).

The Brooke Charity

Eligibility: People in need who live in the parish of Brooke and adjoining parishes.

Types of grants: One-off grants.

Annual grant total: About £7,000.

Applications: In writing to the correspondent. Applications can be submitted directly by the individual or through a social worker, citizen's advice bureau or other welfare agency. They are considered at any time.

Correspondent: Mr Greer, Priory Cottage, Main Street, Brooke, Oakham, Leicester LE15 8DE.

The Elizabeth Clarke Relief-in-Need Fund & The Wigston Relief-in-Need Fund

Eligibility: People in need who live in Wigston Magna, Wigston Fields and South Wigston.

Types of grants: One-off grants towards general relief-in-need, including clothing, safety alarms, special chairs, wheelchairs, orthopaedic footwear, travel costs for medical treatment, bedding, spectacles and so on. No grants for rent arrears, rent, community charge, gas/electric payments, ongoing assistance of any kind, or where trustees feel the need can be met in a better way or through other sources.

Annual grant total: Elizabeth Clarke Relief-in-Need Fund: £1,000. Wigston Relief-in-Need Fund: £2,500.

Applications: In writing to the correspondent, accompanied by a supporting letter from a social worker or other welfare agency if possible. Applications are considered in March, September and November, but exceptions can be made in emergencies.

Correspondent: The Clerk to the Trustees, Bushloe House, Station Road, Wigston, Leicestershire LE18 2DR (0116 288 8961).

Other information: These two trusts work closely together, and often large grants are paid from funds from both trusts. However, people applying for South Wigston are not eligible for grants from the Elizabeth Clarke Relief-in-Need fund, and they receive grants solely from The Wigston Relief-in-Need Fund.

Coalville and District Relief in Sickness Fund

Eligibility: People in need of medical equipment not provided by NHS who live in Coalville and district.

Types of grants: One-off grants in the range of £150 to £1,000 towards medical needs only, such as special mattresses, gas fires, washing machines, reconditioned computers and home alternations.

Annual grant total: In 2000/01 the trust's assets totalled £37,000, it had an income of £2,900 and eight grants were made totalling £2,500.

Applications: In writing directly by the individual to: Mrs N Baxter, Babeny, Beresford Court, Newton Road, Coalville Leicestershire LE76 2RD. Applications are considered throughout the year.

Correspondent: J Dennies, Hon. Treasurer, 33 St David's Crescent, Agar Nook, Coalville, Leicestershire LE67 4ST (01530 836687).

The J Reginald Corah Trust

Eligibility: People in need, especially people who are elderly or employees or former employees of hosiery firms carrying on business in Leicestershire.

Types of grants: One-off and recurrent grants according to need. A wide range of needs can be considered, although there are no grants for educational purposes.

Annual grant total: Grants to individuals and organisations total about £125,000.

Applications: In writing to the correspondent, to be submitted through a social worker, citizen's advice bureau or other third party, to whom the cheque will be sent. Applications are considered every eight to nine weeks.

Correspondent: Mrs Fowle, Harvey Ingram Owston, 20 New Walk, Leicester LE1 6TX (0116 254 5454; Fax: 0116 255 4559; e-mail: hio@plf.co.uk).

Thomas Harley Relief in Need Charity

Eligibility: Clergy widows, people who are divorced or separated from clergy and the dependants of clergy. Individuals must live in England and Wales, but there is a preference for those living in the dioceses of Leicester, then Southwell.

Types of grants: One-off grants ranging from £150 to £500, towards extraordinary day-to-day costs such as TV licences and repairs to electrical appliances including washing machines.

Annual grant total: In 1999/2000 the trust's assets totalled £18,000, it had an income of £53,000 and 41 grants were made totalling £31,000.

Applications: Directly by the individual on a form available from the correspondent, for consideration in March and August.

Correspondent: A M Ward, Mather Jamie Ltd, Rectory Place, Loughborough, Leicestershire LE11 1UR.

Miss Herrick's Annuity Fund & the Herrick Fund for Widows & Single Women Afflicted with Incurable Diseases

Eligibility: In general, women in need who live in Leicestershire.

Specifically for Miss Herrick's Annuity: female members of the Church of England, especially 'ladies over 50 years of age who are widows, daughters or sisters of clergymen or of officers in the armed service of the Crown or of professional men or gentlemen'; for the Herrick Fund: widows or single women aged 30 or over who have incurable diseases (except blindness, deafness or insanity).

Types of grants: One-off and recurrent grants according to need.

Annual grant total: In 1999 one grant from the annuity fund was made of £250, with no grants being given from the Herrick Fund. For the last few years money has been available in both funds with very few applications.

Applications: In writing to the correspondent, to be considered in January, March, May, July, September and November.

Correspondent: Mrs K Jamieson, Clerk, c/o 20 Churchgate, Loughborough LE11 1UD (01509 650572).

The Leicester Charity Organisation Society

Eligibility: People in need who live in the city of Leicester and the vicinity, which includes the whole of Leicestershire and Rutland.

Types of grants: One-off grants and occasionally recurrent grants or pensions. The society makes payments from its own funds, administers funds on behalf of other charities and puts potential beneficiaries into contact with funds and charities which may be able to help. A very wide range of grants is considered from small immediate payments, for example, for food, to larger payments of, for example, £6,500 for a special computer for a disabled man.

Annual grant total: In 1999/2000 a total of 5,000 grants were given to individuals totalling £494,000. A further £23,000 went to organisations.

Applications: Generally through a social worker, health visitor, doctor or welfare agency on an application form.

Correspondent: M A Marvell, Director, 20a Millstone Lane, Leicester LE1 5JN (0116 222 2200; Fax: 0116 222 2201; e-mail: m.marvell@charity-link.org).

Other information: If the organisation awards all its funds available from distribution, there are a number of other trusts they can approach on the applicants behalf or refer applicants on to.

The Leicester Freemen's Estate

Eligibility: Needy freemen of Leicester and their widows who are elderly or infirm. As of July 2002 the trust was working with the Charity Commission to extend certain benefits to the daughters of freemen.

Types of grants: Charitable payments, currently of £12 per week for non-residents and £10 per week for residents, and Christmas bonuses of between £25 and £40.

Annual grant total: In 2001 the trust had assets of £4.4 million and an income of £170,000. The amount given varies each year. In prevous years about £13,000 had been given to individuals.

Applications: On a form available from the correspondent and including proof of status as a freeman/widow of a freeman. Applications can be submitted directly by the individual and are considered throughout the year.

Correspondent: M J Hagger, Estate Office, 32 Freemen's Holt, Old Church Street, Aylestone, Leicester LE2 8NH (0116 283 4017).

Other information: The trust also provides accommodation for needy freemen and their widows. Applications should be made to the above address.

The Leicestershire Coal Industry Welfare Trust Fund

Eligibility: Miners and their dependants working in the British coal mining industry aged over 16, who have not taken up other full-time work.

Types of grants: Grants have been given towards special needs assistance, house repairs, house conversions and televisions.

Annual grant total: In 2000 the fund had an income of £12,000 and a total expenditure of £6,200.

Applications: In writing to the correspondent, including details of the individual's mining connection, proof of their residence in Leicestershire and dependance on the mineworker (in the case of children).

Correspondent: E R Andrews, Welfare Offices, Berry Hill Lane, Mansfield, Nottinghamshire NG18 4JR.

The Leicestershire County Nursing Association

Eligibility: Retired district nurses and people who are sick and in need, who live in Leicestershire or Rutland (excluding the city of Leicester). Priority is given to retired district nurses.

Types of grants: One-off grants ranging from £5 to £100. Grants can be given for any need and in the past have been given towards hospital costs, bedding and convalescence.

Annual grant total: In 2000 the association had assets of £1.2 million and an income of £58,000. The sum of £16,000 was distributed to nine nurses.

Applications: In writing to the correspondent, directly by the individual in the case of retired district nurses or through Leicester Charity Organisation Society (see separate entry) in other cases. Applications are considered in January and October.

Correspondent: Edward Cufflin, Morgan Stanley Quilter, Provincial House, 37 New Walk, Leicester LE1 6TU (0116 249 3000; Fax: 0116 247 1555).

The Loughborough Welfare Trusts

Eligibility: People in need who live in Loughborough and Hathern.

Types of grants: One-off and recurrent grants are given generally to families on low income for decoration costs, second-hand fridges, cookers and so on. Grants are also made towards clothing for primary schoolchildren aged under 11.

Annual grant total: About £9,000 to individuals for relief-in-need.

Applications: In writing to the correspondent for consideration in January, March, May, July, September or November.

Correspondent: Mrs K Jamieson, Bird, Wilford & Sale, Solicitors, 20 Churchgate, Loughborough LE11 1UD (01509 650572).

Other information: This trust administers Miss Herrick's Annuity Fund, The Herrick Fund, The Reg Burton Fund and The Loughborough Community Chest.

The Nicholson Memorial Fund

Eligibility: Young people and children 'who are delinquent, deprived, neglected or in need of care' in Leicestershire.

Types of grants: Usually one-off grants according to need.

Annual grant total: In 1999/2000 the trust had assets of £270,000 and an income of £15,000. Grants to individuals totalled £4,800. Grants to nine organisations totalled £4,700.

Applications: In writing to the correspondent at any time, requesting an application form. As well as donating grants, the fund provides support and advice to applicants, for example through directing them to other suitable funding bodies.

Correspondent: The Clerk, c/o Leicester Charity Link, 20a Millstone Lane, Leicester LE1 5JN (0116 222 2211).

The Royal Leicestershire, Rutland & Wycliffe Society for the Blind

Eligibility: People who are registered blind or partially sighted and live in the county of Leicestershire, the city of Leicester and Rutland.

Types of grants: 1. Special needs grants which can range from replacement of stolen cash to provision of household equipment such as a new/safer cooker. Grants range from £50 to £200.

2. Grants towards holidays whether they are organised by the individual or a group or organisation. They tend to be £75. Holiday grants will not be given in two successive years, unless under exceptional circumstances.

No grants for electricity, gas, rent or community charge arrears, nor for telephone installation, rental or calls.

Annual grant total: About £3,000 a year.

Applications: On a form available from the correspondent, usually through welfare agencies. Applications can be considered at any time and decisions are normally made within three weeks.

Correspondent: The Director, Margaret Road, off Gwendolen Road, Leicester LE5 5FU (0116 249 0909; Fax: 0116 249 8811).

The Rutland Dispensary

Eligibility: People who are poor, old or sick and live in Rutland.

Types of grants: One-off and recurrent grants ranging from £50 to £250.

Annual grant total: In 2001 the trust had assets of £60,000, an income of £2,600 and a total expediture of £1,800. The sum of £1,500 was given in eight grants.

Applications: In writing to the correspondent.

Correspondent: Fred R Bellingall, 8 Holyrood Close, Oakham, Leicestershire LE15 6SF (01572 723480).

The Rutland Trust

Eligibility: Young people who are disabled and live in Rutland and are in need.

Types of grants: One-off and recurrent grants ranging between £200 and £300, to buy equipment.

Annual grant total: In 2001 the trust had assets of £269,000 and an income of £9,600. A total of £9,100 was spent, of which £200 was given in one relief-in-need grant. Educational grants to individuals totalled £1,700, with £6,600 given to organisations.

Applications: An initial telephone call is recommended.

Correspondent: David Parkin, Clerk, 22 Church Road, Egleton, Oakham, Rutland

Midlands – Leicestershire

LE15 8AD (01572 756850; e-mail: parkin_egleton@yahoo.co.uk).

The Thomas Stanley Shipman Charitable Trust

Eligibility: People in need who live in the city and county of Leicester.

Types of grants: One-off and recurrent grants ranging between £75 and £500.

Annual grant total: In 2000/01 the trust had assets of £1.4 million, an income of £70,000 and its total expenditure was £69,000. Relief-in-need grants to individuals totalled £44,000.

Applications: In writing to the correspondent either directly by the individual or via a relevant third party such as a social worker, citizen's advice bureau or other welfare agency, or through Leicester Charity Link. Applications should be submitted in mid-October and mid-May for consideration in November and June.

Correspondent: A R York, 20a Millstone Lane, Leicester LE1 5JN (0116 222 2211; Fax: 0116 222 2201).

Cossington

Rev John Babington's Charity

Eligibility: People in need in the parish of Cossington.

Types of grants: One-off and recurrent grants according to need.

Annual grant total: In 1999 it had an income of £20,000. Grants to individuals totalled £5,100. Grants to four organisations totalled £3,600.

Applications: In writing to: Smith-Woolley, Collingham, Newark, Nottinghamshire NG23 7LG.

Correspondent: G Dickie, Chair, Old Manor House, Cossington, Leicestershire LE7 4UU (01509 812340).

Other information: This entry was not confirmed by the trust, but the address was correct according to the Charity Commission database.

Great Glen

Great Glen Relief in Need Charity

Eligibility: Pensioners and other people in need who live in the parish of Great Glen and have been living there for a number of years.

Types of grants: One-off grants according to need. Pensioners receive grants in the form of vouchers at Christmas.

Annual grant total: In 2000 the charity had an income of £1,800 and a total expenditure of £1,200. It can only make distributions from income.

Applications: In writing to the correspondent. Applications are considered twice a year, usually in November and April.

Correspondent: Mrs H M Hill, Secretary, 35 Ashby Rise, Great Glen, Leicester, Leicestershire LE8 9GB.

Groby

Thomas Herbert Smith's Trust Fund

Eligibility: People who live in the parish of Groby in Leicestershire.

Types of grants: One-off and recurrent grants ranging from £100 to £500.

Annual grant total: In 2000/01 the trust had assets of £349,000 generating an income of £20,000. Grants were given to five organisations and local schools totalling £17,000, with £6,800 given to individuals in need.

Applications: On a form available from the correspondent, for consideration throughout the year. Applications can be submitted either directly by the individual, or through a social worker, citizen's advice bureau or other third party.

Correspondent: A R York, 20a Millstone Lane, Leicester LE1 5JN (0116 222 2211; Fax: 0116 222 2201).

Kegworth

Doctor M A Gerrard's Kegworth Old People's Benevolent Fund

Eligibility: People of retirement age who are in need and live in the parish of Kegworth.

Types of grants: One-off grants according to need. Past grants have included payment for a new gas fire for an older man. Organisations benefiting older people are also supported.

Annual grant total: In 2001/02 the trust had an income of £580 and it did not spend any money in that year.

Applications: In writing to the correspondent, either directly by the individual, or through a welfare worker.

Correspondent: Mrs Lesley Pendleton, 1 London Road, Kegworth, Derby DE74 2EU (01509 670204; Fax: 01509 673500).

Keyham

Keyham Relief in Need Charity

Eligibility: People who live in the parish of Keyham, Leicestershire and are in need. People who have strong family connections with the parish can also be considered.

Types of grants: One-off grants ranging between £100 and £1,000.

Annual grant total: In 2000 the trust had an income of £14,000 and its total expenditure was £9,300.

Applications: In writing to the correspondent, to be submitted directly by the individual, for consideration in March and October. Urgent applications can be considered at other times. If the applicant does not live in Keyham, information about their connection with residents should be provided with the application.

Correspondent: D B Witcomb, Chair, Tanglewood, Snows Lane, Leicester, Leicestershire LE7 9JS.

Other information: If funds are available, grants are made to groups which benefit the parish.

Leicester

The Leicester Aid-in-Sickness Fund

Eligibility: Sick, poor people who live in the city of Leicester.

Types of grants: Almost entirely one-off grants ranging from £5 to £50.

Annual grant total: The fund stated that the amount distributed in any given year depends on the level of income. In 2000/01 it had an income of £17,000 and a total expenditure of £15,000.

Applications: Leicester Charity Organisation Society (see separate entry) acts as agent of the trustees for the purpose of considering and administering grants. Applications are considered continually.

Correspondent: R P Harris, Clerk, 20 New Walk, Leicester LE1 6TX (0116 254 5454).

The Leicester Indigent Old Age Society

Eligibility: People 65 or over who are in need and live in the city of Leicester.

Types of grants: Pensions only of £80 a year, paid in quarterly installments.

Annual grant total: In 2000/01 the society had an income of £2,800 and a total expenditure of £2,300.

Applications: In writing to the correspondent, through a social worker or other welfare agency.

Correspondent: M A Marvell, 20a Millstone Lane, Leicester LE1 5JN (0116 222 2200; Fax: 0116 222 2201; e-mail: m.marvell@charity-link.org).

The Parish Piece Charity

Eligibility: Elderly people in need who live in the city of Leicester.

Types of grants: Pensions only.

Annual grant total: Over £4,000 each year in about 80 small pensions.
Applications: In writing to the correspondent or via Leicester Charity Organisation Society.
Correspondent: J E Adams, 19 Rowley Fields Avenue, Leicester LE3 2ER (0116 289 7432).

St Margaret's Charity

Eligibility: People in need who live in the city of Leicester.
Types of grants: One-off and recurrent grants ranging from £25 to £100.
Annual grant total: About £1,000 a year in 10 to 20 grants.
Applications: In writing to the correspondent or via the Leicester Charity Organisation Society.
Correspondent: J E Adams, Clerk, 19 Rowley Fields Avenue, Leicester LE3 2ER (0116 289 7432).

Sir Edward Wood's Bequest Fund For Gentlewomen

Eligibility: Gentlewomen (either unmarried or widows) at least 55 years old who have lived in the area administered by Leicester City Council for at least 10 years, and who are members of a protestant non-conformist church.
Types of grants: Pensions only of £400 a year, paid quarterly.
Annual grant total: About £4,000 a year.
Applications: On a form available from the correspondent either directly by the individual or via a third party. A reference from a church minister is also needed. There are only a limited number of pensions available and applications can only be considered when a vacancy arises.
Correspondent: The Secretary, 19 The Crescent, King Street, Leicester LE1 6RX (0116 254 1344).

Market Harborough

The Market Harborough & the Bowdens Charity

Eligibility: People in need who live in the former urban council district area of Market Harborough.
Types of grants: Grants are one-off and are wide-ranging, providing they meet with the charity's scheme and geographical area. No grants are given for sport.
Annual grant total: In 2001 the charity had assets of £10 million and a disposable income of about £250,000. About 40 grants to individuals totalled £20,000. Grants are also given to organisations.
Applications: On a form available from the correspondent. Applications can be submitted either directly by the individual or via a relevant third party such as a social worker, citizen's advice bureau or other welfare agency. They are considered bi-monthly. Potential applicants are welcome to contact the correspondent directly for further guidance.
Correspondent: J G Jacobs, Steward, 149 St Mary's Road, Market Harborough, Leicester LE16 7DZ (01858 462467; Fax: 01858 431898; e-mail: mhbc@godfrey-payton.co.uk; website: www.marketharboroughandthebowdens.co.uk).

Markfield

Jane Avery Charity – Markfield

Eligibility: People in need who live in the ancient parish of Markfield.
Types of grants: Normally one-off grants of £25 to £300. Grants have included those towards holiday costs, nursery school fees, a wheelchair and house repairs.

No grants for educational purposes.
Annual grant total: In 2001 the trust had assets of £22,000 and an income of £920. The sum of £350 was given in two grants to individuals in need. The year saw an unusually low number of applicants.
Applications: In writing to the correspondent. Applications can be submitted directly by the individual or through a social worker, citizen's advice bureau, other welfare agency, or through a third party such as a doctor, minister, neighbour or relative. They can be considered at any time.
Correspondent: Canon G T Willett, Secretary, The Rectory, The Nook, Markfield, Leicestershire LE67 9WE (Tel & Fax: 01530 242844).

Mountsorrel

The Mountsorrel Relief-in-Need Charity

Eligibility: People in need who live in the parish of Mountsorrel.
Types of grants: Grants have been given towards invalid chairs, house repairs, essential domestic appliances, emergency telephones, travel costs (e.g. for visiting hospitals, day centres), nursing home fees, house decoration and gardening.
Annual grant total: In 2000/01 grants totalled £52,000.
Applications: On a form available from the correspondent: Mrs J L Allard, 84 Rockhill Drive, Mountsorrell, Loughborough, Leicestershire LE12 7DT.
Correspondent: Paul Roland Blakemore, Godkin & Co., 105 Derby Road, Loughborough, Leicestershire LE11 5AE (01509 214496).

Oadby

The Oadby Educational Foundation

Eligibility: People in need in the parish of Oadby only.
Types of grants: One-off and recurrent grants in the range of £70 and £200.
Annual grant total: In 2001 the foundation had assets of £985,000 and an income and total expenditure of £35,000. Two relief-in-need grants were made totalling £200.
Applications: In writing to the correspondent, to be submitted either through a social worker, citizen's advice bureau or other welfare agency, or directly by the individual. They are considered in March, June and October.
Correspondent: Rodger Moodie, Hon. Secretary, 26 Richmond Way, Oadby, Leicestershire LE2 5TR (0116 271 6279).

Queniborough

Alex Neale Charity

Eligibility: Older people who live in the parish of Queniborough.
Types of grants: One-off grants which are usually distributed every two years. 90% of grants are towards heating bills. In 2001 the trust donated grants of £400 to reimburse people for the bills they had paid in the previous two years.
Annual grant total: In November 2001 the trust donated grants totalling £4,000.
Applications: The trustees publicise the grants, usually every two years, in The Queniborough Gazette. An application form is then available from the correspondent. The trust may ask you to submit copies of your fuel bills for the two years prior to application, and the grant would then be towards reimbursing you for those bills.
Correspondent: Maurice R A Kirk, 6 Ervin Way, Queniborough, Leicester LE7 3TT (0116 260 6851).

Quorn

The Quorn Town Lands Charity

Eligibility: People in need who live in the parish of Quorn.
Types of grants: One-off and recurrent grants of up to £250.
Annual grant total: In 2001/02 the charity had assets of £72,000, an income of £5,400 and a total expenditure of £4,700.
Applications: In writing to the correspondent. Applications should be submitted directly by the individual or through a relevant third party. They are

considered in February, May, August and November and should be submitted in the preceding month.

Correspondent: G B Gibson, Clerk, 2 Wallis Close, Thurcaston, Leicester LE7 7JS (0116 235 0946).

Other information: This charity consists of three different funds: Quorn Town Lands Charity, Quorn Aid in Sickness Fund and Quorn Education Fund.

Shepshed

John Lambert's Charity

Eligibility: People, particularly children, who are in need and live in Shepshed.

Types of grants: One-off grants only.

Annual grant total: £2,000 was recently given to individuals for relief-in-need purposes and £12,000 was given in grants for other purposes. Educational grants to individuals totalled £12,000.

Applications: On a form available from the correspondent submitted directly by the individual. Applications are considered in March, June, September and December.

Correspondent: G S Freckelton, 1 Leicester Road, Loughborough, Leicestershire LE11 2AE (01509 214564).

Smisby

The Smisby Parochial Charity

Eligibility: People in need who live in Smisby.

Types of grants: Christmas hampers to older people.

Annual grant total: In 2000/01 the charity had an income of £46,000. Total expenditure was £3,000.

Applications: In writing to the correspondent. Applications can be submitted either directly by the individual or a relevant third party, or through a social worker, citizen's advice bureau or other welfare agency. They can be considered at any time.

Correspondent: Mrs S Heap, Clerk, Cedar Lawns, Forties Lane, Smisby, Ashby-De-La-Zouch, Leicestershire LE65 2SN (01530 414179; Fax: 01530 414171).

Syston

The H A Taylor Fund

Eligibility: People in need who live in the parish of Syston.

Types of grants: One-off grants in the range of £50 to £500. Grants have been given to help with travel, furniture, clothing, fuel, medical treatment, books and fees, a vehicle for a disabled person, telephone and television costs, repairs and redecoration, and a loan to help with getting a job.

Annual grant total: In 2000/01 the fund had assets of £580,000, an income of £23,000 and a total expenditure of £21,000. The sum of £11,000 was distributed in 38 relief-in-need grants. A further £6,000 was given to organisations.

Applications: On an application form available from the correspondent. Applications can be submitted at any time either through a social worker, citizen's advice bureau or other welfare agency, or directly by the individual. They are considered about every seven weeks.

Correspondent: Andrew York, Administrator, Leicester Charity Link, 20a Millstone Lane, Leicester LE9 6UG (0116 222 2211; Fax: 0116 222 2201).

Wymeswold

The Wymeswold Parochial Charities

Eligibility: People in need who have lived in Wymeswold for the last two years.

Types of grants: Winter gifts to senior citizens, widows and widowers. One-off grants are also given to people who are ill.

Annual grant total: About £4,000 a year.

Applications: In writing to the correspondent at any time.

Correspondent: Mrs P Hubbard, 97 Brook Street, Wymeswold, Loughborough LE12 6TT (01509 880166).

Lincolnshire

The Addlethorpe Parochial Charity

Eligibility: People in need who live in the parish of Addlethorpe, or who previously lived in Addlethorpe and now live in an adjoining parish. Applicants must be either living on a much-reduced income, with limited savings or investments, or be disabled or infirm.

Types of grants: Most grants are in the form of solid fuel or electricity/gas cheques (35 beneficiaries received around £30 three times a year in 2001). One-off grants are given towards funeral expenses (one of £50), household repairs, other necessities (5 beneficiaries totalling £400 in 2001). Grants have also been given for hospital or doctor's visits (one totalling £120 in 2001). Special grants generally range from £25 to £50, but may be given up to three times during the year.

Annual grant total: In 2001/02 the trust had an income of £3,900 and gave £3,200 in grants to individuals and couples.

Applications: In writing to the correspondent, including details of length of residence in Addlethorpe. Applications are considered in September but exceptional cases are dealt with as they come to the notice of the trustees.

Correspondent: J Smedley, Secretary, Carinya, Church Lane, Addlethorpe, Skegness, Lincs PE24 4UN (01754 873940).

The Charity of John Dawber

Eligibility: People in need who live in the city of Lincoln and the parish of Bracebridge.

Types of grants: Christmas grocery vouchers and quarterly payments.

Annual grant total: In 2000/01 the charity had assets of £1.1 million, an income of £45,000 and its total expenditure was £28,000. About £21,000 was given to individuals in need.

Applications: In writing to the John Dawber Committee, Lincoln City Council, City Hall, Beaumont Fee, Lincoln LN1 1DD.

Correspondent: Messrs Andrew & Co., St Swithins Square, Lincoln LN2 1HB (01522 512123; Fax: 01522 546713; e-mail: andsol@enterprise.net).

The Farmers' Benevolent Institution

Eligibility: People living within a 15-mile radius of Grantham and 'having been owners or occupiers of land, but who from losses or other untoward circumstances have become destitute'. Applicants must be 60 if they have been a subscriber of the funds for ten years or more. Otherwise they should be over 65.

Types of grants: Annual payments of £150 in July and a supplementary payment of £250 at Christmas.

Annual grant total: About £2,500 per year.

Applications: In writing to the correspondent.

Correspondent: The Secretary, c/o Duncan & Toplis, 3 Castlegate, Grantham, Lincolnshire NG31 6SF (01476 591200).

The Gainsborough Dispensary Charity

Eligibility: People in need who live in Gainsborough and Morton.

Types of grants: One-off grants towards furniture, domestic appliances, holidays where there is a medical need, clothing etc., up to a maximum of £300.

Annual grant total: In 2001 the charity had assets of £156,000, an income of £7,100 and its total expenditure was £8,600 most of which was given in grants to 40 individuals in need.

Applications: In writing to the correspondent through a social worker, citizen's advice bureau, other welfare agency or through a community nurse or a minister of religion. They are considered every month.

Correspondent: B E Stonehouse, Clerk, 15 Chestnut Avenue, Gainsborough, Lincolnshire DN21 1EX (01427 613067).

The Mayor of Great Grimsby's Fund

Eligibility: People in need who live in north east Lincolnshire.

Types of grants: One-off grants for urgent needs, typically ranging from £75 to £100. No cash grants are given; recent grants include ones towards a new carpet and medical equipment.

Annual grant total: About £1,000 in about 10 grants.

Applications: In writing to the correspondent, with details of the need. Telephone enquiries are not invited; the correspondent will respond to all letters.

Correspondent: John Callison, Civics Manager, Civic Office, Grimsby Town Hall, Town Hall Square, Grimsby DN31 1HX.

Other information: In July 2002 the trust stated that over the next couple of years it would be undergoing major changes, including a merger with two or three other funds. Contact the trust in writing for up-to-date information.

The Hesslewood Children's Trust (Hull Seamen's & General Orphanage)

See entry on page 181

Hunstone's Charity

Eligibility: Gentlemen in need who live in Lincolnshire with preference for 'Decayed gentlemen of the family of Edward Hunstone or of the several families of the Gedneys or of Robert Smith or of the Woodliffes and decayed gentlemen living in the county of Lincoln'. Particular mention is also made of retired clergymen, members of HM Forces, farmers, farm labourers or anyone connected with land, and disabled people. Grants are not given to women.

Types of grants: Recipients receive £250 per year, paid in two instalments of £125 in April and October. The assistance will be given as long as the trustees consider necessary or until the death of the recipient.

Annual grant total: In 2001 the charity had assets of £600,000, an income of £34,000 and a total expenditure of £20,000. The sum of £8,800 was given in 35 relief-in-need grants.

Applications: On a form available from the correspondent. Applications should be submitted either through a social worker, citizen's advice bureau or other welfare agency, or directly by the individual. They are are considered in May each year, but can be considered at other times if urgent. Two references are required with each application.

Correspondent: T Bradley, 58 Eastwood Road, Boston, Lincolnshire PE21 0PH (01205 364175).

The Lincoln General Dispensary Fund

Eligibility: People in need who are sick, convalescent, disabled or infirm and live in the district of Lincoln.

Types of grants: One-off grants for amounts of up to £250, to alleviate suffering or aid recovery 'by providing or paying for items, services or facilities which are calculated to achieve this objective but are not readily available to them from other sources'. Recent grants have been given for orthopaedic beds, alarm systems and recuperative holidays. Grants are also given to local organisations.

Annual grant total: In 2001 the trust had assets of £280,000, an income of £15,000 and a total expenditure of £16,000. A sum of £13,000 was given in 55 relief-in-need grants.

Applications: On a form through a social worker, citizen's advice bureau other welfare agency. They are considered throughout the year.

Correspondent: M Bonass, Durrus Scothern Lane, Dunholme, Lincoln LN2 3QP (01673 860660; Fax: 01673 861701).

Lincolnshire Police Charitable Fund

Eligibility: People in need who are present or former employees of Lincolnshire Police Authority, and their dependants.

Types of grants: One-off grants of up to £3,000.

Annual grant total: About £20,000.

Applications: On a form available from the Welfare Officer at the address below. Applications can be submitted directly by the individual or through a social worker, citizen's advice bureau or other welfare agency. Applications should contain details of income and expenditure, although grants are not means tested. They can be considered in any month.

Correspondent: Mrs Cilla Smith, Lincolnshire Police Welfare Dept, 19 Sixfield Close, Lincoln LN6 0EJ.

The Tyler Charity for the Poor

Eligibility: People in need who live in the parishes of Morton and Thornock.

Types of grants: One-off and recurrent grants according to need.

Annual grant total: In 1999/2000 the fund had an income of £690 and a total expenditure of £460.

Applications: In writing to the correspondent.

Please note, at the time of publication of this guide the correspondent was about to step down, but a new correspondent had not yet been appointed. If you do not receive a reply from the trust we suggest you contact the Charity Commission, to see whether they have an up-to-date correspondent (0870 333 0123; website: www.charity-commission.gov.uk).

Correspondent: H Waring, Secretary, 15 Ludford Crescent, Gainsborough, Lincolnshire DN21 1XB.

The Willingham & District Relief in Sickness Charity

Eligibility: People in need who live in the parishes of Corringham, Heapham, Kexby, Springthorpe, Upton and Willingham.

Types of grants: One-off and recurrent grants according to need, e.g. for one-off items or respite care. Priority is usually given to help with bills.

Annual grant total: About £3,500 a year.

Applications: In writing to the correspondent by 1 April or 1 October for meetings at the end of those months.

Correspondent: Mrs J C Spencer, Secretary, 4 Church Road, Upton, Gainsborough, Lincolnshire DN21 5NS (01427 838385).

Bardney, Tupholme and Bucknall

The Kitchings General Charity

Eligibility: People in need who live in the parish of Bardney, Tupholme and Bucknall.

Types of grants: One-off grants to relieve hardship or distress e.g. holidays/respite care for disabled people (mostly at a special home at Sandringham), specialised nursing equipment and funeral expenses. Grants are usually for amounts of up to £350.

Annual grant total: In 2000 the trust had an income of about £15,000 and a total expenditure of £16,000. Relief-in-need grants to three individuals totalled £1,000. Grants for other purposes totalled £8,000.

Applications: In writing to the correspondent directly by the individual, only basic details are required. Applications should be submitted in May, if possible (but not essential) for consideration in May, October or January.

Correspondent: Mrs J Smith, Secretary, 42 Abbey Road, Bardney, Lincoln LN3 5XA (01526 398505).

Barrow-upon-Humber

The Beeton, Barrick & Beck Relief-in-Need Charity

Eligibility: People who are over 60 and in need and live in the parish of Barrow-upon-Humber.

Types of grants: Christmas vouchers and one-off grants for example for immediate relief following a house fire and travel costs to hospital.

Annual grant total: In 2000/01 the trust had an income of £2,800 and a total expenditure of £2,500.

Applications: On a form available from the correspondent by September/October for consideration in November.

Correspondent: Mrs A Lawe, Barrow Wold Farm, Deepdale, Barton-upon-Humber, North Lincolnshire DN18 6ED.

Barton-upon-Humber

The Barton-upon-Humber Relief-in-Sickness Fund

Eligibility: People who are sick or disabled and who live in the parish of Barton-upon-Humber.

Types of grants: Discretionary grants are given for all kinds of need, but usually for medical aids and equipment.

Annual grant total: Around £2,000 per year.

Applications: In writing to the correspondent. The trustees discuss cases which are known personally to them, although written applications are equally welcome and are considered when received.

Correspondent: H K Ready, Keith Ready & Co., Market Place, Barton-upon-Humber DN18 5DA (01652 632215; Fax: 01652 660036; e-mail: keith@ready.fs.co.uk).

The Charity of John Tripp (Blue Coat)

Eligibility: People in need who live in Barton-upon-Humber.

Types of grants: One-off grants usually of around £25 to £30.

Annual grant total: In 1997/98 the trust had an income of £3,600 and a total expenditure of £990. No further information was available.

Applications: By letter to the correspondent. Unless urgent, applications are considered each November.

Correspondent: H K Ready, Keith Ready & Co., Market Place, Barton-upon-Humber DN18 5DA (01652 632215; Fax: 01652 660036; e-mail: keith@ready.fs.co.uk).

Billingborough

The Billingborough United Charities

Eligibility: People in need who live in the civil parish of Billingborough.

Types of grants: One-off cash grants including those to poor widows at Christmas and people who are disabled. Grants are for a minimum of £30. No payments are made towards statutory liabilities for example council tax, income tax or national insurance.

Annual grant total: In 2002 the charities had an income of £1,300, out of a total expenditure of almost £800, the sum of £480 was distributed in 18 relief-in-need grants. £300 was distributed in other grants.

Applications: Applications should be submitted in writing either by the individual or on their behalf by a vicar, churchwarden, school master, doctor, district nurse, friend, family member, social worker, citizen's advice bureau or other welfare agency.

Correspondent: R F Lovelock, Southways, 1 Folkingham Road, Billingborough, Sleaford, Lincolnshire NG34 0NT (01529 240374).

Colsterworth

The Frederick Ingle Charities

Eligibility: People who are sick and in need and have lived in the parish of Colsterworth for at least five years.

Types of grants: One-off and recurrent grants in the range of £20 to £50 are given towards medical care and aids. No grants are given to people in receipt of funds from other grant-giving organisations, pensions or income support schemes.

Annual grant total: In 2001 the trust had assets of £24,000 and an income of £900. A total of £450 was given in 20 grants to individuals. £350 was given in grants for other purposes.

Applications: In writing to the correspondent either through a third party such as a social worker, citizen's advice bureau or other welfare agency or directly by the individual. Applications are considered at the beginning of March, June and December and should include details of the applicant's financial position and a doctor's report.

Correspondent: Mrs M A Winn, Spring House, 43 Newton Way, Woolsthorpe-by-Colsterworth, Grantham, Lincolnshire NG33 5NP (01476 860404).

Deeping

The Deeping St James United Charities

Eligibility: People who are ill or elderly and live in the parish of St James, Deeping.

Types of grants: One-off and recurrent grants according to need.

Annual grant total: In 2000 the trust had assets of £835,000 and an income of £32,000. Grants totalled £13,000 including £3,400 to widows aged over 60 and £1,900 to individuals for relief of sickness.

Applications: In writing to the correspondent for consideration at the start of March, June, September and December.

Correspondent: R Moulsher, Connell Estate Agents, 3 High Street, Market Deeping, Lincolnshire PE6 8ED (01780 762951).

Other information: This trust also give grants to college and university students and local organisations.

Dorrington

Dorrington Welfare Charity

Eligibility: People in need who live in the village of Dorrington.

Types of grants: One-off grants of £15 to £25 towards, for example, relieving sudden distress; travel expenses to visit family in hospital; heating and lighting costs in cases of real hardship; washing machines for widows with large families; radio or television sets for lonely or housebound people; adaptations to homes of disabled people; domestic coal; and the general relief of sickness, infirmity or need. Grants of £300 can be made towards funeral expenses. Pensioners receive grants of £25 at Christmas. The trust also makes education grants to people under 17.

Annual grant total: In 2001 the charity had assets of £59,000 and an income of £5,200. Out of a total expenditure of £2,400 the sum of £1,600 was distributed in grants to individuals for welfare and educational purposes.

Applications: In writing to the correspondent or a trustee, directly by the individual. Applications are considered in February, July and October. Applications should include a general explanation of assistance required, an estimate of the expenses involved, details of any other assistance received or confirmation that no assistance has been or can be received from the DWP or any other public funds.

Correspondent: Miss K E Griffiths, 59 Main Street, Dorrington, Lincoln LN4 3PX. (01526 832802).

Frampton

The Frampton Town Land & United Charities

Eligibility: People in need over 65 and recently bereaved widows who have lived in the ancient parish of Frampton for at least five years.

Types of grants: Grants towards electricity bills and Christmas gifts for the elderly. People can reapply each year.

Annual grant total: In 1998/99 the charities had an income of £9,800 and a total expenditure of £13,000. Grants to individuals totalled £4,400.

Applications: In writing to the correspondent. Applications are considered in early October.

Correspondent: Mrs J Bailey, Clerk, 52 West End Road, Frampton, Boston, Lincolnshire PE20 1BT (01205 724089).

Friskney

The Friskney United Charities

Eligibility: Elderly people in need who live in Friskney, particularly those who have a connection with agricultural work.

Types of grants: Annual grants of 3cwt of coal and/or £5 each.

Annual grant total: In 2001 the charities had an income of £30,000 and a total expenditure of £13,000.

Applications: In writing to the correspondent. Applications are considered in November. A list of applicants is produced by the trustees based upon their local knowledge.

Correspondent: Mrs A M Bray, Cranberry Lodge, Cranberry Lane, Friskney, Boston, Lincolnshire PE22 8PT.

Other information: This entry was not confirmed by the charities, but the address was correct according to the Charity Commission database.

Grimsby

Sir Alec Black's Charity

Eligibility: Sick poor fishermen who live in the borough of Grimsby.

Types of grants: One-off and recurrent grants according to need.

Annual grant total: In 1998/99 the trust had an income of £77,000 and a total expenditure of £80,000. Grants, mainly to organisations, totalled £65,000. In other years about £1,500 has been given to individuals.

Applications: In writing to the correspondent. The trustees meet twice a year, in May and November, to consider applications.

Correspondent: S Wilson, Trustee, Messrs Wilson Sharpe & Co., 17-19 Osborne Street, Grimsby, North East Lincolnshire DN31 1HA (01472 348315).

Other information: Organisations can also receive grants, although those funded by the health authority are excluded.

The Grimsby Fishermen's Dependants Fund

Eligibility: Widows, children and dependant parents of Grimsby fishermen lost at sea, or dying ashore while still fishermen.

Types of grants: Regular allowances of £13 a week for widows and other dependants and extra quarterly grants of £100 for widows, £250 for orphans and £100 for other dependants.

Annual grant total: In 2000/01 the fund had assets of £1.1 million, an income of £47,000 and its total expenditure was £55,000. £48,000 was given in 48 grants.

Applications: On a form available from the correspondent or from the Port Missioner, to be submitted directly by the individual or through a social worker, citizen's advice bureau or other welfare agency. Applications are considered when received.

Correspondent: J R McLellan, Charities Administrator, 1st Floor, rear of 23 Bargate, Grimsby, Lincolnshire DN34 4SS (01472 347914; Fax: 01472 348341).

Hacconby & Stainfield

Hacconby Poor's Money & Others

Eligibility: People in need who live in Hacconby and Stainfield parish.

Types of grants: One-off and recurrent grants, ranging between £90 and £190. Grants include Christmas grants to people aged over 65, help with home alterations for disabled people and grants towards funeral expenses and hospital travel costs.

Annual grant total: In 2001 the charity had assets of £90,000 and an income of £2,500. Total expenditure was £2,700, all of which was given in 28 grants.

Applications: In writing to the correspondent. Applications can be submitted directly by the individual or through a third party such as a social worker, citizen's advice bureau, welfare agency or neighbour, and can be considered at any time.

Correspondent: Mrs Gillian F Stoneman, 8 Church Street, Hacconby, Bourne, Lincolnshire PE10 0UJ (01778 570607; e-mail: stoneman@beamsend.fq.co.uk).

Kesteven

The Kesteven Children in Need

Eligibility: Children/young people up to the age of 16 who live in Kesteven.

Types of grants: One-off and recurrent grants of up to £500. Examples of grants include clothing, educational holidays, days out, prams/pushchairs, beds/sheets, fireguard, secondhand washing machines, educational toys and playschool fees.

Annual grant total: In 1998/99 the trust had an income of £5,400 and a total expenditure of £3,700, all of which was given in grants.

Applications: Generally through local social workers, health visitors, teachers and education officers. Information should include the family situation, the age of the child and his/her special needs. Applications are considered throughout the year.

Correspondent: Mrs Jane Howard, Nocton Rise, Sleaford Road, Nocton, Lincoln LN4 2AF.

Other information: This entry was not confirmed by the trust, but the address was correct according to the Charity Commission database.

A L Padley Charity Fund

Eligibility: People living in Kesteven who are: couples wishing to get married where the man is 24 years or older and the woman is 21 years or older; pensioners; or people who have been suffering from prolonged illness.

Types of grants: One-off and recurrent grants according to need.

Annual grant total: In 2000/01 the fund had an income of £3,800, no expenditure was recorded in the year.

Applications: In writing to the correpsondent, please mark with ref. HAT. The trust asks applicants to write to the trust first to see if your interests match the trustees.

Correspondent: The Trustees, Fraser Brown Solicitors, 84 Friar Lane, Nottingham NG1 6ED (0115 947 2541).

Lincoln

The Bishop of Lincoln's Discretionary Fund

Eligibility: Ministers of the Church of England who live and work in the Diocese of Lincoln.

Types of grants: One-off grants of £25 to £450 according to need. Grants are usually to assist sick clergy and their families and for holiday grants.

Annual grant total: In 2001 the fund had an income of £16,000 and a total expenditure of £9,700. Grants to individuals total about £5,000 a year.

Applications: In writing by the individual or one of the other local bishops to the Bishop of Lincoln. Applications are considered throughout the year.

Correspondent: Canon Raymond Rodger, Bishop's House, Eastgate, Lincoln LN2 1QQ (01522 534701; Fax: 01522 511095).

The Lincoln Municipal Relief-in-Need Charities

Eligibility: People in need who live in the city of Lincoln.

Types of grants: One-off grants up to a maximum value of £250 each, for all kinds of need except relief with rates, taxes or public funds; improvement to properties; or debts already incurred.

Annual grant total: In 2001/02 the charity had an income of £34,000 and a total expenditure of £26,000. A total of £21,000 was distributed in 69 relief-in-need grants.

Applications: On a form available from the correspondent, to be submitted through a social worker, citizen's advice bureau or other welfare agency. Applications are considered at any time.

Correspondent: M G Bonass, Clerk, Durrus Scothern Lane, Dunholme, Lincoln LN2 3QP (01673 860660; Fax: 01673 861701).

The Herbert William Sollitt Memorial Trust

Eligibility: People in need who are widows or widowers and live in the city of Lincoln.

Types of grants: One-off grants of £75 to £100 for household items and decoration, holidays and telephone installation. Grants are not given to married people or people who live outside the area of benefit.

Annual grant total: In 2000/01 the trust had an income of £1,900 and a total expenditure of £1,700.

Applications: On a form available from the correspondent, through a social worker, citizen's advice bureau or other welfare agency. Applications are considered throughout the year.

Correspondent: Mrs Jacqueline Smith, Secretary, 24 Sunfield Crescent, Birchwood, Lincoln LN6 0LL.

Other information: This entry was not confirmed by the trust, but the address was correct according to infomation on file at the Charity Commission.

Moulton

The Moulton Poors' Lands Charity

Eligibility: People in need, generally older people, who live in the civil parish of Moulton.

Types of grants: Grants can be paid in cash or in kind. Relief-in-need grants are generally paid following a severe accident, unexpected loss or misfortune.

Annual grant total: About £15,000 a year.

Applications: In writing to the correspondent, usually through a trustee. Applications are considered in April and December.

Correspondent: R W Lewis, Clerk for the Charity, Maples & Son, 23 New Road, Spalding, Lincolnshire PE11 1DH (01775 722261).

Navenby

The Navenby Towns Farm Trust

Eligibility: People in need who live in the village of Navenby.

Types of grants: One-off grants according to need.

Annual grant total: In 1999/2000 the trust had an income of £10,000. The trust states that grants are made to both organisations and individuals, with two thirds of the income used for education and the remainder for welfare and other purposes.

Applications: On a form available from the correspondent, the post office, or Smith and Willows the newsagents. Applications are considered in September. Urgent applications may occassionally be considered at other times.

Correspondent: The Secretary, Winton House, Grantham Road, Navenby, Lincoln LN5 0JJ (01522 810868).

South Holland

The Spalding Relief-in-Need Charity

Eligibility: People in need who live in the area covered by South Holland District Council with priority to residents of the parishes of Spalding, Cowbit, Deeping St Nicholas, Pinchbeck and Weston.

Types of grants: One-off grants in the range of £25 to £1,000 towards furniture and domestic appliances, rent arrears and other debts and children's clothing. Food vouchers can also be given.

Annual grant total: In 2000/01 the charity had assets of £502,000 and an income of £30,000. A total of £17,000 was given in 125 relief-in-need grants to individuals.

Applications: On a form available from R W Skells, Deputy Clerk, at the address below. Applications can be submitted directly by the individual or assisted if appropriate by a social worker, citizen's advice bureau, other welfare agency or third party. Smaller grants are considered at any time. Larger grants are considered in March, June, September and December.

Correspondent: R A Knipe, Solicitor, Dembleby House, 12 Broad Street, Spalding, Lincolnshire PE11 1ES (01775 768774; Fax: 01775 725842; e-mail: knipemiller@btclick.com).

Spilsby

The Spilsby Feoffees (Poorlands) Charities

Eligibility: People of retirement age in need who have lived in Spilsby for at least five years.

Types of grants: Grants of about £25 a year.

Annual grant total: In 2001 the charity had an income of £2,300 and an expenditure of £2,200, all of which was given in grants.

Applications: On a form available from the correspondent. Applications must be submitted directly by the individual and are considered in June and December. Applicants must state how long they have lived in Spilsby.

Correspondent: Mrs J Tong, Clerk, Rosedale Lodge, Ashby Road, Spilsby, Lincolnshire PE23 5DW (01790 752885).

Stamford

Winifrede Browne's Charity

Eligibility: People in need who are sick or elderly and live in Stamford.

Types of grants: Grants given include those for clothing, travel to hospital and assistance with funeral expenses.

Annual grant total: About £2,000 a year.

Applications: Application forms are available from the correspondent, to be submitted either through a social worker, citizen's advice bureau or other welfare agency, or directly by the individual. They are considered every month.

Correspondent: N P Fluck, Messrs Stapleton & Son, 1 Broad Street, Stamford, Lincolnshire PE9 1PD (01780 751226; Fax: 01780 766407; e-mail: enquiries@stapletons.com).

Stickford

The Stickford Relief-in-Need Charity

Eligibility: People in need who live in the parish of Stickford.

Types of grants: One-off and recurrent grants for relief-in-need purposes, towards school uniforms, and a Christmas bonus. Further grants are given towards a bus service for older people, youth club outings and so on.

Annual grant total: In 2000 the trust had an income of £15,000 and a total expenditure of £12,000.

Applications: In writing to the correspondent. Applications should be submitted directly by the individual and are considered all year.

Correspondent: Mrs K L Bunting, Clerk, The Old Vicarage, Church Road, Stickford, Boston, Lincolnshire PE22 8EP.

Other information: This entry was not confirmed by the charity but the address was correct according to information on file at the Charity Commission.

Surfleet

The Surfleet United Charities

Eligibility: Retired people in need who have lived in the parish of Surfleet for over ten years (exceptions will be made on the age restriction in cases of extreme need).

Types of grants: Normally grants before Christmas each year of £15 (individuals) and £25 (couples). Other one-off grants according to need.

Annual grant total: In 2001 the charities had an income of £5,600 and a total expenditure of £2,600. The sum of £2,200 was distributed in about 150 relief-in-need grants.

Applications: In writing to the correspondent. Applications can be submitted directly by the individual and are considered in November.

Correspondent: Robert Barlow, 37 Brayfields, Pinchbeck, Spalding, Lincolnshire PE11 3YT (01775 720654).

Sutterton

The Sutterton Parochial Charity Trust

Eligibility: Individuals in need who live in the parish of Sutterton in Boston.

Types of grants: One-off grants of £35 at Christmas.

Annual grant total: In 2000/01 it had assets of £8,700 and an income of £4,500. Total expenditure was £3,400, including 87 grants totalling over £3,000. £400 was given to an organisation.

Applications: In writing to the correspondent for consideration throughout the year.

Correspondent: Mrs S Truman, Golden Lodge, One Way Road, Sutterton, Boston, Lincolnshire.

Sutton Bridge

Sutton Bridge Power Fund

Eligibility: Adults living, and children living or attending schools, in Sutton Bridge, Lincolnshire (very clearly defined boundaries which incorporate Waldpole Cross Keys, Norfolk, Tydd St Giles, Cambridgeshire, Sutton Bridge, Tydd St Mary, Lincolnshire).

Types of grants: One-off and recurrent grants according to need.

Annual grant total: About £15,000 to £20,000 a year.

Applications: In writing to the correspondent.

Correspondent: Anthony Gallagher, Templar House, 81–87 High Holborn, London WC1V 6NU (020 7331 3167).

Sutton St James

The Sutton St James United Charities

Eligibility: People in need who live in the parish of Sutton St James.

Types of grants: One-off and recurrent grants according to need, including bereavement grants, help to people being evicted and those on the breadline.

Annual grant total: The charities have an income of about £7,000. This is divided between education and relief-in-need grants.

Applications: On a form available from the correspondent. Applications are only considered when all other available avenues have been explored.

Correspondent: K Savage, Clerk, 4 Armitage Close, Holbeach, Lincolnshire PE12 7QL.

Swineshead

The Swineshead Poor Charities

Eligibility: People in need who live in the parish of Swineshead.

Types of grants: One-off and recurrent grants and loans according to need.

Annual grant total: In 2000/01 the trust had an income of £11,000 and a total expenditure of £9,000. Grants are made to organisations and individuals.

Applications: In writing to the correspondent.

Correspondent: Mrs D Nundy, Loders, 29 Abbey Road, Swineshead, Boston, Lincolnshire PE20 3EN (01205 820381; e-mail: dohnundy@aol.com).

Other information: This entry was not confirmed by the charities, but the address was correct according to the Charity Commission database.

Northamptonshire

Edmund Arnold's Charity (Poors Branch)

Eligibility: People in need who live in the parish of Nether Heyford, Northamptonshire, the ancient parish of St Giles in Northampton and the parish of Stony Stratford, Buckinghamshire.

Types of grants: One-off and recurrent cash grants of £100 to £300 according to need.

Annual grant total: In 2001 the charity had an income of £1,600 and a total expenditure of £1,200, all of which was given in grants to individuals in need.

Applications: On a form available on written request from the correspondent. Applications are considered in April and October.

Correspondent: Gordon Gee, Clerk, c/o Mssrs Wilson Browne, Solicitors, 60 Gold Street, Northampton NN1 1RS.

The John & Anne Camp's Charity

Eligibility: Widows and spinsters of 'good character' aged 55 or over who have lived in the parliamentary borough of Northampton for at least five years. Preference is given to people born in the borough or county of Northampton.

Types of grants: Up to 20 annuities paid in quarterly payments of £5, with an additional gift paid at Christmas.

Annual grant total: About £500 a year.

Applications: By nomination by one of the trustees.

Correspondent: Mrs Duberry, Hewitson Becke & Shaw, 7 Spencer Parade, Northampton NN1 5AB (01604 233233).

The Valentine Goodman Estate Charity

Eligibility: People in need who live in the parishes of Blaston, Bringhurst, Drayton, East Magna, Hallaton and Medbourne.

Types of grants: One-off or recurrent grants according to need.

Annual grant total: In 2000 the charity had an income of £11,000 and a total expenditure of £5,800.

Applications: In writing to the correspondent. Grants are distributed in February each year.

Correspondent: Norman Paske, Secretary, Samuel Rose, Cottage Farm, Sywell, Northampton NN60 BJ (01604 782700).

The Kettering Charities (Fuel Grants)

Eligibility: People over the statutory retirement age who live alone in Kettering or Baron Seagrave. Applicants with an income under £146.12 a week are guaranteed a grant.

Types of grants: Grants towards winter fuel bills.

Annual grant total: In 2001 the sum of £10,000 was given in 850 grants.

Applications: On a form available from the correspondent which can be obtained after the charity is advertised in local newspapers in November each year. Grants are considered in November. Applicants must include details of income, status, age and address.

Correspondent: David Cook, Municipal Offices, Bowling Green Road, Kettering NN15 7QX (01536 534398; Fax: 01536 410795).

The Henry & Elizabeth Lineham Charity

Eligibility: Women in need, generally widows or spinster daughters of professional men who have died. Applicants must be at least 55 and live in Northampton borough.

Types of grants: Grants of £50 paid in the summer and at Christmas.

Annual grant total: The trust had an income of £35,000 and there were 85 annuitants.

Applications: Through nomination by one of the trustees, mostly councillors or ex-councillors.

Correspondent: Mrs Duberry, Hewitson Becke & Shaw, 7 Spencer Parade, Northampton NN1 5AB (01604 233233).

The Northamptonshire Medical Charity

Eligibility: People in need who have served as medical practitioners in the borough/county of Northampton and their dependants. Medical charities are also supported.

Types of grants: One-off and recurrent grants according to need. Grants have been given to assist with an aircraft flight for a widow to visit her family overseas, a television to a doctor's widow and occasional payments to a widow with very limited resources.

Educational grants are given to medical students and postgraduates, but no grants are made for school fees.

Annual grant total: In 2000 the trust had an income of £12,000 and a total expenditure of £5,700.

Applications: In writing to the correspondent for consideration throughout the year.

Correspondent: Mr Woolmore, Secretary/Treasurer, 457 Wellingborough Road, Northampton NN3 3HW (01604 713908; e-mail: michael@woolymed.demon.co.uk).

Other information: Due to lack of demand, the charity was, in July 2002, reviewing its future regarding grantmaking to individuals.

The Rowlett Trust

Eligibility: Adults with learning difficulties and their carers who live in Corby and surrounding villages.

Types of grants: One-off grants of £100 to £250. Grants are usually for holidays. Recent grants have been given to a carer towards the support of a mentally disabled adult during a holiday at home and towards a bathing aid for a physically and mentally disabled adult.

Annual grant total: In 2000/01 the trust had an income of £910, no funds were expended in the year.

Applications: In writing to the correspondent at any time. Applications can be submitted by a carer or through a social worker, citizen's advice bureau or other welfare agency.

Correspondent: Mrs Janet Jones, 58 Kirby Road, Corby, Northamptonshire NN17 3DB (01536 770625).

Saint Giles Charity Estate

Eligibility: People in need who live in Northamptonshire.

Types of grants: One-off grants and annual Christmas grants to individuals and families towards for example helping to fund individual household requirements such as carpets/washing machines etc. Grants are always made for a specific purpose, not as a financial 'top up'.

The charity does not normally make grants towards paying off debts; tuition fees (although help may be given towards purchase of books/equipment); or for building projects.

Annual grant total: In 2001 the trust had assets of £2.8 million and an income of £347,000. It gave £12,000 in about 60 grants to individuals for relief-in-need and educational purposes. Occasional grants are also made to locally based charities.

Applications: On a form available from the correspondent. The charity will give preference to applications which are submitted through a social worker, citizen's advice bureau or other welfare agency. Details of income, expenditure and purpose for which the grant is required must be given. Applications are considered in February, May, August and November.

Correspondent: A D Lainsbury, Administrator, 15 Churchill Avenue, Northampton NN3 6NY (01604 645539).

Sir Thomas White's Loan Fund

Eligibility: People aged between 21 and 34 years of age who live in the extended borough of Northampton.

Types of grants: One-off grants towards buying a house, home improvements (e.g. central heating/double glazing installation, bathroom improvements), wedding expenses, car expenses, etc. The fund was originally set up for the provision of tools for people setting up in a trade or profession and it also gives nine-year interest-free loans for education and new businesses.

Annual grant total: About 150 loans of about £800, totalling about £100,000 are given for relief-in-need and educational purposes.

Applications: Apply in writing for a form in November, following a public notice advertising the grants.

Correspondent: Mrs Duberry, Clerk to the Trustees, Hewitson Becke & Shaw, 7 Spencer Parade, Northampton NN1 5AB. (01604 233233).

Other information: The fund is currently reviewing its scheme. In future years it plans to make grants as well as loans.

The Yelvertoft & District Relief in Sickness Fund

Eligibility: People in need who live in the parishes of Yelvertoft, West Haddon, Crick, Winwick, Clay Coton and Elkington, who are sick, convalescent, disabled or infirm.

Types of grants: One-off and recurrent grants for hospital visits. Support will not be given for things that the trustees feel is the responsibility of the NHS.

Annual grant total: In 2001 the fund had a total expenditure of £6,000 of which £3,900 was given directly to individuals and £1,600 went on chiropody fees. In the year wheelchairs and other pieces of equipment were also purchased for loan.

Applications: In writing to the correspondent. Applications should be submitted directly by the individual, a relative or district nurse, and can be considered at any time.

Correspondent: Mrs Anne Drewett, Secretary and Trustee, 6 Monks Way, Crick, Northampton NN6 7XB (01788 823499).

Blakesley

The Blakesley Parochial Charities

Eligibility: People in need who live in Blakesley.

Types of grants: One-off and recurrent grants according to need. Grants are given towards the fuel bills of elderly people and as pensions to widows.

Annual grant total: Around £3,000 a year, of which £730 is given for educational purposes.

Applications: In writing to the correspondent. Applications are considered in December.

Correspondent: Patricia Paterson, Secretary, Quinbury Cottage, 35 Quinbury End, Blakesley, Towcester, Northamptonshire NN12 8RF (01327 860424).

Brackley

The Brackley United Feoffee Charity

Eligibility: People in need who live in Brackley.

Types of grants: One-off grants which have helped with buying children's shoes, a washing machine, cooker, dryer and the provision of supplementary heating. No grants for the relief of rates, taxes etc. but the trust may supplement statutory provision. Christmas gifts are given to older people of £20 or £30.

Annual grant total: In 2000/01 the trust had £9,400 available for distribution. It gave one-off grants to eight individuals totalling £2,600 and a further £1,100 in 49 Christmas gifts to pensioners. £1,600 was also given in education grants.

Applications: In writing to the correspondent preferably by the individual or through a social worker, citizen's advice bureau or other welfare agency. The correspondent states: 'When in doubt apply – funds are usually available. Almost any reasonable case succeeds.'

Correspondent: Mrs R Hedges, 7 Easthill Close, Brackley, Northants NN13 7BS (01280 702420).

Braunston

The Braunston Town Lands Charity

Eligibility: People who live in Braunston and have to spend four nights or more in a hospital. Grants are given to patients and to their relatives. The size of grant depends on the distance that has to be travelled to the hospital and the amount of time spent at hospital.

Types of grants: One-off grants in the form of cash donations at Christmas for those over 90 years of age and Christmas gifts for people who are hospitalised or housebound.

Annual grant total: In 2000/01 the trust had an income of £2,900 and a total expenditure of £2,500. The sum of £1,700 was given in relief-in-need grants to individuals. Grants are also made to organisations.

Applications: In writing to the correspondent, directly by the individual.

Correspondent: Miss S M Rowley, 5 Danecourt, Church Road, Brauston, Daventry, Northamptonshire NN11 7HG (01788 890559).

Brington

The Chauntry Estate

Eligibility: Elderly people and other people in need who live in the parish of Brington.

Types of grants: One-off grants to relieve sudden distress or infirmity are made, for example, towards travel expenses for visits to hospital, food, fuel and heating appliances, and comforts or aids not provided by health authorities. In 1998/99 grants were given towards coal for pensioners (£780), spectacles (£820), funeral expenses (£400), electricity bills (£840), lifeline units (£70), sheep shearing equipment (£350) and special needs (£200).

Annual grant total: About £5,000 is given each year in relief-in-need grants.

Applications: In writing to the correspondent.

Correspondent: Rita Tank, Walnut Tree Cottage, Main Street, Great Brington, Northampton NN7 4JA (01604 770809).

Byfield

The Byfield Poors Allotment

Eligibility: People in need who live in the parish of Byfield.

Types of grants: Grants given include those to pensioners at Christmas.

Annual grant total: In 2001 grants to 38 individuals totalled £1,400, mostly for welfare purposes.

Applications: On a form available from the correspondent. Applications can be made directly by the individual or a relevant third party. They can be submitted at any time for consideration in March, June, September and December.

Correspondent: Mrs J M Goddard, 22 Bell Lane, Byfield, Daventry, Northamptonshire NN11 6US (01327 260619).

Chipping Warden

The Reverend W Smart's Charity

Eligibility: People in need who live in the parish of Chipping Warden, Northamptonshire.

Types of grants: One-off and recurrent grants usually of between £50 and £250. Grants can be given to individuals or organisations. Preference is given to elderly people and young people in education.

Annual grant total: In 2001 the trust had an income of £3,200 and a total expenditure of £1,700.

Applications: In writing to the correspondent either directly by the individual or by another third party such as the Parochial Church Council, Parish Council or a relative. Applications are considered all year round.

Correspondent: P T Fenwick, Mill Lane House, Chipping Warden, Nr Banbury, Oxon OX17 1JZ (Tel & Fax: 01295 660243).

Daventry

The Daventry Consolidated Charity

Eligibility: People in need who live in the borough of Daventry.

Types of grants: One-off grants for a specific need such as a special chair for a child with cerebral palsy, travel to hospital for a child 45 miles from home and help with the costs of adaptations to a motability vehicle. No grants towards debts or ongoing expenses.

Annual grant total: In 2000 the trust had an income of £11,000 and a total expenditure of £7,400. Grants to individuals total about £6,000 a year.

Applications: In writing to the correspondent. Trustees meet three times a year in March, July and November. Applications must include financial circumstances and the specific purpose for the grant. Relevant information not included will be requested if required.

Correspondent: Mrs Maggie Dowie, 15 Astbury Close, Daventry, Northants NN11 4RL.

Desborough

The Desborough Town Welfare Committee

Eligibility: People who are elderly, sick or in need and living in Desborough.

Types of grants: One-off and recurrent grants, paid mainly at Christmas.

Annual grant total: Over £1,000 in about 30 grants, plus £2,000 in Co-op vouchers.

243

Applications: In writing to the correspondent, for consideration within two to three months.

Correspondent: Mrs A King, 190 Dunkirk Avenue, Desborough, Kettering, Northants NN14 2PP.

East Farndon

The United Charities of East Farndon

Eligibility: Families in need who live in East Farndon.

Types of grants: The trust provides fuel, normally at Christmas.

Annual grant total: In 2001 the trust had an income of £1,700 and its total expenditure was £1,200.

Applications: In writing to the correspondent or via one of the trustees.

Correspondent: C L Fraser, Linden Lea, Main Street, Market Harborough, Northamptonshire LE16 9SJ (01858 464218; e-mail: fraser-cameron@hotmail.com).

Gayton

The Gayton Relief-in-Need Charity

Eligibility: People of pensionable age who are in need who live in the parish of Gayton.

Types of grants: Monthly pensions and grants towards funeral costs. Grants range from £10 to £100.

Annual grant total: In 2000/01 it had an income of £3,500 and a total expenditure of £3,400.

Applications: In writing to the correspondent, or through the vicar of Gayton Church.

Correspondent: M J Percival, Clerk, Oxford House, Cliftonville, Northampton NN1 5PN (01604 230400).

Harpole

The Harpole Parochial Charities

Eligibility: People in need who live in Harpole and have lived there for more than seven years, with a preference for those over 60.

Types of grants: Recurrent grants ranging from £10 to £50.

Annual grant total: Over £1,000 in 70 grants.

Applications: On a form available from the correspondent. Applications can be submitted either directly by the individual or through a relative. They are considered in December and should be submitted in November.

Correspondent: J Calderwood, 39 Upper High Street, Harpole, Northampton NN7 4DJ.

Kettering

The Stockburn Memorial Trust

Eligibility: People who are sick or poor and live in the borough of Kettering.

Types of grants: One-off and recurrent grants for general purposes.

Annual grant total: In 2000 the trust had an income of £7,000 and a total expenditure of £3,100.

Applications: In writing to the correspondent through a social worker, citizen's advice bureau or other welfare agency. Details should include age, financial situation and health circumstances of the applicant. Applicants will be visited by the trust, usually within a week of applying.

Correspondent: Mrs P M Reynolds, 70 Windermere Road, Kettering, Northants NN16 8UF (01536 524662).

Litchborough

The Litchborough Parochial Charities

Eligibility: People in need who live in Litchborough.

Types of grants: One-off or recurrent grants according to need.

Annual grant total: In 2000/01 the charities had an income of almost £2,000 and a total expenditure of £5,000.

Applications: In writing to the correspondent.

Correspondent: A Harvey, 42 Farthingstone Road, Litchborough, Towcester, Northamptonshire NN12 8JE (01327 830228).

Long Buckby

The Long Buckby United Charities

Eligibility: People who are over 70 and live in the parish of Long Buckby; this also includes people who are not 'in need'.

Types of grants: One-off grants at Christmas. The trust has a policy of giving modest grants of £2.50 to around 360 individuals.

Annual grant total: The charities have an annual income of about £900.

Applications: In writing to the correspondent. Applications should be submitted directly by the individual to be considered in November.

Correspondent: J H Williams, 115 East Street, Long Buckby, Northampton NN6 7RB (01327 842468).

Middleton Cheney

Middleton Cheney United Charities

Eligibility: People in need under pensionable age who live in Middleton Cheney.

Types of grants: One-off grants in the range of £100 and £250.

Annual grant total: In 2001 the trust had an income of £8,000 and a total expenditure of £8,200. The sum of £4,500 was given in 19 relief-in-need grants to individuals. Educational grants to individuals totalled £2,000.

Applications: In writing to the correspondent directly by the individual. Applications are considered at any time.

Correspondent: Mrs Elizabeth Watts, 1 Chacombe Road, Middleton Cheney, Banbury, Oxfordshire OX17 2QS.

Northampton

The Mary Anne & Ruth Blunt Charity

Eligibility: Spinsters over 60 who have lived in the borough of Northampton for at least 20 years.

Types of grants: Annuities paid twice a year, in June and December.

Annual grant total: About £1,000.

Applications: By nomination by one of the trustees.

Correspondent: Mrs Duberry, Clerk to the Trust, Hewitson Becke & Shaw, 7 Spencer Parade, Northampton NN1 5AB (01604 233233).

The Coles & Rice Charity

Eligibility: People in need who are at least 55 years old and live in Northampton.

Types of grants: Recently, one-off grants have seldom been made. Most grants are annual pensions paid in quarterly instalments of £45. Each pensioner also receives a Christmas voucher of around £40.

Annual grant total: In 2001 the trust had assets of £240,000 and an income of £13,000. A total of £8,900 was given in grants to about 40 individuals.

Applications: On a form available from the correspondent. Applications should be made either directly by the individual or through a social worker, citizen's advice bureau or other welfare agency. They are considered around March and November. Details of income and expenditure, age and length of time the applicant has lived in the borough of Northampton must also be included.

Correspondent: Miss Forsyth, Wilson Browne, 60 Gold Street, Northampton NN1 1RS (01604 628131; Fax: 01604 230719).

The Northampton Municipal Church Charities

Eligibility: People in need who live in the borough of Northampton.

Types of grants: People aged over 55 are eligible for payments of £75 a quarter and a Christmas voucher of £30 (over 120 pensioners are supported each year). People of any age can receive one-off grants of up to a maximum of £500.

Annual grant total: In 2000/01 the charities had assets of £4.1 million and an income of £182,000. Out of a total expenditure of £166,000, about £50,000 was given in about 200 donations to individuals in need. A further £74,000 was given in grants for other purposes.

Applications: On a form available from the correspondent. Applications can be submitted either directly by the individual or through a third party such as a social worker, citizen's advice bureau or other welfare agency. They are considered bi-monthly. Applications must include details of age, residence, income, assets and expenditure.

Correspondent: Miss J A Forsyth, Wilson Browne Solicitors, 60 Gold Street, Northampton NN1 1RS (01604 628131; Fax: 01604 230719; e-mail: j.forsyth@wilsonbrowne.co.uk).

Other information: The charity runs a sheltered housing scheme at St Thomas House in St Giles Street, Northampton. It is warden controlled and has 17 one-bedroomed flats for people over 60. For further information, contact the correspondent.

The charities' income must firstly be used for maintaining property belonging to the charities, secondly for the benefit of residents of those properties and thirdly for the relief-in-need of people who live in Northampton.

The Page Fund

Eligibility: People in need who live in the borough of Northampton or within five miles from the Guildhall and have done so for more than five years. Preference is given to older people, and to those with a sudden unforeseen drop in income, for example widows following the death of a husband.

Types of grants: Pensions of £600 per year for people suffering a reduction in income due to widowhood or old age.

Annual grant total: In 2000/01 the fund had assets of £823,000 and an income of £23,000. Out of a total expenditure of £20,000, relief-in-need grants to individuals totalled £9,500. A further £11,000 was given to organisations.

Applications: On a form available from the correspondent. Applications can be submitted either through a social worker, citizen's advice bureau or other welfare agency; or directly by the individual. They are accepted at any time and are considered in May and November.

Correspondent: The Clerk, Messrs Wilson Browne, Solicitors, 60 Gold Street, Northampton NN1 1RS (01604 628131; 01604 230719).

Old

The Old Parish Charities

Eligibility: People in need who live in the parish of Old.

Types of grants: One-off and recurrent grants ranging from £25 to £600. Grants towards education, holidays, Christmas gifts, television rental, hospital visits, funeral expenses etc.

Annual grant total: The trust has assets of about £1 million and an annual income of about £50,000. Some 200 relief-in-need grants are given each year totalling around £17,000. Any remaining income is spent on maintaining six almshouses, and the community centre.

Applications: On a form available from the correspondent. Applications are considered each month.

Correspondent: R Frankham, Clerk, 2 Townson Close, Old, Northampton NN6 9RR (01604 781252).

Pattishall

The Pattishall Parochial Charities

Eligibility: People in need who live in the parish of Pattishall. Preference is given to people who are over 65.

Types of grants: In 2001 grants included the following: 14 widows and widowers received monthly pensions of £15; 46 households received grants for fuel at Christmas (£40 to single people and £55 to couples); and 3 individuals received one-off grants totalling £1,500, towards an electric wheelchair, a walk-in shower and a new path and hand rail.

Annual grant total: In 2001 the charities had an income of £6,400 and a total expenditure of £6,400, all of which was given in 63 grants.

Applications: In writing to the correspondent. Applications are usually considered in November for fuel grants, July for pensions, and throughout the year for other grants. Applications can be submitted either directly by the individual or by anybody who hears of a need such as one of the trustees or the rector of the parish. Receipts (copies will do) should be included for the cost of travel for hospital visits and for the purchases of large equipment, for example wheelchairs.

Correspondent: Mrs Vicki Streten, 4 Home Close, Eastcote, Towcester, Northamptonshire NN12 8NZ.

Ringstead

The Ringstead Gift

Eligibility: People in need who live in the parish of Ringstead.

Types of grants: One-off and recurrent grants of fuel, hospital travel, household items etc. Grants are also given to students. No grants for rent or rates.

Annual grant total: In 2000/01 the charity had an income of £1,400 and a total expenditure of £1,100.

Applications: In writing to the correspondent, to be submitted by June or the end of November.

Correspondent: Mrs D Pentelow, 20 Carlow Street, Ringstead, Kettering, Northamptonshire NN14 4DN.

Other information: This entry was not confirmed by the charity, but the address was correct according to the Charity Commission database.

Roade

The Roade Feoffees & Chivalls Charity

Eligibility: People in need who live in the ancient parish of Roade.

Types of grants: One-off grants ranging from £15 to £100. Grants are given at Christmas and for such things as travel expenses to visit relatives in hospital.

Annual grant total: In 1999 the charity had assets of £273,000 and an income of £10,000. Total expenditure was £7,500, with grants to individuals totalling £1,800 including educational grants.

Applications: In writing to the correspondent specifying the need. Applications are considered at any time.

Correspondent: Mrs Sylvia Mawby, 27 Church Croft, Roade, Northampton NN7 2PG.

Other information: This entry was not confirmed by the charity, but the address was correct according to the Charity Commission.

Scaldwell

The Scaldwell Relief-in-Need Charity

Eligibility: People in need who live in the parish of Scaldwell only.

Types of grants: One-off grants ranging from £50 to £250. Single grants are given to older people and to people with learning difficulties and disabilities.

Annual grant total: In 2000/01 the charity had assets of £17,000, an income of £1,200 and its total expenditure was £1,600. The sum of £1,500 was distributed in 26 relief-in-need grants.

Applications: In writing to the correspondent. Applications can be submitted through a social worker, citizen's advice bureau, other welfare agency or other third party, or directly by the individual. They are considered in November and February.

Correspondent: Mrs L A Goodenough, Scaldwell House, Scaldwell, Northampton NN6 9JS (01604 882136; e-mail: alison.goodenough@btinternet.com).

Silverstone

The Silverstone Poors' Allotment Charity

Eligibility: People in need who live in the parish of Silverstone.

Types of grants: Grants are given as cash or in kind for coal, hospital visiting and travel necessary for treatment etc.

Annual grant total: Between £800 to £1,000 a year.

Applications: In writing to the correspondent. Applications can be submitted directly by the individual or through a social worker, citizen's advice bureau, other welfare agency or another third party such as a neighbour or relative. Applications are considered on receipt.

Correspondent: J Tustian, 11 Towcester Road, Silverstone, Towcester, Northants NN12 8UB (01327 857842).

Towcester

The Sponne & Bickerstaffe Charity

Eligibility: People in need who live in the civil parish of Towcester.

Types of grants: One-off grants according to need. Grants have in the past been given towards the cost of carpets and telephone installation. At Christmas, Gateway vouchers are sent to older people and families who have little income.

Annual grant total: In 1999 about £7,000 was given for educational and welfare purposes.

Applications: In writing to the correspondent, either directly by the individual or through a social worker, citizen's advice bureau or other welfare agency.

Correspondent: Sue Joice, Moorfield, Buckingham Way, Towcester, Northamptonshire NN12 6PE (01327 351206).

Wappenham

The Wappenham Poors' Land Charity

Eligibility: People in need who live in the ecclesiastical parish of Wappenham.

Types of grants: The trust gives a small standard grant to pensioners in need. Grants are also given to widows, widowers and people who are sick or disabled and are in need of specific items e.g. wheelchairs, orthopaedic beds, home improvements, shower installation, redecoration and so on.

Annual grant total: In 2000/01 the charity had an income of £2,400. About £1,000 is given to individuals each year.

Applications: In writing to Cannon F E Pickard at The Vicarage, Lois Weedon, Towcester, Northants NN12 8PN, for consideration throughout the year.

Correspondent: Peter Lawrence Bell, Secretary, 2 Richmond Road, Towcester, Northamptonshire NN12 6EX (01327 350518).

Welton

The Welton Town Lands Trust

Eligibility: People in need who live in Welton.

Types of grants: Each December a payment of about £35 per household is made to deserving older people and others who qualify in terms of need. These may be repeated in subsequent years.

Annual grant total: About £1,400 is paid out annually to individuals in need, although this figure varies greatly dependent on number of applicants and money available.

Applications: On a form available from the correspondent. Applications are considered in November for distribution in December. The clerk states that details of the trust are well publicised within the village.

Correspondent: Mrs M Lovatt, Clerk, Stone House, High Street, Welton, Daventry, Northamptonshire NN11 5JP.

Nottinghamshire

The Arnold Aid in Sickness Fund

Eligibility: Sick and needy people who live in the urban district of Arnold and Daybrook, Nottinghamshire.

Types of grants: One-off grants, up to a maximum of £500, for specific items such as mobility aids within the house, improved shower or bathing facilities and assistance towards larger items such as stairlifts or wheelchairs. Occasionally a grant may be paid for a holiday or other small personal comfort. Grants are also given to organisations supporting individuals in the area.

Annual grant total: In 2001/02 the fund had assets of £25,000 and an income of £1,000. No grants were made in the year.

Applications: In writing to the correspondent, directly by the individual.

Correspondent: Mrs Jean Baird, Secretary, c/o Blythens Chartered Accountants, Haydn House, 309-329 Haydn Road, Sherwood, Nottingham NG5 1HG.

The Beatrice Eveline Bright Trust

Eligibility: Women of the protestant faith who are in need and live within a five-mile radius of the council house in the city of Nottingham.

Types of grants: Quarterly cash payments to supplement income, ranging from £65 to £260 in 2000. Also, payment of telephone/television rentals.

Annual grant total: In 2000/01 the trust had assets of £337,000 and an income of £30,000. Out of a total expenditure of £15,000, £7,200 was distributed in 24 grants.

Applications: In writing to the correspondent (there is no application form). Applicants are likely to be visited by the trust. Applications are considered on an ongoing basis and can be submitted either directly by the individual or a relevant third party such as a social worker, citizen's advice bureau or other welfare agency.

Correspondent: Mr J J Moore, Nelsons, Pennine House, 8 Stanford Street, Nottingham NG1 7BQ (0115 958 6262; Fax: 0115 941 9671).

The Lucy Derbyshire Annuity Fund

Eligibility: People of good character who are in reduced circumstances or of limited means and have lived in Nottingham or Nottinghamshire for at least five years preceding their application.

Types of grants: A yearly allowance of between £39 and £156.

Annual grant total: In 2001/02 the trust had assets of £468,000 and an income £150,000. It spent £158,000, of which £1,700 was given in 11 grants to individuals.

Applications: In writing to the correspondent. Applications can be submitted directly by the individual or through a social worker, citizen's advice bureau or other welfare agency.

Correspondent: P R Moore, c/o Tenon Ltd, Foxhall Lodge, Gregory Boulevard, Nottingham NG7 6LH (0115 955 2000; Fax: 0115 969 1043).

The Mary Dickinson Charity

Eligibility: Widows or the unmarried fatherless daughters of clergymen, gentlemen, professionals or others in trade or agriculture. Applicants must also be members of the Church of England or some other protestant faith or the Roman Catholic Church, and be resident or have at some time been resident in the city or the county of Nottinghamshire. Applicants are usually over 50 years old.

Types of grants: One-off grants for emergency items such as replacing gas fires and safety alarm and telephone systems.

Annual grant total: In 2000/01 the charity had assets of £940,000 and an income of £59,000. A total of £52,000 was spent, of which £11,000 was given in relief-in-need grants to individuals.

Applications: On a form available from the correspondent. Applications should be submitted through a doctor/member of the clergy or directly by the individual, supported by a reference from one of the aforementioned. Applications can be submitted all year round and are considered in March, June, August and December, although emergency cases can be considered at any time.

Correspondent: C N Cullen, Freeth Cartwright, Bramley House, 1 Oxford Street, Nottingham NG1 5BH (0115 936 9369; Fax: 0115 901 5500).

The Fifty Fund

Eligibility: People in need who live in and around Nottingham.

Types of grants: Payments of £65 a quarter and one-off grants and loans. Grants given include those for telephone and television rentals and licences, holidays and medical equipment.

No grants are given for education or sponsorship.

Annual grant total: In 2000 the trust had assets of just over £1 million and an income of £166,000. Out of a total expenditure of £150,000, the sum of £69,000 was given in 75 relief-in-need grants to individuals. A further £69,000 was given in grants for other purposes.

Applications: Applications, in writing to the correspondent, can be submitted either by the individual or through a recognised referral agency (e.g. social worker, citizen's advice bureau or doctor) or another third party. They are considered on an ongoing basis. Applicants are likely to be visited by a member of the trust.

Correspondent: J J Moore, Nelsons, Pennine House, 8 Stanford Street, Nottingham NG1 7BQ (0115 958 6262).

Other information: Grants are also given to other charities with similar objects.

The Sir Stuart & Lady Florence Goodwin Charity

Eligibility: People over 60 and in need who live in the former rural district of East Retford and the Finningly parish of South Yorkshire.

Types of grants: In the past funds have largely been given as Easter payments with remaining money given as one-off grants. These Easter payments are now ending and more will be available for emergency grants.

Annual grant total: In 2000/01 the charity had an income of £10,000 and a total expenditure of £970.

Applications: Applications in writing to the correspondent for consideration twice a year. They can be submitted directly by the individual or through a third party such as Age Concern.

Correspondent: John Brooks, Bassetlaw District Council, Queen's Buildings, Potter Street, Worksop, Nottinghamshire S80 2AH (01909 533174; Fax: 01909 501246).

The Charles Wright Gowthorpe Fund & Clergy Augmentation Fund

Eligibility: (i) The Gowthorpe Fund supports widows and other women in need who live within a 12-mile radius of the Market Square, Nottingham.

(ii) The Clergy Augmentation Fund generally supports clergymen within a 10-mile radius of St Peter's Church, Nottingham.

Types of grants: Grants usually of £100, paid once a year in December.

Annual grant total: (i) £7,500; (ii) £3,000.

Applications: On a form available from local Church of England vicars, to be returned by the end of October. Do not write to the correspondent initially, only send the application form once it has been completed.

Correspondent: Christopher Reid, Lloyds TSB Private Banking Ltd, UK Trust Centre, 22–26 Ock Street, Abingdon, Oxfordshire OX14 5SW (01235 554000).

The Harper Annuities

Eligibility: Women in need who live or have lived in the Nottingham area.

Types of grants: Pensions only of £130 a quarter.

Annual grant total: In 2000 the trust had assets of £244,000, an income of about £13,000 and spent £11,000. It gave 17 pensions totalling £8,800.

Applications: In writing to the correspondent directly by the individual. Applications can be submitted at any time and are considered in May, or as and when a vacancy arises.

Correspondent: M J Witherspoon, Secretary, 6 Weekday Cross, Nottingham NG1 2GF (0115 959 0055; Fax: 0115 959 0099).

The John William Lamb Charity

Eligibility: People in need who have been living for at least one year within the city of Nottingham, or within 20 miles of the Nottingham Exchange.

Types of grants: Annuities of £100 a quarter are given to 38 people.

Annual grant total: About £15,000 a year.

Applications: In writing to the correspondent. Applicants will be visited by a member of the trust.

Correspondent: Mrs Bennett, Cooper Parry Chartered Accountants, 14 Park Row, Nottingham NG1 6GR.

Manor House Trust (incorporating The Charity of Lily Taylor)

Eligibility: People in need, principally those who live in Nottinghamshire. For The Charity of Lily Taylor, applicants must live within a radius of 15 miles of the city of Nottingham.

Types of grants: One-off grants for necessities, in the range of £100 to £300. The charity states that it receives more relevant applications than its resources can meet.

Annual grant total: In 2000/01 about £10,000 was given in about 50 relief-in-need grants to individuals. About £15,000 was given for other purposes.

Applications: In writing to the correspondent, to be submitted by a social worker, citizen's advice bureau or other welfare agency. Direct applications will not be considered.

Correspondent: W F Whysall, Eversheds, Solicitors, 1 Royal Standard Place, Nottingham NG1 6FZ (0115 950 7000; Fax: 0115 950 7111).

The New Appeals Organisation for the City & County of Nottingham

Eligibility: People in need who live in the city and county of Nottingham.

Types of grants: One-off grants to meet needs which cannot be met from any other source. Much of the money is raised for specific projects or people. The trust has a library of equipment for adults and children including electric and sports wheelchairs, computers. Grants are given for a wide variety of needs. The trust does not usually help with debt arrears, building works, wages or educational costs.

Annual grant total: In 2000/01 a total of £71,000 was given in grants to 116 individuals and groups.

Applications: On a form available from the correspondent. Applications should ideally be made through a social worker, citizen's advice bureau, medical establishment or other welfare agency, ahough those submitted directly by the individual are considered. Applications are considered every month.

Correspondent: Philip Everett, Joint Chairman, 4 Rise Court, Hamilton Road, Nottingham NG5 1EU (0115 960 9644).

The Nottingham Annuity Charity

Eligibility: Spinsters or widows of good character who are in need and live in Nottinghamshire.

Types of grants: Regular yearly allowances of up to £208 (paid in quarterly grants).

Annual grant total: In 2000/01 the trust had an income of £14,000 and £9,400 was given in 38 allowances.

Applications: On a form available from the correspondent to be submitted either directly by the individual or via a relevant third party such as a social worker, citizen's advice bureau or other welfare agency. Applications can be submitted at any time and are considered in February, May, September and November.

Correspondent: F B Raven, 3 Beetham Close, Bingham, Nottingham NG13 8EQ (Tel & Fax: 01949 831485).

The Nottingham Children's Welfare Fund

Eligibility: Children under 18, with priority given to young children, who live in Nottinghamshire especially in Nottingham and especially those who have lost either or both of their parents.

Types of grants: One-off grants of £50 to £75 for almost any purpose where there is a need. Recent awards have been made to buy domestic appliances, furniture, furnishings, clothing, toys and contributions to school trips and family holidays.

Applications for a large amount of money where there is no assurance that the remainder is available from elsewhere will not be considered.

Annual grant total: In 2000/01 the fund had an income of £2,500 and a total expenditure of £2,600.

Applications: On a form (which must be completed in full to be considered) available from the correspondent to be submitted by social services, the probation service or another welfare agency or third party e.g. a teacher. Direct applications are not considered. Applications are considered four times a year.

Correspondent: Mrs Gwen Derry, 37 Main Road, Wilford, Nottingham NG11 7AP.

The Nottingham Fuel Fund

Eligibility: People of retirement age who are in need and live in Nottinghamshire.

Types of grants: One-off grants of up to £150 towards heating bills.

Annual grant total: In 2001 between £4,000 and £5,000 was distributed in grants.

Applications: On a form available form the correspondent.

Correspondent: David Lowe, Nottingham Evening Post, Castle Wharf House, Nottingham NG1 7EU (0115 964 4036; e-mail: david.lowe@nottinghameveningpost.co.uk).

The Nottingham General Dispensary

Eligibility: People in need who are sick, convalescent, disabled or infirm and live in the county of Nottinghamshire.

Types of grants: One-off grants have including those for computer equipment for people who are disabled, convalescent holidays, travel expenses for families with terminally ill relatives and specialist equipment for children and adults. No grants are given where funds are already available from other sources.

Annual grant total: In 2000/01 the fund had assets of £1.2 million, an income of £50,000 and a total expenditure of £41,000. The sum of £31,000 was given in relief-in-need grants to individuals.

Applications: In writing to the correspondent through a social worker, citizen's advice bureau, other welfare agency or a professional, for example a doctor or teacher. Individuals can apply directly, but they must include supportive medical evidence with their application. Applications are considered all year round.

Correspondent: D S Corder, Bramley House, 1 Oxford Street, Nottingham NG1 5BH (0115 936 9369; Fax: 0115 985 9652).

Other information: Grants are also given to organisations.

Nottingham Gordon Memorial Trust for Boys & Girls

Eligibility: Children and young people aged up to 25 who are in need and who live in Nottingham and the area immediately around the city.

Types of grants: One-off grants are made for needs such as clothing, bedding, refrigerators, basic equipment for people who are disabled, family holidays and educational courses.

Annual grant total: In 2000 the trust had assets of £1.1 million and an income of £41,000. Out of a total expenditure of £37,000, the sum of £33,000 was distributed in relief-in-need grants. Educational grants to individuals totalled £3,000.

Applications: On a form available from the correspondent preferably through a social worker, health visitor or other welfare agency, although applications can also be submitted directly by the individual in writing including a professional referee. All applications should include full name, date of birth of child/children and details of the financial circumstances of the family. They are considered all year round.

Correspondent: Mrs Colleen Douglas, Bramley House, 1 Oxford Street, Nottingham NG1 5BH (0115 947 5792; Fax: 0115 859 9652).

Nottinghamshire County Council Fund for Disabled People

Eligibility: People who are disabled, live in Nottinghamshire and are in need. This does not include residents of the city of Nottingham.

The fund also gives to voluntary groups working with people with disabilities.

Types of grants: One-off grants of between £50 and £500 towards buying equipment, vehicle adaptations or making a building accessible. The fund does not make grants for: driving lessons, car purchase or mobility deposits; dropped kerbs; decorating, house repairs and general maintenance costs; showers or computers; items available elsewhere, for example from social security or NHS or leisure service departments; or medical equipment. Successful applicants cannot reapply for the next three years. No retrospective grants are made.

Annual grant total: In 2001/02 the fund had an income and total expenditure of £53,000.

Applications: On a form available from the correspondent. Applications can be submitted either through a social worker, citizen's advice bureau, other welfare agency or a relative or friend; or directly by the individual. Letters of support are required from professionals, for example a doctor, social worker or occupational therapist. In certain cases a full assessment is needed from Disabilities Living Centre. Meetings are held on a six-weekly basis.

Correspondent: Mrs Sue Curran, Accounting Services, Policy and Resources Department, County Hall, West Bridgford, Nottingham NG2 7QP (0115 977 3015; Fax: 0115 945 5280).

Other information: 'The Disability Discrimination Act 1995 defines a disabled person as someone who has a disability i.e. "a physical or mental impairment which has a substantial and long-term adverse effect on his/her ability to carry out normal day-to-day activities". This includes people with sensory impairments and learning disabilities; as well as people with physical impairments. It does not include any impairment resulting from or consisting of a mental illness, unless that illness is clinically well-recognised.'

The Nottinghamshire Miners' Welfare Trust Fund

Eligibility: Miners or ex-miners in need living in Nottinghamshire, who were retired or redundant, are still unemployed and who have not worked outside of the industry, and their dependants.

Types of grants: One-off and recurrent grants according to need.

Annual grant total: In 1999 the fund had assets of £1.9 million and an income of £93,000. Grants were given to 39 organisations and totalled £103,000. In the previous year six grants to individuals were made totalling £5,200.

Applications: In writing to the correspondent.

Correspondent: Bob Andrews, Welfare Offices, Berry Hill Lane, Mansfield NG18 4JR.

The Perry Trust Gift Fund

Eligibility: In order of preference: (a) people in need who have lived in the city of Nottingham for at least five years; (b) people in need who have lived in Nottinghamshire for at least five years.

Types of grants: One-off grants of up to £200. Grants are mainly to elderly people with low incomes. Some grants are made to one-parent families through local social services departments.

Annual grant total: In 2000/01 the trust had an income and total expenditure of £18,000. About £15,000 is given in grants each year.

Applications: Applications can be made by the individual, social workers, citizen's advice bureau or other welfare agency on a form available from the correspondent. Applications are considered in May and November.

Correspondent: Mrs B J Martin, 57 Moorsholm Drive, Wollaton, Nottingham NG8 2EF (0115 928 1764).

J D Player Endowment Fund

Eligibility: People who have been professionally employed in nursing in and around Nottingham. Also, other people in need who live in and around Nottingham.

Types of grants: Payments of £65 a quarter and one-off grants and loans. One-off grants can be for telephone rentals, television rentals and licences, holidays and medical equipment. No grants are given for education.

Annual grant total: In 2000 the trust had assets of £821,000 and an income of £95,000. Out a total of £85,000, £19,000 was distributed in 40 grants.

Applications: In writing to the correspondent (there is no application form). Applicants are likely to be visited by the trust. Applications can be submitted directly by the individual or by a relevant third party such as a social worker, citizen's advice bureau or other welfare agency. Grants are considered on an ongoing basis.

Correspondent: S J Moore, Nelsons, Pennine House, 8 Stanford Street, Nottingham NG1 7BQ (0115 958 6262).

The Puri Foundation

See entry on page 114

The Thomas Underwood's Charity

Eligibility: Spinsters and widows with an income of less than £4,000 excluding benefits, who live in the city of Nottingham or within five miles of the city market place and who are at least 45 years old.

Types of grants: Regular yearly allowances of £150 to £250, paid half-yearly. Allowances are paid for life unless circumstances change.

Annual grant total: About £6,000 in around 25 to 30 allowances.

Applications: On a form available from the correspondent, usually after the recommendation of the trustees or other contacts who know of people with financial difficulties. Applications are considered in July and December. All beneficiaries are visited twice-yearly to discuss circumstances and assess needs and so on.

Correspondent: Miss D Rednall, 28 Forsythia Close, Lutterworth, Leicestershire LE17 4FD (01455 554295).

The West Gate Benevolent Trust

Eligibility: People in need who live in Nottinghamshire, although usually grants are given to people living in Retford and Worksop.

Types of grants: Usually one-off items where the DWP has been unable to help, for example for washing machines,

holidays or travel to visit relations in hospital. Individuals can reapply year after year. Grants given have been in the range of £50 to £5,000.

Annual grant total: About £40,000 each year to individuals.

Applications: Through a third party e.g. social services or citizen's advice bureau. Applications directly by the individual will not be considered.

Correspondent: S Carey, Secretary, 17 Storcroft Road, Retford, Nottinghamshire DN22 7EG.

The Williamson Benevolent Trust

Eligibility: Children, young people, the elderly and families who live in Nottinghamshire and who are in need due to hardship, sickness or disability.

Types of grants: One-off and recurrent grants according to need.

Annual grant total: About £12,000 a year.

Applications: In writing to the correspondent.

Correspondent: S Carey, 17 Storcroft Road, Retford, Nottinghamshire DN22 7EG.

Balderton

The Balderton Parochial Charity

Eligibility: People in need who live in the parish of Balderton.

Types of grants: One-off grants include those for cookers, electric wheelchairs, cycle trailers and garden alterations. No donations for the relief of rates, taxes or other public funds.

Annual grant total: In 2001/02 the charity had assets of £94,000 and an income of £5,600. Out of a total expenditure of £3,300, almost £3,000 was distributed in 100 relief-in-need grants. Grants can also be made to local organisations.

Applications: In writing to the correspondent either through a social worker, citizen's advice bureau, or other welfare agency; or directly by the individual. Applications are considered as they are received.

Correspondent: P C Holland, 8 Meadow Road, Balderton, Newark, Nottinghamshire NG24 3BP (01636 682083; e-mail: p.c.holland@ntlworld.com).

Bingham

The Bingham Trust Scheme

Eligibility: People under the age of 21 living in Bingham.

249

Types of grants: One-off and recurrent grants according to need, paid in early January and early July each year.

Annual grant total: Grants total about £1,500.

Applications: In writing to the correspondent for an application form. Applications must be submitted by 30 April and 31 October each year.

Correspondent: Mrs Anita Smith, 36 Gillotts Close, Bingham, Nottingham NG13 8GE (01949 837475).

Bingham United Charities

Eligibility: People in need who live in the parish of Bingham.

Types of grants: One-off grants in the range of £50 to £300. Grants given include those towards: Christmas gifts for a struggling family; carpets for a recently rehabilitated man; respite care; and visiting expenses for local clergy members.

Grants are not given to the same person twice.

Annual grant total: In 2001/02 seven grants to individuals were made totalling £1,300. Grants for other purposes totalled £4,300.

Applications: In writing to the correspondent, preferably directly by the individual; alternatively, they can be submitted through a social worker, citizen's advice bureau or other welfare agency. Applications are considered on the second Tuesday in alternate months, commencing in May. Details of the purpose of the grant and other grants being sought should be included.

Correspondent: Claire Pegg, c/o Bingham Town Council, The Old Court House, Church Street, Bingham, Nottinghamshire NG13 8AL (Tel & Fax: 01949 831445).

Other information: Grants are also given to organisations and individuals for educational purposes.

Calverton

The Jane Pepper Charity

Eligibility: People in need who live in Calverton Village.

Types of grants: One-off and recurrent grants and loans according to need. Help has been given, for example, to provide aids/clothing for people who are disabled. Loans have been granted to buy mobility chairs and electric scooters.

Annual grant total: In 2001 the charity had an income of £3,700 and a total expenditure of £4,000. A total of £2,500 was given in relief-in-need grants to individuals and £1,500 was given for other purposes.

Applications: In writing to the correspondent, or one of the trustees. Applications can be submitted, at any time, by the individual or through a doctor, health visitor or church.

Correspondent: W A Peet, Secretary, 2 Bonner Hill, Calverton, Nottingham NG14 6FR (0115 965 3293; e-mail: bill.peet@talk21.com).

Carlton in Lindrick

The Christopher Johnson & the Green Charity

Eligibility: People in need who live in the village of Carlton in Lindrick.

Types of grants: One-off grants ranging from £50 to £200 towards, for example, an alarm to warn parents of their daughter's epilepsy. It also gives £2 vouchers to all pensioners at Christmas who claim. Other grants are not given to individuals who have received a grant in the recent past.

Annual grant total: In 2001 the trust had assets of £47,000 with an income of £2,100. Expenditure totalled £1,500 including £1,300 in 578 relief-in-need grants.

Applications: In writing to the correspondent either directly by the individual or via a third party such as a social worker, local rector, doctor, district nurse or through a citizen's advice bureau or other welfare agency for consideration throughout the year.

Correspondent: C E R Towle, Hon. Secretary and Treasurer, 135 Windsor Road, Carlton in Lindrick, Worksop, Nottinghamshire S81 9DH (01909 731069; e-mail: robin@towle.screaming.net).

Other information: Grants are also given to local organisations some of whose members are in need i.e. pensioners groups, pre-school nurseries and the disabled riding school. The charity also owns 40 allotments let at a nominal rent of £5 a year and lets two bungalows to elderly people.

Coddington

The Coddington United Charities

Eligibility: People in need who live in the parish of Coddington.

Types of grants: One-off grants according to need.

Annual grant total: The trust had an income of around £7,000 in 1997. No further information was available.

Applications: In writing to the correspondent. Applications can be submitted at any time either through a third party such as a social worker, citizen's advice bureau or other welfare agency, or directly by the individual.

Correspondent: A Morrison, Clerk to the Trustees, Alasdair Morrison Chartered Surveyors, 26 Kirkgate, Newark, Nottinghamshire NG24 1AB (01636 700888; Fax: 01636 700885; e-mail: alasdair@amorrison.co.uk).

Farndon

The Farndon Relief-in-Need Charity

Eligibility: Individuals in need who live in the parish of Farndon.

Types of grants: The trust provides one-off grants, Christmas hampers and clothing vouchers.

Annual grant total: In 2000/01 the trust's income was £1,500 and grants totalled £1,000, including £600 in grants to individuals. The remaining grants were to local organisations.

Applications: In writing to the correspondent directly by the individual, providing full details. The trustees meet twice a year, usually in May and October. Emergency applications can be considered at other times.

Correspondent: L G Aslin, Trustee, Stephenson Nuttall, Ossington Chambers, 6-8 Castle Gate, Newark-on-Trent, Nottinghamshire NG24 1AX (01636 705624; Fax: 01636 640509).

Gotham

Doctor M A Gerrard's Gotham Old People's Benevolent Fund

Eligibility: Older people in need who live in Gotham village.

Types of grants: One-off and recurrent grants according to need.

Annual grant total: In 2000/01 the trust had assets of £28,000, an income of £860 and its total expenditure was £500. Local organisations were the only beneficiaries in that year.

Applications: In writing to the correspondent, submitted directly by the individual or via a third party such as a friend or neighbour. Applications are considered throughout the year.

Correspondent: Mrs P R Dines, 8 Chadborn Avenue, Gotham, Nottingham NG11 0HT (0115 983 0582; e-mail: pat@dinesp.fsnet.co.uk).

Hucknall

The Hucknall Relief-in-Need Charity

Eligibility: Individuals in need who live in Hucknall, with a preference for 'poor householders'.

Types of grants: One-off and recurrent grants according to need. No grants for the relief of rates, taxes or other public funds.

Annual grant total: In 2000/01 the trust's income was £3,900 and grants to organisations totalled £1,900, with £1,200 given to individuals.

Applications: In writing to the correspondent at any time. Individuals should apply through a social worker, minister of religion etc.

Correspondent: C E Thrall, 29 Linby Lane, Papplewick, Nottingham NG15 8FB (0115 963 2941).

Other information: This entry was not confirmed by the trust, but the address was correct according to the Charity Commission database.

Long Bennington and Foston

Long Bennington Charities

Eligibility: People in need who live in the parish of Long Bennington and Foston.

Types of grants: Recurrent grants are given towards hospital travel and garden maintenance for people who are elderly, sick or disabled; television licences for those who are housebound; and fuel at Christmas for widows, widowers and other people on low incomes. Grants range from £850 to £1,700.

Annual grant total: In 2001 the trust had assets of £56,000 and an income of £5,300. A total of £2,000 was given in 175 to 200 grants to individuals.

Applications: In writing to the correspondent directly by the individual. Applications are considered quarterly.

Correspondent: Mrs G Baggaley, Trustee, 6 Lilley Street, Long Bennington, Nr Newark, Nottinghamshire NG23 5EJ (01400 281364).

Other information: The charities also supply aids for disabled people (wheelchairs, wooden ramps and so on).

Mansfield

The Brunts Charity

Eligibility: Elderly people over 60 who are in need and have lived in the the former borough of Mansfield (as constituted in 1958) for at least five years at the time of application.

Types of grants: Regular allowances only, in the form of small pensions.

Annual grant total: About £5,000, but varies from year to year.

Applications: On a form available from the correspondent to be submitted directly by the individual. Applications are considered regularly.

Correspondent: Clerk to the Trustees, Brunts Chambers, 2 Toothill Lane, Mansfield, Notts NG18 1NJ (Tel & Fax: 01623 623055).

Other information: The charity is mainly concerned with running almshouses. Grants may also be made to organisations such as Salvation Army as long as they fulfill the charity's criteria.

George Henry Francis Payling's Charity

Eligibility: People over 60 who are in need and live within the boundary of the former borough of Mansfield.

Types of grants: One-off grants in the range of £100 to £500. Grants are not given for holidays or for anything that the state may fund.

Annual grant total: The annual disposable income is about £5,000, most of which is distributed.

Applications: In writing to the correspondent. Applications can be submitted either through a social worker, citizen's advice bureau, other welfare agency, relative, friend or neighbour or directly by the individual. They should be submitted in February, May, August and November for consideration in the next month, those including letters of support form social service departments, doctors and so on always carry most weight.

Correspondent: T J Lidbury, Clerk to the Trustees, 35 Leas Road, Mansfield Woodhouse, Nottinghamshire NG19 8JH.

Newark

The Stuart Goodwin Charity

Eligibility: People aged 60 or over living in the parish of Newark.

Types of grants: Grants of £5, plus either a meal at the town hall or a packed lunch.

Annual grant total: About £5,000 a year.

Applications: On a form published in the local paper in February. Individuals cannot receive awards in successive years.

Correspondent: Keith Brown, Barclays Bank plc, PO Box 294, Lincoln LN6 7YY (01636 663807; Fax: 01522 343537).

The Newark Municipal (General) Charities

Eligibility: People in need who live in the borough of Newark.

Types of grants: Christmas gifts and other one-off grants usually ranging from £50 to £350, but they can be for as much as £1,000. Grants are given towards holidays for families, medical equipment and household items such as cookers, washing machines and furniture.

Annual grant total: In 1999 the trust had assets of £1 million and an income of £20,000. Grants totalled £42,000 of which £18,000 went to individuals. A further £20,000 went to organisations.

Applications: On a form available from the correspondent submitted through a social worker, citizen's advice bureau or other welfare agency. Applications are considered in March, June, August and November and must include details of the particular need.

Correspondent: M Gamage, Clerk, 48 Lombard Street, Newark, Nottinghamshire NG24 IXP (01636 640649; Fax: 01636 640627).

The Mary Elizabeth Siebel Charity

Eligibility: People over 60 years of age who are ill and live within a radius of 12 miles of Newark town hall.

Types of grants: One-off grants ranging from £50 to £2,500. The trust aims to enable individual applicants to live in their own homes e.g. help with the cost of stairlifts, essential home repairs, aids for disabled people, care at home, relief for carers and so on.

Annual grant total: In 1998/99 it had assets of £2 million, an income of £78,000 and gave 91 grants to organisations and individuals totalling £69,000.

Applications: On a form available from the correspondent, which requires the endorsement of the applicant's doctor.

Correspondent: Mrs F C Kelly, Messrs Tallents Godfrey, 3 Middlegate, Newark, Nottinghamshire NG24 1AQ (01636 671881).

Nottingham

Bilby's and Cooper's Relief in Need Charity

Eligibility: People in need who live in the city of Nottingham.

Types of grants: One-off grants according to need. In 2000 grants were in the range of £100 to £500.

Annual grant total: In 2000 the charity had assets of £57,000 and an income of £2,500. A total of £1,500 was spent during the year, of which £1,200 went to four individuals.

Applications: In writing to the correspondent either through a social worker, citizen's advice bureau or other welfare agency, or directly by the individual. Applications are considered at any time.

Correspondent: Sue Cottee, Blythens Chartered Accountants, 309-329 Haydn Road, Sherwood, Nottingham, NG5 1HG (0115 960 7111; Fax: 0115 969 1313; e-mail: smcottee@blythens.co.uk).

The Frank Hodson Foundation Ltd

Eligibility: People of 60 years of age and older who are in need, are able to care for themselves and live in Nottingham.

Types of grants: One-off and recurrent grants according to need. The foundation also gives rent-free accommodation. The foundation does not provide grants for lifts nor for any nursing or warden-aided assistance.

Annual grant total: In 2000/01 the foundation had assets of £5.6 million, an income of £278,000 and its total expenditure was £164,000. The sum of £5,700 was given to 24 individuals.

Applications: On a form available from the correspondent, submitted directly by the individual. Applications should be sent to: Mrs N Pyatt, 23 Cyprus Road, Mapperley Park, Nottingham NG3 5EB. They are considered at any time.

Correspondent: S J Christophers, 12 Killerton Park Drive, West Bridgford, Nottingham NG2 7SB (0115 984 5377).

George Pendry's Fund for Widows and Spinsters

Eligibility: Women over 60 who are widows or spinsters and live in the city of Nottingham.

Types of grants: Small one-off grants in the range of £50 to £100 are awarded for items, services or facilities. Recent grants have been given towards a tumble dryer (£75), winter clothing (£75), debts (£50) and a TV (£50).

Annual grant total: In 2000/01 the fund had assets of £12,000 and an income of £680. Just one grant was made totalling £50.

Applications: On a form available from the correspondent, to be submitted directly by the individual at any time. Applications are considered twice a year, usually in April and November. The correspondent will assist people in their applications if necessary.

Correspondent: Janet Stapleton, Nottingham City Council, Programmes and Strategy, Development and Environmental Services, 2nd Floor, Exchange Buildings South, Cheapside, Nottingham NG1 2HU (0115 915 7505; Fax: 0115 915 7510; e-mail: jan.stapleton@nottinghamcity.gov.uk).

The Thorpe Trust

Eligibility: Widows and spinsters in need who live within a mile radius of Nottingham city centre. The recipients must be the widows or fatherless daughters of clergymen, gentlemen or professional people or of people engaged (otherwise than in a menial capacity) in trade or agriculture.

Types of grants: Recurrent grants according to need.

Annual grant total: About £12,000 a year.

Applications: On a form available from the correspondent. Applications can be submitted directly by the individual or through a social worker, citizen's advice bureau or other welfare agency. They are considered once during the Summer and at Christmas.

Correspondent: Mrs M Kelly, Actons Solicitors, 2 King Street, Nottingham NG1 2AX (0115 910 0200).

Southwell

The Southwell Charities for the Poor & Sick Poor

Eligibility: People in need who live in the ancient parish of Southwell.

Types of grants: One-off and recurrent grants according to need. Grants are given to people of pensionable age towards winter heating.

Annual grant total: Around £500 per year.

Applications: In writing to the correspondent.

Correspondent: R G Beckett, Clerk, 13 Market Place, Southwell, Notts NG25 0HE (01636 812291).

Warsop

The Warsop United Charities

Eligibility: People in need who live in the urban district of Warsop (Warsop, Church Warsop, Warsop Vale, Meden Vale, Spion Kop and Skoonholme).

Types of grants: One-off grants for necessities and quarterly grants to about 60 individuals.

Annual grant total: In 2000 the trust had an income of £9,600 and a total expenditure of £8,600.

Applications: In writing to the correspondent. Trustees met three or four times a year.

Correspondent: Mrs Denise Fritchley, 7 Bowne Street, Sutton-in-Ashfield, Nottinghamshire NG17 4BH.

Shropshire

The Atherton Trust

Eligibility: People who are widowed, orphaned, sick, disabled or otherwise in need who live in the parishes of Pontesbury and Hanwood and the villages of Annscroft and Hook-a-Gate in the county of Shropshire.

Types of grants: One-off and recurrent grants according to need.

Annual grant total: In 2000/01 the trust had assets of £168,000 and an income of £7,600. The sum of £220 was given in one relief-in-need grant and £5,800 was given in grants for other purposes.

Applications: On a form available from the correspondent submitted directly by the individual. Applications are considered in February, May, August and November.

Correspondent: The Secretary, Whittingham Riddell, Chartered Accountants, 15 Belmont, Shrewsbury SY1 1TE (01743 355785; Fax: 01743 360745; e-mail: wr@whittingtonriddell.co.uk; website: www.whittingtonriddell.co.uk).

Other information: The trust also supports institutions that give support and services to people who need aid due to loss of sight, limb or health by accident or inevitable causes.

The Ellen Barnes Charitable Trust

Eligibility: People in need who live in Weston Rhyn and adjoining parishes.

Types of grants: Although the trust's income is mainly used to run six almshouses, one-off grants are considered.

Annual grant total: About £1,000 a year to individuals.

Applications: In writing to the correspondent either directly by the individual or through a social worker, citizen's advice bureau, doctor or other welfare agency. Applications are considered throughout the year.

Correspondent: Mark Woodward, Messrs Crampton, Pym & Lewis, 47 Willow Street, Oswestry, Shropshire SY11 1PR (01691 653301; Fax: 01691 658699).

The Bridgnorth Parish Charity

Eligibility: People living in Bridgnorth parish, including Oldbury and Eardington, who are in need.

Types of grants: One-off grants of £50 to £750, including those towards playgroup fees, school visits, funeral expenses and heating costs.

Annual grant total: In 2000 grants were made to seven individuals totalling £2,100. The trust had an income of £3,700.

Applications: In writing to the correspondent either directly by the individual or through a doctor, nurse, member of the local clergy, social worker, citizen's advice bureau or other welfare agency.

Correspondent: F Brown, Secretary, 6 Love Lane, Bridgnorth, Shropshire WV16 4HD (01746 762605).

Other information: Grants are also made to organisations.

The Edward's Bequest

Eligibility: Widows in need who have lived in Pant, Porthywaen and Treflach Wood for at least three years.

Types of grants: Single annual cheques of £7.

Annual grant total: The trust had assets of £12,000 in 2000/01 and an income of £520. It gave 68 payments of £7.

Applications: In writing to the correspondent, addressed to the trustees, directly by the individual, including confirmation of widowhood. They should be submitted in early October for consideration in October.

Correspondent: R V Hughes, Bethany, Tregarthen Lane, Pant, Oswestry, Shropshire SY10 8LF (01691 830546).

The Lady Forester Trust

Eligibility: People who live in Shropshire and are sick, disabled, convalescent or infirm.

Types of grants: One-off grants for medical equipment, nursing care, travel to and from hospitals and other medical needs not otherwise available on the NHS. No retrospective grants are made, nor are grants given for building repairs/alterations, home improvements or household bills.

Annual grant total: In 2001 the trust had an income of £112,000. Out of a total expenditure of £117,000, grants to individuals were made totalling £99,000.

Applications: On a form available from the correspondent. Applications should be made through a doctor (or social services in exceptional circumstances) and are considered throughout the year.

Correspondent: The Administrator, Willey Park, Broseley, Shropshire TF12 5JJ (01952 884318; Fax: 01952 883680; e-mail:ladyforesttrust@willeyestates.co.uk).

Dr Gardner's Charity for Sick Nurses

Eligibility: Nurses in need who live in Shropshire.

Types of grants: One-off grants, usually of about £300, to help sick nurses to convalesce or to have further help to enable them to return to work.

Annual grant total: In 2001/02 the trust's income was £1,600 and it made one grant of £300.

Applications: On a form available from the correspondent. Applications can be submitted at any time either through a social worker, citizen's advice bureau or other welfare agency, or directly by the individual or a relevant third party.

Correspondent: Dr P L Boardman, Hon. Secretary, 3 Mayfield Park, Shrewsbury SY2 6PD (01743 232768).

The Oswestry Dispensary Fund

Eligibility: People who are both poor and sick and live in the borough of Oswestry and its surrounding district.

Types of grants: One-off grants, for example, for medical care and equipment and second hand television sets.

Annual grant total: In 2000/01 the fund had an income of £13,000 and grants were made totalling £150.

Applications: In writing to the correspondent either directly by the individual or via a relevant third party such as a social worker, citizen's advice bureau or other welfare agency. Applications should be submitted in April and November for consideration in December and May.

Correspondent: Emyr Richard Lloyd, Brown and Lloyd, The Albany, 37–39 Willow Street, Oswestry, Shropshire SY11 1AQ (01691 659194; Fax: 01691 652755).

The Roddam Charity

Eligibility: People in need who live in the parishes of Newport, Chetwynd, Church Aston, Chetwynd Aston, Woodcote, Edgmond and Longford in Shropshire and Forton in Staffordshire.

Types of grants: One-off grants of between £50 and £200 to help with items, services or facilities that are not available readily from other sources, which will relieve the suffering or assist the recovery of those mentioned above.

Annual grant total: In 2000/01 the charity had assets of £80,000, an income of £4,000 and its total expenditure was £5,400. The sum of £250 was given in relief-in-need grants.

Applications: On a form available from the correspondent to be submitted directly by the individual in February, March, April and November for consideration in March, June, September and November.

Correspondent: Mrs E Watson Todd, Hon. Secretary, 20 Granville Avenue, Newport, Shropshire TF10 7DX (01952 820048).

The Shrewsbury & District Welfare Society

Eligibility: Post Office employees and their dependants who live in Shrewsbury, Wem, Church Stretton and Craven Arms.

Types of grants: Loans and one-off grants according to need. Recurrent grants may be available for people who are long-term sick.

Annual grant total: In 2001 the society had an income of £7,400 and a total expenditure of £7,100.

Applications: In writing to the correspondent.

Correspondent: B Davies, Treasurer, The Sorting Office, Castle Forgate, Shrewsbury, Shropshire SY1 1AA (01743 277274).

The Shrewsbury Municipal Charity

Eligibility: People in need who live in the borough of Shrewsbury and Atcham. 60% of the disposable income is for education/training of people under 25 years of age; the balance is for general relief of need.

Types of grants: One-off grants of £50 to £250.

Annual grant total: In 2000/01 the charity had an income of £1,300 and a total expenditure of £910.

Applications: In writing to the correspondent, either directly by the individual or through a social worker, citizen's advice bureau, welfare agency or other third party. Applications are considered in January, May, and September, but emergencies can be considered at any time. Please include details of any other charities that have been contacted for assistance.

Correspondent: Ian Scott Garrett, 27 The Oval, Bicton, Shrewsbury SY3 8ES.

Other information: This entry was not confirmed by the charity but the address was correct according to information on file at the Charity Commission.

The Shropshire Football Association Benevolent Fund

Eligibility: People in need who live in Shropshire, who are: (i) amateur and professional footballers; (ii) apprentices; (iii) coaches; (iv) managers; (v) any other official or employee of any football team; (vi) referees and referee's assistants and widows and orphans of other persons dependant wholly or partially on any of the above people who may die or be disabled or be unable to earn a living.

Types of grants: One-off grants or recurring grants for absolute necessities.

Annual grant total: Up to £1,000 a year.

Applications: In writing to the correspondent.

Correspondent: David Rowe, The Gay Meadow, Abbey Forgate, Shrewsbury SY2 6AB (01743 362769; Fax: 01743 270494).

The Shropshire Welfare Trust

Eligibility: Individuals in Shropshire with medically-related and disability-related expenses.

Types of grants: One-off grants of between £50 and £300. Grants have in the past been given towards the cost of repairs to an electric wheelchair, to help with household matters which affect health e.g. washing machine or fridge repairs and to help with the expenses of hospital treatment e.g.

travel and occasional accommodation for relatives during major operations.

No grants for educational purposes or building costs.

Annual grant total: In 2001/02 the trust had an income of about £1,500, all of which was distributed in about 100 grants.

Applications: On a form available from the correspondent; advice is also available. Applications can be submitted through a social worker, citizen's advice bureau or other welfare agency; or by the individual, at any time.

Correspondent: Dr P Boardman, Hon. Secretary, 3 Mayfield Park, Shrewsbury, Shropshire SY2 6PD (01743 232768).

Other information: Occasional grants are given to organisations with similar objects.

The St Chads Charity

Eligibility: People in need who have lived in the ecclesiastical districts of St Chad and St George, Shrewsbury, Astley, Kinnerley, Guildsfield, Great Ness and Bicton for not less than five years immediately before their application.

Types of grants: One-off grants of between £35 and £50 to help with the cost of clothes, linen, bedding, tools, medical or other aid in sickness, food or other articles in kind.

Annual grant total: In 2001 the charity's income was £500 and its total expenditure was £400; all of this was given in grants.

Applications: On a form available from the correspondent. Applications should be submitted directly by the individual and they are considered at any time.

Correspondent: L E Smith, Little Garth, 3 Roman Road, Shrewsbury SY3 9AZ (01743 353869).

Other information: The charity also gives support to religious work of the Church of England and to promote education for people under 25.

The Thompson Pritchard Trust

Eligibility: Individuals who live in Shropshire and have medically-related and disability-related expenses and problems. Preference is given to those who have recently been discharged from hospital.

Types of grants: One-off grants in the range of £50 to £300 are given towards: medical equipment e.g. wheelchairs, and their repair; domestic equipment which affects health e.g. washing machine or fridge repairs; expenses incurred during illness including treatment; and travel and occasional accommodation for relatives during major operations.

Annual grant total: In 2001/02 the trust had a total expenditure of about £15,000.

Applications: On a form available from the correspondent. Applications for small grants can be submitted at any time either directly by the individual or via a relevant third party such as a social worker, citizen's advice bureau or other welfare agency. Advice is available from the trust.

Correspondent: P L Boardman, Hon. Secretary, 3 Mayfield Park, Shrewsbury SY2 6PD (01743 232768).

Mrs Wingfield's Charitable Trust

Eligibility: People who live in Shropshire and are in need.

Types of grants: One-off grants, ranging between £100 and £1,000.

Annual grant total: In 2000/01 the trust's assets totalled £373,000, it had an income of £23,000 and its total expenditure was £17,000. A total of £13,000 was distributed to individuals in the year.

Applications: In writing to the correspondent, directly by the individual. Cases are considered at regular meetings of the trustees. Refusals are not always acknowledged due to the cost involved. If a reply is required, please enclose an sae.

Correspondent: John Dodds, Dyke Yaxley, 1 Brassey Road, Old Potts Way, Shrewsbury SY3 7FA (01743 241281; Fax: 01743 235794; e-mail: info@dykeyaxley.co.uk; website: www.dykeyaxley.co.uk).

Other information: Organisations directly supporting individuals are also supported.

Albrighton and Boningale

Albrighton Relief in Need Charity

Eligibility: People in need who live in the parishes of Albrighton and Boningale.

Types of grants: In 2001 grants ranged from £25 to £36. One-off grants can be made towards, for example, individuals attending university interviews, furniture, appliances, shoes or clothing for children, one-off gardening services, repairs and temporary respite provisions.

No grants are made where statutory funds are available.

Annual grant total: In 2001 the trust had assets of £5,100, an income of £1,400 and grants were made to 16 individuals totalling £610.

Applications: In writing to the correspondent directly by the individual, or via a third party such as a social worker, citizen's advice bureau, GP, district nurse or health visitor. Applications are considered throughout the year.

Correspondent: D Beechey, 34 Station Road, Albrighton, Wolverhampton WV7 3QG (01902 372779; e-mail: david.beechey@stnroad.fsnet.co.uk).

Alveley

The Alveley Charity

Eligibility: People in need who live in the parish of Alveley.

Types of grants: One-off grants according to need.

Annual grant total: In 2000/01 the charity had assets of £385,000, an income of £14,000 and a total expenditure of almost £5,000. A sum of £3,100 was distributed in about 10 grants.

Applications: In writing to the correspondent either directly by the individual, or through a social worker, citizen's advice bureau or other welfare agency.

Correspondent: David Bishop, Morton Fisher, 18 Load Street, Bewdley, Worcester DY12 2AB (01299 402221).

Clun

The Earl of Northampton's Charity

See entry on page 369

Farlow

The Farlow James & Williams Charity

Eligibility: People in need who live in the ancient parish of Farlow.

Types of grants: One-off and recurrent grants towards necessities and basic household equipment, e.g. washing machines, log burners, aids for getting up stairs etc.

Annual grant total: In 1998/99, the trust had an income of £6,700 and a total expenditure of £3,100.

Applications: In writing to the correspondent.

Correspondent: Mrs Audrey Hill, Secretary, Hillside Bungalow, Crumps Brook, Hopton Waffers, Kidderminster, Worcs DY14 0HS (01584 890127).

Hodnet

The Hodnet Consolidated Eleemosynary Charities

Eligibility: People in need who live in Hodnet parish.

Types of grants: Grants include Christmas parcels and coal for people of pensionable age.

Annual grant total: In 2000 the charities had an income of £3,300 and a total expenditure of £2,800.

MIDLANDS – SHROPSHIRE/STAFFORDSHIRE

Applications: In writing to the correspondent for consideration throughout the year. Applications can be submitted directly by the individual or through a social worker, citizen's advice bureau or other welfare agency.

Correspondent: Mrs S W France, 26 The Meadows, Hodnet, Market Drayton, Shropshire TF9 3QF.

Other information: This entry was not confirmed by the charities but was correct according to information on file at the Charity Commission.

Hopesay

Hopesay Parish Trust

Eligibility: People in need living in the parish of Hopesay. Priority is given to those under 25 years old.

Types of grants: One-off grants according to need. In 2001 two grants were made to individuals in need, to farming families in cash difficulties because of foot and mouth disease restrictions.

Grants are not made where the funding is the responsiblity of central or local government, whether or not the individual has taken up such provision.

Annual grant total: In 2001 the trust had capital of £126,000, its income was £4,000 and grants were made to seven individuals for educational purposes totalling £2,200, and to two individuals for relief-in-need purposes totalling £500.

Applications: Preferably on an application form, available from the correspondent. The application form covers the essential information required, and the trustees will ask for futher details if necessary. Applications can be made at any time, either directly by the individual, or by a third party on their behalf.

Correspondent: David Evans, Park Farm, The Fish, Hopesay, Craven Arms, Shropshire SY7 8HG (01588 660545).

Other information: The trust gives priority to educational grants. At the trustees' discretion, any surplus income may be applied for other charitable purposes within the parish.

Lilleshall

The Charity of Edith Emily Todd

Eligibility: Pensioners in need who live in the ecclesiastical parish of Lilleshall.

Types of grants: Pensions of £15 a month with a bonus payment at Christmas, this was £75 in 2001, but varies according to funds available.

Annual grant total: In 2000/01 the trust had assets of £173,000 and an income of £7,900. Total expenditure was £12,000, of which £9,600 was distributed in 33 grants to individuals.

Applications: In writing directly by the individual, either to the correspondent or to: Mrs Leila Underwood-Whitney, 51 Ford Road, Newport, Shropshire TF10 7TU. Applications are considered on receipt.

Correspondent: Mrs Mary Heather Ayres, Kenilworth, 4 Willmoor Lane, Lilleshall, Newport, Shropshire TF10 9EE (01952 606053).

Shrewsbury

The Gorsuch, Langley & Prynce Charity

Eligibility: People in need, particularly those with children, who live in the parishes of Holy Cross, Shrewsbury (the Abbey) and St Giles.

Types of grants: One-off and recurrent grants ranging from £50 to £500. Recent grants have been given towards furniture, carpets, washing machines, cookers, fridges, baby clothes and cots.

Annual grant total: In 2001 the trust had assets of £840,000 and an income of £30,000. It spent £29,000, including £25,000 to about 130 individuals and families.

Applications: In writing to the correspondent either directly by the individual or through a social worker, citizen's advice bureau or other welfare agency such as Homestart or Money Advice Service, setting out in full the amount required, reasons for the need and why the trustees should support the application. The secretary will usually visit the applicant. Applications are considered every month.

Correspondent: G Spencer, 44 Underdale Road, Shrewsbury SY2 5DT (01743 232103).

Staffordshire

The Burton-on-Trent Nursing Endowment Fund

Eligibility: People in need who live in the former county borough of Burton-on-Trent and the parishes of Anslow, Branston, Barton-under-Needwood, Dunstall, Rangemore, Rolleston, Stretton, Tatenhill and Tutbury.

Types of grants: Usually one-off grants towards chiropody treatment, bedding, removal costs, replacement of batteries for electric scooters, fridges, freezers and childcare provision.

Annual grant total: In 2000/01 the fund had an income of £6,500 and a total expenditure of £12,000.

Applications: On a form available from the correspondent. Applications can come directly via the individual or through a recognised referral agency (social worker, citizen's advice bureau or nurse, doctor etc.). They are considered in May and November and should be submitted one month prior to this, however grants for emergencies can be considered at any time.

Correspondent: T Bramall, Clerk, Messrs Talbot & Co., Solicitors, 148 High Street, Burton-on-Trent DE14 1JY (01283 564716; Fax: 01283 510861).

Consolidated Charity of Burton-upon-Trent

Eligibility: People in need who live in the former county of Burton upon Trent and the parishes of Branston, Stretton and Outwoods.

Types of grants: One-off and recurrent grants according to need.

Annual grant total: In 2000 it had an income of £416,000. Grants to individuals totalled £44,000 whilst £373,000 was given to organisations.

Applications: On a form available from the correspondent, including quotes for the cost of the item needed using suppliers listed in the trust's guidance sheet, and a supporting letter from a social worker, doctor, health visitor, probation officer, priest or other person in authority. The trustees meet in February, May, August and November.

Correspondent: Miss Theresa Iliff, 148 High Street, Burton upon Trent, Staffordshire DE14 1JY (01283 564716; Fax: 01283 510861; e-mail: consolidatedcharity@talbotandco.freeserve.co.uk).

The Baron Davenport Emergency Grant

Eligibility: Needy widows, spinsters, divorcees or women abandoned by their husbands, who live in the borough of Stafford and neighbouring areas.

Types of grants: One-off grants of £20 to £200 for emergencies only; applications for help with heating bills are not accepted. Grants may be given in cash or in kind, such as electrical equipment.

Annual grant total: A maximum of £2,000.

Applications: On a form to be submitted by a social worker, citizen's advice bureau or other welfare agency such as age concern or a women's refuge. Direct applications by the individual will be considered although they will take longer to process.

Correspondent: Mrs Helen Dart, Stafford District Voluntary Services, 131–141 North

Walls, Stafford ST16 3AD (01785 606670; Fax: 01785 606669).

Other information: For information on Baron Davenport's Charity Trust, see entry in the Midlands general section.

The Baron Davenport's Charity Trust Emergency Fund

Eligibility: Needy widows, spinsters, divorcees (over 55 years) living alone or with school children on a low income with savings of less than £3,000; and children under 21 whose fathers are dead, who live in east Staffordshire.

Types of grants: One-off grants up to a maximum of £200 for emergencies only. Help has been given with a burglar alarm, water leak repairs, a deposit on a flat, a special chair, removal and decoration costs and a replacement gas fire. No grants to pay off debts.

Annual grant total: In 2000/01 the charity had an income of £2,000 and gave nine grants totalling £1,200.

Applications: In writing to the correspondent at any time. Applications can be submitted directly by the individual or through a social worker, citizen's advice bureau or other welfare agency.

Correspondent: Mrs S Hudson, Community Action and Support – East Staffordshire, Voluntary Services Centre, Union Street Car Park, Burton-on-Trent, Staffordshire DE14 1AA (01283 543414; Fax: 01283 512365; e-mail: staff@cases-vol.org.uk).

Other information: For information on Baron Davenport's Charity Trust, see entry in the Midlands general section.

The Heath Memorial Trust Fund

Eligibility: People over 18 and in need who are convalescing and live in North Staffordshire.

Types of grants: One-off grants for a recuperative holiday/convalescence only, of up to £75 per person per week, £95 for two people per week, £115 per person for two weeks, or £130 for two people for two weeks.

Christmas vouchers, for which applications should not be submitted, are distributed by trustees to eligible people.

Annual grant total: In 2001 the trust had an income of £2,500 and a total expenditure of £2,000.

Applications: On a form available from the correspondent, countersigned by a trustee, local councillor, health visitor, social worker or doctor. Applications are considered throughout the year.

Correspondent: Hon. Treasurer, Corporate Services Department, PO Box 632, Swann House, Boothen Road, Stoke-on-Trent ST4 4UJ (01782 232709).

The Fred Linford Charitable Trust

Eligibility: Individuals living in Staffordshire.

Types of grants: One-off and recurrent grants according to need.

Annual grant total: In 2000/01 the trust had an income and total expenditure of £10,000.

Applications: In writing to the correspondent.

Correspondent: D Linford, Trustee, The Kennels, Upper Longdon, Rugeley, Staffordshire WS15 1QF (01543 414234; Fax: 01543 410065; e-mail: dlinford@linfordgroup.co.uk).

Other information: The trust also gives grants to organisations.

The Edward Malam Convalescent Fund

Eligibility: People in need who live in the former urban district of Tunstall (comprising the parishes of Tunstall, Goldenhill and most of Chell), the city of Stoke-on-Trent and its neighbourhood.

Types of grants: One-off grants for convalescence only. Maximum grants are as follows: £75 per person per week; £115 for a couple per week; £95 per person for two weeks; and £130 for a couple for two weeks.

Annual grant total: In 2000/01 the fund had an income of £2,600 and a total expenditure of £3,500. About £3,000 is distributed in grants each year.

Applications: On a form available from the correspondent to be signed by a trustee, local councillor, health visitor or doctor when completed. Applications are considered throughout the year, however, due to limited finance it is best to apply early in the year.

Correspondent: Honorary Treasurer, Stoke-on-Trent City Council, Corporate Resources Department, PO Box 632, Swann House, Boothen Road, Stoke-on-Trent ST4 4UJ (01782 232710).

The North Staffordshire Coalfield Miners Relief Fund

Eligibility: Mineworkers or retired mineworkers who worked in the North Staffordshire coalfield, including ironstone miners, and their widows or dependants. The mineworker must have suffered an industrial accident or disease or died as a result of their duties.

Types of grants: One-off grants according to need.

Annual grant total: In 2000/01 the fund had assets amounting to £109,000 and an income of £4,100. The sum of £4,600 was distributed in four relief-in-need grants.

Applications: In writing to the correspondent or by telephone either directly by the individual or via a third party such as a social worker, citizens advice bureau or other welfare agency. Grants are given after a home visit. Applications are considered throughout the year.

Correspondent: Miss S Wilson, Secretary, c/o Coal Industry Social Welfare Organisation, 142 Queens Road, Stoke-on-Trent, Staffordshire ST4 7LH (01782 744996; Fax: 01782 749117; e-mail: sue.wilson@ciswo.org.uk).

North Staffordshire Convalescent & Relief Fund

Eligibility: Mineworkers or retired mineworkers who worked in the North Staffordshire coalfield and their families, widows or dependants. The mineworker must have suffered an industrial accident or disease or died as a result of their employment.

Types of grants: One-off grants are given towards the cost of convalescent holidays only.

Annual grant total: In 2000/01 the trust had assets of £94,000, an income of £4,500 and a total expenditure of £400. The sum of £250 was distributed in one relief-in-need grant.

Applications: In writing to the correspondent or by phone either directly by the individual or via a third party such as a social worker or citizens advice bureau. Grants are given after a home visit. Applications are considered throughout the year.

Correspondent: Miss S Wilson, Secretary, c/o Coal Industry Social Welfare Organisation, 142 Queens Road, Penkhull, Stoke-on-Trent ST4 7LH (01782 744996; Fax: 01782 749117; e-mail: sue.wilson@ciswc.org.uk).

The Strasser Foundation

Eligibility: Individuals in need in the local area, with a preference for North Staffordshire.

Types of grants: Usually one-off grants ranging from £100 to £200 for a specific cause or need, to help with the relief of poverty and for educational purposes.

Annual grant total: Grants totalling around £4,500 are given for relief-in-need and educational purposes.

Applications: In writing to the correspondent for consideration in March, June, September and December and occasionally at other times.

Correspondent: Tony Bell, c/o Knight & Sons, The Brampton, Newcastle-Under-Lyme, Staffordshire ST5 0QW (01782 619225).

Church Eaton

The Church Eaton Relief-in-Need Charity

Eligibility: People in need who live, and have lived for at least two years, in the parish of Church Eaton.

Types of grants: Payment for, or provision of, items, services or facilities that would reduce the person's need e.g. winter fuel payments, provision of TV licences and provision of lifeline telephones. Grants may also be given to organisations which assist needy residents in the parish of Church Eaton.

Annual grant total: In 2000 the charity had an income of £9,100 and a total expenditure of £5,400.

Applications: In writing to the correspondent. Applications are considered when received.

Correspondent: Stephen Rutherford, 5 Ashley Court, Church Eaton, Stafford ST20 0BJ.

Other information: This entry was not confirmed by the charity, but the address was correct according to the Charity Commission database.

Enville

The Enville Village Trust

Eligibility: People in need who live in the parish of Enville, with a preference for older people.

Types of grants: One-off and recurrent grants ranging from £50 to £250. Grants may not always be given directly to individuals sometimes they may be to provide a service to individuals, which they cannot afford. Grants have been given for telephone installation/connection (including an emergency contact line), emergency medical help, optician bills for partially-sighted people, special dental treatment, food parcels, clothing and for fuel in winter.

Annual grant total: In 2000/01 the trust had assets of £23,000 and an income of £2,100. Its total expenditure was £1,300 most of which was given in relief-in-need grants.

Applications: In writing to he correspondent. Applications can be submitted directly by the individual or through a social worker, citizen's advice bureau, other welfare agency such as the Old People's Welfare Committee, or through the vicar of the parish church. They are considered at any time.

Correspondent: J A Gloss, Walls Cottage, Kinver Road, Enville, Staffordshire DY7 5HE (Tel & Fax: 01384 873691).

Leek

The Carr Trust

Eligibility: People in need of pensionable age, who live in Leek.

Types of grants: Grants of £20 a month, paid on the last Tuesday of each month, towards payment for, or provision of, items, services and facilities that will help to reduce need or hardship. Most beneficiaries also receive a Christmas bonus of £70.

Annual grant total: In 2001 the trust had assets of £500,000 and an income of £26,000. A total of £20,000 was distributed in 79 grants.

Applications: In writing to the correspondent. An advert about the grants appears in a local paper in March each year. The trustees require details of the applicant's age, religion, marital status, income from all sources, savings and details of any property owned.

Correspondent: Mrs Clare Wooley, Tinsdills, 10 Derby Street, Leek, Staffordshire ST13 5AW (01538 399332; Fax: 01538 399100).

Lichfield

The Lichfield Municipal Charities

Eligibility: Individuals in need who live in the city of Lichfield (as it was pre-1974).

Types of grants: One-off grants according to need.

Annual grant total: The trust has an annual income of about £50,000, most of which is given in grants to individuals.

Applications: On a form available from the correspondent. Trustees meet four times a year in March, June, September and December.

Correspondent: Simon R James, Clerk, St Mary's Chambers, 5 Breadmarket Street, Lichfield, Staffordshire WS13 6LQ (01543 263456; Fax: 01543 258603; e-mail: sjames@hadenslc.hadens.co.uk).

Michael Lowe's & Associated Charities

Eligibility: People in need who live in the city of Lichfield, particularly older people in need and those requiring help in an emergency.

Types of grants: One-off grants ranging from £50 to £600. People who are 75 or older can also apply for fuel grants. Grants can be made for household items, but not for carpets.

Annual grant total: In 2000/01 the trust had assets of £1.2 million, an income of £92,000 and its total expenditure was £78,000. Grants, including fuel grants, were made to 197 individuals totalling £40,000.

Applications: On a form available from the correspondent. Applications can be submitted either directly by the individual, or, at the individual's consent, via a third party such as a social worker, citizen's advice bureau or other welfare agency. Trustees usually meet every two months.

Correspondent: C P Kitto, Clerk, Hinckley Birch & Brown, 20 St John Street, Lichfield, Staffordshire WS13 6PD (01543 262491; Fax: 01543 254986).

Other information: Grants are also made to local organisations which assist in relieving need.

Newcastle-under-Lyme

The Newcastle-under-Lyme United Charities

Eligibility: People in need who live in the borough of Newcastle-under-Lyme (as it was before 1974).

Types of grants: Recurrent grants of £12 each, given to people who are poor, infirm etc. No grants to older people living in sheltered housing.

Annual grant total: In 2000/01 the charities had an income and total expenditure of £4,200. Grants of £12 were given to 300 people totalling £3,600.

Applications: In writing to the correspondent. Applications should be submitted either directly by the individual or via a friend or family member. They are considered in November and should be submitted by the end of October.

Correspondent: Miss Caroline Horne, Legal and Democratic Services, Newcastle Borough Council, Civic Offices, Merrial Street, Newcastle-under-Lyme, Staffordshire ST5 2AG (01782 742232; Fax: 01782 711032; e-mail: caroline.horne@newcastle-staffs.gov.uk).

Stoke-on-Trent

The Baron Davenport Emergency Grant

Eligibility: Needy widows, spinsters, and children under 21 whose fathers are dead, who live in Stoke-on-Trent.

Types of grants: One-off grants for emergencies only.

Annual grant total: Generally about £2,000.

Applications: On a form available from the correspondent.

Correspondent: Age Concern North Staffordshire, 6 Albion Street, Hanley, Stoke-on-Trent ST1 1QH.

Midlands – Staffordshire

Other information: For information on Baron Davenport's Charity Trust, see entry in the Midlands general section.

The John Pepper Charity

Eligibility: Elderly people in need who live in the city of Stoke-on-Trent.

Types of grants: £6 recurrent Christmas grants in the form of a postal order.

Annual grant total: The trust has an annual income and expenditure of about £900.

Applications: Applications are considered in November and should be made through a trustee or the housing and health department. Emergency applications cannot be considered.

Successful applicants remain on the list of beneficiaries from year to year. The list is accurately checked each year and the trustees of the housing departments add to the list as they see fit.

Correspondent: Lisa Powell, Civic Centre, PO Box 631, Glebe Street, Stoke-on-Trent ST4 1RG.

The Stoke-on-Trent Children's Holiday Trust Fund

Eligibility: Children aged 5 to 17 who live in Stoke-on-Trent and whose parents are unable to afford a recuperative holiday for them.

Types of grants: One-off grants for children only (which includes travel costs and pocket money) for a recuperative holiday. A holiday can be anything from a day at the seaside to two weeks abroad. The purpose of the grant is to give the child a break from the home environment, away from the pressures of everyday life.

Holidays can be taken with the children's parents or can be organised by schools, and taken either within the UK or Europe. Grants range from £30 to £100.

Annual grant total: In 2000 the fund had an income of £3,700 and a total expenditure of £2,700.

Applications: On a form available from the correspondent. Applications can be submitted directly by the individual or through a teacher, social worker, citizen's advice bureau or other welfare agency. They are considered as received. Applications need to be submitted at least six weeks prior to the date of the holiday and must include details of the date of the child's last holiday, the family's income and expenditure and the reason why the holiday is needed.
It is very rare that the trustees will give retrospective grants.

Correspondent: Hon. Treasurer, Corporate Services Department, PO Box 632, Swann House, Boothen Road, Stoke-on-Trent ST4 4UJ (01782 232709).

Tamworth

Beardsley's Relief-in-Need Charity

Eligibility: People in need who live in the borough of Tamworth.

Types of grants: One-off grants for health and welfare purposes, of between £100 and £1,000.

Annual grant total: In 2000/01 the charity had an income of £9,700 and a total expenditure of £9,200.

Applications: In writing to: F A Yates, c/o Rutherfords Solicitors, 6–9 Laybank, Tamworth, Staffordshire B79 7NF, either directly by the individual or through a social worker, citizen's advice bureau or other welfare agency. Applications are considered continually.

Correspondent: D W Tomkinson, Torview, 95 Main Road, Wiggington, Tamworth, Staffordshire B79 9DU (01543 255612; Fax: 01543 415461).

The Baron Davenport Emergency Grant

Eligibility: (i) Needy widows, spinsters and women who have been abandoned by their partners; and (ii) any children under 21 of women in the first category. Only applicants who have lived in the area of Tamworth for at least 10 years will be considered. Household income must not exceed £134 a week; this figure changes in line with state benefits.

Types of grants: One-off grants of £130 to £250 for emergencies only such as urgent domestic repairs/adaptations, clothing and removal costs. No grants towards fuel bills.

Annual grant total: In 2001/02 the charity gave eight grants totalling £1,400.

Applications: On a form available from the correspondent. Applications should be submitted either directly by the individual; or through a social worker, citizen's advice bureau or other welfare agency. They are considered every six weeks.

Correspondent: The Director, Tamworth Community Service Council, Carnegie Centre, Corporation Street, Tamworth, Staffordshire B79 7DN (01827 709657; Fax: 01827 709660; e-mail: admin.tcsc@virgin.net).

Other information: For information on Baron Davenport's Charity Trust, see entry in the Midlands general section.

The Rawlet Trust

Eligibility: People in need who live in the borough of Tamworth.

Types of grants: One-off and recurrent grants ranging from £150 to £1,000. The larger grants are usually for organisations helping people in need in Tamworth. Grants to individuals have included a portable telephone for school nurse at a special needs school, the installation of a shower for somebody who is disabled, to enable patients at a mental health centre to go on holiday. Help has also been given with Home Link telephone costs for older people.

Annual grant total: About £10,000 in grants to individuals and organisations.

Applications: In writing to the correspondent. Applications can be submitted directly by the individual or through a social worker, citizen's advice bureau or other welfare agency. They are considered in March, October and December.

Correspondent: Mrs C A Gilbert, Clerk, 54 Browsholme, Tamworth, Staffordshire B79 7TY (01827 54975).

The Tamworth Municipal Charities

Eligibility: People in need who live in the borough of Tamworth.

Types of grants: In 2000 one-off grants were mainly given for equipment, household items, and transport for a holiday for a disabled person. Grants are usually in the range of £50 to £400.

Annual grant total: In 2000 the charities had assets of £51,000 and an income of £2,800. Out of a total expenditure of £3,100, £1,100 was given in four relief-in-need grants to individuals. £1,900 was given to eight organisations.

Applications: In writing to the correspondent to be submitted either through a social worker, citizen's advice bureau or other welfare agency, or directly by the individual. There is one main meeting of trustees to allocate funds each year, in early November, applications for smaller grants are considered at other times, while funds last. Details of the financial circumstances of individuals are required.

Correspondent: D J Weatherley, Secretary to the Trustees, Tamworth Borough Council, Marmion House, Lichfield Street, Tamworth, Staffordshire B79 7BZ (01827 709220).

Trentham

The Lady Katherine and Sir Richard Leveson Charity

Eligibility: People in need who live in the ancient parish of Trentham.

Types of grants: One-off and recurrent grants according to need.

Annual grant total: In 2001 the charity had assets of £26,000 and an income of £2,900. A total of £2,100 was distributed in nine education and welfare grants.

Applications: In writing to the correspondent either directly by the individual or a relevant third party, or through a social worker, citizen's advice bureau or other welfare agency. Applications are usually considered in Spring and Autumn.

Correspondent: G C Cooper, 5 Fairway, Trentham, Stoke on Trent ST4 8AS (01782 657988).

The Charity of Edith Emily Todd Deceased

Eligibility: People in need who live in the ecclesiastical parish of St Mary and All Saints, Trentham.

Types of grants: Older people can receive a recurrent grant, which are reviewed twice a year. The trust can also make one-off grants.

Annual grant total: In 2001/02 the charity had assets of £15,000 and an income of £1,300. A total of £1,100 was given in grants.

Applications: In writing to the correspondent at any time. Applications can be submitted either through a third party such as a social worker, citizen's advice bureau or other welfare agency, or directly by the individual.

Correspondent: G C Cooper, Administrator, 5 Fairway, Stoke-on-Trent ST4 8AS (01782 657988).

Tutbury

The Tutbury General Charities

Eligibility: People in need who live in the parish of Tutbury.

Types of grants: One-off and recurrent grants according to need. All residents in the parish who are over 70 receive a birthday card and £2 to be spent at a local shop. Vouchers for fuel or goods at a local store (from £5 to £12.50) are also given to about 200 people in need who live within the parish regardless of their age at Christmas.

Special cases are considered on their merits by the trustees but applicants must live in the parish of Tutbury.

Annual grant total: In 2000/01 the charities had assets of £110,000, an income of £6,500 and spent £4,300, of which £1,200 was given in 170 relief-in-need grants to individuals.

Applications: The trust has application forms, available from the correspondent, which should be submitted for consideration in November for Christmas vouchers. Inclusion in birthday voucher scheme can be done at any time (all that is needed is the name, address and date of birth of the person).

Correspondent: Mrs J M Minchin, 66 Redhill Lane, Tutbury, Burton-on-Trent, Staffordshire DE13 9JW (01283 813310).

Warwickshire

The Sarah Chamberlayne Charity

Eligibility: Widows/unmarried women who are at least 50 years old; older men; physically/visually disabled people of either sex, and children who have lost both parents or children who are mentally/physically disabled or infirm. Applicants must live in Southam and Long Itchington in Warwickshire or Hatfield Broad Oak and Ugely in Essex.

Types of grants: Quarterly annuities of £14 or £15 to 30 individuals.

Annual grant total: In 2000/01 the charity had an income of £3,300 and a total expenditure of £3,400.

Applications: In writing to the correspondent, although it is usually people who know one of the trustees who are recommended for grants.

Correspondent: J M P Hathaway, Clerk, 42 Brook Street, Warwick CV34 4BL.

Other information: This entry was not confirmed by the charity, but it was correct according to information on file at the Charity Commission.

The Baron Davenport Emergency Grant

Eligibility: (i) Needy widows, spinsters, divorcees over 50 years old, and women abandoned by their partners; and (ii) children under the age of 25 whose mothers are in the first category, in the borough of North Warwickshire. Applicants must have been resident in the West Midlands for about 10–15 years, be living alone (except where school age children are living with their mother) and have a bank, building society or Post Office account.

The total income of the household should be no more than £134 a week; this figure changes in line with state benefits.

Types of grants: One-off grants of between £25 and £250 for house reapirs, furniture, school clothes, bedding emergencies and so on. Pensions are also given of either £110 or £90 at each half-yearly distribution.

Annual grant total: In 1998/99 grants totalled £1,300.

Applications: On an form available from the correspondent. Applications should be submitted through a social worker, citizen's advice bureau or other welfare agency. They are considered throughout the year.

Correspondent: The Chief Officer, North Warwickshire Council for Voluntary Service, Community House, Coleshill Road, Atherstone, Warwickshire CV9 1BN (01827 718080; 01827 720416; e-mail: info@nwcvs.org.uk; website: nwcvs.org.uk).

Other information: For information on Baron Davenport's Charity Trust, see entry in the Midlands general section.

The Baron Davenport Emergency Grant

Eligibility: Needy widows, spinsters, divorcees aged 50 and over, women abandoned by their partners and the children (under 25) of young spinsters or young women abandoned by their partners and live in Nuneaton and Bedworth.

No grants are given to adult males over 25.

Types of grants: One-off grants in the range of £100 and £300. Recent grants applied for include those for carpets, washing machines, beds, cookers, security and repair work.

Annual grant total: In 2001/01 the sum of £1,100 was distributed in five grants.

Applications: On a form available from the correspondent to be submitted via a social worker, citizens advice bureau or other welfare agency. Applications are considered every month.

Correspondent: Liz Stuart, Chief Executive, Nuneaton & Bedworth Council for Voluntary Service, 72 High Street, Nuneaton, Warwickshire CV11 5DA (024 7638 5765; Fax: 024 7637 4891; e-mail: lizs@cvsnunbed.co.uk).

Other information: For information on Baron Davenport's Charity Trust, see entry in the Midlands general section.

The Baron Davenport Emergency Grant

Eligibility: Needy widows, spinsters and children under 21 whose fathers are dead. Applicants must live in Warwickshire.

Types of grants: One-off grants for emergencies only, such as for repairs to bathrooms, kitchens, heating systems and windows or doors, including security improvements and double glazing. Grants ranged from £65 to £375 in 2001/02.

Annual grant total: In 2001/02 the charity had an income of £1,900, most of which was distributed in ten grants.

Applications: On a form available from: Citizen's Advice Bureau Manager, 1st Floor, Chestnut House, 32 North Street, Rugby CV21 2AH (01788 541000). Applications can be submitted at any time either through a social worker, citizen's advice bureau or other welfare agency, or directly by the individual.

Correspondent: Rugby Council for Voluntary Service, 19–20 North Street, Rugby CV21 2AG (01788 574258).

Other information: For information on Baron Davenport's Charity Trust, see entry in the Midlands general section.

The Baron Davenport Emergency Grant

Eligibility: Needy widows, spinsters and children under 21 whose fathers are dead and live in Leamington Spa, Kenilworth or Warwick.

Types of grants: One-off grants, generally of £50 to £200, for needs such as new cookers, bath lifts, baby equipment, carpets, telephone extensions, showers and pushchairs.

Annual grant total: About £2,000 each year is available for distribution.

Applications: Applications can be made to the correspondent via CVS Warwick District, 109 Warwick Street, Leamington Spa, Warwickshire. Applications are considered monthly, and can be submitted either directly by the individual or through a social worker, citizen's advice bureau, welfare agency or other third party.

Correspondent: Jean Ball, 11 Godfrey Close, Leamington Spa CV31 1UH (01926 425032).

Other information: For information on Baron Davenport's Charity Trust, see the entry in the Midlands general section.

The Hatton Consolidated Charities

Eligibility: People in need who live in the parishes of Hatton, Beausale and Shrewley. Applications from outside the above areas will not be considered.

Types of grants: One-off grants in cash or in kind. Grants are also given to help students and young people starting work to help buy books and tools.

Annual grant total: About £3,000.

Applications: In writing to the trustees or the correspondent.

Correspondent: Mrs M H Sparks, Clerk, Weare Giffard, 32 Shrewley Common, Warwick CV35 7AP (01926 842533).

The Hatton & District Nursing Fund

Eligibility: People in need who are sick or elderly and live in the parishes of Beausale, Hatton, Haseley, Honiley, Shrewley and Wroxall.

Types of grants: One-off grants, mostly towards the cost of travel to and from hospital, although grants are available for other medical requirements such as heating and electrical bills. Grants are occasionally given to children and local organisations.

Annual grant total: This trust has an annual income of between £900 and £1,000 per year.

Applications: In writing to the correspondent.

Correspondent: Mrs A Pickering, Chair, Ley End Farm, School Road, Beausale, Nr Warwick CV35 7NX (01926 484324).

The Merevale Aid-in-Sickness Fund

Eligibility: People who are sick, convalescing, physically/mentally disabled or infirm and who live in Merevale, Grendon, Baddesley, Ensor, Bentley or Baxterley.

Types of grants: One-off grants of between £5 and £10, and gifts such as fruit, flowers and necessities.

Annual grant total: In 2000/01 the fund had assets of £21,000 and an income of £750. Total expenditure was £420 with 40 grants totalling £300.

Applications: In writing to any of the trustees directly by the individual, at any time.

Correspondent: H J McCranor, Accountant, Merevale, 89 Brinklow Road, Binley, Coventry CV3 2JB (024 7645 8500; e-mail: jim.mcranor@tinyworld.co.uk).

The Charity of Lord Redesdale

See entry on page 293

The South Warwickshire Welfare Trust

Eligibility: People who are sick and in need and live in Warwick district and the former rural district of Southam.

Types of grants: One-off grants of £25 to £300 for items, services or facilities to alleviate suffering or assist recovery for people who are sick, convalescent, disabled or infirm. Recent grants have been given towards household goods such as washing machines, carpets, beds and fridges; school uniforms; and towards larger items such as central heating, conditional upon the full amount being raised elsewhere.

Grants are not repeated and are not given for relief of taxes or other public funds.

Annual grant total: In 2000 the trust had assets of £260,000, an income of £8,000 and its total expenditure was £7,000. About £5,700 was given in 24 grants.

Applications: On an application form available from the correspondent to be submitted through a social worker, citizen's advice bureau or other welfare agency, or through a doctor, church official or similar third party. Applications are considered in January, April, July and October and should be submitted in the preceding months. Details of income/expenditure must be disclosed on the application form.

Correspondent: Mrs V Grimmer, Clerk, 62 Foxes Way, Warwick CV34 6AY (01926 492226).

The Warwickshire Miners Welfare Fund

Eligibility: Mineworkers and former mineworkers who have worked within the coal industry in Warwickshire and their dependants.

Types of grants: One-off grants from £50 to £300 towards convalescent holidays, hospital visits to spouse (or applicant), electrical appliances such as cookers and vacuum cleaners, carpets, beds and other furniture, wheelchairs, inhalors, electric hoists and so on, and medical reports for industrial diseases. No death grants or grants to people who have received redundancy pay in the last 10 years. Grants will not be given for any purpose for which the DNP will pay.

Annual grant total: In 1999 it had assets of £612,000 and an income of £24,000. Grants to 15 individuals totalled £5,900.

Applications: In writing to the correspondent. Applications can be submitted directly by the individual or through a social worker, citizen's advice bureau or other welfare agency or other third party. Applications should include weekly income and medical proof from doctor (if applicable). They are considered at any time.

Correspondent: G R Smith, CISWO, 142 Queens Road, Stoke-on-Trent ST4 7LH (01782 744996).

The Warwickshire Police Benevolent Fund

Eligibility: Police officers of the Warwickshire Constabulary who regularly subscribe to the fund, retired members who take on honorary membership, and their widows or widowers and immediate dependants, who are in need.

Types of grants: Grants are made to members who are proved to be in needy circumstances and interest-free loans may be awarded to subscribing members. Grants may also be made to members to assist with travel and incidental expenditure when attending a police or other convalescent home.

Annual grant total: In 1999/2000 grants totalled £7,400.

Applications: Forms are required to be completed which show a full breakdown of income and expenditure. These are available from the Secretary or Force Welfare Officer who will also advise on the application. Applications are considered at least four times a year. In urgent cases, a grant or loan of up to £1,000 may be awarded by a sub-committee.

Correspondent: G Savage, Secretary, Warwickshire Police, c/o Police Federation Office, Police Station, Kenilworth CV8 1QG.

Atherstone

The Charity of Priscilla Gent & Others

Eligibility: People in need who live in Atherstone, Warwickshire.

Types of grants: One-off grants according to need. Recent grants include those to cover the costs of furniture, carpets, washing machine repairs, clothing and travel to and from hospital.

Annual grant total: In 2001 the trust had an income of about £8,800 and a total of £1,500 was given in nine grants.

Applications: Applications can be submitted in writing by the individual or through a recognised referral agency (e.g. social worker, citizen's advice bureau or doctor). They are considered in May and November but should be received in the preceding month. Emergency applications can be considered at other times.

Correspondent: M L R Harris, Clerk, 42 King Street, Seagrave, Loughborough, Leicestershire LE12 7LY (01509 812366).

Other information: Grants are also made to organisations.

Baginton

The Lucy Price Relief-in-Need Charity

Eligibility: Only people in need who are under 25 and live in the parish of Baginton, Warwickshire.

Types of grants: Grants are given only for the calendar or academic year in which the application is made. All applications for grants spread over more than one year must be submitted annually. Grants are given for specialist tuition not dealt with under the education category. The charity also helps with financing of local organisations such as the swimming club, youth club and specialist events for children organised by Baginton Village Hall.

Annual grant total: In 2000 the charity had an income of £50,000 and a total expenditure of £41,000.

Applications: On a form available from the correspondent. Applications are considered principally at trustees' meetings held quarterly. Applications can be sent by the individual, through a social worker, citizen's advice bureau or other welfare agency, or by the parents if the applicant is under 16 years old. Applications should also include full details of the reason for application and any available printed information.

Correspondent: G Meredith, Clerk, Flat 39, Westbrook Court, Sutherland Avenue, Coventry CV5 7RB.

Other information: This entry was not confirmed by the charity but the address was correct according to information on file at the Charity Commission.

Barford

The Barford Relief-in-Need Charity

Eligibility: People in need who live in the parish of Barford.

Types of grants: One-off or recurrent grants, including Christmas gifts, help in particular financial difficulties, and assistance towards funeral expenses for those recently bereaved. No loans are given.

Annual grant total: About £7,500 each year.

Applications: In writing to the correspondent directly by the individual. Applications are considered in May and November, but at any time in an emergency.

Correspondent: Mrs Janet Bradley, 15a Wellesbourne Road, Barford, Warwick, Warwickshire CV35 8EL (01926 624433).

Bedworth

The Henry Smith Charity

Eligibility: Older people in need who live in Bedworth.

Types of grants: Food vouchers at Christmas of £3 for a local shop.

Annual grant total: Between £900 and £1,200.

Applications: In writing to the correspondent before September, for consideration in December.

Correspondent: Pam Matthews, Legal & Committee Services, Nuneaton & Bedworth Borough Council, Town Hall, Nuneaton, Warwickshire CV11 5AA (024 7637 6204; Fax: 024 7637 6596; e-mail: pam.matthews@nuneatonandbedworth.gov.uk).

Bilton & New Bilton

The Bilton Poors' Land & Other Charities

Eligibility: People in need who live in the ancient parishes of Bilton and New Bilton (now part of Rugby).

Types of grants: One-off grants, generally of between £50 and £100. Grants are often given to older people, students and those referred by social services.

Annual grant total: About £10,000 a year.

Applications: In writing to the correspondent, by the individual or through a third party such as a minister, although often applications are forwarded by social services.

Correspondent: D Lee, Messrs Frederick Fuller, 24 Albert Street, Rugby, Warwickshire CV21 2RT (01788 542288).

Coleshill

The Simon Lord Digby Non-Educational Foundation (Relief-in-Need)

Eligibility: People in extreme hardship who live in the parish of Coleshill.

Types of grants: One-off grants according to need. Recent grants have been given to a multiple sclerosis sufferer towards the cost of electric reclining/rising chair and to a family of an eight year old leukaemia sufferer for help with extra expenses.

Annual grant total: In 2000 the endowment had an income of £14,000 and a total expenditure of £9,700.

Applications: In writing to the correspondent. Applications are decided in March and November although decisions can be made more quickly in an emergency. They should be submitted directly by the individual or through a social worker, citizen's advice bureau or other welfare agency and should give as much detail as possible including information about applications to other organisations/trusts.

Correspondent: Mrs Ann Latimer, The Vicarage Office, High Street, Coleshill, Warwickshire B46 3BP (01675 462188).

Grandborough

The Grandborough & Sutton Charities

Eligibility: People in need who live in the parish of Grandborough.

Types of grants: One-off grants that range from £20 to £100 and have included help with optician's fees and other general needs.
Grants are not given when the need is covered by the Benefits Agency.

Annual grant total: In 2000/01 the charities had an income of £1,100 and a total expenditure of £725, most of which was given in grants.

Applications: In writing to the correspondent either directly by the individual or through a third party on behalf of the individual if the applicant is unable to write. Applications are considered on an ongoing basis. Evidence of expenditure is required.

Correspondent: Mrs P A Cooke, Clerk, Westwood, Sawbridge Road,

Grandborough, Rugby, Warwickshire CV23 8DN (01788 810742).

Kenilworth

The Kenilworth Carnival Comforts Fund

Eligibility: People in need who live in Kenilworth.

Types of grants: Mainly one-off grants of £15 per person or £20 per couple, usually in the form of a grocery voucher redeemable at various shops in Kenilworth, hampers of food or bouquets of flowers. About 100 grants are given at Christmas, the rest are given throughout the year. Grants are not made to charities.

Annual grant total: In 2000 the fund had an income of £1,700 and a total expenditure of £2,100.

Applications: In writing to the correspondent. Applications can be submitted directly by the individual or through a social worker, citizen's advice bureau, other welfare agency or a third party e.g. a friend or relative. They are considered bi-monthly from February.

Correspondent: J A Evans, Treasurer, 7 Queens Road, Kenilworth CV8 1JQ.

The Kenilworth United Charities

Eligibility: People in need who live in the ancient parish of Kenilworth.

Types of grants: Generally grocery vouchers given to one-parent families. Recently one-off grants have also been given e.g. towards a washing machine.

Annual grant total: In 2000/01 the charities had an income of £5,300 and a total expenditure of £2,800.

Applications: On a form available from the correspondent. Applications are considered quarterly, although urgent cases can be considered quarterly.

Correspondent: Damian Joseph Plans, Clerk, 29b Warwick Road, Kenilworth CV8 1HN.

Leamington Spa

The Leamington Relief-in-Sickness Fund

Eligibility: People suffering from ill-health who live in the former borough of Leamington Spa and the neighbourhood and are in need. People with disabilities or mental health problems are especially welcomed.

Types of grants: One-off grants only from around £25, including help with fuel debts, television licence, baby necessities, food for special diets, fares for visiting hospitals or sick relatives, replacing locks after a burglary, children's clothing, and repairs to washing machines and so on.

Annual grant total: About £2,000 a year.

Applications: In writing through a social worker, citizen's advice bureau, health visitor, doctor, probation service, Mind or other welfare agency. Applications submitted by individuals will not be acknowledged or considered. Applications are considered throughout the year, although applicants can only receive one grant each year.

Correspondent: Mrs R Smyth, Clerk, 27 Montrose Avenue, Leamington Spa, Warwickshire CV32 7DS (01926 428796).

Long Lawford

Sir Edward Boughton Long Lawford Charity

Eligibility: People in need who live in the parish of Long Lawford. Applicants for pensions must have lived in the parish for the last five years.

Types of grants: Pensions of £10 a month to about 100 pensioners. One-off grants can also be awarded, with a preference for people who are sick, e.g. grants towards an invalid chair. Small awards have also been made for swimming classes. The trust is hoping to widen its boundaries and increase the amount it can give in educational grants.

Annual grant total: About £12,000 per year.

Applications: On a form available from the correspondent, to be considered in March, June, September and November.

Correspondent: D S Edge, 36 St Leonards Walk, Ryton-on-Dunsmore, Coventry CV8 3FD (024 7630 1352).

Napton-on-the-Hill

The Napton Charities

Eligibility: People in need who live in the parish of Napton-on-the-Hill only.

Types of grants: One-off and recurrent grants of £20 to £25 towards heating (e.g. gas, electricity, solid fuel), footwear or clothing.

Annual grant total: In 2000/01 the charities had an income of £2,800 and a total expenditure of £1,900.

Applications: On a form available from the correspondent, for consideration usually in winter. Applications can be submitted either directly by the individual or by a relative or friend with the consent of the individual. Proof of having lived in Napton for over a year is required.

Correspondent: A Fletcher, Secretary, Endene, Southam Road, Napton-on-the-Hill, Southam, Warwickshire CV47 8NG (01926 812804).

Nuneaton

The Nuneaton Poors' Piece Charity

Eligibility: People in need who live in the borough of Nuneaton. There is a preference for those in need due to serious accident, illness or trauma.

Types of grants: One-off and recurrent grants according to need.

Annual grant total: About £1,000 a year.

Applications: In writing to the correspondent through the social services, citizen's advice bureau or a similar welfare agency.

Correspondent: F L Matts, Clerk, 31 Chartwell Close, Nuneaton, Warwickshire CV11 6SL (024 7634 9401).

Rugby

Rokeby Charitable Trust

Eligibility: People who live in the Rugby area and are in need.

Types of grants: One-off grants ranging between £100 and £250.

Annual grant total: In 2001 the trust had assets of £240,000 and an income of £12,000. No relief-in-need grants were made in the year, although £7,500 was given in educational grants.

Applications: In writing to the correspondent directly by the individual. Applications can be submitted at any time for consideration in February and October.

Correspondent: R M Furber, The Orchards, 259a Bilton Road, Rugby, Warwickshire CV22 7EQ (01788 812839; Fax: 01788 817984).

The Rugby Welfare Charities

Eligibility: People in need who live in the ancient parish of Rugby, which includes St Andrew's and St Matthew's.

Types of grants: One-off grants, usually for people of pensionable age although general relief-in-need grants are also given. Grants are usually paid at Christmas.

Annual grant total: About 100 grants to individuals totalling over £1,000.

Applications: In writing to the correspondent. Applications are generally considered three or four times a year, although urgent cases can be considered at any time.

Correspondent: Mrs Mary Poxon, Clerk, St Andrew's Church, Rugby CV21 3PT.

Stratford-upon-Avon

The Baron Davenport Emergency Grant

Eligibility: Widows, spinsters, older divorced women and children under 21 who are in need and whose fathers are dead. Applicants must live in Stratford-upon-Avon District Council area.

Types of grants: One-off grants of up to £200 for emergencies only, and where state benefit is not available or undue delay would cause hardship.

Annual grant total: About £1,000.

Applications: Applications can be made directly to the correspondent but must include supporting evidence from a third party, such as a health visitor, social worker, doctor or other professional.

Correspondent: The CVS Chief Officer, Stratford-upon-Avon Council for Voluntary Service, The Hospital, Arden Street, Stratford-upon-Avon CV37 6NW (01789 298115).

Other information: For information on Baron Davenport's Charity Trust, see entry in the Midlands general section.

The Mayor's Fund Society of Stratford-upon-Avon

Eligibility: People in need who live in the former borough of Stratford-upon-Avon.

Types of grants: One-off and recurrent grocery vouchers of £15. Loans are not made.

Annual grant total: In 2001/02 the trust gave £2,800 in 164 grocery vouchers.

Applications: In writing to the correspondent. Applications can be submitted directly by the individual or through a social worker, citizen's advice bureau, other welfare agency or other third party such as a member of the clergy. They are considered in September, November and January and should include a general summary of income, other relief received (for example housing benefits) and financial commitments.

Correspondent: Trevor Cox, Hon. Secretary, 7 Keats Road, Stratford-upon-Avon CV37 7JL (01789 204730).

The Stratford-upon-Avon Municipal Charities – Relief in Need

Eligibility: People in need living in the town of Stratford-upon-Avon.

Types of grants: One-off and recurrent grants in the range of £100 and £500. Older people can receive help towards fuel bills, following adverts each year. Lone parents may receive help towards e.g. household items such as washing machines, TVs or clothing. Other grants can also be given to people with different needs. Educational grants are also available.

Annual grant total: About £20,000 is given to individuals for educational and welfare purposes.

Applications: On a form available from the correspondent, including details of the financial circumstances of the applicant and parent(s) if appropriate. There is a separate form for students. Applications for schoolchildren must be made through the school.

Correspondent: Mrs Joan Beningfield, Manor Farm, Shottery, Stratford-upon-Avon, Warwickshire CV37 9HA (Tel & Fax: 01789 263423).

Sutton Cheney

Sir William Roberts Relief in Need Charity

Eligibility: People who live in the village of Sutton Cheney and are in need.

Types of grants: One-off grants according to need for basic necessities only.

Annual grant total: In 2001 the trust had assets of £73,000, an income of £3,500 and its total expenditure was £3,400. The sum of £1,800 was given in 13 relief-in-need grants. Other grants were given to organisations and to individuals for further education totalling £1,500.

Applications: In writing to the correspondent, or any of the trustees. Applications can be submitted directly by the individual at any time.

Correspondent: Miss D A Read, Secretary, Chatsmoth Cottage, Sutton Cheney, Nuneaton, Warwickshire CV13 0AG.

Thurlaston

Thurlaston Poor's Plot Charity

Eligibility: People of pensionable age who are in need and live in Thurlaston.

Types of grants: The charity gives help with the payment of bills.

Annual grant total: In 2001 the charity had an income of £2,200 and a total expenditure of £3,600.

Applications: In writing to the correspondent directly by the individual. Applications are considered in January, September and November.

Correspondent: Mrs K Owen, Clerk, Congreaves, Main Street, Thurlaston, Rugby CV23 9JS.

Other information: Educational grants are also made to students.

Warwick

The Austin Edwards Charity

Eligibility: People living in the old borough of Warwick.

Types of grants: Grants ranging from £250 to £500 for relief-in-need purposes.

Annual grant total: In 1999 grants totalled £10,000. Around £1,000 of this was given to individuals for educational and welfare needs, the rest to organisations.

Applications: In writing to the correspondent. Applications are considered throughout the year.

Correspondent: R Ogg, Wright Hassall & Co, 9 Clarendon Place, Leamington Spa, Warwickshire CV32 5QP (01926 886688; Fax: 01926 885588).

The Warwick Municipal Charities – King Henry VIII Charity

Eligibility: People who live in the old borough of Warwick (CV34 postal district).

Types of grants: One-off grants according to need.

Annual grant total: In 2001 the charity had assets of £23 million generating an income of £1.6 million. Grants to 10 individuals totalled £10,000. Grants to organisations totalled £440,000.

Applications: On an application form available from the correspondent. Applications can be submitted at any time directly by the individual or a relevant third party; or through a social worker, citizen's advice bureau or other welfare agency. They are considered bi-monthly.

Correspondent: R J Wyatt, Clerk & Receiver, 12 High Street, Warwick CV34 4AP (01926 495533; Fax 01925 401464).

The Warwick Provident Dispensary

Eligibility: People who are sick or infirm and live in the town of Warwick.

Types of grants: One-off and recurrent grants for the relief of sickness or infirmity.

Annual grant total: In 1999 it had assets of £228,000, an income of £18,000 and gave 22 grants to organisations and individuals totalling £12,000.

Applications: In writing to the correspondent, directly by the individual or through a social worker, citizen's advice bureau, other welfare agency or other third party. Applications are considered at all times.

Correspondent: Christopher Houghton, Messrs Moore & Tibbits, 34 High Street, Warwick CV34 4BE (01926 491181; Fax: 01926 402692).

Warwick Relief in Need Charity

Eligibility: People in need who live in the town of Warwick.

Types of grants: One-off grants according to need, towards for example washing machines, beds, mattresses, vacuum cleaners, carpets and holidays.

Annual grant total: In 1998/99 the trust had assets of £2.3 million and an income of £40,000. Total expenditure was £32,000 including £22,000 in 38 grants to individuals and organisations.

Applications: In writing to the correspondent.

Correspondent: C E R Houghton, c/o Moore & Tibbits, Solicitors, 34 High Street, Warwick CV34 4BE (01926 491181).

West Midlands

The Avon Trust

Eligibility: Retired Methodist ministers and their dependants with some preference for those living in the West Midlands, and people in residential homes who live in the West Midlands.

Types of grants: One-off and recurrent grants according to need.

Annual grant total: In 2000/01 the trust had an income of £9,300 and a total expenditure of £9,800.

Applications: In writing to the correspondent. The trustees meet once a year in July but can deal with applications at other times.

Correspondent: Mrs A Lawe, Barrow Wold Farm, Deepdale, Barton-upon-Humber, South Humberside DN18 6ED.

Other information: This entry was not confirmed by the charity, but was correct according to information on file at the Charity Commission.

The Badley Memorial Trust

Eligibility: People in need who are sick, convalescent, disabled or infirm and live in the former county borough of Dudley (as constituted in 1953). In certain cases the present metropolitan boroughs of Dudley and Sandwell may be included.

Types of grants: Grants have been made towards medical aids, clothing, beds/bedding, heating appliances, cookers, washing machines, vacuum cleaners, televisions, radios, fuel, respite holidays, and adaptations for disabled people. Recurrent grants are only given in exceptional cases. Grants are not given to pay off debts or for educational fees.

Annual grant total: In 2000/01 the trust had assets of £968,000 with an income of £51,000. A total of 90 relief-in-need grants were made totaling £39,000.

Applications: On a form available from the correspondent to be submitted directly by the individual, or through a social worker, citizen's advice bureau, other welfare agency; or a third party for example a relative, doctor or member of the clergy. Applications are considered in February, May, August and November.

Correspondent: D Underwood, 23 Water Street, Kingswinford, West Midlands DY6 7QA (01384 277463).

The Beacon Centre for the Blind

Eligibility: People who are registered blind or partially sighted and live in the metropolitan boroughs of Dudley (except Halesowen and Stourbridge), Sandwell and Wolverhampton, and part of the South Staffordshire District Council area.

Types of grants: One-off grants towards socials and outings; holidays; and talking books and newspapers. Grants for specific items of equipment can be given to those who are visually impaired.

Annual grant total: In 1999/2000 the charity gave £75,000 in grants to individuals for relief-in-need purposes, and a further £7,200 in educational grants.

Applications: In writing to the correspondent stating the degree of vision and age of the applicant. Applications can be submitted directly by the individual or through a social worker, citizen's advice bureau or other welfare agency and are considered quarterly.

Correspondent: Chief Executive, Beacon Centre for the Blind, Wolverhampton Road East, Wolverhampton WV4 6AZ (01902 880111; Fax: 01902 671889; e-mail: enquiries@beacon4blind.co.uk; website: www.beacon4blind.co.uk).

Other information: This charity also gives grants to organisations.

The Frances Lynn Betteridge Memorial Trust Fund

Eligibility: Children and young people under 18 who are in need and live in, or close to, the city of Birmingham. Preference will be given to those within the city.

Types of grants: One-off grants have been given for outings, holidays, trips, toys and treats.

Annual grant total: About £3,500 a year.

Applications: Applicants must be nominated by a recognised third party such as a teacher or social worker.

Correspondent: Miss L K Alexander, Social Service Department, Birmingham City Council, Louisa Ryland House, 44 Newhall Street, Birmingham B3 3PL (0121 303 4579).

The Birmingham and District Butchers and Pork Butchers Association Benevolent Fund

Eligibility: Past and present members of the association and their dependants and any other person connected with the meat trade in Birmingham and district.

Types of grants: One-off and recurrent grants ranging from £120 to £175 according to need.

Annual grant total: In 2000 the trust had an income of £2,200 and a total expenditure of £1,600.

Applications: In writing to the correspondent. Applications can be submitted directly by the individual or through a social worker, citizen's advice bureau or other welfare agency. They are considered in June and November.

Correspondent: Mrs J P Hemming, Secretary, Office 30, Manor House, 40 Moat Lane, Birmingham B5 5BD (0121 622 4900).

The Birmingham Jewish Community Care

Eligibility: Jewish people in need living in the West Midlands.

Types of grants: Mainly one-off grants ranging from £10 to £260. Grants have been given to a small number of clients at Jewish festivals and for school clothing, music lessons for a gifted child, holidays for disadvantaged children and travel expenses for visiting distant cemeteries and occasionally to provide lifeline telephones and cover monitoring charges where there is no family support. There is also a kosher meals-on-wheels service.

Regular payments are no longer made. Applicants must be prepared to update their circumstances before a second grant is made (other than in the case of regular telephone rental payment in some cases). Grants are not made for setting up businesses.

Annual grant total: In 2000/01 the trust had an income of £1.3 million and a total expenditure of £1.4 million.

Around £2,000 is available each year in grants to individuals. Most of the income is spent on running two residential homes, a day centre and a full social work service.

Applications: In writing to the social worker, including information on length of residence in the area, other applications made and whether or not the applicant is in receipt of income support or support from other charities. Applications are considered monthly and may be submitted directly by the individual or through a social worker, citizen's advice bureau or other welfare agency or third party e.g. rabbi.

No grant is ever made without personal contact with a social worker.

Correspondent: Mrs Sharon Grey, Social Worker, 1 Rake Way, Birmingham B15 1EG (0121 458 6891; Fax: 0121 643 5291).

The Thomas Bromwich Charity

Eligibility: People in need living in Handsworth (i.e. the ecclesiastical parishes of St Mary, St Andrew, St James, St Michael, St Peter and the Holy Trinity, Birdfield and St Paul, and Hanstead); Great Barr (i.e. the ecclesiastical parish of St Margaret), and Perry Barr (i.e. the ecclesiastical parishes of St John the Evangelist, Perry Barr, St Luke, Kingstanding, and St Matthews and Perry Beeches).
Types of grants: One-off grants towards telephone installation, school uniform and payment of gas or electricity bills and so on.
Annual grant total: In 2000/01 the charity had an income of £4,800 and a total expenditure of £4,000. About £4,000 to £5,000 is distributed each year.
Applications: In writing to the correspondent either directly by the individual or through a social worker, citizen's advice bureau or other welfare agency. Applications are considered at any time.
Correspondent: W M Colacicchi, Willcox Lane Clutterbuck, 55 Charlotte Street, St Paul's Square, Birmingham B3 1PX.
Other information: This entry was was not confirmed by the charity but the income was correct according to information on file at the Charity Commission.

The Chance Trust

Eligibility: People in need in the rural deaneries of Warley and West Bromwich.
Types of grants: One-off grants ranging from £50 to £400.
Annual grant total: The trust made grants of between £2,500 and £3,000 a year to individuals for both educational and relief-in-need purposes.
Applications: In writing to the correspondent, outlining need and the money required. Applications are considered in May and November.
Correspondent: Revd Michael Dunk, Trustee, St Hilda's Vicarage, Abbey Road, Smethwick, West Midlands B67 5NQ (0121 429 1384).
Other information: Grants are also given to organisations.

The Coventry Community Cancer Fund

Eligibility: Firstly the patients of Macmillan nurses and secondly people and families of people with cancer or cancer-related diseases living within 15 miles of Coventry city centre.
Types of grants: Grants have been given towards beds, washing machines, specialised medical aids for individuals, as well as towards the cost of nursing care.
Annual grant total: In 1998 the fund had an income of £3,000 and a total expenditure of £2,400; no further up-to-date information was available.
Applications: Applications can only be made through Macmillan nurses. No other referrals and no direct applications will be accepted.
Correspondent: D R Sarginson, Sarginsons, 10 The Quadrant, Coventry CV1 2EL (024 7655 3181).

The Coventry Freemen's Charity

Eligibility: Freemen and their dependants who are in need and live within seven miles of St Mary's Hall, Coventry.
Types of grants: Recurrent grants of £39 to £57 are paid quarterly to individuals who are 67 or over. Lump sum grants are given to other applicants.
Annual grant total: In 2001 the charity had assets of almost £8 million, an income of £449,000 and its total expenditure was £437,000. A total of £283,000 was given in 1,855 grants to individuals in need. £2,000 was given in grants for other purposes.
Applications: On a form available from the correspondent directly by the individual, for consideration bimonthly.
Correspondent: David Evans, Clerk, Abbey House, Manor Road, Coventry CV1 2FW (024 7625 7317; Fax: 024 7655 2845; e-mail: david@foxevans.co.uk; website: www.foxevans.co.uk).

The Dudley Charity

Eligibility: People in hardship or distress who are living in the town of Dudley (as constituted immediately prior to 1 April 1966) and its immediate surroundings including Netherton.
Types of grants: One-off grants according to need.
Annual grant total: In 2001/02 grants totalled £2,400.
Applications: On a form available from the correspondent. Applications can be submitted directly by the individual or through a vicar, a social worker, citizen's advice bureau, other welfare agency or other third party. Applications are considered in January, May and September.
Correspondent: D C Jones, Secretary to the Trustees, St Thomas's Church, King Street, Dudley DY2 8QB (01384 392704).

Grantham Yorke Trust

Eligibility: People under 25 who were born in the old West Midlands metropolitan county area (basically: Birmingham, Coventry, Dudley, Redditch, Sandwell, Solihull, Tamworth, Walsall or Wolverhampton).
Types of grants: One-off grants according to need.
Annual grant total: In 1998/99 the trust had assets of £4.8 million, an income of £351,000 and its total expenditure was £346,000. Grants were made to organisations, and to individuals for welfare and educational purposes.
Applications: On a form available from the correspondent. Applications should be submitted directly by the individual or via a relevant third party such as a social worker, citizen's advice bureau or other welfare agency, in February, May, August and November for consideration in the following month.
Correspondent: Miss Lucy Chatt, St Philips House, St Philips Place, Birmingham B3 2PP (0121 200 3300; Fax: 0121 625 3326; e-mail: lucy.chatt@martjohn.com).

The Harborne Parish Lands Charity

Eligibility: People in need who live in the parish of Harborne, which includes Smethwick.
Types of grants: One-off grants in the range of £100 to £2,000. Grants cover a wide range of needs, including furniture, aids and adaptations, clothing and assistance with transport. It cannot help with taxes and so on.
Annual grant total: In 2000/01 this trust had assets of £11 million and an income of £460,000. A total of £406,000 was spent of which £50,000 was given in 52 grants. £250,000 was given to organisations in the year.
Applications: A short application form is available from the correspondent; all applicants are visited. Applications can be submitted through a social worker, citizen's advice bureau or other welfare agency or directly by the individual at any time.
Correspondent: Lynda Bending, 7 Harborne Park Road, Birmingham B17 0DE (Tel & Fax: 0121 426 1600; e-mail: the clerk@hplc.fednet.org.uk; website: www.harborneparishlandscharity.org.uk).

The CB & AB Holinsworth Fund of Help

Eligibility: People in need who live in or near to the city of Birmingham and are sick or convalescing.
Types of grants: One-off grants ranging from £50 to £300. Grants are given towards the cost of respite holidays, travelling expenses to and from hospital, clothing,

beds and carpets. Generally grants are not given for bills or debt.

Annual grant total: In 2000/01 the fund had an income of £7,300 and a total expenditure of £5,600. Grants are made to individuals and organisations.

Applications: On a form available from the correspondent. Applications are considered throughout the year and should be submitted through a social worker, citizen's advice bureau or other welfare agency. Confirmation of illness is needed, for example a letter from a doctor, consultant or nurse.

Correspondent: Clerk to the Trustee, Room B23, Birmingham City Council, The Council House, Victoria Square, Birmingham B1 1BB (0121 303 2017; Fax: 0121 303 1372).

The Lant Trust

Eligibility: People in need, especially those who are elderly, living in the ecclesiastical parishes of Berkswell (St John the Baptist), Balsall Common (St Peter) and Temple Balsall (St Mary). The trust also augments three clergy stipends, gives grants to residents of Berkswell, Burton Green and Temple Balsall, and helps maintain some playing fields.

Types of grants: One-off and recurrent grants according to need.

Annual grant total: In previous years around £8,000 has been given in grants.

Applications: In writing to the correspondent.

Correspondent: The Clerk, c/o Rotherham & Co., 8–9 The Quadrant, Coventry CV1 2EG (024 7622 7331; Fax: 024 7622 1293).

The James Frederick & Ethel Anne Measures Charity

Eligibility: The following criteria apply:
(i) applicants must usually originate in the West Midlands
(ii) applicants must show evidence of self-help in their application
(iii) trustees have a preference for disadvantaged people
(iv) trustees have a dislike for applications from students who have a full local authority grant and want finance for a different course or study
(v) trustees favour grants towards the cost of equipment
(vi) applications by individuals in cases of hardship will not usually be considered unless sponsored by a local authority, health professional or other welfare agency.

Types of grants: One-off or recurrent grants, usually between £50 and £500.

Annual grant total: In 1999/2000 the trust had assets of £1.3 million and an income of £58,000. Grants were given to 101 organisations totalling £74,000, with six individuals receiving £1,800 in total.

Applications: In writing to the correspondent. No reply to unsuccessful applicants unless an sae is enclosed.

Correspondent: Sally Darby, Clerk to the Trustees, 33 Great Charles Street, Birmingham B3 3JN.

Other information: This entry was not confirmed by the charity but was correct according to information on file at the Charity Commission.

The Pedmore Sporting Club Trust Fund

Eligibility: Individuals in need living in the West Midlands.

Types of grants: One-off grants have included those for medical care equipment, travel to and from hospital, wheelchairs and IT equipment. Christmas and Easter parcels are also given.

Annual grant total: In 2001 the trust had assets of £251,000, an income of £42,000 and grants totalled £61,000. Grants were made to 9 individuals totalling £16,000, with a further £1,800 going on Easter food parcels and £1,900 on Christmas parcels. Grants were made to 19 organisations totalling £46,000.

Applications: Applicants for the Easter food parcels should be recommended by a member of the sporting club. Other applications should be made in writing to the correspondent. Applications are considered in January, May, September and November and should be submitted in the preceding month.

Correspondent: B W J Mann, Secretary, Pedmore House, Ham Lane, Pedmore, Stourbridge, West Midlands DY9 0YA (01384 372727; Fax: 01384 440359).

The Temple Balsall Amalgamated Charities

Eligibility: People in need who live in the ecclesiastical parishes of Temple Balsall and Balsall Common.

Types of grants: Grants are considered 'when, for whatever reason, illness, accident, bereavement etc. a sudden need arises; or when reduced circumstances and rising prices turn necessities into luxuries'. The trust gives about 20 recurrent grants to individuals, five special grants to individuals, and eight grants to local organisations.

Annual grant total: The trust has an annual income of about £8,000.

Applications: In writing to the correspondent at any time. A trustee may then visit the applicant.

Correspondent: D W Hill, Clerk, 74 Broad Oaks Road, Solihull, West Midlands B91 1HZ.

Bilston

The Bilston Relief-in-Need Charity

Eligibility: People in need living in the ecclesiastical parish of Bilston and the area of the former borough of Bilston.

Types of grants: Generally one-off grants for holiday costs, clothes and domestic furnishings and appliances where help cannot be obtained from any other source.

Annual grant total: In 2001/02 the charity gave 14 relief-in-need grants to individuals totalling £500.

Applications: Applications, in writing to the correspondent, can be submitted by the individual or through a recognised referral agency for example a social worker, citizen's advice bureau, doctor or medical worker.

Correspondent: Desmond Smith, 36 Springfield Road, Bilston, West Midlands WV14 6LN (01902 493928).

Birmingham

The Freda & Howard Ballance Trust

Eligibility: People in need who live in Birmingham. Grants are only made to people in need 'who can demonstrate that they are trying to help themselves'.

Types of grants: One-off grants ranging from £50 to £200, for example for clothing or furniture, or as a contribution towards a computer for people with physical disabilities or learning difficulties. Grants are usually not given for educational purposes.

Annual grant total: In 2000/01 the trust had assets of £52,000, an income of £1,700 and grants to 18 individuals totalled £2,000.

Applications: On a form available from the correspondent to be submitted in time for the meetings of the trustees in March, June, September and December. Applications can be made either directly by the individual or via a third party such as a charity, social worker or citizen's advice bureau. Evidence should be included showing that the individual is trying to 'help him/herself'.

Correspondent: M G M Stocks, Appeals Secretary and Trustee, 47 Newhall Street, Birmingham B3 3QU (0121 233 2644; Fax: 0121 233 2196).

Other information: Donations can also be made to organisations, but preference is given to individuals.

The Richard & Samuel Banner Trust

Eligibility: Poor men and widows in need living in the city of Birmingham.

Types of grants: Clothing grants of about £100.

Annual grant total: About £6,000 a year.

Applications: Applicants must be nominated by a trustee, doctor or the Council for Old People. Applications are considered on 1 November and grants are distributed on or after 2 November (All Souls Day).

Correspondent: Mrs A E Holmes, Lee Crowder, 39 Newhall Street, Birmingham B3 3DY (0121 236 4477).

Other information: The trust can also give apprenticing grants to male students under 21, but this is done through certain colleges; applicants should not apply direct.

Birmingham Money Advice Grants (BMAG)

BMAG's work includes: holding endowments to distribute in grants, see (1) below; adminstering a range of trusts, some of which are listed below; applying to third party charities on behalf of individuals in need; and helping to adminster other trusts that are still mainly adminstered by those trusts' trustees.

Applications for all of the following funds, except The George Fentham (Birmingham) Charity, should be made on a BMAG application form available from the correspondent and from the website. Guidelines are also available. An application to BMAG counts as an application to all the trusts.

Option 1 for applicants – submit the following to BMAG: a completed application form; a signed form 'Our standards, your rights' (available from the correspondent or website); photocopied proof of all family income; a letter from the social fund saying that they will not give you a community care grant for the items you are requesting; and medical evidence of any condition you are relying on as part of your case for a grant.

Option 2 – provide your name and address to BMAG and you will be contacted, normally within a few weeks, with an initial appointment. A BMAG officer will then help you to complete the application: you will need to provide all the evidence described in Option 1 in order for your application to be considered.

Applications to The Birmingham Children's Holiday Fund must be made via a social worker from the Birmingham Child Advisory Social Work Service.

All applications are considered throughout the year.

Correspondent: Alan Norman, BMAG, 138 Digbeth, Birmingham B5 6DR (0121 678 8846; Fax: 0121 678 8821; e-mail: manager@b-mag.org.uk; website: www.b-mag.org.uk).

(i) Central endowments

Eligibility: Families and people under pensionable age who are in need and live in Birmingham.

Types of grants: Grants are usually for household appliances, furniture, holidays and 'other one-off expenses for which [their] clients find it hard to budget'. The trust states, 'Even if you have an unusual need it is worth contacting us for advice as to whether we can help'.

Annual grant total: About £200,000 is available in grants each year for individuals and families.

Other information: A similar service is available to people over pensionable age from Age Concern Birmingham.

(ii) The George Fentham (Birmingham) Charity

Eligibility: People in need who have lived in the city of Birmingham.

Types of grants: One-off and recurrent grants to individuals for household equipment.

Annual grant total: In 2000 the charity had an income of £120,000. The annual grant total varies from year to year.

Applications: On a form available from the correspondent. Applications from individuals should be made through a social worker, citizen's advice bureau or other welfare agency and are considered at any time.

Correspondent: Mrs A E Holmes, Secretary, Lee Crowder, 39 Newhall Street, Birmingham B3 3DY (0121 236 4477).

(iii) The Baron Davenport Emergency Grant

Eligibility: Needy widows, spinsters and children under 21 whose fathers are dead, who live in the city of Birmingham. In practice, applications from women who are unmarried but have children are not accepted.

Types of grants: One-off grants of up to £250 depending on the need for household essentials.

Annual grant total: In 2001/02 the trust had an income of £4,000 and gave 18 relief-in-need grants totalling £3,000.

Other information: For information on Baron Davenport's Charity Trust see entry in the Midlands general section.

(iv) The Birmingham Children's Holiday Fund

Eligibility: Children and young people aged 5 to 19 who live in Birmingham.

Types of grants: One-off grants towards holidays/outings for children in need as a result of social, emotional or environmental deprivation, who are known to social workers of Child Advisory Social Work Service in Birmingham. Grants are also given towards day trips, adventure camps, caravan holidays, school/educational and holidays/trips. Grants range from £20 to £150.

Grants are not given to children not known to Child Advisory Social Work Service.

Annual grant total: In 1999/2000 the trust had an income of £1,900.

Friends of Home Nursing in Birmingham

Eligibility: Sick and elderly people who live in Birmingham City and who are patients nursed at home where the district nurse attends.

Types of grants: The trust provides goods, equipment and occasional monetary grants which are not available from other sources. In the past this has included digital thermometers, a dressing trolley, cameras and films for ulcer recordings, and part of the cost of holidays. Grants are usually one-off and range from £50 to £500.

No grants are made for double glazing or electrical work.

Annual grant total: In 2000 the charity had assets of £18,000 and an income of £8,400. Total expenditure was £11,000.

Applications: In writing, via a district nurse, to Mrs J Burns, Hon Treasurer, 46 Underwood Road, Handsworth Wood, Birmingham B20 1JS. Applications can be submitted at any time, for consideration in the spring and autumn, 'but if a real case of need occurs [they] deal with it as soon as possible'.

Correspondent: Mrs C F Massey, 80 Linthurst Road, Barnt Green, Birmingham B45 8JJ.

The Charity of Jane Kate Gilbert

Eligibility: People of at least 60 years of age and in need who have lived in Birmingham for at least two years.

Types of grants: Quarterly pensions, of £15 for three quarters and £40 during the Christmas quarter.

Annual grant total: In 2001/02 the charity had a total expenditure of £2,000.

Applications: On a form available from the correspondent to be submitted through a social worker, citizen's advice bureau or other welfare agency. Applications are considered in March and November.

Correspondent: Clerk to the Trustees, Room B23, Birmingham City Council, The Council House, Victoria Square, Birmingham B1 1BB (0121 303 2017; Fax: 0121 303 1372).

The Handsworth Charities including the Charity of William Stevenson

Eligibility: People in need living in the ancient parish of Handsworth (now in Birmingham) which covers Kingstanding.

Types of grants: Mainly one-off grants according to need.

Annual grant total: In 2000 the charities had an income of £9,900 and a total expenditure of £9,700. The trust regularly has surplus money available for grants.

Applications: In writing to the correspondent.

Correspondent: Jennifer Stetson, Anthony Collins, St Philip's Gate, 5 Waterloo Street, Birmingham B2 5PG (0121 212 7461; Fax: 0121 212 7439).

The Charity of Joseph Hopkins

Eligibility: People who live in the city of Birmingham.

Types of grants: One-off grants are given at the discretion of the trustees. Applications from individuals cannot be considered and grants are only made via registered charities. Grants usually range between £100 and £500.

Annual grant total: In 2000/01 the trust had assets of £762,000 generating an income of £34,000. The total expenditure was £40,000 and grants to individuals in need totalled £6,200.

Applications: On a form available from the correspondent to be submitted directly by the charity. Applications are considered twice yearly, usually in April and October.

Correspondent: H B Carslake, Martineau Johnson, St Philips House, St Philips Place, Birmingham B3 2PP (0121 200 3300; Fax: 0121 625 3326).

Harriet Louisa Loxton Trust Fund

Eligibility: People in need who live in Birmingham, with a preference for older people.

Types of grants: One-off grants ranging from £100 to £2,000, though the average is generally around £300. Examples of grants given include: £500 to an older disabled man for a washing machine and drier, £100 for a vacuum cleaner for an older woman who was ill, £1,700 for central heating for a woman who was blind and £500 towards an electric scooter for a man who was totally immobile.

No grants to pay off debts, relieve public funds or towards the community charge and no grants to organisations.

Annual grant total: In 2001/02 the sum of £26,000 was approved in grants.

Applications: On a form available, with notes of guidance, from: Richard Bateman, Service Contract Section, New Aston House, Alma Street, Newton B19 2RL. The trustees meet four times a year to consider applications. Applications may take some considerable time to process. Immediate decisions on applications cannot be given.

Correspondent: The Administrator, Level 4, Louisa Ryland House, 44 Newhall Street, Birmingham B3 3PL.

Other information: The trust was established from proceeds of the sale of Icknield, a property donated to the city by Harriet Louisa Loxton for use as a home for older people.

The Robert Stevens Charity

Eligibility: Individuals and families in need where statutory help is not available and who live in the ecclesiastical parish of St Mary's, Moseley and 'other districts of Birmingham'.

Types of grants: One-off grants of £30 to £100, averaging about £40. Grants have been given towards winter clothing, decorating materials, new cookers and fridges and holidays for needy families.

Annual grant total: In 2000/01 the charity had an income of £1,700, almost all of which was distributed in relief-in-need grants.

Applications: On a form available from the correspondent, usually on referral by social services and other national or local organisations. Applications are considered in March, June, September and December.

Correspondent: Mrs L J Bullock, 59 Elmfield Crescent, Moseley, Birmingham B13 9TL (0121 449 3571; e-mail: lorraine_bullock@hotmail.com).

The Yardley Great Trust

Eligibility: People living in the ancient parish of Yardley in the city of Birmingham. This includes the wards of Yardley, Acocks Green, Fox Hollies, Billesley, Hall Green and part of the wards of Hodge Hill, Shard End, Sheldon, Small Heath, Sparkhill, Moseley, Sparkbrook and Brandwood. (A map is produced by the trust outlining the beneficial area.)

Types of grants: One-off grants of a minimum of £50. Recent donations have been given towards: washing machines, fridges, cookers, clothing, beds and bedding and household furniture. No grants are given for educational needs or for items that should be met by local authorities, health authorities or social sevices.

Annual grant total: In 2001 the trust had assets of about £5.4 million and an income of around £1.7 million. The trust had a total expenditure of £1.7 million, of which £72,000 was given in relief-in-need grants to individuals.

Applications: On a form available from the correspondent. Applications should be submitted through a social worker, citizen's advice bureau or other welfare agency. They are considered on the second Tuesday of each month.

Correspondent: Mrs V K Slayter, Clerk to the Trustees, Old Brookside, Yardley Fields Road, Stechford, Birmingham B33 8QL (0121 784 7889; Fax: 0121 785 1386; e-mail: enquiries@yardley-great-trust.org.uk).

Bushbury

The Bushbury United Charities

Eligibility: People in need living in the ancient parish of Bushbury.

Types of grants: Annual grants paid at Christmas.

Annual grant total: In 2000 the charities had an income of £8,200 and a total expenditure of £8,000.

Applications: The charities stated in July 2002 that funds were fully committed.

Correspondent: Mr Hilton, Dallow & Dallow, 23 Waterloo Road, Wolverhampton, West Midlands WV1 4TJ (01902 420208).

Castle Bromwich

The Dame Mary Bridgeman Charity

Eligibility: People in need living in the ecclesiastical parishes of St Mary and St Margaret, and St Clement, Castle Bromwich.

Types of grants: One-off grants have in the past been used to meet the cost of heating bills or respite care.

Grants are not given if they will affect any statutory benefits.

Annual grant total: In 2000/01 the charity had an income of £1,000 and a total expenditure of £1,100. The grant total has varied between £50 and £1,000 in recent years.

Applications: In writing to the correspondent, directly by the individual or through a social worker, welfare agency or other third party such as a parent, partner or relative. Applications should include the applicant's income and expenditure. They are considered mainly in May and November.

Correspondent: P B Jackson, Secretary, 147 Chester Road, Castle Bromwich, Birmingham B36 0AE (0121 747 2498).

Coventry

The Children's Boot Fund

Eligibility: Schoolchildren in the city of Coventry, aged 4 to 16.

Types of grants: Grants for school footwear for children in need. No other type of help is given. Grants are made direct to footwear suppliers in the form of vouchers.

Annual grant total: In 2000/01 the fund made grants totalling £12,000.

Applications: On a form available from schools. Referrals are made by local schools to the executive committee which meets three or four times a year. Application forms are available from schools in the area. Applications are considered in September, December, March and May, or as the need arises.

Correspondent: P R H Hancock, Hon. Secretary, 19 Priorsfield Road, Kenilworth CV8 1DA (01926 854818).

The Coventry Nursing Trust

Eligibility: People in need living in and who have been patients in the city of Coventry.

Types of grants: Grants for the relief of sickness are mainly given to help with night sitting costs, although day sitting is also provided for. A large proportion of the grant total is also given towards convalescence recommended by a doctor or social worker and may occasionally include the cost of the patient's travel to and from the convalescent home. Help with day-to-day expenses is not given.

Annual grant total: In previous years £17,000 has been given in grants; £12,000 towards sitting costs and £5,000 towards convalescent care.

Applications: In writing to the correspondent. For grants towards convalescent care applications can only be made by a social worker on a form available from the trust and payments are made directly to convalescent homes.

Correspondent: Mrs E A Martin, Clerk, 44 Madeira Croft, Chapelfields, Coventry CV5 8NY.

Other information: This entry was not confirmed by the trust, but the address was correct according to the Charity Commission.

The Dunsmoor Charity

Eligibility: Expectant mothers, mothers with babies under one year old, and children under 16 who live in Coventry.

Types of grants: One-off grants ranging from £50 to £250 for baby equipment, beds, bedding, pushchairs, maternity clothes and children's clothes and other family necessities etc. No repeat grants within 12 months and no payments towards debts.

Annual grant total: In 1999 the trust had assets of £125,000 and an income of £6,700. 64 grants to individuals totalled £4,500.

Applications: On a form available from the correspondent, thorough a social worker, health visitor or other welfare agency. Applications, which should include the family's financial details, are considered in January, April, June and September (and at other times if funds are available).

Correspondent: The Chair, Church Office, 10 Warwick Row, Coventry CV1 1EX.

The General Charities of the City of Coventry

Eligibility: People in need living in the city of Coventry.

Types of grants: One-off and recurrent grants, but not cash grants, towards e.g. gas bills, washing machines, carpets or clothing. Freemen of the city of Coventry can be given interest-free loans up to a maximum of £300. Recurrent grants of £39 a quarter can be given to a maximum of 650 pensioners.

Annual grant total: In 1997 the charities had assets of £4.9 million and an income of £1.7 million. Out of a total expenditure of £294,000 the sum of £76,000 was distributed in 289 relief-in-need grants to individuals and £88,000 was given in 570 gifts to pensioners. A further £24,000 was given for relief-in-need purposes to three organisations. Up-to-date information was not available.

Applications: Applications should be made through social workers, probation officers, citizen's advice bureaux or other welfare agencies.

Correspondent: The Clerk, Old Bablake, Hill Street, Coventry CV1 4AN.

Other information: The charities receive income from Sir Thomas White's Charity including the allocation for the Sir Thomas White's Loan Fund in Coventry.

This entry was not confirmed by the charities but was correct according to information on file at the Charity Commission.

The Dr William MacDonald of Johannesburg Trust

Eligibility: People in need who live in Coventry. Preference is given to under 18 year olds.

Types of grants: One-off welfare grants, typically about £50, usual maximum £200. No educational grants or grants for the relief of debt.

Annual grant total: About £2,000.

Applications: In writing to the Lord Mayor. Applications can be submitted directly by the individual and are usually considered within two weeks.

Correspondent: The Lord Mayor's Secretariat, Lord Mayor's Office, Council House, Earl Street, Coventry CV1 5RR (024 7683 3100; Fax: 024 7683 3078).

The Charity of John Moore

Eligibility: People in need, generally older people, living in the city of Coventry.

Types of grants: Grants of up to £20 given in December.

Annual grant total: About £2,500 a year.

Applications: The charity has five trustees, each of whom selects 25 recipients either directly or through local churches.

Correspondent: C Adams, Assistant Secretary, Sarginsons, 10 The Quadrant, Coventry CV1 2EL (024 7655 3181).

The Samuel Smith Charity, Coventry

Eligibility: People in need who live in Coventry and the ancient parish of Bedworth.

Types of grants: Pensions and one-off grants.

Annual grant total: In 2001 grants to individuals totalled £44,000.

Applications: Applications can be made in writing to the correspondent, but most beneficiaries are referred by the charity's almoner.

Correspondent: Mrs E A Martin, Clerk, 44 Madeira Croft, Chapelfields, Coventry CV5 8NY.

Spencer's Charity

Eligibility: Older ladies in need living in the city of Coventry.

Types of grants: Pensions of £10 a month.

Annual grant total: About £20,000 to between 160 and 170 beneficiaries.

Applications: In writing to the correspondent.

Correspondent: G T W Foottit, Mander Hadley & Co. Solicitors, 1 The Quadrant, Coventry CV1 2DW.

The Tile Hill & Westwood Charities for the Needy Sick

Eligibility: People who are both sick and in need and live in the parish of Westwood and parts of the parish of Berkswell, Kenilworth and Stoneleigh and elsewhere within a three and a half mile radius of 93 Cromwell Lane, Coventry.

Types of grants: One-off grants according to need.

Annual grant total: Around £15,000 per year.

Applications: In writing to the correspondent.

Midlands – West Midlands

Correspondent: J C Ruddick, Clerk, 444 Westwood Heath Road, Coventry CV4 8AA (024 7653 1532; Fax: 024 7630 1300).

The Harry Weston Memorial Fund

Eligibility: Pensioners living in the city of Coventry.

Types of grants: Contribution to the cost of television licences and rental for black and white television sets. The fund can provide the equivalent towards colour licences. Grants range from £30 to £35 and are recurrent.

Annual grant total: In 2001 the fund had an income of £3,900 and a total expenditure of £1,300.

Applications: In writing to Osborne Clewett Partnership, 8 Eaton Road, Coventry CV1 2FJ either directly by the individual, or through a third party such as a social worker, citizen's advice bureau, other welfare agency such as Age Concern Coventry or a relative or a neighbour. Applications must include information on the applicants age, circumstances and date of TV licence renewal if relevant.

Correspondent: G C D Osborne, Secretary, 4 Styvechale Avenue, Coventry CV5 6DX (024 7671 3942; Fax: 024 7655 5309).

Dudley

The Baron Davenport Emergency Grant

Eligibility: Widows, spinsters, divorcees (aged 50 years or over) or women who have been abandoned by their partners; also the children of these women, aged under 25, who live in Dudley.

Applicants must have been resident in the West Midlands for about 10–15 years, be living alone (except where school age children are living with their mother) and have a bank, building society or Post Office account. The total income of the household should be no more than £134 a week; this figure changes in line with state benefits.

Types of grants: One-off emergency grants of £100 to £350. pensions of £90 or £110 are made at each half-yearly distribution.

Annual grant total: About £1,000.

Applications: On a form available from the correspondent. Applications are usually made through a social worker or a citizen's advice bureau, but they can be made directly by the individual and are considered at any time. Distributions take place at the end of May and the end of November.

Correspondent: Mrs G C Cooper, General Secretary, Dudley Council for Voluntary Service, 7 Albion Street, Brierly Hill, West Midlands DY5 3EE (01384 78166 or 01384 573381).

Other information: For information on Baron Davenport's Charity Trust, see entry in the Midlands general section.

The Reginald Unwin Dudley Charity

Eligibility: Mainly elderly and chronically sick people in need who live in the area administered by Dudley Metropolitan Council.

Types of grants: Grants for emergency needs ranging from £30 to £500.

Annual grant total: In 2000/01 the trust's income was £4,200 all of which was given in grants.

Applications: On a form available on written request from the correspondent.

Correspondent: R J Little, 27 Priory Close, Dudley, West Midlands DY1 3ED (01384 256006; e-mail: regjohn@ic24.net).

Mr Thomas Griffiths and Miss Rebecca Griffiths Charity

Eligibility: People in need who live in the parish of St Thomas and St Luke (in Dudley). Applicants must be in receipt of some kind of state benefit, such as unemployment benefit, 100% housing benefit, and so on.

Types of grants: Clothing vouchers are donated (in 2001 they were of the value of £50 each).

Annual grant total: In 2000 the trust had an income of £760 and an expenditure of £180. About £750 is available each year to distribute in the form of vouchers.

Applications: In the first instance contact the trust requesting an application form. Applications must include evidence that the individual is in receipt of benefits. They are usually considered in the autumn.

Correspondent: Janet Fulljames, The Vicarage, King Street, Dudley, West Midlands DY2 8QB (01384 252015; e-mail: janet@fullj.freeserve.co.uk).

Sandwell

The Fordath Foundation

Eligibility: People in need living in the borough of Sandwell.

Types of grants: Usually about 50 one-off grants ranging from £50 to £200 to cover a wide range of needs including holidays, funeral expenses, furniture, heating bills, essential clothing and equipment.

Annual grant total: The trust had assets of £64,000 and an income of £6,500 in 1998. All income is dispensed as grants.

Applications: Applications are usually made through Sandwell Social Services. They are considered throughout the year, funds permitting.

Correspondent: J Sutcliffe, 33 Thornyfields Lane, Stafford ST17 9YS.

The Mayor's General Fund

Eligibility: People in need living in the area covered by Sandwell Metropolitan Borough Council.

Types of grants: Generally small grants (usually about £25, but up to £100) to help with one-off financial needs (e.g. clothing and fuel bills).

Annual grant total: Around £2,500 a year.

Applications: In writing to the correspondent through a social worker, citizen's advice bureau or other welfare agency. Applications are considered at any time.

Correspondent: The Mayor, Mayor's Parlour, Sandwell Council House, PO Box 2374, Oldbury, Sandwell, West Midlands B69 3DE (0121 569 3041; Fax: 0121 569 3050).

The George & Thomas Henry Salter Trust

Eligibility: People in need living in the borough of Sandwell.

Types of grants: One-off grants of £50 to £1,000 towards clothing and household equipment. No grants are given for the repayment of debt, individual holidays, items of capital expenditure, childcare or nursery costs.

Annual grant total: In 2001 the trust had assets of £1.4 million and an income of £59,000. Welfare grants to individuals totalled £5,200.

Applications: On a form available from the correspondent, to be submitted through a social worker, citizen's advice bureau or other welfare agency. Applications are considered in February, April, June, September, November and December.

Correspondent: Mrs J S Styler, Clerk, Lombard House, Cronehills Linkway, West Bromwich B70 7PL (0121 553 3286; Fax: 0121 500 5204).

Other information: Grants are also given for educational purposes and to organisations.

Solihull

The Baron Davenport Emergency Grant

Eligibility: Women who are widowed, single or divorced over 55 years old and are living alone, and their children who are under 25. In special cases, where a woman has been abandoned by her partner, the applicant and her child would be eligible regardless of age. Please note, applicants must live in Solihull and have lived in the West Midlands for at least ten years.

Types of grants: One-off emergency grants.
Annual grant total: About £2,000.
Applications: Applications can only be made through voluntary and statutory organisations in the borough of Solihull.
Correspondent: Andrew Moore, Director, Solihull Council for Voluntary Service, Church Hill Road, Solihull, West Midlands B91 3LF (0121 704 1619).
Other information: For information on Baron Davenport's Charity Trust, see entry in the Midlands general section.

Stourbridge

The Palmer & Seabright Charity

Eligibility: Elderly people in need living in the parish of Stourbridge.
Types of grants: Weekly grants are made. Educational grants can also be given.
Annual grant total: In 2000 the trust had an income of £47,000 and a total expenditure of £33,000.
Applications: In writing to the correspondent.
Correspondent: Roger Kendrick, Wall James & Davis, 15–23 Hagley Road, Stourbridge, West Midlands DY8 1QW (01384 371622; Fax: 01384 374057).

The Stourbridge Relief in Sickness Charity

Eligibility: People in need who are sick, convalescent, disabled or infirm and live in the Stourbridge District, Dudley.
Types of grants: Providing or paying for items, services or facilities which will alleviate the suffering or assist the recovery of such people where funds are not available from any other source. Grants may be given towards holidays, clothing, heating, adaptation to home and so on.
Annual grant total: About £400 is given each year.
Applications: In writing to the correspondent stating a brief outline of the case, confirmation of financial circumstances, reason for the request and what other avenues have been followed. Applicants should be referred by a caring agency and applications should be submitted through a social worker, citizen's advice bureau or other welfare agency.
Correspondent: Peter Pinfield, Secretary & Treasurer, Stourbridge Social Services, Wollescote Hall, Wollescote Road, Stourbridge DY9 7JG (01384 813150; Fax: 01384 813151).

Sutton Coldfield

The Sutton Coldfield Municipal Charities – General Charity

Eligibility: People in need living in the Four Oaks, New Hall and Vesey wards of Sutton Coldfield. Applicants need to have lived in the area of benefit for at least five years (except for school clothing, where this time limit does not apply).
Types of grants: One-off grants are given to individuals in the range of £100 and £1,500. Grants to individuals are given for special needs e.g. wheelchairs, school clothing etc. and essential household equipment e.g. carpets, washing machine, cooker etc.

Grants are not given to people in receipt of benefits from other sources, for example social services, family, DHSS etc.
Annual grant total: In 2000/01 the charity had assets of £27.4 million and an income of £1.3 million. Total expenditure was £1.1 million with 48 relief-in-need grants totalling £25,000.
Applications: On a form available from the correspondent. Applications should be made directly by the individual or through a parent or carer. They are considered every month, except April, August and December. Telephone enquiries are welcomed.
Correspondent: Andrew Macfarlane, Lingard House, Fox Hollies Road, Sutton Coldfield, West Midlands B76 2RJ (0121 351 2262; Fax: 0121 313 0651).
Other information: The principal objective of the charities is the provision of almshouses, the distribution of funds and other measures for the alleviation of poverty and other needs for inhabitants and other organisations within the boundaries of the former borough of Sutton Coldfield.

Tettenhall

The Tettenhall Relief-in-Need & Educational Charity

Eligibility: People in need living in the parish of Tettenhall as constituted on 22 June 1888.
Types of grants: Grants are given mainly for clothing and food and range from £25 to £50.
Annual grant total: In 2000/01 the trust had assets of £69,000, an income of £2,400 and its total expenditure was £2,400. Grants to individuals in need totalled £1,500.
Applications: In writing to the correspondent. Applications should be made through a social worker, citizen's advice bureau or other welfare agency, doctor or senior citizen's organisation. They should be submitted in October for consideration in November.
Correspondent: K J Gollings, 10 Greenacres, Tettenhall, Wolverhampton WV6 8SR (01902 744304).

Walsall

The Baron Davenport Emergency Grant

Eligibility: Needy widows, spinsters, divorcees and children under 21 whose fathers have died and who live in the borough of Walsall area and district.
Types of grants: One-off emergency grants ranging from £10 to £100. Grants have been given towards heating bills, minor urgent repairs to property (especially where safety is a factor), bedding, winter clothes and other essential items.

The trust's aims are to 'alleviate hardship, with special concern for basic necessities, health and education'.
Annual grant total: About £2,000 a year.
Applications: On a form available from the correspondent. Applications are considered in January, March, May, July, September and December. Applications should also include details of social background and hardship or reduced circumstances (in particular following illness).
Correspondent: K Buckler, Chief Officer, Age Concern Walsall (Walsall Guild for Voluntary Service), 50 Lower Hall Lane, Walsall WS1 1RJ (01922 638825; Fax: 01922 615713).
Other information: For information on Baron Davenport's Charity Trust, see entry in the Midlands general section.

Willenhall Area Relief, Rehabilitation & Nursing Trust (WARRANT)

Eligibility: People in need who live in the metropolitan borough of Walsall and former urban district of Willenhall.
Types of grants: One-off grants for the provision of equipment to alleviate need, such as nebulisers, and for disability educational aids.
Annual grant total: In 1999 the trust had assets of £1.4 million and an income of £43,000. It spent £22,000, of which £2,000 was given in two grants to individuals.
Applications: In writing to the correspondent. Applications are considered in April and October and must include details as to whether funding is available from any other source e.g. public funds. Applications can be submitted through a social worker, citizen's advice bureau or other welfare agency, through another third party or directly by the

individual with the support of one of the above.

Correspondent: John Laidlaw Ward, Clerk, 1 New Road, Willenhall, West Midlands WV13 2AH (01902 366571).

The Blanch Woolaston Walsall Charity

Eligibility: People in need living in the borough of Walsall. Educational grants will only be given to those under 21 years of age. There is no age limit for relief-in-need grants.

Types of grants: Small one-off grants. No grants towards the payment of rates, taxes or other public funds (including gas, electricity and so on). The trustees cannot undertake to repeat/renew any grants.

Annual grant total: Around £1,000 each year.

Applications: On a form available from the correspondent. Applications are considered four times a year.

Correspondent: Clerk to the Trustees, Constitutional Services, Walsall Metropolitan Borough Council, Civic Centre, Darwall Street, Walsall WS1 1TP (01922 650000; Fax: 01922 720885).

Wednesfield

The Wednesfield Parochial Charity

Eligibility: People in need living in the team parish of Wednesfield. The connection with the parish must be a current one.

Types of grants: One-off or recurrent grants ranging from £15 to £40. The charity also gave £800 to various welfare organisations and also provides pastoral care (e.g. bereavement counselling).

Annual grant total: In 2001 the trust had an income of £2,400 and a total expenditure of £940.

Applications: In writing to the correspondent either directly by the individual or through a social worker, citizen's advice bureau, other welfare agency or other third party. Applicants must also include full details of their need.

Correspondent: Revd John Points, Wednesfield Rectory, 9 Vicarage Road, Wednesfield, Wolverhampton WV11 1SB (01902 731462).

West Bromwich

The Charity of Jane Patricia Eccles

Eligibility: Elderly women in need, living within the old West Bromwich boundary.

Types of grants: Generally one-off grants to meet specific needs e.g. phone installation, showers and braille reader machines for the blind.

Annual grant total: In 1999/2000 the trust had an income of £640 and a total expenditure of £290.

Applications: In writing to the correspondent for consideration in December. Applications must be made through, and include, a letter of support from a doctor, church minister or welfare agency.

Correspondent: Mrs Ann Nicholls, Orchard House, Wyken, Bridgnorth, Shropshire WV15 5NN.

Wolverhampton

The Greenway Benefaction Trust

Eligibility: Children in need living in the Bradley area of the city of Wolverhampton.

Types of grants: One-off grants towards the cost of holidays, convalescence, toys, entertainment and so on.

Annual grant total: In 2001/02 the trust had assets of £21,000 and an income of £900. Due to a lack of applications, no grants have been given.

Applications: Applications should be sent to: The Members of the Council, Wolverhampton City Council, Civic Centre, St Peter's Square, Wolverhampton WV1 1RL. They can be submitted either by the individual or a relevant third party for example a parent, social worker, citizen's advice bureau or other welfare agency. They are considered as received.

Correspondent: Mr G Entwistle, Finance and Physical Resources, Wolverhampton City Council, Civic Centre, St Peter's Square, Wolverhampton WV1 1RL (01902 554432; Fax: 01902 554437).

The Power Pleas Trust

Eligibility: Mainly young people, under 18 years, with muscular dystrophy and similar diseases living in the borough of Wolverhampton.

Types of grants: Grants are given primarily towards the purchase and provision of outdoor electric powered wheelchairs and other aids.

Annual grant total: In 2000/01 the trust had an income of £16,000 and a total expenditure of £17,000. £6,000 was given in grants to individuals.

Applications: In writing to the correspondent directly by the individual.

Correspondent: Mrs Valerie Rendell, Secretary, 14 Foley Avenue, Wolverhampton WV6 8NL (01902 754868).

The Wolverhampton Trust Fund

Eligibility: People in financial or physical need in the borough of Wolverhampton, and for educational purposes.

Types of grants: One-off and recurrent grants according to need.

Annual grant total: In 2000/01 the trust had an income of £2,700 and a total expenditure of £2,200.

Applications: In writing to the correspondent via a social worker, school or other welfare agency.

Correspondent: Mrs R Jones, Mayor's Office, Civic Centre, St Peters Square, Wolverhampton WV1 1RR (01902 554090).

Other information: This fund has lots of funds within it; applying to one fund is an application to all the funds.

Worcestershire

The Astley and Areley Kings Sick Fund

Eligibility: People who are disabled who live in the parishes of St Peter Astley, St Bartholomew Areley Kings, St Michael & All Angels Stourport-on-Severn and All Saints Wilden.

Types of grants: One-off grants are made towards specialist equipment for home-care, disabled facilities and additional home support.

Annual grant total: In 2000/01 the trust had assets of £20,000, an income of £1,900 and a total expenditure of £78. No grants were made to individuals in this year.

Applications: In writing to the correspondent. Applications can be submitted either directly by the individual, or through a social worker, citizen's advice bureau or another third party. Trustees meet regularly throughout the year.

Correspondent: Revd A Vessey, The Rectory, Rectory Lane, Areley Kings, Stourport-on-Severn, Worcestershire DY13 0TB (Tel & Fax: 01299 822868).

Other information: Grants are occasionally made to local organisations (£78 in total in 2000/01).

The Baron Davenport Emergency Fund

Eligibility: Divorcees over 55, young spinsters/women abandoned by their partners, fatherless children under 25 and widows who live in the Malvern Hills district. Beneficiaries must have an income of less than £129 per week and savings of less than £3,000,

Types of grants: One-off grants (£100 to £250) for emergencies only. Grants have been given towards telephone debt, removal expenses and a recuperative holiday.

Annual grant total: In 2001/02 the sum of £420 was given in grants.

Applications: On a form available from the correspondent. Applications can be made through a social worker, citizen's advice bureau or other other welfare agency, or directly by the individual. or other welfare agency. They are considered in January, April, July and October, or at other times in emergencies.

Correspondent: The Coordinator, Community Action Malvern District, 28-30 Belle Vue Terrace, Worcestershire WR14 4PZ (01684 580638; Fax: 01684 575155; e-mail: comact@malvernca.solis.co.uk).

Other information: For information on Baron Davenport's Charity Trust, see entry in the Midlands general section.

Pershore United Charity

Eligibility: People in need who live in private or rented dwellings (not residential or nursing homes) in the parishes of Pershore and Pensham. Priority to older and needy people who have lived in the town for several years.

Types of grants: Recurrent and occasional one-off grants to help with heating costs at Christmas. In 1999/2000 the award was £30.

Annual grant total: In 2000/01 the charity had an income of £4,100. Each year about £3,000 is given in grants to over 100 individuals.

Applications: In writing to the correspondent. Applications are considered in October.

Correspondent: Ken Myers, Town Council Offices, Belle House, 5a Bridge Street, Pershore, Worcestershire WR10 1AJ (01386 561561; Fax: 01386 561996).

The Ancient Parish of Ripple Trust

Eligibility: People in need living in the parishes of Ripple, Holdfast, Queenhill and Bushley.

Types of grants: Small one-off cash grants are made. Ongoing Christmas grants can also be made to older people.

Annual grant total: In 1999/2000 the trust had an income of £16,000. A total of £2,500 was given to individuals in need and £1,000 to students in higher education. A further £100 was given at the discretion of the rector of the parish.

Applications: In writing to the correspondent. Grants are considered at any time of year.

Correspondent: John Willis, Secretary, 7 Court Lea, Holly Green, Upton upon Severn, Worcestershire WR8 0PE.

Other information: Grants are also made to registered charities that serve local people.

The Worcestershire Cancer Aid Committee

Eligibility: People with cancer who live in the old county of Worcestershire.

Types of grants: Assisting cancer patients in financial distress with home nursing, transport to hospital, specialist equipment and so on.

Annual grant total: In 2000/01 the trust had assets of £32,000 and an income of £8,600. A total of 200 relief-in-need grants were made totalling £11,000.

Applications: In writing to the correspondent only through a third party such as a social worker, citizen's advice bureau, other welfare agency or a doctor or district nurse. Applications are considered within one week.

Correspondent: Anthony T Atkinson, c/o Kennel Ground, Gilberts End, Hanley Castle, Worcestershire WR8 0AJ (01684 310408).

Cropthorpe

Randolph Meakins Patty's Farm & the Widows Lyes Charity

Eligibility: People in need who live in the village of Cropthorne (Worcestershire).

Types of grants: As well as general welfare grants, Christmas parcels are also given.

Annual grant total: In 1998/99 the trust had assets of £63,000 generating an income of £4,900. Grants to individuals and organisations totalled £3,800.

Applications: In writing to the correspondent.

Correspondent: G Cropper, Chair, Corner Bungalow, Blacksmith Lane, Cropthorne, Worcester WR10 3LX.

Evesham

John Martin's Charity

Eligibility: People in need living in the town of Evesham. There is a limited scope and special criteria for people living just outside Evesham.

Types of grants: Grants to individuals and organisations, to further religious activities and for the relief of poverty. Recent grants include allowances to pensioners, general relief-in-need grants, emergency relief-in-need grants and relief-in-need grants in cash, food vouchers or the supply of goods or payment for services. Grants are one-off and range from £10 to £100.

No grants towards nursing home fees, or for businesses or rates and taxes.

Annual grant total: In 2001/02 the trust had assets of £17 million and an income of £700,000. Expenses totalled £78,000 and grants totalled £571,000. About £67,000 was given in about 600 relief-in-need grants.

Applications: On a form available from the correspondent, on written or personal request. Applications can be submitted directly by the individual or through a social worker, citizen's advice bureau or other welfare agency. They are considered twice monthly.

Correspondent: The Clerk, 16 Queen's Road, Evesham, Worcester WR11 4JP (01386 765440; Fax: 01386 765340).

Kidderminster

The Kidderminster Aid In Sickness Fund

Eligibility: People who are sick and poor and live in the borough of Kidderminster.

Types of grants: One-off grants towards fuel expenses, equipment, furniture, beds, bedding and so on.

Annual grant total: In 2000 the fund had an income and total expenditure of £13,000. On average, under £10,000 is given each year.

Applications: In writing to the correspondent. Applications can be considered at any time.

Correspondent: F P G Hill, 19 York Street, Stourport on Severn, Worcester DY13 9EH (01299 827827; Fax: 01299 827012).

Worcester

Armchair

Eligibility: People in need who live in Worcester.

Types of grants: The charity provides recycled second hand furniture, crockery and cutlery rather than cash. Electrical goods and bedding are not given nor are cash grants made.

Annual grant total: In 2001/02 the trust had cash assets of £20,000, an income of £20,000 and its total expenditure was £27,000.

Applications: Applications should be submitted through a social worker, citizen's advice bureau or other welfare agency, they are considered all year round.

Correspondent: Paul Griffiths, (Tel & Fax 01905 456080).

Other information: The trust owns its own warehouse and van and employs two part-time staff.

The Mary Hill Trust

Eligibility: People in need who live within the boundaries of the city of Worcester.

Types of grants: One-off grants in the range of £50 to £400.

Annual grant total: In 2001 the trust had assets of £75,000, an income of £7,400 and a total expenditure of £12,000. A total of £3,100 was given in grants to 14 individuals. Further grants were given to organisations.

Applications: In writing to the correspondent either through a third party such as a social worker, citizen's advice bureau or other welfare agency, or directly by the individual. Applications should include as much information as possible as to why the grant is needed, current financial position, income/expenditure and so on.

Correspondent: A G Duncan, Clerk, 16 The Tything, Worcester WR1 1HD (01905 731731).

The Charity known as The Mayors Fund

Eligibility: People in need who live within the Worcester city boundary.

Types of grants: Usually one-off grants of between £30 and £100 for things such as: school books and clothing, single beds, carpets, decorating materials, pushchairs, spectacles, washing machines and vacuum cleaners.

No support for course fees for students.

Annual grant total: In 2001/02 the trust had assets of £34,000 and an income of £1,800. It gave around 30 grants to individuals totalling £1,500.

Applications: Applications can be submitted by the individual, or through a third party such as a social worker, citizen's advice bureau or other welfare agency. Applications should be on a form available from the correspondent for consideration in March, June, September and December.

Correspondent: Stephen Taylor, Clerk, The Guildhall, Worcester WR1 2EY (01905 723471; Minicom: 01905 722516; e-mail: staylor@cityofworcester.gov.uk).

The Shewringe's Hospital & Robert Goulding's Charities

Eligibility: People in need who live in the city of Worcester.

Types of grants: One-off and recurrent grants according to need.

Annual grant total: In 2000 the charity had an income of £11,000 and a total expenditure of £10,000.

Applications: In writing to the correspondent by mid-February.

Correspondent: Mr Mullins, Clerk, 8 Sansome Walk, Worcester WR1 1LW (01905 723561; Fax: 01905 723812; e-mail: pmullins@marchedwards.co.uk).

Other information: It has been the policy of this charity to make donations only in the form of vouchers. In spring 2002, when this guide was being researched, they were unsure if this was going to continue.

The Henry Smith Charity

Eligibility: People in need who live in the ecclesiastical parish of St John-in-Bedwardine. Priority is usually given to people who are older or in need and have lived in the parish for several years.

Types of grants: Recurrent and occasional one-off grants ranging from £20 upwards, such as towards fuel, medical care and equipment, clothing and food.

Annual grant total: In 2001 the trust had an income of £910, all of which was given in over 30 relief-in-need grants to individuals.

Applications: In writing to the correspondent to be submitted by October/November for consideration in December. Applications can be submitted through a social worker, citizen's advice bureau or other welfare agency, or directly by the individual.

Correspondent: The Vicar, The Parish Office, 1a Bromyard Road, Worcester WR2 5BS (01905 420490; Fax: 01905 425569; e-mail: vicar@stjohn34.freeserve.co.uk).

The United Charity of Saint Martin

Eligibility: People in need who live in the parish of St Martin, Worcester.

Types of grants: One-off grants and pensions, according to need.

Annual grant total: About £3,000 a year.

Applications: Contact the rector of the church at St Martin.

Correspondent: Keith Johnson, 1 Stuart Rise, Worcester WR5 2QQ.

The Henry & James Willis Trust

Eligibility: People who are convalescing and live within the city boundary limits of the city of Worcester.

Types of grants: One-off grants of an average of £250 a week for up to six weeks at the seaside or a health resort. Travel costs and accommodation are included and in special cases the cost of a carer. Patients are asked for a £25 per week contribution.

Annual grant total: About £5,000 a year.

Applications: On a form obtainable from: The Red Cross, Greenhill, London Road, Worcester. Applications can be submitted directly by the individual, through a social worker, citizen's advice bureau or other welfare agency. They are considered throughout the year and should include a medical certificate.

Correspondent: John Wagstaff, Clerk, 4 Norton Close, Worcester WR5 3EY (01905 355659).

The Worcester Consolidated Municipal Charity

Eligibility: People in need who live in the city of Worcester.

Types of grants: One-off grants of £20 to £1,000, principally towards electrical goods, carpets, household items, clothing and so on.

Annual grant total: In 2001 the charity had assets of £7.1 million and an income of £537,000. Out of a total expenditure of £415,000, £43,000 was given in 229 relief-in-need grants to individuals. Grants to organisations totalled £136,000.

Applications: Applications are usually through a social worker, citizen's advice bureau or other welfare agency. Statutory sources must have first been exhausted. Applications are submitted on a form available from the correspondent and are considered every month.

Correspondent: I C Pugh, Clerk to the Trustees, 4 & 5 Sansome Place, Worcester WR1 1UQ (01905 726600; Fax: 01905 613302; e-mail: icp@hallmarkslaw.co.uk).

7. SOUTH WEST

The Christina Aitchison Trust

See entry on page 175

Viscount Amory's Charitable Trust

Eligibility: People in need in the south west of England, with a preference for Devon (due to limited funds).

Types of grants: One-off and recurrent grants according to need.

Annual grant total: In 1999/2000 the trust had assets of £8.8 million and an income of £376,000. Grants to 29 individuals totalled £13,000, of which £1,300 was given for relief-in-need purposes, the rest was given for educational purposes. Grants to organisations totalled £442,000.

Applications: In writing to the correspondent, for consideration every month.

Correspondent: Ther Trust Secretary, The Island, Lowman Green, Tiverton, Devon EX16 4LA (01884 254899; Fax: 01884 255155).

Children's Leukaemia Society

See entry on page 165

The Duke of Cornwall's Benevolent Fund

Eligibility: People who are in need. In practice funds are steered towards the West Country and areas related to duchy lands, which are principally in Cornwall.

Types of grants: One-off and recurrent grants according to need.

Annual grant total: In 1999/2000 the trust had assets of £2.8 million and an income of £85,000. Grants to three individuals totalled £16,000. Grants to 158 organisations totalled £130,000.

Applications: In writing to the correspondent.

Correspondent: R G Mitchell, 10 Buckingham Gate, London SW1E 6LA (020 7834 7346).

The Haymills Charitable Trust

Eligibility: People in need in the UK, but particularly in the west of London and Suffolk, where the Haymills group is sited.

Types of grants: Welfare grants are made to those who are considered to be 'in necessitous circumstances' or who are otherwise distressed or disadvantaged. A small number of grants were also made to Haymills pensioners.

Annual grant total: In 1999/2000 the trust's assets stood at £2 million and the income was £132,000. Grants totalled £85,000 and were mostly made to organisations.

Applications: Trustees meet at least twice a year, usually in March and October. Applications are not acknowledged.

Correspondent: I W Ferres, Secretary, Wesley House, 1/7 Wesley Avenue, London NW10 7BZ (020 8951 9700).

Other information: This entry was not confirmed by the trust, but the address was correct according to the Charity Commission database.

The Douglas Martin Trust

See entry on page 303

The Pirate Trust

Eligibility: People in need living within the Pirate FM 102 broadcast area (Cornwall, Plymouth and west Devon). Preference is given to people with special needs.

Types of grants: One-off and recurrent grants according to need.

Annual grant total: In 1999/2000 it had an income of £22,000. Grants totalled £25,000, of which £6,000 went to individuals and the rest to organisations.

Applications: In writing to the correspondent at any time.

Correspondent: Jane Atken, Secretary, Pirate FM Ltd, Carn Brea Studios, Barncoose Industrial Estate, Redruth, Cornwall TR15 3XX.

The Plymouth & Cornwall Cancer Fund

Eligibility: People in need who have cancer, or who have a dependant or relative with cancer, and live in the county of Cornwall and within a radius of 40 miles of Plymouth Civic Centre in Devon, and in-patients or out-patients of any hospital controlled by Plymouth Hospital NHS Trust.

Types of grants: One-off grants to relieve hardship which is caused by cancer, for example, towards the cost of travel to hospital for patients and visitors, telephone bills or home alterations.

Annual grant total: In 1999/2000 the trust had an income of £80,000 and its total expenditure was £11,000. About £5,000 is given in hardship grants to individuals each year, with the rest given towards major research and building projects. (In 2001 for example, about £100,000 was given to Plymouth Hospital NHS Trust for a building.)

Applications: In writing to the correspondent.

Correspondent: D H Spencer, Hon. Secretary, Whiteford Crocker, 28 Outland Road, Plymouth PL2 3DE (01752 550711).

The Portishead Nautical Trust

Eligibility: Young people aged under 25 who are disadvantaged and live in Bristol and North Somerset.

Types of grants: One-off grants ranging from £50 to £750.

Annual grant total: In 20001/02 the trust had an income of £75,000 and its total expenditure was £77,000. Grants to organisations totalled £58,000 and 20 grants were made to individuals totalling £6,800.

Applications: On a form available from the correspondent. Applications are considered at quarterly meetings: the dates vary each year. Applications should be submitted through a third party such as a social worker, citizen's advice bureau or a professional healthcare/resettlement worker.

Correspondent: P C Dingley-Brown, Secretary, 108 High Street, Portishead, Bristol BS20 6AJ.

Other information: Grants are also made to organisations that provide services for young people who have physical disability, emotional problems, educational needs, family breakdown or behavioural problems.

The Christine Woodmancy Charitable Foundation

Eligibility: Children and young people up to the age of 21, who live in the Plymouth area and are in need.

Types of grants: One-off grants according to need, usually ranging between £50 and £2,500. Grants can be for special equipment to people in need and people who are disabled, or for 'enterprising' events such as the tall ships race. No grants for holidays.

Annual grant total: In 2000/01 the trust had assets of £316,000 and its income was £16,000. Total expenditure was £15,000, made for welfare and educational purposes.

Applications: In writing to the correspondent, directly by the individual or via a social worker or citizen's advice bureau, and so on. Applications should include background information and provide evidence of financial need.

Correspondent: Vicky Bligh, Foot Anstey Sargent Solicitors, Foot & Bowden Building, 21 Derry's Cross, Plymouth, Devon PL1 2SW (01752 675000; Fax: 01752 671802; e-mail: vicky.bligh@foot-ansteys.co.uk).

Other information: Schools, hospitals and charities that benefit children are also supported.

Avon

Avon Local Medical Committee Benevolent Fund

Eligibility: Medical practitioners who are practising or have practised in the former county of Avon, and his or her dependants who are in need.

Types of grants: One-off and recurrent grants according to need.

Annual grant total: In 2000/01 the trust's income was £9,200 and its total expenditure was £9,600.

Applications: In writing to the correspondent.

Correspondent: Dr J C D Rawlins, Acacia House, Chew Magna, Bristol BS40 8PW (01275 332344).

Other information: This entry was not confirmed by the trust, but the information was correct according to the Charity Commission database.

Avon & Somerset Constabulary Benevolent Fund

Eligibility: Mainly serving and retired members of the Avon & Somerset Constabulary. Their dependants may also be supported.

Types of grants: One-off grants for equipment and house repairs; interest free loans to cover debts or other urgent needs.

No grants for private medical treatment, legal representation or private education.

Annual grant total: In 2001/02 the trust's assets totalling £636,000 and its income was £56,000. Grants to individuals totalled £33,000.

Applications: Applications must be submitted with a report and recommendation by a force welfare officer. They can be considered at any time.

Correspondent: P Roberts, Force Counselling & Welfare Officer, Avon & Somerset Constabulary Headquarters, Valley Road, Portishead, Bristol BS20 8QJ (01275 818181).

Bath Dispensary Charity

Eligibility: People who are sick and in need who live in or very near Bath.

Types of grants: One-off grants only, generally not for more than £750, usually towards medical equipment, but other requests are considered.

Annual grant total: About £7,300 in 2001.

Applications: On a form available from the correspondent. Applications should be made either by the individual or through a social worker, citizen's advice bureau or other welfare agency, most of which have copies of the application form. The Almoner may visit an applicant at home and meets with trustees, allocated to deal with cases weekly to decide awards.

Correspondent: Mrs C Bayntun-Coward, Almoner, Bath Municipal Charity, 4 Chapel Court, Bath BA1 1SL (01225 486413).

The John & Celia Bonham Christie Charitable Trust

Eligibility: People in need in the former county of Avon.

Types of grants: One-off and recurrent grants according to need.

Annual grant total: In 2000/01 the trust had an income of £37,000 and its total expenditure was £70,000. Further information was not available for this year. In 1996/97 grants to four individuals totalled £1,500 and organisations received £37,000 in total.

Applications: In writing to the correspondent.

Correspondent: P R Fitzgerald, Trustee, Wilsons, Steynings House, Fisherton Street, Salisbury SP2 7RJ.

The Grateful Society

Eligibility: Women who are single (divorced or widowed), over 50, have lived in Bristol and the surrounding area, for at least 10 years and would benefit from financial assistance in order to pursue an independent life in their own home.

Types of grants: Regular allowances of £420 to £780 a year, paid in quarterly instalments. Occassional gifts can be made towards, for example, holidays, new furniture, washing machines, kitchen equipment and maintaining gardens.

Annual grant total: In 2001 the trust had assets of £540,000, its income was £76,000 and its total expenditure was £79,000. Grants were made to 100 individuals totalling £57,000.

Applications: In writing to the the correspondent, submitted directly by the individual, or through a recognised referral agency (e.g. social worker, citizen's advice bureau or doctor), or a friend or colleague. Applications are considered throughout the year. Applicants must provide confirmation that they have lived in the beneficial area for 10 years, are over 50 and are female. Details of income and level of savings should also be included.

Correspondent: Joyce Liddiard, Administrator, Royal Oak House, Royal Oak Avenue, Bristol BS1 4GB (0117 989 7738; Fax: 0117 989 7740).

The Peter Herve Benevolent Institution

Eligibility: People aged 60 and over who live within a 25-mile radius of Bristol city centre, own their own homes and have fallen on hard times.

Types of grants: Recurrent grants, on average of £170 a quarter and one-off emergency grants of up to £200, for example, £200 towards a new boiler.

Annual grant total: In 2000 the trust had an income of £95,000 and its total expenditure was £102,000, nearly all of which was given in grants to individuals.

Applications: In writing to the correspondent, for consideration throughout the year.

Correspondent: Mrs June Moody, Administrator, PricewaterhouseCoopers, 31 Great George Street, Bristol BS1 5QD (0117 929 1500).

Nailsea Community Trust Ltd

Eligibility: People of any age or occupation who are in need due, for example, to hardship, disability or sickness, and who live in the town of Nailsea and the immediate area in North Somerset.

Types of grants: One-off grants, usually up to £200, towards items, services or facilities.

Annual grant total: In 1999/2000 grants for educational and welfare purposes totalled £2,100. The income was £4,700 and the total expenditure was £5,600.

Applications: An application form and guidelines are available from the correspondent upon receipt of an sae. Applications should be made through people 'of standing in the community', for example clergy or social workers, who know the details and circumstances of the individual.

Correspondent: Mrs A J Codrington, Secretary, Advent Rise, 10 Harptree Close, Nailsea, Bristol BS48 4YT.

The Portishead Nautical Trust

Eligibility: People in need, usually under 25, who live in Bristol or North Somerset. Preference is given to people who are: homeless; unemployed; experiencing problems related to drug or solvent abuse; being ill-treated; being neglected, in the areas of physical, moral and educational well-being; or 'people who have committed criminal acts, or are in danger of doing so'.

Types of grants: Small grants and bursaries, 'where such a grant will enable a young person to realise their full potential'.

Annual grant total: In 2000/01 the trust had an income of £75,000 and its total expenditure was £80,000. Grants were made to individuals totalling £6,800 and to organisations totalling £58,000.

Applications: On a form available from the correspondent. Applications must be supported by a sponsor, such as a welfare officer or health visitor.

Correspondent: P C Dingley-Brown, Secretary, 108 High Street, Portishead, Bristol BS20 6AJ.

Ralph and Irma Sperring Charity

Eligibility: People in need who live within a 5-mile radius of the Church of St John the Baptist in Midsomer Norton, Bath.

Types of grants: One-off and recurrent grants according to need.

Annual grant total: In 2000/01 the trust had an income of £75,000 and its total expenditure was £94,000. In the previous year around £40,000 was available in grants to both individuals and organisations for both educational and welfare purposes.

Applications: In writing to the correspondent, to be considered quarterly.

Correspondent: The Clerk to the Trustees, Thatcher & Hallam Solicitors, Island House, Midsomer Norton, Bath BA3 2HJ (01761 414646).

Other information: This trust also supports local organisations in the area.

Almondsbury

Almondsbury Charity

Eligibility: People in need in the old parish of Almondsbury.

Types of grants: One-off grants according to need, for instance for household appliances. Grants are not given towards fuel bills.

Annual grant total: In 1999/2000 the charity had assets of £2 million and an income of £46,000. Grants to 56 individuals and families for relief-in-need and educational purposes totalled £9,800. Grants to organisations totalled £60,000.

Applications: On a form available from the correspondent. Cash grants are never made directly to the individual; the grant is either paid via a third party such as social services, or the trust pays for the item directly and donates the item to the individual.

Correspondent: T Davies, Secretary, 18 Coape Road, Stockwood, Bristol BS14 8TN (01275 833026).

Bath

Bath Abbey Charities

Eligibility: Individuals in need who live in the ecclesiastical parish of St Peter and St Paul with St James.

Types of grants: One-off and recurrent grants according to need.

Annual grant total: In 2000 the trust's income was £1,400 and its total expenditure was £1,000.

Applications: In writing to the correspondent.

Correspondent: Robin H Kirkland, The Abbey Office, 13 Kingston Buildings, Bath BA1 1LT (01225 422462).

Bath and District Spastics Society

Eligibility: People with cerebral palsy and its allied conditions, and their parents and carers, who live in Bath and district.

Types of grants: One-off grants from £200, for example to buy a special bed or chair.

Annual grant total: In 2000/01 the trust's income was £2,600 and its total expenditure was £7,400. Each year about £3,000 is available to give in grants to individuals.

Applications: In writing to the correspondent. Most applications are made on the recommendation of a local physiotherapist.

Correspondent: W W Hedley, The Court, Wingfield House, Wingfield, Trowbridge, Wiltshire BA14 9LF (01225 767598).

Bath Holiday Trust

Eligibility: People who are physically disabled and their carers, who live in Bath.

Types of grants: One-off grants towards holiday accommodation.

Annual grant total: In 1999/2000 the trust's income was £9,600 and its total expenditure was £3,800.

Applications: In writing to the correspondent.

Correspondent: A D Bendall, 12 Lansdown Place East, Bath BA1 5ET.

Other information: This entry was not confirmed by the trust, but the address was correct according to the Charity Commission database.

Bath Nursing Association Charity

Eligibility: People who are sick and in need who live in the city of Bath.

Types of grants: One-off and recurrent grants according to need.

Annual grant total: In 2001 the trust's income was £2,700 and its total expenditure was £760.

Applications: In writing to the correspondent.

Correspondent: Mrs C Bayntun-Coward, Almoner, Bath Municipal Charities, 4 Chapel Court, Bath BA1 1SL (01225 486413).

The Mayor of Bath's Relief Fund

Eligibility: People in need who live in Bath.

Types of grants: One-off grants for a wide range of needs, usually ranging from £50 to £150.

Annual grant total: In 2001/02 the trust had an income of £5,000 and gave £4,000 in grants.

Applications: On a form available from the correspondent. Applications must be submitted through a social worker, citizen's advice bureau, health visitor, doctor or other welfare agency. They are considered throughout the year. Grants are only made when all other agencies have been tried.

Correspondent: Edward Barrett, Mayor's Office, Guildhall, High Street, Bath BA1 5AW (01225 477411; Fax: 01225 477408).

The Monmouth Street Society, Bath

Eligibility: The 'deserving poor' who live in Bath and have done so for at least two years.

Types of grants: One-off and recurrent grants up to £150, for example, for food, children's clothing, reconditioned washing

machines, beds, television licences and very occasionally towards bills and debts.
Annual grant total: About £8,000.
Applications: Preference for personal applications, but will accept any received through social workers and such like. All cases are investigated by a member of the society, and are considered throughout the year.
Correspondent: Mrs Vicky Carr, Clerk, 4–6 Chapel Court, Bath BA1 1SQ (01225 312799).

The St John's Hospital, Bath

Eligibility: People in need living in Bath. There are no age restrictions.
Types of grants: Grants, which may be made up of several payments, but generally not for more than a total of £750. Help is given towards utility debts and domestic equipment, and other requests are considered.
Annual grant total: In 2002 425 relief-in-need grants were given, totalling £121,000. The budget for 2002 was £132,000.
Applications: On a form available from most agencies, such as citizen's advice bureaux, Housing Advice Centre and Social Services. This will be forwarded with a recommendation to the correspondent (below). The almoner may visit applicants at home and meets with one of the two trustees once or twice-weekly to decide on awards.
Correspondent: Mrs C Bayntun-Coward, Almoner, St John's Hospital, 4 Chapel Court, Bath BA1 1SL (01225 486413).

Bath and North East Somerset

Archdeaconry of Bath Clerical Families Fund

Please see entry on page 56

Combe Down Holiday Trust

Eligibility: People who are disabled and their families and carers, who live in Bath and North East Somerset.
Types of grants: One-off grants ranging from £240 to £750, towards the cost of a holiday.
Annual grant total: In 2000/01 the trust's assets totalled £952,000, its income was £41,000 and the total expenditure was £51,000. Grants were made to 152 individuals totalling £37,000.
Applications: On a form available from the correspondent, submitted either directly by the individual or through a social worker, citizen's advice bureau or other welfare agency.
Correspondent: Richard Osborn, Combe Down House, The Avenue, Combe Down, Bath BA2 5EG (01225 837181; e-mail: richard.osborn@care4free.net).

North East Somerset Trust (NEST) for Children

Eligibility: Children who are in need and live in the North East Somerset area and their families. Preference is given to children who have experienced physical, emotional or sexual abuse and children of families who are in financial need for whatever reason.
Types of grants: Grants are of up to £75 for each application. Several applications can be made each year. Grants can be towards, for example, basic clothing, shoes, birthday presents, Christmas presents, Easter eggs and safety equipment such as stairgates and fireguards.
Annual grant total: In 2000/01 the trust's income was £15,000 and its total expenditure was £12,000, spent on grants to individuals and outings organised by the trust.
Applications: On a form available from the correspondent, or by letter, either directly by the individual, or through a social worker, school, probation officer or other welfare agency worker. Applicants may receive a home visit and assessment from an officer of the trust.
Correspondent: Mrs Jennifer Pearce, Kelson House, Tilley Lane, Cold Bath, Farmborough, Bath BA2 0BD (01761 470165).

Batheaston

Henry Smith's Charity (Longney)

Eligibility: People in need who live in Batheaston.
Types of grants: One-off and recurrent grants towards the cost of coal.
Annual grant total: In 2000 the trust's income was £700 and its total expenditure was £600, all of which was given in grants to individuals.
Applications: In writing to the correspondent.
Correspondent: Janet Jackson, 4 Wayfield Gardens, Batheaston, Bath BA1 (01225 859843).

Bristol

The Anchor Society

Eligibility: Women over 60 and men over 65 who are in need and live in the Greater Bristol area.
Types of grants: One-off and recurrent grants according to need (usually up to £500).
Annual grant total: About £4,000 in one-off grants; about £14,000 is given in annuities. The income is about £75,000 a year, and grants are also made towards sheltered accommodation projects.
Applications: On a form available from the correspondent.
Correspondent: Honorary Secretary, BMC House, Orchard Street, Bristol BS1 5EQ (0117 927 9546).

Thomas Beames' Charity

Eligibility: People in need who live in the ancient parish of St Augustine with St George in Bristol.
Types of grants: Grants are made at the discretion of the trustees, towards, for example, bedding, food and electrical cookers.
Annual grant total: About £5,000.
Applications: In writing to the correspondent including details of why help is needed. Applications are usually considered quarterly.
Correspondent: Alan Stevenson, Clerk, c/o the Rector's Room, St Stephen's Street, Bristol BS1 1EQ.
Other information: This entry was not confirmed by the trust, but the address was correct according to information at the Charity Commission.

The Bristol Benevolent Institution

Eligibility: Older people living in their own homes with small fixed incomes and little or no capital. Applicants must be over 60 and have lived in Bristol for 15 years or more.
Types of grants: Mostly small recurrent grants paid quarterly in advance within the level disregarded by the DWP when calculating benefits. Also for people aged 70 or over who own their own house, free of mortgage, interest free loans of £1,500 p.a can be given against the security of their deeds. Loans to be repaid on death or the sale of property. No charges of any kind are made at any time.

About 540 annuitants receive between £260 and £1,500 a year maximum.
Annual grant total: In 2000 the trust had an income of £380,000 and its total expenditure was £400,000, including £335,000 given to individuals.
Applications: Referrals to the correspondent or directly by the individual in writing for consideration in March, June, September and December. Applicants are asked to provide details of income and expenditure. All applicants are visited.
Correspondent: Mrs Maureen Nicholls, 45 High Street, Nailsea, Bristol BS48 1AW (01275 810365).

The Bristol Municipal Charities

Eligibility: People in need who for the last five years have lived within a 10-mile radius of Bristol city centre.

Types of grants: One-off grants, generally of £35 to £200 for emergencies, clothing (especially for children), household equipment, furniture, bedding, medical equipment and aids for disabled people. No grants for debts or rent arrears. Only one grant is given per applicant per year and there is a limit of three grants per person.

Annual grant total: In 2000/01 the charities' income and total expenditure both totalled about £1 million.

Each year about £200,000 is given to about 1,500 individuals, including about £40,000 for educational purposes. A further £50,000 is given to organisations.

Applications: On a form available from social workers, health visitors, citizen's advice bureaux, housing associations, and so on, who make the application on behalf of the individual. Applications are considered daily.

Correspondent: D W Jones, Chief Executive, Orchard Street, Bristol BS1 5EQ (0117 930 0302; Fax: 0117 925 3824; e-mail: djones@bristol-mc.co.uk).

The Lord Mayor of Bristol's Christmas Appeal for Children

Eligibility: Children under 16 who are in need and who live in the city of Bristol.

Types of grants: One-off grants in the form of £24 worth of vouchers for food, clothes and toys at Christmas.

Annual grant total: In 2000/01 the trust had an income of £48,000 and gave grants totalling about £44,000.

Applications: Through a social worker, citizen's advice bureau, welfare agency or other third party such as parents or a person who can vouch for the individual's needs.

Correspondent: B N Simmonds, Hon. Treasurer, Priestlands, Hambrook, Bristol BS16 1RN (0117 956 6010 am or 0117 970 1610 any other time).

The Charles Dixon Pension Fund

See entry on page 219

The Dolphin Society

Eligibility: People in need and/or at risk through sickness, ill-health, disability or poverty and who live in Bristol. Preference is given to older people whom the society aims to help by maintaining their independence in their own homes whilst having contact through the telephone, or immediate help with a pendant alarm.

Types of grants: Help towards telephone installations and pendant alarms.

Annual grant total: In 1999/2000 the trust had an income of £58,000 and its total expenditure was £73,000, all of which was spent on grants to individuals.

Applications: Can be returned through the social services. If directly from the individual the application must be supported by a doctor, clergy etc. (not necessary if elderly). Applications are considered throughout the year.

Correspondent: Maureen Nicholls, Administrator, 45 High Street, Nailsea, Bristol BS48 1AW (01275 810365).

The Federation of Master Builders (Bristol Branch) Benevolent Fund

Eligibility: Elderly and infirm members of the building trade who live or have worked in Bristol, and their dependants. New entrants training in the construction industry in the Bristol area are also eligible.

Types of grants: Pensions and one-off grants.

Annual grant total: About £1,000.

Applications: In writing to the correspondent. Applications can be submitted directly by the individual and are considered quarterly.

Correspondent: J W A Chapman, Regional Director, 83 Alma Road, Clifton, Bristol BS8 2DP (0117 973 6891).

The Redcliffe Parish Charity

Eligibility: People in need who live in the city of Bristol.

Types of grants: One-off grants usually of £25 to £50. 'The trustees generally limit grants to families or individuals who can usually manage, but who are overwhelmed by circumstances and are in particular financial stress rather than continuing need.' Grants are typically given for cooker repairs, items for a new baby, children's school trips and school uniforms and after burglary/fire etc.

No support for adult education, school fees or repetitive payments.

Annual grant total: In 2000/01 the trust had an income of £8,300 and donated £7,000 in grants to 130 individuals, for welfare needs and school trips and uniform.

Applications: In writing to the correspondent. Applications should be submitted on the individual's behalf by a social worker, doctor, health visitor, citizen's advice bureau or appropriate third party, and will be considered early in each month. Ages of family members should be supplied in addition to financial circumstances and the reason for the request.

Correspondent: Mrs M Jardine, Jowayne, Hobbs Wall, Farmborough, Bath BA2 0BJ (01761 471713).

The Unity Fund for the Elderly

Eligibility: People over 60 in need in the Bristol area.

Types of grants: One-off grants ranging between £40 to £500, towards small building repairs, cookers, fridges and other household items. No grants for residential care or nursing home fees.

Annual grant total: In 2001 the trust had assets of £285,000, an income of £22,000 and a total expenditure of £17,000. Grants were given to 68 people and totalled £17,000.

Applications: In writing to the correspondent. Applications should be submitted through a social worker, citizen's advice bureau or other welfare agency. They are considered at any time.

Correspondent: D H T Rowcliffe, Secretary, 5 Bishop Road, Emersons Green, Bristol BS16 7ET (0117 956 1289).

Wraxall Parochial Charities

Eligibility: People living in the parish of Wraxall and Failand, Bristol who are in need due to hardship or disability.

Types of grants: One-off grants.

Annual grant total: In 2001 the trust had an income of £9,900 and made grants to individuals in need totalling £6,000. Grants for educational purposes totalled £350.

Applications: In writing to the correspondent, directly by the individual.

Correspondent: Mrs A Sissons, Clerk to the Trustees, 2 Short Way, Failand, Bristol BS8 3UF.

Langford

Charles Graham Stone's Relief-in-Need Charity

Eligibility: People in need who live in Langford, North Somerset.

Types of grants: One-off grants, for example, towards travel expenses of visiting relatives in hospitals or nursing homes and fuel bills. No grants for payment of government taxes and local or water rates.

Annual grant total: In 2001 the trust's assets totalled £99,000, its income was £5,000 and its total expenditure was £16,000. Grants were given to organisations and individuals for welfare and educational purposes.

Applications: In writing to the correspondent for consideration in March and September (applications should be submitted by the end of February and August). Please note, initial approaches must be made in writing, not by telephone.

Correspondent: M A Endacott, Hill Cottage, Worlebury Hill Road, Weston-Super-Mare, North Somerset BS22 9TL (01934 628230).

South Gloucesteshire

The Chipping Sodbury Town Lands

Eligibility: People in need who live in Chipping Sodbury or Old Sodbury.

Types of grants: One-off and recurrent grants according to need.

Annual grant total: In 2000 the trust had assets of £8.9 million, an income of £228,000 and a total expenditure of £181,000. Grants to individuals and organisations totalled £53,000.

Applications: In writing to the correspondent.

Correspondent: Mrs Nicola Gideon, Clerk, Town Hall, 57–59 Broad Street, Chipping Sodbury, South Gloucestershire BS37 6AD.

Cornwall

J H Beckly Handicapped/Sick Children's Fund

Eligibility: Children under 18 who live in the city of Plymouth or district of Caradon, Cornwall and who are sick or disabled and in need.

Types of grants: Generally one-off grants according to need.

Annual grant total: In 2000/01 the trust's income was £8,800 and its total expenditure was £6,700. Further information was not available for this year.

In 1998/99 the trust had assets of £161,000, an income of £8,600 and its total expenditure was £7,100. £4,200 was given in 19 grants to individuals.

Applications: In writing to the correspondent giving brief details of income and outgoings of the applicant's parent/guardian and a description of the child's need. Applications should be made preferably through a social worker, citizen's advice bureau or other welfare agency but can also be made directly by the individual or through another third party. They are considered on an ongoing basis.

Correspondent: Miss Louise Widley, Foot Anstey Sargent, 21 Derry's Cross, Plymouth, Devon PL1 2SW (01752 675000; Fax: 01752 671802).

Other information: The fund occasionally give to charities/organisations who support such children.

The Blanchminster Trust

Eligibility: People who live in the parishes of Bude, Stratton and Poughill (the former urban district of Bude-Stratton).

Types of grants: Generally one-off grants (with no real minimum or maximum size) for the relief of need, hardship or distress, for example for clothing, food, medical care and equipment, and travel to and from hospital.

Annual grant total: In 2001 the trust's assets totalled £6.2 million, it had an income of £360,000 and its total expenditure was £380,000. Relief-in-need grants were made to 29 individuals, totalling £11,000.

Applications: On a form available from the correspondent. Applications are considered monthly and should be submitted directly by the individual. Where possible the application should include a request for a specific amount and be supported with quotes for the costs of items etc. needed and/or written support from a social worker or other welfare agency.

Correspondent: Owen A May, Clerk, Blanchminster Building, 38 Lansdown Road, Bude, Cornwall EX23 8EE (Tel & Fax: 01288 352851).

Other information: Grants are also made for educational purposes and to community projects.

The Lizzie Brooke Charity

Eligibility: People in need who live in West Cornwall: not people living in other parts of Cornwall.

Types of grants: One-off grants of £50 to £150 for the necessities of everyday living and for assistance to help provide mobility for disabled people. No grants for students for fees.

Annual grant total: In 2000 the trust had an income of £7,400 and its total expenditure was £9,700, most of which was given in grants.

Applications: On a form available from the correspondent and completed by a sponsor. Applications should be submitted through a social worker, citizen's advice bureau or other welfare agency. They are considered at any time.

Correspondent: Mrs W A Stone, Hon. Secretary, Woodside, 8 Tredarvah Road, Penzance TR18 4LE (01736 364908).

The Cornwall Retired Clergy, Widows of the Clergy and their Dependants Fund

Eligibility: Retired clergymen, usually over 65 years, and their relatives who live in Cornwall or on the Isles of Scilly.

Types of grants: Grants are one-off and occasionally recurrent according to need. Recent grants have been made towards plumbing, heating bills, spectacles, dentist fees and wheelchairs.

No grants for assistance with school fees or university fees.

Annual grant total: In 2001 the trust's assets totalled £130,000 and it had an income of £4,600 and it made seven grants totalling £2,000 to individuals.

Applications: In writing to the correspondent. Applications can be submitted directly by the individual or through a relative or a carer. They are considered throughout the year.

Correspondent: Revd O R M Blatchly, 1 Rose Cottages, East Road, Stithians, Truro, Cornwall TR3 7BD (01209 860845).

Cornwall Seamen's Benevolent Trust

Eligibility: Distressed merchant seamen, fishermen or lifeboatmen who live in Cornwall or their widows and dependants.

Types of grants: One-off and recurrent grants of £100.

Annual grant total: In 2001 the trust had assets of £78,000, an income of £19,000 and its total expenditure was £23,000. It gave £21,000 in grants to 94 individuals.

Applications: On a form available from the correspondent. Applications can be submitted by the individual, or through a third party such as a social worker, citizen's advice bureau or the trust's representative.

Correspondent: C C Jago, 25 Budock Terrace, Falmouth, Cornwall TR11 3ND (01326 311782).

The United Charities of Liskeard

Eligibility: For the relief-in-need fund, people in need who live in the town of Liskeard (formerly the borough of Liskeard). For the relief-in-sickness fund, people in need who live in Liskeard, the parish of Dobwalls with Trewidland (formerly the parish of Liskeard) and the parishes of Menheniot and St Cleer.

Types of grants: One-off and recurrent grants according to need.

Annual grant total: In 2000 the trust had an income of 31,000 and its total expenditure was £1,400, most of which was given in grants.

Applications: In writing to the correspondent.

Correspondent: A J Ball, Tremellick, Pengover Road, Liskeard, Cornwall PL14 3EW (01579 343577).

Gunwalloe

The Charity of Thomas Henwood

Eligibility: People who are unemployed, sick and retired and live in the parish of Gunwalloe.

Types of grants: One-off or recurrent grants according to need, and grants for the provision of nurses and to assist people recovering from illness. All by periodic distribution. Grants range from £60 to £100. Income is also used to care for graves in the churchyard if no relatives are still alive.

Annual grant total: In 2000 the trust had an income of £5,800 and its total expenditure was £6,200. Further information was not available for this year. In the previous year its income was £7,700 and it made grants totalling £2,800.

Applications: In writing to the trustees. Applications are considered in March and December.

Correspondent: Mrs B Pollard, 1 Jubilee Terrace, Gunwalloe, Helston, Cornwall TR12 7PZ.

Other information: This entry was not confirmed by the trust, but the information was correct according to its file at the Charity Commission.

Gwennap

Charity of John Davey

Eligibility: Ex-miners over 70 years of age, or their widows, who live in the ancient parish of Gwennap, near Redruth in Cornwall and are in need.

Types of grants: Recurrent grants of £10 to £40 a quarter for general living expenses.

Annual grant total: In 2000/01 the trust had an income of £7,900 and its total expenditure was £8,900, most of which was given in grants.

Applications: Initial telephone calls to the correspondent are welcome and application forms are available on request.

Correspondent: E T Pascoe, 13–15 Commercial Road, Hayle, Cornwall TR27 4DE (01736 753357).

Helston

The Helston Welfare Trust

Eligibility: People in need who live in the area administered by Helston Town Council.

Types of grants: One-off grants for all kinds of need including help with fuel bills, television licence fees, furniture, clothing, travel expenses for hospital visiting, telephone installation, food for special diets and equipment for disabled people. Grants have been given in the past towards repair work on uninsured property and a visit to France for a youth club member.

Annual grant total: In 2000/01 the trust had an income of £2,300 and its total expenditure was £840.

Applications: In writing to the correspondent. Applications should be submitted directly by the individual. They should include details of need and the financial circumstances of the applicant. Applications are considered as they are received.

Correspondent: Ginette Cardew, Town Clerk, Guildhall, Helston, Cornwall TR13 8ST (01326 572063; Fax: 01326 565761).

Penzance

Mayor's Welfare Fund

Eligibility: People who live in Penzance and who are suffering from hardship.

Types of grants: One-off and recurrent grants according to need.

Annual grant total: In 2001/02 the trust had assets totalling £6,400, and both an income and a total expenditure of around £2,000. Grants were made to individuals and organisations.

Applications: In writing to the correspondent at any time, directly by the individual or through a third party on their behalf.

Correspondent: D J L Gallie, Town Clerk, Town Clerk's Office, Alverton Street, Penzance, Cornwall TR18 2QP (01736 363405; Fax: 01736 330221).

Devon

Bideford Bridge Trust

Eligibility: People in need who live in Bideford and neighbourhood.

Types of grants: One-off grants ranging from £150 to £500. Grants are not given for computers for personal use.

Annual grant total: In 2001 the trust had assets of £7.1 million and an income of £539,000. Total expenditure was £405,000; information about how much was given to individuals was not available for this year.

In 2000 grants to organisations totalled £565,000 and £12,000 was given to individuals in book and social grants.

Applications: On a form available from the correspondent, to be submitted at any time during the year by the individual, although a sponsor is usually required.

Correspondent: P R Sims, 24 Bridgeland Street, Bideford, Devon EX39 2QB (01237 473122).

Edward Blagdon's Charity

Eligibility: People in need who live in Tiverton and Washfield in Devon.

Types of grants: One-off grants only, usually of £150, but can be for up to £450.

Annual grant total: In 1998/99 the charity had assets of £130,000, an income of £7,000 and its total expenditure was £11,000. Grants to individuals totalled £2,900.

Applications: Directly by the individual or through a social worker, citizen's advice bureau or other welfare agency. People in Tiverton should apply to: D R Gibling, 29 Park Road, Tiverton, Devon EX16 6AY; and people in Washfield should apply to: C C J French, Lower Woodgates, Washfield, Tiverton, Devon EX16 8PD. Applications are considered bi-monthly.

Correspondent: Mrs B M Randell, Clerk to the Trustees, 7 William Street, Tiverton, Devon EX16 6BJ (01884 254465; Fax: 01884 243451).

The Mrs E L Blakeley Marillier Annuity Fund

See entry on page 175

The Brownsdon & Tremayne Estate Charity (also known as the Nicholas Watts Trust)

Eligibility: For the Brownsdon Fund, men in need who live in Devon, with a preference for Tavistock applicants, preferably owner/occupiers. For the Tremayne Estate Charity, people in need who live in Tavistock.

Types of grants: One-off grants. In addition to general relief of need, the trustees prefer to help towards the maintenance of homes owned by beneficiaries, for example, providing new carpets, grants towards the costs of roof repairs and occasionally supplying computers to people with disabilities. The trust does not assist with mortgage repayments. Grants range from £60/£100 to £3,000/£5,000.

Annual grant total: In 2000/01 the trust had an income of £16,000 and its total expenditure was £12,000.

It makes grants totalling about £11,000 a year to between 5 and 15 individuals.

Applications: On a form available from the correspondent. The trustees advertise for applications in July, to be considered in September, but at other times for emergencies. Applications can be submitted directly by the individual.

Correspondent: A D Carr, Denmarian, 3 Deer Park Close, Tavistock, Devon PL19 9HE (01822 613040).

Devon County Football League Benevolent Fund

Eligibility: People in need who live in the county of Devon who are or were involved with a club in the Devon County Football League, and referees in the league. Grants are given to people who are disabled, have a serious illness, or who have experienced personal misfortune.

Types of grants: One-off and recurrent grants ranging from £50 to £250. A recent grant was made to a player who suffered a depressed cheekbone fracture.

No grants to people with short term injuries, or anyone not considered to be 'in need'.

Annual grant total: In 2001/02 the trust's assets totalled £3,200, it had an income of £1,200 and grants were made to about 16 individuals totalling £1,400.

Applications: In writing to the correspondent either directly by the individual, or through a social worker, citizen's advice bureau, or other third party such as the club secretary. The trustees meet to consider applications on the first Thursdays in January, March, May, September and November. Applications should include the individual's marital and employment status, number of children and length of incapacity.

Correspondent: P A Hiscox, 19 Ivy Close, Exeter EX2 5LX (Tel & Fax: 01392 493995; e-mail: pahiscox@hotmail.com; website: www.devonleague.co.uk).

The Exeter Nursing Association Trust

Eligibility: People in need who are receiving or in need of medical/nursing care, or needy employees or ex-employees of the association and those who have been employed in nursing, who live in the city and county of Exeter. Grants are also given to charities connected with nursing in the beneficial area.

Types of grants: Providing and supplementing nursing services of any kind. One-off grants are also made.

Annual grant total: In 2000/01 the trust's income was £9,700 and it had an expenditure of £8,900, most of which was given to individuals in need.

Applications: In writing to the correspondent. Patients should write via their attending health visitor or district nurse; nurses should write via a senior nurse at Community Nursing Services Exeter Localities.

Correspondent: G M Jarman, 4 Curlew Close, Upcott, Okehampton, Devon EX20 1SE (01837 53501).

The Heathcoat Trust

Eligibility: People who are disabled and in financial need and live and study in Tiverton and the mid-Devon area.

Types of grants: One-off and recurrent grants according to need.

Annual grant total: In 2001/02 grants to individuals for welfare purposes totalled £30,000. Further grants were made to individuals for education totalling £140,000, and to organisations for welfare purposes totalling £216,000.

Applications: In writing to the correspondent.

Correspondent: E W Summers, Secretary, The Factory, Tiverton, Devon EX16 5LL (01884 254949).

The Christopher Hill Charity

Eligibility: People in need who live in the former parish of Netherexe or in the surrounding parishes in Devon.

Types of grants: One-off and recurrent grants according to need. All aspects of individual's circumstances are considered, particularly the elderly living alone including grants towards transport (e.g. taxis for visits to Health Centre, to village social events, church meeting etc.). No loans are made. Grants are not given to occupants of cottages who are known to be only short-term lets.

Annual grant total: In 2000/01 the trust had both an income and total expenditure of about £1,500. Further information was not available for this year.

In 1997/98 the charity had assets of £4,700 and an income of £1,400. It gave £600 in four grants of £150.

Applications: In writing to the correspondent or any trustee. Applications can be submitted directly by the individual or through another third party on behalf of the individual. They should include details of financial circumstances and health and are considered in May and November.

Correspondent: Colin Bond, Trustee, Fortescue Crossing, Thorverton, Exeter EX5 5JN (01392 841512).

Other information: This entry was not confirmed by the trust, but the information was correct according to its file at the Charity Commission.

The Maudlyn Lands Charity & Others

Eligibility: People who live in the Plympton St Mary and Sparkwell areas.

Types of grants: One-off or recurrent grants, usually ranging between £250 and £500.

Annual grant total: In 2000/01 the trust had assets ot £178,000, its income was £9,000 and its total expenditure was £7,400. Grants totalled about £4,000 and included those made to five individuals in need.

Applications: In writing to the correspondent. Applications are considered in November.

Correspondent: Anthony Peter Golding, Clerk to the Trustees, Blue Haze, Down Road, Tavistock, Devon PL19 9AG (Tel & Fax: 01822 611027; e-mail: amza36@dial.pipex.co.uk).

Northcott Devon Foundation

Eligibility: People living in Devon who are distressed or in need as the result of illness, injury, bereavement or exceptional disadvantages.

Types of grants: One-off and recurrent grants of up to £1,000, can be given towards, for example, computers for physically disabled children, adaptations, repairs, holidays, clothing, furniture and wheelchairs.

No grants towards long-term educational needs, funeral expenses or to relieve debts.

Annual grant total: In 2001/02 the trust's assets were £5.5 million, it had both an income and total expenditure of £220,000 and grants to individuals totalled £200,000.

Applications: On a form available from the correspondent. Applications can be submitted through a social worker, citizen's advice bureau, welfare agency or a third party such as a doctor, health visitors or SSAFA. Applications should include the individual's name and address, and details of income and expenditure, type of household, age and children. They are considered every month.

Correspondent: G Folland, 1b Victoria Road, Exmouth, Devon EX8 1DL (Tel & Fax: 01395 269204).

Other information: The trust also gives to local organisations.

The Ritchie Charitable Trust

Eligibility: People in need who live in North Devon.

Types of grants: One-off and recurrent grants are given for relief of hardship, social and educational welfare.

Annual grant total: In 1999/2000 the trust's income was £3,700 and its total expenditure was £4,100.

Applications: In writing to the correspondent.

Correspondent: Dr J E Crabtree, Chair, Postaway, Higher Park Road, Braunton, North Devon EX33 2LG.

Other information: This charity also gives grants for medical research.

The Tavistock, Whitchurch & District Nursing Association Trust Fund

Eligibility: Sick or needy people living in Tavistock, Whitchurch, Brentor, Mary Tavy and Peter Tavy, Gulworthy and Lamerton.

Types of grants: Mainly one-off grants of £35 to £100 initially according to need, for example, to help with heating and water bills, travel to medical appointments or to help people stay in their own homes; also towards stairlifts, a wheelchair and an alarm system. Grants can occasionally be recurrent.

Annual grant total: In 1998/99 the trust made 65 grants totalling £1,700.

Applications: In writing to the correspondent, submitted by the individual or through a social worker, citizen's advice bureau, doctor, district nurse, health visitor, church or town councillor. Applications are considered in May and November.

Correspondent: John Montgomery, 24 Chollacott Close, Tavistock, Devon PL19 9BW (01822 612837).

Other information: Grants are also given to assist carers in caring for spouses.

Barnstaple

The Barnstaple Municipal Charities (The Poors Charity Section)

Eligibility: People in need living in Barnstaple.

Types of grants: One-off grants.

Annual grant total: The trust's income is £1,390 a year and all of this is available in grants: about 50% goes to people in need and 50% to students and people starting work.

Applications: In writing to the correspondent. Applications are considered quarterly.

Correspondent: M Steele, 29 Carrington Terrace, Yeo Vale, Barnstaple, North Devon EX32 7AF (01271 346354).

The Barnstaple & North Devon Dispensary Fund

Eligibility: Sick and poor people who live in the borough of Barnstaple and district (i.e. within a seven mile radius of the centre of Barnstaple).

Types of grants: One-off grants according to need. In 1998, grants were made as follows: £150 to coal and heating bills, £300 to holidays and convalescence, £3,000 to medical costs, £1,300 to bedding and clothing and £2,300 to travel and food.

Annual grant total: In 2000 the trust's income was £9,300 and its total expenditure was £8,000.

Applications: In writing to the correspondent, through a doctor, health visitor or social worker and so on.

Correspondent: Miss I G Hibbs, Clerk, 28 Beaufort Walk, Gorwell, Barnstaple, North Devon EX32 7JB (01271 375013).

Other information: This entry was not confirmed by the trust, but the address was correct according to the Charity Commission's database.

Bridge Trust

Eligibility: People who live in the borough of Barnstaple, Devon, with a preference for disabled, elderly and young people.

Types of grants: One-off and recurrent grants according to need. Educational grants are not given.

Annual grant total: In 1999 the trust had assets of £411,000 and an income of £248,000. Grants totalling £132,000 were given to a wide range of causes, mainly to organisations.

Applications: In writing to the correspondent. Applications must be made via a social worker, citizen's advice bureau or other welfare agency or third party.

Correspondent: C J Bartlett, Clerk to the Trustees, 7 Bridge Chambers, Barnstaple, Devon EX31 1HB (01271 343995).

Bratton Fleming

The Bratton Fleming Relief-in-Need Charity

Eligibility: People in any kind of need living within the parish of Bratton Fleming.

Types of grants: One-off or recurrent grants between £35 and £70. Grants can be, for example, towards extra expenses caused by children going to new schools, heating during the winter or illness expenses.

Annual grant total: In 2000 the trust had an income of £2,100 and its total expenditure was £2,000. Information on grants was not available in this year. In 1997 the trust made 18 relief-in-need grants totalling £880.

Applications: In writing to the correspondent or by word of mouth by the individual or a third party on their behalf, to be considered in early June and early December.

Correspondent: T Squire, Haxlea, Threeways, Bratton Fleming, Barnstaple, Devon EX31 4TG (01598 710526).

Other information: This entry was not confirmed by the trust, but the address was correct according to the Charity Commission's file.

Brixham

John Mitchelmore's Charity

Eligibility: People who live in Brixham who are in need, for example due to hardship, disability or sickness.

Types of grants: One-off or recurrent grants according to need.

Annual grant total: In 2000 the trust had an income of £1,600 and its total expenditure was £1,000. In 2002 the trust stated that grants had not recently been made to individuals, since no suitable individuals had applied. Grants had been made to organisations.

Applications: In writing to the correspondent.

Correspondent: C Sumner, 8 Trafalgar Terrace, Higher Furzeham Road, Brixham, Devon TQ5 8QT.

Brixton

The Brixton Feoffee Trust

Eligibility: People in need who live in the parish of Brixton, near Plymouth.

Types of grants: One-off or recurrent grants (for a minimum of £50) according to need. Grants have in the past been given, for example, towards gardening assistance, a medic-alert pendant, clothing, household appliances, telephone installation, a motor scooter, care visits, building a ramp for disabled access, childcare costs, an electric wheelchair and an electric rise/recliner chair. The charity cannot give grants where the funds can be obtained from state sources.

Annual grant total: In 2000/01 the trust had assets of £674,000 and an income of £21,000. Total expenditure was £14,000, including £6,300 to St Mary's Church, £2,300 to individuals in need, £4,600 to local organisations and groups and £930 to the Car Scheme (see below).

Applications: In writing to the correspondent. Applications can be submitted directly by the individual or through a social worker, citizen's advice bureau or other welfare agency or third party. They are considered throughout the year. Applications must give as much detail as possible.

Correspondent: Mrs S Axell, Clerk to the Trustees, 15 Cherry Tree Drive, Brixton, Plymouth PL8 2DD (01752 880262).

Other information: The trust's scheme states that its net income should be shared equally between people in need in the parish of Brixton and a local church, St Mary's in Brixton, for its upkeep and maintenance. If any of the allotted money is unspent at the end of the financial year it is transferred to a third fund which is distributed to charitable schemes that benefit Brixton parish as a whole. This fund enables the trustees to fund a Car Scheme, helping parishioners who have restricted access to convenient travelling provision.

Broadclyst

The Broadclyst Relief-in-Need Charity

Eligibility: People in need who live in the parish of Broadclyst. In particular people on fixed incomes with no other resources and students whose parents are unemployed, on Income Support or invalidity benefit.

Types of grants: Mostly annual grants to older people. One-off grants may also be made, ranging from £20 to £100.

Annual grant total: In 2000/01 the trust had an income of £420 and it gave £1,100 in grants.

Applications: On a form available from the village post office or the correspondent. Applications should be submitted directly by the individual. They are considered in December, following local publicity, but also at any other time when appropriate.

Correspondent: Revd A J Mortimer, The Rectory, 9 Church Hill, Pinhoe, Exeter, EX4 9ER (01392 467541; e-mail: themortimers@totalise.co.uk).

Broadhempston

The Broadhempston Relief-in-Need Charity

Eligibility: People in need who live in the parish of Broadhempston.

Types of grants: One-off or recurrent grants ranging from £40 to £100. Recent grants have included assistance with food and fuel for older people, residential school trips for special needs families and aids for older people and disabled people. Grants are also made towards children's educational trips and aids for educational purposes.

Annual grant total: In 2000/01 the trust had assets of £6,000, its income was £1,200 and its total expenditure was £1,300. Grants to 48 individuals totalled £1,100, mainly for relief-in-need purposes.

Applications: In writing to the correspondent directly by the individual to be considered in June and December.

Correspondent: Mrs R H E Brown, Meadows, Broadhempston, Totnes, Devon TQ9 6BW (01803 813130).

Budleigh Salterton

The Budleigh Salterton Nursing Association

Eligibility: People who live in the parish of Budleigh Salterton and are sick, convalescent, disabled or infirm.

Types of grants: One-off grants of between £20 and £500 for medical items, services and facilities that will alleviate the suffering, or assist the recovery of sick persons. Recent grants have been given for a wheelchair, raised bed, stair lift, several commodes and an access ramp. Assistance will not be given towards rates or council/government taxes.

Annual grant total: In 2000/01 the trust had an income of £3,200 and its total expenditure was £2,300, all of which is likely to have been given in grants.

Applications: In writing to the correspondent at any time including details of the nature of the illness, doctor's name, an indication of why funds are unavailable and family details, such as the number of children to help, spouse disabled and unemployed or separated. Applications can be submitted directly by the individual, through a social worker, citizen's advice bureau or other appropriate third party (such as a doctor) and are considered all year round.

Correspondent: Mrs Mary Perriam, Hillcrest, Hayes Lane, Otterton, Budleigh Salterton, Devon EX9 7JS (01395 568410).

Fryer Welfare and Recreational Trusts

Eligibility: People in need living in the local authority boundary of Budleigh Salterton.

Types of grants: One-off grants of £200 to £500 for recreational and welfare purposes.

Annual grant total: In 2000/01 the trusts had joint assets of £71,000, joint incomes of £2,800 and £900 was given in grants to individuals.

Applications: In writing to the correspondent at any time. Applications can be submitted directly by the individual or through a social worker, citizen's advice bureau or other welfare agency.

Correspondent: W K H Coxe, Council Chambers, Budleigh Salterton, Devon EX9 6RL (01395 442223).

Colyton

The Colyton Parish Lands Charity

Eligibility: People in need in the ancient parish of Colyton.

Types of grants: One-off and recurrent grants according to need.

Annual grant total: In 2000 grants to organisations and individuals totalled £3,900.

Applications: In writing to the correspondent.

Correspondent: J Chambers, Colyton Chamber of Feoffees, Town Hall, Market Place, Colyton, Devon EX24 6JR (01297 553593).

Colyton Sick and Poor Fund

Eligibility: People who are poor and ill in the ancient parish of Colyton.

Types of grants: One-off and recurrent grants according to need.

Annual grant total: In 2000/01 the trust had an income of £600 and a total expenditure of £1,000.

Applications: In writing to the correspondent.

Correspondent: J Chambers, Colyton Chamber of Feoffees, Town Hall, Market Place, Colyton, Devon EX24 6JR (01297 553593).

Cornwood

Reverend Duke Yonge Charity

Eligibility: People in need who live in the parish of Cornwood.

Types of grants: One-off grants for general relief-in-need purposes. Recent grants have included help with playgroup attendance fees, a sit-in shower facility, a support chair and winter heating costs.

Annual grant total: In 2000 the trust had assets of £44,000, its income was £12,000 and its total expenditure was £17,000. Grants were made to 14 individuals for relief-in-need and educational purposes, totalling £6,400.

Applications: In writing to the correspondent via the trustees, who are expected to make themselves aware of any need. Applications are considered in March and November.

Correspondent: Mrs J M Milligan, 8 Chipple Park, Lutton, Nr Cornwood, Ivybridge, Devon PL21 9TA.

Other information: Grants are also made to the community bus service, playgroup, village hall and students.

Crediton

The Crediton Relief-in-Need Charity

Eligibility: People in need who have been resident in Crediton town and the parish of Crediton Hamlets for at least 12 months.

Types of grants: One-off grants, for example, towards nursery school costs, second hand washing machines, travel

SOUTH WEST – DEVON

expenses to see a specialist doctor, furnishings for a new home, and medical equipment.

Grants are not given towards house improvements or to repay exisiting debts.

Annual grant total: In 2001/02 the trust had assets of £260,000, its income was £9,000 and its total expenditure was £5,500. Grants were made to 15 individuals in need, totalling £2,600 and over 70 'benefit tickets' of £5 were issued.

Applications: On a form available from the correspondent. Applications can be submitted directly by the individual, or through a social worker, citizen's advice bureau or other welfare agency. Applications are considered monthly.

Correspondent: Mike Armstrong, The Organ House, Church Lane, Crediton, Devon EX17 2AH (01363 776529).

Culmstock

Culmstock Fuel Allotment Charity

Eligibility: People in need who live in the ancient parish of Culmstock.

Types of grants: Recurrent grants, towards electricity and solid fuel bills, and gifts for older people who live in the parish.

Annual grant total: In 2000/01 the trust's assets totalled £1,700, it had an income of £3,800 and its total expenditure was £3,600. It made 53 grants to individuals for relief-in-need and to students for books and equipment, totalling £3,200.

Applications: In writing to the correspondent, directly by the individual in September or October for consideration in November.

Correspondent: Mrs Elaine Artus, Clerk, Pendle, Culmstock, Cullompton, Devon EX15 3JQ (Tel & Fax: 01884 840577)

Dartmouth

The Saint Petrox Trust Lands

Eligibility: People in need who live in the ancient parish of St Petrox, Dartmouth.

Types of grants: One-off grants of £100 to £500. Recent grants have included support to widows, orphans and other people in need, for example: a low income widower by providing upgraded facilities in home (i.e. a shower); towards expenses whilst receiving treatment for cancer; and towards curtains and flooring.
Grants are also given towards the upkeep of ancient buildings within the ancient parish of St Petrox.

Annual grant total: In 2000/01 the trust had an income of £48,000 and its total expenditure was £17,000. All of the trust's income is available to be given in grants each year – to individuals and for the upkeep of buildings.

Applications: In writing to the correspondent either directly by the individual or through a social worker, citizen's advice bureau, other welfare agency, or other third party on behalf of the individual. Applications should include purpose of grant, proof of need and estimates of costs. They are considered in January, April, July and October.

Correspondent: H D Bastone, Clerk, 30 Rosemary Gardens, Paignton, Devon TQ3 3NP (Tel & Fax: 01803 666322).

Dunsford & Doddiscombe Leigh

Cranbrook Charity

Eligibility: People in need who live in the parishes of Dunsford and Doddiscombe Leigh.

Types of grants: Ongoing grants are made to about 45 people, of about £80 every six months.

Annual grant total: In 2000/01 the trust had an income of £8,600 and a total expenditure of £6,600. It usually makes grants totalling about £8,000 to individuals each year.

Applications: In writing to the correspondent. There are two distributions a year, in June and December.

Correspondent: Stephen Purser, Venn Farm, Bidford, Exeter EX6 7LF (01647 252328; e-mail: stephen.purser@tinyworld.co.uk).

Other information: This entry was not confirmed by the trust, but the information was correct according to its file at the Charity Commission.

Exeter

The Central Exeter Relief-in-Need Fund

Eligibility: People in need who live in Exeter, with a preference for the parish of Central Exeter.

Types of grants: One-off grants usually of £50 to £150 for basic needs such as furniture, assistance with heating bills, children's clothing and mobility aid. Grants are not made for educational and training needs.

Annual grant total: In 2000/01 the trust had an income of £1,900 and its total expenditure was £1,600; most of this was given in grants.

Applications: In writing to the correspondent with the support of a social worker, health visitor or other welfare agency. Applications are considered in June and December.

Correspondent: Revd Alison Beever, The Rectory, 3 Spicer Road, Exeter EX1 1SX (Tel & Fax: 01392 272450).

Exeter Dispensary & Aid-in-Sickness Fund

Eligibility: Sick or disabled poor people who live in the city of Exeter.

Types of grants: One-off grants for day-to-day needs including convalescence breaks, help with fuel or telephone bills, cooking or heating appliances, clothing, food, medical care, bedding, travel to and from hospitals, etc. The average such grant is £100. Larger grants are made towards medical appliances and aids. Grants are not given for items which are available from public funds or for structural alterations to property.

Annual grant total: The charity's usual income is about £30,000. In 2001 it spent or pledged £30,000, of which almost £13,000 was given in grants to 122 individuals.

Applications: Applications should be made through a social worker, citizen's advice bureau, other welfare agency or other third party such as a doctor. They should include brief details of the medical condition, the financial circumstances and the specific need. Applications are considered throughout the year for day-to-day needs and in March and November for medical appliances and so on.

Applications should be sent to: A R Gladstone, 'Blanchland', 18 Streatham Drive, Exeter EX4 4PD for day-to-day needs; otherwise, in writing to the correspondent.

Correspondent: D W Fanson, Hon. Secretary, 85 Beacon Lane, Whipton, Exeter EX4 8LL (01392 256381).

Other information: Grants are also given to other organisations with similar objectives.

The Exeter Relief-in-Need Charity

Eligibility: People in need who live in the city of Exeter.

Types of grants: One-off grants of between £50 and £150; individuals can reapply in subsequent years. Clothing vouchers are given throughout the year and sometimes vouchers can be given to buy furniture or furnishings. In winter, fuel vouchers are also available. Grants are also made for travel expenses. No grants for debt repayment, interest on loans, rent, mortgage, or council tax arrears.

Annual grant total: In 2000 the trust's assets totalled £140,000, it had an income of £5,600 and its total expenditure was £5,400. Grants were made to about 50 individuals in need totalling £4,000.

Applications: On a form available from the correspondent, submitted directly by the individual, or through a social worker, citizen's advice bureau or other welfare agency. Applications should include details of the income, including benefits and outgoings of the applicant. Three references must normally be supplied. Awards are usually made following interviews of the applicants by trustees. Applications are considered in February, May, August and November.

Correspondent: M R King, Clerk, Exeter Municipal Charities, 22 Southernhay East, Exeter EX1 1QU (01392 201550; Fax: 01392 201551; e-mail: properties@cbandm.co.uk).

Other information: This charity is part of Exeter Municipal Charities.

The St Edmunds & St Mary Major Charity

Eligibility: People in need who live in the parishes of St Edmunds on the Bridge and St Mary Major, Exeter.

Types of grants: Small one-off grants generally of £60 to £150 and recurrent grants according to need.

Annual grant total: £1,000.

Applications: In writing to the correspondent at any time. Applications can be submitted directly by the individual or through a social worker, citizen's advice bureau or appropriate third party. Applications must include full name, address and telephone number of the individual, details of any other grant applications made, amounts received and the individuals own contribution towards the full costs (if any).

Correspondent: A J D Firth, 12 West Street, Exeter EX1 1BA.

Exminster

Exminster Feoffes

Eligibility: People in need living in the parish of Exminster.

Types of grants: One-off grants usually of £200 each. Grants have previously included cash grants and goods in kind.

Annual grant total: In 2001 the trust's assets totalled £25,000, it had an income of £1,300 and its total expenditure was £340, all of which was given in grants to individuals.

Applications: In writing to the correspondent. Applications are usually made through a doctor's surgery, social worker or primary school. They are dealt with by the trust upon immediate receipt.

Correspondent: K A Beer, Highfield, 3 Higher Aboveway, Exminster, Nr Exeter EX6 8BW (01392 832674).

Exmouth

Exmouth Welfare Trust

Eligibility: People living in the former urban district of Exmouth, comprising the parishes of Withycombe Raleigh and Littleham-cum-Exmouth who are convalescent, disabled, infirm or in need.

Types of grants: One-off grants according to need, for example, for food, clothing, medical care and equipment, convalescent holidays, beds and bedding, cookers, washers, refrigerators and travel to and from hospital. No grants for rents, rates, debts and outstanding liabilities.

Annual grant total: In 2000 the trust had an income of £18,000 and its total expenditure was £22,000. Grants were made to individuals totalling £21,000.

Applications: On a form available from the correspondent, submitted through an independent third party (not a relative) such as a social worker, citizen's advice bureau, other welfare agency, or another professional or well experienced person with detailed knowledge. Applications are considered throughout the year.

Correspondent: The Secretary, PO Box 16, Exmouth, EX8 3YT.

Gittisham

Elizabeth Beaumont Charity

Eligibility: People in need who live in the parish of Gittisham.

Types of grants: Quarterly pensions in March, June, September and December with a bonus at Christmas. One-off grants have been given for holidays and a mobile telephone for a disabled beneficiary. Grants and pensions range between £50 and £100.

Annual grant total: In 2001 the trust had an income of £3,900 and a total expenditure of £5,200. Information was not available about grants to individuals for this year.

The last edition of the guide stated that about 70 relief-in-need grants are made each year totalling £2,300.

Applications: In writing to the correspondent at any time throughout the year. Applications can be submitted directly by the individual or through a third party.

Correspondent: Mrs Paula S Land, 130 High Street, Honiton, Devon EX14 1JR (01404 41221; Fax: 01404 44976; e-mail: paula.land@everys.co.uk).

Great Torrington

The Great Torrington Town Lands Poors Charities

Eligibility: People in need who live in the former borough of Great Torrington.

Types of grants: Usually one-off grants according to need.

Annual grant total: In 2000/01 the trust made grants totalling £3,400 to individuals in need and £27,000 to organisations.

Applications: In writing to the correspondent, with all relevant personal information.

Correspondent: C J Styles, The Town Hall Office, High Street, Torrington, Devon EX38 8HN (01805 623517).

Other information: This entry was not confirmed by the trust, but the information was correct according to its file at the Charity Commission.

Highweek

Highweek Charities

Eligibility: People in need over the age of 65 who live in the ancient parish of Highweek.

Types of grants: One-off Christmas grants of £60 and other grants of up to £300 or £500.

Annual grant total: In 2000 the trust's income was £7,200 and grants totalled £2,600, including £2,100 to individuals.

Applications: In writing to the correspondent, directly by the individual. Applications should be submitted in September or October, for consideration in October.

Correspondent: T Keen, Clerk and Collector, Parkhill, Coombeshead Road, Highweek, Newton Abbot TQ12 1PY (01626 206675).

Holsworthy

The Peter Speccott Charity

Eligibility: People in need who live in Holsworthy and Holsworthy Hamlet.

Types of grants: Grants and loans are given to provide temporary relief for people facing unexpected loss or sudden destitution.

Annual grant total: The trust has an income of £2,100 a year, of which £1,500 is disbursed to about 50 people, for relief of need and also for people starting work. In 2000 its total expenditure was £2,300.

Applications: In writing to the correspondent. The trust also advertises in local colleges, careers offices, social services and so on.

Correspondent: Denzel C Blackman, 8 Fore Street, Holsworthy, Devon EX22 6ED (01409 253262).

Honiton

Honiton United Charities

Eligibility: People in need, aged 65 or over (men) or 60 or over (women), who live in the borough of Honiton.

Types of grants: Pensions of £10 a quarter for single people, and £15 a quarter for married couples. Any additional funds can also be given in one-off payments towards, for example, shoes, clothing or holidays.

Annual grant total: In 2000 the trust's income and total expenditure were both of about £7,800. Over 400 quarterly grants were made to individuals totalling £6,500.

Applications: In writing to the correspondent including details of income and savings. Applications can be submitted directly by the individual or through a social worker, citizen's advice bureau or other welfare agency, and are considered throughout the year.

Correspondent: Mrs Paula Land, 130 High Street, Honiton, Devon EX14 1JR (01404 41221; Fax: 01404 44976; e-mail: paula.land@everys.co.uk).

Kingsbridge

The Parish Charity (Dodbrook Feoffees)

Eligibility: People in need who live in the parishes of Dodbrook and Kingsbridge.

Types of grants: One-off grants and pensions to elderly people.

Annual grant total: In 2000 the trust had an income of £18,000 and its total expenditure was £16,000.

Applications: In writing to the correspondent. Applications are considered in January, March, June and September.

Correspondent: D Tucker, 6 Alvington Terrace, Westville, Kingsbridge, Devon TQ7 1HD.

Other information: This entry was not confirmed by the trust, but the information was correct according to its file at the Charity Commission.

Litton Cheney

The Litton Cheney Relief-in-Need Trust

Eligibility: People in need who live in the parish of Litton Cheney.

Types of grants: Grants ranging from £100 to £220 are distributed once a year at the beginning of December. One-off emergency grants can be made at any time, for example, where there is a serious illness in the family.

Annual grant total: In 2000 the trust had an income of £2,900 and its total expenditure was £3,700, all of which was given in grants to people in need, university students and people starting work.

Applications: Applications, on a form available from the correspondent, should be submitted directly by the individual, and are considered throughout the year.

Correspondent: Mrs Betty Champkins, Pins Knolls, Chalk Pit Lane, Litton Cheney, Dorchester, Dorset DT2 9AN.

Other information: Grants of £100 are made each year for 16 year old people who are about to start a career and to 18 year olds who are about to start at university. Grants are towards books and equipment.

Newport

The Newport Charity

Eligibility: People in need who are 65 or over and live in the ecclesiastical parish of Newport.

Types of grants: In 2002 this trust was carrying out changes in the way it managed its assets and no grants had been made for a number of years. It had previously donated vouchers, paid in December and June to spend in local shops and anticipated that this programme would be running again in 2004. In the meantime emergency one-off grants can possibly be made.

Annual grant total: See above.

Applications: In writing to the correspondent.

Correspondent: D Pickard, Lawnswood, 17 Hillcrest Road, Barnstaple, Devon EX32 9EP (01271 343738).

Ottery St Mary

The Non-Ecclesiastical Charity of Thomas Axe

Eligibility: Sick and poor people living in Ottery St Mary.

Types of grants: One-off grants ranging from £25 to £200 in 'marriage portions', and aids for elderly and disabled people. Recurrent support cannot be given.

Annual grant total: In 2001 the trust's income was £2,000, all of which was given in grants to individuals: £1,800 for relief-in-need purposes and £200 for educational purposes.

Applications: In writing to the correspondent directly by the individual, or through a social worker, citizen's advice bureau or other welfare agency. Applications are considered in March, June, September and December although urgent requests can be considered at any time. Requests for marriage portions should be submitted on an application form available from the correspondent.

Correspondent: D B Roberts, Eminence, Otter Close, Tipton St John, Sidmouth, Devon EX10 0JU (01404 813961).

The Ottery Feoffee Charity

Eligibility: People in need who live in the ancient parish of Ottery St Mary.

Types of grants: One-off or recurrent grants according to need.

Annual grant total: In 2000 the trust had an income of £32,000 and its total expenditure was £27,000, mainly spent on the upkeep of the charity's almshouses. £400 was given in grants to individuals. In the following year few applications were received from individuals, and no grants were made.

Applications: In writing to the correspondent.

Correspondent: J E Akers, 7 Broad Street, Ottery St Mary, Devon EX11 1BS (01404 812228; e-mail: mossop&whitham@eclipse.co.uk).

Paignton

Paignton Parish Charity

Eligibility: Poor people who are long-term residents of Paignton.

Types of grants: Cash payments of £50 are given twice a year for use as the recipient wishes. Payments are not made for any recurring expenditure, such as rent, mortgage or child support.

Annual grant total: In 2000/01 the trust's assets totalled £120,000, it had an income of £9,200 and its total expenditure was £7,000. Grants were made to 40 individuals totalling £4,000. The trust also makes annual donations to surgery support groups, and in 2000/01 these totalled £1,500.

Applications: On a form available from the correspondent, submitted via one of the trustees, for consideration at meetings in May and December.

Correspondent: c/o Mrs A Palmer, 12 Monastery Road, Paignton, Devon TQ3 3BU (01803 556680).

Plymouth

J H Beckly Handicapped/Sick Children's Fund

See entry on page 280

The Joseph Jory's Charity

Eligibility: Widows over 50 who are in need and have lived in the city of Plymouth for the last seven years.

Types of grants: Pensions paid quarterly. Amounts vary according to available income. In 2001 the amount was £177 a quarter. At the time of printing the vacancies were all filled, the trust said that when vacancies arise, they will be advertised locally.

Annual grant total: In 2001 the trust had an income of £10,000 and its total expenditure was £12,000, all of which was given in grants.

Applications: The trust advertises when funds are available: because ongoing grants are made funds only become available to new applicants when someone leaves the fund's list of beneficiaries. New applications made are, however, kept on file.

Correspondent: Julie Watson, 62–64 North Hill, Plymouth PL4 8EP (01752 663295).

The Ladies Aid Society and Eyre Charity

Eligibility: Widows and spinsters who were born, have lived or now live in Plymouth. Women who are divorced are not eligible for grants.

Types of grants: Annuities of £100 quarterly to each recipient.

Annual grant total: In 2001 the trusts had assets of £255,000, an income of £9,400 and its total expenditure was £13,000. Annuities were made totalling £11,000.

Applications: Applications are considered in March and September. They should be submitted on a form available from the correspondent, through a social worker, citizen's advice bureau, clergy, doctor, solicitor or similar third party.

Before applying to the trust, the applicant should have obtained any statutory help they are entitled to.

Correspondent: Mrs J M Stephens, 14 Court Park, Thurlestone, Kingsbridge, Devon TQ7 3LX (01548 560891).

Plymouth Charity Trust

Eligibility: People in need who live in the city of Plymouth.

Types of grants: Grants are one-off and can be towards the cost of clothes for children of families with very limited income and to relieve sudden distress, sickness or infirmity. No grants are given to other charities, to clear debts or for any need that can be met by Social Services. Grants are of between £50 and £150. The trust usually makes the donation in the form of vouchers, credit at the Co-op or payment into a voluntary grants account. They prefer not to give payment directly to the applicant to prevent mis-use of funds.

Annual grant total: In 2001/02 the trust made grants totalling £1,000 to 12 individuals for relief-in need purposes and £500 to 5 individuals for educational purposes.

Applications: On a form available from the correspondent, to be submitted directly by the individual or through a social worker, citizen's advice bureau or other third party. Applications are considered every month except August. Applications must include financial details.

Correspondent: Mrs J Gibbons, Charity Trust Office, 41 Heles Terrace, Prince Rock, Plymouth PL4 9LH (Tel & Fax: 01752 663107; e-mail: jg@charity-trust.demon.co.uk).

Sandford

The Sandford Relief-in-Need Charity

Eligibility: Pensioners in need who live in Sandford parish.

Types of grants: One-off grants usually of £10 to £50 to repair broken/damaged household items, towards bereavement expenses etc. or recurrent grants of £12 a month (to about 30 households). Two pensioners have also received donations for their Lifelines. Winter grants are given in December towards fuel bills to be exchanged at local suppliers.

Annual grant total: In 2001 the trust had an income of £5,700 and its total expenditure was £5,800. Grants were made totalling £4,600 to 399 individuals in need.

Applications: In writing to the correspondent either directly by the individual or through a social worker, citizen's advice bureau, or other welfare agency. Applications are usually considered in March, September and November, but they can also be considered outside of these times.

Correspondent: Mrs H D Edworthy, 7 Snows, Sandford, Crediton, Devon EX17 4NJ (01363 772550).

Sheepwash

The Bridgeland Charity

Eligibility: Older people in need who live in the parish of Sheepwash.

Types of grants: One-off grants ranging from £25 to £100.

Annual grant total: In 2000/01 the trust had assets of £60,000, its income was £3,200 and its total expenditure was £2,700. No grants were given to individuals for relief in need, but £1,900 was given for other purposes.

Applications: In writing to the correspondent directly by the individual, for consideration throughout the year.

Correspondent: P M Whittaker, Littlewoods, East Street, Sheepwash, Beaworthy, North Devon EX21 5NW (01409 231534).

Other information: The trust also supports local schools and community projects.

Sidmouth

Sidmouth Consolidated Charities

Eligibility: People in need who live in Sidmouth.

Types of grants: One-off grants of up to £1,000, towards for example new cookers, washing machines and stairlifts, and to help with travel expenses to visit someone in hospital,

Annual grant total: In 2000 the charities' assets totalled £390,000, their joint income was £58,000 and their total expenditure was £46,000. Grants were made to 12 individuals in need totalling £3,600. Grants were made to 11 individuals for education totalling £7,000.

Applications: In writing to the correspondent, either directly by the individual, or through a social worker, citizen's advice bureau or welfare agency. Applications are considered at monthly meetings.

Correspondent: Mrs Ruth Rose, 22 Alexandria Road, Sidmouth, Devon EX10 9HB (01395 513079; e-mail: ruth.rose@eclipse.co.uk).

Silverton

Silverton Parochial Charity

Eligibility: People in need in the parish of Silverton.

Types of grants: One-off grants, with no minimum or maximum limit. Grants are towards anything that will help to relieve the hardship or need, such as alarms for people who are infirm, stairlifts, hospital travel costs, heating costs, children's clothing and wheelchairs.

No grants are made towards state or local authority taxes.

Annual grant total: In 2001 the trust had assets of £253,000, its income was £20,000 and its total expenditure was £22,000, including £10,000 given in 52 grants to individuals in need. £10,000 was given in grants for other purposes, including for the carers of people in need.

Applications: Application forms can be obtained from the Silverton Post Office or the Community Hall, or prospective beneficiaries can write or speak to the correspondent at the address below. Completed forms can be submitted to the correspondent by the individual or by a carer or welfare department, and so on. The trustees will need details of the applicant's financial situation. Applications are considered monthly.

Correspondent: C A Williams, Henbury, Old Butterleigh Road, Silverton, Devon EX5 4JE (01392 860408).

Other information: Grants are also made to organisations providing assistance to people in need who live in the parish, and for educational purposes.

South Brent

The South Brent Parish Lands Charity

Eligibility: People in need who live in the parish of South Brent.

Types of grants: One-off or recurrent grants and Christmas gifts. Grants can be £25 to £300 and can be for a variety of needs including hospital transport/travel costs and special treatment to adults and/ or children where the family is desperately in need of help.

Annual grant total: In 2000 the trust had an income of £38,000 and its total expenditure was £11,000. It stated that it usually donates about £13,000 in about 50 grants to individuals for both welfare and educational purposes.

Applications: On a form available from the correspondent which can be submitted by the individual or through a local health centre/social worker/educational welfare officer.

Correspondent: J I G Blackler, Luscombe Maye, 6 Fore Street, South Brent, Devon TQ10 9BQ (01364 73651; Fax: 01364 73885; e-mail: luscombe@ukonline.co.uk).

Sowton

Sowton In Need Charity

Eligibility: People in need who live in the parish of Sowton.

Types of grants: One-off grants for any specific educational or personal need. Grants have been given towards funeral expenses in the past.

Annual grant total: In 1999 the charity had an income and a total expenditure of £1,000.

Applications: In writing to the correspondent, to be submitted either directly by the individual or through a social worker, citizen's advice bureau, other welfare agency or any third party.

Correspondent: Dr N S Alcock, The Old Rectory, Sowton, Exeter EX5 2AG (01392 367423).

Other information: Grants are also given to organisations.

Topsham

The Charity of John Shere & Others

Eligibility: People in need who have lived in the parish of Topsham (as its boundaries were in 1966) for at least three years.

Types of grants: According to the correspondent, sums vary depending on the number of applications received. In 2001 grants of £150 were given to 22 individuals.

Annual grant total: In 2000/01 the trust's assets totalled £11,000, it had an income of £5,300 and its total expenditure was £4,200. Grants were made to 22 individuals totalling £3,300.

Applications: On a form available from the correspondent. Applications should be submitted directly by the individual in May, for consideration in June each year.

Correspondent: David Tucker, 25 White Street, Topsham, Exeter EX3 0AE (01392 873168).

Torbay

The Leonora Carlow Trust Fund

Eligibility: Children up to 18 who have physical or mental disabilities and live in Torbay.

Types of grants: One-off grants ranging from £100 to £500 for special equipment such as wheelchairs, bath hoists and car seats. No grants for telephones.

Annual grant total: In 2000/01 the trust had assets of £13,000, an income of £870 and gave three grants to individuals in need totalling £850.

Applications: On a form available from the correspondent, through a social worker, citizen's advice bureau or other welfare agency. Applications are considered throughout the year except during August, and should include details of help sought from any other source and the outcome.

Correspondent: Caroline Jane Shaw, Administration Assistant, Social Services Directorate, Oldway Mansion, Torquay Road, Paignton TQ3 2TS (01803 208412; Fax: 01803 208408; e-mail: carolineshaw@torbay.gov.uk).

Torquay

The Annie Toll Bequest

Eligibility: Elderly or sick women in need who live in Torquay.

Types of grants: Recurrent grants of up to £20 a month and one-off payments for special needs ranging from £100 to £300. Grants may be given towards the hire costs of equipment, for example a television.

Annual grant total: In 2000 the trust's income was £3,000 and its total expenditure was £3,900. Grants were made to 12 individuals totalling £3,600.

Applications: In writing to the correspondent. Applications can be made directly by the individual, through a social worker, citizen's advice bureau, other welfare agency or other third party on behalf of the individual.

Correspondent: A C Grant, 3 Monterey Close, Torquay, Devon TQ2 6QN.

Totnes

The Dart Valley Medical Trust

Eligibility: People in need who are sick and live in Dart Valley (Totnes, Buckeastleigh or Ashburton).

Types of grants: Provision of equipment, materials (usually as a loan) and services not provided by the Health Authority or doctors. Occasionally electric wheelchairs are bought and loaned to beneficiaries. Wheelchairs are serviced and re-issued on the death of the beneficiary. Grants are also given for bath lifts, special beds, wheelchairs and computers for people who are disabled.

Annual grant total: In 2000/01 the trust had an income of £3,200 and its total expenditure was £4,200. Information about how much was given in grants was not available for this year.

In 1998/99 the trust had an income of £6,600 and spent £5,100, of which £370 (excluding loans) was given in grants.

Applications: In writing to the correspondent either directly by the individual or through a doctor, social worker, citizen's advice bureau or other welfare agency. Applications are considered four to six times a year by a board that includes members of social services and medical practices.

Correspondent: P D Bethel, Tingrith, Ashburton Road, Totnes, Devon TQ9 5JU (01803 862021).

Dorset

The Beaminster Charities

Eligibility: People in need who live in Beaminster, Netherbury and Stoke Abbott.

Types of grants: One-off and recurrent grants according to need. The trustees will consider any application.

Annual grant total: In 2000 the trust's income was £14,000 and grants made to

South West – Dorset

individuals totalled £9,900, including grants to schoolchildren for school trips.

Applications: Applications can be submitted in writing to the correspondent by the individual or through a recognised referral agency (social worker, citizen's advice bureau or doctor etc).

Correspondent: J Groves, 24 Church Street, Beaminster, Dorset DT8 3BA (01308 862313).

The Boveridge Charity

Eligibility: Poor single people, widows/widowers or spinsters/bachelors, who are in need and have lived in the ancient parish of Cranborne (which includes the present parishes of Cranborne-cum-Boveridge, Wimborne St Giles, Alderholt, Verwood, Ferndown, West Farley and Edmondsham) for at least two years.

People in need who live outside the beneficial area may also be supported in exceptional circumstances.

Types of grants: Monthly pensions and one-off grants for any type of need, of up to £750. Grants have previously been given for holiday recuperation after sickness, alterations to a cottage to provide ground floor facilities for an infirm older person, a computer for a disabled child, coal for a single mother, and for help with electricity bills.

Annual grant total: In 2001/02 the trust's assets totalled £130,000, it had an income of £7,000 and its total expenditure was £4,800. It gave 14 grants to 8 individuals totalling £4,000.

Applications: In writing to the correspondent, submitted directly by the individual, or through a third party. Applications are considered throughout the year and should contain details of the individual's income and capital.

Correspondent: Mrs R D Hunt, Abernant, Bessomer Drove, Redlynch, Salisbury, Wiltshire SP5 2PM (Tel & Fax: 01725 510508).

The Pitt-Rivers Charity

Eligibility: People who live in the parish of Hinton St Mary and the surrounding area who are in need, for example due to hardship, disability or sickness.

Types of grants: One-off grants, ranging between £100 and £1,000.

Annual grant total: Grants totalled £29,000 in 2001 and were mostly given to organisations.

Applications: In writing to the correspondent.

Correspondent: G A Pitt-Rivers, Hinton St Mary Estate Office, Sturminster Newton, Dorset DT10 1NA.

Other information: The trust stated that because of the geographical limitations of this trust, grants are only occasionally given to individuals.

The Poole Children's Fund

Eligibility: Children up to 18 who are disadvantaged, disabled or otherwise in need and live in the borough of Poole.

Types of grants: One-off grants of £10 to £50 towards the cost of holidays, educational or recreational opportunities.

Preference for children with behavioural and social difficulties who have limited opportunities for leisure and recreational activities of a positive nature, for schoolchildren with serious family difficulties so the child has to be educated away from home and people with special education needs.

Annual grant total: In 1999 the trust had an income of £1,800 and its total expenditure was £1,300, most of which was given in grants for both welfare and educational purposes.

Applications: On a form available from the correspondent completed by a third party such as a social worker, health visitor, minister or teacher. Applications are considered throughout the year. They should include details of family structure including: ages; reason for application; family income and any other sources of funding which have been tried; what agencies (if any) are involved in helping the family; and any statutory orders (for example, care orders) relating to the child or their family members.

Correspondent: Ms Jacqui Crump or Joan Hart, 14a Commercial Road, Park Stone, Poole, Dorset BH14 0JW (01202 735046/01202 745110).

Tollard Trust

Eligibility: (i) People living in Bournemouth, Poole and elsewhere in Dorset who are older or disabled and who live in their own homes and are affected by hardship and sickness. Applicants should be, or have been: chemists; members of the clergy; ex-services and service people; farmers; legal professionals; masons; medical professionals; musicians; research workers; seafarers and fishermen; and textile workers and designers.
(ii) People from Asia and Africa who are disabled or in financial need.

Types of grants: Recurrent grants of about £100, towards items, services or facilities. No grants are made for education and training, including expeditions or scholarships.

Annual grant total: In 2000/01 the trust had an income of £9,900 and its total expenditure was £11,000. Further information was not available for this year. The trust has previously stated that it makes grants totalling about £7,000 a year.

Applications: Grants are made once a year, usually in November. Most grants are in answer to requests from charities, for example, Salvation Army, Pramacare, RUKBA, Greenhill, McDougall and other local charities. Very occasionally grants are made directly to individuals in need who live locally.

Correspondent: R J Carlyle-Clarke, Tollard Green Farm, Salisbury, Wiltshire SP5 5PX (01725 516323).

Other information: Up-to-date information was not provided by the trust, but the address was correct according to the Charity Commission database.

The William Williams Charity

Eligibility: People in need who live in the ancient parishes of Blandford, Shaftesbury or Sturminster Newton.

Types of grants: One-off grants according to need.

Annual grant total: In 2000 the trust's income and total expenditure were both £258,000. Educational grants to individuals totalled about £100,000. Further grants were given to individuals in need, possibly totalling about £20,000. Grants are also given to organisations.

Applications: Applicants should apply directly to one of the trustees; in the first instance contact the correspondent to find which of the trustees is most relevant, and what their address is. The trustees meet quarterly to discuss applications.

Correspondent: Ian Winsor, Steward, Stafford House, 10 Prince of Wales Road, Dorchester, Dorset DT1 1PW (01305 264573; e-mail: wwc@kennedylegg.demon.co.uk).

Bournemouth

Bournemouth Society for the Visually Impaired (formerly The Bournemouth Blind Aid Society)

Eligibility: People who are registered blind or partially sighted and who live within the borough boundary of Bournemouth.

Types of grants: Grants of £8 are given towards holiday expenses. Larger grants may be given towards the cost of special equipment and special aids.

Annual grant total: In 1999/2000 the trust had an income of £91,000. Its total expenditure was £60,000 and included: £1,800 to holidays, outings and events, £1,800 on chiropody, £1,400 towards handicraft materials, £540 in subscriptions and donations and £174 in other grants.

Applications: Applications are considered throughout the year and can be made either directly by the individual or through a social worker, citizen's advice bureau, other welfare agency or other third party on behalf of the individual. Applicants will need to declare their income for means-testing.

Correspondent: Mrs Angela Ross, Director, Centre for the Visually Impaired,

5 Victoria Park Road, Moordown, Bournemouth, Dorset BH9 2RB (01202 546644).

The MacDougall Trust

Eligibility: People in need who live in Bournemouth and the surrounding area, in the county of Dorset.

Types of grants: One-off grants of up to £200 to £300, for all kinds of personal need, including debts. Grants are not given to organisations, or for educational purposes or sponsorship, or where statutory or other help is still available.

Annual grant total: In 2000/01 the trust had assets totalling £188,000, its income was £13,000 and it made grants to individuals in need totalling £14,000.

Applications: Applicants should ensure all statutory funding has been accessed before making an aplication to the trust.

Applications should be made on a form available from Mrs A Kirby, 7 Minterne Grange, Crichel Mount Road, Poole, Dorset BH14 8LU, preferably with the backing of a recognised agency, for example a GP or social services. Applications are considered quarterly.

Correspondent: P D Malpas, 7 Church Road, Parkstone, Poole, Dorset BH14 8UR (01202 730002).

Charmouth

The Almshouse Charity

Eligibility: People in need who, or whose immediate family, live in the parish of Charmouth.

Types of grants: One-off and recurrent grants, generally of £40 to £200. Grants have been given for hospital travel, funeral expenses, special needs, health, sports and general expenses. Grants can also be towards the total or part payment of the costs of equipment, such as electric chairs and cars, arthritic supports, shopping trolleys, washing machines and nebulisers. Annual grocery vouchers are given to selected people ranging from £40 to £60. The trust also makes interest-free loans.

Annual grant total: In 2001 the trust had assets of £69,000 and its income was £2,500. Total expenditure was £3,600, including £1,900 in grants to 44 individuals for both relief-in-need and educational purposes, and £1,800 in other grants.

Applications: In writing to the correspondent or other trustees. Applications can be submitted directly by the individual or through a third party such as a rector, doctor or trustee. They are usually considered in February, June and November; emergencies can be considered at other times. Applications should include details of the purpose of the grant, the total costs involved, and an official letter or programme/itinerary.

Correspondent: D H M Carter, Secretary, 2 Parkway, Lower Sea Lane, Charmouth, Bridport, Dorset DT6 6LP (01297 560910).

Other information: Grants are also given to individiuals for further and higher education and overseas voluntary work, and to youth clubs for specific purposes.

Christchurch

Legate's Charity

Eligibility: People in need who live in Christchurch borough.

Types of grants: Allowances of £3.50 a week for individuals and £5.50 a week joint allowance, to help with household bills and so on. One-off grants may be awarded depending on circumstances, for example, towards domestic items and clothing. Funds are not given to pay off debts to public bodies (income or council tax debt).

Annual grant total: In 2001 the trust had assets of £170,000, an income of £7,100 and its total expenditure was £6,900, all of which was given in grants and allowances.

Applications: On a form available from the correspondent submitted either directly by the individual or through a friend, relative, social worker, citizen's advice bureau or other welfare agency. New applications are considered quarterly.

Correspondent: Lee Abraham, Clerk to the Trustees, Civic Offices, Bridge Street, Christchurch, Dorset BH23 1AZ (01202 495141; Fax: 01202 482060; e-mail: l.abraham@christchurch.gov.uk).

Mayor's Goodwill Fund

Eligibility: People in need who live in the borough of Christchurch.

Types of grants: Food parcels at Christmas to elderly people and other people in need who cannot afford extras at Christmas. Potted plants are given to lonely and alone people at Christmas. Sweets and chocolates are given to children who are disabled or ill.

Annual grant total: In 2000/01 the trust had assets of £2,100, an income of £1,300 and it made 310 grants to individuals in need totalling £2,400.

Applications: On a form available from the correspondent preferably through a social worker, citizen's advice bureau, other welfare agency, friend, neighbour or clergy. Applications should be submitted in October and November, and are considered in November. They should include the applicant's name and address and details of their circumstances.

Grants are not made where full details of the individual's needs are not supplied.

Correspondent: The Mayor's Secretary, Civic Offices, Bridge Street, Christchurch, Dorset BH23 1AZ (01202 495134; Fax: 01202 482060; e-mail: l.jamieson@christchurch.gov.uk).

Other information: Grants can also be made to local organisations which provide Christmas activities for people in need, such as Age Concern.

Corfe Castle

Corfe Castle Charities

Eligibility: People in need who live in the parish of Corfe Castle, including the village of Kingston.

Types of grants: One-off grants or interest-free loans to relieve sickness, infirmity or distress, e.g. rental of emergency lifelines, help with recuperative hospital costs and payment of travel expenses for patients/visiting relatives to hospital.

Annual grant total: In 2001/02 the trust made relief-in-need grants totalling £17,000.

Applications: On a form available from the correspondent, to be submitted directly by the individual. The trustees meet monthly, but emergency requests are dealt with as they arise.

Correspondent: Mrs J Wilson, The Spinney, Springbrook Close, Harmans Cross, Dorset BH20 5HS (01929 480873; Fax: 01929 481271).

Dorchester

Dorchester Relief-in-Need Charity

Eligibility: People in need who live in the ecclesiastical parish of Dorchester.

Types of grants: One-off grants of up to £250, for example, for redecoration of a room or flat, household equipment e.g. fridge or cooker, repair of a wheelchair and playschool fees.

Annual grant total: In 2000/01 the trust's assets totalled £16,000, its income was £2,800 and its total expenditure was £2,100, all of which was given in 11 grants, for both relief-in-need and educational purposes.

Applications: Applications should be submitted through a social worker, health visitor, citizen's advice bureau, clergy, school or similar third party. There is a form and applications are considered throughout the year.

Correspondent: R C Burnett, 48 Herringston Road, Dorchester, Dorset DT1 2BT (01305 265496).

Shaftesbury

John Foyles Charity

Eligibility: People in need who live in the town of Shaftesbury.

Types of grants: One-off and recurrent grants and loans, including those for educational toys for people who are disabled, moving expenses, fuel meter money, equipment, carpets and decoration.

Annual grant total: In 2002 the trust stated that in a recent year, its assets were £140,000, it had an income of about £3,000 and its total expenditure was £250, all of which was given to individuals in need.

Applications: In writing to the correspondent at any time. Applications can be submitted directly by the individual or through an appropriate third party; and should show evidence of need, for example, benefit record, and proof of address. They can be submitted at any time, for consideration at the discretion of the trustees.

Correspondent: Simon Rutter, Grosvenor House, Bleke Street, Shaftesbury, Dorset SP7 8AW (01747 851881; 01747 851081).

Sturminster Newton

The Sturminster Newton United Charities

Eligibility: Pensioners in need who live in the parish of Sturminster Newton.

Types of grants: Recurrent grants are made at Christmas in the form of tokens.

Annual grant total: In 2001 the trust had assets of £16,000, its income was £790 and its total expenditure was £900.

Applications: In writing to the correspondent by the individual or an appropriate third party. The trustees meet in mid-November and decide on the amount to be given before Christmas in the form of food and fuel tokens.

Correspondent: G Allen, 9 Durrant, Sturminster Newton, Dorset DT10 1DQ (01258 473296).

Wimborne Minster

Brown Habgood Hall and Higden Charity

Eligibility: Usually retired people on low income living in the ancient parish of Wimborne Minster, in Dorset.

Types of grants: One off grants, but mainly quarterly payments. Grants are not usually for more than £200, and are mainly for smaller amounts.

Annual grant total: About 38 regular grants are given, approximately four each month, plus one-off grants.

In 2000 the trust had an income of £12,000 and its total expenditure was £11,000.

Applications: In writing to the correspondent either directly by the individual, through a social worker, citizen's advice bureau, other welfare agency or through another third party such as a doctor, health visitor or clergy. The applicant's full name, address, age and employment should be included.

Correspondent: Mrs M A Brace, 2 Cobbs Road, Colehill, Wimborne, Dorset BH21 2RL (01202 885932).

Gloucestershire

The Barnwood House Trust

Eligibility: People in need who have a serious and non-remedial physical or mental disability and have lived in the county of Gloucestershire for at least 12 months.

Types of grants: One-off grants ranging from £50 to £300, are given for house adaptations, equipment, respite care breaks, holidays, clothes, selected bills and so on.

No grants for private education, private medicine/therapies, council tax or other taxes or fines, funeral related expenses, recurring grants, non-disabled dependants and no grants for anything there is state provision for. Loans are rarely given.

Annual grant total: In 2001 the trust gave £315,000 in 1,116 grants to individuals.

Applications: By referral only to the Grants Administrator at the address below. The key professional (such as social worker, doctor etc.) who knows the applicant's circumstances and need should complete the trust's application form. A financial assessment is made. Applications are considered weekly.

Correspondent: Grant Administrator, The Manor House, 162 Barnwood Road, Gloucester GL4 7JX (01452 611292 & 614429; Fax: 01452 372594).

Other information: Grants are also given to organisations in Gloucestershire who work with the beneficial group.

Dame Ann Cam's Charity

Eligibility: People who as a result of age, ill health or some other infirmity can no longer support themselves and who live within a 20 mile radius of Dymock.

Types of grants: Pensions of about £120 a year paid half yearly.

Annual grant total: About £1,600 is given in grants each year. In 2000/01 the trust had an income of £1,600 and its total expenditure was £1,300.

Applications: On a form available from the correspondent. Applications should be submitted before June each year.

Correspondent: W H Masefield, Secretary, R & C B Masefield, Worcester Road, Ledbury, Herefordshire HR8 1PN (01531 632377; Fax: 01531 633904).

Cheltenham Aid-in-Sickness & Nurses Welfare Fund and the Cheltenham Family Welfare Association – Gooding Fund

Eligibility: (i). Domiciliary nurses, past or present, who are in need and have worked or lived in the Cheltenham area.
(ii). People in need who are sick, convalescent, disabled or infirm who live in Cheltenham and neighbourhood.
(iii). (Gooding Fund) Individuals or families in need, where no illness is involved.

Types of grants: One-off grants, up to £100, towards clothing, essential items of furniture, beds and bedding, washing machines, cookers, floor covering, appliances for disabled people, telephone installation and so on. 'Pensions' are also given.

Annual grant total: About £8,000 is given in grants to around 140 individuals, including pensions for 3 nurses.

Applications: On a form available from the correspondent. Applications should be submitted through a social worker, citizen's advice bureau, health visitor, community nurse or other welfare agency. They are considered monthly.

Correspondent: Mrs K Fleming, Secretary, Cheltenham Family Welfare Association, 21 Rodney Road, Cheltenham, Gloucestershire GL50 1HX (Tel & Fax: 01242 522180; e-mail: cfwa@fish.co.uk).

Other information: Occasionally grants are made for educational trips for local schoolchildren in need and to local organisations working with people in need.

The Fluck Convalescent Fund

Eligibility: Women of all ages and children (both sexes) under 16 who live in the city of Gloucester and its surrounding area, being the former rural district of Gloucester, who are poor, sick or convalescent after illness or surgical operation.

Types of grants: One-off grants between £50 and £350 for recuperative holidays, clothing, bedding, furniture, fuel, food, household equipment, domestic help and medical or other aids. Grants will not be made for the repayment of a debt already incurred or recurrent payments such as rent, electricity, taxes and other public funds.

Annual grant total: In 2000/01 the fund had assets of £940,000, an income of £33,000 and its total expenditure was £27,000. It gave 118 grants totalling £25,000.

Applications: Applications in writing to the correspondent must be submitted through a social worker, citizen's advice bureau or other welfare agency or through another third party such as a health visitor or doctor. Applications are considered throughout the year.

Correspondent: The Clerk, c/o Whitemans Solicitors, Second Floor, 65 London Road, Gloucester GL1 3HF (01452 411601; Fax: 01452 300922).

The Gloucester District Nursing Charities

Eligibility: People in need who live in the city of Gloucester and the immediately adjoining parishes.

Types of grants: One-off and recurrent grants ranging from £50 to £100. Examples of recent grants include those towards a special bed, electric wheelchair, specially adapted tricycle, a microwave and two chests of drawers.

Annual grant total: In 2000/01 the trust had an income of £38,000 and its total expenditure was £32,000. Information on grants was not available this year.

In 1999 the trust had assets of £45,000, an income of £32,000 and its total expenditure was £27,000. It gave £700 in grants to three individuals.

Applications: In writing to the correspondent for consideration throughout the year.

Correspondent: The Clerk to the Trustees, Office 8, Hewmar House, 120 London Road, Gloucester GL1 3PL (01452 524915).

Gloucestershire Bowling Association Benevolent Fund

Eligibility: Bowlers, ex-bowlers and their immediate dependants, who are in need and are present or past members of the association.

Types of grants: One-off and recurrent grants towards, for example, hospital visits.

Annual grant total: In 1998/99 the trust had an income of £2,300 and its total expenditure was £1,000.

Applications: In writing to the correspondent.

Correspondent: J Hinds, Beech Corner, Sheepscombe, Nr Stroud, Gloucestershire GL6 7QZ (01452 813368).

Gloucestershire Football Association Benevolent Fund

Eligibility: Amateur football players who were injured while playing football in 'recognised' matches and are affiliated to Gloucestershire Football Association.

Types of grants: One-off and recurrent grants according to need.

Annual grant total: In 2000 the trust had an income of £12,000 and its total expenditure was £6,700.

Applications: In writing to the correspondent.

Correspondent: The Clerk to the Trustees, Gloucestershire Football Association Limited, Oaklands Park Stadium, Gloucester Road, Almondsbury, Bristol BS32 4AG (01454 615888; e-mail: gloucestershire.fa@dial.pipex.com).

Sylvanus Lyson's Charity

Eligibility: Clergy of the Church of England and their widows and dependants who are in need and are serving in or retired from the diocese of Gloucester.

Types of grants: One-off grants according to need.

Annual grant total: In 2000/01 the trust's assets totalled £5.2 million, it had an income of £240,000 and its total expenditure was £280,000. Grants were made to individuals in need totalling £30,000, and to churches in the diocese, for their religious and charitable work, totalling £200,000.

Applications: In writing to the correspondent, directly by the individual, for consideration in March, July, September and November.

Correspondent: N A M Smith, Morroway House, Station Road, Gloucester GL1 1DW (01452 301903; Fax: 01452 411115).

The Prestbury Charity (also known as The Prestbury United Charities)

Eligibility: People in need who live in the ecclesiastical parish of St Mary, Prestbury and the adjoining parishes of Southam and Swindon village.

Types of grants: One-off grants towards, for example, clothing, food, medical care, equipment travel to and from hospital and repairs to homes.

Annual grant total: In 2001 the trust's assets totalled £310,000, it had an income of £10,000 and total expenditure was £6,100. Grants to three individuals totalled £1,600. Grants to organisations totalled £3,700.

Applications: In writing to the correspondent, either directly by the individual, or via a social worker, citizen's advice bureau or other welfare agency or third party. Applications should include the individual's home address, so that the trust can see that they live in the area of benefit.

Correspondent: K J Gyles, 7 Old Hall Close, Aston Somerville, Broadway, Worcester WR12 7JN (01386 852881).

Other information: Local organisations are also supported.

The Charity of Lord Redesdale

Eligibility: Members of the Church of England or people in regular attendance at divine service, who are in need and living in the ancient parishes of Batsford, Bourton-on-the-Hill, Blockley, Great Wolford, Moreton-in-Marsh, Little Wolford, and Snowshill.

Types of grants: Grants have been given towards help in bereavement, illness and loss of possessions in fire, for example, for medical costs, fuel or respite care.

Annual grant total: In 2000 the trust had an income of £1,600 and its total expenditure was £480.

Applications: In writing to the vicar of the parish, who will nominate applicants to the trustees.

Correspondent: c/o The Trustees, Lemington Grange, Moreton-in-Marsh, Gloucestershire GL56 9NN (01608 650547; Fax: 01608 651677).

Bisley

The Bisley Charities for the Poor

Eligibility: People in need who live in the ancient parish of Bisley.

Types of grants: One-off or recurrent grants according to need.

Annual grant total: In 2000/01 the trust had an income of £8,000 and its total expenditure was £8,100.

Applications: In writing to the correspondent.

Correspondent: Mrs M R Hartwell, Secretary, Prospect Cottage, Bisley, Stroud, Gloucestershire GL6 7AB (01452 770600).

Charlton Kings

Charlton Kings Relief in Need Charity

Eligibility: People in need who live in the parish of Charlton Kings or have a connection with the parish.

Types of grants: Grants of £50 to £1,000, according to need.

Annual grant total: In 2000/01 the trust had an income of £3,800 and its total expenditure was £2,700.

Applications: An initial telephone call is welcomed, although formal application should be by letter to the correspondent, submitted either directly by the individual or through a third party. Applications are considered five times a year.

Correspondent: M J Mitchell, Clerk, 11 Chestnut Terrace, Charlton Kings, Cheltenham, Gloucestershire GL53 8JQ (01242 572810).

Cirencester

The Smith's Cirencester Poor Charity

Eligibility: People in need who live within five miles of Cirencester town centre.

Types of grants: One-off grants of £150 to £200 towards, for example, items for people with disabilities or kitchen equipment, furniture and so on for young single mothers and families on low incomes. Recurrent grants are made to six beneficiaries each year, paid quarterly, to help with heating or living expenses.

Annual grant total: In 2000/01 the trust's assets were £13,000 and its income was £300. Its total expenditure was £3,600 and grants were made to 16 individuals totalling £2,700. Other grants totalled £200.

Applications: On a form available from the correspondent, submitted either directly by the individual or through a third party such as a landlord, teacher, doctor or social worker. Applications are considered in January, April, July and October.

Correspondent: Mrs Maria Ann Bell, 7 Dollar Street, Cirencester, Gloucestershire GL7 2AS (01285 650000).

Other information: Grants are also made to the social serivces to help set up groups to educate in 'life skills' such as parenting and cooking.

Gloucester

The United Charity of Palling Burgess

Eligibility: People in need who live in the city of Gloucester.

Types of grants: One-off and recurrent grants according to need. Grants may be made for almost any purpose except the payment of debts or fines. Grants are not usually made in cash.

Annual grant total: 25 grants totalling about £1,100.

Applications: In writing to the correspondent. Applications should be submitted through a social worker, nurse, health visitor, minister of religion or similar third party and are considered twice a year in March and October. Only applications submitted in February and September will be considered.

Correspondent: Mrs G E L Jones, Saith-Deg, 70 Oxstalls Drive, Longlevens, Gloucester GL2 9DE.

Minchinhampton

Albert Edward Pash Charitable Trust Fund

Eligibility: People who live in the civil parish of Minchinhampton, of any age or occupation, who are in need due, for example, to hardship, disability or sickness.

Types of grants: One-off grants.

Annual grant total: In 2001/02 the trust's assets totalled £32,000 and it had both an income and total expenditure of £1,200. A minimum of 25% of the income must be given towards hospital research each year, with the rest donated to individuals.

Applications: In writing to the correspondent, directly by the individual. Grants are distributed yearly in April.

Correspondent: Mrs Diana Wall, Clerk, The Parish Office, School Road, Minchinhampton, Gloucestershire GL6 9BP (Tel & Fax: 01453 731186; e-mail: minch@parish4.fsnet.co.uk).

Tewkesbury

Gyles Geest Charity

Eligibility: People in need who live in the town of Tewkesbury.

Types of grants: Annual distribution in December of £25 vouchers to be used in local shops for groceries etc. Recipients are generally retired or pensioners.

Annual grant total: In 2000/01 the trust had an income of £7,100. Gifts to people in need totalled £7,900 and other expenditure came to £490.

Applications: On a form available from the correspondent. Applications should be submitted directly by the individual before October each year, to be considered in November.

Correspondent: E A Hughes, Clerk, 23 Elmvil Road, Newtown, Tewkesbury, Gloucestershire GL20 8DD (01684 294493).

Thornbury

Thornbury Consolidated Charities (administered by Thornbury Town Trust)

Eligibility: People in need who live in the parish of Thornbury. Beneficiaries are often of pensionable age or disabled but anyone in the parish can apply.

Types of grants: One-off grants usually ranging from £60 to £100 to help with the extra expense of Christmas but they are also given at other times. Grants are also given to organisations. No grants for educational purposes. Grants are not given where the need is covered by statutory authorities.

Annual grant total: In 2001 donations totalled £7,600, including 87 grants to individuals totalling £5,200.

Applications: On a form available from the correspondent. Applications can be submitted directly by the individual or through a social worker, citizen's advice bureau or other welfare agency and should include details of income. They are considered in November for Christmas but applications for special needs can be made at any time.

Correspondent: J F Gibbon, Clerk, 7 Charles Close, Thornbury, Bristol BS35 1LN (01454 413857).

Wotton under Edge

Edith Strain Nursing Charity

Eligibility: Older people who live in the town of Wotton under Edge and who are in need due to sickness or infirmity.

Types of grants: One-off and recurrent grants normally ranging between £50 and £100. Grants are not made where statutory money is available.

Annual grant total: In 2000/01 the trust's assets totalled £56,000, it had an income of £2,200 and made 18 grants totalling £1,100 to individuals. Grants to organisations totalled £950.

Applications: In writing to the correspondent, either directly by the individual, or via a social worker, citizen's advice bureau or other welfare agency. An sae is required. Applications are usually considered in May and November.

Correspondent: R V Cartwright, The Charities Office, Perry and Dawes Almshouses, Church Street, Wotton under Edge, Gloucestershire GL12 7HE (01453 842944).

Other information: Grants are also made to local organisations which care for people who are sick.

Somerset

J A F Luttrell Memorial Charity

Eligibility: People in need who live in Edington, Catcott, Chilton Polden and Burtle.

Types of grants: One-off grants ranging from £100 to £750, towards, for example, hospital travel grants, vehicle maintenance, gardening, educational grants and medical care.

Annual grant total: In 2000/01 the trust's assets totalled £100,000, its income was £5,400 and it made 58 grants to individuals in need totalling £5,600.

Applications: In writing to the correspondent, directly by the individual.

Correspondent: Mrs A Auld, West Close, Church Road, Edington, Bridgwater, Somerset TA7 9JT (01278 722418).

The Somerset County Bowling Association Benevolent Fund

Eligibility: Bowlers from Somerset (pre-1965 borders) who are or have been members of subscribing clubs affiliated to the county association and their widows who are in need.

Types of grants: One-off grants ranging from £100 upwards.

Annual grant total: In 2000/01 the trust had an income of £1,600 and its total expenditure was £450. All of the income is available each year to be given in grants.

Applications: Applications should be made through the club secretary on the form available, and are considered throughout the year. There is an assessment of need.

Correspondent: J D Durston, 196 Newbridge Road, Bath, North East Somerset BA1 3LF (01225 480996; Fax: 01225 318954; e-mail: scba@newbridge-fine-wines.freeserve.co.uk).

The Somerset Local Medical Benevolent Fund

Eligibility: General medical practitioners who are practising or have practised in Somerset and their dependants, who are in need.

Types of grants: One-off or recurrent grants according to need. Recently a quarterly grant was given to the widow of a Somerset GP and another grant was given to cover expenses incurred by a doctor who was involved in a serious accident.

Annual grant total: In 2000/01 the trust had an income of £18,000 and its total expenditure was £6,800. About £9,000 is given in two grants every year.

Applications: In writing to the correspondent. Applications can be submitted directly by the individual, or by any person on their behalf.

Correspondent: Dr J H Yoxall, Secretary to the Trustees, Somerset Local Medical Committee, c/o Somerset Health Authority, Wellsprings Road, Taunton, Somerset TA2 7PQ (01823 344314; Fax: 01823 344390; e-mail: medsec@somersetlmc.demon.co.uk).

Axbridge

The William Spearing Charity & Others

Eligibility: People in need who live in the town of Axbridge.

Types of grants: Annual Christmas gifts of about £25 to elderly people.

Annual grant total: About 33 grants are given at Christmas totalling around £1,000. In 1999 the trust's income totalled £1,400.

Applications: At a meeting in November the trustees meet to assess the list of regular beneficiaries: looking at who to take off the list and adding any new people who have moved to the town.

Correspondent: William Simms, Clerk and Treasurer, Bethel, Moorland Street, Axbridge, Somerset BS26 2BA (01934 732705).

Bridgwater

The Manchip Trust

Eligibility: People in need aged 70 years or over, who live in Bridgwater, are in receipt of means-tested benefits, and have capital of less than £1,500 (single person) or £3,000 (couple).

Types of grants: Regular grants are paid quarterly: £242 for single people and £160 each for couples. Bedding parcels are given on acceptance as a regular beneficiary. The trust stated in March 2002 that it had room to support five more eligible beneficiaries. Individuals who already receive regular grants can apply for modest one-off grants for specific purposes.

Annual grant total: In 2001 the trust's income was £4,100 and it made four grants to individuals in need totalling £796. Grants are up to £242 a year.

Applications: Applications should be submitted on a form available from the correspondent, and should give details of age and income/expenditure. Applications are considered every two months and can be submitted either directly by the individual, or through a social worker, citizen's advice bureau or other third party such as a GP or a friend.

Correspondent: The Applicants Officer, c/o Universal Beneficent Society, 6 Avonmore Road, London W14 8RL (020 7605 4202; Fax: 020 7605 4201; e-mail: ubs@rukba.org.uk).

The Tamlin Charity

Eligibility: Older people over 65 years of age who are in need and live in Bridgwater.

Types of grants: Quarterly instalments of £10 (£40 a year).

Annual grant total: In 2001 the trust had an income of £1,800 and gave payments to 38 beneficiaries totalling £1,500.

Applications: On a form available from a trustee or from the correspondent. Applications can be submitted directly by the individual or through a third party such as a social worker, citizen's advice bureau or other welfare agency. They are considered in March, June, September and December.

Correspondent: Richard Young, Clerk, 5 Channel Court, Burnham on Sea, Somerset TA8 1NE (01278 789859).

Cannington

The Cannington Combined Charity

Eligibility: People in need who live in the parish of Cannington.

Types of grants: Grants to meet regular or one-off bills where applicants cannot receive additional assistance from any other source. Recent grants have been towards a shower for a woman following major surgery, help with household expenses and travel expenses to a special school. There may be a preference for older and disabled people.

Annual grant total: In 2000/01 the trust had an income of £5,800 and its total expenditure was £3,600.

Applications: On a form available from the correspondent. Applications can be submitted directly by the individual, through a social worker, family member, doctor or similar third party. Trustees meet quarterly in January, April, August and November.

Correspondent: Mrs Betty Edney, Clerk to the Trustees, Down Stream, 1 Mill Close, Cannington, Bridgwater, Somerset TA5 2JA (01278 653026; e-mail: betty@edneybfsnet.co.uk).

Compton Martin

The William Webb's Charity

Eligibility: State pensioners who live in the ancient parish of Compton Martin in Somerset.

Types of grants: One-off grants of a minimum of £15.

Annual grant total: In 2001 the trust had an income of £462 and it made grants totalling £450.

Applications: In writing to the correspondent. Grants are advertised on noticeboards in the parish requesting applications. Applications are considered in December and can be submitted directly by the individual.

Correspondent: Mrs Margaret A J Vaughan, Clerk, Priors Farm House, The Street, Compton Martin, Bristol BS40 6JF (01761 221232).

Draycott

Charity of John & Joseph Card (also known as Draycott Charity)

Eligibility: People in need who live in the hamlet of Draycott, near Cheddar, with a preference for those who receive a pension from the charity.

Types of grants: Pensions usually range from £100 to £500 a year and are made to people of pensionable age on low incomes (i.e. basic pensions). One-off hardship payments range from £50 to £250 and can be made to people of all ages. One-off grants have recently been made for clothing and travel to and from hospital.

Annual grant total: In 2000/01 the trust's assets totalled £86,000, its income was £5,400 and grants were made to 29 individuals totalling £4,400.

Applications: For pensions apply on a form available from the correspondent, for hardship grants apply in writing. Applications are considered in November. They can be submitted either directly by the individual, or via a third party such as a warden of sheltered accommodation or a neighbour.

Correspondent: Mrs Helen Dance, Leighurst, The Street, Draycott, Nr Cheddar, Somerset BS27 3TH (01934 742811).

Other information: Grants are also made to organisations such as playgroups, churches and so on.

Ilchester

Ilchester Relief-in-Need and Educational Charity

Eligibility: People in need who live in the parish of Ilchester.

Types of grants: One-off grants according to need.

Annual grant total: In 2001 the trust had assets totalling £144,000 and its income was £23,000. Total expenditure was £13,000 and 69 grants were made to individuals totalling £7,400, for both welfare and educational purposes.

Applications: On a form available from the correspondent. Applications can be submitted directly by the individual or through a social worker, citizen's advice bureau or other welfare agency or third party.

Correspondent: Mrs Wendy Scrivener, Milton House, Podimore, Yeovil, Somerset BA22 8JF (01935 840070).

Newton St Loe

The Henry Smith Charity

Eligibility: People in need who live in Newton St Loe, and have done so for at least five years.

Types of grants: Annual grants of food vouchers and clothing tickets.

Annual grant total: In 1993 the trust had £1,350 income allocated by Henry Smith's (General Estate) Charity. All of this was given in grants. Up-to-date information was unavailable.

Applications: In writing to the correspondent. Applications should be submitted directly by the individual by September 25th, for payment in November/December each year.

Correspondent: Mrs J Ringham, 51 Claysend Cottages, Newton St Loe, Bath BA2 9DE.

Other information: We were unable to confirm the information for this entry with the trust.

Pitminster

Allotments for the Labouring Poor of Pitminster

Eligibility: People who live or have lived recently in the parish of Pitminster who are in need.

Types of grants: One-off grants for items, services or facilities to reduce need.

Annual grant total: In 1998/99 the trust had an income of £2,100 and total expenditure of £2,900, including £1,200 in grants to individuals.

Applications: In writing to the correspondent. Please include an sae.

Correspondent: P Jones, 2 Westview, Sellicks Green, Blagdon Hill, Taunton, Somerset TA3 7SA.

Other information: The trust also supports the upkeep of a recreation ground in the parish.

Porlock

The Henry Rogers Charity (Porlock Branch)

Eligibility: Pensioners who live in the rectorial manor of Porlock and have done so for five years or more.

Types of grants: Monthly grants of £12 are made to 11 pensioners. One-off grants are not made.

Annual grant total: In 2001 the trust had both an income and a total expenditure of £1,800. Monthly grants were made totalling about £1,600.

Applications: On a form available from the correspondent, submitted directly by the individual.

Correspondent: Mrs C M Corner, Tyrol, Villes Lane, Porlock, Minehead, Somerset TA24 8NQ (01643 862645).

Rimpton

The Rimpton Relief-in-Need Charities

Eligibility: People in need who live in the parish of Rimpton only.

Types of grants: One-off or recurrent grants according to need.

Annual grant total: In 2000 the trust had an income of £1,900 and its total expenditure was £2,100. Information about how much was given in grants was not available for this year.

In 1998 the trust had assets of £48,000 and an income of £3,000. £1,000 was given to five individuals. Organisations in the village also receive grants.

Applications: In writing to the correspondent. Applications are considered at any time.

Correspondent: G L Burrows, Treasurer, Old Hall House, Rimpton, Yeovil, Somerset BA22 8AD (01935 851300).

Other information: This entry was not confirmed by the trust, but the address was correct according to the Charity Commission database.

Shapwick

The Shapwick Relief in Need Charity

Eligibility: People in need who live in Shapwick.

Types of grants: One-off and recurrent grants of £10 to £50.

Annual grant total: In 2000 the trust had an income of £690 and its total expenditure was £710.

Applications: In writing to the correspondent.

Correspondent: Mrs M Motum, The Linhay, 8 Blacksmiths Lane, Shapwick, Bridgwater, Somerset TA7 9LZ (01458 210998).

Other information: This charity is made up of The Henry Smith Charity and Alexander's Charity for the Poor.

Stanton Prior

The Henry Smith Charity (Longnet Estate)

Eligibility: People in need who have lived in Stanton Prior for more than three years.

Types of grants: Marks and Spencer vouchers are donated on a one-off basis.

Annual grant total: In 2001 the trust had both an income and total expenditure of £700.

Applications: In writing to the correspondent, directly by the individual, for consideration by the trustees in November and December.

Correspondent: Ron Hardwick, Poplar Farm, Stanton Prior, Bath BA2 9HX (Tel & Fax: 01761 470382).

Street

The George Cox Charity

Eligibility: People in need who live in the parish of Street. No applications from people living outside the parish can be considered.

Types of grants: Generally one-off grants of £50 to £100, paid through the social services to all deserving cases. Help is given towards, for example, holidays; repair of domestic appliances such as washing machines and cookers; equipment for the frail elderly such as visual aids and helping hand; second hand furniture and carpets; hospital visiting travel costs.

Annual grant total: In 2000/01 the trust had assets of £9,300, an income of £2,900 and a total expenditure of £1,800. Grants were made to 35 individuals in need, totalling £1,600.

Applications: In writing to the correspondent. Applications are usually submitted through a social worker, citizen's advice bureau or other welfare agency, or through one of the trustees or someone known to the trustees. They are considered at any time.

Correspondent: P A Preston, Clerk, 10 Seymour Road, Street, Somerset BA16 0SP (01458 443501).

The Victoria Homes Relief in Need Charity

Eligibility: People in need who live in the urban district of Street.

Types of grants: One-off grants ranging from £30 to £75 towards holiday activities for young children, bedding and furniture, washing machine, visit to hospital, telephone installation and wheelchair.

Annual grant total: £1,200 a year.

Applications: In writing to the correspondent. Applications can be submitted directly by the individual or through a social worker, citizen's advice bureau or other welfare agency. They are considered at any time.

Correspondent: B Cremieu-Alcan, Huckham House, Berhill, Ashcott, Bridgwater, Somerset TA7 9QN (01458 210231).

Taunton

The Taunton Aid in Sickness Fund

Eligibility: Sick poor people who live within a four mile radius of St Mary's Church Taunton, with priority for those living in the old borough of Taunton and the civil parish of Trull.

'Grants are not given to those who do not fit into the description of 'sick poor' (i.e. long-term Sickness Benefit, recurring family credits and with no other means of support).'

Types of grants: One-off grants, ranging from £30 to £400 according to need. The trustees may consider larger grants in cases where they consider that more is required. Examples of recent grants given include those towards: holidays, travel costs, outings and entertainments, laundering, furniture, food for special diets, help with child care costs, and many other benefits for the sick.

Grants cannot be used in place of public/statutory funds, but can be used as a supplement to support those where need is proven. The trustees are not limited to assisting people who receive state benefits.

Grants cannot be made on a recurring basis.

Annual grant total: In 2001/02 the trust made 94 grants totalling £17,000 to individuals in need. Further grants were made to organisations totalling £6,000.

In 1998/99 the trust had assets of £138,000, an income of £21,000 and a total expenditure of £26,000. It gave 80 grants to individuals totalling £8,800.

Applications: On a form available from the correspondent. Grant applications should be made and signed by recognised referral agencies writing on behalf of the applicant, and to whom the grant can be paid. If the cheque is to be made out to an individual, please ensure that the person has a bank account.

The recognised form should be used so that all relevant information is provided to the trustees. It is important that all applications to other charities or other sources of help such as state grants like the Family Fund or the Social Fund are brought to the notice of the trustees.

Applicants must provide details of the type and amount of benefits being paid into the applicant's household.

Specific items of basic need should be costed and the actual amount required should be given. Electrical goods should be sought from reputable outlets offering warranties and should normally be second-hand.

Applications are considered throughout the year.

Correspondent: Mrs Nan Williams, Clerk, c/o A C Mole and Sons, 10 Billetfield, Taunton, Somerset TA1 3NL (01823 251311; Fax: 01823 336398).

Taunton Deane

Taunton Town Charity

Eligibility: People who live in the borough of Taunton Deane.

Types of grants: One-off grants for specific items to people in need, this includes furniture and clothing. No help towards clearing debts.

Annual grant total: In 2001 the trust made grants to 122 individuals for welfare purposes totalling £28,000. Grants to 101 individuals for educational purposes totalled £12,000.

Applications: On a form available from the correspondent, for consideration throughout the year. Applications should be submitted through a third party, such as a social worker, citizen's advice bureau or other welfare agency. The third party should verify that the applicant is in receipt of all statutory benefits to which they are entitled.

Correspondent: Sheila Naylor, Clerk to the Trustees, The Committee Room, Huish Homes, Magdalene Street, Taunton, Somerset TA1 1SG (01823 335348).

Other information: The prime role of the charity is to provide sheltered accommodation for older people. Grants are also made for educational purposes.

Trull

The Trull Parish Lands Charity

Eligibility: People in need who live in the parish of Trull (including part of Comeytrowe).

Types of grants: One-off or recurrent grants according to need.

Annual grant total: In 2001 the trust had an income of about £6,000 available.

Applications: In writing to the correspondent.

Correspondent: W P Morris, Clerk, Porter Dodson Solicitors, 11 Hammet Street, Taunton TA1 1RJ (01823 331293).

Yeovil

The Marsh Trust

Eligibility: Children and young people in need who live in the ecclesiastical parishes of Holy Trinity and St Michael and All Angels, and the ecclesiastical parish of St John the Baptist, all in Yeovil.

Types of grants: One-off grants only.

Annual grant total: £770 in 2000/01.

Applications: In writing to the correspondent.

Correspondent: Miss Sue Clarke, Porter Dodson Solicitors, Central House, Church Street, Yeovil BA20 1HH (01935 424581).

Wiltshire

Brave Hearts (formerly Children's Relief Fund Association)

See entry on page 301

R J Harris Charitable Settlement

Eligibility: Individuals in need who live in West Wiltshire, with particular emphasis on Trowbridge, and in North Wiltshire, south of the M4 motorway.

Types of grants: One-off and recurrent grants according to need.

Annual grant total: In 2000/01 the trust's assets totalled £1.7 million and its income was £74,000. The total expenditure was £92,000 and included 25 relief in need grants to individuals totalling £5,000. In the past, grants have also been made to individuals for education and to organisations; in 2000/01 'other grants' totalled £76,000.

Applications: In writing to the correspondent, either directly by the individual, or through a social worker, citizen's advice bureau or another third party. An sae should be enclosed with the application. Trustees meet to consider applications, in February, May/June and September/October.

Correspondent: J J Thring, Secretary, Thring Townsend Solicitors, Midland Bridge, Bath BA1 2HQ (01225 340099; Fax; 01225 319735).

Dr C S Kingston Fund

Eligibility: People in need who live in urban district of Trowbridge and those who are closely connected with the district. Most applicants are in receipt of Income Support.

Types of grants: One-off grants only, ranging between £15 and £500, for example, towards equipment, washing machines and occasionally for school uniforms.

Annual grant total: In 2000/01 the trust had an income of £5,000 and made grants totalling £3,500.

Applications: In writing to the correspondent including details of the need, the applicant's resources and other benefits available. Applications can be submitted directly by the individual in exceptional cases, but are generally made through a social worker, doctor, citizen's advice bureau or other welfare agency. They are considered at any time.

Correspondent: Matthew Ridley, c/o Messrs Sylvester & Mackett, Castle House, Castle Street, Trowbridge, Wiltshire BA14 8AX.

Malmesbury Community Trust

Eligibility: Older people, of any occupation, who are suffering from hardship and live in Malmesbury or its surrounding villages.

Types of grants: One-off grants.

Annual grant total: In 2000/01 the trust had an income of £21,000 and its total expenditure was £1,200. The trust relies for its income on the receipt of legacies; its income therefore varies substantially from year to year. Grants normally total about £1,500.

Applications: On an application form available from the correspondent.

Correspondent: A C Neve, 3 Common Road, Malmesbury, Wiltshire SN16 0HN (01666 823864; e-mail: tony@nevet.fsnet.co.uk).

Salisbury City Almshouse & Welfare Charities

Eligibility: People in need who live in Salisbury and district.

Types of grants: One-off grants of between £100 and £300, to meet all kinds of emergency or other needs that cannot be met from public funds. Grants can be towards, for example, essential items such as reconditioned cookers, washing machines, refrigerators, school clothing, shoes, moving costs, beds/bedding, holidays and wheelchairs.

Grants are not normally made for relief in sickness.

Annual grant total: In 2001 the trust had assets of £10 million, an income of £1 million and its total expenditure was £64,000. 110 grants were made to individuals totalling £15,000. £20,000 was available in 2002.

Applications: Applications are considered on the first Friday of each month. Application forms should be submitted at least 15 days before and should be sponsored by a recognised professional who is fully aware of statutory entitlements and is capable of giving advice/supervision in budgeting and so on. Application forms, together with guidance notes, are available from the clerk.

Correspondent: Clerk to the Trustees, Trinity Hospital, Trinity Street, Salisbury SP1 2BD (Tel & Fax: 01722 325640; e-mail: clerk@almshouses.demon.co.uk).

Wiltshire Ambulance Service Benevolent Fund

Eligibility: Serving and retired members of the Wiltshire Ambulance Service and their dependants.

Types of grants: One-off and recurrent grants according to need.

Annual grant total: In 2000/01 the trust had an income of £24,000 and its total expenditure was £18,000.

Grants usually total about £20,000 each year.

Applications: Applicants should contact their station benevolent fund representative, who will then contact the chairman on their behalf.

Correspondent: A C Newman, Treasurer, 39 Forest Road, Melksham, Wiltshire SN12 7AA (01225 790203).

Aldbourne

Aldbourne Poors' Gorse Charity

Eligibility: Older people in need over the age of 65 who live in the parish of Aldbourne.

Types of grants: One-off grants of £20, distributed at Christmas.

Annual grant total: In 2001 the trust had an income of £2,100 and it gave 94 grants to individuals in need totalling £1,900.

Applications: In writing to the correspondent, directly by the individual, usually on the charity's invitation. Applications should be submitted at any time before November, for consideration in November.

Correspondent: Terry Gilligan, Secretary, 9 Cook Road, Aldbourne, Nr

Marlborough, Wiltshire SN8 2EG (01672 540205).

Ashton Keynes

The Ashton Keynes Charity

Eligibility: Older people in need who live in Ashton Keynes.

Types of grants: Grants to pensioners.

Annual grant total: In 2000 the trust had an income of £6,400 and an unusually high expenditure of £14,000, due to a grant made to the village hall. Grants to individuals usually total around £5,500.

Applications: In writing to the correspondent.

Correspondent: R E Smith, Clerk, Amberley, 4 Gosditch, Ashton Keynes, Swindon, Wiltshire SN6 6NZ (01285 861461; Fax: 01285 861461).

Chippenham

Chippenham Borough Lands Charity

Eligibility: People in need who have lived in the civil parish of Chippenham for a minimum of two years.

Types of grants: One-off and occasionally recurrent grants and loans are made, according to need. Recent grants have included help with bills or rent arrears, mobility aids, domestic appliances and/or furniture and clothing.

Grants are not given in any circumstances where the trustees consider the award to be a substitute for statutory provision.

Annual grant total: In 2000/01 the charities had assets of £9.6 million which generated an income of £390,000. Total expenditure was £410,000. £99,000 was given in 169 grants to individuals for relief in need purposes. Educational grants were made to 15 people totalling £25,000. Grants to organisations totalled £150,000.

Applications: On a form available from the correspondent. Applications are considered every month and can be submitted directly by the individual or though a social worker, citizen's advice bureau, other welfare agency or other third party such as a doctor.

Correspondent: Maggi Roynon, Administrator, Jubilee Building, 32 Market Place, Chippenham, Wiltshire SN15 3HP (01249 658180; Fax: 01249 446048; e-mail: cblc@lineone.net).

East Knoyle

The East Knoyle Welfare Trust

Eligibility: People in need who live in the parish of East Knoyle.

Types of grants: One-off grants only, usually for heating bills.

Annual grant total: About £1,500 for both relief-in-need and educational purposes.

Applications: At any time to the correspondent or any other trustee.

Correspondent: Mrs L A Jolliffe, Clerk, Horseshoe Cottage, East Knoyle, Salisbury, Wiltshire SP3 6AR (01747 830412).

Marlborough

Herbert Leaf Bequest

Eligibility: People in need who live in the parish of Marlborough and are on the electoral roll.

Types of grants: One-off grants only.

Annual grant total: In 1999 the trust had assets of £56,000 generating an income of £1,500. Total expenditure was £3,000, some of which was given in grants to organisations.

Applications: In writing to the correspondent. Applications are considered in July each year and can be submitted directly by the individual.

Correspondent: G Gittins, Marlborough Town Council, 5 High Street, Marlborough, Wiltshire SN8 1AA (01672 512487; Fax: 01672 512116; e-mail: marltc@btinternet.com).

Salisbury

The William Botley Charity

Eligibility: Women in need who live in the city of Salisbury.

Types of grants: One-off grants ranging from £100 to £250, to meet all kinds of emergency and other needs that cannot be met from public funds. Grants have been made, for example, for guaranteed secondhand white goods, clothing for mothers and children, carpets and floor coverings and holiday costs. Payment for debts will not be made.

Annual grant total: In 2000/01 the trust had assets of £210,000, an income of £8,400 and grants were made to 59 individuals in need totalling £7,800.

Applications: Application forms, together with guidance notes, are available from the clerk. Applications are considered every month and should be submitted through a recognised professional who is fully aware of statutory entitlements and is capable of giving advice/supervision on budgeting and so on (such as a social workers, citizen's advice bureau workers or primary care team workers).

Correspondent: Clerk to the Trustees, Trinity Hospital, Trinity Street, Salisbury SP1 2BD (Tel & Fax: 01722 325640; e-mail: clerk@almshouses.demon.co.uk).

Trowbridge

The Cecil Norman Wellesley Blair Charitable Trust

Eligibility: People in need who live in the civil parish of Trowbridge.

Types of grants: One-off grants only, mainly in the form of Christmas vouchers for food, fuel and clothing.

Annual grant total: In 2002 the trust made 500 grants totalling £6,500.

Applications: The trust advertises the date of distribution each year in the local press – usually the first Friday in December. It issues vouchers via two distribution points and beneficiaries must go to those points and show their pension book, as proof that they are in receipt of statutory benefits.

Correspondent: M Ridley, Sylvester & Mackett, Castle House, Castle Street, Trowbridge, Wiltshire BA14 8AX (01225 755621).

Other information: In very exceptional circumstances, when surplus money is available, the trust gives grants to local organisations.

Westbury

The Henry Smith Charity

Eligibility: People in need who live in Westbury and are aged over 40 years.

Types of grants: Grants of £30 are given towards, for example, fuel, food or clothing.

Annual grant total: In 2001 the trust had an income of £1,000 and its total expenditure was £1,100. Grants were made totalling £780.

Applications: In writing to the correspondent.

Correspondent: Messrs Pinniger Finch & Co., Solicitors, Church Street, Westbury, Wiltshire BA13 3BZ.

8. South East

Anglia Care Trust

Eligibility: People in need who live in East Anglia and are experiencing or have experienced a legal restriction on their liberty, and their families.

Types of grants: One-off grants towards rehabilitation and education. Grants usually range from £10 to £70. Sums of money are not usually paid direct, but itemised bills will be met directly.

Applicants are usually already being supported by, or are known to, ACT and should have exhausted all possible sources of statutory funds. Grants are not given towards payment of debts, fines or legal costs.

Annual grant total: Up to £5,000 if funds allow*.

Applications: In writing to the correspondent. All applications must be supported by a probation officer or other professional person and are considered quarterly.

Correspondent: E Battle, Chief Executive, 65 St Matthew's Street, Ipswich, Suffolk IP1 3EW (01473 213140; Fax: 01473 219648; e-mail: admin@angliacaretrust.org.uk).

Other information: * For this entry, the information relates to the money available from ACT. For more information on what is available throughout East Anglia, contact the correspondent.

The Anglian Water Trust Fund

See entry on page 105

The Berkshire Nurses & Relief-in-Sickness Trust

Eligibility: 1. People in need through sickness or disability who live in the county of Berkshire and those areas of Oxfordshire formerly in Berkshire.

2. Nurses and midwives employed as district nurses in the county of Berkshire and those areas of Oxfordshire formerly in Berkshire and people employed before August 1980 as administrative and clerical staff by Berkshire County Nursing Association.

Types of grants: One-off grants only towards household accounts (excluding those below), holidays, some medical aids, special diets, clothing, wheelchairs, electronic aids for disabled people, hospital travel costs, prescription season tickets etc.

No grants for rent or mortgage payments, community charge, water rates, funeral bills, on-going payments such as nursing home fees or any items thought to be the responsibility of statutory authorities.

Annual grant total: About £50,000 a year to individuals.

Applications: On a form available from the correspondent. Applications should be made through a social worker, citizen's advice bureau or other welfare agency and supported by a member of the statutory authorities. They are considered as received. Applications are not accepted from members of the public.

Correspondent: Mrs R Pottinger, Honorary Secretary, 26 Montrose Walk, Fords Farm, Calcot, Berkshire RG31 7YH (0118 942 4556).

Brave Hearts (formerly Children's Relief Fund Association)

Eligibility: Children in need who are 16 or under and live in the Hampshire, Wiltshire, Salisbury and Kennet districts.

Types of grants: Grants towards the cost of recreational facilities for children or young people and the care, welfare and treatment of physically disabled people. Grants are one-off and range from £20 to £500. Recent grants to children included £85 towards transport, £60 towards special equipment and £350 towards a special cycle.

Annual grant total: In 2000/01 the fund had an income of £2,700 and a total expenditure of £2,600.

Applications: In writing to the correspondent either directly by the individual or through a social worker, citizen's advice bureau, other welfare agency or third party such as a doctor or hospital. Applications are considered monthly.

Correspondent: R N Bennett, 11 Vespusian Road, Andover, Hampshire SP10 5JP.

Other information: This entry was not confirmed by the trust, but the address was correct according to the Charity Commission database.

The Brighton Housing Trust Charitable Trust

Eligibility: People in need who live in East or West Sussex.

Types of grants: Grants to relieve problems of setting up house after being homeless or having to move to new accommodation.

Annual grant total: In 2000/01 the trust had an income of £5,500 and a total expenditure of £5,700.

Applications: In writing to the correspondent, via projects such as First Base Day Centre.

Correspondent: R C H Allen, Trustee, 144 London Road, Brighton BN1 4PH (01273 694939; Fax: 01273 675852).

The Buckle Family Charitable Trust

Eligibility: People in need in Suffolk or Essex.

Types of grants: One-off and recurrent grants according to need.

Annual grant total: In 2000 the trust gave £5,000 to individuals and £66,000 to organisations

Applications: In writing to the correspondent.

Correspondent: G W N Stewart, Trustee, 9 Trinity Street, Colchester, Essex CO1 1JN (01206 544434).

The Derek & Eileen Dodgson Foundation

Eligibility: People in need over 60, who live in East and West Sussex, with preference for connections with Brighton and Hove.

Types of grants: One-off grants and loans of £50 to £1,500, mainly to older people. Most of the funds are given to local non-governmental organisations to pass on to individuals.

Annual grant total: In 2000/01 the foundation had assets of £1 million and an income of £50,000. A total of £41,000 was given in over 400 grants to individuals.

Applications: On a form available from the correspondent. Applications can be submitted either through a social worker, citizen's advice bureau, welfare agency or a third party, or directly by the individual.

Correspondent: I W Dodd, 61 Church Road, Hove, East Sussex BN3 7QS (01273 229500; Fax: 01273 229515; e-mail: solicitors@rdlaw.uk.com).

East Sussex Farmers Union Benevolent Fund

Eligibility: People in need who are farmers, farmworkers or their dependants, with priority for those who live in the county of East Sussex. When funds are available eligible people living in Kent, Surrey and West Sussex may also be supported.

Types of grants: One-off and recurrent grants according to need.

Annual grant total: In 2000/01 the income of the trust was £29,000 and its total expenditure was £9,500, all of which was given in grants to individuals.

Applications: In writing or by telephone to the correspondent.

Correspondent: G Fowle, Harper & Eede Ltd, Broyle House, Ringmer, Lewes, East Sussex BN8 5NN (01273 812707).

Eastbourne and District Police Court Mission

Eligibility: People in prison or on probation, and their dependants, who live in Eastbourne and district and are in need.

Types of grants: One-off or recurrent grants according to need.

Annual grant total: In 2001 a total of £3,500 was distributed.

Applications: The probation services at Hastings, Eastbourne and Lewes, each have a representative who applies on behalf of the individual to the trust. Applications should only be made to the trust via these probation officers.

Correspondent: Mrs Gillian Grimmond, (See above.)

The German Society of Benevolence

Eligibility: People in need who are or were citizens of Germany and their dependants. Applicants must live in Greater London, Essex, Hertfordshire, Kent or Surrey.

Types of grants: Small one-off and recurrent grants for heating, clothing and other needs, but not for relief of rates and taxes. The society can make no commitment to renew payments.

Annual grant total: In 1999/2000 the society had an income of £7,600 and a total expenditure of £1,400.

Applications: Applications are considered from individuals or from agencies acting on their behalf.

Correspondent: D F Heydorn, Old Cornstore, London Road, Westerham TN16 1DR.

The Handicapped Children's Aid Committee

Eligibility: Disabled children, under 19, who live in London and the Home Counties.

Types of grants: Cash grants are NOT given. Rather, specific items are purchased on behalf of the individual in need.

Annual grant total: Between £1,000 and £2,000 per year for individuals.

Applications: On a form available from the correspondent. Applications can be made directly by individuals or via a social worker/medical staff and must be backed up with medical recommendations. Applications are considered monthly, although urgent cases can be quicker.

Correspondent: Paul Maurice, Amberley Lodge, 13 Beechwood Avenue, Finchley, London N3 3AU (020 8346 1147).

Other information: The committee supplies equipment etc. for schools, hospitals and clubs for disabled and underprivileged children, as well as for individuals. Please note that in no case does the committee make any grants in cash. All equipment, clothing etc. is purchased by the committee and supplied by them to the recipient.

The Hunstanton Convalescent Trust

Eligibility: People who are on a low income, physically or mentally unwell and in need of a convalescent or recuperative holiday, with a preference for those living in Norfolk and Cambridgeshire.

Types of grants: Grants ranging from £100 to £350 are given to provide or assist towards the expenses of recuperative holidays, including for carers. The trust can sometimes provide other items, services or facilities which will help the individual's recovery.

Annual grant total: In 1999/2000 the trust had assets of £306,000, an income of £9,400 and a total expenditure of £5,000. Grants were made to 15 individuals, totalling £2,700.

Applications: On a form available from the correspondent, through a social worker, doctor or other welfare workers. Applications should be submitted at least one month before the proposed holiday. The full board of trustees meet in January, June and September.

Correspondent: Mrs J J Littler, Secretary, Windfall House, 60 Holt Road, North Elmham, Norfolk NR20 5JQ (01362 668143).

Jewish Care

Eligibility: Members of the Jewish faith who are elderly, mentally ill, visually impaired or physically disabled, and their families, who live in London and the south east of England.

Types of grants: Jewish Care (includes the former Jewish Welfare Board, Jewish Blind Society and the Jewish Home and Hospital at Tottenham) is the largest Jewish social work agency, providing a range of services, both domiciliary and residential. Financial assistance is not a normal part of the board's work, though some such expenditures are inevitably associated with its social work service. (See also the Egerton Fund at the same address.)

No help with burial expenses or education fees.

Annual grant total: In 1998 the trust had assets of £79 million and an income of £33 million, the majority of which went in the provision and administration of Jewish social services. Some direct financial help was, however, provided in the form of grants. These ranged between £5 and £1,000, were given to 1,000 people and totalled £34,000.

Applications: In writing to the correspondent either direct by the individual or through a social worker.

Correspondent: J Oppenheim, Chief Executive, Head Office, Stuart Young House, 221 Golders Green Road, London NW11 9DQ (020 8922 2000).

The Elaine & Angus Lloyd Charitable Trust

Eligibility: Individuals in need with a preference for those who live in Essex and Surrey.

Types of grants: One-off and recurrent grants according to need.

Annual grant total: In 2000/01 the trust had an income of £73,000 and a total expenditure of £62,000. Grants were made to organisations totalling £44,000 and to individuals totalling £12,000.

Applications: In writing to the correspondent. The trustees meet regularly to consider grants.

Correspondent: J S Gordon, Trustee, Brewin Dolphin, 5 Giltspur Street, London EC1A 9VD (020 7248 4400).

The B V MacAndrew Trust

Eligibility: People in need who live in East and West Sussex.

Types of grants: One-off grants for a variety of needs including emergencies and household appliances.

Annual grant total: The amount given each year depends upon income (£25,000 in 2000/01).

Applications: In writing to the correspondent at any time. Applications can be made directly by the individual, although the trust prefers them to be made through a social worker, citizen's advice bureau or other welfare agency.

Correspondent: D J E Diplock, Hon. Solicitor & Treasurer, 79 Church Road, Hove, East Sussex BN3 2BB (01273 722532; Fax: 01273 326347).

The Douglas Martin Trust

Eligibility: People in need who live in southern England and are personally known to the trustees.

Types of grants: One-off grants of up to £250 for items such as bedding, furniture, children's holidays, debt relief and educational grants. Grants are never made to organisations.

Annual grant total: In 2000/01 the trust had assets of £282,000 and an income of £69,000. Relief-in-need grants to individuals totalled £49,000.

Applications: Applicants must be known by the trustees or referred by an organisation known by the trustees.

Correspondent: David Evans, 45 Burnards Field Road, Colyton, Devon EX24 6PE (Fax: 01297 553007; e-mail: dorevans@tiscali.co.uk).

The Middlesex King Edward VII Memorial Fund

Eligibility: Children in need aged between 6 and 16 and who live in Greater London, Buckinghamshire, Essex, Hampshire, Hertfordshire, Kent, Surrey, East Sussex or West Sussex.

Types of grants: Grants for holidays or convalescence at the seaside or in the country (holidays must be in the UK). Grants range on average from £50 to £100 per individual.

Annual grant total: About £10,000.

Applications: On a form available from the correspondent. Applications should be submitted through a third party such as a social worker, welfare agency or a head teacher. Information should include details of the financial circumstances of the parent(s)/guardians(s), and cost and location of the proposed holiday. Applications may be considered at any time but the main allocation occurs in April and June.

Correspondent: A J G Moore, Hon. Secretary, King Edward VII Memorial Fund, PO Box 249, Orpington BR5 1ZL (01689 877009).

The Ogilvie Charities

See entry on page 67

The Pusinelli Convalescent & Holiday Home

Eligibility: People who are or were citizens of the German Federal Republic, the German Democratic Republic or Austria and dependants of the above. Applicants must live in Greater London, Essex, Hertfordshire, Kent or Surrey.

Types of grants: Grants of not more than £500 for families who would not otherwise be able to have a holiday and who did not have one the year before.

Annual grant total: About £5,000 a year.

Applications: Applications should be made to the correspondent directly from the individual or from any welfare agency on their behalf.

Correspondent: D F Heydorn, Old Cornstore, London Road, Westerham, Kent TN16 1DR (01959 561103; Fax: 01959 564945).

The Florence Reiss Trust for Old People

See entry on page 118

The E E Roberts Charitable Trust

Eligibility: People in need in the UK with a preference for Sussex and Kent.

Types of grants: One-off and recurrent grants according to need.

Annual grant total: In 2000/01 the trust had an income of £38,000 and grants totalled £28,000, including grants totalling £1,000 made to three individuals.

Applications: In writing to the correspondent. The trustees meet twice a year in January and July. Unsuccessful applications will not be acknowledged.

Correspondent: Robert B McKillop, Secretary to the Trustees, Messrs Cripps Harries Hall, Windsor House, 6–10 Mount Ephraim Road, Tunbridge Wells, Kent TN1 1EG (01892 515121).

Stoke Poges United Charities

Eligibility: People in need who live in the parish of Stoke Poges, including parts of the parish of Slough Borough – Stoke wards. Preference is given to widows and people who are sick.

Types of grants: Grants can be given for clothing, food, household necessities, medical care and equipment.

Annual grant total: In 2001 the trust had assets of £133,000, an income of £9,700 and a total expenditure of £1,100. No grants were given.

Applications: In writing to the correspondent, to be submitted either directly by the individual or through a social worker, citizen's advice bureau, other welfare agency or any third party.

Correspondent: A P Levings, The Cedars, Stratford Drive, Wooburn Green, High Wycombe, Buckinghamshire HP1 0QH (01628 524342).

Other information: This charity consists of five separate funds which provide grants for relief-in-need or educational purposes.

The Sussex Police Welfare Fund

Eligibility: Serving Sussex police officers and their immediate families; retired Sussex police officers and their widowed spouses or dependants.

Types of grants: One-off grants for any type of need such as equipment (e.g. stairlift, wheelchair), travel to hospital, subsistence and short term home, nursing or child care support. Discretionary loans may be given to serving officers subscribing to the fund who are facing financial difficulties. Loans are repayable from salary at source per pay period. No loans to pay charges or taxes by central or local government. No grants towards debt repayment. There are specific exceptions to this for retired staff/widowed spouses e.g. funeral costs where there is a real need.

Annual grant total: In 2001 the fund had assets of £1.5 million and an income of £119,000. It spent £211,000 and 329 grants to individuals totalled £110,000.

Applications: In writing to the correspondent. Applications can be submitted directly by the individual, through a social worker, citizen's advice bureau or other welfare agency or through a welfare liaison officer for retired staff or widowed spouses. These are considered monthly or at any time in cases of emergency. For equipment and services, an estimate of costs is necessary. Serving officers approaching the fund for loans will receive financial advice and complete an income/expenditure form.

Correspondent: Mrs C A MacFie, Fund Secretary, Sussex Police Headquarters, Welfare Department, Malling House, Church Lane, Lewes, East Sussex BN7 2DZ (01273 404144; Fax: 01273 404283).

The Wantage District Coronation Memorial & Nursing Amenities Fund

Eligibility: People who are sick, convalescent, disabled or infirm and who live in the parishes of Wantage, East Challow, Grove, Letcombe Regis, Letcombe Bassett, West Challow, Childrey, Denchworth, Goosey, East Hanney, West Hanney and Lockridge in the county of Oxfordshire and the parishes of Farnborough and Fawley in the county of Berkshire.

Types of grants: The provision of, or payment for, items, services or facilities which will alleviate the suffering or assist the recovery of such people, which are not readily available to them from any other source. Grants are one-off and recurrent and are given in the range of £20 to £100.

The income of the charity is not to be applied directly for the relief of taxes, rates or other public funds, but may be applied in supplementing relief or assistance provided out of public funds.

Annual grant total: In 2000/01 the fund had an income of £3,700 and a total expenditure of £3,200. Over £1,000 was given to 29 individuals.

Applications: In writing to the correspondent.

Correspondent: Mrs Carol Clubb, 133 Stockham Park, Wantage, Oxfordshire OX12 9HJ (01235 765366).

Other information: Grants are also made to organisations.

Bedfordshire

Mary Lockingtons Charity

Eligibility: Individuals living in the parishes of Dunstable, Leighton Buzzard and Hockliffe who are in need, for example due to hardship, disability or sickness.

Types of grants: One-off and recurrent grants towards items, services or facilities.

Annual grant total: In 1999/2000 the charity had an income of £8,500 and a total expenditure of £5,800.

Applications: In writing to the correspondent.

Correspondent: Mrs M J Bradley, Clerk, Grove House, 76 High Street North, Dunstable, Bedfordshire LU6 1NF.

Other information: This entry was not confirmed by the charity, but the address was correct according to the Charity Commission database.

The Sandy Charities

Eligibility: People who live in Sandy and Beeston and are in need.

Types of grants: One-off grants only ranging from £100 to £1,000, towards, for instance, motorised wheelchairs, nebulisers, bedding, and a rent deposit deed.

Annual grant total: In 2000/01 the trust had an income of £7,500 and its total expenditure was £6,900. Welfare grants were made to nine individuals totalling £3,200.

Applications: In writing to the correspondent who will supply a personal details form for completion. Applications can be considered in any month, depending on the urgency for the grant; they should be submitted either directly by the individual or via a social worker, citizen's advice bureau or other welfare agency.

Correspondent: P J Mount, Clerk, c/o Messrs Leeds Day, 6 Bedford Road, Sandy, Bedfordshire SG19 1EN (01767 680251; Fax: 01767 691775).

Other information: Grants are also made to organisations, and to individuals for educational purposes.

Bedford

The Municipal Charities & the Bedford & District Aid in Sickness Charity

Eligibility: People in need who live in the borough of Bedford.

Types of grants: Pensions; annual grants towards fuel bills and other necessities; occasional one-off grants for special purposes, and emergency Christmas bonuses.

Annual grant total: About £40,000.

Applications: In writing to the correspondent at any time of year. Individual applicants are usually visited to assess the degree of need.

Correspondent: c/o Clerk to the Trustees, Bedford Borough Council, Town Hall, St Paul's Square, Bedford MK40 1SJ (01234 227203; Fax: 01234 221606).

Clophill

Clophill United Charities

Eligibility: People who live in the parish of Clophill and are in need.

Types of grants: One-off and recurrent grants according to need. No grants where statutory funds are available.

Annual grant total: In 2001 annual payments to pensioners totalled £4,000, and other relief in need grants were made to individuals totalling £820, including £270 for school trips. Grants for the general benefit of the village were made to groups totalling £790.

Applications: On a form available from the correspondent. The trustees meet every two months to consider applications.

Correspondent: T Goddard-Mason, Clerk to the Trustees, 35 Reads Hill, Clophill, Bedford MK45 4AG.

Dunstable

The Dunstable Poor's Land Charity

Eligibility: People, usually pensioners, in need who live in the area of the parish of Dunstable as previous to 1907.

Types of grants: Grants are made annually on Maundy Thursday mostly to older people on Income Support or other benefit.

Annual grant total: About £4,000 a year in around 200 grants.

Applications: Personal application to the trustees after the annual distribution on Maundy Thursday morning. Applicants must provide evidence of their income.

Correspondent: Mrs M J Bradley, Grove House, 76 High Street North, Dunstable, Bedfordshire LU6 1NF.

The Dunstable Welfare Trust

Eligibility: People in need who live in Dunstable.

Types of grants: One-off grants ranging from £50 to £100. Grants are not given for relief of rates, taxes or other public funds.

Annual grant total: About £500.

Applications: In writing to the correspondent through a social worker, citizen's advice bureau or other welfare agency or clergy. Applications are considered quarterly.

Correspondent: Revd G Newton, Chews House, 77 High Street South, Dunstable, Bedfordshire LU6 3SF (01582 703271).

Flitwick

The Flitwick Town Lands Charity

Eligibility: People in need who live in the parish of Flitwick.

Types of grants: Usually one-off grants.

Annual grant total: Approximately £3,100 for relief-in-need purposes, and the same in educational grants.

Applications: On a form available from the correspondent.

Correspondent: David William Epsom, 28 Orchid Way, Flitwick MK45 1LF (01525 718145).

Husborne Crawley

The Husborne Crawley Charities of the Poor

Eligibility: People in need who live in the ancient parish of Husborne Crawley.

Types of grants: Grants of £100 are given to all pensioners for fuel and a Christmas gift, in death grants to relatives and to other people in need.

Annual grant total: In 2000/01 the trust had an income of £4,000 and a total expenditure of £3,800.

Applications: In writing to the correspondent either directly by the individual or via a third party. Applications are considered throughout the year.

Correspondent: Charles Lousada, Estate Office, Crawley Park, Husborne Crawley, Bedford MK43 0UU (01908 282860; Fax: 01908 282861).

SOUTH EAST – BEDFORDSHIRE/BERKSHIRE

Kempston

The Kempston Charities

Eligibility: People in need who live in Kempston (including Kempston rural).

Types of grants: On-off grants according to need. No recurrent grants are made.

Annual grant total: In 2001 the trust had both an income and a total expenditure of £8,000.

Applications: In writing to the correspondent. Applications should be made either directly by the individual or through a social worker, citizen's advice bureau or other welfare agency. They are considered in March, July and November.

Correspondent: Mrs N Darwood, 113 High Street, Kempston, Bedford MK42 7BP.

Other information: Grants are also given to local schools and other local institutions.

Luton

The Emily Ada Sibthorpe Trust

Eligibility: Women over 60 and men over 65 who are in need and live in Luton.

Types of grants: One-off grants which have been given towards household items, electric scooters and specialist items. Sometimes a contribution is made towards cost of an item, rather than to cover the full amount.

Annual grant total: About £2,500 a year.

Applications: In writing to the correspondent through the social services department.

Correspondent: Helen Knightley, Finance Manager, Housing and Social Services, Luton Borough Council, Unity House, 111 Stuart Street, Luton, Bedfordshire LU1 5NP (01582 547532).

Ravensden

The Ravensden Town & Poor Estate

Eligibility: People in need and widows who live in the parish of Ravensden.

Types of grants: Annual grants of £30 to £35 are given to widows, widowers and others in need at Christmas. One-off grants are also given for special needs.

Annual grant total: In 2000 the trust had an income of £3,100 and a total expenditure of £3,400. In previous years two-thirds of this has been distributed in grants to individuals, the remaining third going to a school.

Applications: In writing to the correspondent. Applications can be submitted directly by the individual. They are considered in November, although urgent cases can be responded to at any time.

Correspondent: R O Watson, The Plantation, Ravensden, Bedfordshire MK44 2RL.

Berkshire

The Earley Charity

Eligibility: People in need who have lived in Earley and central, east and south Reading, or the immediate neighbourhood, for at least six months.

Types of grants: One-off grants for relief of poverty, sickness, disability and for housing needs.

Grants range from £50 to £2,500.

Annual grant total: In 2000 the trust had assets of £13 million and a total income of £440,000. Over £100,000 was given in relief-in-need grants to individuals.

Applications: On a form available from the correspondent either directly by the individual or through a social worker, citizen's advice bureau, another third party or other welfare agency and signed by the applicant. Applications are considered every six weeks.

Correspondent: John Evans, The Liberty of Earley House, Strand Way, Earley RG6 4EA (0118 975 5663; Fax: 0118 975 2263).

The Finchampstead & Barkham Relief-in-Sickness Fund

Eligibility: People in need who are sick, convalescent, mentally/physically disabled or infirm and who live in the civil parishes of Finchampstead and Barkham.

Types of grants: Usually one-off grants towards the cost of medical, nursing and domestic sevices, and for appliances. Help is also given for those caring for or visiting sick or disabled people. 'The terms of the trust do not permit the offer of continuing support but the committee is always glad to consider a repeat application where need recurs or continues.'

Annual grant total: The fund has an income and total expenditure of £2,500.

Applications: Application can be made directly by the individual through any member of the committee who will be personally responsible for assessing eligibility. They can also be made through a social worker, citizen's advice bureau or other welfare agency or through a third party on behalf of the individual. Applications can be submitted throughout the year.

Correspondent: Dr J K Dewhurst, Fourwinds, The Ridges, Finchampstead, Wokingham, Berkshire RG40 3SY (0118 973 2783); P Jourdan (01344 772687); Revd Sheila Nunn (0118 973 0030); Mrs Claire Markham (0118 973 2632); or Revd Carol Edwards (0118 973 0030).

The Polehampton Charity

Eligibility: People in need who live in Twyford and Ruscombe.

Types of grants: One-off grants for clothing, domestic appliances, holidays and medical equipment. Grants range from £100 to £200.

Annual grant total: In 2000 the charity had assets of £1 million, an income of £65,000 and a total expenditure of £44,000. A total of 75 relief-in-need grants to individuals were made totalling £6,500.

Applications: Applications should be made either directly by the individual or through a social worker, carer etc. to: Liz Treadwell, Assistant Clerk, 14 Victoria Road, Wargrave, Berkshire RG10 8AE. Applications can be made at any time and are considered at trustee meetings held in February, May and October and by a sub-committee in between meetings.

Correspondent: Peter M Hutt, Clerk, 1 London Street, Reading, Berkshire RG1 4QW (0118 951 6322; Fax: 0118 950 2704; e-mail: huttp@fsp-law.com)

Other information: Grants totalling £19,000 were made to schools.

Trustees of the Reading Dispensary Trust

Eligibility: People in need who have a physical or mental disability or infirmity and who live in Reading and the surrounding area (roughly within a seven-mile radius of the centre of Reading).

Types of grants: One-off grants including those given for clothing and footwear, beds and bedding, holidays and travel, house adaptations and repairs, respite care, washing machines, wheelchair equipment, scooters, expeditions and so on.

Grants are not made when help is available from statutory sources.

Annual grant total: In 2001 the trust had assets of £1 million, an income of £49,000 and a total expenditure of £43,000. A total of £23,000 was given in 169 grants to individuals. Grants to organisations totalled £7,900.

Applications: On a form available from the correspondent. Applications should be submitted either through a social worker, citizen's advice bureau or another welfare agency or third party, or directly by the individual. Applications are considered every month.

Correspondent: The Clerk to the Trustees, 16 Wokingham Road, Reading RG6 1JQ (0118 926 5698).

305

South East – Berkshire

The Reading Municipal Church Charities

Eligibility: People below the age of 24.

Types of grants: A number of different charities operate from the same address; one is for relief-in-need purposes:

Archbishop Laud's Marriage Portions Charity – grants to girls, who were born or live in the district of Reading or the parish of Wokingham and are about to get married.

Grants usually range between £50 and £100.

Annual grant total: About £2,000 in total is available each year for grants to individuals.

Applications: In writing to the correspondent.

Correspondent: Philip Wickens, St Mary's Church House, Chain Street, Reading, Berkshire RG1 2HX (0118 957 1057; Fax: 0118 958 7041).

The Slough and District Community Fund

Eligibility: People in need who live in and around the borough of Slough.

Types of grants: One-off grants are made towards household items, food, fuel costs, clothing, the needs of babies and children and so on. No grants for educational purposes or expeditions.

Grants are only paid to the recommending agency or a third party and, wherever possible, are for specific items.

Annual grant total: In 2001 the fund had assets of £94,000, an income of £9,500 and its expenditure was £9,600. Grants to 162 individuals totalled £8,700.

Applications: On a form available from the correspondent, to be considered monthly. Applications must be made through a social worker, citizen's advice bureau or other third party, such as a teacher or councillor. Full details of the case are required, including income and expenditure.

Correspondent: Rosemary Brown, The Day Centre, William Street, Slough SL1 1XX (01753 536347).

Other information: This new trust was formed by the amalgamation of 'All Good Causes' and 'The Slough Nursing Fund'.

The Wokingham United Charities

Eligibility: People in need who live in the civil parishes of Wokingham, Wokingham Without, St Nicholas, Hurst, Ruscombe and that part of Finchampstead known as Finchampstead North.

Types of grants: One-off grants between £25 and £150. Grants have been given towards household items, utility arrears and clothing.

Annual grant total: In 1998/99 the trust gave 15 grants for both welfare and educational purposes totalling £1,700.

Applications: On a form available from the correspondent. Applications are considered each month (except August) and can be submitted directly by the individual, or through a social worker, headteacher or similar third party.

Correspondent: P Robinson, Clerk, 66 Upper Broadmoor Road, Crowthorne, Berkshire RG45 7DF.

Other information: This entry was not confirmed by the charity but the address was correct according to the Charity Commission.

Binfield

The Fritillary Trust

Eligibility: People in need who live in Binfield.

Types of grants: One-off and recurrent grants ranging from £300 to £1,500.

Annual grant total: In 2000/01 the trust had an income of £8,400 and a total expenditure of £8,900.

Applications: In writing to the correspondent.

Correspondent: The Trustees, SG Hambros Trust Company Limited, 41 Tower Hill, London EC3N 4SG.

Burnham

The Cornelius O'Sullivan Fund

Eligibility: People in need who are sick, convalescent, disabled or infirm and live in or near the parish of Burnham.

Types of grants: One-off grants of about £500 for pilgrimages or towards specialist medical equipment.

Annual grant total: In 2000/01 the trust had an income of £580 and a total expenditure of £720.

Applications: Applications can be submitted by the individual, through a recognised referral agency (e.g. social worker, citizen's advice bureau or doctor) or other third party. They are considered in September and January.

Correspondent: Our Lady of Peace RC Junior School, Derwent Drive, Slough, Berkshire SL1 6HW.

Datchet

The Datchet United Charities

Eligibility: People in need who live in the ancient parish of Datchet, with a preference for older people.

Types of grants: 80 to 90 individuals receive heating grants ranging from £90 to £150 each. Additional one-off grants are given.

Annual grant total: About £14,000 to individuals. The charity also gives money to organisations.

Applications: In writing to the correspondent either directly by the individual or through a social worker, citizen's advice bureau or other welfare agency. All applicants will be visited by the charities' social worker.

Correspondent: Gwenna Mary Howard, 59 London Road, Datchet, Berkshire SL3 9JY (Tel & Fax: 01753 541883; e-mail: gwenna@gulenna.freeserve.co.uk).

Hedgerley

The Tracy Trust

Eligibility: Pensioners who are in need and live in the parish of Hedgerley.

Types of grants: In 2000/01 grants were divided as follows:

TV licences	£1,900
Christmas vouchers	£4,300
Holidays/outings	£2,600
Mini-bus service	£5,000
Bus passes	£200
Aid call alarm	£2,300
Welfare/medical equipment	£6,200
Telephones	£70
Hospital taxis	£1,100

Annual grant total: In 2000/01 the trust had an income of £89,000 and grants were made to individuals totalling £27,000.

Applications: In writing to the correspondent.

Correspondent: Mr G Shedden, Charsley Harrison, 8 Sheet Street, Windsor, Berkshire SL4 1BD.

Other information: This entry was not confirmed by the trust, but the address was correct according to the Charity Commission database.

Newbury

Newbury & Thatcham Welfare Trust

Eligibility: People in need who are sick, disabled, convalescent or infirm and live in the former borough of Newbury as constituted on 31 March 1974 and the parishes of Greenham, Enborne, Hampstead, Marshall, Shaw-cum-Donnington, Speen and Thatcham.

Types of grants: One-off grants up to £250. Grants given include those for medical aids, food, holidays, respite care, travel, special equipment, TV licences, furniture and appliances. Grants are not given towards housing or rent costs and debts.

SOUTH EAST – BERKSHIRE/BUCKINGHAMSHIRE

Annual grant total: About £2,500 was distributed in 17 grants to individuals.

Applications: By application form submitted either through a social worker, citizen's advice bureau or other welfare agency or through a third party on behalf of an individual i.e. doctor, health visitor or other health professional. They can be considered at any time.

Correspondent: Mrs Heather Codling, September Cottage, Stoney Lane, Ashmore Green, Thatcham, Berkshire RG18 9HD (01635 861625; Fax: 01635 869325).

Reading

St Laurence Charities for the Poor

Eligibility: People in need who live in the area of the ancient parish of St Laurence in Reading. Surplus money can be given to people living in the county borough of Reading.

Types of grants: One-off and annual grants are awarded according to need. Grants are not made to students for training research grants. The minimum grant is £100.

Annual grant total: In 2001 grants totalling £600 were awarded to individuals. The Charities had an income of £66,000 and a total expenditure of £89,000.

Applications: In writing to the correspondent, directly by the individual including details of requirements. Applications are considered at any time.

Correspondent: John Michael James, c/o Vale West, Victoria House, 26 Queen Victoria Street, Reading RG1 1TG (0118 957 3238).

Other information: They also give money to charities provided they benefit individuals in need. For more information see *A Guide to Local Trusts in the South of England.*

Shinfield

The Edmund Godson Charity

See entry on page 369

Sunninghill

The Sunninghill Fuel Allotment

Eligibility: People in need who live in the civil parish of Sunninghill.

Types of grants: One-off grants only up to £1,000 e.g. to relieve sudden distress, to purchase essential equipment or household appliances, to meet bills from utilities etc. Grants given include payment for: telephone charges; a recliner chair; conversion costs.

Annual grant total: In 2000/01 the trust had assets of £2.2 million, an income of £78,000 and a total expenditure of £89,000, of this £960 was distributed to three individuals.

Applications: In writing to the correspondent through a social worker, citizen's advice bureau or other welfare agency or through a doctor or district or practice nurse. Applications are considered in February, April, July and November. Applicants should be prepared to provide documentary evidence or arrange independent corroboration of their difficulties and circumstances.

Correspondent: Richard J Dugdale, 101 Victoria Road, Ascot, Berkshire SL5 9DS (01344 620614).

Other information: Grants are also made to organisations including hospices, community facilities and schools.

Buckinghamshire

1067 Trust Fund

Eligibility: People in need who live in the parishes of Wooburn, Little Marlow, Flackwell Heath, Hedsor, Bourn End and Loudwater (south of the A40).

Types of grants: One-off grants in the approximate range of £30 to £500. In 2000/01 grants were made as follows:
Hospital travel £100
Insurance costs £250
Playgroup costs £65
Goods £90
Holidays £100
Computers and other equipment £470
Other £30

Annual grant total: In 2000/01 the trust's assets totalled £17,000, it had an income of £950 and eight relief-in-need grants were made totalling £1,100.

Applications: In writing to: Brian Spires, 1 Highlands, Flackwell Heath, Buckinghamshire HP10 9BT. Applications should be made either through a social worker, citizen's advice bureau or other welfare agency or directly by the individual or a third party on behalf on an individual. Applications can be submitted at any time for consideration in March, June, September or December. Emergency applications can be considered at any time.

Correspondent: D E Tracey, Uplands, New Road, Bourne End, Buckinghamshire SL8 5BY (01628 528699).

The Iver Heath Sick Poor Fund

Eligibility: People who are sick, convalescent, physically or mentally disabled or infirm and who live in the Iver Heath ward of the parish of Iver and part of the parish of Wexham.

Types of grants: Usually one-off grants for clothing, medical needs, home help, fuel, lighting, chiropody and other necessities, although recurrent grants will be considered.

Annual grant total: About £2,000.

Applications: In writing to the correspondent. Applications are considered twice a year in spring and autumn, although in emergencies they can be considered at other times.

Correspondent: The Rector, The Rectory, 2 Pinewood Close, Iver Heath, Buckinghamshire SL0 0QS (01753 654470).

Iver United Charities

Eligibility: People in need who live in the parishes of Iver, Iver Heath and Richings Park.

Types of grants: One-off grants and hampers.

Annual grant total: In 2000/01 the charities had an income of £4,100 and a total expenditure of £4,600.

Applications: In writing to the correspondent by a social worker, health visitor, vicar, district nurse or other appropriate third party on behalf of the individual. Applications must include details of the applicant's weekly income, housing and sick benefit, council tax benefit and any other income.

Correspondent: Robert Penn, 26 Chequers Orchard, Iver, Buckinghamshire SL0 9NH (01753 655839).

The Salford Town Lands

Eligibility: People in need who live in the parish of Hulcote and Salford.

Types of grants: Usually one-off grants ranging from £60 to £200, including those for older people at Christmas and children's Christmas tokens.

Annual grant total: In 2001 the charity had an income of £6,200. A total of £3,700 was given in relief-in-need grants. Educational grants totalled £3,700.

Applications: In writing to the correspondent. Applications can be submitted directly by the individual or through any other parishioner.

Correspondent: Bill Oldhams, Fendene, Wavingdon Road, Salford, Milton Keynes MK17 8BD.

Other information: Grants are also made to organisations supporting the community.

The Stoke Mandeville & Other Parishes Charity

Eligibility: People in need who live in the parishes of Stoke Mandeville, Great and Little Hampden and Great Missenden.

Types of grants: Annual Christmas grants to people over 70 and one-off grants to

307

people who are disabled for specific needs such as wheelchairs or stairlifts.
Annual grant total: In 1999 the trust's assets totalled £2.2 million and the income was £190,000. Grants to organisations and individuals totalled £88,000.
Applications: On a form available from the correspondent, considered in January, April, July and October.
Correspondent: G Crombie, Secretary, Blackwells, Great Hampden, Great Missenden, Buckinghamshire HP16 9RJ.
Other information: This entry was not confirmed by the charity but was correct according to information on file at the Charity Commission.

Tyringham Pension Fund for the Blind

Eligibility: People in need who are blind and live in the former Newport Pagnell or Wolverton rural or urgan district councils' areas.
Types of grants: Pensions of £20 per quarter.
Annual grant total: In 2000/01 the trust had an income of £5,400 and a total expenditure of £1,000.
Applications: Applications should not be made directly to the trust. Individuals should contact Buckinghamshire Association for the Blind, who approach the trust on their behalf.
Correspondent: Mrs Sylvia Eales, Secretary, 148 Wolverton Road, Newport Pagnell, Buckinghamshire MK16 8JQ (01908 612897).

Wooburn, Bourne End & District Relief-in-Sickness Charity

Eligibility: People who live in the parishes of Wooburn, Bourne End, Hedsor or parts of Little Marlow who are sick, convalescent, physically or mentally disabled or infirm.
Types of grants: One-off grants in the range of £30 to £600 for telephone installation, help with nursing costs, convalescence, holidays, home help and other necessities. All items for which a grant is requested must have a direct connection with the applicant's illness. No recurrent grants are given.
Annual grant total: In 2001 the charity had assets of £53,000, an income of £8,900 and a total expenditure of £8,500. A total of £7,500 was distributed in 40 relief-in-need grants to individuals.
Applications: In writing to the correspondent through a doctor, health visitor, priest or other third party. Applications are usually considered at half-yearly meetings, but in emergency cases applications can be considered sooner.

Correspondent: Mrs D A Heyes, 11 Telston Close, Bourne End, Buckingham SL8 5TY (01628 523498).

Aylesbury

Elizabeth Eman Trust

Eligibility: Women in need in the following order of priority: (1) widows born in the former borough of Aylesbury as constituted immediately before 1st April 1974; (2) widows living in the present district of Aylesbury Vale; (3) women living in the present district of Aylesbury Vale.
Types of grants: Allowances of £65 per quarter. Grants are for life.
Annual grant total: In 2000 the trust had an income of £36,000 and a total expenditure of £29,000. A total of £28,000 was given to individuals.
Applications: On a form available from the correspondent after a public advertisement. Applications can be submitted directly by the individual or through a social worker or other welfare agency, or by a member of the individual's immediate family. Original birth, marriage and husband's death certificates should be included as appropriate. Applications are normally considered in May and November each year, although they can be considered at other times.
Correspondent: N Freeman, Horwood James, 7 Temple Square, Aylesbury, Buckinghamshire HP20 2QB (01296 487361; Fax: 01296 427155; e-mail: enquiries@horwoodjames.co.uk).

William Harding's Charity

Eligibility: People in need who live in the town of Aylesbury.
Types of grants: One-off grants are given for general relief-in-need.
Annual grant total: In 2000 the trust had assets of £20 million and an income of £525,000. A total of £414,000 was awarded in grants to individuals and organisations for welfare and educational purposes.
Applications: On a form available from the correspondent to be submitted directly by the individual. Trustees meet 10 times each year to consider applications.
Correspondent: John Leggett, Clerk to the Trustees, Messrs Parrott & Coales, Solicitors, 14 Bourbon Street, Aylesbury HP20 2RS (01296 318500).

Bletchley

Bletchley Fuel Allotment Charity

Eligibility: People in need who live in the MK3 area of Bletchley. Beneficiaries tend mainly to be people who are elderly.

Types of grants: Christmas grants of £20 and upwards.
Annual grant total: About £1,300.
Applications: In writing to the correspondent.
Correspondent: Mrs P Clark, 25 Warwick Road, Bletchley, Milton Keynes MK3 6AN.

Calverton

Calverton Apprenticing Charity

Eligibility: People in need, particularly those over 65, who live in the parish of All Saints, Calverton.
Types of grants: Recurrent grants in the range of £75 to £150. Grants given include those for clothes, heating and so on.
Annual grant total: In 2000/01 the charity had an income of £3,200 and a total expenditure of £3,000. A total of £2,100 was distributed in 14 relief-in-need grants. Three educational grants totalled £330.
Applications: On a form available from the correspondent. Applications are considered in May and November.
Correspondent: Miss K Phillips, 78 London Road, Stony Stratford MK11 1JH (01908 563350; e-mail: karen.phillips@virgin.net).

Cheddington

Cheddington Town Lands Charity

Eligibility: People in need who live in Cheddington.
Types of grants: One-off and recurrent grants according to need.
Annual grant total: In 1999/2000 the sum of £29,000 was distributed to the parish church and other organisations and individuals.
Applications: In writing to the correspondent.
Correspondent: W G King, 5 Chaseside Close, Cheddington, Leighton Buzzard, Bedfordshire LU7 0SA (01296 668608).

Denham

The Denham Nursing Fund

Eligibility: People in need who are sick and infirm and who live in the parish of Denham.
Types of grants: One-off grants given at Christmas only, except in emergencies.
Annual grant total: About £800 a year.
Applications: In writing to the correspondent.
Correspondent: Mrs B J Greenfield, Chair, 38 Skylark Road, Denham,

Buckinghamshire UB9 4HS
(01895 833047).

Emberton

Emberton United Charity

Eligibility: Older people in need who live in the parish of Emberton.

Types of grants: One-off and recurrent grants, usually of up to £250.

Annual grant total: About £5,000 was given in grants to older people, and young people for educational purposes.

Applications: In writing to the correspondent, direcly by the individual.

Correspondent: George Davies, Secretary to the Trustees, 59 Olney Road, Emberton, Olney, Buckinghamshire MK46 5BU (Fax: 0870 164 0662; e-mail: george@taipooshan.demon.co.uk).

Great Linford

Great Linford Relief in Need Charity

Eligibility: People in need who live in the parish of Great Linford.

Types of grants: One-off grants of up to £200. Grants have been given towards educational activities and to assist with the cost of sheltered housing.

Annual grant total: In 2001 the charity had assets of £17,000, an income of £460 and a total expenditure of £1,200. One grant of £200 was made for relief-in-need purposes.

Applications: On a form available from: David Enticknap, 52 Graves End, Great Linford, Milton Keynes MK14 5DX. Applications can be submitted either directly by the individual or through a social worker, citizen's advice bureau, other welfare agency or a third party such as a relative, teacher or carer. Applications are considered in January, June and September.

Correspondent: The Vicar, The Rectory, Great Linford, Milton Keynes, Buckinghamshire MK14 5BD (01908 605892).

Other information: Grants are also given to organisations.

High Wycombe

The High Wycombe Central Aid Society

Eligibility: People in need who live in the old borough of High Wycombe, usually people on benefits or people who are elderly.

Types of grants: One-off grants in times of crisis towards fuel debts, clothes, holidays, spectacles, telephone installation, decorating materials and so on. Grants range from £50 to £150.

The trust also has a second-hand furniture warehouse and clothes and soft furnishings store.

Annual grant total: In 2001 the society gave grants totalling £700 per month.

Applications: In writing to the correspondent. Applications can be submitted directly by the individual or through a social worker, citizen's advice bureau or other welfare agency. They are considered on the first Monday of each month with the exception of August.

Correspondent: Mrs M Mitchell, Secretary, 1–3 Cornmarket, High Wycombe, Buckinghamshire HP11 2BW (01494 535890; Fax: 01494 538256).

Other information: The society also runs a Pensioners Pop-In for people over 50 twice a week.

Hitcham

Hitcham Poor Lands Charity

Eligibility: People in need who live in the parish of Hitcham.

Types of grants: One-off and recurrent grants according to need.

Annual grant total: About £5,000.

Applications: In writing to the correspondent.

Correspondent: Mrs Pam Reay, 45 Nursery Road, Taplow, Maidenhead, Berkshire SL6 0JX.

Other information: This entry was not confirmed by the charity, but the address was correct according to the Charity Commission database.

Pitstone

The Pitstone Town Lands Charity

Eligibility: People in need who live in Pitstone.

Types of grants: One-off grants for fuel, bus fares, outings, travel to or from hospital, spectacles, chiropody and other necessities.

Annual grant total: In 1999/2000 the sum of £13,000 was given in grants.

Applications: In writing to the correspondent through a social worker, citizen's advice bureau or other welfare agency or third party, or directly by the individual. Applications are considered throughout the year and must include full information to support the application.

Correspondent: Mrs C Martell, 22 Chequers Lane, Pitstone, Leighton Buzzard, Bedfordshire LU7 9AG (01296 668389).

Other information: The charity also gives grants to organisations in the area.

Radnage

Radnage Poor's Land Estate (Poors Branch)

Eligibility: People in need who live in the parish of Radnage.

Types of grants: One-off and recurrent grants of around £50 to £200. Recent grants have been given towards hospital visits and food.

Annual grant total: In 2001 the trust had an income of £3,900 and made grants to 50 individuals totalling £3,600.

Applications: In writing to the correspondent through a social worker, citizen's advice bureau or other welfare agency, directly by the individual, or through a relevant third party i.e. a local parishioner. Applications are considered in February, June, September and December.

Correspondent: I K Blaylock, Clerk to the Trustees, Hilltop, Green End Road, Radnage, High Wycombe, Buckinghamshire HP14 4BY.

Stony Stratford

The Ancell Trust

Eligibility: People in need in Stony Stratford.

Types of grants: Grants are given to older people at Christmas as well as one-off payments throughout the year.

Annual grant total: In 1999 it had an income of £12,000. Grants to 8 individuals totalled £1,300. Grants to organisations totalled £9,700.

Applications: In writing to the correspondent at any time.

Correspondent: Roger Borley, Secretary, 79 High Street, Stony Stratford, Milton Keynes MK1 1AU (01908 563232).

Water Eaton

Water Eaton Poors Land Charity

Eligibility: People of pensionable age who live in Water Eaton.

Types of grants: Pensions of between £10 and £12.

Annual grant total: In 1998/99 the charity had an income of £2,300 and a total expenditure of £1,700. No recent financial information was available.

Applications: In writing to the correspondent for consideration in November.

Correspondent: Mrs E A Cumberland, 9 Katrine Place, Betchley, Milton Keynes MK2 3DW.

Other information: This entry was not confirmed by the charity, but the address was correct according to the Charity Commission database.

Wingrave

Wingrave United Charities

Eligibility: People in need who live in the parish of Wingrave.

Types of grants: One-off and recurrent grants according to need.

Annual grant total: About £1,000, mainly to individuals.

Applications: In writing to the correspondent.

Correspondent: Mrs E P Morgan, 12 Nup End Close, Wingrave, Aylesbury, Buckinghamshire HP22 4QA (01296 681101).

Wolverton

The Catherine Featherstone Charity

Eligibility: People in need who live in the ancient parish of Wolverton.

Types of grants: One-off and recurrent grants ranging from £50 to £500.

Annual grant total: In 2001 the charity had assets of £171,000, an income of £7,700 and a total expenditure of £7,100. A total of £6,000 was distributed in 25 relief-in-need grants to individuals.

Applications: In writing to the correspondent, either directly by the individual, through a social worker, citizen's advice bureau or welfare agency. Applications should be received in January, April, July and September for consideration in the following month.

Correspondent: Miss K Phillips, Secretary, 78 London Road, Stony Stratford, Milton Keynes, Buckinghamshire MK11 1JH (01908 563350; e-mail: karen.phillip@virgin.net).

Cambridgeshire

Cambridgeshire County Bowling Association – Benevolent Fund

Eligibility: Bowlers who are or have been affiliated members of Cambridgeshire County Bowling Association and their dependants. Applicants must be in need.

Types of grants: One-off and recurrent grants according to need.

Annual grant total: In 1999/2000 the trust had an income of £530 and its total expenditure was £680.

Applications: In writing to the correspondent.

Correspondent: Barry Grimwood, 108 Northfield Road, Soham, Ely, Cambridgeshire CB7 5XA (01353 722781).

Other information: This entry was not confirmed by the fund, but the address was correct according to the Charity Commission database.

The Farthing Trust

Eligibility: People in need, with a priority given to those either personally known to the trustees or recommended by those personally known to the trustees. This is a national trust although grants are usually given to people in Cambridgeshire.

Types of grants: One-off and recurrent grants according to need.

Annual grant total: In 2000/01 the trust had assets of £2.1 million and an income of £344,000. Out of a total expenditure of £191,000 the sum of £12,000 was given to individuals in need in the UK.

Applications: In writing to the correspondent. Applicants will only be notified of a refusal if an sae is enclosed.

Correspondent: Heber Martin, 48 Ten Mile Bank, Littleport, Ely, Cambridgeshire CB6 1EF (01353 860586).

Other information: The trusts states that it receives up to 20 letters a week and is able to help about one in a 100. There would seem little point in applying unless a personal contact with a trustee is established.

This entry was not confirmed by the trust, but the address was correct according to the Charity Commission database.

The Leverington Relief-in-Sickness Fund

Eligibility: People in need who live in the villages of Leverington and Gorefield and are sick, convalescing, disabled or infirm.

Types of grants: One-off grants towards, for example, medical expenses, household items or bills.

Annual grant total: About £1,500 per year.

Applications: In writing to the correspondent. An advert is usually placed in the local press near the time when applications are considered (around September time).

Correspondent: Mrs C A Gray, 41 Milton Drive, Leverington, Wisbech, Cambridgeshire PE13 5DF (01945 463113).

The Leverington Town Lands Charity

Eligibility: People in need who live in the parishes of Leverington, Gorefield and Newton.

Types of grants: One-off grants towards, for example, glasses, new teeth or household appliances.

Annual grant total: About £15,000.

Applications: On a form available from the correspondent. Applications are considered in May and November.

Correspondent: Mrs C A Gray, 41 Milton Drive, Leverington, Wisbech, Cambridgeshire PE13 5DF (01945 463113).

The Foundation of Edward Storey

See entry on page 60

The Swaffham Prior Parochial Charities

Eligibility: People in need who live in the parishes of Swaffham Prior and Reach.

Types of grants: One-off and recurrent grants ranging from £10 to £100. Grants are usually given for childrens' clothing, although anything where need can be proven will be considered.

Annual grant total: About £6,500 a year for both educational and welfare purposes.

Applications: In writing to the correspondent or any of the trustees, including details of need and sources of existing aid. Applications can be submitted directly by the individual or through a third party such as a social worker, citizen's advice bureau, relation or friend. Applications are generally considered three times a year although emergency cases can be considered immediately.

Correspondent: S G Hewitt, Clerk, St Mary's, 63 High Street, Swaffham Prior, Cambridge CB5 0LD (01638 741337).

Other information: Grants are also given to local organisations for equipment and so on.

The Charities of Nicholas Swallow & Others

Eligibility: People in need who live in the parish of Whittlesford (near Cambridge) and adjacent area.

310

Types of grants: One-off cash grants at Christmas; help can also be given towards hospital travel and educational costs.
Annual grant total: Over £3,000 in 2002 for educational and welfare purposes.
Applications: Directly by the individual in writing to the correspondent.
Correspondent: Nicholas Tufton, Clerk, 11 High Street, Barkway, Royston, Hertfordshire SG8 8EA (01763 848888).

The Upwell (Cambridgeshire) Consolidated Charities

Eligibility: People in need who are over 65 (unless widowed) and live in the parish of Upwell (on the Isle of Ely) and the parish of Christchurch, and have done so for at least five years.
Types of grants: Annual grants usually range from £10 to £40.
Annual grant total: In 2001 the trust had an income of £3,500 and a total expenditure of £3,300. A total of 101 relief-in-need grants totalled £2,600.
Applications: In writing to the correspondent. Applications should be submitted directly by the individual and are considered in December.
Correspondent: Mrs W J Judd, Clerk, 27 Hallbridge Road, Upwell, Wisbech, Cambridgeshire PE14 9DP (01945 773668).

Balsham

The Balsham Parochial Charities

Eligibility: People in need who live in Balsham.
Types of grants: One-off grants including Christmas bonuses to people in need.
Annual grant total: In 2000/01 the charities had an income of £2,300 and a total expenditure of £2,100.
Applications: In writing to the correspondent.
Correspondent: Ian Creek, 6 Trinity Close, Balsham, Cambridge CB1 6DW.
Other information: This trust also gives grants to local youth organisations such as schools, scouts and guides.

Cambridge

The Cambridge Community Nursing Trust

Eligibility: Poor or sick people living in the boundaries of the city of Cambridge only.
Types of grants: Grants of up to about £300 are given to provide extra care, comforts and special aids which are not available from any other source. Grants are also given to organisations.

Annual grant total: Around £7,000. Any money unclaimed by individuals is given to local charities.
Applications: In writing or by telephone to the correspondent. The trustees meet three times a year to discuss applications, but grants can usually be arranged without delay.
Correspondent: Mrs M Hoskins, 11 Rutherford Road, Cambridge CB2 2HH (01223 840259; e-mail: mhos24992@aol.com).

Chatteris

The Chatteris Feoffee Charity

Eligibility: People who are 'poor and needy' and have lived in Chatteris for at least 10 years.
Types of grants: £25 grants given annually in January.
Annual grant total: In 2000/01 the charity had an income of £3,700 and a total expenditure of £3,300.
Applications: In writing to the correspondent, or upon recommendation of a trustee.
Correspondent: The Clerks, Messrs Brian, Hawden & Co., Solicitors, 1 Wood Street, Chatteris, Cambridgeshire PE16 6AB (01354 692212).

Downham

The Downham Feoffee Charity

Eligibility: People in need who live in the ancient parish of Downham.
Types of grants: One-off and recurrent grants according to need.
Annual grant total: About £5,000.
Applications: In writing to the correspondent.
Correspondent: W D Crawley, Clerk, 14 Vineyard Way, Ely, Cambridgeshire CB7 4QQ.

Elsworth

The Samuel Franklin Fund

Eligibility: Children, young people, older people and families, who are in need and who live in the parish of Elsworth.
Types of grants: One-off or recurrent grants according to need.
Annual grant total: About £6,000 for educational and welfare purposes.
Applications: In writing to the correspondent.
Correspondent: Mrs Lynda Hogan, Secretary, 46 Boxworth Road, Elsworth, Cambridge CB3 8JQ.

Ely

The Ely District Nursing Trust

Eligibility: People in need who are sick and live in the city of Ely (excluding the hamlet of Prickwillow).
Types of grants: One-off grants in the range of £100 to £1,000. Grants given include those for medical care and equipment and travel expenses to hospital.
Annual grant total: In 2000/01 the trust had an income of £3,300 and gave grants to individuals totalling £2,200.
Applications: In writing to the correspondent either directly by the individual or through a social worker, citizen's advice bureau or other welfare agency. Applications are considered on the first Friday of each month.
Correspondent: The Trustees, Hall Ennion & Young, 8 High Street, Ely, Cambridgeshire CB7 4JY (01353 662918; Fax: 01353 662747).

Thomas Parson's Charity

Eligibility: People in need who live in the City of Ely.
Types of grants: One-off and occasionally recurrent grants and loans, ranging from £1,000 to £4,000.
Annual grant total: In 2000/01 the trust had assets of £2.1 million and an income of £138,000. Grants to individuals totalled £5,600 whilst £4,000 was given to organisations. It has a usual surplus of about £11,000 which is used towards repairs to its almshouses.
Applications: In writing to the correspondent, for consideration on the first Friday in each month. Applications can be submitted either directly by the individual, or through a social worker, citizen's advice bureau or other welfare agency.
Correspondent: J M Smith, Secretary, Messrs Hall Ennion & Young, 8 High Street, Ely, Cambridgeshire CB7 4JY (01353 662918; Fax: 01353 662747; e-mail: jms@heysolicitors.co.uk).

Fenstanton

The Fenstanton Town Trust

Eligibility: People in need who live in Fenstanton.
Types of grants: One-off grants for specific needs. Grants have been given to allow a girl guide to attend a festival abroad, to allow an ill couple to adapt their car, and towards utility bills.
Annual grant total: In 1999 a couple of hundred pounds was available due to a low income that year.
Applications: In writing to the correspondent. Applications can be

submitted directly by the individual or by an appropriate third party, to be considered at the trustees' meeting in February (although decisions can be made throughout the year if necessary).

Correspondent: Ann Sinclair-Russell, Westmoor House, London Road, Chatteris, Cambridgeshire PE16 6AS (Tel & Fax: 01354 692136).

Other information: This trust also makes grants for educational purposes and local organisations such as a drama society.

Grantchester

The Grantchester Relief in Need Charity

Eligibility: People in need who live in the ancient parish of Grantchester.

Types of grants: One-off grants according to need.

Annual grant total: In 2001 the charity had an income of £3,800 and 77 grants to individuals were made totalling £2,400.

Applications: In writing to the correspondent.

Correspondent: Mrs D M Pauley, 7 Burnt Close, Grantchester, Cambridge CB3 9NJ (01223 840361).

Hilton

Hilton Town Charity

Eligibility: People who live in the village of Hilton, Cambridgeshire, of any age or occupation, who may have unforeseen needs, due for example, to hardship, disability or sickness.

Types of grants: One-off or recurrent grants according to need.

Annual grant total: £4,500 in 2001 for both welfare and educational purposes.

Applications: In writing to the correspondent.

Correspondent: R Slayter, Treasurer, The Old Rectory, Hilton, Cambridgeshire PE28 9NA.

Other information: Grants are also available for organisations who serve the direct needs of the village.

Ickleton

The Ickleton United Charities (Relief-in-Need Branch)

Eligibility: People in need who live in the parish of Ickleton, Cambridgeshire.

Types of grants: One-off grants of about £40 towards fuel costs and necessities, and gift vouchers at Christmas.

Annual grant total: In 2001 the trust had an income of £7,400 and its total expenditure was £2,100. The sum of £1,500 was distributed among 35 individuals.

Applications: In writing to the correspondent to be submitted directly by the individual.

Correspondent: D H Isaac, 6 Church Street, Inkleton, Saffron Waldren, Essex CB10 1SL (01799 530618).

Landbeach

Rev Robert Masters Charity for Widows

Eligibility: People in need who live in the parish of Landbeach, with a preference for widows.

Types of grants: One-off and recurrent grants according to need.

Annual grant total: About £500 a year.

Applications: In writing to the correspondent.

Correspondent: G Hayward, Secretary, North Farm, Landbeach, Cambridge CB4 8ED (01223 860038).

Little Wilbraham

The Johnson Bede & Lane Charitable Trust

Eligibility: People in need who live in the civil parish of Little Wilbraham.

Types of grants: One-off grants usually between £40 and £100. Recent awards have included small Christmas grants and help with heating costs for older people, help with playgroup fees and special equipment for a disabled child. The trust also makes educational grants.

Annual grant total: About £3,000 a year.

Applications: In writing to the correspondent directly by the individual or by a third party such as a social worker, citizen's advice bureau or neighbour. Applications are usually considered in February, June and November.

Correspondent: Davis Taylor, 66 High Street, Little Wilbraham, Cambridge CB1 5JY.

Pampisford

Pampisford Relief-in-Need Charity

Eligibility: People in need who live in the parish of Pampisford.

Types of grants: People who are elderly or disabled may receive Christmas gifts or individual grants of up to £250. Contributions are also made for the improvement of village amenities, which can then be enjoyed by people who are elderly or disabled.

Annual grant total: In 2001 the charity had both an income and a total expenditure of £12,000. £2,700 was distributed to individuals.

Applications: In writing to the correspondent directly by the individual. Applications can be considered at any time.

Correspondent: A J S Rogers, Clerk, 7 Hammond Close, Pampisford, Cambridgeshire CB2 4EP (01223 835954).

Other information: Half of the charity's income goes to the Pampisford Ecclesiastical Charity.

Peterborough

The Florence Saunders Relief-in-Sickness Charity

Eligibility: People who live in the area of the former city of Peterborough and who are sick, convalescent, infirm or disabled.

Types of grants: Usually one-off grants between £100 and £500. No grants for repayment of debts.

Annual grant total: About £8,000 a year.

Applications: In writing to the correspondent throughout the year.

Correspondent: Clerk to the Trustees, Stephenson House, 15 Church Walk, Peterborough PE1 2TP (01733 343275).

Sawston

John Huntingdon's Charity

Eligibility: People in need who live in the parish of Sawston in Cambridgeshire.

Types of grants: One-off grants, usually ranging from £50 to £250 and occasionally up to £500 or more. Grants can be for essential household items such as cookers, beds or fridges, TV licences, holidays, medical equipment, debts, transport costs, decorating costs and childcare fees.

Annual grant total: In 2000 the trust had assets of £6.8 million, its income was £258,000 and its total expenditure was £149,000. Grants were made to 92 individuals in need totalling £16,000, mostly for welfare purposes. £58,000 was given in grants for other purposes.

The amount given to individuals each year has since increased, and in 2002 the trust anticipated donating about £20,000 to £30,000 in total to individuals each year.

Applications: In writing to the Sawston Support Services at the address below, or by telephone. Office opening hours are 9am to 2pm Monday to Friday. All grants are means tested.

Correspondent: Revd Mary Irish, Clerk to the Trustees, John Huntingdon House, Tannery Road, Sawston, Cambridge CB2 4UW (Tel & Fax: 01223 830599;

Sawston Support Service Tel: 01223 836289; e-mail: johnhuntingdonscharity@care4free.net).

Soham

Soham United Charities

Eligibility: People in need of all ages who live in the parish of Soham.

Types of grants: One-off grants have been given to individuals recommended by the citizen's advice bureau and Cambridgeshire Social Services to pay pressing debts, buy clothing for adults and children and to provide equipment for people on courses. No grants towards education.

Annual grant total: In 2000 the trust had an income of £18,000. It gave grants totalling £11,000 to organisations and individuals.

Applications: In writing to the correspondent directly by the individual. Applicants should include a financial statement giving details of assets and liabilities, and reasons in support of the application. They are considered in November and February. There is also an emergency committee which can meet during the rest of the year.

Correspondent: Mrs J Hobbs, Clerk, 3 Churchgate Street, Soham, Ely, Cambridgeshire CB7 5DS (01353 720317; Fax: 01353 24161).

Other information: The trustees will discuss and investigate in detail the circumstances arising for the grant to be requested before making any award.

Stetchworth

The Stetchworth Relief-in-Need Charity

Eligibility: People in need who live in the parish of Stetchworth and have done so for at least two years.

Types of grants: One-off grants ranging from £20 to £60 according to need. Grants have been given towards, for example, electricity bills, fuel, groceries (through an account at the local community shop), transport to hospital and educational needs.

Annual grant total: Over £1,000.

Applications: On a form available form the correspondent or the Ellesmere Centre, Stetchworth which should include details of income, expenditure and any other applications for help, rebates or discounts. Applications are considered at any time. The charity says, 'We welcome information from anyone who knows someone in need.'

Correspondent: Mrs F R L Swann, 19 Ditton Green, Woodditton, Newmarket, Suffolk CB8 9SG (01638 730859).

Other information: Grants are available at any time of the year, although many of the elderly applicants tend to apply for a Christmas bonus in December. Whilst it is not the policy of the charity to give Christmas bonuses, it is happy to be used in this way.

Stretham

Stretham Charity

Eligibility: People who live in the parish of Stretham who are in need.

Types of grants: One-off grants, exceptionally of up to £10,000, but normally under £1,000.

Annual grant total: About £1,800 each year, for both welfare and educational purposes.

Applications: In writing to the correspondent. Prospective applicants may telephone on 01353 648079.

Correspondent: Miss V Baylis, 5 Hay Fen Close, Streatham, Ely, Cambridgeshire CB6 3NE.

Other information: Local organisations are also supported.

Sutton

The Sutton Poors' Land Charity

Eligibility: People in need who live in the parish of Sutton.

Types of grants: Generally Christmas vouchers of £10 to £50 and occasional one-off grants to people in need or for further education.

Annual grant total: About 100 grants totalling up to £4,500, a small proportion of which is given for educational purposes.

Applications: In writing to the correspondent, considered at any time.

Correspondent: Ann Sinclair-Russell, Westmoor House, London Road, Chatteris, Cambridgeshire PE16 6AS (Tel & Fax: 01354 692136).

Swaffham Bulbeck

The Swaffham Bulbeck Relief-in-Need Charity

Eligibility: People in need who are over 65 and have lived in the parish of Swaffham Bulbeck for at least a year.

Types of grants: One-off and annual grants in kind or in cash, usually for not more than £20 each.

Annual grant total: In 2001 the charity had an income of £5,000. Grants totalled £1,500.

Applications: In writing to the correspondent.

Correspondent: Mrs C Ling, 43 High Street, Swaffham Bulbeck, Cambridge CB5 0HP (01223 811733).

Other information: Grants are also made to local clubs, schools and churches.

Swavesey

Thomas Galon's Charity

Eligibility: People in need who live in the parish of Swavesey, who are 70 or over, single or widowed; married couples when one partner reaches 70 and widows and widowers with dependent children up to 18 years old.

Types of grants: An annual gift, to be agreed in November for people in need. One-off grants for hospital travel expenses, fuel costs and other needs. Grants of at least £35 are generally made. No grants for capital projects such as buildings.

Annual grant total: Each year 100 to 120 grants are made totalling about £4,000.

Applications: In writing to the correspondent for consideration in November; grants will be delivered in December.

Correspondent: Linda Miller, Clerk, 10 Carters Way, Swavesey, Cambridgeshire CB4 5RZ (01954 202982).

Walsoken

The Walsoken United Charities

Eligibility: People in need who are 60 or over and have lived in Walsoken for at least two years.

Types of grants: One-off grants in the form of cash (usually £5 to £8 per household) and gifts in kind.

Annual grant total: Between £2,500 and £3,000.

Applications: In writing to the correspondent directly by the individual for consideration in December.

Correspondent: D Mews, Clerk, Fraser Southwell, 28–29 Old Market, Wisbech, Cambridgeshire PE13 1ND (01945 582664).

Whittlesey

The Whittlesey Charity

Eligibility: People in need who live in the ancient parishes of Whittlesey Urban and Whittlesey Rural only.

Types of grants: Small annual cash grants, plus the occasional one-off grant.

Annual grant total: In 1999 the relief-in-need fund of this charity had assets of £117,000 and an income of £34,000. Total expenditure was £17,000, all of which was given in grants.

Applications: In writing to the correspondent. Applications are considered in February, May and September, but urgent applications can be dealt with at fairly short notice. Please note, the trust will not respond to ineligible applicants.

Correspondent: P S Gray, 34 Gracious Street, Whittlesey, Peterborough PE7 1AR (01733 205180).

East Sussex

The Catharine House Trust

Eligibility: Sick people of limited means in need of medical or surgical treatment and convalescent or other accommodation. Priority is given to people living in the Hastings and St Leonards area of East Sussex.

Types of grants: One-off grants towards the cost of treatment, convalescence, accommodation and travel.

Annual grant total: About £25,000.

Applications: In writing to the correspondent. Previous applicants are not considered.

Correspondent: Mrs P M Hawke, Secretary, 9 Brading Close, Hastings, East Sussex TN34 2HT (01424 426543).

Hart Charitable Trust

Eligibility: Individuals in need who live in East Sussex, with a preference for people in the Hastings and Rother districts.

Types of grants: One-off grants, on average of £100 each, towards clothing, bedding and travel etc. Usually small amounts are given to meet immediate needs. No grants are made for the payment of debts or for carpets or curtains.

Annual grant total: In 2000/01 the trust had assets of £700,000, its income totalled £27,000 and grants to organisations totalled £600, with a further £13,000 going in total to 156 individuals.

Applications: On a form available from the correspondent. Applications should be submitted, at any time of year, through a social worker, citizen's advice bureau or other welfare agency.

Correspondent: Michael R Bugden, Clerk to the Trustees, Gaby Hardwicke, 2 Eversley Road, Bexhill on Sea, East Sussex TN40 1EY (01424 730945; Fax: 01424 730043).

Other information: On rare occasions, the trust makes grants to small local organisations helping those in need.

The Doctor Merry Memorial Fund

Eligibility: People who are ill and who live in the Eastbourne area Health Authority.

Types of grants: One-off grants for nursing home care, help with Lifeline rentals and medical equipment.

Annual grant total: In 2000/01 the trust had an income of £7,300 and a total expenditure of £14,000.

Applications: Individuals should apply via their doctor on a form available from the correspondent. Applications are considered throughout the year.

Correspondent: R E Langford, Treasurer, 4 Crown Street, Eastbourne, East Sussex BN21 1NX.

Other information: This charity was founded in 1922 as a memorial to Dr Merry who died of exhaustion after caring for the people of Eastbourne in the 'flu epidemic of that time'.

This entry was not confirmed by the fund, but the address was correct according to information on file at the Charity Commission.

The Relief – Hastings Area Community Trust

Eligibility: People in need who are under 60 and live in Hastings and St Leonards-on-Sea. People aged 60 or over are only eligible if Age Concern are unable to help them.

Types of grants: One-off grants in the form of payments to suppliers for essential furniture and household items, including cookers, washing machines, beds, baby items, bedding and travel costs to or from hospital. Grants are in the range of £100 to £150.

Annual grant total: In 2001/02 a total of £22,000 was given in 235 individual grants.

Applications: On a form available from the correspondent. Applications can only be accepted from a recognised referral agency (e.g. social worker, citizen's advice bureau or doctor) and are considered throughout the year.

Correspondent: Ms Janice Evans, Clerk, Hastings Area Community Trust, 49 Cambridge Gardens, Hastings, East Sussex TN34 1EN (Tel & Fax: 01424 718880).

The Mrs A Lacy Tate Trust

Eligibility: People in need who live in East Sussex.

Types of grants: One-off and recurrent grants according to need.

Annual grant total: In 1999 the trust had an income of £49,000 and grants totalled £48,000, including £20,000 in grants to 79 individuals.

Applications: In writing to the correspondent.

Correspondent: I Stewart, Trustee, Heringtons Solicitors, 39 Gildredge Road, Eastbourne, East Sussex BN21 4RY (01323 411020).

Other information: Grants are also made to individuals for educational purposes and to organisations.

Battle

The Battle Charities

Eligibility: People in need who live in Battle.

Types of grants: Grants are usually made towards fuel costs and clothing costs in respect of children and range between £15 and £100. One-off and recurrent grants are considered.

Annual grant total: In 2000 the charities had an income of £2,100 and a total expenditure of £1,700.

Applications: Applications will be considered which are sent directly by individuals or by a suitable third party. Full details are required.

Correspondent: T P Roberts, 1 Upper Lake, Battle, East Sussex TN33 0AS (01424 772401).

Brighton & Hove

The Brighton District Nursing Association Trust

Eligibility: People in need who are sick and live in the county borough of Brighton and Hove or are patients of doctors in the same county borough.

Types of grants: One-off grants up to £250 for items in respect of medical treatment and for convalescence; some limited allowances for nurses.

Annual grant total: The trust has about £50,000 available for distribution each year to organisations and individuals. In previous years about £3,000 has been given to individuals.

Applications: In writing to the correspondent, preferably supported by a doctor or health visitor.

Correspondent: Anthony Druce, Hon. Sec, Fitzhugh Gates, 3 Pavilion Parade, Brighton BN2 1RY (01273 686811).

The Mayor of Brighton and Hove's Welfare Charity

Eligibility: Individuals in need living in the old borough of Hove and Portslade for welfare purposes.

Types of grants: One-off and recurrent grants, to a maximum of £200. No retrospective grants are made. The committee will only consider one grant for each applicant and successful applicants should not reapply.

Annual grant total: In 2000/01 the charity had assets of £70,000 and an income of £3,500. A total of £2,100 was distributed in 20 relief-in-need grants.

Applications: In writing to the correspondent. Applications should be submitted directly by the individual or a relevant third party i.e. friend, carer or professional (social worker, health visitor). Grants are considered bi-monthly, in January, March, May, July, September and November.

The charity needs to know the following: full name and address; the circumstances leading to the request and why the grant is needed; and the exact sum of money being requested, including estimates and/or price lists.

No money is given directly to the applicant, but rather directly to settle invoices.

Correspondent: Michael Hill, Selborne Centre, 5 Selborne Place, Hove BN3 3EJ (01273 779432; Fax: 01273 208668; e-mail: michaelhill@supanet.com).

Eastbourne

The Mayor's Discretionary Fund & The Mayor's Fund, Eastbourne

Eligibility: Adults and children in need who live in the borough of Eastbourne.

Types of grants: One-off grants for urgent needs, usually between £25 and £500. No grants for education or travel costs.

Annual grant total: In 2000/01 the fund had an income of £940 and a total expenditure of £880.

Applications: Considered on receipt, usually but not necessarily from social workers or health visitors on behalf of the individual. Applications must include all relevant information.

Correspondent: The Mayor's Secretary, The Town Hall, Grove Road, Eastbourne, East Sussex BN21 4UG (01323 415020).

Hastings

William Shadwell Charity

Eligibility: People in need who are sick and live in the borough of Hastings.

Types of grants: One-off and recurrent grants, ranging from £75 to £300. No grants are given for the payment of debt, taxes etc.

Annual grant total: In 2001 the charity had assets of £162,000 and an income of £6,400. Total expenditure was £5,700, including £4,000 in 36 relief-in-need grants to individuals.

Applications: In writing to the correspondent to be submitted in March and September for consideration in April and October, but urgent cases can be considered at any time. Applications can be submitted directly by the individual or through a third party.

Correspondent: C R Morris, 4 Barley Lane, Hastings, East Sussex TN35 5NX (Tel & Fax: 01424 433586).

Mayfield

The Mayfield Charity

Eligibility: People in need who live in the ancient parish of Mayfield.

Types of grants: One-off grants according to need. Grants have been given towards hospital travel and outings and Christmas gifts for older people.

Annual grant total: In 2001 the charity had assets of £120,000, an income of £5,500 and gave £3,500 in 23 grants for welfare purposes and £650 in grants to 3 individuals for educational purposes.

Applications: In writing to the correspondent directly by the individual. Applications are considered at any time.

Correspondent: John Logan, Little Broadhurst Farm, Broad Oak, Heathfield, East Sussex TN21 8UX.

Other information: Grants are also given to groups to set up a local hospital/community care service and for educational trips.

Newick

The Newick Distress Trust

Eligibility: People in need who live in the village of Newick.

Types of grants: One-off or recurrent grants according to need.

Annual grant total: About £1,000 a year, but depends on the number of requests.

Applications: In writing to the correspondent or one of the trustees.

Correspondent: G L Clinton, Dolphin Cottage, 3 High Hurst Close, Newick, East Sussex BN8 4NJ (01825 722512).

Rotherfield

Henry Smith (Rotherfield share)

Eligibility: People in need who live in the ancient parish of Rotherfield.

Types of grants: One-off and recurrent grants according to need.

Annual grant total: About £700 a year.

Applications: In writing to the correspondent.

Correspondent: M S Tollit, Ghyll Mead South, Ghyll Road, Crowborough, East Sussex TN6 1SU (01892 664922).

St Leonards-on-Sea

The Sarah Brisco Charity

Eligibility: People in need who live in the parish of St Peter and St Paul, St Leonards-on-Sea.

Types of grants: One-off cash grants between £25 and £100 and gifts in kind (e.g. £100 at Christmas, £25 vouchers etc.).

Annual grant total: In 2000 the charity had an income of £7,200 and a total expenditure of £9,500.

Applications: In writing to the correspondent. Applications should be submitted directly by the individual and are considered at any time.

Correspondent: D A Ray, 6 Clarence Road, St Leonards-on-Sea, East Sussex TN37 6SD (01424 439556)

Warbleton

The Henry Smith Charity

Eligibility: People in need who live in the parish of Warbleton.

Types of grants: Christmas grants for fuel, plus a food parcel.

Annual grant total: About £1,000 a year; some grants are given for educational purposes.

Applications: In writing to the correspondent, to be submitted either through a social worker, citizen's advice bureau or other welfare agency, or directly by the individual or a relevant third party. Applications are considered every two months.

Correspondent: A R Baldock, Mountain Side, Unde Road, Magham Down, Hailsham BN27 1QD (01323 831514; Fax: 01323 832642; e-mail: c.baldock@virgin.net).

Essex

The Sarah Chamberlayne Charity

See entry on page 259

The Colchester Catalyst Charity

Eligibility: People who are disabled or sick and live in north east Essex, and who cannot get what they need from statutory organisations.

Types of grants: One-off and recurrent grants for special equipment not available from statutory organisations, provided such needs are properly assessed by an appropriate professional practitioner (GP, occupational therapist, district nurse etc.).

Items can include wheelchairs and other mobility aids, special beds or chairs, pressure relieving mattresses and cushions, computers for specifc needs and communication aids. In cases of extreme need the charity may also contribute to specialist therapy.

Annual grant total: In 1999/2000 the trust had assets of £8.9 million, an income of £341,000 and a total expenditure of £555,000. Grants to individuals totalled £40,000.

Applications: In writing to the correspondent.

Correspondent: The Trustees, Lodge Lane, Langham, Colchester CO4 5NE (01203 231740).

Other information: The trust also: provides respite care for carers and the person being cared for; will consider supporting projects helping sick and disabled people; and makes loans of disability equipment.

Essex Police Support Staff Benevolent Fund

Eligibility: People in need who work or worked full-time or part-time for Essex Police Authority, and their dependants.

Types of grants: One-off grants or loans for essential needs such as travel expenses for hospital visits and unforeseen bills such as car repairs. No grants towards medical treatment.

Annual grant total: In 2001/02 the fund had an income of £7,700 and a total expenditure of £4,500. The amount given each year depends on the number of applications.

Applications: Individuals should apply via the benevolent fund representative of their division or subdivision of Essex Police Authority. Applications are considered quarterly, although this can be sooner in emergencies.

Correspondent: Ann Ackland, Hon. Secretary, Essex Police Headquarters, PO Box 2, Chelmsford, Essex CM2 6DA (01245 452990).

Help-in-Need Association (HINA)

See entry on page 360

The Kay Jenkins Trust

Eligibility: People in need, especially older or disabled people, who live in Great and Little Leighs.

Types of grants: One-off, mainly small, grants to help with household expenditure, medical aids and equipment. Occasionally we wll give up to £1,000 for a large item. No loans are made.

Annual grant total: In 2001/02 the trust gave a total of £3,000 in grants to 20 individuals.

Applications: In writing to the correspondent directly by the individual or through a relative. Grants are considered throughout the year.

Correspondent: Diana Tritton, Lyons Hall, Great Leighs, Chelmsford, Essex CM3 1PL (01245 361204; e-mail: dstritton@yahoo.com).

The Palmer Brother Trust for the Elderly

Eligibility: Pensioners living in the districts of Colchester and Tendring, who are ill or in need.

Types of grants: One-off and recurrent grants according to need. Grants have in the past been given as food parcels, and the trust also arranges Christmas lunches and summer outings for local pensioners.

Annual grant total: In 2000/01 the trust had an income of £1,800 and no grants were made in the year.

Applications: In writing to the correspondent.

Correspondent: Mrs Mary Worsfold, Secretary, 9 Cambridge Road, Colchester, Essex CO3 3NS (01206 573096).

Basildon

Basildon Sports Council Benevolent Fund

Eligibility: People in need who live in Basildon and have been injured while engaged in sporting activities, and their dependants.

Types of grants: One-off and recurrent grants according to need.

Annual grant total: In 1997/98 the trust had an income of £1,000 and its total expenditure was £1,100. Up-to-date information was not available.

Applications: In writing to the correspondent.

Correspondent: Jenny Burton, 1 Quendon Road, Basildon, Essex SS14 3PE.

Braintree

The Braintree United Charities

Eligibility: People in need who live in the parishes of St Michael's and St Paul's, Braintree; usually those in receipt of an old age pension.

Types of grants: One-off and recurrent grants ranging from £40 to £100. Annual grants are given at Christmas to people in need who are registered with the charity: £70 to couples and £40 to single people. Loans are not made.

Annual grant total: In 2000/01 the charities had assets of £82,000 and an income of £4,400. A total of £2,100 was distributed in relief-in-need grants to 44 individuals.

Applications: On a form available from the correspondent. Applications should be submitted through a social worker, citizen's advice bureau, other welfare agency or other third party, or directly by the individual, and are considered between May and October.

Correspondent: Miss S Carlile or Mrs C Harris, Gordon House, 22 Rayne Road, Braintree CM7 2QW (01376 321311; Fax: 01376 559239; e-mail: charris@hjsmith.co.uk).

Broomfield

Broomfield United Charities

Eligibility: People in need who live in the civil parish of Broomfield.

Types of grants: One-off grants according to need and vouchers at Christmas.

Annual grant total: In 2000/01 the trust had an incme of £7,000 and a total expenditure of £5,100.

Applications: In writing to the correspondent directly by the individual for consideration at any time.

Correspondent: Mrs P M MacDonald, 42 Berwick Avenue, Broomfield, Chelmsford, Essex CM1 4AS.

Chigwell and Chigwell Row

The George and Alfred Lewis (of Chigwell) Memorial Fund

Eligibility: 'Those men and women who served in HM Forces or the Merchant Service during the 1939/45 War, and who lived in the parishes of Chigwell and Chigwell Row at the time of their enlistment, who are suffering hardship as a result of such service or who are in necessitous circumstances.'

Types of grants: One-off payments or loans, to help with hospital or funeral bills or to people who have exceptional financial demands due to family illness, old age, domestic emergencies etc. The maximum grant is usually £500. Recent grants have been made towards house repairs, funeral expenses and new spectacles.

Annual grant total: In 2001 the fund had an income of £7,000 and made 35 relief-in-need grants to individuals totalling £7,300.

Applications: In writing to: Miss Enid Smart, 16 Forest Terrace, High Road, Chigwell, Essex IG7 5BW. Applications can be made either directly by the individual or through a third party on behalf of the individual i.e. spouse or child, and should include as much detail of personal circumstances as is deemed appropriate. Applications are considered at any time.

Correspondent: J R Redfern, Chair, 14 Mount Pleasant Road, Chigwell, Essex IG7 5ER (020 8500 2914).

Colchester

The Colchester Lying-In Charity

Eligibility: Women in Colchester who are at least six months pregnant or with a child under six months, and who are in receipt of means tested benefits with savings of less than £250 for a single person or £500 for a family.

Types of grants: One-off grants, up to a maximum £250, towards cots, prams or other items needed before, during or after childbirth. The grant must directly benefit the baby or mother, and not be a service provided by a statutory authority or which can be bought by other means.

Annual grant total: In 2000/01 the charity had an income of £1,000 and a total expenditure of £3,900.

Applications: On a form available from the correspondent. Applications are considered on an ongoing basis.

Correspondent: Lynne Woods, Social and Economic Regeneration, PO Box 5215, Town Hall, Colchester, CO1 1GG (01206 282573; Fax: 01206 500331; e-mail: lynne.woods@colchester.co.uk; website: www.colchester.gov).

The Colchester Society for the Blind

Eligibility: Blind people living in Colchester and district only.

Types of grants: One-off or recurrent grants according to need.

Annual grant total: In 2000/01 the society had an income of £10,000 and a total expenditure of £12,000.

Applications: In writing to the correspondent.

Correspondent: Barbara Gilhooly, 15 Finchingfield Way, Colchester CO2 0AY (01206 533711).

Dovercourt

The Henry Smith Charity

Eligibility: People in need who live in the parish of All Saints, Dovercourt.

Types of grants: The trust prefers to contribute towards the total cost of items and services rather than cash grants i.e. the purchase of a buggy for a disabled person, TV licence costs, food, and washing machine purchase and fitting. Donations are for up to £250.

Annual grant total: In 2000/01 the charity had assets of £2,800, an income of £800 and its total expenditure was £910.

Applications: In writing to the correspondent for consideration at any time. Applications can be submitted directly by the individual, through a social worker, citizen's advice bureau or other welfare agency or through a third party such as a priest who can recommend the applicant. After receiving a letter, the trustees usually visit the applicant. Applications are considered throughout the year.

Correspondent: A N Peake, 2 Kings Court, Kings Road, Dovercourt, Harwich, Essex CO12 4DT (01255 502209).

East Bergholt

The East Bergholt United Charities

Eligibility: People in need who live in East Bergholt.

Types of grants: One-off grants according to need. Recent grants have included one for a special computer for a child who is disabled. If no cases of hardship are brought to the attention of the trustees, they usually give £20 each at Christmas to about 10 to 20 older people who are known to have small incomes. These are not given to the same person two years running, though additional help can be given if needed.

Annual grant total: In 2000/01 the charities had an income of £8,000 and a total expenditure of £7,800. The sum of £325 was distributed in 13 relief-in-need grants to individuals.

Applications: In writing to the correspondent, although most cases are brought to the attention of the trustees. Applications can be submitted directly by the individual or by a relative at any time. Proof of the financial situation of the applicant is required.

Correspondent: Mrs G Abbs, 31 Fiddlers Lane, East Bergholt CO7 6SJ (01206 299822).

East Tilbury

East Tilbury Relief-in-Need Charity

Eligibility: People in need who live in the parish of East Tilbury.

Types of grants: One-off and recurrent grants have been given towards hospital visits and children in need.

Annual grant total: Between £5,000 and £6,000 a year.

Applications: In writing to the correspondent, to be considered in November.

Correspondent: R F Fowler, Treasurer, 27 Ward Avenue, Grays, Essex RM17 5RE (01375 372304).

Halstead

Helena Sant's Residuary Trust Fund

Eligibility: People in need who live in the parish of St Andrew with Holy Trinity, Halstead who have at any time been a member of the Church of England.

Types of grants: One-off or recurrent grants according to need. Grants can be given in money or gifts in kind, but are not given to pay rates, taxes or public funds.

Annual grant total: In 2001 the trust had an income of £6,400 and a total expenditure of £5,100.

Applications: In writing to the correspondent either directly by the individual or through a social worker, citizen's advice bureau or other welfare agency. Applications are considered at any time.

Correspondent: M R R Willis, Trustee, Greenway, Church Street, Gestingthorpe, Halstead, Essex CO9 3AX.

Harlow

The Harlow Community Chest

Eligibility: Individuals and families in desperate financial need, particularly where a small financial contribution will help to arrest the spiral of debt. Applicants must live in Harlow.

Types of grants: One-off main grants up to around £250 for the payment of outstanding bills such as fuel and telephone bills for people in special need, clothing (e.g. for unemployed young people going for a job interview), household items (e.g. repair of cooker) and help towards funeral expenses, removal costs, lodging deposits and nursery fees. Emergency payments of up to £30 can be applied for by phone and are made within 24 hours.

Only one main grant to an individual/family can be made in any one year. No grants for housing rents or rates.

Annual grant total: In 2000/01 the charity had an income of £19,000 and a total expenditure of £27,000. Grants totalling £26,000 were given to 350 individuals.

Applications: Applications, on a form available from the correspondent, should be submitted through a recognised referral agency (e.g.. social worker, citizen's advice bureau or doctor) or other third party, and are considered on the first Wednesday of each month. Emergency payments of up to £25 can be made between meetings.

Correspondent: Gaynor Watson, Secretary, 33 Guilfords, Harlow, Essex CM17 0HU (Tel & Fax: 01279 429995; e-mail: gaynor@glenford.fsworld.co.uk).

Hutton

Ecclesiastical Charity of George White

Eligibility: People in need who live in Hutton. Particular favour is given to children, young adults and older people.

Types of grants: Pensions and one-off grants towards necessary living expenses.

Annual grant total: In 2001 the charity had an income of £1,100 and a total expenditure of £1,000.

Applications: Initial telephone calls are welcomed.

Correspondent: Revd Chair, c/o St Peter's Parish Office, Hutton, Brentwood, Essex CM13 1JS (01277 362864).

Saffron Walden

The Saffron Walden United Charities

Eligibility: People in need who live in Saffron Walden.

Types of grants: All types of help can be considered, except help with council or income tax. Grants have been given towards rent arrears, disabled equipment and fees for nursery schools.

Annual grant total: In 2001 the trust had an income of £34,000 and a total expenditure of £54,000.

Applications: In writing to the correspondent. Applications are considered as they arrive.

Correspondent: Jim Ketteridge, Community Hospital, Radwinter Road, Saffron Walden, Essex CB11 3HY.

Springfield

The Springfield United Charities

Eligibility: Individuals in need living in the parish of Springfield.

Types of grants: One-off grants according to need.

Annual grant total: In 1997/98 the charities had an income of £9,600 and a total expenditure of £6,500. No recent information was available.

Applications: In writing to the correspondent.

Correspondent: Clive Willetts, Hon. Treasurer, Corporate Services, Civic Centre, Chelmsford, Essex CM1 2YJ.

Other information: This entry was not confirmed by the charities, but the address was correct according to the Charity Commission database.

Thaxted

Lord Maynard's Charity

Eligibility: People who live in the parish of Thaxted.

Types of grants: One-off and recurrent grants for general relief-in-need.

Annual grant total: In 1999/2000 the charity had an income and total expenditure of £2,600.

Applications: In writing to the correspondent. Applicants traditionally queue in the local church on 1 August for the money to be handed out, but postal applications prior to this are accepted.

Correspondent: Mr Chapman, Messrs Wade & Davies, Solicitors, 28 High Street, Great Dunmow, Essex CM6 1AH (01371 872816).

The Thaxted Relief-in-Need Charities

Eligibility: People in need who live in the parish of Thaxted.

Types of grants: One-off and recurrent grants according to need.

Annual grant total: In 2000 the charities had an income of £12,000 and a total expenditure of £6,900. This trust also runs three almshouses.

Applications: In writing to the correspondent.

Correspondent: M B Hughes, Secretary, Yardley Farm, Thaxted, Essex CM6 2RQ (01371 830642).

Other information: This entry was not confirmed by the charities, but the address was correct according to the Charity Commission database.

Hampshire

The Bordon Charity

Eligibility: Any individual or organisation in the area of Bordon and the surrounding regions.

Types of grants: One-off grants of between £25 and £5,000 can be awarded. The trustees consider a wide range of applications including heating and rent arrears.

Annual grant total: In 2001 the sum of £37,000 was given to individuals and organisations.

Applications: Applications can be made either directly by the individual or through a social worker, citizen's advice bureau, other welfare agency, health visitor or district nurse. Applications are considered monthly, and the trust reserves the right to commission a social worker's report.

Correspondent: C J A Tantum, Fulford, Headley Fields, Headley, Bordon, Hampshire GU35 8PS (01428 714958; Fax: 01428 712511; e-mail: ctantum@aol.com).

Other information: Funding is also available for local organisations.

Dibden Allotments Charity

Eligibility: People in need who live in the parish of Fawley Hythe and Marchwood, with a priority to families with children of school age.

Types of grants: One-off grants according to need, for the relief of hardship or distress. Grants range from £10 to £2,000 and are made towards items and services such as the provision of household goods to families, travel costs to hospital, assistance with gardening for older people, childcare costs for full-time students and support initiatives by health visitors and social workers e.g. parenting/job skills courses.

No grants for direct repayment of debts; funeral and memorial costs, holidays unless linked to health or sponsorship of sport or the arts.

Annual grant total: In 2000/01 the sum of £135,000 was given to individuals for relief-in-need purposes. A further £4,100 was given for educational purposes.

Applications: On a form available from the correspondent, with a reference from a professional. Applications are considered weekly.

Correspondent: Barrie Smallcalder, Clerk to the Trustees, 25 St John's Street, Hythe, Hampshire SO45 6BZ (Tel & Fax: 023 8084 1305).

The Farnborough (Hampshire) Welfare Trust

Eligibility: People in need who live in the Cove and Farnborough area.

Types of grants: One-off and recurrent grants mainly to older people at Christmas. Grants are generally between £20 and £50.

Annual grant total: In 2000 the trust's income was £2,900. 90 relief-in-need grants totalled £2,700.

Applications: In writing to the correspondent either directly by the individual or by a third party. Applications are considered in early December.

Correspondent: M R Evans, Bowmarsh, 45 Church Avenue, Farnborough, Hampshire GU14 7AP.

Hampshire Ambulance Service Benevolent Fund

Eligibility: Serving and retired members of Hampshire Ambulance Service and their dependants.

Types of grants: One-off grants according to need, although individuals can reapply each year.

Annual grant total: About £10,000 a year.

Applications: In writing to M Wratten, Treasurer, 3 Avlan Court, St Cross Road, Winchester SO23 9RD.

Correspondent: P Kail, Chair, 11 Test Mill, Holman Drive, Mill Lane, Romsey, Hants SO51 8EP (01794 502249).

Hampshire Association for the Care of the Blind (HACB)

Eligibility: People who are visually impaired, in need and live in Hampshire, excluding the cities of Portsmouth and Southampton.

Types of grants: One-off grants of up to £500 each to aid independent living for eligible people, e.g. towards special equipment, aids to daily living, holiday costs and costs incurred when moving into independent living. No grants are given for educational purposes or to groups.

Annual grant total: A total of £8,000 was given in the year.

Applications: On a form available from the correspondent. Applications can be made directly by the individual or through a third party (as long as it is signed by the individual). The trust encourages a supporting statement from the individual. Applications are considered every two months.

Correspondent: Bob Newport, Hampshire Association for the Care of the Blind, 25 Church Road, Bishopstoke, Eastleigh, Hampshire SO50 6BL (023 8064 1244; Fax: 023 8061 6535; e-mail: info@hacb.org.uk; website: www.hacb.org.uk).

The Hampshire Constabulary Welfare Fund

Eligibility: Members, pensioners, and civilian employees of the Hampshire Constabulary and their dependants.

Types of grants: One-off or recurrent grants or loans according to need. Grants have been given towards such things as stairlifts and bathlifts for older people and chairlifts and wheelchairs for disabled people.

Annual grant total: In 2000/01 the fund had an income of £262,000 and a total expenditure of £214,000.

Applications: Through local police welfare officers. Applications are considered immediately if less than £500, and a little longer if over £500.

Correspondent: Mike King, Treasurer, Police Federation Office, Police Headquarters, Romsey Road, Winchester, Hants SO22 5DB (01962 841500; Fax: 01962 842005).

Hampshire Football Association Benevolent Fund

Eligibility: People in need who have been injured while playing football, and others who have 'done service' to the game of football. Applicants must be playing for a team afilated with Hampshire Football Association.

Types of grants: One-off and recurrent grants according to need.

Annual grant total: In 1998/99 the trust had an income of £8,200 and its total expenditure was £7,200.

Applications: In writing to the correspondent.

Correspondent: The Secretary, William Pickford House, 8 Ashwood Gardens, Winchester Road, Southampton SO16 7PW.

Hampshire Golfers Benevolent Fund

Please see entry on page 42

The Kingsclere Welfare Charities

Eligibility: People in need who live in the parishes of Ashford Hill, Headley and Kingsclere.

Types of grants: The provision or payment for items, services or facilities such as medical equipment, expenses for travel to hospitals and grants to relieve hardship. Grants are mostly one-off, but recurrent grants can be considered. They range from £120 to £2,500.

Annual grant total: About £7,000 a year.

Applications: In writing to the correspondent. Applications are considered in February, April, June, September and November.

Correspondent: C R Forth, 'Rostaq', Winston Ave, Tadley, Hampshire RG26 3NN (0118 981 1602).

The Lord Rank 1958 Charity

Eligibility: Older people from in and around the Sutton Scotney area of Hampshire.

Types of grants: Small monthly payments are given.

Annual grant total: In 2001 the trust had an income of £74,000 and made grants totalling £75,000, most of which was probably to individuals. Assets amounted to £2.3 million.

Applications: The trust states that 'it consistently spends in excess of its income and has identified other beneficiaries which it would support if funds were available. Unsolicited applications are not invited and any applications that are received are met with a 'standard decline letter'.

Correspondent: John Wheeler, Trustee, 11a Station Road West, Oxted, Surrey RH8 9EE (01883 717919; Fax: 01883 717411; e-mail: jrbt@btopenworld.com).

The New Forest Keepers Widows Fund

Eligibility: Retired keepers or widows and children of deceased keepers who are in need and live in the New Forest.

Types of grants: Regular payments according to need.

Annual grant total: In 2000/01 the trust had assets of £319,000, an income of £8,400 and a total expenditure of £1,700. A sum of £1,400 was distributed in three grants.

Applications: In writing to the correspondent. Applications can be submitted at any time.

Correspondent: Mrs E Tilling, Secretary, 17 Provost Street, Fordingbridge, Hampshire SP6 1AY (01425 655562).

The Penton Trust

Eligibility: People in need who are 65 or over and live in Hampshire on a limited income. Applicants should either live in their own homes or be in sheltered accommodation.

Types of grants: Regular allowances to enable people to live in comfortable rented accommodation or, for those living in their own home, to be able to afford domestic help. Grants range from £25 to £550, although most grants are of £434.

Annual grant total: In 2000/01 the trust had an income of £11,000 and a total expenditure of £12,000.

Applications: In writing to the correspondent, for consideration throughout the year.

Correspondent: R Innes-Ker, Chair, Wills Chandler, 76 Bounty Road, Basingstoke, Hampshire RG21 3BZ (01256 322911).

The Portsmouth Victoria Nursing Association

Eligibility: People in need who are sick and live in the Portsmouth and South East Hampshire area.

Types of grants: One-off grants according to need, often for medical requisites that are not available from the NHS.

Annual grant total: In 2001 the association had an income of £32,000. The income is utilised in paying for nurses' welfare and administration expenses as well as grants to individuals.

South East – Hampshire

Applications: All aplications must be made through the community nursing staff and help is confined to those on whom the nurses are in attendance. Referrals are made by the district nurses on a form which is considered by the committee at monthly meetings.

Correspondent: J A Restall, Secretary, 7 Upper House Court, Winchester Road, Wickham, Hampshire PO17 5LH (01329 834357).

The Lord Mayor of Portsmouth's Charity

Eligibility: Individuals in need who live in the City of Portsmouth, Havant, Waterlooville, Fareham or Droxford, or who have a Portsmouth connection.

Types of grants: Grants range between £20 and £300. Educational fees or scholarships are not funded.

Annual grant total: About £15,000 a year, including grants to local organisations.

Applications: Application forms are available from the correspondent.

Correspondent: The Lord Mayor's Administrative Officer, Portsmouth City Council, Guildhall, Guildhall Square, Portsmouth, Hampshire PO1 2AJ (023 9283 4057).

The Scale Charitable Trust Fund

Eligibility: People who are blind and in need over 30 who were born and have lived in Hampshire for at least five years.

Types of grants: Grants to aid independent living for eligible people, for example, towards equipment, course fees or transport costs.

Annual grant total: In 2000/01 the trust had both an income of £3,300 and a total expenditure of £3,300.

Applications: Portsmouth City Council still administer the trust, however, people living in Hampshire, excluding those living in Portsmouth, should apply in writing directly to: B Richards, Hampshire Association for the Blind, 25 Church Road, Bishopstoke, Eastleigh, Hants SO5 0BL (01703 641244).

People living in Portsmouth should apply in writing directly to: Ian Howard-Harwood, Portsmouth Association for the Blind, 48 Stubbington Avenue, North End, Portsmouth PO2 0HY (01705 661717).

Correspondent: Director of Corporate Services, Portsmouth City Council, Committee Services, Floor 3, Civic Offices, Guildhall Square, Portsmouth PO1 2AL (023 9283 4057).

The Southampton Charitable Trust

Eligibility: People who are sick and poor and who live in Southampton and the immediate surrounding area.

Types of grants: One-off grants only ranging from £50 to £250. Recent grants have been given for bedding, food, fuel and specialist equipment to alleviate an existing condition or assist with day-to-day living. No grants towards general living expenses or relief from debt.

Annual grant total: In 2000/01 the trust had both an income and a total expenditure of £12,000.

Applications: In writing to the correspondent. Applications should preferably be submitted through a social worker, citizen's advice bureau or other welfare agency. The trustees meet in early April and October, but applications can be dealt with outside these meetings. Applicants must clearly demonstrate that they are both sick and poor (such as evidence of Income Support or other state benefits).

Correspondent: Clerk to the Trustees, Charter Court, Third Avenue, Southampton SO15 0AP (023 8070 2345; Fax: 023 8070 2570).

The Earl of Southampton Trust

Eligibility: People in need who live in the ancient parish of Titchfield (now subdivided into the parishes of Titchfield, Sarisbury, Locks Heath, Warsash, Stubbington and Lee-on-the-Solent). Groups catering for the needy are sometimes considered.

Types of grants: One-off grants in the range of £20 and £500.

In 2000/01 grants were broken down as follows:
household equipment £3,600 (14 grants)
home help and child minding £2,100 (12)
mortgage and rent arrears £2,500 (4)
medical equipment £1,400 (4)
preschool fees £1,400 (11)
holiday activities £890 (6)
courses, equipment and transport £790 (5)
building costs £960 (3)
legal fees £750 (3)
famiiy holidays £840 (2)
clothing £260 (2)
buggy purchase £310 (2)
medical visits £850 (1)
contribution to stair lift £1,000 (1)
furniture storage £350 (1)
various £230 (3).

Annual grant total: In 2000/01 grants totalling £18,000 were made to 77 individuals. The trust had an income of £57,000 and assets of £1.4 million with a total expenditure of £52,000.

The trust runs 16 almshouses and a day centre for old people.

Applications: In writing to the correspondent, either through a social worker, citizen's advice bureau, other welfare agency or third party (e.g. doctor, district nurse, clergy or councillor). Applications must include details of medical/financial status. Applications are considered on the last Tuesday of every month.

Correspondent: J J B Caldicott, Clerk to the Trustees, 24 The Square, Titchfield, Hampshire PO14 4AF (Tel & Fax: 01329 513294; e-mail: earlstrust@yahoo.co.uk).

Other information: Other information:

The Three Parishes Fund

Eligibility: People in need who live in the parishes of Headley, Whitehill, Grayshott and Lindford.

Types of grants: One-off grants.

Annual grant total: In 2000 the fund had an income of £9,900 and a total expenditure of £7,400.

Applications: In writing or by application form available from the correspondent. Applications are considered at any time and can be submitted directly by the individual, or by a social worker, doctor, clergy or similar third party.

Correspondent: G Wilson, Fremont, 23 Taylor's Lane, Lindford, Bordon, Hampshire GU35 0SW (01420 472899; e-mail: threeparishesfund@care4free.net).

Twyford and District Nursing Association

Eligibility: People living in the parishes of Twyford, Compton and Shawford, Colden Common and Owslebury and Morestead, who are sick, disabled, convalescent or infirm.

Types of grants: One-off grants including those for medical equipment, respite care, transport to and from nursing home, nursing care and the provision of specialist items for care in the home.

Retrospective grants will only be considered after consultation with two trustees.

Annual grant total: In 2001 the association had assets of £119,000, an income of £7,800 and a total expenditure of £6,000. The sum of £5,000 was distributed in relief-in-need grants.

Applications: On an application form available from the correspondent with information showing that other sources of funding have been sought. Applications are usually made through the medical practices in the area (mainly the Twyford Practice) and people can also apply through the social services, a doctor or community nurse, or if they do not have a direct medical contact, directly to the correspondent or a relevant third party.

Correspondent: Mrs A V Sowton, Bourne Cottage, Twyford, Winchester SO21 1NX (e-mail: veronicasowton@ukgateway.net).

The Winchester Children's Holiday Trust

Eligibility: Children under 18 who live in the area administered by Winchester City Council and surrounding districts who are experiencing some sort of social disadvantage.

Types of grants: Grants to help with the cost of holidays and adventure expedition. No grants are given directly to individuals.

Annual grant total: In 2000/01 the trust had an income of £6,000 and a total expenditure of £9,000.

Applications: In writing to the correspondent through a social worker, citizen's advice bureau or other welfare agency or through a third party professional. Applications are considered throughout the year.

Correspondent: David Pearcey, Waterside Cottage, Worthy Road, Headbourne Worthy, Winchester, Hampshire SO23 7JR (01962 880063).

The Winchester Rural District Welfare Trust

Eligibility: People in need who live in Winchester Rural District. This includes the parishes of Beauworth, Bighton, Bishops Sutton, Bramdean, Cheriton, Chilcomb, Compton, Crawley, Headbourne Worthy and Abbotts Barton, Hursley, Itchen Stoke and Ovington, Itchen Valley, Kilmeston, Kings Worthy, Littleton, Micheldever, New Alresford, Northington, Old Alresford, Olivers Battery, Owslebury, Sparsholt, Tichborne, Twyford, and Wonston. It does NOT include the city of Winchester.

Need as far as the trust is concerned may arise where assistance required is not available from public funds, or not available in time from public funds.

Types of grants: One-off grants towards, for example, bedding, clothing, special food, fuel and heating appliances, telephone, nursing requirements, house repairs, transport and convalescent care.

Immediate assistance may be obtained in any particular parish from the local trustee. The names and addresses of these trustees are widely circulated. If in doubt contact local clergy or the correspondent.

Annual grant total: In 2000/01 the trust had an income of £2,900 and a total expenditure of £3,000.

Applications: In writing to the correspondent who will pass the application on to the trustees to make a decision. They should be submitted through a social worker, citizen's advice bureau or other welfare agency and are considered at any time.

Correspondent: Anthony Stacey, 48 Compton Way, Winchester, Hampshire SO22 4HW (01962 866244).

Other information: This trust was formed by merging the endowments of 26 charities in 25 parishes in the Winchester Rural District. The trust has an information sheet outlining the area of benefit and support available.

Alverstoke

The Alverstoke Trust

Eligibility: People in need who live in Alverstoke or nearby.

Types of grants: One-off grants, usually of £200 to £600. The trust does not make loans, grants to other charities or recurring awards.

Annual grant total: In 2001 the trust had an income of £1,200 and a total expenditure of £1,400. Grants totalling £1,400 were made to five individuals. The trust had assets amounting to £12,000.

Applications: In writing to the correspondent, either directly or through a third party such as a citizen's advice bureau, social worker, welfare agency or other third party. Applications are considered at any time.

Correspondent: Edward T Genge, Hon. Clerk, 25 Beechcroft Road, Alverstoke, Gosport, Hampshire PO12 2EP (023 9264 7369).

Brockenhurst

The Groome Trust

Eligibility: People in need who live in the parish of Brockenhurst.

Types of grants: One-off grants for any need, particularly medical and financial problems.

Annual grant total: About £5,000.

Applications: In writing to the correspondent, although often the applicant is known to the trustees. Applications are considered as received.

Correspondent: Mrs P Dunkinson, 'Belmont', Burford Lane, Brokenhurst SO42 7TN (01590 622303).

Fareham

The Fareham Welfare Trust

Eligibility: People in need who live in the ecclesiastical parishes of St Peter & Paul, St John and Holy Trinity, all in Fareham.

Types of grants: One-off and recurrent grants to a maximum of £250 a year. Grants can be given towards clothing, furniture, food, cookers, washing machines and other essential electrical items.

Grants are not given where a statutory award is an entitlement/available.

Annual grant total: Between £8,000 and £9,000 a year.

Applications: Applications should be submitted through a recognised referral agency (e.g. social worker, health visitor, citizen's advice bureau or doctor) or trustee. They are considered throughout the year. Details of the individuals income and circumstances must be included.

Correspondent: Mrs Anne Butcher, Clerk, 44 Old Turnpike, Fareham, Hampshire PO16 7HA (01329 235186).

Gosport

Thorngate Relief-in-Need and General Charity

Eligibility: People in need who live in Gosport.

Types of grants: One-off grants mostly of between £100 and £250.

Annual grant total: In 2001/02 the trust made grants to 11 individuals totalling £2,000. Grants to local charities totalled £12,000.

Applications: On a form available from the correspondent. Applications can be made either directly by the individual or through a social worker, citizen's advice bureau, probation service or other welfare agency.

Correspondent: A E Donnelly, 16a Palmerston Way, Gosport, Hampshire PO12 2LZ (023 9258 0485).

Hawley

The Hawley Almshouse & Relief-in-Need Charity

Eligibility: People in need who have lived in the parish of Hawley for at least one year. Beneficiaries are generally women aged 60 or over and men aged 65 or over.

Types of grants: Generally one-off grants for needs that cannot be met from any other source. Help is given towards very high heating bills during extremely cold weather and the installation of equipment such as chair-lifts.

Annual grant total: In 2000/01 the trust had an income of £62,000 and a total exenditure of £77,000.

Applications: Considered in February, May, August, and November, but grants of up to £100 can be made at any time in emergencies. Applications can be submitted directly by the individual or by an appropriate third party such as a social worker or close family member.

Correspondent: Mrs C Spence, Secretary, Trustees' Office, Ratcliffe House, Hawley Garden Cottages, Hawley Road, Blackwater, Camberley, Surrey GU17 9DD (01276 33515).

Hordle

The Hordle District Nursing Association

Eligibility: People in need who live in the parish of Hordle (New Forest).

Types of grants: Grants are given to help with the costs incurred by illness. They are usually one-off.

Annual grant total: In 2000/01 the trust had an income of £980, a total of £500 was given in one grant

Applications: Applications can be made in writing, either directly by the individual or by anyone with a knowledge of the applicant's need. They are considered at any time throughout the year.

Correspondent: Mrs A Hill, 7 Firmount Close, Everton, Lymington, Hampshire SO41 0JN (01590 642272).

Isle of Wight

The Broadlands Home Trust

Eligibility: Widows of pensionable age who are in need living on the Isle of Wight.

Types of grants: Pensions of £6 a week paid every two months.

Annual grant total: In 2000/01 the trust had assets of £239,000, an income of £9,100 and a total expenditure of £10,000. Grants totalling £6,600 were made to individuals in need. Eductional grants to 27 individuals totaled £3,100.

Applications: In writing to the correspondent, either directly by the individual or through a social worker, citizen's advice bureau or other welfare agency. Applications are considered at any time.

Correspondent: Mrs L Hayden, 3 Winchester Close, Newport, Isle of Wight PO30 1DR (01983 521368).

The Mary Pittis Charity for Widows

Eligibility: Widows who are aged 60 and over, who live on the Isle of Wight and express Christian beliefs.

Types of grants: One-off grants ranging from £50 to £200, towards heating bills, contribution to new cookers and rental for the WightCare emergency telephone system.

Annual grant total: In 2000/01 the charity had both an income and a total expenditure of £9,000.

Applications: On a form available from the correspondent. Applications can be made directly, through a welfare agency or a minister of religion. They are considered at any time.

Correspondent: Messrs Roach Pittis, Trustees' Solicitors, 62–66 Lugley Street, Newport, Isle of Wight PO30 5EU (01983 524431; Fax: 01983 525970).

Lyndhurst

The Lyndhurst Welfare Charity

Eligibility: People in need, who live in the parish of Lyndhurst.

Types of grants: Grants are normally one-off and are made towards items, services or facilities, e.g. household items, respite care and counselling. Grants usually range between £50 and £500.

Annual grant total: In 2001/02 the trust's assets totalled £98,000, it had an income of £3,400 and made one grant totalling £500. Total expenditure was £2,000.

Applications: Applicants should telephone or write to the correspondent, either directly themselves, or through a social worker, citizen's advice bureau or other welfare agency. Applications are usually considered in April and October, but emergency applications can be considered in between those times.

Correspondent: A G Herbert, Clerk, 59 The Meadows, Lyndhurst, Hampshire SO43 7EJ (023 8028 3895).

Other information: Grants are also made to organisations.

Portsmouth

The Isaac & Annie Fogelman Relief Trust

Eligibility: People of the Jewish faith aged 40 and over who live in Portsmouth.

Types of grants: One-off and recurrent grants according to need.

Annual grant total: Between £3,000 and £3,500 a year.

Applications: In writing to The Secretary, Portsmouth & Southsea Hebrew Congregation, The Thicket, Elm Grove, Southsea PO5 2AA. Applications are considered quarterly.

Correspondent: S J Forman, 48 Portland Place, London W1B 1AJ (020 7323 6600).

Thomas King Trust (also includes The John Wallace Peck Trust)

Eligibility: People in need who live in Portsmouth and have lived there for 10 years.

Types of grants: Mainly one-off and recurrent grants according to need.

Annual grant total: About £3,000 a year.

Applications: Application forms are available from the correspondent and are considered in October and November for decisions in December. They can be submitted either directly by the individual, or through a social worker, citizen's advice bureau or other third party.

Correspondent: Mrs Joanne Wildsmith, Committee Services, Floor 3, Civic Offices, Portsmouth City Council, Guildhall Square, Portsmouth PO1 2AL (023 9283 4057; Fax: 023 9283 4076).

Other information: The John Wallace Peck Trust and three other local charities were amalgamated with this trust in 1999.

The Montagu Neville Durnford & Saint Leo Cawthan Memorial Trust

Eligibility: People over 60 who are in need and who live in the city of Portsmouth. Preference to ex-naval personnel and their dependants/ widows.

Types of grants: Annual grants of £50 given by the Royal Naval Benevolent Trust (RNBT) and to those recommended by Age Concern.

Annual grant total: In 2000/01 the trust had an income of £13,000 and a total expenditure of £11,000.

Applications: In writing to RNBT. Grants are made to the RNBT and Age Concern in October, for redistribution.

Correspondent: Director of Corporate Services, Committee Services, Floor 3, Civic Offices, Portsmouth City Council, Guildhall Square, Portsmouth PO1 2AL (023 9283 4057).

The E C Roberts Charitable Trust

Eligibility: Poor children and orphans of the city of Portsmouth only, with preference for people who are blind or who have other disabilities.

Types of grants: One-off or recurrent grants to help feed, care for, and clothe local children in need.

Annual grant total: About £10,000 a year.

Applications: The trust states that: 'Most of the income is currently committed to grants supporting the Portsmouth Children's Society /Community Team through the children's society.'

Correspondent: Miss H A G Tyler, Trustees' Solicitor, Messrs Brutton & Co., West End, 288 West End House, Fareham, PO16 0AJ (01329 236171).

Ryde

The Ryde Sick Poor Fund (also known as Greater Ryde Benevolent Trust)

Eligibility: Sick people in need who live in the former borough of Ryde.

Types of grants: One-off grants only. The trust is unable to give recurrent grants.

Annual grant total: In 2000 the trust had an income of £3,600 and its expenditure was £3,700.

Applications: In writing to the correspondent.

Correspondent: A Searle, Clerk, 1 The Girdlers, 39 St Thomas' Street, Ryde, Isle of Wight PO33 2DL (01983 615636; Fax: 01983 565809; e-mail: twssearle@aol.com).

Southampton

The Southampton (City Centre) Relief-in-Need Charity

Eligibility: People in need who live in the ecclesiastical parish of Southampton (in practice, the city centre).

Types of grants: One-off grants for a wide range of needs such as travel to hospital, convalescence, heating, medical equipment, holidays, special food or equipment, book recordings and chiropody. No grants towards rent, debts or council tax.

Annual grant total: About £10,000 a year.

Applications: In writing to the correspondent submitted through a social worker, citizen's advice bureau, health visitor or other welfare agency. Applications made directly by the individual will not be considered.

Correspondent: Dorothy Alderson, 8 Westgate Street, Southampton SO14 2AY (023 8063 1804).

Sway

The Sway Welfare Aid Group

Eligibility: People who are sick, disabled, older or in need who live in the civil parish of Sway and its immediate neighbourhood.

Types of grants: One-off and recurrent grants according to need.

Annual grant total: Between £6,000 and £7,000 a year.

Applications: In writing to the correspondent or by personal introduction. Meetings are held quarterly.

Correspondent: K M Hamilton, Southlings, St James Road, Sway, Lymington, Hampshire SO41 6AJ.

Winchester

The Winchester Welfare Charities

Eligibility: People who are in need or distress, or who are sick, convalescing, disabled or infirm and live in Winchester and its immediate surroundings.

Types of grants: The trust gives winter fuel payments in December and emergency grants throughout the year. These one-off grants (typically £25 to £50) have been towards repairs to an electric wheelchair, special shoes for disabled people, repairs to a washing machine and so on. Help can also be given for furniture, bedding, clothing, food, fuel and nursing requirements.

Annual grant total: Between £1,200 to £1,300 each year.

Applications: Recipients of Christmas vouchers are nominated by the trustees and local agencies. Applications for emergency payments should be made through a social worker, citizen's advice bureau or similar third party.

Correspondent: D Shaw, Hon. Clerk, Winchester Council, City Offices, Colebrook Street, Winchester, Hampshire SO23 9LJ (01962 848221).

Other information: A leaflet is available from the correspondent.

Hertfordshire

The Bowley Charity for Deprived Children

Eligibility: Disadvantaged children up to 16 years (or 18 if in full-time education) who live in Watford and Three Rivers District.

Types of grants: Small one-off grants of between £50 and £500 (the upper limit is for larger families), for items such as cookers, beds, bedding, prams, cots and other essential household items. Grants are also given for essential items of clothing for children but not for school uniforms.

Annual grant total: In 2000/01 a total of £9,200 was given in 66 grants, benefiting 140 children.

Applications: On a form available from the correspondent. Applications should be made through a social worker, citizen's advice bureau or other welfare agency. Trustees meet quarterly to consider grants.

Correspondent: Ms Fiona Brown, Clerk, c/o HCC, 39 Oxhey Drive, South Oxhey, Hertfordshire WD19 7SD (01923 354510; Fax: 01923 354505; e-mail: fiona.brown@hertscc.gov.uk).

Boxmoor and Berkhamsted (Post Office) Benevolent Society

Eligibility: Post Office servants who are in need; probably those who work in Boxmoor and Berkhamsted. The dependants of such people may possibly be supported, but this was not confirmed by the society.

Types of grants: One-off and recurrent grants according to need.

Annual grant total: In 2000 the trust's income was £4,200 and its total expenditure was £7,300.

Applications: In writing to the correspondent.

Correspondent: Fiona O'Donnell, C P O"Donnell & Co., Homeland, Hempstead Road, Bovingdon, Hemel Hempstead, Hertfordshire HP3 0HF (01442 269527).

The Hertfordshire Charity for Deprived Children

Eligibility: Disadvantaged children up to the age of 17 living in Hertfordshire (excluding the Watford area).

Types of grants: One-off grants generally for holidays (not overseas), clothing (e.g. school or cub uniforms or general clothing), and equipment (e.g. a baby buggy, cot, washing machine or cooker, where this would improve the quality of life for the child). Grants range between £30 and £300.

Annual grant total: In 2000/01 the trust had an income of £11,000 and a total expenditure of £7,700.

Applications: On a form available from the correspondent. Applications should be made through a health visitor, social worker, probation officer or similar third party. Trustees meet in June and November, but applications can be considered between meetings and can be approved on the agreement of two trustees.

Correspondent: Richard Errington, Clerk, 42 Wrensfield, Hemel Hampstead HP1 1RP (01442 264804).

Hertfordshire Community Foundation

Eligibility: People up to 18 years of age who live in Hertfordshire and are disabled, disadvantaged or who have been in care.

Types of grants: One-off grants in the range of £50 to £200 for cookers, washing machines, specialist software and beds and bedding. No grants are given for holidays or one-off events.

Annual grant total: In 2000/01 the foundation had assets of £20,000 and an income of £3,000. A total of £2,200 was distributed in 13 relief-in-need grants to individuals.

Applications: Applications can be made at any time through a social worker, citizen's advice bureau or other welfare agency or though a healthcare professional. Evidence of income and expenditure should be provided.

Correspondent: Christine Mills, Sylvia Adams House, 24 The Common, Hatfield, Hertfordshire AL10 0NB (01707 251351; Fax: 01707 251133; e-mail: hcf@care4free.net).

The Hertfordshire Convalescent Trust

Eligibility: People who are sick and their carers, who live in Hertfordshire.

Types of grants: One-off grants for 'the chronic sick, the carers and the cared for' of any age. Grants are for fees for short care only (not for equipment or transport costs); for convalescence at convalescent homes, short stay at nursing homes and holidays for carers and cared for and families, who are in need. Awards usually range between £300 and £450.

Annual grant total: In 2001 the trust had an income of £28,000 and made relief-in-need grants totalling £25,000.

Applications: Applications are considered throughout the year and can be made by the individual or through a social worker, doctor, citizen's advice bureau or other appropriate third party. An application form is available from the correspondent.

Correspondent: Mrs Janet Bird, Administrator, 140 North Road, Hertford SG14 2BZ (01992 505886; Fax: 01992 582595).

The Hertfordshire County Nursing Trust

Eligibility: Nurses working in the community, either practising or retired, who work or have worked in Hertfordshire.

Types of grants: One-off and recurrent grants according to need.

Annual grant total: In 2000/01 the trust had an income of £54,000 and a total expenditure of £31,000.

Applications: In writing to the correspondent.

Correspondent: Alasdair Shand, Timber Hall, Cold Christmas, Ware, Hertfordshire SG12 7SN (01920 466086).

Other information: This trust also makes grants for educational purposes and to organisations.

Buntingford

The Buntingford Relief in Need Charity

Eligibility: Older people on state registered pensions who live in Buntingford and have lived there for 10 years.

Types of grants: £20 per household given in early December towards fuel.

Annual grant total: In 2000 the charity had an income of £6,200 and a total expenditure of £6,400. In 1999 grants to 184 individuals totalled £3,700.

Applications: In writing to the correspondent.

Correspondent: Mrs J W Bailey, Clerk, Longmead, Buntingford, Hertfordshire SG9 9EF (01763 271208).

Dacorum

The Dacorum Community Trust

Eligibility: People in need who live in the borough of Dacorum.

Types of grants: Generally one-off grants up to £500 towards welfare purposes and educational trips.

Grants are not normally given for the costs of further education and only in exceptional circumstances for gap-year travel.

Annual grant total: In 2000/01 the trust had both an income and a total expenditure of £19,000. Grants totalling £8,400 were made to individuals.

Applications: On a form available from the correspondent. Applications can be submitted by the individual, through a recognised referral agency (e.g. social worker or citizen's advice bureau) or through an MP, doctor or school. Applications are considered in March, June, September and December. The trust asks for details of family finances. A preliminary phonecall is always welcome.

Correspondent: Mrs Margaret Kingston, 48 High Street, Hemel Hemstead, Hertfordshire HP1 3AF (01442 231396; website: www.dctrust.org.uk).

Other information: The trust also gives grants to organisations within the borough.

Harpenden

The Harpenden Trust

Eligibility: People in need who live in the 'AL5' postal district of Harpenden, with a preference for younger and older people.

Types of grants: One-off grants for up to £500 are made, for example, for large and unexpected bills, medicine expenses involving children, and staircases and similar equipment. Water rate grants can be made to people of pensionable age.

Annual grant total: In 2001 the trust's assets totalled £784,000, its income was £62,000 and the total expenditure was £56,000. Grants to 352 individuals in need totalled £20,000. The total amount given in grants for other purposes totalled £28,000.

Applications: In writing to the correspondent, either directly by the individual, or through a third party such as a social worker or citizen's advice bureau. The trust aims to give a speedy reponse to 'calls for help'.

Correspondent: The Chairman, 90 Southdown Road, Harpenden, Hertfordshire AL5 1PS (01582 460457).

Other information: Grants are also made to organisations which benefit local people.

Hatfield

Wellfield Trust

Eligibility: People in need who are on a low income and live in the parish of Hatfield.

Types of grants: One-off grants, towards household goods, bill arrears, equipment for people who are disabled, carpets, and so on.

Annual grant total: In 2000/01 the trust's income was £58,000 and its total expenditure was £86,000. The trust's grants budget was £25,000 to individuals for welfare and educational purposes, with a further £25,000 available for organisations.

Applications: On a form available from the correspondent only via a third party such as social services or citizen's advice bureaux. Most of the local appropriate third parties also have the application form. The trustees meet to consider applications every month.

Correspondent: Mrs Karen Richards, Birchwood Leisure Centre, Longmead, Hatfield, Hertfordshire AL10 0AS (01707 251018; e-mail: wellfieldtrust@aol.com).

Letchworth Garden City

The Letchworth Civic Trust

Eligibility: People who are in need, sick or require accommodation and live in Letchworth Garden City, and have lived there for two years or more.

Types of grants: Grants are one-off and range from £50 to £250. Grants have previously been towards, for example, to an ex-prisoner on recommendation from a probation officer, and towards a city-wide appeal for an individual who was undergoing dialysis and could not travel to hospital: the appeal was raising money for an extension to her house so the medical care could take place in her home.

Annual grant total: In 2000/01 the trust's assets totalled £159,000, its income was £40,000 and 92 grants totalling £26,000 were made to students and other individuals in need.

Applications: By letter or on an application form available from the correspondent. Applications can be made at any time, either directly by the individual or through a third party such as a probation officer or social worker.

Correspondent: Peter Jackson, Secretary, Broadway Chambers, Letchworth Garden City, Hertfordshire SG6 3AD (01462 484413; Fax: 01462 641258; e-mail: peterjackson32@btinternet.com).

Other information: Grants are also made to schoolchildren and students, and to groups and societies, but not religious or political groups.

Watford

The Watford Health Trust

Eligibility: People in need who have medical needs or physical disabilities and live in the borough of Watford and neighbourhood.

Types of grants: One-off and recurrent grants according to need.

Annual grant total: In 2000 the trust had an income of £27,000 and assets of £667,000. Grants totalling £16,000 were made to individuals with a further £1,700 to organisations.

Applications: In writing to the correspondent. The trust predominantly makes grants via social services/SSAFA etc.

Correspondent: Peter Spivey, Clerk, Flat 3, Nutfield House, 56 Stratford Road, Watford WD17 4NZ (01923 220188).

Wormley

The Wormley Parochial Charity

Eligibility: People in need who live in the parish of Wormley as it was defined before 31 March 1935, particularly those who are elderly, sick or newly bereaved.

Types of grants: One-off and recurrent grants up to a maximum of £75 can be given in response to a specific need. In the past they have included Christmas parcels, grants towards fuel bills, or for the cost of travel to visit a relative in hospital.

Annual grant total: In 2000 the trust had an income of £3,900 and a total expenditure of £2,000. Grants are awarded dependent on need, and can be given for educational or welfare purposes.

Applications: In writing to the correspondent, either directly by the individual, through a social worker, citizen's advice bureau, welfare agency, or a third party such as a friend who is aware of the situation. Applications are considered in November.

Correspondent: Mrs S White, 13 Westlea Road, Wormley, Hertfordshire EN10 6JH.

Kent

The Appleton Trust (Canterbury)

Eligibility: People in need connected with the Church of England in the diocese of Canterbury.

Types of grants: One-off grants ranging between £50 and £2,000. Recent grants include those made to youth workers and clergy wives. Grants are not given for further education.

Annual grant total: In 2001 the trust had assets of £692,000, an income of £33,000 and it spent £36,000. Grants totalling £13,000 were given to 13 individuals.

Applications: In writing to the correspondent. Applications should be submitted directly by the individual or a church organisation, to be considered in March, June, September and November.

Correspondent: Miss R A Collins, Clerk, Diocesan House, Lady Wootton's Green, Canterbury, Kent CT1 1NQ (01227 459401; Fax: 01227 450964; e-mail: rcollins@diocant.org).

Other information: Organisations connected to the Church of England in Canterbury Diocese are also supported.

The Christmas Gift Fund for the Old City of Canterbury

Eligibility: Older people in need who live in the former county borough of Canterbury (as it was in March 1974) and the surrounding villages.

Types of grants: Christmas parcels.

Annual grant total: In 2000/01 the fund had an income and total expenditure of £16,000.

Applications: In writing to the correspondent.

Correspondent: Clerk to the Trustees, Robert Brett House, Milton Manor Farm, Ashford Road, Canterbury CT4 7PP (01227 829000; Fax: 01227 829025).

R V Coleman Trust

Eligibility: People who live in Dover and the immediate neighbourhood and who are sick, convalescing, mentally or physically disabled or infirm.

Types of grants: Grants given according to need, for amounts up to £740. Grants have been given for periods in nursing homes, for specific needs such as wheelchairs, telephone facilities and convalescent holiday breaks. Grants are not given for repairs to properties.

Annual grant total: In 2000/01 the trust had assets of £868,000, an income of £66,000 and total expenditure of £87,000. A total of 94 relief-in-need grants were made totalling £47,000. Grants to local hospices totalled £20,000.

Applications: Applications should be made through a social worker, citizen's advice bureau, welfare agency, doctor or consultant. Applications are considered continuously and should be sent to: Mrs Barbara Godfrey, Welfare Officer, 41 The Ridgeway, River, Dover, Kent CT16 1RT.

Correspondent: P W Sherred, The Clerk, 'Copthorne', Dover Road, Guston, Dover CT15 5EN (01304 824781; e-mail: copthorne@talk21.com).

Other information: Grants are also made to local hospices.

Cornwallis Memorial Fund

Eligibility: People in need who live in Kent. Only those who were born in, or have lived in Kent for some time will be considered.

Types of grants: One-off grants of £50 to £300 for items, services or facilities.

Annual grant total: In 2000/01 the trust had an income of £12,000 and made grants to 34 individuals totalling £7,500.

Applications: On a form available from the correspondent, on receipt of an sae. Applications can be made either directly by the individual, or through a social worker, citizen's advice bureau or other third party. They should provide as much detail as possible, including extra information sheets with the application as relevant. Applications are considered on receipt.

Correspondent: G H Pierce, Secretary, 204a Edwin Road, Rainham Mark, Gillingham, Kent ME8 0JL (Tel & Fax: 01634 362722).

Other information: Grants are also made to self-help groups.

Headley-Pitt Charitable Trust

Eligibility: Individuals in need who live in Kent with a preference for Ashford. There is also a preference for older people.

Types of grants: One-off grants of about £500 each.

Annual grant total: In 2000/01 the trust's income was £57,000. Grants totalled £38,000 and included about £1,500 in grants to three individuals.

Applications: In writing to the correspondent at any time.

Correspondent: Mrs S D Pitt, Secretary, Summerville, Ulley Road, Kennington, Ashford, Kent TN24 9HX (01233 623831).

Other information: Grants are also made for educational purposes and to organisations.

The Kent Children's Trust

Eligibility: Children and young people up to the age of 21, who are in need and live in Kent County Council area.

The trust is keen to support children and young people who have not had the opportunities that most children and young people enjoy, either because they have physical or learning disabilities, a sensory impairment, or difficult social circumstances.

Types of grants: Usually one-off grants up to £1,000. Grants must be of direct benefit to the child or young person. The trust is particularly keen to enable children and young people to pursue activities, hobbies and interests which cannot be financed through usual sources, i.e. local authorities, schools and community groups and where applicants show self-help through fundraising. Grants may be for equipment for personal development, or to allow the opportunity to learn new skills, or being involved in an expedition or outing.

Annual grant total: About £12,000 in 2002/03

Applications: On a form available from Jean Howland at the address below. Applications must be made on behalf of individuals by a charity, an organised group, society or professional. This includes schools, youth, and community groups and so on.

Correspondent: Mike Ballard, Kent County Council, Social Services Directorate, Sessions House, County Hall, Maidstone, Kent ME14 1XQ (01622 694270; Fax: 01622 694305).

Other information: This trust was set up by Kent Social Services using proceeds from a staff club lottery.

The Kent County Football Association Benevolent Fund

Eligibility: People living in the area of Kent as at 1908, who have an injury or illness which was caused by football, or who are officials and in need. Any surplus grants can be given to other people living in the area who are in need and are involved in football.

Types of grants: One-off or recurrent grants according to need.

Annual grant total: In 2000 the fund had an income of £7,400 and a total expenditure of £4,000.

Applications: On a form available from the correspondent.

Correspondent: K T Masters, Chief Executive, 69 Maidstone Road, Chatham, Kent ME4 6DT (01634 843824; Fax: 01634 815349).

Kent Nursing Institution

Eligibility: People in need who are sick, convalescent, disabled or infirm and live in Kent.

Types of grants: One-off grants. Previous grants have been given in cases of known hardship caused by family illness (to help cover the costs of hospital visits etc.) and to assist in buying specialist equipment to relieve discomfort (special beds, ultrasound matching etc.).

Annual grant total: In 2001 the trust had assets of £1,500 and an income of £3,200. It spent £2,700, of which £2,300 was given in nine grants.

Applications: In writing to the correspondent either through a social worker, citizen's advice bureau or other welfare agency or through other third party such as a doctor or clergy. Applications are considered all year round.

Correspondent: Mrs M Balfour, Walnut Tree Farm, Birling, West Malling, Kent ME19 5JL.

The Pearl Newman Memorial Fund in Aid of Cancer Relief

Eligibility: People in need who have cancer and their carers, local to Kent only.

Types of grants: Grants are given to 'improve quality of life for carer and patient'. Grants have been given towards, for example, a family holiday, telephone bills, council tax and new beds.

Annual grant total: About £50,000.

Applications: On a form available from the correspondent, to be signed by a member of the medical profession.

Correspondent: P J Newman, Chair of the Trustees, The Pearl Suite, Unit 1B, Eddington Business Park, Thanet Way, Herne Bay, Kent CT6 5UJ (01227 742624; Fax: 01227 365123).

The Dorothy Parrott Memorial Trust

Eligibility: People in need who live in the area administered by Sevenoaks Town Council and adjoining parishes. Young children and older people are given preference.

Types of grants: Usually one-off grants ranging from £25 to £100 according to need. Grants have been given towards educational purposes, a fridge, school outing for a child of a single parent, house decoration, boots, ballet shoes, mattress for twins and project trips such as Operation Raleigh.

Annual grant total: About £3,000 a year, depending on income received.

Applications: Either direct to the correspondent or through a social worker, citizen's advice bureau or similar third party, including a general history of the family. Applications are considered on the last Monday of January, April, July and October.

Correspondent: C F Coston, Secretary, 11 Kingwood Road, Dunton Green, Sevenoaks, Kent TN13 2XE (01732 462248).

Sir Thomas Smythe's Charity

Eligibility: People of pensionable age who are in need and live within the 25 parishes of Tonbridge and Tunbridge Wells. Grants are not made to people in residential care.

Types of grants: All pensions are £380 a year.

Annual grant total: About £11,000 a year.

Applications: Applications are only recommended via local trustees.

Correspondent: Charities Department, The Skinners' Company, Skinners' Hall, 8 Dowgate Hill, London EC4R 2SP (020 7236 5629).

Richard Watts and The City of Rochester Almshouse Charities

Eligibility: People in need who live in Rochester city and Strood town.

Types of grants: Pensions for retired people and one-off grants towards needs such as school uniforms, washing machines and helpline costs. Educational grants are also available.

Annual grant total: In 2001 the charity had assets of £13 million and an income of £739,000. Total expenditure was £602,000 with grants and pensions to individuals totalling £106,000.

Applications: In writing to the correspondent. Applications can be submitted at any time.

Correspondent: Mrs B A Emerry, Watts Almshouses, Maidstone Road, Rochester, Kent ME1 1SE (01634 842194; Fax: 01634 409348).

Other information: Grants are also given to local organisations which benefit the local community. The charity also runs an almshouse.

Borden

William Barrow's Eleemosynary Charity

Eligibility: People in need who live in the ancient ecclesiastical parish of Borden or have lived in the parish and now live nearby. There is a preference for people of 60 years or over and disabled people.

Types of grants: One-off grants and twice-yearly allowances to people who are pensioners, disabled or in need, hardship or distress. Grants may be given towards vouchers for those attending Age Concern for meals and transport; payments of bathing allowances; grants for children's clothing and outings; and help towards the purchase of specialist equipment for disabled people. Further grants may be made to organisations. Grants typically range from £200 to £400 a year.

Annual grant total: In 2000 the trust had a joint income with William Barrow's Educational Foundation of £43,000 and an expenditure of £36,000. No further information was available.

Applications: On a form available from the correspondent. Applications are considered in April/May and October but may also be considered in February and July in urgent cases.

Correspondent: S J Mair, Clerk, c/o George Webb & Co., 43 Park Road, Sittingbourne, Kent ME10 1DX (01795 470556; Fax: 01795 470769).

Canterbury

The Canterbury United Municipal Charities

Eligibility: People in need who have lived within the boundaries of what was the old city of Canterbury for at least two years.

Types of grants: One-off and recurrent grants and pensions. Annual pensions of £100 are given to about 20 needy older people. Also at Christmas, vouchers/tokens of £25 are given for: clothing for children aged 6 to 16 (30 children); and people who are elderly and in need (120 adults).

Annual grant total: In 2000 the trust had an income of £7,000 and a total expenditure of £4,800. No further information was available. In previous years about £1,500 has been distributed in relief-in-need grants to individuals.

Applications: In writing to the correspondent through a social worker, citizen's advice bureau or other welfare agency or directly by the individual. Applications are considered on an ongoing basis and should include a brief statement of circumstances and proof of residence in the area.

Correspondent: G B Cotton, Clerk, 2 Castle Street, Canterbury CT1 3NA (01227 456731; Fax: 01227 451018).

Other information: Grants are also given for educational purposes and to organisations with similar objects.

Streynsham's Charity

Eligibility: People who live in the ancient parish of St Dunstan's.

Types of grants: One-off grants, up to a maximum of about £300.

Annual grant total: In 2001 a total of £18,000 was given to individuals in relief-in-need and educational grants.

Applications: In writing to the correspondent. Applications should be made directly by the individual. They are usually considered in March and October but can be made at any time and should include an sae and telephone number if applicable.

Correspondent: Mrs J L McCulloch, Clerk, Langley, 13 South Canterbury Road, Canterbury, Kent CT1 3LH (01227 761624).

Chatham

Chatham District Masonic Trust

Eligibility: Freemasons and their widows and children, living in Chatham.

Types of grants: One-off and recurrent grants according to need.

Annual grant total: In 2000/01 the trust had an income of £35,000 and a total expenditure of £33,000.

Applications: In writing to the correspondent.

Correspondent: N Stephney, 5 Manor Road, Chatham, Kent ME4 6AG (01634 842419).

Other information: This entry was not confirmed by the trust but the address was correct according to the Charity Commission database.

Cliffe-at-Hoo

Cliffe-at-Hoo Parochial Charity

Eligibility: People in need who live in the ancient parish of Cliffe-at-Hoo.

Types of grants: One-off grants according to need.

Annual grant total: In 2001/02 the trust had assets of £30,000 and an income of £5,000. A total of £3,000 was distributed in 50 relief-in-need grants.

Applications: In writing to the correspondent, to be submitted directly by the individual. Applications are considered throughout the year.

Correspondent: P Kingman, Clerk, 52 Reed Street, Cliffe, Rochester, Kent ME3 7UL (01634 220422).

Dover

The Casselden Trust

Eligibility: People in need who live in the Dover Town Council area.

Types of grants: One-off and recurrent grants, up to a maximum of £250.

Annual grant total: About £1,500 to individuals for both educational and welfare purposes and a further £1,000 to organisations.

Applications: In writing to the correspondent.

Correspondent: Leslie Alton, 26 The Shrubbery, Walmer, Deal, Kent CT14 7PZ (01304 375499).

Folkestone

The Folkestone Municipal Charities

Eligibility: People in need, particularly older people and single parent families, who live in the area of the former borough of Folkestone.

Types of grants: One-off and recurrent grants of £30 to £400 for most types of need (e.g. telephone installation, help after a burglary, loss of a purse/wallet, shoes for disadvantaged children, gas/electricity bills, beds/bedding, prams, clothing and household repairs).

Annual grant total: In 2000/01 the trust had assets of £2.4 million and both an income and a total expenditure of £88,000. A total of £81,000 was given in relief-in-need grants to individuals.

Applications: On a form available from the correspondent. Applications should be through a social worker, citizen's advice bureau or other welfare agency, and are considered monthly.

Correspondent: Michael A Cox, Romney House, Cliff Road, Hythe CT21 5XA (01303 260144).

Fordwich

The Fordwich United Charities

Eligibility: People in need who live in Fordwich.

Types of grants: One-off grants have included those given for heating and Lifeline costs. Grants are for £125.

Annual grant total: In 2001 a total of six grants for welfare purposes totalled £750. Education grants to seven individuals totalled £700.

Applications: In writing to: M Beck, 1 The Willows, Spring Lane, Fordwich, Canterbury CT2 0DJ. Grants are disbursed in September each year.

Correspondent: C B Wacher, Furley Page Fielding & Barton Solicitors, 39 St Margaret's Street, Canterbury CT1 2TX (01227 763939).

Gillingham

Dobson Trust

Eligibility: Older people who receive a state pension or (in exceptional circumstances) those over 50 and retired from full-time employment, and who live in the former borough of Gillingham.

Types of grants: One-off grants towards: exceptional outgoings; unexpected bills, e.g. to repair or replace an essential domestic appliance or furniture; specialist equipment associated with disability or impairment; or the costs associated with the death of a partner (excluding funeral costs). Recent grants included £115 towards a nebuliser; £100 towards roof repairs and £45 towards a pair of special shoes.

Annual grant total: In 2000/01 the trust's assets totalled £154,000, it had an income of £2,600 and its total expenditure was £14,000. Grants were made to one individual totalling £220.

Applications: Application forms and guidelines are available on request from: Mrs Louise Curr, Medway Council, Democratic Services, Civic Centre, Strood, Rochester, Kent ME2 4AU. Applications are usually considered in June.

Correspondent: Mrs Margaret Taylor, Charities/Treasury Management Officer, Resources Directorate, Medway Council, Finance and Corporate Services, Civic Centre, Strood, Rochester, Kent ME2 4AU (01634 332144; Fax: 01634 732876; e-mail: margaret.taylor@medway.gov.uk).

Other information: Local organisations are also supported.

Godmersham

Godmersham Relief in Need Charity

Eligibility: People in need, due to hardship and distress who live in the ancient parish of Godmersham.

Types of grants: Usually one-off grants towards items, services or facilities.

Annual grant total: In 2001 the charity had an income of £8,800, of which £350 was given in two relief-in-need grants to individuals. Educational grants to 14 individuals totalled £3,400.

Applications: Applications should be by letter, or exceptionally by telephone if the need is urgent.

Correspondent: David T Swan, Feleberge, Canterbury Road, Bilting, Ashford, Kent TN25 4HE (01233 812125).

Gravesham

William Frank Pinn Charitable Trust

Eligibility: People of pensionable age who live in the borough of Gravesend.

Types of grants: One-off grants for specific purposes only, such as clothing, furniture, holidays and fuel.

Annual grant total: In 2000/01 the trust had an income of £255,000 and gave grants to individuals totalling £224,000.

Applications: On a form available from the correspondent. Applications should be submitted directly by the individual and are considered monthly.

Correspondent: Trust Controller, HSBC Trust Co. (UK) Ltd, Norwich House, Commercial Road, Southampton SO15 1GX (023 8072 2220; Fax: 023 8072 2250).

Herne Bay

The Herne Bay Parochial Charity

Eligibility: People in need who live in Herne Bay. Applicants preferably should be on income support or in receipt of similar financial assistance.

Types of grants: Both one-off and regular grants during the year and at Christmas. The usual grant to individuals consists of:
(i) monthly voucher for £5 which can be exchanged at certain shops or the local council office
(ii) cash grant of £20 at Christmas
(iii) cash grant of £10 in February towards fuel and
(iv) cash grant of £10 in November towards fuel.

The charities make a £10 Christmas grant to several other individuals. Examples of other grants are to purchase a particular necessary item such as providing a telephone or to clear a debt e.g. electricity bill.

Annual grant total: In 2001 the charity had assets of £54,000 and an income of £3,800. A total of £1,600 was distributed in 34 grants.

Applications: In writing, or by telephone in an emergency, to the correspondent through a social worker, citizen's advice bureau or other welfare agency or directly by the individual or some relevant third party. Applications are considered in April and October and ideally, should be received in the preceding month. The charities have to be satisfied that the applicant is financially in need, such as with supporting evidence of income support, housing benefit and so on.

Correspondent: J Craig King, Clerk, 158 High Street, Herne Bay, Kent CT6 5NP (01227 373874; Fax: 01227 365897).

Other information: Grants are also made to organisations helping people in need.

Hildenborough

Helen Georgie Hills Charity

Eligibility: People in need who are sick and in Hildenborough.

Types of grants: One-off grants according to need. Grants are not given to replace statutory responsibilities.

Annual grant total: In 2000 the charity had assets of £117,000, an income of £3,900 and its total expenditure was £3,200, all of which was given in grants to individuals in need.

Applications: In writing to the correspondent. Applications can be submitted directly by the individual, or through a social worker, citizen's advice bureau or other welfare agency or another third party. Grants are considered at any time.

Correspondent: M Armstrong, Durham's Farm, Egg Pie Lane, Hildenborough, Kent TN11 8PE (01732 833241; Fax: 01732 838121).

Hothfield

The Thanet Charities

Eligibility: People in need who live in the parish of Hothfield.

Types of grants: One-off grants according to need.

Annual grant total: About £3,000.

Applications: In writing to the correspondent.

Correspondent: Mrs Pat Guy, The Garden House, Bethesden Road, Hothfield, Ashford TN26 1EP.

Hythe

Anne Peirson Charitable Trust

Eligibility: People who live the parish of Hythe and are in need, due for example to hardship, disability or sickness.

Types of grants: One-off grants ranging from £50 to £300. Recent grants were made towards nursery school fees, special needs for people who are homeless, and furnishings etc.

Annual grant total: In 2000 the trust's assets totalled £250,000, it had an income of £7,200 and made grants for educational and welfare purposes to 32 individuals totalling £3,600.

Applications: In writing to the correspondent via a social worker, citizen's advice bureau, health visitor or school headteacher etc. Grants are considered on an ongoing basis.

Correspondent: Miss Ina Barker, Trustee/Secretary, 34 Sene Park, Hythe, Kent CT21 5XB (01303 260779; Fax: 01303 238660).

Other information: Grants are also made to local organisations.

Leigh

The Leigh United Charities

Eligibility: People in need who live in the ancient parish of Leigh.

Types of grants: Christmas gifts and grants for food and fuel of £25 to £100.

Annual grant total: In 2001/02 the trust had an income and total expenditure of £47,000. A total of 140 relief-in-need grants were made to individuals totalling £30,000.

Applications: In writing to the correspondent directly by the individual. Applications are considered throughout the year.

Correspondent: W S Crocker, Eastern Bungalow, High Street, Leigh, Tonbridge, Kent TN11 8RP (01732 832580).

Maidstone

The Edmett & Fisher Charity

Eligibility: People in need, preferably over 60, who live in the former borough of Maidstone (as it was before April 1974).

Types of grants: Christmas gifts and about 22 pensions of £5 a week paid quarterly.

Annual grant total: In 2000/01 the charity had an income of £7,500 and a total expenditure of £7,900. Over £5,000 is given in grants every year.

Applications: On a form available from the correspondent either directly by the individual, through a social worker, citizen's advice bureau, welfare agency or other third party on behalf of the individual. Applications must include full income details. They are considered in May and November.

Correspondent: R P Rogers, 72 King Street, Maidstone, Kent ME14 1BL (01322 698000).

The Hollands-Warren Charitable Trust

Eligibility: People in need of temporary medical and nursing services in their own homes and/or domestic help, who live in the old borough of Maidstone.

Types of grants: Grants towards the cost of such services and/or domestic help.

Annual grant total: In 2000/01 the trust had an income of £54,000 and a total expenditure of £66,000.

Applications: In writing to the correspondent. Applications should be submitted directly by the individual.

Correspondent: Mrs Kim Harrington, Somerfield House, 59 London Road, Maidstone, Kent ME16 8JH.

Other information: The trust states: 'The trustees do not have funds to monitor individual applications. Accordingly funds are allocated in bulk and individual applications are only considered via personal recommendation by a trustee.'

The Maidstone Relief-in-Need Charities

Eligibility: People in need, hardship or distress who live in the former borough of Maidstone.

Types of grants: One-off grants towards gas or telephone bills, household items and to meet a wide variety of other needs.

Annual grant total: In 2000/01 the charities had an income of £3,600 and a total expenditure of £2,100.

Applications: Applications must be made through a social worker, health visitor, doctor or similar third party on a form available from the clerk. Applications are considered three or four times a year, although grants under £200 can be made at shorter notice.

Correspondent: The Clerk, The Directorate of Client and Support Services, Maidstone Borough Council, London House, 5–11 London Road, Maidstone, Kent ME16 8HR (01622 602030; Fax: 01622 692246).

Margate

Margate and Dr Peete's Charity

Eligibility: People in need who live in the former borough of Margate as constituted before 31 March 1974.

Types of grants: One-off and quarterly grants of between £35 and £250 recent grants include those given at Christmas and for the purchase of a washing machine. No grants are given for loan repayments.

Annual grant total: In 2000/01 the charity had assets of £184,000 and an income of £7,900. Total expenditure was £7,800 with 47 grants totalling £6,900.

Applications: On a form available from the correspondent, to be submitted either directly by the individual or through a social worker, citizen's advice bureau or other welfare agency. Applications can be submitted at any time and are considered in January, April, July and October.

Correspondent: The Secretary, c/o 39 Hawley Square, Margate CT9 1NZ (01843 220567; Fax: 01843 228540).

Rochester

The William Mantle Trust

Eligibility: People in need who are over 60 and who were either born in that part of Rochester which lies to the south and east of the River Medway, or have at any time lived in that part of the city for a continuous period of not less than 15 years.

Types of grants: Pensions of £10 a week.

Annual grant total: In 2000/01 the trust had assets of £186,000 and an income of £7,300. It spent £6,200, of which £5,800 was given in 15 grants.

Applications: On a form available from the correspondent either directly by the individual or through a third party on their behalf. Applications are considered at any time; they should include details of their income and expenditure. If the annual grant maximum is reached, no more applicants will be considered unless a vacancy occurs.

Correspondent: Mrs B A Emery, Clerk, Administrative Offices, Watt's Almshouses, Maidstone Road, Rochester, Kent ME1 1SE (01634 842194; Fax: 01634 409348).

Sevenoaks

The Kate Drummond Trust

Eligibility: People in need who live in Sevenoaks, preference is given to young people.

Types of grants: The majority of grants are one-off.

Annual grant total: In 1999/2000 the trust had an income of £6,600 and a total expenditure of £4,100.

Applications: In writing to the correspondent, with an sae if a reply is required.

Correspondent: The Rector, St Nicholas Rectory, Rectory Lane, Sevenoaks, Kent TN13 1JA (01732 740340).

Sutton Valance

William Lambe (Pension) Trust

Eligibility: People who are in need, over retirement age and live in the parish of Sutton Valance, Kent or one of the adjacent parishes.

Types of grants: Grants are awarded as extra pensions twice yearly.

Annual grant total: In 2000/01 the trust made grants totalling £14,000.

Applications: Applicants can either write to or telephone the welfare services department for an application form. Applications can be submitted at any time either directly by the individual or through a social worker, citizen's advice bureau, other welfare agency or other third party.

Correspondent: Mrs B Hollidge, Friends of the Elderly, 40–42 Ebury Street, London SW1W 0LZ (020 7730 8263; Fax: 020 7259 0154; e-mail: bridget.hollidge@forte.org.uk).

Tunbridge Wells

Miss Ethel Mary Fletcher's Charitable Bequest

Eligibility: Older people in need who live in the Tunbridge Wells area.

Types of grants: One-off and recurrent grants according to need.

Annual grant total: In 2000/01 the trust had an income of £15,000 and a total expenditure of £14,000. No further information was available.

Applications: In writing to the correspondent, through a social worker, citizen's advice bureau or other welfare agency. The charity stated 'funds are fully committed, although consideration will be given to extreme applications'.

Correspondent: Mrs J Mills, Thomson, Snell & Passmore, 3 Lonsdale Gardens, Tunbridge Wells, Kent TN1 1NX (01892 510000).

Other information: Occasional grants are made to organisations with similar objects.

Wilmington

The Wilmington Parochial Charity

Eligibility: People in need, living in the parish of Wilmington, who are receiving income support or help towards their council tax.

Types of grants: Recurrent grants are available as follows: grocery vouchers of £30, cash grants of £10 at Christmas and heating grants of £60 at Easter.

Annual grant total: In 2000/01 just over £10,000 was given in relief-in-need grants. However, the grant total varies according to income.

Applications: Applications should be submitted by the individual, or through a social worker, citizen's advice bureau or other welfare agency.

Correspondent: S J Stringer, 13 Meadow Walk, Wilmington, Dartford, Kent DA2 7BP (01322 226335).

Other information: Grants are also given to students and local schools.

Norfolk

The Blakeney Twelve

Eligibility: Individuals who are elderly, infirm or disabled and who live in the parish of Blakeney, Morston and district.

Types of grants: One-off and recurrent grants, donations of coal and the payment of insurance and licences.

Annual grant total: In 2000/01 the trust had an income of £15,000 and a total expenditure of £12,000.

Applications: In writing to the correspondent.

Correspondent: M Curtis, Secretary, Molehill, Kinsway, Blakeney, Norfolk NR25 7PL (01263 712023).

The Calibut's Estate & the Hillington Charities

Eligibility: People in need who live in Hillington and East Walton.

Types of grants: One-off and recurrent grants considered according to need. Grants range from £15 to £75.

Annual grant total: Between £600 and £800 a year.

Applications: In writing to the correspondent, either directly by the individual or by another third party for consideration in November.

Correspondent: Mr W J Tawn, Trustee/Chair, 2 Wheatfields, Hillington, King's Lynn, Norfolk PE31 6BH (01485600641).

The Anne French Memorial Trust

Eligibility: Members of the Anglican clergy in the diocese of Norwich.

Types of grants: Holiday grants and other relief-in-need grants.

Annual grant total: In 1999/2000 the trust's income was £276,000 and grants totalled £191,000, including £16,000 to charities, with the rest given to members of the clergy and for other church-related purposes.

Applications: In writing to the correspondent. The trust states 'In no circumstances does the Bishop wish to encourage applications for grants other than those which are dealt with locally'.

Correspondent: C H Dicker, c/o Lovewell Blake, 66 North Quay, Great Yarmouth, Norfolk NR30 1HE (01493 335100).

The King's Lynn & West Norfolk Borough Charity

Eligibility: People in need who live in the borough of King's Lynn and West Norfolk.

Types of grants: One-off grants only up to £250 or £300. Recent grants include those for furniture (such as beds), washing machines, carpets, bedding, cookers and an electric scooter.

Grants are not given to relieve public funds.

Annual grant total: In 2001 the charity had an income of £8,700 and a total expenditure of £9,900, all of which was distributed in 46 grants to individuals.

Applications: On a form available from the correspondent. Applications should be submitted through a social worker, citizen's advice bureau or other welfare agency. They are usually considered in March, June, September and December and should be received in the preceding month.

Correspondent: Mrs Veronica Stiles, Secretary to the Trustees, 54 Park Road, Hunstanton, Norfolk PE36 5DL (01485 533352).

Other information: This charity also gives grants to organisations.

The Saham Toney Fuel Allotment & Perkins Charity

Eligibility: People in need who have lived in Saham Toney, Saham Hills or Saham Waite for at least two years.

Types of grants: Recurrent grants of between £40 and £110, to help with the cost of fuel.

Annual grant total: In 2001 a total of 66 grants totalling £6,100 were awarded. The income for the charity was £10,000.

Applications: On a form available from the correspondent, submitted directly by the individual, giving details of dependants and income. Applications should be submitted in May for consideration in June.

Correspondent: Mrs J S Glenn, 7 Pound Hill, Saham Toney, Thetford, Norfolk IP25 7HN (01953 882731).

The Shelroy Trust

Eligibility: Residents and charities of East Norfolk and Norwich with Christian, medical or community emphasis.

Types of grants: One-off grants, ranging from £100 to £500.

Annual grant total: In 2000/01 the trust gave grants totalling £16,000 to individuals and organisations.

Applications: In writing to the correspondent. Applications can be made directly by the individual or through a social worker, citizen's advice bureau or other third party. They are considered at the trustees' quarterly meetings in March, June, September and December.

Correspondent: R Wiltshire, 4 Brandon Court, Brundall, Norwich NR13 5NW.

The Southery, Feltwell & Methwold Relief in Need Charity

Eligibility: People in need who live in the parishes of Southery, Feltwell and Methwold.

Types of grants: One-off grants in the range of £50 to £100. Grants are often given towards the costs of travel to and from hospital.

Annual grant total: In 2000/01 the trust had an income of £1,200 and a total

SOUTH EAST – NORFOLK

expenditure of £940, of which £900 was distributed to 13 individuals.

Applications: In writing to the correspondent. Applications are to be submitted by a third party such as a parishioner or committee member, and are considered throughout the year, but mainly in February or March.

Correspondent: Mrs J K Hodson, 36a Lynn Road, Southery, Downham Market, Norfolk PE38 0HU (01366 377303).

The West Winch Town Yard Charity

Eligibility: People in need, mainly over 65, who live in West Winch and Setchey.

Types of grants: 5cwt of coals at Christmas.

Annual grant total: The total given in grants to individuals each year depends on the price of 5cwt of coal, and the number of applicants. Grants are also made to village senior citizens' organisations.

Applications: In writing to the correspondent to be considered in September/October. Applications should be submitted directly by the individual and should indicate whether the applicant is retired or unemployed.

Correspondent: F H Fuller, Meadow Farm, 42 Hall Lane, West Winch, King's Lynn, Norfolk PE33 0PP (01553 842256).

The Witton Charity

Eligibility: Pensioners and other people in need who live in Witton and Ridlington.

Types of grants: Grants of coal twice a year and food parcels at Christmas.

Annual grant total: About £2,000.

Applications: In writing to the correspondent.

Correspondent: Mrs L F Tompkins, Shootersway, Heath Road, Ridlington, North Walsham, Norfolk NR28 9NZ.

Banham

The Banham Parochial Charities

Eligibility: People in need who live in the parish of Banham.

Types of grants: One-off grants according to need. Grants have been given towards such things as heating bills, clothing and funeral expenses.

Annual grant total: About £6,800.

Applications: In writing to the correspondent. Applications can be considered at any time.

Correspondent: Martin Baglin, Norfolk House, The Green, Banham, Norwich NR16 2AA (01953 887216).

Barton Bendish

The Barton Bendish Poor's Charity

Eligibility: Widows and people in need who live in Barton Bendish, including Eastmoor.

Types of grants: Grants of £40 towards funeral expenses, travel to hospitals, Christmas payments for fuel costs and other cases of special hardship.

Annual grant total: In 2001/02 the charity had an income and total expenditure of £1,100, all of which was given in grants.

Applications: The five trustees are well known and can be approached in writing. Applications can also be submitted in writing to the correspondent at any time throughout the year.

Correspondent: Mrs Freda E Rumball, Clerk, 45 Church Road, Barton Bendish, King's Lynn, Norfolk PE33 9DP (01366 347324).

Beeston

The Beeston Fuel Charity

Eligibility: Older people over 65 and in need who live in the parish of Beeston and have done so for at least five years.

Types of grants: Fuel grants of between £20 and £25 given at Christmas.

Annual grant total: About £1,100 a year.

Applications: In writing to the correspondent, for consideration in December.

Correspondent: Brian Potter, The Old Cottage, Syers Lane, Beeston Village PE32 2NJ (01328 701698).

Burnham Market

The Harold Moorhouse Charity

Eligibility: Individuals in need who live in Burnham Market in Norfolk only.

Types of grants: One-off grants are made ranging from £50 to £200 for heating, medical care and equipment, travel to and from hospital, education equipment and school educational trips.

Annual grant total: In 2000/01 the trust had assets of £403,000, its income was £16,000 and total expenditure was £14,000. Grants to individuals totalled £7,300. Grants to organisations totalled £6,100.

Applications: In writing to the correspondent. Applications should be submitted directly by the individual in any month.

Correspondent: R J Utting, Trustee, Angles House, Station Road, Burnham Market, King's Lynn, Norfolk PE31 8HA.

Buxton with Lammas

Picto Buxton Charity

Eligibility: People in need who live in the parish of Buxton with Lamas.

Types of grants: One-off and recurrent grants according to need.

Annual grant total: In 2000/01 the trust had an income of £16,000 and a total expenditure of £10,000. In the year one grant totalling £20 was made to an individual.

Applications: In writing to the correspondent directly by the individual. Applications are considered at any time.

Correspondent: Dick W Smithson, Clerk, Avandix, Crown Road, Buxton, Norwich NR10 5EN (01603 279203).

Other information: Educational help for needy families is also available. Grants are also made to organisations or groups within the parish boundary.

Diss

The Diss Parochial Charities Poors Branch

Eligibility: People in need who live in the town and parish of Diss.

Types of grants: One-off grants ranging between £30 and £100. Recent grants included bereavement grants of £100 each and grants towards the cost of 'Life Line' (£37). Grants towards fares to college (£105) and grants towards school trips (£320). Grants are one-off.

Annual grant total: In 2001 the charity had an income of £16,000 and a total expenditure of £14,000.

Applications: In writing through DWP, CAB, Diss Health Centre, Diss Town Hall or directly to the correspondent. They are considered upon receipt.

Correspondent: J H Scoggins, Highpoint, Brewers Green Lane, Diss, Norfolk IP22 4QP.

Downham Market and Downham West

Downham Aid in Sickness

Eligibility: People who are sick, convalescent or infirm and live in the district of Downham Market or the parish of Downham West.

Types of grants: One-off and recurrent grants according to need.

Annual grant total: In 2001/02 the trust had assets of £40,000 and an income of £2,300. Grants to individuals and organisations totalled £1,100.

Applications: In writing to the correspondent for consideration in May and November.

Correspondent: John Clarke, 21 London Road, Downham Market, Norfolk PE38 9AP (01366 387387; Fax: 01366 383638; e-mail: john.clarke@londonroadoffice.demon.co.uk).

The Hundred Acre Charity – Dolcoal

Eligibility: People in need who live in Downham Market and Downham West parishes.

Types of grants: Fuel vouchers of £15 or £16.

Annual grant total: In 2000 the charity had an income of £5,800 and a total expenditure of £6,300.

Applications: In writing to the correspondent, after local advertisements are placed in shops in the village. Applications can be submitted directly by the individual and are usually considered at the end of November.

Correspondent: Jean Markwell, Northfield, The Rows, Wereham, KIng's Lynn, Norfolk PE33 9AY.

Other information: This entry was not confirmed by the charity, but the address was correct according to the Charity Commission database.

East Dereham

The East Dereham Relief-in-Need Charity

Eligibility: People in need who live in East Dereham.

Types of grants: Recurrent grants ranging from £35 to £100 including payments of coal and clothing vouchers.

Annual grant total: In 2000/01 the charity had an income of £7,400 and a total expenditure of £9,300.

Applications: On a form available from the correspondent, submitted either directly by the individual or through a social worker, citizen's advice bureau or other welfare agency. They are considered in December.

Correspondent: R H Parker, Secretary, 130 Norwich Road, Dereham, Norfolk NR20 3AU (01362 691412).

Other information: One-off grants are also made to organisations helping people in the community.

East Tuddenham

The East Tuddenham Charities

Eligibility: People in need who live in East Tuddenham.

Types of grants: Christmas grants for fuel and occasional one-off grants.

Annual grant total: About £15,000 a year is distributed to individuals for educational and relief-in-need purposes.

Applications: In writing to the correspondent.

Correspondent: Mrs Janet Guy, 7 Mattishall Road, East Tuddenham, Dereham, Norfolk NR20 3LP (01603 880523).

Feltwell

The Edmund Atmere Charity

Eligibility: People, generally aged over 70, (except in special cases of dire need) who have lived in Feltwell for at least 10 years. Grants have been made to people with multiple sclerosis or a similar condition and children who are sick.

Types of grants: One-off grants in the range of £9 to £250.

Annual grant total: In 2001/02 the trust had assets of £14,000 and an income of £2,100. A total of £2,200 was distributed in 139 grants.

Applications: In writing to: G Broadwater, Treasurer, 16 Nightingale Lane, Feltwell, Norfolk IP26 4AR. Applications can be submitted between 1 October and 1 November either directly by the individual or through a relevant third party. Applications are considered in November.

Correspondent: E A S Lambert, Hill Farm, Feltwell, Thetford, Norfolk IP26 4AB (01842 828156).

Sir Edmund Moundeford's Educational Foundation

Eligibility: Individuals in need who live in Feltwell.

Types of grants: One-off and recurrent grants according to need.

Annual grant total: In 2000 the trust's income was £100,000. About £5,000 was given in grants to individuals for both relief-in-need and educational purposes.

Applications: In writing to the correspondent.

Correspondent: B L Hawkins, The Estate Office, Lynn Road, Downham Market, Norfolk PE38 9NL (01366 387180; Fax: 01366 386626; e-mail: barry@barryhawkins.freewire.co.uk; website: www.barryhawkins.freewire.co.uk).

Foulden

The Foulden Parochial Charities

Eligibility: People in need who live in Foulden.

Types of grants: One-off and recurrent grants according to need. Grants given have included those towards orthopaedic beds, dentures and books for students.

Annual grant total: About £2,000 a year, depending on income.

Applications: In writing to the correspondent, directly by the individual or through a welfare agency. Applications are considered as and when necessary.

Correspondent: Karen Stephenson, 7 School Road, Foulden, Thetford, Norfolk IP26 5AA (01366 328446).

Garboldisham

The Garboldisham Parish Charities

Eligibility: People in need who live in the parish of Garboldisham. Generally, this is covered by the Relief-in-Need Fund, although widows and those over 65 who have lived in the parish of Garboldisham for over two years may qualify for allowances given by the Fuel Allotment Charity.

Types of grants: One-off and recurrent grants of £40 each. Awards are made annually from the Fuel Allotment Charity; only one grant per household can be made.

Annual grant total: In 1999 a total of 51 grants of £35 each were distributed to widows and those over 65.

Applications: Applications can be submitted directly by the individual including specific details of what the grant is required for. They are usually considered in July and December.

Correspondent: P Girling, Treasurer, Smallworth, Garboldisham, Diss, Norfolk IP22 2QW (01953 681646).

Gayton

The Gayton Fuel Allotments

Eligibility: People in need or distress who live in the administrative parish of Gayton, which includes the village of Gayton Thorpe.

Types of grants: One-off and recurrent grants from £25 according to need.

Annual grant total: About £700 a year.

Applications: In writing to the correspondent. Applications should be submitted directly by the individual or through a third party such as a relative or a neighbour for consideration in November. Urgent requests are considered at any time.

SOUTH EAST – NORFOLK

Correspondent: N F Bradshaw, Clerk, 14 Birch Road, Gayton, King's Lynn, Norfolk PE32 1UN (01553 636321).

Gaywood

The Gaywood Poors' Fuel Allotment Trust

Eligibility: Older people in need who live in the ecclesiastical parish of Gaywood.

Types of grants: Individual hardship grants and distributions of £5 per person at Christmas to people of pensionable age who live in the parish.

Annual grant total: In 2000/01 the trust had an income of £3,400 and gave grants totalling £2,900. Assets amounted to £97,000.

Applications: In writing to the correspondent through social services.

Correspondent: Frank Walker, 1 Grantley Court, Gayton Road, King's Lynn, Norfolk PE30 4TN (01553 774887).

Great Hockham

The Great Hockham Fuel & Furze Trust

Eligibility: People in need who live in the parish of Great Hockham.

Types of grants: Grants to help with the cost of fuel (e.g. cheque payable to local electricity board).

Annual grant total: Up to £1,500.

Applications: Directly by the individual in writing to the correspondent or through a third party on their behalf (eg. relative or neighbour). Applications are considered towards the end of the year, following an advert in a local paper.

Correspondent: Chris Wiltshire, Clerk, 8 Little Hockham Lane, Great Hockham, Thetford, Norfolk IP24 1NR.

Harling

Harling Fuel Allotment Trust

Eligibility: People in need living in Harling.

Types of grants: The trust's primary objective is to provide fuel; and secondly to make cash grants or to provide or pay for items, services or facilities. A recent grant included the purchase of two custom-made beds.

Annual grant total: In 2001/02 the sum of £650 was distributed in 13 awards of £50 each.

Applications: In writing to the correspondent at any time from any source; a brief financial statement will be required.

Correspondent: David Gee, Cerk, Hanworth House, Market Street, East Harling, Norwich NR16 2AD (01953 717652; Fax: 01953 717611).

The West Harling Road Allotment Gardens Trust

Eligibility: Women in need who live in the parish of Harling. Women living immediately outside the parish will be considered in exceptional circumstances.

Types of grants: One-off grants according to individual merits. Recent grants have been for building repairs, education costs and assistance with mortgage payments.

Annual grant total: In 2001/02 the trust had an income of £680; no applications were received.

Applications: In writing to the correspondent at any time, either directly by the applicant or by a third party. Applications should include a brief financial statement and the reason a grant is needed.

Correspondent: David Gee, Clerk, Hanworth House, Market Street, East Harling, Norwich NR16 2AD (01953 717652; Fax: 01953 717611).

Hilgay

The Hilgay Feoffee Charity

Eligibility: People in need who live in the parish of Hilgay.

Types of grants: One-off and recurrent grants according to need (including coal).

Annual grant total: The grant total varies each year.

Applications: In writing to the correspondent, directly by the individual. Applications are considered in October and should be received in the preceding month.

Correspondent: Mrs P Golds, Reeve Cottage, Wards Chase, Stow Bridge, King's Lynn, Norfolk PE33 3NN.

Horstead with Stanninghall

The Horstead Poor's Land

Eligibility: People in need who live in Horstead with Stanninghall.

Types of grants: One-off and recurrent grants according to need, from £10 upwards.

Annual grant total: In 2000/01 the trust had an income of £8,900 and a total expenditure of £5,600.

Applications: Applications, in writing to the correspondent, can be submitted directly by the individual, through a recognised referral agency (e.g. social worker, citizen's advice bureau or doctor) or other third party, and are considered throughout the year.

Correspondent: W B Lloyd, Watermeadows, 7 Church Close, Horstead, Norwich NR12 7ET (01603 737632).

Other information: This trust also makes grants for educational purposes.

King's Lynn

The King's Lynn Charities for the Poor

Eligibility: People in need who live in King's Lynn.

Types of grants: One-off grants according to need.

Annual grant total: The trust has an income of about £600.

Applications: In writing to the correspondent.

Correspondent: A J Cave, Clerk, 11 King Street, King's Lynn, Norfolk PE30 1ET (01553 761316).

Little Dunham

The Little Dunham Relief-in-Need Charities

Eligibility: People in need who live in Little Dunham.

Types of grants: Grants are given according to need.

Annual grant total: In 2000/01 the charities had an income of £2,900 and a total expenditure of £2,400.

Applications: The trustees usually depend on their local knowledge, but also consider direct approaches from village residents.

Correspondent: Mrs L A Wrighton, Candlestick Cottage, Burrows Hole Lane, King's Lynn, Norfolk PE32 2DP.

Other information: Grants are also given to local primary schools, churches and community organisations.

Lyng

The Lyng Heath Charity

Eligibility: People in need living in the parish of Lyng for at least one year.

Types of grants: One-off and recurrent grants between £20 and £50, primarily for fuel.

Annual grant total: In 2001/02 the trust's income was £1,600 and a total of £1,200 was distributed in 26 grants to individuals.

Applications: On a form available from the correspondent or any member of the committee at any time. Applications can be submitted directly by the individual or through another third party on behalf of the individual i.e. carer, home help, friend. Applicants should include their date of birth, how long they have lived in the village, the reason they are applying and any other relevant information. Applications are considered in November, or any time if necessary.

Correspondent: Mrs S A Broad, Clock House, The Street, Lyng, Norwich NR9 5AL (01603 872234).

Other information: Grants are occasionally made to village organisations.

Marham Village

The Marham Poors Land's Trust

Eligibility: Women over 60 and men over 65 who are pensioners and who live in Marham Village.

Types of grants: One-off vouchers of £35 to be spent in village shops.

Annual grant total: In 1999 the trust had assets of £16,000, an income of £3,600 and expenditure was £2,500.

Applications: In writing to the correspondent. Applications are considered in October.

Correspondent: Mrs W Steeles, Jungfrau Main Street, Marham, Kings Lynn, Norfolk PE33 9JQ (Tel & Fax: 01760 337286).

Northwold

The Northwold Combined Charities and Edmund Atmere Charity

Eligibility: People in need who live in the parish of Northwold.

Types of grants: One-off and recurrent grants in the range of £40 to £100.

Annual grant total: In 2001 the charities had an income of about £9,000 and a total expenditure of £8,000, all of which was given in relief-in-need grants to individuals.

Applications: In writing to the correspondent directly by the individual. Applications should be received in November for consideration in December.

Correspondent: Mrs J A Norris, Secretary, 25 West End, Northwold, Norfolk IP26 5LE.

Norwich

Benevolent Association for the Relief of Decayed Tradesmen, their Widows and Orphans

Eligibility: People who live in Norwich and are in need. Preference is given to those who have carried out a trade in the area of benefit and their dependants.

Types of grants: One-off and recurrent grants according to need.

Annual grant total: In 2000 the trust's income was £4,300 and it did not spend any money.

Applications: In writing to the correspondent.

Correspondent: Joan Emilia Orford, League of St Bartholomew's Nurses, c/o St Bartholomew's School of Nursing and Midwifery, West Smithfield, London EC1A 7QN (01603 629871).

Other information: This entry was not confirmed by the association, but the address was correct according to the Charity Commission database.

Norwich Consolidated Charities

Eligibility: People on low incomes who are permanent residents of the city of Norwich. Grants are generally only made to those with dependants, unless the application is supported by a social worker. Applicants, if eligible, must have evidence that they have applied, and been rejected, for a social fund loan.

Types of grants: One-off grants for welfare in the range of £50 to £500. Grants given include those for carpets, cookers, beds, washing machines as well as childcare costs for low income, single parents. Some assistance is given towards medical items if supported by a doctor and social worker and all other avenues of help have been explored.

Annual grant total: In 2001 the charities had assets of £16 million and an income of £1.1 million. Total expenditure totalled £1.4 million, including £41,000 to 117 individuals.

Applications: On a form available from the correspondent either through a social worker, citizen's advice bureau or other welfare agency or directly by the individual. Please ring or write to the office to confirm eligibility. Applications are considered by the trustees at five committee meetings each year.

Generally applicants will be asked to attend for an interview or they will be visited.

Correspondent: Mrs S A Franklin, Head of Finance and Administration, 10 Golden Dog Lane, Norwich NR3 1BP (01603 621023).

Other information: Grants are also made to charitable institutions within Norwich for welfare purposes.

Norwich Town Close Estate Charity

Eligibility: Freemen of Norwich and their families who are in need.

Types of grants: One-off grants, for example towards decorating costs, house repairs, carpets, spectacles and dental work. Grants are occasionally given for holiday costs. Small regular pensions have also been made to older people.

Annual grant total: In 2000/01 the charity had assets of £12 million, an income of £677,000 and a total expenditure of £638,000. A total of £4,000 was given in about 20 grants to individuals for welfare purposes. Grants totalling £66,000 were given to individuals for educational purposes and £398,000 was given to organisations.

Applications: On a form available from the correspondent. Applications are considered throughout the year. Applicants living locally will usually be required to attend for interview.

Correspondent: Ms S A Franklin, Head of Finances and Administration, 10 Golden Dog Lane, Magdalen Street, Norwich NR3 1BP (01603 621023).

Old Buckenham

The Old Buckenham United Eleemosynary Charity

Eligibility: People in need who live in Old Buckenham, Norfolk. Preference for pensioners (over 65) but others are considered.

Types of grants: Normally recurrent grants in coal or cash in lieu for those without coal fires. Grants are currently 400kg or £48 and distributed yearly in early December. Cases considered to be of exceptional need can be given more.

Annual grant total: In 2001 the charity had an income of £2,500 and a total expenditure of £2,600.

Applications: For new applicants, in writing to the correspondent following posted notices around the parish each autumn. Applications are usually considered in early November and can be submitted either directly by the individual, or through another third party such as any of the ten trustees. Any relevant evidence of need is preferred, but not essential.

Correspondent: D C Hardy, 4 Sutherland Chase, Blythewood, Ascot, Berkshire SL5 8TF.

Other information: This entry was not confirmed by the charity, but the address was correct according to information on file at the Charity Commission.

Pentney

The Pentney Charities

Eligibility: People over 65 who have lived in the parish of Pentney for the last two years.

Types of grants: One-off grants to individuals and organisations for the general benefit of the inhabitants of Pentney. Fuel grants are offered to all eligible people. Grants given include those for: travel to and from hospital; funeral expenses; medical expenses; and fuel costs. No grants are given where help is available from the social services.

Annual grant total: In 2001/02 the trust had an income of £11,000. Relief-in-need grants to 70 individuals totalled £6,000 and £1,900 was given to organisations.

Applications: In writing to the correspondent either through a social worker, citizen's advice bureau or other welfare agency or directly by the individual or a third party on behalf on the individual i.e. a neighbour or relative. Applications are considered in May and November.

Correspondent: Mrs Susan Smalley, Falgate Farm, Narborough Road, Pentney, King's Lynn, Norfolk PE32 1JD (Tel & Fax: 01760 337534).

Saham Toney

The Ella Roberts Memorial Charity for Saham Toney

Eligibility: People in need who are aged, sick or disabled and live in Saham Toney.

Types of grants: One-off cash grants usually up to a maximum of £200 to buy or hire additional necessary equipment, facilities and care that is not provided by the local authority.

Annual grant total: In 1999/2000 the trust had an income of £1,800 and a total expenditure of £1,700.

Applications: On a form available from the local post office, including details of applicant's income and reasons why assistance is needed. Applications are considered at any time, usually including an individual assessment from a sub-committee.

Correspondent: Mrs R E Benton, Treasurer, 36 Richmond Road, Saham Toney, Thetford, Norfolk IP25 7ER (01953 881844).

Saxlingham

The Saxlingham Nursing Charity

Eligibility: People who have a nursing need and a financial need who live in Saxlingham Nethergate and Saxlingham Thorpe.

Types of grants: One-off grants are given to eligible applicants for medical and other needs, including grants towards fuel at Christmas.

Annual grant total: Over £2,000 is available.

Applications: In writing to the correspondent, to be considered as they arrive.

Correspondent: Dr J Fox, Chairman, Ivy Farm, Foxhole, Saxlingham Thorpe, Norfolk NR15 1UG (01508 499468).

The Saxlingham United Charities

Eligibility: People in need aged 70 or over who have lived in the village of Saxlingham Nethergate for five or more years.

Types of grants: Recurrent grants for coal and electricity of £100 and one-off grants for widows and widowers.

Annual grant total: In 2001 grants totalling £2,000 were made to 21 people. A further £300 was given in educational grants.

Applications: In writing to the correspondent. Applications can be submitted directly by the individual and are usually considered in October.

Correspondent: Mrs Jane Turner, 47 The Street, Saxlingham, Nethergate NR15 1AJ (01508 498396).

Other information: Grants are also made to individuals in education.

Shipdham

The Shipdham Parochial & Fuel Allotment

Eligibility: People in need who have lived in Shipdham for two years.

Types of grants: One-off grants of £60.

Annual grant total: In 2000/01 the trust had an income of £7,200. Total expenditure was £9,300, of which £6,400 was given in 107 grants. Grants were also given to organisations.

Applications: On an application form available from the correspondent. Applications are considered in November.

Correspondent: A R Aram, 7 Pound Green Lane, Shipdham, Thetford, Norfolk IP25 7LF (01362 821034).

Shotesam

The Earl of Northampton's Charity

See entry on page 369

South Creake

The South Creake Charities

Eligibility: People in need who live in South Creake.

Types of grants: Mostly recurrent annual grants towards fuel of between £35 and £100 per year. No grants are given to people in work.

Annual grant total: In 2001/02 the sum of £3,100 was given in 66 educational grants.

Applications: In writing to the correspondent. Applications should be submitted directly by the individual and are considered in November; they should be received before the end of October.

Correspondent: Miss E M Sands, 2 Bluestone Crescent, South Creake, Fakenham, Norfolk NR21 9LZ (01328 823433).

Other information: Grants are also given to schools and playgroups.

Stow Bardolph

The Stow Bardolph Town Lands & Poors Charity

Eligibility: People in need who live in the parish of Stow Bardolph. Households where one person is working or where anyone receives income other than their state pension are excluded unless experiencing particular hardship.

Types of grants: Fuel vouchers for people in need. In recent years the vouchers have been worth £35 to £50 each.

Annual grant total: In 1999, the trust gave 58 relief-in-need grants totalling £2,900.

Applications: Applications should be submitted directly by the individual in September/October and are considered in November.

Correspondent: P Golds, Reeve Cottage, Wards Chase, Stowbridge, King's Lynn, Norfolk PE34 3NN.

Swanton Morley

Thomas Barrett's Charity

Eligibility: Older people in need who live in Swanton Morley.

Types of grants: One-off and recurrent grants according to need.

Annual grant total: In 2000/01 the charity had both an income and total expenditure of £2,800.

Applications: In writing to the correspondent directly by the individual. Applications are considered in November or December.

Correspondent: Nicholas Saffell, Old Bank of England Court, Queen Street, Norwich NR2 4TA (01603 629871).

Thetford

The Henry Smith Charity

Eligibility: People who are elderly and live in Thetford.

Types of grants: Grants of about £11 to £20 at Christmas only for heating.

Annual grant total: In 2001 the trust received £1,300 income, allocated by Henry Smith's (General Estate) Charity, all of which was given in grants.

Applications: An advertisement is placed in the Thetford & Watton Times in October inviting applications. Applications are considered in November and should be submitted directly by the individual.

Correspondent: Christine Mason, Clerk, 2 The Walled Garden, Nunnery Place, Thetford, Norfolk IP24 2PZ (01842 750386).

Thurne

Thurne Charity Trustees

Eligibility: People in need who live in Thurne (mainly older people).

Types of grants: Grants are given around Christmas time usually in the form of coal, otherwise cash to the same value is given towards other fuel costs. Grants are recurrent and range from £100 to £200.

Annual grant total: In 2001/02 the trust had an income of £2,700 and a total of 216 grants were given totalling £3,000.

Applications: In writing to the correspondent directly by the individual in November, for consideration in December.

Correspondent: D W George, Abbey Farm, Thurne, Great Yarmouth, Norfolk NR29 3BY (01692 670336; Fax 01692 671940).

Tilney All Saints

The Tilney All Saints Parish Lands Charity

Eligibility: People in need who live in the ancient parish of Tilney All Saints.

Types of grants: Christmas grants to widows and widowers and grants for the general relief-in-need of other parishioners.

Annual grant total: About £1,000.

Applications: In writing to the correspondent.

Correspondent: Mrs E Constable, Elm House, Station Road, Clenchwarton, King's Lynn, Norfolk PE34 4DH (01553 764003).

Walpole

The Walpole St Andrew Dole Charity

Eligibility: People in need who are over 65 and live in Walpole St Andrew and Walpole Cross Keys.

Types of grants: One-off grants ranging from £50 to £150. Loans are not made.

Annual grant total: In 2001 the charity had an income of £7,000 and a total expenditure of £2,800.

Applications: In writing to the correspondent. Applications should be submitted directly by the individual. They are considered in April.

Correspondent: Mrs A Buckle, Clerk, Merrydown, Church Road, Walpole St Peter, Wisbech, Cambridgeshire PE14 7NU (01945 780046).

The Walpole St Peter Poor's Estate

Eligibility: Older people over 65 who are in need and live in the old parishes of Walpole St Peter, Walpole Highway and Walpole Marsh.

Types of grants: Recurrent grants of £10 to individuals over the age of 65, limited to one per household.

Annual grant total: About £1,300 to £1,400 a year.

Applications: In writing to the correspondent. Applications should be submitted directly by the individual and are considered in November.

Correspondent: Jack Bowers, Chairman, Birchwood, Mill Road, Walpole Highway, Wisbech, Cambridgeshire PE14 7QW.

Other information: Grants are also made to college or university students for books.

Watton

The Watton Relief-in-Need Charity

Eligibility: People in need who live in Watton. The charity actively considers help for young people (who live in the area of benefit) such as one parent families.

Types of grants: One-off grants only, generally from £10 to £200, although larger grants are available. Grants are given to older people at Christmas and have been given towards medical equipment, funeral expenses, clothing, carpets and kitchen and household expenses.

Grants are not given for the relief of taxes, rates or other public funds. The charity cannot commit to repeat or renew relief given.

Annual grant total: In 2000/01 the trust had assets of £27,000, an income of £3,000 and a total expenditure of £5,100. A total of £2,800 was distributed in 52 grants.

Applications: In writing to the correspondent either directly by the individual, or through a social worker, citizen's advice bureau, welfare agency or through a friend or neighbour. Applications are considered in March, July and December, but extraordinary meetings are possible.

Correspondent: Derek I Smith, 39 Dereham Road, Watton, Norfolk IP25 6ER (01953 884044).

Other information: Grants are also made to organisations with similar objects.

Welney

The Bishop's Land Charity

Eligibility: People in need (men over 65 years and women over 60 years) who live in the parish of Welney.

Types of grants: Grants of £12 per person each year.

Annual grant total: In 2001/02 the trust had an income of £1,000. The sum of £910 was given in 76 relief-in-need grants to individuals.

Applications: Applicants should be made by personal attendance or a signed note, to St Mary's Church – Welney on the second Saturday of December between 10.30 am and 11.30 am.

Correspondent: Mrs P A Copeman, 1 Chestnut Avenue, Welney, Wisbech, Cambridgeshire PE14 9RG (01354 610226; Fax: 01354 610418; e-mail: g85ww@aol.com).

William Marshall's Charity

Eligibility: Widows in need who live in the parish of Welney.

Types of grants: Grants of £100 paid quarterly.

Annual grant total: In 2001 the charity had assets of £129,000 and an income and total expenditure of £31,000.

Applications: In writing to the correspondent. The list of recipients is reviewed quarterly.

Correspondent: Lynda Clarke-Jones, The Barn, Main Street, Littleport, Cambridgeshire CB6 1PH (01353 860449; Fax: 01353 860441; e-mail: littleportpc@btconnect.com).

Other information: The local church receives an annual grant out of the net income from land rents.

Wereham

Wereham Relief-in-Need Charity

Eligibility: Pensioners in need who live in Wereham and have done so for at least one year. Men must be over 65, women over 60. Applications are restricted to one per household. Applicants must be householders and permanent residents.

Types of grants: Cheques made out to post office counters. Grants can be recurrent.

Annual grant total: In 2001 the charity had an income of £1,300 all of which was given in 42 grants.

Applications: In writing to the correspondent, to be submitted in October for consideration in November.

Correspondent: Mrs E Baddock, Clerk, Chile House, Wereham, King's Lynn, Norfolk PE33 9AN (01366 500233).

West Walton

The West Walton Poors' Charity

Eligibility: Widows or single women over 60, or men over 65, who are not employed and are deserving and in need of financial assistance who have lived in the parish of West Walton for at least five years.

Types of grants: Grants are given at Christmas on a yearly basis, i.e. qualifying individuals must reapply each year.

Annual grant total: About £3,000 a year.

Applications: The grants are advertised locally every year, giving a closing date for applications.

Correspondent: Mrs J E Johnson, Clerk, c/o Frasers Solicitors, 29 Old Market, Wisbech, Cambs PE13 1ND (01945 582664; Fax: 01945 468709).

Wiveton

Ralph Greneway Charity

Eligibility: People in need who are over 60 and have lived in the parish of Wiveton for at least three years. Preference is given to widows.

Types of grants: Small weekly pensions and one-off fuel grants.

Annual grant total: In 2000/01 the trust had an income of £2,400 and a total expenditure of £2,100.

Applications: Applications, on a form available from the correspondent, should be submitted directly by the individual and are considered in June and November. The names of two referees and details of the purpose of the grant should be included.

Correspondent: Mrs Margaret L Bennett, 4 The Cottages, Blakeney Road, Wiveton, Holt, Norfolk NR25 7TN (01263 741384).

Other information: Educational grants are also available from a subsidiary charity, for young people up to university age, including young people who are starting work.

Woodton

Woodton United Charities

Eligibility: People in need who live in the parish of Woodton.

Types of grants: One-off and recurrent grants according to need.

Annual grant total: In 2000/01 the trust had assets of £22,000, an income of £2,200 and a total expenditure of £2,900. Relief-in-need and educational grants to 30 individuals were made totalling £2,600. A local hospice was given £200.

Applications: In writing to the correspondent directly by the individual; applications can be submitted at any time.

Correspondent: J V Cowan, Long Barn, Hempnall Road, Woodton, Bungay, Suffolk NR35 2LR (01508 482624).

Wretton

The Jane Forby Charity

Eligibility: People in need who live in the parish of Wretton.

Types of grants: One-off and recurrent grants according to need.

Annual grant total: In 1998/99 the charity had an income of £2,500 and a total expenditure of £1,600.

Applications: In writing to the correspondent, directly by the individual or by a third party aware of the circumstances. Applications are considered in November.

Correspondent: Stanley James Saunders, 2 Cottage Farm Mews, The Street, Marham, King's Lynn, Norfolk PE33 9JQ (01760 338966).

Oxfordshire

The Bampton Welfare Trust

Eligibility: People who live in the parishes of Bampton, Aston, Lew and Shifford, of any occupation, who are in need. Preference is given to children, young people and older people.

Types of grants: One-off grants which can be repeated in subsequent years at the discretion of the trustees. Grants given include food vouchers for a family awaiting benefit payment, heating allowance for older people in need and assistance in purchasing a washing machine for a single parent with multiple sclerosis.

Annual grant total: In 2001 the trust had assets of £170,000, an income of £6,000 and a total expenditure of £6,900. A total of £3,600 was distributed in 32 grants.

Applications: Applicants are advised to initially discuss their circumstances with the welfare officer, Janet Newman (01993 850755) or any of the trustees, who will advise the applicant on which steps to take. This initial contact can be made directly by the individual, or by any third party, at any time.

Correspondent: David Pullman, Clerk, Millgreen Cottage, Bampton, Oxfordshire OX18 2HF (01993 850589).

Other information: Grants are also made to organisations operating in the area.

The Banbury Charities – Bridge Estate

Eligibility: People in need who live within a five mile radius of Banbury.

Types of grants: The trust can support 'any charitable purposes for the general benefit of the inhabitants of Banbury'.

Annual grant total: Around £17,000 to individuals.

Applications: In writing to the correspondent either directly by the individual or through a social worker, citizen's advice bureau, other welfare agency or third party.

Correspondent: A Scott Andrews, Clerk, 36 West Bar, Banbury, Oxfordshire OX16 9RU (01295 251234).

Other information: In addition to the above, the trustees are also in charge of two smaller trusts which each give grants totalling £200 a year.

The Burford Relief-in-Need Charity

Eligibility: People in need who live within five miles of the Tolsey, Burford.

Types of grants: One-off grants of £200 to £1,000. The trust may give grants to relieve sudden distress, travel expenses for hospital visiting, towards fuel and telephone bills, television licences, furniture, bedding, clothing, essential household items, services such as decorating, repairs, meals on wheels etc. and recuperative holidays, and for training leading to a career.

Annual grant total: In 2001 the trust had an income of £5,000 and made 15 grants totalling £4,300. Assets amounted to £97,000.

Applications: In writing to the correspondent either directly by the individual or through a social worker, citizen's advice bureau or other welfare agency including full name, address, age, and the number of years the applicant has lived in Burford or their connection with Burford. Receipts are required for grants towards the cost of equipment. Applications are considered in February, May, August and November, urgent cases can be dealt with immediately.

Correspondent: Mrs E L Cornick, Swan Bank, Swan Lane, Burford, Oxfordshire OX18 4SH (01993 823866).

Cozens Bequest

Eligibility: Widows or spinsters in need who live in the parishes of Tetsworth, Great Hasley, Lewknor, Stoke Talmage, Wheatfield, Adwell, South Weston and Ashton Rowant.

Types of grants: One-off grants according to need given at the discretion of the trustees.

Annual grant total: In 1999/2000 the trust had an income of £5,100 and a total expenditure of £1,400.

Applications: In writing to the correspondent, or the chair of the parish council.

Correspondent: Mr C Trotter, Attington Stud, Tetsworth, Thame, Oxfordshire OX9 7BY (01844 281206).

Ducklington & Hardwick with Yelford Charity

Eligibility: People in need or hardship who live in the villages of Ducklington, Hardwick and Yelford.

Types of grants: One-off grants in the range of £50 to £150. Grants given include those towards heating for older people, assistance with playgroup fees, furniture, funeral expenses, conversion of rooms for people who are older or disabled, provision of telephones, spectacles, school holiday assistance and assistance with rent arrears.

Annual grant total: In 2001 the trust had assets of £105,000, an income of £4,200 and a total expenditure of £5,600. A total of £2,600 was given in 19 grants to individuals. Four educational grants totalled £200.

Applications: In writing to the correspondent. Applications are considered in March and November, but emergency cases can be dealt with at any time.

Correspondent: Mrs A P Shaw, Clerk, 127 Abingdon Road, Standlake, Witney, Oxfordshire OX29 7QN (01865 300615).

Other information: Grants are also made to organisations such as clubs, schools and so on.

The Faringdon United Charities

Eligibility: People in need who live in the parishes of Faringdon, Littleworth, Great and Little Coxwell, all in Oxfordshire.

Types of grants: One-off grants for: clergy expenses for visiting the sick, domestic appliances and pre-school fees.

Grants cannot be given for nursing/retirement home fees or the supply of equipment that the state is obliged to provide.

Annual grant total: In 2001/02 the charity had assets of £233,000 and both an income and a total expenditure of £13,000. A total of £7,200 was distributed to individuals for education and welfare purposes.

Applications: In writing to the correspondent throughout the year. Applications can be submitted either through a social worker, citizen's advice bureau or other third party, directly by the individual or by a third party on their behalf i.e. neighbour, parent or child.

Correspondent: W R Jestico, Clerk, Critchleys, 10 Marlborough Street, Faringdon, Oxfordshire SN7 7JP (01367 240226; Fax: 01367 242747).

Other information: Grants are also made to organisations helping people in need.

Doris Field Charitable Trust

Eligibility: People in need who live in Oxfordshire.

Types of grants: One-off and recurrent grants according to need. In the past, for example, a grant was given towards the cost of a high-chair for a boy with disabilities. No grants are made to students.

Annual grant total: In 1999/2000 the trust had an income of £225,000 and a total expenditure of £203,000. Around £60,000 is given in grants to individuals.

Applications: In writing to the correspondent in the first instance, requesting an application form. Applications are considered twice a year, usually in March and September.

Correspondent: Morgan Cole Solicitors, Buxton Court, 3 West Way, Oxford OX2 0SZ (01865 262600; Fax: 01865 721367).

The Lockinge & Ardington Relief-in-Need Charity

Eligibility: People in need who live in the parish of Lockinge and Ardington.

Types of grants: One-off and recurrent grants between £30 and £60.

Annual grant total: About £3,000 a year.

Applications: In writing to the correspondent by the individual. Applications are considered in March, July and November although urgent cases can be considered at any time.

Correspondent: Mrs A Ackland, c/o Lockinge Estate Office, Ardington, Wantage, Oxon OX12 8PP (01235 833200).

Ellen Rebe Spalding Memorial Fund

Eligibility: Women and children who live in Oxfordshire.

Types of grants: One-off and recurrent grants according to need.

Annual grant total: About £1,000.

Applications: Applications should be made through Oxfordshire Social Services.

Correspondent: The Secretary, PO Box 85, Stowmarket IP14 3NY.

Other information: This entry has not been confirmed by the fund, but the address was correct according to the Charity Commission database.

The Thame Welfare Trust

Eligibility: People in need who live in Thame and immediately adjoining villages, and to clubs, groups etc. which support them.

Types of grants: Mainly one-off but some recurrent grants according to need, where help cannot be received from statutory organisations. Recent grants have been given towards e.g. a single parent's mortgage payment and a wheelchair for a person who is disabled.

Annual grant total: The charity's income is over £2,000 a year. This money is given to individuals and organisations for relief-in-need and education.

Applications: In writing to the correspondent mainly through social workers, probation officers, teachers, or a similar third party but also directly by the applicant.

Correspondent: J Gadd, Pearce Court, Windmill Road, Thame, Oxfordshire OX9 2DJ (01844 212564).

The Town Estate Charity

Eligibility: Grants are given to people in need who live in the civil parish of Sibford Gower and the hamlet of Burdrop.

Types of grants: One-off and recurrent grants towards essential items and services such as telephone provision. The trust also provides free home chiropody treatment.

Annual grant total: Between £1,000 and £2,000 a year.

Applications: In writing to the correspondent, to be considered as they are received.

Correspondent: P H Baadsgaard, Quince Cottage, Sibford Gower, Banbury, Oxfordshire OX15 5RT (01295 780378).

Abingdon

The Appleton Trust (Abingdon)

Eligibility: People in need who live in Appleton or Eaton.

Types of grants: One-off and recurrent grants in the range of £50 to £100, towards needs such as fuel and bereavement costs.

Annual grant total: In 2001 the trust had assets of £115,000, an income of £4,200 and it spent £4,100, of which £2,600 was given in 36 grants to individuals in need. Grants to organisations totalled £1.500.

Applications: In writing to the correspondent, either directly by the individual or through an appropriate third party.
Correspondent: D J Dymock, 73 Eaton Road, Appleton, Abingdon, Oxfordshire OX13 5JS (01865 862458).
Other information: Grants are also given for educational purposes to former pupils of Appleton Primary School.

Bletchingdon

The Bletchington Charity

Eligibility: People in need who live in the parish of Bletchington, in particular people who are elderly or infirm.
Types of grants: Grants to people who are elderly and infirm at Christmas and Easter towards fuel bills and other needs. Help is given for travel, chiropody and television licences. Otherwise one-off grants for social welfare, education and relief-in-sickness according to need.
Annual grant total: Relief-in-need grants totalling £4,200 were made in 2001, while educational grants totalled £1,500.
Applications: Generally as the trustees see a need, but applications can be made in writing to the correspondent by the individual or by a social worker, doctor or welfare agency.
Correspondent: J A Hayward, Chair, 2 Valentia Close, Bletchington, Kidlington, Oxfordshire OX5 3DF (01869 350507).
Other information: The charity also seeks to support any educational, medical and social needs that will benefit the village community as a whole.

Eynsham

The Eynsham Consolidated Charity

Eligibility: People in need who live in the ancient parish of Eynsham (which covers Eynsham and part of Freeland).
Types of grants: One-off grants usually in the range of £50 and £200, mainly to older people to help with winter heating costs. Grants are also given, for example, towards playgroup fees, equipment for those with disabilities and financial help following bereavement. The trust does not give recurrent grants or loans, nor does it relieve rates, taxes or other public funds.
Annual grant total: In 2000 the trust had an income of £3,500. Out of a total expenditure of £2,000 the sum of £1,600 was distributed in 25 relief-in-need grants.
Applications: In writing to the correspondent. Applications can be made through a social worker, citizen's advice bureau or other welfare agency; or by the individual or a neighbour, friend etc. They are considered in February, May, September and November and should be submitted in the preceding month. Applications should include details of the value of grant required.
Correspondent: R N Mitchell, 20 High Street, Eynsham, Witney, Oxfordshire OX29 4HB (01865 880665).

Over Norton

The Over Norton Trust

Eligibility: People in need who live in the ancient hamlet of Over Norton.
Types of grants: One-off grants of electricity stamps or coal vouchers to the value of £45 to £60.
Annual grant total: In 1999/2000 the trust had an income of £3,300 and a total expenditure of £3,200.
Applications: In writing to the correspondent. Applications are considered at a meeting in October so must be received in good time.
Correspondent: Mrs D Macrae, 4 The Penn, Over Norton, Oxon OX7 5QZ (01608 642499).

Oxford

The City of Oxford Charities

Eligibility: People in need who have lived in the city of Oxford for at least three years, and who have a low income.
Types of grants: One-off grants of up to £600. Priority is given to children and people who are elderly, disabled or have a medical condition. Grants have been awarded for furniture to people moving home; washing machines; recuperation holidays for people with disabilities or medical problems and/or their carers; baby equipment; and wheelchairs and mobility scooters. Applications for electrical appliances will be given an appliance of the trust's choice unless specifically requested.
Annual grant total: In 2001 a total of 136 grants totalling £34,000 were awarded.
Applications: Application forms are available from the correspondent, and should be submitted through a social worker, citizen's advice bureau or other welfare agency, and are considered every six weeks. Applications should specify exactly what the money is for and the cost as applications without exact costings will be delayed. There can be a quick response for emergency applications for amounts of less than £150.
Correspondent: David Wright, 11 Davenant Road, Oxford OX2 8BT (Tel & Fax: 01865 553043; e-mail: david@oxfordcitycharities.fsnet.co.uk; website: www.oxfordcitycharities.org).
Other information: Grants for educational purposes to schoolchildren, school leavers and people on vocational courses are also available.

The Stanton Ballard Charitable Trust

Eligibility: Individuals in need who live in the city of Oxford and the immediate area.
Types of grants: One-off grants according to need.
Annual grant total: In 2000/01 the trust had an income of £83,000 and a total expenditure of £94,000.
Applications: On an application form available from the correspondent on receipt of an sae. Applications should be made via social services, probation officers or other bodies, and are considered six times a year.
Correspondent: Mrs M J Tate, PO Box 81, Oxford OX4 4ZA (01865 778391).

Souldern

The Souldern United Charities

Eligibility: People in need who live in the parish of Souldern.
Types of grants: One-off and recurrent grants according to need.
Annual grant total: About £2,000 a year.
Applications: In writing to the correspondent.
Correspondent: Thomas Jordan, Cheviot Fox Hill Lane, Souldern, Oxon OX27 7JZ (01869 345479).
Other information: Grants have also been awarded to local schools and to help a PhD student.

Steventon

The Steventon Allotments & Relief-in-Need Charity

Eligibility: People in need who live in Steventon.
Types of grants: One-off grants for provision of food, fuel and personal items such as clothing, repair or replacement of faulty domestic equipment or furniture, loans of electric wheelchairs, provision of special equipment to chronically sick people and grants or loans for unforeseen difficulties. Large loans will need to be secured as a percentage of a second mortgage.
Annual grant total: In 2000 the trust had assets of £2.7 million and an income of £58,000. Total expenditure was £147,000 with grants to individuals in need totalling £5,800. This charity also gives money to organisations in the area of benefit.

South East – Oxfordshire/Suffolk

Applications: In writing to the correspondent. The trust advertises regularly in the local parish magazine. Applications should include full details of income and expenditure, and will be treated in strictest confidence.

Correspondent: Mrs P Effer, 19 Lime Grove, Southmoor, Abingdon, Oxfordshire OX13 5DN.

Other information: This entry was not confirmed by the charity, but the address was correct according to the Charity Commission database.

Wallingford

The Wallingford Municipal & Relief-in-Need Charities

Eligibility: People in need who live in the former borough of Wallingford.

Types of grants: One-off grants for necessities including the payment of bills, shoes, cookers, fridges and so on. Payments are made to local suppliers, cash grants are not made directly to the individual.

Annual grant total: In 2000/01 the trust had an income of £6,500 and a total expenditure of £6,900. Grants totalled about £6,000.

Applications: On a form available from the correspondent. Trustees meet about every three months, although emergency cases can be considered. Urgent cases may require a visit by a trustee.

Correspondent: A Rogers, Town Clerk, 9 St Martin's Street, Wallingford, Oxfordshire OX10 0AL.

Suffolk

The Cranfield Charitable Trust

Eligibility: People who live in Suffolk and are in need.

Types of grants: One-off and recurrent grants according to need.

Annual grant total: In 1999/2000 the trust had assets of £170,000 and an income of £14,000. Grants totalled £10,000, mostly to organisations.

Applications: In writing to the correspondent.

Correspondent: H S Cranfield, The Red House, Wrentham, Beccles, Suffolk NR34 7NE (01502 675278).

The John Dorkin Charity

Eligibility: People in need who live in the ancient parish of St Clement, Ipswich (broadly speaking the south-eastern sector of Ipswich bounded by Back Hamlet/Foxhall Road and the River Orwell). Preference for the widows and children of seamen.

Types of grants: One-off cash grants have been given for such things as domestic and electrical goods, clothes and for other cases of need.

Annual grant total: About £9,000 is given in grants each year.

Applications: In writing to the correspondent at any time, giving details of financial circumstances.

Correspondent: 32 Lloyds Avenue, Ipswich, Suffolk IP1 3HD (01473 213311).

The Mills Charity

Eligibility: Individuals in need who live in Framlingham and the surrounding district.

Types of grants: One-off grants ranging from £50 to £550.

Annual grant total: In 2001/02 the trust had an income of £79,000 and its expenditure totalled £72,000. £59,000 was distributed in grants to organisations, and £13,000 in total to 35 individuals.

Applications: In writing to the correspondent, either directly by the individual or through a social worker, citizen's advice bureau or other welfare agency.

Correspondent: M E Ashwell, Chair, 38 Pembroke Road, Framlingham, Suffolk IP13 9HA (01728 723525).

Mrs L D Rope's Third Charitable Settlement

Eligibility: People who are on a low income and live in the Ipswich area.

Types of grants: One-off grants according to need. Grants given include those for food, clothing and furnishings/furniture. No grants are given for new overseas projects, individuals working overseas, replacement of statutory funding, debt relief, health/palliative care or educational fees.

Annual grant total: In 2000/01 the trust had assets of £23 million, an income of £746,000 and a total expenditure of £639,000, of which £51,000 was distributed in 104 relief-in-need grants to individuals.

Applications: In writing to the correspondent either directly by the individual or through a social worker, citizen's advice bureau or other welfare agency. Apply in a concise letter, saying what is needed and how the trust may be able to help. It helps to include details of household income (including benefits) and expenses, and a daytime telephone number.

Correspondent: C M Rope, Crag Farm, Boyton, Woodbridge, Suffolk IP12 3LH (01473 288987; Fax: 01473 217182).

Other information: Grants are also made to organisations.

Aldeburgh

Aldeburgh United Charities

Eligibility: People in need who live in the town of Aldeburgh.

Types of grants: One-off and recurrent grants according to need.

Annual grant total: In 2001 the trust had an income of £3,000 and the total expenditure was £3,100.

Applications: In writing to the correspondent.

Correspondent: Hugo Herbert-Jones, Priors Hill, 48 Park Road, Aldeburgh, Suffolk IP15 5ET (01728 453335; e-mail: hugo@herbertjones.fsnet.co.uk).

Other information: This entry was not confirmed by the trust, but the address was correct according to the Charity Commission database.

Assington

Assington Charity

Eligibility: People who live in the parish of Assington who are in need.

Types of grants: One-off and recurrent grants according to need.

Annual grant total: In 2000 the trust's income was £8,500 and its total expenditure was £8,300.

Applications: In writing to the correspondent.

Correspondent: Mrs L J Britcher, Old School House, The Street, Assington, Sudbury, Suffolk CO10 5LH.

Other information: This entry was not confirmed by the charity, but the address was correct according to the Charity Commission database.

Brockley

The Brockley Town & Poor Estate (Brockley Charities)

Eligibility: Older people in need who have lived in Brockley village for at least three years.

Types of grants: Recurrent grants of £70, usually as rebates on electricity bills.

Annual grant total: In 2001 the trust had assets of £1,200 and both an income and a total expenditure of £1,500, of which £1,300 was distributed in 18 grants to individuals.

Applications: In writing to the correspondent. Applications are considered in December and should be submitted in November. They can be submitted directly by the individual or through relatives or family friends. Details of the electricity supplier or method of payment (i.e. metres) are required.

Correspondent: Mrs M A Morley, Fundin, Chapel Lane, Brockley, Bury St Edmunds, Suffolk IP29 4AS (01284 830543).

Bungay

Bungay Charities

Eligibility: People in need who live in the parish of Bungay.

Types of grants: One-off grants on average of £200, to meet a wide range of needs. Older people, for example, can receive help with the costs of telephone installation, heating costs or travel to hospital, children from needy families can receive grants to pay for school trips or clothing and single parents can be given grants to help pay for furniture, washing machines etc.

Annual grant total: £1,000 to £2,000.

Applications: In writing to the correspondent.

Correspondent: Peter Morrow, 11 Wharton Street, Bungay, Suffolk NR35 1EL (01986 892361).

Scott Charity

Eligibility: People who live in the urban district of Bungay and are sick, convalescent, disabled or infirm.

Types of grants: One-off grants usually ranging from between £250 to £1,000 including those to cover the costs of care, equipment and travel to hospitals.

Annual grant total: In 2000/01 the charity had an income of £4,900 and made three relief-in-need grants to individuals totalling £4,700.

Applications: In writing to the correspondent either directly by the individual or through a third party on behalf of an individual i.e. doctor, nurse or family member. Applications are considered on an ongoing basis.

Correspondent: H R G Pulford, 12 Flixton Road, Bungay, Suffolk NR35 1HQ (01986 892438; e-mail: harold@pulfordh.freeserve.co.uk).

Other information: Grants are also made to medical institutions.

Bury St Edmunds

The Bury St Edmunds Old School Fund Foundation

Eligibility: Widows in need who live in Bury St Edmunds.

Types of grants: One-off and recurrent grants according to need, ranging from £50 to £100.

Annual grant total: About £4,000 is given in grants each year for education and welfare purposes.

Applications: In writing to the correspondent.

Correspondent: M C Dunn, Clerk, 80 Guildhall Street, Bury St Edmunds, Suffolk IP33 1QB (01284 762211; Fax: 01284 705739).

Carlton and Carlton Colville

The Carlton Colville Fuel & Poors Allotment Charity

Eligibility: People in need, aged over 70 who live in the ancient parish of Carlton and Carlton Colville, with a preference for those who only receive the basic state pension.

Types of grants: Recurrent grants (£82 in 2001) for fuel and heating costs and exceptionally for transport to/from places of worship and outings for residents of sheltered housing in the area. Occasionally, one-off grants towards specific items/equipment such as boiler repair, heater etc.

Annual grant total: In 2001 the trust had assets of £333,000, an income of £13,000 and spent £12,000; 126 individual grants totalled over £10,000.

Applications: On a form available from the correspondent or to the other four trustees, or the treasurer. Applications can be submitted directly by the individual or through a social worker, citizen's advice bureau or other welfare agency for consideration at any time. Applicants should provide confirmation that their income is restricted to the state pension, although other income may not mean an application will be rejected.

Correspondent: M Soloman, 59 The Street, Carlton Colville, Lowestoft, Suffolk NR33 8JP (01502 586102).

Cavendish

The George Savage Charity

Eligibility: People over 60 in need who live in Cavendish, or who are connected with the village and wish to return.

Types of grants: One-off and recurrent grants according to need.

Annual grant total: About £1,000 a year is given in grants.

Applications: Application forms are available from the correspondent, to be submitted directly by the individual for consideration in January.

Correspondent: Mrs A Wayman, Colt's Hall, Cavendish, Sudbury, Suffolk CO10 8BS (01787 280439).

Chediston

The Chediston United Charities, Town & Poors' Branch

Eligibility: People in need who live in the civil parish of Chediston.

Types of grants: One-off and recurrent grants according to need ranging from £5 to £100. Grants are given for alarm systems for older people, hospital transport, Christmas gifts, and to every child of school age or younger.

Annual grant total: In 2000/01 the charities had an income of £2,300 and a total expenditure of £2,200.

Applications: In writing to the correspondent. Applications are considered throughout the year, although mainly in November. The trust has no formal application procedure as requests are usually made personally to the trustees.

Correspondent: Michael Stanton, Clerk, Hedgerows, Chediston, Halesworth, Suffolk IP19 0AZ (01986 875514).

Chelsworth

The Chelsworth Parochial Charity

Eligibility: People in need who live in the parish of Chelsworth.

Types of grants: One-off grants or payment for items, services and facilities that will reduce the person's need, hardship or distress.

Annual grant total: In 2000 the charity had both an income and a total expenditure of £1,600.

Applications: In writing to the correspondent.

Correspondent: Mrs S Buckeridge, The Summer House, Chelsworth, Ipswich, Suffolk IP7 7HU

Corton

The Corton Poors' Land Trust

Eligibility: People in need who live in the ancient parish of Corton.

Types of grants: Grants have included Christmas gifts for older people, grants for chiropody treatment, taxi fares to hospital, and payment for home alarm installation and rent.

Annual grant total: About £4,500 to £5,000 each year.

Applications: In writing to the correspondent. Applications can be submitted at any time directly by the individual or by an appropriate third party, to be considered monthly.

Correspondent: B N H Blake, 28 Long Lane, Lowestoft, Suffolk NR32 5HA (01502 730665).

Other information: Grants are also made to organisations which carry out the charity's aims within the area of benefit.

Dennington

The Dennington Consolidated Charities

Eligibility: People in need who live in the village of Dennington.

Types of grants: One-off and recurrent grants according to need including travel expenses for hospital visiting of relatives, telephone installation for emergency help calls for people who are elderly and infirm, and Christmas grants to older people. Grants range from £50 to £250. The trust does not make loans, nor does it make grants where public funds are available unless they are considered inadequate.

Annual grant total: About £3,000 is given each year for educational and welfare purposes.

Applications: In writing to the correspondent. Applications are considered throughout the year and a simple means test questionnaire may be required by the applicant.

Correspondent: W T F Blakeley, Clerk, Thorn House, Saxtead Road, Dennington, Woodbridge, Suffolk IP13 8AP.

Dunwich

Dunwich Pension Charity

Eligibility: People in need who live in the parish of Dunwich.

Types of grants: One-off grants are usually of around £250. Christmas grants for fuel can be made, in the form of electricity stamps or coal. Other payments can be made for telephone bills, water and sewage charges, personal alarm rental, senior railcards, household energy efficiency surveys and pre-school children costs.

Annual grant total: Between £10,000 and £15,000 is given in grants each year.

Applications: In writing to the correspondent, including reasonable proof of need, hardship or distress. Applications can be made directly by the individual or through a third party and are considered at any time.

Correspondent: John W Saunders, The Old Smithy, Dursham Road, Westleton, Saxmundham, Suffolk IP17 3AX (01728 648259).

Earl Stonham

Earl Stonham Trust

Eligibility: People in need who live in the parish of Earl Stonham.

Types of grants: One-off grants in the range of £50 to £240.

Annual grant total: In 2000/01 the trust had an income of £3,300 and a total expenditure of £2,400. Relief-in-need grants to individuals totalled £240, with a further £380 being given to individuals in educational grants.

Applications: In writing to the correspondent, to be submitted either by the individual or through a social worker, citizen's advice bureau or other third party. Applications are considered in March, June, September and December.

Correspondent: S R M Wilson, College Farm, Forward Green, Stowmarket, Suffolk IP14 5EH.

Felixstowe

Alexandrine De La Roche Relief in Need Charity

Eligibility: Children and women in need who live in the urban district of Felixstowe.

Types of grants: One-off and recurrent grants according to need.

Annual grant total: In 2000 the trust had an income of £2,700 and no money was spent.

Applications: In writing to the correspondent.

Correspondent: Mrs Susan C Robinson, Clerk to the Charity, Town Hall, Felixstowe, Suffolk IP11 2AG (01394 282086).

Framlingham

The Florence Pryke Charity

Eligibility: People in need who live in the ecclesiastical parish of Framlingham.

Types of grants: One-off grants in the range of £30 and £50. Grants given include those for travel to hospital and medical care.

Annual grant total: In 2000/01 the charity had assets of £24,000, an income of £2,000 and an expenditure of £960. Relief-in-need grants to 24 individuals totalled £790.

Applications: In writing to the correspondent either directly by the individual or through a relevant third person. Applications are considered monthly.

Correspondent: Mrs B Hall, Llanelli, Saxted Road, Framlingham, Woodbridge, Suffolk IP13 9HF.

Gisleham

The Gisleham Relief in Need Charity

Eligibility: People in need who live in the parish of Gisleham.

Types of grants: Recurrent grants according to need, usually of £50 to £60 and occasional one-off grants for people in severe need. A luncheon club for the elderly is held at the local school once a month during term time. Those that are deemed not able to pay, are paid for by the trust.

Annual grant total: About £4,000.

Applications: In writing to the correspondent for consideration by a minimum of two trustees. Applications can be submitted directly by the individual, through a social worker, citizen's advice bureau or other welfare agency or through other third party such as a relative or a friend. Applications are considered in November.

Correspondent: Mrs E Rivett, 2 Mill Villas, Black Street, Gisleham, Lowestoft, Suffolk NR33 8EJ (01502 743189).

Gislingham

The Gislingham United Charity

Eligibility: People in need who live in Gislingham.

Types of grants: Usually one-off grants according to need towards, for example, the cost of hospital travel for older people, playgroup fees and for specific items or equipment. Grants usually range from £50 to £100. No regular payments are made.

Annual grant total: In 2001 the charities had assets of £34,000 and an income of £2,200. A total of £930 was distributed in six relief-in-need grants.

Applications: In writing to the correspondent. Applications should be submitted directly by the individual. They are considered on the third Friday of alternate months – January, March, May, July, September and November, although extra meetings may be called in urgent cases.

Correspondent: R Moyes, 37 Broadfields Road, Gislingham, Eye, Suffolk IP23 8HX (Tel & Fax: 01379 788105; e-mail: rmoye@onetel.net.uk).

Other information: The charity also gives educational grants and supports village organisations.

Halesworth

The Halesworth United Charities

Eligibility: People in need who live in the ancient parish of Halesworth.

Types of grants: One-off grants according to need. Recent examples include travel abroad for educational purposes, medical equipment or tools needed for a trade.

Annual grant total: In 1999/2000 the charities had an income of £1,200 and a total expenditure of £2,300.

Applications: In writing to the correspondent, directly by the individual or through a social worker, citizen's advice bureau or other welfare agency. Applications can be submitted at any time for consideration in January, July and December, or any other time if urgent.

Correspondent: Janet Staveley-Dick, Clerk, Messrs Rodwell & Co., 52 The Thoroughfare, Halesworth, Suffolk IP19 8AR (01986 872513; Fax: 01986 875484).

Kirkley

Kirkley Poor's Land Estate

Eligibility: Individuals in need who live in the parish of Kirkley.

Types of grants: One-off grants according to need.

Annual grant total: In 1999/2000 the trust's income was £63,000 and grants totalled £51,000, including £21,000 to individuals.

Applications: In writing to the correspondent.

Correspondent: Ian R Walker, Clerk, 4 Station Road, Lowestoft, Suffolk NR32 4QF (01502 514964).

Lakenheath

The Charities of George Goward & John Evans

Eligibility: People in need who live in the parish of Lakenheath in Suffolk only.

Types of grants: One-off grants according to need. No help is given for the relief of public funds.

Annual grant total: In 2001 the charities had assets of £250,000, an income of £12,000 and a total expenditure of £20,000. A total of £830 was distributed in three relief-in-need grants to individuals. Educational grants to 33 individuals totalled £6,500.

Applications: Applications must come through a social worker, citizen's advice bureau or other welfare agency and are considered in March and September. Grants are not made in cash, invoices are settled by the trust.

Correspondent: Mrs Mary Crane, 3 Roughlands, Lakenheath, Brandon, Suffolk IP27 9HA (01842 860445).

The Lakenheath Consolidated Charities

Eligibility: People over 65 in need who live in Lakenheath parish, Sedge Fen and Undley.

Types of grants: Usually one-off grants ranging from £30 to £40.

Annual grant total: In 2001 the sum of £11,000 was given in grants.

Applications: On a form available from the correspondent for consideration in November/December.

Correspondent: P Crane, Clerk, 28 Roughlands, Lakenheath, Suffolk IP27 9HA.

Lowestoft

The Lowestoft Church and Town Relief in Need Charity

Eligibility: People in need who live in the area of the old borough of Lowestoft.

Types of grants: One-off grants only ranging from £25 to £500 for items and services such as furniture, childcare costs, help for disabled people, debt relief, help with funeral costs and so on.

Annual grant total: In 2000/01 the trust had assets of £32,000, an income of £5,200. Total grant expenditure was £3,300.

Applications: In writing to the correspondent to be submitted either by the individual or through a social worker, citizen's advice bureau or other welfare agency.

Correspondent: John M Loftus, Clerk, Lowestoft Charity Board, 148 London Road North, Lowestoft, Suffolk NR32 1HF (01502 533000; Fax: 01502 533001).

The Lowestoft Fishermen's & Seafarers' Benevolent Society

Eligibility: Children and dependants of fishermen and seamen lost at sea from Lowestoft vessels, who are in need.

Types of grants: Monthly payments and one-off grants.

Annual grant total: About £30,000 a year.

Applications: In writing to the correspondent.

Correspondent: H G Sims, Secretary, Star Buildings, 10 Waverley Road, Lowestoft, Suffolk NR32 1BN (01502 574312; Fax: 01502 565752).

The Lowestoft Maternity & District Nursing Association

Eligibility: People in a nursing or caring profession and retired nurses/carers who live in the borough of Lowestoft and either (a) are retired and on a low income, (b) have a long-term disability or (c) are experiencing short-term hardship, usually through illness.

Types of grants: One-off and recurrent grants according to need, ranging from £30 to £100.

Annual grant total: About £1,700 is given in grants each year.

Applications: In writing to the correspondent through community nurses or carers. Applications are usually considered in October.

Correspondent: Mrs V A Holmes, 50 Somerleyton Road, Lowestoft NR32 4DR (01502 565818).

Other information: Grants can also be given to charitable organisations.

Melton

The Melton Trust

Eligibility: People living in Melton who are in need, hardship or distress.

Types of grants: One-off and recurrent grants according to need. All pensioners in the parish can receive Christmas grants.

Annual grant total: About £7,000.

Applications: The trust states that they 'don't want people to apply', but they 'try to give to everyone' (who is eligible).

Correspondent: David Petley, 1 St Johns Hill, Woodbridge, Suffolk IP12 1HS (01394 380584).

Other information: The trust also gives grants to organisations.

Mendlesham

Mendlesham Town Estate Charity

Eligibility: People who are elderly, disabled or otherwise in need, and who live in the parish of Mendlesham, Suffolk.

Types of grants: One-off grants towards heating, hospital visiting and associated special needs, including bereavement. Grants are in the range of £60 to £120.

Annual grant total: In 2001 the trust had an income of £4,700 and made grants to 38 individuals totalling £2,600.

Applications: In writing to the correspondent or any other trustee via a local church minister or similar third party.

Correspondent: Mrs P Colchester, Clerk, Ashes Farm, Mendlesham, Stowmarket, Suffolk IP14 5TE (Tel & Fax: 01449 766330).

Mildenhall

The Mildenhall Parish Charities

Eligibility: Pensioners and widows in need who live in the parish of Mildenhall.

Types of grants: One-off grants.

Annual grant total: In 2001 the charities had an income of £17,000 and a total expenditure of £22,000.

Applications: In writing to the correspondent either directly by the individual or a recognised third party. Applications are considered in May and October.

Correspondent: T Coombs, Clerk, 39 Mulberry Close, Mildenhall, Bury St Edmunds IP28 7LL.

Pakenham

The Pakenham Charities for the Poor

Eligibility: People in need who live in Pakenham.

Types of grants: One-off and recurrent grants, usually to older people, although other people can receive grants according to need. Grants range from £20 to £250.

Annual grant total: About £2,000 to £3,000 a year.

Applications: In writing to the correspondent either directly by the individual or through a friend or neighbour. Applications are considered in November.

Correspondent: Maggie Cohen, Clerk, 5 St Mary's View, Pakenham, Nr Bury St Edmunds, Suffolk IP31 2ND (01359 232965).

Other information: Grants are also made to organisations which benefit the elderly, the sick or the poor of the parish.

Reydon

The Reydon Trust

Eligibility: People in need who live in the parish of Reydon.

Types of grants: One-off and recurrent grants according to need. Grants have been given for travel expenses to hospital for treatment or visiting, school meals, college fees/travel, stairlift, powered wheelchair, Christmas hampers, fuel, cooking stove, medical supplies and equipment.

No grants can be given for the relief of rates, taxes or other funds but may be applied in supplementing relief or assistance provided out of public funds.

Annual grant total: In 2000/01 the trust had an income of £5,800 and a total expenditure of £5,500.

Applications: In writing to the correspondent. Applications can be submitted directly by the individual or through a third party. They are considered at any time.

Correspondent: H C A Freeman, 22 Kingfisher Crescent, Reydon, Southwold, Suffolk IP18 6XL (01502 723746).

Other information: The charity will also give donations or subscriptions to institutions or organisations which provide such items, services or facilities for people who are eligible.

Risby

The Risby Fuel Allotment

Eligibility: People in need who live in the parish of Risby.

Types of grants: Annual grants, primarily to buy winter fuel, although also for other needs.

Annual grant total: Around £9,000, with £3,000 being given in fuel grants.

Applications: In writing to the correspondent. Applications can be submitted by the individual and are considered in March and October.

Correspondent: Mrs P Wallis, 3 Woodland Close, Risby, Bury St Edmunds, Suffolk IP28 6QN (01284 810649).

Rushbrooke

Lord Jermyn's Charity

Eligibility: People in need who are over 60 and live in Rushbrooke.

Types of grants: One-off or recurrent grants according to need.

Annual grant total: In 2000/01 the trust had an income of £5,000 and £3,500 was given in grants to individuals in need.

Applications: In writing to the correspondent.

Correspondent: Mrs W Cooper, Estate Office, Rushbrooke, Bury St Edmunds, Suffolk IP30 0ED.

Stanton

The Stanton Poors' Estate Charity

Eligibility: People in need who live in the parish of Stanton, who are in receipt of statutory benefits. Grants are made to people on means-tested benefit such as Family Credit, Income Support, Job-Seekers Allowance, Rent Rebate or Housing Benefit. Grants can be made in special cases of need or hardship outside this criteria at the trustees' discretion.

Types of grants: Grants generally range between £40 and £90, although larger applications may be considered.

Annual grant total: In 1999/2000 the trust had assets of £7,200 and an income of £5,000. Total expenditure was £5,500, almost all of which was given in 66 grants.

Applications: In writing to the correspondent, for consideration in November.

Correspondent: G E Cawthorne, Hon. Treasurer, The Lodge, Stanton, Bury St Edmonds, Suffolk IP31 2DJ (Tel & Fax: 01359 250554).

Stowmarket

The Stowmarket Relief Trust

Eligibility: People in need who live in the town of Stowmarket. Also subject to the availability of income, people who live in the civil parishes of Stowupland, Creeting St Peter, Badley, Combs, Great Finborough, Onehouse, Haughley and Old Newton with Dagworth.

Applicants must have approached all sources of statutory benefit. People on Income Support will normally qualify. People in full-time paid employment will not normally qualify for assistance, but there are possible exceptions. People with substantial capital funds are also ineligible.

Types of grants: Normally one-off, but recurrent grants have been given in exceptional circumstances. Grants are available for virtually any purpose for which a need can be established. Examples of recent grants given include those for or towards: family and recuperative holidays; expenses to visit people in hospital; electricity or gas accounts; sewerage and water charges; council tax; rent arrears; buying or repairing electrical appliances; beds, bedding, clothing and footwear; adapting homes for disabled people; telephone installation charges and rental; wheelchairs for disabled people; and decorating or repairing houses/fixtures and medical aids. Grants range from £15 to £500.

Annual grant total: In 2000/01 the trust had assets of £915,000, an income of £52,000 and a total expenditure of £39,000. A total of £32,000 was distributed in 161 relief-in-need grants.

Applications: On a form available from the correspondent. Applications are accepted from organisations or individuals on behalf of the prospective beneficiary, who have knowledge of his/her needs and family and financial circumstances e.g. social worker, probation officer, citizen's advice bureau, doctor, welfare organisations etc. Applications are usually dealt with within 10 to 14 days of receipt.

Correspondent: C Hawkins, Kiln House, 21 The Brickfields, Stowmarket, Suffolk

IP14 1RZ (01449 674412; Fax: 01449 677595).

Other information: Grants are also given to other charities with similar aims.

Stutton

The Charity of Joseph Catt

Eligibility: People in need who live in the parish of Stutton only.

Types of grants: One-off grants and loans to help with fuel, hospital travel expenses, convalescent holidays, household goods and clothing. The maximum grant in 2001 was £1,800.

Annual grant total: In 2001 the trust had assets of £73,000, an income of £9,000 and a total expenditure of £7,000. Grants totalling £6,700 were given in eight grants, including grants for schoolchildren.

Applications: Applications can be submitted by the individual, or through a recognised referral agency (e.g. social worker, citizen's advice bureau or doctor) and are considered monthly. They can be submitted to the correspondent, or any of the trustees at any time, for consideration in May and November.

Correspondent: K R Bales, Chair, 34 Cattsfield, Stutton, Ipswich, Suffolk IP9 2SP (01473 830055).

Other information: The charity also supports local almshouses.

Sudbury

The Sudbury Municipal Charities

Eligibility: People in need who are aged 70 or over and live within the old borough boundaries of Sudbury.

Types of grants: Ascension day gifts for men and women aged 70 or over; Christmas day gifts for men aged 70 or over, and special consideration to one-off cases of hardship. Grants range from £100 to £300.

Annual grant total: In 2001 the trust had an income of £5,800; it gave £720 in Ascension Day gifts and £750 in Christmas Day gifts. A further £2,100 was given in grants to organisations.

Applications: To apply for an Ascension day gift, complete the application form that appears annually in the local free newspaper. For Christmas day gifts, reply in writing to the advertisement appearing in the local free newspaper.

Correspondent: A C Walters, Clerk, Longstop Cottage, The Street, Lawshall, Bury St Edmunds IP29 4QA (01284 828219).

Walberswick

The Walberswick Common Lands

Eligibility: People in need who live in Walberswick.

Types of grants: Grants include quarterly payments to 17 individuals, towards gardening, telephone rental and television licence payments and Christmas cash and vouchers. One-off grants are also made for larger items and other emergencies.

Annual grant total: In 2001 the charity had an income of £35,000 and a total expenditure of £36,000. The sum of £5,000 was distributed in relief-in-need grants. One educational grant totalled £660, whilst £18,000 was given to organisations.

Applications: In writing to the correspondent through a social worker, citizen's advice bureau or other welfare agency, or directly by the individual or through a relative or neighbour. Applications are considered in February, April, June, August, October and December.

Correspondent: Mrs Jayne Tibbles, Lima Cottage, Walberswick, Southwold, Suffolk IP18 6TN (01502 724448; Fax: 01502 722469).

Surrey

Banstead and District Benevolent Fund

Eligibility: People in need who live in Banstead, Burgh Heath or Woodmansterne.

Types of grants: One-off and recurrent grants according to need.

Annual grant total: In 2000/01 the trust's income was £3,600 and its total expenditure was £2,800.

Applications: In writing to the correspondent.

Correspondent: Edward J T Newcomb, 9 Chalmers Road, Banstead, Surrey SM7 3HF (01737 355612; Fax: 01737 370036).

John Beane's Eleemosynary Charity

Eligibility: People in need living in the administrative county of Surrey.

Types of grants: One-off or recurrent grants according to need.

Annual grant total: About £30,000 a year.

Applications: On a form available from the correspondent, submitted through a social worker, health visitor, citizen's advice bureau or other welfare agency.

Correspondent: B W France, PO Box 607, Guildford GU2 6WR (01483 822952).

The Bookhams, Fetcham & Effingham Nursing Association Trust

Eligibility: People in need who are sick, convalescent, disabled or infirm who live in Great Bookham, Little Bookham, Fetcham & Effingham.

Types of grants: Providing or paying for items, services or facilities which will alleviate the discomfort or assist the recovery of such people, where these facilities are not available from any other sources.

Annual grant total: About £7,000 a year.

Applications: Applications should be referred through medical or social services, not directly from the public.

Correspondent: Mrs M E Blow, Secretary, 1a Howard Road, Great Bookham, Leatherhead, Surrey KT23 4PW.

The Churt Welfare Trust

Eligibility: People in need, hardship and distress who live in the parish of Churt and its neighbourhood.

Types of grants: One-off grants according to need.

Annual grant total: In 2000/01 the trust had an income of £11,000 and a total expenditure of £16,000. The sum of £10,000 was given in grants to individuals and organisations.

Applications: In writing to the correspondent.

Correspondent: Mrs E Kilpatrick, Hale House, Hale House Lane, Churt, Farnham, Surrey GU10 2JQ (01428 712238).

The Cranleigh & District Nursing Association

Eligibility: People in need who are sick and poor and live in the parishes of Cranleigh and Ewhurst.

Types of grants: One-off and recurrent grants in the range of £20 to £500. Recent grants have been given towards carpets, phone rental, MedicAlert bracelets, chiropody, hospital visits and pavement vehicles.

Annual grant total: In 2001 the association had an income of £2,300 and gave 14 grants totalling £1,900. Assets amounted to £47,000.

Applications: In writing to the correspondent either directly by the individual or through a social worker, citizen's advice bureau or other welfare agency.

Correspondent: Mrs P H Gallagher, Secretary, The Slade, New Park Road, Cranleigh, Surrey GU6 7HN (01483 273193).

SOUTH EAST – SURREY

The Deakin Charitable Trust

Eligibility: People in need who live in Surrey, particularly Woking.

Types of grants: One-off and recurrent grants according to need.

Annual grant total: In 1999/2000 the trust had assets of £455,000 and an income of £43,000. Grants totalled £36,000, including £7,000 to individuals for relief-in-need purposes.

Applications: In writing to the correspondent.

Correspondent: W A Hodgetts, Herbert Parnell, Kingsway House, 123–125 Goldsworth Road, Woking, Surrey GU21 1LR.

Other information: This entry was not confirmed by the trust, but the information was correct according to the Charity Commission database.

The Dempster Trust

Eligibility: People in need, hardship or distress who live in Farnham and the general neighbourhood.

Types of grants: One-off grants or help for limited periods only. Grants have in the past been given towards nursing requisites, to relieve sudden distress, travelling expenses, fuel, television and telephone bills, clothing, washing machines, televisions, radios, alarm systems and so on. Grants range from £50 to £500. Help is not given towards rent, rates or house improvements.

Annual grant total: About £10,000 in more than 100 grants.

Applications: On a form available from the correspondent to be submitted through a doctor, social worker, hospital, citizen's advice bureau, or another welfare agency. Applications can be considered at any time.

Correspondent: Mrs J P Baker, Clerk, Stream Cottage, 73 Bridgefield, Farnham, Surrey GU9 8AW (01252 722826).

The Ewell Parochial Trusts

Eligibility: People in need who live, work or are being educated in the ancient ecclesiastical parish of Ewell and the liberty of Kingswood.

Types of grants: One-off or recurrent grants according to need.

Annual grant total: In 2001 the trust had an income of £60,000, it is not known how much of this was given in grants to individuals.

Applications: In writing to the correspondent. Applications which do not meet the above criteria will not be acknowledged.

Correspondent: Geoffrey Berry, 2 Portway Crescent, Ewell, Epsom, Surrey KT17 1SX (Tel & Fax: 020 8393 5979).

The Frimley Fuel Allotments Charity

Eligibility: People in need who live in the wards of Old-Dean Town, St Michaels, St Pauls, Watchetts, Frimley, Frimley-Green, Mytchett, Heatherside and Parkside. Priority is given to people who are elderly or disabled (physically or mentally) and those who care for them.

Types of grants: One-off grants ranging from £100 to £1,500 (average £300) generally given directly to people in need and not to organisations providing a service. Help has been given towards fuel bills, to enable 250 elderly people to live in their own homes, and to provide discretionary funds for head teachers for the direct benefit of pupils from poor families.

Annual grant total: In 1998 the charity had an income of £95,000. It spent £103,000, of which £82,000 was given in 350 grants to individuals in need.

Applications: On a form available from the citizen's advice bureau or from the social service centres. Applications should be returned to the respective social service centre by 15 November and can be made directly by the individual. Urgent applications can be considered at any time if supported by a vicar, parish priest, GP, Councillor, citizen's advice bureau, Social Services, district nurse or health visitor.

The charity employs no staff. Accurate and complete data on the form is essential.

Correspondent: Mrs Kim Murray, Hon. Secretary, 2a Hampshire Road, Camberley, Surrey GU15 4DW (01276 23958).

Other information: The trust's income is derived from the Pine Ridge Golf Centre, an 18-hole golf course and driving range developed on 164 acres of land leased from the charity trustees.

The trust also make grants to local scout groups, youth groups and cadets.

The trust also provides a useful 'Notes for applicants' on the back of the application form and a leaflet about the charity.

A book *200 Years of Frimley's History – The Story of Frimley Fuel Allotments Charity and Pine Ridge Golf Course* has just been published by Gordon Wellard, Camberley's historian. The book is available in local book shops and at the Golf Centre.

The Godstone United Charities

Eligibility: People in need who live in the local authority boundary of the parish of Godstone (Blindley Heath, South Godstone and Godstone Village).

Types of grants: Food vouchers are given in December and February. One-off payments are given mainly for urgent medical attention, though also towards, for example, school uniforms and household items such as cookers. Grants are in the range of £25 to £50.

Grants are not given to those who are in debt due to criminal activity or for any reasons other than unemployment or sickness.

Annual grant total: In 2001/02 the charities had an income of £9,500 and a total expenditure of £7,500. The sum of £4,600 was distributed in 85 grants.

Applications: In writing to the correspondent or through a relevant third party or a social worker, citizen's advice bureau or other welfare agency. Applications should include relevant details of income, outgoings, household composition and reason for request. They are considered in November and February.

Correspondent: Mrs P A Rodgers, Bassett, Oxted Road, Surrey RH9 8AD (01883 742625; Fax: 01883 744767).

Other information: The charities also give grants to local charities for the benefit of people who are elderly or disabled.

The Shere Charity for Relief-in-Need

Eligibility: People in need who live in the parish of Shere (this includes Gomshall, Peaslake and Holmbury St Mary).

Types of grants: One-off or recurrent grants according to need, where assistance cannot be obtained elsewhere.

Annual grant total: In 2000 the charity had an income of £14,000 and a total expenditure of £11,000.

Applications: On a form available from the correspondent. Applications can be submitted directly by the individual or through a third party on behalf of the individual. They are considered at any time.

Correspondent: R C Callingham, Clerk, 3 Pilgrims Way, Shere, Guildford, Surrey GU5 9HR (01483 202450).

The Henry Smith Charity

Eligibility: People in need who live in Camberley, Deepcut, Frimley, Frimley Green and Mytchett.

Types of grants: Usually one-off grants in the range of £100 to £300. Grants have been given for clothing, furniture and special needs equipment.

Annual grant total: In 1999/2000 the trust had an income of £1,100 and gave four grants to individuals totalling £900.

Applications: In writing to the correspondent either directly by the individual or through a social worker, citizen's advice bureau or other welfare agency.

Correspondent: R J Ivory, Clerk to the Trustees, Surrey Heath Borough Council, Surrey Heath House, Knoll Road, Camberley, Surrey GU15 3HD (01276 707315; Fax: 01276 707446; e-mail: borough_secretary@surreyheath.gov.uk; website: www.surreyheath.gov.uk).

SOUTH EAST – SURREY

The Henry Smith Charity

Eligibility: People in need who live, work or are being educated in the ancient ecclesiastical parish of Ewell and the liberty of Kingswood.

Types of grants: One-off or recurrent grants according to need.

Annual grant total: In 2001 the trust received £12,000, allocated by Henry Smith's (General Estate) Charity.

Applications: In writing to the correspondent. Applications which do not meet the above criteria will not be acknowledged.

Correspondent: G Berry, 2 Portway Crescent, Ewell, Epsom, Surrey KT17 1SX (Tel & Fax: 020 8393 5979).

The Henry Smith Charity

Eligibility: People in need who live in Ash and Normandy.

Types of grants: One-off or recurrent grants according to need.

Annual grant total: In 2001 the trust received £3,000 income, allocated by Henry Smith's (General Estate) Charity.

Applications: In writing to the correspondent, either directly by the individual or through a social worker, citizen's advice bureau or other welfare agency. Applications are considered as they arrive.

Correspondent: J G Ades, 87 Oxenden Road, Tongham, Surrey GU10 1AR (Tel & Fax: 01252 323909; e-mail: adesj@remote.guildford.gov.uk).

The Henry Smith Charity

Eligibility: Widows or people over 60 who are in need, of good character and have lived in the parishes of Long Ditton and Tolworth for the past five years.

Types of grants: Grants of £28 to be spent on coal, clothing and electricity bills at named retailers.

Annual grant total: In 2001/02 the charity had £3,000 available for grants, about £2,200 of which was actually given.

Applications: In writing to the correspondent. Applications are considered in December and January and must include details of the applicant's age and length of residence in the parish.

Correspondent: R L Howard, 4 Cholmley Terrace, Portsmouth Road, Thames Ditton, Surrey KT7 0XY (020 8398 6852).

The Henry Smith Charity

Eligibility: People in need who live in Send and Ripley, and have done so for five years.

Types of grants: One-off annual grants of £30 a year to around 50 or 60 in Send and a similar number in Ripley. Other grants are available from any remaining funds, and have included money towards a wheelchair for a disabled student.

Annual grant total: The annual income is about £4,000, all of which is available in grants.

Applications: In writing to the correspondent. Applications can be submitted directly by the individual, through a social worker, citizen's advice bureau or any other welfare agency or third party on behalf of the individual. Applications are considered as they arrive.

Correspondent: G A Richardson, Emali, 2 Rose Lane, Ripley, Surrey GU23 6NE (01483 225322).

The Henry Smith Charity

Eligibility: People in need who live in Albury, including Farley Green and Little London.

Types of grants: One-off or recurrent grants according to need.

Annual grant total: In 1993 the trust received £3,600 income, allocated by Henry Smith's (Warbleton Estate) Charity.

Applications: In writing to the correspondent.

Correspondent: Revd Ken Hobbs, Yeoman's Acre, Farley, Guildford GU5 9DN (01483 202165).

Other information: We were unable to contact this trust. This information was included in the last edition of the guide.

The Henry Smith Charity

Eligibility: People in need who live in Puttenham and Wanborough parishes.

Types of grants: One-off or recurrent grants ranging from £30 to £45. Grants are not given to people who are working or who own their house.

Annual grant total: The charity receives around £1,000 a year, allocated by Henry Smith's (General Estate) Charity. In 2001 it gave £900 in grants to individuals.

Applications: In writing to the correspondent, submitted in October for consideration in November.

Correspondent: David Knapp, No 2 Old School House, School Hill, Seale, Surrey GU10 1HY (01483 887772; Fax: 01483 887757; e-mail: dsk@hartbrown.co.uk).

Other information: Grants are also given for the benefit of the parish as a whole.

The Henry Smith Charity (I Wood Estate)

Eligibility: People over 60 who are in need and live in Chertsey, Addlestone, New Haw and Lyne, Surrey.

Types of grants: Recurrent fuel vouchers of £35 to older people in need which can be used as part payment of fuel bills.

Annual grant total: In 2000/01 the trust had an income of £19,000, allocated by Henry Smith's (General Estate) Charity. All of this was given in 548 donations.

Applications: In writing to the correspondent either through a social worker, citizen's advice bureau or other third party or directly by the individual. Applications can be considered at any time during the year.

Correspondent: B A Fleckney, c/o Committee Section, Civic Offices, Runnymede Borough Council, Station Road, Addlestone, Surrey KT15 2AH (01932 425620).

The Surrey Association for Visual Impairment

Eligibility: People who are blind or partially-sighted and who live in the administrative county of Surrey.

Types of grants: One-off grants for most kind of need. General grants have a set maximum of £500 but most are much lower than this. Grants are given for equipment required to overcome a sight problem or a sudden domestic need. Interest-free loans are occasionally made.

Annual grant total: In 2000/01 the association had an income of £997,000 and a total expenditure of £805,000. Relief-in-need grants were made to 70 individuals totalling £6,800.

Applications: On a form available from the correspondent. Applications can be submitted at any time by the individual or through a social worker, welfare agency, club or any recognised organisation for blind or partially-sighted people. Priority will be given where income support is being received or, in the case of clubs, low income prevents service delivery.

Correspondent: Lance Clarke, Chief Executive, Rentwood, School Lane, Fetcham, Surrey KT22 9JX (01372 377701; Fax: 01372 360767; e-mail: lclarke@svab.org.uk; website: www.surreywebsight.org.uk).

The Windlesham United Charities & Poors Allotment Charities

Eligibility: People in need living in the parishes of Bagshot, Lightwater and Windlesham.

Types of grants: One-off grants mainly in the form of small heating grants.

Annual grant total: In 2000 the trust had an income of £36,000, its total expenditure was £29,000 and it made grants to individuals in need totalling £5,400.

Applications: In writing to the correspondent at any time. Applications should include full particulars.

Correspondent: Mrs D V Christie, Clerk to the Trustees, 67 Keswick Drive, Lightwater, Surrey GU18 5XE (01276 471140; Fax: 01276 489335).

Other information: This entry was not confirmed by the trust, but the

SOUTH EAST – SURREY

information was correct according to the Charity Commission file.

Witley Charitable Trust

Eligibility: Children and young people aged under 20 and older people aged over 60 who are in need and who live in the parishes of Witley and Milford.

Types of grants: One-off grants of £20 to £300, towards, for example, telephone, electricity and gas debts (up to about £150) usually paid via social services, and medical appliances not available through the Health Service. At Christmas about 25 grants/hampers are given. Grants are also given for educational purposes and to organisations.

The trust does not give loans or to people who should be supported by statutory services.

Annual grant total: In 2001 the trust had assets of £26,000 and an income of £3,300. £2,000 was spent in the year, all of this was distributed in 32 relief-in-need and educational grants to individuals.

Applications: In writing to the correspondent, to be submitted through nurses, doctors, social workers, the clergy, citizen's advice bureaux etc. but not directly by the individual. Applications are usually considered in February and September, although emergency applications can be considered throughout the year.

Correspondent: Daphne O'Hanlon, Triados, Waggoners Way, Grayshott, Hindhead, Surrey GU26 6DX (01428 604679).

The Wonersh Charities

Eligibility: People in need who live in the parish of Wonersh, Shamley Green and Blackheath. (There is a preference for elderly people.)

Types of grants: A cash grant of £75 is given to each of the named people at Christmas. One-off grants are also available.

Annual grant total: Each year about £4,000 is received from Henry Smith's (General Estate) Charity, most of which is given in grants.

Applications: In writing to the correspondent preferably through a third party such as a citizen's advice bureau, trustee of the charity, local clergy or other organisation. Applications are usually considered in early July and early December.

Correspondent: Mrs Juliet Cummings, Arthur's Cottage, Shamley Green, Guildford, Surrey GU5 0UP.

Abinger

The Henry Smith Charity

Eligibility: People in need who live in the ancient parish of Abinger.

Types of grants: One-off or recurrent grants according to need.

Annual grant total: In 2000 the trust had an income of £10,000 and a total expenditure of £13,000, of which £12,000 was distributed in about 45 grants.

Applications: In writing to the correspondent.

Correspondent: Mrs L Childs, 6 Wellers Court, Shere, Surrey GU5 9JU (01483 203431).

Other information: Grants are also made to organisations with similar objects.

Alford

The Alfold Smith's Charity

Eligibility: People in need, generally people of pensionable age, who live in Alfold and have done so for at least five years.

Types of grants: Vouchers for the village shop worth £30 to £40, usually given at Christmas.

Annual grant total: £2,000, allocated by Henry Smith's (General Estate) Charity.

Applications: The correspondent states that 'no application necessary' as the committee and trustees know the eligible people from the village.

Correspondent: Mrs L Enticknap, Sethern, Rams Lane, Dunsfold, Godalming, Surrey GU8 4NR.

Other information: This entry was not confrmed by the charity, but the address was correct according to the Charity Commission database.

Ashford

Ashford Relief in Need Charities

Eligibility: People in need who live in the ancient parish of Ashford.

Types of grants: One-off grants according to need.

Annual grant total: In 2000/01 the trust's income was £6,900 and its total expenditure was £8,700. Grants to individuals in need totalled £3,700, and a further £5,000 was given in grants for other purposes.

Applications: In writing to the correspondent at any time, including the usual income of the applicant, his or her age and details of any disabilities or health problems. Applications can be made either directly by the individual, or through a third party such as a social worker, citizen's advice bureau or relative.

Correspondent: Charles Merry, 47 Manor Road, Ashford, Middlesex TW15 2SL (01784 252393; Fax: 01784 246309).

Banstead and Kingswood

The Banstead United Charities

Eligibility: People in need who live in the ancient parish of Banstead and Kingswood.

Types of grants: One-off grants, usually up to £500. Grants have been given towards funeral expenses, equipment for people who are disabled, travel for hospital treatment and rehabilitation, children's clothing and a small number of educational grants.

Annual grant total: About £3,500.

Applications: In writing to the correspondent. Applications can be submitted directly by the individual or through a social worker, citizen's advice bureau or other welfare agency. They are considered throughout the year.

Correspondent: Bryan Wright, Heath Dene, 20 Tadworth Street, Tadworth KP20 5RN (01737 351982).

Betchworth

Betchworth United Charities & Henry Smith Charity

Eligibility: Strictly limited to people in need who live in the ancient parish of Betchworth (which includes the parish of Brockham). People living off private pensions are not eligible (unless the amount received is nominal).

Types of grants: Up to £100 in recurrent grants, also grocery, fuel or clothing vouchers worth around £60 to £75.

Annual grant total: In 2001 the trust had an income exceeding £10,000, most of which was given in grants to individuals.

Applications: In writing to the correspondent to be submitted by a third party, such as a shopkeeper, doctor, minister or social worker. Applications are consider twice a year in May and November.

Correspondent: Mrs V F Houghton, Clerk, Brick Field, 20 Kiln Lane, Betchworth, Surrey RH3 7LX (01737 843342).

Bisley

The Henry Smith Charity

Eligibility: People in need who live in Bisley and have done so for at least three years.

Types of grants: Vouchers to assist with food cost are distributed twice a year (£20 at Christmas and £100 in February) for use in local shops.

No grants are given to single people earning over £6,000 per year, or couples earning over £10,000 per year.

Annual grant total: In 2001 the charity had an income of £1,000 and a total expenditure of £960.

Applications: On a form available from the correspondent to be submitted directly by the individual. Applications should be received by 31 December, for consideration in January.

Correspondent: A J Harris, 21 Cobbetts Walk, Bisley, nr Woking, Surrey GU24 9DT (01483 476637).

Bletchingley

The Bletchingley United Charities

Eligibility: People in need who live in the parish of Bletchingley.

Types of grants: One-off grants in the range of £20 to £200. Donations have been given for: clothing; food; medical equipment; gas, electricity and telephone bills; and essential equipment, such as cookers and fridges. Grants are not given for rates, taxes or other public funds.

Annual grant total: In 2000/01 the trust had an income of £9,700 and a total expenditure of £10,000. Grants totalling £6,400 were made to 172 individuals.

Applications: In writing to the correspondent at any time, through a social worker, citizen's advice bureau or other welfare agency.

Correspondent: Mrs C A Bolshaw, Cleves, Castle Street, Bletchingley, Surrey RH1 4QA (01883 743000; Fax: 01883 744788); or D Martin, 94 High Street, Bletchingley, Surrey (01883 743144).

Other information: Care organisations working locally are also considered.

Bramley

The Henry Smith Charity

Eligibility: People in need who live in the parish of Bramley, Surrey.

Types of grants: One-off grants according to need.

Annual grant total: The income is normally about £2,400, allocated by Henry Smith's (General Estate) Charity.

Applications: In writing to the correspondent, there are no application forms. The letter should contain as much information as possible about why support is required and why the person has been unable to manage this him/herself.

Correspondent: D Morley, Clerk to Bramley Parish Council, Village Hall, Hall Road, Bramley, Surrey GU5 DAX (01483 894138).

Byfleet

The Byfleet United Charities

Eligibility: People in need who have lived in the parish of Byfleet (as it was on 1 November 1918) for at least one year before applying.

Types of grants: Monthly pensions of £86 a household. One-off grants can also be given to individuals or families for items such as cookers, heaters, vacuum cleaners, nursery schools fees etc.

Annual grant total: In 2001 the trust had an income of £239,000, and gave £243,000 in pensions and £43,000 in grants to individuals.

Applications: By letter or telephone to the correspondent. Applicants will be visited and assessed.

Correspondent: The Administrator, Stoop Court, Leisure Lane, West Byfleet, Surrey KT14 6HF (01932 340943; Fax: 01932 340532).

Other information: This charity is an amalgamation of smaller charities, including the Byfleet Pensions Fund. The charity also gives money to local charities who work in a similar field.

Capel

The Henry Smith Charity

Eligibility: People in need who live in Capel parish, with a preference for older people.

Types of grants: Christmas bonuses of vouchers for the local store.

Annual grant total: The trust receives an income from the Henry Smith's (General Estate) Charity. In 2001 the sum of £2,200 was given in grants.

Applications: In writing to the correspondent.

Correspondent: Mrs J Richards, Old School House, Coldharbour, Dorking, Surrey RH5 6HF (01306 711885).

Charlwood

John Bristow and Thomas Mason Trust

Eligibility: People who are in need, hardship or distress, or are sick, convalesent, disabled or infirm who live in the parish of Charlwood as constituted on 17 February 1926.

Types of grants: Grants given include those for: the annual service charge for community alarms for older people; riding lessons for individuals who are disabled; and new shoes for a child.

Annual grant total: in 2001 the trust had assets of £2 million and an income of £69,000. Total expenditure on grants was £38,000 with three relief-in-need grants totalling £750. A further £4,800 was given in educational grants and £33,000 to organisations.

Applications: On a form available from the correspondent. Applications can be submitted directly by the individual or through another third party on behalf of the individual. They are considered at any time.

Correspondent: Mrs P J Assender, Trust Secretary, 54 Churchfield Road, Reigate, Surrey RH2 9RH (Tel & Fax: 01737 226008).

Other information: This trust is an amalgamation of the Thomas Alexander Mason Trust and Revd John Bristow's Charity.

Smith & Earles Charity

Eligibility: Disabled people or those over 65 and in need who live in the old parish of Charlwood.

Types of grants: One-off and recurrent grants from £70 upwards towards food and fuel.

Annual grant total: In 2000/01 the charity had an income of £5,700. It spent £5,200 and £3,800 was given in 62 grants to individuals.

Applications: On a form available from the correspondent. Applications for one-off (usually larger) grants should be submitted through a recognised referral agency (e.g. social worker, citizen's advice bureau or other welfare agency). Applications for recurrent grants can be submitted directly by the individual. They are considered in November. Details of any disability or special need should be given.

Correspondent: Robin Pacey, Ivy Cottage, Russ Hill Road, Charlwood, Horley, Surrey RH6 0EJ (01293 863933).

Other information: Help is also given towards the hiring of halls for meetings for older people, hospices and school requirements.

Cheam

Cheam Consolidated Charities

Eligibility: People in need who live in Cheam.

Types of grants: One-off and recurrent grants, of £50 to £200.

Annual grant total: In 2001 the trust had an income of £6,000 and a total expenditure of £5,600. A total of £3,000 was given to individuals with a further £2,600 going to organisations.

Applications: In writing to the correspondent, for consideration in May and November. Applications can be made either directly by the individual, or via a social worker, citizen's advice bureau or other welfare agency.

Correspondent: Mrs P Shaw-Davis, Secretary, 55c North Street, Carshalton, Surrey SM5 2HG (020 8669 1039).

Chertsey

The Chertsey Combined Charity

Eligibility: People in need who live in the electoral divisions of the former urban district of Chertsey.

Types of grants: Grants are given in the form of fuel vouchers, Christmas grants and one-off grants.

Annual grant total: In 1999/2000 the trust had an income of £51,000 and its expenditure was £35,000. Grants were given for educational and welfare purposes.

Applications: On a form available from the correspondent.

Correspondent: M R O Sullivan, Secretary, PO Box 89, Weybridge, Surrey KT13 8HW.

Other information: This entry was not confirmed by the trust, but was correct according to information on file at the Charity Commission.

Chessington

The Chessington Charities

Eligibility: People in need who live in the parish of St Mary the Virgin, Chessington.

Types of grants: Recent grants included those given to older people (with low income) at Christmas; grants for special food; grants for furniture and grants for cookers. Grants are given in the range of £30 to £200 and are usually one-off.

Grants are not given 'as a dole', or to pay debts.

Annual grant total: In 2001 the charities had assets of £42,000, an income of £4,000 and a total expenditure of £3,800. A total of 51 relief-in-need grants were made to individuals totalling £2,700.

Applications: On a form available from the correspondent to be submitted either directly by the individual or through a social worker, citizen's advice bureau or other agency. Christmas gifts are distributed in November. Other applications are considered throughout the year. A home visit will be made by a trustee to ascertain details of income and expenditure and to look at the need.

Correspondent: Mrs A M Hollis, 26 Bolton Road, Chessington, Surrey KT9 2JB (020 8397 4733).

Other information: Grants are also given to local organisations which help people who are elderly or disabled e.g. Chessington Voluntary Care, Arthritis Care.

Chobham

Henry Smith Charity

Eligibility: People in need who live in the ancient parish of Chobham only, which includes the civil parishes of Chobham and West End.

Types of grants: Vouchers of £20 to £30 to be exchanged for goods in local shops are given to over 200 people at the annual distribution.

Annual grant total: In 2000/01 the charity had an income of £5,000 and a total expenditure of £5,200.

Applications: On a form available from the correspondent for consideration in January.

Correspondent: R V Steer, 37 Cedar Close, Bagshot, Surrey GU19 5AB (01276 473689).

Chobham & West End

The Chobham Poor Allotment Charity

Eligibility: People in need who live in the ancient parish of Chobham which includes civil parishes of Chobham and West End.

Types of grants: Grants are given in the form of vouchers of between £25 and £45, as payment towards fuel bills, solid fuel, and equipment for people who are disabled.

Annual grant total: In 2000/01 the charity had an income of £55,000 and a total expenditure of £64,000. About £20,000 is given to individuals.

Applications: On a form available from the correspondent. Applications should be submitted directly by the individual at any time.

Correspondent: Jenny Ellis, 6 Ashley Way, West End, Surrey GU24 9NJ (01483 475548).

Other information: Grants are also made to organisations which benefit the local community.

Crowhurst

Crowhurst Relief-in-Need Charities

Eligibility: People in need or distress, especially the elderly, disabled and unemployed who live in Crowhurst (Surrey).

Types of grants: One-off grants mainly to help with fuel bills and travel to or from hospital, usually ranging from £100 to £150. A grant of £250 was given to the parents of a severely ill young child to help with transport and other costs.

Annual grant total: In 2000/01 the trust had assets of £1,000, an income of £2,300 and a total expenditure of £2,500. Grants to 12 individuals were made totalling £1,800.

Applications: On a form available from the correspondent, submitted directly by the individual, for consideration mainly in November, but requests are considered at any time of the year.

Correspondent: Mrs P Cook, Church Farm Cottage, Crowhurst, Lingfield, Surrey RH7 6LR (01342 834121).

Other information: Grants are also given to local charities with similar objects.

Dorking

The Dorking Charity

Eligibility: People in need who live in the old parish of Dorking.

Types of grants: One-off or recurrent grants have been given to single parents and pensioners who are receiving benefits, for repairs, bills and heating costs.

Annual grant total: Around £450.

Applications: In writing to the correspondent either directly by the individual or through a third party. Applications are considered at any time.

Correspondent: D Matanle, Homefield, 5 Fortyfoot Road, Leatherhead, Surrey KT22 8RP (01372 370073; Fax: 01372 361466; e-mail: luchar@btinternet.com).

Dunsfold

The Henry Smith Charity (Dunsfold)

Eligibility: People in need who live in Dunsfold and who have done so for the past five years.

Types of grants: Grocery vouchers for £40 to £50 exchangeable in the village store.

Annual grant total: Around £2,000.

Applications: In writing to the correspondent. They are considered in December.

Correspondent: Mrs L Enticknap, Sethern, Rams Lane, Dunsfold, Godalming, Surrey GU8 4NR.

Other information: This entry was not confrmed by the charity, but the address was correct according to the Charity Commission database.

East and West Horsley

Lady Noel Byron's Nursing Association

Eligibility: People in need of medical or welfare assistance who live in the parishes of East and West Horsley.

Types of grants: One-off or recurrent grants according to need for medical or welfare related purposes only. This has included grants towards holidays, equipment and such like.

Annual grant total: In 2000/01 the association had an income of £2,500 and a total expenditure of £1,800. Grants are made to organisations and individuals.

Applications: In writing to the correspondent. Applications can be made directly by the individual or through a social worker, other welfare agency or third party. They are considered at any time.

Correspondent: J R Miles, Postboys, Cranmore Lane, West Horsley, Leatherhead, Surrey KT24 6BX.

Other information: This entry was not confirmed by the association but the address was correct according to the Charity Commission database.

The Henry Smith Charity

Eligibility: People in need who live in West Horsley.

Types of grants: One-off or recurrent grants according to need.

Annual grant total: About £800 a year.

Applications: In writing to the correspondent.

Correspondent: Mrs Mollie Lewendon, Secretary, Lansdowne, Silkmore Lane, West Horsley, Surrey KT24 6JB (01483 284167).

Henry Smith's Charity

Eligibility: People in need who have lived in East Horsley for at least two years and are disabled or in need.

Types of grants: One-off or recurrent grants according to need.

Annual grant total: The trust receives about £1,000 a year, allocated by Henry Smith's (General Estate) Charity.

Applications: In writing to the correspondent at any time. The main meeting is held in November/December, but applications are considered at any time.

Correspondent: Mrs A Jackson, Sable Lodge, Pine Walk, East Horsley, Surrey KT24 5AG (01483 281148).

East Molesey

The Henry Smith Charity

Eligibility: People in need who live in the parish of St Mary, East Molesey.

Types of grants: One-off grants are given, including those for the care of children, support for parents and travel for people who are elderly.

Annual grant total: In 2001 the charity had an income of £800; the sum of £250 was given in one grant.

Applications: In writing to the correspondent through a social worker, citizen's advice bureau or other welfare agency. They are considered at any time.

Correspondent: Revd Don J Adams, The Vicarage, St Mary's Road, East Molesey, Surrey KT8 0ST (Tel & Fax: 020 8979 1441).

Other information: The charity also gives grants to local organisations which assist individuals in the area of benefit.

The Henry Smith Charity

Eligibility: People who are in need in East Molesey St Paul.

Types of grants: Grants according to need

Annual grant total: Between £800 and £900.

Applications: In writing to the correspondent.

Correspondent: E Mallett, 20 Walton Road, East Molesey, Surrey KT8 0DF (020 8979 6446).

Effingham

The Henry Smith Charity

Eligibility: People in need who live in Effingham.

Types of grants: One-off or recurrent grants according to need. Grants are generally of £50 to £100; many grants are given at Christmas.

Annual grant total: About £2,000 divided between 20 to 30 people.

Applications: In writing to the correspondent.

Correspondent: C E W Crouch, 85 Woodlands Road, Little Bookham, Leatherhead, Surrey KT23 4HL (01372 452232).

Egham

The Egham United Charity

Eligibility: People in need who live in the ancient parish of Egham.

Types of grants: One-off grants to alleviate immediate need.

Annual grant total: About £10,000 a year.

Applications: On a form available from the correspondent, submitted directly by the individual or through an appropriate third party. Applications are considered every six weeks.

Correspondent: Ann Brown, The Moorings, 6 Riverside, Egham, Surrey TW20 0AA (01784 472742).

Epsom

Epsom Parochial Charities

Eligibility: People in need who live in the ancient parish of Epsom.

Types of grants: One-off grants ranging from £100 to £500 according to need. Grants given included those for clothing, food, medical care and equipment and household appliances.

Annual grant total: In 2000 the charities gave six relief-in-need grants to individuals totalling £1,000.

Applications: On a form available from the correspondent. Applications can be submitted by the individual or through a social worker, citizen's advice bureau or other welfare agency. They are usually considered in March, June, September and December but should be submitted in the preceding month.

Correspondent: Mrs M West, Clerk to the Trustees, 38 Woodcote Hurst, Epsom, Surrey KT18 7DT (01372 721335; Fax: 01372 748665).

Other information: Grants totalling £1,000 were made to local organisations in 2000.

Esher

The Henry Smith Charity

Eligibility: People in need who live in the ancient parish of Esher.

Types of grants: Annual grants of around £60 towards fuel bills for elderly or sick people or families with young children who are living on low pensions or Income Support. Emergency grants of up to £200 towards, for example, nursery school fees, renovation of a bathroom and gas bill arrears.

Annual grant total: The trust has an income of about £2,000, allocated by Henry Smith's (General Estate) Charity, all of which is given in grants.

Applications: In writing to the correspondent through a social worker, citizen's advice bureau or other third party. Details of the applicant's financial circumstances should be included. Annual grants are considered in December, emergency grants at any time.

Correspondent: Mrs G B Barnett, Clerk, 24 Pelhams Walk, Esher KT10 8ED (01372 465755).

Gatton

The Henry Smith Charity

Eligibility: People in need who live in the parish of Gatton.

Types of grants: One-off grants for help with fuel costs, respite care, bedding, clothing, tools of the trade for apprentices and educational grants. Christmas bonuses are also available, traditionally in the form of food vouchers although this is being phased out due to a lack of stores who accept them. Grants are not given for rates or taxes.

Annual grant total: The trust receives £2,300 income, allocated by Henry Smith's (Worth Estate) Charity. However, the charity receives more money than it can give in grants and always has much more money available.

Applications: In writing to the correspondent either directly or through a third party such as a doctor, minister of religion, councillor etc. Applications are generally considered twice a year, but urgent applications can be considered within four weeks. The charity advertises before Christmas, whilst the trustees are well known within the community and know of people who are in need.

Correspondent: M S Blacker, Chair, 6a Orpin Road, Merstham, Surrey RH1 3EZ.

Other information: This entry was not confirmed by the charity but the address was correct according to the Charity Commission.

Godalming

The Margaret Jeannie Hindley Charitable Trust

See entry on page 108

Guildford

The Guildford Aid in Sickness Fund

Eligibility: Sick or disabled people who are recognised as being in need and who live in the borough of Guildford as constituted prior to 31 March 1974.

Types of grants: One-off grants between £100 and £400 for: convalescent holidays; clothing; furniture for people who are mentally illl and moving into the community; and medical appliances not available through the NHS.

Annual grant total: In 2000 the fund had assets of £131,000, an income of £4,100 and a total expenditure of £3,500, all of which was given in 25 grants to individuals in need.

Applications: On a form available from the correspondent either directly by the individual, through a social worker, citizen's advice bureau or other welfare agency, or through a friend or relative. Applications are considered every month.

Correspondent: C E Fullagar, 56 Quarry Street, Guildford, Surrey GU1 3UE (Tel & Fax: 01483 533184).

The Guildford Poyle Charities

Eligibility: People in need who live in the borough of Guildford as constituted prior to 31 March 1974.

Types of grants: Mainly one-off grants between £60 to £250 for clothing, food, furniture, floor coverings, holidays and other necessities.

Debts are paid, but only when circumstances are extreme.

Annual grant total: In 2000 the charities had assets of £1.2 million, an income of £55,000 and an expenditure of £56,000. A total of £38,000 was given in 251 grants to individuals in need.

Applications: On a form available from the correspondent directly by the individual or through a social worker, citizen's advice bureau or other welfare agency or through a relative or friend. Applications are considered every month.

Correspondent: C E Fullagar, 56 Quarry Street, Guildford, Surrey GU1 3UE (Tel & Fax: 01483 533184).

The Mayor of Guildford's Christmas & Local Distress Fund

Eligibility: People in need who live in the borough of Guildford.

Types of grants: One-off grants according to need. Grants are limited to £100.

Annual grant total: In 2000/01 the fund had an income of £12,000 and a total expenditure of £16,000. Over £10,000 is given in grants each year.

Applications: In writing to the correspondent either through a social worker, citizen's advice bureau or another welfare agency or through a doctor or a relevant third party.

Correspondent: The Mayor's Secretary, Millmead House, Millmead, Guildford, Surrey GU2 5BB (01483 444041).

Hambledon

The Henry Smith Charity

Eligibility: Older people in need who live in Hambledon.

Types of grants: Grocery vouchers at Christmas, of around £35 per household.

Annual grant total: In 2001 the trust had an income of £830 and made 24 grants totalling £860.

Applications: In writing to the correspondent.

Correspondent: Jane Woolley, Clerk, Hambleton Parish Council, Cobblers, Hambledon, Godalming, Surrey GU8 4HL (01428 684213; e-mail: jane.woolley1@btopenworld.com).

Hascombe

The Henry Smith Charity

Eligibility: People in need, generally pensioners who live in Hascombe. The trustees will consider giving grants to other residents of Hascombe in cases of real need or emergency whatever their age and not necessarily only at Christmas.

Types of grants: Generally grants are given at Christmas of £50 each.

Annual grant total: The trust receives an income of £1,200 each year, allocated by the Henry Smith's (General Estate) Charity, plus the interest on the capital.

Applications: In writing to the correspondent.

Correspondent: Mrs Lynn Enticknap, Sethern, Rams Lane, Dunsfold, Surrey GU8 4NR (01483 200532).

Other information: This correspondent is also connected with The Henry Smith Charities in Alfold and Dunsfold.

Headley

The Henry Smith Charity

Eligibility: People in need who live in the parish of Headley.

Types of grants: One-off and recurrent grants are available to help with electricity, groceries, TV licences and hospital travel. They can be given in vouchers or cash and average £70.

Annual grant total: In 2000/01 the charity had an income of £4,700 and gave grants totalling £2,700. A further £150 was given in educational grants.

Applications: In writing directly by the individual to the correspondent or any trustee, giving the reasons for making the application. Applications are considered in October/November or any time if urgent.

Correspondent: Mrs Yvonne Stovell, 8 Broome Close, Headley, Epsom, Surrey KT18 6LW (01372 377353).

Other information: Grants are also made to university students and organisations.

Horley and Salfords

The Henry Smith Charity

Eligibility: Single people and married couples aged 75 or over and who have lived in the parish of Horley and Salfords for a minimum of 25 years.

Types of grants: Christmas bonuses are given as vouchers for Waitrose Ltd at the start of December.

Annual grant total: In 2001 the sum of £5,700 was given in grants.

Applications: On a form, to be collected from The Help Shop, Consort Way, Horley. Application forms are available from early November.

Correspondent: Miss A Middlecote, Clerk, Eton Chambers, 95 Victoria Road, Horley, Surrey RH6 7QH (01293 782425; Fax: 01293 775833).

Other information: Grants of £100 are also given to first year students for books, usually to two or three students a year.

Horne

The Henry Smith Charity

Eligibility: People in need who have lived in the ancient parish (i.e. the old boundaries) of Horne for at least one year.

Types of grants: One-off grants are available, although recurrent grants can be considered. Group applications are not considered.

Annual grant total: The trust receives an income of about £6,000 each year, allocated by Henry Smith's (General Estate) Charity.

Applications: On a form available from Trustees Henry Smith Charity at Yew Tree House. Applications can be submitted either directly by the individual or through a social worker and should include details of the applicant's level of income; they are available in April and October for consideration in May and November (meetings are held around three weeks after notices are posted within the parish).

Correspondent: Mrs Pam Bean, Hon. Secretary, Yew Tree Cottage, Smallfield Road, Horne, Horley, Surrey RH6 9JP (01342 843173).

Horsell

The Henry Smith Charity

Eligibility: People in need who live in the parish of Horsell. Most support is given to older members of the parish.

Types of grants: The trust distributes cash grants (typically £40) to assist with food, clothing and domestic bills.

Annual grant total: In 2001 the trust had an income of £1,100. A total of £1,200 was given in 25 grants to individuals.

Applications: In writing to the correspondent. Applications can be made directly by the individual or through a social worker, citizen's advice bureau or other welfare agency or third party e.g. vicar. They are usually considered in December.

Correspondent: R E Jarvis, Lyndhurst Lodge, Ridgeway, Horsell, Woking, Surrey GU21 4QR (01483 762064).

Kingston-upon-Thames

Ann Elizabeth Savage's General Charities

Eligibility: Mainly widows in need who live in the borough of Kingston-upon-Thames.

Types of grants: Mainly recurrent grants.

Annual grant total: In 2001 the trust gave grants to 12 widows totalling £1,200. Other grants totalled £800 and were made to local groups.

Applications: The trustees usually support individuals known via their contacts at All Saints Parish Church in Kingston-upon-Thames. It is unlikely grants would be available to support unsolicited applications.

Correspondent: Mrs Rosemary Gout, 19 Fairfield East, Kingston-upon-Thames, Surrey KT1 2PT.

Leatherhead

The Leatherhead United Charities

Eligibility: People in need who live in the area of the former Leatherhead urban district council.

Types of grants: One-off grants towards heating bills for older people, unexpected expenditure (e.g. damage caused by fire/flooding) and children's clothing. Pensions are also given.

Annual grant total: About £10,000 is given in welfare and educational grants. A further £40,000 is given in pensions.

Applications: On a form available from the correspondent and submitted through a recognised referral agency (e.g. social worker, citizen's advice bureau or doctor) giving details of income and the names of two referees. Applications are considered throughout the year.

Correspondent: David Mantale, Homefield, 5 Fortyfoot Road, Leatherhead, Surrey KT22 8RP (01372 370073).

Leigh

The Henry Smith Charity

Eligibility: People in need who live in Leigh.

Types of grants: The trust has a list of all people over 65; each receives support at Christmas in the form of food vouchers, or help with gas and electricity. Gifts may also be given at Easter in the years when the trust receives more income.

Annual grant total: In 2000/01 the trust had an income and total expenditure of £4,600.

Applications: In writing or by telephone to the correspondent, or through a third party.

Correspondent: Mrs J Sturt, Fortune Farmhouse, Mynthurst, Leigh, Reigate, Surrey RH2 8RJ.

Merstham and South Merstham

The Henry Smith Charity

Eligibility: People in need who live in the parish of Merstham and South Merstham, mainly older people.

Types of grants: One-off and recurrent grants typically of £50 each.

Annual grant total: In 2000/01 the charity had assets of £1,800 and an income of £3,500. A total of £3,000 was distributed in 59 grants.

Applications: On a form available from the correspondent to be submitted directly by the individual. Applications are considered in December/January.

Correspondent: C C Morris, The Cottage, Quality Street, Merstham, Surrey RH1 3BB (01737 642012).

Newdigate

The Henry Smith Charity

Eligibility: People in need who live in the parish of Newdigate.

Types of grants: One-off grants for a variety of needs. Grants are given to widows on the death of a partner and payments towards bills can be made up to half the full amount. A grant has been given to allow a prospective university student to visit open days in five different towns and to help towards purchasing a boat to help somebody qualify for the Olympics.

Vouchers are given annually or fuel, if funds allow.

Annual grant total: The trust receives around £5,000 income, allocated by Henry

SOUTH EAST – SURREY

Smith's (General Estate) Charity, although this figure varies each year.
Applications: In writing to the correspondent.
Correspondent: Diana Salisbury, 'Langholm', Village Street, Newdigate, Dorking, Surrey RH5 5DH (01306 631435).

Nutfield

Smith's Charity-Parish of Nutfield

Eligibility: People in need who live in the parish of Nutfield.
Types of grants: One-off and recurrent grants ranging from £35 to £45. Vouchers for local shops are given. The charity also makes some grants to village organisations.
Annual grant total: The trust receives about £5,000 income a year, allocated by Henry Smith's (General Estate) Charity.
Applications: In writing to the correspondent. Applications can be submitted either directly by the individual or by any of the four trustees and are considered in December.
Correspondent: Miss N E Kempsell, 1 Church Hill, Nutfield, Redhill, Surrey RH1 4JA.

Ockley

United Charities Ockley (Henry Smith Charity)

Eligibility: People in need who live in Ockley (primarily people of pensionable age).
Types of grants: Recurrent annual cash gifts of £85.
Annual grant total: In 2000/01 the charity had an income of £7,000. It spent £8,800, of which £3,900 was given in 46 grants.
Applications: In writing to: G E Lee-Steere, Chair, Jayes Park, Ockley, Surrey RH5 5RR. Applications can be submitted either directly by the individual or through a social worker, citizen's advice bureau or other welfare agency. They are considered in November.
Correspondent: Timothy Pryke, Danesfield, Ockley, Dorking, Surrey RH5 5SY (01306 711511).
Other information: The charity also supports certain local organisations.

Oxted

The Oxted United Charities

Eligibility: People in need who live in the parish of Oxted.
Types of grants: One-off grants in the range of £20 to £500. Donations given include those for clothing, food, education, utility bills, television licences, furniture and floor covering.

No grants are given for council tax, rent payments and so on.
Annual grant total: In 2001/02 the charities had an income of £4,700 and gave 121 grants to individuals totalling almost £7,000.
Applications: In writing to the correspondent. Applications are considered at any time and should be submitted through a social worker, citizen's advice bureau or other welfare agency; or directly by the individual.
Correspondent: C J Berry, Trustee, Robinslade, Wilderness Road, Oxted, Surrey RH8 9HS (01883 714553).

Peper Harow

The Peper Harrow Charities

Eligibility: People in need who live in Peper Harow.
Types of grants: Grants of about £50 paid at Christmas, Easter and Michaelmas.
Annual grant total: About three people receive grants totalling £500.
Applications: In writing to the correspondent or by word of mouth through the trustees, local shopkeepers, doctor, social services and so on.
Correspondent: Mrs S Cole, Royal Farmhouse, Elstead, Godalming, Surrey GU8 6LA (01252 702460).

Pirbright

The Pirbright Relief-in-Need Charity

Eligibility: People in need, hardship or distress who live in the parish of Pirbright.
Types of grants: One-off or recurrent grants for a variety of items, services or facilities that will reduce the need, hardship or distress of the individual, including buying or renting medical equipment to use at home.

Grants will not be given for taxes, rates or any other public funds. The trustees must not commit themselves to repeating or renewing any grant.
Annual grant total: About £1,400.
Applications: In writing to the correspondent or any of the trustees.
Correspondent: P B Lawson, Stanemore, Rowe Lane, Pirbright, Surrey GU24 0LX (01483 472842).

Pyrford

The Pyrford United Charities (Henry Smith Charity)

Eligibility: People in need who live in the ancient parish of Pyrford.
Types of grants: Vouchers given for food, fuel or clothing. Other one-off grants are made according to need.
Annual grant total: About £1,500.
Applications: In writing to the correspondent either directly by the individual or through a third party. Applications are usually considered in October.
Correspondent: Mrs D Mossini, Treasurer, Charleroi, 1 Floyds Lane, Pyrford, Woking, Surrey GU22 8TF (01932 400089).

Shalford

Smiths Charity

Eligibility: People in need who live in Shalford parish.
Types of grants: One-off and recurrent cash grants of £100, to relieve financial problems.
Annual grant total: In 2000/01 the charity had an income of £3,000 and an expenditure of £2,900, all of which was given in 29 grants to individuals in need.
Applications: In writing to the correspondent, either directly by the individual or through a social worker, citizen's advice bureau or other welfare agency or directly by the individual or a relevant third party. Applications are considered in March, after the grants are advertised locally.
Correspondent: J D Surrey, 39 Summersbury Drive, Shalford, Guildford, Surrey GU4 8JG (01483 574473; e-mail: shalparish@yahoo.co.uk).

Shottermill

Shottermill United Charities (Henry Smith and Others)

Eligibility: People in need who live in the parish of Shottermill.
Types of grants: Grants usually ranging from £30 to £50 according to need. The charity distributes gift vouchers at Christmas and has also helped a local resident with costs associated with moving house.
Annual grant total: In 2000/01 the trust had an income of £1,100 and a total expenditure of £990. All of this was distributed in 28 relief-in-need grants to individuals.
Applications: In writing to the correspondent. Applications can be

submitted directly by the individual or through a social worker, citizen's advice bureau or other welfare agency or third party. They are considered at any time, but particularly at Christmas.

Correspondent: Mrs Hilary Bicknell, 7 Underwood Road, Haslemere, Surrey GU27 1JQ (01428 651276).

Staines

The Staines Parochial Charity

Eligibility: Older people who live in the parish of Staines and occasionally other people in need who live in the area of the former urban district of Staines.

Types of grants: One-off and recurrent grants according to need for payment of gas or electricity bills. Grants are usually around £70.

Annual grant total: In 2001/02 the charity had an income of £4,900 and a total expenditure of £5,300. In previous years about £5,000 has been given to 80 individuals.

Applications: In writing to the correspondent either directly by the individual, through a social worker, citizen's advice bureau, welfare agency or other third party. The application must be sent via a trustee who must countersign the application. Applications are normally considered in September.

Correspondent: Mrs A Davey, Assistant Chief Executive, Council Offices, Knowle Green, Staines, Spelthorne, Middlesex TW18 1XB (01784 451499; Fax: 01784 446333; e-mail: a.davey@spelthorne.gov.uk).

Other information: Eligibility for housing benefit or Income Support is taken as an indication of need.

Stoke D'Abernon

The Henry Smith Charity

Eligibility: People in need who live in the ancient parish of Stoke D'Abernon (which includes Oxshott).

Types of grants: One-off and recurrent grants according to need, ranging from £20 to £50.

Annual grant total: In 2001/02 the charity had an income of £1,200 and a total expenditure of £1,400; most of this was distributed in 39 relief-in-need grants to individuals.

Applications: In writing to the correspondent, through a social worker, citizen's advice bureau or other welfare agency. They are considered at any time.

Correspondent: Mrs H C Lee, Beggars Roost, Blundel Lane, Stoke D'Abernon, Cobham, Surrey KT11 2SF (01932 863107).

Tandridge

The Henry Smith Charity

Eligibility: People in need who live in the parish of Tandridge.

Types of grants: One-off grants of about £100.

Annual grant total: In 2001/02 the trust had an income of £4,600. A total of £3,400 was distributed in 34 relief-in-need grants to individuals.

Applications: In writing to the correspondent. Applications should be submitted in October either directly by the individual or through another third party if the individual is unable to apply. Applications should include the address and the amount of money needed; they are considered in November.

Correspondent: Mrs C Scott, Goulds Farm, Hare Lane, Lingfield, Surrey RH7 6JA (01342 832376).

Other information: The charity also makes grants to individuals in education and grants to organisations providing education, health and social services to residents.

Thorpe

The Thorpe Parochial Charities

Eligibility: People in need who live in the ancient parish of Thorpe, especially those over 60.

Types of grants: Grants of solid fuel or contributions to gas or electricity accounts and 'aids to the sick'. Grants are for £35 to £45. Educational grants are also available.

Annual grant total: In 2001/02 the trust had an income of £2,000 and made 41 grants totalling £1,800.

Applications: In writing to the correspondent by the end of October. Applications are usually considered in November.

Correspondent: Mrs A C Price, Clerk, 29 Grange Road, Egham, Surrey TW20 9QP (01784 433416).

Thursley

The Thursley Charities

Eligibility: People in need who live in the parish of Thursley in Surrey.

Types of grants: One-off and recurrent grants according to need.

Annual grant total: The trust receives about £1,300 income, allocated by Henry Smith's (Warbleton Estate) Charity.

Applications: In writing to the correspondent.

Correspondent: P Coles, Upper Ridgeway, Hyde Lane, Thursley, Surrey GU8 6QP (01428 604508).

Other information: The charities are the Charities of Anthony Smith and Henry Smith.

Walton-on-the-Hill

The Henry Smith Charity

Eligibility: People in need who live within the parish of Walton-on-the-Hill.

Types of grants: One-off or recurrent grants according to need.

Annual grant total: In 2000/01 the trust received £2,300 income, allocated by Henry Smith's (General Estate) Charity.

Applications: In writing to the correspondent.

Correspondent: Mrs J E Turnbull, Little Orchard, Egmont Park Road, Walton-on-the-Hill, Tadworth, Surrey KT20 7QG (01737 814681).

West Clandon

The Henry Smith Charity

Eligibility: People in need who live in West Clandon.

Types of grants: One-off cash grants of £20 to £40 are distributed annually in November. Grants are generally based on personal knowledge of the trustees.

Annual grant total: About £1,500 is awarded each year.

Applications: In writing to the correspondent for consideration in October/November.

Correspondent: M C Tosh, Little Clandon, The Street, West Clandon, Guildford, Surrey GU4 7ST.

Other information: Funding is also available for organisations and amenities which provide services for eligible parishioners.

West Molesey

The Henry Smith Charity

Eligibility: People in need who live in West Molesey.

Types of grants: Small one-off grants, usually under £50.

Annual grant total: The trust usually receives £1,000 income each year, allocated from Henry Smith's (General Estate) Charity.

Applications: In writing to the correspondent.

Correspondent: Revd Peter Tailby, 518 Walton Road, West Molesey, Surrey KT8 2QF (020 8979 3846).

Weybridge

The Henry Smith Charities and Others

Eligibility: People in need who live in the ancient parish of Weybridge.

Types of grants: One-off grants towards the cost of necessary and essential equipment. Recent grants have been given to a family with young children to replace their broken cooker and older people who are disabled to improve their mobility and quality of life. No grants are given for existing debts.

Annual grant total: In 2001/02 the trust had an income of £2,400 and a total expenditure of £700, all of which was given in four grants.

Applications: On a form available from the correspondent, to be submitted either directly by the applicant or through a social worker, citizen's advice bureau, other welfare agency or any other third party. Applications should be submitted in April or October or any other time.

Correspondent: Terry Oatley, Clerk to the Trustees, Elmbridge Borough Council, Civic Centre, High Street, Esher, Surrey KT10 9SD (01372 474178; Fax: 01372 474980; e-mail: toatley@elmbridge.gov.uk).

Other information: This trust formerly gave Christmas grants of £6 to £8, but had a change of policy in June 2000 and now gives grants for larger items.

Weybridge Land Charity

Eligibility: People in need who live in Weybridge.

Types of grants: Grants given are categorised as follows:
General grants of £50 to residents in need, living in sheltered unit accommodation.
General grants of £65 to residents in need, living in other accommodation.
Special additional grants of between £50 and £500 upwards to those in need who have a special requirement e.g. to buy a microwave, furniture etc.

Annual grant total: In 2001 the trust had assets of about £1.3 million, an income of £81,000 and a total expenditure of £61,000. The sum of £18,000 was distributed in 190 relief-in-need grants to individuals. Grant aid of £25,000 was budgeted for 2002.

Applications: On a form available from: Weybridge Land Charity, PO Box 730, Woking, Surrey GU23 7LD. Applications can come directly from the individual or through a relevant third party and are considered in November and should be submitted in September and October.

Correspondent: Howard Turner, Little Knowle, Woodlands, Send, Surrey GU23 7LD (01483 211728; Fax: 01483 224467).

Other information: Grants are also made to organisations.

Woking

The Henry Smith Charity

Eligibility: People in need who live in the ancient parish of Woking.

Types of grants: One-off grants only. Grants are not given for the relief of rates, taxes and other public funds.

Annual grant total: About £5,000.

Applications: In writing to the vicar of the parish, either directly by the individual or through a social worker, citizen's advice bureau or other welfare agency.

Correspondent: David Bittleston, Pin Mill, Heathfield Road, Woking, Surrey GU22 7JJ (01483 828621).

Worplesdon

Worplesdon Parish Charities (including the Henry Smith Charity)

Eligibility: People in need who live in the parish of Worplesdon.

Types of grants: Vouchers to buy coal, clothing or groceries at Christmas.

Annual grant total: In 2000/01, 55 vouchers of £40 were distributed.

Applications: Apply when the distribution is advertised within the parish (normally in October/ November each year). Emergency grants can be considered at any time.

Correspondent: S A Morgan, 21 St Michaels Avenue, Guildford, Surrey GU3 3LY (01483 233344).

Wotton

The Henry Smith Charity

Eligibility: People in need who live in the ancient parish of Wotton.

Types of grants: One-off according to need, ranging from £100 to £500. Grants have in the past been given to older people of the parish towards fuel and lighting bills and holidays, young people taking part in schemes such as The Duke of Edinburgh Award which will enhance their job prospects, and help towards the cost of independent projects or travel costs.

Annual grant total: In 2001 the sum of £5,700 was given in grants.

Applications: In writing to the correspondent. Applications are considered in March and September. They can be submitted directly by the individual or through other third party on their behalf.

Correspondent: Mrs R A Wakefield, Secretary, 2 Brickyard Cottages, Hollow Lane, Wotton, Dorking RH5 6QE (01306 730856).

West Sussex

Ashington, Wiston, Warminghurst Sick Poor Fund

Eligibility: People in need who live, firstly in the village of Ashington, Wiston and Warminghurst, and secondly in West Sussex.

Types of grants: One-off grants according to need. Grants are given to provide or pay for items or services which will alleviate the need or assist the recovery of beneficiaries where assistance is not readily available from any other source.

Annual grant total: In 2001 the fund had an income of £3,800 and made two grants totalling £380.

Applications: On a form available from the correspondent. Applications can be submitted directly by the individual or a relevant third party, or through a third party such as a social worker, citizen's advice bureau or other welfare agency. They are mainly considered in May and November although emergency cases can be considered between meetings.

Correspondent: Mary Slade, c/o St Richard's Hospital, Royal West Sussex NHS Trust, Spitalfield Lane, Chichester PO19 4SE (01243 788122).

The Chichester Welfare Trust

Eligibility: People who are in need, sick, disabled or infirm and live in the city of Chichester and environs.

Types of grants: Cash grants or provision of items such as furniture, bedding, clothing, food, fuel, loan of services or facilities. Care is taken not to duplicate benefits provided by social services. A limited amount of cash is held for immediate use in cases of emergency. No financial support is given towards rent arrears.

Annual grant total: The trust's income is about £4,500 and its expenditure is about £3,000.

Applications: All applications must come through third parties such as social services, citizen's advice bureaux, health visitors and so on.

Correspondent: Cliff Spawton, Honorary Secretary, 6 Norwich Road, Chichester, West Sussex PO19 5DF (01243 789301).

The East Grinstead Relief in Sickness Charity

Eligibility: People in need who are sick, convalescent, disabled or infirm and live in the parish area of East Grinstead and the immediate outside area.

Types of grants: Usually one-off grants ranging from about £10 to £100. Grants have been given towards childcare during illness and comfort aids for people who are disabled.

Grants are not given towards housing, council tax or anything the statutory services should provide. Also grants are not given towards the ongoing expenses for articles that have been provided i.e. they may help install a telephone but will not pay for future rental.

Annual grant total: In 2000/01 the trust had an income of £500 and about £550 was given in 11 grants.

Applications: On a form available from the correspondent. Applications can be made directly by the individual, through a social worker, citizen's advice bureau or other welfare agency or by a third party on behalf of an individual i.e. relative, health professional, friend or church contact. They are considered at any time and must include evidence of need due to illness, disability or poverty and the cost of the service or object required.

Correspondent: Mrs M Hooker, Treasurer, 61 Fulmar Drive, East Grinstead, West Sussex RH19 3NN (01342 321292).

The Mitford Foulerton Charitable Trust

Eligibility: People who live in West Sussex and are running training courses concerned with the preservation and conservation of buildings of historical, architectural, artistic or scientific interest.

Types of grants: One-off and recurrent grants according to need.

Annual grant total: In 1999/2000 the trust had an income of £6,800 and a total expenditure of £16,000. Information about how much was given in grants to individuals was not provided.

Applications: In writing to the correspondent.

Correspondent: Christopher Noel Butcher, Trustee, 5 East Pallant, Chichester, West Sussex PO19 1TS (01243 786111; Fax: 01243 775640).

The West Sussex County Nursing Benevolent Fund

Eligibility: Firstly, retired community nursing staff in need who have worked in West Sussex. Secondly, people who are sick, convalescent, disabled or infirm and live in West Sussex.

Types of grants: One-off grants ranging from £40 to £800. Grants are given to provide or pay for items or services which will alleviate the suffering or assist the recovery of beneficiaries in cases where assistance is not readily available from any other source. Recent grants include those towards wheelchairs, tricycles for disabled children and respite holidays for a severely mentally disabled child. Chirstmas gifts are also given.

Annual grant total: In 2001 the fund had an income of £12,000 and made 80 grants totalling £7,500

Applications: On a form available from the correspondent. Applications can be submitted directly by the individual, or through a third party such as a social worker, citizen's advice bureau or other welfare agency. They are mainly considered in May and November.

Correspondent: Mary Slade, c/o St Richard's Hospital, Royal West Sussex NHS Trust, Spitalfield Lane, Chichester PO19 4SE (01243 788122).

Horsham

The Innes Memorial Fund

Eligibility: People who are poor, sick and in need and who live in Horsham.

Types of grants: One-off grants according to need. In 2000/01 grants were given towards wheelchairs, cookers, holidays, alarms, domestic help, school uniforms and chiropody costs.

Annual grant total: In 2000/01 the fund had an income of £18,000 and a total expenditure of £20,000.

Applications: In writing to the correspondent, to be submitted through a doctor or social worker.

Correspondent: Mrs P C Eastland, Administrator, 12 Coolhurst Lane, Horsham, West Sussex RH13 6DH (01403 263289).

Midhurst

The Midhurst Pest House Charity

Eligibility: Poor, sick and needy people of the parish of Midhurst.

Types of grants: One-off in the range of £60 to £500. Grants have been given towards transport and holiday costs.

Annual grant total: In 2000/01 the trust had assets of £192,000 and income of £13,000. A total of £1,200 was distributed in five grants to individuals.

Applications: In writing to the correspondent either directly by the individual or through a social worker, citizen's advice bureau or other welfare agency. Applications are considered in April and October and should be received in the preceding month.

Correspondent: Tim Rudwick, Clerk, 31 Pretoria Avenue, Midhurst, West Sussex GU29 9PP (01730 812489; e-mail: tim.rudwick@hants.gov.uk).

Other information: Grants are also occasionally made to a local school.

Wisborough Green

The Elliott Charity

Eligibility: People who are elderly or disabled in Wisborough Green.

Types of grants: One-off grants according to need.

Annual grant total: In 2000 it had an income of £2,300 and a total expenditure of £900.

Applications: In writing to the correspondent.

Correspondent: Mrs Rosmund Felicity Tidman, 5 Forrest Place, Loxwood Road, Wisborough Green RH14 0DS (01403 700354).

Other information: Grants are also made to community causes.

9. London

Arsenal Charitable Trust

Eligibility: People in need including those injured whilst playing sport or their dependants who live in Greater London, with a preference for Islington and Hackney.

Types of grants: Grants and loans according to need.

Annual grant total: In 2000/01 the trust had an income of £61,000. Grants to organisations totalled £51,000 with a further £3,000 going to eight individuals.

Applications: In writing to the correspondent.

Correspondent: The Trustees, Arsenal Stadium, Highbury, London N5 1BU (020 7704 4000; Fax: 020 7704 4001).

Benevolent of Strangers' Friend Society

Eligibility: People in need, particularly 'strangers not entitled to parochial relief', that is people who have exhausted all other possible sources of funding. Beneficiaries must live in London, mainly inner London.

Types of grants: One-off and recurrent grants according to need.

Annual grant total: In 2000 the trust had an income of £500 and its total expenditure was £1,100. Grants to individuals total about £1,000 a year.

Applications: Applications should not be made to the society since it does not make grants directly to individuals. It allocates funds to certain Methodist ministers living in most areas of inner London and some areas of outer London, who in turn distribute the funds to individuals in need of whom they become aware.

Correspondent: C Linford, Room 314, 1 Central Buildings, Westminster, London SW1H 9NH (020 7222 8010).

The Benevolent Society for the Relief of the Aged and Infirm Poor

Eligibility: People over 60 years of age who are needy and infirm and live in the London area.

Types of grants: Commonly grants are given for the replacement or acquisition of essential personal or household items such as clothing, shoes, cookers, heaters and so on. Also for assistance with the cost of optical and orthopaedic items that are not available free on the NHS and gas/electricity bills that can no longer be managed. Grants typically range from £50 to £250.

Annual grant total: Around £7,000.

Applications: In writing to the correspondent including a full statement of income, expenditure, assets, liabilities, the need and estimates of cost together with details of other applications pending. Applications can be submitted by the individual, their spouse, a family member or friend, or through a recognised referral agency (social worker, citizen's advice bureau or doctor etc.) and are considered on an ongoing basis. Please note that in August 2002 the trust stated that, due to a lack of funds, very few new grants were being made.

Correspondent: G S Hutton, Trustee, St Mary Moorfields, 4–5 Eldon Street, London EC2M 7LS.

Other information: This entry was not confirmed by the trust, but the address is correct according to the Charity Commission database.

The Cripplegate Foundation

Eligibility: People in need who live or work in the ancient parish of St Giles, Cripplegate, and the former parish of St Luke's, Old Street (the north of the City of London and the southern part of the borough of Islington respectively). Individuals must have lived or worked there for a minimum of 12 months. These residential qualifications are waived for asylum seekers and people who are homeless.

Types of grants: One-off grants of up to £500 for holidays (in the UK only), clothing, respite care and household items such as cookers, fridges and essential furniture. No grants are given towards housing costs, items already purchased, education and funeral costs.

Annual grant total: In 2001 the trust had assets of £29 million and both an income and a total expenditure of £1.2 million. Grants to 195 individuals totalled £57,000.

Applications: On a form available from the correspondent. Decisions are usually made within three weeks of the receipt of completed forms. People who are unsure of whether they live in the beneficial area should telephone the trust before making an application.

Correspondent: The Clerk to the Governors, 76 Central Street, London EC1V 8AG (020 7336 8062; Fax: 020 7336 8201; e-mail: grants@cripplegate.org.uk).

Other information: Grants are also made to organisations.

The Isaac Davies Trust

Eligibility: People of the Jewish faith who live in London.

Types of grants: One-off grants according to need.

Annual grant total: The trust's income is about £11,000. Most of the income is given in grants to organisations, but around £2,000 is given to individuals, some of which is for educational purposes.

Applications: In writing to the correspondent.

Correspondent: The Secretary, United Synagogue, Adler House, 735 High Road, London N12 0US (020 8343 8989).

The Charles Dixon Pension Fund

See entry on page 219

The Emanuel Hospital Charity

Eligibility: People over 56 who are in need, members of the Church of England and for at least two years have lived in one of the following areas: (i) the city of Westminster (with priority for the area north of the Thames river but south of Oxford Street and Bayswater Road), (ii) the royal borough of Kensington & Chelsea (with priority for the area north of the Thames river and east of Chelsea Creek) or (iii) the borough of Hillingdon (with priority for the area known as the parish of Hayes).

Types of grants: Pensions of £504 a year, paid in monthy instalments.

London – General

Annual grant total: In 2000/01 the charity had assets of £1.9 million and an income of £61,000. The sum of £62,000 was distributed in 111 relief-in-need grants.

Applications: Application forms can be obtained from the correspondent and should be returned along with evidence of their need. They should be submitted directly by the individual. Applications are considered in May and November.

Correspondent: David Haddon, Clerk, Town Clerk's Office, Corporation of London, PO Box 270, London EC2P 2EJ.

Other information: The charity publicises its activities and details of pension vacancies in local papers, through welfare agencies and churches within the beneficial areas.

Sir John Evelyn's Charity

Eligibility: People in need who are in receipt of state benefits and live in the ancient parish of St Nicholas, Deptford and St Luke, Deptford.

Types of grants: Grants, such as for domestic items, and pensions. Beneficiaries can receive grants for up to five years, subject to review each year.

Annual grant total: In 1999 the charity had assets amounting to £3.9 million and an income of £116,000. Grants to organisations totalled £44,000 with a further £18,000 going on pensions, £9,800 in grants to individuals, and £8,800 towards pensioners' holidays run by the charity.

Applications: On a form available from the correspondent. Applications are considered every two months.

Correspondent: Collette Saunders, Clerk's Office, 11 Blanindon Drive, Bexley, Kent DA5 3BS (Tel & Fax: 020 8303 5260).

The German Society of Benevolence

See entry on page 302

The Ronnie Gubbay Memorial Fund

Eligibility: Jewish people of Spanish and Portuguese origin, living in Greater London.

Types of grants: One-off and recurrent grants according to need.

Annual grant total: In 2000/01 the fund had an income of £8,000, all of which was given in grants.

Applications: The trust has a limited income and is not seeking further applications.

Correspondent: The Secretary, 2 Ashworth Road, London W9 1JY (020 7289 2573).

Other information: This fund is one of the several trusts administered by the Spanish & Portuguese Jews Congregation and was established in 1944.

The Hampton Fuel Allotment Charity

Eligibility: Primarily people in need who are sick, convalescent, disabled or infirm and live in the ancient town of Hampton, i.e. the present areas of Hampton, Hampton Hill and also the former borough of Twickenham and the remainder of the present borough of Richmond-upon-Thames.

Types of grants: One-off grants ranging from £50 to £280 for heating costs, lifeline alarm systems and other items. No cash grants are made

Annual grant total: The trust had assets of £41 million and an income of £1.7 million in 2000/01. Out of a total expenditure of £1.5 million, the sum of £574,000 was distributed in 1,497 grants to individuals. Grants to organisations totalled about £700,000.

Applications: On a form available from the correspondent either directly by the individual or through a social worker, citizen's advice bureau, other welfare agency or other third party, such as a partner or friend (with the individual's consent). Applications are considered every second month.

Correspondent: Michael Ryder, 15 Hurst Mount, High Street, Hampton, Middlesex TW12 2SA (020 8979 5555).

Other information: Grants are also given to organisations which support those in need or provide community benefit, in the area outlined above.

The Handicapped Children's Aid Committee

See entry on page 302

Help-in-Need Association (HINA)

Eligibility: People in need who live in the area surrounding hospitals affiliated to St Bartholomew's and The Royal London Medical School (i.e. east London and areas in south Essex).

Types of grants: One-off and recurrent grants, usually up to £300 each. Recent grants were made to a child with learning disabilities to cover the costs of an IT course (£100) and a lady with small children for toys (£50).

Annual grant total: In 2000/01 the trust had assets totalling £15,000, its income was £1,800 and total expenditure was £2,000. No grants were made to individuals in this year; grants to organisations totalled £1,500.

Applications: On a form available from the correspondent via a third party such as social services or a citizen's advice bureau. Applications can be submitted at any time during the year and should include financial information.

Correspondent: Abigail Fogo, St Bartholomew's and the Royal London, School of Medicine and Dentistry, The Royal London Hospital Clubs Union, London E1 2AD (020 7377 7641; e-mail: hina@bartslondon.com).

Other information: Grants are also made to organisations.

The Hornsey Parochial Charities

Eligibility: People in need who live in the ancient parish of Hornsey in Haringey and Hackney which comprises N8 and parts of N2, N4, N6, N10 and N16.

Types of grants: One-off grants for all kinds of need provided funding is not available from statutory or other sources, such as clothing, bedding or essential items and the costs of heating and lighting.

Annual grant total: In 2000 the trust had an income of £129,000 and a total expenditure of £48,000. Grants were made for educational and welfare purposes.

Applications: Individuals can write requesting an application form which, on being returned, can usually be dealt with within a month.

Correspondent: Lorraine Fincham, PO Box 22985, London N10 3XB (Tel & Fax: 020 8352 1601; e-mail: hornseypc@aol.com).

Inner London Fund for the Blind and Disabled

Eligibility: People who are blind, partially sighted or disabled who live or are regularly employed in the borough of Greenwich, and people who are blind or partially sighted who live within the London area. Preference will be given to applicants who live alone.

Types of grants: Grants of £130 to £500 towards e.g. travel expenses, washing machines, wheelchairs, cookers and home improvements. No grants towards rent arrears, rates, food, clothing/footwear, heating or lighting, except in exceptional circumstances.

Annual grant total: In 1998/99 the trust had an income of £16,000 and a total expenditure of £13,000. Seven grants totalled £2,000.

Applications: On a form available from the correspondent. Applications can be made directly by the individual or through a social worker. Details of income/expenditure and charitable assistance received within the past year must be included.

No application will be considered where an alternative statutory source of funding is available.

Correspondent: Alan Johnson, 55 Kenilworth Gardens, London SE18 3JB.

Other information: This entry was not confirmed by the trust, but the information was correct according to the file at the Charity Commission.

Jewish Care

See entry on page 302

William Kendall's Charity (Wax Chandlers' Company)

Eligibility: People in need who live in Greater London or members of the Wax Chandlers' Company and their relatives or dependants.

Types of grants: One-off and recurrent grants according to need.

Annual grant total: In 2001/02 the charity had assets of £2.3 million, an income of £104,000 and a total expenditure of £106,000. Grants to individuals and organisations totalled £97,000.

Applications: On a form available from the correspondent, submitted by a welfare organisation, for consideration in February, May, August and November. No grants are made directly to individuals.

Correspondent: R J Percival, Assistant Clerk, Wax Chandlers' Hall, Gresham Street, London EC2V 7AD (020 7606 3591; Fax: 020 7600 5462;
e-mail: info@waxchandlershall.co.uk;
website: www.waxchandlershall.co.uk).

The London Bereavement Relief Society

Eligibility: Widows and widowers in need who live within London postal districts.

Types of grants: One-off small cash grants to help with the initial problems of bereavement. Grants range from £100 to £200.

Annual grant total: In 2001 the society had assets of £14,000, an income of £3,000 and a total expenditure of £4,100. The sum of £3,400 was given in 25 grants.

Applications: In writing via a social worker, citizen's advice bureau, other welfare agency or through any other responsible person such as a minister or a priest. Applications must be submitted within four months of bereavement. A meeting will then be arranged with the society's visitor. Letter of application should include name, address and telephone number to arrange a visit.

Correspondent: W N Barr, Secretary, 175 Tower Bridge Road, London SE1 2AH (020 7234 3581; Fax: 020 7403 6711).

London East Aids Network (LEAN)

Eligibility: People in need who are living with HIV in east London, i.e. the London boroughs of Hackney, Newham, Tower Hamlets, Redbridge, Waltham Forest, Barking and Dagenham and Havering. People who are affected by HIV, i.e. the partner, primary carer or dependant of an infected person, are also eligible for grants. 'Affected' people are eligible for up to three months after the death of someone with HIV.

Unless there are exceptional circumstances (e.g. sudden bereavement/sudden and unexpected change), the following people are not eligible:
(a) individuals in receipt of Disability Living Allowance at the middle and higher rates and the maximum qualifying premiums for income support
(b) individuals whose income is in excess of the amount as would be received as outlined above (a).

Types of grants: Grants of up to £100 each, and of up to £200 within a year, which form part of a sustainable reponse to the financial hardship of the applicant.

Priority is given to making grants for the following: essential household items; food; fuel bills; subsistence (see below); travel (to solicitors, treatment centres, collect food vouchers); reasonable telephone bills.

Grants will only be made for utility costs on receipt of the bill, when proof is received that the remaining balance has been paid or the award will prevent disconnection of the service.

Subsistence
Grants can be made to people who have no access to money for their subsistence; for example asylum seekers who have received a negative decision on their asylum application, or people who are waiting for their social security benefits to start or re-start.

Grants cannot be made to people who have a long-term funding problem. Grants can be for subsistence for up to a week at a time, for a maximum of four weeks – i.e. until social security benefits are received or clients gain access to support from social services.

Destitute clients can receive awards of up to: £5 a day if aged 18 or over, or aged between 16 and 18 and he/she is no longer a dependant; £2.50 a day if aged under 18 and he/she is a dependant.

Grants are not made for: air fares, alternative therapies, any cost associated with a car, council tax and community charge arrears, car insurance, all credit debts such as credit/charge cards/loan/catalogues and so on, driving lessons, holidays, home care and domestic assistance, investments, medical items, parking fines, payments towards credit cards and loans, rent arrears, respite care, school/college fees, tv licences and water rates arrerars.

Annual grant total: In 2001/02 the trust had an income of £20,000, all of which was given in grants to 415 individuals.

Applications: In the first instance, applicants should contact LEAN at the address below to make an appointment to meet with a member of staff. All applications must be made through completion of LEAN's hardship form, completed by a member of LEAN staff with the applicant. Decisions on applications are made within three working days from the date of application; cash awards are confirmed verbally and awards made by cheque are confirmed in writing.

Awards will only be made to individuals when LEAN is in receipt of an original medical letter of diagnosis confirming HIV status of the infected person. In an emergency, verbal confirmation will be accepted.

Correspondent: Fiona Clarke, 35 Romford Road, London E15 4LY (020 8519 9545; Fax: 020 8519 6229;
e-mail: info@lean.org.uk;
website: www.lean.org.uk).

The Metropolitan Society for the Blind

Eligibility: Blind and partially sighted people who live on a permanent basis in one of the 12 central London boroughs or the City of London with a preference for registered blind people.

Types of grants: One-off grants up to a maximum value of £250. The society can also help with a wide variety of aids, equipment (including loan of radios), holidays, furniture and fittings.

Awards are not normally made for the following: payment of outstanding debts, holidays outside the UK (although help with associated costs could be considered), payment of council tax/rent arrears, educational grants (although help with associated costs may be considered), installation of a telephone service where the applicant is in short-term or temporary accommodation, or payments of deposit to telephone company in respect of installation of telephone service if the applicant has no former 'track record'. Grants are not given when statutory provision is available.

Annual grant total: In 2001 the trust had assets of £4.2 million and an income of £427,000. The sum of £17,000 was distributed in 98 grants.

Applications: On a form available from the correspondent. Applications should be made through a welfare or voluntary agency, church, registered charity or similar organisations. The secretary can be contacted between 9.30 am and 4 pm on weekdays.

Applicants should first apply to the social fund whenever eligibility exists, and a check should be made to make sure that the applicant is in receipt of all the state benefits they are entitled to.

Correspondent: Frank Luck, Secretary, Lantern House, 102 Bermondsey Street, London SE1 5UB (020 7403 6184/6571; Fax: 020 7234 0708;
e-mail: enquiries@msb.gb.com).

LONDON – GENERAL

Other information: The society's primary function is as a full-time home-visiting agency on which it spends almost half its income; it also offers a small-scale escort service conducted by volunteer car drivers, normally in the London area.

The society also supports organisations helping visually impaired people such as social clubs.

The Metropolitan Visiting & Relief Association

Eligibility: People in need who live in the boroughs of Camden, Greenwich, Hackney, Hammersmith & Fulham, Islington, Kensington & Chelsea, Lambeth, Lewisham, Southwark, Tower Hamlets, Wandsworth, Westminster and the City of London.

Types of grants: One-off grants for almost every kind of need, but not fines, rent arrears, council tax, water rates and funeral expenses. The most common requests are for help with fuel bills, children's clothing and holidays, but more unusual needs can also be met. Grants usually range from £100 to £300.

Annual grant total: £8,600 in 1999/2000.

Applications: Via a professional person initially in writing, then on a form available from the correspondent. These forms must be signed by the Church of England vicar of the applicant's parish (although the applicant need not be a church-goer). Applications are considered throughout the year.

Correspondent: The Grants Manager, Family Welfare Association, 501–505 Kingsland Road, London E8 4AU (020 7254 6251; Fax: 020 7249 5443).

Other information: The Family Welfare Association administers a wide variety of funds that can potentially meet most cases of individual need nationally. See the entry in the National and general charities section of the book.

The Middlesex King Edward VII Memorial Fund

See entry on page 303

Mary Minet Trust

Eligibility: People who are sick, disabled or infirm and live in the borough of Southwark or Lambeth.

Types of grants: One-off grants for household items such as washing machines, fridges, microwaves, cookers, essential furniture, carpets, clothing, beds, bedding and respite care. No grants are given for holidays or for statutory payments, rent, council tax, gas and electricity.

Annual grant total: In 2000/01 the trust had assets of £441,000, an income of £18,000 and a total expenditure of £19,000. Grants totalled £16,000.

Applications: In writing to the correspondent either directly by the individual, or through a social worker, citizen's advice bureau, welfare office or a third party such as a doctor, advice centre or Victim Support. Applications should include details of income, particulars of illness or disability, age and family circumstances. They are considered in March, June, September and December.

Correspondent: Dr A Clark-Jones, 54–56 Knatchbull Road, London SE5 9QY.

Arthur and Rosa Oppenheimer Fund

Eligibility: Jewish people who live in London and are sick or disabled. Preference is given to older people.

Types of grants: One-off grants and also grants for a longer period, for instance, for nurses salaries. Grants range between £100 and £1,000, for example, towards nursing care, other amenities and holidays for deprived children.

Annual grant total: In 2000/01 the trust had an income of £3,500 and a total expenditure of £730.

Applications: In writing to the correspondent, either directly by the individual, or via a social worker, citizen's advice bureau or other third party. They are considered at any time.

Correspondent: Arnold S Oppenheimer, Trustee, 9 Ashbourne Avenue, London NW11 0DP.

Other information: Organisations are also supported.

Port of London Authority Police Charity Fund

Eligibility: Former officers who have served in the port authority's police force, and their dependants. It is the charity's policy to establish a genuine need.

Types of grants: One-off and recurrent grants according to need. Grants are usually towards unexpected bills, travel to/from hospital, medical care, clothing, essential household items, optical needs and so on.

Annual grant total: In 2000/01 the trust had assets of £41,000 and an income of £15,000. Almost £12,000 was given in 58 grants to individuals.

Applications: In writing to the correspondent either directly by the individual or a relevant third party. They are considered at quarterly meetings, or when necessary.

Correspondent: Insp. Roger Elliott, Hon. Secretary, Port of Tilbury Police, Port of Tilbury, Tilbury, Essex RM18 7DU (01375 857633; Fax: 01375 852404; e-mail: teri.spencer@potll.com).

The Pusinelli Convalescent & Holiday Home

See entry on page 303

Betty Rhodes Fund

See entry on page 94

The Royal Scottish Corporation (also known as The Scottish Hospital of the Foundation of King Charles II)

Eligibility: Scottish people, and their children and widows, who are in now and live within a 35-mile radius of Charing Cross. Beneficiaries are usually in receipt of state benefits.

Types of grants: The trust gives pensions (of £9.95 per week in 2000/01) and one-off grants (averaging £543 in 2000/01) for essential household items and training needs. Small grants can also be made following a visit by the trust and Christmas and summer grants are also available.

Annual grant total: In 2000/01 the trust had assets of £34 million, an income of £1.5 million and a total expenditure of £1.4 million. Pensions totalled about £145,000. 141 one-off grants totalled £83,000. Small discretionary grants from home visits totalled £60,000. Christmas and summer grants totalled £42,000. Expenditure on holidays and day trips run by the corporation totalled £43,000.

Applications: On a form available from the corporation by posting, e-mailing or telephoning contact details including telephone number and date and place of birth. Upon receiving the completed form, which should include birth/wedding certificates, the corporation decides whether to submit the application for consideration at the trustees' monthly meeting, or may decide to visit the applicant to discuss the application.

Correspondent: Willie Docherty, Chief Executive, 37 King Street, Covent Garden, London WC2E 8JS (020 7240 3718; Fax: 020 7497 0184; e-mail: enquiry@royalscottish corporation.org.uk; website: www.royalscottishcorporation.org.uk).

Other information: The corporation also runs holiday schemes and other services for eligible beneficiaries.

The Sheriffs' & Recorders' Fund

Eligibility: People on discharge from prison, and families of people imprisoned. Applicants must live in the Metropolitan Police area or Greater London area.

Types of grants: One-off grants according to need. Educational grants are also available.

Annual grant total: In 2001/02 the fund gave £85,000 in grants, broken down as follows: household items £26,000; clothing £25,000; education £23,000; other £10,000.

Applications: Must be on a form available from the correspondent, submitted through probation officers or social workers. They are considered throughout the year.

Correspondent: Mrs Richard Saunders, Chair, c/o Central Criminal Court, Old Bailey, London EC4M 7BS (020 7248 3277).

The Society for the Relief of Distress

Eligibility: People in need who live in the boroughs of Camden, Greenwich, Hackney, Hammersmith & Fulham, Islington, Kensington & Chelsea, Lambeth, Lewisham, Southwark, Tower Hamlets, Wandsworth, Westminster and the City of London.

Types of grants: One-off grants, usually of £25 to £100, for 'any cases of sufficient hardship or distress, whether mental or physical'. Grants may be given towards essential household items and clothing but seldom convalescent holidays, funeral expenses or debts.

Annual grant total: About £12,000 a year.

Applications: Through social workers, citizen's advice bureaux, registered charities and church organisations only. Applications submitted by individuals will not be considered.

Correspondent: Mrs S L McCulloch, 57 Bowerdean Street, London SW6 3TN.

The South London Relief-in-Sickness Fund

Eligibility: People in need through sickness, disability or infirmity who live in the boroughs of Lambeth and Wandsworth.

Types of grants: One-off grants up to £100, towards, for example, furniture, furnishings, clothing and holidays. No grants towards taxes.

Annual grant total: In 2001/02 about £6,000 was given in grants.

Applications: In writing to the correspondent through a citizen's advice bureau, social worker or other welfare agency. Applications are considered quarterly. They should include details of the applicant's name, address, age, family composition, disability/illness, source of income and benefits, purpose of the grant, if any funding is being applied for and if any previous applications have been made to the fund.

Correspondent: Rachel Williamson, Room 110, Wandsworth Town Hall, Wandsworth High Street, London SW18 2PU (020 8871 6035; Fax: 020 8871 6036; e-mail: rlwilliamson@wandsworth.gov.uk).

The Spanish Welfare Fund

Eligibility: People in need, of Spanish nationality who live in London, and their dependants.

Types of grants: One-off and recurrent grants according to need.

Annual grant total: In recent years the fund has had a regular income and expenditure of £10,000.

Applications: In writing to the correspondent.

Correspondent: John Scanlan, Landau & Scanlan, 35 North Audley Street, Mayfair, London W1Y 2LS (020 7629 3214).

The St George Dragon Trust

Eligibility: People in need who live in Greater London and are moving, or have recently moved, from supported housing into independent accommodation.

Types of grants: One-off grants ranging from £50 to £300 for buying essential household equipment and furniture. Applicants should not be eligible for a grant from the Social Fund/community care grants and must have only minimal resources.

Annual grant total: In 2001/02 the trust had an income of £5,500 and a total expenditure of £5,000, most of which was given to 21 individuals.

Applications: In writing through a social or housing worker, citizen's advice bureau or other welfare agency, addressed to the trustees at the address below. They are considered monthly. Applications should be typed wherever possible and should be made on the headed notepaper of the organisation through which the application was made.

The application should include name, age and sex of the applicant; address and time spent there; address of new accommodation where applicable; social and financial circumstances; when an application was made to the social fund and why it was refused; whether the appeal process has been finalised; amount requested and its purpose; signature of the applicant; how long the referring worker has personally known the applicant and the worker's appraisal of this application; signature and status of referring worker and the work telephone number and address if different from that shown on the headed paper; date of application.

Correspondent: Alison Barraball, Clerk to the Trustees, 68 Chaucer Road, London SE24 0NU (Tel & Fax: 020 7274 7830).

St Luke's Parochial Trust

Eligibility: People in need from the former parish of St Luke, Old Street (just outside the City of London) who have either lived there for five years and continue to live there, or who have previously lived there for 15 consecutive years.

Types of grants: Pensions are distributed.

Annual grant total: In 2001 the trust had an income of £885,000 and a total expenditure of £976,000. Grants were made to 305 individuals totalling £65,000.

Applications: In writing to the correspondent.

Correspondent: David Green, 76 Central Street, London EC1V 8AG (020 7336 8062).

The Benevolent Society of St Patrick

Eligibility: People irrespective of creed or politics who are Irish or whose parents or grandparents are Irish and who live in the London postal area.

Types of grants: Grants ranging from £50 to £150 for clothing, essential household items, fuel bills, convalescent holidays, visits to families at a time of bereavement and general assistance for hardship caused by illness or unemployment. Help has also been given towards summer outings for children and older people.

Annual grant total: About £10,000.

Applications: In writing to the correspondent, through welfare organisations, charitable institutions or local authorities only.

Correspondent: The Clerk, Family Welfare Association, 501–505 Kingsland Road, Dalston, London E8 4AU (020 7254 6251; Fax: 020 7249 5443).

The Paul Stephenson Memorial Trust

Eligibility: People who have served at least two years of imprisonment and are near the end of their sentence or have been released recently. Applicants must be in need and live or intend to live in the Greater London area.

Types of grants: One-off grants of up to £100. Grants can be in cash or in kind for a particular rehabilitative need of the applicant or their immediate family, e.g. home furnishings, clothing, tools for work or assistance with college expenses.

Grants are not given for recreational activities, setting up small businesses or becoming self employed, or for existing debts.

Annual grant total: In 2000 the trust had an income of £1,300 and a total expenditure of £720. Grants were made for welfare and educational purposes.

Applications: On a form available from the correspondent, which must be submitted via a probation officer, prison education officer or voluntary associate. Applicants should mention other trusts or organisations that have been applied to and other grants promised or received, including any statutory grants. Trustees usually meet monthly.

Correspondent: Mrs Hood, PO Box 294, Esher KT10 9WS.

Other information: This entry was not confirmed by the trust, but was correct according to the Charity Commission database.

The Vacher's Endowment

Eligibility: People in need who are over 50 and live or have lived in Greater London, and their dependants. Preference has to be given to those who have been engaged in some trade or profession on their own account in Greater London, and to people who either live or have lived in the area of the united parishes of St Margarets and St John Westminster. Preference also to members of, or regular worshippers at, a Protestant Christian church.

Types of grants: Quarterly pensions of £50 and one-off grants.

Annual grant total: In 2001 the trust had assets of £602,000 and an income of £26,000. Out of a total expenditure of £19,000 the sum of £8,100 was paid in 34 pensions and £8,000 directly to 26 individuals.

Applications: Further information may be obtained from the correspondent in writing.

Correspondent: Roger Walker, Palmer's House, 42 Rochester Row, London SW1P 1BU (020 7828 3131).

The Matthew Wistrich Trust

Eligibility: Children and young people up to the age of 25 who are physically disabled or have learning difficulties, and their families.

Types of grants: Grants for clothing, travel, holidays and equipment, usually ranging from £100 to £200.

Annual grant total: In 1999/2000 the trust had an income of £3,000. Grants totalled £1,100.

Applications: By referral from a professional person initially by letter, then on an application form. Applications are considered all year.

Correspondent: The Grants Manager, Family Welfare Association, 501-505 Kingsland Road, Dalston, London E8 4AU (020 7254 6251; Fax: 020 7249 5443).

Barking & Dagenham

The Barking & Dagenham Mayor's Fund

Eligibility: People in need who live in Barking and Dagenham.

Types of grants: One-off grants, usually between £20 and £50. Examples include Christmas gifts for pensioners, travel expenses in cases of hardship, holiday expenses for children in need, clothing, washing machines and beds and the payment of debts incurred by people on probation. Also every year each individual Mayor nominates a charity to be supported; this comes from a separate fund.

Annual grant total: About £500.

Applications: In writing to the correspondent, either directly by the individual, or through a social worker, citizen's advice bureau, other welfare agency or other third party. Applications are considered throughout the year.

Correspondent: The Mayor's Personal Assistant, London Borough of Barking & Dagenham, Mayor's Parlour, Civic Centre, Dagenham RM10 7BN (020 8227 2121; Fax: 020 8227 2162; e-mail: janet.allen@lbbd.gov.uk; website: www.barking-dagenham.gov.uk).

The Dagenham United Charity

Eligibility: People in need who live in the ancient parish of Dagenham (as it was 1921 to 1924).

Types of grants: Gift vouchers at Christmas. The vouchers were £50 in 2001, but this changes each year since it depends on the charity's income and the number of applicants.

Annual grant total: About £1,500.

Applications: In writing to the correspondent either directly by the individual or through a social worker, citizen's advice bureau, other welfare agency or other third party. Details of any disability should be included if appropriate, along with information about the applicant's income, age and so on. Applications are considered in October/November.

Correspondent: Barry Ray, Civic Centre, Dagenham RM10 7BN (020 8227 2134; Fax: 020 8227 2171).

Other information: This charity is an amalgamation of the William Ford & Dagenham United Charities.

Barnet

The Milly Apthorp Charitable Trust

Eligibility: People who live in the London borough of Barnet.

Types of grants: Grants are given for a range of needs, such as holidays for people with physical disabilities and their carers/families, and holidays for young people towards adventurous expeditions and character building activities.

Annual grant total: £630,000 to organisations and individuals, including grants to individuals for educational purposes.

Applications: On a form available from the correspondent. Applications are considered in March, June, September and December and should be made through a registered charity in the preceding month. The trust does not invite applications, and will not reply to unsuccessful applicants.

Correspondent: Mrs A Corbett, Grants Unit, Borough Treasurer's Service, London Borough of Barnet, Town Hall, The Burroughs, London NW4 4BG (020 8359 2092; Fax: 020 8359 2685).

The Mayor of Barnet's Benevolent Fund

Eligibility: People who are on an income-related benefit and who live in the London borough of Barnet and have done so for at least six months.

Types of grants: One-off grants of up to £100 towards essential household items, such as cookers, children's clothing, furniture, items for schoolchildren and one-off debts such as telephone bills.

Annual grant total: In 2001/02 grants to 78 individuals totalled £4,000.

Applications: In writing to the correspondent. Applications should preferably be submitted directly by the individual with a supporting letter from an appropriate agency. Applications must also include a quote for the cost of purchases and so on. They are considered at any time. Applicants may only apply for help twice.

Correspondent: The Borough Treasurer, London Borough of Barnet, Town Hall, The Burroughs, Hendon, London NW4 4BG (020 8359 2020; Fax: 020 8359 2685).

The Finchley Charities

Eligibility: People in need who live in the former borough of Finchley (as it was before 1 April 1965); now in the borough of Barnet.

Types of grants: One-off grants only. No educational grants.

Annual grant total: The charities have a budget of £25,000 a year allocated to organisations and individuals.

Applications: In writing to the correspondent either directly by the individual, through a social worker, citizen's advice bureau or welfare agency. Applications must include details of the amount being asked for and the reason for the application. Individuals can reapply year after year but grants are not necessarily repeated or renewed.

Correspondent: Mrs Jean Field, Manager, 41a Wilmot Close, East Finchley, London N2 8HP (020 8346 9464; Fax: 020 8346 9466).

Other information: The trust also provides 167 flatlets for elderly people in the area. Grants may be given to organisations which provide items, services or facilities for those considered as deserving assistance.

The William Jackson Trust

Eligibility: Poor widows over 60 who live in East Barnet and have done so for at least 20 years.

Types of grants: An annual grant is given rather than a fixed pension.

Annual grant total: In 2000 the trust had an income of £1,600 and a total expenditure of £5,500.

Applications: On a form available from the correspondent for consideration in November.

Correspondent: The Rector, The Rectory, Church Hill Road, East Barnet, Hertfordshire EN4 8XD.

Other information: This entry was not confirmed by the trust but the address was correct according to the Charity Commission database.

Jesus Hospital Charity

Eligibility: People in need, hardship or distress who live in the former district of Barnet, East Barnet and Friern Barnet as constituted immediately prior to 1 April 1965.

Types of grants: One-off grants between £100 and £1,000 towards, for example, reducing electricity and gas bills for those living on low incomes; winter clothing, shoes, food vouchers, fridges/freezers, beds, gas cookers and utensils for single parent families and couples living on low incomes; and holidays for the disabled.

Annual grant total: In 1999 the charity's assets were £7 million, it had an income of £321,000 and grants totalled £65,000. Support is mainly given to local organisations; in previous years about £8,000 has been given to individuals.

Applications: On a form available from the correspondent through a social worker, citizen's advice bureau, welfare agency, a minister or doctor. Applications should state whether the applicant is in receipt of Income Support or housing benefit and whether applications have been made to other charitable organisations. Applications are considered in January, March, May, July, September and November.

Correspondent: Mrs E Payne, Clerk to the Visitors, Ravenscroft Lodge, 37 Union Street, Barnet EN4 9QT (020 8440 4374; Fax: 020 8275 0655; e-mail: jesushc@care4free.net).

Eleanor Palmer Trust

Eligibility: People in need who live in the former urban districts of High Barnet and East Barnet.

Types of grants: One-off grants up to £1,000 towards, for example, carpets, furniture and clothing. (The trust concentrates on running its own almshouses and a residential home for older people). No grants to pay for taxes.

Annual grant total: In 2000/01 the trust had assets of £3.5 million and an income of £1 million. The sum of £6,200 was distributed in 15 grants to individuals.

Applications: In writing to the correspondent either directly or through an appropriate third party. Applications are considered every two months. They should include the names of any other charities to which applications have been made.

Correspondent: Richard Peart, Clerk, 106b Wood Street, Barnet, Hertfordshire EN5 4BY (020 8441 3222; Fax: 020 8364 8279; e-mail: richard.peart.ept@care4free.net).

The Valentine Poole Charity

Eligibility: People in need who live in the former urban districts of Barnet and East Barnet.

Types of grants: One-off grants are given towards essential items such as household items, children's clothing and food.

Annual grant total: In 2001 the trust had assets of £448,000, an income of £49,000 and a total expenditure of £71,000. Grants to 110 individuals totalled £27,000. Grants to organisations totalled £32,000.

Applications: On a form available from the correspondent for consideration in March, July and November. Applications should be submitted by a social worker, citizen's advice bureau or other third party or welfare agency, not directly by the individual.

Correspondent: Mrs M G Lee, The Forum Room, Ewen Hall, Wood Street, Barnet, Hertfordshire EN5 4BW (020 8441 6893).

The Henry Smith Charity

Eligibility: People in need who live in Chipping Barnet.

Types of grants: Vouchers of £15 to £20 to spend in local supermarkets are given to people in need at Christmas.

Annual grant total: In 2001/02 the charity had an income of £1,400, the sum of £1,300 was given in grants to individuals.

Applications: In writing to the correspondent. Applications should be submitted through a social worker, citizen's advice bureau or other welfare agency or through a parish priest, minister of church etc. They shoud be submittd in September/October and are considered in November.

Correspondent: Mrs P M Chatterton, 60 Cedar Lawn Avenue, Barnet, Hertfordshire EN5 2LN (020 8449 8991).

Bexley

The Bexley Mayor's Fund

Eligibility: People in need who live in the borough of Bexley.

Types of grants: Grants, usually in the range of £50 to £100, for a variety of needs (for example towards an electric wheelchair for a severely disabled man and to buy new clothes for an elderly person whose home had been damaged in a fire). There can be an immediate response in emergency cases.

Annual grant total: Around £3,000 to individuals and organisations.

Applications: In writing to the correspondent. In practice, many applications are referred by the council's social services department who also vet all applications from individuals. Applications can be submitted at any time.

Correspondent: The Mayor, London Borough of Bexley, Civic Offices, Broadway, Bexleyheath, Kent DA6 7LB (020 8303 7777; Fax: 020 8301 2661).

The Samuel Edward Cook Charity for the Poor

Eligibility: People in need who live in Bexleyheath.

Types of grants: About 10 one-off grants a year to individuals and families. Grants range from £100 to £400 and in recent cases have been given towards the provision of a cooker and towards the cost of a holiday.

Annual grant total: In 2000/01 the charity had an income of £760 and made three grants totalling £1,100.

Applications: In writing to the correspondent, directly by the individual or through a social worker, citizen's advice bureau or other welfare agency. Allocation of the funds is at the discretion of the Minister of Trinity Baptist Church.

Correspondent: Revd T M Griffith, 75 Standard Road, Bexleyheath, Kent DA6 8DR (020 8303 5858; e-mail: terry.griffith@lineone.net).

The John Payne Charity

Eligibility: Older people who live in the ancient parish of East Wickham.

Types of grants: Grants of up to £100 towards gas, electricity and water and for holidays for carers.

Annual grant total: In 2001 the charity had assets of £60,000 and an income of £1,200. The sum of £790 was distributed in eight grants to individuals.

Applications: On a form available from the correspondent, to be submitted either directly by the individual or through a social worker, citizen's advice bureau, Age Concern or a similar agency. They are considered in March and October. Details of sources of income, rent and so on are required.

Correspondent: Bill Price, Clerk, Foster's Primary School, Westbrooke Road, Welling, Kent DA16 1PN (020 8317 8142; Fax: 020 8317 8142).

Other information: Grants are also made to the British Polio Fellowship to be given as grants for holiday relief for carers.

Brent

The Kingsbury Charity

Eligibility: People in need who live in the ancient parish of Kingsbury.

Types of grants: One-off grants according to need. Most of the charity's expenditure is on almshouses. Grants to individuals have previously included £100 towards the cost of a trip to Lourdes for a terminally ill woman, and £100 to help a family with a six-year-old child with leukaemia.

Annual grant total: £700 in 2000 including grants to organisations.

Applications: In writing to the correspondent, either directly by the individual or through a social worker, citizen's advice bureau, other welfare agency or other third party. They are considered every six weeks.

Correspondent: J B Jordan, Hon. Secretary, 55 Grove Crescent, Kingsbury, London NW9 0LS (020 8205 2101).

The Wembley Samaritan Fund

Eligibility: People who have lived in the electoral ward of Wembley Central, Tokyington, Alberton, Barham, Sudbury or Sudbury Court for at least two years and are sick or in need.

Types of grants: Grants of £200 to £300 towards, for example, bedding, clothing, heating appliances and bills, food, equipment, holidays and support for carers.

Annual grant total: About £5,000.

Applications: By telephone or in writing to the correspondent. A visit by two trustees to the applicant will be arranged.

Correspondent: The Chair, c/o Sudbury Neighbourhood Centre, 809 Harrow Road, Wembley, Middlesex HA0 2LP (020 8908 1220).

Bromley

The Bromley Relief-in-Need Charity

Eligibility: People in need who live in the ancient borough of Bromley.

Types of grants: One-off grants of up to £100. Twice-yearly seasonal grants are also available.

Annual grant total: About £2,500.

Applications: Only through social services or a similar welfare agency or a citizen's advice bureau, doctor, health worker, headteacher and so on.

Correspondent: The Clerk, Lavender House, 11 Alexandra Crescent, Bromley, Kent BR1 4ET (020 8460 5242).

Camden

The Bloomsbury Dispensary

Eligibility: Sick or ill people who live in Bloomsbury.

Types of grants: One-off grants for the relief of sickness and illness (this does not include pregnancy). No grants for debt repayments.

Annual grant total: In 1999 grants totalled £4,500.

Applications: In writing to the correspondent.

Correspondent: Mrs J Rustage, Secretary, 17a Macklin Street, Drury Lane, London WC2B 5NR.

Other information: This entry was not confirmed by the trust but the address was correct according to the Charity Commission database.

The Mayor of Camden's Charity Trust Fund

Eligibility: People in need who live in the borough of Camden.

Types of grants: One-off grants according to need.

Annual grant total: In 2000/01 the trust had an income of £59,000 and a total expenditure of £41,000.

Applications: On a form available from the correspondent, with a letter of support from e.g. a social worker or citizen's advice bureau. Individuals can only apply once a year.

Correspondent: Margaret Humphrey, Charity Secretary, The Mayor's Office, Town Hall, Judd Street, London WC1H 9JE (020 7278 4444).

The Dibdin Brand Charity

Eligibility: Older people in need who live in the former metropolitan borough of Holborn.

Types of grants: Pensions of £15 a month.

Annual grant total: About £1,000.

Applications: In writing to the correspondent.

Correspondent: Mrs J Rustage, Secretary, 17a Macklin Street, Drury Lane, London WC2B 5NR.

Other information: This entry was not confirmed by the charity, but the address was correct according to the Charity Commission database.

Hampstead Wells & Campden Trust

Eligibility: People who are sick, convalescent, disabled, infirm or in conditions of need, hardship or distress and who live in the former metropolitan borough of Hampstead.

Types of grants: Pensions of £10 a week and one-off grants. In 2001 grants were broken down in the accounts as follows:

category	number	total
holidays	22	£5,900
education	8	£2,600
clothing	90	£19,000
furniture	515	£72,000
help with debts	27	£8,300
removals and transport	13	£3,100
gas, electricity and fuel	3	£610
TV and telephone	14	£2,200
Christmas	400	£17,000
medical	6	£1,500
security	2	£480
pensioners' birthday hampers	162	£3,000
miscellaneous	6	£1,500

Annual grant total: In 2000/01 the trust had assets of £12 million, an income of £558,000 and a total expenditure of £532,000. One-off grants to 1,300 individuals for welfare purposes totalled £137,000, with a further £112,000 given in 172 pensions. Organisations received £177,000 in total.

Applications: Applications should normally be sponsored by a statutory or voluntary organisation, or by a person familiar with the circumstances of the case e.g. a social worker, doctor or clergyman.

Applications for pensions are made on a form available from the correspondent. Applications for one-off grants can be made in writing and should include the client's name, date of birth, occupation, address and telephone number, details of other household members, other agencies and charities applied to, result of any application to the Social Fund, household income, and details of any savings and why these savings cannot be used. Decisions are usually made within two weeks.

Correspondent: Mrs Sheila A Taylor, 62 Rosslyn Hill, London NW3 1ND (020 7435 1570; Fax: 020 7435 1571; e-mail: hwct@ndirect.co.uk).

Other information: The trust also assists organisations or institutions providing services and facilities for the relief of need or distress. There is a leaflet available from the above address which further outlines the objectives and procedures of the trust.

Charities Administered from the Guild Church of St Andrew Holborn

Correspondent: M Charlotte Maizels, Grants Coordinator, St Andrew's Holborn, 5 St Andrew Street, London EC4A 3AB (020 7583 7394; Fax: 020 7583 3488).

(i) The City Foundation

Eligibility: People in need who have lived or worked in the city of London or in the London WC1 postal area and part of EC1 west of Farringdon Road. Beneficiaries must usually have lived in the area for more than three years.

Types of grants: One-off grants of between £80 and £700 for a wide range of items such as household appliances, furnishings and travel costs. Grants can be given in-kind, usually as cheques payable to the relevant stores.

Annual grant total: In 1999 the charity had assets of £176,000 and an income of £28,000. Total expenditure was £9,700 with 15 grants totalling £5,000. Four grants for educational purposes totalled £1,500.

Applications: On a form available from the correspondent, to be submitted either directly by the individual or through a social worker, citizen's advice bureau or other welfare agency. Applications can be submitted at any time, and will be considered within 21 days.

(ii) Isaac Duckett Charity

Eligibility: People in need who are working or have worked in the London WC1 postal area and part of EC1 west of Farringdon Road, and who are now unfit for employment due to age, illness, accident or infirmity and who have difficulty maintaining themselves.

Types of grants: Pensions of £500 per year, and one-off grants of between £100 and £6,500 towards household appliances, medical items, furnishings, clothing and so on. Grants are not made towards education and rarely towards holidays or redecoration.

Annual grant total: In 1999 the charity had assets of £1.9 million and an income of £65,000. Total expenditure was £36,000 with 60 grants totalling £20,000.

Applications: On a form available from the correspondent, to be submitted either directly by the individual or through a social worker, citizen's advice bureau or other welfare agency. Applications can be submitted at any time, and will be considered within 21 days.

(iii) The Hoxton Charity

Eligibility: People in need who have lived for at least the past three years in the London WC1 postal area and part of EC1 west of Farringdon Road.

Types of grants: Pensions of £500 per year, and one-off grants of between £100 and £650 towards household appliances, furnishings, carpets, winter clothing, beds, mattresses, medical equipment and redecoration.

Annual grant total: In 1999 the charity had assets of £632,000 and an income of £28,000. Total expenditure was £19,000 with 47 grants totalling £18,000.

Applications: On a form available from the correspondent, to be submitted either directly by the individual or through a social worker, citizen's advice bureau or other welfare agency. Applications can be submitted at any time, and will be considered within 21 days.

(iv) The Stafford Charity

Eligibility: People in need who have lived in the Holborn and East Bloomsbury areas in the borough of Camden for at least three years and are unemployed due to age, accident, illness or infirmity and are in financial need.

Types of grants: One-off grants of between £50 and £650, and pensions of £500 per year. Grants have been given towards kitchen appliances, furnishings, carpets, medical equipment, clothing and redecoration costs.

Annual grant total: In 1999/2000 the charity had assets of £2.8 million and an income of £120,000. Total expenditure was £89,000 with 164 grants totalling £62,000.

Applications: On a form available from the correspondent, to be submitted either directly by the individual or through a social worker, citizen's advice bureau or other welfare agency. Applications can be submitted at any time, and will be considered within 21 days.

(v) The William Williams Charity

Eligibility: People in need who have lived for at least the past three years in the London WC1 postal area and part of EC1 west of Farringdon Road.

Types of grants: Pensions of £500 per year, and one-off grants of between £100 and £650 towards household appliances, furnishings, carpets, winter clothing, beds, mattresses, medical equipment and redecoration.

Annual grant total: About £7,500 is given each year to individuals and organisations.

Applications: On a form available from the correspondent, to be submitted either directly by the individual or through a social worker, citizen's advice bureau or other welfare agency. Applications can be submitted at any time, and will be considered within 21 days.

The St Pancras Welfare Trust

Eligibility: People in need who are sick, convalescent, disabled or infirm, who live or work in the old metropolitan borough of St Pancras (NW1, NW5, N6, N19 and parts of WC1 and NW3).

Types of grants: One-off grants, usually between £100 and £200, for a wide range of needs. No grants are made for educational purposes.

Annual grant total: In 2000/01 the trust had assets of £921,000, an income of £53,000 and a total expenditure of £80,000. The sum of £45,000 was distributed in 260 grants.

Applications: The trustees will only consider applications made through statutory, community or voluntary organisations. Applications are considered in March, June, September and December.

Correspondent: John Knights, Secretary to the Trustees, c/o 212 Eversholt Street, London NW1 1BD (Tel & Fax: 020 8881 7773; e-mail: spwt@btinternet.com; website: www.spwt.org.uk).

Other information: Occasional grants are given to organisations with similar objects.

City of London

The Aldgate Freedom Foundation

Eligibility: People over 65 who are in need who live in the parish of St Botolph's, Aldgate. Applicants must have less than £5,000, and a limited income i.e. a government pension.

Types of grants: One-off and recurrent grants of £156 a year plus a £30 Christmas gift. Help is also given to hospitals within the city and St Botolph's church project.

Annual grant total: About £6,000 to individuals.

Applications: On a form available from the correspondent, directly by the individual, through a social worker, citizen's advice bureau or through a councillor or an alderman. Details of income/capital/expenditure and length of residence in the parish must be included. Applications are considered at any time.

Correspondent: C Wright, St Botolph's Church, Aldgate, London EC3N 1AB (020 7480 5884).

The City Chapter & Percy Trentham Charity

Eligibility: People at least 60 years old who are ill or in financial need and live or have lived or worked in the City of London including Glasshouse Yard.

Types of grants: One-off cash grants and ongoing grants of £300.

Annual grant total: About £4,000 a year.

Applications: In writing to the correspondent via a local clergyman. Applications for regular grants are processed twice a year, all other applications are dealt with as they are received.

Correspondent: Revd David Burgess, St Lawrence Jewry, Next Guildhall, London EC2V 5AA (020 7600 9478).

The Charity of John Land for Widows & Children (Widows Branch)

Eligibility: Children under the age of 25 and widows, of Freemen of the City of London, who are in need.

Types of grants: Pensions to widows of £65 a quarter, or one-off grants according to need.

Annual grant total: Around £1,000 is given each year, although more is available.

Applications: In writing to the correspondent.

Correspondent: The Clerk to the Trustees, St Dunstan's Vestry, 186a Fleet Street, London EC4A 2EA (020 7973 6513).

The Ada Lewis Winter Distress Fund

Eligibility: Poor and distressed people who live or work, or have lived or worked, in the City of London, and their dependants.

Types of grants: Grants to people who are poor during the winter months (November to March). Christmas hampers are also available to people who have already received a grant from the fund.

Annual grant total: In 2001 total expenditure was just over £4,000.

Applications: In writing to the correspondent, throughout the year.

Correspondent: Paul Debuse, The Town Clerk's Office, Corporation of London, PO Box 270, Guildhall, London EC2P 2EJ (020 7606 3030).

The Mitchell City of London Charity

Eligibility: Men over 65 and women over 60 who are in need and who live or work, or have lived or worked, in the City of London for at least five years, and their widows or children.

Types of grants: Usually quarterly pensions of £75.

Annual grant total: In 2000/01 the trust had assets of £1.7 million, an income of £74,000 and a total expenditure of £74,000. Grants totalled £59,000.

Applications: On a form available from the correspondent. Applications are considered in March, June, September and November.

Correspondent: John Keyte, Clerk, Fairway, Round Oak View, Tillington, Hereford HR4 8EQ (Tel & Fax: 01432 760409).

Charities Administered from the Guild Church of St Andrew Holborn – The City Foundation

See entry on page 367

The St John the Baptist Charitable Fund

Eligibility: People in need through poverty or sickness who live in the parish of St John the Baptist, Purley.

Types of grants: One-off grants, usually ranging from £100 to £500. Assistance in the past has been given towards trips to Lourdes, towards the needs of a disabled parishioner and for other cases of financial need.

Annual grant total: About £1,500 to individuals and organisations.

Applications: In writing to the correspondent, either directly by the individual or through the parish priest of St John the Baptist Church, a welfare agency or other third party. Applications are considered in any month.

Correspondent: P Bunce, 4 Highclere Close, Kenley, Surrey CR8 5JU (020 8660 7301; Fax: 020 8668 4777).

Croydon

Charity of Annie Jane Knowles

Eligibility: People who are visually impaired and live in the London borough of Croydon.

Types of grants: Recurrent pensions of about £65 per year.

Annual grant total: In 1999/2000 the charity had an income of £6,300 and a total expenditure of £390.

Applications: In writing to the correspondent directly by the individual. Applications should include details of age and financial circumstances. Trustees meet once a year in November.

Correspondent: Hilary Bowles, Committee Division, Democratic Services Department, Taberner House, Park Lane, Croydon CR9 3JS.

Ealing

Acton (Middlesex) Charities

Eligibility: People in need who have lived in the former ancient parish of Acton for the last five years.

Types of grants: One-off grants of between £13 and £200.

Annual grant total: In 2002 the trust had an income of £10,000.

Applications: On a form available from the clerk or the rector, by referral from clergy, doctors, health visitors or other professional people. Applications are considered in May and November, and should include the length of time the applicant has lived in Acton.

Correspondent: Mrs D Young, Clerk, 42 Creswick Road, Acton, London W3 9HF (Tel & Fax: 020 8992 6385).

Other information: The trust also gives grants towards education and the arts, supporting individuals and local schools and carnivals.

The Ealing Aid-in-Sickness Trust

Eligibility: People in need who live in the old metropolitan borough of Ealing.

Types of grants: One-off or recurrent grants according to need.

Annual grant total: Just under £1,000 is available each year.

Applications: On a form available from the correspondent.

Correspondent: M J Barber, Secretary, 25 Golden Manor, Hanwell, London W7 3EE (Tel & Fax: 020 8579 2921).

Ealing Philanthropic Institution

Eligibility: People who are elderly, sick or otherwise in need and live in Ealing W5 and W13 postal districts.

Types of grants: Christmas gifts and one-off grants, are usually, but not exclusively given to older people. Grants range from £10 to £50.

Annual grant total: In 2000/01 the institution had an income of £4,900 and a total expenditure of £5,700. The sum of £400 was given in 31 grants to individuals. A further £1,100 was given for Christmas gifts and £3,200 in summer and Christmas outings.

Applications: In writing to the correspondent either directly by the individual or through a social worker, citizen's advice bureau or other welfare agency. Applications are considered at any time.

Correspondent: P F Jacobsen, Hon. Secretary, 137 Coldershaw Road, West Ealing, London W13 9DU (020 8567 7482).

Other information: Grants are also occasionally given to organisations which exist to help the individuals described above.

The Eleemosynary Charity of William Hobbayne

Eligibility: People in need who live in the Hanwell (London W7) area.

Types of grants: One-off or recurrent grants according to need.

Annual grant total: About £42,000 is available each year.

Applications: Local sponsoring bodies apply on an application form which has to be completed by the sponsor and sent in the first instance to the correspondent.

Correspondent: M J Barber, Secretary, 25 Golden Manor, Hanwell, London W7 3EE (Tel & Fax: 020 8579 2921).

Other information: Grants are also made to organisations.

Enfield

The Edmonton Aid-in-Sickness & Nursing Fund

Eligibility: People in need who are sick or experiencing ill-health and live in the old borough/parish of Edmonton. The fund cannot support individuals who are living temporarily in the area.

Types of grants: One-off grants up to £300 for clothing, furniture, household necessities, convalescence, household bills and debts and medical equipment not covered by NHS provision. The trust will not subsidise public funds, therefore applicants should have sought help from all public sources before approaching the trust.

Annual grant total: In 2000/01 the fund had assets of £126,000 and an income of £5,200. The sum of £5,300 was distributed in 35 grants.

Applications: In writing either directly by the individual or through social services, citizen's advice bureau or other welfare agency. Applications can be received at any time and are dealt with immediately and without formality.

Correspondent: David M Firth, Hon. Secretary, 9 Crossway, Bush Hill Park, Enfield, Middlesex EN1 2LA (020 8372 3014).

The Old Enfield Charitable Trust

Eligibility: People in need, hardship or distress who live in the ancient parish of Enfield.

Types of grants: The first priority of the charity is relief of need and grants are given for a wide range of needs.

Annual grant total: In 2000/01 £285,000 was available in welfare grants. A further £81,000 was available for educational purposes.

Applications: On a form available on written request from the correspondent. Applications can be made either directly by the individual or through social services, probation service, hospitals, clinics or clergy. Applicants who write directly are visited and assessed. Grants are distributed either directly to individuals or through a welfare agency or suitable third party.

Correspondent: Mrs P Taylor, Clerk, The Old Vestry Office, 22 The Town, Enfield, Middlesex EN2 6LT (020 8367 8941; Fax: 020 8366 7898; e-mail: toect@ic24.net; website: www.toect.org.uk).

Other information: The Enfield Parochial Charities and the Hundred Acres Charity were merged to form this charity on 1 April 1994.

Greenwich

The Charity of Sir Martin Bowes

Eligibility: People in need who live in the boroughs of Woolwich and Greenwich. Applicants must have lived in London for a minimum of ten years, and all statutory services must have been tried.

Types of grants: One-off grants.

Annual grant total: In 2000/01 the trust had assets of £97,000 and an income of £4,500. No grants were made in the year.

Applications: Applications should be made to: The Director of London Borough of Greenwich Social Services and Education Welfare, Nelson House, 50 Wellington Street, London SE18 6PY. Do not write to the correspondent.

Correspondent: Clerk of the Goldsmiths Company, Secretary, Goldsmith's Hall, Foster Lane, London EC2V 6BN (020 7606 7010; Fax: 020 7606 1511).

The Edmund Godson Charity

Eligibility: People in need who wish to emigrate and who currently live in Woolwich, Shinfield near Reading, north east Herefordshire and Tenbury in Worcestershire. Grants are especially given to people who have a new job to go to.

Types of grants: One-off grants ranging from £1,000 to £1,500.

Annual grant total: In 2000/01 the trust gave one grant of £690 to an individual.

Applications: Directly by the individual on a form available from the correspondent. Details of the proposed destination, occupation, eligibility of emigration and financial circumstances must be given. Applications are normally considered at the annual meeting in May, although they can also be considered as they are received.

Correspondent: Karen Forbes, Clerk to the Charity, c/o Godson & Company, 6–7 Pollen Street, W1S 1NJ (020 7495 5916; Fax: 020 7495 5918).

Other information: Grants of up to £750 can also be given to local charities for the relief of hardship in the above areas.

The Greenwich Charity

Eligibility: People in need who live in the ancient parish of Greenwich.

Types of grants: One-off and recurrent grants according to need.

Annual grant total: In 1999/2000 the trust had an income of £11,000 and made grants totalling £14,000, most of which was given to organisations.

Applications: In writing to the correspondent.

Correspondent: R H Crudington, Grant Saw & Sons Ltd, 181-183 Trafalgar Road, London SE10 9EH (020 8858 6971).

The Earl of Northampton's Charity

Eligibility: Preference is given to older people in need who live in Castle Rising and Shotesham in Norfolk, Clun in Shropshire and Greenwich, London.

Types of grants: Pensions of £18 a week.

Annual grant total: In 2000/01 the charity had assets of £11.6 million, an income of £501,000 and its total expenditure was £448,000. A total of £18,000 was given in 17 pensions during the year. A further £207,000 was given to organisations.

Applications: In writing to the correspondent. Pensions are given to individuals introduced to the Mercers' Company by approved agencies or others already known to the Company. Applications are considered monthly.

Correspondent: Grants Manager, Mercers' Company, Mercers' Hall, Ironmonger Lane, London EC2V 8HE (020 7726 4991; Fax: 020 7600 1158;

e-mail: mail@mercers.co.uk;
website: www.mercers.co.uk).

Other information: The Mercers' Company also administers the Whittington Charity (210293) which also gives grants to individuals in need (recommended by a social worker or a health visitor) ranging from £50 to £100.

The charity also supports almshouses and makes charitable grants to organisations helping older people.

The Woolwich & Plumstead Relief-in-Sickness Fund

Eligibility: People in need who have a physical illness or a disability or who have mental health needs. They must live in the borough of Greenwich, with an emphasis on the Woolwich and Plumstead areas.

Types of grants: One-off grants up to about £350 to help with needs linked to the illness or disability of the applicant and the problems these can cause. The trust has in the past given grants towards household goods, beds and bedding, clothing, holidays, equipment not readily available from other sources, electric wheelchairs and at Christmas, grocery vouchers to families with a sick or disabled member. It cannot help with debts, rates, gas or electric bills, recurrent expenditure, structural works or rent.

Annual grant total: In 2000/01 the fund had assets of £34,000, an income of £8,500 and a total expenditure of £8,100, all of which was given in 20 grants and 250 Christmas vouchers.

Applications: On a form available from the correspondent either directly by the individual or through health visitors, district nurses, social services or welfare agencies. The application should include the applicant's income and expenditure, a health professional's letter supporting the diagnosis and the resulting problems and the reason for request of the grant. Applications can be dealt with as and when received.

Correspondent: Ms S Zachariah, Secretary, 167 Crookston Road, Eltham SE9 1YG.

Hackney

Mr John Baker's Trust

Eligibility: Poor widows and unmarried women over 70 who have lived for at least five years in the parish of Christchurch, Spitalfields in the borough of Hackney.

Types of grants: Pensions.

Annual grant total: In 2000 the trust had an income of £4,600. Pensions totalling about £5,000 were paid to 14 individuals.

Applications: In writing to the correspondent.

Correspondent: The Clerk to the Brewers' Company, Brewers' Hall, Aldermanbury Square, London EC2V 7HR (020 7606 1301).

Hackney Benevolent Pension Society

Eligibility: People who are elderly and in need and who have lived in Hackney for at least seven years.

Types of grants: Gifts to pensioners are made, consisting of £30 at Christmas, £30 on the individual's birthday and £30 distributed at the society's annual general meeting.

Annual grant total: In 2000/01 the trust had an income of £5,300 and its total expenditure was £4,300. Each year it can make grants totalling a maximum of £5,400, to 60 pensioners at £90 each.

Applications: In writing to the correspondent. Please note, the society may not have any places for new pensioners available on its list of beneficiaries since it keeps pensioners on the list for life, unless they move out of the area.

Correspondent: Mrs J Cassell, Larch Corner, Coopers Lane, Crowborough, East Sussex TN6 1SN (01892 667416).

The Hackney District Nursing Association

Eligibility: Nurses and midwives in need who live in the London borough of Hackney.

Types of grants: Pensions and the provision of medical aids.

Annual grant total: In 1999 £9,000 was given for educational and welfare purposes to both individuals and hospital departments.

Applications: In writing to the correspondent.

Correspondent: Charlotte Ashburner, c/o Homerton University Hospital, Homerton Row, Homerton, London E9 6SR (020 8510 5555).

Other information: Homes for nurses and midwives, clinics for child welfare and other relief and assistance can also be given to people in need in the area of benefit.

The Hackney Parochial Charities

Eligibility: People in need who live in the former metropolitan borough of Hackney (as it was before 1970).

Types of grants: Grants are given to people who are sick, disabled or elderly for bedding, clothing, heating appliances and furniture, and towards the cost of aid and treatment (but not when this should be the responsibility of the statutory authorities, such as provision of essential wheelchairs). The cost of fares to visit long-stay patients can also be met in the case of close relatives. Grants have also been given for holidays for widows with small children and single parent families, and for gifts at Christmas for children in need.

Grants are one-off, generally of £100 to £250, although individuals can apply annually. No grants for statutory charges, rent, rates, gas, electricity or telephone charges.

Annual grant total: In 1999/2000 the charities gave about £75,000 in grants, of which £30,000 went to organisations and about £45,000 to over 150 individuals for educational and welfare purposes.

Applications: In writing to the correspondent. The trustees meet in March, June, September and November and as grants cannot be made between meetings it is advisable to make early contact with the correspondent.

Correspondent: Robin Sorrell, Craigen Wilders & Sorrell, 2 The Broadway, High Street, Chipping Ongar, Essex CM5 9JD (01277 365532).

Hammersmith & Fulham

Dr Edwards' & Bishop King's Fulham Charity

Eligibility: People in need who live in the old Metropolitan borough of Fulham.

Types of grants: One-off grants are made towards essential items.

Annual grant total: In 2000/01 grants totalled £294,000.

Applications: On a form available from the correspondent submitted either directly by the individual or through social welfare agencies. Applications are considered monthly.

Correspondent: Mrs Maria Blackmore, Clerk to the Trustees, Percy Barton House, 33-35 Dawes Road, London SW6 7DT (020 7386 9387; Fax: 020 7610 2856).

Other information: The charity also gives some educational grants to people who live in Fulham for vocational training, and grants to organisations whose work benefits people in need who live in Fulham.

The Fulham Philanthropic Society

Eligibility: Individuals in need who live in the borough of Fulham.

Types of grants: One-off grants ranging from £50 to £200 to assist, for example, poorer families or single mothers for baby/

child clothing, cots, buggies or for school clothes or shoes for older children. Support has also been given towards the special needs of people who are elderly or sick.

Bills will not be paid under any circumstances and grants will not be given towards expenditure that has already been incurred, settlement of debts/arrears, holidays or education costs. Grants are given mostly through social services. No grants to organisations.

Annual grant total: In 1998 the trust's assets totalled £11,000, it had an income and expenditure of £1,500 and the total amount given in grants to 22 individuals was £1,400.

Applications: In writing to the correspondent. Applications can be submitted directly by the individual, through a social worker, citizen's advice bureau or other welfare agency or through other third party. Applications are considered monthly, with the exception of January and August.

Correspondent: L J Lapham, 20 Philpot Square, Fulham, London SW6 3HT.

Other information: This entry was not confirmed by the trust, but the address was correct according to the Charity Commission database.

The Mayor of Hammersmith & Fulham's Appeal Fund

Eligibility: People in need who live in the borough of Hammersmith and Fulham.

Types of grants: Grants are given for general relief-in-need, ranging from £25 to £50.

Annual grant total: About £2,000.

Applications: In writing to the correspondent through a social worker, citizen's advice bureau or other third party.

Correspondent: The Mayor, Mayor's Office, Room 201, Hammersmith Town Hall, King Street, London W6 9JU (020 8748 3020).

The Hammersmith Relief-in-Sickness Fund

Eligibility: People in need with low income and savings who are disabled or physically or mentally ill, and who have lived in the former metropolitan borough of Hammersmith for at least one year.

Types of grants: One-off grants of up to £60 towards thermal or warm clothing, shoes, underwear, nightwear, bedding, necessary household goods, smoke alarms, microwaves, refrigerators, washing machines, heating appliances, draughtproofing materials, lens for spectacles, surgical, medical and special diet necessities, wheelchairs, and essential furniture (although this cannot be considered if an applicant is entering a new flat owned by the council or a housing association that has its own furniture

store). Additionally, help towards telephone installation, fares for hospital visits, reasonable fuel arrears, cooker connection, household appliance repair and servicing, removals, and funeral costs in exceptional cases, can also be considered. Lastly, help towards recuperative holidays in this country, or fares to stay with relatives, are also eligible.

No grants for telephone, fuel or council tax bills, television licences, arrears or debts, decorating materials or tools, educational fees, unnecessary household goods or luxury items, unnecessary clothing, subsistence, or unsubstantiated holidays.

Annual grant total: In 2000/01 the fund had assets of £75,000, an income of £4,600 and an expenditure of £4,400, of which £2,000 was paid to individuals via third parties.

Applications: On a form available from the correspondent to be submitted through a recognised referral agency (e.g. social work department, another charity, citizen's advice bureau, housing association, hospital or medical centre) or other third party. They are considered by the trustees at the end of every month, except June.

Applications are best supported by a letter from a doctor confirming the applicant's illness or disability and the extent of their need. Details of other charities or official sources which have been approached for assistance should be included, together with details of the income and expenditure of both the applicant and their partner, the size of the family and how long they have been at their current Hammersmith address.

Correspondent: Mrs J O'Loughlin, Secretary, 196a Blythe Road, West Kensington, London W14 0HH (020 7602 1221).

Haringey

The Tottenham District Charity

Eligibility: People in need, especially the elderly, who have lived in the urban district of Tottenham (as constituted on 28 February 1896 which is largely the postal districts of N15 and N17) for at least three years prior to applying.

Types of grants: One-off grants to people who are poor, elderly, sick or disabled to reduce need, hardship or distress. Grants are to help with clothes, carpets and essential household items and range from £50 to £400. Pensions of £10 a month are paid quarterly to elderly people. Christmas and Easter gifts are also given.

No grants for education or debts.

Annual grant total: In 1998/99 the trust's income was £86,000. Expenditure was £119,000, of which grants totalled £40,000.

Applications: On a form available from the correspondent, which can be submitted directly by the individual or through social services, citizen's advice bureau, other welfare agency or any other third party. Applications are considered usually within a month.

Correspondent: Mrs Carolyn Banks, Hon. Clerk, c/o Civic Centre, High Road, Wood Green, London N22 8LE (020 8489 2919; Fax: 020 8489 2985).

The Wood Green (Urban District) Charity

Eligibility: People in need who have lived in the urban district of Wood Green (as constituted in 1896, roughly the present N22 postal area) for at least seven years.

Types of grants: Pensions and small one-off grants ranging from £50 to £300. Grants have in the past been given towards household items such as beds, fridges and clothes.

Annual grant total: About £2,000 a year towards relief-in-need and apprenticeships.

Applications: On a form available from the correspondent, to be submitted directly by the individual or via a social worker, citizen's advice bureau or other welfare agency or third party. Applications are considered all year round.

Correspondent: Mrs Carolyn Banks, Clerk, c/o Civic Centre, High Road, Wood Green, London N22 8LE (020 8489 2919; Fax: 020 8881 5218).

Harrow

The Mayor of Harrow's Charity Fund

Eligibility: People in need who live in the borough of Harrow.

Types of grants: One-off grants usually up to a maximum of £250 are given for basic items such as beds, cookers, clothing.

Annual grant total: In 2000/01 the fund had an income of £8,000 and it gave about £7,000 in grants to 35 individuals. A further £870 went to organisations.

Applications: On a form available from the correspondent. Most applications come through a social worker, citizen's advice bureau or other welfare agency, although this does not preclude individuals from applying directly. They are considered at any time. Applicants must demonstrate that the individual/family are experiencing financial hardship and that the grant will alleviate or improve essential living conditions, ill health or poverty.

Correspondent: Eunice Morren, Chief Executive's Department, PO Box 57, Civic Centre, Harrow, Middlesex HA1 2XF (020 8424 1628; Fax: 020 8420 9635; e-mail: eunice.morren@harrow.gov.uk).

Hillingdon

The Harefield Parochial Charities

Eligibility: People in need who live in the ancient parish of Harefield, especially people who are sick or elderly.

Types of grants: One-off and recurrent grants according to need.

Annual grant total: About £4,000.

Applications: In writing to the correspondent either directly by the individual or through a social worker, citizen's advice bureau or other welfare agency.

Correspondent: Joyce Willis, 95 Newdigate Road East, Harefield, Middlesex UB9 6ES (01895 822657).

The Hillingdon Partnership Trust

Eligibility: People in need who live in the borough of Hillingdon.

Types of grants: One-off gifts of equipment, furniture, clothes and toys. Grants have included a computer donated to a disabled girl.

Annual grant total: Between £70,000 and £80,000 a year to organisations and individuals.

Applications: On a form available from the correspondent.

Correspondent: Chair of Trustees, Marketing Executive, Room 22–25, Building 219, Epsom Square, Easton Business Park, London Heathrow Airport, Hillingdon, Middlesex TW6 2BW.

Other information: This entry was not confirmed by the trust, but the address was correct according to the Charity Commission database.

Uxbridge United Welfare Trusts

Eligibility: People in need who are physically or mentally disabled and people on low incomes (such as families with young children or people who are elderly) who live in the Uxbridge area (bordered by Harefield in the north, Ickenham in the east, Uxbridge in the west and Cowley/Colham Green in the south).

Types of grants: One-off grants either in cash or for services or specific items such as furniture, equipment, clothing and help with fuel bills. No grants are given for rent or rates.

Annual grant total: Between £40,000 and £50,000 a year; about £5,000 of this is given for educational purposes and a small amount to organisations.

Applications: On a form available from the correspondent. Applications can be submitted directly by the individual or through a social worker, citizen's advice bureau or other welfare agency. They are considered each month.

Correspondent: Mrs S M Pritchard, Chair, Trustee Room, Woodbridge House, New Windsor Street, Uxbridge UB8 2TY (01895 232976; Fax: 01895 231538).

Hounslow

The Brentford Relief-in-Need Charity

Eligibility: People in need who live in the parish of Brentford.

Types of grants: One-off or recurrent grants for items such as removal expenses, medical equipment, holidays, cookers, washing machines and decorating materials.

Annual grant total: The trust has an annual income of about £2,500.

Applications: Preference is given to applications made through a recognised referral agency (social worker, citizen's advice bureau, doctor etc.) and are considered upon receipt.

Correspondent: Margaret Todd, Clerk, St Paul's Centre, St Paul's Road, Brentford, Middlesex TW8 0PN (020 8568 7442).

The John Fielder Haden (Isleworth) Relief in Sickness Charity

Eligibility: People in need in the ancient parish of Isleworth.

Types of grants: One-off grants according to need.

Annual grant total: In 2001 the trust had an income of £1,400 and an expenditure of £1,200. Grants total about £1,000 a year and are mainly given to individuals.

Applications: On a form available from the correspondent. Applications are considered throughout the year.

Correspondent: Mrs J H Worboys, Clerk, Clerk's Office, Toison Lodge, North Street, Old Isleworth, Middlesex TW7 6BY (020 8569 9200).

Other information: Grants are also made to organisations.

Islington

Richard Cloudesley's Charity

Eligibility: People in need who are sick or disabled and live in the ancient parish of St Mary's Islington (roughly the modern borough, excluding the area south of the Pentonville and City Roads).

Types of grants: One-off grants, typically up to £200, to help with cases of sickness or disability only.

Annual grant total: In 1999/2000 the charity's assets stood at £2.3 million and it had an income of £537,000. Grants totalled £796,000 of which £158,000 was set aside for the charity's welfare fund which made emergency grants to over 900 individuals. A further 91 grants amounted to £642,000, divided between churches and medical/welfare charities.

Applications: Applications should be made in writing through the social services, a doctor, citizen's advice bureau or similar agency to: Miss Kerala Thompson, Honorary Almoner, c/o 166 Upper Street, London N1 1XU.

Correspondent: Keith Wallace, Clerk, c/o Richards Butler, Beaufort House, 15 St Botolph Street, London EC3A 7EE (020 7772 5703; Fax: 020 7247 5091).

The Finsbury Relief-in-Sickness Charity

Eligibility: People in need who live in Finsbury.

Types of grants: One-off grants ranging from £50 to £100. Help has been given towards the cost of clothing, gas and electric bills, bedding, furniture, cookers and washing machines. Grants will not be given towards holidays, telephone bills, rent, council tax, television licences, cars or electric wheelchairs.

Annual grant total: In 2000/01 the charity had an income of £2,500 and a total expenditure of £2,300.

Applications: In writing to the correspondent, submitted through social services, hospitals, citizen's advice bureaux or similar agencies. They are considered quarterly from January onwards.

Correspondent: Miss Doreen Scott, c/o IVAC, 322 Upper Street, London N1 2XQ.

Lady Gould's Charity

Eligibility: People in need who live in Highgate (i.e. the N6 postal district and part of the N2, N8, N10 and N19 districts).

Types of grants: One-off grants between £300 and £500. Very exceptionally recurrent grants will be considered.

Annual grant total: In 2001 a total of 81 grants were made totalling £25,000.

Applications: On a form available from the correspondent.

Correspondent: Andrew Couch, Bircham Dyson Bell, 50 Broadway, Westminster, London SW1H 0BY (020 7227 7116; Fax: 0207 222 3480; e-mail: andycouch@bdb-law.co.uk).

Dame Alice Owen's Eleemosynary Charities

Eligibility: Poor widows who are over 50 and live in the parishes of St Mary, Islington and St James, Clerkenwell and have done so for at least seven years. There is a preference for people over 70 years old.

Types of grants: Pensions.

Annual grant total: In 2000 the charities had assets of £45,000, an income of £1,700 and made grants totalling £1,100.

Applications: The local vicar and social services are told when vacancies arise, but direct applications can be made.

Correspondent: The Clerk, The Worshipful Company of Brewers, Brewers' Hall, Aldermanbury Square, London EC2V 7HR (020 7606 1301).

The St Sepulchre (Finsbury) United Charities

Eligibility: People over 60 who are in need who live in the parish of St Sepulchre, Islington (EC1 and N1).

Types of grants: Pensions and one-off grants ranging from £100 to £300.

Annual grant total: In 2000/01 the trust had assets of £1.2 million and an income of £52,000. Total expenditure was £21,000 with distributions to individuals totalling £1,400.

Applications: In writing to the correspondent either directly by the individual or through a social worker, citizen's advice bureau or other welfare agency.

Correspondent: P S Rust, Clerk, Boundary House, 91–93 Charterhouse Street, London EC1M 6PN (020 7253 3757).

Kensington & Chelsea

The Campden Charities

Eligibility: People in need who live in the old parish of Kensington, north of the Fulham Road.

Types of grants: Pensions to people in need who are over 70 and who have lived in the parish for at least seven years. Christmas and birthday presents, television licences, holidays and other sundries are distributed. The average pension in 2001 was £500.

Grants are also given to individuals through agencies, for needs such as children's clothing, equipment, settling of debts and so on.

Annual grant total: In 2001 the charities had assets of over £60 million and an income of £2.6 million. Pensions to 575 individuals totalled £287,000. Educational grants to 626 individuals totalled £440,000. Grants to organisations totalled £1.1 million.

Applications: Preliminary telephone enquiries are welcomed. Specific application forms are available for social work organisations seeking pensions or charitable relief for individuals in the parish. Applications are considered by the case committee, the education committee or the board of trustees as appropriate. Each of these meets monthly (except during August).

Correspondent: C Stannard, Clerk, 27a Pembridge Villas, London W11 3EP (020 7243 0551; Fax: 020 7229 4920; e-mail: chris-stannard@campdencharities.org.uk; website: www.campdencharities.org.uk).

Other information: The charities also make grants to organisations. (See *A Guide to the Major Trusts, Volume 1.*)

The Kensington District Nursing Trust

Eligibility: People who are older and frail and people who are physically or mentally ill who are in need who have lived for at least two years in the former borough of Kensington.

Types of grants: One-off grants up to £1,000 for domestic appliances, medical and nursing aids and equipment, beds, bedding and other furniture and clothing. Up to 60 heating allowances of £100 are also made. Some grants are also given to local organisations.

Annual grant total: In 2000/01 the trust had assets of £1.5 million, an income of £73,000 and a total expenditure of £91,000. The sum of £24,000 was given in 98 grants.

Applications: On a form available from the correspondent. Applications must be submitted through a social worker, citizen's advice bureau or other welfare agency. Applications are considered each month.

Correspondent: Margaret Rhodes, 27a Pembridge Villas, London W11 3EP (020 7229 3538; Fax: 020 7229 4920).

Kingston-upon-Thames

The Kingston-upon-Thames Association for the Blind

Eligibility: Blind and partially sighted people who live in the royal borough of Kingston-upon-Thames.

Types of grants: Grants are one-off and have been given to help towards the cost of a gas boiler, spectacles, a bed, a family holiday, a CCTV system and an X-pand system.

Annual grant total: About £10,000 to individuals and organisations.

Applications: On a form available from the correspondent submitted either directly by the individual or through a social worker, citizen's advice bureau or other welfare agency. Applications are considered every other month from January onwards.

Correspondent: John Walmsley, 26 Manor Crescent, Surbiton KT5 8LQ (020 8399 3022).

Other information: The association employs a part-time volunteer coordinator for its home visiting scheme. Support is also given to satellite clubs for the blind and to talking newspapers.

William Nicholl's Charity

Eligibility: People in need who live in the former borough of Kingston-upon-Thames as constituted until 1964.

Types of grants: Recurrent pensions and fuel vouchers, ranging from £12 to £312.

Annual grant total: In 2001 the charity had assets of £37,000 and an income of £1,900. The sum of £2,200 was distributed in 71 grants to individuals.

Applications: In writing to the correspondent. Applications can be submitted either directly by the individual or through a social worker, citizen's advice bureau, welfare agency or any other third party. Applications should be submitted in December and are considered in April.

Correspondent: Andrew Bessant, Royal Borough of Kingston-upon-Thames, The Guildhall, High Street, Kingston-upon-Thames, Surrey KT1 1EU (020 8547 4628; Fax: 020 8547 5032; e-mail: andrewbessant@rbk-kingston.gov.uk; website: www.kingston.gov.uk).

Lambeth

The Brixton Dispensary

Eligibility: People on a low income who are in need through acute and chronic illness, disability, learning difficulties or mental ill-health who live in the nine ecclesiastical parishes around Brixton.

Types of grants: One-off grants between £50 and £100, towards personal or household items, special equipment, or holidays, where they have a direct impact on the illness or disability or contribute towards improvements in the applicant's health or general well-being.

No grants towards debts, or costs which can be met by statutory sources.

Annual grant total: In 2001 the trust had an income of £3,000 and a total expenditure of £1,600.

Applications: On a form available from the correspondent. Applications should be submitted through a recognised referral agency (social worker, citizen's advice bureau, doctor or teacher) and are considered by the trustees four times a year. The Chair can deal with emergency applications at any time.

Applicants need to provide details of name and address, living situation, information about health and income and the reason for the application.

Correspondent: Paul Shepherd, Clerk to the Trustees, St John's Angell Town CE School, 85 Angell Road, Brixton SW9 7HH.

Other information: This entry was not confirmed by the charity, but the address was correct according to the Charity Commission database.

The Clapham Relief Fund

Eligibility: People in need who live in the former parish of Clapham.

Types of grants: Grants typically ranging from £75 to £400 are made towards domestic appliances, beds and bedding, redecoration, clothing, educational expenses, convalescent holidays, particularly to older people, asylum seekers and to local institutions caring for those needs. No grants will be given where sufficient help is available from public sources.

Annual grant total: In 2000/01 the fund had assets of £464,00 and an income of £18,000. A total of £17,000 was given in grants to organisations and individuals.

Applications: On a form available from the correspondent. Applications should be submitted through a social worker, citizen's advice bureau, welfare agency or another third party such as a district nurse, charitable agency worker, parish priest or doctor. They are considered in February, May, July and November.

Correspondent: Clerk to the Trustees, c/o Holy Trinity Church, Clapham Common North Side, London SW4 0QZ (020 8671 2592; Fax: 020 8627 5065).

The Lambeth Endowed Charities (The Walcot Non-Educational Charity & The Hayles Charity)

Eligibility: People in need who live in the borough of Lambeth.

Types of grants: *The Walcot Non-Educational Charity*
One-off grants for individuals under 29 or families who have urgent needs that cannot be met from statutory sources. Grants range from £50 to £150 and can be made towards the cost of furniture, clothing, household equipment and respite holidays. Larger grants up to a maximum of £400 will be considered in exceptional circumstances.

No grants can be made towards bills and debts, funeral expenses or childcare costs. No more than one application per individual or family in a twelve month period.

The Hayles Charity
The majority of grants made by the Hayle's Charity are to projects and organisations (see *A Guide To The Major Trusts Volume 1*). However, grants can be made to individuals who, due to to illness or disability, require specialised aids, equipment or services not available from statutory sources.

Annual grant total:
The Walcot Non-Educational Charity
In 2000 the charity gave 580 grants to individuals totalling £78,000 and 58 grants to organisations totalling £35,000.

The Hayles Charity
In 2000 the charity gave 147 grants totalling £24,000.

Applications: Applications must be made by a recognised referring social/welfare agency, e.g. social services, citizen's advice bureau, doctor or minister of religion. They must be made on a form available from the correspondent and are considered on an on-going basis. The agency will be expected to administer the grant on behalf of the client and the trustees may ask for copies of receipts for items purchased.

The Walcot Non-Educational Charity also makes grants to projects and organisations (see entry in *A Guide To The Major Trusts Volume 1*).

Correspondent: Robert Dewar, Director and Clerk, 127 Kennington Road, London SE11 6SF (020 7735 1925; Fax: 020 7735 7048).

Lewisham

The Deptford Pension Society

Eligibility: People over 60 who have lived in the former London borough of Deptford for at least seven years.

Types of grants: Pensions of £10 a month to about 40 individuals.

Annual grant total: In 2000 the society had an income of £7,800 and a total expenditure of £4,900.

Applications: On a form available from the correspondent, for consideration throughout the year.

Correspondent: John Dolding, 2 Hunts Mead Close, Chislehurst, Kent BR7 5SE.

Other information: This entry was not confirmed by the society but the address was correct according to the Charity Commission database.

The William Hatcliffe Non-Educational Charity

Eligibility: People in need, particularly people who are elderly or disabled, who have lived in the ancient parish of Lee in Lewisham for at least five years.

Types of grants: Regular allowances (currently £146 a year).

Annual grant total: In 1998 the trust had an income of £7,800 and a total expenditure of £2,900.

Applications: In writing to the correspondent.

Correspondent: Mr Hillier, 27 Beechwood Rise, Chislehurst, Bromley, Kent BR7 6TF (Tel & Fax: 020 8467 8724).

Lewisham Relief in Need Charity

Eligibility: People who live in the ancient parish of Lewisham, which does not include Deptford or Lee, who are elderly, disadvantaged or disabled and in need.

Types of grants: Small one-off grants for specific purposes rather than general need. Christmas grants are also made to older people of £25 each. No grants are made where statutory assistance is available.

Annual grant total: In 2000/01 grants totalled £2,900.

Applications: In writing to the correspondent, for consideration throughout the year.

Correspondent: Mrs Alison Murdoch, Clerk, Lloyd Court, Slagrave Place, London SE13 7LP (020 8690 8145).

Other information: Grants are also made to small organisations aiding the people of Lewisham.

Merton

Wimbledon Guild of Social Welfare (Incorporated)

Eligibility: Individuals in need who live primarily in Wimbledon but also in the borough of Merton, with some preference for older people.

Types of grants: One-off grants according to need. Examples of grants include assisting older people with heating bills, and paying for a holiday for a terminally ill child.

Annual grant total: In 2001/02 the guild's income totalled £1.9 million and its expenditure was £1.8 million. Grants to individuals are only a small part of the charity's work and in 2001/02 totalled £22,000.

Applications: On a form available from the correspondent. Applications are considered monthly.

Correspondent: Russell Humphreys, 30–32 Worple Road, Wimbledon, London SW19 4EF (020 8946 0735; e-mail: rhumphreys@wimbledonguild.co.uk; website: www.wimbledonguild.co.uk).

Other information: Grant-making is only a small part of this charity's work.

Newham

The Mary Curtis' Maternity Charity

Eligibility: People under 21; mainly pregnant women or mothers with newborn babies, otherwise women who have babies or children. Applicants must live in Newham and can be asylum seekers, or pregnant underage.

Types of grants: One-off grants ranging from £50 to £100 towards, for instance, cots, pushchairs and baby clothes.

Annual grant total: Up to £1,000.

Applications: In writing to the correspondent, through a doctor, vicar, teacher, midwife or social worker. Applications are considered every month and should include details about the area in which the individual lives and how many children she is responsible for.

Correspondent: Paul Regan, Durning Hall, Earlham Grove, London E7 9AB.

Redbridge

The Ethel Baker Bequest

Eligibility: People in need who live in the parish of Woodford Baptist Church in the London borough of Redbridge.

Types of grants: One-off and recurrent grants according to need.

Annual grant total: Between £4,000 to £5,000.

Applications: In writing to the correspondent, although the trust states that its funds are already allocated.

Correspondent: K R Hawkins, Treasurer, 41 Bressey Grove, South Woodford, London E18 2HX (020 8643 1166).

The George and Alfred Lewis (of Chigwell) Memorial Fund

Eligibility: 'Those men and women who served during the 1939/45 War, and who lived in the parishes of Chigwell and Chigwell Row at the time of their enlistment, who are suffering hardship as a result of such service or who are in necessitous circumstances.'

Types of grants: Grants are given as one-off payments including those to help towards funeral costs, new spectacles, new dentures, electric wheelchairs and domestic emergencies and so on. The maximum grant is usually £500. Grants are not given for the purchase of items deemed by the trustees to be luxuries or for overseas holiday expenses.

Annual grant total: In 2001 the fund had assets of £120,000 and an income of £7,200. The sum of £7,300 was distributed in 35 grants to individuals.

Applications: In writing to the correspondent including dates of service in the forces, residence at date of enlistment and main source of current income. Applications are considered at any time.

Correspondent: Miss E E A Smart, Hon. Secretary, 16 Forest Terrace, High Road, Chigwell, Essex IG7 5BW.

Richmond-upon-Thames

The Barnes Relief-in-Need Charity and The Bailey & Bates Trust

Eligibility: People in need who live in the London SW14 postal district.

Types of grants: Grants, on average for £150, towards household items, bills etc.

Annual grant total: About £3,800.

Applications: Applications should be made through a social worker, citizen's advice bureau or other welfare agency, on an application form.

Correspondent: J P Walsh, Clerk, 1 Rocks Lane, Barnes, London SW13 0DE (020 8876 8811/2/3).

The Barnes Workhouse Fund

Eligibility: People in need who are elderly, poor, sick or distressed and live in the ancient parish of Barnes (in practice SW13).

Types of grants: One-off grants of up to £350, for example to provide items such as carpets, domestic appliances, children's clothing and school trips and assistance with the costs of medical needs not available from the National Health Service.

Annual grant total: In 2000 the trust had assets of £5.1 million and an income of £214,000. £38,000 was given in 148 welfare grants and 17 educational grants to individuals. Grants to 33 organisations totalled £74,000.

Applications: Applications can be submitted by the individual or preferably through a recognised referral agency (such as social worker, health visitor, citizen's advice bureau or doctor) on a form available from the correspondent. Applications are considered every other month, starting with January.

Correspondent: J P J Walsh, 1 Rocks Lane, Barnes, London SW13 0DE (020 8876 8811; Fax: 020 8878 4425).

The Hampton and Hampton Hill Philanthropic Society

Eligibility: People in need in Hampton and Hampton Hill.

Types of grants: Grants of £200 each are made to people who have suddenly come into financial need.

Annual grant total: In 1998/99 the trust had an income of £1,300 and gave grants totalling £600. Priority is given each year to making grants to individuals, any surplus funds left over at the end of the year are donated to local organisations.

Applications: In writing to the correspondent throughout the year.

Correspondent: Mrs Joan Barnett, Waverley, Old Farm Road, Hampton, Middlesex TW12 3RL.

Other information: Grants are also made to organisations.

The Hampton Wick United Charity

Eligibility: People in need who live in Hampton Wick and most of South Teddington, within the parishes of St John the Baptist, Hampton Wick and St Mark, South Teddington.

Types of grants: One-off grants (with the possibility of future reapplication).

Annual grant total: In 2000/01 the charity had assets of £354,000. Welfare grants to individuals totalled £8,000. Educational grants to individuals and organisations totalled £17,000.

Applications: In writing to the correspondent. The trustees normally meet three times a year to consider applications.

Correspondent: Roger Avins, 241 Kingston Road, Teddington, Middlesex TW11 9JJ (020 8977 1322).

The Petersham United Charities

Eligibility: People in need who live in the ecclesiastical parish of Petersham, Surrey.

Types of grants: Pensions and grants of £50 to £500, including Christmas and birthday gifts and grants towards heating.

Annual grant total: In 2000 the trust had assets of £125,000 and an income of £4,600. It gave 19 grants totalling £4,700.

Applications: In writing to the correspondent. Applications are considered in January, April, July and October and can be submitted either directly by the individual or through a social worker, citizen's advice bureau or other welfare agency.

Correspondent: R M Robinson, Clerk, Dixon Ward, 16 The Green, Richmond, Surrey TW9 1QD (020 8940 4051; Fax: 020 8940 3901).

The Richmond Aid-in-Sickness Fund

Eligibility: People in need who live in the borough of Richmond.

Types of grants: One-off grants ranging from £25 to £350 for bedding, fuel bills, funeral expenses, recuperative holidays and other small cash grants for the relief of the sick.

Annual grant total: In 2001 the trust had an income of £4,100 and £3,300 was given in grants to 14 individuals.

Applications: Applications should be submitted through a social worker, citizen's advice bureau or other welfare agency. They are considered on the first Wednesday of February, March, May, June, September, November and December.

Correspondent: Mrs C Rumsey, The Richmond Charities, 8 The Green, Richmond, Surrey TW9 1PL (020 8948 4188; Fax: 020 8948 6224; e-mail: richmondcharities@compuserve.com).

The Richmond Parish Lands Charity

Eligibility: People in need who have lived in Richmond, Kew, Ham, Petersham, North and East Sheen or Central Mortlake (NOT the whole borough of Richmond) for at least six months prior to application and have no other possible sources of help.

Types of grants: i. Small grants for people in financial need, up to a maximum of £250, towards a wide range of needs, such as furniture, cookers, fridges and other essential items for the home, utility bills and food.
ii. Grants for people with physical disabilities. Each case is considered on its merits, there is no stated maximum.
iii. Warm campaign: heating vouchers for older people on low incomes.
iv. Provision of housing to those in need.

Annual grant total: In 2000/01 the trust had assets of £35 million, an income of £848,000 and a total expenditure of £771,000. One-off grants to 267 individuals totalled £50,000. Heating vouchers to 1,000 people totalled £40,000. Educational grants to individuals totalled £87,000.

Applications: On a form, submitted through nominated welfare organisations – mainly citizen's advice bureau and social services. No direct applications are considered. Applications are considered in January for the warm campaign and at any time for other grants.

Correspondent: The Clerk to the Trustees, The Vestry House, 21 Paradise Road, Richmond, Surrey TW9 1SA (020 8948 5701; Fax: 020 8332 6792).

Other information: The charity also supports organisations in the area of benefit, please see *A Guide to Local Trusts in Greater London*, published by DSC, for further information.

The Richmond Philanthropic Society

Eligibility: People in need who live in the borough of Richmond.

Types of grants: Small one-off grants up to a maximum of £250 including those for washing machines, cookers and fridges, prams, beds and bedding, TV licences, rent arrears and utility bills. No grants are given for educational purposes or for the payment of council tax. No cash grants.

Annual grant total: In 2000/01 the trust had assets of £290,000 and an income of £12,000. A total of £7,500 was given in 34 grants.

Applications: Preferably through citizen's advice bureaux, social services, district nurses, health visitors and so on.

Correspondent: Derrick Schauerman, Hon. Treasurer, 29 Maze Road, Kew, Richmond, Surrey TW9 3DE (020 8940 0778; Fax: 020 8948 5432).

The Henry Smith Charity

Eligibility: People experiencing hardship or distress who live in the old borough of Richmond.

Types of grants: One-off grants ranging from £100 to £400. Recently the greatest number of grants have been made to unemployed single parents, towards children's clothing and fuel bills.

Annual grant total: In 2001 the trust received £2,200 income, allocated from Henry Smith's (General Estate) Charity. Almost £3,000 was distributed in 10 grants to individuals.

Applications: In writing to the correspondent, from referring bodies such as social services, health authority or a citizen's advice bureau. Applications are considered at trustees' meetings in February, March, May, June, September, November and December.

Correspondent: Mrs C Rumsey, The Richmond Charities, 8 The Green, Richmond, Surrey TW9 1PL (020 8948 4188; Fax: 020 8948 6224; e-mail: richmondcharities@compuserve.com).

Southwark

The Camberwell Consolidated Charities

Eligibility: Older people in need who live in the old metropolitan borough of Camberwell, including Peckham and Dulwich.

Types of grants: 245 pensions of £10 a quarter. Hardship grants are available for emergency items.

Annual grant total: In 2000/01 the charities had an income of £12,000 and a total expenditure of £15,000.

Applications: Vacancies are advertised by social services area offices, Age Concern and so on. Application forms are also available at the town hall. Applications are considered in February, May, July, September and November.

Correspondent: Clerk to the Trustees, Town Hall, Peckham Road, London SE5 8UB.

The Christ Church United Charities

Eligibility: Older people in need who live in the former metropolitan borough of Southwark.

Types of grants: Grants to eligible people in the form of pensions (about £180,000), Christmas parties (about £8,500), and summer holidays (about £30,000).

Annual grant total: About £200,000.

Applications: In writing to the correspondent.

Correspondent: P E McSorley, Clerk, 151–153 Walworth Road, London SE17 1RY (020 7525 2129).

Other information: Christ Church United Charities also administer almshouse

LONDON – SOUTHWARK/SUTTON

charities, Edward Edward's Charity, St George the Martyr Charities, St Mary Newington United Charities, Vaughans Pension Charity and Walworth United Charities.

The Joseph Collier Holiday Fund

Eligibility: People of pensionable age who live in the former metropolitan borough of Southwark (i.e. the northern part of the present borough of Southwark).

Homeowners are excluded, whether the house was bought by themselves or on their behalf.

Types of grants: Yearly one-off grants towards the cost of recuperative holidays in the UK or travel expenses to visit a relative.

Annual grant total: In 2000/01 the fund had an income of £5,600 and a total expenditure of £4,700.

Applications: Applicants should collect a form, in person from the office. Applications are considered all year round. Forms are not issued to any other party.

Correspondent: P E McSorley, Charities Section, Municipal Offices, 151–153 Walworth Road, London SE17 1RY (020 7525 2128).

The Peckham & Kent Road Pension Society

Eligibility: People who have lived in Peckham, SE15, for at least five years, receive Income Support and are over 60 (women) or 65 (men).

Types of grants: Monthly pensions of £7. The correspondent states that the trust's resources are already stretched by its pension commitments.

Annual grant total: No recent financial information was available.

Applications: In writing to the correspondent.

Correspondent: C Hutchins, c/o Sandom Solicitors, 4 Ye Market, Selsdon Road, South Croydon CR2 6PW (020 8680 7885).

Rotherhithe Consolidated Charities

Eligibility: People over 65 and in need who live in the ancient parish of St Mary's, Rotherhithe.

Types of grants: The trust pays an annual pension of £91 and provides holidays to about 40 pensioners, and gives other one-off grants.

Annual grant total: £6,000 to £7,000.

Applications: In writing to the correspondent. Applications can be submitted directly by the individual or through a third party. They are considered at any time.

Correspondent: B D Claxton, Hardcastle Burton, Amwell House, 19 Amwell Street, Hoddesdon, Hertfordshire EN11 8TS (01992 444466).

The Mayor of Southwark's Common Good Trust (The Mayor's Charity)

Eligibility: People in need who live in the borough of Southwark.

Types of grants: One-off grants, paid in cash or kind. The trust states that 'every application is individual' and that each case is taken on its own merits.

Annual grant total: About £4,500.

Applications: In writing to the correspondent. Applications can be made either directly by the individual or through a social worker, citizen's advice bureau or other welfare agency, a family member, MP, doctor or other third party. Any third party must undertake to have personally visited the applicant to verify that there is a genuine need. Applications should include full details of family/financial/health background and details of other sources of funds, including whether a previous application has been made to this trust. Applications are considered every month, usually in the first week.

Correspondent: Mrs N Hammond, Secretary to the Trust, c/o Room 33 West House, The Town Hall, 31 Peckham Road, Southwark, London SE5 8UB (020 7525 7347; Fax: 020 7525 7277).

Other information: The trust does not encourage applications from other registered charities.

The United Charities of St George the Martyr

Eligibility: Older people in need in the parish of St George the Martyr (in north Southwark SE1).

Types of grants: One-off grants according to need, usually of up to £300, towards buying items such as fridges. Pensions and Christmas parcels are also given.

Annual grant total: In 2000 the charities had assets of £4.8 million and an income of £255,000. Direct charitable expenditure totalled £147,000. A total of £84,000 was spent on summer holidays organised by the trust, £38,000 on pensions and £16,000 on Christmas parcels and parties. A further £2,300 was given in grants to local schools.

Applications: In writing to the correspondent. In June 2002 the trust stated that all its grants and pensions were fully committed, and its list of beneficiaries was closed. In such instances its policy is to keep new applications on file and contact relevant applicants when the list reopens.

Correspondent: Mrs J N Fox, Clerk to the Trustees, St Alphege Church, Kings Bench Street, London SE1 0QX (020 7401 3829).

St Olave's United Charity, incorporating the St Thomas & St John Charities

Eligibility: People in need who live in Bermondsey (i.e. SE1).

Types of grants: Pensions of £100 a year and a further grant towards holidays once every year or every two years. Depending on additional income, other one-off grants can be made for a wide variety of needs, including clothes, musical instruments and holidays.

Annual grant total: In 1998/99 the trust had an income of £413,000. £142,000 was given to individuals for welfare purposes, with a further £77,000 given for educational purposes.

Applications: Applications for pensions should be made in writing to the correspondent and are considered four times a year. There is currently a waiting list for applicants.

Correspondent: Mrs S Broughton, Secretary, 6–8 Tooley Street, London SE1 2EU (020 7407 2530).

The Emily Temple West Trust

Eligibility: People under 19 or their parents in need who live in the SE1 London area.

Types of grants: One-off cash grants only ranging from £150 to £500. Grants are given for clothing, shoes, holidays and so on.

Annual grant total: About £2,000.

Applications: On a form available from the correspondent directly by the individual or individual's parents or through a third party such as a church, social services, advice centre etc. Applications are considered in May and November.

Correspondent: The Administrator, Christchurch Industrial Centre, 27 Blackfriars Road, London SE1 8NY (020 7928 4707).

Sutton

The Sutton Nursing Association

Eligibility: People who are sick or in need and live in and around the London borough of Sutton.

Types of grants: One-off grants, up to a maximum of £2,000, according to need.

Recurrent grants and matters relating to ongoing liabilities are not considered. Generally, requests for property improvements are not considered although some exceptions may be made if such grants would primarily provide some relief from sickness.

Annual grant total: In 2001 the association had assets of £664,000, an income of £31,000 and a total expenditure of £29,000. The sum of £16,000 was distributed to individuals.

Applications: Applications should come through a social worker, citizen's advice bureau or other welfare agency. They are considered bi-monthly and must include as much information as possible, such as the cost involved, funds available from other sources and the ability of the individual to contribute.

Correspondent: D N Skingle, 3 Glebe Road, Cheam, Sutton, Surrey SM2 7NS (020 8642 6485).

Other information: The association also assists the community nursing services and local hospitals with requests for help towards the cost of much needed equipment not available from NHS Trusts.

Tower Hamlets

Bishopsgate Foundation

Eligibility: People of pensionable age who live in the parishes of St Botolph, Bishopsgate; Christchurch, Spitalfields; and St Leonard's, Shoreditch – all in the borough of Tower Hamlets.

Types of grants: Pensions of £130 per quarter, plus a Christmas box of £30. Beneficiaries are also provided with a monthly pensioners' lunch and four outings a year.

Annual grant total: In 2000/01 the trust's assets totalled £11 million, its income was £960,000 and the total expenditure was £860,000. Grants were made to 40 individuals totalling £18,000.

Applications: On a form available from the correspondent for consideration in October. Applications can be submitted either directly by the individual or through a social worker, citizen's advice bureau or other welfare agency.

Correspondent: Andrew Fuller, 230 Bishopsgate, London EC2M 4QH (020 7247 6844; Fax: 020 7375 1794; e-mail: afuller@bishopsgate.org.uk).

Other information: Grants are also made to organisations that help relieve need.

The Henderson Charity

Eligibility: Pensioners who live in the hamlets of Ratcliff and Shadwell, and the parish of St George's-in-the-East, Stepney. Applicants must be longstanding residents of the beneficial area and there is a maximum income requirement.

Types of grants: Pensions of £20 a month for single people and £30 a month for married couples.

Annual grant total: About £13,000.

Applications: Vacancies are advertised locally and through social services and appropriate welfare agencies. When a pension is available, application forms can be obtained from social services or the correspondent.

Correspondent: Jonathan Woodbridge, Ringley Park House, 59 Reigate Road, Reigate, Surrey RH2 0QT (01737 221911; Fax: 01737 221677)

The Trevor Huddleston Fund for Children

Eligibility: Children in need who live on the Isle of Dogs.

Types of grants: About 100 one-off grants a year, up to £100 each, towards basic needs, particularly winter clothes and shoes.

Annual grant total: In 2000/01 the fund had an income of £4,100 and a total expenditure of £3,200.

Applications: In writing to the correspondent on behalf of the individual child by schools, social services, churches or other community agencies for consideration at any time. Applications made by individuals or their families are not considered.

Correspondent: The Secretary, c/o Christ Church Vicarage, Manchester Road, London E14 3BN.

The Ratcliff Pension Charity

Eligibility: Older people in financial need who live in the London borough of Tower Hamlets, with a preference for the Stepney area

Types of grants: One-off and recurrent grants according to need.

Annual grant total: In 1998/99 the charity had an income of £44,000. Grants were made totalling £42,000 of which more than £5,000 was paid to over 50 individuals. The charity also made 49 grants to welfare and community organisations.

Applications: In writing to the correspondent.

Correspondent: J A Newton, Clerk, Cooper's Hall, 13 Devonshire Square, London EC2M 4TH (020 7247 9577).

Other information: This entry was not confirmed by the trust, but the address was correct according to the Charity Commission database.

Stepney Relief-in-Need Charity

Eligibility: People in need who live within the boundaries of the following area in Stepney: Jubilee Street on the west, Mile End Road on the north, Grand Union Canal on the east and Commercial Road on the south.

Types of grants: One-off grants of £100 to £500 are given for items such as bedding, furniture, clothing, hoovers, washing machines, holidays, food, TVs and radios, hospital travel, wheelchairs and so on. No grants are made towards the repayment of debts, including rent and rates.

Annual grant total: In 2000/01 the trust had an income of £12,000. Total expenditure was £5,000, of which £4,700 was given in 18 grants, mostly for welfare purposes.

Applications: On a form available from the correspondent, submitted either directly by the individual, or through a relative, social worker or other welfare agency. Applicants should state whether any other body has been approached for help. The trustees usually meet four times a year, but applications can be considered between meetings.

Correspondent: Mrs J Partleton, Clerk, Rectory Cottage, 5 White Horse Lane, Stepney, London E1 3NE (020 7790 3598).

Miss Vaughan's Spitalfields Charity

Eligibility: People in need who live in the ecclesiastical parishes of Christchurch with All Saints in Spitalfields, St Matthew in Bethnal Green and St Leonard, Shoreditch.

Types of grants: Originally clothing and support was given to poor mechanics and weavers in Spitalfields who were unable to work. Now grants are given to individuals and families who are convalescing, unemployed or disabled and also to large families on a low income.

Annual grant total: In 2000/01 grants totalled £850.

Applications: To a member of the clergy from the above mentioned parishes.

Correspondent: Philip Whitehead, 45 Quilter Street, Bethnal Green, London E2 7BS.

Wandsworth

The Harold Carter Bequest

Eligibility: People in need who live in the postal district of SW11.

Types of grants: One-off grants ranging from £25 to £100 a year towards the cost of washing machines, bedding, redecorating materials and short holidays for carers who need a break. Grants are not given for ongoing financial aid, for example, educational grants or debt repayment.

Annual grant total: About £1,500 to individuals. Grants are also made to organisations.

Applications: In writing through social services, charities, citizen's advice bureaux or schools. A preliminary phone call to discuss the application is welcomed. Applications are considered throughout the year.

Correspondent: D Jesson-Dibley, 52 Worfield Street, Battersea, London SW11 4RA (020 7228 7604).

The Peace Memorial Fund

Eligibility: Children aged 16 or under who live in the borough of Wandsworth.

Types of grants: Grants of £40 to £75 towards holidays and school trips.

Annual grant total: In 2001 the trust had assets of £153,000, an income of £8,000 and a total expenditure of £8,400. Grants to 126 individuals totalled £7,500.

Applications: Through a welfare agency on a form available from the correspondent. Applications should be submitted in February/March and May/June.

Correspondent: Gareth Jones, Town Hall, Room 153, Wandsworth High Street, London SW18 2PU (020 8871 7520).

The Putney Creche

Eligibility: Mothers with children up to the age of seven who live in the Putney and Wandsworth areas.

Types of grants: One-off grants to mothers who might have experienced matrimonial problems and are now experiencing financial difficulties in bringing up infant children. Grants up to £50 where there is one child in the family and up to £100 where there are two or more. If help is still needed after six months, a further payment of up to half the above values can be made. Grants are made specifically for those items which will directly benefit the children, such as clothing, shoes, bed linen or a pushchair. No grants for such things as the payment of electricity bills and such like.

Annual grant total: In 2001 the sum of £13,000 was given in grants to individuals.

Applications: On a form available from the correspondent. Applications that come directly from individuals are not considered. They must be submitted through a social worker, citizen's advice bureau or other welfare agency, for consideration at any time.

Correspondent: Mrs A M Smalley, Messrs Russell-Cooke, 2 Putney Hill, London SW15 6AB (020 8789 9111).

Other information: The creche also makes grants to local schools and organisations, and have in the past donated toothbrushes to nursery children to allow a health visitor to give talks.

Supporting Children of Wandsworth Trust (SCOWT)

Eligibility: Children aged between 3 and 18 who live in the borough of Wandsworth and have lived there for at least two years.

Types of grants: Grants to a maximum of £200 towards items such as musical instruments, sporting equipment, special clothing and educational trips. Grants are made for educational and welfare purposes to 'help children to achieve their full potential'.

Annual grant total: In 1998/99 the trust had assets of £27,000 and an income of £12,000. Total expenditure was £3,200, all of which was given in 16 grants to individuals.

Applications: On a form available from the correspondent. Applications should include recommendation letters from clubs, social workers and so on if possible. The trustees meet every two to three months, although urgent applications can be considered between meetings.

Correspondent: Cllr Mrs Lois Lees, The Secretary, 12 Roedean Cresecent, Roehampton SW15 5JU (020 8876 3851; Fax: 020 876 4951).

The Wandsworth Combined Charity

Eligibility: Older people in need who live in the ancient parish of Wandsworth, ie. the present wards of Fairfield, Earlsfield, Southfield, West Hill, Springfield, part of Thamesfield and part of East Putney.

Types of grants: Discretionary grants of £20 a month, except for December when there is a bonus payment. No one-off grants are made.

Annual grant total: About £12,000 in 60 pensions.

Applications: In writing to the correspondent, either directly by the individual or via social services, Age Concern or local clergy.

Correspondent: A V Rashbrook, Clerk, H E Rashbrook & Son, 91 East Hill, Wandsworth, London SW18 2QD (020 8874 2211; Fax: 020 8877 1370).

Westminster

The Bengough Charity (also known as The United Westminster Almhouses Group of Charities)

Eligibility: Women in need or distress, with preference for those who live in the parish of St Matthew, Westminster.

Types of grants: Giving grants or paying for items, services or facilities.

Annual grant total: In 2001 the trust had assets of £866,000 and an income of £37,000. Out of a total expenditure of £28,000 the sum of £25,000 was distributed in 67 grants.

Applications: In writing to the correspondent.

Correspondent: The Clerk to the Trustees, Palmer's House, 42 Rochester Row, London SW1P 1BU (020 7828 3131).

Other information: Grants may occasionally be given to institutions or organisations which provide for the above mentioned beneficiaries or for women who are communicants of the Church of England and regular attenders at the Church of St Matthew, Westminster.

The Charity of A J G Cross

Eligibility: People who are sick, convalescent, disabled or infirm and in need and live in South Westminster (i.e. south of Oxford Street).

Types of grants: One-off grants ranging from £50 to £100 including those for clothing, furnishings, holidays and medical equipment. No grants are given towards arrears.

Annual grant total: In 2000/01 the charity had an income of £6,000 and a total expenditure of £5,100. Grants to 52 individuals were made totalling £3,800.

Applications: On a form available from the correspondent to be submitted through a social worker, citizen's advice bureau or other welfare agency. They are considered once a month.

Correspondent: Miss Janet Dain, 10a Culford Mansions, Culford Gardens, London SW3 2SS (020 7589 7180).

Isaac Duckett's Charity (St Clement Danes Branch)

Eligibility: People who are or have been employed in the London borough of the City of Westminster, with preference for the parish of St Clement Danes and St Mary le Strand. Preference for people who are qualified as, who are or have been domestic servants, housekeepers or resident caretakers, or, who have served in a service capacity, for example, busdrivers and road sweepers. Applicants must be over 21, but more usually are of pensionable age.

Types of grants: One-off grants and pensions. In 2001/02 pensions of £100 a quarter were given and one-off grants of up to £600.

Annual grant total: In 2001/02 the charity had an income of £78,000 and gave grants totalling £65,000 of which £51,000 was given in pensions and £10,000 in one-off grants. A further £4,500 was given to organisations.

Applications: On a form available from the correspondent. Applicants must show their eligibility and demonstrate their needs.

Correspondent: Frank Brenchley-Brown, 169 Strand, London WC2R 2LS (020 7836 3205).

The Hyde Park Place Estate Charity (Civil Trustees)

Eligibility: People in need who are residents of the borough of Westminster.

London – Westminster

Refugees and asylum seekers are not eligible.

Types of grants: One-off grants to individuals and families for all kinds of need including educational. No recurrent grants are given, but beneficiaries can reapply if there is further need.

Annual grant total: In 1999/2000 the trust had assets of £10 million, an income of £416,000 and gave grants to individuals and organisations totalling £169,000.

Applications: In writing to the correspondent. Applications on behalf of individuals need the recommendation of a third party such as a social worker, priest or representative of a welfare organisation. Applications are often processed within a few days but may be held over to the next quarterly meeting if large-scale funding is involved.

Correspondent: Mrs J Roberts, Clerk, St George's Vestry, 2a Mill Street, London W1S 1FX (020 7629 0874).

The Paddington Welfare Charities

Eligibility: People who are sick or in need who live in the former metropolitan borough of Paddington (roughly the north-west corner of the city of Westminster, bounded by Edgware Road and Bayswater Road).

Types of grants: These charities operate a number of schemes. One-off grants are made towards specific needs, including furniture, other household equipment, clothing and essential bills such as telephone, gas and electric. Monthly pensions with a small Christmas bonus are available to 75 older people in Paddington. Social work agencies and clergy are provided with food and fuel coupons to distribute to the people they can most assist. Clergy are also eligible to select 10 individuals to receive a gift of £10, and can request £50 each to give as immediate aid to people in need without having to report back to the trust how this money is spent. The city council's social service department receives funds to make grants or loans of up to £50 in cases of specific need.

Annual grant total: In 2001 grants totalled: £4,000 in one-off grants; £15,000 in pensions; £1,800 in fuel and food coupons; £1,100 in gifts and immediate aid: and £600 in grants through social services.

Applications: For one-off grants applications must be made in writing via social services or a welfare agency, and will generally be considered within three weeks. None of the other types of grants are administered directly by the trust. Pensions are given via Age Concern. Local clergy should be contacted for fuel and food grants, gifts and immediate aid, although welfare organisations may be able to help with fuel and food coupons. Social services can also consider urgent applications.

Correspondent: Helen Ashworth, Assistant Clerk, 17th Floor, Westminster City Hall, 64 Victoria Street, London SW1E 6QP (020 7641 2667).

Sarah, Duchess of Somerset

Eligibility: People, particularly those who are older, who live in Westminster. Special reference is given to those who live in the former united parishes of St Margaret and St John the Evangelist.

Types of grants: Quarterly pensions and grants.

Annual grant total: In 2001 the fund had assets of £103,000 and an income of £4,300. Out of a total expenditure of £2,400 the sum of £730 was given in 3 grants and 24 pensions.

Applications: In writing to the correspondent.

Correspondent: Roger Walker, Palmer's House, 42 Rochester Row, London SW1P 1BU (020 7828 3131)

The St Clement Danes Parochial Charities

Eligibility: People who live in the parish of St Clement Danes in Westminster, but if there are no suitable applicants, the city of Westminster.

Types of grants: One-off grants to a maximum of £200 and quarterly pensions. In 2001 the charity gave 13 pensions of £100 a quarter.

Annual grant total: In 2001 the charities had an income of £12,000, the sum of £7,000 was given in grants and pensions.

Applications: On a form available from the correspondent.

Correspondent: Frank Brenchley-Brown, 169 Strand, London WC2R 2LS (020 7836 3205).

The St Mary-le-Strand Charity

Eligibility: People in need who have lived in the City of Westminster for more than a year.

Types of grants: One-off grants of about £150 to individuals in need and regular allowances to older people in need. In 2001 four pensions of £400 a year were given.

Annual grant total: In 2001 the charity had an income of £86,000. Grants were made totalling £92,000 of which £26,000 was given to individuals.

Applications: Applications must come from social workers or welfare agencies where a case worker is already working with the potential beneficiary.

Correspondent: Frank Brenchley-Brown, 169 Strand, London WC2R 2LS (020 7836 3205).

The St Marylebone Health Society

Eligibility: Families with children of school age and under who live in the former borough of St Marylebone in the city of Westminster i.e. east of Edgware Road and north of Oxford Street in NW8, NW1 or W1.

Types of grants: Holidays for parents and their children are arranged and paid for. Grants are usually sufficient to pay for one week at a holiday centre, including fares and food allowance if self-catering. The applicant should have lived in the beneficial area for two years. Overseas holidays and families without children cannot be funded.

Other grants (length of residence qualification not necessary) are made for beds, bedding, household equipment, children's equipment, clothing and so on. Grants average between £250 and £300. Christmas grants are made in the form of grocery vouchers.

Grants are not given to adults not caring for children, to assist elderly people or to students. Cash grants are rarely given.

Annual grant total: £17,000 in 2000, allocated as follows: £6,600 in holiday grants, £7,500 in general grants and £1,600 in Christmas grants.

Applications: Via social workers, educational welfare officers and health visitors, using the application form available from the correspondent. Holiday applications by February if possible. Other applications at any time.

Correspondent: Mrs Sue Webber, 17 St Paul's Cresent, London NW1 9XN.

The United Charities of St Paul's, Covent Garden

Eligibility: People in need who live in the city of Westminster.

Types of grants: One-off grants ranging from £50 to £150. Monthly payments are made to about 12 people. Grants can be paid directly or through hospitals, health authorities, family service units or an early intervention service.

Annual grant total: About £3,000.

Applications: In writing to the correspondent.

Correspondent: C G Snart, Clerk, c/o 31 Manor Wood Road, Purley, Croydon CR8 4LG (020 8660 2786).

United Westminster Almshouses Charity

Eligibility: People in need over 60 who live in the City of Westminster. Preference is given to individuals who have resided in the former parishes of St Margaret and St John the Evangelist.

Types of grants: Quarterly pensions and one-off grants.

Annual grant total: In 2001 the trust had assets of £14 million, an income of £430,000 and a total expenditure of £385,000. The sum of £4,500 was given in 24 relief-in-need grants.

Applications: In writing to the correspondent.

Correspondent: Roger Walker, Palmer's House, 42 Rochester Row, London SW1P 1BU (020 7828 3131).

Other information: The charity provides accommodation in 38 single bedroom flats. A permanent endowment provides services to the residents and some of the costs of maintaining the property. Surplus funds are used for the relief of need of people who qualify for almshouse accommodation but who continue to live independently.

The Waterloo Parish Charity for the Poor

Eligibility: People in need who live in the parish of Waterloo, St John & St Andrew.

Types of grants: Small grants for living expenses and domestic items. Grants range from £20 to £100.

Annual grant total: About £800 was given in 15 grants in 2000/01.

Applications: Applications can be submitted either through a social worker, citizen's advice bureau or other welfare agency, or directly by the individual or a relevant third party.

Correspondent: Canon R Truss, 1 Secker Street, London SE1 8UF
(Tel & Fax: 020 7928 4470).

The Westminster Amalgamated Charity

Eligibility: People in need who live, work or study in the borough of Westminster (Soho, Covent Garden, The Strand, Mayfair, Victoria, Pimlico and part of Kensington but not Bayswater or Paddington). Applicants who used to live in this area must have done so for a total of five years or more, in order to be eligible to receive a grant.

Types of grants: One-off grants are given for holidays and holiday fares, clothing, household equipment and furnishing, and other forms of real need. Grants normally range from £50 to £350.

Annual grant total: In 2001 the trust's income was £316,000. Grants to 693 individuals totalled £60,000.

Applications: On a form available from the correspondent submitted through a welfare agency, doctor, social services or similar third party. They are considered throughout the year.

Correspondent: Mrs J A Turner, Clerk and Chief Executive, School House, Drury Lane, London WC2B 5SU (020 7395 9460; Fax: 020 7395 9479).

Advice Organisations

The following lists the names and contact details of voluntary organisations that offer advice and support to individuals in need. The list is split into two sections: general welfare needs; and sickness and disability. Each section begins with an index, before listing the organisations by category.

The listings provide a source of reference about organisations where individuals can discuss their situation and receive advice and support. These organisations will have experience in tackling the sorts of problems that other individuals have faced, and will know the most effective and efficient ways of dealing with them. They may also be able to arrange for people to meet others in a similar situation. As well as providing advice and support, many of the organisations will be happy to help individuals submit applications to the trusts included in this guide. They may also know of other sources of funding available.

Some of the organisations included in this list have their own financial resources available to individuals. We have marked these with an asterisk (*). This list should not be used as a quick way of identifying potential funding – the organisations will have criteria and policies which may mean they are unable to support all needs under that category and the guide will include many more potential sources of funding than there are organisations here.

Some organisations have local branches, which are better placed to have a personal contact with the individual and have a greater local knowledge of the need. We have only included the headquarters of such organisations, which will be happy to provide contact details for any relevant branches.

It is helpful for the organisations listed if any request for information includes an sae.

This list is by no means comprehensive, and should only be used as a starting point. It only contains national organisations rather than local groups, and does not include organisations that provide general advice and support solely to members of a particular religion, country or ethnic grouping. For further details of groups working in your local area, look for charitable and voluntary organisations in your local phone book, or contact your local Council for Voluntary Service (sometimes called Voluntary Action) which should be listed in the phone book.

Welfare

General   383
Bereavement   383
   Children   383
   Parents   384
Carers   384
Children and young people   384
   Bullying   384
   Young people leaving care   384
Families   384
Housing   384
Legal   384
Men's Rights   384
Missing people   384
Offenders and ex-offenders   384
   Families of offenders   384
   Women offenders and ex-offenders   384
Older people   384
Parenting   385
   Abduction   385
   Adoption and fostering   385
   Childcare   385
   Divorced parents   385
   Expectant mothers   385
   Grandparents   385
   Mothers   385
   Single parents   385
Poverty   385
Refugees and asylum seekers   386
Relationships   386
Social isolation   386
Squatters   386
Victims of accidents and crimes   386
   Abuse   386
   Crime   386
   Disasters   386
   Domestic violence   386
   Medical Accidents   386
   Rape   386
   Road Accidents   386
Widows   386
Work issues   386
Women   386

General

National Association of Citizens Advice Bureaux (NACAB), Myddelton House, 115–123 Pentonville Road, London N1 9LZ (020 7833 2181; e-mail: info@nacab.org.uk; website: www.nacab.org.uk).

* *The Salvation Army*, Territorial Headquarters, 101 Newington Causeway, London SE1 6BN (020 7367 4500; e-mail: thq@salvationarmy.org.uk; website: www.salvationarmy.org.uk).

Bereavement

Cruse Bereavement Care, 126 Sheen Road, Richmond-upon-Thames, Surrey TW9 1UR (020 8939 9530; Helpline: 0870 167 1677; e-mail: info@crusebereavementcare.org.uk; website: www.crusebereavementcare.org.uk).

Natural Death Centre, 6 Blacklock Mews, Blacklock Road, London N4 2BT (Helpline: 020 8208 2853 – 9.30am–5.30pm weekdays; e-mail: rhino@dial.pipex.com; website: www.naturaldeath.org.uk).

Survivors of Bereavement by Suicide (SOBS), Centre 88, Saner Street, Anlaby Road, Hull HU3 2TR (01482 610728; Helpline: 0870 241 3337, 9am–9pm daily; e-mail: sobs.support@care4free.net; website: www.uk-sobs.org.uk).

Children

Winston's Wish, The Clara Burgess Centre, Gloucestershire Royal Hospital, Great Western Road, Gloucester GL1 3NN (01452 394377; Helpline: 0845 203 0405 – Monday–Friday 9.30am–5pm; e-mail: info@winstonswish.org.uk; website: www.winstonswish.org.uk).

Advice Organisations

Parents

Child Death Helpline, Great Ormond Street Hospital for Children, Great Ormond Street, London WC1N 3JH (020 7813 8551; Helpline: 0800 282 986; e-mail: contact@childdeathhelpline.org; website: www.childdeathhelpline.org.uk).

The Compassionate Friends, 53 North Street, Bristol BS1 3EN (0117 966 5202; Helpline: 0117 953 9639 – 10am–4pm and 6.30pm–10.30pm seven days a week; e-mail: info@tcf.org.uk; website: www.tcf.org.uk).

Foundation for the Study of Infant Deaths, Artillery House, 11–19 Artillery Row, London SW1P 1RT (020 7222 8001; Helpline: 020 7233 2090; e-mail: fsid@sids.org.uk; website: www.sids.org.uk/fsid).

Carers

Carers UK, Ruth Pitter House, 20–25 Glasshouse Yard, London EC1A 4JT (020 7490 8818; e-mail: info@ukcarers.org; website: www.carersonline.org.uk).

Leonard Cheshire, 30 Millbank, London SW1P 4QD (020 7802 8200; e-mail:info@london.leonard-cheshire.org.uk; website: www.leonard-cheshire.org.uk).

Children and young people

ChildLine, Studd Street, London N1 0QW (020 7239 1000; Helpline: 0800 1111 – 24 hours daily; e-mail: info@childline.org.uk; website: www.childline.co.uk).

The Children's Society, Edward Rudolf House, Margery Street, London WC1X 0JL (020 7841 4400; Helpline: 020 7841 4436 – Monday-Friday 10am–noon and 2pm–4pm; e-mail: info@childrenssociety.org.uk; website: www.childrenssociety.org.uk).

Get Connected, The Carphone Warehouse Support Centre, North Acton Business Park, Wales Farm Road, London W3 6RS (020 8896 4774; Helpline: 0808 808 4994 1pm–11pm, seven days a week; e-mail: admin@getconnected.org.uk; website: www.getconnected.org.uk).

NCH (Action for Children), 85 Highbury Park, London N5 1UD (020 7704 7000; Helpline: 0845 762 6579; website: www.nch.org.uk).

Save the Children UK, 17 Grove Lane, London SE5 8RD (020 7703 5400; e-mail: enquiries@scfuk.org.uk; website: www.savethechildren.org.uk).

The Who Cares? Trust, Kemp House, 152-160 City Road, London EC1V 2NP (020 7251 3117; Helpline: 0500 564570 – Monday, Wednesday and Thursday 3.30pm–6pm; e-mail: mailbox@thewhocarestrust.org.uk; website: www.thewhocarestrust.org.uk).

Bullying

Anti-Bullying Campaign, 185 Tower Bridge Road, London SE1 2UF (020 7378 1446; Helpline: 020 7378 1446; e-mail: anti-bullying@compuserve.com).

Kidscape Campaign for Children's Safety, 2 Grosvenor Gardens, London SW1W 0DH (020 7730 3300, Helpline: 0845 1205 204 – Monday–Friday 10–4; e-mail: info@kidscape.org.uk; website: www.kidscape.org.uk).

Young people leaving care

First Key (National Leaving Care Advisory Service), Oxford Chambers, Oxford Place, Leeds LS1 3AX (0113 244 3898; e-mail: fkeyslds@aol.com; website: www.first-key.co.uk).

Families

Home-Start UK, 2 Salisbury Road, Leicester LE1 7QR (0116 233 9955; e-mail: info@home/start.org uk; website; www.home/start.org.uk).

Housing

Shelter, 88 Old Street, London EC1V 9HU (020 7505 2000; Helpline: 0808 800 4444 – 24 hour; e-mail: info@shelter.org.uk; website: www.shelter.org.uk).

Legal

Advice Services Alliance (ASA), 4 Deans Court, St Paul's Churchyard, London EC4V 5AA (020 7236 6022; e-mail: asa@asauk.org.uk; website: www.asauk.org.uk).

Bar Pro Bono Unit, 7 Gray's Inn Square, London WC1R 5AZ, (020 7831 9711; e-mail: enquiries@barprobonounit.org.uk; website: www.barprobono.org.uk).

Men's Rights

Mankind, Suite 367, 2 Lansdown Row, Berkley Square, London W1X 8HL (Helpline: 01643 863352; e-mail: head.office@mankind.org.uk; website: www.mankind.org.uk).

Missing people

Message Home Helpline, PO Box 28908, London SW14 7ZU (020 8392 4550; Helpline: 0800 700740 – 24 hours; e-mail: info@missingpersons.org; website: www.missingpersons.org).

National Missing Persons Helpline. PO Box 28908, London SW14 7ZU (020 8392 4590; Helpline: 0500 700 700; e-mail: admin@missingpersons.org; website: www.missingpersons.org)

Offenders and ex-offenders

APEX Trust, St Alphage House, Wingate Annexe, 2 Fore Street, London EC2Y 5DA (020 7638 5931; Helpline: 0870 608 4567 – Monday–Friday 10–4; e-mail: jobcheck@apextrust.com; website: www.apextrust.com).

* *National Association for the Care and Rehabilitation of Offenders (NACRO)*, 169 Clapham Road, London, SW9 0PU (020 7582 6500; Helpline: 020 7840 6464 – Monday–Friday 9am–5pm; e-mail: communications@nacro.org.uk; website: www.nacro.co.uk).

Prisoners Abroad, 89–93 Fonthill Road, London N4 3JH (020 7561 6820; e-mail: info@prisonersabroad.org.uk; website: www.prisonersabroad.org.uk).

Families of offenders

Aftermath, PO Box 414, Sheffield S4 7RT (0114 275 8520; e-mail: callaftermath@hotmail.com).

Partners of Prisoners and Families Support Group (POPS), Suite 4b, Building 1, Wilsons Park, Monsall Road, Newton Heath, Manchester M40 8WN (Helpline: 0161 277 9066; e-mail: mail@partnersofprisoners.co.uk; website: www.partnersofprisoners.co.uk).

Prisoners' Families and Friends Service, 20 Trinity Street, London SE1 1DB (020 7403 4091; Helpline: 0800 808 3444 – Monday–Friday 10am–5pm and Wednesday 10am–8pm; e-mail: pffs@btclick.com; website: http://home.btclick.com/pffs.index.html).

Women offenders and ex-offenders

Creative and Supportive Trust (CAST), 37–39 Kings Terrace, London NW1 0JR (020 7383 5228; e-mail: info@castcamben.uk).

Older people

Action on Elder Abuse (AEA), Astral House, 1268 London Road, London SW16 4ER (020 8765 7000; Helpline: 0808 808 8141 – Monday–Friday 10am–4.30pm; e-mail: aea@ace.org.uk; website: www.elderabuse.org.uk).

* *Friends of the Elderly*, 40–42 Ebury Street, London SW1W 0LZ (020 7730 8263; e-mail: enquiries@fote.org.uk; website: www.fote.org.uk).

Help the Aged, 207–221 Pentonville Road, London N1 9UZ (020 7278 1114; Helpline: 0808 800 6565 – Monday–Friday 9am–4pm; e-mail: info@helptheaged.org.uk; website: www.helptheaged.org.uk).

Third Age Employment Network, 207–221 Pentonville Road, London N1 9UZ (020 7843 1590; Helpline: 020 7843 1590; e-mail: taen@helptheaged.org.uk; website: www.taen.org.uk).

ADVICE ORGANISATIONS

Parenting

Parentline Plus, 520 Highgate Studios, 53–79 Highgate Road, London NW5 1TL (020 7284 5500; Helpline: 0808 800 2222; e-mail: centraloffice@parentlineplus.org.uk; website: www.parentlineplus.org.uk).

Stillbirth and Neonatal Death Society (SANDS), 28 Portland Place, London W1B 1LY (Helpline: 020 7436 5881 – Monday–Friday 9.30am–4pm; e-mail: support@uk-sands.org; website: www.uk-sands.org).

Twins and Multiple Births Association (TAMBA), 2 The Willows, Gardener Street, Guilford, Surrey GU1 4PG (0870 121 4000; Helpline: 01732 868000 – weekdays 7pm–11pm, weekends 10am–11pm; e-mail: enquiries@tamba.org.uk; website: www.tamba.org.uk).

Abduction

Reunite (National Council for Abducted Children), PO Box 4, London E1 6FR (0116 2556 234, Helpline: 0116 2555 345).

Adoption and fostering

Adoption UK, Manor Farm, Appletree Road, Chipping Warden, Banbury, Oxfordshire OX17 1LH (01295 660121; Helpline: 0870 770 0450; e-mail: admin@adoptionuk.org.uk; website: www.adoptionuk.org.uk).

After Adoption, 12–14 Chapel Street, Manchester M3 7NH (0161 839 4932; Helpline: 0800 056 8578; e-mail: information@afteradoption.org.uk; website; www.afteradoption.org.uk).

Fostering Network, 87 Blackfriars Road, London SE1 8HA (020 7620 6400; Helpline: 020 7620 2100; e-mail: info@fostering.net).

National Stepfamily Association, Chapel House, 18 Hatton Place, London EC1N 8RU (0990 168388 – 2pm–5pm and 7pm–10pm daily).

National Organisation for Counselling Adoptees and Parents, 112 Church Road, Wheatley, Oxfordshire OX33 1LU (Helpline: 01865 875000, Monday–Friday 10am–1pm and 1.30–3pm; e-mail: enquiries@norcap.org; website: www.norcap.org.uk).

Post-Adoption Centre, 5 Torriano Mews, Torriano Avenue, London NW5 2RZ (020 7284 0555, Helpline: 020 7485 2931; e-mail: advice@postadoptioncentre.org.uk; website: www.postadoptioncentre.org.uk).

Childcare

Daycare Trust (National Childcare Campaign), 21 St George's Road, London SE1 6ES (020 7840 3350; e-mail: info@daycaretrust.org.uk; website: www.daycaretrust.org.uk).

Family Rights Group, The Print House, 18 Ashwin Street, London E8 3DL (020 7923 2628; Helpline: 0800 731 1696 – Monday–Friday 1.30pm–3.30pm; e-mail: office@frg.org.uk; website: www.frg.org.uk).

Divorced parents

Both Parents Forever, 39 Cloonmore Avenue, Orpington, Kent BR6 9LE (Helpline: 01689 854343 – 8am–9pm seven days a week).

Families Need Fathers, 134 Curtain Road, London EC2A 3AR (020 7613 5060; Helpline: 020 8295 1956/01920 462825 – 24 hours every day; e-mail: fnf@fnf.org.uk; website: www.fnf.org.uk).

National Family Mediation, 9 Tavistock Place, London WC1H 9SN (020 7485 9066; Helpline: 020 7485 8809; e-mail: general@nfm.org.uk; website: www.nfm.u-net.com).

* *NCDS Trust (National Council for the Divorced and Separated Trust)*, PO Box 6, Kingswinford, West Midlands DY6 8YS (020 8529 8778; e-mail: info@ncds.org.uk; website: www.ncds.org.uk).

Expectant mothers

ARC (Antenatal Results and Choices) (formerly Support around Termination for Abnormality), 73 Charlotte Street, London W1T 4PN, (020 7631 0280; Helpline: 020 7631 0285 – Monday–Friday 10am–6pm; e-mail: arcsatfa@aol.com; website www.arc-uk.org).

British Pregnancy Advisory Service (BPAS), Austy Manor, Wootton Wawen, Solihull, West Midlands B95 6BX (01564 793225; Helpline: 0845 730 4030 – seven days a week; e-mail: info@bpas.org; website: www.bpas.org).

Brook (formerly Brook Advisory Centre), 421 Highgate Studios, 53–79 Highgate Road, London NW5 1TL (020 7284 6040; Helpline: 0800 018 5023; e-mail: admin@brookcentres.org.uk; website: www.brook.org.uk).

Caesarean Support Network, 55 Cooil Drive, Douglas, Isle of Man IM2 2HF (01624 661269 – 6pm–9pm; e-mail: shiddingfold@hotmail.com).

Disability Pregnancy and Parenthood International (DPPI), National Centre for Disabled People, 89–93 Fonthill Road, London N4 3JH (020 7263 3088; Helpline: 0800 018 4730; e-mail: info@dppi.org.uk; website: www.dppi.org.uk).

National Childbirth Trust, Alexandra House, Oldham Terrace, London W3 6NH (020 8896 1677; Helpline: 0870 444 8707 – Monday–Thursday 9am–5pm and Friday 9am–4.30pm; e-mail: enquiries@national-childbirth-trust.co.uk; website: www.netpregnancyandbabycare.com).

Grandparents

Grandparents Association, Moot House, The Stow, Harlow, Essex CM20 3AG (01279 428040; Helpline: 01279 444964 – Monday–Thursday; e-mail: info@grandparentsassociation.org.uk. website: www.grandparents-association.org.uk).

Mothers

Maternity Alliance, 5th Floor, Murray House, 45 Beech Street, London EC2P 2LX (020 7588 8583; Helpline: 020 7588 8582 – Monday–Thursday working hours: e-mail: info@maternityalliance.org.uk; website: www.maternityalliance.org.uk).

Mothers Apart from their Children (MATCH), BM Problems, London WC1N 3XX (e-mail: enquiries@match1979.co.uk; website: www.match1979.co.uk).

Single parents

Gingerbread, 1st Floor, 7 Sovereign Close, Sovereign Court, London E1W 3HW (020 7488 9300; Helpline: 0800 018 4318 – Monday–Friday 10am–4pm; e-mail: office@gingerbread.org.uk; website: www.gingerbread.org.uk).

National Council of One Parent Families, 255 Kentish Town Road, London NW5 2LX (020 7428 5400; Helpline: 0800 018 5026 – Monday–Friday 9am–5pm; e-mail: info@oneparentfamilies.org.uk; website: www.oneparentfamilies.org.uk).

Poverty

Care International, 10–13 Rushworth Street, London SE1 0RB (020 7934 9334 – Monday–Friday 9am–5pm; e-mail: info@ciuk.care.org; website: www.careinternational.org.uk).

Counselling, 39 Warwick Road, Atherton, Manchester M46 9TA (07974 942798; e-mail: info@counsellingcharity.freeserve.co.uk; website: www.counsellingcharity.freeserve.co.uk).

Counselling and Advisory Service, The Dellow Centre, 82 Wentworth Street, London E1 7SA (020 7422 6393 – am only).

* *Family Welfare Association (FWA)*, 501–505 Kingsland Road, London E8 4AU (020 7254 6251; e-mail: fwa.headoffice@fwa.org.uk; website: www.fwa.org.uk).

National Debtline, Birmingham Settlement, 318 Summer Lane, Birmingham B19 3RL (0121 248 3000; Helpline: 0808 808 4000 – 24 hours; website: www.birminghamsettlement.org.uk).

ADVICE ORGANISATIONS

OPAS (Pensions Advisory Service), 11 Belgrave Road, London SW1V 1RB (020 7630 2250; Helpline: 0845 6012 923; e-mail: enquiries@opas.org.uk; website: www.opas.org.uk).

Refugees and asylum seekers

ARHAG Housing Association, 2nd Floor, 122–124 High Road, Wood Green, London N22 6HE (020 8365 7170).

Asylum Aid, 28 Commercial Street, London E1 6LS (020 7377 5123; e-mail: info@asylumaid.org.uk; website: www.asylumaid.org.uk).

Immigration Advisory Service, County House, 190 Great Dover Street, London SE1 4YB (020 7967 1330; Helpline 020 7378 9191 – 24 hours every day; e-mail: advice@iasuk; website: www.iasuk.org).

Migrants Helpline, Room 65, 1 Control Building, Eastern Docks, Dover, Kent CT16 1JA (01304 203977; e-mail: info@migranthelpline.org; website: www.migranthelpline.org).

Refugee Action, 3rd Floor, The Old Fire Station, 150 Waterloo Road, London SE1 8SB (020 7654 7700; e-mail: waterloo@refugee-action.org.uk).

Refugee Council, Bondway House, 3–9 Bondway, London SW8 1SJ (020 7820 3000; e-mail: info@refugeecouncil.org.uk; website: www.refugeecouncil.org.uk).

Refugee Support Centre, 47 South Lambeth Road, London SW8 1RH (020 7820 3606).

Relationships

Albany Trust Counselling, c/o The Art of Health and Yoga, 280 Balham High Road, London SW17 7AL (020 8767 1827).

Family Planning Association, 2–12 Pentonville Road, London N1 9FP (020 7837 5432; Helpline: 0845 310 1334 – 9am–7pm Monday–Friday; website: www.fpa.org.uk).

Relate (National Marriage Guidance), Herbert Gray College, Little Church Street, Rugby, Warwickshire CV21 3AP (01788 573241; e-mail: enquiries@national.relate.org.uk; website: www.relate.org.uk).

Social isolation

Meet-a-Mum Association (MAMA), 77 Westbury View, Peasedown St John, Bath, Avon BA2 8TZ (01761 433598; Helpline: 020 8768 0123 – Monday–Friday 7pm–10pm; e-mail: meet-a-mum.assoc@blueyonder.co.uk; website: www.mama.org.uk).

Rural Stress Information Network (RSIN), Arthur Rank Centre, Stoneliegh Park, Warwickshire CV8 2LZ (024 7641 2916; e-mail: enquiries@rusin.org.uk; website: www.rsin.org.uk).

Single Concern Group, PO Box 40, Minehead, Somerset TA24 5YS (01643 708008).

Write Away, 1 Thorpe Close, London W10 5XL (020 8964 4225; e-mail: info@write-away.org; website: www.write-away.org).

Squatters

Advisory Service for Squatters (ASS), 2 St Paul's Road, London N1 2QN (020 7359 8814; Helpline: 020 7359 8814 – Monday–Friday 2pm–6pm).

Victims of accidents and crimes

Abuse

Childwatch, 19 Spring Bank, Hull HU3 1AF (Helpline: 01482 325552 – Monday–Friday 9am–5pm; e-mail: info@childwatch.org.uk; website: www.childwatch.org.uk).

National Society for the Prevention of Cruelty to Children (NSPCC), 42 Curtain Road, London EC2A 3NH (020 7825 2500; Helpline: 0808 800 5000 – 24 hours daily; e-mail: info@nspcc.org.uk; website: www.nspcc.org.uk).

POPAN (Prevention of Professional Abuse Network), 1 Wyvil Court, Wyvil Road, London SW8 2TG (020 7622 6334; Helpline: 0845 450 0300 – Monday–Friday 10am–4.00pm (closed 12.30 to 1.30); e-mail: info@popan.org.uk: website: www.popan.org.uk).

Crime

Victim Support, Cranmer House, 39 Brixton Road, London SW9 6DZ (020 7735 9166; Helpline: 0845 3030 900 – Monday–Friday 9am–9pm and Saturday–Sunday 9am–7pm; e-mail: contact@victimsupport.org.uk; website: www.victimsupport.org).

Disasters

Disaster Action, PO Box 849, Woking, Surrey GU21 8WB (Tel & Fax: 01483 799066; website: www.disasteraction.org.uk).

Domestic violence

First Step Centre, The Crowndale Centre, 218 Eversholt Street, London NW1 1BD (Helpline: 0800 281281 – Monday–Friday 9am–8pm, Saturday 11am–4.30pm and Sunday 2pm–5pm).

Men's Advice Line and Enquiries (MALE), PO Box 402, Sutton, Surrey SM1 3TG (020 8644 9914 – Monday and Wednesday).

Medical Accidents

Action for Victims of Medical Accidents (AVMA), 44 High Street, Croydon, London CR0 1YB (020 8686 8333).

Rape

Rape Crisis Federation, Unit 7, Provident Works, Newdigate, Nottingham NG7 4FD (0115 900 3562; e-mail: info@rapecrisis.co.uk; website: www.rapecrisis.co.uk).

Women Against Rape (WAR), PO Box 287, London NW6 5QU (Helpline & Minicom: 020 7482 2496 – Monday–Friday 1.30pm–4pm; e-mail: crossroadswomencentre@compuserve.com).

Road Accidents

RoadPeace, PO Box 2579, London NW10 3PW (020 8838 5102; Helpline: 020 8964 1021 – 9am–9pm daily; e-mail: info@roadpeace.org; website: www.roadpeace.org).

Widows

National Association of Widows, 48 Queens Road, Coventry CV1 3EH (024 7663 4848; e-mail: enquiries@nawidows.org; website: www.nawidows.co.uk.).

Work issues

Employment Tribunals Enquiry Line, 100 Southgate Street, Bury St. Edmunds IP33 2QA (0345 959775, Monday–Friday 9am–5pm, website: www.ets.gov.uk).

Public Concern at Work, Suite 306, 16 Baldwins Gardens, London EC1N 7RJ (020 7404 6609; e-mail: eo@pcaw.co.uk; website: www.pcaw.co.uk).

Women Against Sexual Harassment (WASH), Wesley House, Wild Court, Kingsway, London WC2B 4AU (Helpline: 020 7405 0430 – Monday–Tuesday 10.30am–3.30pm).

Women

Refuge, 2–8 Maltravers Street, London WC2R 3EE (020 7395 7700; Helpline: 0870 599 5443; e-mail: info@refuge.org.uk).

Women and Girl's Network, PO Box 13095, London W14 0FE (020 7610 4678; Helpline: 020 7610 4345).

Women's Health, 52–54 Featherstone Street, London EC1Y 8RT (020 7251 6333; Helpline: 0845 125 5254 – Monday–Friday 9.30am–1.30pm; e-mail: health@pop3.poptel.org.uk; website: www.womenshealthlondon.org.uk).

ADVICE ORGANISATIONS

Sickness and disability

Sickness/Disability (General)   387
Addiction   388
Ageing   388
AIDS/HIV   388
Alcohol   388
Allergy   388
Alopecia Areata   388
Alzheimer's Disease   388
Angelmann Syndrome   388
Ankylosing Spondylitis   388
Arthritis/Rheumatic Diseases   389
Arthrogryposis   389
Asthma   389
Ataxia   389
Autism   389
Back Pain   389
Behcet's Syndrome   389
Blepharospasm *(See Dystonia)*
Blindness/Partial Sight   389
Bone Marrow   389
Bowel Disorders   389
Brain Injury   389
Brittle Bones   389
Burns   389
Cancer and Leukaemia   389
Cerebral Palsy   389
Chest/Lungs   389
Child Growth   389
Cleft Lip/Palate Disorder   389
CMT   389
Coeliac Disease   390
Colostomy   390
Cot Death   390
Counselling   390
Craniosynostosis or Craniostenosis   390
Crohn's Disease   390
Crying/Restless Babies   390
Cystic Fibrosis   390
Deafblind   390
Deafness/Hearing Difficulties   390
Dental Health   390
Depression   390
Diabetes   390
Disfigurement   390
Down's Syndrome   390
Drugs   391
Dyslexia   391
Dysphasia *(See Speech/Language Difficulties)*
Dyspraxia   391
Dystonia   391

Eating Disorders   391
Eczema   391
Endometriosis   391
Epidermolysis Bullosa   391
Epilepsy   391
Feet   391
Friedreich's Ataxia *(See Ataxia)*
Gambling   391
Gastro Intestinal Disease *(See Digestive Complaints)*
German Measles *(See Rubella)*
Glaucoma *(See Blindness/Partial Sight)*
Growth Problems   391
Guillain Barre Syndrome   391
Haemophilia   391
Head Injury   391
Heart Attacks/Heart Disease (General)
Hemiplegia   391
Hepatitis B *(See Liver Disease)*
Herpes   391
Hodgkin's Disease   391
Huntington's Disease   391
Hydrocephalus *(See Spina Bifida)*
Hyperactive Children   391
Hypertension   391
Hypogammaglobulinaemia   392
Incontinence   392
Industrial Diseases   392
Infantile Hypercalcaemia   392
Infertility   392
Irritable Bowel Syndrome   392
Kidney Disease   392
Leukaemia *(See Cancer and Leukaemia)*
Limb Disorder   392
Literacy/Learning Difficulties   392
Liver Disease   392
Lowe Syndrome   392
Lungs *(See Chest/Lungs)*
Lupus   392
Lymphoederma *(See Cancer)*
Marfan Syndrome   392
Mastectomy   392
Meniere's Disease   392
Meningitis   392
Menopause   392
Mental Health and Disability   392
Metabolic Disorders   392
Migraine   392
Miscarriage   393
Motor Neurone Disease   393
Multiple Sclerosis   393
Muscular Dystrophy   393
Myasthenia Gravis   393
Myotonic Dystrophy   393
Narcolepsy   393
Neurofibromatosis   393

Organ Donors   393
Osteoporosis   393
Paget's Disease   393
Parkinson's Disease   393
Perthes Disease   393
Phobias   393
Pituitary Disorders   393
Poliomyelitis   393
Post-natal   393
Prader-Willi Syndrome   393
Pre-Eclampsia   393
Pre-Menstrual Syndrome   393
Psoriasis   393
Raynaud's Disease   393
Retinitis Pigmentosa   393
Rett Syndrome   393
Reye's Syndrome   393
Rheumatic Diseases *(See Arthritis/Rheumatic Diseases)*
Rubella   393
Sacroidosis   394
Schizophrenia   394
Scoliosis   394
Seasonal Affective Disorder   394
Sickle Cell Disease   394
Sjogren's Syndrome   394
Sleep Disorders   394
Sleepless Children *(See Crying/Sleepless Children)*
Smoking   394
Solvent Abuse   394
Sotos Syndrome   394
Spastics *(See Cerebral Palsy)*
Speech & Language Difficulties   394
Spina Bifida   394
Spinal Injuries   394
Stress   394
Stroke   394
Thalassaemia   394
Thrombocytopenia with Absent Radii   394
Tinnitus   394
Tourette Syndrome   394
Tracheo-Oesophageal Fistula   394
Tranquillizers   394
Tuberous Sclerosis   394
Turner Syndrome   394
Urostomy   395
Vaccine Damage *(See Victims of Medical Accidents)*
Williams Syndrome   395

Sickness/Disability (General)

Action Research, Vincent House, North Parade, Horsham, West Sussex RH12 2DP (01403 210406;

387

Advice Organisations

e-mail: info@actionresearch.org.uk;
website: www.actionresearch.org.uk).

Contact a Family, 209–211 City Road, London EC1V 1JN (020 7608 8700; Helpline: 0808 808 3555, Monday–Friday 10–4; e-mail: info@cafamily.org.uk; website: www.cafamily.org.uk).

DIS – Disability Information Service, Harrowlands, Harrowlands Park, Dorking, Surrey RH4 2RA (01306 875156; website: www.dis.org.uk).

Disabled Living Foundation (DLF), 380–384 Harrow Road, London W9 2HU (020 7289 6111; Helpline: 0845 130 9177; e-mail: advice@dlf.org.uk; website: www.dlf.org.uk).

Disabled Parents' Network, National Centre for Disabled Parents, 89–93 Font Hill Road, London N4 3JH (020 7263 3088; Helpline: 0870 241 0450; e-mail: information@disabledparentsnetwork.com; website: www.disabledparentsnetwork.com).

Disablement Income Group (DIG), Unit 5, Archway Business Centre, 19–23 Wedmore Street, London N19 4RZ (020 7263 3981).

Disabilities Trust, 32 Market Place, Burgess Hill, West Sussex RH15 9NP (01444 239123; e-mail: info@disabilities-trust.org.uk; website: www.disabilities-trust.org.uk).

Disability Alliance, 1st Floor East, Universal House, 88–94 Wentworth Street, London E1 7SA (020 7247 8776; Helpline: 020 7247 8763 – Mon & Wed 2pm–4pm; e-mail: office.da@dial.pipex.com; website: www.disabilityalliance.org).

Disability Law Service (DLS), 39–45 Cavell Street, London E1 2BP (020 7791 9800; e-mail: advice@dls.org.uk).

Disability Pregnancy and Parenthood International (DPPI), National Centre for Disabled Parents, Unit F9, 89–93 Fonthill Road, London N4 3JH (020 7263 3088; Helpline: 0800 018 4730; Text Line 0800 018 9949; e-mail: info@dppi.org.uk; website: www.dppi.org.uk).

Invalid Children's Aid Nationwide (I CAN), 4 Dyer's Buildings, Holborn, London EC1N 2QP (0870 010 4066; website: www.ican.org.uk).

* *Jewish Care*, 221 Golders Green Road, London NW11 9DQ (020 8922 2000; e-mail: info@jcare.org; website: www.jewishcare.org).

Kidsactive, Pryor's Bank, Bishop's Park, London SW6 3LA (020 7736 4443; Helpline: 020 7731 1435; e-mail: office@kidsactive.org.uk; website: www.kidsactive.org.uk).

Mobility Information Service, National Mobility Centre, Unit B1, Greenwood Court, Shrewsbury SY1 3TB (01743 463072; e-mail: mis@mncuk.freeserve.uk; website: www.mis.org.uk).

PHAB England, PHAB Centre, Summit House, Wandle Road, Croydon CR0 1DF (020 8667 9443; e-mail: info@phabengland.org.uk; website: www.phabengland.org.uk).

Queen Elizabeth's Foundation (QEFD), Leatherhead Court, Woodlands Road, Leatherhead, Surrey KT22 0BN (01372 841100; website: www.qefd.org.uk).

Royal Association for Disability & Rehabilitation (RADAR), Unit 12, City Forum, 250 City Road, London EC1V 8AF (020 7250 3222; e-mail: radar@radar.org.uk; website: www.radar.org.uk).

Addiction

Addaction, 67–69 Cowcross Street, London EC1M 6PU (020 7251 5860; e-mail; info@addaction.org.uk; website: www.addaction.org.uk).

Tacade (Advisory Council on Alcohol and Drug Education), 1 Hulme Place, The Crescent, Salford, Greater Manchester M5 4QA (0161 745 8925; e-mail: ho@tacade.demon.co.uk; website: www.tacade.com).

Ageing

Age Concern England, Astral House, 1268 London Road, London SW16 4ER (020 8679 8000; e-mail: ace@ace.org.uk; website: www.ageconcern.org.uk).

* *Counsel & Care*, Twyman House, 16 Bonny Street, London NW1 9PG (020 7485 1550; Helpline: 0845 300 7585 – Mon–Fri 10am–12.30pm & 2pm–4pm; e-mail: advice@councilandcare.org.uk; website: www.councilandcare.org.uk).

AIDS/HIV

Terrence Higgins Trust, 52–54 Grays Inn Road, London WC1X 8JU (020 7831 0330; Helpline: 020 7242 1010 [12pm–10pm]; Advice & Support: 0845 1221 200 [7 days a week, 11am–8pm]; e-mail: info@tht.org.uk; website: www.tht.org.uk).

National Aids Trust, New City Cloisters, 188–196 Old Street, London EC1V 9FR (020 7814 6767; e-mail: info@nat.org.uk; website: www.nat.org.uk).

Alcohol

ACCEPT SERVICES UK, 724 Fulham Road, London SW6 5SE (020 7371 7477).

Al-Anon Family Groups UK & Eire (AFG), 61 Great Dover Street, London SE1 4YF (020 7403 0888; e-mail: alanonuk@aol.com; website: www.hexnet.co.uk/alanon).

Alcohol Concern, Waterbridge House, 32–36 Loman Street, London SE1 0EE (020 7928 7377; e-mail: contact@alcoholconcern.org.uk; website: www.alcoholconcern.org.uk).

Alcohol Counselling & Prevention Service, 34 Electric Lane, London SW9 8JT (020 7737 3579; e-mail: info@acaps.co.uk; website: www.acaps.co.uk).

Alcohol Recovery Project (ARP), 68 Newington Causeway, London SE1 6DF (020 7403 3369; website: www.arp-uk.org).

Alcoholics Anonymous (AA), General Service Office, PO Box 1, Stonebow House, Stonebow, York YO1 7NJ (01904 644026; Helpline: 0845 7697 555; website: www.alcoholics-anonymous.org.uk).

Drinkline, 1st Floor, Cavern Court, Mathew Street, Liverpool L2 6RE (Helpline: 0800 917 8282, 11am–11pm Monday–Friday).

Turning Point, New Loom House, 101 Back Church Lane, London E1 1LU (020 7553 5502; website: www.turning-point.co.uk).

Allergy

Action Against Allergy, PO Box 278, Twickenham TW1 4QQ (020 8892 2711).

Allergy UK, Deepdene House, 30 Bellgrove Road, Welling, Kent DA16 3PY (020 8303 8525; Helpline: 020 8303 8583 [Mon–Fri 9am–9pm, Sat & Sun 10am–1pm]; e-mail: info@allergyuk.org.uk; website: www.allergyuk.org.uk).

Alopecia Areata

Hairline International/The Alopecia Patients' Society, Lyons Court, 1668 High Street, Knowle, West Midlands B93 0LY (01564 775281 [9am–4.30pm] or 01564 782270 [emergency, after 4.30pm]; website: www.hairlineinternational.co.uk).

Alzheimer's Disease

* *Alzheimer's Society*, Gordon House, 10 Greencoat Place, London SW1P 1PH (020 7306 0606; website: www.alzheimers.org.uk).

Angelmann Syndrome

Angelmann Syndrome Support Group, c/o Mrs S Woolven, 15 Place Crescent, Waterlooville, Hampshire PO7 5UR (023 9226 4224).

Ankylosing Spondylitis

National Ankylosing Spondylitis Society (NASS), PO Box 179, Mayfield, East Sussex TN20 6ZL (01435 873527; e-mail: nass@nass.co.uk; website: www.nass.co.uk).

Arthritis/Rheumatic Diseases

Arthritis Care, 18 Stephenson Way, London NW1 2HD (020 7916 1500; website: www.arthritiscare.org.uk).

Arthritis Research Council (ARC), Copeman House, St Mary's Court, St Mary's Gate, Chesterfield S41 7TD (01246 558033; e-mail: info@arc.org.uk; website: www.arc.org.uk).

Arthrogryposis

Arthrogryposis Group (TAG), 1 The Oaks, Gillingham, Dorset SP8 4SW (01747 822655; e-mail: info@tagonline.org.uk; website: www.tagonline.org.uk).

Asthma

National Asthma Campaign (NAC), Providence House, Providence Place, London N1 0NT (020 7226 2260; Helpline: 0845 7010 203 [Mon–Fri 9am–7pm]; website: www.asthma.org.uk).

Ataxia

* *Ataxia UK* (formerly Friedrich's Ataxia Group), 10 Winchester House, Kennington Park, Carnmer Road, London SW9 6EJ (020 7820 3900; website: www.ataxia.org.uk).

Autism

National Autistic Society (NAS), 393 City Road, London EC1V 1NG (020 7833 2299; e-mail: nas@nas.org.uk; website: www.oneworld.org/autism_uk/).

Back Pain

Back Care, 16 Elm Tree Road, Teddington, Middlesex TW11 8ST (020 8977 5474; e-mail: info@backcare.org.uk; website: www.backcare.org.uk).

Behcet's Syndrome

Behcet's Syndrome Society, 3 Church Close, Lambourn, Hungerford, Berkshire RG17 8PU (01488 71116; e-mail: info@behcets-society.fsnet.co.uk; website: www.behcets.org.uk).

Blindness/Partial Sight

British Retinitis Pigmentosa Society (BRPS), PO Box 350, Buckingham MK18 5EL (01280 821334; Helpline: 01280 860363).

CALIBRE (Cassette Library of Recorded Books), Aylesbury, Buckinghamshire HP22 5XQ (01296 432339; website: www.calibre.org.uk).

International Glaucoma Association (IGA), 108c Warner Road, Camberwell, London SE5 9HQ (020 7737 3265; website: www.iga.org.uk).

Listening Books, 12 Lant Street, London SE11QH (020 7407 9417; e-mail: info@listening-books.org.uk; website: www.listening-books.org.uk).

National Federation of the Blind of the UK, Sir John Wilson House, 215 Kirkgate, Wakefield WF1 1JG (01924 291313; e-mail: nfbuk@nufbk.org; website: www.nfbuk.org).

Partially Sighted Society, PO Box 322, Doncaster DN1 2XA (01302 323132).

* *Royal National Institute for the Blind (RNIB)*, 105 Judd Street, London W1CH 9NB (020 7388 1266; e-mail: helpline@rnib.org.uk; website: www.rnib.org.uk).

Bone Marrow

Anthony Nolan Bone Marrow Trust, The Royal Free Hospital, London NW3 2QG (020 7284 1234 [24-hours]; e-mail: heathgate@anthonynolan.com; website: www.anthonynolan.com).

Bowel Disorders

National Advisory Service for Parents of Children with a Stoma (NASPCS), 51 Anderson Drive, Darvel, Ayrshire KA17 0DE (01560 322024).

National Association for Colitis & Crohn's Disease (NACC), 4 Beaumont House, Sutton Road, St Albans, Hertfordshire AL1 5HH (01727 830038; Helpline: 0845 130 2233 [Mon–Fri 10am–1pm]; e-mail: nacc@nacc.org.uk; website: www.nacc.org.uk).

Brain Injury

British Institute for Brain-Injured Children (BIBIC), Knowle Hall, Bawdrip, Bridgwater, Somerset TA7 8PJ (01278 684060; e-mail: info@bibic.org.uk; website: www.bibic.org.uk).

Brittle Bones

* *Brittle Bone Society*, 30 Guthrie Street, Dundee DD1 5BS (01382 204446; e-mail: bbs@brittlebone.org; website: www.brittlebone.org).

Burns

British Burn Association, Dr K Judkin, Regional Burns Centre, Pinderfields Hospital, Wakefield WF1 4DG (01924 201688).

Cancer and Leukaemia

Action Cancer, 1 Marlborough Park South, Belfast BT9 6HQ (028 9066 1081).

BACUP, 3 Bath Place, Rivington Street, London EC2A 3JR (020 7613 2121; e-mail: info@cancerbacup.org.uk; website: www.cancerbacup.org.uk).

* *Cancer & Leukaemia in Childhood Trust (CLIC)*, Unit 6, Emma-Chris Way, Abbey Wood, Bristol BS34 7JU (0117-311 2600; website: www.clic.uk.com).

Marie Curie Foundation, 89 Albert Embankment, London SE1 7TP (020 7599 7777; website: www.mariecurie.org.uk).

* *Leukaemia Care Society*, 2 Shrubbery Ave, Worcester WR1 1QH (01905 330003; website: www.leukaemiacare.org.uk).

* *Macmillan Cancer Relief*, 89 Albert Embankment, London SE1 7UQ (020 7840 7840; e-mail: postmasters@macmillan.org.uk; website: www.macmillan.org.uk).

Tak Tent Cancer Support, Flat 5, 30 Shelly Court, Gart Navel Complex, Glasgow G12 0YN (0141 211 0122; e-mail: tak.tent@care4free.net; website: www.taktent.org).

* *Tenovus Cancer Information Centre*, 43 The Parade, Cardiff CF24 3AB (029 2048 2000; e-mail: mail@tenovus.com; website: www.tenovus.com).

Cerebral Palsy

International Cerebral Palsy Society, 19 St Mary's Grove, Chiswick, London W4 3LL (020 8994 6386).

SCOPE, PO Box 833, Warren Farm Village, Wolverton Mill, Milton Keynes MK12 5NW (01908 231047; 24 Hour Helpline: 0808 800 3333; e-mail: cphelpline@scope.org.uk; website: www.scope.org.uk).

Chest/Lungs

British Lung Foundation, 78 Hatton Garden, London EC1N 8LD (020 7831 5831; E-mail: info@britishlungfoundation.com; website: www.lunguk.org).

Child Growth

Child Growth Foundation, 2 Mayfield Avenue, London W4 1PW (020 8995 0257; e-mail: cgf@aol.com; website: www.heightmatters.org.uk). Also contactable through the above address: *Growth Hormone Insufficiency; Russel Silver Syndrome; Bone Dysplasia Group; Sotos; PSM (Premature Sexual Maturation – Precocious Puberty)*.

Cleft Lip/Palate Disorder

Cleft Lip & Palate Association (CLAPA), 235–237 Finchley Road, London NW3 6LS (020 7431 0033; e-mail: info@clapa.com; website: www.clapa.com).

CMT

CMT International United Kingdom, PO Box 5089, Christchurch, Dorset BH23 2WJ (029 2070 9537;

Advice Organisations

e-mail: secretary@cmt.org.uk;
website: www.cmt.org.uk).

Coeliac Disease

Coeliac UK, PO Box 220, High Wycombe, Buckinghamshire HP11 2HY (01494 437278;
website: www.coeliac.co.uk).

Colostomy

British Colostomy Association (BCA), 15 Station Road, Reading RG1 1LG (0118 939 1537; Advice line: 0800 3284 257 – Mon–Thurs 9am–5pm, Fri 9am–3pm, Sat–Sun 3pm–9pm;
e-mail: sue@bcass.org.uk;
website: www.bcass.org.uk).

Cot Death

Compassionate Friends, 53 North Street, Bristol BS3 1EN (0117 966 5202; 24–hour Helpline: 0117 953 9639;
e-mail: info@tcf.org.uk;
website: www.tcf.org.uk).

Cot Death Society, 4 West Mills Yard, Kennet Road, Newbury, Berkshire RG 14 5LP (01635 38137; Helpline: 0845 601 0234 – Mon–Fri 9.30am–5.30pm;
e-mail: fundraising@cotdeathsociety.org.uk; website: www.cotdeathsociety.org.uk).

Foundation for the Study of Infant Deaths (Cot Death Research and Support), Artillery House, 11–19 Artillery Row, London SW1P 1RT (020 7222 8001; Helpline: 020 7233 2090 – 24 hours; e-mail: fsid@sids.org.uk;
website: www.sids.org.uk/fsid).

Counselling

British Association for Counselling and Psychotherapy, 1 Regent Place, Rugby CV21 2PJ (0870 443 5252;
e-mail: bacp@bacp.co.uk;
website: www.counselling.co.uk).

Careline, Cardinal Heenan Centre, 326–328 High Road, Ilford, Essex IG1 1QP (020 8514 5444; Helpline: 020 8514 1177).

Samaritans (The Samaritans), The Upper Mill, Kingston Road, Ewell, Surrey KT17 2AF (020 8394 8300; Lo-call 24-hour helpline: 08457 90 90 90; see phone book for local number;
website: www.samaritans.org).

SupportLine, PO Box 1596, Ilford, Essex IG1 3FW (020 8554 9006; Helpline: 020 8554 9004;
e-mail: info@supportline.org.uk;
website: www.supportline.org.uk).

Trauma Aftercare Trust, Buttfields, The Farthings, Withington, Gloucestershire GL54 4DF (01242 890306; Helpline: 0800 169 6814;
e-mail: tact@tacthq.demon.co.uk;
website: www.tacthq.demon.co.uk).

Craniosynostosis or Craniostenosis

Headlines, 44 Helmsdale, Leamington Spa, Warwickshire CV32 7DW (01926 334629;
e-mail: info@headlines.org.uk;
website: www.headlines.org.uk).

Crohn's Disease

Crohn's in Childhood Research Association (CICRA), Parkgate House, 356 West Barnes Lane, Motspur Park, Surrey KT3 6NB (020 8949 6209; Fax: 020 8942 2044; e-mail: support@cicra.org; website: www.cicra.org).

National Association for Colitis & Crohn's Disease (NACC), 4 Beaumont House, Sutton Road, St Albans AL1 5HH (01727 830038; Advice Line: 0845 130 2233 – Mon–Fri 10am–1pm;
e-mail: nacc@nacc.org.uk;
website: www.nacc.org.uk).

Crying/restless babies

The CRY-SIS Helpline, BM Box CRY-SIS, London WC1N 3XX (Helpline: 020 7404 5011, 9am–10pm;
website: www.our-space.co.uk/serene.htm).

Cystic Fibrosis

* *Cystic Fibrosis Trust*, 11 London Road, Bromley, Kent BR1 1BY (020 8464 7211; e-mail: enquiries@cftrust.org.uk;
website: www.cftrust.org.uk).

Deafblind

* *Deafblind UK*, 100 Bridge Street, Peterborough, Cambridgeshire PE1 1DY (01733 358100;
website: www.deafblind.org.uk).

* *Sense*, 11–13 Clifton Terrace, Finsbury Park, London N4 3SR (020 7272 7774; e-mail: enquiries@sense.org.uk;
website: www.sense.org.uk).

Deafness/Hearing Difficulties

British Deaf Association (BDA), 1–3 Worship Street, London EC2A 2AB (020 7588 3520; Text: 0800 652 2965; Voicemail: 0870 770 3300; Videophone: 0207 496 9539;
e-mail: helpline@bda.org.uk;
website: www.bda.org.uk).

* *National Deaf Children's Society*, 15 Dufferin Street, London EC1Y 8UR (020 7490 8656; Helpline: 0808 800 8880 [Mon–Fri 10am–5pm and until 7pm on Tuesday]; website: www.ndsc.org.uk).

Royal Association for Deaf People (RAD), Walsingham Road, Colchester CO2 7BP (01206 509509; Text: 01206 577090; Videophone: 01206 710064; e-mail: info@royaldeaf.org.uk;
website: www.royaldeaf.org.uk).

Royal National Institute for the Deaf (RNID), 19–23 Featherstone Street, London EC1Y 8SL (Voice: 020 7296 8000; Text: 020 7296 8001; Helpline: 0808 808 6666 [Voice] 0808 808 0007 [Text];
e-mail: informationonline@rnid.org.uk; website: www.rnid.org.uk).

Dental Health

British Dental Association, 64 Wimpole Street, London W1G 8YF (020 7935 0875; website: www.bda-dentistry.org.uk).

British Dental Health Foundation (BDHF), 2 East Union Street, Rugby, Warwickshire CV22 6AJ (01788 546365; Helpline: 0870 770 4014;
website: www.dentalhealth.org.uk).

Depression

Befrienders, 26–27 Market Place, Kingston-upon-Thames KT1 1JH (020 8541 4949;
e-mail: admin@befrienders.org;
website: www.befrienders.org).

Depression Alliance, 35 Westminster Bridge Road, London SE1 7JB (020 7633 0557;
e-mail: information@depressionalliance.org; website: www.depressionalliance.org).

Fellowship of Depressives Anonymous, Box FDA, Self Help Nottingham, Ormiston House, 32–36 Pelham Street, Nottingham NG1 2EG (01702 43383; e-mail: fdainfo@aol.com).

Manic Depression Fellowship Ltd, 8–10 High Street, Kingston-upon-Thames, Surrey KT1 1EY (020 8974 6550).

The Samaritans, The Upper Mill, Kingston Road, Ewell, Surrey KT17 2AF (020 8394 8300; Helpline: 0845 790 9090 – 24 hours; e-mail: jo@samaritans.org; website: www.samaritans.org).

Diabetes

Diabetes UK, 10 Parkway, London NW1 7AA (020 7424 1000;
website: www.diabetes.org.uk).

Diabetes Foundation, 177a Tennison Road, London SE25 5NF (020 8656 5467 – 9am–9pm).

Disfigurement

Disfigurement Guidance Centre, PO Box 7, Cupar, Fife KY15 4PF (01337 870281; website: www.dgc.org.uk).

Let's Face It, Support Network for the Facially Disfigured, 14 Fallowfield, Yately, Hampshire GU46 6LW (01252 879630 – Mon–Fri 9am–9pm; e-mail: chrisletsfaceit@aol.com;
website: www.letsfaceit.force9.co.uk).

Down's Syndrome

Down's Syndrome Association, 155 Mitcham Road, Tooting, London

SW17 9PG (24-hour helpline: 020 8682 4001; e-mail: info@downs-syndrome.org.uk; website: www.downs-syndrome.org.uk).

Drugs

ADFAM National, Waterbridge House, 32–36 Loman Street, London SE1 0EH (020 7928 8898; e-mail: admin@adfam.org.uk).

Chemical Dependency Centre, 11 Redcliffe Gardens, London SW10 9BG (020 7351 0217; Helpline: 020 7351 0217, Monday–Friday 9–5; e-mail: info@thecdc.org.uk; website: www.thecdc.org.uk).

Community Drug Project, 9a Brockley Cross, London SE4 2AB (020 8692 4975; e-mail: mel@communitydrugproject.org; website: www.communitydrugproject.org).

DrugScope, Waterbridge House, 32-36 Loman Street, London SE1 0EE (Helpline: 020 7928 1211; e-mail: services@drugscope.org.uk; website: www.drugscope.org.uk).

Families Anonymous, Doddington and Rollo Community Association, Charlotte Despard Avenue, Battersea, London SW11 5HD (0845 1200 660; Fax: 020 7498 1990; e-mail: office@famanon.org.uk; website: www.famanon.org.uk).

Narcotics Anonymous (NA), 202 City Road, London NC1V 2PH (020 7730 0009 [10am–10pm]; website: www.ukna.org).

National Drugs Helpline, PO Box 5000, Glasgow G12 8BR (0800 77 66 00 – 24 hours).

Turning Point, New Loom House, 101 Back Church Lane, London E1 1LU (020 7553 5502; website: www.turning-point.co.uk).

Dyslexia

British Dyslexia Association, 98 London Road, Reading RG1 5AU (0118 966 2677; Helpline: 0118 966 8271; website: www.bda-dyslexia.org.uk).

Dyslexia Institute Ltd (DI), 133 Gresham Road, Staines, Middlesex TW18 2AJ (01784 463851 [8.30am–5.30pm]; website: www.dyslexia.inst.org).

Dyspraxia

Dyspraxia Foundation, Administrator, 8 West Alley, Hitchin, Hertfordshire SG5 1EG (01462 454986; website: www.dyspraxiafoundation.org.uk).

Dystonia

Dystonia Society, 46–47 Britton Street, London EC1M 5UJ (020 7490 5671; e-mail: info@dystoniasociety.org.uk; website: www.dystoniasociety.org.uk).

Eating Disorders

Eating Disorders Association, 1st Floor, Wensum House, 103 Prince of Wales Road, Norwich NR1 1DW (01603 619090; Helpline: 0845 634 1414 [8.30am–8.30pm]; Youth Helpline: 0845 634 7650 [4–6pm]; website: www.edauk.com).

Eczema

* *National Eczema Society*, Hill House, Highgate Hill, London N19 5NA (020 7281 3553; Helpline: 0870 241 3604).

Endometriosis

National Endometriosis Society, Suite 50, Westminster Place Gardens, 1-7 Artillery Row, London SW1P 1RL (020 7222 2781; Crisis Helpline: 0808 808 2227 [7–10pm]).

Epidermolysis Bullosa

Dystrophic Epidermolysis Bullosa Research Association (DEBRA), Debra House, 13 Wellington Business Park, Dukes Ride, Crowthorne, Berkshire RG45 6LS (01344 771961; e-mail: debra.uk@btinternet.com; website: www.debra.org.uk).

Epilepsy

Epilepsy Action, New Anstey House, Gateway Drive, Yeadon, Leeds LS19 7XY (0113 210 8800; Helpline: 0808 800 5050 [Mon–Thurs 9am–4.30pm; Fri 9am–4pm]; website: www.epilepsy.org.uk).

Feet

Sole-Mates, 46 Gordon Road, London E4 6BU (020 8524 2423).

Gambling

Gamblers Anonymous (GANON), PO Box 88, London SW10 0EU (Helpline: 020 7384 3040, 24 hours daily; e-mail: pro@gamblersanonymous.org.uk: website: www.gamblersanonymous.org.uk).

GamCare, 1 Catherine House, 25–27 Catherine Place, London SW1E 6DU (020 7233 8988; Helpline: 0845 600 0133, Seven days a week; 10am–10pm; e-mail: director@gamcare.org.uk; website: www.gamcare.org.uk).

Growth Problems

Restricted Growth Association (RGA), PO Box 8, Countesthorpe, Leicestershire LE8 5ZS (0116 247 8913).

Guillain Barre Syndrome

Guillain Barre Syndrome Support Group (GBS), Lincolnshire County Council Offices, Eastgate, Sleaford, Lincolnshire NG34 7EB (0800 374803; e-mail: admin@gbs.org.uk; website: www.gbs.org.uk).

Haemophilia

* *Haemophilia Society*, 3rd Floor, Chesterfield House, 385 Euston Road, London NW1 3AU (020 7380 0600; e-mail: info@haemophelia.org.uk; website: www.haemophelia.org.uk).

Head Injury

Headway – National Head Injuries Association Ltd, 4 King Edward Court, King Edward Street, Nottingham NG1 1EW (0115 924 0800; e-mail: enquiries@headway.org.uk; website: www.headway.org.uk).

Heart Attacks/Heart Disease (General)

British Heart Foundation, 14 Fitzhardinge Street, London W1H 6DH (020 7935 0185; website: www.bhf.org.uk).

HeartLine Association, Rossmore House, 26 Park Street, Camberley, Surrey GU15 3PL (01276 707636).

Hemiplegia

Hemi-Help, 2nd Floor, Bedford House, 215 Balham High Road, London SW17 7BQ (020 8767 0210 [Mon–Fri 10am–8pm]; e-mail: support@hemihelp.org.uk; website: www.hemihelp.org.uk).

Herpes

Herpes Viruses Association (SPHERE), 41 North Road, London N7 9DP (Helpline: 020 7609 9061).

Hodgkin's Disease

Hodgkin's Disease & Lymphoma Association, PO Box 386, Aylesbury, Buckinghamshire HP20 2GA (01296 619400; Helpline: 0808 808 5555 [Mon–Fri 9am–5pm]; website: www.lymphoma.org.uk).

Huntington's Disease

* *Huntington's Disease Association*, 108 Battersea High Street, London SW11 3HP (020 7223 7000; website: www.hda.org.uk).

Hyperactive Children

Hyperactive Children's Support Group, 71 Whyke Lane, Chichester, West Sussex PO19 2LD (01903 725182 [10am–1pm]; e-mail: web@hacsg.org.uk; website: www.hacsg.org.uk).

Hypertension

Coronary Artery Disease Research Association (CORDA), 121 Sidney Street, London SW3 6NR (020 7349 8686;

Advice Organisations

e-mail: corda@rbh.nthames.nhs.uk; website: www.corda.org.uk).

Hypogammaglobulinaemia

Primary Immunodeficiency Association, Alliance House, 12 Caxton Street, London SW1H 0QS (020 7976 7640; e-mail: info@pia.org.uk; website: www.pia.org.uk).

Incontinence

Association for Continence Advice (ACA), 102A Astra House, Arklow Road, London SE14 6EB (020 8692 4680; e-mail: info@aca.uk.com; website: www.aca.uk.com).

Industrial Diseases

Occupational & Environmental Diseases Association (OEDA), PO Box 26, Enfield EN1 2NT (020 8360 8490; website: www.oeda.org.uk).

Repetitive Strain Injury Association (RSIA), Chapel House, 152-156 High Street, Yiewsley, West Drayton, Middlesex UB7 7BE (01895 431134 [11.30am–4pm]).

Infantile Hypercalcaemia

Williams Syndrome Foundation, 161 High Street, Tonbridge, Kent TN9 1BX (01732 365152).

Infertility

Child, the National Infertility Support Network, Charter House, 43 St Leonards Road, Bexhill-on-Sea, East Sussex TN40 1JA (01424 732361 – 24 hours; e-mail: office@child.org.uk; website: www.child.org.uk).

Irritable Bowel Syndrome

Irritable Bowel Syndrome Network (IBS), Northern General Hospital, Sheffield S5 7AU (0114 261 1531; Helpline: 01543 492192 – Mon–Fri 6pm–8pm & Sat 10am–12am; website: www.ibsnetwork.org.uk; if writing, please enclose an sae and the charity recommends a donation of È1).

Kidney Disease

* British Kidney Patient Association (BKPA), Bordon, Hampshire GU35 9JZ (01420 472021/2).

National Kidney Federation, 6 Stanley Street, Worksop, Nottinghamshire S81 7HX (01909 487795; e-mail: nkf@kidney.org.uk; website: www.kidney.org.uk).

Limb Disorder

British Limbless Ex-Servicemen's Association (BLESMA), 185–187 High Road, Chadwell Heath, Romford RM6 6NA (020 8590 1124; e-mail: blesma@btconnect.com; website: www.blesma.org).

Limbless Association, Roehampton Rehabilitation Centre, Queen Mary's Hospital, Roehampton Lane, London SW15 5PR (020 8788 1777; e-mail: enquiries@limbless-association.org; website: www.limbless-association.org).

Reach – The Association for Children with Hand or Arm Deficiency, 12 Wilson Way, Earles Barton, Northamptonshire NN6 0NZ (0845 130 6225; website: www.reach.org.uk).

STEPS (A National Association for Families of Children with Congenital Abnormalities), Lymm Court, 11 Eagle Brow, Cheshire WA13 0LP (01925 757525; e-mail: info@steps-charity.org.uk; website: www.steps-charity.org.uk).

Literacy/Learning Difficulties

Basic Skills Agency, 7th Floor, Commonwealth House, 1–19 New Oxford Street, London WC1A 1NU (020 7405 4017; e-mail: enquiries@basic-skills.co.uk; website: www.basic-skills.co.uk).

Liver Disease

British Liver Trust, Central House, Central Avenue, Ransomes Europark, Ipswich IP3 9QG (01473 276326; e-mail: info@britishlivertrust.org.uk; website: www.britishlivertrust.org.uk).

Lowe Syndrome

Lowe's Syndrome Association (UK Contact Group) (LSA), 29 Gleneagles Drive, Penwortham, Preston PR1 0JT (01772 745070; website: www.lowestrust.org.uk).

Lupus

Lupus UK, St James House, Eastern Road, Romford RM1 3NH (01708 731251; website: www.lupusuk.com).

Raynaud's & Scleroderma Association, 112 Crewe Road, Alsager, Cheshire ST7 2JA (01270 872776; e-mail: webmaster@raynauds.demon.co.uk; website: www.raynauds.demon.co.uk).

Marfan Syndrome

Marfan Association UK, Rochester House, 5 Aldershot Road, Fleet, Hampshire GU51 3NG (01252 810472; e-mail: marfan@tinyonline.co.uk; website: www.marfan.org.uk).

Mastectomy

Breast Cancer Care (BCC), Kiln House, 210 New King's Road, London SW6 4NZ (020 7384 2984; Helpline: 0808 800 6000 [Mon–Fri 10am–5pm]; e-mail: info@breastcancercare.org.uk; website: www.breastcancercare.org.uk).

Meniere's Disease

Meniere's Society, 98 Maybury Road, Woking, Surrey GU21 5HX (01483 740597; e-mail: info@menieres.org.uk; website: www.menieres.org.uk).

Meningitis

Meningitis Trust, Fern House, Bath Road, Stroud, Gloucestershire GL5 3TJ (01453 768000; e-mail: info@meningitis-trust.org; website: www.meningitis-trust.org).

Menopause

Women's Nutritional Advisory Service, PO Box 268, Lewes, East Sussex BN7 1QN (01273 487366; website: www.wnas.org.uk).

Mental Health and Disability

CARE, 9 Weir Road, Kibworth, Leicester LE8 0LQ (0116 279 3225; e-mail: carecentral@freeuk.com).

Mencap, Mencap National Centre, 123 Golden Lane, London EC1Y 0RT (020 7454 0454).

Mental Health Foundation, 83 Victoria Street, London SW1H 0HW (020 7802 0300; e-mail: mhf@mhf.org.uk; website: www.mentalhealth.org.uk).

MIND (National Association for Mental Health), Granta House, 15–19 Broadway, London E15 4BQ (020 8519 2122; Mind information line: 0845 766 0163; e-mail: info@mind.org.uk; website: www.mind.org.uk).

SANE (The Mental Health Charity), 1st Floor, Cityside House, 40 Adler Street, London E1 1EE (Helpline: SANELINE: 0845 767 8000 [2pm–12 midnight, 365 days]; e-mail: info@saneline.org; website: www.sane.org.uk).

Metabolic Disorders

Research Trust for Metabolic Diseases in Children, Golden Gates Lodge, Weston Road, Crewe, Cheshire CW2 5XN (01270 259375).

Migraine

Migraine Action Association (formerly British Migraine Association), Unit 6, Oakley Hay Lodge Business Park, Great Folds Lane, Great Oakley, Northamptonshire NN18 9BE (01932 352468; website: www.migraine.org.uk).

Migraine Trust, 45 Great Ormond Street, London WC1N 3HZ (020 7831 4818;

Advice Organisations

e-mail: info@migrainetrust.org.uk;
website: www.migrainetrust.org.uk).

Miscarriage

The Miscarriage Association, c/o Clayton Hospital, Northgate, Wakefield, West Yorkshire WF1 3JS (01924 200795; Helpline: 01294 200799, – Monday–Friday 9am–4pm;
e-mail: info@miscarriageassociation.org.uk;
website: wwww.miscarriageassociation.org.uk).

Motor Neurone Disease

* *Motor Neurone Disease Association (MND)*, PO Box 246, Northampton NN1 2PR (01604 250505;
e-mail: enquiries@mndassociation.org.uk;
website: www.mndasssociation.org.uk).

Multiple Sclerosis

* *Multiple Sclerosis Society of Great Britain & Northern Ireland*, MS National Centre, 372 Edgware Road, London NW2 6ND (020 8438 0700; Helpline: 0808 800 8000 [Mon–Fri 9am–9pm];
e-mail: info@mssociety.org.uk;
website: www.mssociety.org.uk).

Muscular Dystrophy

Muscular Dystrophy Group of Great Britain & Northern Ireland, 7–11 Prescot Place, London SW4 6BS (020 7720 8055;
e-mail: info@muscular-dystrophy.org.uk;
website: www.muscular-dystrophy.org.uk).

Myasthenia Gravis

Myasthenia Gravis Association, Keynes House, Chester Park, Alfreton Road, Derby DE21 4AS (01332 290219; Free 24-hour helpline: 0800 919922;
e-mail: mg@mgauk.org.uk;
website: www.mgauk.org.uk).

Myotonic Dystrophy

Myotonic Dystrophy Support Group, 35a Carlton Hill, Carlton, Nottingham NG4 1BG (0115 987 0080;
e-mail: mdsg@tesco.net;
website: www.mdsguk.org).

Narcolepsy

Narcolepsy Association (UK) (UKAN), 1 Brook Street, Stoke-on-Trent, Staffordshire ST4 1JN (01782 832725).

Neurofibromatosis

The Neurofibromatosis Association, 82 London Road, Kingston-upon-Thames, Surrey KT2 6PX (020 8547 1636;
e-mail: nfa@zetnet.co.uk).

Organ Donors

British Organ Donor Society (BODY), Balsham, Cambridge CB1 6DL (Helpline: 01223 893636;
e-mail: body@argonet.co.uk;
website: www.argonet.co.uk/body).

Voluntary Transcribers' Group, 8 Segbourne Road, Rubery, Birmingham B45 9SX (0121 453 4268, 9am–9pm;
e-mail: brail@blueyonder.co.uk).

Osteoporosis

National Osteoporosis Society, Camerton, Bath BA2 0PJ (01761 471771; Helpline: 01761 472721 [9.30am–5pm];
e-mail: info@nos.org.uk;
website: www.nos.org.uk).

Paget's Disease

National Association for the Relief of Paget's Disease, 323 Manchester Road, Walksden, Worsley, Manchester M28 3HH (0161 799 4646;
e-mail: narpd@aol.com;
website: www.paget.org.uk).

Parkinson's Disease

* *Parkinson's Disease Society of the United Kingdom*, 215 Vauxhall Bridge Road, London SW1V 1EJ (020 7931 8080; Helpline: 0808 800 0303 [8am–6pm];
website: www.parkinsons.org.uk).

Perthes Disease

Perthes Association, 15 Recreation Road, Guildford, Surrey GU1 1HE (01483 534431; Helpline: 01483 306637 – Mon–Fri 9am–1pm;
e-mail: help@perthes.org.uk;
website: www.perthes.org.uk).

Phobias

First Steps to Freedom (FSTF), 22 Randall Road, Kenilworth, Warwickshire CV8 1JY (Helpline: 01926 851608 [10am–10pm]).

National Phobics Society, Zion Community Resource Centre, 339 Stretford Road, Hulme, Manchester M15 4ZY (0870 770 0456;
e-mail: natphob.soc@good.co.uk;
website: www.phobics-society.org.uk).

Pituitary Disorders

Pituitary Foundation (PIT-PAT), PO Box 1944, Bristol BS99 2UB (0870 774 3355;
e-mail: helpline@pituitary.org.uk;
website: www.pituitary.org.uk).

Poliomyelitis

British Polio Fellowship, Eagle Office Centre, The Runway, South Ruislip, Middlesex HA4 6SE (020 8842 4999;
e-mail: info@britishpolio.org;
website: www.britishpolio.org).

Post-natal

Association for Post-Natal Illness, 145 Dawes Road, London SW6 7EB (Helpline: 020 7386 0868; e-mail: info@apni.org;
website: www.apni.org).

Prader-Willi Syndrome

Prader-Willi Syndrome Association (UK), 125A London Road, Derby DE1 2QQ (01332 365676;
e-mail: admin@pwsa-uk.demon.co.uk;
website: www.pwsa-uk.demon.co.uk).

Pre-Eclampsia

Pre-Eclampsia Society, Meadowside, 185 Greensward Lane, Essex SF5 5JN (01702 205088;
e-mail: dawnjones@clara.net;
website: www.dawnjones.clara.net).

Pre-Menstrual Syndrome

Women's Nutritional Advisory Service, PO Box 268, Lewes, East Sussex BN7 1QN (01273 487366;
website: www.wnas.org.uk).

Psoriasis

Psoriasis Association, Milton House, 7 Milton Street, Northampton NN2 7JG (01604 711129;
e-mail: mail@psoriasis.demon.co.uk).

Raynaud's Disease

Raynaud's Scleroderma Association, 112 Crewe Road, Alsager, Cheshire ST7 2JA (01270 872776;
e-mail: webmaster@raynauds.demon.co.uk; website: www.raynauds.demon.co.uk).

Retinitis Pigmentosa

British Retinitis Pigmentosa Society (BRPS), PO Box 350, Buckingham MK18 5EL (01280 860363 [Office hours and 6pm–10pm]).

Rett Syndrome

Rett Syndrome Association UK, 113 Friern Barnet Road, London N11 3EU (020 8361 5161;
e-mail: info@rettsyndrome.org.uk;
website: www.rettsyndrome.org.uk).

Reye's Syndrome

National Reye's Syndrome Foundation of the UK (NRSF), 15 Nicholas Gardens, Pyrford, Woking, Surrey GU22 8SD (01932 346843 [8am–6pm];
website: www.reyessyndrome.co.uk).

Rubella

* *Sense*, 11–13 Clifton Terrace, Finsbury Park, London N4 3SR (020 7272 7774;
e-mail: enquiries@sense.org.uk;
website: www.sense.org.uk).

Sacroidosis

Sacroidosis and Interstitial Lung Association, Chest Clinic Office, Victoria and Albert Ward, King's College Hospital, Denmark Hill, London SE5 9RS (e-mail: info@sarcoidosis.org.uk; website: www.sarcoidosis.org.uk).

Schizophrenia

Rethink Severe Mental Illness, 30 Tabernacle Street, London EC2A 4DD (020 7330 9100; Advice Line: 020 8974 6814 [Mon–Fri 10am–3pm]; e-mail: info@rethink.org; website: www.rethink.org).

Scoliosis

Scoliosis Association (UK) (SAUK), 2 Ivebury Court, 323–327 Latimer Road, London W10 6RA (020 8964 5343; Helpline: 020 8964 1166 – Mon–Fri 10am–5pm; e-mail: sauk@sauk.org.uk; website: www.sauk.org.uk).

Seasonal Affective Disorder

SAD Association (SADA), PO Box 989, Steyning, West Sussex BN44 3HG (01903 814942).

Sickle Cell Disease

Sickle Cell Society (SCS), 54 Station Road, London NW10 4UA (020 8961 7795; e-mail: sicklecellsoc@btinternet.com; website: www.sicklecellsociety.org).

Sjogren's Syndrome

British Sjogren's Syndrome Association (BSSA), 20 Kingston Way, Nailsea, Bristol BS19 2RA (01275 854215 [Tues & Thurs 10.30am–3.30pm]).

Sleep Disorders

British Snoring & Sleep Apnoea Association (BSSAA), 52 Albert Road North, Reigate RH2 9EL (0800 085 1097; e-mail: information@britishsnoring.co.uk; website: www.britishsnoring.co.uk).

Smoking

QUIT (National Society of Non-Smokers), 121 Old Street, London EC1 9NR (020 7388 5775; Helpline: 0800 00 22 00; e-mail: quit@clara.net; website: www.quit.org.uk).

Solvent Abuse

Re-Solv, 30a High Street, Stone, Staffordshire ST15 8AW (01785 817885; website: www.re-solv.org).

Sotos Syndrome

Sotos Syndrome Support Group, c/o Child Growth Foundation, 2 Mayfield Avenue, London W4 1PW (020 8995 0257;
e-mail: cgflondon@aol.com; website: www.heightmatters.org.uk).

Speech & Language Difficulties

Association for All Speech-Impaired Children (AFASIC), 50–52 Great Sutton Street, London EC1V 0DJ (020 7490 9410; e-mail: info@afasic.org.uk; website: www.afasic.org.uk).

British Stammering, 15 Old Ford Road, London E2 9PJ (020 8983 1003; e-mail: mail@stammering.org; website: www.stammering.org).

Royal Association in Aid of Deaf People (RAD), Walsingham Road, Colchester CO2 7BP (01206 509509; e-mail: info@royaldeaf.org.uk; website: www.royaldeaf.org.uk).

Speakability, 1 Royal Street, London SE1 7LL (020 7261 9572; e-mail: speakability@speakability.org.uk; website: www.speakability.org.uk).

Spina Bifida

* *Association for Spina Bifida and Hydrocephalus (ASBAH)*, 42 Park Road, Peterborough PE1 2UQ (01733 555988; e-mail: postmaster@asbah.org; website: www.asbah.org).

Spinal Injuries

Spinal Injuries Association, 76 St James' Lane, London N10 3DF (020 8444 2121; Counselling: 0800 980 0501 – Mon–Fri 9.30am–4.30pm; e-mail: sia@spinal.co.uk; website: www.spinal.co.uk).

Stress

The Coronary Artery Disease Research Association (CORDA), PO Box 9353, 121 Sidney Street, London SW3 6NR (020 7349 8686; e-mail: corda@rbh.nthames.nhs.uk; website: www.corda.org.uk).

'Unwind' Pain and Stress Management, Melrose, 3 Alderlea Close, Gilesgate, Durham DH1 1DS (0191 384 2056; e-mail:marie_unwind@compuserve.com).

Stroke

* *Stroke Association*, Stroke House, Whitecross Street, London EC1Y 8JJ (020 7490 7999; Helpline: 0845 303 3100 – Mon–Fri 9am–5pm; website: www.stroke.org.uk).

Thalassaemia

United Kingdom Thalassaemia Society (UKTS), 19 The Broadway, Southgate Circus, London N14 6PH (020 8882 0011; e-mail: office@ukts.org; website: www.ukts.org).

Thrombocytopenia with Absent Radii

TAR Syndrome Support Group, Little Wings, Whatfield Road, Elmsett, Ipswich IP7 6LS (01473 657535; e-mail: tarsupport@telia.com; website: www.ivh.se/tar).

Tinnitus

British Tinnitus Association (BTA), Ground Floor, Unit 5, Acorn Business Park, Woodseats Close, Sheffield S8 0TB (0114 250 9933; Helpline: 0800 018 0527 – 24 hours; e-mail: info@tinnitus.org.uk; website: www.tinnitus.org.uk).

Royal National Institute for the Deaf (RNID), 19–23 Featherstone Street, London EC1Y 8SL (Voice: 020 7296 8000; Text: 020 7296 8001; Helpline: 0808 808 6666 [Voice] 0808 808 0007 [Text]; e-mail: informationonline@rnid.org.uk; website: www.rnid.org.uk).

Tourette Syndrome

Tourette Syndrome (UK) Association (TSA UK), PO Box 26149, Dunfermline KY12 9WT (01892 669151; website: www.tsa.org.uk).

Tracheo-Oesophageal Fistula

Aid for Children with Tracheostomies (ACT), 72 Oakridge, Thornhill, Cardiff CF14 9BQ (029 2075 5932; e-mail: claire@claire-act.fsnet.co.uk; website: www.actfortrachykids.com).

Tracheo-Oesophageal Fistula Support Group (TOFS), St George's Centre, 91 Victoria Road, Netherfield, Nottingham NG4 2NN (0115 961 3092; e-mail: office@tofs.org.uk; website: www.tofs.org.uk).

Tranquillizers

First Steps to Freedom (FSTF), 22 Randall Road, Kenilworth, Warwickshire CV8 1JY (Helpline: 01926 851608 – 10am–10pm).

Tranquilliser Anxiety Stress Help Association (TASHA), 241 High Street, Brentford, Middlesex TW8 0NE (020 8569 9933; Helpline: 020 8560 6601 – Mon–Fri 5pm–1am, Sat–Sun 9pm–1am; e-mail: tashaf@freenetname.co.uk; website: www.tasha-foundation.org.uk).

Tuberous Sclerosis

* *Tuberous Sclerosis Association*, Little Barnsley Farm, Catshill, Bromsgrove, Worcestershire B61 0NQ (01527 871898).

Turner Syndrome

Turner Syndrome Support Society, 1/8 Irving Court, Hardgate, Clydebank,

Glasgow G81 6BA (01389 380385;
e-mail: turner.syndrome@tsss.org.uk;
website: www.tsss.org.uk).

Urostomy

Urostomy Association,
18 Floxglove Avenue, Uttoxeter,
Staffordshire ST14 8UN
(0870 770 7931; Fax: 0870 770 7932;
e-mail: ua@centraloffice.fsnet.co.uk).

Williams Syndrome

Williams Syndrome Foundation,
Infantile Hypercalcaemia Foundation Ltd,
161 High Street, Tonbridge, Kent
TN9 1BX (01732 365152).

Index

1067:
1067 Trust Fund *307*

1930:
1930 Fund for District Nurses *46*

1940:
1940 Dunkirk Veterans Association *86*

5th
5th Royal Inniskilling Dragoon Guards Association *84*

A

Abbott:
Abbott Memorial Trust *175*

Aberdeen:
Aberdeen Disabled Person's Trust *143*
Aberdeen Indigent Mental Patients' Fund *143*
Aberdeen Widows & Spinsters' Benevolent Fund *143*

Abergwili:
Abergwili Relief-in-Need Charity *170*

ABTA:
ABTA Benevolent Fund *69*

Accrington:
Accrington & District Helping Hands Fund *212*

Action:
Action for Blind People *97*

Acton:
Acton (Middlesex) Charities *368*

Actors':
Actors' Benevolent Fund *26*
Actors' Charitable Trust *26*

Adamson:
Adamson Trust *133*

Addlethorpe:
Addlethorpe Parochial Charity *236*

Adjutant:
Adjutant General's Corps Regiment Association *81*

Aged:
Aged Christian Friend Society of Scotland *133*

Ainslie:
Ainslie, Sir Samuel Chisholm & Fraser Hogg Bequests *156*

Airborne:
Airborne Forces Security Fund *71*

Aircrew:
Aircrew Association Charitable Fund *71*

Airth:
Airth Benefaction Trust *133*

Aitchison:
Christina Aitchison Trust *175*

AJEX:
AJEX Charitable Foundation (formerly known as The Association of Jewish Ex-Servicemen & Women) *71*

AJR:
AJR Charitable Trust *121*

Albrighton:
Albrighton Relief in Need Charity *254*

Alchemy:
Alchemy Foundation *105*

Aldborough:
Aldborough, Boroughbridge & District Relief-in-Sickness Fund *183*

Aldbourne:
Aldbourne Poors' Gorse Charity *298*

Aldbrough:
Aldbrough Poor Fields *182*

Aldeburgh:
Aldeburgh United Charities *340*

Aldgate:
Aldgate Freedom Foundation *367*

Aldo:
Aldo Trust *120*

Aldridge:
Aldridge Charitable Trust *90*

Alexander:
Alexander Mortification Fund *153*

Alexis:
Alexis Trust *120*

Alfold:
Alfold Smith's Charity *348*

Alfreton:
Alfreton Welfare Trust *228*

Allotments:
Allotments for the Labouring Poor of Pitminster *296*

Almondsbury:
Almondsbury Charity *277*

Almshouse:
Almshouse Charity *291*

All:
All Saints Relief-in-Need Charity *230*

Allan:
James Allan of Midbeltie *143*

Allen:
Mary Ellen Allen Charity *229*

Alnwick:
Alnwick & District Relief-in-Sickness Fund *186*

Alverstoke:
Alverstoke Trust *321*

Alzheimer's:
Alzheimer's Society *96*

Amalgamated:
Amalgamated Engineering & Electrical Union *35*

Ambleside:
Ambleside Welfare Charity *206*

Ambulance:
Ambulance Services Benevolent Fund *37*
Ambulance Service Workers Hardship Fund *47*

Ancell:
Ancell Trust *309*

Anchor:
Anchor Aid *185*

Ancient:
Ancient Parish of Ripple Trust *273*

Anderson:
Anderson Trust *149*
Andrew Anderson Trust *69*

Andrew:
Frederick Andrew Convalescent Trust *90, 123*

Anglian:
Anglian Care Trust *301*
Anglian Water Trust Fund *105*

Appleton :
Appleton Trust (Abingdon) *338*
Appleton Trust (Canterbury) *325*

Apthorp:
Milly Apthorp Charitable Trust *364*

Arbib:
Arbib Lucas Fund *123*

Archdeaconry:
Archdeaconry of Bath Clerical Families Fund *56*

INDEX

Architects:
   Architects Benevolent Society 22
Architecture:
   Architecture & Surveying Institution Benevolent Trust 23
Argyll:
   Argyll and Sutherland Highlanders' Regimental Association 81
Armchair:
   Armchair 273
Armstrong:
   Elizabeth Armstrong Charitable Trust 158
Armthorpe:
   Armthorpe Poors Estate Charity 188
Army:
   Army Air Corps (Parachute Regiment and Glider Pilot Regiment) pre-1957 81
   Army Air Corps Fund (post Sept 1957) 81
   Army Benevolent Fund 72, 87
   Army Catering Corps Benevolent Association 72
   Army Cycle Corps 81
   Army Physical Training Corps Association 81
Arnold:
   Arnold Aid in Sickness Fund 246
   Edmund Arnold's Charity (Poors Branch) 241
Arsenal:
   Arsenal Charitable Trust 359
Arthritic:
   Arthritic Association 96
Artists':
   Artists' Rifles Aid Fund 81
   Artists' General Benevolent Institution 23
Ashby-de-la-Zouch:
   Ashby-de-la-Zouch Relief-in-Sickness Fund 231
Ashford:
   Ashford Relief in Need Charities 348
Ashington:
   Ashington, Wiston, Warminghurst Sick Poor Fund 356
Ashton:
   Ashton Keynes Charity 299
   Frances Ashton's Charity 56
   John Ashton Charity (including the Gift of Ellis Smethurst). 196
ASPIRE:
   ASPIRE (Association for Spinal Injury Research Rehabilitation and Reintegration) Human Needs Fund 90
Assington:
   Assington Charity 340
Associated:
   Associated Society of Locomotive Engineers & Firemen (ASLEF) Hardship Fund 56

Association:
   Association for Spina Bifida & Hydrocephalus (ASBAH) Welfare Grant 103
   Association for the Relief of Incurables in Glasgow & the West of Scotland 157
   Association of Her Majesty's Inspectors of Taxes Benevolent Fund 66
   Association of Principals of Colleges Benevolent Fund 66
   Association of Professional Foresters Education and Provident Fund 21
   Association of Royal Navy Officers (ARNO) 72
   Association of Teachers & Lecturers Benevolent Fund 66
   Association of University Teachers Benevolent Fund 66
Assyrian:
   Assyrian Charity and Relief Fund of UK 114
Astley:
   Astley and Areley Kings Sick Fund 272
Aston-cum-Aughton:
   Aston-cum-Aughton Charity Estate 188
Ataxia:
   Ataxia UK (formerly Friedreich's Ataxia Group) 97
Atherton:
   Atherton Trust 252
Atmere:
   Edmund Atmere Charity 332
ATS:
   ATS & WRAC Benevolent Fund 72
Attlee:
   Attlee Foundation 90
Auchray:
   Auchray Fund 149
Authors':
   Authors' Contingency Fund 27
Auto:
   Auto Cycle Union Benevolent Fund 51
Auxiliary:
   Auxiliary Fund of the Methodist Church 56
Avenel:
   Avenel Trust 152
Avery:
   Jane Avery Charity – Markfield 235
Avon:
   Avon & Somerset Constabulary Benevolent Fund 276
   Avon Local Medical Committee Benevolent Fund 276
   Avon Trust 264
Axe:
   Non-Ecclesiastical Charity of Thomas Axe 287
Ayrshire:
   Ayrshire Yeomanry Charitable Trust 81

B

Backhouse:
   Backhouse Fund 206
Badley:
   Badley Memorial Trust 264
Bagri:
   Bagri Foundation 106
Bailey:
   Ernest Bailey Charity 229
Baines:
   Baines Charity 212
Baker:
   Ethel Baker Bequest 375
   Mr John Baker's Trust 370
   Bakers' Benevolent Society 38
Balderton:
   Balderton Parochial Charity 249
Ballance:
   Freda & Howard Ballance Trust 266
Balmanno:
   Miss Christian Balmanno's Mortification 160
Balsham:
   Balsham Parochial Charities 311
Baltic:
   Baltic Exchange Charitable Society 62
Bampton:
   Bampton Welfare Trust 337
Banbury:
   Banbury Charities – Bridge Estate 337
Banham:
   Banham Parochial Charities 331
Bankers:
   Bankers Benevolent Fund 28
Banner:
   Richard & Samuel Banner Trust 267
Banstead:
   Banstead and District Benevolent Fund 345
   Banstead United Charities 348
Barbers':
   Barbers' Amalgamated Charity 42, 47
Barford:
   Barford Relief-in-Need Charity 261
Barham:
   Barham Benevolent Foundation 38
Barking:
   Barking & Dagenham Mayor's Fund 364
Barnes:
   Barnes Relief-in-Need Charity and The Bailey & Bates Trust 375
   Barnes Samaritan Charity 207
   Barnes Workhouse Fund 375
   Ellen Barnes Charitable Trust 252
   William Clayton Barnes Trust 231
Barnsley:
   Barnsley Prisoner of War Fund 188
   Barnsley Tradesmen's Benevolent Institution 188

INDEX

Barnstaple:
Barnstaple & North Devon Dispensary Fund 283
Barnstaple Municipal Charities (The Poors Charity Section) 283

Barnwood:
Barnwood House Trust 292

Barony:
Barony Charitable Trust 106

Barrett:
Thomas Barrett's Charity 335

Barristers':
Barristers' Benevolent Association 44

Barron:
Thomas Metcalfe Barron Charity 180

Barrow:
Barrow Thornborrow Charity 205
William Barrow's Eleemosynary Charity 326

Barton:
Barton Bendish Poor's Charity 331

Barton-upon-Humber:
Barton-upon-Humber Relief-in-Sickness Fund 238

Basildon:
Basildon Sports Council Benevolent Fund 316

Bates:
John Heggs Bates' Charity for Convalescents 251

Bath:
Bath Abbey Charities 277
Bath and District Spastics Society 277
Bath Dispensary Charity 276
Bath Holiday Trust 277
Bath Nursing Association Charity 277

Batley:
Batley Town Mission 194

Battle:
Battle Charities 314

Baxter:
John Boyd Baxter Charitable Trust 133

Bayne:
James Bayne Charitable Trust 207

BCOP:
BCOP 116

Beacon:
Beacon Centre for the Blind 264

Beames:
Thomas Beames' Charity 278

Beaminster:
Beaminster Charities 289

Beane:
John Beane's Eleemosynary Charity 345

Beardsley:
Beardsley's Relief-in-Need Charity 258
Maud Beattie Murchie Charitable Trust 220

Beaumont:
Beaumont & Jessop Relief-in-Need Charity 196
Elizabeth Beaumont Charity 286
Charity of Letitia Beaumont 204

Becket:
Becket Bulmer Charitable Trust 230

Beckly:
J H Beckly Handicapped/Sick Children's Fund 280

Bedale:
Bedale Welfare Charity 183

Bedfordshire:
Bedfordshire and Hertfordshire Regiment Association 81

Beeston:
Beeston Fuel Charity 331

Beeton:
Beeton, Barrick & Beck Relief-in-Need Charity 238

Beighton:
Beighton Relief-in-Need Charity 189

Belfast:
Belfast Association for the Blind 129
Belfast Central Mission 129
Belfast Sick Poor Fund 129

Bell:
Sir Hugh & Lady Bell Memorial Fund 175

Ben:
Ben – Motor & Allied Trades Benevolent Fund 51

Benevolent:
Benevolent Association for the Relief of Decayed Tradesmen, their Widows and Orphans 334
Benevolent Fund for Nurses in Scotland 133
Benevolent Fund of the British Psychoanalytical Society 47
Benevolent Fund of the College of Optometrists and the Association of Optometrists 48
Benevolent Fund of the Engineering Employers' Federation (including the Dyer Memorial Funds) 35
Benevolent Fund of the Institution of Civil Engineers 36, 50
Benevolent Fund of the Institution of Mechanical Engineers 36
Benevolent Fund of the Institution of Mining & Metallurgy 50
Benevolent Fund of The Society of Chiropodists 50
Benevolent Fund of the South Wales Institute of Engineers (Incorporated) 169
Benevolent of Strangers' Friend Society 359
Benevolent Society for the Relief of the Aged and Infirm Poor 359
Benevolent Society of St Patrick 363
Benevolent Society of the Licensed Trade of Scotland 137

Bengough:
Bengough Charity (also known as The United Westminster Almhouses Group of Charities) 379

Berkshire:
Berkshire and Westminster Dragoons Association 81
Berkshire Nurses & Relief-in-Sickness Trust 301
Berkshire Regiment 81

Bertha:
Bertha Trust 149

Berwick-upon-Tweed:
Berwick-upon-Tweed Nursing Amenities Fund 187

Bestway:
Bestway Foundation 113

Betard:
Betard Bequest 97

Betchworth;
Betchworth United Charities & Henry Smith Charity 348

Betteridge:
Frances Lynn Betteridge Memorial Trust Fund 264

Betton:
Thomas Betton's Charity for Pensions & Relief-in-Need 106

Bexley:
Bexley Mayor's Fund 365

Bibby:
Elizabeth Bibby Bequest 133

Bible:
Bible Preaching Trust 56

Bideford:
Bideford Bridge Trust 281

Biggart:
Biggart Trust 134

Bilby:
Bilby's and Cooper's Relief in Need Charity 251

Billingborough:
Billingborough United Charities 238

Bilston:
Bilston Relief-in-Need Charity 266

Bilton:
Bilton Poors' Land & Other Charities 261
Percy Bilton Charity 90, 116

Bingham:
Bingham Trust Scheme 249
Bingham Trust 228
Bingham United Charities 250

Bingley:
Bingley Diamond Jubilee Relief-in-Sickness Charity 194

Bircham:
Bircham Dyson Bell Charitable Trust – The Crossley Fund 123

Birchington:
Birchington Convalescent Benefit Fund 90

Birkenhead:
Birkenhead Relief-in-Sickness Charities 218

399

INDEX

Birmingham:
  Birmingham & Midland Cinematograph Trade Benevolent Fund 223
  Birmingham & Three Counties Trust for Nurses 223
  Birmingham and District Butchers and Pork Butchers Association Benevolent Fund 264
  Birmingham Children's Holiday Fund 267
  Birmingham Jewish Community Care 264
  Birmingham Money Advice Grants (BMAG) 267

Bishop:
  Bishop of Lincoln's Discretionary Fund 239
  Bishop's Land Charity 336

Bishopsgate:
  Bishopsgate Foundation 378

Bisley:
  Bisley Charities for the Poor 293

Black:
  Black Horse Association (7th Dragoon Guards) 81
  Black Watch Association 134
  Black's Bequest 156
  Dr James Black's Trust 157
  Sir Alec Black's Charity 239

Blackpool:
  Blackpool Borough Council Services Welfare Fund (formerly The Mayor of Blackpool's Welfare Services Fund) 214
  Blackpool Ladies' Sick Poor Association 214
  Blackpool, Fylde & Wyre Society for the Blind 212

Blackstock:
  Blackstock Trust 152

Blagdon:
  Edward Blagdon's Charity 281

Blair:
  Cecil Norman Wellesley Blair Charitable Trust 299
  J T Blair's Charity 207

Blakeley-Marillier:
  Blakeley-Marillier Annuity Fund 175

Blakeney:
  Blakeney Twelve 330

Blakesley:
  Blakesley Parochial Charities 243

Blanch:
  Blanch Woolaston Walsall Charity 272

Blanchminster:
  Blanchminster Trust 280

Bletchingley:
  Bletchingley United Charities 349

Bletchington:
  Bletchington Charity 339

Bletchley:
  Bletchley Fuel Allotment Charity 308

Bloomsbury:
  Bloomsbury Dispensary 366

Blues:
  Blues and Royals Association 81

Blunt:
  Mary Anne & Ruth Blunt Charity 244

Blyth:
  Blyth Benevolent Trust 134

Boath:
  Boath & Milne Trust 146

Bolton:
  Bolton & District Nursing Association 208
  Bolton Poor Protection Society 208

Bond:
  James Bond Charity 215

Book:
  Book Trade Benevolent Society 28

Bookbinders':
  Bookbinders' Charitable Society 28

Bookhams:
  Bookhams, Fetcham & Effingham Nursing Association Trust 345

Booth:
  Booth Charities 211

Border:
  Border Regimental Benevolent Fund 81

Bordon:
  Bordon Charity 318

Botley:
  William Botley Charity 299

Boughton:
  Sir Edward Boughton Long Lawford Charity 262

Bournemouth:
  Bournemouth Society for the Visually Impaired (formerly The Bournemouth Blind Aid Society) 290

Boveridge:
  Boveridge Charity 290

Bowcocks:
  Bowcocks Trust Fund for Keighley 197

Bowes:
  Charity of Sir Martin Bowes 369

Bowley:
  Bowley Charity for Deprived Children 323

Bowness:
  Bowness Trust 207

Boxmoor:
  Boxmoor and Berkhamsted (Post Office) Benevolent Society 323

Boyack:
  Boyack Fund 146

Brackley:
  Brackley United Feoffee Charity 243

Bradford:
  Bradford & District Children's Charity Circle 194
  Bradford & District Wool Association Benevolent Fund 192
  Bradford Jewish Benevolent Fund 192
  Bradford Tradesmen's Homes 194

Braemar:
  Braemar Charitable Trust 143

Braintree:
  Braintree United Charities 316

Bramhope:
  Bramhope Trust 197

Bramley:
  Bramley Poors' Allotment Trust 189

Brampton:
  Brampton Bierlow Welfare Trust 187

Bratton:
  Bratton Fleming Relief-in-Need Charity 283

Braunston:
  Braunston Town Lands Charity 243

Brave:
  Brave Hearts (formerly Children's Relief Fund Association) 301

Brechin:
  Brechin Victoria Nursing Association 147

Brecknock:
  Brecknock Association for the Welfare of the Blind 165
  Brecknock Welfare Trust 166

Brecknockshire:
  Brecknockshire Regiment 81

Brentford:
  Brentford Relief-in-Need Charity 372

Brentwood:
  Brentwood Charity 212

Brideoake:
  Charity of Miss Ann Farrar Brideoake 175

Bridge:
  Bridge Trust 283

Bridgeland:
  Bridgeland Charity 288

Bridgeman:
  Dame Mary Bridgeman Charity 268

Bridgnorth:
  Bridgnorth Parish Charity 252

Bridlington:
  Bridlington Charities 182

Bright:
  Beatrice Eveline Bright Trust 246

Brighton:
  Brighton District Nursing Association Trust 314
  Brighton Housing Trust Charitable Trust 301

Brisco:
  Sarah Brisco Charity 315

Bristol:
  Bristol Benevolent Institution 278
  Bristol Corn Trade Guild 34
  Bristol Municipal Charities 279

Bristow:
  John Bristow and Thomas Mason Trust 349

INDEX

British:
British Airline Pilots' Association Benevolent Fund (BALPA) 22
British Antique Dealers' Association Benevolent Fund 22
British Association of Former United Nations Civil Servants Benevolent Fund 30
British Athletics Benevolent Fund 27
British Dental Association Benevolent Fund 47
British Fire Services Association Widows Orphans and Benevolent Fund 37
British Jewellery & Giftware Federation Benevolent Society 44
British Kidney Patient Association 100
British Korean Veterans (1981) Relief Fund 86
British Limbless Ex-Service Men's Association (BLESMA) 72
British Motor Cycle Racing Club Benevolent Fund 51
British Motoring Sport Relief Fund 52
British Office Systems & Stationery Federation Benevolent Fund 65
British Polio Fellowship 103
British Racing Drivers Club (BRDC) Benevolent Fund 52

Brittle:
Brittle Bone Society 98

Brixton:
Brixton Dispensary 374
Brixton Feoffee Trust 283

Broadclyst:
Broadclyst Relief-in-Need Charity 284

Broadhempston:
Broadhempston Relief-in-Need Charity 284

Broadlands:
Broadlands Home Trust 322

Brockley:
Brockley Town & Poor Estate (Brockley Charities) 340

Bromley:
Bromley Relief-in-Need Charity 366

Bromwich:
Thomas Bromwich Charity 265

Brook:
Charles Brook Convalescent Fund 197

Brooke:
Brooke Charity 232
Lizzie Brooke Charity 280

Broomfield:
Broomfield United Charities 316

Brotherton:
Brotherton Charity Fund 199

Broughton:
Broughton, Kirkby & District Good Samaritan Fund 183

Broughty:
Broughty Ferry Benevolent Fund 147

Brown:
Brown Habgood Hall and Higden Charity 292

Browne:
Winifrede Browne's Charity 240

Brownlow:
Lawrence Brownlow Charity 207

Brownsdon:
Brownsdon & Tremayne Estate Charity (also known as the Nicholas Watts Trust) 281

Bruce:
Bruce Charitable Trust 151

Brunts:
Brunts Charity 251

BT:
BT Benevolent Fund 67

Buchanan:
Buchanan Society 134

Buckingham:
Buckingham Trust 56

Buckinghamshire:
Buckinghamshire, Berkshire & Oxfordshire Yeomanry and Artillery Trust 81

Buckle:
Buckle Family Charitable Trust 301

Budleigh:
Budleigh Salterton Nursing Association 284

Buffs:
Buffs Benevolent Fund 81

Builders':
Builders' Benevolent Institution 29

Bungay:
Bungay Charities 341

Buntingford:
Buntingford Relief in Need Charity 324

Burford:
Burford Relief-in-Need Charity 337

Burma:
Burma Star Association 72

Burton:
Burton Breweries Charitable Trust 223

Burton-on-Trent:
Burton-on-Trent Nursing Endowment Fund 255

Bury:
Bury Relief-in-Sickness Fund 208
Bury St Edmunds Old School Fund Foundation 341

Bushbury:
Bushbury United Charities 268

Butchers':
Butchers' & Drovers' Charitable Institution 38

Butterfield:
Butterfield Trust 194

Buttle:
Buttle Trust 112

Byfield:
Byfield Poors Allotment 243

Byfleet:
Byfleet United Charities 349

C

Calder:
Dr John Calder's Fund 144

Calibut:
Calibut's Estate & the Hillington Charities 330
Calverley:
Calverley Charity 192

Calverton:
Calverton Apprenticing Charity 308

Cam:
Dame Ann Cam's Charity 292

Camberwell:
Camberwell Consolidated Charities 376

Cambrian:
Cambrian Educational Trust Fund 165

Cambridge:
Cambridge Community Nursing Trust 311

Cambridgeshire:
Cambridgeshire County Bowling Association – Benevolent Fund 310
Cambridgeshire County Remembrance Fund 86
Cambridgeshire Regiment Association 81

Cameron:
Cameron Fund 47, 144

Cameronians:
Cameronians (Scottish Rifles) Benevolent Association 81

Camp:
John & Anne Camp's Charity 241

Campden:
Campden Charities 373

Canadian:
Canadian Veterans' Affairs 86

Cancer:
Cancer & Leukaemia in Childhood Trust (CLIC) 98

Cannington:
Cannington Combined Charity 295

Canterbury:
Canterbury United Municipal Charities 327

Cantley:
Cantley Poor's Land Trust 189

Capital:
Capital Charitable Trust 152

Caravan:
Caravan (the trading name of The National Grocers Benevolent Fund) 38

Card:
Charity of John & Joseph Card (also known as Draycott Charity) 296

Cardiff:
Cardiff Caledonian Society 170
Cardiff Charity for Special Relief 170

INDEX

Carlee:
Carlee Ltd *121*

Carlisle:
Carlisle Sick Poor Fund *206*

Carlton:
Carlton Colville Fuel & Poors Allotment Charity *341*

Carlow:
Leonora Carlow Trust Fund *289*

Carmichael:
Mrs Agnes W Carmichael's Trust (incorporating Ferguson and West Charitable Trust) *149*

Carnegie:
Carnegie Hero Fund Trust *106*

Carperby:
Carperby Poor's Land Charity *184*

Carr:
Carr Trust *257*

Carter:
Harold Carter Bequest *378*

Casselden:
Casselden Trust *327*

Catenian:
Catenian Benevolent Association *119*

Catharine:
Catharine House Trust *314*

Catholic:
Catholic Clothing Guild *106*

Catt:
Charity of Joseph Catt *345*

Cattle:
Joseph & Annie Cattle Trust *181*

Cavell:
Edith Cavell & Nation's Fund for Nurses *47*

Central:
Central endowments (BMAG) *267*
Central Exeter Relief-in-Need Fund *285*

Century:
Century Benevolent Fund *30*

Ceramic:
Ceramic Industry Welfare Society *30*

Certified:
Certified Accountants' Benevolent Association *21*

Chalker:
Henry & Ada Chalker Trust *199*

Challenger:
Challenger Children's Fund *134*

Chalmers:
George, James & Alexander Chalmers Trust *144*

Chamberlain:
Chamberlain Foundation *106*

Chamberlayne:
Sarah Chamberlayne Charity *259, 315*

Champney:
Margaret Champney Rest & Holiday Fund *90*

Chance:
Chance Trust *265*

Channel:
Channel – Supporting Family Social Work in Liverpool *219*

Chapel:
Chapel Allerton & Potternewton Relief-in-Need Charity (Leeds) *197*

Chapman:
Adele Chapman Foundation *91*
John William Chapman Charitable Trust *189*

Charitable:
Charitable trusts administered by East Ayrshire Council *159*

Charities:
Charities Administered by Angus Council *146*
Charities Administered by Dumfries and Galloway Council *158*
Charities adminstered by Edinburgh City Council *153*
Charities Administered by Fife Council (West Fife Area) *151*
Charities Administered by Midlothian Council *156*
Charities Administered by Rochdale Borough Council *210*
Charities Administered by the City of Aberdeen *143*
Charities administered by the Educational Institute of Scotland *135*
Charities Administered by the Moray Council Welfare Grants *149*
Charities Administered from the Guild Church of St Andrew Holborn *367*
Charities administrated by The City of Glasgow Society of Social Service *160*
Charity known as The Mayors Fund *274*

Charlton:
Charlton Kings Relief in Need Charity *293*

Chartered:
Chartered Accountants' Benevolent Association *21*
Chartered Institute of Building Benevolent Fund *29*
Chartered Institute of Journalists Orphan Fund *46*
Chartered Institute of Library and Information Professionals (CILIP) (formerly known as The Library Association Benevolent Fund) *45*
Chartered Institute of Loss Adjusters Benevolent Fund *45*
Chartered Institute of Management Accountants Benevolent Fund *21*
Chartered Institute of Patent Agents' Incorporated Benevolent Association *52*
Chartered Institution of Building Services Engineers Benevolent Fund *35*
Chartered Society of Physiotherapy Members' Benevolent Fund *47*
Chartered Society of Queen Square *102*

Chasah:
Chasah Trust *57*

Chatham:
Chatham District Masonic Trust *327*

Chatteris:
Chatteris Feoffee Charity *311*

Chauntry:
Chauntry Estate *243*

Cheam:
Cheam Consolidated Charities *349*

Cheddington:
Cheddington Town Lands Charity *308*

Chediston:
Chediston United Charities, Town & Poors' Branch *341*

Chelsworth:
Chelsworth Parochial Charity *341*

Cheltenham:
Cheltenham Aid-in-Sickness & Nurses Welfare Fund and the Cheltenham Family Welfare Association – Gooding Fund *292*

Chemical:
Chemical Engineer's Benevolent Fund *30*

Chepstow:
Chepstow Charity Amalgamated *171*

Chertsey:
Chertsey Combined Charity *350*

Cheshire:
Cheshire Provincial Fund of Benevolence *202*
Cheshire Regiment Association *81*
Cheshire Yeomanry Association Benevolent Fund *81*

Chessington:
Chessington Charities *350*

Chester:
Chester Parochial Relief-in-Need Charity *203*

Chesterfield:
Chesterfield General Charitable Fund *228*
Chesterfield Municipal Charities *227*

Chevras:
Chevras Ezras Nitzrochim *122*

Cheyne:
Gordon Cheyne Trust Fund *144*

Chichester:
Chichester Welfare Trust *356*

Children:
Children of the Clergy Trust *57*
Children's Boot Fund *269*
Children's Leukaemia Society *165*

Chindits:
Chindits Old Comrades Association *86*

Chippenham:
Chippenham Borough Lands Charity *299*

Chipping:
Chipping Sodbury Town Lands *280*

Chobham:
Chobham Poor Allotment Charity *350*

Christ:
　Christ Church Fund for Children *218*
　Christ Church United Charities *376*

Christadelphian:
　Christadelphian Benevolent Fund *120*

Christie:
　Christie Fund *156*
　John & Celia Bonham Christie Charitable Trust *276*
　Robert Christie Bequest Fund *152*

Christmas:
　Christmas Gift Fund for the Old City of Canterbury *325*

Chronicle:
　Chronicle Cinderella Fund *212*
　Church Eaton Relief-in-Need Charity *257*
　Church of England Pensions Board *57*
　Church School Masters and School Mistresses Benevolent Institution *66*

Church:
　Church of England Pensions Board *57*
　Church School Masters and School Mistresses Benevolent Institution *66*

Churt:
　Churt Welfare Trust *345*

Cinema:
　Cinema & Television Benevolent Fund *46*

City:
　City Chapter & Percy Trentham Charity *368*
　City Foundation *367*
　City of Bradford Fund for the Disabled *194*
　City of Edinburgh Charitable Trusts *153*
　City of Glasgow Native Benevolent Association *160*
　City of Glasgow Regiment *81*
　City of London Linen and Furnishings Trades Association *68*
　City of Oxford Charities *339*
　City of Salford Relief-in-Distress Fund *211*

Civil:
　Civil Service Benevolent Fund *31*

Clackmannan:
　Clackmannan District Charitable Trust *150*

Clapham:
　Clapham Relief Fund *374*

Clark:
　James Clark Bequest Fund *135*

Clarke:
　Elizabeth Clarke Relief-in-Need Fund & The Wigston Relief-in-Need Fund *232*

Clayton:
　Clayton, Taylor & Foster Charity *192*

Cliffe-at-Hoo:
　Cliffe-at-Hoo Parochial Charity *327*

Clitheroe:
　Clitheroe District Nursing Association Fund *214*

Clophill:
　Clophill United Charities *304*

Closehelm:
　Closehelm Ltd *121*

Cloudesley:
　Richard Cloudesley's Charity *372*

Clover:
　Emily Clover Trust *218*

Coal:
　Coal Industry Benevolent Trust *32*
　Coal Trade Benevolent Association *33*

Coalville:
　Coalville and District Relief in Sickness Fund *232*

Cochrane:
　Matthew Cochrane Bequest *159*

Cockermouth:
　Cockermouth Relief-in-Need Charity *206*

Cockpen:
　Cockpen Lasswade & Falconer Bequest *156*

Coddington:
　Coddington United Charities *250*

Cohen:
　Myrtle Cohen Trust Fund *45*

Colchester:
　Colchester Catalyst Charity *315*
　Colchester Lying-In Charity *317*
　Colchester Society for the Blind *317*

Coldstream:
　Coldstream Guards Association *81*

Cole:
　Charities of Susanna Cole & Others *223*

Coleman:
　R V Coleman Trust *325*

Coles:
　Coles & Rice Charity *244*

Collier:
　Collier Charitable Trust *57*
　Joseph Collier Holiday Fund *377*

Colvile:
　J I Colvile Charitable Trust *112*

Colvill:
　Colvill Trust *147*

Colyton:
　Colyton Parish Lands Charity *284*
　Colyton Sick and Poor Fund *284*

Combe:
　Combe Down Holiday Trust *280*

Combined:
　Combined Services Association (Wakefield) Benevolent Fund *192*

Commandos':
　Commandos' Benevolent Fund *73*

Commercial:
　Commercial Travellers of Scotland Benevolent Fund for Widows & Orphans *134*
　Commercial Travellers' Benevolent Institution *33*

Common:
　Common Lands of Rotherham Charity *189*

Commonwealth:
　Commonwealth Ex-Services League *73*

CommunicAbility:
　CommunicAbility – The John Powell (UK) Trust *91*

Community:
　Community Foundation (Serving Tyne & Wear and Northumberland) *175*
　Community Foundation for Calderdale *195*
　Community of the Presentation Trust *91*
　Community Shop Holiday Fund *197*
　Community Shop Trust *198*

Concert:
　Concert Artistes' Association Benevolent Fund *24*

Confectioners':
　Confectioners' Benevolent Fund *38*

Congleton:
　Congleton Town Trust *203*

Connaught:
　Connaught Rangers Association *81*

Conroy:
　Conroy Trust *220*

Conservative:
　Conservative and Unionist Agents' Benevolent Association *106*

Consolidated:
　Consolidated Charity of Burton-upon-Trent *255*

Constable's:
　Constable's Fund *81*

Conwy:
　Conwy Welsh Church Acts Fund *167*

Cook:
　Samuel Edward Cook Charity for the Poor *365*

Cooper:
　Cooper & Lancaster Annuities *187*
　Brian & Margaret Cooper Trust *142*
　William Alexander Coopers Liverymen Fund *34*

Corah:
　J Reginald Corah Trust *232*

Corbett:
　Thomas Corbett's Charity *223*

Corfe:
　Corfe Castle Charities *291*

Corkhill:
　John Lloyd Corkhill Trust *220*

Corn:
　Corn Exchange Benevolent Society *34*

Cornwall:
　Cornwall Retired Clergy, Widows of the Clergy and their Dependants Fund *280*
　Cornwall Seamen's Benevolent Trust *280*

Cornwallis:
　Cornwallis Memorial Fund *325*

INDEX

Corporation:
　Corporation of London Benevolent Association 55
　Corporation of London Staff Association Benevolent Fund 55
　Corporation of the Sons of the Clergy 57

Corps:
　Corps of Army Music Trust 81

Corstorphine;
　Corstorphine & Cramond Bequests 153

Corton:
　Corton Poors' Land Trust 341

Corwen:
　Corwen College Pension Charity 166

Cottam:
　Cottam Charities 214

Cotton:
　Cotton Districts' Convalescent Fund 201
　Cotton Industry War Memorial Trust 68

Counsel:
　Counsel & Care for the Elderly 116

County:
　County of London Yeomanry (3rd/4th) (Sharpshooters) 81

Coventry:
　Coventry Community Cancer Fund 265
　Coventry Freemen's Charity 265
　Coventry Nursing Trust 269

Cowbridge:
　Cowbridge with Llanblethian United Charities 172

Cox:
　George Cox Charity 297
　Mary Morrison Cox Fund 145

Cozens:
　Cozens Bequest 338

Craigcrook:
　Craigcrook Mortification 134

Cranbrook:
　Cranbrook Charity 285

Cranfield:
　Cranfield Charitable Trust 340

Cranleigh:
　Cranleigh & District Nursing Association 345

Crediton:
　Crediton Relief-in-Need Charity 284

Crerar:
　Alastair Crerar Trust for Single Poor 134

Cresswell:
　Eliza Ann Cresswell Memorial 228

Cricketers:
　Cricketers Association Charity 34

Cripplegate:
　Cripplegate Foundation 359

Crisis:
　Crisis Fund of Voluntary Service Aberdeen 144

Croatian:
　Croatian Relief Fund 114

Crosby:
　Crosby Ravensworth Relief-in-Need Charities 206

Crosland:
　Crosland Fund 209

Cross:
　Charity of A J G Cross 379
　Cross House Trust 57

Crowhurst:
　Crowhurst Relief-in-Need Charities 350

Crusader:
　Crusader Benevolent Fund 43

Crusaid:
　Crusaid Hardship Fund 95

Culmstock:
　Culmstock Fuel Allotment Charity 285

Cumbria:
　Cumbria Constabulary Benevolent Fund 205
　Cumbria Miners' Welfare Trust Fund 205

Cummings:
　Robert Cummings Bequest 159

Curtis:
　Mary Curtis' Maternity Charity 375

Customs:
　Customs & Excise Family Fund 34

Cwmbran:
　Cwmbran Trust 172

Cystic:
　Cystic Fibrosis Trust 99

D

Dacorum:
　Dacorum Community Trust 324

Dagenham:
　Dagenham United Charity 364

Dahl:
　Roald Dahl Foundation 102

Dance:
　Dance Teachers' Benevolent Fund 24

Dargie:
　Mrs Marie Dargie Trust 147

Dart:
　Dart Valley Medical Trust 289

Datchet:
　Datchet United Charities 306

Davenport:
　Baron Davenport Emergency Fund 272
　Baron Davenport Emergency Grant 224, 255, 257-260, 263, 267, 270-271
　Baron Davenport's Charity Trust Emergency Fund 256
　Baron Davenport's Charity 224

Daventry:
　Daventry Consolidated Charity 243

Davey:
　Charity of John Davey 281

Davidson:
　Davidson Charity Trust 191
　Elisabeth Davidson Memorial Benevolent Trust 144
　George Davidson's Benevolent Fund 144

Davies:
　Charity of Arthur Vernon Davies for the Poor 209
　Isaac Davies Trust 359
　Mark Davies Injured Riders Fund 123

Dawber:
　Charity of John Dawber 236

Deafblind:
　Deafblind UK 100

Deakin:
　Deakin Charitable Trust 346
　Deakin Institution 121

Deeping:
　Deeping St James United Charities 238

Deiro:
　Margaret de Sousa-Deiro Fund 91

De La Roche:
　Alexandrine De La Roche Relief in Need Charity 342

Dempster:
　Dempster Trust 346

Denham:
　Denham Nursing Fund 308

Dennington:
　Dennington Consolidated Charities 342

Denton:
　Denton Relief in Sickness Charity 208

Deptford:
　Deptford Pension Society 374

Derby:
　Derby City Charity 229

Derbyshire:
　Derbyshire Special Constabulary Benevolent Fund 227
　Lucy Derbyshire Annuity Fund 246
　Derbyshire Yeomanry Old Comrades Association 81

D'Erlanger:
　Late Baron F A D'Erlanger's Charitable Trust 107

Desborough:
　Desborough Town Welfare Committee 243

Devon:
　Devon County Football League Benevolent Fund 282

Devonshire:
　Devonshire and Dorset Regiment Association 81
　Devonshire Regiment Old Comrades' Association 81

Dewsbury:
　Dewsbury & District Sick Poor Fund 192
　Dewsbury Relief in Sickness Fund 196

Dibden:
　Dibden Allotments Charity 318

Dibdin:
　Dibdin Brand Charity 366

Dibs:
Dibs Charitable Trust *107*

Dickinson:
Mary Dickinson Charity *247*

Diss:
Diss Parochial Charities Poors Branch *331*

Dixon:
Charles Dixon Pension Fund *219*

Dobson:
Dobson Trust *327*

Dodgson:
Derek & Eileen Dodgson Foundation *301*

Dolphin:
Dolphin Society *279*

Domestic:
Domestic Servants Benevolent Institution *34*

Domine:
Domine Trust *57, 112*

Donald:
Donald Trust *144*

Door:
Door of Hope Christian Trust *227*

Dorchester:
Dorchester Relief-in-Need Charity *291*

Dorkin:
John Dorkin Charity *340*

Dorking:
Dorking Charity *350*

Dorrington:
Dorrington Welfare Charity *238*

Dorset:
Dorset Regiment Old Comrades Association *81*

Downham:
Downham Aid in Sickness *331*
Downham Feoffee Charity *311*

Dragoon:
Dragoon Guards *81*

Drake:
Francis Drake Fellowship *123*

Drexler:
George Drexler Foundation *33*

Driving:
Driving Instructors Accident & Disability Fund *35*

Dronfield:
Dronfield Relief-in-Need Charity *227*

Drummond:
Kate Drummond Trust *329*

Duckett:
Isaac Duckett Charity *367*
Isaac Duckett's Charity (St Clement Danes Branch) *379*

Ducklington:
Ducklington & Hardwick with Yelford Charity *338*

Dudley:
Dudley Charity *265*

Dugdale:
Henry Percy Dugdale Charity *197*

Duke:
Duke of Albany's Seaforth Highlanders *82*
Duke of Cambridge's Own Middlesex Regiment *82*
Duke of Cornwall's Benevolent Fund *275*
Duke of Cornwall's Light Infantry Association *82*
Duke of Edinburgh's Royal Regiment Association (Berkshire & Wiltshire) *82*
Duke of Wellington's (West Riding) Regimental Association *82*

Dumbarton:
Dumbarton Children's Trust *162*

Duncan:
G M Duncan Trust *158*

Dundee:
Dundee Indigent Sick Society *148*

Dunn:
W E Dunn Trust *224*

Dunnachie:
W J & Mrs C G Dunnachie's Charitable Trust *73*

Dunsmoor:
Dunsmoor Charity *269*

Dunstable:
Dunstable Poor's Land Charity *304*
Dunstable Welfare Trust *304*

Dunwich:
Dunwich Pension Charity *342*

Durham:
Durham Light Infantry Charitable Fund *82*

Durnford:
Montagu Neville Durnford & Saint Leo Cawthan Memorial Trust *322*

E

Ealing:
Ealing Aid-in-Sickness Trust *368*
Ealing Philanthropic Institution *368*

Earl:
Earl Haig Fund Scotland *135*
Earl of Northampton's Charity *369*
Earl of Southampton Trust *320*
Earl of Stair Bequest *156*
Earl Stonham Trust *342*

Earley:
Earley Charity *305*

East:
East Africa Women's League (UK) Benevolent Fund *107*
East Anglian Regiments *82*
East Bergholt United Charities *317*
East Chevington Mining Community Aged & Sick Persons Fund *187*
East Dereham Relief-in-Need Charity *332*
East Grinstead Relief in Sickness Charity *357*
East Kent Regiment *82*
East Knoyle Welfare Trust *299*
East Lancashire Regiment Benevolent Fund *82*
East Surrey Regiment *82*
East Sussex Farmers Union Benevolent Fund *302*
East Tilbury Relief-in-Need Charity *317*
East Tuddenham Charities *332*
East Yorkshire Regimental Association *82*

Eastbourne:
Eastbourne and District Police Court Mission *302*

Eaton:
Eaton Fund for Artists, Nurses & Gentlewomen *26, 48, 123*

Ebb:
Ebb and Flow Charitable Trust *112*

ECAS:
ECAS – Challenger Children's Fund *134*
ECAS (Access/Holiday Fund) *152*

Eccles:
Charity of Jane Patricia Eccles *272*

Ecclesfield:
Ecclesfield Welfare Charities *189*

Eddleston:
John Eddleston's Charity *218*

Edinburgh:
Edinburgh Merchant Company Endowment Trust *152*
Edinburgh Royal Infirmary Samaritan Society *154*
Edinburgh Society for Relief of Indigent Old Men *155*
Edinburgh Voluntary Organisations' Trusts *152*

Edmett:
Edmett & Fisher Charity *329*

Edmonds:
William Edmonds Fund *219*

Edmonton:
Edmonton Aid-in-Sickness & Nursing Fund *369*

Edridge:
Edridge Fund *54*

Educational:
Educational Institute of Scotland Benevolent Fund *135*

Edwards:
Austin Edwards Charity *263*
Edward's Bequest *253*
Dr Edwards' & Bishop King's Fulham Charity *370*

Egerton:
George Julian Egerton Fund *121*

Egham:
Egham United Charity *351*

Egyptian:
Egyptian Community Association in the United Kingdom *114*

Electrical:
Electrical and Electronics Industries Benevolent Association *35*

INDEX

Electronic:
Electronic Aids for the Blind *97*

Elliott:
Elliott Charity *357*

Ely:
Ely District Nursing Trust *311*

Eman:
Elizabeth Eman Trust *308*

Emanuel:
Emanuel Hospital Charity *359*

Emberton:
Emberton United Charity *309*

Emmandjay:
Emmandjay Charitable Trust *195*

EMMS:
EMMS International Hawthornbrae Trust *155*

English:
English National Opera Benevolent Fund *25*

Entertainment:
Entertainment Artistes' Benevolent Fund *23*

Enville:
Enville Village Trust *257*

Environmental:
Environmental Health Officers Welfare Fund *37*

Epsom:
Epsom Parochial Charities *351*

Equity:
Equity Trust Fund *23*

Essex:
Essex Police Support Staff Benevolent Fund *316*
Essex Regiment Association *82*

Ethel:
Ethel Mary Fund For Nurses *48*

Evelyn:
Sir John Evelyn's Charity *360*

Ewell:
Ewell Parochial Trusts *346*

Exeter:
Exeter Dispensary & Aid-in-Sickness Fund *285*
Exeter Nursing Association Trust *282*
Exeter Relief-in-Need Charity *285*

Exminster:
Exminster Feoffes *286*

Exmouth:
Exmouth Welfare Trust *286*

Ex-Service:
Ex-Service Fellowship Centres *86*
Ex-Services Mental Welfare Society (Combat Stress) *86*

Eynsham:
Eynsham Consolidated Charity *339*

F

Faculty:
Faculty of Advocates 1985 Charitable Trust *135*

Falkirk:
Falkirk Temperance Trust *150*

Family:
Family Fund Trust *91*
Family Holiday Association *115*
Family Welfare Association *107*

Far:
Far East (Prisoners of War and Internees) Fund *86*

Fareham:
Fareham Welfare Trust *321*

Faringdon:
Faringdon United Charities *338*

Farlow:
Farlow James & Williams Charity *254*

Farmers
Farmers' Benevolent Institution *236*

Farnborough:
Farnborough (Hampshire) Welfare Trust *318*

Farndon:
Farndon Relief-in-Need Charity *250*

Farrar:
Mary Farrar's Benevolent Trust Fund *192*

Farrell:
Farrell Charitable Trust *92*

Farthing:
Farthing Trust *107, 310*

Fearnside:
Susannah Fearnside's Charity *176*

Featherstone:
Catherine Featherstone Charity *310*

Federation:
Federation of Master Builders (Bristol Branch) Benevolent Fund *279*

Feltmakers:
Feltmakers Charitable Foundation *32*

Fenstanton:
Fenstanton Town Trust *311*

Fentham:
George Fentham (Birmingham) Charity *267*

Ferryhill:
Ferryhill Station, Mainsforth & Bishop Middleham Aid-in-Sickness Charity *180*

Field:
Doris Field Charitable Trust *338*
Olive & Norman Field Charity *176*

Fife:
Fife and Forfar Yeomanry Association *82*
Fife Council – Common Good Funds and Trusts (East) *151*
Fife, Kinross & Clackmannan Charitable Society *160*

Fifty:
Fifty Fund *247*

Finchampstead:
Finchampstead & Barkham Relief-in-Sickness Fund *305*

Finchley:
Finchley Charities *364*

Finn:
Elizabeth Finn Trust *107*

Finnart:
Finnart House School Trust *121*

Finnie:
David Finnie & Alan Emery Charitable Trust *92*

Finsbury:
Finsbury Relief-in-Sickness Charity *372*

Fire:
Fire Services National Benevolent Fund *37*

Fisher:
Fisher Institution *187*
Jane Fisher Trust *206*
Jane Fisher's Gift *189*

Fishmongers:
Fishmongers' & Poulterers' Institution *38*

Fleetwood:
Fleetwood Fishing Industry Benevolent Fund *215*

Fleming:
Fleming Bequest *151*

Fletcher:
Miss Ethel Mary Fletcher's Charitable Bequest *330*

Flitwick:
Flitwick Town Lands Charity *304*

Fluck:
Fluck Convalescent Fund *292*

Flynn:
Paul Flynn Memorial Fund *96*

Fogelman:
Isaac & Annie Fogelman Relief Trust *322*

Folkestone:
Folkestone Municipal Charities *327*

Football:
Football Association Benevolent Fund *40*

Footwear:
Footwear Benevolent Society (formerly The Boot Trade Benevolent Society) *32*

Forbes:
Forbes Fund *144*
Dr Forbes (Inverness) Trust *163*
Trust of Mrs Mary Anne Forbes *149*

Forby:
Jane Forby Charity *337*

Forces:
Forces Pensions Society *86*

Ford:
Joseph Ford's Trust *184*

Fordath:
Fordath Foundation *270*

Fordwich:
Fordwich United Charities *327*

INDEX

Foreigners:
Foreigners' Relief Fund *160*

Forres:
Forres Poor Fund & Others *149*

Forth:
Forth Valley Medical Benevolent Fund *151*

Foster:
Alfred Foster Settlement *28*

Foulden:
Foulden Parochial Charities *332*

Fountain:
Fountain Nursing Trust *188*

Four:
Four Winds Trust *57*

Fox:
Fox Memorial Trust *92*

Foxton:
Foxton Dispensary *213*

Foyle:
Charles Henry Foyle Trust *224*

Foyles:
John Foyles Charity *292*

Frampton:
Frampton Town Land & United Charities *239*

Franklin:
Sir George Franklin's Pension Charity *190*
Samuel Franklin Fund *311*

Fraser:
Emily Fraser Trust *135*
Miss Jane Campbell Fraser's Trust *155*

Freeman:
Freeman Evans St David's Day Denbigh Charity *168*

French:
Anne French Memorial Trust *330*

Friends:
Friends Hall Farm Street Trust *224*
Friends of Home Nursing in Birmingham *267*
Friends of the Clergy Corporation *57*
Friends of the Elderly *116*

Friendship:
Friendship Community Trust *108*

Frimley:
Frimley Fuel Allotments Charity *346*

Friskney:
Friskney United Charities *239*

Fritillary:
Fritillary Trust *306*

Frodsham:
Frodsham Nursing Fund *203*

Fryer:
Fryer Welfare and Recreational Trusts *284*

Fuel:
Fuel Fund of Voluntary Service Aberdeen *146*

Fulham:
Fulham Philanthropic Society *370*

Fund:
Fund for Human Need *108, 114, 116*

Fur:
Fur Trade Benevolent Society *41*

Furness:
Furness Seamen's Pension Fund *180*

Furnishing:
Furnishing Trades Benevolent Association *41*

Fusiliers:
Fusiliers Aid Society *82*

G

Gainsborough:
Gainsborough Dispensary Charity *236*

Galon:
Thomas Galon's Charity *313*

Garboldisham:
Garboldisham Parish Charities *332*

Garden:
Garden Nicol Benevolent Fund *144*

Gardeners:
Gardeners' Royal Benevolent Society *41*

Gardner:
Grace Gardner Trust *185*
Dr Gardner's Charity for Sick Nurses *253*
Gardner's Trust for the Blind *97*

Gargrave:
Gargrave Poor's Land Charity *183*

Garlthorpes:
Garlthorpes Charity *182*

Garrett:
Dr Garrett Memorial Trust *209*

Garthgwynion:
Garthgwynion Charities *166*

Gateshead:
Gateshead Blind Trust Fund *191*
Gateshead Relief-in-Sickness Fund *191*

Gayton:
Gayton Fuel Allotments *332*
Gayton Relief-in-Need Charity *244*

Gaywood:
Gaywood Poors' Fuel Allotment Trust *333*

Geest:
Gyles Geest Charity *294*

General:
General Charities of the City of Coventry *269*

Gent:
Charity of Priscilla Gent & Others *261*

George:
Ruby & Will George Trust *33*

Georgeson:
Georgeson Charitable Trust *164*

German:
German Society of Benevolence *302*
German Welfare Council *114*

Gerrard:
Doctor M A Gerrard's Gotham Old People's Benevolent Fund *250*
Doctor M A Gerrard's Kegworth Old People's Benevolent Fund *234*

Gibson:
Gibson, Simpson & Brockbank Annuities Trust *215*

Gilbert:
Charity of Jane Kate Gilbert *267*

Gilbertson:
Gilbertson Trust *164*

Gild:
Gild of Freemen of Haverfordwest *172*

Gill:
Francis Butcher Gill's Charity *224*

Girls:
Girls Welfare Fund *216*

Gisleham:
Gisleham Relief in Need Charity *342*

Gislingham:
Gislingham United Charity *342*

Glasgow:
Glasgow Angus & Mearns Benevolent Society *160*
Glasgow Benevolent Society *161*
Glasgow Bute Benevolent Society *158*
Glasgow Dumfriesshire Society *161*
Glasgow Dunbartonshire Benevolent Association *161*
Glasgow Kilmarnock Society *161*
Glasgow Kilmun Society *161*
Glasgow Regiment *82*
Glasgow Society of the Sons of Ministers of the Church of Scotland *135*

Glasspool:
R L Glasspool Charity Trust *108*

Glebe:
Glebe Charitable Trust *112*

Glider:
Glider Pilot Regimental Association Benevolent Fund *82*

Gloucester:
Gloucester District Nursing Charities *293*

Gloucestershire:
Gloucestershire Bowling Association Benevolent Fund *293*
Gloucestershire Football Association Benevolent Fund *293*
Gloucestershire Regimental Association *82*

Godmersham:
Godmersham Relief in Need Charity *328*

Godson:
Edmund Godson Charity *369*

Godstone:
Godstone United Charities *346*

Golborne:
Golborne Charities *209*

Goldie:
Grace Wyndham Goldie (BBC) Trust Fund *46*

407

Index

Goldminers:
  Goldminers OAP Outing & Christmas Fund 227
Goldsborough:
  Goldsborough Poor's Charity 183
Goldsmiths:
  Goldsmiths', Silversmiths' & Jewellers' Benevolent Society 44
Goodall:
  Goodall Trust 196
Goodman:
  Valentine Goodman Estate Charity 241
Goodwin:
  Sir Stuart & Lady Florence Goodwin Charity 247
  Stuart Goodwin Charity 251
Goore:
  John Goore's Charity 220
Goosnargh:
  Goosnargh & Whittingham United Charity 213
Gordon:
  Gordon District Charities 144
  Gordon Highlanders' Association 82
Gorsuch:
  Gorsuch, Langley & Prynce Charity 255
Gourock:
  Gourock Coal & Benevolent Fund 162
Governesses:
  Governesses' Benevolent Society of Scotland 135
Gow:
  Neil Gow Charitable Trust 142
Goward:
  Charities of George Goward & John Evans 343
Gowland:
  Ralph Gowland Trust 180
Gowthorpe:
  Charles Wright Gowthorpe Fund & Clergy Augmentation Fund 247
Grampian:
  Grampian Police Diced Cap Charitable Fund 142
Grand:
  Grand Charity (of Freemasons under the United Grand Lodge of England) 119
  Grand Lodge of Antient, Free & Accepted Masons of Scotland 135
  Grand Order of Water Rats Charities Fund 23
  Grand Prix Mechanics Charitable Trust 52
Grandborough:
  Grandborough & Sutton Charities 261
Grant:
  Grant, Bagshaw, Rogers & Tidswell Fund 201
Grantchester:
  Grantchester Relief in Need Charity 312

Grantham:
  Grantham Yorke Trust 265
Grateful:
  Grateful Society 276
Gratrix:
  Gratrix Charity 209
Gray:
  Miss Margaret Gray's Trust 145
Great:
  Great Glen Relief in Need Charity 234
  Great Hockham Fuel & Furze Trust 333
  Great Linford Relief in Need Charity 309
  Great Torrington Town Lands Poors Charities 286
Green:
  Green Howards Benevolent Fund 82
  Green Jackets 1st, 2nd, 3rd, 43rd & 52nd 82
Greenway:
  Greenway Benefaction Trust 272
Greenwich:
  Greenwich Charity 369
  Greenwich Hospital 73
Greggs:
  Greggs Trust Hardship Fund 176
Gregson:
  Gregson Memorial Annuities 201
Grenadier:
  Grenadier Guards Association 82
Greneway:
  Ralph Greneway Charity 337
Griffiths
  Megan and Trevor Griffiths Trust 92
  Sir Percival Griffiths' Tea Planters Trust 39
  Mr Thomas Griffiths and Miss Rebecca Griffiths Charity 270
Grimsby:
  Grimsby Fishermen's Dependants Fund 239
Groome:
  Groome Trust 321
Groves:
  Groves Charitable Trust 58
  Groves Trust for Nurses 48
Grut:
  Grut Charitable Trust 108
Gubbay:
  Ronnie Gubbay Memorial Fund 360
Guild:
  Guild of Air Pilots Benevolent Fund 22
  Guild of Benevolence of The Institute of Marine Engineering Science and Technology 36
  Guild of Motoring Writers Benevolent Fund 23
  Guild of Registered Tourist Guides Benevolent Fund 69
Guildford:
  Guildford Aid in Sickness Fund 352
  Guildford Poyle Charities 352

Guildry:
  Guildry Incorporation of Perth 149
Gurkha:
  Gurkha Brigade Association Trust 82
  Gurkha Welfare Trust 82
Gurney:
  Gurney Fund for Police Orphans 53
Gurunanak:
  Gurunanak Charitable Trust 108

H

Hacconby:
  Hacconby Poor's Money & Others 239
Hackney:
  Hackney Benevolent Pension Society 370
  Hackney District Nursing Association 370
  Hackney Parochial Charities 370
Haden:
  John Fielder Haden (Isleworth) Relief in Sickness Charity 372
Haemophilia:
  Haemophilia Society 100
Haendler:
  Nathan and Adolphe Haendler Charity 122
Haig:
  John & Margaret Haig Bequest 156
Halesworth:
  Halesworth United Charities 343
Halifax:
  Halifax Childrens Welfare League 195
  Halifax Society for the Blind 195
  Halifax Tradesmen's Benevolent Institution 195
Hall:
  George & Clara Ann Hall Charity 187
Hamilton:
  Janet Hamilton Memorial Fund 160
Hammersmith:
  Hammersmith Relief-in-Sickness Fund 371
Hampshire:
  Hampshire & Isle of Wight Military Aid Fund (1903) 73
  Hampshire Ambulance Service Benevolent Fund 319
  Hampshire and Isle of Wight Military Aid Fund (1903) 82
  Hampshire Association for the Care of the Blind (HACB) 319
  Hampshire Constabulary Welfare Fund 319
  Hampshire Football Association Benevolent Fund 319
  Hampshire Golfers Benevolent Fund 42
Hampstead:
  Hampstead Wells & Campden Trust 366
Hampton:
  Hampton and Hampton Hill Philanthropic Society 375
  Hampton Fuel Allotment Charity 360
  Hampton Wick United Charity 375

INDEX

Hamsterley:
Hamsterley Poors' Land Charity *180*

Handicapped:
Handicapped Children's Aid Committee *302*

Handsworth:
Handsworth Charities including the Charity of William Stevenson *268*

Happy:
Happy Days Children's Charity *92, 113*

Harborne:
Harborne Parish Lands Charity *265*

Harding:
William Harding's Charity *308*

Hardwick:
Ben Hardwick Fund *100*

Harefield:
Harefield Parochial Charities *372*

Harley:
Thomas Harley Relief in Need Charity *58, 232*

Harling:
Harling Fuel Allotment Trust *333*

Harlow:
Harlow Community Chest *317*

Harnish:
Harnish Trust *58*

Harpenden:
Harpenden Trust *324*

Harper:
Harper Annuities *247*

Harpole:
Harpole Parochial Charities *244*

Harris:
Harris Charity *213*
James Edward Harris Trust *168*
R J Harris Charitable Settlement *298*

Harrison:
Margaret Harrison Trust *227*
Harrison & Potter Trust (incorporating Josias Jenkinson Relief-in-Need Charity) *198*

Harrogate:
Harrogate Good Samaritan Fund *184*

Harrow:
John Harrow's Mortification *145*

Hart:
Hart Charitable Trust *314*
Robert Hart Trust *157*

Hartley:
N & P Hartley Memorial Trust *92, 176*

Hastings:
Hastings Benevolent Fund *48*

Hatcliffe:
William Hatcliffe Non-Educational Charity *374*

Hatton:
Hatton & District Nursing Fund *260*
Hatton Consolidated Charities *260*

Hawley:
Hawley Almshouse & Relief-in-Need Charity *321*

Hay:
Douglas Hay Trust *136*

Haymills:
Haymills Charitable Trust *275*

Hayward:
R S Hayward Trust *156*

Head:
Francis Head Bequest *27*

Headley-Pitt:
Headley-Pitt Charitable Trust *325*

Headmasters:
Headmasters' Association Benevolent Fund *66*

Heath:
Heath Memorial Trust Fund *256*

Heathcoat:
Heathcoat Trust *282*

Heckmondwike:
Heckmondwike & District Fund for the Needy Sick *193*

Helena:
Helena Benevolent Fund *48*

Help:
Help a South Wales Child *165*

Help-in-Need:
Help-in-Need Association (HINA) *360*

Helston:
Helston Welfare Trust *281*

Henderson:
Henderson Charity *378*
Dr William Henderson's Mortification *150*

Henwood:
Charity of Thomas Henwood *281*

Herd:
Anne Herd Memorial Trust *142*

Hereford:
Hereford Corn Exchange Fund *230*
Hereford Municipal Charity *231*
Hereford Society for Aiding The Industrious *230*

Herne:
Herne Bay Parochial Charity *328*

Herrick:
Miss Herrick's Annuity Fund & the Herrick Fund for Widows & Single Women Afflicted with Incurable Diseases *232*

Hertfordshire:
Hertfordshire Charity for Deprived Children *323*
Hertfordshire Community Foundation *323*
Hertfordshire Convalescent Trust *324*
Hertfordshire County Nursing Trust *324*

Herve:
Peter Herve Benevolent Institution *276*

Hesslewood:
Hesslewood Children's Trust (Hull Seamen's &General Orphanage) *181*

Heywood:
Heywood Relief-in-Need Trust Fund *210*

High:
High Wycombe Central Aid Society *309*

Highland:
Highland Children's Trust *163*
Highland Council – Ross & Comarty Area *163*
Highland Light Infantry *82*

Highlanders:
Highlanders (Seaforth, Gordons & Camerons) Regimental Association *82*

Highweek:
Highweek Charities *286*

Hilgay:
Hilgay Feoffee Charity *333*

Hill:
Christopher Hill Charity *282*
Mary Hill Trust *273*
Rowland Hill Memorial And Benevolent Fund *54*

Hillingdon:
Hillingdon Partnership Trust *372*

Hills:
Helen Georgie Hills Charity *328*

Hilton:
Hilton Town Charity *312*

Hindley:
Margaret Jeannie Hindley Charitable Trust *108*

Hitcham:
Hitcham Poor Lands Charity *309*

HM:
HM Inspectors of Schools Benevolent Fund *61*

Hobbayne:
Eleemosynary Charity of William Hobbayne *369*

Hodgson:
Bill & May Hodgson Charitable Trust *176*

Hodnet:
Hodnet Consolidated Eleemosynary Charities *254*

Hodson:
Frank Hodson Foundation Ltd *252*

Hogg:
George Hogg Trust *136*

Holford:
John Holford Charity *202*

Holinsworth:
CB & AB Holinsworth Fund of Help *265*

Hollands-Warren:
Hollands-Warren Charitable Trust *329*

Hollon:
Mary Hollon Annuity & Relief-in-Need Fund *187*

409

INDEX

Holt:
Charity of Ann Holt *196*

Holywood:
Holywood Trust *159*

Home:
Home Warmth for the Aged *116*

Honiton:
Honiton United Charities *287*

Honourable:
Honourable Artillery Company Benevolent Fund *82*
Honourable Company of Master Mariners *62*

Hoper-Dixon:
Hoper-Dixon Trust *122*

Hopesay:
Hopesay Parish Trust *255*

Hopkins:
Charity of Joseph Hopkins *268*

Hordle:
Hordle District Nursing Association *322*

Horley:
Honourable Miss Frances Horley Charity *169*

Hornsby:
Hornsby Professional Cricketers Fund Charity *34*

Hornsey:
Hornsey Parochial Charities *360*

Horstead:
Horstead Poor's Land *333*

Horticultural:
Horticultural Trades Association Benevolent Fund *42*

Hospital:
Hospital Fund and Johnston Bequest *148*
Hospital of God at Greatham *177*
Hospital Saturday Fund Charitable Trust *92*

Hospitality:
Hospitality Action (formerly Hotel And Catering Benevolent Association) *43*

Hounsfield:
Hounsfield Pension *121*

Household:
Household Division Queens Jubilee Trust *74*

Housing:
Housing the Homeless Central Fund *116*

Hoxton:
Hoxton Charity *367*

Hucknall:
Hucknall Relief-in-Need Charity *250*

Huddersfield:
Huddersfield and District Army Veterans' Association Benevolent Fund *193*
Huddersfield School Children's Trust *197*

Huddleston:
Trevor Huddleston Fund for Children *378*

Hull:
Hull Aid in Sickness Trust *181*
Hull Fisherman's Trust Fund *182*

Humberside:
Humberside Police Welfare and Benevolent Fund *181*

Hume:
Elizabeth Hume Trust *156*

Hundred:
Hundred Acre Charity– Dolcoal *332*

Hunstanton:
Hunstanton Convalescent Trust *302*

Hunstone:
Hunstone's Charity *237*

Hunt:
Hunt & Almshouse Charities *108*
Michael and Shirley Hunt Charitable Trust *120*

Hunter:
John Routledge Hunter Memorial Fund *177*
William Hunter's Old Men's Fund *136*

Huntingdon:
John Huntingdon's Charity *312*

Huntington:
Huntington's Disease Association *100*

Hurst:
Arthur Hurst Will Trust *58*

Husborne:
Husborne Crawley Charities of the Poor *304*

Hussars:
Hussars *82*

Hutchinson:
Joseph Hutchinson Poors Charity *206*

Huyton:
Huyton with Roby Distress Fund *219*

Hyde:
Hyde Park Place Estate Charity (Civil Trustees) *379*

Hylton:
Hylton House Fund *99, 177*

I

Ibero-American:
Ibero-American Benevolent Society *114*

Ickleton:
Ickleton United Charities (Relief-in-Need Branch) *312*

Ilchester:
Ilchester Relief-in-Need and Educational Charity *296*

Imperial:
Imperial Yeomanry *82*

Incorporated:
Incorporated Association of Organists Benevolent Fund *25*
Incorporated Association of Preparatory Schools Benevolent Fund *66*
Incorporated Benevolent Fund of The Institution of Electrical Engineers *35*
Incorporated Brewers' Benevolent Society *39*

Independent:
Independent Living (1993) Fund *92*

India:
India Welfare Society *114*

Indian:
Indian Army Association *82*
Indian Police Benevolent Fund *53*

Ingle:
Frederick Ingle Charities *238*

Injured:
Injured Jockeys Fund *42*

Inner:
Inner London Fund for the Blind and Disabled *360*

Innes:
Innes Memorial Fund *357*

Inns:
Inns of Court Regimental Association *82*

Institute:
Institute of Chartered Secretaries & Administrators Benevolent Fund *64*
Institute of Clayworkers Benevolent Fund *32*
Institute of Company Accountants Benevolent Fund *21*
Institute of Financial Accountants & International Association of Book-Keepers Benevolent Fund *21*
Institute of Football Management & Administration Charity Trust *40*
Institute of Healthcare Management Benevolent Fund *48*
Institute of Legal Executive Benevolent Funds *44*
Institute of Petroleum 1986 Benevolent Fund *53*
Institute of Physics Benevolent Fund *61*
Institute of Quarrying Educational Development and Benevolent Fund *55*

Institution:
Institution of Gas Engineers Benevolent Fund *36*
Institution of Plant Engineers Benevolent Fund *37*
Institution of Structural Engineers Benevolent Fund *37*

Insurance:
Insurance Charities – The Benevolent Fund *43*
Insurance Charities – The Orphans' Fund *43*

Intelligence:
Intelligence Corps Association *82*

International:
International Dance Teachers' Association Benevolent Fund *24*

Invalids-at-Home:
Invalids-at-Home *93*

Iprovision:
Iprovision (formerly The Institute of Public Relations Benevolent Fund) *55*

INDEX

Irish:
  Irish Ex-Service Trust 86
  Irish Guards Association 82
Irving:
  Irving Fund to Relieve Distress 214
ISM:
  ISM Members Fund (The Benevolent Fund of The Incorporated Society of Musicians) 25
Iver:
  Iver Heath Sick Poor Fund 307
  Iver United Charities 307

J

Jackson:
  William Jackson Trust 365
Jamieson:
  Jamieson Charity 147
  George Jamieson Fund 136
Jay:
  Jay Foundation 113
Jeffcock:
  Jeffcock Memorial Aid In Sickness Trust 187
Jenkins:
  Kay Jenkins Trust 316
Jenkinson:
  David Jenkinson Memorial Fund Child Cancer Concern 98
Jennifer:
  Jennifer Trust 103
Jesus:
  Jesus Hospital Charity 365
Jewish:
  Jewish Aged Needy Pension Society 122
  Jewish AIDS Trust 96
  Jewish Care Scotland 136
  Jewish Care 302
Johnson:
  Johnson Bede & Lane Charitable Trust 312
  Christopher Johnson & the Green Charity 250
Johnston:
  Johnston Family Fund 108
  William Johnston Trust Fund 109, 117
Johnstone:
  Johnstone Wright Fund 136
Joicey:
  Rose Joicey Fund 177
Joint:
  Joint Committee of St John & Red Cross 79
  Joint Industrial Council & the Match Manufacturing Industry Charitable Fund 46
Jones:
  Owen Jones Charity 166
Jopp:
  Henry John Jopp Fund 145

Jordison:
  Jordison and Hossell Animal Welfare Charity 109
Jory:
  Joseph Jory's Charity 288
Juckes:
  Florence Juckes Memorial Trust Fund 109

K

Kangas:
  Kangas Trust 109
Kay:
  Louisa Alice Kay Fund 208
Kelly:
  Kelly Holdsworth Artillery Trust 73
Kempston:
  Kempston Charities 305
Kendall:
  John Kendall Trust 185
  William Kendall's Charity (Wax Chandlers' Company) 361
Kenilworth:
  Kenilworth Carnival Comforts Fund 262
  Kenilworth United Charities 262
Kensington:
  Kensington District Nursing Trust 373
Kent:
  Kent Children's Trust 325
  Kent County Football Association Benevolent Fund 326
  Kent Nursing Institution 326
Kesteven:
  Kesteven Children in Need 239
Kettering:
  Kettering Charities (Fuel Grants) 242
Key:
  Key Trust 136
Keyes:
  Ursula Keyes' Trust 203
Keyham:
  Keyham Relief in Need Charity 234
Kidderminster:
  Kidderminster Aid In Sickness Fund 273
King:
  King George VI Youth Awards 129
  King George's Fund for Sailors 87
  King James VI Hospital Fund 150
  Thomas King Trust (also includes The John Wallace Peck Trust) 322
King's:
  King's Lynn & West Norfolk Borough Charity 330
  King's Lynn Charities for the Poor 333
  King's and Manchester Regiments' Association (Liverpool Branch) 82
  King's Own Royal Border Regimental Association 82
  King's Own Royal Regiment 82
  King's Own Scottish Borderers Association 82
  King's Own Yorkshire Light Infantry Regimental Association 82
  King's Royal Rifle Corps 82
  King's Shropshire and Herefordshire Light Infantry Association 83
Kingsbury:
  Kingsbury Charity 366
Kingsclere:
  Kingsclere Welfare Charities 319
Kingston:
  Dr C S Kingston Fund 298
Kingston-upon-Thames:
  Kingston-upon-Thames Association for the Blind 373
Kinloch:
  Kinloch Bequest 74
Kirkby:
  Kirkby Lonsdale Relief-in-Need Charity 206
Kirkcaldy:
  Kirkcaldy Charitable Trust 151
Kirke:
  Kirke Charity 198
Kirkley:
  Kirkley Poor's Land Estate 343
Kitchings:
  Kitchings General Charity 237
Knaresborough:
  Knaresborough Relief-in-Need Charity 184
Knight:
  Knight's House Charity 205
Knowles:
  Charity of Annie Jane Knowles 368
Knox:
  James and Jane Knox Fund 162
Kroch:
  Heinz & Anna Kroch Foundation 93
Kyd:
  John Normansell Kyd's Trust for Walton & Rashiewell Employees 148

L

Labour:
  Labour Corps 83
Ladies:
  Ladies Aid Fund 216
  Ladies Aid Society and Eyre Charity 288
Lady:
  Lady Alice Shaw-Stewart Memorial Fund 162
  Lady Crosthwaite Bequest Fund 185
  Lady Elizabeth Hastings' Non-Educational Charity 58
  Lady Forester Trust 253
  Lady Gould's Charity 372
  Lady Hewley Trust 58
  Lady Katherine and Sir Richard Leveson Charity 258
  Lady McCorquodale's Charity Trust 117
  Lady Noel Byron's Nursing Association 351
  Lady Peel Legacy Trust 59

411

INDEX

Lakenheath:
Lakenheath Consolidated Charities *343*

Laleston:
Laleston Relief-in-Sickness Charity *170*

Lamb:
John William Lamb Charity *247*

Lambe:
William Lambe (Pension) Trust *329*

Lambert:
John Lambert's Charity *236*

Lambeth:
Lambeth Endowed Charities (The Walcot Non-Educational Charity & The Hayles Charity) *374*

Lancashire:
Lancashire County Nursing Trust *213*
Lancashire Football Association Benevolent Fund *213*
Lancashire Fusiliers' Compassionate Fund *83*
Lancashire Infirm Secular Clergy Fund *201*
Lancashire Regiment (Prince of Wales's Volunteers) Regimental Association *83*

Lancaster:
Lancaster Charity *215*

Lancers:
Lancers *83*

Land:
Charity of John Land for Widows & Children (Widows Branch) *368*

Langhorn:
Richard Langhorn Trust *113, 123*

Lant:
Lant Trust *266*

LATCH:
LATCH (Llandough Aim to Treat Children with Cancer and Leukaemia with Hope) *173*

Lathom:
Peter Lathom's Charity *213*

Lavender:
Lavender Trust *120*

Lavender's:
Lavender's Charity *229*

Law:
Law Society of Scotland Benevolent Fund *136*

Leaf:
Herbert Leaf Bequest *299*

League:
League Managers Benevolent Trust *40*
League of the Helping Hand *93*

Leamington:
Leamington Relief-in-Sickness Fund *262*

Leather:
Leather & Hides Trades' Benevolent Institution *44*

Leatherhead:
Leatherhead United Charities *353*

Leeds:
Leeds Benevolent Society for Single Ladies *198*
Leeds District Aid-in-Sickness Fund *198*
Leeds Jewish Welfare Board *177*
Leeds Poors Estate *198*
Leeds Tradesmen's Trust *199*

Lees:
Sarah Lees Relief Trust *209*

Legate:
Legate's Charity *291*

Leicester:
Leicester Aid-in-Sickness Fund *234*
Leicester Charity Organisation Society *232*
Leicester Freemen's Estate *233*
Leicester Indigent Old Age Society *234*

Leicestershire:
Leicestershire Coal Industry Welfare Trust Fund *233*
Leicestershire County Nursing Association *233*
Leicestershire Regiment *83*

Leigh:
Leigh United Charities *328*

Leinster:
Leinster Regiment (for those resident in UK) *83*

Leith:
Leith Aged Mariners Fund *155*
Leith Benevolent Association Ltd *155*
Leith Holiday Home Committee *155*

Lemon:
Claude Lemon Memorial Fund *65*

Lennox:
Lennox Childrens Trust *163*

Letchworth:
Letchworth Civic Trust *324*

Lethbridge:
Lethbridge – Abell Charitable Bequest *161*

Leukaemia:
Leukaemia Care Society *98*

Leverington:
Leverington Relief-in-Sickness Fund *310*
Leverington Town Lands Charity *310*

Lewis
Ada Lewis Winter Distress Fund *368*
Christian Lewis Trust *99*
George and Alfred Lewis (of Chigwell) Memorial Fund *316, 375*

Lewisham:
Lewisham Relief in Need Charity *374*

Lichfield:
Lichfield Municipal Charities *257*

Life:
Life Guards Association *83*

Lifespan:
Lifespan Trust *117*

Light:
Light Dragoons Charitable Trust *83*
Light Infantry Benevolent Association *83*

Lighthouse:
Lighthouse Club Benevolent Fund *29, 37*

Lincoln:
Lincoln General Dispensary Fund *237*
Lincoln Municipal Relief-in-Need Charities *240*

Lincolnshire:
Lincolnshire Police Charitable Fund *237*
Lincolnshire Regiment *83*

Lindow:
Lindow Workhouse Trust *205*

Lindsay:
Misses Elizabeth & Agnes Lindsay Fund *148*

Lineham:
Henry & Elizabeth Lineham Charity *242*

Linford:
Fred Linford Charitable Trust *256*

Linnecar:
Trust of Arthur Linnecar *169*

Lionheart:
Lionheart (The Royal Institution of Chartered Surveyors Benevolent Fund) *30*

Lipton:
Francis Lipton Memorial Fund *161*

Litchborough:
Litchborough Parochial Charities *244*

Little:
Andrew & Mary Elizabeth Little Charitable Trust *161*
Little Dunham Relief-in-Need Charities *333*

Littleborough:
Littleborough Nursing Association Fund *215*

Litton:
Litton Cheney Relief-in-Need Trust *287*

Liverpool:
Liverpool Caledonian Association *216*
Liverpool Children's Welfare Trust *216*
Liverpool Corn Trade Guild *219*
Liverpool Governesses' Benevolent Institution *66*
Liverpool Ladies Institution *216*
Liverpool Merchants' Guild *216*
Liverpool Provision Trade Guild *217*
Liverpool Queen Victoria District Nursing Association (LCSS) *217*
Liverpool Queen Victoria Nursing Association (PSS) *217*
Liverpool Regiment *83*
Liverpool Wholesale Fresh Produce Benevolent Fund *219*

Liversage:
Liversage Trust *229*

Livesey:
Harry Livesey Charity *117*

Llandenny:
Llandenny Charities *171*

Llanidloes:
Llanidloes & District Community Nurses' Comfort Fund Committee *166*

Index

Llanidloes Relief-in-Need Charity 166
Lloyd:
Elaine & Angus Lloyd Charitable Trust 302
Lloyd Thomas Charity for Women & Girls 116
W M & B W Lloyd Trust 214
Lloyd's:
Lloyd's Benevolent Fund 43
Lloyd's Patriotic Fund 74
Local:
Local Aid for Children & Community Special Needs 169
Lockerbie:
Lockerbie & District Sick Benevolent Assocation 159
Lockerbie Trust 158
Lockinge:
Lockinge & Ardington Relief-in-Need Charity 338
Lockingtons:
Mary Lockingtons Charity 304
London:
London Bereavement Relief Society 361
London East Aids Network (LEAN) 361
London Irish Rifles Benevolent Fund 83
London Metal Exchange Benevolent Fund 51
London Regiment 83
London Scottish Regiment Benevolent Fund 83
London Shipowners' & Shipbrokers' Benevolent Society 62
Londonderry:
Londonderry Methodist City Mission 129
Long:
Long Bennington Charities 251
Long Buckby United Charities 244
Longfields:
Longfields Trust 109
Longmore:
John A Longmore's Trust 137
Lord:
Lord Buckland Trust 171
Lord Crewe's Charity 176
Lord Jermyn's Charity 344
Lord Maynard's Charity 318
Lord Mayor of Bristol's Christmas Appeal for Children 279
Lord Mayor of Portsmouth's Charity 320
Lord Provost Charities Fund, the D M Stevenson Fund & the Lethbridge Abell Fund 161
Lord Rank 1958 Charity 319
Lothian:
Lothian & Border Regimental Association (1st Lothians & Border Yeomanry, 2nd Lothians & Border Horse) 83
Loudoun:
Loudoun Bequest 162
Loughborough:
Loughborough Welfare Trusts 233

Lovat:
Lovat Scouts Regimental Association 83
Lovell:
P & M Lovell Charitable Settlement 109
Lowe:
Michael Lowe's & Associated Charities 257
Lowestoft:
Lowestoft Church and Town Relief in Need Charity 343
Lowestoft Fishermen's & Seafarers' Benevolent Society 343
Lowestoft Maternity & District Nursing Association 343
Lowton:
Lowton Charities 215
Loxton:
Harriet Louisa Loxton Trust Fund 268
Loyal:
Loyal Regiment (North Lancashire) Regimental and Old Comrades' Association 83
Lund:
Lucy Lund Holiday Grants 193
Luttrell:
J A F Luttrell Memorial Charity 295
Lyall:
Lyall Bequest 58
Lyndhurst:
Lyndhurst Welfare Charity 322
Lyng:
Lyng Heath Charity 333
Lyson:
Sylvanus Lyson's Charity 293
Lytham:
Lytham Sick Aid Fund 215
Lytham St Anne's Relief-in-Sickness Charity 215

M

MacAndrew:
B V MacAndrew Trust 302
McCallum:
Catherine McCallum Memorial Fund 135
Macdonald:
Macdonald Bequest 151
Dr William MacDonald of Johannesburg Trust 269
McDonald:
Henry McDonald Trust 158
MacDougall:
MacDougall Trust 291
Macfarlane:
Macfarlane Trust 96
McGibbon:
John McGibbon Fund 154
MacKenzie:
William MacKenzie Trust 164
McKenzie:
George McKenzie Fund 137

McKenna:
McKenna Charitable Trust 109
Mackichan:
Catherine Mackichan Trust 137
Mackie:
John Mackie Memorial Ladies' Home 209
McKune:
James McKune Mortification 159
McLaren:
McLaren Fund for Indigent Ladies 137
McLean:
Annie Ramsay McLean Trust for the Elderly 137
George McLean Trust 137
Macleod:
Agnes Macleod Memorial Fund 137
Macmillan:
Macmillan Cancer Relief – Patients Grants Scheme 99
McRobert:
McRobert Mortification– Gamrie & Forglen 145
MacWatt:
MacWatt Bequest 157
Macclesfield:
Macclesfield Relief-in-Sickness Fund 203
Machine:
Machine Gun Corps Old Comrades Association 83
Maerdy:
Maerdy Children's Welfare Fund 170
Magic:
Magic Circle Benevolent Fund 24
Maidstone:
Maidstone Relief-in-Need Charities 329
Mair:
Miss Annie Smith Mair Bequest 160
Malam:
Edward Malam Convalescent Fund 256
Malcolm:
Malcolm Fund 145
Malmesbury:
Malmesbury Community Trust 298
Manchester:
Manchester District Nursing Institution Fund 207
Manchester Jewish Federation 207
Manchester Jewish Soup Kitchen 208
Manchester Regiment Aid Society and Benevolent Fund 83
Manchester Relief-in-Need Charity and Manchester Children's Relief-in-Need Charity 209
Manchip:
Manchip Trust 295
Mann:
Victor Mann Trust (also known as The Wallsend Charitable Trust) 192
Manor:
Manor House Trust (incorporating The Charity of Lily Taylor) 247

413

INDEX

Mantle:
William Mantle Trust 329

Manx:
Manx Marine Society 212

Margate:
Margate and Dr Peete's Charity 329

Marham:
Marham Poors Land's Trust 334

Marillier:
Mrs E L Blakeley Marillier Annuity Fund 281

Marine:
Marine Society 62

Market:
Market Harborough & the Bowdens Charity 235
Market Research Benevolent Association 45

Marsh:
Marsh Trust 298

Martin:
Douglas Martin Trust 303
John Martin's Charity 273

Massey:
Dr Isaac Massey's Charity 225

Master:
Master Tailors' Benevolent Association 32

Matthew:
Matthew Trust 101

Maudlyn:
Maudlyn Lands Charity & Others 282

Mayfield:
Mayfield Charity 315

Mayor:
Mayor of Barnet's Benevolent Fund 364
Mayor of Bath's Relief Fund 277
Mayor of Bebington's Benevolent Fund 218
Mayor of Brighton and Hove's Welfare Charity 314
Mayor of Camden's Charity Trust Fund 366
Mayor of Great Grimsby's Fund 237
Mayor of Guildford's Christmas & Local Distress Fund 352
Mayor of Hammersmith & Fulham's Appeal Fund 371
Mayor of Harrow's Charity Fund 371
Mayor of Southwark's Common Good Trust (The Mayor's Charity) 377
Mayor of Tameside's Distress Fund 211

Mayor's:
Mayor's Discretionary Fund & The Mayor's Fund, Eastbourne 315
Mayor's Fund for Necessitous Children 191
Mayor's Fund Society of Stratford-upon-Avon 263
Mayor's General Fund 270
Mayor's Goodwill Fund 291
Mayor's Welfare Fund 281

Measures:
James Frederick & Ethel Anne Measures Charity 266

Mellor:
Mellor Fund 208

Melton:
Melton Mowbray Building Society Charitable Foundation 225
Melton Trust 343

Mendlesham:
Town Estate Charity 343

Meningitis:
Meningitis Trust 101

Mercer:
Alexander Darling Silk Mercer's Fund 153

Merchant:
Merchant Navy Welfare Board 81
Merchant Taylors of York Charity 178

Merchants:
Merchants House of Glasgow 157

Mercian:
Mercian Volunteers Regimental Association 83

Merevale:
Merevale Aid-in-Sickness Fund 260

Merry:
Doctor Merry Memorial Fund 314

Mersey:
Mersey Mission To Seafarers 217

Merseyside:
Merseyside Jewish Community Care 219
Merseyside Police Orphans' Fund 217

Merthyr:
Merthyr Mendicants 171

Metcalfe:
Metcalfe Shannon Trust 74
Metcalfe Smith Trust 199

Methodist:
Methodist Child Care Society 129
Methodist Local Preachers Mutual Aid Association 58

Metropolitan:
Metropolitan Police Civil Staff Welfare Fund 53
Metropolitan Police Combined Benevolent Fund 53
Metropolitan Society for the Blind 361
Metropolitan Visiting & Relief Association 362

Micklegate:
Micklegate Strays Charity 186

Middlesex:
Middlesex King Edward VII Memorial Fund 303
Middlesex Regiment (Duke of Cambridge's Own) Regimental Association 83

Middleton:
Charity of Miss Eliza Clubley Middleton 182
Middleton Cheney United Charities 244
Middleton Relief-in-Need Charity 210

Middleton-on-the-Hill:
Middleton-on-the-Hill Parish Charity 231

Midgley:
William & Sarah Midgley Charity 193

Midhurst:
Midhurst Pensions Trust 109
Midhurst Pest House Charity 357

Mildenhall:
Mildenhall Parish Charities 344

Military:
Military Police 83
Military Provost Staff Corps Association 83

Mills:
Mills Charity 340

Minet:
Mary Minet Trust 362

Mining:
Mining Institute of Scotland Trust 33

Ministers:
Ministers' Relief Society 58

Mitchell:
Mitchell City of London Charity 368

Mitchelmore:
John Mitchelmore's Charity 283

Mitford:
Mitford Foulerton Charitable Trust 357

Mobility:
Mobility Trust II 93

Molyneux:
Ann Molyneux Charity 219

Monk:
Joseph & Lucy Monk's Trust 204

Monke:
Thomas Monke's Charity 225

Monmouth:
Monmouth Charity 171
Monmouth Street Society, Bath 277

Monmouthshire:
Monmouthshire Regiment 83
Monmouthshire Welsh Church Acts Fund 171

Montgomery:
Montgomery Welfare Fund 166

Moonzie:
Moonzie Parish Trust 151

Moore:
Charity of John Moore 269

Moorhouse:
Harold Moorhouse Charity 331

Morar:
Morar Trust 163

Morden:
Morden College 117

Morgan:
Junius S Morgan Benevolent Fund for Nurses 48

Morison:
  Morison Bequest *137*

Morpeth:
  Morpeth Dispensary *186*

Morris:
  Morris Beneficent Fund *123*

Morval:
  Morval Foundation *121*

Moser:
  Moser Benevolent Trust Fund *195*

Motability:
  Motability *93*

Mother:
  'Mother Humber' Memorial Fund *182*

Motor:
  Motor Neurone Disease Association *101*

Mottram:
  Mottram St Andrew United Charities *204*

Moulton:
  Moulton Poors' Lands Charity *240*
  Non-Ecclesiastical Charity of William Moulton *191*

Moundeford:
  Sir Edmund Moundeford's Educational Foundation *332*

Mountsorrel:
  Mountsorrel Relief-in-Need Charity *235*

Multiple:
  Multiple Sclerosis Society of Great Britain and Northern Ireland *101*

Municipal:
  Municipal Charities & the Bedford & District Aid in Sickness Charity *304*

Murchie:
  Maud Beattie Murchie Charitable Trust *220*

Murdoch:
  John Murdoch Trust *61*

Murray:
  Matilda Murray Trust *145*
  Colonel Peter Murray Bequest– Clan Gregor Fund *113*

Musicians:
  Musicians Benevolent Fund *25*
  Musicians' Social & Benevolent Council *25*

MYA:
  MYA Charitable Trust *122*

Mylne:
  Mylne Trust *122*

N

NABS:
  NABS *21*

Nadezhda:
  Nadezhda Charitable Trust *59*

Nafferton:
  Nafferton Feoffee Charity Trust *181*

Nailsea:
  Nailsea Community Trust Ltd *276*

Napton:
  Napton Charities *262*

Nash:
  Janet Nash Charitable Trust *94*
  Nash Charity *74*

National:
  National Amalgamated Stevedores & Dockers Union Building & Benevolent Fund *182*
  National Association for Colitis and Crohn's Disease *94*
  National Association for the Care & Resettlement of Offenders (NACRO) *120*
  National Association of Cooperative Officials' Benevolent Fund *33*
  National Association of Master Bakers *39*
  National Association of Schoolmasters Union of Women Teachers Benevolent Fund *67*
  National Benevolent Institution *117*
  National Benevolent Society of Watch and Clockmakers *69*
  National Blind Children Society *97*
  National British & Irish Millers' Benevolent Society *39*
  National Caravan Council Benevolent Fund *29*
  National Council for the Divorced & Separated Trust (NCDS) *109*
  National Dairymen's Benevolent Institution *39*
  National Ex-Prisoners of War Association *86*
  National Federation of Fish Friers Benevolent Fund *39*
  National Federation of Retail Newsagents Convalescence Fund *52*
  National Federation of Sub-Postmasters Benevolent Fund *54*
  National Union of Journalists Provident Fund *46*

Navenby:
  Navenby Towns Farm Trust *240*

Navy:
  Navy Special Fund *74*

Naysmyth:
  Alexander Naysmyth Fund *138*

NCDS:
  NCDS (National Council for the Divorced & Separated Trust) *109*

Neale:
  Alex Neale Charity *235*
  Neale Trust Fund for Poor Children *173*

Nelson:
  Nelson District Nursing Association Fund *216*

Netherlands:
  Netherlands Benevolent Society *114*

New:
  New Appeals Organisation for the City & County of Nottingham *248*
  New Forest Keepers Widows Fund *319*
  New Masonic Samaritan Fund *119*

Newark:
  Newark Municipal (General) Charities *251*

Newbury:
  Newbury & Thatcham Welfare Trust *306*

Newcastle-under-Lyme:
  Newcastle-under-Lyme United Charities *257*

Newfield:
  Newfield Charitable Trust *225*

Newick:
  Newick Distress Trust *315*

Newman:
  Pearl Newman Memorial Fund in Aid of Cancer Relief *326*

Newport:
  Newport Charity *287*

Newspaper:
  Newspaper Press Fund *46*

NewstrAid:
  NewstrAid Benevolent Society *52*

Newton:
  Newton on Derwent Charity *183*

Newtownabbey:
  Newtownabbey Methodist Mission *130*

NHS:
  NHS Pensioners' Trust *48*

Nicholl:
  William Nicholl's Charity *373*

Nicholson:
  Nicholson Memorial Fund *233*

NICHS:
  NICHS (Northern Ireland Children's Holiday Schemes) *130*

Nightingale:
  Florence Nightingale Aid-in-Sickness Trust *94*

Nimmo:
  William Brown Nimmo Charitable Trust *155*

Nithsdale:
  Nithsdale District Charities *159*

Nivison:
  Nivison Trust *159*

Norfolk:
  Norfolk Regiment *83*

Normandy:
  Normandy Veterans Association Benevolent Fund *86*

Norris:
  Norris (Penarth, Cogan, Llandough) Charity *173*
  Evelyn Norris Trust *24*

North:
  North East Area Miners Welfare Trust Fund *178*
  North East Area Mineworkers' Convalescent Fund *178*
  North East Somerset Trust (NEST) for Children *278*

INDEX

North Eastern Prison After Care Society 178
North Lancashire Regiment 83
North of Scotland Quaker Trust 138
North Staffordshire Coalfield Miners Relief Fund 256
North Staffordshire Convalescent & Relief Fund 256
North Staffordshire Regiment 83
North Wales Association for Spina Bifida & Hydrocephalus 167
North Wales Fund for Needy Psychiatric Patients 166
North Wales Police Benevolent Fund 167
North Wales Society for the Blind 167
North West Customs and Excise Benevolent Society 201
North West Police Benevolent Fund 201

Northampton:
Northampton Municipal Church Charities 245

Northamptonshire:
Northamptonshire Medical Charity 242
Northamptonshire Regiment Benevolent Fund 83
Northamptonshire Yeomanry Association (1st and 2nd Regiments) 83

Northcott:
Northcott Devon Foundation 282

Northern:
Northern Counties Orphans' Benevolent Society 178
Northern Counties' Charity for the Incapacitated 202
Northern Ireland Children's Holiday Schemes (NICHS) 130
Northern Ladies Annuity Society 179, 202
Northern Police Orphans' Trust 53

Northwold:
Northwold Combined Charities and Edmund Atmere Charity 334

Norton:
Norton Canon Parochial Charities 231
Norton Foundation 225

Norwich:
Norwich Consolidated Charities 334
Norwich Town Close Estate Charity 334

Norwood:
Norwood (formerly Norwood Ravenswood) 122

Not:
'Not Forgotten' Association 74

Nottingham:
Nottingham Annuity Charity 248
Nottingham Children's Welfare Fund 248
Nottingham Fuel Fund 248
Nottingham General Dispensary 248
Nottingham Gordon Memorial Trust for Boys & Girls 248

Nottinghamshire:
Nottinghamshire and Derbyshire Regiment 83
Nottinghamshire County Council Fund for Disabled People 248
Nottinghamshire Miners' Welfare Trust Fund 249

NUMAST:
NUMAST Welfare Fund 62

Nuneaton:
Nuneaton Poors' Piece Charity 262

Nurses:
Nurses Fund for Nurses 49
Nurses Memorial to King Edward VII Edinburgh Committee 138
Nurses' Benefit Fund 210

Nutter:
Joseph Nutter's Foundation 195

O

Oadby:
Oadby Educational Foundation 235

Officers':
Officers' Association Scotland 138
Officers' Association 75

Ogilvie:
Ogilvie Charities 67

Old:
Old Buckenham United Eleemosynary Charity 334
'Old Contemptibles' 83
Old Enfield Charitable Trust 369
Old Parish Charities 245
Old Park Ward Old Age Pensioners Fund 229

Oldham:
Oldham Distress Fund 210
Oldham United Charities 210

Oliver:
Ada Oliver Will Trust 99

Open:
Open House Darts League 230

Oppenheimer:
Arthur and Rosa Oppenheimer Fund 362

Organists':
Organists' Benevolent League 25

O'Sullivan:
Cornelius O'Sullivan Fund 306

Osborn:
Sir Samuel Osborn's Deed of Gift (Relief Fund) 190

Oswestry:
Oswestry Dispensary Fund 253

Ottery:
Ottery Feoffee Charity 287

Ottringham:
Ottringham Church Lands Charity 183

Ouchterlony:
Ouchterlony Old Men's Indigent Society 148

Over:
Over Norton Trust 339

Overseas:
Overseas Civil Service Benevolent Fund 31
Overseas Service Pensioners' Benevolent Society 31

Owen:
Dame Alice Owen's Eleemosynary Charities 373

Oxfordshire:
Oxfordshire and Buckinghamshire Light Infantry Regimental Association 83
Oxfordshire Yeomanry Trust 83

Oxted:
Oxted United Charities 354

P

Paddington:
Paddington Welfare Charities 380

Padley:
A L Padley Charity Fund 239

Page:
Page Fund 245

Paignton:
Paignton Parish Charity 287

Pakenham:
Pakenham Charities for the Poor 344

Palmer:
Palmer Brother Trust for the Elderly 316
Eleanor Palmer Trust 365
Palmer & Seabright Charity 271

Pampisford:
Pampisford Relief-in-Need Charity 312

Panton:
Mrs Jeane Panton and Miss Anne Stirling Trust 138

Parachute:
Parachute Regiment 83

Pargeter:
Pargeter & Wand Trust 225

Parish:
Parish Charity (Dodbrook Feoffees) 287
Parish Piece Charity 234

Parkinson's:
Parkinson's Disease Society 102

Parrott:
Dorothy Parrott Memorial Trust 326
James Parrott Charity 202

Parson:
Thomas Parson's Charity 311

Parsons:
Geoffrey Parsons Memorial Trust 25

Pash:
Albert Edward Pash Charitable Trust Fund 294

Paterson:
James Paterson's Trust 157

Paton:
Paton Trust 59

Patrick:
Joseph Patrick Memorial Trust 102

Pattishall:
Pattishall Parochial Charities 245

INDEX

Pattullo:
Gertrude Muriel Pattullo Trust for Handicapped Boys *142*
Gertrude Muriel Pattullo Trust for Handicapped Girls *143*
Gertrude Muriel Pattullo Trust for the Elderly *143*

Patty:
Randolph Meakins Patty's Farm & the Widows Lyes Charity *273*

Pawnbrokers:
Pawnbrokers' Charitable Institution *52*

Payling:
George Henry Francis Payling's Charity *251*

Payne:
John Payne Charity *366*

Peace:
Peace Memorial Fund *379*

Pearson:
Pearson's Holiday Fund *116*

Peckham:
Peckham & Kent Road Pension Society *377*

Pedmore:
Pedmore Sporting Club Trust Fund *266*

Peirson:
Anne Peirson Charitable Trust *328*

Pendlebury:
Sir Ralph Pendlebury's Charity for Orphans *211*

Pendry:
George Pendry's Fund for Widows and Spinsters *252*

Pentney:
Pentney Charities *334*

Penton:
Penton Trust *319*

Peper:
Peper Harrow Charities *354*

Pepper:
Jane Pepper Charity *250*
John Pepper Charity *258*

Performing:
Performing Right Society Members' Fund *25*

Perry:
Perry Fund *117*
Perry Trust Gift Fund *249*

Persehouse:
Persehouse Pensions Fund *226*

Pershore:
Pershore United Charity *273*

Perth:
Perth Indigent Old Men's Society *150*

Peter:
Peter Benevolent Fund *148*

Peterhead:
Peterhead Coal Fund *145*

Petersham:
Petersham United Charities *376*

Petrie:
Mrs Margaret T Petrie's Mortification *148*

PGA:
PGA European Tour Benevolent Trust *42*

Phace:
Phace Scotland – Crusaid Hardship Fund In Scotland *138*

Pickles:
A Pickles Charitable Trust *196*
H T Pickles Memorial Benevolent Fund *51*

Picto:
Picto Buxton Charity *331*

Pinn:
William Frank Pinn Charitable Trust *328*

Pirate:
Pirate Trust *275*

Pirbright:
Pirbright Relief-in-Need Charity *354*

Pitstone:
Pitstone Town Lands Charity *309*

Pitt-Rivers:
Pitt-Rivers Charity *290*

Pittis:
Mary Pittis Charity for Widows *322*

Player:
J D Player Endowment Fund *249*

Plymouth:
Plymouth & Cornwall Cancer Fund *275*
Plymouth Charity Trust *288*

Podde:
Podde Trust *59*

Polehampton:
Polehampton Charity *305*

Police:
Police Aided Clothing Scheme of Edinburgh *155*
Police Dependants' Trust *53*

Police-Aided:
Police-Aided Children's Relief-in-Need Fund *204*

Polish:
Polish Air Force Association Benevolent Fund *75*
Polish Soldiers Assistance Fund *75*

Poole:
Valentine Poole Charity *365*
Poole Children's Fund *290*

Poor:
Poor's Charity of Margaret Evans *170*

Port:
Port of London Authority Police Charity Fund *362*

Portishead:
Portishead Nautical Trust *275, 277*

Portsmouth:
Portsmouth Victoria Nursing Association *319*

Post:
Post Office Rifles *83*

Pottery:
Pottery & Glass Trade Benevolent Institution *54*

Power:
Power Pleas Trust *272*

Pratt:
Pratt Charity *208*

Presbyterian:
Presbyterian Old Age Fund, Women's Fund & Indigent Ladies Fund *130*
Presbyterian Orphan and Children's Society *130*

Presbytery:
Presbytery of Gordon Benevolent Fund *145*

Prestbury:
Prestbury Charity (also known as The Prestbury United Charities) *293*
Prestbury, Harehill & District Nursing Association *204*

Preston:
Preston Relief-in-Need Charity *216*

Price:
Lucy Price Relief-in-Need Charity *261*

Priestman:
Sir John Priestman Charity Trust *179*

Prime:
Prime Charitable Trust *64*

Primrose:
John Primrose Trust *159*

Prince:
Prince of Wales Leinster Regiment *83*
Prince of Wales' Royal Volunteers *83*
Prince of Wales's Own (West & East Yorkshire) Regimental Association *83*

Princess:
Princess Louise's Kensington Regimental Association *83*
Princess Mary's Royal Air Force Nursing Services (PMRAFNS) Trust *81*
Princess of Wales's Royal Regiment Association and Benevolent Fund *83*
Princess Royal Trust for Carers *49*

Printers:
Printers' Charitable Corporation *54*

Pritt:
Pritt & Corlett Funds *220*

Professional:
Professional Billiards & Snooker Players Benevolent Fund *65*
Professional Classes Aid Council *110*
Professional Footballers Association Accident Insurance Fund *40*
Professional Footballers Association Benevolent Insurance Fund *41*
Professional Hair and Beauty Benevolent Fund (formerly British Hairdressers' Benevolent & Provident Institution) *42*

417

INDEX

Prospects:
Prospects Benevolent Fund (formerly The Institution of Professionals, Managers & Specialists Benevolent Fund and The Engineers' & Manager's Association (EMA) Benevolent Fund) *31*

Protestant:
Protestant Orphan Society for the Counties of Antrim & Down (Inc) *130*

Provision:
Provision Trade Charity *39*

Provost:
Provost's Fuel Fund *162*

Pryke:
Florence Pryke Charity *342*

Public:
Public and Commercial Services Union Benevolent Fund *31*

Purey:
Purey Cust Fund *184*

Puri:
Puri Foundation *114*

Pusinelli:
Pusinelli Convalescent & Holiday Home *303*

Putney:
Putney Creche *379*

Pyncombe:
Pyncombe Charity *59*

Pyrford:
Pyrford United Charities (Henry Smith Charity) *354*

Q

Qarnns:
Qarnns Trust Fund *81*

Queen:
Queen Adelaide Naval Fund *75*
Queen Alexandra's Royal Army Nursing Corps Association *83*

Queen's:
Queen's Nursing Institute *49*
Queen's Bay (2nd Dragoon Guards) *83*
Queen's Bodyguard *83*
Queen's Dragoon Guards *83*
Queen's Lancashire Regiment Association *83*
Queen's Own Buffs, The Royal Kent Regiment Benevolent Fund *84*
Queen's Own Cameron Highlanders' Regimental Association *84*
Queen's Own Highlanders (Seaforth and Camerons) Regimental Association *84*
Queen's Own Royal West Kent Regiment Compassionate Fund *84*
Queen's Own Yorkshire Dragoons *84*
Queen's Regimental Association *84*
Queen's Royal Hussars (incorporating 3rd The King's Own Hussars, 7th Queen's Own Hussars, 8th King's Royal Irish Hussars, The Queen's Own Hussars and Queen's Royal Irish Hussars) *84*
Queen's Royal Lancers (incorporating 16th Lancers, 5th Lancers, 17th Lancers, 21st Lancers, 16th/5th The Queen's Royal Lancers, 17th/21st Lancers and The Queen's Royal Lancers) *84*
Queen's Royal Regiment (West Surrey) *84*
Queen's Royal Surrey Regiment Regimental Association *84*

Quorn:
Quorn Town Lands Charity *235*

R

Racing:
Racing Welfare *43*

Radio:
Radio Clyde – Cash for Kids at Christmas *157*
Radio Forth Help A Child Appeal *138*
Radio Tay – Caring for Kids (Radio Tay Listeners Charity) *139*

Radnage:
Radnage Poor's Land Estate (Poors Branch) *309*

Railway:
Railway Benevolent Institution *56*
Railway Housing Association & Benefit Fund *56*

Ramsay:
Peggy Ramsay Foundation *26*
Sir William Ramsay Watson Bequest *154*

Ramsbottom:
Ramsbottom Aid-in-Sickness Fund *210*

Ramsden:
Edward Ramsden Charitable Trust *179*

Rank:
Joseph Rank Benevolent Fund *182*

Ratcliff:
Ratcliff Pension Charity *378*

Rathbone:
Rathbone Moral Aid Charity *230*

Ravensden:
Ravensden Town & Poor Estate *305*

Rawlet:
Rawlet Trust *258*

Raygill:
Raygill Trust *184*

React:
React (Rapid Effective Assistance for Children with Potentially Terminal Illness) *94*

Reading:
Reading Municipal Church Charities *306*

Reconnaisance:
Reconnaisance Corps *84*

Red:
Red House Home Trust *155*

Redcliffe:
Redcliffe Parish Charity *279*

Redesdale:
Charity of Lord Redesdale *293*

Referees':
Referees' Association Members Benevolent Fund *41*

Regular:
Regular Forces Employment Association *86*

Reid:
John Reid Mortification Fund *154*

Reiss:
Florence Reiss Trust for Old People *118*

Relief:
Relief – Hastings Area Community Trust *314*

REME:
REME Benevolent Fund *75*

Removers:
Removers Benevolent Association *60*

Retail:
Retail Trust (formerly Cottage Homes) *60*

Retired:
Retired Ministers' and Widows' Fund *59*
Retired Ministers' House Fund *130*

Rev:
Rev Dr George Richards Charity *59*
Rev John Babington's Charity *234*
Rev Robert Masters Charity for Widows *312*

Reverend:
Reverend Alexander Barclay Bequest *133*
Reverend Duke Yonge Charity *284*
Reverend Matthew Hutchinson Trust (Gilling and Richmond) *184*
Reverend W Smart's Charity *243*

Reydon:
Reydon Trust *344*

Rhodes:
Betty Rhodes Fund *94*

Rhodesians:
Rhodesians Worldwide Assistance Fund *115*

Rhymney:
Rhymney Trust *170*

Richmond:
Richmond Aid-in-Sickness Fund *376*
Richmond Parish Lands Charity *376*
Richmond Philanthropic Society *376*

Rifle:
Rifle Brigade *84*

Riflemen's:
Riflemen's Aid Society *84*

Rimpton:
Rimpton Relief-in-Need Charities *296*

Ringstead:
Ringstead Gift *245*

Risby:
Risby Fuel Allotment *344*

Ritchie:
Ritchie Charitable Trust *282*

INDEX

RMT:
RMT (National Union of Rail, Maritime & Transport Workers) Orphan Fund *56*

RN:
RN & RM Children's Fund *75*

Road:
Road Haulage Association Benevolent Fund *61*

Roade:
Roade Feoffees & Chivalls Charity *245*

Roberts:
E C Roberts Charitable Trust *303, 322*
Ella Roberts Memorial Charity for Saham Toney *335*
Evan & Catherine Roberts Home *167*
Sir William Roberts Relief in Need Charity *263*

Robertson:
Mair Robertson Benevolent Fund *148*

Robinson:
J C Robinson Trust No. 3 *110*
Rebecca Guest Robinson Charity *188*
Thomas Robinson Charity *218*

Rochdale:
Rochdale Fund for Relief-in-Sickness *210*
Rochdale United Charity *210*

Roddam:
Roddam Charity *253*

Rogers:
Henry Rogers Charity (Porlock Branch) *296*

Rokeby:
Rokeby Charitable Trust *262*

Rope:
Mrs L D Rope's Second Charitable Settlement *110*
Mrs L D Rope's Third Charitable Settlement *340*

Ropner:
Ropner Centenary Trust *180*

Ross:
Esther Ross' Bequest *161*

Rosslyn:
Rosslyn Park Injury Trust Fund *95*

Ross-Shire:
Ross-Shire Buffs, Duke of Albany's Seaforth Highlanders *84*

Rotherhithe:
Rotherhithe Consolidated Charities *377*

Rothschild:
Alfred de Rothschild Charity *91*

Rowland:
Emma Rowland Fund *208*

Rowlandson:
Rowlandson & Eggleston Relief-in-Need Charity *184*

Rowlett:
Rowlett Trust *242*

Roxburghshire:
Roxburghshire Landward Benevolent Trust *156*

Royal:
Royal Agricultural Benevolent Institution *21*
Royal Air Force and Dependants Disabled Holiday Trust *81*
Royal Air Force Benevolent Fund (Scottish Branch) *139*
Royal Air Force Benevolent Fund *76, 87*
Royal Air Forces Association *76*
Royal Air Forces Ex-POW Association Charitable Fund *81*
Royal Alfred Seafarers Society *81*
Royal Anglian Regiment Association *84*
Royal Antediluvian Order of Buffaloes, Grand Lodge of England War Memorial Annuities *119*
Royal Armoured Corps War Memorial Benevolent Fund *76*
Royal Army Chaplains' Department Centre *84*
Royal Army Dental Corps Association *84*
Royal Army Educational Corps Association *84*
Royal Army Medical Corps Charitable Fund 1992 *76*
Royal Army Ordnance Corps Charitable Trust *84*
Royal Army Pay Corps Regimental Association *84*
Royal Army Service Corps & Royal Corps of Transport Benevolent Fund *77*
Royal Army Veterinary Corps Benevolent Fund *84*
Royal Artillery Charitable Fund *77*
Royal Ballet Benevolent Fund *24*
Royal Belgian Benevolent Society *115*
Royal Berkshire Regiment Old Comrades' Association *84*
Royal Blind Society for the UK *98*
Royal British Legion *77*
Royal British Legion Women's Section *77*
Royal College of Midwives Benevolent Fund *49*
Royal College of Nursing Charitable Trust *49*
Royal Dragoon Guards Association *84*
Royal Dublin Fusiliers Old Comrades' Association *84*
Royal Dublin Fusiliers *84*
Royal East Kent Regiment *84*
Royal Eastern Counties Schools Limited *113*
Royal Engineers Association *84*
Royal Fusiliers Aid Society *84*
Royal Gardeners' Orphan Fund *42*
Royal Gloucestershire Hussars *84*
Royal Gloucestershire, Berkshire & Wiltshire Regiment Association *84*
Royal Green Jackets *84*
Royal Hampshire Regiment Comrades' Association *84*
Royal Highland Fusiliers Regimental Benevolent Association *84*
Royal Horse Guards (Blues) Comrades' Association *84*
Royal Incorporation of Architects in Scotland *139*
Royal Inniskilling Fusiliers Benevolent Fund *84*
Royal Institution of Naval Architects Benevolent Fund *52*

Royal Irish Fusiliers (Princess Victoria's) Regimental Association *84*
Royal Irish Rangers Association *84*
Royal Irish Regiment & South Irish Horse Old Comrades' Association *84*
Royal Irish Regiment Benevolent Fund *84*
Royal Irish Rifles *84*
Royal Leicestershire Regiment Royal Tigers Association *85*
Royal Leicestershire, Rutland & Wycliffe Society for the Blind *233*
Royal Lincolnshire Regiment Association *85*
Royal Literary Fund *27*
Royal Liverpool Seamen's Orphan Institution *63*
Royal Logistic Corps Association Trust *85*
Royal London Aid Society *120*
Royal Marines Benevolent Fund *81*
Royal Masonic Benevolent Institution *119*
Royal Medical Benevolent Fund *49*
Royal Medical Foundation *50*
Royal Metal Trades Benevolent Society *51*
Royal Military Academy Sandhurst Band *85*
Royal Military Police Central Benevolent Fund *78*
Royal Munster Fusiliers Charitable Fund *85*
Royal National Institute for the Blind *98*
Royal National Mission to Deep Sea Fishermen *63*
Royal Naval Association *81*
Royal Naval Benevolent Society for Officers *78*
Royal Naval Benevolent Trust *78, 87*
Royal Naval Reserve (V) Benevolent Fund *78*
Royal Norfolk Regimental Association *85*
Royal Northumberland Fusiliers Aid Society and Regimental Association *85*
Royal Observer Corps Benevolent Fund *81*
Royal Opera House Benevolent Fund *24*
Royal Patriotic Fund Corporation *78*
Royal Pharmaceutical Society's Benevolent Fund *50*
Royal Pioneer Corps Association *78*
Royal Regiment of Fusiliers *85*
Royal Regiment of Wales (24th/41st) Benevolent Fund *85*
Royal Scots Benevolent Society *85*
Royal Scots Dragoon Guards Association (Carabiniers & Greys) *85*
Royal Scots Fusiliers Benevolent Association *85*
Royal Scots Greys (2nd Dragoons) *85*
Royal Scottish Agricultural Benevolent Institution *139*
Royal Scottish Corporation (also known as The Scottish Hospital of the Foundation of King Charles II) *362*
Royal Seamen's Pension Fund *63*
Royal Signals Benevolent Fund *79*
Royal Society for Home Relief to Incurables, Edinburgh (General Fund) *139*
Royal Society for the Relief of Indigent Gentlewomen of Scotland *123, 139*

INDEX

Royal Society of Chemistry Benevolent Fund 62
Royal Society of Musicians of Great Britain 26
Royal Sussex Regimental Association 85
Royal Tank Regiment Association and Benevolent Fund 85
Royal Theatrical Fund 26
Royal Tigers' Association 85
Royal Ulster Constabulary Benevolent Fund 130
Royal Ulster Rifles Benevolent Fund 85
Royal United Kingdom Beneficent Association (RUKBA) 95, 118
Royal Warwickshire Regimental Association 85
Royal Welch Fusilier Comrades' Association 85
Royal West Kent Regiment 85
Royton Sick & Needy Fund 211

RTRA:
RTRA Benevolent Fund 35

Ruabon:
Ruabon & District Relief-in-Need Charity 168

Rugby:
Rugby Football Union Charitable Fund 61, 95
Rugby Welfare Charities 262

Runcorn:
Runcorn General War Relief Fund 204

Rural:
Rural, Agricultural & Allied Workers' Benevolent Fund 22

Rutland:
Rutland Dispensary 233
Rutland Trust 233

Rycroft:
Rycroft Children's Fund 202

Ryde:
Ryde Sick Poor Fund (also known as Greater Ryde Benevolent Trust) 323

S

SACRO:
SACRO Trust 140

Saddlery:
Saddlery and Leather Goods Retailers Benevolent Fund 44

Saffron:
Saffron Walden United Charities 318

Saham:
Saham Toney Fuel Allotment & Perkins Charity 330

Sailors':
Sailors' Families' Society 63
Sailors' Orphan Society of Scotland 140

Saint:
St Andrew's Scottish Soldiers Club Fund 79
St Andrew's Society for Ladies in Need 124
St Andrews Welfare Trust 151
St Chads Charity 254
St Clement Danes Parochial Charities 380
St Cyrus Benevolent Fund 147
St Dunstan's 79
St Edmunds & St Mary Major Charity 286
St George Dragon Trust 363
Saint Giles Charity Estate 242
St John the Baptist Charitable Fund 368
St John's Hospital, Bath 278
St Laurence Charities for the Poor 307
St Leonards Hospital Charity 196
St Luke's Parochial Trust 363
St Margaret's Charity 235
St Martin-in-the-Fields' Vicar's Relief Fund 111
St Marylebone Health Society 380
St Mary-le-Strand Charity 380
Charity of St Michael-le-Belfry 186
St Olave's United Charity, incorporating the St Thomas & St John Charities 377
St Pancras Welfare Trust 367
Saint Petrox Trust Lands 285
St Sepulchre (Finsbury) United Charities 373
St Vincent de Paul Society (England & Wales) 111

Salford:
Salford Town Lands 307

Salisbury:
Salisbury City Almshouse &Welfare Charities 298

Salt:
Sir Titus Salt's Charity 193

Salter:
George & Thomas Henry Salter Trust 270

Salvation:
Salvation Army 110

Sandal:
Sandal Magna Relief-in-Need Charity 199

Sanders:
William Sanders Charity 172

Sanderson:
Sanderson Charity for Women 193

Sandford:
Sandford Relief-in-Need Charity 288

Sandy:
Sandy Charities 304

Sant:
Helena Sant's Residuary Trust Fund 317

Sarah:
Sarah, Duchess of Somerset 380

Sargent:
Sargent Cancer Care for Children 99

Saunders:
Florence Saunders Relief-in-Sickness Charity 312
Mr William Saunders Charity for the Relief of Indigent Gentry and Others 110

Savage:
Ann Elizabeth Savage's General Charities 353
George Savage Charity 341

Saxlingham:
Saxlingham Nursing Charity 335
Saxlingham United Charities 335

Scaldwell:
Scaldwell Relief-in-Need Charity 246

Scale:
Scale Charitable Trust Fund 320

Scandinavian:
Scandinavian Benevolent Society 115

Scarborough:
Scarborough District Nursing Trust 185
Scarborough Municipal Charities 185

Scheme:
Scheme of Winter Payments to the Elderly and Disabled 163

Schoolmistresses:
Schoolmistresses & Governesses Benevolent Institution 67

Scientific:
Scientific Relief Fund of the Royal Society 61

Scones:
Scones Lethendy Mortifications 150

Scots:
Scots Guards Association 85

Scott:
Archie Scott Benevolent Fund for Bookmakers' Employees 29
Scott Charity 341

Scottish:
Scottish Artists' Benevolent Association 24, 140
Scottish Association of Master Bakers Benevolent Fund 140
Scottish Chartered Accountants' Benevolent Association 140
Scottish Cinematograph Trade Benevolent Fund 140
Scottish Grocers' Federation Benevolent Fund 140
Scottish Hide & Leather Trades Provident & Benevolent Society 140
Scottish Hydro Electric Community Trust 141
Scottish Mining Disasters Relief Fund 141
Scottish National Institution for the War-Blinded 141
Scottish Nautical Welfare Society 141
Scottish Prison Service Benevolent Fund 141
Scottish Retail Credit Association Benevolent Fund 68
Scottish Rifles 85
Scottish Secondary Teachers' Association Benevolent Fund 141
Scottish Solicitors' Benevolent Fund (incorporating The Scottish Law Agents' Society Benevolent Fund) 141
Scottish Women's Land Army Benevolent Fund 141

Seaforth:
Seaforth Highlanders' Regimental Association 85

Seamans:
Seamans' Friend Charitable Society 162
Seamen's Hospital Society 63

INDEX

Secretary:
Secretary Heads Association Benevolent Fund 64

Sedgefield:
Sedgefield District Relief-in-Need Charity 180

Semple:
Mairi Semple Fund for Cancer Relief & Research 158

Sense:
Sense, the National Deaf-Blind & Rubella Association 100

Severn:
Severn Trent Trust Fund 226
Severn Trent Water Charitable Trust 110

Sewing:
Sewing Machine Association Trade Benevolent Society 64

Shadwell:
William Shadwell Charity 315

Shanks:
Shanks Bequest 150

Shapwick:
Shapwick Relief in Need Charity 297

Sharpshooters:
Sharpshooters Yeomanry Association (3rd/4th County of London Yeomanry) 85

Shaw:
Shaw Charities 213

Shearer:
Shearer Bequest 160

Sheffield:
Sheffield Church Burgesses Trust 190
Sheffield West Riding Charitable Society Trust 188

Shelroy:
Shelroy Trust 330

Shepherd:
Patricia and Donald Shepherd Trust 110
W H Shepherd Trust 145

Shere:
Charity of John Shere &Others 289
Shere Charity for Relief-in-Need 346

Sheriffs':
Sheriffs' & Recorders' Fund 362

Sherwood:
Sherwood and Waudby Charity 183
Sherwood Foresters 85
Sherwood Rangers Yeomanry Regimental Association 85

Shetland:
Shetland Islands Council Charitable Trust 164

Shewringe:
Shewringe's Hospital & Robert Goulding's Charities 274

Shipdham:
Shipdham Parochial & Fuel Allotment 335

Shipman:
Thomas Stanley Shipman Charitable Trust 234

Shipwrecked:
Shipwrecked Fishermen & Mariners' Royal Benevolent Society 64

Shottermill:
Shottermill United Charities (Henry Smith and Others) 354

Show:
Show Business Benevolent Fund (Scotland) 141

Shrewsbury:
Shrewsbury & District Welfare Society 253
Shrewsbury Municipal Charity 253

Shropshire:
Shropshire Football Association Benevolent Fund 253
Shropshire Welfare Trust 253

Sibbald:
Dr J R Sibbald's Trust 142

Sibthorpe:
Emily Ada Sibthorpe Trust 305

Sidmouth:
Sidmouth Consolidated Charities 288

Siebel:
Mary Elizabeth Siebel Charity 251

Silverstone:
Silverstone Poors' Allotment Charity 246

Silverton:
Silverton Parochial Charity 288

Silverwood:
Silverwood Trust 59

Sim:
James Sim of Cornhill Trust 146

Simmons:
Sydney Simmons Pension Fund 68

Simon:
Simon Lord Digby Non-Educational Foundation (Relief-in-Need) 261

Simpson:
Simpson Trust 146

Sinclair:
Mrs Mary Sinclair's Trust 162

Skelton:
Skelton Swindells Trust 214

Slough:
Slough and District Community Fund 306

Small:
Small Arms School Corps Comrades' Association 85

Smedley:
Richard Smedley's Charity 226

Smisby:
Smisby Parochial Charity 236

Smith:
Charity of Frederick William Smith 172
Henry Smith (Rotherfield share) 315
Henry Smith Charities and Others 356
Henry Smith Charity (Dunsfold) 350
Henry Smith Charity (Longnet Estate) 297
Henry Smith Charity 59, 261, 274, 296, 299, 315, 317, 335, 346-349, 350, 351-353, 355-356, 365, 376
Henry Smith Charity (I Wood Estate) 347
Henry Smith's Charity (Longney) 278
Henry Smith's Charity 351
Smith & Earles Charity 349
Mrs Smith & Mount Trust 363
Samuel Smith Charity, Coventry 269
Smith's Charity-Parish of Nutfield 354
Smith's Cirencester Poor Charity 294
Thomas Herbert Smith's Trust Fund 234

Smiths:
Smiths Charity 354

Smorthwaite:
Smorthwaite Charity 185

Smythe:
Sir Thomas Smythe's Charity 326

Snowball:
Snowball Trust 226

Social:
Social Workers' Benevolent Trust 65

Society:
Society for Mucopolysaccharide Diseases 101
Society for Relief of Widows & Orphans of Medical Men 50
Society for the Assistance of Ladies in Reduced Circumstances 123
Society for the Orphans and Children of Ministers & Missionaries of the Presbyterian Church in Ireland 130
Society for the Relief of Distress 363
Society for the Relief of Poor Clergymen 60
Society of Authors Pension Fund 27
Society of Friends of Foreigners in Distress 115
Society of Licensed Victuallers 40
Society of Motor Manufacturers & Traders Charitable Trust Fund 51
Society of Radiographers Benevolent Fund 50
Society of Schoolmasters and Schoolmistresses 67

Soham:
Soham United Charities 313

Solicitor:
Solicitor's Benevolent Association 45

Sollitt:
Herbert William Sollitt Memorial Trust 240

Solomons:
Jack Solomons' Charity Fund 29

Somerset:
Somerset County Bowling Association Benevolent Fund 295
Somerset Light Infantry Regimental Association 85
Somerset Local Medical Benevolent Fund 295

Index

Souldern:
Souldern United Charities 339

South:
South Atlantic Fund 86
South Brent Parish Lands Charity 289
South Creake Charities 335
South Lancashire Regiment (Prince of Wales's Volunteers) 85
South London Relief-in-Sickness Fund 363
South Moss Foundation 217
South Shields Indigent Sick Society 191
South Staffordshire Regiment 85
South Wales Association for Spina Bifida & Hydrocephalus 169
South Wales' Borderers 85
South Wales Police Benevolent Fund 169
South Warwickshire Welfare Trust 260

Southampton:
Southampton (City Centre) Relief-in-Need Charity 323
Southampton Charitable Trust 320

Southery:
Southery, Feltwell & Methwold Relief in Need Charity 330

Southport:
Southport & Birkdale Provident Society 220

Southwell:
Southwell Charities for the Poor & Sick Poor 252

Sowton:
Sowton In Need Charity 289

Spalding:
Ellen Rebe Spalding Memorial Fund 294, 338
Spalding Relief-in-Need Charity 240

Spanish:
Spanish Welfare Fund 363

Speak:
Paul and Nancy Speak's Charity (formerly The Bradford Gentlewomen's Pension Fund) 195

Spearing:
William Spearing Charity & Others 295

Speccott:
Peter Speccott Charity 286

Special:
Special Air Service Regimental Association (Benevolent Fund SAS) 85
Special Forces Benevolent Fund 87

Speck:
Speck Walker Annuity Fund 179

Spence:
Miss Caroline Jane Spence's Fund 146

Spencer:
Spencer's Charity 269

Sperring:
Ralph and Irma Sperring Charity 277

Spilsby:
Spilsby Feoffees (Poorlands) Charities 240

Spittal:
Spittal Trust 150

Spondon:
Spondon Relief-in-Need Charity 229

Sponne:
Sponne & Bickerstaffe Charity 246

Springboard:
Springboard Charitable Trust 111

Springfield:
Springfield United Charities 318

SSAFA:
SSAFA Forces Help 79

Stafford:
Stafford Charity 367

Staffordshire:
Staffordshire Regiment (Prince of Wales's) Regimental Association 85
Staffordshire Yeomanry 85

Staines:
Staines Parochial Charity 355
Staines Trust 31

Stanford:
Miss Doreen Stanford Charitable Trust 95

Stanley:
Stanley St Peter Relief-in-Sickness Fund 199

Stanton:
Stanton Ballard Charitable Trust 339
Stanton Charitable Trust 227
Stanton Poors' Estate Charity 344

Starfish:
Starfish Trust 95

Stationers:
Stationers Social Society Benevolent Fund 65

Stead:
Stead Benefaction Trust 142

Steel:
Sir James Steel's Trust 154

Stephen:
Miss Margaret J Stephen's Charitable Trust 148

Stephenson:
Paul Stephenson Memorial Trust 363

Stepney:
Stepney Relief-in-Need Charity 378

Stetchworth:
Stetchworth Relief-in-Need Charity 313

Stevens:
Robert Stevens Charity 268

Steventon:
Steventon Allotments & Relief-in-Need Charity 339

Stewart:
Sydney Stewart Memorial Trust 131

Stickford:
Stickford Relief-in-Need Charity 241

Stock:
Stock Exchange Benevolent Fund 65
Stock Exchange Clerks Fund 65

Stockburn:
Stockburn Memorial Trust 244

Stockport:
Stockport Sick Poor Nursing Association 211

Stoddart:
Stoddart Samaritan Fund 189

Stoke:
Stoke Mandeville & Other Parishes Charity 307
Stoke Poges United Charities 303

Stoke-on-Trent:
Stoke-on-Trent Children's Holiday Trust Fund 258

Stone:
Charles Graham Stone's Relief-in-Need Charity 279

Storey:
Foundation of Edward Storey 60

Stourbridge:
Stourbridge Relief in Sickness Charity 271

Stow:
Stow Bardolph Town Lands & Poors Charity 335

Stowmarket:
Stowmarket Relief Trust 344

Strain:
Edith Strain Nursing Charity 294

Straits:
Straits Settlement & Malay States Benevolent Society 111

Strand:
Mary Strand Charitable Trust 111

Strasser:
Strasser Foundation 256

Stratford-upon-Avon:
Stratford-upon-Avon Municipal Charities – Relief in Need 263

Strathclyde:
Strathclyde Police Benevolent Fund 158

Stretham:
Stretham Charity 313

Streynsham:
Streynsham's Charity 327

Stroke:
Stroke Association 103

Stuart:
Miss M C Stuart's Legacy 163

Sturminster:
Sturminster Newton United Charities 292

Sudbury:
Sudbury Municipal Charities 345

Suffolk:
Suffolk Regimental Old Comrades Association 85

Sumner:
Sir John Sumner's Trust 111

INDEX

Sunderland:
  Sunderland Guild of Help 190
  Sunderland Orphanage & Educational Foundation 190
  Samuel Sunderland Relief-in-Need Charity 194

Sunninghill:
  Sunninghill Fuel Allotment 307

Sunshine:
  Sunshine Society Fund 131

Support:
  Support Paraplegics in Rugby Enterprise – SPIRE 95

Supporting:
  Supporting Children of Wandsworth Trust (SCOWT) 379

Sure:
  Sure Foundation 120

Surfleet:
  Surfleet United Charities 241

Surplus:
  Surplus Fire Fund 154

Surrey:
  Surrey Association for Visual Impairment 347

Sussex:
  Sussex Police Welfare Fund 303
  Sussex Regiment 85

Sutherland:
  Dr Sutherland's Fund 164

Sutterton:
  Sutterton Parochial Charity Trust 241

Sutton:
  Sutton Bridge Power Fund 241
  Sutton Coldfield Municipal Charities – General Charity 271
  Sutton Nursing Association 377
  Sutton Poors' Land Charity 313
  Sutton St James United Charities 241

Swaffham:
  Swaffham Bulbeck Relief-in-Need Charity 313
  Swaffham Prior Parochial Charities 310

Swallow:
  Charities of Nicholas Swallow & Others 310

Swallowdale:
  Swallowdale Children's Trust 214

Swansea:
  Swansea & District Friends of the Blind 172

Sway:
  Sway Welfare Aid Group 323

Swineshead:
  Swineshead Poor Charities 241

Swiss:
  Swiss Benevolent Society 115

T

Tailors:
  Tailors' Benevolent Institute 32

Tamlin:
  Tamlin Charity 295

Tamworth:
  Tamworth Municipal Charities 258

Tancred:
  Tancred's Charity for Pensioners 60, 79

Tate:
  Mrs A Lacy Tate Trust 314

Taunton:
  Taunton Aid in Sickness Fund 297
  Taunton Town Charity 297

Tavistock:
  Tavistock, Whitchurch & District Nursing Association Trust Fund 283

Taylor:
  Archibald Taylor Trust 160
  H A Taylor Fund 236
  Miss M O Taylor's Trust 142

Teacher:
  Teacher Support Network (formerly The Teachers Benevolent Fund – TBF) 67

Teesside:
  Teesside Emergency Relief Fund 179

Temple:
  Temple Balsall Amalgamated Charities 266

Tenbury:
  Tenbury & District Nursing Association 226

Tenby:
  Tenby Relief-in-Need & Pensions Charity 172

Tenovus:
  Tenovus Cancer Information Centre 99

Tettenhall:
  Tettenhall Relief-in-Need & Educational Charity 271

Textile:
  Textile Benevolent Association (1970) 68
  Textile Industry Children's Trust 68

Thame:
  Thame Welfare Trust 338

Thanet:
  Thanet Charities 328

Thaxted:
  Thaxted Relief-in-Need Charities 318

Theatrical:
  Theatrical Guild (formerly The Theatrical Ladies Guild of Charity) 27

Thompson:
  Thomas Thompson Poors Rate Gift 190
  Thompson Pritchard Trust 254

Thomson:
  Hannah & Margaret Thomson Trust 149
  Joseph Thomson Mortification 153
  Miss Jessie Ann Thomson's Trust 146

Thornbury:
  Thornbury Consolidated Charities (administered by Thornbury Town Trust) 294

Thorngate:
  Thorngate Relief-in-Need and General Charity 321

Thornton:
  Thornton Fund 60

Thorpe:
  Thorpe Parochial Charities 355
  Thorpe Trust 252

Three:
  Three Parishes Fund 320

Thurlaston:
  Thurlaston Poor's Plot Charity 263

Thurne:
  Thurne Charity Trustees 336

Thursley:
  Thursley Charities 355

Tile:
  Tile Hill & Westwood Charities for the Needy Sick 269

Tilney:
  Tilney All Saints Parish Lands Charity 336

Timber:
  Timber Trades Benevolent Society 22

Tobacco:
  Tobacco Trade Benevolent Association 68

Tod:
  Tod Bequest 156

Todd:
  Charity of Edith Emily Todd Deceased 259
  Charity of Edith Emily Todd 255

Todmorden:
  Todmorden Needy Sick Fund 199

Toll:
  Annie Toll Bequest 289

Tollard:
  Tollard Trust 290

Tottenham:
  Tottenham District Charity 371

Town:
  Town Estate Charity 338
  Town Moor Money Charity 191

Townend:
  Ethel Maude Townend Charity 181

Townrow:
  Arthur Townrow Pensions Fund 120, 228

Towries:
  Robert Towries Charity 181

Tracy:
  Tracy Trust 306

Trades:
  Trades House of Glasgow 161

Trained:
  Trained Nurses Annuity Fund 50

Transport:
  Transport Benevolent Fund 55

INDEX

Trinity:
Trinity Homes and Mariners' Charities 64
Trinity Hospital Fund 154

Tripp:
Charity of John Tripp (Blue Coat) 238

Troughton:
Mrs S H Troughton Charitable Trust 142

Trull:
Trull Parish Lands Charity 298

Trustees:
Trustees of the Reading Dispensary Trust 305

Trusts:
Trusts administered by the Scottish Borders Council 156

Tuberous:
Tuberous Sclerosis Association Benevolent Fund 103

Tullochan:
Tullochan Trust 158

Tutbury:
Tutbury General Charities 259

Twyford:
Twyford and District Nursing Association 320

Tyler:
Tyler Charity for the Poor 237

Tyne:
Tyne Mariners' Benevolent Institution 190

Tyre:
Charles & Barbara Tyre Trust 158

Tyringham:
Tyringham Pension Fund for the Blind 308

U

UBA:
UBA Benevolent Fund 27

Ulster:
Ulster Defence Regiment Benvolent Fund 85

Underwood:
Thomas Underwood's Charity 249

UNIFI:
UNIFI Benevolent Fund 28

UNISON:
UNISON Welfare 55

United:
United Charities Ockley (Henry Smith Charity) 354
United Charities of East Farndon 244
United Charities of Liskeard 280
United Charities of St George the Martyr 377
United Charities of St Paul's, Covent Garden 380
United Charity of All Saints (Relief-in-Need Branch) 231
United Charity of Palling Burgess 294
United Charity of Saint Martin 274

United Law Clerks Society 45
United Westminster Almshouses Charity 380

Unity:
Unity Fund for the Elderly 279

Universal:
Universal Beneficent Society 118

Unwin:
Reginald Unwin Dudley Charity 270

Upwell:
Upwell (Cambridgeshire) Consolidated Charities 311

Ure:
Ure Elder Fund for Widows 161

Uxbridge:
Uxbridge United Welfare Trusts 372

V

Vacher:
Vacher's Endowment 364

Valance:
George Valance Bequest 154

Valentine:
Valentine Memorial Pension Fund 24

Vaughan:
Miss Vaughan's Spitalfields Charity 378

Vardy:
Vardy Foundation 111

Vawer:
William Vawer's Charity 172

Vegetarian:
Vegetarian Charity 123

Verden:
Verden Sykes Trust 146

Veterinary:
Veterinary Benevolent Fund 69

Victoria:
Victoria Convalescent Trust 95
Victoria Homes Relief in Need Charity 297
Victoria Homes Trust 131

Vincent:
Eric W Vincent Trust Fund 226

Viscount:
Viscount Amory's Charitable Trust 275

Visual:
Visual Impairment Services South East Scotland 153

W

Walberswick:
Walberswick Common Lands 345

Walker:
Angus Walker Benevolent Fund 147

Wallingford:
Wallingford Municipal & Relief-in-Need Charities 340

Walpole:
Walpole St Andrew Dole Charity 336
Walpole St Peter Poor's Estate 336

Walsh:
John Walsh Fund 190

Walsoken:
Walsoken United Charities 313

Wandsworth:
Wandsworth Combined Charity 379

Wansbeck:
Wansbeck Appeal Fund Trust 187

Wantage:
Wantage District Coronation Memorial & Nursing Amenities Fund 303

Wappenham:
Wappenham Poors' Land Charity 246

War:
War Widows Association of Great Britain 87

Warbrick:
Richard Warbrick Charities 218

Warrington:
Warrington Sick & Disabled Trust 204

Warsop:
Warsop United Charities 252

Warwick:
Warwick Municipal Charities – King Henry VIII Charity 263
Warwick Provident Dispensary 263
Warwick Relief in Need Charity 264

Warwickshire:
Warwickshire Miners Welfare Fund 260
Warwickshire Police Benevolent Fund 260

Water:
Water Conservators Charitable Trust Fund 69
Water Eaton Poors Land Charity 309

Waterloo:
Waterloo Parish Charity for the Poor 381

Watford:
Watford Health Trust 325

Watson:
Watson Bequest 157
John Watson of Saughton Fund 154

Watt:
John Watt's Trust 153

Watton:
Watton Relief-in-Need Charity 336

Watts:
Richard Watts and The City of Rochester Almshouse Charities 326

Weaverham:
Weaverham & Acton Bridge Sick Poor Fund 203

Webb:
William Webb's Charity 296

Webster:
William Webster's Charity 193

Wednesfield:
Wednesfield Parochial Charity 272

Welch:
Welch Regiment 85

INDEX

Wellfield:
Wellfield Trust *324*

Welsh:
Welsh Guards Association & Benevolent Fund *85*
Welsh Rugby Charitable Trust *165*

Welton:
Welton Town Lands Trust *246*

Wembley:
Wembley Samaritan Fund *366*

Wereham:
Wereham Relief-in-Need Charity *336*

West:
West Gate Benevolent Trust *249*
West Glamorgan County Blind Welfare Association *169*
West Harling Road Allotment Gardens Trust *333*
West Kent Regiment *85*
West Kirby Charity *220*
West Riding Distress Fund *193*
West Riding Regiment *85*
West Surrey Regiment *85*
West Sussex County Nursing Benevolent Fund *357*
Emily Temple West Trust *377*
West Walton Poors' Charity *337*
West Winch Town Yard Charity *331*
West Yorkshire Police (Employees) Benevolent Fund *194*
West Yorkshire Regimental Association *85*

Westgarth:
Clara Westgarth Trust *204*

Westminster:
Westminster Amalgamated Charity *381*

Weston:
Harry Weston Memorial Fund *270*

Weybridge:
Weybridge Land Charity *356*

Wheatcroft:
Julie Wheatcroft Trust *163*

White:
Ecclesiastical Charity of George White *318*
Sir Thomas White's Loan Fund *242*

Whittlesey:
Whittlesey Charity *313*

Whittuck:
Whittuck Charity *196*

Widows:
Widows Fund *60*
Widows', Orphans' & Dependants' Society of the Church in Wales *165*

Wigan:
Wigan Town Relief-in-Need Charity *212*

Wilde:
Edward Wilde Foundation *111*

Willenhall:
Willenhall Area Relief, Rehabilitation & Nursing Trust (WARRANT) *271*

Williams:
Elizabeth Williams Charities *167*
Marjorie Williams Bequest Fund *170*
William Williams Charity *290*
William Williams Charity *367*

Williamson:
Williamson Benevolent Trust *249*
Jessie Williamson Bequest *162*
Williamson Memorial Trust *118*

Willingham:
Willingham & District Relief in Sickness Charity *237*

Willis:
Henry & James Willis Trust *274*

Wilmington:
Wilmington Parochial Charity *330*
Wilmington Trust *182*

Wilmslow:
Wilmslow Aid Trust *205*

Wilson:
John Wilson Bequest Fund *153*
Wilson & Peter Bequest *147*

Wiltshire:
Wiltshire Ambulance Service Benevolent Fund *298*
Wiltshire Regiment Old Comrades' Association *85*

Wimbledon:
Wimbledon Guild of Social Welfare (Incorporated) *375*

Winchester:
Winchester Children's Holiday Trust *321*
Winchester Rural District Welfare Trust *321*
Winchester Welfare Charities *323*

Windlesham:
Windlesham United Charities & Poors Allotment Charities *347*

Wine:
Wine & Spirits Trades' Benevolent Society *40*
Wine Trade Foundation *40*

Wingfield:
Mrs Wingfield's Charitable Trust *254*

Wingrave:
Wingrave United Charities *310*

Winham:
Francis Winham Foundation *118*

Winterscale:
Robert Winterscale Charity *185*

Wireless:
Wireless for the Bedridden *95, 119*

Wirksworth:
Wirksworth and District Trust Fund *228*

Wirral:
Wirral Sick Children's Fund *221*

Wistrich:
Matthew Wistrich Trust *364*

Withers:
Withers Pensions *190*

Witley:
Witley Charitable Trust *348*

Witting:
S C Witting Trust *112*

Witton:
Witton Charity *331*

Wokingham:
Wokingham United Charities *306*

Wolverhampton:
Wolverhampton Trust Fund *272*

Women:
Women's Royal Army Corps Benevolent Fund *85*

Wonersh:
Wonersh Charities *348*

Wooburn:
Wooburn, Bourne End & District Relief-in-Sickness Charity *308*

Wood:
Sir Edward Wood's Bequest Fund For Gentlewomen *235*
James Wood Bequest and the James Wood & Christina Shaw Bequests *157*
John Theodore Wood Charity *167*
Wood Green (Urban District) Charity *371*

Woodmancy:
Christine Woodmancy Charitable Foundation *276*

Woodthorpe:
Woodthorpe Relief-in-Need Charity *228*

Woodton:
Woodton United Charities *337*

Woolwich:
Woolwich & Plumstead Relief-in-Sickness Fund *370*

Worcester:
Worcester Consolidated Municipal Charity *274*

Worcestershire:
Worcestershire & Sherwood Foresters Regiment Welfare and General Charitable Fund *85*
Worcestershire Cancer Aid Committee *273*
Worcestershire Regiment *85*

Wormley:
Wormley Parochial Charity *325*

Worplesdon:
Worplesdon Parish Charities (including the Henry Smith Charity) *356*

Worshipful:
Worshipful Company of Carmen Benevolent Trust *55*
Worshipful Company of Cordwainers *107*
Worshipful Company of Engineers Charitable Trust Fund *36*
Worshipful Company of Farriers Charitable Trust *37*
Worshipful Company of Launderers Benevolent Trust *44*

Wraxall:
Wraxall Parochial Charities *279*

Index

Wrenbury:
Wrenbury Consolidated Charities *203*

Wrexham:
Wrexham & District Relief in Need Charity *168*

Wright:
Charity of Jane Wright *186*

WRNS:
WRNS Benevolent Trust *79*

WRVS:
WRVS Benevolent Trust *124*

Wybunbury:
Wybunbury United Charities *205*

Wylde:
Anthony & Gwendoline Wylde Memorial Charity *226*

Wylie:
Eliza Haldane Wylie Fund *142*

Wymeswold:
Wymeswold Parochial Charities *236*

Y

Yardley:
Yardley Great Trust *268*

Yelvertoft:
Yelvertoft & District Relief in Sickness Fund *242*

Yeoman:
Yeoman of the Guard – Queen's Bodyguard *86*
Yeoman Warders *86*

Yeomanry:
Yeomanry Benevolent Fund *86*

York:
York and Lancaster Regimental Association *86*
York City Charities *186*
York Dispensary Charitable Trust *184*
York Division Medical Association Charities Fund *179*
York Fund for Women & Girls *186*

Yorkshire:
Yorkshire County Bowling Association Benevolent Fund *179*
Yorkshire Hussars Regimental Association *86*
Yorkshire Regiment (Alexandra, Princess of Wales's Own) *86*
Yorkshire Water Community Trust *179*

Yorkston:
Mrs E W Yorkston Bequest *156*

You:
You and Your Community Millennium Awards *112*

Young:
Jonathan Young Memorial Trust *227*
Roger Pilkington Young Trust *94, 118*

Z

Zimbabwe:
Zimbabwe Rhodesia Relief Fund *115*

ZSV:
ZSV Trust *122*